THE BRUTAL FRIENDSHIP

Sir William Deakin was born in 1913. He studied modern history at Christ Church, Oxford. Through his long career he was a Fellow at Wadham College, and Warden at St Anthony's College, Oxford. In 1939 he joined the army and was later seconded to Special Operations at the War Office. In 1943 he led the first British Military Mission to Tito, and in 1945 and 1946 was First Secretary at the Embassy in Belgrade. He holds the DSO, the Grosse Verdeinstkreuz, the Yugoslav Partisan Star (1st class), and is a member of the Russian Order of Valour and a Chevalier of the Légion d'Honneur.

Also by F. W. Deakin

The British Political Tradition
The Case of Richard Sorge [with G. R. Storry]
The Oxford History of Modern Europe
The Embattled Mountain
A History of World Communism

THE
BRUTAL
FRIENDSHIP

*Mussolini, Hitler and
the Fall of Italian Fascism*

F. W. Deakin

**PHOENIX
PRESS**

5 UPPER SAINT MARTIN'S LANE
LONDON
WC2H 9EA

A PHOENIX PRESS PAPERBACK

First published in Great Britain
by Weidenfeld & Nicolson in 1962
This paperback edition published in 2000
by Phoenix Press,
a division of The Orion Publishing Group Ltd,
Orion House, 5 Upper St Martin's Lane,
London WC2H 9EA

A CIP catalogue record for this book is
available from the British Library.

Printed and bound in Great Britain by
Clays Ltd, St Ives plc

ISBN 1 84212 049 2

This book is dedicated to my wife

'My attachment to the person of the Duce has not changed
. . . but I regret not having listened to reason, which imposed
on me a brutal friendship in regard to Italy.'

Adolf Hitler, April 1945

CONTENTS

CONTENTS

Book III

Book IV

PART TWO
THE FORTY-FIVE DAYS OF MARSHAL BADOGLIO

PART THREE
SALÒ: THE SIX HUNDRED DAYS

Book I

CONTENTS

Book II

PREFACE

This is a book by an Englishman, in part based on German documents, on the fall of the Fascist government in Italy. It has grown in labour out of a short study of the events leading up to the meeting of the Grand Council on July 24, 1943, which seemed to give a deceptively tidy illustration of the technique of the coup d'état in contemporary history. Further and lengthy investigation destroyed the neatness of the original interpretation, and, as material accumulated, it became clear to me that I should attempt to marshal and select the massive, and at the same time fragmentary, unpublished evidence, which might throw new and detailed light on the collapse of Italian Fascism under the impact of military disaster. The study of contemporary history is fraught with the temptation of uttering premature personal judgments, and with the snare of the uncritical assembly of excessive material. In spite of the uneven wealth of written sources, much has been destroyed by chance of war, and perhaps more buried by the death of leading witnesses or withheld by the living. In spite of such hazards, which are the lot of the historian, it seems that the prime and humble duty of the student of contemporary history is to establish the elementary record before it is dissipated.

In the case of this work, the author has deliberately attempted to unfold with a minimum of apocalyptic commentary the account of the disintegration of the régime in Italy from the moment when military events from the autumn of 1942 onwards reacted savagely and progressively on the internal structure of Italian Fascism, and he trusts that the reader will be patient with such a direct and first-hand presentation of the evidence, of which most is original, and much is tempered by numerous discussions with surviving witnesses.

The weighing of oral evidence in such an enterprise is risky and imprecise, and perhaps its only justification is that from time to time vital fragments are snatched from oblivion. One word on this subject belongs to Dr Johnson. 'Nothing but experience could evince the frequence of false information, or

enable any man to conceive that so many groundless reports should be propa-
gated . . . Some men relate what they think, as what they know; some men of
confused memories and habitual inaccuracy, ascribe to one man what belongs
to another; and some talk on, without thought or care. A few men are
sufficient to broach falsehoods, which are afterwards innocently diffused by
successive relators.'

This portentous warning should not however deter the contemporary
historian from seeking confirmation or denial of matters arising from the
plethora of documents with which he is confronted. His work at best is the
provisional creation of a pioneer.

ACKNOWLEDGMENTS

•••

In the writing of this book I am indebted to friends and colleagues in England, the United States, and Italy and my formal expression of thanks would be inadequate. Any views expressed, however, or errors committed, are mine.

In the early stages of the work, I have a special debt to the Hon. Margaret Lambert who led me with a sure and experienced hand into the jungle of the German diplomatic records, and encouraged me to undertake a detailed study of the subject; to Professor Howard M. Smyth, now of the Historical Division of the State Department, who put at my disposal, with a rare generosity, the drafts of his invaluable forthcoming official American history of the war in Italy; and to their Excellencies Dr Manlio Brosio and Count Vittorio Zoppi, successively the envoys of the Republic of Italy at the Court of St James for persuading me that my task was not, as a foreigner, a total impertinence, and for the courtesy of introducing me to certain leading Italian witnesses.

I am grateful to my colleagues at St Antony's College, Oxford, for their patience over an excessively long period, and in particular to Sir John Wheeler-Bennett, Mr James Joll and Mr David Footman for their helpful criticism.

I have also profitably inflicted the draft manuscript on friends in the University, and my warm thanks are due to Professor Sir Isaiah Berlin, Professor A J. Ayer, Professor Sir Ronald Syme; the Master of St Catherine's, Mr A. L. C. Bullock; and the Warden of Rhodes House, Mr E. T. Williams. I have an equal debt to the Earl of Birkenhead, Count Julian Dobrski and the Hon. Anthony Samuel.

It is a special pleasure to pay tribute to the late Professor Federico Chabod for his serene and perceptive advice; to Professor Mario Toscano, the Director of the Italian Foreign Office Archives, for his courteous assistance; to my Oxford friend, Professor Count Alessandro Passerin D'Entrèves; to Professor Franco Venturi; and to Dr Leo Valiani.

I was fortunate to have the benefit of talks with the German Ambassador to the Republic of Salò, Dr Rudolf von Rahn, who patiently submitted to interrogation, and to correspond with the former Japanese Ambassador to Italy, Dr Hidaka, who was good enough to answer importunate questions. I would also wish to thank Count Dino Grandi for the courtesy of discussing with me the central theme of this work, and for permission to publish certain correspondence.

Finally this book would never have been completed without the sturdy and uncomplaining labours beyond the call of duty of my secretary, Mrs Patricia Kirkpatrick, of Miss Mary Worthington, and their colleagues on the staff of St Antony's College, and to them I would like to express my specially warm thanks. My task has been lightened by the helpful efficiency of Miss Margaret Carlyle and Miss Jill Myford in handling documentary material.

PART ONE

THE CRISIS OF THE SYSTEM

'A régime never falls for internal reasons, moral questions, economic stresses. Party struggles do not hazard the existence of a system. A régime, of whatever kind, collapses only under the weight of defeat.'

Mussolini, The History of a Year

PART ONE

Book I

CHAPTER ONE

'THE FOURTH PUNIC WAR'

THE AUTUMN of 1942 marked for Italy the crisis of the Second World War. By that time all the assumptions upon which she had entered the conflict just over two years previously had been destroyed. The war aims of Italian Fascism had been outlined by the Duce in private at a meeting of the Grand Council on February 4, 1939. His speech was drafted to guide this supreme consultative body in Italian foreign policy 'for a short or for a long, even very long, term'; it summarized the aspirations of his government and was a quintessence of its foreign aims since the take-over of political power in October 1922.

'The premise from which I argue is the following: States are more or less independent according to their maritime position . . . Italy is bordered by an inland sea which communicates with the ocean through the Suez Canal—an artificial means of communication which is easily blocked even by accident—and by the Straits of Gibraltar, dominated by the government of Great Britain. Italy has in fact no free access to the oceans. She is really a prisoner in the Mediterranean, and the more populous and powerful she becomes, the more will she suffer from her imprisonment. The bars of this prison are Corsica, Tunisia, Malta, and Cyprus. Its sentinels are Gibraltar and Suez.'

From this situation Mussolini drew the following deductions. The task of Italian policy 'which has not and never can have as objectives continental European territory except Albania, is in the first place to break the prison bars'. Once this was done, Italy could have only one watchword: 'The March to the Ocean. Which Ocean? The Indian Ocean linking across the Sudan and Libya to Abyssinia; or the Atlantic Ocean across French North Africa? In the first, as in the second, hypothesis we find ourselves face to face with Anglo-French opposition. To brave the solution of such a problem without having secured our backs on the Continent would be absurd. The policy of the Rome-Berlin Axis therefore answers the historical necessity of a fundamental order. The same applies to our conduct in the Spanish Civil War.' [1]

The conception of an Italo-German alliance, apart from its ideological significance, was therefore, from the Italian point of view, to cover and secure by treaty with the greatest European land power the continental position of Italy, and free her to pursue her 'vital interests' in the Mediterranean and in Africa. As Mussolini expressed it three years later in a speech to senior Party officials, 'The question of our land frontiers was settled by the war of 1915–18. We are faced today with the problem of the maritime frontiers, and this conflict has for us a very special character, that of the Fourth Punic War.' [2] The weakness of any alliance between Germany and Italy must be, as he realized at the Munich Conference in September 1938, that Italy might be dragged into a major war, the timing of which would be decided by Germany in her own political and strategic interests, before her ally was in a condition to fight. The Czech crisis was a warning.

As Mussolini analysed the position to the Grand Council, 'Are we today, February 1939, in ideal conditions to engage on a war? No State is ever in ideal conditions to make war, when by this you mean to imply the mathematical assurance of victory . . . But there is no doubt that our preparations will be better in a few years' time, and more exactly when we have renewed all our artillery (during 1941–2), when we have in service eight battleships and perhaps double the existing number of submarines, when the empire is completely pacified, self-sufficient, and can provide us with a native army, when we have realized at least fifty per cent of our autarchic plans and when we have held at the end of 1942 the Exhibition, which should reinforce our reserves.' This last plan of marking the twentieth anniversary of the March on Rome by a celebration of the achievements of Fascist rule was thus established, with a neat symbolism, as the most appropriate and convenient date for an Italian entry into a war.

The progress of events in Europe moved harshly in the following months, and with little relation to Italy's position or interests. The signing of the Axis Pact in the following May brought little change.[a] This treaty was the personal creation of Hitler and Mussolini, and the alliance between the two countries rested essentially on the relationship between the two men. Hitler's admiration of his Italian colleague was of long standing. As he told his entourage on one occasion, the Duce had overcome Bolshevism 'not by military force but by superior intellect, and we have to thank him for showing for the first time, by his decisive defeat of the inner power of Bolshevism, that even in this twentieth century it is possible to recall a people to a sense

a. For a brilliant and exhaustive account of these negotiations see Toscano "*Le Origini Diplomatiche del Patto D'Acciaio*" (Second edition, 1956).

of purely national pride'.[3] The Duce had been therefore the precursor of the original crusade. The master of the technique of modern mass dictatorship, he had also inspired a new conception of rule, and Hitler regarded himself as his pupil. 'When I read the history of Fascism I feel as if I am reading the history of our movement.' In Germany 'things had developed spontaneously and subsequently acquired a speed comparable with that of developments in Italy. The Duce himself has told me that at the moment when he undertook the struggle against Bolshevism, he didn't know exactly where he was going . . . What crowns these parallel destinies is that today we are fighting side by side against the same Powers and against the same personages. At the same period, the Duce and I were both working in the building-trade. This explains that there is also a bond between us on the purely human level. I have a deep friendship for this extraordinary man.' [4]

The historical and temperamental differences between the two peoples could not conceal, in Hitler's mind, the identity of outlook of the two dictators. But such a conception was cerebral and spurious, and onlookers observed during the summit meetings between the two men a lack of real understanding and comprehension. There was no familiar intercourse between them, and their successive encounters created an increasingly distorted image of their relationship.[b] The only reality of the personal bond between them lay in their mutual and lonely isolation at the summit of supreme power. There was an artificiality also about the political and ideological bond which they had forged between their two countries, and this arbitrary and fragile structure could ill stand the reality of war. Hitler perhaps more than Mussolini was aware of its personal nature. As he told his generals as early as August 1939. 'There will never be in the future a man who possesses more authority than I do. My very existence is also a great factor of value. But I can be put out of the way at any time either by a criminal or a lunatic. The second personal factor is the Duce. His existence also is decisive. If anything happened to him, the loyalty of Italy to the alliance would be no longer secure.' [5]

Mussolini was more realistic than Hitler as to the limitations of the Pact. He never completely lost sight of the fact that the power interests of Italy were both distinct from those of Germany and in some instances conflicting. From the military point of view, the treaty laid down prior consultation between the allies in event of one or the other being engaged in armed conflict, which was regarded as inevitable. The occupation of Czechoslovakia in March 1939 by Nazi Germany as a forward base for any eventual assault in the East, was countered on the Italian side by the occupation of Albania a

b. In 1926 or 1927 the Italian Embassy in Berlin received a request from a certain Mr Adolf Hitler for a signed photograph of the Duce, which was forwarded to Rome. The Embassy were instructed to transmit a polite refusal. See Donosti, *Mussolini e L'Europa*, p. 80.

few days later, in order to mark Italy's separate, if limited, interests in Europe which were not confined, as Mussolini had stated to the Grand Council in February, to Albanian territory, but which included the 'unfinished business' of the First World War in the Adriatic and at the expense of Yugoslavia. Control of this inland sea was essential to Italy's conception of her position as a Mediterranean power, and the Peace Treaties of 1919 had left Italy unsatisfied in this direction.

But her ultimate success in achieving her objectives might be achieved by the diplomatic ability of Mussolini in restraining Hitler from pursuing immediate German interests which might endanger the peace of Europe. He had acquired at Munich in the previous year a view of his position as an arbitrator, and in terms of prestige and ideology he was quick to grasp one aspect of this crisis. In a private address to a gathering of Italian Prefects at the end of 1938 he had shouted: 'The word Munich means that for the first time since 1861 Italy has played an extremely prominent and decisive role in an event of world importance (loud applause) . . . What happened in Munich was simply colossal, and I use the word advisedly as it is one of ours. What happened at Munich spelt the end of Bolshevism in Europe, the end of all Russian political influence on our continent. Prague was the principal headquarters of democracy and of Bolshevism. Prague housed the archives of the Third International. With the conquest of Prague we had already practically captured Barcelona.'[6] The connection between Munich and the events of the Spanish Civil War was that it gave Mussolini the pretext to withdraw the Italian contingent from Spain and to liquidate this commitment prior to the gathering storm in central Europe. But whatever the 'moral' victory, there remained the brutal inadequacies of Italian armament and industry. After the signature of the Axis Pact, Mussolini sent one of his generals, Ugo Cavallero, the future Chief of the General Staff, to Germany with a personal note to Hitler dated May 30, 1939, outlining Italy's position in the event of a European war, and repeating, in some passages word for word, his speech to the Grand Council in the previous February. Mussolini recognized that war was inevitable, but added: 'The two European powers of the Axis need a period of peace lasting not less than three years. It is from 1943 onwards that a war effort will have the greatest prospects of victory . . . Fascist Italy, although convinced that it is inevitable, has no desire to anticipate a European war . . . Italy can mobilize proportionately more men than Germany. But with its abundance of manpower there is a corresponding modesty of materials.'[7]

The Axis Pact did not lead to corresponding Staff talks, or to any serious consideration of building up Italy's war potential from German sources. Hitler had no intention of preparing for a long conflict, and at no time did he show any interest in Italian military co-operation in the event of a major war. Her role at best would be to neutralize by the threat of intervention British and French forces in the Mediterranean and North Africa, if Germany were to be involved in hostilities with the Western Powers as a result of German action in the East.

The steps leading to the Nazi-Soviet Pact were taken by the German leaders without any reference to Rome or any consideration of Italian interests. The German attack on Poland in September 1939 equally was not a subject of prior consultation as laid down in the Axis Pact between the two partners. The German conception of a Blitzkrieg in Europe presented certain dangers for Fascist Italy, and overwhelming German power on the Continent, and possible German expansion, in the event of the total defeat of Britain and France, in their imperial possessions in Africa, would be at the expense of the long-term aims of Italian policy.

Until the spring of 1940, however, Mussolini reluctantly maintained a neutral position. On September 17 the King had telegraphed to him, 'I would like to hope that, when Poland has been liquidated, you will be able to negotiate diplomatically, and if, in spite of the sinking of their merchant shipping, the British want to treat, one can perhaps reach a good solution'.[8] But Mussolini's basic assumptions underwent successive changes as events developed. On March 31, 1940, in a memorandum sent to the King, Mussolini referred to the inevitability of Italian entry into the conflict, but in 'a war parallel to that of Germany to obtain our objectives, which can be summed up in this phrase: liberty on the seas; a window on the ocean'.[9] Hitler had also discussed such an action at a meeting on the Brenner earlier that month, and it was established that the timing of such a decision concerned Italy alone. His conception of Italy's role was somewhat contemptuous. At the moment of an Anglo-French collapse Italy should be allowed a modest pound of flesh, acquired by a nominal show of force.

The original Italian time-table for entering the conflict in 1942 was rendered meaningless by the march of the German armies. Their successes in Norway, then in the Low Countries and France in the late spring and early summer of 1940 revolutionized the whole position. At a meeting of the Italian military leaders in the Duce's room at the Palazzo Venezia on May 29 the die was cast. The decision to go to war had already been outlined in the Duce's memorandum to the King on March 31. 'That left the date, the most important problem to settle in connection with the tempo of a war. This date had originally been fixed for the spring of 1941. After the easy conquest of Norway and the domination of Denmark, I had already brought this date forward to early September 1940. Now, after the conquest of Holland, the fall of Belgium, the invasion of France and the resultant general situation, I have brought the date still further forward, and consider that any day from June 5 next is suitable for entering the war. The present situation rules out any further delay, as otherwise we run the risk of greater dangers than would have resulted from a premature intervention. Moreover, in my opinion, the situation is—so far as the so-called allies are concerned—decisive. If we delayed two weeks or a month, we should not improve the situation, while we might give Germany the impression of arriving after the *fait accompli* when the risk is slight; besides the fact that it is not in our moral code to strike a man when he is down. Finally, all this could be important when peace is signed.' [10]

Mussolini's decision to enter the war on June 5 was accepted by Hitler without enthusiasm. There was no co-ordinated military planning to meet such an event. A nominal and ineffectual Italian assault on the French advance positions in the Western Alps was to have the intended effect of giving Italy a place in the armistice negotiations with France. Even before this attack was launched, the French armies had collapsed.

On June 17 Marshal Pétain from Bordeaux sought an armistice in Berlin, and Hitler called at once for a meeting with the Duce, who was taken by surprise, without a pondered solution and without a token victory. When the Italo-German conference opened at Munich on June 18 the real subject of debate was the cutting down of any eventual Italian claims against France in order to permit Germany to seek a working compromise with the new Vichy government. The German attitude was conditioned by the fear that a French government-in-exile might be set up in North Africa, and the hope that England might be persuaded to consider a compromise peace. Although Hitler seems to have agreed in his first private talk at Munich with Mussolini that Italian claims would be respected, there was little conviction in his tone.

It was not only a question of territorial claims, but also of the fate of the French Fleet which, as both belligerent parties realized, held the balance of not only the Mediterranean but also the war at sea throughout the world. As Hitler expressed it, 'the best thing that we can hope for is that the French will sink it. The worst is that the fleet should go over to the British'. This would enable the latter to protect their convoys, and garrison and supply their bases 'from Egypt to Portugal, keeping alive or creating a series of theatres of operations, thus leading to a long war and the impossibility of hitting the enemy decisively. I far prefer a compact and concentrated enemy as France was, which I can grasp and beat, to enemies who may be weak, but who are scattered here and there.' It would be impolitic therefore to ask the French to hand over their fleet to the Axis powers, but it should be concentrated 'in a position where it could neither move nor fire', either in French or neutral (preferably Spanish) ports. 'On the whole, there was agreement with the Fuehrer's point of view.' Italian territorial demands were to be shelved 'until peace negotiations are started'.[11] The evidence as to how this fatal step was taken is contained in an unpublished letter of June 22, from Mussolini to Hitler: 'With the aim of making it easier for the French to accept the armistice conditions, I have not included in the clauses the occupation of (French) territory on the left bank of the Rhône, of Corsica, Tunisia, or Djibouti, which we agreed on at Munich. I confined myself to the minimum—i.e. to demanding a demilitarized zone of 50 kms. I think this minimum is indispensable for avoiding incidents. For all the rest, I adopted the clauses of the German armistice.' [12]

These decisions set the future frame of 'the French problem' in Axis policy, and had been taken on the assumption of a rapid military victory over Great Britain or of an early negotiated settlement with her. But if Italy were to pursue in earnest hostilities against the British in the Mediterranean, such concessions from France were essential to the conduct of this campaign. The Italian General Staff pointed this out in a memorandum drafted for the Munich conference, and Mussolini agreed to press them. Why did he change his mind? The significance of this meeting with Hitler was that the latter was able to persuade the Duce of the imminent collapse of Great Britain and that, given this assumption, the importance of the immediate neutralization of France in the Mediterranean, of her fleet and her North African possessions, was vital to the successful and quick conclusion to the war.

The notes taken at the conference by the Vice-Chief of the Italian Army Staff, General Roatta, read: 'The Duce sent for me and told me the following: "The Fuehrer, who is not anxious to see the appearance of American intervention and to pass a second winter at war, has given the clear impression that he wishes to conclude in the shortest space of time peace with England. He only referred vaguely to offensive action against her, and in completely hypothetical terms."' [13] When Ciano presented the Italian claims to Ribbentrop, the latter said: 'One must be moderate and not have eyes bigger than one's stomach . . . but Ciano has formed the conviction that Germany is in the state of mind of a poker player who, far beyond his hopes, finds himself in front of a pile of chips. Would it not be better to close the game?' [14]

Mussolini's decision to enter the war had been a calculated risk. A token campaign on the Western Alpine frontier would bring him to the conference table with the French, and make it possible to settle, at least in part, the historic claims to Nice, Corsica, and Tunis. An operation on the Libyan border against the British in Egypt would entitle the Italians to take their seat at the armistice with the British which, it was calculated, would rapidly follow Operation 'Sea-Lion' and the invasion of the British Isles. In August Marshal Badoglio, the Chief of the Italian General Staff, was still hoping 'for a quick end to the war through the activities of the German Air Force and a landing in Great Britain. There is only sufficient food in (Italian) East Africa until the spring. An offensive against Egypt can only achieve *tactical* success.' [15]

Mussolini had received over many months due warning of the state of the Italian armed forces and of the economy of the country in the event of war. No decrees or reorganization could change the brutal reality of this position. The Italian army was neither a highly equipped and trained élite striking force, nor a Napoleonic conscript army. Italy was totally deficient in anti-aircraft defence. In 1940 she possessed two searchlights and some 230 anti-aircraft batteries for the defence of the mother country. There were only 42,000 vehicles for the whole metropolitan army in July 1940; she possessed no modern artillery or tanks. Much out of date equipment and war material at the disposal of the Italian armed forces had been lost in Ethiopia and in Spain. These stocks had not been replenished, and she had not the industrial machinery to maintain an effective Air Force whose plans and training were far behind that of the Western Powers. The Navy, though better equipped, possessed no battle experience and was dependent for oil supplies on forces beyond her control. The closing of Suez and Gibraltar at the outbreak of war with Britain meant that Italy would henceforward be totally dependent on Germany for the transport of raw materials to Italian industry. According to reports from the Italian Commission of War Production, which reached Mussolini at the end of 1939, Italian industry could begin to meet in full the needs of the three armed services by 1944, and in order to enter the war with sufficient stocks to maintain hostilities for one year only the date would be 1949. By February 1940 General Favagrossa, head of the Commission, was able to report that the former date could be brought forward to 1943.[16]

This was the background of Mussolini's gamble. In any event, however short the period of the war might be, Italy would be dependent during the ensuing months in transport, communications and supplies of raw materials on her German ally. Nevertheless, the Duce was determined to fight his own 'parallel war', to achieve the aims which he had outlined to the Grand Council in the previous year and at the same time, somewhat unrealistically, to seek liberation from economic dependence on Germany and to bolster up the Italian system of economic autarchy. The incorrigible slowness of the British to surrender, and the limited tasks and resources allotted to Graziani in Libya, thereby excluding any decisive results in the African theatre, led Mussolini, prompted by Ciano, to snatch at quick profits in another region where Italian interests were traditionally involved, and before the Germans could further extend their control. Mussolini was not only determined to pursue his own war without German military aid, but also if necessary at the expense of certain German interests.

The Fascist mission to complete the unachieved war aims of 1915–18 was specially linked with the whole Balkan area. Even if Italy had not come into the war on the side of Germany in 1940 against the British and French, she would probably have sought compensation at the expense of Yugoslavia in a separate and distinct expedition. As Graziani put it at his post-war trial, referring to the time when he had been Chief of the Italian Army Staff which was planning for such an enterprise in April 1940, 'they wanted to make a little war for the mines as they had done in Albania, and not a large-scale war alongside the Germans which they hoped to avoid'.[17]

Italy's interest in Yugoslavia was both historic in terms of Dalmatia and the Adriatic coast and economic in regard to the valuable copper and bauxite. The attack on Yugoslavia was stood down temporarily until after the fall of France, when 37 Italian divisions were again put on the alert for this purpose. If Mussolini's time-table were accurate, and the French armistice were followed by negotiations with the British, and Italian aims in Egypt and East Africa were fulfilled, the acquisition of parts of Yugoslav territory and her economic resources would round off Italian claims in the Mediterranean, and complete the cycle of Italy's 'parallel war'. But as so often in the past the Duce, perhaps discouraged by the frigid German attitude to the Yugoslav adventure, cancelled the operation and orders were given to demobilize 600,000 men. The war, it seemed, was practically over, and the Italians could be resigned to collecting their pieces of silver from the French and the British.

As the first winter of the war drew on, however, there were no signs of a British collapse, and Ciano, in particular, thought to snatch a further lightning compensation for the Italian Mediterranean empire in the form of a sudden attack on Greece, in spite of the recent disorganization and demobilization of a large part of the Italian army which had just begun. It could be argued that in military terms the Greek expedition was linked with the stalemate on the Libya–Egypt border and by tempting the British into Greece a far more important decision might follow in the direction of Egypt and Suez. But the Greek campaign, and the failure of the Italians to defeat the Greek armies extended German intervention in the Balkans—an area which the Italians hoped to keep for themselves, and brought a stage nearer the Italo-German combined military operations which Mussolini hoped so much to avoid. The Axis occupation of Greece, bringing with it a wave of Italian profiteers and dubious businessmen to exploit the resources of the country in the interests of Italian economy, as had happened the previous year in Albania, also increased the Italian military commitment overseas to garrison and contain the Greek peninsula.

A separate Italian adventure against Yugoslavia, in light of the Greek experience, was now out of the question. By joint diplomatic pressure Yugoslavia might be forced into the Axis camp, thus completing control of the whole of the European fortress. Yugoslavia represented the last remaining neutral power in Europe outside the Iberian peninsula and Switzerland. The failure of these diplomatic moves, and the Yugoslav rising in March 1941, caught both the Italians and the Germans by surprise. The planning of the Russian campaign was now far advanced, although as usual unknown to the

Italians and Hitler was about to embark on his major gamble. The sharp Yugoslav campaign, which followed in April, led to the destruction of the State of Yugoslavia, the partition of the country to include the setting up of the independent satellite state of Croatia, German military government in Serbia, and Italian military occupation of Montenegro and the annexation of Dalmatia. This situation was to produce one of the main frictions between the Axis allies in the conduct of the war, and to feature at intervals henceforward at every summit conference between the two dictators. In fragile fashion the Italians had achieved their territorial aims in the Adriatic, but the physical presence of the Germans in these regions brought with it the revival of the historical ghosts of the Habsburgs and their claims on former Austrian territory in the Balkans, and in particular in Slovenia and Croatia. The copper-mines in Serbia and the bauxite deposits in Herzegovina became of central concern to the German aircraft industry. An inevitable clash with Italian economic interests followed.

The German attack on Russia brought a further revolution in the position in the Balkans. The Germans were now actively allied to Roumania, and the supplies of wheat, and oil from Ploesti and the other Roumanian oilfields vital to the Axis war effort, could reach Germany and Italy only along the main railways running through Yugoslavia and Hungary. These communications were now of major importance to both Axis Powers, and in addition represented the supply route to the Piraeus and thence to the Italian and German garrisons in Greece and to Rommel in North Africa. They were the main life-line of the Axis.

The German attack on Russia changed the face of the war, and precluded any major German military effort in the Mediterranean theatre as an alternative operation to the assault on the British Isles itself which had now been indefinitely postponed. Italy alone was incapable of reaching a decision against the British Mediterranean positions. Spain could not be brought into the war except at the expense of the French, and Hitler's Montoire policy towards the Pétain government precluded any such sacrifice. The Italian possessions in East Africa, cut off from all supplies and contact with the mother country, fell piecemeal into British hands. After the wholesale surrender of the Italian armies in Ethiopia, and with the see-saw campaigns in North Africa, the Italians were unable to achieve a temporary decision, let alone a victory.

Although the main German attention was now directed towards an Eastern Blitzkrieg, the German High Command realized that limited military reinforcements to Africa might just tip the balance. In any event it would be but a secondary episode. As General Ambrosio, the future Chief of the General Staff, wrote later, 'The politico-military conduct of the present war is characterized on the German side by a completely continental strategy and a total incomprehension of the decisive importance of the Mediterranean theatre. In fact, apart from the episode of the air assault on England and the battle of the Atlantic—to which can probably in the main be attributed a secondary role in favour of the battle for Northern Europe—the whole German effort has always and only been directed against the continental Powers.' But Mussolini's initial obstinacy in fighting his own 'parallel war' led to the rejection on more than one occasion of German armoured reinforcements for the Libyan Front. The German appreciation of the military value of the Italian army was such that appeals for more tanks and material alone were never met. As Ambrosio wrote: 'From 1940 onwards armoured equipment was requested for the Italian troops in Italian North Africa to put them in a condition to undertake a rapid offensive against the British forces in Egypt. The requests for material were not conceded, in spite of the fact that during the whole of the second half of 1940 and the first quarter of 1941 the German army was not engaged in any operations of war. A few hundred tanks at that time would have probably been enough to occupy the zone of Suez.' [18]

Mussolini had been dazzled by the mirage of a cheap triumph in 1940. His justification for entering into the war, apart from reasons of prestige and a sense of inferiority in regard to the might of Nazi Germany, was to secure sufficient gains for Italy to counter-balance total German supremacy in Europe. But such calculations, which had been quickly disproved by the military events following the French armistice, were swept away by the German attack on Russia, and Mussolini rapidly conceived of a new set of false premises. The Italian 'parallel war' which had been begun to seek limited aims in the Mediterranean, the Balkans and Africa, was now incongruously merged in a German crusade against a Bolshevik East. Mussolini's pose as the leading prototype of the anti-Bolshevist leader was now put to a rude and brutal test. Just as he had felt compelled to enter the war in June 1940 to gain some territorial advantage in face of a German victory in the West, so now in 1941 he could hardly stand aside from this fateful extension of the conflict.

The Libyan campaign was conceived of as a token operation which would strengthen Italy's position at the conference table. Mussolini telegraphed to Graziani in North Africa in October 1940, 'We must bring home to the peace conference our military conquests; it is not worth the trouble of having sixteen months' time in which to prepare and equip fifteen divisions just in order to bring home Sidi El Barani.' [19] In similar fashion he forced on a reluctant Hitler, in the winter of 1941, the Italian Expeditionary Corps on the Russian front to take part in the victorious march to the East as a claim on the economic resources of the Soviet Union at yet another triumphant peace, and told the Italian Commander, General Messe, 'We cannot count less than Slovakia and the other minor states. I must be at the side of Hitler in Russia as he was at mine in the war against Greece, and is henceforward in Africa. The destiny of Italy is intimately bound up with that of Germany.' [20]

In 1940 his calculations were destroyed by the continued resistance of Great Britain, and those of 1941 were shattered by that of the Soviet Union. The myth of the invincibility of the German army on which both dictators had staked their régimes lay derelict. They could only hope, by desperate and co-ordinated efforts, to achieve sufficient initiative on the Eastern Front and in the Mediterranean, to create a stalemate which would form the basis for a compromise peace. Such was the reality of the situation facing the Axis powers in 1942. Hitler and Mussolini, who had never discussed at their sporadic meetings a joint overall politico-military strategy, were reluctant to face such a logic. The Duce drew the conclusion that Italy was at war primarily with England backed by the United States, and that he could not conduct such an effort without German aid in terms of troops, air force, armaments, and supplies in the Mediterranean theatre. Hitler was driven fatally to seek at whatever the cost a victorious solution of his crusade in the East.

His gamble with Operation 'Barbarossa' included a complementary plan to strike, after the rapid defeat of the Soviet armies, through the Caucasus and to form a massive concentration on the highlands of Anatolia—with or without Turkish consent—whence to strike a decisive blow at the British Empire in the Middle East through Iraq, and onwards to a Napoleonic rendezvous with the Italians and Rommel's Africa Corps at Alexandria and Suez. He outlined this strategic task in his Directive of June 30, 1941. 'Prosecution is envisaged of the fight against the British position in the Mediterranean and the Near East by a concentrated attack from Libya through Egypt, from Bulgaria through Turkey, and also, under certain circumstances, from Transcaucasia through Iran.' [21] With the failure to reach a decision on the Russian Front by the winter of 1941, any operational planning, other than that for the Russian Front itself, was abandoned. The Germans and Italians were faced at the beginning of 1942 with the bankruptcy of the whole conception of a Blitzkrieg against either the West or the East and with the added, and indeed decisive, burden of the entry of the United States into the war, counterbalanced inscrutably by the declaration of war by Japan on the Axis side. It was not only the myth of the Blitzkrieg but also of the Italian 'parallel war' which had vanished by the end of 1941.

Speaking at the Italian Council of Ministers in December 1941, Mussolini made this reluctant admission: 'The war will last long—three to four years. The situation of the Eastern Front will gradually be stabilized. Germany will occupy those territories which she regards as essential. Russia will be liquidated as an opponent. To win the war, Great Britain must be defeated;

either by invasion or the capture of her world bases. The key is the Suez Canal; the attack must come not only from one side, but "also from the East".' c

The entry of the United States into the war produced a threat of massive Anglo-American intervention in the Western Mediterranean and on the Atlantic coast of French West Africa, and with it the increased possibility of the ultimate defection of Vichy and the fading chance of Spanish intervention on the Axis side. An early decision in the North African theatre was now not only imperative for Italy, but also for the Germans, and, for the first time since the outbreak of hostilities, the German High Command was forced to pay increased attention to the Mediterranean war. Mussolini for his part was forced to withdraw his opposition to direct German military aid. The German Air Force had, since October 1940, been operating from Sicily against Alexandria, and after a temporary transfer to Greece for the Crete operation in the summer of 1941, Field Marshal Kesselring, with a German Air Fleet based on Sicily, set up a permanent command at Frascati outside Rome. At the turn of the year the German Expeditionary Corps in Africa under General Rommel was sent to stiffen the Italian positions in Libya and Tripolitania, with a view to achieving a military decision in the direction of Egypt before an Anglo-American threat in the Western Mediterranean might materialize.

The fortunes of the see-saw fighting in the North African desert were linked with the ability to maintain air superiority over the battlefield, and a preponderance of supplies in fuel, munitions, and men at the front. Secure in their bases at Gibraltar, Malta and Alexandria, the British were able to control the skies, and decimate Axis shipping on the sea routes between Italy and North Africa to a sufficient degree to emasculate any serious offensive which might be mounted in the direction of Egypt. The Italian Supreme Command decided therefore to concentrate on Malta, and began planning in earnest early in 1942 for what was christened 'Operation Hercules' to carry out an air-sea combined operation against the island to open on June 10. [22] If this could be timed to coincide with a thrust southwards from the Caucasus in the direction of Egypt, the balance of power in the Mediterranean might be decisively altered in favour of the Axis.

The Germans showed at first little enthusiasm for 'Operation Hercules'. The losses in the Crete operation of 1941 were not forgotten, and, although there were now two German Air Corps in the Mediterranean theatre, one in Sicily and Southern Italy, and another in Greece and on Crete and Rhodes, there was no clear Axis superiority in the air. It was not until April 21, 1942,

c. German Collection, Rome telegram, January 2, 1942. The meeting had taken place on December 27. The Germans received regular reports of these sessions 'through a reliable and well-known source'.

that the German General Staff agreed in principle to the plan. [23] At Berchtesgaden, however, on April 30, the German and Italian leaders met in a military conference, which followed the political discussions at Salzburg on the previous day.[d] The main issue under discussion between the representatives of the Axis General Staffs was the relation between the planned operation against Malta and the opening of the offensive along the North African coast in the direction of the Nile Delta. The thesis of Marshal Cavallero, who had succeeded Badoglio as Chief of the Italian General Staff after the Italian fiasco in Greece in December 1940, was that Malta must be taken before marching on Tobruk, which guarded the eastward land route to Egypt. The German military leaders insisted however that, unless Tobruk were first occupied and the Axis forces reached at least the Egyptian border, the British would take the initiative in the desert with the decisive support of the Royal Air Force based on Malta. Cavallero was forced as usual to accept the German plan. Rommel was to move against Tobruk and up to the frontier of Egypt, starting at the end of May and in a campaign of two weeks. The Malta operation would then begin. Cavallero recorded the debate in his diary: 'As to Malta, the Fuehrer is of the opinion that it must be taken from the British. I point out the difficulties in regard to means and preparations to such an end. The Fuehrer envisages an operation based on the use of troops landed from gliders, who will pave the way for parachutists . . . One must go into action in Libya at the end of May, and on Malta in the middle of June. As an item of curiosity, I show the Fuehrer Napoleon's plan of 1798 for the conquest of the island.' [24]

German air activity in the ensuing weeks of May over the Central Mediterranean enabled the Axis to build up sufficient supplies in North Africa for Rommel to move eastwards from his Libyan bases. [25] He launched his offensive on May 26, by which time the convoy battle in the Central Mediterranean was being lost by the Axis, and the British position in Malta strengthened by reinforcements at heavy sacrifice. On June 21 the Duce wrote to Hitler: 'At the centre of our strategic plan is the problem of Malta . . . August is the last period of the year for carrying out the operation; after that we would have to wait until the summer of 1943, with consequences of which you are fully aware. Besides solving the problem of Mediterranean traffic, the operation against Malta would allow us to dispose freely once more of our air forces, which today are tied to the Mediterranean sector, and will remain so as long as the enemy has Malta. The freeing of the air forces together with the other advantages of taking Malta would mean that our freedom of manoeuvre would be restored—a factor of prime importance for victory.' [26]

The rapid advance of Rommel, however, threw out of gear the strategy of a simultaneous action against Malta and towards Egypt. On June 21 Tobruk

d. For the records of this Salzburg meeting see the translation of the German minutes in the State Department Bulletin No. 367, July 14, 1946, pp. 57–63.

fell to the Axis forces. On the following day Cavallero obtained Mussolini's agreement to issue orders limiting the Axis advance to the Egypt frontier line, and withdrawing a proportion of the air forces for the pending Malta operation. On June 23 Rommel, on receiving Mussolini's directions, told the senior Italian liaison officer attached to his staff that he intended to continue his advance into Egypt, and press on to the Persian Gulf. On the same day Rintelen in Rome informed Cavallero that he had instructions to this effect from the German General Staff. As Kesselring wrote later: 'Rommel at this time had an almost hypnotic influence on Hitler, which made the latter incapable of an objective judgment on the military situation.' [27]

The fatal confirmation that Hitler had personally ordered the abandonment of the Malta operation came on June 23 in his letter to Mussolini. [28] 'Destiny has offered us a chance which will never be repeated in the same theatre of war. The main military objective must be, in my opinion, to exploit it as totally and rapidly as possible. So far I have always had every defeated enemy followed as far and as completely as our forces allowed. The British Eighth Army is practically destroyed. In Tobruk, whose port installations are almost intact, you possess an auxiliary base, Duce, which is all the more important since the British themselves have built a railway from there almost as far as Egypt. If the remnants of this British Army are not now followed by every soldier to his last breath, the same thing will happen which deprived the British of success when, within a very short distance of Tripoli, they suddenly stopped in order to send troops to Greece.e Only this capital error on the part of the British Command made it possible for our efforts to be crowned with the reconquest of Cyrenaica.

'If our forces do not now advance into the heart of Egypt as far as is humanly possible, we shall see first of all an influx of American long-range bombers which will be able to reach Italy easily. Moreover this will be followed by a concentration of all British and American forces, wherever they can be assembled. The situation will very shortly turn against us. But if we pursue the enemy mercilessly they will be undone. This time, under certain conditions, Egypt could be wrested from England. The consequences of such a stroke would be of world-wide importance. Our offensive for which we are opening the road by conquering Sebastopol, will contribute to the fall of the whole Eastern structure of the British Empire. Therefore, Duce, if in this historic hour, which will not be repeated, I can give you a piece of advice straight from my eager heart, it would be: "Order operations to be continued until the British forces are completely annihilated, as far as your Command, and Marshal Rommel, think that they can do it militarily with their forces."

'The goddess of fortune passes only once close to warriors in battle. Anyone who does not grasp her at that moment can very often never touch her again.'

e. In March 1941.

B.F.—2

The gamble was irresistible, and the prize a revolution in the balance of the whole war. Reserves were strained recklessly to the limit. The warnings both of Cavallero, and of Kesselring went unheeded. If Rommel outran his supplies, the disaster would be irretrievable, with the British falling back on their bases at Alexandria and Suez, and the Axis forces stretching their lines of supply and air cover to breaking point.

On June 26, at a conference at his headquarters, Rommel gave his analysis of the tactical situation. The objective of the advance was the position of El Alamein. 'If today the army succeeds in breaking the enemy position, we shall be at Cairo or Alexandria on June 30.'[f]

The Duce crossed to Africa for the final parade, accoutred with the Sword of Islam, while Hitler launched his armies for the long-awaited thrust on the Southern Russian Front. Plans for the administration of an occupied Egypt were already being discussed through diplomatic channels. An Italian civil administrator was nominated,[g] and Hitler agreed that Egypt 'would belong to the Italian zone of influence'. But disappointment was swift, and the doubters were proved to have been justified in their caution. Rommel, now a Field Marshal and military commander designate of Egypt, came to a halt at the Alamein positions.

On his return from the African front, Mussolini wrote to Hitler to explain the reasons for the 'hold up' at El Alamein. They 'could be summed up in one word: the physical exhaustion of the troops, particularly of the Italian infantry'. In an enclosure to his letter dated July 22, Mussolini amplified his views. 'The battle which began on May 26 and which can be called the battle of Tobruk, ended in the first days of July in front of the line of Bir el Alamein. The results of the battle were impressive for a whole enemy army was destroyed, but the objectives hoped for—Cairo and Alexandria—were not attained because, after chasing the enemy for over five hundred kilometres, the Axis troops arrived exhausted. One (Allied) air group and the appearance of a small number of fresh forces sufficed to stop an advancing army which had no reserves to throw into the line . . . The battle of Tobruk is over: the battle of tomorrow will be the battle of the Delta. The time needed to prepare for this new battle must be counted in weeks, but not a single moment must be lost in this competition of speed between the enemy and ourselves.' [29]

In order to carry out Mussolini's instructions on his return from Africa to

f. This optimism was heightened by the climate of deep insecurity in Cairo as reported in the telegrams of the American Mission there, and intercepted by the Italian Military Intelligence. The morale of the British troops was reported low; 1,009 tanks had been lost out of 1,142, and in all the Middle East depots scarcely a hundred remained. (See Faldella, *L'Italia e la Seconda Guerra Mondiale*, p. 451.)

g. Count Mazzolini, a senior diplomatic officer then serving in Italian-occupied Montenegro. After September 1943 he was put in charge of the Foreign Office at Salò.

reinforce the Alamein front and strengthen the Axis hold on the advanced bases and ports in Libya, the Italian reserves of men and shipping intended for the Malta operation were diverted to Rommel. 'Operation Hercules' was abandoned, and with it any hope of regaining the initiative by the Axis in the Mediterranean.

On August 4 Hitler replied sympathetically to Mussolini's comments on the position at El Alamein. 'However long it takes to consolidate our position, I have, like you, given orders to throw into North Africa everything of value in the way of support, reinforcements and replacements . . . It will be difficult and complicated for us to do this. The formation and maintenance of such a strong group of air transport for Africa at the moment of our big offensive in the Caucasus means slowing up the advance of our armoured divisions out there. In the eastern bend of the Don particularly our movements will automatically slow down, because in a vast unroaded zone the necessary fuel supplies can in bad weather often only be brought up by air. There are in addition certain precautionary measures which I am compelled to adopt or keep up in the West.' [30]

The advance of Rommel to the Egyptian border coincided with the launching of the main German offensive on the Russian Front. In order to drive southwards to the oilfields of the Caucasus, it was essential as a first step to establish the German armies in a central strategic position at Stalingrad on the Volga and thus to cover the left flank of the German armies and hold a strong front protecting the southern advance against an eventual Russian counter-offensive. Just as Rommel over-extended his lines of communication and supply in a race for Egypt in June, so the Germans pressed deep into the Caucasus in August, diverting forces needed for the capture of the keypoint of Stalingrad.

Once irretrievably committed on the Southern Russian front, Hitler turned to his Italian ally for reinforcements. Since the dispatch of the first Italian units to Russia in July 1941 as a symbolic counter-aid to the German expeditionary force of Rommel in North Africa, the Germans had been sceptical of the value of an Italian contribution to the war on the Eastern Front. The failure to reach a military decision against Russia by the winter modified this reluctance on the part of Hitler. Ciano had pressed, on Mussolini's instructions, during his visit to Berlin in November 1941, for sending Alpine divisions, and Hitler admitted that especially after the passage into the Caucasus, the intervention of Italian forces would be most useful. The moment had now arrived.

In his letter of August 4 to Mussolini, Hitler wrote: 'I would now like to suggest, Duce, that you allow the three Alpine divisions to be employed alongside our mountain and light divisions on the Caucasus front. This is the more important because the forcing of the Caucasus will bring us into territories which do not belong to the German sphere of interests, and where, therefore, on psychological grounds it would be better if we were accompanied by Italian detachments—if possible by the Alpine Corps, which is the most suitable for this purpose . . . For the rest, I fervently hope that in a few weeks Russia will have lost her most important source of petrol supplies, while in consequence our own disastrous lack of these supplies will be definitely eliminated.'

Mussolini had already been preparing since the previous winter to send the Italian Eighth Army to Russia in spite of gloomy warnings from General Messe, commanding the original Italian force on the Eastern front. Late in July came a formal German request to send Alpine reinforcements to the Caucasus. The proposed move of Italian Alpine troops from the Italo-French frontier to Russia reveals the basic weakness of the Axis military position in the Mediterranean. The failure of a quick gamble to occupy Egypt and gain supremacy in the Eastern Mediterranean exposed the lack of balance of Italy's front in the West. If the Italian Eighth Army went to Russia, the French frontier would be uncovered, and at a moment when there might be an Allied landing in North Africa—an obvious riposte to Rommel's eastward advance—or a coup d'état in France which would create a situation long overdue, in which the unoccupied zone must be taken over by the Axis and the one remaining northern shore of the Mediterranean finally sealed against enemy invasion.

As autumn approached, the military scene on the Axis side was thus dominated by two failures: Russia and Egypt, and a threat: an Allied attack in the Western Mediterranean on North Africa.

The Germans could not afford another indecisive winter in the East.[h] But the personal commitment of Hitler to the Russian war was obsessive and limitless. Everything depended on the early fall of Stalingrad, to which action on other fronts must be subordinated. Just as control of the Ukraine was vital to the Axis in terms of food supplies, so the possession of the Caucasian oilfields was indispensable for the further decisive conduct of the war against the Anglo-Americans. A sinister aspect of the Egyptian gamble had been the exhaustion of stocks. As Keitel had telegraphed to Cavallero on June 27: 'The handing over of 160,000 tons of fuel oil to the Italian Navy has effectively exhausted the last remaining (German) reserves.' [31] After the Italian capture of Mersa Matruh two days later, Cavallero noted in his diary: 'There is no more fuel for the destroyers at Tripoli . . . The oil tanks are empty and two cruisers as well.' [32]

In pressing the Italian Ambassador in Berlin, Alfieri, for three Alpine divisions for the Caucasus, 'a region which interests Italy more than

h. For Hitler's frank review of the German failure in the winter of 1941 see his two hours' conversation alone with Mussolini in the following April at Salzburg. The latter's minutes is in the Hitler-Mussolini Correspondence, *op cit* pp. 119–20.

Germany', Hitler was merely underlining this stark reality. [33] The Caucasian mirage was to dominate Hitler's military thinking through the year. As he told the Italian Fascist Party Secretary, Vidussoni, during the latter's visit to his headquarters, his plan was: 'to push forward from West to East into the South Caucasus in order to reach the oil regions of the British. Once this was accomplished, the British would be prevented further from operating in the Mediterranean.' [34]

With the failure of Rommel to reach Suez, the initiative in the North African theatre passed to the Allies. It was too late in the year to mount the Malta operation, nor indeed would the supply position or the state of Axis air power, after the Egyptian effort, permit it. The Italian parachutists destined for Malta were now fighting as infantry in Egypt. The Italian Command was strangled and tied by the Egyptian front on which, as Cavallero plaintively noted, 'depends the fate of the Middle East'. [35]

It was inconceivable that the Western Allies should not act in such a situation. Both Hitler and Mussolini were, however, convinced that they would not have to face a second front in Europe in 1942.

In a memorandum headed 'Considerations on the military situation', addressed to Cavallero on July 19, Mussolini had expressed his view of Allied strategic intentions. There would be a mounting air offensive against German cities, and on land a front would not be opened 'in Norway nor in any of the countries bordering the Atlantic, nor even in the African territories on the shores of the same ocean (Morocco). The Second Front will take place in the Middle East, that is, in Egypt, Palestine, Syria, Iraq, in countries in which men and equipment can land without fighting in lands which constitute the great crossroads of the British Empire.' [36] As the Fuehrer wrote to Mussolini at the beginning of August, 'I think this Second Front is quite mad. However, since in democracies it is the majority and therefore human folly which makes the decisions, we must reckon with the possibility that madmen will take control and will try to open a Second Front . . . I have nevertheless decided to leave a large number of first-class divisions in the West and even to take more over there so as to have compact armies always at hand for counter-attacks. . . . If the English and Americans really make this mad attempt, they will get unpleasant technical surprises, which from 1942 onwards will make them lose all desire to repeat this experiment on the European continent.

'Unfortunately, for the moment I am not able to leave General Headquarters even for a few days. But as soon as joint operations on the Eastern Front are under way, I hope to make you my promised visit. I am convinced that by then the picture will have become much clearer and will have changed in our favour.' [37]

The summer of 1942 proved to be the watershed of the war, or rather of the two 'parallel wars' fought by the Germans and Italians in the East and in the Mediterranean. It witnessed the end of the last hopes of a Blitzkrieg. On August 17 the American Strategic Air Force began operating against Germany on a massive scale and three weeks earlier, on July 24, after bitter and obstinate staff talks on the highest level, the Allied leaders had decided to launch the planning of a major operation against French North Africa, under the code name of 'Torch', as the first stage of a grand design to liquidate the war in the Mediterranean and a prelude to opening a Second Front in Europe in 1943. Only a drastic revision of a grand strategy together with careful joint planning and a survey of existing military commitments could re-establish the military initiative of the Axis. Both dictators were victims of their own strategic obsessions.

Although Hitler was correct in his view that no landing would take place in the West in 1942, and Mussolini in his in regard to the opening of the Allied air offensive against Germany, neither grasped the intentions of the Allies in the Mediterranean, and their failure to do so changed the course of the war.

Apart from the basic strategic errors of the Axis leadership, the absence of a co-ordinated machinery of military and political consultation was fatal to the conduct of the war. There were no secret military clauses in the Axis Pact, and no formal machinery of consultation on a General Staff level set up after the entry into the war in June 1940. The experts on both sides in practice only met as part of the delegations to summit conferences between the two leaders called hastily and irregularly in moments of crisis.

On the German side neither Keitel nor Jodl visited Italy before the collapse of the Fascist régime in July 1943. Goering, as head of the Air Force and a self-appointed specialist on Italian affairs, was the main channel of intermittent high-level contact. When the Germans were forced to pay urgent and anxious attention to the supply problems of the African Front at the turn of the year 1942, Admiral Doenitz was sent twice on a special mission to Rome. Apart from these sporadic and infrequent visits, the channel of communication ran through the Military Attachés in the two Embassies in Berlin and Rome and the German commanders in Italy to their respective ministries and chiefs in Berlin. The German Military Attaché in Rome, General Enno von Rintelen, was the main and most reliable and perceptive source of information on Italian affairs. He had been in this post since 1936, and was by far the best observer of the Italian scene. His reports and dispatches form the most accurate picture of events as seen from Rome during these years.

Field Marshal Kesselring had been transferred from the Eastern Front to command the German Air Force based on Sicily in November 1941, and was the senior German officer in the Mediterranean theatre. His meetings with Mussolini were held on a more or less regular basis, and in times of crisis almost daily. His headquarters at Frascati just outside Rome was in theory an expeditionary force under Italian command, and nominally directly under the Duce himself, but any real decision in regard to the African war was made in correspondence between Mussolini and Hitler, or by direct orders issued by the latter to the Commander of the German Afrika Corps.

On the Italian side the conduct of the war was the personal province of Mussolini. His meetings with his Chief of the General Staff, Cavallero, and the heads of the Armed Services, although held regularly, bore little resemblance to the equivalent machinery on the Allied side. Marshal Cavallero had succeeded Badoglio in December 1940 after the Greek fiasco. He was both efficient and unpopular in carrying out his functions.

After the First World War he had abandoned his military career to work for the Pirelli rubber company. In 1925 Mussolini appointed him Undersecretary of War, but three years later he returned to business life as a director of the giant Ansaldo shipbuilding yards, and there were certain scandals relating to contracts for building cruisers which were hushed up at the time by the veteran Costanzo Ciano, but which were widely known in Italian military circles.[i] Cavallero was, nevertheless, a man of outstanding gifts of organization and a brilliant administrator.

These characteristics led him inevitably to admire the efficiency of the German war production and military structure, and on his return to active service on the Italian General Staff he became identified at an early stage with the pro-Axis party in Italy. After the outbreak of war, Cavallero headed the liaison office of the Italian High Command with the German military missions in the country. His appointment as Chief of the General Staff in December 1940 was regarded in Berlin as an encouraging sign of future improvement in the Italian conduct of the war and of closer co-operation between the two allies. Cavallero, with his own experience of industry, also made his influence felt in the chaotic sector of Italian war production. His future position would in fact depend largely on relations with the Germans. As Rintelen reported later to Berlin, 'Within the bounds of possibility he (Cavallero) is fulfilling all German wishes.'

From the Italian side, however, as Chief of the General Staff, he was at the mercy of Mussolini's changing attitudes, and the intrigues of the clans within the Italian service ministries. Unless the war in the Mediterranean could be won in the ensuing months, Cavallero would be sacrificed. He was the symbol of the idea of an Italian Blitzkrieg in the Mediterranean, and time was running out. By the beginning of 1942 his position had reached the point of weakening. Rintelen reported on February 13 that this was now endangered.

i. I am specially indebted for the lucid account of the Italian High Command, and also for these facts about Cavallero, to Professor Howard Smyth's article in *Military Affairs* XV, Spring 1951. On the Ansaldo scandal see also Armellini, *Diario di Guerra*, p. 188.

'Cavallero has carried through, in a fashion hitherto unknown in the Italian Armed Forces, a strong military leadership, and in particular he has forced the Navy—in spite of opposition from them—to take action in supplying Libya. He has used his influence with the various military and civilian officials to increase war production. He is working in a close and trustworthy manner with the German military agencies, which is regarded in some circles as going too far.' The Duce was beginning, however, to lose confidence in him, and his career would henceforth increasingly depend on German protection. [39]

Diplomatic relations between the two Powers were also seldom conducted in traditional style. The German Embassy in Rome and the Italian Embassy in Berlin would normally have been regarded as fulfilling such a function. But as the war progressed an unofficial network of contacts grew up between individual Ministers in both countries, Party politicians and specialists, which bedevilled the work of both diplomatic missions to such an extent as to sabotage any efficient conduct of business. The Italian Ambassador in Berlin, Dino Alfieri, was in particular exposed to this climate. He had been nominated to his post as the successor to Count Attolico, who had fought with all his skill and experience to preserve Italian neutrality after September 1939. Alfieri should have been, in theory, a central pivot of contact in the wartime affairs of the two countries. A lawyer from Milan, he had made his career in the Fascist Party along conventional lines, firstly in the Ministry of Corporations at intervals between 1929 and 1936, and then as the first Minister of Popular Culture dealing with press and propaganda from June 1936 until his appointment to Berlin in May 1940. He came to his post with no training in diplomacy, but was viewed by the Nazi leaders as an adequate representative of Italian Fascism. He had established good relations with Goebbels during his period at the Ministry, and Hitler had special regard for him as Alfieri had, at the time of the Austrian crisis in 1934, warmly supported German policy.

Baron Hans Georg von Mackensen, the German Ambassador in Rome, came from a different school. He had succeeded Ulrich von Hassell as Ambassador in Rome in April 1938, and his predecessor, like Attolico in Berlin, had striven both to avoid the outbreak of hostilities in Europe and to avert the fatal commitments which led to the Axis Pact. Hassell was later to perish as one of the civilian leaders in the July Plot in 1944. Mackensen was an old-world diplomat, son of the Field Marshal of the First World War, and his innate correctness of approach to the problems of diplomacy made it difficult for him to interpret with any subtlety or skill the irresponsible and often contradictory mechanism of Roman politics.

The real decisions relating to the conduct of the war by the Axis did not pass, however, through such channels. They were made at irregular summit conferences between the two dictators, and initiated and implemented by unofficial visitors at all levels from both sides; from Berlin, in particular by Goering or Ribbentrop and occasionally Himmler, and from Rome by Ciano and on occasion special economic or military missions.

The two Embassies in Berlin and Rome operated therefore in an atmosphere of resentment and confusion, plagued by sporadic personal visits of political and military figures of varying importance reflecting a criss-cross of private intrigues and conflicting organs of power, bedevilling and impeding the routine business of the official representatives. In addition, each political organ and Party boss in both countries established his own unofficial agents. As Alfieri wrote on one occasion in a private letter to Ciano:

'I commend to you our famous colleagues who arrived from Italy in Germany—a real plague with their self-advertisement without limits or decency . . . They write, report, try to unsettle the Embassy, better themselves with the Germans and work for their masters. I can assure you that I keep my eye on all of them, otherwise I would need my own *homme d'affaires*. I think the best *homme d'affaires* for me remains my dear and good Galeazzo in Rome.' [40]

In a further letter to the head of Ciano's private office, D'Ajeta, Alfieri complained of the way in which the visit of the Italian Minister of Agriculture to Berlin had been arranged by the latter through the Agricultural Attaché in the German Embassy in Rome without anybody's knowledge. 'All this is in conflict with the agreement between the two foreign ministries, the basis of which is that the visits of Italians to Germany must be organized through the Italian Embassy in Berlin and visits of Germans through the German Embassy in Rome. If this system had been followed, a great many misunderstandings would have been avoided.' [41]

The lengthening of the conflict had also revealed the artificiality of the Axis alliance. The longer the war lasted the greater the aversion towards Germany in political circles in Italy. In Italian eyes the justification of the Axis Pact and the linking of the destiny of Fascist Italy to that of Germany could only be the achievement of quick results, of historic Italian aims in the Mediterranean, the Adriatic, and Africa, as the appendix of a German victory in Western Europe. Such a programme failed even before it could be implemented. By the autumn of 1942 the temporary optimism which had marked Italy's declaration of war two years earlier had evaporated, and a sense of fear and frustration pervaded the Italian scene. Historically Italy had always sought freedom of action; to ally with one great power or another. The basic principle of her foreign policy had always been freedom of choice. What alternative now lay ahead if only Germany were left in Europe as a great power? And if Germany were defeated, what would be the fate not only of the Fascist régime, but of Italy herself? There was also a strong feeling that Germany did not sincerely regard Italy as an equal partner, and that the war was being conducted without any regard for Italy's susceptibilities or interests. In spite of protestations to the contrary, Germany had penetrated economically into the one Italian sphere of influence in Europe, namely the Balkans. Italy was now totally dependent on Germany both militarily and economically for the continuance of her war effort, and there was no frank discussion or even propaganda as to the future construction of a New Europe in event of victory, nor of Italy's place in such a world.

Disillusionment in Italy in regard to the German ally in its turn stimulated criticism of the régime itself, calling in question the prestige and personal authority of the Duce.

CHAPTER TWO

TWENTY YEARS AFTER

ON JULY 21, 1942 the Duce returned from his African expedition, leaving behind him a tactical and strategic stalemate. As he wrote in a memorandum the next day, 'We must rake up everything that can be taken without danger from Libya and send for everything else from Italy.' [1] But he knew intuitively that a final chance had been missed to redress the balance of military power in favour of the Axis in Africa. His sense of an irretrievable loss of initiative in the conduct of the war in the Mediterranean extended to a profound weariness in the management of affairs at home. For the first time in his career, the burden of responsibility became unbearable and was outwardly manifested in a breakdown in health.

At the end of July, Mussolini left Rome for the Adriatic resort of Riccione, and spent the remainder of the summer there, partly with his mistress Clara Petacci, whose existence and the activities of whose family were at last precipitating a political scandal on the fringes of government circles. The physical crisis in the Duce's health intensified during the ensuing months, coming to a head in October. Apart from three brief visits to Rome, he was either at Riccione or his retreat in the Romagna at La Rocca delle Caminate, between the end of July and the middle of October. Such absences of the Head of State from the seat of authority inevitably disturbed the routine of administration, and the confusion was the greater because of the peculiar climate of Mussolini's personal rule.

Throughout the twenty years of the régime, the traditional organs of rule had atrophied or been abolished, and a strange and unique amalgam of uncoordinated bodies and conventions had taken their place, all stemming from the immanent authority of one man. The formal structure of Fascist power lay in the national machinery of a totalitarian party. Its roots as a revolutionary movement had been in origin regional. The organization of the March on Rome, and the capture of the State machine in October 1922 had been the work of the provincial organizations. Both the strength and the weakness of the Party in its early history was its loose and decentralized structure. The authority of the original Milan Fascio, for example, was never imposed on groups outside that city. As Mussolini wrote in July 1919, 'The Fasci are not, do not wish to be, and cannot become a Party. Fascism has neither statutes nor rules.' [2] It was not until November 1921 that a Party statute and a national directorate were set up and a Director-General appointed to curb the activities of the regional Action Squads. Indeed, underlying and permeating the whole history of Italian Fascism were two opposed conceptions of party organization within the ranks of the leaders of the first generation: the Jacobins of Italian Fascism, represented by Roberto Farinacci, who believed in a highly organized revolutionary machine to safeguard the permanent revolution: and the believers, such as Giuseppe Bottai, in an opposition within the Party which should be a decentralized system of discussion clubs with voluntary membership and freedom of speech. The issue between these two opposing views of the nature of Party government was settled early in the history of the movement. With the parliamentary crisis after the murder of the Socialist leader Matteotti in 1924, and the vertiginous decline in popularity of the Fascist Party throughout Italy, the extreme elements of the Action Squads now incorporated in the Party Militia, and with Farinacci as their spokesman, won the day—and decisively. It was he who, as Party Secretary after the crisis of January 1925, broke the original Fascist Party machine which had carried through the political revolution three years earlier. He also set the frame for the future development of the whole movement, and the effects of his draconian actions were never basically reversed. By massive purges of the membership, he broke the strength of the provincial bosses and their organizations, and the political fiefs of the city states of Northern Italy, which had been the strength of the early Fascist movement, lost their independence. The elements of a centralized Party machinery in Rome were now set up. It is therefore primarily due to Farinacci that the Italian Fascist Party assumed a rigid frame. His successors followed his example. The Party machine became increasingly organized on lines of military discipline, and it was the Party Secretary himself who now controlled all local appointments at all levels of the Party hierarchy, with power to dismiss any nominee. The general result of such a procedure was to replace the provincial 'tyrants' by local clans, whose existence and enjoyment of office depended on the favours of a central secretariat in Rome.[a]

In the inter-war years the functions of the Party Secretary extended into the machinery of government. Already in 1932 he had exclusive control of Party affairs, and the selection of the central Party directorate lay in his hands. He himself was always a personal nominee of the Duce. The Party

a. For instance, Starace who was Party Secretary from 1931 to 1939, appointed half the new provincial secretaries in a purge in 1929.

Directorate itself was a body meeting weekly, consisting of three Vice-Secretaries, the Administrative Secretary, and eight nominated members, acting as a sort of Party Cabinet. Below this body lay a National Council, consisting of the 92 provincial secretaries, the members of the Directorate, certain honorary nominees, and a number of national inspectors. The essential function of this body was to impress upon the provinces the unity of the Party through directives issued at the meetings held usually once or twice a year, and often presided over by the Duce himself. In 1938 the Party statute was again revised, and the Secretary now became both Secretary of State in the Council of Ministers, Secretary of the Grand Council, leader of the youth organizations, and of para-Party organizations. In addition he had in practice a certain control over the activities of the Fascist syndicates. With the outbreak of war in 1940 the activities of the Party, under the direct control of the Secretary, extended into such fields as the mobilization of shop-workers in agriculture, and setting up committees—as at the time of the Ethiopian war—to attempt to regulate and control prices.

The Party machine had its own liaison office with the Militia and its own political police organization. Through the provincial secretaries a machinery characteristic of Italian Fascism developed alongside that of the Prefects and of the traditional civil administration, and through the Party national headquarters from time to time it would send out requests for secret information on local reactions to Party politics, just as in the same way the Prefects would report to the Ministry of the Interior.

Throughout the twenty years of Fascist rule there was a continuous debate on the concept of Party membership, and thus on the relationship of the Party to the population as a whole. The three early tests of membership had been: participation in the March on Rome, membership of the Party during the Matteotti crisis, or later training in the Party youth organizations and special schools. The original apparatus was manned by the pre-1922 generation, and as late as 1934 two-thirds of the provincial organizations were still controlled by members of the old guard of the Action Squads. In 1923 recruitment was halted and a temporary stop put to the election of new members. The lists were open again after the murder of Matteotti the following year. In 1932 regulations were enforced whereby civil servants, school and university teachers, and officers in the Army were obliged to take out Party cards, thus widening the circle of membership; but it was seldom that any member of this generation reached any responsible office within the Party itself. In 1938, in an endeavour to meet the basic problem of the second generation of Fascists, Party membership was thrown open to the graduates of the now massive youth organizations under Party control. In 1940 the lists were opened to all members of the armed forces, with the result that the total figures reached over three and a half million, in addition to the now highly developed youth cadres of nearly eight million.

From the time of the take-over of power in October 1922 until the outbreak of war in 1940, the organs of Fascist control had been gradually extended and perfected, invading the jurisdiction and prerogatives of the traditional State machinery. Throughout the whole system of government ran a basic dualism of authority and activity, ranging from the undefined relations between Mussolini as Prime Minister, appointed with all legal propriety in 1922, and the King as constitutional monarch, through the ill-defined and parallel existence of the Party and the Civil Service, the Militia and the Army, to the provincial Party secretaries and the Prefects.

Finally, as a cornerstone of a supreme collective authority within the régime developed the functions of the Grand Council of Fascism. This unique body was to play a decisive part in the history of the movement. It was set up originally early in 1923 as a sort of central committee of the Party, and indeed as 'shadow Cabinet'. In 1932 it was transformed from a Party institution into the highest governing authority of the Fascist State, by-passing the traditional Council of Ministers or Government, and co-ordinating and integrating all the activities of the régime. As Farinacci put it, 'The State and the Party have, in the Grand Council . . . the unifying centre through which the antithesis between Party and government is rendered no longer possible.' [3] There was even a touch of Platonic ritual in the conception of a nocturnal council to make the Laws of the State. The Party Secretary acted, among his other functions, as secretary of the Grand Council, and, in the absence of the Duce, as its Chairman. The Grand Council, among its many functions, regulated the succession to the Party leadership, and just before the war—to the controlled fury of the Sovereign—that of the Crown itself. The membership of the Grand Council consisted of some twenty individuals who represented the élite of Fascism. There were the life members, and these were the survivors of the Quadrumvirs, the leaders of the columns in the March on Rome; then the holders of key offices, such as the Cabinet Ministers, the President of the Special Tribunal, the Party Secretary and vice-Secretary, selected members of the Party Militia, and the President of the Institute of Fascist Culture. Finally, certain special members were appointed for three years; four Ministers and Party Secretaries, and 'eminent men'; of the revolution. The Grand Council provided the audience for the historic decisions of the Fascist government, and it was at a meeting on December 8, 1939, that the principle of Italian non-belligerency in the war was enunciated. But no minutes were ever kept or any vote taken. The body had not been summoned since that date.

The machinery of the Fascist Party, together with its armed embodiment in the Militia and with the Grand Council of Fascism as its apex, governed

Italy through its own special organs and by extensive and persistent penetration of the three traditional pillars of administration and authority—the Army, the Police, and the Civil Service.

The Legislature had survived the shock of the March on Rome, and with the revised electoral procedure of a single list, continued even after the Matteotti crisis and the secession from Parliament of the 'Aventini'—the opposition deputies in 1924—as a rump assembly. But the fiction of such an elective body was eliminated in December 1938, and replaced by a nominated Chamber, the deputies being National Councillors of the Fascist Party and appointed as such partly by the Party machine and partly from the various professional Corporations of employers, technicians, the professions, and the workers. To these were added *ex officio* the high officials of the Party, the holders of ministerial office, and the Undersecretaries of State. In violation of the constitutional statute of the Kingdom of Italy, this legislative body was sanctioned by a law passed by the expiring Chamber of Deputies and ratified by the Senate and the King.[b] Indeed, the continued existence of the Senate and undefined privileges of the Crown were the sole remaining fragments of the edifice of the Albertine Statute of 1848. It was primarily against these two surviving historical enclaves that the Fascist revolution stopped short of a totalitarian frame.

The entry of Italy into the war in 1940 produced first hidden and then revealed pressures, which brought to light the essential flaws in the whole structure of Fascism. By 1942, when the conflict approached its military crisis, the internal weakness of the régime became manifest. Apart from the inconveniences of the highly personal rule and style of government of the Duce himself, the rigid and conformist structure of a mammoth Party machine became progressively exposed. As in the field of State administration, so in the higher levels of the Party, Mussolini's inevitable solution was a series of 'changes of the guard', exhausting the cadres and depressing their morale. After twenty years of government, and according to paper planning, a new and enthusiastic generation trained in the youth organizations, the Militia, and the Party schools, should be awaiting in the wings, in fervent Fascist enthusiasm, their summons onto the stage. Their absence was only too painfully apparent, and the exigencies of the war effort, quite apart from the peculiar mentality of the Duce himself, made any drastic reform of the Party machine out of the question. It was this problem of the second generation, or as it was called 'the second wave', which was the recurrent and central theme in Party discussions in the late 1930's and again during the first two

b. As Federzoni wrote later: 'The salient episode in the demolition of the monarchy was the inauguration of the Chamber of Fasci and Corporations.' Federzoni, *Memorie*. XIX. July 16, 1946, extracts in the weekly paper 'Indipendente'.

years of the war. With the failure of the long-expected élite cadres of Fascist youth to appear, the only temporizing recourse in each crisis within the Party would be a search for the ghosts of the old discarded leaders of the Action Squads of the 1920's, whose enthusiasm could not be recaptured and whose very existence was difficult to trace. The fluctuating history of the Fascist Party in the later months of its life revolves round this antithesis and the unreal choice between the survivors of the revolutionary generation and the 'second wave'.

In December 1941 Mussolini appointed as Party Secretary a young man called Vidussoni. He was 28 years old, and had not yet finished his Law studies. He came from the model provincial Fascist world of Trieste. As a Militia officer he had been wounded in the fighting during the Civil War in Spain and decorated with the military Gold Medal. As Ciano put it, 'One cannot say more about him.' (Ciano, *op cit*. December 26, 1941.) He was not intelligent, but equally not disloyal, and he was to act as a kind of cheerful and eager aide-de-camp to Mussolini. As the latter expressed it in his speech to the Party Directorate on January 3, 1942,[c] the nomination of Vidussoni was 'a symbol of youth and heroic commitments. One has now reached a point where the generation which made the Fascist revolution has become old, feeble, or ill, and is on the decline, while the new generation is on the move . . . The tasks of the Party are in the first place of a moral nature, and lie in a purely political sphere, and these tasks, from the point of view of the State, are above all a police function. The more successful the work of the Party in the moral sphere, the less work for the police.'

The Duce drew attention to the essential importance of the millions of members of the Fascist youth organizations, where 'the loss of 400,000 Party members is unimportant in itself'. In accordance with customary rhetoric, mention of the faithful was followed by that of the enemy within, in this case the too familiar caricature and butt—the Italian middle classes—together with the external scarecrow, international capitalism. Regarding the first, 'We will bring these fat sheep into the pen and shear him'; as to the second, 'On January 3, 1925, we were faced with the internal opposition of the Aventine.[d] Today we have to deal with a much more powerful Aventine, which stretches from Moscow to Washington and is created by capitalism. The inner relationship between Bolshevism and capitalism has not surprised me.'

c. These speeches of Mussolini to the Party Directorate were usually kept secret, although the Germans always had a reliable informer. The date of at least one of the two or three meetings of this body held each year was fixed on January 3—the anniversary of Mussolini's ferocious speech in the Chamber after the Matteotti crisis announcing the establishment of totalitarian government. The above quotations come from the German Collection, Mackensen telegram, January 14, 1942, reported 'from a reliable source'.

d. The parliamentary opposition which walked out of the Italian Chamber as a consequence of the events following the murder of the Socialist leader, Matteotti.

Early in 1942 the Duce reviewed the activities of the Fascist Party in a tour through the main regions of Italy. A summary of these speeches reveals a familiar series of propaganda themes; the need for a link between the first and second generations of the movement, and the resistance of the middle classes to integration within the system. For example, when addressing the provincial secretaries in the following month in Umbria and Tuscany, the Duce sounded this note. 'The youth of Italy has been softened by too many favours from Fascism, and in the main the intellectuals have contributed by their abstention from the régime.' And again, 'We must, and with desperation, become a serious people.'

This last grand tour of the Duce is a vivid illustration of his lightning changes of mood and alternating gusts of exultation, cynicism, and pessimism. When speaking in the historical Fascist territory of Emilia and the Romagna he declared his faith in the world of the Action Squads. 'There is no doubt that the region between Piacenza, the Apennines and the Po is a region which has always had a decisive importance in the history of Italy. One must bear in mind that the population lives for the main part in the plain, and that the road system is highly developed. One can mobilize the whole population of Emilia in four hours [e] . . . It is a mass of decided, strong, intelligent men, who are always available. Today it is clear that whoever possesses the mass of this quality has, one can say, in his hands the key to the general critical situation.'[4]

At the conclusion of this tour, the Duce presided over two meetings of the Party Directorate at the end of May 1942. By this time he was speaking under the influence of an unbalanced internal economy, rising prices, and evidence of corruption. 'I have no longer any doubt in regard to lack of discipline, sabotage, and passive resistance all along the line. The régime is exhausting itself, wearing itself out, and literally consuming scores of comrades in the Party organizations and the Ministries, and we are almost back where we were.' But in time of war, and particularly at a period of imminent decline in military fortunes, there was little chance of considering a basic purge within or outside Party circles. This outburst was in itself an implied criticism of the Party hierarchy on whom should, in principle, depend the enforcement of civil discipline and obedience, and the fight against corruption.

The maintenance of the Italian war effort was dependent not only on massive German aid, but also on the resistance of the Home Front. 'New military disasters could only be borne if the whole nation were prepared to face up to them.'[5] Effective political control was in turn bound up with the morale and prestige of the Party, and in the last resort of the Militia. At the same time the whole structure of Italian government was characterized by an ill-defined

e. It was a historical irony that this type of mobilization was carried out later on by the partisans.

dyarchy ranging from the relations and balance of authority between the King and Mussolini, to the respective functions of the Party regional machine headed by the Federal secretaries and the civil administration represented by the Prefects nominated by the Crown; the competing roles of the Militia and the royal military police in keeping public order, and the position of the Army in relation to both bodies. Within the confusion of these rival organs of control and unresolved dualisms, Mussolini had imposed his own supreme authority, and in a sense his unique position, as he conceived it, depended on its continuance.

By 1942 Benito Mussolini embodied the following attributes of power. As Duce of Fascism he controlled in the last resort all manifestations of the Party, changing its Secretary at will; packing the National Directorate, and presiding over the supreme organ and symbol of Fascist power, the inner conclave of the leadership, the Grand Council, whose theoretical functions had no counterpart in the traditional structure of the Italian State, regulating not only the life of the Party and its armed embodiment in the Militia, but even charged with deciding the succession to the Duce, and to the Throne itself.

In keeping with conventional usage, however, the Duce of Fascism was also Prime Minister of a government, appointed with due form by the King in October 1922. In virtue of such an office, Mussolini was received in audience twice a week, and the Monarch was duly informed of the progress of public affairs, keeping his own counsel and stretching to the limit the fiction that he was dealing with a constitutional Prime Minister. Throughout twenty years the main rôle of King Victor Emmanuel had been to keep up appearances, and when the inevitable crisis of the régime came, it was Mussolini who proved to be the self-deluded victim of the fictitious relationship between the two men.

It was, however, not only as President of the Council, or Prime Minister, that Mussolini held supreme executive authority. On the outbreak of war he assumed the office of Minister of War and the Commandership in Chief of the Armed Forces, a position constitutionally held by the Monarch. The service Ministries were thus directly subordinate to him, and the ultimate responsibility for the conduct of the war lay exclusively in his hands.

In dealing with routine affairs, civilian and military, Mussolini had evolved over the years his own peculiar and highly personal style. He was methodical in planning his day and his time-table rarely varied, but he was capricious in employing any machinery of consultation, and destructive of any ordered dispatch of business. As Bottai put it, 'Investiture to office by rotation and changes of the guard were his highly personal method. Names were chosen by chance, often from the parliamentary directory, and often even mistakes of name were made.' Italy was governed by clans of functionaries and not by a ruling class. 'If three Ministers agree on a subject, it is a conspiracy . . .

the balcony of the Palazzo Venezia has completely substituted the Council of Ministers and even the Grand Council itself.' [6]

The Council of Ministers was a disjointed body of subordinates, summoned on paper to meet at 10.30 on the last Saturday morning of every month at the Viminale,[f] but the date was never fixed in practice and meetings were often postponed at the last moment. In principle an agenda of draft legislation was prepared for discussion between the Ministers. In practice the intermittent occasions on which the Council of Ministers was summoned were employed by Mussolini to clarify in confidence his thoughts aloud, and usually a second meeting had to be summoned to deal with the routine business.

One such session is refreshingly described by Giuseppe Gorla, who was Minister of Public Works from October 1940 to February 1943.[7] 'Suddenly the door of the President's study opened, and Mussolini appeared. Everyone was silent, and saluted in Roman fashion . . . In front of each Minister was placed a sheet containing the agenda, which is very long. It contains a list of draft legislation to be introduced for the approval of the Ministers. Mussolini having sorted out the documents in front of him begins to speak, but does not follow the agenda, and announces that he has confidential statements to make to the Council alone.' Gorla, seeing that the secretary of the office of the President was keeping no record, began to take notes. 'Mussolini notices almost at once and asks me what I am doing. I tell him. I stop for a moment. "Do not do so. You can see that even the secretary of the Council is keeping no record, on my orders. Because I want to talk freely and I can only do so in this body which alone can keep a secret. Not even in the Grand Council can I speak openly, as the walls seem to have ears . . . Yes, in eighteen years, nothing has been repeated outside this room. Perhaps because the ministers share the responsibility. So no records." '[g]

The Council of Ministers was thus a private sounding-board rather than a consultative body. The effective conduct of business radiated from the Duce's private office, the Sala del Mappamondo in Palazzo Venezia, in individual audiences and myriad telephone calls. On a normal morning when in Rome, Mussolini would usually receive the head of the political police (the OVRA), the Foreign Minister, the Minister of Popular Culture who controlled the Press, the Secretary of the Party, the head of the Ministry of the Interior, and the Chief of the Armed Forces. In addition a mass of reports and memoranda would filter on to his desk through the private secretariat, police and spy reports from the competing and rival agencies of the Interior, the Chief of Police, the special offices of the Party and—separate again—of the Militia and of the Military Intelligence; reports of the Prefects from the provinces, the telegrams of the Foreign Office, and the war bulletins and memoranda

f. The building of the Ministry of the Interior.
g. Gorla continued to take notes under the table, and at subsequent meetings.

from the Chief of the General Staff. These documents would be scrutinized without minuted comment, and returned with a bare majestic 'M' in blue pencil. Decisions would usually be taken verbally or by telephone.

The reading of the Italian and foreign press occupied a central position in this activity, and the daily directives to the Ministry of Popular Culture were the essence and revelation of the personal direction of the Duce.[h] A study of these directives would give a detailed picture at any given moment of the shifts and trends of Italian policy. A change in headlines or pagination in the totally-controlled Press would indicate imminent and future developments and recent decisions. This was Mussolini's real world, and the measure of his genius lay essentially in the manipulation of the masses by the written and spoken word. But his increasing isolation in recent years from the public arena had led to a certain loss of contact with the Italian people. His last public appearance of national importance had been on the balcony of Palazzo Venezia to announce the declaration of war in June 1940. The explanation of the 'mission' of the Fascist government came to depend increasingly on the written directives to the Press, but the brutal reality of military defeat and stalemate, of Allied bombing and short rations deprived words of their meaning, and under such an impact Fascism began at last to exhaust its vocabulary. In a sense Mussolini governed Italy as if he were running a personal newspaper single-handed, setting the type, writing the leaders, interviewing everybody, chasing the reporters, paying the informers, sacking staff incessantly, defining the policy to be adopted and the causes to be defended, and basically ignoring the supreme responsibility of political power as extraneous to the business.

The twentieth anniversary of the March on Rome fell on October 28, 1942. It had been hoped to celebrate the occasion with due pomp and to demonstrate to the Italian people the fruits of twenty years of the Party and the Régime. There had indeed been plans initiated in 1938 for a world exhibition, and even for a moment a tidy and artistic notion of the Duce to enter the conflict at such a moment. But under existing circumstances the ceremonies were by his orders to be muted. The historical significance of the occasion was unhappily dwarfed by the harsh realities of war and the first perceptible signs of the disintegration of the very structure of the régime, whose creation was to be the solemn subject of celebration.

Hitler wrote with turgid rhetoric to excuse his absence from the celebrations of the sister revolution. 'Comrade and Reichsleader Dr Ley,[i] who has been chosen, at the invitation of the Fascist Party, to lead the German delegation to Italy, will hand you this letter. In it I wish above all to express my

h. See Ciano's remarks on these activities. Castellano, *Come Firmai L'Armistizio*, p. 34.
i. Ley was head of the Labour Front, the organization of the Nazi Trades Unions.

own indissoluble links with you and those of the National-Socialist and the
Fascist movements. I am quite clear that your historic March, twenty years
ago, introduced a turning-point in world history. The fact that our democratic
opponents do not grasp this is not exclusively due to their ill-will, nor is it
based on the selfish interests which they represent. For just as the deaf can
hardly understand the greatness of a musical genius or the blind the beauty
of a picture and thereby appreciate the significance of its creator, even less
can the average and spiritually hidebound leaders of the ordinary middle-
class parliamentary system, even with the best will in the world, judge the
greatness of an historical turning-point and its leading personalities, through
whom one period of history is brought to an end and a new one opened.

'While you, Duce, led your Fascist revolution to victory, I was still fighting
for power with varying degrees of fortune. The prelude to my struggle ended
in a grave collapse and for me personally and with over a year's imprisonment.
Although the paths by which the two revolutions came to power were so
different, yet I am perfectly convinced, Duce, that you were the first man to
succeed in combating Marxism not by police methods, but by overcoming it
through a force able to create a new state and community. You removed the
mass of its followers and bound them to a new idea.

'I am perhaps, Duce, better able than any other man of our time to
appreciate the historic greatness of your struggle, having had, like you, to
battle against a current which is called public opinion, and which embraces
all existing interests, including human folly and cowardice, unhappily so
deeply rooted. This is not a conviction acquired after the event, but only the
reiteration of what has motivated me ever since, in 1921 and 1922, I saw
from afar the emergence and finally the acceptance of you and your
movement. That this appreciation of your personality, Duce, came so late, is
to be found simply in the fact that the destiny of my own people weighed so
terribly on us and on myself, that we were so engaged in a life and death
struggle in our own country, that the outside world and its problems seemed
to have little importance for us.

'But Duce, ever since in your heroic struggle for power you became a
symbol for the whole world and for me in particular, you have acquired at
least one sincere admirer, besides the millions of supporters in your own
country—and I can add, also a follower in the outside world—and that is
myself. I have often studied in retrospect the phases of your Fascist revolution, and I am always convinced anew that fate must have willed that two
men and two revolutions in Europe should determine the features of the New
Age. What separates us are only those racial characteristics, whose imprint is
given us by blood and history and by the limits of vital space defined by
geopolitics. What repeatedly brings us together is not only the conviction of
the need to defend in common our ancient continent against a world which
threatens it, but a vast sum of past historical events and finally the common

struggle which we have to sustain for the very existence of our two revolutions.

'By this common struggle we hand on to posterity a heritage which, more than anything else, binds together not only both our Revolutions, but also our peoples. I am convinced that later generations in Italy and in Germany, so long as they are reared and led in a National-Socialist and Fascist framework, will be influenced mutually in their mental attitudes by the joint and mighty struggle of today, and above all, Duce, by the friendship of men which will one day be historic. Thus, in these days, I feel to be personally with you and your work, and with the warmest good wishes. I would so much have liked to come and tell you this myself.

'But, in the first instance, on this twentieth anniversary of your March on Rome, your people should consecrate themselves wholly to their Duce and not be in any way distracted from this. In the second place, the situation in the East is not yet such as to allow me to be away from here for a relatively long period with a clear conscience . . . Although I am surrounded here at my headquarters by so many people, I am living in the Ukraine in solitude, as befits the essence of my task; and you will understand, Duce, that it would be a real rest for me to spend a few days in a more beautiful country. But, since I took over direct command of the army, I am unhappily more and more tied to the telephone and tape-machine and above all to the eventuality of having to intervene in the East or West at any time in the space of a few hours.' [8]

In thanking Hitler for his congratulatory message Mussolini wrote: 'The arrival of the mission headed by Doctor Ley, and the participation of the German press and people in our twentieth anniversary celebrations, created a profound and welcome impression not only in Fascist circles, but among the Italian people at large. Unfortunately our enemies took pleasure in disturbing this solemn occasion—on purpose—by massive bombardments on Milan, Genoa, and Savona.' [9]

Mussolini had intended to make a speech to a mass gathering of the Party leaders on October 29, but orders were given to cancel everything. Ciano noted in his diary: 'Three current interpretations: that the doctors have forbidden the strain of a long speech; that Mussolini does not wish to say anything until the Libyan offensive is decided; that he intends to make big changes in the Party and, as would be logical, he wants to speak to the new leaders.' [10]

The only public ceremony held to celebrate the March on Rome was the inauguration of the Museum of the Revolution. It was the first time that Mussolini had appeared in public since his illness. It was a cool and hollow occasion, but with a harsh significance. It was an implicit and unexpressed indictment of the Party, whose triumphant accession to power twenty years earlier was the formal subject of commemoration. As Ciano wrote, 'The organization of the ceremony was far from coming up to par, lacking even the least sense of comradeship among its members. The fact is that the present secretariat of the Party is made up of obscure men, to whom we are in turn unknown . . . On this very day of the recurrence of the Fascist celebration, the inefficiency of the Party is felt more strongly than ever.' [11]

The real celebrations of the historical triumph of Italian Fascism in 1922 were marked by the British in Libya and the Royal Air Force over the towns of Northern Italy.

CHAPTER THREE

THE PROBLEM OF THE SUCCESSION

•-•

'FROM OCTOBER 1942 onwards I had a constant and growing presentiment of the crisis which was to overwhelm me. My illness greatly influenced this.'[a] The rumour in informed circles in Rome that expert medical diagnosis showed that the Duce had no more than four or five months to live produced consternation. On September 26 Ciano received a letter from his wife, who had just arrived at the Rocca delle Caminate, and which 'disturbs me a great deal . . . Under the circumstances, for the Duce to be ill would be really disastrous.'[1] Bottai saw Mussolini on the evening of October 7 on his return to Rome: 'His face grey and ashen, the cheeks sunken, his look troubled and tired, his mouth expressing a sense of bitterness, and thus revealing clearly the illness which, according to rumour, has attacked him again. But the man does not seem to be so much ill as dejected and saddened, no longer fighting triumphantly against age . . . He has in himself killed the man that he was. All bonds of confidence are broken. Even to ask after his health makes him suspicious.'[2]

The physical incapacity of the Duce created a vacuum at the summit of power and a crisis of leadership which coincided with a weakening of national confidence in the régime, both in its handling of internal affairs and in view of the mounting tide of military defeat. For the first time since 1924 there were spreading doubts as to the continued viability of the personal rule of the Duce, and agitated speculation as to the political succession in the event of his disappearance or demise.

The machinery of Fascism provided in theory for such a situation. It was one of the functions of the Grand Council to maintain a list of deputy leaders, the senior of whom would receive formal and automatic nomination. Such a convention had been under cursory review in the months following

a. *Pontine Notes.* Written during the internment of Mussolini at Ponza after July 26, 1943. See p. 547.

the first grave crisis of Fascism in 1924. It was in no way geared to the political realities of the régime, but was conceived in a moment of fleeting danger. The only personality designated was Count Costanzo Ciano, who had been intimately concerned with the inner councils of the movement at the time of the March on Rome and was one of the leading figures of the early Party. He had been nominated the first President of the Fascist Chamber on its inauguration, but died shortly afterwards in the summer of 1939. He had been an honorific figure, trusted by Mussolini, and unhampered by a following in the Party machine. His very designation as the official successor to the Duce signified his lack of political significance. The Grand Council met after his death, in December 1939, but to discuss the realities of Italian policy in regard to the outbreak of war in Europe. The theoretical issue of the succession was not raised, and the Council itself ceased to meet.

The trusted intimacy of Count Costanzo Ciano with the Duce was perhaps more significant in forwarding the career of his son, Galeazzo.[3] After brilliant high school and law studies in Rome, the young man sought to make his mark in the journalistic and literary clans of the capital which passed for the intellectual circles of the régime. The young Ciano was soon at ease in this café society [b] of political leader-writers, critics, and writers, and marked by his contact with this climate of licensed comment on the régime. Coming from a prosperous Leghorn family with widespread shipping interests he typified that upper middle class which had viewed with benevolence the rise to power of Fascism, but which did not seek advancement through the channels of the Party. His ambitions, unfulfilled as a playwright, soon changed direction. He sat for the regular Foreign Service examination in 1925, and passed among the first successful candidates. He was first posted to Brazil and then to China. In 1929 Ciano returned to Rome on his appointment as secretary at the Vatican Legation. It was at this time, through his sister, that he met Edda Mussolini, and his marriage to the Duce's daughter the following year was to launch him into the centre of the government.

His career henceforth was the personal creation of the Duce. In August 1933 he was appointed head of the Press Office in the Foreign Ministry and a year later Undersecretary in the newly created Ministry of Press and Propaganda. In 1935 he was appointed Minister. In this capacity he was the intimate spokesman of Mussolini in a characteristic field of Fascist activity, and the channel of interpretation, through the organs of a controlled Press, of the manifestations of the régime. The young unsuccessful playwright had become the intimate interpreter of the veteran journalist. Mussolini gave his affection easily, but his confidence rarely. Since the death of his brother

---

b. See a brief description of this world—for example, the 'third room' of the Café Aragno in Rome—in Bastianini, *Uomini Cose Fatti*, pp. 228–9. This meeting place was later closed on Mussolini's orders.

Arnaldo he had accepted no collaborator. His son-in-law seemed destined to fill the void.

In June 1936, at the age of 33, Ciano became Foreign Minister, a post hitherto held by his father-in-law.

The influence and prestige of Ciano in Italian politics was both subtle and fragile. He was in the last resort immutably dependent on his father-in-law, and possessed no constant personal following of his own, although at any given moment he commanded a series of fleeting loyalties. In general the upper ranks of the Fascist Party were hostile to him. He did not belong to the generation of the March on Rome, and was thus alien to the core of Party bosses, and on the whole he was indifferent to the vagaries of internal Party intrigue. His meteoric rise had not been through the channels of the Party, but by family accident, and inevitably multifarious jealousies concentrated around him. However, his position as Foreign Minister brought with it closer access than any other public figure to the Duce, on whom every decision depended not only in foreign affairs but throughout the whole machinery of government. It was this that gave Ciano a special and unique importance, but at the same time any action by him was totally circumscribed by the will and indeed the whims of Mussolini.

Ciano's support was constantly enlisted from every quarter, and his agile, imaginative mind was perpetually active in creating shifting alliances of mutual and usually temporary convenience within the political and social world of Rome. At the beginning of 1942, for example, he was in close and constant touch with Buffarini, who controlled the working of the all-important Ministry of the Interior. Colonel Dollmann, Himmler's representative in Rome, reported that Ciano was in a leading position, before the Greek campaign, 'not in popularity but in influence'. He was followed hand in glove by Buffarini. Both men had succeeded in winning over the Duce's private secretaries 'which means in Italian politics the suppression of every disagreeable report'. [4] Ciano was, as Acquarone put it, 'a man badly viewed and attacked by all' [5] and his essential weakness was his basic isolation. He seemed cast by nature for the eventual role of scapegoat, and although the basic decisions of policy, which had led to the entry of Italy into the war, had been the personal responsibility of Mussolini, in the popular mind Ciano was intimately identified with them. The mounting crisis of the conduct of the war in the autumn of 1942 represented a potential threat to his personal position, and the illness of the Duce affected him even more immediately and acutely. It might also, however, create an opportunity.

One of the characteristics of Mussolini's political technique of rule was to regard his collaborators of the moment as both immediately expendable and always available. He was not concerned with creating a loyal team, but maintaining a reservoir of clients, totally dependent on him for the favours and fruits of office, awaiting their turn or return and thus circumscribed in their loyalties to each other, and reluctant to establish more than an effusive camaraderie among themselves, or to push a momentary cabal beyond private consultations.

Nor would Mussolini allow even the outline of a rival personality to appear in his vicinity. As Italo Balbo once remarked: 'As soon as he sees too much light shining on us, he turns off the switch.'[c] This deliberate fragmentation of the Fascist governing class ultimately brought about its self-destruction. Each leading figure was contained in his activities by a direct relationship to the Duce, to which every other position or office which he might hold was secondary, even in the Fascist movement itself.

Dino Grandi was perhaps both the most outstanding product and victim of this 'system'. His early career was like that of his generation in the Fascist movement. A gallant officer in an Alpine regiment in the First World War, a law student who completed his studies, an early member of the local Fascist organization and a leader of the Action Squads in Emilia. The pattern of his local position follows that of his contemporaries: a leading rôle in the squads in the region and then in the Party machine in Bologna; an editor of the local paper *Il Resto del Carlino*, an activity essential to the influence and prestige of a successful politician; and then a member of the Party Directorate by 1921.

By the time of the March on Rome, Grandi in Bologna, like Balbo in Ferrara, could answer for his regional clan, and was in a position to exercise a certain influence on the direction of the movement. In this early period, when Mussolini's authority was not absolute over his followers, Grandi clashed with him openly both over the former's attempt to make a pact with the Socialists, and again in opposing the leader's short-lived anti-monarchical campaign. Although designated as a member of the 'General Staff', set up to organize the March on Rome, Grandi, who had already opposed the idea of insurrection on the grounds that the battle could be won without effort by legal means, stayed in Rome to take a leading part in the intricate negotiations with Antonio Salandra, the interventionist Prime Minister of the First World War, and other Liberal politicians, in order to bring about a coalition ministry with the Fascists, a plan approved by the Crown and rejected by Mussolini. Grandi claims that this action on his part 'excluded him from any political activity for nearly two years'.[d] He

c. There had always been three collaborators, of whose political intelligence and independence of view the Duce had been wary, Grandi, Bottai, and Balbo. The last had been killed in North Africa, shot down over Tripoli harbour by the guns of an Italian warship.

d. Grandi's own brief and provisional account is given in *Dino Grandi Racconta* (August 1943), an Italian translation of an article published in the American magazine, 'Life'.

was, however, summoned to Rome in March 1923, and his official career begins with his appointment as Undersecretary at the Ministry of the Interior. Two years later, he transferred to the same post in the Foreign Office to become Foreign Minister in 1929.

Grandi was now imprisoned in the 'system'. 'What should I have been if I had not met you? At the very most, an obscure provincial lawyer.' A series of such letters from Grandi was published by Mussolini in his thrashing booklet first issued in August 1944 as a supplement to the Milan paper *Il Corriere della Sera*. There is no reason to doubt their authenticity, and they illustrate the style of 'double-talk' which became increasingly and inevitably a familiar part of every dialogue between the Duce and his collaborators, containing an element of genuine effusion within a general convention of language, which was not intended wholly to deceive the recipient.

During the years in which Grandi controlled the Foreign Ministry, and after 1932 when he was sent as Ambassador to Great Britain, he was influenced by the necessity, in the interests of Italy, of avoiding a clash with the Western Powers and he devoted much energy, charm, and persistence, particularly when in London, to improving relations between the Italian and British governments. Grandi was recalled in the early summer of 1939 and nominated, without his prior knowledge, Minister of Justice,[e] and in December he was appointed President of the new Fascist Chamber, on the death of the first holder of this office, Ciano's father.[f] The former post brought Grandi into the Council of Ministers; the latter provided an as yet unexplored political sounding-board, and made him an *ex-officio* member of the Grand Council.

In the desperate controversy in Italian political circles over the attitude to be taken by Italy after the outbreak of war in Europe, Grandi openly favoured Mussolini's immediate and reluctant declaration of non-belligerency. In March 1940, when Mussolini began talking openly of entering the war on the side of Germany, Ciano noted, 'Against the adventure are Grandi and Bottai.'[6] In the following month, on April 21, 1940, Grandi expressed his views in a wide-ranging personal letter to Mussolini.[g] It was a forceful plea that Italy should remain neutral in existing circumstances. 'It is never "late" to enter a war. Italy has not the means equal to those of any of the protagonists in the present European drama, but could, under certain conditions, become "the decisive weight" . . . These conditions depend on what

e. Grandi's own account reads: 'I went to Rome and asked to see Mussolini at once. He told me, "The Germans are after your head, and I have my own reasons for not entirely agreeing. Besides I need a lawyer in my government."' *Dino Grandi Racconta* p. 26.

f. Having first favoured Farinacci to succeed his father, Ciano spoke to Mussolini 'in favour of the appointment of Grandi'. (See Ciano, *op cit* pp. 113 and 178.)

g. This letter was printed for the first time in an Italian weekly *Il Borghese*, September 10, 1959.

Russia does or does not do, the third great absentee power. Depending on the future attitude of Russia the future position of Italy can be judiciously considered . . . Until such a time, let us remain as we are, neutral, non-belligerent, abstainers. The formulae are irrelevant provided that Italy keeps out. In the meantime let us prepare and arm ourselves in a serious manner.'

With the news, however, of the vertiginous collapse of the Western Front in May, no single leading figure in Italy was exempt from the ensuing wave of euphoria. Grandi made an anti-Allied speech in the Chamber, which he seems promptly to have regretted. Ciano maliciously recorded that Grandi only received three telegrams of congratulation: two from well-known Fascist figureheads, 'and one from an inmate of a lunatic asylum in Catania, who offered to put the speech into verse for one hundred lire'.[7] But as the general optimism as to a war of weeks evaporated and after the fiasco of the 'parallel' war in Greece in the winter of 1940, the muted chorus of critical comment recovered its voice.

In the months leading up to Italy's entry into the war, Mussolini had noticeably and exceptionally made use of the formal machinery of government. The Council of Ministers met frequently, major policy decisions regarding non-belligerency were discussed in the Chamber, and recorded solemnly in the Grand Council at the beginning of December 1939. There was, however, no consultation on the declaration of war. This step was the supreme personal act of the Duce himself, and as abruptly as he had previously taken soundings, henceforward—apart from irregular meetings of the Council of Ministers where he was accustomed to think aloud and unreported—the administrative and executive organs of the State, apart from working technical committees, ceased to function. Such was his conception of government that, in moments of panic or in an atmosphere of pessimism, he regarded each body as merely a potential forum of criticism and discontent, however passing and impotent.

The Greek fiasco had generated just such a climate. As Grandi put it 'Parliament virtually vanished.'[8] It was so in a literal sense, as most of the Ministers, and National Councillors of the Party, were mobilized and sent to the Albanian-Greek front as a puckish means of dissipating incipient plotting. This move of Mussolini's was greeted with anxious astonishment. Some people, such as Bottai, went so far as to speak of 'a real coup d'état by the Duce in order to get rid of Fascism and place his reliance on other political currents'.[9] Bottai, who was at the time Minister of Education, received without warning a telephone call from Mussolini telling him that he was mobilized. The Duce was said to be in excellent humour. 'I will show the country how one governs with only senior civil servants.' Bottai commented, 'We are the object of a new dictatorial experiment.' The same fate befell Grandi later in the month, and he too found himself on the Greek front. Ironically, it was here that the discontented caballed. As Grandi put it, with a certain telescoped and grandiloquent exaggeration, 'I made contact with my friends, and jotted down, there in the trenches of Greece, the plan of the resolution which later marked the end of Mussolini.' [10]

There have been numerous references in contemporary memoirs and documents to Grandi's 'circle' or 'Grandi and his friends', implying the existence of a shadowy but coherent political group.[h] Such a concept is at the same time too precise and misleading. But with two men of his own political generation Grandi enjoyed a particular intimacy and an interchange of ideas, which became increasingly marked after his return from Greece and which intensified in the late autumn of 1942. They were Giuseppe Bottai, and Luigi Federzoni, both in distinct ways leading personalities in the formative years of Fascism and drawn together subsequently by a similar approach to the problems created by Fascist rule. They both held a series of high offices, and were, in the prevailing climate of the régime, both beneficiaries and critics. Grandi was the diplomatic expert; Bottai the theoretician of 'constitutional' Fascism; and Federzoni the elder statesman, and potentially, as in October 1922, a respected link with the Crown.

Bottai, like Grandi, had been a young officer at the front and had fought in those commando units—the *Arditi*—which supplied so many recruits to D'Annunzio's adventure at Fiume, and to the early Action squads of Fascism. In 1919 he had taken part in the founding of the Rome Fascio, and led its detachment in the March on Rome. Unlike many of his companions he had literary pretentions beyond the immediate field of local journalism, and possessed serious intellectual qualities. 'Even if I have always recognized the origins of Fascism as being neither theoretical nor logical . . . I have never believed that intelligence was absent from those origins.' [i] Through the pages of his review 'Critica Fascista', founded in Rome after 1922, he made obstinate and not entirely forlorn attempts to enunciate a 'moderate' programme for a triumphant Fascism, of fundamental reform by legal revolution, achieved and modified by constant self-criticism and revision within the élite of the Party. 'I pleaded for an opposition on interior lines.' Bottai was arguing for formal acceptance by the Party leadership of such an approach, but the weakness of his case was that the essential problem created by the occupation of the State machine by Fascism—namely the demarcation of the frontiers between illegality and legitimacy in the exercise of power—could never be faced owing to the limits, both in terms of brute strength and moral ascendancy in the country as a whole, of the very Fascist movement itself. He glimpsed this at one early moment. 'In a certain

h. The Germans often use the term after 1942 of 'The Fronde of Grandi'. See for example German Collection, Rome telegram, December 12, 1942.

i. Bottai, *Vent' Anni e Un Giorno* p. 11. This book is the most serious attempt by his political generation to analyse critically, after defeat, the historical experience of Fascism.

sense one can say that it is not that Fascism is in a state of crisis, but that Fascism is a synthesis of the crisis of Italian life as a whole, a crisis of formation, of growth, and of a definition of values.' [11] Between the ultra-revolutionary conception of Farinacci and the 'slow but sure revolution' by legal process of Bottai, developed the personal dictatorship of Mussolini. The historic dilemma of Fascism was that it did not possess the vital force or the united will to achieve a total political and social revolution, nor the coherence and discipline to be compressed into the role of a governing political party in a traditional constitutional frame, however modified by reform.

In 1936 Bottai became Minister of Education and occupied himself with the formation of a second generation, more comprehending than his contemporaries in his conceptions of the structure of the Fascist régime. He still held this office in the autumn of 1942.

Luigi Federzoni represented in the history of the Fascist movement the later arrival of an older political grouping, the Nationalist Party, which he had founded with Enrico Corradini at the time of the Libyan war, and which formed the advance guard of the interventionist campaign in 1914–15. In the years immediately following the armistice, Federzoni and his party were rivals of and hostile to the early manifestations of Fascism, and the temporary allies of D'Annunzio. The Nationalist and pro-monarchist 'Blue Shirts' were also a particular source of disquiet to Mussolini in the regions of Italy south of Rome, where the Fascist hold was weak. The personal relations between Federzoni and Grandi dated from the intricate negotiations in the capital preceding the March on Rome, and the latter played a role in the subsequent absorption of the Nationalist group into the ranks of Fascism. Federzoni formally joined the Party in 1923, but with mental reserves, which survived his appointments as Minister of the Colonies, of the Interior, and President of the Senate. Like Bottai, he possessed marked intellectual gifts. In 1942 he was President of the Italian Academy, and as such was also a member of the Grand Council.

This private grouping of Grandi and his friends, however, did not constitute a distinct political force. As Bottai put it, 'We are consumed with inactivity. We are only isolated individuals: we do not form a governing class, nor even a government team.' [12] It was nevertheless among these 'isolated individuals' that a programme and a platform were conceived which, in July 1943, as Grandi put it, 'marked the end of Mussolini'. The essence of Grandi's solution was the ultimate intervention of the Crown, the revival of the constitutional organs of government, the setting up of a 'moderate' Fascist administration, the resumption by the King, as head of the Nation, of the supreme command of the Armed Forces, and a probing search for contacts with the Western Allies with a view to a separate peace. Its implementation depended exclusively on the action of the King, and in the absence of any sign from him no move could be made. It was a time for analysis and definition rather than action.

The continued existence of the institution of the Monarchy under Fascism was a tacit reminder that the Fascist revolution had its limits set, and that in the event of any disputed succession to the Duce the ultimate decision could only lie with the King. As Hitler on one occasion told his advisers: 'In Rome I saw what Fascism is like. It could not prevail over the Court circle . . . The Fascists and the Quirinal crowd are all jumbled together . . . How does he judge Italy's chances in the event of a waning of the Fascist revolution, or of the Royal House? . . . For either the Royal House supersedes the Fascist Revolution—how would he judge the prospects of his people in that case? . . . Or how does he judge them if the Royal House alone should take over power? It is hard to say. In Klessheim he made a remark while we were having dinner together. He suddenly said, "My Fuehrer, I don't know; I have no successor in the Fascist revolution. A chief of state can be found to succeed me, but no one who will continue the Fascist revolution." That is certainly a tragedy.' j

The decline or disappearance of Mussolini must inevitably lead to a reactivation of the prerogatives of the Crown. Much turned on the personality of the Monarch. As he told General Puntoni, the head of his military household, 'In 1922 I had to call on "these people" to govern, as all the others, some in one way and some in another, had abandoned me. For forty-eight hours I had to give orders direct to the Police Commissioners of Rome and the Corps Commander to prevent Italians killing each other.' [13] Twenty years of Fascist rule had progressively shorn the royal prerogative, but in spite of the tacit complicity of the Monarchy with the régime, the prestige of the Crown survived. The ultimate sanction of Italian politics, as in 1922, still lay in the constitutional intervention of the King. He was a close taciturn man, both obstinate and diffident, secretive and distrustful, keeping absolutely his own counsel. His attitude to public affairs was conditioned by his rigid and formalistic conception of his duties as a constitutional monarch. Even if Fascist rule had circumscribed and diminished the royal authority, the outward forms remained intact.

It was also of salient importance that, although Mussolini had assumed nominal command of the Armed Forces in June 1940—the latest violation of the royal prerogative—the oath of loyalty of every officer was to the King, and in a major political crisis the Army would not only be the decisive factor, but would also as in October 1922, obey and await the orders of the Crown. Just as at the time of the March on Rome the Army accepted the new

j. Gilbert, *Hitler Directs His War*, pp. 36–7. Military conference of May 20, 1943. The reference to Klessheim is to the meeting of April 29–30, 1942.

régime following the example of the Monarchy, there was every reason to believe that, in changed circumstances, the military power might become the loyalist instrument for the overthrow of Fascism. According to Hitler, 'The work of the Duce is mainly hampered by the fact that his power is limited by the Crown. One cannot lead a nation when the army, for example, has sworn fealty to another who is not the effective head of the state. Just as a man cannot run a commercial firm if others hold a majority of the shares and thus have the power to cancel all his decisions.' [14]

But in spite of the mounting internal weaknesses of the Fascist system, the growing loss of contact of the Party with the masses, and the declining authority of the Duce, only two events, together or separately, could lead to the collapse of the régime: the disappearance of Mussolini or total defeat in war. The military situation, though grave, was not hopeless so long as the African front could be held and the invasion of the Italian mainland averted. But the crisis of the Duce's health must inevitably endanger the existence of his rule, and excite speculation and anxiety in every quarter. 'Must hold one's tongue. Spies on the Staff . . . Political situation not clear. Duce ill.' This entry appears in the diary of General Ambrosio, Chief of the Italian Army Staff, on October 17, 1942.[k] The course of the war and the internal state of the country gave further cause for alarm. Intensive Allied bombardment of Italian cities, the problems of evacuation of damaged areas and of rationing, added to the war-weariness of the population a sharp pervasive criticism of the régime.

The King was aware that any move which he might make would be decisive not only for the country but also for the future of the Monarchy. He was conscious of his exclusive and unique role which could be played only once, and its manner and timing would depend on him alone. He also knew that, with the exception of a few Party extremists, every circle and clan in Italian public life looked in the last resort for such action as the supreme catalyst. General Puntoni recorded, 'They all hope for an intervention of the Crown and think it necessary for the Sovereign to be in close union with the Army, which, in the event of a crisis, can alone save the situation.' [15]

The King, as was his nature, proceeded with secretive caution. Early in October he had retired to San Rossore, one of the Royal estates near Pisa. Since the declaration of war in 1940 he had avoided appearing in public or receiving in audience more often than his routine duties as monarch required. His main confidant and link with the world of public affairs was

k. Quoted by Mussolini in his memoirs written at Salò in 1944 under the title 'Story of a Year', quoted henceforth as *Memoirs* (English translation), p. 26. This private diary of Ambrosio was apparently handed by the Germans to Mussolini. It has not since come to light. The Italian Collection only contains lists of his appointments after his nomination as Chief of the General Staff in February, 1943.

the Duca Acquarone, who since 1939 had held the post of Minister of the
Royal Household. The King, slow to give his confidence, was impressed by
Acquarone's grasp of business and his handling of the Royal finances and
estates. The Minister was a wealthy Genoese aristocrat and former cavalry
officer, loyal, discreet, ambitious, and active. Victor Emmanuel came to
rely on him more and more as a source of political information and as an
intermediary behind the political scene. By the winter of 1942 not only was
this special role of Acquarone assured, but the Monarchy might well require the widest possible personal contacts in the event of an internal crisis
transcending the Fascist régime.

On October 10 the King was considering a visit to Rome. Acquarone
telephoned to fix an audience with the Duce, but was told that the latter
intended to meet Hitler in Russia. Two days later it appeared that Mussolini
was suffering again from the internal malady which had followed his recent
North African trip, and had postponed his journey. There were rumours of
cancer. The King, however, appears to have been less concerned about
the gravity of the Duce's condition than other observers. As he said to
Puntoni, 'Mussolini's womenfolk complain that he is a bizarre invalid and
does not want to look after himself. I would advise him to take care and
remember that he is sixty years old.' [16]

On October 27 the King came to Rome, and received Mussolini the
same morning. He learnt 'nothing particular' from his Prime Minister, but
'spoke to him clearly about the internal position'. It is not without significance that the main informant of the Court for some time had been
General Hazon, one of the senior officers of the military police, the very
body responsible for the maintenance of public order and incidentally by
tradition and sentiment deeply royalist. In the event of any disturbance,
their role would be of prime importance. Any weakening of control would
be the precursor of a national crisis, and to this threat the King, with his
clear memories of the events following the end of the First World War,
turned his attention. In his methodical way, he addressed himself to one
problem at a time.

The internal malaise of 1942 indeed presented certain features in common
with the grave tensions in Italian affairs in 1917; the same picture of military disaster as at Caporetto, and of war-weariness and political strains on
the Home Front. As this latter situation had been the political school of
King Victor Emmanuel his judgment of the former must be to some extent inevitably influenced by a particular historical pattern. The recurrence of the
same stresses might lead to the revival of the role of the Crown in Italian
affairs, but under conditions totally modified by twenty years of Fascism.
The destruction of all organizational forms of a parliamentary opposition
after 1924 had also removed the means of appointing an alternative govern-

ment by constitutional process. The open removal of the Duce would now be a revolutionary act, and this the King intended to avoid at all costs. He was by temperament and training opposed to radical solutions, and in particular because the chances of a successful counter-coup by the Fascist Party aided by the Germans were difficult to estimate or at least analyse with any certainty.

But the danger of the disintegration of the Fascist State as the direct result of the death, by natural causes or violence, of Mussolini, or through a military collapse followed by enemy invasion, or both, had in the autumn of 1942 become real and menacing. The candidates for the succession, in the absence of any system of political parties, might be found among the 'moderates' of the older generation of the Fascist movement itself, men like Grandi, Bottai, and Federzoni, who had always regarded themselves in part as a self-elected opposition within the system, or from the exiguous band of survivors of the political and military élite of pre-Fascist Italy.[8] It was unlikely that any of these elements, even in an emergency, could form into an administration by themselves, but they were in a sense possible candidates to the succession; and each had his own particular solution and in every case this depended in the final resort on the action of the Monarchy.

Any new government, formed from whatever elements, and in the shadow of military defeat, would need the prestige of a senior military figure in order to ensure the political support of the Army and to create some psychological basis of support and confidence among the masses, the extent of whose allegiance to the cult of the Duce was another undefined element in the situation. One aspect of the case, therefore, was the appearance in the wings of the Marshals of the First World War, and the abrupt prospect of a vacancy at the summit of political power, for which they might be competitors. The least retired and most obvious candidates were Badoglio and Caviglia, linked in an ironic and mutual hatred in the historical controversy over the responsibility for the Caporetto disaster in 1917, the Italian Gallipoli of the First World War. Their subsequent careers too had sharply diverged.

It was Caviglia who had suppressed D'Annunzio's rebellion at Fiume in 1920, after Badoglio had displayed his natural wariness. Caviglia had regarded the successful march of Fascism with a consistent and distant sarcasm, and both D'Annunzio and Mussolini were in his eyes 'the charlatans of power'.[1] He commanded a certain following among the older generation of survivors in the Senate, the only enclave of murmured and

---

1. For the following see a fragmentary but illuminating file on Caviglia in the Italian Collection. A reference in his published diary for August 1942 reads, 'I made a mistake in 1919 in going against the Fiume enterprise. It alienated me from Italian youth.' Caviglia *Diario*, p. 369.

licensed discontent under Fascism, but he remained aloof, independent, and untouchable. A police report suggested that in the first politico-military crisis of the war—in October 1940—Caviglia was 'prepared to assume the liquidation of the régime'.[17] There is no reliable evidence to elucidate or confirm this, but it does appear that in the succeeding months he was received by the King on more than one occasion.

Badoglio, on the other hand, although by legendary account he had in October 1922, as Farinacci put it, 'boasted that in five minutes of machine-gun fire he would clear away all the Black Shirts', [18] had become a major beneficiary of the régime, ennobled and enriched by Mussolini, the victorious commander in Ethiopia, Duca di Addis Ababa, and Chief of the General Staff at the outbreak of war. His direct responsibilities, however, made him closer than Caviglia to leading Army circles, and his position in regard to the war, though he retained his functions, was unequivocally opposed to Italy's entry. With the Greek disaster in the winter of 1940, his abrupt dismissal modified the impression of his Fascist past. He had thus closer and more recent links than Caviglia with the upper ranks of the Army, and a special advantage in the virulent personal hatred of Farinacci and thereby of those extremist Fascist elements compromised with and bound to the German ally.

On the eve of the war there is a fleeting but unconfirmed indication that the King had proposed to both Caviglia and Badoglio that action should be taken by them against Mussolini. They both evaded the hint, and as the police report added, 'These Marshals have no contacts between themselves.'

In any event, both rivals were by the autumn of 1942 active and expectant observers of the political scene.

The Germans in their turn were alerted. Against the opposition of his rival Ribbentrop, Himmler announced that he would visit Rome in early October.[m] It appears to have been a private move inspired by Ciano, as a plaintive telegram from Alfieri, the Italian Ambassador in Berlin, shows: 'The rumours which have been circulating in recent weeks in Germany, and I imagine also in Italy, over Himmler are certainly known there. This morning I learnt from a reliable German source that Himmler will be visiting Rome at the invitation of Minister Ciano on the 10th or 11th of this month. It would have been very interesting for me, if at the same time as this news had been given by you to the German Embassy, I had received a confidential indication, and in fact for several reasons which I will pass on to you another time.' [19]

It was natural that Himmler should wish to sniff the political air in view of

m. Ciano, *op cit* p. 508. Ciano also says that in the previous July Himmler had already suggested making such a visit 'in October to talk things over with me after the offensive in Russia'. (*Ibid* p. 471.)

the increasing reports of the decline in Mussolini's health, and to investigate the intricate balance of forces behind the scenes which might follow a disappearance of the Duce from public life. Ciano's motives in encouraging such a visit are less clear. Perhaps he was anxious to quieten Himmler's suspicions as to the fragility of the Italian political scene, and as to the attitude of the Italian royal house—and in particular the Prince of Piedmont —with whom Ciano seems to have been increasingly in contact as a possible ally in the event of a hiatus of power.

On October 11 Ciano, by an unusual protocol, went to the station to meet the head of the German SS. In a later conversation, he found that 'what counts is the extremely reserved tone of his conversation . . . He wanted to find out a good deal about Italy. In particular he wanted to know about the Monarchy and the Vatican . . . I praised the loyalty of the first and the discretion of the second.' [20]

In a subsequent report to the Fuehrer, Himmler described his formal reception by Mussolini, who seems to have made a special effort for the occasion. The memorandum has the mark of a prissy schoolmaster.[n] 'The Duce gave me a very cordial reception. He was in civilian clothes and looking particularly well, extremely fresh and in the best of humours . . . (He) gave me, in the course of conversation, an outline of the Italian political situation. He described the mood of the population as not enthusiastic, but as resolute. The Italian people was well aware of what was at stake in the war. He, the Duce, and the Party had the people well in hand, and there were no grounds for misgivings of any kind. The only question that was serious, though neither dangerous nor catastrophic, was the food position . . . Italy had, in general, a good many problems to face; and one of these problems was of course the fact that, as he phrased it, "there are three of us in Rome: myself, the King, and the Pope." In spite of this things were better than was generally thought. The Pope was not going to make things too difficult for him, and he was, after all, an Italian at heart. He added that the lower ranks of the Italian clergy were moreover very patriotic, though some of the higher clergy dabbled in politics. Referring to the Royal Family, the Duce said that "the King was of course very old, but he remained loyal, and had indeed been loyal to him from the very first days of his Premiership. The Crown Prince was a Fascist and had completely subordinated himself to him, the Duce; he was equally loyal." I replied that this struck me not merely as gratifying, but also as good policy on the Crown Prince's part, since the House of Savoy owed its throne in the last resort to the Duce, whose intervention had alone rescued Italy from Bolshevism and upheld

n. German Collection. 'Notes on my interview with the Duce at 5 p.m. on Sunday October 11, 1942, in the Palazzo Venezia.' These documents have also been printed in Italian translation in *Movimento di Liberazione in Italia* No. 47 (April–June, 1957); and in *Viertelgahrsheft für Zeitgeschichte* (October 1956).

the monarchy. I said that it was to be hoped that the House of Savoy would be duly grateful and never forget this fact. The Duce, however, rejoined that one should never expect gratitude from princes, for they were not as other men: princes were the last International.'

Himmler's reference to his talk with Ciano is laconic and unilluminating. 'The conversation which took place during my visit with Count Ciano dealt with substantially the same themes as with the Duce. Count Ciano likewise laid great stress on the supply problem.'

But the real purpose of his visit becomes clear from the rest of his report. Himmler spent three days in Rome touring the city, sometimes in mufti, and accompanied on different occasions by Buffarini, who controlled the Ministry of the Interior, Senise, the Chief of Police, and Ricci, the Minister of Corporations—and, in the background, his own representative in Rome, Colonel Dollmann. These were his main sources of information. Buffarini at the Interior had long been such a source and a key through the intermediary of Dollman. Senise was a professional expert on police affairs, and, although his loyalties may have lain elsewhere, his duties required that he should brief the distinguished visitor. Ricci, apart from being in charge of the important Party stronghold, the Ministry of Corporations, had close links with the Militia, which would be the essential element in an internal crisis.

During this visit, which was primarily to gain a first hand impression of the Italian political scene, there was clearly speculation in private conclave of the possible course of events if the Duce should disappear from the stage, and the establishing of confidential contacts with reliable Italian Fascists to act in such an event. It is significant that just after Himmler's departure Dollmann should report in the following terms: 'May I begin these lines by emphasizing the deep and enduring impression which the Rome visit of the Reichsfuehrer SS has left behind everywhere here. I can best summarize this fact in the statement made repeatedly to me by Excellency Ricci. "The best offensive of this autumn in the Axis camp is called Heinrich Himmler in Rome." Again Ricci recently stressed how vitally necessary this contact was for the friends of the Axis in Rome, whose positions are undermined from so many sides.' [21]

The reserve nucleus of an eventual Fascist counter-coup, among the leaders of which can be identified Buffarini and Ricci, can for the first time be discerned, and indeed their later role after the events of the following July provides such a confirmation.

Apart from rallying internal support to maintain a pro-German régime in power in event of a sudden collapse, Himmler was anxious to study the immediate situation of Mussolini. 'I am convinced that so long as the Duce is alive, Italy will hold firmly and steadfastly to the Axis, and will fight the war to the finish.' But if an untoward event occurred, the only rallying point of opposition to Italian Fascism could, in German eyes, come from the circle of the Royal House. This had always been the basic interpretation of Italian affairs both by Hitler and his entourage. Himmler's particular interest was therefore focused on this aspect of the Roman world. He was but half convinced by the Duce's assurances. 'The good relations maintained with the Royal Family and with Crown Prince Umberto were stressed with quite striking unanimity by most Italian ministers and dignitaries. However, I heard *through links confidentially established with Italian circles*° that despite this external emphasis the Italian police are busily compiling a dossier on the Crown Prince, as in fact he is still not quite trusted.' Rumours continued to cluster round the Prince of Piedmont as a possible successor to the régime, and as the leader of such a movement, but as a result of his visit to Rome Himmler would now be better informed, and able to observe more closely the labyrinthine moves of Italian affairs.

o. Author's italics.

CHAPTER FOUR

'TORCH'

• •

ON OCTOBER 17 the German Embassy in Rome sent a report on the views of Italian political and military circles on the Mediterranean war. 'A considerable intensification of military activity' must be expected. The Italian Foreign Office had already at the beginning of the year felt that, in the event of an Axis failure in Egypt in the summer, they must reckon with an American landing either at Dakar or at a Moroccan port. Since the Italians had been halted at El Alamein, 'these anxieties have increased. Although the Italian General Staff are quietly awaiting the British offensive, there are other disturbing factors: an English air superiority of three to one; and Axis shipping losses and supply difficulties in North Africa. An English flanking attack at El Alamein is expected, coupled with the certainty of American operations against Dakar. I learn reliably,' the German Ambassador wrote, 'that the Italian High Command has decided to make at once the necessary preparations to occupy Tunis, if military developments require.' [1][a]

From the Italian strategic point of view, the Western Front ran from the French Alpine frontier through the islands of Corsica and Sardinia and Sicily to the Tripolitanian and Tunisian borders. As the Duce put it in a survey of the war to his service advisers at a meeting on October 1 at Palazzo Venezia: 'This front could become active at any moment, in all probability in relation to the attitude of France, which seems ambiguous. That is so much the case that our Allies have already agreed on ways and means of occupying the whole country should the government be forced to go over to the enemy. If this should happen, it is for us to occupy Southern

---

a. On October 10, at a Council of Ministers, the Duce gave orders to prepare and carry out an advance to the Tunisian border 'in order to be ready for counter-action in Tunis in event of enemy operations in West Africa'. Such enemy action was, however, not thought to be practical 'until early next year'. (German Collection. Mackensen telegram, October 17, 1942.)

France and Corsica; such a task, if one considers the experience of the Germans in France, and ours in the Balkans, will not be easy. The assault on the cities will be particularly difficult, and we will have to attack Toulon and Marseilles . . . We must also take into account that, if we proceed to the total occupation of France, the French government may go to settle in Algiers and become the ally of the Anglo-Saxons, thus opening to them those landing areas which today it asserts that it wishes to defend. French Equatorial Africa is also threatened. For this reason, I have decided to send one division into Tripolitania to be followed by two others . . . We should try to have sufficient forces in Tripolitania to extend our occupation up to the western frontier of Tunisia before enemy forces could land in strength.

'Above all it seems to be the Allied intention to launch an offensive against Libya simultaneously from Egypt and from West Africa. It is certain that Churchill and Roosevelt regard the North African theatre as Front Number One. Their plan is to destroy Italy as the weaker Axis partner.' [2] But several months must elapse before such an enemy operation could be mounted. The Italian High Command reckoned on, first an attack by the British at El Alamein, followed by a simultaneous assault from both sides on Libya. The Duce however was optimistic. 'He still has not written off a decisive thrust against Egypt. If the Americans set foot first in Morocco, he will march into Tunis and occupy Tunisia, irrespective of whether Vichy reacts.' Preparations against this must be made on the Alpine frontier. No Italian initiative as such would be taken in this region, except possibly in the direction of Nice. 'Under present circumstances, Italy will take no action against France. The emphasis of the war has moved to the Mediterranean. The need is to strengthen the Axis positions there and to step up the U-boat war in the Atlantic.' [3]

On October 19 Goering had arrived in Rome to review with the Duce the war situation on both the Eastern and Mediterranean fronts. As head of the German Air Force, he had a major interest in the Italian contribution to the war, both because of the stationing of the German Second Air Fleet under Marshal Kesselring in Italy, and its role in supporting the North African campaign, and also because on the successful resistance of Italy depended the air defence of Germany herself. It was also Goering, rather than his other colleagues, who came to Rome as the personal envoy of the Fuehrer in times of particular stress, and as the interpreter of the latter's immediate preoccupations.

Hitler and Mussolini had met on the Russian Front in the autumn of 1941. There was still a year later no sign of a German breakthrough to the oilfields of the Caucasus, and the mirage of a Middle Eastern meeting linking up the two war fronts of Russia and the Mediterranean was still beyond the horizon. A critical battle was now imminent on the Don, and the German advance into the Donetz basin was barred at Stalingrad. Until this major deadlock was broken, Hitler could hardly turn his attention to the other problems of the war, which Goering was now sent to discuss in Rome. He arrived in the Italian capital on October 19 on the heels of Himmler, but business was delayed by an attack of dysentery which as Ciano noted 'did not permit him to leave his throne even for ten minutes'.[b] His meeting with Mussolini took place on October 23, and lasted for two hours, with the assistance of the inevitable interpreter Schmidt.[4]

Goering's first duty was to describe the situation on the Eastern front. The Russians must be driven out of the Caucasus, and the Stalingrad battle should be over in the next eight days. As Goering said subsequently at breakfast in the German Embassy, he had been deliberately optimistic as the Duce had a pessimistic impression from Rommel of the African Front—a view which was supported by the British assault at El Alamein on the day of this conversation at the Palazzo Venezia.

The regrettable pause at Stalingrad had nevertheless increased the danger of the British and Americans being 'forced' by the Russians to open a Second Front in the West. Goering stressed that there were crack German divisions on the West Wall in France and that it was also unlikely that the enemy would land in Spain or Portugal. 'The main anxiety arises in the Mediterranean, in an eventual attack on French Africa, Libya, Sardinia or Crete. He (Goering) did not reckon on a landing in Italy. Crete and the Peloponnese, as well as the endlessly long Mediterranean coast of Africa were threatened, but the question of a landing in the Adriatic or in Croatia did not arise.'

The Axis armies in Africa could again become operative only if adequately supplied. 'If a major landing in the Mediterranean does not happen in another area (than Libya) and if supplies via Greece and Crete can be assured, which has proved useful in contrast to earlier experience in supplying Tobruk, the Axis need not fear anything from the direction of Egypt.'

Mussolini's main preoccupation was inevitably with the situation in North Africa, where the decisive military engagement was already in progress. He summarized the results of the Axis failure in the Mediterranean since 1940, and he was talking under the shadow of a fatal and decisive reckoning— the omission to occupy Tunis, to take Malta, and to protect the supply lines to the battle front in Libya. 'The Duce continued that he wanted to discuss one internal and two military problems. The latter were the question of oil supplies and Malta. To protect the convoys the fleet escorts required certain quantities of oil, and to safeguard the supply routes Malta must be neutralized . . . Then the routes from Italy to Tripoli and from Greece to Tobruk could be safeguarded. The Duce was preparing to send three further divisions to Africa. One division had already been moved by air to meet a

b. Ciano, *op cit* p. 512. This is Ciano's only reference to the visit.

threat from the Sahara to the south. The other two, whose presence in Africa raised again a supply problem, he would station on the Tunisian frontier and would occupy Tunis at once in the event of an Anglo-American landing in French Africa. For if they occupied Tunis there arose the possibility of an English landing in Italy, even if it were not successful. The French population was adopting a waiting attitude . . . In event of an Anglo-American attack France would only put up a token defence as in Syria and Madagascar, to save its honour. One should not forget that the Axis had released much war material to the French and that all Frenchmen hated the two Axis allies. They hated the Germans with respect, and the Italians with contempt.

'In this connection the Reichsmarshal expressed his regret that Tunis was not in the hands of the Axis, to which the Duce answered that naturally if this had been the case the question of supply would be absolutely assured.' Goering then asked 'why at the time of the armistice negotiations with France the occupation of Tunis had not been demanded. After some hesitation the Duce replied that he must admit that this had been a failure by omission. Italy had been too modest.' c

In general the Duce said that 'he was optimistic as to the outcome of the war. The next year would be decisive. Nevertheless one must prepare for a long war and work for a longer endurance.' Goering agreed. 'Theoretically one must prepare for thirty years in order to win the struggle in a shorter time.'

The conversation ended with Goering expressing the hope of the Fuehrer that he could meet the Duce next month, as he must in any case be in Munich on November 8.

While the two men were in conclave in Palazzo Venezia, the British Eighth Army opened its long-planned and awaited assault on Rommel's positions at El Alamein. During the night of November 2, after a decisive Allied breakthrough, he ordered a general retreat, in spite of orders and counter-orders from above. As Rintelen wrote later in his memoirs, 'It is not possible to interfere in tactical decisions from East Prussia, or even from Rome, in a battle in Egypt.' 5 The 'battle for the Delta' was over, and the remnants of the Axis army in North Africa were disengaging at speed from the British assault.

On November 5, the Italian Supreme Command received precise intelligence of a large Allied convoy in readiness to leave Gibraltar. Cavallero, at a meeting of the Italian Chiefs of Staff, commented on the news. 'One does not know whether this will be to supply Malta or whether it has an operational purpose: a landing at Casablanca or Oran. Our surface naval forces cannot

---

c. Prince Bismarck, the German Minister in Rome, in reporting this conversation to Berlin, wrote that, when Goering asked this question, 'the Duce was embarrassed and had no proper answer'. (German Collection. Rome telegram, October 23, 1942.)

take action owing to lack of fuel.' [6] At 8.30 that evening, the Italian Naval Chief of Staff reported to Cavallero that the convoy had left Gibraltar half an hour earlier. 'One did not yet know in which direction.' The Duce summoned his service advisers on the following morning. It was agreed that if the Allies landed in French North Africa, the Italians must occupy Corsica immediately, and be prepared to move into the unoccupied zone of Southern France. At a meeting that evening Rintelen was present. The Duce had a presentiment of disaster and talked at length of the sacrifices in men and material which had been made in Libya.[7] The 'omission' of Tunis at the time of the Franco-Italian armistice might now cost the Italians their North African territories.[d] As Mussolini told Rintelen: 'We must settle the French question. Otherwise the further conduct of the war will be difficult. I shall speak to the Fuehrer at the end of November.' [8]

The Germans were also considering the reports of the moves of the Allied armada. Jodl had already telephoned to Rintelen to instruct him to emphasize to Mussolini that Hitler was personally convinced that the Allied intention was to land in Rommel's rear at Tripoli or Benghazi.[9] This was confirmed in a telephone conversation between Goering and Kesselring, which had been intercepted on the same day, November 6, by the Italian Intelligence:

'*Goering*: In my view, they will attempt a landing in Corsica or Sardinia, at Derna or Tripoli.
Kesselring: It is more likely to be in a North African port.
Goering: Yes, but not in a French one.' [10]

Hasty orders were issued to concentrate all air and naval forces in an attack on the convoy. But the main German U-boat packs were operating in the Atlantic in anticipation of an Allied operation against West Africa, and, thanks to this strategic error, the 'Torch' convoys passed unscathed in their appointed direction.[e]

In the small hours of November 8, reports from the Italian Intelligence in Algiers confirmed landings throughout French North Africa. At 5.30 a.m., Ribbentrop woke Ciano from his sleep to tell him the first news on the telephone. In the next crucial hours it was vital to the Italians and to the Germans to form an accurate assessment of French reactions to the Allied landings, and to reach with speed an agreed line of action in regard to France.

d. See p. 11.
e. General Vacca Maggiolini, head of the Italian Control Commission, had been reporting continuously on the activities of American agents in North Africa and warned his German colleagues of Allied threats to the area. In September 1942, at a joint Italo-German meeting, the latter refused to consider recommending any plans to move into Tunisia in a crisis. On the evening of November 7 the senior German Staff Officer on the Commission maintained that the Allied convoys now identified were bound for Tripoli. (See Faldella, *L'Italia e la Seconda Guerra Mondiale* p. 531 note.)

During the course of the morning of November 8, the Duce formed his own preliminary view of the situation, and at noon summoned Rintelen who sent at once the following personal message from Mussolini to Hitler.

'If the French government is seriously prepared to fight with us together against the English and Americans, I am ready to agree. It seems to me requisite that France should not only break off diplomatic relations with America, but also declare war both on England and the United States, as would be obvious in the case of an attack on her own territory. In order to defend aggression against the North African theatre, agreement to a landing of ground troops in Tunisia is absolutely necessary. If these conditions are not met, and there is no question of a common struggle as an ally, I think it is essential to occupy immediately the rest of France and Corsica. At all costs Corsica must not fall into enemy hands, for a threat from Corsica would be fatal to Italy. Of these two possibilities, I prefer collaboration with the French.' [11]

The immediate balance of power in the Mediterranean lay, as in 1940, with the French battle fleet. The first reports led Cavallero to note in his diary on November 8: 'The French fleet is ready to put out from Toulon in an hour. I do not dare to hope, but if this collaboration comes off, we have won the war. I am a convinced partisan of collaboration with the French, although I have no friendly feelings towards them . . . But today we must seek for this collaboration by every means.' [12]

During the day, Hitler confirmed his agreement with the Duce's appreciation of the French attitude, and Rintelen had a further meeting with the latter that evening. 'The Duce summoned me again on November 8 at 7 p.m., together with Marshal Cavallero. After I had reported that the Fuehrer agreed with the Duce's analysis (as outlined in the above message), the latter made the following points: "In this morning's talk I omitted to draw attention to one point, namely, supposing that the Vichy government accepts an agreement with the Axis powers and then the population rebels against the government? In this case, too, nothing remains but to occupy the rest of France and Corsica.

' "If the French government raises the question of what to expect after the war, my view is that we should not discuss it. Territorial issues do not play the same role as at the beginning of the war, we are now fighting for our existence. It is a matter of winning and postponing all territorial questions until later. When we have won, there will be sufficient points of compensation for the French. Whatever decisions are made, I am determined to defend Libya to the last man." ' [f]

f. German Collection. Rome telegram, November 9, 1942. In the Italian Collection is a minute by the Duce dated November 8, 1942, on the same theme. It reads as follows: '*Memorandum* (A movement against Vichy in France?) According to reports which we have received so far, two hypotheses are possible, namely: (1) Vichy France asks loyally for the help of the Axis and it is my strong conviction that it is in the

That night, Ribbentrop again telephoned to Ciano to say that it was essential that either the Duce or Ciano came at once to Munich for talks with Hitler, and that Laval would also be summoned. 'It is time to consider our line of conduct towards France,' wrote Ciano in his diary on November 9. He does not seem to have been present at the various meetings held by Mussolini the previous day, and there is no evidence to show that he was directly aware of the Duce's views as expressed to Rintelen and Cavallero. Ciano now told the Duce of his conversation with Ribbentrop. 'I wake the Duce. He is not very anxious to leave, especially since he is not yet feeling at all well. I shall go, and on the instructions: if France is ready to collaborate loyally, she will receive all possible aid from us; if, on the other hand, she plays hot and cold, we are going to adopt preventive measures: the occupation of the Free Zone and a landing in Corsica.' [13]

The picture of events, as seen in Munich and Rome, and in French metropolitan and African territory, was changing hourly. There was no further news of the French fleet, except that the French Admiralty, on November 9, had asked the Italian Armistice delegation for collaboration with the Axis forces in Sardinia, and a French Naval Mission had arrived in Rome for talks.[g] It was not clear how far Pétain and Laval were in active agreement with such a move, or whether the French naval authorities were seeking their own revenge for the sinkings by the British at Oran in 1940. The Germans had already made certain preliminary demands at Vichy. Even before the landings in North Africa they had asked for permission to send German aircraft across the Unoccupied Zone for reconnaissance in the Western Mediterranean. At 3 a.m. on November 8, they offered the support of the Axis air force based on Sicily and Sardinia.[h] The French Cabinet met at 11 a.m. that morning. Laval was opposed to military collaboration with the Germans, but careful not to give a categorical refusal.

At 2 p.m. the German request for bases in Tunisia, so long delayed, was handed in by the Control Commission at Wiesbaden. An hour later a message from Hitler to the French government asked whether they were prepared to fight on Germany's side against the Anglo-Saxons. Otto Abetz, the German representative at Vichy, specified that all that was required was military collaboration in Africa. Early that evening, Laval received the invitation to meet Hitler and Ciano at Munich. Just before midnight the German General

---

highest interest of the Axis to offer such help without hesitation. It is in the interests of the Axis to prevent the building of a second front in the Mediterranean. (2) If this hypothesis is not valid, it is an absolute and urgent necessity for the Axis to proceed to occupy the whole of France and Corsica.'

g. See Cavallero, op cit p. 381. The naval mission left Vichy on November 9 'pour étude'. (See Mallet, Laval II, p. 103. The author was Laval's private secretary.)

h. For details see Mallet, op cit p. 101. Laval was in favour of waiting until the balance of support and defection was clearer in North Africa.

Staff insisted on immediate agreement for the use of the Tunisian airfields and requested a reply within an hour. Consent was by now a grudging formality.

On the morning of November 9, Ciano arrived at the station at Munich to find Ribbentrop awaiting him 'tired out, thin and courteous. Laval, who is making a long journey by car, will arrive during the night.' [14] Ciano's first conversation with Hitler took place that evening. [15] The latter immediately launched into a ranging monologue, minimizing the present dangers, and sketching an apologia for his past attitude towards France. 'Generally from the point of view of the military expert, the American landing in North Africa was not so dangerous as that of the English in Norway (in 1940) . . . At that time the landing took place in an area where both the military and the civil population were firmly on the English side. The present situation in North Africa was different: the country was half-heartedly co-operating with the Americans and nevertheless offering some resistance. If in addition the enemy were decided on a Second Front such as the present one in North Africa, the military dispositions to be adopted by Germany and Italy would be easier. It would no longer be necessary to maintain a large number of troops along a gigantic front which could be attacked at any point—no one knew where. Fifty-two armoured and infantry divisions were concentrated in France. The moment it transpired that danger no longer threatened, they could disperse all the troop concentrations there.'

The situation had been much worse in the winter of 1940–1. The threat to Germany from the East was only a few hundred miles from the frontier of the Reich. No one then knew from what quarter the attack from the East would come: through Roumania, the Balkans, or with the help of Yugoslavia. At the same time the British were in Crete and in Greece and had almost reached the Syrte in North Africa. Hitler stressed that he had not changed his attitude towards France. 'The French loved neither Germany nor Italy. Some admitted this with brutal openness, others were rather more reserved, and a third category sought slyly to hide it.'

In regard to French affairs, he had always tried to get the best out of each situation. 'Whether, in the present situation, much or little was to be obtained from the French it was not yet possible to judge.' In agreement with the Italian General Staff, Germany had demanded from the French the evacuation of their air bases in Tunis, and had sent in two wings of Stukas. It was unlikely that a direct attack from the sea by the Allies would follow in view of the proximity of the Axis air bases in Sicily. The Americans would attempt to advance on Tunis from the land side. It was therefore important that the Axis should be installed in Tunis beforehand.

If the Allied landing was in effect a Second Front, the military situation of the Axis in Africa would be held and improved. 'This would be especially true if the French really defended themselves against the Americans.

In Western Morocco and Southern Algeria this seemed to be the case, where-as in the city of Algiers itself there was treachery, and Darlan and Juin appeared to have been arrested. Here it was certainly a case of a plot. Even Marshal Pétain was to have been lured to Africa, and would in fact have been there if the Germans had not declared his journey inopportune.'

The decisive point was that the advance of German infantry and armoured divisions up to the French demarcation line [i] would have been completed by midnight, so that, if the French should collapse, these troops could march in at dawn the following morning. Hitler had asked the Duce also to make arrangements to move into Southern France, and to occupy Corsica whose importance for the air protection of Italy was immense. If this were not done with lightning speed and the Americans were to establish themselves there, this would be a catastrophe for Italy. 'One could not predict what would come out of the conversations with Laval. Whether he would bring an offer of alliance, or request deliveries of weapons or demand further release of war prisoners, one could not foresee. Hitler thought it right that an Italian representative should be present at these talks, since quick decisions would probably have to be taken to which the Italian Foreign Minister, in case of doubt, could seek the Duce's agreement by telephone.'

Ciano then summarized Mussolini's first reactions to the Allied landings in Africa. 'If the French asked for help, and fought with a minimum of loyalty, the Duce would be ready to accord them such assistance.' If they were 'ambiguous', rapid decisions must be made. Above all, Corsica must be occupied at once.[j]

As Ciano explained, 'either co-operation or occupation—that was the Duce's standpoint—and he was now waiting to know what measures the Fuehrer intended to take. The Duce would also be ready at any time of the day or night to telephone the Fuehrer if the latter wished to speak to him direct.' Ribbentrop then referred to rumours that Weygand was to take over control in French Africa. Hitler was strongly distrustful of the latter, and added, 'Laval must take a clear stand tomorrow. The French knew anyway that Germany was decided to go to the limit. They could certainly not be unaware of the troop movements. In the course of the last six weeks alone a further eighteen divisions had been sent to France'. Ciano noted in his diary: 'Hitler has not built up any illusions about the French desire to fight. . . . He will listen to Laval. But whatever he says will not modify his already definite point of view: the total occupation of France, a landing in Corsica, a bridgehead in Tunisia. Hitler is neither nervous nor restless, but he does not underrate American initiative, and he wants to meet it with all

i. Between the Occupied and Unoccupied Zones of France as laid down in the 1940 armistice.

j. These views of Mussolini were essentially a repetition of his earlier remarks to Rintelen in Rome. See p. 63.

the resources at his disposal. Goering does not hesitate to declare that the occupation of North Africa represents the first point scored by the Allies since the beginning of the war.'[16]

Laval was travelling by car from Vichy to Munich because of the hurry, but had been stopped on the way by fog, and could not reach the Bavarian capital until about four in the morning. Joint conversations with him were postponed therefore until about noon on the following day. Ciano met Hitler again briefly the next morning. News had come in that, during the night of November 9/10, both German and Italian air units had arrived in Tunisia. The French reception of the Italians had been 'cool, almost hostile'. The Germans had also been very coldly received. On the basis of the latest reports of the fighting in North Africa, Ciano pressed hard for the occupation of Corsica by the Italians, and the Fuehrer warmly concurred. It was decided to telephone to the Duce the Fuehrer's agreement.[17]

While Ciano was telephoning to Rome, and Laval, who in the meantime had arrived at the Fuehrerbau,[k] was on the line to Vichy on the latest developments in North Africa, Hitler was briefed on the partly contradictory reports on the attitude of the French in Africa, particularly events in Algiers and the arrest of Darlan and Juin. Abruptly the meeting with Laval was postponed until the afternoon. There had been a sudden and dramatic change in the position in North Africa. Darlan had opened negotiations with the Americans. Early in the afternoon Pétain had disavowed him over the radio, and assumed command of the French armed forces.[l]

This news reached Laval only in Munich. He had already had a brief preliminary talk with Ribbentrop and rejected the formal offer of an alliance.[m] Early in the afternoon Abetz, the German political representative with the Vichy government, who had come with Laval, showed him the German monitoring of Darlan's cease-fire order, and the Frenchman telephoned to

k. The official building used by Hitler on public occasions when in Munich.

l. For Pétain's secret code messages to Darlan approving of the latter's action, see Mallet, *op cit* II, pp. 107–8.

m. A draft treaty exists in the German Collection. The text reads as follows: 'Draft—Munich, November 1942. Not handed over.

'The government of the Reich and the Royal Italian government on the one hand, and the French government on the other hand are in agreement on the following points:
  (1) Following Anglo-American aggression against French North Africa, France will take an active part, and with all the resources at her disposal, in the Axis war against England and the United States.
  (2) The government of the Reich and the Royal Italian government give to the French government the following assurance:
    (a) France will keep her territorial possessions on the European continent in conformity with the position in 1914.
    (b) France will keep her possessions in North Africa. (Altered in one draft to "Africa".) Certain changes which might also prove necessary concerning French colonial possessions in the frame of a definite general settlement of African territories, will be compensated for on at least an equal basis by the Axis powers.'

Rochat, the head of the Vichy Foreign Ministry. The Germans were recording the conversation. 'I shall be received presently by Hitler: therefore do
nothing for the moment. Everything will be broken off and I shall resign, if
you negotiate with the Americans without my having got back and been
able to talk to you. I want to know what is the Marshal's decision.' A
second telephone call from Vichy informed Laval that Pétain had given
formal orders to defend Africa.[18] Such was the latest position when Laval,
who had been already waiting over two hours in the Fuehrerbau, was shown
into the main salon. It was in this room that Daladier and Chamberlain had
been received by Hitler in September 1938. Ciano observed the entry. 'Laval,
with his white tie and middle class French peasant attire, is very much out
of place in the great salon among so many uniforms. He tries to speak in a
familiar tone about his journey, and his long sleep in the car, but his words
are unheeded. Hitler treats him with frigid courtesy.' [19]

Hitler began curtly. 'A situation had arisen that he had always feared . . .
There were two courses open to France: either to lean definitely and clearly
on the Axis or to lose her entire colonial empire. At Montoire [n] he had
explained to Marshal Pétain that someone had to pay for this war, France
or Britain, anyway not Germany, who had not wanted the war, had not
begun it, and deeply regretted its outbreak.' Hitler nevertheless still wanted
to work with France, and to help to maintain the French colonial empire.
'It was clear that France alone could not effectively oppose the Americans
and British in North Africa, but would need strong Axis support. Fundamentally it was desirable that the whole European stake in Africa should be
guaranteed and defended in common. The question therefore arose as to
whether France was prepared to accept such support. The Fuehrer asked
Laval to tell him how he judged the situation in Africa and whether France
were ready to accept Axis aid.'

Laval began his exposition. His presence at the head of the French
government since the previous April meant in itself a policy of understanding and reconciliation between Germany and France. But this could not be
promoted by routine political contact, and he had repeatedly sought a personal
meeting. He thanked Hitler for agreeing to such a talk, 'and only regretted
that, owing to its late realization, it was being held under the shadow of
unfavourable events'.[o] It was not only in the interest of France but also of
the whole of Europe if France were allowed to arm herself more effectively
for her defence. The situation in Africa was serious. According to report,
Darlan had ordered the cessation of hostilities. Under these circumstances
it was as well that no conversations had taken place in Munich that morn-

n. The meeting between Hitler and Pétain in October 1940, which created the basic
premises of Franco-German 'collaboration'.
o. It seems that another reason for the delay in holding the meeting until the afternoon of November 10 was Hitler's annoyance at Laval's rejection of the offer of alliance
when talking to Ribbentrop in the morning. Mallet, *op cit* II, p. 108.

ing, so that Laval could press Vichy the whole time on the telephone, and finally induce Marshal Pétain himself to take over command of the three armed forces, to disavow Darlan's order, and to strengthen anew his own (Pétain's) instructions whereby resistance should be offered to the Allies. He feared, however, that all this coming and going had produced much confusion in the minds of the senior officers. He had no doubts as to the loyalty of General Noguès, who was defending Morocco. Governor-General Chatel, who had returned to his post in Southern Algeria since Algiers was occupied, was equally reliable . . . and hoped to rally the whole population to obedience to Vichy. In Morocco resistance had been more effective, because there was more equipment and better leadership. Casablanca had not yet fallen . . . Admiral Esteva in Tunisia had acted very loyally and had told the American Consul that he only took orders from Marshal Pétain. It was not yet clear what had happened with Darlan . . . It was unlikely that, being a prisoner, he had any further freedom of decision. Nevertheless Laval was surprised that Darlan should have given the order to cease hostilities. Since his arrest Darlan had so far sent only one telegram in which he intimated that he would negotiate through the Americans for the handing over of the administration in Algiers. A reply was sent that he should undertake nothing. This cable crossed with a further telegram from Darlan saying that he had already ordered all units to cease fighting. Whereupon, persuaded by Laval on the telephone, the Marshal himself after a talk with the War, Navy and Air Ministers, had taken over command of the Armed Forces, and in this way had firm control of the three services together. Laval stressed the need 'for very great and urgent counter-measures' against the danger in North Africa. Hitler interposed at once a demand that 'the harbours of Tunis and Bizerta must be placed at the disposal of the Axis as a prerequisite to building up a counter-offensive.' Had this happened earlier, there would never have been a landing in West Morocco.

Laval then spoke of the meeting at Montoire, 'which represented a generous gesture of the victor to the vanquished, which was certainly unique in history. He must say quite sincerely that France would not have so behaved if she had beaten Germany.' Hitler went on: 'The fate of France lay in her own hands . . . If she pursued the wavering path which she had so far followed, she would lose all her colonial territory.'

There could be no doubt that Germany would vanquish England. It was true that Germany had to make 'an excursion to the East', but this was also in France's interest. Because of this, the reckoning with England was at the most postponed. The East would certainly be liquidated. This would have happened earlier if France had shown herself to be more understanding. And then Germany would have devoted her attention to England.

Laval then turned to the question of political collaboration in Europe.

'Whereas earlier wars had been waged from village to village, and later from country to country, now a whole continent ought to be organized for peace. This would of course not be possible if each country insisted on putting forward claims to satisfy its natural greed. Such a way meant rejecting the possibility of organizing Europe on a solid enduring foundation.' He 'spoke of these things with great passion as a man whose heart lay not only in his own country but also in Europe. As such he did not want certain egoisms (sic) to hinder the erection of the structure for which the peoples of Europe longed.' He had taken a great personal risk in coming out publicly in favour of a German victory, and had done so because he wanted to save his country from Communism. But in order to further his intention he needed the help of the victors 'in creating a suitable atmosphere'.

Hitler curtly interrupted this disquisition. 'Time was pressing and at the moment it was a question of whether it was possible to provide safe ports of disembarkation for the Axis forces in Tunis and Bizerta, and to give the air force bases in Tunis, from which they could inflict crushing defeats on the enemy. If this was not possible, that was the end of collaboration . . . They must consider what practical steps should be taken to carry out these plans.'

Laval answered that he could not give a binding reply to the Fuehrer's precise question, which must be decided through Marshal Pétain. But he himself would support the fulfilment of the German request. In any event 'he must express one or two considerations, and would be glad if this discussion could take place in the presence of Count Ciano. Germany had never demanded any French colonies and only called for the return of former German territory. At Montoire France had been given a clear assurance that her colonial empire would be preserved in the fullness of its strength. Laval had always interpreted this to mean that it related to the colonial empire in its present context.'

Hitler became agitated. 'France had received no such comprehensive assurance at Montoire. The German and Italian claims had been markedly small and reasonable. If necessary they could consult the German minutes of that meeting . . . from which it would emerge that no such all-embracing and absolute guarantee had been given.' Laval slipped off the subject and back to the Italians. He stressed that Italy had never officially claimed Tunis from France. She had confined herself to bringing forward in a polemical manner on the radio and in the press claims on Corsica, Nice, and Tunis. 'In France he had often been asked—and had answered—that he knew nothing definite and could only state that at no stage had Italy made a formal claim on France, for which he was very pleased. He would like to express himself very clearly on this point . . . France would not accept such a demand from Italy. He said this as a politician who had shown how strongly he felt about French-Italian understanding. For this very reason he had sacrificed himself politically and had been overthrown by the Popular Front.[p] Even now he wanted once more to search for other formulas in order to achieve a French-Italian understanding.'

Laval was seeking a pretext to prevaricate over the Axis demand for the use of the bases of Bizerta and Tunis, which would be followed by Italian territorial claims. 'He could not predict the answer of the French ministers to the request for the admission of combined German-Italian forces. The population and the army would doubtless be very hesitant. If Italy had not broadcast her familiar propaganda in a partly insulting form and supported subversive movements in Tunis, he would be the last man in France to have second thoughts about such a request. He had the greatest admiration for Mussolini, above all because of his fight against Communism, but he feared that it would be held against him in France if, by inviting Italian troops to Tunis, he really accepted the above-mentioned Italian claims.' Hitler answered that Germany and Italy were after all allies, and that France should draw the consequences from the fact and accept combined units. 'The possession of bases in Tunis would permit the reconquest of the whole of French North Africa.' In the eyes of the Fuehrer, future German policy towards France would be conditioned by Laval's attitude to the militarily vital request for these bases.

But at this first conference since Montoire between the victors and vanquished some political concessions must be made to the French if Laval was to be able to maintain his own line of support for collaboration in general terms with Germany and Italy. 'He felt it his duty to try to obtain more favourable conditions of support from Germany, which would also be in the interests of Europe.'

Hitler's attitude was categorical. 'If Germany lost the war, Bolshevism would overrun Europe: no Atlantic Charter could be erected against the wild eastern storm of the Soviet savages. There had been a time when France too had seen the situation in this light. There was much talk then in French circles representing the view that France should devote herself to her colonial empire and that Germany should be given a free hand in the East. Among others, Monsieur Flandin, who hitherto had been an opponent of Germany, shared this view. In recognizing the extent of the threatening danger from the East, every nationally-minded Frenchman must wish fanatically for the victory of Germany . . .' Laval retorted: 'Nevertheless it was not entirely easy to convince the French of this obvious truth. The country had existed a very long time in happy peaceful conditions and had been poisoned by the doctrines of the Popular Front.'

The Frenchman's persuasive advocacy reached its peroration. The Fuehrer must help 'in creating the moral conditions in France in favour of collaboration with Germany. The present state of German-French relations was pictured by many Frenchmen as a one way street.' Laval asked for a gesture

p. In January 1936.

by Germany to lighten his task, and for more frequent personal contacts. Hitler's only answer was that 'he hoped that it would be realized in France that the Anglo-Saxons were aiming at world supremacy.'

Laval now took his leave and expressed again, 'with obvious emotion, the wish to do all in his power to collaborate and also the hope that in future Germany and France would between them find a relationship of friendly co-operation'. [20] He had never in his career played so hard for time, nor from such a position of weakness. His dialogue with Hitler, brilliant in form, neither altered nor modified a single decision, in particular the total occupation of France. As Ciano wrote, 'Not a word was said to Laval about the impending action. The orders to occupy France were being given while he was smoking his cigarette and conversing with various people in the next room. Ribbentrop told me that Laval would only be informed next morning at eight o'clock that, because of information received during the night Hitler had been obliged to proceed to the total occupation of the whole country.' [21] That evening Ciano returned to Rome.

The Allied landing in North Africa had forced on the Axis powers, in unplanned and barely co-ordinated haste, the decisions originally taken at the conference in Munich in June 1940.[q] As in the past, the Germans acted first and on their own. Marshal von Rundstedt, commanding the German armies in France, transmitted a letter to Marshal Pétain on the morning of November 11—there was a fortuitous irony in the date—announcing the crossing of the demarcation line by his forces. On the same day, German armoured units were landed at Tunis and Bizerta. German and Italian air units were already in occupation of the Tunisian airfields.

The Italian war machine was less highly geared to such lightning action. The decision to occupy Corsica was made on November 10, and orders given to move that night. The expedition was delayed by rain and heavy seas, and ultimately put to sea, in part literally in sailing cutters, the following afternoon. The Italian Fourth Army on the French frontier was 'a little behindhand', [22] and eventually began to move the same evening. An Italian convoy was due to arrive in Tunisian ports on November 12. As Cavallero noted in his diary: 'The Duce says if we do not gain time, the game is lost. It is not enough to occupy France, we must not lose Libya.' [23] But Rommel was withdrawing so fast that Cavallero, on a lightning trip to Africa, was unable to locate his headquarters three days later. 'Now Mussolini thinks,' wrote Ciano in his diary on his return from Munich, 'that we shall have God to thank if we can succeed in stopping at the old Agedabia line. I see a few people, and gather the impression that the events of the last few days have been a sad blow for the country which, for the first time, is asking many questions without finding answers.' [24]

q. See pp. 10–11.

CHAPTER FIVE

THE AXIS AND NORTH AFRICA

● ●

THE MENACING presence of the Anglo-American forces in North-West Africa created a military revolution in the Mediterranean, shattered the structure of German relations with France as defined at Montoire, and drove both Axis powers to occupy positions and undertake commitments regardless of the political consequences at Vichy. Having resisted Italian claims on Nice, Corsica, and Tunis in 1940, Hitler was now obliged from military necessity to press for their fulfilment by the French. Even so, there was a note of meanness.

Following the Munich Conference on November 9/11, 1942, Ribbentrop asked the German Ambassador in Rome to summarize the present Italian attitude to eventual claims against France, insinuating that perhaps Germany had no ultimate obligations in this respect towards her ally. Mackensen minuted the conversation: 'There was no evidence to show that the Duce had in any way changed in regard to Italian claims on Djibouti, Tunis, Corsica and Nice, but there were certain signs that, at least seen from outside at a given moment they would be upheld in their entirety . . . In addition I wanted to point out that the Fuehrer had repeatedly and also in his letters to the Duce, plainly stated that he would support Italian claims against France as presented by the Duce. As I saw it, there could be no question of giving the Italians to understand even by a hint that on our side there was any desire for a reduction of these claims. With these four demands the Duce had brought his people into the war and had firmly relied on the Fuehrer's word. The whole Italian population had still lively memories of the gulf between the promises of the Allies in May 1915 and that which was in reality conceded to them in November 1918, so that their trust in their present Ally would be shattered even by a hint. The German Foreign Minister agreed with my presentation completely and answered that for him it was beyond any discussion and that we had to abide unswervingly by the Fuehrer's assurances.' [1]

The psychological effect of the North African landings on Italian public opinion had been depressive, and it was a necessary reaction that emphasis should be made at once on these Italian claims. On November 18 Alfieri in Berlin protested to the German Undersecretary of State, Weizsäcker, against 'two reproaches against Italy now current in German circles: that Rommel's retreat was blamed on the lack of resistance of Italian units on the Egyptian border, and that Italian claims on Nice, Corsica, and Tunis lead to the criticism that the Italians did not conclude peace in time with France'. Weizsäcker replied that he had not heard of the first reproach and that as to the second 'he was astonished at the time of the Italo-French armistice that the Duce renounced the occupation of the three mentioned territories— Nice, Corsica, and Tunis'. Alfieri retorted that he believed that this renunciation by the Duce was due on his side to a wish to meet a plea from the Fuehrer in this sense. The German denied any knowledge of such a hint; on the contrary, he recalled that Hitler gave Mussolini 'a completely free hand, . . . and told him that the Franco-German armistice would only come into force after France had agreed armistice terms with Italy'. Weiszaecker admitted however that Italian claims must be settled if a final peace settlement with Vichy were made. [2]

The immediate issues, vital to the future conduct of the war in the Mediterranean, were the exploitation in time of the Tunis bridgehead and the fate of the French fleet. On November 13 Rintelen reported an optimistic conversation with Mussolini: 'The Duce summoned me at 8.30 p.m. on November 13 and instructed me to convey the following to the Fuehrer: — "Now that five days have passed since the American landing in North Africa, I do not view unfavourably the development of the situation in the interval. It is particularly good that we have taken possession of Tunis and Bizerta. The occupation of Tunis is of decisive importance for the further conduct of hostilities in the Mediterranean and therefore our first and most urgent task is to build up the Tunis bridgehead . . . I regard it as an excellent measure to have obtained the word of honour of the French fleet at Toulon." ' [3]

On the immediate credit side, also, the French merchant fleet was to be handed over to the Axis.[a] This acquisition might prove decisive in the battle of the African convoys. It was agreed at once that the bulk of the ships would be transferred to the Italians. But since the events of November 8/9, the attitude of the French Navy to the course of the war in the Mediterranean had been menacingly obscure. The Axis powers were now faced with a situation not unlike that of the British at the time of the 1940 armistice, and the grim solution was similar.

On the evening of November 26 Kesselring delivered to the Duce an urgent letter from Hitler. It was an announcement, without previous consultation, of the entry of German troops into Toulon. 'The information from the Italian

a. 159 ships totalling 645,000 tons (including Danish, Greek and Norwegian ships) in French Mediterranean ports. They were taken over by the Germans on November 18.

Consul in Toulon about the incidents in the French fleet, which was passed on to me on your instructions, confirms numerous reports from other sources and, together with the treachery of North Africa, gives now incontestable proof of the disloyal attitude of all the French Armed Forces, including the Fleet. After the appeal which Darlan broadcast over the wireless, we must particularly expect political sedition in the Toulon fleet. Not only will the latter not oppose an enemy attack, but from now on there is great danger that it will suddenly leave port and join the enemy. The same can be said for the French Army and Air Force. As an uncertain factor they constitute a threat to our rear for which I think I can no longer be responsible. I have therefore decided to disarm the French Army and Air Force as far as is necessary, and to occupy Toulon suddenly so as to make sure of the French fleet. German submarines are already off the French naval base with instructions to attack immediately every French warship which may attempt to escape.

'Duce, Marshal Kesselring will give you the details of my orders. Likewise I have asked General Field Marshal von Rundstedt to inform the Italian Fourth Army promptly and seek its support. And now, Duce, I would like to ask you, in support of these—in my opinion—absolutely necessary measures, to issue general orders to your Armed Forces authorizing them to co-operate with Field Marshal von Rundstedt. Since the success of this plan, which may well be of decisive importance for the war, depends on complete secrecy, I would ask you, Duce, to inform as few people as possible and above all not to give telephoned or more precise orders, but, as I have done with my Armed Forces, only to direct your Army to collaborate.' Instructions had also been given to distribute the French merchant fleet, 'so as to take into account in the fullest possible way the heavy Italian losses'. The Germans only needed relatively few ships for North African, Cretan and Black Sea convoys. 'As for the French Navy, I fear that it will not come to us intact, but if this does happen, Italy is the only lawful possessor.' The Germans required only temporarily light escort vessels for convoys which would be returned after the war. 'I hope, Duce, that the motives which I have given for my action seem reasonable to you.' [4]

The Axis was confronted in the following hours with the total sabotage by the French of their Mediterranean fleet in Toulon, and the dragging commitment of a military occupation of Southern France, thus tying down divisions needed in Russia and North Africa. Such was the final result of Montoire. The concept of a strong collaborationist French Government neutralizing the Western Mediterranean had disappeared. The German army in the West was now forced to garrison the Unoccupied Zone of France with inevitable adverse political repercussions at Vichy. The stationing of the Italian Fourth Army on the Southern coast of France came at a moment when the battle of North Africa was reaching a decisive stage, and such an extension of

Italian military commitments represented a dangerous stretching of her resources.

The Allied invasion of French North Africa also brought into sharp relief the issue of Spain's continued neutrality in the war, and forced equally on both belligerent parties a reappraisal of their own policies towards the Spanish government. The Allies, at the moment of the 'Torch' landings, had given formal assurances to respect Spanish territory, both European and African. On the other hand, the Axis might well have an interest in reviving the strategy of Hendaye, when in October 1940, at the meeting between Hitler and Franco, the former had pressed for Spanish co-operation in a German advance across Spain against Gibraltar. The Spanish demands had been excessive, and the guarantees of military co-operation unsatisfactory. Mussolini's attempt to appeal to Franco's sense of obligation for the decisive support given by Italy during the Civil War in Spain met with little success when the two men met at Bordighera early in 1941, and this failure on the part of the Axis to inveigle Spain into the war deprived them of any means to liquidate the British base at Gibraltar, or establish themselves in Spanish Morocco, and thus control the Western entry into the Mediterranean. As the Italian minutes of the meeting in April 1942 with Hitler at Salzburg read: 'Regret for not having carried out the operation of Gibraltar for which everything was ready, including a mountain in the Jura which looked like Gibraltar, and round which innumerable exercises had been carried out.' [5] Just as Hitler had met the nemesis of his French policy in the fracas of the North African landings, so Ciano was driven to face, under the same impact, the bankruptcy of the whole assumption underlying that Italian intervention in the Spanish Civil War, of which he had been the instigator.

The reactions of Franco to the new revolution in the balance of forces in the Mediterranean were carefully and ably reviewed by the German Ambassador in Madrid, Stohrer, in a telegram to Berlin on November 16. His initial assumption was that in spite of Party and Army talk in Spain about burning boats and intervening on the Axis side, Franco and his government were determined to avoid war. 'Spanish fears of being drawn unwillingly into the war are not only based on the threatening new power position of the Anglo-Saxons, but also in the recognition that Germany could have an interest in threatening the enemy flank in North Africa and in blocking the Straits of Gibraltar by an advance through Spain . . . Did we intend to attack through Spain?'

The Spaniards saw in a further success of Allied plans a grave threat to Italy, whose powers of resistance 'one does not estimate very highly here since the experience in the Spanish Civil War. The Government and public opinion reject entry into the war either on the side of the Anglo-Saxons or the Axis. Spain would attempt to resist attack on the Spanish motherland. She would fight the Anglo-Americans with weapons in her hand. In the event of a German invasion, orders for military resistance would be given, but it is not likely to come to this. In any case we must reckon with an active opposition from Red elements, which would receive supplies from the enemy. A German invasion would mean total war for Spain . . . An early breakdown of the food situation would be inevitable; in view of the strong Red elements present in Spain one must reckon with severe sabotage by stages. Spain has made no preparations for a war . . . There is also no spiritual mobilization. Even in the event of small landing operations by the enemy, one must reckon with the rising of the Spanish population, especially in the separatist (Basque and Catalan) and Red regions. The Spanish government is however *at the moment* probably still strong enough to quell such revolts.

'I stress however that these objections are only valid for the present military and political situation. The position can change. If, for example, we should succeed in driving the enemy from Algiers and parts of Oran, the Spaniards might well be tempted to make territorial conquests in North Africa and fight for such increase of their zone. It is also possible to conceive of a change in the situation, which would enable us to advance with strong forces through Spain and then drag the Spaniards along with us.'

The main need was military aid, both to strengthen Spain, and to discourage the Allies from regarding her as 'a glacis for their offensive against Europe'. If things developed better for the Allies in Africa, an increase in armaments to Spain would help her to resist pressure. This was the best means to prevent her sliding on to the other side. In any case, conversations should be held. 'We must not today allow the Spaniards to give themselves up.' [6]

Four days later, the German Ambassador had an interview with Franco, and the latter referred to the Allied guarantee as 'a piece of paper' and proceeded to outline Spanish requirements for military aid. There was however little implication that such requests would herald any active intervention by Spain in the war. As Stoehrer reported, 'Towards the end of the conversation of November 20, Franco asked me quite abruptly how we viewed the attitude of Italy. It seemed to him that Italy's powers of resistance were not very great . . . I answered of course reassuringly that we were firmly convinced that Italy possessed every requisite power of resistance, and that there was no demoralization, nor was it to be expected. But as there is no doubt that, by asking this question, Franco wanted to give a hint, and as naturally an unfavourable appreciation of Italy's will to resist must influence Franco's judgment of the whole situation, I thought that I should report the above.' [b]

b. German Collection. Madrid telegram, November 21, 1942. Franco repeated these doubts in a further meeting with the German Ambassador on January 24, 1943. 'The war has lasted longer than one had originally thought. He (Franco) must also say that this information as to the state of opinion in Italy begins to give him anxiety.' (German Collection. Madrid telegram, January 24, 1943.)

The German government, although dubious of the advantages of Spanish belligerency, demanded a guarantee from Franco that, if he was supplied with war material, he would at least fight if attacked by the Allies. Hitler was not prepared to be rushed. At a meeting on December 3, he decided after a lengthy exposition that 'it would be best for our conduct of the war if Spain remains neutral. An invasion of Spain under present conditions, both military and economic, would place exceptional demands on us.' Hitler would equip Spain with modern weapons only if she would fight with them. 'If she only wants to preserve her neutrality, let her seek equipment in America. We do not intend to attack Spain, hence we are indifferent as to where Spain obtains weapons to preserve her neutrality.' [7]

Mussolini had already reached the same conclusion independently, but as always tentatively. 'Spain will move increasingly in the direction of complete neutrality. Nothing much has been lost, as the entry of Spain into the war would require a very strong support in weapons and other things.' [8] And again on December 9 he told Ciano that 'he does not intend to move a finger to accelerate Spain's intervention in the war, because it could be more of a hindrance than a help'.[9]

The Allied landings in North Africa had created a new war front on the Tunisian border. The other lay, separate and unco-ordinated, along a rapidly disintegrating line in Libya as a consequence of the British victory at Alamein. If the shrinking Axis bridgehead in Africa were to be held—and the politico-military consequences of its loss would be incalculable—major strategic decisions at the highest level must be taken. A conference between Hitler and Mussolini on Africa might have led to a revision of Axis strategy, but the former was nailed in isolation in East Prussia with his maps of the Eastern Front, and the Duce confined by ulcers in Rome.

Rommel was by now sceptical of any stand being made, even in Tunisia. He had no hope of parrying a British outflanking drive. Only one-third of his fighting power was left and all reserve stocks and supply dumps had been lost. On November 11, having failed to persuade Cavallero or Kesselring to come to Africa, he had sent one of his officers to the Fuehrer's headquarters in the hopes of getting a precise directive. The officer 'met with little understanding. The Fuehrer had instructed him to inform me that I should leave Tunis out of my calculations and simply act on the assumption that the bridgehead would be held.' [10] In writing to Mussolini on November 20, in answer to requests for aircraft and artillery to defend Tripolitania on the Agheila line, Hitler assured him that guns would be sent 'as and when each gun is produced' and 'everything possible' would be done to strengthen the air force. But the immediate German interest was concentrated in Tunis. 'The aim of operations in Tunisia should in my opinion be that of advancing towards the west in order to break up the North African-Mediterranean positions of the Franco-Anglo-American troops.' [11] This was small comfort to Rommel. He had received orders from the Duce to hold on at all costs. His own conviction was that the only purpose of a delayed withdrawal would be to evacuate the remnants of an élite corps for action in Europe. 'In the long run neither Libya nor Tunisia could be held, for the African war was being decided by the battle of the Atlantic.' [12]

An Italo-German staff conference on November 24 revealed that the Afrika Korps now consisted of only one weak German division. It also showed a profound divergence of view between Rommel and Kesselring, the latter being obsessed with the consequences of Allied air bases being set up in Tunisia, and the creation of an air triangle Malta-Algiers-Tripoli which would control communications in the Central Mediterranean. In final exasperation, Rommel decided abruptly to fly in person to Hitler's headquarters to ask for a strategic decision and request as a long-term policy the evacuation of North Africa. The Fuehrer received him on the evening of November 28 in a thunderous mood. Rommel was barely able to state his case, and was lectured on the political necessity of holding a major bridgehead in Africa. Hitler was at last and belatedly convinced that the continued participation of Italy in the war depended on such action. The effect of Rommel's visit was at least to force the Fuehrer to take some decision. As a personal meeting with Mussolini was for the moment impracticable, Goering was sent to Rome, together with Rommel, and full powers to negotiate with the Italians.[13] As Ciano put it, 'Goering comes to Rome without advance notice. From what was said by members of the General Staff, the visit was prompted by the fact that Rommel left Libya secretly to see the Fuehrer. We protested, and the assistant German Military Attaché has been told that if an Italian General had behaved in this way he would have been brought before a court martial. Now Goering comes to settle the trouble, but this discord is not a matter of form . . . We shall see what decisions emerge from the conference that is to be held today at Palazzo Venezia.' [14]

It was a grumpy journey in Goering's special train. Rommel suspected Goering of wishing to supplant him, and of creating a private army and air force under his own command in Africa. The two men quarrelled all the way to Rome, which they reached on November 30, preceded by a telegram from Hitler to Mussolini complaining blandly of Italian delays in supplying Rommel's forces.[15] On arrival Goering, Kesselring and Rommel first attended a meeting at the Italian Supreme Command Headquarters to review the military position, particularly in regard to supplies for the African front.[c]

c. Rommel also refers to this conference, but writes that it took place on December 2. *The Rommel Papers* (edited by Captain Liddell Hart) p. 368. There is some confusion as to the dates of these meetings. According to the German military records, there was one meeting at Palazzo Venezia on November 30, and another at the Italian Supreme Command, at which Goering spoke, on the following day.

Goering's speech on this occasion was a blustering lecture. 'We no longer have in Africa one battlefield divided into two separate sectors, but one united zone. The enemy is, as is known, superior there in numbers, material, and principally in tonnage. Our submarines will from now on act with particular energy against these new enemy supply routes. For us the central problem is that of supplies. For the first time we are not far away from our battlefield—a mere "panther's leap". Hence we can ship rapidly men and material to Tunisia . . . Both for Tunisia and for Rommel one thing is certain and that is: if the supplies continue to be sent at the present rhythm we cannot hold either Tunisia or Tripolitania. Air transport is out of the question . . . The normal route is thus by sea. There is the question of mines, and in a meeting held by the Fuehrer there was a long discussion about these mines. We have the example of the British, which is the most eloquent of all. The English minefield which runs from Scapa Flow to the Thames has made it impossible for German U-boats to approach the English coast . . . We must without fail produce a similar one between Sicily and Tunis. This is the view of the Fuehrer and he will make available the necessary material, including mines.' [16]

One of Goering's staff officers was instructed at the meeting to order 500,000 mines immediately. The fact that only one minelayer was available was no deterrent to the Reichsmarshal who declared that 'he did not admit that such difficulties should be raised'.[17]

Rommel took a grudging part in this discussion. 'I had already drawn attention to the fact that practically the whole of our shipping space was being used for the Fifth Armoured Group in Tunisia, and that my army was not even receiving the necessities of life though it was carrying the main burden of the fighting.' [18]

At least one member of the German leadership understood his position. On December 12 Jodl, with a rare burst of independence, told Hitler at a military conference, 'I think that one cannot say anything against his (Rommel's) measures there. It is like asking a man, who has been nourished on a little bread and milk, to participate in the Olympic games. He has not received anything for weeks; in the East they scream if they are two trains short.' [19]

At a further conference with the Duce, Goering emphasized that the Germans were sending three armoured divisions to Africa, the Adolf Hitler, the Hermann Goering, and the Deutschland, 'three names which mean much to German honour'. This news seems to have heartened Mussolini, whom Ciano found 'optimistic both as regards the war and the internal situation',[d] and it was in this mood that the Duce supported Rommel when the latter

d. Ciano, op cit December 1, 1942, p. 530. It is noticeable that Ciano was not present at the meeting. There is no record available of the talk, though Ciano mentions 'the Duce sent me a report of his conversation with Goering'.

was openly attacked by Goering at the meeting for leaving the Italians in the lurch at Alamein. 'Before I could make a worthy reply to this monstrous statement,' Rommel recorded, 'Mussolini said, "That's news to me; your retreat was a masterpiece, Marshal Rommel." ' [20]

The main and public aim of Goering's mission was to hector and push the Italians into total mobilization of their war effort, civil and military, to save North Africa.

His visit to Southern Italy was taken up with inspections of port installations, and contacts with Italian officials. Sicily might well be the next threatened objective in the Mediterranean strategy of the Allies, and in any event its defence must play a decisive role in Goering's own personal policy to press for a continuing hold on North Africa. But the effort to translate German methods in an emergency into southern terms proved frustrating. As Dollmann wrote in his private report to Himmler: 'The Reichsmarshal was visibly influenced by German ability to make a supreme effort in moments of crisis—the final involvement of all Party members, the appeal to the Party—points of view which I endeavoured to relate to a somewhat different set of conditions here.' There was the old Italian Admiral at Messina, for example, 'who whispered in my ear that in the last resort the way out lay in no sense with the Party, but in a military dictatorship'.[21] The whole machinery of Fascist administration was fast reaching the point of decisive strain, but in the last resort the capacity for resistance depended on the civilian prefects as much as on the military commanders.

On December 5 Goering had a final meeting with Cavallero and the Italian military experts. He wished to stress the lessons of his trip to the South, the main practical purpose of which had been to form an idea of how the loading of ships for the Africa run was working. The main anxiety would be relieved 'when the French shipping in Marseilles would be brought unhindered to Italian ports'. Loading and repair facilities must be improved and speeded up. He had seen one ship in Naples which had been lying idle for months with damaged propellers and steering-gear. 'The dock workers must be spurred to greater efforts.' Sublimely unaware of Neapolitan habits, Goering announced that he would arrange for field kitchens so that the dockers could be fed while at work. 'He also stressed the use of the Fascist Party and its organizations for a speedy remedying of the lack of labour.' [22]

Ciano had watched Goering's visit to Italy with distant asperity. D'Ajeta, the head of Ciano's private office, reported to him a private talk with the German Minister in Rome, Prince Bismarck, who was quoted as saying: 'The Germans themselves are convinced that there is nothing more to be done in Africa, and that all Goering's promises are destined to remain in the kingdom of the clouds. But it is a matter of saving Rommel's reputation . . . Goering's principal task therefore is to create confusion and prove that the fault lies with our defective organization of shipping . . .' Bismarck added that the military experts of the German Embassy were amazed at the number of stupidities which the Reichsmarshal could accumulate. 'Can it be that Goering is really thinking of appointing himself the Reichsprotektor of Italy?' [23]. It is not inconceivable that Goering may have considered such a project in the event of a sudden disappearance of the Duce from the scene, through illness or a political coup. The defence of the Italian mainland would then become a German responsibility and form the outer bastions covering the fortress of Europe and possibly more effectively organized by direct military government, backed by the divisions now being sent to Italy which, together with the Air Force, were closely connected with Goering. A similar thought had occurred to Rommel on the train journey to Rome. 'Goering also possessed inordinate ambition and had no scruples about the means he used to advance it. Thus he thought that there were easy laurels to be earned on the African Front, and was angling to manoeuvre the Air Force into control of it. Units of his Praetorian Guard, the Armoured division "Hermann Goering", were already on their way to Tunis.' [24]

In any event, Goering now appeared as the leading exponent, on the German side, of bolstering up the Mediterranean theatre. He presided over meetings of Italian civilians and technical experts, creating confusion, obstruction and resentment.[25] Rommel noted: 'Particularly interesting was Goering's political attitude towards the Italians in relation to the difficult situation in Africa. Although we had always been forbidden to say a word to the Italians about the shortcomings of their Army and State, or to demand improvements, Goering now began to talk to Cavallero about really fundamental questions, such as the poor Italian armament, their sea strategy and similar thorny subjects. The only result, of course, was that he put their backs up without having any hope of getting anything put right . . . Many Italians felt very deeply that the Axis was a sham, and consequently believed that in final victory we would have scant regard for their interests. It was generally felt that, if Tripolitania were lost, Mussolini would be threatened by a political crisis in Italy. His position may well have been further weakened by Goering's sudden heavy-handed behaviour. A great many Italians had had enough of the war, and were considering how best they could get out of it.' [26]

CHAPTER SIX

'THE BERESINA WIND'

• •

'THE FUEHRER wanted to bring the battle for Stalingrad to a conclusion. This would probably happen in the next eight days, as already eight-tenths of the city was in German hands . . . Then the fighting on the Volga in this region would be closed.' [1] These remarks by Goering during his talk with Mussolini in Rome on October 23 masked the real situation on the Eastern Front.

Hitler was counting to reach a final decision within the year 1942 in the Russian war, which tied down over 200 German and satellite divisions and 70 per cent of the total German armed forces. He had set himself a two-fold and simultaneous task: firstly a thrust south-eastwards to the Caucasus which would bring into German hands the granaries of the Kuban, the industrial regions of the Donetz Basin, and the oilfields of the Caucasus; secondly, having achieved this conquest, a final flanking assault on the main concentration of the Russian armies in Central Russia ending with the occupation of Moscow—an operation which had failed in the blitzkrieg of the previous winter. By the middle of August the southern advance had already been carried out according to plan, and the concentration of oil fields at Maikop was already in German hands. But the communications of their armies were now stretched to the limits, and the mountainous terrain of the southern Caucasus lay ahead of them, and beyond that the Grozny oil fields and the ultimate objective, Baku. The limit of the southern advance was reached during the first days of November.

The first stages of the second part of the German plan consisted of a major thrust conducted by forty German divisions to break through from the Southern Don to the Volga, and towards the industrial keypoint of Stalingrad lying on that river, the possession of which would cut off Central Russia from the Caucasus. From here the northern offensive along the right bank of the Volga would be pursued against the main Russian armies protecting the approaches to Moscow. The attack against Stalingrad was launched and the outskirts of the city were reached on September 3. In the early planning of the German campaign Stalingrad had not been a major target, except in the sense that the city lay on the main axis of the ultimate gigantic German flanking manoeuvre against Moscow. The fatal diversion to the Caucasus resulted in neither the Central, Northern, nor the Southern offensives being successful. The Russians were able to withdraw their forces on the central sector behind the Don, and create a Stalingrad front. During September and October the issue of the Russian war, and indeed that of one of the major fronts of the world conflict, was fought out in and around the city.

From the beginning of September the German air forces were flying up to 2,500 sorties a day over the battle area. The climax of the campaign was sudden and dramatic. During these weeks of grim fighting, the Russians had massed sufficient forces east of the Volga to launch an encircling offensive against the German armies in front of embattled Stalingrad. On November 19 the Russians attacked the German forces north of the city, and on the following day assaulted the positions to the South. Within five days, 22 German divisions were encircled and another 14 destroyed. By the end of the month the German 6th Army under General Paulus was totally surrounded, and the whole operational plan of the Germans for 1942 lay shattered. Meanwhile the Caucasus offensive had come to a standstill, and the German Commander, von Manstein, was ordered to divert forces in a combined move to liberate the Stalingrad pocket. On December 12 this abortive thrust from the south was launched, together with a similar operation due eastwards from positions on the Don. On December 16 the Russians struck southwards from their positions east of Stalingrad against Mannstein's divisions, and he was driven rapidly southwards. By the second half of December another 22 German satellite divisions had been broken to pieces.

The catastrophic course of the war on the Eastern Front had coincided with the destruction of the Axis position in North Africa at El Alamein. The mirage of a rendezvous at Suez had been brutally dispersed, and the initiative lost on the two land fronts of the war.

On the evening of November 6, after the Alamein battle, Mussolini had told Rintelen, 'I would like to convey to you personally my impression that we must make a separate peace with Russia as soon as possible.' [2] Only in such a manner could the deadlock of the war be broken on the Axis side, and the only person who could raise such an issue personally with Hitler was the Duce himself. Unless such a drastic summit decision were made, there would be a total strategic disaster.

On December 4 Goering came again to Rome, and in private conversation with Mussolini, at which no interpreter was present, the latter pursued this delicate and vital theme. 'The Duce believed that, one way or another, the henceforth pointless chapter of the war against Russia should be closed. If it should prove possible to arrive at a second Brest-Litovsk [a]—and this one could do by giving Russia territorial compensation in Central Asia— care must be taken to set up a defensive line which will destroy all enemy initiatives and with the minimum commitment of Axis forces. Goering says this would be Hitler's ideal.'[b]

The attitude of Goering on this occasion is unresolved. No German leader could openly express scepticism at the victorious outcome of the Russian campaign. This would amount to treason. The only hope, however meagre, of persuading Hitler even to consider a compromise peace with the Russians, must lie in the subtle pattern of relations between the Fuehrer and the Duce. Hence the intense, wary, and at times alarmed, speculation in certain German circles during the autumn and winter of 1942, and again in the spring of 1943, as to the very political existence and future of Mussolini. The historic role of the Duce might be to persuade Hitler to come to such a decision, and there are signs, even though as yet, in the present state of the evidence, faint, that Mussolini was cast in just such a political part, not only by his own entourage, but also in certain German quarters.

There is a posthumous account by Ribbentrop, which is understandably not corroborated in any formal minutes of diplomatic talks during these weeks, but coincides in time with the first indication of the Duce's own intention to approach Hitler on the subject. 'When the Anglo-American landing in North Africa took place in November 1942, I happened to be in Berlin. The very first reports showed the remarkable tonnage employed—four million was mentioned. Clearly, an operation of such vast dimensions was very serious, and we had apparently been very wrong in our estimates of enemy tonnage. Indeed, Hitler later admitted as much. Since fortunes in the African theatre had always swayed backwards and forwards, I now feared the worst concerning the Axis position in the Mediterranean.

'After contacting the Fuehrer I invited Count Ciano to come to Munich immediately for a conference; the Duce could not be spared to leave Italy. I flew to Bamberg, where I boarded the Fuehrer's special train, which arrived there from the East. I briefly reported as follows: the Anglo-American landing was serious, for it showed that our estimates of enemy tonnage, and therefore of the prospects of our U-boat war, had been radically wrong. Unless we could expel the British and Americans from Africa, which seemed very doubtful in view of our transport experiences in the Medi-

a. The Treaty of Brest Litovsk was signed between the Central Powers and Russia on March 3, 1918.
b. Italian Collection. Duce-Goering conversation, December 4, 1942. In his diary Ciano notes, 'The Duce has dictated to me a brief summary of his conferences with Goering, which I have preserved elsewhere.' (Ciano, *op cit* p. 532. December 6, 1942.)

terranean, Africa and the Axis army there were lost, the Mediterranean would be open to the enemy, and Italy, already weak, would be confronted with the gravest difficulties. In this situation the Fuehrer needed a decisive reduction of his war commitments, and I asked for authority to make contact with Stalin through Madame Kollontay, the Soviet Ambassadress in Stockholm. I suggested that, if need be, most of the conquered territories in the East would have to be given up. To this the Fuehrer reacted most strongly. He flushed, jumped to his feet and told me with indescribable violence that all he wanted to discuss was Africa—nothing else. His manner forbade me to repeat my proposal.' [3] It does however appear that on December 14 an agent of Ribbentrop's, Edgar Clauss, first contacted Madame Kollontay.[c]

On December 15, on the eve of the forthcoming talks with the Germans, Mussolini aired his views to Bottai on a possible settlement with Russia, which to him was now the cardinal issue of the war. Mussolini seemed 'worn out, unshaven, his face livid and shrunken. I referred to the . . . fixation of German thoughts on the Russian front, which they now call the Soviet sphinx. He reacted at once, reminding me that he had already attempted on one occasion to draw the attention of Hitler and "that dilettante Foreign Minister of his" to the "decisive" Mediterranean front. But in vain. It would have been better if we had dealt with the Russians. Having swallowed the Non-Aggression Pact, it was better to reach an alliance. And he alluded to the expediency, even today, of making peace with the Russians.' [4]

But one brutal set of facts was seldom reviewed. The basic raw materials of the Italian war economy, steel, iron, and oil must also come from German-controlled territories. Here again the vital sources of supplies lay in occupied Russia, and on the imminent possession of the Donetz Basin and the Caucasus, in spite of any wishful thinking in Rome of a separate peace with the Russians, depended the future successful maintenance of the Axis war effort. Negotiations had just taken place on December 14 in Berlin between German and Italian technicians on the failure of the Germans to maintain their steel deliveries essential to keep even a minimum level of production by the Italian war industry. The Italian representative, General Favagrossa, the Undersecretary at the Ministry of War Production, was received by Ribbentrop, and treated to a survey of the war. The weight of the German forces lay in the East: 1,000,000 men as against less than 50,000 in Africa. But there would be no early Russian collapse. It had taken two and a half years in the First World War. In regard to oil, there was an unfortunate dependence on

c. Kleist, *Zwischen Hitler und Stalin*, pp. 235 ff. It is also not without interest to note Canaris' pessimistic talk with Amé at this time. The heads of the two Military Intelligence Services met at Nice in early December. See Ciano, *op cit* p. 533, December 9, 1942.

Roumania, but the Caucasus fields were in sight. 'Next year the oil problem will be solved.'d

The military crisis on the Russian front, and the revolution in the position of the Axis in the Mediterranean, now forced Hitler to call a summit meeting with his Italian ally. The two leaders had not met since the previous April at Salzburg. On December 6, the German Ambassador in Rome, Mackensen, officially extended the long-postponed invitation to the Duce to come to Germany. Laval was to be summoned for the second part of the meeting. According to Ciano, Mussolini was prepared to go 'but without enthusiasm'. He said that he would want his meals alone 'because he does not want a lot of ravenous Germans to notice that he is compelled to live on rice and milk only'.5

The Germans had suggested that the meeting should be held at Klessheim where the Axis leaders had last met in April 1942, but late on December 15 Mackensen called on Ciano to say Hitler 'cannot leave the High Command, nor can he postpone the meeting'. He therefore asked that, as the journey would be long for the Duce, Ciano should come, together with Cavallero, to East Prussia.e The Duce agreed that Ciano should go 'and this time provided with exact instructions'. The Germans had given no precise indication as to an agenda. Mackensen had merely told Ciano that 'the conversations would be important and last a few days'. Bismarck however told D'Ajeta, the head of Ciano's private office, that Hitler had tried to avoid the meeting with the Duce, because he did not want to enter into general political discussions. 'It seems,' wrote Ciano, 'that we shall speak only of France, and that Laval will be present.'

On December 16 Ciano received his instructions for the conference, 'Mussolini is especially anxious that Hitler should know, as he had already spoken of it to Goering, that he considers it extremely advisable to come to an agreement with Russia, or at least to fix upon a defensive line which could be held by small forces. 1943 will be the year of the Anglo-Saxon effort. Mussolini considers that the Axis must have the greatest number of divisions possible to defend itself in Africa, the Balkans, and perhaps in the West.' 6

It appears that Ciano placed 'elsewhere' a copy of his instructions, and although this document has not yet come to light, a page of notes clearly made from them, possibly on the journey to East Prussia, is among his papers.

d. German Collection. Ribbentrop-Favagrossa December 14, 1942, and Favagrossa, *Perché perdemmo la guerra*, pp. 227 ff. In the subsequent talks with experts, Italy was to be kept going with 85,000 tons of steel a month.

e. Relations between Ciano and Cavallero were nearing a crisis. 'Notwithstanding the fact that we told the Germans that we did not consider Cavallero's presence advisable at the coming meeting at Klessheim, they have still insisted that he should come. It becomes more and more obvious that they consider him their man.' Ciano, *op cit* December 13, 1942, p. 534.

The main entries read: 'Policy—1943. Effort of the Anglo-Americans—North Africa and also West Africa. If we do not want two fronts—Brest-Litovsk is necessary, if possible; if not, at least a systemization of the Eastern Front—withdrawal of strongest Axis units. War with Russia has no point. See if one can use intervention by Japan.[f]

'1943. Italy will make military effort and in January call up 1907 and 1923 age-groups; in March, 1924; and after the harvest, 1925. 1,000,000—weapons and equipment. Without a stable air superiority which makes provisioning possible, the position in North Africa will become uncertain and in the end untenable.' [7]

While Mussolini was brooding on the consequences of the war in the East, Hitler was obsessed with the impossibility of retreat from the clash of armies at Stalingrad and was cut off from all reality save the impulse to endure all the implications of his anti-Bolshevist crusade. Living in the physical isolation of a secret headquarters on the East Prussian front, where it was dark early in the afternoon, he had retreated mentally from every other preoccupation with the war save the imperative need to avoid military disaster in the East.

Neither the Germans nor the Italians seem to have been able to face up to the problems of joint planning and command. The occupation of the Tunis bridgehead had at once created such an issue. Should there be a unified command in Africa for both the Eastern and Western fronts, Libya and Tunisia, and if so, under whom? At a military conference at Hitler's headquarters on December 1, Jodl touched on the matter and the ensuing dialogue lights up the German reaction to their Italian allies. 'May I add something on the question of leadership in Africa? Of course that is a question of organization. This is a very touchy point with the Italians: before long they will say, "of course we must have full command in this theatre of war". Up to now they have not raised the question.' Hitler retorted, 'At the moment we are handling the show, and if we do start another offensive you can be sure that there will be no Italians in it.' Jodl added that 'this was also the reason why they never spoke of the fact that we are quietly in command' in the African theatre. 'How can they?' Hitler answered. 'With seven divisions we are running the war alone anyway. They are not running it.' [8]

On December 12, at a further meeting with his military advisers Hitler, talking of the misfortunes of Rommel in North Africa, referred to 'the tragic distractions with the Italians, the eternal uncertainty. We are expecting that too; I didn't sleep last night; that's the feeling of uncertainty. If I had a German front, it would still be possible that something might happen, but I would have the feeling that it would be made up again. At least a whole army

f. See Appendix B to this chapter.

would not fall apart in a day . . . We won't succeed with the Italians anywhere. Therefore, if anybody breaks through there, there will be a catastrophe.' [9]

It was to study this 'uncertainty' that the present conference had been summoned, although the formal reason was the new situation in France. 'The Germans want to study thoroughly our will to resist.' [g]

The Italian delegation led by Ciano and Cavallero, and accompanied by Mackensen, left Rome by train on the evening of December 16. They were joined in Berlin by the Italian Ambassador, Alfieri, and by Lanza, his senior Embassy official. The journey has been described by the latter.

'Thursday, December 17. Travelling since last night. Sumptuous train. Ciano, Mackensen, Cavallero; each has a special carriage. Then there is a "radio" car, full of the most ingenious contraptions, which at the critical moment never work; then a carriage for the General Staff which is so cold, dark, and abandoned that no one dare put their feet inside. The train seems to be dragging with difficulty a dead weight behind it. The food is refined, the service perfect, and there are fresh flowers at each meal. At each stop in the railway stations in Germany, radio contact is made in a few minutes with Rome. But Rome has nothing to say, and our Minister (Ciano) does not believe that he has any succulent meditations to expound. His table talk, brilliant and amusing, is disconcertingly vacuous and extremely monotonous. The Germans seem to be his favourite target and he enjoys himself by talking of them in the worst possible way. Mackensen must be used to hearing every kind of insult, for he keeps quiet with dignity at the all too open asides against his country. One never sees Cavallero. Ciano, whenever he refers to him, calls him "that bum with short legs". Bum here, bum there; imbecile Germany here, cretinous Germans there; "that delinquent Ribbentrop"; "that criminal Hitler" and so on. Slowly, to the rhythm of these phrases, the train carries us, without bumping or deviating, towards the goal.' [h]

The following day, the train reached a siding beyond Rastenburg, where Ribbentrop and Keitel were awaiting their Italian colleagues. The formal conference was preceded by a brief private talk between Hitler and Ciano.[i] The former expressed anxiety at the Duce's state of health on which so much depended. Ciano explained that 'the Duce, as the result of his stomach trouble, has lived for a long time almost exclusively on milk, but he is now

g. Simoni, *Berlino Ambasciata D'Italia*, p. 296. Simoni is the pseudonym of the Italian Minister at the time in Berlin, Baron Michele Lanza, who accompanied Alfieri to the conference.

h. Simoni, *op cit* p. 297–8. The atmosphere of this Italian delegation to Hitler was not unlike that of the mission to Mussolini of Goering and Rommel a fortnight earlier.

i. For the following see: German Collection, Schmidt minutes for December 18, 19, 20, 1942; Italian Collection. Ciano's report, 'Summary of the conversations at Headquarters on December 18, 19, 20, 1942'; and Cavallero, *op cit* pp. 412–22 based on Ciano's report.

able to take some nourishment again and it is hoped that he will be fully recovered in two or three months. The Fuehrer answered that he had followed the course of the Duce's illness with special sympathy as he himself had suffered for a time from a stomach complaint which had indeed been of nervous origin and caused by overwork.'

At noon the two men were joined by Ribbentrop, Keitel, Jodl and Cavallero. The Fuehrer opened the meeting by saying that it had not been possible to work out a formal agenda. 'He would probably be called away many times during the talks in order to make military decisions . . . It would therefore be a matter of a business discussion without formalities or a conventional frame.' j

Hitler began by reviewing in detail the reasons which had led him to begin the Russian campaign; 'a struggle for the existence not only of the totalitarian régime but of our very countries'. The greatest danger which now threatened them was that of Bolshevism. If the Axis were to suffer defeat from Bolshevism, all Europe would be infected by it, because the Democracies, who had not had the strength to bring it to a halt in Russia itself in 1920, would not now be capable of hindering its westward march.

'The balance sheet of the war up to date showed, as all balance sheets, a credit and debit.' On the credit side, Italy and Germany had completely liberated Europe from bridgeheads held by the enemy except 'if our mistakes allow the Anglo-Saxons to regain a renewed footing there'. In the autumn of 1938, at the moment when the war really began, the opposing forces had the following military strength: Czechoslovakia 35 divisions, Poland 60, Denmark and Norway 8–10, Holland 18–22, Belgium 24, France 136, Jugoslavia 30–34, Greece over 20, Russia 260–270. 'We may now claim that all these enemies have been beaten and the Russians driven back 1,500–2,000 kilometres, and that in comparison with the past they represent a much smaller danger.

'And we must not forget the successes of the U-boat war which has sunk 25 million tons of Allied shipping; when to this is added the shipping blockaded in the ports of France and Norway, in Russia, in the Black Sea and the Baltic, it amounts to a total of 30 million tons. Now, more than ever before, since events have proved that the war is closely bound up with the transport problem, the enemy can be considered to be more blockaded than ourselves.'

On the debit side, the severing of overseas communications had led to the loss of the Italian Empire and now the temporary loss of Cyrenaica and a part of Tripolitania, which had nevertheless been compensated by the occupation of Tunisia and Bizerta.

j. The Schmidt minute of this first meeting runs to fifty-five pages of typescript. Ciano's report to Mussolini is more succinct. The former document has been quoted to show only important additions or striking phrases omitted by Ciano.

Speaking of the military position, Hitler postulated the existence of four fronts: the Eastern, the South-Eastern, the North African, and the Far Eastern.

The Eastern Front, 'which represents the protective front of Europe. Its purpose is to destroy the Bolshevik colossus and to assure ourselves living space from which Europe can draw not only the necessary foodstuffs, but also the indispensable raw materials for the prosecution of the war, such as coal, petroleum, and iron . . . Russia is now making a desperate effort to wrest from us the advantages already gained. . . . Countermeasures have already been taken, and we are sure that the situation will be controlled and corrected.' [10]

The South-Eastern Front. Hitler did not know how many Anglo-American divisions were marching on Tripoli, but they might be in a position simultaneously to bring forces to Syria and prepare to attempt a landing in the Balkans. 'It is obvious that, as long as we have bases in the Dodecanese, Rhodes, the Peloponnese, Crete, Greece, and Dalmatia, all efforts to make a landing will fail, on the condition that together with the bases we also control the rear.

'The following measures are basic in order to avoid the threat of a Balkan front: the strengthening and securing of communication between the Dodecanese, Crete, Rhodes, the Peloponnese; the building of a striking force;[k] contacts with Hungary and Bulgaria, to work out eventual action with them; taking all measures to ensure order in the Balkan hinterland as well as supplies to our forward bases. It cannot yet be said whether the Anglo-Saxons will launch such an enterprise, but we must take steps to meet the worst eventuality.'

The North African Front. German policy towards France was based on the experiment of Montoire. 'Then began the so-called collaboration which was regarded by the Germans simply as a business proposition. Germany has gained certain advantages but it must be recognized that in reality she has paid a higher price than France, and even more so as the French have only partly carried out their obligations. Hitler has never believed in the sincerity of France and now believes therein even less. It is clear that Pétain himself has conducted a policy only based on gaining time, on thus obtaining advantages for his country, and on sowing discord between Germany and Italy. On this all Frenchmen including Laval are united, and Hitler never again wants to receive Laval alone. This mistrust of France has had the effect that Hitler has never forgotten that, while he has been placing his troops on the Atlantic coast in a defensive role against England, he has in his rear a France which is at the same time an unknown quantity and a

k. See Cavallero's diary, *op cit* p. 415. 'We also thought for this purpose of a division for the Eastern Front.'

B.F.—4*

threat. When it came to the events in North Africa, it was clear that there must be no ultimatum, in order above all to avoid the Fleet going to Algiers and taking up a position against us. In any event it is better to know that the Fleet is sunk in Toulon rather than intact in Algiers. He is by no means convinced that the Generals and Admirals betrayed Pétain. There is evidence that the Marshal himself was aware beforehand, was essentially in agreement, and had in mind a trip to Algiers himself. The German government refused permission for such a journey although he had stated that he would not go to Tunisia in order not to "annoy" the Italians.'

Hitler emphasized the importance of the whole of French territory and particularly of Corsica, Tunisia and Bizerta. 'Tunis was strategically of great importance to the Axis. It was no coincidence that the first Punic War had been fought for Tunis, and the domination of ancient Rome in the Mediterranean was only completed by the conquest of Tunis. And now the Axis was here faced with a series of decisive tasks. First in importance was the transport question. If this could not be solved, Tunis could not be held. If it could, then Germany could and would send her best divisions to Tunis and drive the British and Americans from these regions. If it proved possible to bring to Tunis supplies, oil, and men, Algeria would be lost to the Anglo-Saxons and the Axis would be soon outside Melilla, which might well bring about a change in the attitude of Spain. If the transport problem could not be solved, it would be a waste of each man and each item of equipment brought to Tunis. One could not answer for sending further troops there. If the operation succeeded, the efforts and commitments of the Anglo-Saxons would be in vain and they would have to supply their positions in the Eastern Mediterranean by the long route via the Cape, where they were again threatened by U-boats. It was clear that on both sides the problem of transport was basic. To solve the Axis problem of supplies to Africa there must in any event be a widespread sacrifice on the part of the civilian population [11] . . . The Italian Navy must be impelled beyond the bounds of the possible to assure communications with Tunis and Bizerta. The solution of this problem was of the greatest importance for the conduct of the war itself, and one must not shrink from the possibility of losing ships, for either the war was won and the ships could easily be replaced, or the war was lost and then one need have no illusions about the fate of the fleet, even if it had been carefully spared during the conflict.' [12]

In conclusion Hitler said that 'he was determined to give of his best, because he regarded the North African question as decisive for the war, and wanted to stand by Italy out of warm friendship towards the Duce. The enemy was seeking advantages each for himself, while Germany and Italy had no conflicting interests and existed in completely separate living spaces.'

At five o'clock that evening, December 18, the meeting reassembled. Ciano, speaking from his instructions, placed squarely before the conference the main proposal of Mussolini.

'The Duce took the view that the British and Americans would in 1943 carry out large-scale operations in North Africa, in South-East Europe, and in Western Europe. Under these circumstances he wondered whether it was not possible to avoid the war on two fronts by making a political settlement with Russia. An ideal solution seemed to him to be a new "Brest-Litovsk Treaty", although he was also aware that it would be exceptionally hard to reach such an agreement with Russia. If it did turn out to be too difficult to arrive at that sort of arrangement, he would be of the opinion that they should take up a position on the Russian Front which would allow the Axis to transfer greater numbers of troops as soon as possible from East to West. Ciano emphasized that these considerations were mere hypotheses which had not assumed any concrete shape. The Duce believed that one could possibly use Japan to explore the chances of a political solution with Russia. By these means Russian dynamism must be steered in another direction—towards Central Asia.'[1]

Ciano recorded in his subsequent memorandum for the Duce: 'When I spoke of the possibility of a separate peace with Russia, Hitler expressed his own negative point of view in the following words. Germany had already in the past posed the problem of coming to an understanding with Russia, and precisely in the winter of 1940–41 every attempt was made to push the Russians into Central Asia. This was particularly discussed at the time of Molotov's visit to Berlin. But the Russians did not follow this course. Instead they brought up their historic claims on Finland and the Dardanelles, against Roumania, and in the direction of Bulgaria. If Germany had given way at that time, the Russians would first have attacked Finland, and then after they had taken over the Roumanian oil, the Axis would have been placed in an untenable position.

'The Russia of Stalin still follows the path chosen by Peter the Great for the expansion of his people to the North and South-West. Russia has in no way shown herself prepared to follow the course proposed to her towards India and the Persian Gulf because she regards these aims as secondary. If she were first assured of hegemony over Europe, the rest would follow of its own accord.

'The break between Germany and Russia arose out of the increasing danger which this latter threat presented. When Hitler knew for certain that nine hundred airfields, an enormous quantity of war material and numerous

1. Schmidt minute, *op cit* pp. 23–4. Ciano does not record his own words in his minute to the Duce, presumably because he was merely amplifying the text of the latter's instructions to him before leaving Rome.

troops were concentrated on the frontier, he had to take defensive measures. Can yet another attempt now be made to reach a settlement of the struggle with Russia? The Fuehrer asked himself this question some months ago, when the rumour was spreading that Japan had sounded the Fuehrer in this sense.[m] But, as we had assumed, we learnt that these rumours had been artificially spread by the Russians themselves to bring pressure on their allies to give more support in armaments, and to obtain the opening of the Second Front.

'What would the position be today if we somehow came to an agreement? It is certain that the Russians would devote six months to a complete overhaul of their equipment and strength in order to fall on our rear again. The Brest-Litovsk line is out of the question. These are regions which represent indispensable reserves of foodstuffs and raw materials for Germany and Russia alike. Thus any line drawn which might satisfy the requirements of one people would sacrifice the needs of the other.

'Even if we came to an understanding with Russia, we would not be able to move larger forces to Africa, because the only reason for the crisis which has arisen in Africa is to be found in our transport difficulties and not at all from lack of material and troops.' Also in regard to air strength an understanding with Russia would bring no noticeable gain. 'No air force could be moved effectively to another front in under six months . . . but in any case, the removal of these forces from Russia would be disquieting as their deployment in the event of a treacherous Russian attack would need many months.' There was only one great advantage, the reduction of losses in manpower; but the risk was too great. In short, Hitler saw no advantage in ending the war in the East. Finland would then probably sever with the Axis and join the enemy. The forces required for the security of Norway and France need not be taken away from the Russian front. Four divisions were already prepared for Africa and could be sent as soon as transport was assured. These divisions would, together with the Italo-German forces already available in Tunisia and Libya, amount to a total of four hundred thousand men, whose maintenance produced transport problems of enormous size, and this number certainly could not be increased.

Ciano broke into the conversation by saying that 'he had taken down the interesting observations of the Fuehrer exactly and would make an exhaustive report to the Duce. The latter had incidentally made no proposal, but only wanted to know the Fuehrer's opinion on certain matters.'[n]

On her side Italy would do everything possible to make a major military effort in 1943. Between January and the summer one million men would be

m. In the Schmidt minute the text reads, 'Some time ago the question was raised by Japan as to whether it was not possible to reach agreement with the Russians on a workable basis.' On this question see Appendix B to this chapter.

n. See Schmidt minute, pp. 34–6. Again Ciano's remarks are not recorded in his own report, but his statements follow the notes on his instructions.

under arms. There would be the problem of equipping them, and Cavallero must talk about this separately to Keitel. As to the situation in North Africa, Mussolini thought it essential to protect the supply routes through the establishment of a permanent air superiority. Without such superiority, the transport position would become increasingly precarious and finally untenable.

Ciano then turned to the French situation. 'The Duce had from the beginning had the gravest mistrust of, and a very modest and limited confidence in, the Laval government,' which certainly represented the real France to a far less degree than the Darlan administration now set up by the Allies in Algiers.

Laval was due to arrive at the conference on the following day. Hitler told Ciano that, 'after Laval has been heard' decisions would be taken about France. He agreed with Mussolini's view. 'The French are eighty per cent *attentistes,* five per cent collaborationists in more or less good faith, and the rest follow Darlan and de Gaulle. All are united in the thought of freeing themselves from the Germans. One must make an exception only for those few who, like Laval, have completely compromised themselves, and know that on the day the Germans leave France they will be shot. The greatest reservations are also made as to the loyalty of Pétain.' But in any case it was proper to support a French government since it at least could neutralize the action carried out by Darlan in North Africa. 'The majority of Frenchmen are not without spirit or enthusiasm. Darlan calls on them to fight; Pétain invites them to avoid battle. Many Frenchmen prefer to live with Pétain rather than die with Darlan ... Germany is only ready to give way on a few formal questions without giving the Laval government any real element of strength.'

Hitler warmed to his own defence of his French policy. 'Pétain ought to be kept peacefully going as a kind of ghost, inflated from time to time by Laval when he appears to be sinking too low.' [13] Hitler did not know what kind of requests Laval wished to bring forward. In any case he would only talk to him in Ciano's presence. Laval would probably want a sort of final peace treaty, but of this there could be no question while Darlan and de Gaulle were sitting in North Africa. 'As to internal concessions Laval will probably put forward requests for a new army. This must be discussed with Field Marshal Keitel. Fundamentally France should not be allowed to have much more than a kind of fire brigade.'

Hitler now invoked his special bogey—the menace of partisan warfare in the Balkans. 'He stressed again the utmost importance of the pacification of these regions in face of an eventual British front in the Balkans. Every measure must be taken to prevent the outbreak of fire in our rear in case an Anglo-Saxon landing takes place. For otherwise all the heroic courage of the Axis troops in Crete and the Peloponnese (in 1941) would have been in vain;

for apart from the above-mentioned railway line, no other route was available. If this was lost the Balkans were finished for the Axis. The recent blowing up of a bridge had shown how disagreeable for supplies such a disruption of traffic could be ° . . . The enemy must therefore be prevented from continuing with their partisan war against Axis communications, otherwise a catastrophic situation would arise. The partisans, with Mihailović at their head, were working closely with England, whence they received material from submarines at night on the Dalmatian coast, and also information and gold from parachutists . . .' [14] Owing to weather conditions in the Balkans, no troops could be sent there to undertake bigger operations before March. The Axis would therefore be helpless in the event of an Allied landing.

The conference was punctuated throughout its proceedings by the disintegration of the whole German front in the East. The line of the river Don from the north of Stalingrad, stretching to the German armies on the sector facing Voronezh, was held by Roumanian and Italian armies. It was here during these December days that the Russians launched a massive thrust, scattering in particular the Italian 2nd Armoured Corps which formed the main body of the Italian force in Russia, and rupturing the whole line.[p]

On the evening of December 18 Ciano returned to his carriage on the official train, and noted in his diary: 'The atmosphere is heavy. Perhaps one should add to the bad news the sadness of this damp forest and the boredom of collective existence in the huts of the High Command. There is no touch of colour, no lively note . . . a smell of kitchen, uniforms and boots . . . Since my arrival no one has hidden from me and my collaborators the uneasiness caused by the news of collapse on the German front in Russia. They seek openly to make us responsible. Hewel,[q] who lives in Hitler's immediate circle, had the following conversation with Panza.[r]

Panza: "Had our army many losses?"

Hewel: "No losses at all; they are running."

Panza: "Like you did in front of Moscow last year?"

Hewel: "Exactly." ' [15]

The Fuehrer went so far as to insist that the Duce should be asked 'personally to telegraph to the Italian troops in Russia not to yield an inch of territory'. Throughout the day Hitler hammered on this theme. That evening Ciano cabled to Mussolini that the situation appeared grave, and there was little possibility of persuading Germany to come to terms with Russia.[16]

o. The Gorgopotamos bridge by a British-led party of Greek partisans, on the main railway line to Piraeus—the supply route to North Africa.

p. For details see the official Italian account '*L'8 Armata nella seconda Battaglia defensiva del Don*' (Rome, 1946).

q. The Liaison officer of the German Foreign Ministry with the Fuhrer's staff.

r. The Vice-Chief of Protocol at the Italian Foreign Office.

Throughout December 18–19 informal conversations continued between the German and Italian delegations. As Ciano wrote in his subsequent report to the Duce on his talks with Ribbentrop: 'In regard to our sector on the Russian front, he asked me to seek the Duce's personal intervention to stress to the Italian troops the necessity that they should fight and die at their posts. In the interests of truth I must say that he did this with great moderation and, as far as is possible with him, with tact. But I cannot conceal that, particularly on that first day of our meeting, Ribbentrop returned more than once to emphasize how serious the situation was in the Italian sector. As he said, some units fought with the utmost bravery, while others "had withdrawn too quickly".

'On the evening of the 18th in my train he brought up a second request, which could be regarded as disagreeable. After he had repeated at length the Fuehrer's arguments about the need to ensure transports to Tunisia, he said that the German navy had had particular experience in this respect during the Norwegian campaign, and that one should surely make use of such experience. He therefore asked—and he said that he was speaking entirely on his own initiative—whether the Italian navy would be prepared to hand over to the German fleet some of its light vessels, which could be manned in the first instance with German crews and then handed back to us when our fleet had gained the necessary experience. I did not fail to point out to Ribbentrop the delicate nature of the question, at which he asked me not to speak about it to the Duce, particularly as the German navy felt that they could use certain light vessels from Toulon for the same purpose.

'Finally Ribbentrop talked about the situation in Croatia. He repeated more or less what the Fuehrer had said, but handled the problem with great energy and wanted me to telephone the Duce to ask for a basic agreement to an aggressive action against the četnik groups of Mihailović and any other Nationalists or Communist elements which could be a threat to our rear in the Balkans. Ribbentrop did not hide his criticism of the attempts of some of our headquarters to solve the problem politically. He is of the opinion that any agreement with the Slavs in the Balkans is a fraud and that we shall pay very heavily in the future for any concession or deal . . . He said that not only the rebels but the whole civil population which had any kind of contact with the četniks must be massacred in their entirety. He also repeated several times that one must exploit the warm relations which existed between some of our commands and the četnik elements to lay a trap for Mihailović and to hang him as soon as he fell into our hands.' [17]

Although Ciano had also shown himself abrupt and unhelpful over the situation in Yugoslavia, he could not avoid being the channel of Hitler's insistence. The talk with Ribbentrop was broken off so that Ciano could telephone to Rome. Mussolini agreed that 'the Croat affair (*sic*) should be settled by force. He had naturally not taken up any position about details, but was completely in favour of the idea of co-operating with Germany.' [18]

In a short conversation between the Fuehrer and Ciano on December 19 the tone of the former's remarks betrayed the lack of confidence in the Italian will to resist.[s] He again turned to the importance of the transport problem in maintaining the Tunisian base. 'He called it a question of life and death that this area should be held, and stated that no technical difficulties should remain unsolved in carrying through supplies.' By this phrase, Hitler made it clear that he was thinking of the need to impose sacrifices on the Italian civilian population. If the railways of Southern Italy were exploited to the full, not only could Tunis be held but the Axis forces could reach Algiers. 'Italy must first of all think of her future.'

The Italian delegates seemed unimpressed and even resentful. 'Count Ciano and Marshal Cavallero listened to the Fuehrer's statements carefully and apparently with inner agreement, without however taking up a position.'

Laval had now arrived at German headquarters. That evening the Frenchman was received by Hitler in the presence of Ciano and the other Axis leaders. Ciano recorded that the ensuing talks 'were without the slightest political interest. They took place first round a tea-table and then at a dinner table. Thus the French Premier, whose journey took him eighty hours, had only three hours with the Fuehrer, during which, when it came to the point, he was able to speak for twenty minutes. The Fuehrer repeated his view about France and avoided every precise demand on the part of Laval. The latter had a long list of questions written on a piece of paper. But he only got out the first one: the request to be able to dissolve the other parties and to found a united party. When this was refused, he did not find the courage to produce the others. Basically he confined himself to seeking a proof of confidence from the German side, as he is aware that this is the only positive element on which he can base his tenure of office, which he recognizes as very difficult. In one of his own phrases, "It is very hard for him to govern a France in which he only hears shouted: Laval to the scaffold."'

Hitler confirmed his general confidence of a personal kind in Laval, 'and a complete mistrust of all his colleagues. It could not be otherwise since during the short conference in Munich Laval had personally stood guarantee for men such as Noguès and Darlan, who in the course of a few hours had shown their true faces.' [19]

'Nevertheless,' wrote Ciano in his diary, 'how the Germans respond to the charm of the French, even of this Frenchman! Except for Hitler, all the others were crowding round him trying to talk to him or to get close to him;

s. German Collection. Schmidt minute. Ribbentrop, Keitel, Jodl and Cavallero were present at this conversation.

it looked like the entrance of an erstwhile great lord into a circle of new-rich parvenus. Ribbentrop also did his best, but he ended with a gaffe. He reminded Laval that his "eminent compatriot" Napoleon had once been in the same forest. If I am not mistaken, Napoleon was there under entirely different conditions.' [20]

The final meeting of the conference took place on the morning of December 20.[t] Hitler announced that he could not come to Italy, 'but Count Ciano had seen for himself how much the Fuehrer was committed to his tasks at Head-quarters'. He then commented on the talks of the last days. 'There was complete agreement between Germany and Italy in their judgment of the so-called French government and on the methods to be employed in France. The aim was to maintain at least the fiction of a French government and to leave Pétain as Head of the State, because this made operations in North Africa easier.' The problem of the French fleet had been settled one way or the other at Toulon. 'As to the problem of the East, the Fuehrer referred to it as a purely military matter. The question of a settlement of the Eastern problem by an agreement with Russia was not ripe for discussion.' According to Hitler, the German-Italian talks on securing the south-eastern flank had been completely successful. In the event of an Anglo-Saxon landing, assisted by the Balkan Nationalists, the situation would be irretrievable. If disorders and sabotage broke out in the area, this would be sufficient for the Axis bases on Crete, in the Peloponnese and on the Dodecanese to be gravely menaced. The possibility of major troop movements, apart from the railways, was out of the question in this area before the month of March, owing to weather conditions. Under such circumstances it would be better to liquidate the bands now rather than be obliged later to launch a major action against British and American supply and air bases, which the Nationalists would concede. This would be a catastrophe, whose consequences did not bear thinking about. It would already be bad enough in economic terms if, instead of running the bauxite and copper trains, one had to transport troops by rail. Whether or not these fears were grounded, or the intentions of the Anglo-Saxons lay in this direction, was irrelevant. The possibility of a landing and the setting up of Anglo-Saxon air bases in the Balkans imposed a categorical duty to do everything to prevent it. In this connection he wanted to emphasize once again that, apart from the problem of communications imposed by the war, Germany was only concerned in this area with the supply of chrome, bauxite and copper. She had no political interest there, and was indifferent as to who ruled in Croatia.

t. See German Collection, Schmidt minute. This talk was held in the presence of Ribbentrop; General Jodl; General Marras, the Italian Military attaché in Berlin; Alfieri and Mackensen. In the Italian Collection there is also an Italian record of the Fuehrer's final summary which follows closely the German text.

Turning to the war in North Africa, Hitler repeated the historical importance of the area for Italy. 'The possession of North Africa was also essential to Italy on grounds of military geography. Thus North Africa was vitally necessary to the Axis for the successful conduct of the war. One might well say that the Axis could withdraw to the fortress of Europe. But in the long run one could not put up with such a self-contraction, but must, through the possession of North Africa, compel the enemy to commit his forces and above all his shipping, which was his very lifeline . . . For this reason alone the transport problem of supplying North Africa must not go unsolved. It was decisive for the war, and every conceivable effort must be made. Moreover, when peace was concluded, Italy would find herself in a more favourable position to claim territories in North Africa if she already held them. Events after 1918 could only strengthen this view.'

Even in the German minutes, Ciano's words strike a distant note. 'Count Ciano thanked the Fuehrer for his statement, of which he would give an exact report to the Duce. The days spent at the Fuehrer's headquarters would be for him an interesting and pleasant memory. He was particularly pleased that the several questions under discussion had been settled in complete agreement.'

A series of further military talks had been conducted during these days between the two delegations headed by Keitel and Cavallero respectively.[21] Much of the argument was a repetition of the political discussions, but in more precise and detailed terms. Some of the points were also taken from the general meetings. Cavallero stressed his special theme that 'in order to maintain oneself in Africa, air supremacy is essential. This could surely be obtained by sending a reinforcement of 500 aircraft to garrison the great air fortress Sardinia-Sicily-Tunisia.' On the subject of Croatia, it was agreed to hold a military conference in Rome of the Italian and German commanders in the Balkans to work out a common plan against the četniks. The shortage of Italian military equipment was catastrophic. 'Marshal Keitel showed that, at this moment, German production is entirely absorbed with the needs of the operational fronts, firstly the Eastern, and then the South-Eastern. She can only hand over to Italy captured war material.' Cavallero hoped that he could obtain 70–80 French seventy-fives, and the Germans undertook to 'examine the matter favourably'.[u]

Among the Italian documents relating to these meetings is a paper headed 'Military situation according to the German appreciation', dated December 19, 1942.[22] It appears to be a summary of a meeting of the Italian and German military leaders on that day. It is an effective and unvarnished survey of the war.

On the Eastern front, even the 1942 campaign had not weakened Russian

u. French guns manufactured in 1918!

resistance. 'As it has not been possible to prepare an "East Wall" in time, it is to be expected that the winter of this year will be even worse than the last. The enemy has now taken the initiative in a dangerous direction behind the Don line. There are not sufficient reserves to counter the break-through on the front of the Italian 8th Army, in spite of the fact that this offensive had been foreseen. The first reserve units, a motorized division, are on the move, but will not have any noticeable impact for three or four days.' Seven German divisions were being moved by rail from France, but would not reach the area for at least a week! 'Nevertheless we are confident of being able to overcome the crisis, especially as the enemy does not seem to have large forces at his disposal or to follow up vigorously. As to the counter-offensive to re-establish communications with Stalingrad there is a momentary pause, perhaps due to the uncertainty of the situation and therefore the need to be sparing in the use of forces. As to the break up of the Italian 8th Army, the Germans have attempted to mount an alibi, accusing our troops—quite without foundation—of not having fought, so as to justify a lack of preventive measures, which was all the more inexplicable since the Italian High Command did not fail to draw the attention of the German General Staff to the weakness of the sector after all the reserves had been diverted to Stalingrad, and to the consequent danger.'

In North Africa 'Rommel's army is in a critical state, but to abandon Tripolitania at this moment, as Rommel proposes, would be very serious and would also compromise our position in Tunisia. We must continue fighting in Libya and reinforce Rommel at all costs, with the chief aim of gaining as much time as possible in order to consolidate ourselves in Tunisia. In Tunisia we must complete the transport of the four specially chosen motorized divisions, which the German General Staff has assigned here, as quickly as possible, and after expanding the bridgeheads we must take offensive action towards the West at the first opportunity.'

In the Eastern Mediterranean, 'the conquest of Cyrenaica has strengthened the enemy position in the Middle East so that it is now more possible than ever that he will attempt a landing in Europe, particularly in an area which would seem to be the least defended (Peloponnese-Crete-Rhodes), and where the enemy can count on the goodwill of the population and the support of those bands which infest the Balkans at the present time. It is therefore necessary and urgent to put an immediate end to the activities of these bands by resolute and ruthless action, while at the same time taking steps to reinforce our defences in Greece, Crete and Rhodes.'

In conclusion, the general military situation was viewed with anxiety 'in that we are still far from a solution of the war, while on the one hand there is the beginning of a shortage of manpower and a decline in the potential of war production, and on the other the availability of oil and raw materials shows no signs of increasing. It seems that our main hope now lies in attacking enemy shipping by every means and especially submarines, so as to neutralize the enemy's advantage of higher war production as far as possible, and to create a supply crisis for him. The maintenance of our position in Africa is of essential importance for this, as well as for avoiding the siege of Axis forces in Europe. But to keep our hold on Africa we must in the next few weeks use every available means to transport men and materials over there, without any kind of interruption. This is the explanation of Marshal Keitel's words: "The outcome of the war depends on the Royal Italian Navy!"'

Ciano returned to Rome on December 22. 'I find considerable panic over the news from the Russian front, especially since the Duce, in speaking to people of a possible peace with Russia, has kindled many hopes . . . In my verbal comments I do not conceal any unfavourable impressions.' [23]

The Goerlitz visit had sharply affected Ciano's spirit and he had come back with a sense of frustration and failure. The 'Beresina Wind',[v] fatal to Napoleon, was blowing across Europe from the steppes of Asia, and the barometer was falling at a remorseless speed.

APPENDIX A

Goering-Duce Conversation in Rome
(December 6, 1942)

ON December 6 Goering called on the Duce, and the two men reviewed the war situation alone. At Mussolini's request neither Schmidt nor Dollmann was present.[w] It seems that the Duce himself drafted a brief note the following day which summarized the talk, and this hitherto unpublished document exists among those of Ciano's papers later captured by the Germans.[x]

During the talk between the Duce and Marshal Goering the following subjects were discussed:
'1. Russia: The Duce believes that, one way or another, the chapter of the war against Russia, which has no more purpose, must be closed. If it should prove possible to arrive at a second Brest-Litovsk (and this one could do by giving Russia territorial compensation in Central Asia), it must be so provided that a defensive line is reached that destroys any enemy initiative and with a minimum of commitments of the Axis forces. Goering says that this would be Hitler's ideal.'

v. A phrase of Grandi's.
w. See Dollmann's report, German Collection, December 16, 1942. The conversation lasted three hours, 5–8 p.m.
x. Italian Collection. 'Note' dated December 6 (in German translation).

'2. All resources must be directed to the West and the Mediterranean, as it is clear that enemy number one is still England and the industrial effort of the United States is such that she will produce an air superiority on the Anglo-Saxon side. Goering says that the Axis can count on a joint monthly production of 5,000 machines.

'3. *Croatia*: The Duce considers the situation very precarious, and foresees the need for a joint command, that will group and exploit all available Italian, German and Croat forces. Goering agrees that Pavelić is still the man the Axis must use.

'4. *Spain:* The Duce suggests that arms should be delivered gradually to Spain (Goering says that Germany is doing this), but she should not be pressed to intervene prematurely as this would be more of a burden than an advantage.

'5. *Turkey*: From the latest reports it seems that Turkey fears Russia, but also is anxious about the Anglo-Saxons who have extended their occupation of Iran and the Middle East.

'In order to bring about a decisive change in Turkish policy it is necessary: (a) to drive down from the Caucasus; (b) to strengthen the Bulgarian army, which will never be used against Russia but can represent a threat to Turkey.'

APPENDIX B

The Concept of a separate Peace in 1942
between Russia and the Axis, with Japan as Mediator

IN the Goerlitz talks on December 18–20, 1942, Hitler revealed for the first time publicly at a conference, and in answer to the Italian view that a separate peace with Russia must be explored, that the Japanese had approached the German government earlier in the year with a similar proposal. Hitler's words were: 'Some time ago the question was raised by Japan as to whether it was not possible to reach agreement with the Russians on a workable basis.'[y]

Ever since the Japanese had entered the war they considered the German campaign in Russia solely in relation to whether or not it contributed to the ultimate victory of the Tripartite powers against England and the United States. If the German plan of a lightning and decisive campaign on the Eastern Front succeeded, there would be no cause for Tokyo to comment; and the Far Eastern War was parallel to that in Europe in the sense that the Italians strove to regard the Mediterranean theatre and their war activities as separate from the German conduct of the war in the East, North and West of Europe. But the failure of the German offensive in Russia in the winter of 1941–2 caused the Japanese leaders to reflect with some concern on the whole course of the war.

y. German Collection. Schmidt minute. December 18, 1942. See p. 94.

Soundings as to the possibilities of a contact between the Germans and the Russians seem to have begun early in 1942, and continued through the summer and autumn. The available evidence is fragmentary.

The first cautious hint appears to have been made by the Japanese Navy, whose clear concern was to interest their European partners in concentrating their war effort against the British and Americans in the Atlantic and Mediterranean. On March 14, 1942, the German Ambassador in Tokyo had sent the following telegram to Berlin: 'Naval attaché has informed the Japanese Admiralty that "Germany from her point of view does not see the possibility of making a peace with Russia, which would establish those conditions essential to cover Germany's rear in her further pursuance of the war against the Anglo-Saxons and would safeguard her in the East. In any event it is felt in Berlin that Russia will suffer further blows this year which will force the Russians to seek peace. The representative of the Japanese Admiralty was receptive to these explanations."

'Naval attaché informed his Japanese colleagues that no information existed in Berlin to show that the Soviet government intended to treat with Germany. But as the communications from the Japanese Navy suggest a change in the attitude of the Soviet government in regard to the continuation of the war with Germany, Berlin would be interested to know what caused the Japanese Navy to hold this view, and in particular did the Soviets, directly or indirectly, take the initiative in bringing to the knowledge of the Japanese their wish to make peace now with Germany?

'German Naval Attaché stressed that Germany would never undertake any such initiative, and received the answer that naturally Japan would never take such action unless requested to do so by Germany.

'The Japanese official concerned pointed out that "the desire" of the Japanese Navy that Germany should postpone her differences with Soviet Russia, and reach an agreement with the Russians, stemmed from the wish that Germany could then turn all her efforts to destroying British forces in the Middle East, and the British position in the Eastern Mediterranean, and in this way and as quickly as possible implement a direct collaboration between the Axis powers and Japan.'

The failure of Rommel's attack in Egypt in the summer of 1942, and of the hopes of an early German break-through in the Caucasus, prompted the Japanese to put out further feelers, in particular through their Ambassador in Russia. The Italians seem to have been aware of these moves. On July 30, Mussolini told the King 'that it seems confirmed that Japan is working to conclude a separate peace between Germany and Russia'.[a]

On August 31 Ribbentrop expressed his irritation at these 'rumours' in a conversation with General Oshima, the Japanese Ambassador in Germany.

z. German Collection. Tokyo telegram, March 14, 1942.
a. Puntoni, *op cit* p. 94.

'The rumour in the world of a separate peace between Germany and Russia has not died down. Unfortunately we have to state that once again it was also Japanese sources which nourished this rumour. It gives strong support to Stalin's propaganda, and he uses it to spur the English to greater efforts. If Japan is using the rumour as cover, to lull the Russians into false security before attacking them, then Ribbentrop has nothing against it. But if not, would Oshima tell his government that "rumour of a separate peace merely helps our enemy". A separate peace was impossible for Germany "for Stalin could not accept the conditions which we would put to him, and which—thanks to our military position—we feel strong enough to make". Also there was, Oshima added, a group in Tokyo, who thought for example that a separate peace between Germany and Russia would be politically useful.'[b]

In September the German Embassy in Tokyo reported that the plan to mediate a peace between Germany and Russia 'has not come to the fore again since the feeler put out earlier this year'. On December 11, Oshima was able to tell Ribbentrop that, 'The theme of a separate peace between Germany and Russia had been very strongly (*sic*) handled at the conference of Japanese Ambassadors in Europe in Berlin, as very many rumours were in circulation. He did not believe himself that Stalin could make peace because of the conditions which Germany would have to make, but in the event of Stalin—having been militarily thoroughly beaten—being finally ready to do so because of the fear of internal revolt, his Japanese government asked to be speedily informed . . . This would be very important to Tokyo as the Army under Yamashida, the conqueror of Singapore, stood on the permanent alert in Manchuria.'[c]

b. German Collection. Tokyo telegrams, September 19, 1942.
c. German Collection. German Foreign Office minute, September 19, 1942.

CHAPTER SEVEN

THE WINTER CRISIS

THE CRISIS on the Home Front in the winter months of 1942, which opened with the illness of the Duce, was also closely bound up with the deterioration of the position of Italy in the military theatres overseas, and the contracting menace of war closing in on the mother country. The collapse of the Axis front at Alamein brought home to the Italian public the threat of invasion of the islands and mainland of Italy itself. The failure of Hitler's gamble in the East, demonstrated by the opening of the great Russian offensive on the Stalingrad front on November 19, marked the end of a grand illusion of a short and victorious war conducted out of sight and almost of mind.

The King returned to Rome from San Rossore on November 13. He had prepared a note for the Duce. 'Serious steps must be taken for the defence of Italy by concentrating the maximum forces on metropolitan territory . . . Everything must be done to obtain the repatriation of our units in Russia . . . starting with the Alpine divisions.' The next day the Duce had an audience of the King, and promised to study this question with care. [1]

In mid-November the seeming recovery in health of the Duce relaxed the political climate. On November 16 the King said, 'I have the impression that Mussolini has entirely recovered, and has a reasonably clear head. His judgment on certain men appeared to me to be clear and precise.' [2] Victor Emmanuel was by instinct opposed to violent change, and his natural preference lay in supporting his Prime Minister in striving to redress the balance of the military situation, and using his royal authority, which Mussolini had always accepted as a political factor, to such an end. As the anonymous Italian informer of the German Embassy reported, 'The state of feeling in the Royal Family is "preoccupied", though the King is co-operating with the Duce in unaltered fashion in the hope of final victory. As to the question whether this preoccupation in the Royal House is related to any desire to

ventilate feelers towards the enemy, (B) thinks that "we have not y͜
this point".'ᵃ

But, in event of a stalemate on the war fronts, the King was awarᵉ
possible contribution which he alone could make in seeking a negotiated ͵
with the Allies, both by exploiting the international connections of royᵉ
and by stressing his role, uncompromised by the present and untouch ͜
by the responsibilities of Fascism. In this sphere he would take no separate initiative. The threat to the internal stability of the country, however,
which had stemmed from the temporary incapacity of the Duce, implied at
least an examination by the Crown of the eventual possibilities of a breakdown of the machinery of administration, and the study of preliminary
counter-measures.

On November 26, for example, the Undersecretary of War, General Scuero,
cautiously warned the King's aide-de-camp, General Puntoni.ᵇ He 'spoke of
the perils of the internal situation. I get the impression that the Undersecretary seeks to learn from me what the Sovereign thinks. He assured me of his
devotion to the King, and expressed his conviction that the Army is closely
bound to the Crown. Scuero is urgently worried that the Grenadier Division
should be recalled to Rome, and I calm him by saying that it is on the way at
the King's express desire.'ᶜ The King's personal intervention in the early
stages of the winter crisis was thus limited to securing the stationing of one
élite army division in Rome, and, in the same line of thought, pressing Mussolini to withdraw the Italian Expeditionary Force from Russia, especially the
Alpine units.

There is evidence, however, that with or without express instructions from
the King, Acquarone had moved further in the direction of precautionary
measures. The role of the Police, particularly the Public Security, in event of
an internal threat, would be as vital as that of the Army. The Director-General
of Security, Carmine Senise, was peculiarly fitted for such special duties. He
had begun his career in the Ministry of the Interior, and at the time of the
March on Rome was head of its Press Office, and in the confidence of the
Minister in Facta's government, Taddei, who was foremost in resisting the

a. German Collection. Bismarck telegram, December 19, 1942, enclosing a report
dated December 12 from 'our known confidant'. It seems almost certain that '(B)' was
Buffarini.

b. Puntoni, *op cit* p. 107. Puntoni had seen the same day the Vice-Commandant of
the Military Police, General Hazon. On the activities of Scuero see Jo di Benigno,
Occasioni Mancate, passim. This book is based on personal contacts with the circles of
the Italian War Office.

c. This action of the King, clearly connected with a potential threat to public order,
is his first and apparently only direct intervention in the existing situation. In conversation with Ciano on November 19 the King referred to 'the scarcity of troops in Italy,
and especially in Rome, where even the Grenadiers have been taken away'. (Ciano, *op
cit* p. 526). On November 23 at a royal audience Mussolini assured him that this
division would return to Rome as soon as possible. (Puntoni, *op cit* pp. 105–6.)

Fascist assault. Senise had thus acquired invaluable experience in the technique of the coup d'état, which proved to be a decisive element in the historical reversal of these events twenty years later.

During the 1930's he had served under a brilliant technician in the person of Arturo Bocchini, who controlled as Chief of Police the security of the régime until his death in November 1940.[d] Cynical, corrupt, observant, and ruthless, the latter built up the Police as an independent arm of the State, extending its powers with the creation of the OVRA as a special branch to protect the person of the Duce against assassination, and in suppressing anti-Fascist agitation and organization inside and outside the country. His supreme achievement was to block any attempt by the Fascist party to penetrate or control the Italian police. It was characteristic of Mussolini that he should both accept and encourage such a situation, and also permit within the Ministry of the Interior, of which he retained the nominal control as Minister, a standing rivalry between the Undersecretary and the Chief of Police.

Since 1933 the former office had been held by Guido Buffarini Guidi, a Tuscan lawyer, elusive, subtle, effusive, obsessed by the political game. [3] It was he, already in the years immediately preceding the war, who held in his hand the private links between the Italian and German security organs, and he had established close contacts, in particular with Himmler. Unlike Bocchini, he sought to play a political role and was in a perpetual search for allies, of whom one was Ciano. He also intrigued in Party circles, and there was much pressure on him from this quarter to appoint a Party nominee to the Police on Bocchini's death in 1940. Senise, however, had paid careful attention to his relations with his Undersecretary even to the extent of enlisting the backing of Himmler's representative in Rome, Dollmann, [4] and it was Buffarini who secured Mussolini's consent to Senise's appointment as Bocchini's successor. Senise's powers of deception exceeded even those of his volatile chief. Ciano, in his flippant and self-revealing way, described the new Chief of Police after the first lengthy meeting between the two men: 'He is a Neapolitan, a queer mixture of intelligence and ignorance; he follows his natural instincts and is a blackmailer; fundamentally he is easy-going, a chatterbox, superficial, and a gesticulator. It is enough to think that such a man is Chief of Police in the twentieth year of Fascism to be convinced that, in this country, *plus ça change, plus c'est la même chose*. He might better have been a Minister under the Bourbons . . . I shall see him more often because it is amusing.' [5]

It was characteristic of Ciano that he should be unaware of and incurious as to Senise's real abilities and attitude. Not only was the new Chief of Police a brilliant administrator and organizer, a planner with a gift of detailed preparation, but he was untouched by any myth of the régime, and was by tem-

d. See the coloured account of Bocchini's personality in Dollmann, *op cit* pp. 60–75. Bocchini and Senise had been colleagues in the Press Office of the Ministry of the Interior during the First World War.

perament a pre-1922 Monarchist, by inclination devoid of any fundamental allegiances.

According to his own account, Senise seems to have considered at an early stage after his appointment in 1940 the precautions to be taken in event of a crisis of the régime. The police was kept independent of the Party; the force was increased by twelve thousand men; in October 1942 the Questore of Rome, the official controlling order and security in the capital, was replaced by the former head of the Milan OVRA, a nominee of Senise's; close relations were established with the Military Police Headquarters, particularly with General Hazon, its vice-commander; help was forthcoming from the Minister of Finance. Thaon de Revel,[e] and General Scuero at the War Office provided equipment for the Police units.[6] Senise claims that he had established close relations with the latter since the summer of 1942 in order to study counter-measures in event of 'a Fascist coup'.[f] Cavallero was also aware of these moves, and sent Senise a message offering arms to the Police. 'Evidently the reason for reviving the plans to maintain public order, on which Scuero and myself had agreed, had not escaped him, and he indicated that he shared our view.'[7]

It appears that by November 1942 therefore some elementary liaison plans between the Police and the Army had been discussed, and that the routine directives to both bodies in event of a crisis of public order had been subject to revision. The only source of reaction on the part of the régime in an emergency lay in the heads of the command of the Party Militia. In theory this protecting force of the régime should be able to act in twenty-four hours.

Senise seems to have probed the intentions of the Militia Commander, General Galbiati, in such an event, and sought to establish the semblance of a combined security plan. Galbiati made it clear that he would make separate arrangements. His concern, as head of the armed formations of the Party, was the internal protection of the régime. Like other public figures he was aware of the feverish and disjointed speculation in all circles during these weeks as to the succession of the Duce. The testing enquiries of the Under-secretary of War and the Chief of Police on the dusty standing instructions for the maintenance of public order drawn up by the Ministry of the Interior years before, and even linking with measures designed originally to combat the predecessors of the Militia, the Action Squads of the days before the March on Rome, could not but arouse his suspicions. Incipient and pre-cautionary plotting in the Ministries of War and the Interior was a minor alarm signal.

e. By 1942 the secret funds at the disposal of the Police exceeded half a million lire. (Senise, *Quando Ero Capo della Polizia*, p. 95.)

f. General Magliano, Scuero's chef de cabinet, was the main link between the offices. He was also an informant of the King's military secretary, General Puntoni. See the latter's Diary, November 26, 1942. 'I see General Magliano who talks openly of a military dictatorship.' (Puntoni, *op cit* p. 107.)

Early in December, Galbiati addressed the Militia Commanders in the presence of Buffarini and Vidussoni. According to Scuero's alarmed report to Puntoni, 'special groups of the members of the former Action Squads have been formed to keep internal order, and the Militia Command has insisted with Senise to have control of the radio-telegraph stations.'[8]

It was typical of the climate of the régime that the Militia should maintain its own political office, and that one of its main functions should be to report to Mussolini on the activities of the Police, particularly in the light of its permanent vendetta with the Public Security authorities. These reports reveal the depth of these feuds. Since January 1941 secret instructions had been issued by the Director of Public Security to the local Chiefs of Police to keep an eye on their opposite numbers, the Federal Secretaries, and particularly to report any matters of a scandalous nature. There was 'in effect a real system of espionage'. Party activities were everywhere obstructed. Senise's contacts with anti-Fascist groups in the Ministries, and in particular the War Office, were reinforced. Scuero, the Undersecretary of War, had a complete plan of action in the event of a 'disturbance of public order which might follow the imminent collapse of the régime, which is regarded as certain, or on the death of the Duce. In such an event all the Party bosses will be immediately arrested, and the combined forces of the Police and the Army used to suffocate any attempts at Fascist insurrection. The Chief of Police, master of the situation, has offered to the King the possibilities of setting up a constitutional government . . . Everything that happens at Militia Headquarters is under surveillance and particularly anything which might be organized for the defence and maintenance of the régime.'[9]

By November 1942 Senise appeared to share the widespread view of the imminent disintegration of the Fascist structure. He was by now in touch with the Minister of the Royal Household, Duca Acquarone, and the latter's confidential secretary and stenographer was one of Senise's agents. On the other hand, his relations with Buffarini at the Ministry of the Interior had declined and he had been unable to maintain regular and direct contact with the Duce and the private secretariat at Palazzo Venezia.

Although the activities in the shadows of the Court could in no way be defined as a Palace conspiracy, it is clear from fragments of evidence that the lineaments of a cabal can be traced, involving, with the active knowledge of Acquarone, leading individuals in the Police, the Army and the Military Police, and indeed, as in the case of Thaon de Revel, in the government ministries, with the object of enabling the Crown to intervene in the event of a political breakdown. But any advance in this direction must depend on the personal decision of the King alone, and in spite of the apparent seriousness of the situation at the end of 1942, there is no sign that the King had as yet any intention of making such a move. As Puntoni explained to Scuero, 'Only in a desperate case will the Crown be able to intervene. At the moment it is as well that His Majesty should be above everything in order to be one day the arbiter of events.' [10]

The origins of Badoglio's search for a 'personal solution' during these weeks is still obscured by lack of convincing evidence. According to his own account, the first appeal to him came from the Princess of Piedmont in the summer of 1942. He 'advised her to report to her father-in-law and husband what she had told him, as he could not ever take by surprise and overthrow the government without a suitable organization, nor would he lend himself to it without orders from the King'.[11]

His notorious prudence is sarcastically depicted by Caviglia. Badoglio told a private gathering at the beginning of 1941, 'I am like the flag that is presented when the regiment is on parade. At that moment I take command and one moves off. You prepare everything, acting like a kind of secret society, and think of me as the leader.' The others present told him, 'No one can organize something on the lines which you propose. One must take an organization which exists, and that is the army. You could take that in hand and we will prepare the country.' Badoglio, as Caviglia commented, 'did not want to take any initial responsibility, he wanted everything fixed and then he would put himself at the head'. [12]

Badoglio's lawyer, Guido Cassinelli, took notes of their frequent private conversations during these months.[g] In November Badoglio apparently told him, 'The succession of Fascism must be prepared. Events are pressing. One must think of names.' At the beginning of December the cryptic reference occurs in Ambrosio's diary: 'Badoglio's proposition—H.M.'s abdication —The Prince—Weapons—Cavallero'. Mussolini later claimed 'this was the first hint of the coup d'état'. [13] It at least indicated an approach by Badoglio to Ambrosio, and implied a certain complicity of the Prince of Piedmont.[h] As early as June the German Legation in Lisbon had reported from sources in the Portuguese Foreign Ministry secret moves from Italy for a separate peace. Discontent was allegedly led by the Crown Prince and Badoglio. There were rumours of a coup d'état planned for June 22. Badoglio would be protected by the King against any action by the Duce. [14]

Whatever lay behind these moves, they had as yet no direct connection with Acquarone or the King. On December 12 the 'known informant' of the German Embassy reported to Bismarck: 'Badoglio has withdrawn further into himself. Rumours of a renewal of his relations with the Royal House are

g. Cassinelli. *Appunti sul 25 Luglio*, p. 13. These entries contain no dates. Badoglio's own memoirs throw no light on these weeks.

h. Little evidence has yet appeared as to the activities of the Crown Prince and his wife at this time.

enemy propaganda.'[i] A police report, dated a few days earlier, repeated a conversation of Badoglio with his family lawyer, Cassinelli. The former 'as a shrewd and suspicious politician has almost always avoided talking politics and avoided any reference to the régime'. [15]

Caviglia had as yet not ventured to make any soundings and was content to observe. Mysteriously, in November, his country house was searched by the Italian police, and almost at the same moment the German War Office asked Rintelen in Rome for his curriculum vitae.[16]

Both Marshals were the subject of discreet German interest. The recent example of Darlan in North Africa could be infectious, and had perhaps been noted in comparable quarters in Rome.

'My anxiety is for the present internal situation. From my last conversation with you, I formed the impression that you were not well informed, and I do not know for what reason . . . Honest Italians are suffering a momentary lack of confidence . . . There are traitors who would willingly see our armies defeated in order to strike at Fascism.' [17]

Farinacci wrote to the Duce on November 19 in these terms. To him the present climate of alarm and discontent in these winter months stemmed logically from the mistaken direction taken over the years by the Fascist movement under Mussolini's leadership. The violent and polemical interventions of Farinacci were a familiar feature of the régime, and his career was symbolic of the defeat of the early extremism of the regional Action Squads. He was the only genuine National Socialist of the Revolution, whose conception of the future of Fascism was totalitarian. It was significant that he came into the movement from the ranks of Anarcho-Syndicalism. He was also one of the few who were really present at the foundation of the Milan Fascio on March 23, 1919. He started life as a station master near Cremona, had struggled to educate himself. He created in his area his own action squads, and Cremona, a Socialist stronghold, was literally taken by assault, and organized as a 'model' fief. He became the natural spokesman of the renegade Left extremist elements of militant Fascism, republican, proletarian, national-socialist, preaching the abolition not only of parliamentary government but of the State, pressing for an all-embracing, all-powerful, party machine led by an incorruptible dedicated élite, the guardian of a permanent revolution.

The inevitable clash with Mussolini had come soon after the accession of Fascism to power, and it was savage and final. The March on Rome, in Mussolini's view, marked for the moment the historic limits of Fascist illegality, and after his arrival in office it became increasingly clear to his

i. German Collection. Bismarck telegram, December 12, 1942. The informant was probably Buffarini, who was observing closely the indiscreet rumblings within the Italian War Office.

followers that he intended to govern with a minimum violation of existing practice, accepting the continued existence of the Monarchy, and—subject to good behaviour—the presence of a parliamentary opposition. Such an attitude, on the part of the Leader, must arouse the puzzled hostility of the extreme elements among the inchoate mass of the provincial Party organizations, and it was Farinacci who crystallized this reaction into a formidable pressure group, aided by the armed formations of the Party now legalized as the Militia, with the official task of preparing the Revolution and with the deliberate purpose of forcing Mussolini back into the path of totalitarian dictatorship.

The murder of the Socialist deputy Matteotti in 1924, after two years of Mussolini's personal experiment in compromise, gave Farinacci his chance. The Leader was driven back into the arms of the faithful by the nation-wide reaction to this political assassination.[j] Mussolini's speech of January 3, 1925, under the impact of this unexpected disaster, marked the historic beginning of Fascist rule. Farinacci became Secretary of the Party. This was his only opportunity, and it never recurred. In one year, during the temporary weakening of Mussolini's personal position and prestige following the Matteotti crisis, Farinacci conducted a large-scale purge of the whole machine, striving to give shape to his own apocalyptic vision. In reality Farinacci, with uncontrolled violence, aimed at a detailed and planned attempt to create a party machine in his own image, which was intended to be the decisive and dominating factor in the political scene. His activities had, however, the effect of breaking the spirit and enthusiasm and indeed the idealism which had been an intrinsic element of the early movement. All that he had built was an imperfect clientele.[k]

By 1926 Mussolini had recovered his nerve and prestige as the Duce of Fascism. Farinacci was removed, and was never to hold active office again outside nominal membership of the Grand Council. He was now relegated to Cremona and through his local paper *Regime Fascista*, conceiving of himself as the conscience of the Party, he became an impotent Cassandra, dangerous and violent in his pursuit of personal feuds, a dissolving and demoralizing influence, bombarding Mussolini with advice in bitter frustration and recrimination at his expulsion into the wilderness. In January 1932, for example, he referred in such a letter to the fact that the Duce 'publicly deplores my existence as a member of the Grand Council, as a Deputy, journalist and lawyer'.[18]

Throughout his correspondence in the succeeding years, he evolved the elements of a personal political programme. His relations with Mussolini were soured for ever, but coloured by a reluctant and disapproving admiration for the figure of the Duce, and the obstinate hope that circumstances would force the Leader again to expel the traitors from within the gate and to march

j. Farinacci had defended Matteotti's assassins at their mock trial.
k. See p. 30.

at the head of the revolution. In the same letter of January 1932 to Mussolini, he wrote 'I am and always will be a faithful soldier of the cause, and if dark times for our country came tomorrow, you would find me at my battle station, my enthusiasm unchanged, and my loyalty intact.'

The political future of Farinacci lay, if at all, only 'in dark times' and he remained remorselessly and almost hopefully the prophet of disaster—in Spain, in Ethiopia, and after the outbreak of war in 1940. The deficiencies of the Italian war effort and the tragi-comedy of the Greek Campaign in October 1940 brought new life to his polemical outbursts. With the pent-up violence of his temperament Farinacci now pursued his longstanding vendetta with the real culprits in his eyes, the Army leaders. His organ of attack, his paper *Regime Fascista,* launched this campaign in November 1940 in an article directed against the incompetence of the General Staff and particularly of Badoglio.[1] As he also wrote to Mussolini at the time: 'If our Revolution has marched into every sector, it has been absent in one and that the most delicate and important—the Army. The old Italy is still at the head of the army with an obstinately anti-Fascist mentality or better still, to describe Badoglio more exactly, with the mentality of a Gamelin.'[19]

The winter crisis of the war in 1942 and the anxieties on the Home Front, together with the Duce's illness, offered Farinacci the promise of a wider field of action. On the problem of the succession, he had written on the same theme nearly ten years before, at Mussolini's request. The latter himself had said that there could not be a second Duce. But there must be strong safe men to carry on the work; where were they? 'The supreme duty is to prepare the governing cadres' though the best members of the régime had been discredited and set aside by the political police (the OVRA). One day Mussolini would realize the harm done by this body to his work of material and spiritual reconstruction. 'What is the State? Faith in Mussolini.'[20]

In the winter of 1942 the country and the régime were in mortal danger. But Farinacci must seek also his personal solution. The axiom of his programme was that Fascism could only survive in close and loyal alliance with National Socialist Germany, and by a heightened and purified joint war effort. It was, however, an implicit peril in the situation at hand that the personal structure of Mussolini's rule might disintegrate before a counter-action could be organized. Quite apart from the possibility of his death, there was always the obsessive theme, in Farinacci's mind, of an all-pervading treachery in the air, of the Royal House, the Army leaders, and within the Party itself. He was by now convinced that even if the Duce survived it was too late to save Fascism except by drastic measures, perhaps even including the sacrifice of Mussolini himself.

Although he had no close allies, Farinacci still could perhaps count on

1. Entitled 'Lower middle-class junk'—'*Zavorra piccolo-borghese*'.

well placed supporters in the Party hierarchy, most of them former political clients. His first step, therefore, was to renew these connections with a view to a 'revival' of the Party on the pattern of 1925. His veteran enemies, the police, were close behind. 'Excellency Farinacci continues his activities aimed at increasing the number of proselytes to carry out his programme of removing the Duce at an opportune moment. He has a house in Rome where his henchmen, having worked on picked Party bosses, invite them to lunch.' His political influence was concentrated in Lombardy. Apart from his personal fief of Cremona, he was assured of support in Milan, Bergamo and Brescia. He had come to terms with the former Party Secretary, Starace, whose activities in office, by creating an elephantine bureaucratic machine, has been as disastrous as his own. The police report continues: 'Starace has recognized Farinacci as the leader, so that the tiny group of the followers of Starace (consisting exclusively of Party bosses favoured by him), has gone over bag and baggage to the Farinacci group.'ᵐ

Apart from attending to his relations within the Party machine, Farinacci must seek support in military circles. Here he had no choice. He had conducted a standing feud with the whole military caste, as anti-Fascist, anti-German, inefficient and disloyal. The only figure who had shown himself willing to fall in with the German conception of the struggle was the Chief of the General Staff, Marshal Cavallero. But the latter had achieved this reputation rather out of passivity of character and fatalism than deliberate intent, and his position was also under mounting attack from Ciano and in Army circles.

It might be that, as Farinacci may have calculated, an alliance between himself and Cavallero, backed by the Germans, provided the other possible alternative solution to the eventual collapse of the régime. But there is no evidence to show that Cavallero was prepared to commit himself to such a desperate plan. Farinacci was a disaster candidate, and Cavallero had observed too long and closely the march of political events in Italy in recent years to compromise himself with such a perilous companion.

Of the several legends which have grown up round the person of Cavallero, one of the most persistent is of such an alliance between the two men. In the interests of Italy such action was allegedly forced upon them in view of the conspiracy of Ciano, Grandi and Ambrosio to overthrow Mussolini and make a separate peace with the Allies, thus bringing the country to disaster. The Farinacci-Cavallero 'plot' was also a later alibi for the others and might have been in part at least originated in another camp. The atmosphere was charged with mutual fears and suspicions, and talk of disloyalty and treason. For instance, in a conversation with Ciano, Galbiati was told that Cavallero 'will

m. Italian Collection. Public Security report, December 10, 1942. Farinacci was reported again on January 5 as being in Milan 'bringing the Federal Secretaries to heel'.

betray because he does not believe any more in victory. He must be replaced, because he is intelligent and will betray well.'[21]

Caviglia's comment is rather a noting of rumour than evidence: 'Farinacci and Cavallero seem to be in close accord. The other Fascist chiefs are worked up against Farinacci, and they fear him because he has the Germans with him. They are all men who are solely concerned with their own personal interests and would like to put Farinacci in a position of not counting for anything, but he knows how to make use of Hitler's support.' [22]

In so far as there is any evidence of Cavallero's activities at this time, it points to a somewhat modified and more cautious sounding, in keeping with his temperament. General Hazon, of the Military Police, told Puntoni already at the end of October 1942 that 'the illness of the Duce has let loose the appetites of the competitors for his succession, some of whom have revealed their hands to Cavallero to find out what he thinks and how he would behave if Mussolini should disappear or in event of a coup d'état'. Cavallero, according to Hazon, had replied that 'his attitude would be that just as he had also loyally served the Duce so he would be prepared to serve the head of the government who would be appointed by the King'.[23]

During November Cavallero voiced his fears in a talk with the commander of the Fascist Militia, General Galbiati, and sounded him on the possible attitude of the Militia and the Party in event 'of the take-over of power on the part of the Germans'. [24] Or was Cavallero rather thinking in terms of his own personal position? The version of this episode given by Puntoni in his diary on November 26 is somewhat different in emphasis and more in this latter sense. The Undersecretary of War, General Scuero, was his source. 'He told me of the conversation which had taken place between Cavallero and Galbiati, and which had ended in the latter's refusal of the request by the Chief of the General Staff to put at the disposal of the Army Corps in Rome several battalions of the Militia to preserve internal order. Galbiati had replied that he had studied the proposition on his own account.' [25]

In his 'Memorandum' dictated after his arrest by Badoglio in August 1943, Cavallero gave his own version of these moves made by him, and part at least is confirmed by Hazon's remarks to the King's military secretary.[n] 'In November 1942, when Mussolini was seriously ill, it was necessary to consider the worst eventuality. I was anxious about this, and gave instructions in such an event to General Magli,[o] to General Ambrosio, Chief of the Army Staff, and to General Scuero, Undersecretary for War. There were two meetings for this purpose; I said clearly that they must be prepared to ensure a co-ordinated solution for the country, and first of all for Rome, in order to hand it over to the Sovereign, who had decided to whom to entrust both the Government and

n. This mysterious document is discussed below. See p. 639.
o. General Magli was a senior staff officer of the War Ministry, attached to the Italian General Staff.

the High Command. I foresaw that the person would be Marshal Badoglio at whose orders, I said to my subordinates, we would all place ourselves.

'An unexpected intervention of the Militia in the affair slightly spoilt things. The situation was however overcome by the recovery of the invalid.'

There is significantly no evidence from German sources of a Farinacci-Cavallero conspiracy at this stage. Such a political solution could only be considered to be the result of a German-planned coup backed by military intervention, and the assessment of the present crisis by the Germans was similar to that of everyone else.

Amid the rumours of plot and counter-plot, the most positive activity that could be attributed to Ciano were his moves, particularly in Army circles, to secure the fall of Cavallero. Towards the end of October to this end he had already sought personal contacts in Army circles, and within the Army General Staff. In his function as Foreign Minister dealing with the Balkans, he had been brought in contact with General Ambrosio as commander of the Italian army in Croatia until January 1942, when he became Chief of the Army Staff, and also with General Roatta, who preceded the latter in the same command.[p] At the same time Ciano came in touch with two young and ambitious Generals, Carboni and Castellano, and a small circle formed to promote the candidature of General Ambrosio as Cavallero's successor.[q]

According to Castellano, he first met Ciano in the latter's office at the beginning of April 1942, and 'the meeting had been prepared by General Carboni'. The purpose of the meeting was to bring Ciano into direct touch with Ambrosio to whom Castellano was a kind of private military secretary. But Ambrosio was not anxious to make the first move.[r] On Ciano's return in November from the Munich Conference, he saw Castellano again, and the question of Cavallero's successor was mentioned. Roatta, the predecessor of Ambrosio as Chief of the Army Staff, was considered as a candidate, but Mussolini was hostile and it was agreed to press for Ambrosio, though nothing was to be said to him. [26]

On November 12 General Puntoni noted, 'Cavallero has gone to Tripoli. His Majesty spoke to me of a conversation with the Prince of Piedmont who reported to him that, among other things, Cavallero was in a critical situation, as the leading representatives of the Army were against him.' [27] On November 22 the Duce appears to have told Ciano that even the King had spoken to

p. Ciano also knew Roatta well as former chief of the Italian Military Intelligence and commander of the Italian forces in Spain.

q. See the not wholly plausible account of Canevari—*La Fine del Maresciallo Cavallero*, passim.

r. Castellano, *op cit* p. 22. Carboni had been dismissed as head of the Italian Military Intelligence under German pressure (see Ciano, *op cit* p. 475).

him about replacing Cavallero, but Mussolini 'who is again optimistic these days, finds that it is not the moment to proceed to a change while we are engaged on two fronts'.[28]

Cavallero had never been popular in military circles, and the intrigues against him in the political world had their counterpart in the army: young ambitious generals like Carboni, who with his personal contacts with Ciano was a link between both worlds, and the general staff officers who resented his personal dictatorship and the planting of his own clan in the Supreme Command; Ambrosio, who although Chief of the Army Staff, was never able to report alone either to the King or the Duce; and his old rival and enemy, Badoglio. All were awaiting him in the shadows.

Just as Cavallero had shown such reluctance to leave Rome in November to go to Africa, so he feared what might happen during his absence the following month at Hitler's headquarters. He saw the King in the afternoon of December 16 on the eve of his departure for East Prussia. The latter's comment to Puntoni was that he 'found the Chief of the General Staff more worried about his political position than about military operations'. But at least Cavallero was taking with him his main enemy, Count Ciano. It appears that the King received the Duce the same day, and repeated his impression. 'The Duce took the opportunity to attack fundamentally Cavallero, whose position appears shaken.' [29]

Ciano, who had been originally one of the latter's supporters in replacing Badoglio as Chief of the General Staff in December 1940, had long since turned against him. On returning from their joint mission to Germany in December 1942, Ciano had reported on his servility to the Germans and Mussolini had said, 'Henceforward Cavallero is finished'.[30]

Two days later, on December 24, Ciano wrote a letter to Carboni, in answer to the latter's impatient proposals for military changes, which had been prompted, it seems, by renewed cautious soundings from Ciano himself. There was speculation already on a possible successor to Cavallero, and Ciano seems to have been thinking of the Italian Commander in Russia, General Messe, as a candidate.[s] The King seems to have been firmly against such an appointment, and Ciano thought again of Ambrosio.[t] In his letter to Carboni, Ciano wrote obscurely 'As to the demand which you have in view (the removal of Cavallero) it is necessary to develop organic (sic) action. There are several difficulties and you can imagine from what quarters.' [31]

These moves were not unknown to the Court. Puntoni had noted in his diary as early as November 26: 'Ciano is said to be working in accord with

s. General Messe had returned from Russia to report in the middle of November. He saw Ciano on December 14. See Ciano, op cit p. 524.

t. Simultaneously Cavallero was planning to remove Ambrosio as Chief of the Army Staff. See Puntoni Diary, op cit p. 111, December 17, 1942.

a senior officer to whom he has assured his protection in the case of "great happenings".'[u]

In the political world of Rome, consultation between Ciano and Grandi had its own special advantages. The latter was perhaps the leading 'elder statesman' of the régime in political intelligence and his knowledge of foreign affairs. The misfortunes of the Axis alliance were bringing Ciano remorselessly into line with Grandi's own appreciation of Italy's external position. There is no doubt that, particularly after the diplomatic conversations with the Germans at Munich in November and at Goerlitz in December, Ciano had few illusions as to the course of events in Africa and Russia, but 'without finding the answers'.[v] He was now eagerly receptive to such persuasive counsel as Grandi was ready to offer. The latter was pressing for a preliminary and private sounding of the Western Allies, at least to discover on what terms, if any, they would talk. At the end of November he suggested that he himself should visit Spain in the hopes of getting in touch with the British Ambassador in Madrid, Sir Samuel Hoare, whom Grandi had known well in London. At the last minute the journey was postponed by Mussolini, who apparently told Ciano that Grandi's presence in Spain might displease 'our German Allies', and the trip was to be postponed 'until the end of the war'.[w] Mussolini was prepared to attempt, as he did through Ciano at Goerlitz in December, to persuade Hitler to settle the Russian war and to concentrate on the Mediterranean Front and in the West against the British and Americans. He was not however ready to consider any reverse proposal of an approach to the Western Allies in order to seek a settlement whereby the united strength of the Axis could be concentrated in the East.

A discreet and preliminary approach to the Allies could henceforth only be made by individuals at their personal risk. The relations between Grandi and Ciano had never been intimate. Apart from the fact that they belonged to different political generations, Ciano had succeeded Suvich, Grandi's successor as Foreign Minister; he had been identified with the major decisions of Italian policy since 1936, intervention in Spain, the Axis Pact, Albania, the entry of Italy into the war, the attack on Greece, and all the consequences of the wartime alliance with Germany. It was true that each step taken had been the personal decision of the Duce, but whatever reserves or doubts Ciano might personally, and indiscreetly, express as to the course which events had taken, he was committed to them. If the Duce was abruptly to change course and seek a dramatic exit from the impasse created by his own now bankrupt gamble of June 1940 on triumphant and lightning military intervention, the obvious suc-

u. Puntoni, *op cit* p. 107. November 26, 1942. His source was General Scuero. As Carboni also boasted of his close ties with the Prince of Piedmont, this may also have been another channel of 'indiscretion'.

v. His own words after the Munich Conference. See p. 72.

w. Grandi, *op cit* p. 38. There is no mention of this episode in Ciano's Diary.

cessor to Ciano as Foreign Minister to conduct such an operation would be Grandi. Whatever the latter might conceive in private cabal, such a possibility could be and was mooted in each moment of stress, possibly encouraged by Mussolini himself. Grandi might well have been both troubled and tempted by such a solution, and the thought of it inevitably increased his caution. It was both a threat and an alternative, and in either case commanded deep attention.

The lineaments of such a position had already been discussed in the first such political crisis in the winter of 1940, which was a precursor to the present one, and produced an outline pattern of it. In the diary of General Puntoni for December 6, 1940, there is the following entry:

'The radio has announced the dismissal of Badoglio and the appointment of Cavallero as Chief of the General Staff. Insistent rumours are circulating in the capital of changes in high quarters. The name of Grandi has come anew to the surface and His Majesty is favourably disposed. The liquidation of Ciano is forecast (to go as Ambassador to Berlin or as Minister of Italian Africa), and in his place Grandi as Foreign Minister. Such items are, however, hardly to be expected to be true, and it is not improbable that they have been put about deliberately by those who out of natural interest desire a radical change in the ministerial structure.' [32]

These rumours were revealing of the recurrent political climate. On January 2, 1941, Farinacci thought it necessary to write to Grandi in his usual brutal style: 'As you know, we are both at this moment the designated victims of public opinion. I am supposed to be working and plotting to set up a German government in Italy, and you, on the other hand, are working for a government favourable to all those currents which would willingly see the eclipse of Mussolini and many of us, including naturally Ciano. Your absence had aroused some criticism, as you were seen on the previous day in Rome by several people; no one believes in your illness.

'My dear Grandi, in your own interests I advise you to choose the first good occasion to come out of your reserve. You are too much on everybody's lips, and an anti-Fascism is deliberately exploiting your name. When Italy declared war on France and England, the news spread in Italy that Farinacci would replace Ciano at the Foreign Ministry. What did I do then? I went to the Duce, and asked him to send Ciano to Cremona, where I organized an impressive manifestation for him.'[x] The warning was clear, and a repetition must be avoided.

There were also other reasons for closer association between Grandi and his friends and Ciano. He represented to them the main source of information and intelligence on the political and military conduct of the war, and,

---

x. Italian Collection. Farinacci to Grandi, January 2, 1941. The letter is referred to in Ciano's diary. 'Grandi is annoyed and frightened by a letter from Farinacci asking him to come out of the equivocal reserve which he had imposed on himself during these last two months.' *op cit* p. 324.

perhaps even more important, he could be the chief interpreter of the condition and moods of the Duce and the lightning shifts of his darting mind.

Ciano was also an ideally placed channel for conveying Grandi's analysis of the situation to the Sovereign. As Foreign Minister the former had constant access to the King, with whom his relations were at this time also closer. For instance, on November 19, the day of the massive Russian assault on the Stalingrad front, 'the Sovereign received Grandi and Ciano. Grandi stayed a few minutes with the King; Ciano, on the other hand, remained in conversation for more than an hour. The King told me that he found Ciano rather well au fait with the situation.' [33] According to the latter, the Sovereign 'wanted to be informed particularly about Spain, Switzerland, and Turkey. He spoke a little of what had happened and is happening in the Mediterranean, but he is particularly concerned with our lack of forces in Italy, and especially in Rome, where even the grenadiers of the Royal Guard have been withdrawn. He requested me to intervene with the Duce to recall troops to Italy from the Russian Front, advising me at the same time not to say that it was he who had spoken to me of this "so that one should not get the impression of secret manoeuvres". As always there is an anti-German touch in his words. He showed a perfunctory confidence in the development of the war, but questioned me closely on Washington and London, and advised me to hold carefully on to any thread which might be renewed "even if it is as thin as a spider's web".' [34]

The Germans were already disturbed by rumours that Ciano was seeking contacts with the Allies and there were vague reports of a secret understanding between him and the Crown Prince as to a political deal in Italy. On November 7, 1942, Admiral Canaris, the head of the German military Counter-Intelligence, circulated a report referring to conversations between American representatives and the Italian Minister and Military Attaché in Lisbon. It was stated that Ciano was 'completely in the picture'. [35] A German telegram from Madrid dated two days later referred to the Crown Prince and to Ciano as 'anti-German'. [36] The purported Lisbon negotiations were based on the evidence of the Portuguese police in a report on November 9 from the German Legation in Lisbon, and the whole affair was summarized in a Berlin telegram circulated to the interested diplomatic posts on December 3, stressing Ciano's active knowledge of these secret talks and adding that it was also intended that the Crown Prince should become King of Italy, in event of success. [37]

These reports were circulated as a routine to the German Ambassador in Rome, Mackensen, and his comments were consistently sceptical of such rumours. On December 4 he telegraphed to Berlin summarizing his impressions. He doubted whether there was any such 'anti-Fascist' circle in touch with the enemy through the Italian Legation in Lisbon. Such rumours had been rife, however, since the North African landings. In any case Ciano was the last person to initiate such feelers. 'It is possible that Count Ciano today, when he is in power, has behind him a group of Fascists . . . It is also a fact that he is by far the most unpopular man in the country. He may be unclear about the extent of his unpopularity, but he must be living on the moon if he has any illusions that he has behind him the mass of the population in whose eyes he is precisely the champion of the Axis. Count Ciano would, however, be clear that in thinking of a separate peace the German factor could not be ignored . . . The Fuehrer would take lightning counter-measures. Ciano was aware also of the size of the German forces in Italy, and was in a position to judge what it would mean if the Reich should suddenly withhold coal deliveries. A separate peace aimed at keeping the war away from the Italian mainland would automatically make it a theatre of war.' [38]

Ciano was ceaselessly chattering at the Golf Club and in the salons of Rome. Many of these conversations were reported to Mussolini. His son-in-law was not, however, the head of a planned conspiracy, but rather a symbol of defeatism and discontent, and the voluble spokesman of the anti-German sentiments of the upper middle class and the aristocracy.

Nor did Grandi and his friends constitute an active opposition group. The impressions of the German Embassy were given in a Rome telegram dated December 19. 'There are no definite plans of action behind the Fronde of Grandi. Both Grandi and Bottai, whose tendencies today are spoken of as pro-Bolshevik, are above all only seeking for an alibi later. Also the attitude of Federzoni cannot be considered otherwise. As yet there are no signs of any other plans of action.' [39]

The physical recovery of the Duce had put an end to the Winter Crisis, but the weaknesses of the Fascist structure after twenty years of existence had been sharply and totally revealed. The future of the régime and of the Axis alliance, as Hitler had always said, depended alone on the personal survival of the Duce. The private murmurings of these months were the precursory signs of the final dissolution, which was to be prolonged until the following summer.

On December 16 Dollmann analysed the Roman scene. 'Everyone who studies and watches must over and over again, in connection with the Duce's health, be confronted with the thunderously dark question: what is going to happen if it leads to a catastrophe here? That the Monarchy stands imperiously in the foreground cannot be denied; the struggle of the Diadochs between Count Ciano—sure of the testamentary succession but most unpopular, and Count Grandi—cool-headed and uncompromised,[y] can only be kept under control by the Crown itself, which today more than ever can be certain of a life and death alliance with the Curia.

'Looking back over these eventful days, I would again suggest that there can

y. Literally 'with clean linen'.

be no talk of a sudden dramatization of the situation. Italy as an ally stands and falls militarily with the fate of North Africa, and the political future of the Axis is and remains bound up with the life of the Duce. If Germany wishes to think of the alliance beyond the lifetime of the Duce, then a weighty and most delicate problem arises; in which direction must channels of contact already explored and established, and which are secure for the future, now be built up?' [40]

CHAPTER EIGHT

THE POLITICAL RECOVERY OF THE DUCE

•—

'ONE RINGING of the bell, and they will all turn out down there to applaud me.' [1] Farinacci repeated this phrase of Mussolini's in mid-November after a conversation in the latter's study at Palazzo Venezia. Gathering together his physical strength, though by no means recovered, the Duce was preparing to ring the bell. On November 19 Bottai saw him. 'People want to know whether he, Mussolini, is in a position to confront the situation, and if he can do so, in what concrete terms.' [2] His first answer was to summon on November 21 the Council of Ministers. His reappearance was awaited tensely. As on previous such occasions the Minister of Public Works, Gorla, kept careful notes. 'When Mussolini entered the room, he looked like a dying man . . . who might faint at any minute. He had a number of sheets of paper in his hand containing . . . a report of the British General Staff describing the development of the Ethiopian campaign. Mussolini began by giving a summary in the following words: "A small army of not more than 40,000 men, belonging to all the Dominions of the Commonwealth, was able to deal with 100,000 Italians and 200,000 native troops . . . The report confirms brutally that the campaign was conducted with such rapidity because of the ingenious practice of the British Command in proposing to the commanders of the various Italian sectors a surrender with all honours of war . . . These facts show a deficiency in the race, which in twenty years I have been unable to change." According to Bottai the Duce added: 'I have invented a neologism, the *bracaioli*,[a] for those who stand around holding up their trousers, and, when faced with any difficulty, babble that there is nothing to be done.' [3]

Gorla noticed that these asides provoked protestations from certain ministers: 'It was the first occasion on which I have seen such a thing, and the confusion is such that one cannot hear what is being said, but the Prime Minister remains impassive as if the matter had nothing to do with him. He

a. Untranslatable literally. *Brache* means in Italian trousers or breeches.

looks at certain papers, and then continues.' [4] Bottai's notes add a further picturesque touch. Presumably during the confused interruption in the course of Mussolini's extempore remarks, the latter had interjected: 'I am making a collection of all the rumours in current circulation. I have inaugurated a special file for them, or a folder as we civil servants say. And on the cover I have written "Documents of human stupidity".' [5]

A brief account followed, in the Duce's words, of the military position in North Africa. The Axis forces at El Alamein had been shattered by the enormous superiority of the enemy, particularly in the air and in artillery. But the retreat of Rommel had been 'a masterpiece' and Mussolini predicted that he would stand on the Agedabia-El Agheila line. There was also every hope of holding Tunisia.

As to the attitude of the Vichy government, 'I consider it to be definitely hostile. I have several times advised Hitler to keep his eyes open, but I fear that Germany still nourishes illusions in regard to France . . . which is now under the dictatorship of Laval, who enjoys the confidence of the Germans. I do not share this at all. I know the man, and cannot make myself see him in the guise of a dictator . . . I have constantly reminded Hitler to keep an eye on Toulon, and under the menace of his guns, as I have not the slightest confidence in the Admiral commanding the French Fleet. The future will prove me right.' Within six days Mussolini had this satisfaction. The Toulon squadron was ordered to scuttle itself.

As to the internal position in Italy, the food situation 'was better than last year. But the public spirit had been strongly affected in recent weeks by massive air bombardments to which the Northern cities had been subjected.' There followed a significant hint to those present. 'I confirm my faith in the Italian people, and regard them as too intelligent not to understand that it would be folly to think of a change of government at this moment . . . because, of whatever complexion, this could not alter our situation in regard to the British and Americans.' He was now able to report to those present that, to meet the massive Allied air attacks, Hitler had promised one hundred anti-aircraft batteries. The consequences of Allied air bombardment on the Italian cities represented the most serious and immediate aspect of the war situation, raising the whole issue of the resistance of the Home Front, and the increase in dependence on Germany, in particular for anti-aircraft defence. This German aid 'has been a proof of solidarity, which we must take into account, and also because of the promptness with which our appeal has been answered. At any rate, it is the direct interest of Germany that Italy keeps on her feet, because if we collapse the Germans, too, will have to lay down their arms.'

The Duce finished speaking and abruptly left the room. There was a moment of silence among the ministers. 'As soon as they began to talk, the comments were sarcastic.' [6] But Mussolini had played his first card.

The first move by Mussolini to re-establish his personal authority took its physical toll. On November 26 the Germany Embassy reported that the Duce was in bed with a cold, and, as Bottai anxiously noted, 'he does not reveal his state of mind or a plan of any kind to anyone'. With his peculiar deceiving humour, Mussolini, speaking of oil deliveries, said to Ciano, who as usual repeated it, 'Next year, for reasons you are not unaware of, we shall need a good deal less.' [7]

It was an external stimulus and personal challenge which now jerked Mussolini again to his feet. On November 30 Churchill, speaking over the radio, announced to the world that the Axis would soon be driven right out of Africa. On the same day Gorla noted, 'Mussolini has not yet returned to work at Palazzo Venezia, but has however summoned the Chamber in plenary session.' [8] A resuscitated Duce must speak to the Italian nation and reply both to the taunts of the enemy, and to the murmurings within the gate. He must also tranquillize German doubts as to the internal situation in Italy. The same evening Goering arrived in Rome.[b]

On December 2 Mussolini made his first public speech since his announcement from the balcony of Palazzo Venezia on Monday, June 10, 1940, of the entry of Italy into the war. On this occasion he chose the forum of the Chamber.[c] 'After eighteen months of silence—we have now entered the thirtieth month of the war—I have the vague impression that a good part of the Italian people would like to hear my voice again.' He referred briefly and inadequately to the social benefits of twenty years of the régime only to launch into an equally cursory justification of the Russian campaign. He, Mussolini, had foreseen the need to prevent a Russian attack on Germany's back and the Eastern war had assured to the Axis vast and fertile territories, rich in raw materials. These remarks were clearly inspired by his talks with Goering.

The main theme, however, of his harangue was a requisitory against Churchill in particular, and the British people in general, quoting Carlyle: 'No human race since Adam is covered in such dirty rags of lies as ours', and then, 'The Italians may have forgotten the abject conduct of Admiral Nelson, who hanged from the yard-arm of the frigate "Minerva" the Neapolitan Admiral Caracciolo, having first betrayed him . . . Gentlemen, one does not wage war without hating the enemy from morning to night . . .' The unique task was to fight to win, 'otherwise the Pax Britannica will be a Versailles multiplied a hundredfold'.

On returning to the Palazzo Venezia he received the retiring Japanese Ambassador. The Duce was still in a state of exaltation from his speech. The

b. See pp. 79–82.

c. For the text of this speech, see E. and D. Susmel. Edition of the *Opera Omnia* of Mussolini, XXXI, pp. 118 *et seq.*

only words of farewell which the diplomat could bring himself to utter were, 'You, Duce, you worn out, very worn out, too worn out.'[9] Mussolini terminated the interview with some abruptness.

The anglophobe outburst of Mussolini propelled him to his next appearance. Later on the same day, he addressed the National Directorate of the Fascist Party as the next deliberate move in his political return to the centre of the scene. He had last taken the chair at a session of this docile gathering in the previous May. Bottai was watching the reactions of this audience. 'Mussolini mounts the rostrum. He gives a kind of footnote to his speech of the morning. Then he gives the order to the Party. It is the hour of the Party because it is the hour of revolution. There are those who have lapsed into administration, and those who have remained faithful to the revolution. It is the spirit of the latter that must be kept alive against the weapons of the Reaction. The Party relies on the morale of the people to avoid being poisoned. There is a human category in itself, the evacuees, who are in this war like the refugees in the other of '15.[d] They must be succoured with full and open fraternal generosity. This mixing together of regions, provinces, and classes will only do good, and assist our unity. The minimum of bureaucracy, that is the way to help them. The final bill will be paid in due course and England will pay it. We will repay terror with terror. I do not tell you by what means, but I might use some which will make England reflect.' [10] With this first public reference to secret weapons, the flight from reality gathers speed.

That evening Mussolini telephoned to the leading Party paper *Il Popolo d'Italia* for the latest news. The revival of this daily habit was a symbolic measure of his recovery. He had not done so for a year. He summoned the editor to Palazzo Venezia, and in the course of conversation remarked, 'Tell me, does it seem to you as if I were already dead?' [11]

On December 19 the German Embassy in Rome forwarded a report to Berlin from their 'known confidant' on the Italian political scene following the Duce's speech to the Chamber. 'The first impression was very strong, but not profound.' The feeling in Palazzo Chigi was that 'a compromise peace with favourable conditions was no longer possible.' War would not last at least until 1944. Belief in victory had much declined throughout the country in the last five or six weeks, although feeling in regard to counteraction in Tunisia and early successes there had been reassuring. The reaction to air bombing had been counteracted however by the news from Tunis. The importance of German anti-aircraft reinforcements was vital, but there was a growing fear of Allied victory. In educated circles scepticism was rife as to the intentions, volume, and extent of German help. The same was true in certain Party circles.[e]

d. There were over one million refugees from the invaded provinces of Northern Italy in the 1915–18 war.

e. Presumably from Buffarini. The enclosed report was dated December 12. German Collection. Bismarck to Weiszaecker, December 19, 1942.

In a further telegram the German Minister in Rome, Prince Bismarck, added: 'The Duce's last speech has made a good impression after so long a silence, but the effect of the speech was quickly dissipated.' Instructions for the evacuation of the Italian cities increased the alarm. 'The population, in its majority, has always remained aloof from the war.' They looked in vain in the speech for any reference to food rationing, price control, the black market, and measures against it.

The German Consul-General in Milan had reported that there was 'a deterioration, the chaos of which I do not need to portray'. But 'the wind has been taken out of the sails of all rumours and "deals" which have sur-rounded the person of the Duce'. There was, however, disillusionment at the Duce's lack of reference to the food situation, and increased disquiet at his orders to evacuate the cities. The arrival of German anti-aircraft units in Milan had been greeted with mixed feelings. They might attract Allied bombing. There were also historic memories from the past Hapsburg occupa-tion of Lombardy! There was no question of any improvement in public opinion as a result of the Duce's speech, but equally no blow to the Duce's authority by recent criticisms.[12]

An acute summary of the feeling in Genoa is contained in a telegram from the German Naval Attaché in Rome. The effect of the air bombardment of the previous October had produced a moral collapse like that in the winter of 1940–41. There was 'much opposition but as yet little organization, no leadership, little confidence in the government but also little self-confidence. Military circles are not interested or are without political influence.' [13]

It seemed as if the only initiative in Italian affairs still lay exclusively in the hands of Mussolini. In a less public manner, the Duce had been prodding the Party Secretary. The latter had been ordered to de-bureaucratize the Party, to reactivate the local organizations, to set aside for the moment the 'technical' activities, which were absorbing its more essential tasks, such as gathering the harvest, and to make a maximum effort 'in view of the reality of the hour'. Vidussoni, taking his cue, responded with a boy-scout enthu-siasm, to defend 'the flag of honesty, which at this moment the Party must unfurl, alongside that, even higher, of faith . . . The Party cannot and must not, be a zone of influence. I allow myself to say it . . . The Party is yourself.'

Either the Party Secretary himself, or more probably the more schooled of his intimates, had sensed a contrary wind. 'I think that a broadening of the cadres of the national leaders, with the admission of members of the Old Guard, alongside the young of the new guard to which you confided the Party, would introduce a panoramic and more up-to-date vision of the Revolution, and would condense the Fascist generations in an indestructible union and continue their fusing.'

Vidussoni therefore himself proposed a reconstruction of the National Directorate, enlarging its membership to embrace the old guard and the young, the Federal Secretaries and the honorary members. 'The enlarged body will have more influence on the national leaders, more contact with the periphery; the Party will everywhere be spurring on the provincial gerarchs.' [14] Confronted with a resuscitated Duce, Vidussoni had received sage advice in the corridors, and the Young Guard was for the moment saved from dismissal.

This reconstruction of the Fascist Party Directorate was announced on December 19. It represented a limited move away from the younger generation, represented by Vidussoni, back to the Action Squad leaders of the March on Rome. The representative in Rome of the German Nationalist Socialist Party reported to Berlin on these changes in the following terms: 'From a point of view of personalities, what is important is the nomination of two new Vice-Secretaries, namely Carlo Scorza and the Militia General Tarabini. Both belong to the circle of Action Squads. Scorza is known as a journalist of the Fascist Party press. He is head of the press section of the Ministry of Popular Culture. Of the existing Vice-Secretaries have remained: Mario Farnesi, who counts as a coming man, and Ravasio.[f] Of the remaining members of the Party Directorate, the appointment of the Federal Secretaries of the large cities threatened by air bombardment—Genoa, Milan, Turin, Palermo, Ferrara, and Leghorn—should be particularly emphasized. The Press has underlined these appointments as indicating that the Party has been summoned to special activity and immediate organizational action at threatened points on the Home Front. Also striking among the new nominations is the appearance of the older generation of Fascist fighters in contrast to the former tendency, since the appointment of Vidussoni, to place the younger generation in leading roles.' [15]

It remained for Mussolini, now strengthened and stimulated by the nervous effort of regaining an audience and a platform, to attempt to dominate and illumine by his oratory the crucial events of the past months. On January 3, he spoke, in his inimitable style, persuasive, caustic, and compelling, to the new Party Directorate.

'I chose the third of January as a date for the meeting of the new National Directorate for obvious reasons [g] . . . The situation today has certain analogies with those of the second half of 1924. These analogies belong not to home affairs but to international. We are faced by an Aventine much more important than that of 1924, but containing the same elements and pursuing the same objects. In order to discover what we ought to do we must examine critically the development of recent events in order to draw the necessary conclusions. The first part of our present war shows the following characteristics. It took place in distant countries: in Ethiopia, in Africa

f. Ravasio was the editor of the Party's intellectual organ *Gerarchia*. Farnesi was a native of Trieste, and nominee of Vidussoni.

g. The anniversary of his speech on January 3, 1925.

(there were only three days' fighting on the Western Front), in Greece—always on the other side of the sea. The Italian people are accustomed to this war which is not too close, and have acquired the habit of indifference under these circumstances. They have come to the conclusion that war will always be far off, that it will be fought and settled in areas which are distant from metropolitan territory.

'All this changed after October 23, 1942, when the Supreme Command discussed the date on which the British would attack. I maintained that the attack would take place at the end of October, partly because the British would wish to benefit by the fact that this would spoil the celebrations of our Twentieth Anniversary . . . That in fact is what happened. In August 1942 the Italo-German offensive at El Alamein failed. Not because the soldiers failed to fight as splendidly as always. But we must remember that in war, victory is won or lost at sea rather than on land. We have lost a very large number of tankers laden with petrol and oil, both necessary fuels without which our motorized divisions cannot function . . . On October 23 the British took the initiative for the first time and obtained a success which they could never have had in the three preceding years. At the same time the terrorist ("scientific" according to Churchill) bombardment of our Italian cities began. This combination was planned so as to exert moral pressure on the Italian people at the time of the lack of success in the land war.

'But the date of November 8 is still more important. On November 8 there happened something which required no prophet but which any ordinary observer of human affairs could have foretold: North Africa was occupied by the North Americans. Only people deliberately wishing to deceive themselves could have expected any effective result from showing political favour to France. France hated us, hates us still and will do so until the end of time, hence all this policy of "petting" (as sailors call it) France is absolutely barren of results . . . This disembarkation of November 8 had certain psychological effects even upon many Italians . . . Events had made these somewhat feeble spirits lose their balance. It was thought impossible that the Anglo-Americans would not reach Ostia in a few days. Then the balance was restored because we replied to the Anglo-Saxon move. We occupied all France, Corsica and Tunisia. The occupation of France is important because at any rate in Metropolitan France misunderstandings have ceased. France no longer has its metropolitan territory; it has no colonial territory; it has no gold, it has no navy, army or air force; it has nothing. The French people does not even possess its own soul, and this is perhaps its most serious loss because sometimes this means the final decline of a people.

'How did it come about that the battle of El Alamein was decisive? Because the other arm of the pincers was lacking. The German troops should have poured down from the Caucasus. But this was not possible because anyone who has some knowledge of geography knows that the valleys there run parallel to the sea, one after the other, and we needed to get down to Batum. In the absence of this strategic manoeuvre it was clear that the battle was bound to end as it did.

'Who is going to win this war? You will say the best armed people. That is not enough. The people with the largest supplies of raw materials. Still not enough. The people with the greatest generals: not even this. This war will be won by the armed forces with the deepest political understanding. The days have gone by in which it was said that the soldier must not be a politician; no, that is a mistake. This could be said at the time when there were ten or fifteen parties. You could not allow ten or fifteen different kinds of political propaganda in barracks. But now there is only one party and one régime, consequently the armed forces can never be too political or too strongly Fascist. If they are not political we cannot win. We need Fascist soldiers to fight for Fascism because this is a war of religion and of ideas. Today all territorial objectives take second place. This does not mean that these objectives are not always in our minds, but that they have become of secondary importance. They are always present with us, because they enter into the general European settlement which must recognize our rights to living space.

'But today's problem is a problem of ideas; this is an authentic war of religion . . . Now we are facing the year 1943 which will be a year of fundamental importance in Italian history. It will be a year in which the régime must show its strength and the Italian people must pass a very serious test. There is no doubt that the international Aventine will bring its whole forces to bear upon Italy. This too could be foreseen. I have always regarded it as more important to occupy Egypt than to occupy England. If England were occupied, the problem would not be solved; but once the hinge of three continents constituted by Egypt had been occupied, and we had come down to the Indian Ocean, and had made contact with the Japanese, we should have broken the back of British Imperialism. This has not happened because each one holds ideas which derive from his historical situation. Ours has always been a Mediterranean one, the German a continental one . . . This has allowed us to take possession of huge areas rich in raw materials which we can use to prolong our resistance, but there is no doubt that at a certain moment we must throw our weight towards the West because the war will be decided in the West, in the Mediterranean.

'We are therefore privileged to foresee that an enemy attack will be directed particularly against Italy. Why? Because it is thought that Italy is the weaker of the two allies, but particularly because the enemy counts on a failure of our morale. For this reason it was thought that under enemy bombardment the people would at a certain moment show a desire for peace, any sort of peace, a separate peace. It is essential that everyone should be convinced, that every Fascist should be convinced, that this would be the most catastrophic solution and would dishonour us for centuries ...

'I do not believe that they (the Allies) will try to open a land front against us. It is too late; we have already taken our measures. Therefore the enemy must seek a place where conditions are more favourable. I believe that it is probable that the Anglo-Saxon attack will take place in the Balkans.

'Hitherto we have seen the following situation: the great power of resistance in Germany. From time to time there have been rumours in Italy about German morale; they always start with a misunderstanding. Because there are no signs of enthusiasm in Germany, it is thought that the German people does not want victory. The German people from the highest to the lowest knows what is at stake because it is clear that the Anglo-Saxons would tomorrow impose on Germany those conditions which were imposed by the Treaty of Versailles; that is, Germany would be paralysed for generations ... As regards the German anti-aircraft batteries which have been sent to Italy and which have already proved excellent, Fascists must be friendly to these men who have come to live with us. A certain excessive susceptibility is a weakness, a negative feature of the Italian character; Italians are unwilling to be helped by anyone. This is going too far.

'The Italian people now has the chance to show what it is made of. The problem is a serious one for us. We must ask ourselves whether twenty years of the Fascist régime have changed things only on the surface, leaving them much the same below. We shall see in the course of 1943. If you ask me "What is your opinion?" it is this: the Italian people will stand firm and astound the world ... By the end of 1943, which will not be the last year of war but will be a decisive year during which we shall see whether the balance will fall, the Italian people will have surmounted every test.

'The Party must be the instrument through which our armed forces become steadily more politically minded. Propaganda must fit in with time and place. Then there is propaganda carried on by everyone belonging to the Party: in the family circle, in the local Party Headquarters, in the social organizations, in conversation ... It is not necessary for the Fascists in Italy to number four millions. It is not even a bad thing, because it is impossible to govern a big country if you are shut up in an ivory tower. The important thing is that there should be a few hundred thousand well-informed, decided, ready, united Black Shirts, all absolutely dependable men, ideologically speaking. I believe that the Italian people has the qualities enabling it to resist, to hold firm and to conquer. At the end of 1943 we shall be able to say proudly that we have in fact realized our aims. At the present moment we have transformed the Italian people if not altogether, at least in part; this was the supreme task of our revolution ... This year will decide whether the Italian people must resign itself to being a land of tourists, a large Switzerland ... I look forward to these months with passionate interest and absolute certainty

... These are the directives which I give on this third of January. In addition, every month a meeting of the entire Directorate, including the inspectors, will be held at Palazzo Venezia, and I will preside. Thus we will work together.' [16]

This speech, projecting the now receding image of the Duce of the triumphant days, alert and confident, taxed his physical and nervous resources. But the cycle of the Winter Crisis was closed.

CHAPTER NINE

'THE EXPULSION
OF THE DISCONTENTED'

ON JANUARY 11 Mussolini was due to make his weekly report to the King, but decided abruptly to break away from the atmosphere of Rome to his retreat at La Rocca delle Caminate in Romagna. He was still unable to throw off the effects of nervous strain with its accompanying internal disorders, and he was driven to yield to medical advice. He left in a special train accompanied by his daughter-in-law Gina, the widow of his son Bruno who had been killed in 1941 in an air crash; his medical attendant, Professor Pozzi; 'General' of the Militia, Ridolfi, a picturesque old gentleman who had been his fencing and riding master years before, and now at the age of seventy-four accompanied the Duce as a personal bodyguard; Professor Vigoler, who gave Mussolini daily lessons in German; and Irma, his private maid, the wife of the porter at Villa Torlonia. The Duce travelled uncomfortably, doubled up with stomach cramps, and conversing about his symptoms and politics with the doctor. On arrival at La Rocca, two specialists were called in. In simple language, their joint opinion was that their patient was suffering from acute gastritis due to nervous tension.[1]

'The Ministers and generals are trembling because usually the isolations of the Duce are a prelude to vast changes of the guard.' [a] Whether this was or was not his purpose, the machinery of government came each time to a standstill. Now the routine royal audience had been cancelled, and the meeting of the Council of Ministers, due on January 16, postponed. In Rome there was a rash of speculation. On January 9 Marshal Caviglia wrote in his diary: 'I know from many directions that the Royal House sees a solution

a. Puntoni, *op cit* p. 114, January 11, 1943. See also Paolo Monelli, *Roma 1943*, p. 36. A brilliant study of the political climate. 'When the Duce left for La Rocca delle Caminate, or on tours of inspection, it was disastrous. Ministers did not dare to make a decision, the most low-level matters were left stranded, the Minister of Popular Culture ceased instructions to the papers and stopped all new handouts.'

near, more near than one thinks. It seems that the King is studying what to do. He will probably leave the ministry as it is and put at the head of the government Federzoni, or Grandi in his capacity as President of the Chamber. It will be a caretaker government pending a normal solution through elections, but holding the balance between the pressures of various groups and of not un-numerous pretenders.' And later again, 'The situation seems to me insoluble by peaceful means, either internally, or vis-a-vis our enemies or our ally. The latter will want to have no say regarding such a government, and will probably support his own candidate—Farinacci.' [b]

In spite of such unchained speculation and the physical absence of the Duce from Rome, his presence had returned to the centre of the political scene. Although Ciano had said that the departure of Mussolini could be explained by his ill-health, it was a reasonable suspicion that he had retired deliberately to his mountain and that his descent would be a signal for an unpredictable reshuffle. Meanwhile rumours were circulating 'of pending changes in the whole structure of the hierarchy'.[2]

On January 8 Ciano lunched with Bottai and Farinacci. 'They are exasperated. Bottai, speaking of the loss of Libya, said, "At bottom we have achieved another aim: in 1911 Mussolini declared, 'Let us get out of Libya.' He has kept his word—thirty years too late." ' [3] This private meeting did not escape the notice of the Party Headquarters. On January 19 Buffarini, together with the Party Secretary Vidussoni, seems to have visited Mussolini at La Rocca to tell him of the activities of the Ciano group.[4] A minute was also sent to the Duce on the day of his departure for La Rocca. 'I have to inform you that on Friday last Farinacci invited to lunch in his Roman villa Ministers Ciano and Bottai, the Party Vice-Secretaries Scorza and Tarabini . . . I have, however, reason to think that no views of a political character were expressed . . .'[5] Nevertheless the Duce telephoned Ciano some days later to ask whether it were true that this luncheon had in fact taken place.[6]

Ciano's next move suggests more than a hint of active caballing. On January 16 he sought out the German Ambassador, in a long private conversation, ostensibly to give him news of the state of the Duce's health. He asked for his remarks to be treated in the strictest confidence. Ciano explained that he based his remarks on the assertion that 'certain rumours would certainly reach me as a result of the Duce's recent journey to La Rocca delle Caminate, which had become known, and of the official announcement that the meeting of the Council of Ministers had been postponed *sine die*. These rumours would be full of the serious nature of the Duce's illness, and Ciano wished to place them in the right proportion.

b. Caviglia, *op cit* pp. 383–5, January 15, 1943. The value of these passages in his diary seems to be primarily as a summary of political rumour, circulating among the Senators.

'Foremost among his utterances—and twice repeated—was the sentence "The Duce is not very well". The pain in the intestines, which had ceased for a few days, had now come back, and the cause was unknown to the doctors . . . The first signs of discomfort had appeared in June, just before the Duce's trip to North Africa. On his return he had been treated by Professor Castellani for amoebic dysentery, which he had never had, and as a result valuable weeks had been lost. Professor Frugoni inclined to the view, which seemed plausible to Count Ciano, that the pain was in the first place of nervous origin. The Duce, as Ciano expressed it, was so constructed that he devoured all worries within himself, and even if he appeared outwardly calm he tore himself to pieces inwardly without being able to lighten the burden by talking. He had, for example, after the advance to El Alamein on the eve of the occupation of Egypt, believed a great victory to be near and, at the further development of events up to very recently, had suffered a heavy moral blow which, as usual with him, took the form of physical pain. In Ciano's view the surest remedy would be good news of decisive importance, which however could not be expected at the moment.

'The Duce's voice, from one telephone conversation which he had had with him,[c] was strong and fresh, his interest in affairs and his delight in making decisions was lively and undiminished. Nevertheless his absence from Rome had already had a noticeably disturbing effect in certain sectors.

'What the retirement of the Duce, on whom everything rested and who was the very driving force of Italy, would mean, Ciano went on, visibly moved, I need not tell you. But we could with absolute certainty rely on the fact that if grounds for serious anxiety should arise, the Fuehrer was the very first person whom he would inform, for he would be fully conscious of the enormous extent of the consequences of a change for the worse in the Duce's condition . . . Even though in conclusion Count Ciano once again underlined the fact that, with X-rays and blood tests, and two frank medical opinions, the thought of a mortal illness was out of the question, nevertheless the emotion with which he spoke clearly showed that he was very worried.' [7]

How far Ciano's worries were of a political order is not clear. If he were actively grasping at the succession, his telephone conversation of the previous day with Mussolini might well have made him reflect. There is no evidence of a concrete private plot, but rather of a despairing and final diplomatic move as Foreign Minister aware of the familiar signs of a possible changing of the guard.

Details of disaster on the Russian front accumulated during those days in Rome, together with depressing evidence of the climate at German headquarters. On January 19 Bottai, who was in constant contact with Ciano,

c. On January 15, to ask whether Ciano had been lunching with Bottai and Farinacci!

noted the content of certain news which the latter showed him in his office. 'Further reports on the German situation. The first of a military character . . . refers to the first break through on the Russian front, in which, through a German collapse on the flanks, our divisions have been overwhelmed. A real and proper rout with all the familiar details of such a collapse. The second, from our liaison officer at German headquarters, shows that henceforth everything is concentrated in Hitler's hands on whom the slightest initiative depends, even the most modest posting of units. The General Staff has no longer any voice in the matter, is forced to let things go and submit . . Finally, of much greater importance, a report from our Minister in Bucharest who had been invited to talk with the younger Antonescu, President of the Council. The latter wanted Mussolini and Ciano to know that the internal Roumanian position was desperate and untenable to such a point as to require not military but political measures, and that is peace negotiations, which he thought possible, and at this moment of definite use, even to the Germans.' [8]

Since the beginning of December the Italian Minister in Bucharest, Baron Bova Scoppa, had been reporting on the increasingly nervous reactions in Roumanian political circles to the outcome of the Don battle. His personal relations with Mihai Antonescu were close, and as early as the autumn of 1941 the two men had discussed informally the idea of a 'Latin Axis' based on Italy, France, Spain, Portugal and Roumania, a bloc 'destined to contain German expansion and Slav impulses'.[9] There was no reaction in Rome to such ideas at the time. But by January 1943 the military, and therefore diplomatic, situation of the Axis was revolutionized. Both Italy and Roumania were closely linked in a catastrophe on the Russian front; the Western Powers were in North Africa, and their advance towards Italy and the Balkans was threatening. Marshal Antonescu had in his turn been summoned to Hitler's headquarters, from January 10–12, to discuss the complete reorganization and further reinforcement of the Roumanian armies in Russia.[d] Three days later, on returning to Bucharest, the Roumanian President of the Council summoned the Italian Minister. The latter was so excited by this talk that he at once took the train to Rome, and on the journey drafted his report summarizing the conversation, and quoting extensively the words of Mihai Antonescu.[10]

The Roumanian leaders had found Hitler 'obsessed with the Russian question, and we had the clear impression of a man tortured by grave preoccupations. He spoke to us at length of his past, of his loneliness, of his revolution . . . He seemed to draw strength from the great memories of his past to neutralize the bitterness of the present hour. In his fixation on the

d. Nineteen new Roumanian divisions were to be raised. See A. Hillgrueber, *Hitler, König Carol, und Marshall Antonescu*, pp. 152–3.

Russian problem, he fails to take account of America and England. He sees the Europe of tomorrow as a citadel, which will have to find its own means to defend itself in the Russian space. General Hauffe [e] even showed us a map of the "citadel of Europe", whose confines ran along the frontier actually occupied by the troops of the Axis, and exclude Africa. The Fuehrer is perfectly aware of the gravity of the external situation, but told us that he was convinced that he would be able to meet it. Exactly how one does not know. When Marshal Antonescu posed to him the problem that if one considers the Russian Front to be decisive, all forces must then be concentrated to occupy Moscow, Leningrad, and the line of the Volga, the Fuehrer answered that what counts is to hold out, to organize Russian industry and agriculture, and to neutralize the air offensive of the Anglo-Saxons.

'Thus we are passing from the offensive war of the Blitzkrieg to the concept of the total defence of that abstraction which is the European citadel. For the eastern defence of this citadel the flower of European infantry is being thrown into the whirlpool.

'On the orders of the Fuehrer (who is the only one to give orders. Jodl seems to me too petrified since last year, and the new Chief of the General Staff, Zeitzler,[f] has nothing of the old Prussian tradition) all the scanty reserves of the Russian Front were either withdrawn or transported to the front line to thicken it. Thus it has happened that once the Russian attack has broken the front, it has found a void. The obstinacy in defending Stalingrad has consumed whole armies. To the not very amiable reproach of Ribbentrop that the Italian and Roumanian infantry had not held on, I replied that they had done so extremely well for many days but that it was not our fault if they had not been equipped with armoured and anti-tank weapons ...

'The front is now vulnerable at every point. The situation is serious in the Caucasus, very bad between the Don and Donetz, and also at Voronezh. At the German headquarters there is a mad centralization which has become a system. Our enemies are preparing major operations with formidable resources. The Fuehrer is not much concerned with Africa. He said that the difficulties in this area were due to lack of oil supplies, but now—he added— "one does not know how we can get out".

'Faced with this nightmare conception of war in the East, which will attract all our resources in this direction, I felt that it was my duty to ask Ribbentrop if it were not opportune also to think of those gigantic problems of a moral political order comprised together under the name of Europe. Ribbentrop replied that his experience led him to believe that one could not discuss this problem "until Russia had been beaten". Europe *must* hold out—he specified—"and that is all". But in the meantime Europe is being

e. Head of the German military mission in Roumania.
f. Zeitzler replaced Halder in September 1942.

shipwrecked, and without losing an ounce of my faith I must make it clear that our intuition is that the chaotic defence of the East at all costs and the absolute lack of comprehension in regard to all the political and above all moral problems in Europe will bring us to the abyss.

'Under these circumstances I think that one should assist the German leaders to clarify the situation. If the position in the East gets still worse, Hitler will send all his reserves to that Front, and then the state of affairs in the Mediterranean and the Balkans will deteriorate. My conviction is that England and America have no interest in letting the Russians into Europe and I have precise information to that effect. The Turkish Ambassador [g] came specially to tell me that America and particularly England were pressing on into Europe in order to bring the war to an end, but that they wished at all costs to avoid the collapse of the European system in favour of Russia. I have received similar reports from Portugal. I have the impression that, as things are at the moment, Germany would be content to expand to the East at the expense of certain Russian territories without putting forward any other great claims.

'I base such an appreciation . . . also on the fact that the internal situation in Germany is very serious. We have noted a certain uneasiness in the High Command, a crisis of confidence. In general, a crisis in the endurance of public opinion, in the system; a crisis above all of manpower and strategic reserves. The German army is tired. The troops who have been through four or five campaigns are as if under the influence of drugs. I think therefore that the moment has come to do something by complete agreement among ourselves. Please tell Count Ciano that it is out of common interest that I justify informing him of this and that it is essential at this decisive moment for our future to make direct contacts. Germany is obsessed with her own problems, and will not see those of Europe . . . If Count Ciano thinks that such an action is not opportune, I shall for my part continue to remain loyal to my commitments . . . Do not damage Germany by indiscretions to Germans . . . If things get worse, Italy is our only point of support, and we must help each other on a mutual basis. Will Count Ciano let me know the Italian point of view through yourself, if it is impossible for him to see me?'[h]

On January 10 Bova Scoppa delivered this document to Ciano at the Palazzo Chigi. The latter noted, 'I shall take the report to the Duce and shall make it the subject of conversation, which I have been planning for some time.' [11]

On the following day Ciano went to La Rocca to call on the Duce, who

g. Tanroier, the Turkish Minister in Bucharest. According to Bova Scoppa (*op cit* pp. 89 ff) Tanroier returned to his post from Ankara in February 1943 with instructions to sound the Roumanians on the chances of a 'Balkan solidarity' against the Slav menace. See p. 303.

h. The conclusion of the memorandum is somewhat repetitive and has been omitted.

listened attentively. Ciano's first impressions were, as was often the case, optimistic. 'Naturally, he rejected Antonescu's offer, "The Danube is not the route we must follow." But he did not jump in the air when I said openly that, at a certain point, we too should try to make some direct contact.'

The next day, however, Mussolini's reaction had altered. He described Antonescu's language as tendentious and 'confirmed in even firmer terms than yesterday his decision to march with Germany to the end'.[12]

Ciano does not seem to have appreciated the import of the Duce's last remark as the rejection of the whole Ciano-Grandi political analysis.

For weeks past, Ciano had been in touch with Grandi and his circle of friends with a view to clarifying the political atmosphere. There was no question, and no possibility, of independent action in any form. The immediate issue, in their eyes, was to persuade Mussolini to raise again with Hitler the liquidation of the war in the East and to concentrate on an all-out effort in the Mediterranean, at the same time emphasizing the need to take cautious preliminary steps to reinsure against total disaster on the lines of Bova Scoppa's memorandum.

A few days later Ciano received similar impressions in a hand-written letter from his former chef de cabinet, Filippo Anfuso, now Italian Minister in Budapest.

'What has happened to the Hungarian Army in Russia has been as swift as it is weighty and in many respects irremediable. All the equipment which was assembled with such effort is lost, the artillery has vanished, the troops are downcast at having been taken by surprise, and are now holding new, long, and insecure lines. You know this country well, and can judge how it must have been here. The middle classes, in so far as they are not Jewish, look silly; the Jews are rubbing their hands, the ruling class—that small political group which in Europe is characterized as feudal—has begun to examine its conscience.'

On the previous day Anfuso had received indirectly a report of certain remarks made by the Hungarian Regent, Admiral Horthy, 'in his good-natured Hapsburg jargon. "We are told that we are an appendage of Germany: fine. But if Germany is not in a position to defend us from the Slavs, what will become of us? I had thought vaguely in recent months of finding a territorial link with Italy, a kind of bridge which would unite us with our allies. This has never been discussed, but I have not given up thinking about it; that in this great German-Slav sea, a common frontier with Italy would be a certain guarantee for us. In any case we shall continue fighting, but we are wracked with alarm." '

The Italian Minister speculated as to whether Hungary was 'sounding out the ground with the Anglo-Americans, as some people are muttering. I know nothing definite. Everything leads one to believe that it is possible. Kallay, perhaps naïvely, said this to me: "As far as I know, Italy is the only country at war with the Anglo-Americans which has not made any approaches for a safe peace." I am forced to believe that the Premier on his side has done so, but perhaps this is a rash thought of mine, as Kallay has many times had his own peculiar way of expressing himself . . .

'The Hungarians are hanging out of the windows of their Ark, floating in the flood of their little parliamentary feelers (the Parliament is there and functions) in the hope of sighting just a strip of land. And this is the first proof of the existence of God, as the scholastic writers would say. Anything else? There is no serious man concerned in politics here who after five minutes' conversation does not take you to one side and say in private, "And what is Italy doing?" That means, "Have you got a good introduction for us? Will our alliance outlast the immediate fate of Europe?" In these questions, which I have presented theatrically, lies the naturally understandable anxiety of those who ask themselves whether the Slavs of the South and North will not slaughter the ten or twelve million Magyars before any English, American, Italian or German military police arrive to save them. In order to imagine this panic state of affairs, it is sufficient to reflect on what has happened recently; the bulls of the Danube and the dogs and cats of the Carpathian plain—in other words, the Hungarians and the Roumanians— have decided to negotiate with each other again, for they realize that they are neither Germans nor Slavs, and fear to be devoured by them . . .[i]

'As you see, Excellency, the situation is a gloomy one; but it is our duty to follow it closely just because we are neither Slavs nor Germans. Sympathy towards us is unimpaired . . . and an Italy which is strengthened by its own experience and which is spiritually prepared to defend European interests and thereby its own, in the hard struggle for the shape of the Europe of tomorrow, can make use of Hungarian friendship . . .

'Summing up. Deep inside there are no serious wounds, but the anxieties are too acute for the ruling class not to believe that it must find a way before the water gets into their shoes. In these last days their activities have been incoherent and now, for the first time, a certain cohesion is noticeable.

'I wanted to say this not to the Minister, but to the arbitrator of Belvedere,[j] who loves and is loved by this romantic group of Asiatics who have boldly settled on the Danube.' [13]

The possibility of forming a bloc of Axis satellites in the Balkans under Italian leadership in the hopes of pressing through a separate peace was the last pipe-dream of Ciano's diplomacy. Such elements of a coherent foreign

i. Ciano himself was less impressed by this move. On January 10 he had written in his diary, 'This sudden desire (of Mihai Antonescu) for conciliation with Hungary is suspect to me. All this would not have happened if the Russian offensive had not been successful.' Ciano, *op cit* p. 545, January 10, 1943.
j. To Ciano in his rôle at the time of the Vienna award in August, 1940.

policy as he had attempted to establish since the outbreak of war lay shattered in his hands. He had always been fertile in quick solutions, and always subject to sudden gusts of optimism in moments which called for cautious pessimism. And his success in any move depended in the last resort on being able to carry the Duce with him.

Having failed to move the Germans, at the December meeting in East Prussia, to consider a compromise peace with Russia, Ciano was equally unsuccessful in persuading Mussolini on his return either to intervene personally with Hitler in the same sense or to consider separate and drastic action. This feeling of personal defeat propelled Ciano into sterile cabals in the company, among others, of Bottai and Grandi. If Mussolini was not prepared to press to the utmost the German ally to negotiate with Russia, it was even more unlikely that he would listen to the similar vague proposals emanating from Bucharest or Budapest, which seemed to have so impressed Ciano and his friends. As Grandi told Bova Scoppa, the latter's report of January 19 was 'the most interesting and important diplomatic document which he had read recently. It was of capital value. Given the mentality of Mussolini, it is destined not to be followed up immediately, but it will be.' [14]

It was now clear that Ciano's credit as Foreign Minister had evaporated, and he was unable to carry the case for a negotiated peace or even secret feelers.[k] It was equally certain that, especially since the December talks at Goerlitz, the Germans too had their reservations about him.

On January 21 the Duce had returned from La Rocca delle Caminate to Rome, refreshed and secretive. The following morning the King received him in audience, and found him 'to be positively cheerful'. He had hinted to the King at 'an imminent reconstruction of the administration'.[15] His 'political design' would soon be apparent, and Bottai's comment that 'people have the impression that there is no longer a central government' was to be corrected.[16]

Marshal Caviglia noted in his diary, 'Perhaps Mussolini will begin to feel the ground slipping under his feet; he cannot understand that his Party bosses, those most beholden to him, are falling away from him. They are

k. Grandi had hoped, as a preliminary move, to send Casardi, one of the former members of his staff when Ambassador in London, to Lisbon. Ciano seems to have hesitated (see Ciano, *op cit* p. 552, January 29, 1943). According to German sources, at the beginning of February and allegedly on Ciano's instructions, the Italian Minister in Bucharest, Bova Scoppa, was sent on a special secret mission to contact British circles in Zurich, but 'the changes in Italian Government made the task superfluous'. (German Collection. Weiszaecker telegram, March 13, 1943.) Bova Scoppa told the author that he went to Switzerland at this time, and met socially the British Consul-General, whom he had known when he had been Italian Minister at Berne. He had no instructions from Ciano, but reported the episode to him on his return to Rome in the general hope that any such personal contact might at some time be used.

all seeking to recreate for themselves a non-Mussolinian virginity.'[17] Precisely for such reasons, the Duce was contemplating an Italianate purge.

The Duce's intentions were apparently also strengthened by information from the Germans. They were aware of the activities of the Italian Foreign Minister and his friends, and not only from Italian sources. According to Mr Allen Dulles, who was at that time head of the American Office of Strategic Services in Switzerland, he learnt early in February 1943 from Gisevius, his main contact with underground resistance groups in Germany, that the German security services had broken one of the American codes in use between Berne and Washington. One of the deciphered messages gave a picture of 'the dissension in the Italian ranks and of the anti-German group which, even early in 1943, formed around Badoglio, Grandi, Ciano and others. According to Gisevius, this deciphered telegram had been laid on Hitler's desk and sent by him to Mussolini with his compliments. A few days later Ciano disappeared from his post as Foreign Minister and went to the Vatican. I was never able to discover whether this was coincidence or whether this cable was the cause.'[1]

During the next days Mussolini gave active attention to public business. The Council of Ministers met on January 23. Each session usually coincided with ill tidings, and on this occasion with the news of the evacuation of Tripoli by the Axis, and further details of the disaster which had struck the Italian army in Russia.

The scene is described by Gorla, the Minister of Public Works. The formal agenda for the meeting was confined to the presentation of the budget by the Finance Minister, Thaon de Revel. 'This is one of the most important acts of government, but the atmosphere is poisoned.' All anxieties were focussed on events taking place in Russia and Africa. Having disposed of the agenda, Mussolini addressed his Ministers.

'While I am speaking to you, Tripoli is being evacuated. One must not however forget that our present objective is to preserve our available forces and as far as possible to concentrate them in Tunisia. For these reasons I agreed to abandon Tripolitania as proposed by the General Staff, despite the fact that I am perfectly aware of the immense repercussion which the news will have on the masses.'

Rommel had conducted 'a masterly retreat . . . Six Italian divisions and three German can be concentrated in Tunisia, representing the advance guards of the Libyan army, besides ninety thousand men already sent direct. These combined forces, and others as well, are needed there because, as all

1. See Allen Dulles, *Germany's Underground*, pp. 130–1. There is no evidence which has as yet come to light, of any moves by Ciano or Grandi in Switzerland at this time, but Badoglio, who had no connection with this group, seems to have established such contacts at the beginning of the year.

hope of breaking through to the East is lost, the objective of extending ourselves westwards may be realized in order to link up with Spanish Morocco, and to provoke the intervention of Spain on the side of the Axis...'

The Duce then turned to the Russian Front, where the dire implications of the Stalingrad disaster were now clear. 'I regard the situation of the German army as very serious. This negative view is not only induced by the loss of Stalingrad and the whole army of von Paulus, but above all because of the fact that the Russian Command has taken firmly in hand the conduct of operations and the Germans are not in a position to reverse the situation.' The Italian divisions in Russia had been obliged to hold too lengthy a front. The German units had given way on either flank under the Russian assault, and the Italian positions had been surrounded. The situation was 'fluid' and 'very serious', but not 'irreparable'.

The monologue terminated in an unprovoked and abrupt attack on the Vatican 'which is becoming the centre of all opposition to Fascism' and a 'revision of judgment' on Christianity itself. 'Islam has perhaps had an even greater influence.'

On this unexpected theme, Mussolini in his usual manner rose and left the room.[18] This outburst was the prelude to changes within the whole hierarchy of the Italian leadership.

It was no secret that Cavallero was marked down for removal. He had complained formally to the Duce on January 10 of Ciano's manoeuvres against him, and met with no satisfaction.[19] Ciano himself had pressed the final case against the Chief of the General Staff in his talk with Mussolini on January 20.[20]

The news of the loss of Tripoli, and Rommel's withdrawal towards the Mareth line provided the timing and the public pretext. The consequences of the disaster on the Eastern Front were as yet incalculable, but the early German reactions were to increase their control and penetration at staff level of the Italian armed forces on every front with a view to a totalitarian effort. The liaison officer of the Italian Foreign Office attached to the High Command reported to Ciano on January 25:

'The (Italian) Eighth Army in Russia has been practically destroyed in the recent fighting. One can, in general terms, reckon that fifty per cent of the troops can be saved, but material and supplies have for the most part been lost. On the German side, it has been proposed to our Command that the remaining elements should be sent back on the long route (eight hundred kilometres on foot) to be re-formed, while the remaining elements still able to fight should remain on the front under German command. The question will be discussed with the Germans. On our side, the so-called requests were rejected. On the part of the Duce, who has talked to Hitler about this, it has been pointed out that General Gariboldi was responsible to the Duce for his troops, that these had not been withdrawn from his command, and that the proposal to transport them to the rear can only be accepted if they go by train. I will follow up the question and report again. I have learned about it only personally and confidentially.'

Hitler was also planning to give orders to the German commander in South-Eastern Europe, General Loehr, to take over both Italian and German forces in the Balkans. And in Africa 'the authority of our Command is now very much restricted and has become an empty formula. The Germans plan a joint Italian-German staff for the African sector. The executive authority of Kesselring and the German commander in Tunis will in effect be complete, although formally staff organizations will be mixed.' [21]

On the same day, January 25, Mussolini was again received by the King, and launched another outburst against Cavallero, and in the early morning of January 31 the King learnt that the latter had been replaced by Ambrosio.

It seemed as if Ciano and his friends had scored a signal victory. The succession of Ambrosio to Cavallero was not unconnected with Ciano's ill-concealed soundings in military and political circles around the end of the year, and on the day of his appointment as Chief of the General Staff there is a note in Ciano's diary. 'In a conversation with me, Ambrosio confirms what we said the last time we met. He is an honest man who will act in the interests of his country rather than in his own.' [m]

Mussolini's decision was characteristic. He could not bring himself to rebel against Hitler, and Cavallero would not do it for him. He could not accept responsibility for the military disaster in Africa, and the imminent collapse of the Russian front. Military defeat in Africa and Russia had now been conveniently erased by the dismissal of the Italian Chief of the General Staff. The Duce must be infallible in the eyes of the nation.

Apart from Ambrosio's divergent views from the Germans on strategy, his appointment, following the dismissal of Cavallero, must modify adversely the relations between the German and Italian General Staffs. Ciano was at pains to tell Prince Bismarck at breakfast at the Golf Club that 'the dismissal of Cavallero has no political background. It is a purely administrative measure.' And that 'Ambrosio is the best type of Italian officer'.[22] But Ciano, with all his facile arrogance, could hardly have thought that such statements would mollify the Germans, and in fact on February 3, after a conversation with the Duce, he recorded: 'Cavallero. His replacement has alarmed the Germans. He was their servant. Now they fear that with his going the whole system will be changed. I reassure Bismarck, but I think it would be well if the Duce wrote to Hitler on the matter.' [23]

On January 31, Ciano also sent his private secretary, Marchese D'Ajeta

m. Ciano, *op cit* p. 553. The previous conversation had apparently been on January 20, when Ambrosio expressed his conviction that Germany would lose the war.

Lanza, to inform the German Embassy of Cavallero's dismissal, which was to be announced later in the day, and to give an explanation. He was received by Prince Bismarck, who reported the news to Berlin:

'The first rift in the relationship between the Duce and Cavallero had happened this summer when the Duce, on the advice of Cavallero, had gone to the Libyan front. A telegraphic code word had been agreed between them which Cavallero would send to the Duce when he judged that the moment had come for the Duce to go to Libya. Cavallero sent the code word twice. The Duce nevertheless waited, and only when Cavallero had telegraphed a third time did he go to Libya. The hoped-for military success was not forthcoming. From this time on the relationship deteriorated, and the Duce was very sensible of the fact that, during the retreat of the Italo-German forces in North Africa, Cavallero continually described the situation in too optimistic terms. Each time a new position was taken up, he represented to the Duce that it could be held against the British. Now that the whole Italian Empire has been lost, the Duce was compelled for political reasons to draw the consequences in the form of a change in the Supreme Commander. Apart from the personal attitude of the Duce towards Cavallero, the latter had always been unpopular in the Italian army in that he embodied the type of "political general" which had never existed in Italy. Cavallero's successor, General Ambrosio, had been chosen as the most senior among the Generals who came into consideration. He was a quiet, balanced military personality.'

Bismarck added his own comment: 'Cavallero's dismissal, from the German point of view, is very regrettable. Because of his energy, intelligence and gift for making quick decisions, co-operation with him was particularly smooth and characterized by the fact that he fell in willingly with the German requests and attempted to implement them with an energy unusual in conditions here . . .' [24]

General Ambrosio took up his duties as Chief of the Italian General Staff on January 31.[n] He had been summoned unexpectedly by the Duce. 'My first reaction was this: Today I am sacked.' He declined the new appointment, but was told that 'in a Fascist régime, orders are obeyed. In any case, I shall share with you the grave responsibility of the post.' Mussolini then asked what he intended to do. Ambrosio's version of his reply was: 'Three things: firstly to bring back to the Mother Country the maximum number of divisions (Mussolini seemed to me to be vexed); secondly, to dig one's toes in with the Germans (Mussolini exclaimed "Fine"); thirdly, to lighten the High Command of all the superstructures which my predecessors had built on it.' [25]

According to Ambrosio, the Duce agreed with the last two points, but was

n. Ambrosio had been Chief of the Italian Army Staff since January 1942, having previously commanded the Italian Second Army in Croatia.

against the first. He gave his reasons. It would be a blow to the prestige of the country abroad, would arouse German suspicions, and encourage the enemy.

The grand design of the Duce was not complete. On the afternoon of February 5, Mussolini sent for his son-in-law. The latter describes the scene in his diary. 'On entering his office, I notice that he is very embarrassed, and I grasp what he is trying to tell me. "What would you like to do at the moment?" he begins, and then adds in a low voice that he has changed the whole government. I understand the reasons, and do not intend to raise the least objection. Among the numerous solutions which he proposes to me . . . I choose the Embassy to the Holy See. It is a place of rest, which however holds many possibilities for the future. And more than ever, the future is in the hands of God.' 26

The next day Mussolini had second thoughts and wished to suspend the nomination. But Ciano had already taken steps to ensure the agrément of the Vatican. The Duce accepted the fait accompli 'with indifference'. Acquarone who seems to have been in touch with Ciano at this time, told him that the King did not know, when Ciano was received in audience on February 4, that he would be dismissed. 'The King is happy that I am going to the Vatican, and personally Acquarone is delighted.' 27

On February 7, he wrote an autograph letter of farewell to his father-in-law: 'The Pope has given his agrément to my nomination. Please permit me now, and all the more since out of understandable emotion I was unable to do so the day before yesterday, to repeat to you my unalterable gratitude for having allowed me to follow so closely your task in such difficult times for Fascism and the Country. It is not without great sadness that one is parted from you as an immediate collaborator and this sadness is especially alive to me. I only wish to repeat to you that I am pleased at the new post which you have conferred on me, and in which, though more at a distance but in the same spirit, I will be able to serve under your orders.' 28

At seven o'clock on February 5 the Italian radio announced the complete reconstruction of the Government.° The Duce himself took over the Foreign Ministry with Bastianini as Undersecretary. Bottai was removed from the Ministry of Education. Grandi was dismissed as Minister of Justice, but retained the office of President of the Chamber. This disposed of the so-called 'Ciano circle'.

The key Ministry of the Interior was also retained nominally by Mussolini himself. He now appointed in place of Buffarini as Undersecretary, the Prefect of Naples, Umberto Albini. At the Finance Ministry Thaon de Revel handed over to Giacomo Acerbo. In order to strengthen the conduct of the

o. For details of these changes, see the Appendix to this chapter. Ciano and Bottai remained members of the Grand Council by decree for three years.

war effort, a new Ministry of War Production was set up under the expert, who had already been struggling with such problems as a co-ordinating Undersecretary, General Favagrossa; and the prominent industrialist, Count Cini, was called in, with the greatest reluctance on his part, to infuse new energy and technical experience into the Ministry of Communications, whose work had come under such clumsy fire from Goering the previous December.[p] The old 'squadrists' Ricci and Pavolini vanished from their respective ministries, the Party strongholds of Corporations and Popular Culture.

This changing of the guard in February 1943 was a supreme example of Mussolini's method and style of personal government. In two cases he had seen outgoing ministers on the day of the public announcement. Bastianini had reported to him in the morning on business regarding Dalmatia, where he was Italian Governor, and announced his departure for Zara that evening. 'Two hours later my private secretary rushed to my hotel to tell me that the Stefani agency [q] was about to issue a communiqué on a complete change in the government. Mussolini was taking over the Ministry of Foreign Affairs with myself as Undersecretary. I regarded this news as incredible until seven o'clock that evening when the radio confirmed it.' [29]

The experience of Gorla, the Minister of Public Works, was more original. [30] He had been received by Mussolini on February 1, and instructed to go to Sicily to enquire into the whole situation on the defence works, but 'in reality to sound public opinion and present a realistic picture as he (Mussolini) needed a first-hand account from someone whom he could trust'.

On arrival in Naples, Gorla perceived that his special ministerial carriage was being unhooked from the train, and he was informed by the railwaymen that, as they had heard over the radio, he was no longer Minister. On his return to Rome he found a letter on his desk marked 'Urgent'. 'I have decided to modify the structure of the government, and would be glad if you would place your office at my disposal. Mussolini.'

When Gorla saw Mussolini three days later, the latter greeted him, 'standing and avoiding looking at me', and explained that there was nothing personal in the dismissal. 'It was a measure of a general character which I had to take and which had to include you.' And then, to Gorla's astonishment, Mussolini went on: 'You should know that, in a first moment you were exempt, but then I had to make the change to give the measure wider character.'

Naturally puzzled, the outgoing minister called on Grandi. 'The latter shook his head. The style still gives me offence. The measure has only one significance: in order to liquidate Ciano and Buffarini all the ministers were

p. Cini was skiing at Cortina D'Ampezzo where he heard on the radio the news of his appointment, and attempted to decline the honour.

q. The official government news agency.

dismissed as a wrapping round the removal of the two elements which he wanted to get rid of.'

At Court, Puntoni also referred by implication to the changes in this way. 'The official news of the reconstruction of the government has been announced. Ciano and Buffarini have been liquidated.' [31] r

The action of the Duce gave rise to myriad speculations, but Grandi's view was essentially correct. Ciano was not only the most unpopular figure in the public eye but had become the symbol of the war-weariness and murmuring, and his dismissal would be quickly understood by the Italian people as a sign that the Duce was again at the helm, and that the climate of defeatism would not be tolerated.

The removal of Buffarini was the subject of less reliable comment. As effective head of the Ministry of the Interior, he was responsible for studying closely the public mood, and for assembling and interpreting political intelligence and information on all aspects of the Home Front. It seems, however, that his dismissal was more a family affair, and due to feminine influence. He had long been deeply involved with Mussolini's mistress, Clara Petacci, and her family, whose financial transactions were a source of scandal in public and Party circles. 'The Petacci affair' had been the source of open comment at a meeting of the provincial secretaries of the Fascist Party in the previous October.

It was natural, therefore, that Buffarini should incur the virulent enmity of Countess Ciano, who had ample opportunity to bully the Duce during his recent retirement at La Rocca. As Dollmann put it, 'The chief danger zone of Buffarinin's today is represented by the ladies of the House of Mussollini who are by no means taken in by him.' [32]

The removal of the other Ministers had been interpreted 'officially' as due to connections with Ciano 'and his friends'.s It is clear however that the explanation of Grandi, and that given by the Duce to Gorla, expressed the real motive. The 'Changing of the Guard' was a domestic affair, and bore no relation to any impending alteration of policy at home or abroad. It was a tactic of distraction, of the liquidation of demoralizing rumours and their

r. There was no political connection between the two men at this time. Mussolini was in familiar style simultaneously breaking two separately caballing personalities.

s. Anfuso, the Italian Minister in Budapest, made a lightning switch of loyalties. In conversation with a German Foreign Office official on February 7 he praised Bastianini and pointed out that Ciano had been unpopular for a long time 'with the Italian people'. He added, as a misleading simplification, that the other dismissed Ministers 'almost all belonged to Count Ciano's circle of friends'. As to the nomination of Ciano to the Vatican, this was 'a clever move by the Duce'. No one could accuse Ciano of being pro-Vatican, but his position as former Foreign Minister and son-in-law meant that the Duce by appointing him 'recognizes the Vatican as a political institution' but will not put up with Vatican interference in Italian affairs. German Collection. Foreign Office minute to Ribbentrop, February 11, 1943.

deliberate replacement by new ones, an exploitation of the Italian people's love of change, and a demonstration of the Duce's renewed vigour.

As Bottai put it: 'A whirl of comments and rumours; what has Mussolini been trying to do? Firstly, I think, to achieve exactly that, and to distract people from the great interrogation marks of the hour with these questionings in the gossip columns. And then, to show his power over men.' [33]

The German Ambassador learnt by chance of Ciano's dismissal. He had been asked to call on the latter at seven o'clock on the evening of February 5. 'He surprised me with the statement that he was no longer Foreign Minister. Today the Duce has carried out a changing of the guard in grand style which included practically all the members of the cabinet . . . Ciano let it be understood that he is taking up a senior post in Rome, although perhaps not at once.' [34]

On February 8 Mackensen had an interview with the Duce and the point was made by Mussolini himself, with the comment that 'he hoped that I had seen to it that the change of government had been regarded by us as a normal internal Italian event. It in no way affected our mutual relations. His completely unambiguous and unmistakable line of policy had nothing to do with the questions as to what men he worked with. For him there was only *one* [t] way. He had destroyed all the bridges behind him. For the rest, many of the retiring ministers had borne the burden of office for five years or more, and were tired, and therefore had better be replaced with new elements. I answered that from the Fuehrer downwards there was no German who had the slightest doubt as to the Duce's clear line. I was nevertheless surprised by this changing of the guard. The Duce capped this remark, laughing, with the words, "That is once again just my way. You must gradually get to know it."' [35]

Hitler's characteristic comments on a previous occasion a year earlier are a revealing measure of the different character of the two men as displayed in such a situation.

'The changing of the guard at Rome is not good news, I think. In my view, too frequent changes of leading figures are a mistake. A responsible chief who knows that he probably will not have time to complete a job that he would like to embark on, generally sticks to routine. I don't understand why one should create such situations. In that way one merely aggravates one's troubles.

'The reason why I can carry the new responsibilities I am undertaking is that gradually I have been freed from certain responsibilities, by colleagues to whom I have given the chance to reveal themselves, and who have succeeded in deserving my trust. It is possible that the Duce cannot find amongst his advisers the sort of collaboration he needs. For my part, I have had the luck to do so.' [36]

t. Underlined in the original text.

On February 10, the German Ambassador in Rome reported in greater detail and accuracy on the Italian cabinet changes.

The impact of bad news from the different theatres of war in recent months had undermined the Italian people's will to resist and their readiness to hold out. 'Even the loss of Tripoli had no longer produced in them the reaction for which the Duce had hoped. To these impressions were added reports which reached him from all parts of Italy of the increasing disorganization of the administration, of symptoms of inflation and a marked decline in willingness to work among the industrial workers in the North. Hand in hand with these phenomena there appeared particularly in the provinces an ever sharper criticism of the Italian government, which no longer stopped at the person of the Duce. The main complaints were directed at the lack of technical knowledge and the tight rigidity in management of those ministries which were the most important in the organization of the country—namely the Interior, Corporations, Foreign Trade and Communications. The old attacks against Count Ciano, about his way of life and his alleged financial deals also played a considerable rôle again. The attempt to tighten up the administration, which had made itself felt through the reconstruction of the Party Directorate,[u] had not had any lasting effect owing to the impact of military events.'

The Duce was aware of this state of affairs, and he concluded that, 'in order to take the reins of government firmly in hand again and re-establish his own prestige, it was high time to show public opinion clearly that he still had power incontestably in his hands and that it only needed a stroke of the pen to replace his existing collaborators by others. It is also certain that there had recently been increasing attempts to try to influence the Duce, and make it clear to him that several of his ministers were conducting too independent a policy and seeking to create for themselves their own spheres of interest.

'A particular part in these interpretations seems to have been played by certain incautious statements made by Count Ciano recently in the circle of his friends . . . Since the Duce did not want to dismiss only Count Ciano and two or three other ministers whom he felt he must get rid of on such grounds, he has changed the whole Cabinet with the exception of the ministers of Colonies and Agriculture.[v]

'The decision to remove Count Ciano and the other ministers was reached by the Duce quite independently and suddenly without consulting other persons, and particularly not the newly appointed ministers. Only Count Ciano and Pavolini were informed direct of his decision—and that on the afternoon of February 5 . . . and immediately afterwards the publication of an official announcement was arranged so that the retiring ministers first learnt

u. In December 1942, see p. 129.
v. Teruzzi and Pareschi.

of their dismissal, and those newly appointed of their nomination, through this public statement—in the case, for instance, of the Minister of Education, Bottai, through the radio, and others the next day in the papers.

'The change of ministers appears from the reports reaching me to be a measure taken by the Duce to eliminate the serious crisis of confidence in which the government found itself and which threatened to direct itself against the Duce himself, by placing in the control of technical specialists those ministries which had hitherto been predominantly in the hands of Party politicians. And Count Ciano, who for a long time had been a burden to the Duce from the point of view of popular confidence, was recalled from the front of the political stage.

'It is not surprising that in Rome political circles this change of practically every Italian minister in circumstances of, for here, surprising suddenness has given rise to a series of false rumours, particularly in connection with the appointment of Count Ciano to the Italian Embassy to the Vatican. The entire Cabinet change, so runs one rumour, "is only a put-up job in which Count Ciano is nominated Italian Ambassador to the Vatican in order to be more easily in a position to establish links with our opponents". In the case of this rumour it is a question of a malicious invention of those circles who, intentionally or out of stupidity, want to throw doubt on the Axis policy of the Duce . . .

'In deciding to accept the Vatican Embassy, it may have weighed with Count Ciano that he wanted to stay in Rome in order not to lose his connections with Italian internal politics. But I think it false to assume that in making this choice he had the prior intention to conduct from this post his own foreign policy. In the circle of his personal and political friends there are certainly many who are of the opinion that he is the man to renew these relations at a given moment, and in these circles a certain satisfaction will reign that he has taken the post at the Vatican, which can offer to him as to no one else such possibilities. Only the future will show whether Count Ciano is prepared to play such a rôle or not.' [37]

On the following day, February 11, the Press Section of the German Foreign Office sent to Ribbentrop's private office a particularly well informed and accurate report on the recent political changes in Rome.[w]

'The intention of the Duce to undertake a thorough clean up goes back to the autumn of last year; even before the last visit, therefore, which Ciano made to German headquarters. In September and October already the Duce had received a series of personalities in order to test them out as heirs presumptive to certain ministers. A large proportion of these have now in fact been appointed.

w. This minute was based on impressions collected from 'friendly' members of the Italian Embassy in Berlin.

'The relations between the Duce and his son-in-law appear not to have been of the best for a long time. They reached an acute crisis after Ciano returned from his last visit to Germany. The Foreign Minister had at that time drawn near to the circle round Grandi and Bottai in order to seek their advice on the foreign political situation. A standpoint had crystallized out of these mutual contacts, which was in favour of substituting the hitherto unconditional co-operation with Germany by one of a restricted kind. Ciano appeared to represent the conviction—and in this was above all supported by Grandi—that the war in the East could not be won militarily, and that the right thing to do would be to seek an agreement with Stalin or at least confine oneself to a defensive conduct of the war in the East. In such a way one would release forces in order to try to reach an offensive decision in the Mediterranean. The German command would have nothing to do with such a proposal. Even if Italy did not succeed in persuading Germany of the validity of this conception, Italian policy must nevertheless be developed independently of Germany. This was all the more necessary as the numerous forecasts which were given to the Italians on the German side as to their military prospects in the East had not been borne out. The latest developments in particular contradicted the optimism so frequently shown by the Germans over the position on the Eastern Front.

'When Ciano was certain that his views were identical with those of Grandi and Bottai, he made clear to the Duce their attitude.[x] The Duce sharply opposed Ciano's views, and declared that the fate of Fascist Italy was indissolubly linked with that of National Socialist Germany, and that even in the future he considered that a hundred per cent joint policy was the only possible line.

'When the Duce had ascertained that this point of view was not shared by Ciano, Bottai, Grandi and other ministers, he decided with lightning speed on a reconstruction of the administration.[y] In spite of the foregoing discussions, this change came as a complete surprise to those concerned.

'The further employment of Ciano as Ambassador to the Vatican is explained by the fact that Mussolini is very well aware of the influence of his son-in-law in certain Roman circles, and intends therefore to keep him under observation. Under no circumstances did he want to leave him unemployed, since this would have increased the possibilities for intrigues under Ciano's leadership.

'One could say in conclusion that the Cabinet reconstruction ensures a hundred per cent Axis line in Italy. On the other hand, one must not underestimate the future rôle of Ciano. He is gravely hindered by corrupt person-

x. At his meeting with the Duce on January 20.
y. Presumably on January 20 after Ciano had revealed, in connection with Bova Scoppa's report of January 19, his general conception of the need for a negotiated peace. Ciano had already discussed the implications of this report with Grandi and Bottai.

alities whom he frequents and is not particularly popular with the people. On the other hand he has powerful friends, who are aware of his marked political ability.' [38]

Mussolini seemed to have succeeded in his purpose. By dismissing Ciano, and covering this move by eliminating almost the whole administration, he had given the impression that politically the new team of technicians would give increased efficiency to an invigorated Italian war effort as a loyal Axis ally, and remove any suspicion of a diplomatic weakening in Italian policy. At the same time the replacement of the pro-German Cavallero by Ambrosio, as Chief of the General Staff, was neatly obscured in its possible military significance by this dramatic realization of a general 'Changing of the Guard'.

APPENDIX

The 'Changing of the Guard' on February 5, 1943

Ministry of Foreign Affairs

Mussolini took charge as Minister.

Ciano was succeeded by Bastianini, who held the rank of Under-Secretary. Ciano, by special decree, remained a member of the Grand Council for three years. Bastianini, at the time of his appointment, was Governor of Dalmatia. He had succeeded Grandi as Ambassador in London in 1939.

Ministry of the Interior

Mussolini remained as nominal Minister.

Buffarini was replaced by Albini as Under-Secretary.

Albini was a career official, and until this appointment Prefect of Naples.

Ministry of Justice

Grandi was replaced by De Marsico. The latter was a Professor of Law in Rome University, and a high-ranking member of the Fascist Party.

Grandi remained President of the Chamber, and a member of the Grand Council.

Ministry of Finance

Thaon de Revel was replaced by Acerbo. Acerbo had been the leading Fascist organizer in Southern Italy (the Abruzzi), and had been involved in the negotiations preceding the March on Rome. He had been Minister of Agriculture from 1929–35.

Ministry of Education

Bottai was replaced by Biggini. The latter was Rector of the University of Pisa and Professor of Law.

Ministry of Public Works

Gorla was succeeded by Benini, formerly Under-Secretary for Albanian affairs.

Ministry of Communications

Host Venturi was replaced by Cini, a leading figure in the world of Italian industry.

Ministry of Corporations

Ricci was replaced by Tiengo. The latter was a career Prefect. He was removed to a clinic shortly after his appointment, and replaced in April 1943 by Cianetti.

Ministry of Popular Culture

Pavolini was replaced by Polverelli. The former became editor of the Rome paper 'Il Messagero'.

Polverelli had been head of Mussolini's Press Office (1932–3) and was Under-Secretary of the Ministry of Popular Culture at the time of his appointment.

Ministry of Exchange and Currency

Riccardi was replaced by Oreste Bonomi.

A new Ministry of War Production was set up, with General Favagrossa at its head. Two Ministers had survived the changes: the Minister of Italian Africa, Teruzzi, and the Minister of Agriculture, Pareschi.

PART ONE

Book II

CHAPTER ONE

THE MILITARY SCENE

• •

THE STATE of the Italian Armed Forces was seldom brought under co-ordinated and detailed review. The initiative of summoning any formal meeting of Chiefs of Staff and their advisers lay with Mussolini as Minister of the three Armed Services and as Commander-in-Chief. Such a meeting had, for example, been held on October 1, 1942.[a] Routine arrangements were confined to the frequent contacts of the Duce with Marshal Cavallero as Chief of the General Staff, when the former was in sufficiently good health, or with Cavallero, Kesselring, and Rintelen as the immediate situation required. Mussolini had little direct relationship with the Chiefs of the three Armed Services, and indeed Cavallero strove to prevent any such contacts being established. Ambrosio appears to have seen the Duce alone on only one occasion during his time as Chief of the Army Staff. There was, therefore, no regular use of any machinery of high-level consultation on military, or on political, affairs in the system of Fascist administration.

The loss of Italian North Africa with the fall of Tripoli, the threat to Tunisia, and the collapse on the Eastern Front, however, forced Mussolini to call a meeting of his military advisers to review the situation in each theatre of war. It took place on January 28 at Palazzo Venezia, and was the last to be attended by Cavallero.[1] It was conducted by Mussolini in similar style to that which he adopted with the Council of Ministers; a long monologue followed by a ragged debate. The discourse of the Duce was unusually thin and facile, and confined largely to political generalities.

'One would logically suppose that when the enemy reach the sea, they will try and cut into two the Italo-German forces in Tunisia. On grounds of logic, if the Anglo-Americans wish to create a second front, the most convenient door is not Sicily. It is not certain that through this door one can reach Germany.

a. See pp. 58–9.

'It would be more appropriate for the enemy to land in Greece where the population is starving, and where the enemy would find help from the army of Mihailović (*sic*). The British and Americans are not yet in agreement about this army, but we all know they are against us. The Greeks cannot take the initiative against us as they had 100,000 dead and wounded in the war against Italy. For the time being they are only active with nuclei of armed bands who have the mask of brigands but in reality are Communists . . . But if the Allies land, every Greek will make common cause with them.

'The Albanian sector is deteriorating, and the population is in a state of agitation . . . I regard Albania as a key position. It is of fundamental importance in safeguarding the Adriatic and because it is the link between the Slav and Hellenic worlds.

'Montenegro is quiet, but there is no cause for confidence as this has only been reached through political agreements . . . In the Croatian sector, the situation is confused. The new State has grown up accompanied by many difficulties, and in the early stages conducted a mistaken policy aimed at destroying two million individuals of Orthodox religion and Serb race, who have lived for centuries in Croat territory . . .

'In Russia we have suffered the consequences of an absurd deployment, all the more since it was not imposed by necessity. One Italian division ought to be holding a front of thirty kilometres. The Russians first attacked the Roumanians, who were thin on the ground, and came forward. They then attacked our sector where we could only confront them with 18 battalions to 70 of theirs . . . I do not think that the Germans will succeed in holding the Caucasus. If they had crossed the Caucasus, we should still today be at El Alamein. It must be remembered that, contrary to the original German view, the Russian General Staff has good possibilities operationally and in matters of supply. On a front of 300 kilometres, their troops lack nothing. The Russian soldier is resistant and brave, and his equipment good. The population has not rebelled. Communism has attached itself to the fighting tradition of ancient Russia.

'The situation in Southern France is more disturbing. Here too we are detested. A part of the population tries to suborn our soldiers, but I do not think with much success, drawing attention to the fact that the Germans are better clothed and eat better than ours, saying "Germany takes away everything. You will take second place, while we shall come back as the great France." There is no absence of Communist propaganda. It is a troubled and morbid atmosphere, as there is corruption by the rich and degenerate. For this reason, when there was a question of occupying Marseilles, I opposed it as I did not want to send Italian troops into that city. I knew that they would be exposed to every kind of propaganda. The French didn't fight in 1940. They are all *attentistes*, beginning with Laval. Perhaps also even Pétain. We would react in the same manner to occupation—with outrages and disturbances. But France has her backbone so weakened that only a very successful landing in force could put her on her feet, and not earlier. The French do not want to compromise themselves prematurely.'

Such was Mussolini's contribution to the discussion. He was prepared, with an effort, to listen to the technical problems raised by his professional advisers. Matters of grand strategy would be discussed as always with Kesselring, and usually in the presence of the Chief of the General Staff only, and subsequently in correspondence with Hitler. This was strictly in accordance with the facts of the situation; the Italian war effort was totally dependent on the Reich for essential war material, equipment, and military backing on the major fronts. The myth of a 'parallel' Italian war had disappeared in Greece in 1940, and with the arrival of Rommel in North Africa the following year.

The order of battle of the Italian army was approximate in the sense that the state of efficiency and equipment of each division was seldom, if ever, analysed or discussed outside the routine committees of the War Office.

After the North African landings, Rintelen had sent the following statement to Berlin, dated November 18, 1942.[2] The number of Italian divisions was listed as follows:

France, Corsica, Tunis	9	
Italy and the Islands	26	(12 Coastal Defence)
Balkans and Dodecanese	33	
Russia	10	
Libya	12	
	—	
	90	

The precise state of these divisions in January 1943 was not discussed in detail at the Palazzo Venezia meeting.

The Italian Army production programme for 1943 had been drawn up in September 1942, and did feature in a document presented at this conference, which was in effect a progress report. 'The programme drawn up in September 1942 for 1943 envisages the bringing up to efficiency of thirty operational divisions of a standard type . . . tank production at maximum capacity, supplies for the above-mentioned thirty divisions.

'It should be noted that the 1943 programme is not related to the real requirements which the army needs to adapt itself to up-to-date fighting, but is a much reduced programme, geared to the amount of raw materials at our disposal, and the capacity of our industry. The programme also takes into account the scale of production which it is effectively possible to achieve in 1943, and which in certain sectors is noticeably inferior to our minimum requirements (for example, anti-aircraft ammunition, tanks).'

'The Ministry of War Production has allocated up to one hundred per cent supplies of ferrous metals, tin and zinc. It has not been able to satisfy entirely the requirements for copper, aluminium, antimony and lead.

'The beneficial effects of these quotas will not be felt for at least 6–7 months. In general, production should improve as from July/August, 1943.

'Between September 1942 and today, the general situation has changed considerably. Requirements which were not then of major importance have now become pre-eminent, such as all the provisions needed for the defence of the Mother Country, which is now directly threatened, and those arising out of the Russian situation.

'The entire tank production for the next four months is commissioned for the reconstruction of the Second Army Corps in Russia with a small margin available for North Africa and Russia.[b]

'Tank units do not exist in Italy. There are only two semi-mobile groups, of which one is destined for Sardinia and the other is at the disposal of the General Staff.

'Taking into account production as planned for 1943, it should be possible to satisfy totally the requirements of coastal defence, except for artillery, which can be only met by half.' [3]

These basic data set the frame within which General Ambrosio was now called on to plan, as Chief of the General Staff, the future conduct of the war by Italy.

His view of Italy's military prospects was more sober than that of Cavallero, and less liable to be swayed by gusts of German optimism. The North African front might be held for two or three months, depending on the extent of German supplies and reinforcements, and the maintaining of the sea route to the North African ports. The battle in Tunisia must be prolonged primarily in order to prepare the defence of Italy and the offshore islands against invasion, and detailed and coherent requests for German military aid for this purpose must be formulated.

Ambrosio had little confidence in a German military recovery on the Eastern Front, and had obstinately opposed the Italian commitment in Russia. He had failed to prevent the dispatch of three Alpine divisions there in the late summer of 1942, but now hoped to be able to liquidate the whole adventure and to persuade the Duce, after the Don battle and the Stalingrad disaster, to withdraw the remnants of the Italian Expeditionary Corps.[c]

b. 'The production of 324 "M" tanks was to begin in December and be completed in August 1943. 60 *may* be ready in January, and 22 in February. No further forecast can be made.'
Cavallero had made attempts to standardize Italian tank production with that of German, but met with the opposition of Italian industrialists.

c. The Italian losses in the Don battle were 4,300 officers and 110,000 men killed, wounded and missing. These figures represented 60 per cent of the officers and 50 per cent of the other ranks. see also Galbiati *op cit* p. 146. 18 out of 20 generals were safe, and only 5 out of 50 Staff Officers were missing.

As to the Italian deployment through the Balkans, Greece, and the Aegean islands, Ambrosio was prepared, if supported, to bring back for the defence of the Italian peninsula the bulk of the thirty divisions which were scattered throughout the area, and which represented half the effective strength of the whole Italian army. His experience of anti-partisan warfare in Yugoslavia had convinced him of the futility of the Italian military occupation in those regions, and he regarded the defence of the Balkans against an Allied threat of invasion as a secondary danger compared with an all-out assault on Metropolitan Italy, which was his basic concern. The fate of the continued Italian participation in the war turned on successful resistance to such a menace.[d]

After the cabinet reconstruction which followed Ambrosio's appointment, the Duce charged Kesselring on February 13, 'to tell the Fuehrer and Marshal Goering that the recent changes in the structure of the ministry in no way modify the goal which Italy has fixed'.[4] But the Germans were bound to interpret the removal of Cavallero as a stiffening by the Italians against German supremacy in the conduct of the war. When on February 7 Mussolini referred to German disquiet in a conversation with Ambrosio, the latter had commented laconically, 'The answer to that: it is normal.' [5]

General Rintelen, as Chief German Liaison Officer with the Italian Command, was the best informed and most responsible witness. 'Ambrosio saw himself faced with a difficult situation. The Royal House and the Officer Corps required of him greater independence in regard to the Germans. The Duce too was tired of this tutelage. On the other hand, his own machine was breaking down and one had to accept and request further German help and support.' [6] In Rintelen's view, relations between the two High Commands would from now on be increasingly strained.

During the days following his nomination as Chief of the General Staff, Ambrosio paid and received a round of official calls, thus gathering wider impressions of Italy's war effort in general.

On February 4, he held a meeting with the head of the Navy, Admiral Riccardi, to review the state of the Fleet. There could be no question of offensive action. 'Operations are thus imposed by the movements of the enemy. The means at our disposal are such that we are not able to organize counter-action against all those enemy movements which have been signalled.'

Ambrosio's main concern was the reinforcement of Tunisia. Italian naval resources were glumly reviewed: twenty destroyers, thirty motor torpedo boats, thirty submarines, and six heavy cruisers which were immobilized by

d. As he had told Caviglia on January 27, just prior to his new appointment: 'Cavallero only thinks of sending new forces out of Italy, and maintains that everything is going well in Tunis. For my part I want to have at least seven divisions in Italy, four in Sicily, and three in Sardinia.' Caviglia *op cit* p. 390.

lack of fuel and, above all, of escorts. Eight light cruisers were under repair. The essential task confronting the Navy was to transport ten thousand German troops to Tunis by the end of February, and thirty-six thousand more in due course. Admiral Riccardi reckoned that this operation alone would take four months. Italy was totally dependent on Germany for fuel oil. The naval consumption was 65–80,000 tons a month, of which 42–44,000 had been received through Roumania and Germany. The oil had to be brought by rail to Fiume and shipped in tankers along the Italian coast to avoid burdening the railways.[7]

In a talk on February 18 with the new Minister of Communications, Count Cini, on the transport situation, Ambrosio was told that, 'if we continue with the present organization, within six months we shall be in a major crisis'.[8]

A discussion with General Favagrossa, the Minister of War Production, revealed a similar picture. That such a department was only given a ministerial head in February 1943, after three years of war, was a measure of the lack of co-ordination of the Italian war effort.

The Duce, however, was seldom impressed by logistics. In his excitement at the prospects of developing the bridgehead in Tunisia as a base for a westward advance, he was ready to liquidate the Libyan adventure. Everything would be concentrated on a new grand operation to the West to remove the disagreeable memories of the failure to sweep eastwards to Egypt in the previous year. Enthusiasm for novelty was a constant characteristic of the Duce, and at most times his optimism was shared by Kesselring.

On February 5, at a meeting with the Duce and Ambrosio, Kesselring had reported that the German commander in Tunis, General von Arnim, talked of the need 'to initiate as soon as possible an offensive towards the West,' and thought that one could start 'in about two weeks'.[e]

The Duce pointed out that the situation of the Anglo-Americans was not of the best: he read out in this connection a telegram from Lisbon and commented on it. In discussing enemy intentions regarding a landing attempt in the Aegean, and eventually in Italy, he expressed doubts.

The Germans were even thinking of considering the political situation in French North Africa with a view to seeking support in French and Arab circles for an eventual Axis occupation of French North Africa, and at this meeting Mussolini, for once cautious, agreed to allow the Germans to deal directly with the French and the Arabs without referring to the Italian government.[9]

---

e. There were two German armies in Tunisia: that of Rommel and the Fifth Panzer Army under von Arnim. The latter had been in North Africa since the previous December, and was to take over the whole German command from Rommel on March 8.

It was this brief mirage of 'a race to Casablanca', as logistically unreal as Rommel's ill-fated dash for Egypt of the previous summer, to which Hitler referred in talking to Rommel on March 10. This mood was not shared by the latter. On February 12, Ambrosio noted in his diary that such a step also removed an obstinate critic of the new 'combined operations' to be directed from Tunisia to the West. As Rommel was under the nominal command of the Italian General Staff, he was dismissed by Mussolini. There was no prior written exchange of views with Hitler.

On January 26 the last gesture of Cavallero as Chief of the Italian General Staff had been to telegraph Rommel that, for health reasons, the latter would be relieved of his command when the Axis forces reached the Mareth line. He would be replaced by General Messe [f], former Corps Commander of the Italian Expeditionary Corps in Russia. By mid-February, the last German rearguards withdrew on to the Mareth line. The retreat from Alamein to Tunisia was over. Mussolini wrote to Hitler on February 11, 'Field Marshal Erwin Rommel has laid down the Command of the Italo-German Armoured Corps. The events of the war in North Africa after spring 1941 will always be linked with his name and actions as Commander; later developments have not detracted from the importance of his repeated brilliant successes there. He always knew how to win the unbounded trust and lively affection of the troops under him; officers and men, Italians and Germans alike, admired in him the brave, just and wise Commander. The Italian forces in Africa were genuinely sorry to see him go. Field Marshal Rommel therefore also deserves credit for having done much to strengthen the bonds of comradeship between the fighting forces of our two countries.' [10]

Hitler did not reply.

Rommel was to conduct one final attack against the Americans at Kasserine, and then, on February 23, to his astonishment, he was appointed commander of a new unified Army Group 'Afrika'. This was a move by Hitler without consulting his Italian ally [g] to support in public the reputation of one of his most popular and able generals, while rejecting in private the latter's earlier appeals for the total evacuation of North Africa. 'For the Army Group to remain longer in Africa was now plain suicide.' [11]

At the end of February, Rommel produced his final report on the situation in Tunisia, after consulting his Army Commanders. He concluded, 'In view of the gravity of the situation, I request that an early decision be reached

f. Possibly to remove the latter from Rome as a rival candidate to the imminent succession of Cavallero. See also Ciano *op cit* p. 552.

g. There is no trace of this decision in the existing Italian records, in particular of the frequent meetings between the Duce, Kesselring, and Ambrosio, which appear to be reasonably complete. According to the German military records, the appointment was made formally by the Italian Supreme Command on February 23. Hitler's directive to the German High Command was issued on the following day.

on the plan for the future long-term conduct of the campaign in Tunisia. We can expect the enemy's offensive to open with the next full moon.' [12]

The whole issue of joint command and future strategy in North Africa was urgently in need of review at the summit.

Ambrosio's first study of the war situation is contained in two minutes to the Duce dated February 17 and 21.

The Germans must shorten their front in the East, and organize during the thaw. Defensive operations would be more rewarding this year than offensive, 'for lack of adequate forces'. Nothing was to be gained by the conquest of space. The occupation of the Caucasus and the industrial zones of Russia was problematical, and not decisive. 'The Russians have organized their industries and oil-wells beyond the Urals. If the Germans rest on the defensive, this is to the advantage of the Mediterranean Front.

'In the Mediterranean, too, the initiative in operations cannot for the moment be wrested from the enemy.' Tunisia must be held as long as possible. 'If Tunisia goes, the enemy will attempt landings on the coast of Europe . . . This cannot happen before May or June. We have therefore two to three months to build up in Tunisia.'

'The Germans must act during this period; decide to grant Italian requests for material to put the defence of their coasts and those of Greece in order; and facilitate as soon as possible the disengagement of Italian divisions operating in Croatia, permitting their withdrawal to the coast to a line enabling them to hold the key points there. These troops in the Balkan peninsula must then be set up as a strategic reserve. Mobile forces should be sent to Greece giving added flexibility, and also to watch the approaches to Salonica.

'Finally, the Italian air forces in the Mediterranean must be built up to resist enemy action adequately, and the number of Axis submarines in the Mediterranean increased. Above all, this is the moment in which the ally must give up fighting a war of his own, and understand that for his own salvation it is equally important to stand fast on the Dnieper as in Sicily or the Peloponnese. In conclusion, the Germans must change their operational objectives and must come to our aid, *otherwise we shall not be obliged to follow them in their erroneous conduct of the war.'* [h]

In the second memorandum to the Duce on February 21, Ambrosio elaborated in more detail this personal assessment of the war. 'There is no sign of a blunting of Russian effort. The Germans have to fight bitterly to contain enemy offensives . . . Germany is making a major effort to reconstitute her units. This will enable her to dominate the position in the East in the spring. But the troops which she will be enabled to put into the field in the

h. Author's italics.

summer "represent her last reserve". They must be used economically to face not only Russian attacks but sooner or later the Anglo-American Second Front.

'There are no decisive strategic objectives in the East. If the Germans attempt a reconquest of the industrial regions of the Don and the oil area of the Caucasus, they will only be back in the same position as in October 1942. Such a struggle would use up their last resources. They would not have the effectives to continue the fight in 1944.

'Committed as she is to a current offensive in the East, Germany cannot, for lack of reserves, meet simultaneously an attack in force by the Anglo-Americans, which will develop at the same time at a point as yet unknown on the European coast line, without seriously compromising the Eastern Front.

'The coasts which are most threatened are the Italian and the Balkan peninsula, to which should be added the shores of Provence . . . As a first priority one should consider an attack on the coast of Southern France, an attack which could be supported by another co-ordinated one against the North Sea coast of France. This operation could also be considered separately from the conquest of Tunisia and will develop independently of the operations in Africa. It might however involve Sardinia and Corsica. It is therefore considered dangerous to withdraw troops beyond a certain limit from France, which although provided with an effective coastal defence in the North, is not equally protected in the South . . .

'The threat to the Italian and Balkan shores . . . is further away in time, because, without the conquest of Tunis, the enemy is not in a position to mount an operation in grand style. The essential point therefore is to hold on to Bizerta as long as possible. The Italian High Command will make every effort, but . . . this is the moment to consider the position in the event of the loss of Tunisia. Should this happen, our islands, the Italian peninsula, and the Balkan coastline, are directly threatened.

'Our assessment is that Sardinia [Corsica] [i] and Sicily are equally exposed because, if the occupation of the first is the necessary premise on the enemy side for an occupation of the peninsula, the possession of the third gives him freedom of transit from the Central to the Eastern Mediterranean and thus the possibility of action in the Balkan peninsula.

'As to an attack against the Balkans, we think that the lack of suitable ports on the Western coastline, the impenetrable nature of the hinterland, and the great distance from the principal objective—the Roumanian oilfields—could lead the enemy to act against Salonica with a view to occupying Crete and the Archipelago.

'However, since it is dangerous in war to attribute to the enemy only the most logical solution, which is often not adopted by them, we must be ready

i. Inserted in the draft later.

to meet all eventualities and to take into account the necessary defence measures, which are: to bring up to strength the coastal defences (of Italy); and the creation of an adequate striking force to be moved at an opportune moment.

'We cannot carry out either on our own. In this context, as we are not entering into detail as to what we require, *it suffices to state that it is absolutely necessary for us to withdraw our forces from less important fronts (Croatia), to increase the garrisons of the islands, to build up a reserve in the mother country, to bring up to strength* j the Western and Eastern Alpine frontiers. In addition we cannot contribute to a strategic reserve in the Balkan peninsula.

'To complete the general picture: the Italian Supreme Command has little confidence in the support, even indirect, which Japan will be able to give the war in Europe. She will not attack Russia, and even if she did, the exhausting spaces of Siberia k would form in themselves the best and most efficient Russian defence. She will not attack India because she lacks the means to get involved in such a distant and vast operation without having first eliminated the enemy in the Indian Ocean. Her action will, in the nature of things, be limited to striking at the Anglo-American fleet in her own waters, an action which however cannot bring us any effective or timely help.

'In summary: the enemy whom Germany has so far sought to destroy, in a magnificent effort, is not beaten to the ground; in the East, we cannot see the possibility of decisive offensive action, but only the probability of holding up the Russians in a series of defensive battles which will however take a long time; the creation of a Second Front in Europe is a grave and imminent danger. If one thinks in terms of manoeuvring on inner lines from the Russian front to the French or to the Italian Peninsula, one may run the risk of not arriving in time or sufficient strength. This danger should be faced with resolute decision and timely advance planning, which must be worked out between the two Supreme Commands.

'The operational plan must be a unified one, and must take our forces and those of the Allies into account globally on the basis that, as he tightens the circle round Europe, the enemy will involve both ourselves and the Germans increasingly in the same common danger.

'The conduct of the war must in the first instance be defensive in order to recuperate our strength, must wear down the enemy and cause his plans to fail, must be able to take the counter-offensive at any moment when a favourable opportunity arises, and, in any case, when the process of attrition will place us in favourable moral and material conditions.' [13]

j. Underlined in the original text.
k. Note the similar phrasing of Mussolini's letter of March 26 to Hitler. (Hitler-Mussolini Correspondence, p. 152.)

These two memoranda contained the essence of Ambrosio's military thought as crystallized since his appointment, and as a basis for staff talks with the Germans, now so long overdue.

For the Italians it was of urgent importance to get agreement to their demands for reinforcements and supplies for the Mediterranean theatre. The Duce had already said to Kesselring, who had been summoned to Berlin by Goering on February 13, that he was awaiting the Reichsmarshal in Italy at an early date, and briefly sketching the problem, he added: 'As for the Mediterranean front, there will be need of submarines, planes and artillery rather than tanks. The British have most up-to-date artillery whereas ours is very antiquated. Besides, numerous submarines are required for the struggle against the enemy fleet, and aircraft to protect our convoys.' [14]

But, presumably on Hitler's direct instructions, Goering's visit was to be preceded by that of Ribbentrop. The technicalities of Mediterranean strategy, as always with the Fuehrer, were secondary to those considerations on the general balance of the conduct of the war which Ribbentrop was to present to the Duce.

At five o'clock on the evening of February 23, Bastianini called on Ambrosio to announce Ribbentrop's visit. The Italian Chief of Staff noted that Bastianini 'assumes that the general situation of the war will be discussed. He is told that the Italian point of view is: defensive on the Eastern Front and predominant importance of the Mediterranean theatre.' [1]

1. Italian Collection. Manuscript War Diary (in fact only notes of appointments) of General Ambrosio (from February 3 to July 26, 1943). The following day at a meeting of the Italian Chiefs of Staff, the two memoranda of February 17 and 21, which had been sent to the Duce were discussed as the basis for the forthcoming talks with the Germans. It was agreed that in regard to the Balkans, which would be the central point of discussion, the Italians must insist on the withdrawal of one division from the area, and a united command in Greece. Italian collection. Ambrosio and the Chiefs of Staff, February 24, 1943.

CHAPTER TWO

THE DIPLOMATIC FRONT

BASTIANINI had learnt of his appointment to the Foreign Ministry over the Italian radio on the evening of February 5. He had been out of touch with the conduct of Foreign Affairs since his return from London in June 1940 where he had succeeded Grandi as Ambassador. His present preoccupations were understandable. He locked himself in his hotel room in Rome for two days before taking over formally from Ciano, and only on the morning of February 10 did he call on the Duce at Palazzo Venezia.

In seeking a reason for his appointment, Bastianini might well have assumed that his previous experience at the Foreign Ministry as Under-Secretary from 1936–40, and briefly as Ambassador in London, which had led him to doubt the wisdom of the whole policy of alignment with the Axis, was now in some way relevant. He was swiftly corrected in this impression. At the first official interview with Mussolini he asked whether the latter wished that he 'should examine thoroughly the situation of Italy both in regard to the ally and the enemy take into account every factor, and determine whether, how, and for what length of time those forces which we know and would dispose of, would permit us to continue to fight this war, which I, as you well know, deprecated without avoiding my duty of participating in it'.

Mussolini replied in substance: 'It seems to me that you are making a mistake; my intentions are not those which you imagine. We are at war. I am the Foreign Minister. You have specific duties to carry out, but the direction of foreign affairs is in my hands, and my conception is very simple; when one is at war, one stays with the ally until the end.' [1]

On February 13 the Duce left Rome for La Rocca, where he stayed for the next eleven days with a recurring bout of ill-health, and during this lull, the new Undersecretary sought to brief himself on the diplomatic and military situation.

There seems to have been an immediate change of tone in the functioning of the Italian Foreign Ministry. There were regular meetings of the heads of departments, and frequent consultations with the retired veteran diplomats of the pre-Fascist school, in particular the former Secretary-General of Palazzo Chigi, Salvatore Contarini, who had continued to guide Italian foreign policy in the years after 1922, but had not set foot in the building since his retirement.[2] Here were the elements of a team to advise on and to formulate planning of a more professional kind, which had been lacking in recent years.

The diplomatic scene as surveyed from Rome was set and circumscribed by the passing of the strategic initiative in the conduct of the war on all fronts throughout Europe to the enemy. A drastic review must be made by both Axis powers, not only of their future strategy on each war front, but also of their failure hitherto to face the political consequences in Axis-occupied Europe, among both the neutrals and the satellite allies, of the disasters of Alamein, the 'Torch' landings, Stalingrad, and finally the loss of all Italian Africa.

On January 27, at Casablanca, the Western Allies had broadcast their communiqué on Unconditional Surrender. The implications of this fateful statement also needed careful analysis in Berlin and Rome, and heightened the need for some counter measure of political warfare and propaganda by the Axis powers to revive declining morale within the European fortress, now threatened directly for the first time by invasion.

The precarious Axis foothold in Tunisia represented the frontline of Europe. It could only be held by massive support from Germany, and at the expense of the Russian Front. If it fell, the Allies could strike in a number of directions from African bases at the southern shores of Europe, on a front stretching from Spain to Turkey, with each area involving delicate issues of diplomacy. The shadow of war now hung over the neutral capitals, involving the Allies and the Axis in grim and relentless underground competition in preserving or infringing the neutrality of these states.

The Allied landings in North Africa had in particular raised the problem of Spain, and on both sides the risks of bringing about Spanish intervention in the conflict were under active and cautious review.

So long as Tunisia could be held, it was unlikely that the Italian mainland or the Balkans would be immediately threatened, but advance precautions must be taken. With the lack of any German strategic reserve of divisions on the continent, in view of the total commitment on the Russian Front, and the need to lock up considerable forces in the West against the threat of a future Second Front based on the British Isles, an error in calculation as to the direction of an Allied assault on Southern Europe would be irreparable.

The Allied declaration on Unconditional Surrender was followed at the end of January by the visit of the British Prime Minister, Mr Winston

Churchill, to the Turkish President at Adana. This could be interpreted as a move by the Western Allies to bring Turkey into the war as a first step towards the invasion of the Balkans, which would vitally affect the whole German conduct of the war in the East. A wrong analysis of the Adana Conference could have a disastrous effect on Axis planning.

The repercussions of this Turkish visit of the British Prime Minister were first felt in the capitals of Southern Europe, and together with the shadow of Stalingrad added to the series of threatening and unresolved menaces to be faced by the German and Italian leaders.

The most pressing of these issues were those concerned with the future relations of the two Axis powers with the two leading neutrals, Spain and Turkey, each placed in key strategic positions at each end of the Mediterranean, the possession of either or both of which could tip the whole balance of the war.

German policy towards Spain at the turn of the year was confused and contradictory, and as usual conducted without any close consultation with Rome.

There was alarm at the apparent success of recent Allied political manoeuvres in Madrid, and an exaggerated fear of Anglo-American military intervention in the Peninsula. Ribbentrop's personal agent in Madrid reported on January 20 1943 that the official Allied policy of supporting Spanish neutrality was proving successful. Its visible result was the maintenance of British control over Gibraltar. The next step would however be to set foot in Spain. 'If there is no decisive change in the general war situation, the Anglo-Saxons will attempt to jump into the Spanish no-man's land, which they have prepared politically. All Red Spanish circles are well organized and determined not to let slip the opportunity offered. A second Civil War . . . would face Germany with the choice either of supporting Nationalist Spain with military help or reckoning with a front on the Pyrenees. In some Spanish circles it is thought that such an event could give the signal for a general revolt in the whole of Europe against the Axis.

'Franco's policy, which he will not alter unless he is obliged to do so, is the attempt of the Church to find a way out in Europe and bring about in an impoverished and unbelieving continent a Roman and reactionary peace. This policy could make Spain a battlefield and face Germany with new complications in the Mediterranean.' German military aid to Spain would be a condition of improvement in German-Spanish relations.[3]

The long standing operation under the code-name 'Gisela' for the occupation of Gibraltar was subject to routine review by the German General Staff. Its implementation would inevitably mean drawing on troops from France, and it was unlikely that such a move would be made unless Spain were directly threatened by an Allied assault and gave guarantees that she would resist. In Franco's letter to Hitler of January 19 no such clear assurances were stated.[4] [a]

On January 24 Franco slyly pointed out to the German Ambassador: 'The war has lasted much longer than one had originally thought. He must also say that his information as to the state of opinion in Italy begins to give him anxiety.' [5]

The Allied declaration at Casablanca on Unconditional Surrender at the end of January seems to have encouraged Franco for a moment to consider adopting the rôle of mediator between the belligerents. But having resisted German pressure to take up a clear position, he must also avoid a similar situation in relation to the Allies. The basic attitude and interests of the latter in Spain were identical with those of the Axis. The Iberian peninsula was a no-man's land or a battlefield. Both parties shunned the prospects of another Balkan commitment, and both sought guarantees of a defined and aggressive neutrality on the part of Spain, short of which neither party would commit itself to economic and military aid.

Franco could not resist exploiting this situation by seeking supplies and equipment on both sides, neither being able to afford an absolute refusal; and by repeating the menaces and conditions of each party to the other.

By exploiting American hints that they might have to act in Spanish Morocco, Franco forced a secret agreement out of the Germans on February 9 whereby, on the basis of war deliveries by Germany, Spain would agree to oppose an Allied move into Spain or Spanish Morocco.[6] This treaty was not disclosed to the Italians, and precisely at this moment Franco turned to Rome to seek Italian backing for further military aid on the basis of the same American pressure.

On February 13 at a meeting with Kesselring, the Duce charged him 'to point out to the Fuehrer that a new element is maturing in the political situation. America is trying to force Spain to take up a decisive attitude and disagreeable facts might emerge in Morocco.' The Duce had received a letter from Franco in which the latter revealed his preoccupation at the situation and considered that American assurances towards him were formal rather than substantial. 'In any event, the Caudillo, in anticipation of a new development, is completing the efficiency of his armed forces. The Duce asserts that he has replied to the Caudillo welcoming his intentions, but pointing out that an intervention by Spain in the conflict must only take place if she is completely prepared.' [7]

If Mussolini could persuade Hitler to concentrate attention on a combined Mediterranean strategy, then the possible contribution of Spain to future Axis planning must be defined, and in the event of a German and Italian west-

a. On January 22, Admiral Canaris summed up an intelligence report by saying that, 'Spain is not capable of taking part in the war.' German Collection, War Diary of the German General Staff.

ward counter-offensive being launched in North Africa, her benevolent co-operation must be sought.

The German and Italian strategic approaches to eventual Spanish intervention were distinct. Hitler conceived of the operation primarily, and in any event reluctantly, as an advance into the Peninsula from the Pyrenees to Gibraltar. Whereas Mussolini saw it as a counter 'Torch'—a race for Casablanca from Tunisia to take the American positions in Morocco in the rear, and from Spanish African bases to launch an assault on Gibraltar.[b] From the immediate military point of view neither plan was practical in operational terms.

In August 1942, Hitler had told the Turkish Ambassador in Berlin, that he 'regarded Turkey as the southern protective flank of Germany. The Reich had no kind of territorial interests which could bring her into conflict with Turkey, and economically relations were developing wonderfully.' [8]

Turkish copper and chrome were as vital to the German war effort as Spanish iron ore, manganese and quicksilver, and a threat of the loss of either source was a standing preoccupation of German policy.

As Hitler stressed, 'Stalin's intentions were now clearer . . . the Bolshevisation of the Balkans.' Germany could not accept this owing to her important economic interest in the region. 'This was the reason why Germany had helped Spain against the Bolsheviks . . . and equally an attempt by Russia to seize the Balkans and the Straits would be unbearable for Germany for economic reasons.' [9]

The basic assumption of both German and Italian policy towards Turkey was that the latter would seek at all costs to preserve her resources in order to face a possible Russian threat to the Straits and the Balkans, and at the same time would seize every opportunity to check by any means such a Soviet advance.

The Allied landings in North Africa in early November 1942, however, revolutionized the strategic position, and concentrated immediate attention on future Anglo-American plans equally in the Eastern and in the Western Mediterranean.

For some time past, the Allies had been discreetly building up supply dumps and improving communications in Turkey. They might attempt to go one stage further, and bring persuasive pressure to bear on the Turkish authorities for the leasing of air bases as a first step towards a Balkan campaign.

On November 20, that skilful veteran politician, von Papen, the German Ambassador in Ankara, sent to Berlin a 'report on the political attitude of Turkey after the North African landings'.

b. It was 'these operations against Casablanca' which Hitler fleetingly referred to in his talk with Rommel on March 10.

He was optimistic. 'There is now as earlier no reason for Turkey to take part in this war preventively on one side or the other . . . In the end we shall win the game in Turkey if our military position in the spring enables us to bring quick and effective help to Turkey if need arises. In this connection the potential of the unweakened Bulgarian army is of vital importance, if we can strengthen it with motorised and air units.' [10]

The situation of Bulgaria in regard to the general frame of the war had until now received little marked attention on the Axis side. Her role as a signatory of the Tripartite Pact in 1941 had been limited by tacit understandings; she would not be asked, as a Slav power, to break off formal relations with the Soviet Union; she would continue in her military occupation of Southern Serbia, undertaken after the Yugoslav campaign of 1941, and play her part in the plans of 'pacification' in that region and on the borders of Albania; her frontier disputes with Greece in Macedonia and Thrace would be shelved pending a peace settlement. In the event of major Allied landings in the Balkans, her potential military support must be mobilized and her relations with Turkey clarified. The latter might join the Western Allies, or, as Papen had hinted, take part in a long-term defensive operation in the Balkans, both against the Anglo-Americans and eventually the Russians.

Towards the end of December 1942, in conversation with the Italian governor of Albania, Mussolini had said that 'he reckoned that in 1943 the enemy would open an early Balkan front. In this connection special importance would be laid on Bulgaria at whose territorial expense the other side, according to reports here, had already given assurances to Greece. Just as in North Africa, the enemy would attempt, under the motto of liberating the oppressed Greeks through the arrival of the Americans, to cover their activities under a mantle of idealism. It appeared from a reliable source that a strong Greek division had been raised in Syria for this purpose.

'In regard to Bulgaria, one could not ask her to take part in the war against Soviet Russia, but all the more therefore to take over the defence against Anglo-American attempts at landings in the Balkans. It was therefore necessary to handle Bulgaria carefully and he instructed the Governor of Albania, in regard to Albanian-Bulgarian frontier questions, to meet Bulgaria half way.

The position of Bulgaria in such circumstances needed study, and her War Minister was summoned to meet Hitler in early January. These talks are of particular value in throwing a revealing light on the Fuehrer's appreciation of the potential Allied threat to the whole Balkan region.

'The Bulgars had hitherto been on the fringe of the war, and had made few requests to the Germans for military supplies. But now they were disturbed by reports from Turkey of the building with British help of railways, airfields, and stores dumps. The Turkish army might move against

Bulgaria. The situation in Turkey was the same in several ways as that of Bulgaria when the German army in Bulgaria planned (in 1940–1) a camouflaged march into Greece and Yugoslavia. In Iran and Iraq there was a concentration of seventy thousand Americans (*sic*). *And, in addition, Salonica had for a long time played a rôle in the strategic plans of Churchill.*' c [11]

Hitler, like the Bulgars, was equally drawn to the historical pattern of British strategy in the First World War, and the shadow of the Dardanelles and the Macedonian campaign lay heavily across his thinking. It was inconceivable to him that Churchill could not be obsessed by the desire to prove in 1943 the validity of his grand strategy of 1915, of a decisive assault against enemy occupied Europe from the South-East. This was the central fear of the Fuehrer, which now coloured his planning against the Western Allies, often in defiance of the appreciations of his military experts.

In the immediate situation, the Bulgarian War Minister told Hitler that if pressed the Turks would agree to the passage of Anglo-American troops. In such an event the Bulgarian army must take the offensive and occupy Thrace. Serbia and Croatia could be cleaned up and pacified in due course. The Greek government must be distrusted. 'In the daytime they were for the Axis and at night they were for the enemy.'

Hitler was less alarmed at the threat of imminent action by Turkey. 'He thought that the most dangerous area in the Balkan region was the Peloponese, particularly as up till then it had not been possible to pacify the hinterland.' British and American troops would only land on Turkish soil if the Turkish army actively collaborated. Nevertheless Bulgaria must have a strong army both for the present and for the future, for Bulgaria was also likely to have the future task of maintaining order in the Balkans. He had, therefore, given orders for the delivery of weapons urgently to the Bulgarian army.

In the worst case Germany would take over the common defence of the area and command of the sixteen Bulgarian divisions. German units would be sent to help. As soon as the German troops could be released from other fronts they would be sent to the Balkans. They would not, in the first instance, be sent to Bulgaria; he was thinking much more of Serbia, particularly the area of Nish as well as that of Salonica. A plan of attack in the direction of Istanbul must be worked out between the two General Staffs.[12]

In the staff talks with the Bulgarian delegation, which followed the next day, they were informed of the intended action in the whole of former Yugoslav territory. This would be carried out in close co-operation with the Italians and would have the intention of moving against the rebel movements with energy. The German commander South East (General Loehr) would, in the event of the Balkans becoming a theatre of war, take command of all forces

c. Author's italics.

including the Bulgarians. It was not intended to send German troops to Bulgaria at this stage. Sufficient reserves lay in Germany and France; but in the event of invasion, a forward concentration area around Nish would be organized.

The Bulgarian view was that the attitude of Turkey would change either in the spring or summer, and it was clearly in their own interest to stress the point. Hitler admitted that one must be prepared for such an eventuality, but for the moment 'the German Army Staff did not think in terms of an Allied landing in Salonica, which was made impossible by the fortified position of Crete'.[13]

But the visit of Churchill to Adana at the end of the month might be the prelude to the Allied invasion of the Balkans which so preoccupied Hitler. He was, in a sense, fighting a personal war with the British Prime Minister. It was vital to penetrate his thinking, and these Anglo-Turkish talks provided the occasion to probe British intentions.

On February 2 Papen reported on his first conversations with Numan Menemjoglu the Turkish Foreign Minister. The latter was a specialist in neutrality. According to him, 'the British had expressed themselves content with the present Turkish attitude, and emphasised that Turkey should strengthen this policy and be armed for all eventualities in the post-war period. No demand of any kind was made with regard to direct or indirect support to the Russians. There was naturally no question of transit through Turkey. But Numan had found it necessary to establish that Turkey in all and every circumstance stood by the treaty of Montreux in regard to the Straits, and would admit no infringement, and that if Allied aircraft in the future flew over the area one would not be satisfied with protests, but would open fire.'

Churchill was convinced that Stalin had no aims which meant 'endangering' Europe, and such Turkish fears were groundless. But as Numan told the German Ambassador, on this point Churchill could in no way convince Turkey.

Churchill had also said 'that Germany must finally be liquidated. He regarded Italy with special hatred and wished to destroy her. General Alexander's view was that one need not reckon any further with the Italians and that Tunis could only be held for a limited period . . . When asked about his conception of post-war Europe, Churchill only expressed vague views. One wanted a political community of interest between several stateless federations, which could form a balance against Russia; the Nordic bloc, the Central European (the Baltic states, Poland, Czechoslovakia, Hungary), and the Balkan bloc. When Numan replied that behind such a concept lay no real power to hinder the planned march of Bolshevism into Europe, Churchill answered that the increasing strength of the Allies in aircraft would enable them to bring the necessary support to any point. Numan remarked that he considered this view completely erroneous, and in general the Turkish attitude to the future organisation of Europe was the farthest apart from that of Churchill.

'From the Turkish point of view the conference had been very welcome. Numan was convinced that the integrity of Turkey would not be violated by the Allies and that they needed rather a strong Turkey for all eventualities against Russia. And he discerned a real mistrust of Russia.'

The purported summary of Churchill's remarks, as conveyed to the Germans, was not only deliberately coloured by Turkish thinking, but is a falsification of the record.[d]

Papen summarized his immediate impressions as follows: 'The programme of Casablanca to bring the remaining neutrals into the war has failed. My conviction is confirmed that Turkey will not move from her strict neutrality even in the event of a deterioration in the position of the Axis, and this has valuable implications for us in our concentration of forces.' [14]

On February 3 Papen reported further on conversations which took place at a farewell lunch for the retiring head of the Italian mission. 'One must assume that the very probable decisions taken at Casablanca include operations against the Dodecanese, Crete, and the Aegean islands, and that it must have been important for Churchill to learn the attitude of Turkey to such an operation and whether they would lend moderate assistance.' No territorial aims had been suggested by the Allies. Possibly after an Aegean operation 'an attack on Greece is planned and possibly through the Adriatic against the Balkans. This would anyway mean more effective aid to the Russians.' [15]

Ribbentrop was not convinced by Papen's buoyant interpretation of the Adana talks, nor did he accept Numan's version of Churchill's attitude. On February 3 he telegraphed to Ankara sourly that no one had really informed Papen about the meeting. 'It is hardly possible that they only talked about the weather.

'As for Turkey's misgivings about Russia, I take it that Churchill pointed out that at the first opportunity, for example after the opening up of the Mediterranean to British shipping, a new front would be established in the Balkans. The presence of British and American troops in the Balkans in connection with later plans for a Danube Federation would also be for Turkey a guarantee against a Russian thrust into the Balkans and towards the Straits.'

As Ribbentrop conveyed to Papen, the Italian Minister in Ankara had also reported that Numan had told foreign diplomats at the same luncheon that Turkish neutrality had not been changed by the Adana Conference 'in

d. See the account of the Adana Conference based on the British official records in W. S. Churchill's *The Second World War*, Vol. 4, pp. 623 *et seq.*

any essential point', and had added that, 'in the event of the Axis position in Tunisia deteriorating (and it appeared that in the long run the Axis could offer no resistance), one must reflect that a serious position would arise for Turkey and that then the pressure of the British and Americans would later take a more concrete and, for Turkey, unavoidable form.'

Ribbentrop's message concluded, 'I express my view that Turkey has preserved her neutrality in these talks. Her further attitude however depends exclusively on the future development of military operations. The military position in the Ukraine and at Tunis is here decisive.[e] If in the forseeable future we have successes in both these theatres of war, Turkey will harden her policy of neutrality. If, on the other hand, the Axis suffers a serious set-back, either in Southern Russia or in Africa, Turkey will join the British and Americans and try through the presence of their troops to resist the threatening demands of the Russians for bases in the Straits. I cannot share your view that Turkey is not to be drawn out of her policy of neutrality even in the event of a deterioration of the Axis position.' [16]

In his reply to Ribbentrop, Papen emphasized that 'in judging the future course of Turkey one must start from the fact that the destruction of the Central European Powers and the realization of English plans for Europe would for Turkey be the most disagreeable outcome of the war. She would find herself hemmed in for centuries between a strong Britain in the Mediterranean and a Russia capable of unlimited action.' This basic assumption of German policy towards Turkey in Papen's view remained unassailable.

On February 6, Ribbentrop replied in milder terms to Papen that he too accepted this concept, and that everything must be done to strengthen Turkish neutrality. It was, after all, Germany's strength which ultimately secured Turkey against Russia.[17]

In summarizing the results of Numan's talks with neutral diplomats in Ankara, Papen noted the reasons why Churchill apparently wanted a strong Turkey. Firstly, 'the failure of Germany to obtain Russian oil means that she must try again and will march through Turkey to Iraq. The Turkish leaders disagreed. And secondly 'if the war goes against Germany, there will be chaos in the Balkans. Turkey must be in a military position to meet this problem and to play a leading part in a future Balkan Federation.'

To Numan's question: 'if, as a consequence of an Allied victory, the Soviets behave in Roumania and Bulgaria in the same manner as in the Baltic states . . . what would be the standpoint of England? Churchill was said to have answered that he was determined not to accept this.' [18]

In completing his comments, Papen added on February 8, 'I have the

e. The Italians, too, had reported that 'Turkey would be in a grave position if the Tunis bridgehead is not held', and as Papen commented on February 5, 'I suggest that the Italian Minister hopes to give an impulse in Rome to the strengthening as far as possible of the Tunis front.' German Collection. Ankara telegram, February 4 and 5, 1943.

B.F.—7

impression that the assault on Italy, anticipated next summer or autumn, has caused considerable anxiety there, and one would probably prefer to see the theatre of war transferred to Turkey and the Balkans. But this must not divert us from a correct assessment of Turkey's position. From a subsequent assembling of reports on Adana [f] . . . it clearly stands out that a basic theme of discussion was the future order in the Balkans.' [19]

The present position of the Axis in South Eastern Europe had been affected by the military disaster on the Don in January 1943, which provoked a grim reappraisal among the European allies of the Axis of the whole conduct of the war by Hitler. Apart from major repercussions on relations with Italy, historically and diplomatically the senior partner, the whole future military and diplomatic position of the satellite powers was threatened, and in particular Roumania and Hungary, whose forces had suffered so heavily in the recent battle.

The rôle of Roumania in German war strategy was vital. Geographically she dominated the whole southern front against Russia, and her defection would throw open the historic land route of invasion of the Huns and the Mongols into the heart of Central Europe, and would inexorably and swiftly lead to a collapse of the whole German military position in the East. Her military contribution to the Eastern campaign was superior to that of any other ally, including Italy. Her losses in the Don battle alone amounted to 9,000 officers and 270,000 men killed, apart from wounded and missing.

Without the oil deliveries, German industry and her armed forces would be unable to function, and with the fading prospect of seizing the Russian oilfields of the Caucasus, Germany would remain totally dependent on the Ploesti region, north of Bucharest. Italy too, in a lesser degree, relied on grain from Roumania, and the Italian Navy was totally at the mercy of arbitrary and fitful German allocations of Roumanian petroleum. A collapse or defection of Roumania would therefore inevitably cripple the German war effort.

Confronted with a deep crisis of confidence throughout the whole of German-controlled Europe, Hitler and his advisers were forced into a series of personal interventions in an attempt to restore the position.

It was logical to begin with the Roumanians, and the 'Conducator' [g] and his Foreign Minister, Mihai Antonescu, were summoned on January 10/11 to Berchtesgaden. They were at once exposed to an excessive blast of optimism

f. The Germans obtained possession of the military protocol of the Adana conference through Intelligence channels. Ribbentrop gave a summary of these in his telegram of March 25 to Papen with the comment *that perhaps Numan had not previously been told the truth about these discussions*!

g. Marshal Antonescu's title as Head of State. Mihai Antonescu, the Foreign Minister, was not a relation.

from Hitler. 'The whole region controlled by Germany and her Allies was highly organized for the struggle. There was only one open wound, and it was at the moment the triangle Rostov, Stalingrad and the Caucasus, the most important area. This main fact must be kept in mind, and in judging the situation one must not be influenced by minor phases of the great drama but, particularly in time of crisis, keep an iron nerve. If Germany were to lose two-thirds of her iron ore, 80–85 per cent of her oil, as well as her entire supplies of coke, and in addition had to overcome a shortage of rubber, the situation would be desperate. This was precisely the position in which Russia found herself today. It was true that she possesed iron ore in the Urals but she could not extract from this iron ore the coke for the production of steel.' [20]

Such a picture, in contradiction with the evidence, could hardly impress the listeners, although Marshal Antonescu, like the Duce, was convinced that there was no solution to the war other than triumphant victory in the East.

This view was not shared by either Foreign Minister, Mihai Antonescu or Ciano, and before leaving for Germany the former sent to Ciano through the Italian Minister in Bucharest his preliminary reflections on possible diplomatic action with a view to a compromise peace with the West or at least on the lines of mutual political consultation within the Axis camp.

At this January meeting in Berchtesgaden, Marshal Antonescu in conversation with Ribbentrop, brought up again an earlier proposal made by Mihai Antonescu for 'holding periodic diplomatic meetings of the Axis powers and their Allies. *Faites vivre l'Europe par l'activité des réunions.*'

Ribbentrop replied that this would be difficult while the war was on. It would raise problems in regard to France, Holland and other such countries, in which during the course of the war severe measures must still be enforced. One might examine the plan when the situation in the East improved. Mihai Antonescu repeated his proposal with the words that 'one must gather Europe together like a family'.[21]

This was precisely what Ribbentrop feared: a coalition within the frame of the Tripartite system of pacts, escaping German leadership, and eventually passing over to the Western Allies. If Italy were to give a lead to such a manoeuvre, the maintenance of the whole German position in Europe would be decisively threatened.

It was to avoid such a complete disaster that the whole diplomatic action of Germany in the early months of 1943 was directed. Before reviewing and sounding the reactions of the smaller partners, it was essential to study in careful detail the repercussions in Italy of the defeat of the Axis armies both in Russia and Africa, and also the significance of the recent government changes in Rome in regard to Italy's attitude to the future conduct of the war.

With such intentions in mind, Ribbentrop decided to make a personal visit to Italy.

CHAPTER THREE

RIBBENTROP IN ROME

•••

ON FEBRUARY 19 Ribbentrop sent instructions to Mackensen in Rome to ask the Duce to receive him 'to discuss certain important current questions'. Two days later, the Italian Ambassador in Berlin, Alfieri, called on the German Foreign Minister to probe the reasons for his trip.

Alfieri, 'who was apparently carrying out instructions, emphasized that the change of ministers in Italy meant nothing more than a confirmation of the Duce's habit of changing his collaborators from time to time. The most that one could say was that the will to work with Germany had therefore been even more strongly emphasized by the Duce.'

Ribbentrop's reply was abrupt and curious. He said that 'he regretted that Count Ciano was no longer his colleague and invited Alfieri to come with him on his visit to Italy where he would talk to the Duce, to Ciano and to Bastianini'. The German Foreign Minister clearly wished to form his own view of recent events in Rome. This talk with the Italian Ambassador was a rehearsal of the forthcoming conference, and set an informal agenda for Alfieri to report to his government.

Ribbentrop would bring a letter from the Fuehrer outlining the latter's views on the general situation 'as well as explanations on specific political and military questions'. A military expert, 'in the shape of a General', would accompany Ribbentrop. These questions related 'to the Mediterranean area, and in particular the problem of Croatia'.

Ribbentrop expounded to Alfieri, whom he was now accustomed to patronizing and thus rehearsing his thoughts, the main points in the current German interpretation of the state of the war. The general situation on the Eastern Front had 'stabilized'. The Fuehrer had decided to destroy the Russians at all costs. There could be no question of finding a solution 'in a diplomatic-political direction'. The German assault along the Russian Front 'would take place in the spring or early summer'.

The real point of Ribbentrop's journey soon emerged. 'The Reich Foreign Minister turned the conversation to the Balkan area. On the German side, there was a certain anxiety about the attitude of the Italian army in Croatia, about which the Duce was already informed.' The whole problem had been discussed in detail with Ciano and Cavallero. 'Both gentlemen had agreed to all Germany's requests, but nothing had happened. Between three and four divisions of the Italian army were needed to achieve really decisive results. Roatta [a] thought that he could play off one party against another, but overlooked the fact that the seemingly mutual warring elements such as the Tito bands, the četniks and Mihailović followers were all united in their hatred of the Italians . . . The situation which had now arisen in Croatia, through Roatta's policy, caused the Fuehrer grave anxiety. The Germans understood that Roatta wanted to spare Italian lives, but they also thought that with his policy he was in a sense trying to drive out the Devil with Beelzebub. The bands must be destroyed, men, women, and children, because their continued existence endangered the lives of German and Italian men, women and children.[b]

'The great worry of our adversaries, who have to consider landing operations, is to find points where the minimum of shipping is required. As possible areas for the British and Americans, the Reich Foreign Minister indicated the Adriatic coast of Serbia, Corsica, Sardinia, and even Sicily and Norway . . . In any case, the Axis must take special care during the next six to nine months, as the enemy was convinced that the U-boat war was going against them and would tend towards rapid action . . . For Italy, it was particularly a question of Corsica and Sardinia, while Germany would ensure the security not only of the Norwegian and Atlantic coasts but also of the island of Crete. Under these circumstances one of the most important tasks of the German and Italian troops—and the Duce should give categorical orders—was to destroy the bands in Serbia before the British attempted a landing. In the latter event one could eventually count on the Bulgars.'

Ribbentrop's monologue mounted in tone. 'If the breath went out of the Russians in the East, which might perhaps happen this year, and the British and Americans suffered even greater shortages in tonnage and heavy losses in their landing attempts, then Germany could finally come to military grips with the British Isles.'[1]

Hitler's 'grave anxiety' to which Ribbentrop had referred, stemmed from his chiromantic belief that the ultimate Allied assault would come from the

---

a. The Italian commander in Croatia. He had replaced General Ambrosio as Commander of the Second Army there in January 1942, the latter succeeding him as Chief of Staff of the Army. At the end of May 1943, Roatta returned again to this latter post. See Roatta, *Otto Milioni di Baionette*, pp. 161–83.

b. Alfieri undertook not to report to Rome on this question before the talks between the Duce and the German Foreign Minister took place, 'but afterwards would do all in his power to press for a development in the sense desired by Germany'.

South-East—the personal revenge of Churchill for the Dardanelles failure in 1915. Through the Balkans lay the direct route of attack against the whole southern flank of the German armies on the Russian front, where the Stalingrad disaster had—for the moment—endangered the life work of the Fuehrer, the crusade against Bolshevism. The challenge was total, and the call to supreme sacrifice must be totalitarian. Final victory in the East was the goal, and the nightmare of a rendezvous of the three enemy belligerents on the Balkan road must be exorcised. Hence the intensity of Hitler's neurotic obsession with these regions, and of his pressure on the Italian ally on this subject. The priority of the Russian front must be absolute. The myth of a destructive and mounting U-boat war must compensate for the absence of German offensive action in Western or Southern Europe, and would furnish the main deterrent against the Allied invasion in these areas.

It was the task of Ribbentrop to translate this obsessive vision into diplomatic terms. Hitler had outlined in Wagnerian language a massive and highly personal survey of the war in the form of a letter to Mussolini. This revealing document was to constitute Ribbentrop's instructions for the forthcoming Rome meeting, which was to be a preliminary to a summit conference between the two Axis leaders as soon as the Russian situation permitted. As Hitler wrote,[c] 'You can hardly imagine how much I want to spend a couple of days personally with you . . . For what I am to Germany, Duce, you are to Italy; and what we both are to Europe, posterity alone can judge . . . No episode on any front can be considered and examined in isolation, since they are all part of a vast chain of events which will ultimately be decisive for the destiny of the whole of Europe, decisive in the sense of those great historical upheavals like the Persian and Punic wars, the invasions of the Huns, the expansion of Islam and the Mongol raids. But I can assure you that I am happy to be alive at such a time and to be able to fight in defence of those immortal values which have taken shape on our continent from the earliest times to the present day. And not only in the narrow racial sense, but also in the comprehensive cultural sense. It does not therefore sadden me that I was chosen to bear this destiny, but I am proud and happy that it should be so.

'The struggle against the West is being fought only in part on land: but to an important degree at sea. As in almost every war, this one too is to a great extent a problem of shipping. The final collapse of such a victorious offensive in Libya against the British was definitely due to the impossibility of solving the supply problem from Italy or from Crete to Tobruk and Mersa Matruh. The attainment of more or less temporary success is thus of little importance. It is only of decisive value if the military gains can be held from the supply

c. The original text, which is nearly sixty typewritten pages long, is in the German Collection and dated February 16. An Italian translation is printed in Hitler e Mussolini *op cit* pp. 128 ff, but it is cut into fragments and wrongly dated.

point of view. America and England may achieve some sort of advantage by acquiring temporary footholds, but what matters is if they succeed in the long run in holding such points by keeping them supplied . . . The continued menacing and obstruction of their sea supply lines is bound sooner or later to lead to catastrophe. I have therefore taken all possible steps to put our U-boat warfare on a virtually indestructible footing . . . The struggle in North Africa and for Western Europe has of course an equally decisive influence on the success of the war as a whole. But the holding and extension of the Tunis and Bizerta bridgehead is obliging England and America to transport their troops and supplies to the Near and Far East by a long detour round the Cape.'

So much for the myth of German superiority at sea. Hitler then disclosed his central anxiety. 'I regard the situation in the Balkan peninsula itself with the gravest concern . . . I was told that the Italian political leaders had counted on risings in Greece in support of the Italian invading forces.[d] No such thing occurred. Not only did the hostile forces, at this very moment, rise as one man against the Italian troops, even the Albanians were only reliable up to a point. If a landing takes place tomorrow, Duce, anywhere in the Balkans, then Communists, followers of Mihailović, and all the other irregulars will be in accord on one thing: launching an immediate attack on the German or Italian armed forces (as the case may be) in support of the enemy landings. I consider it disastrous, Duce, that after we have conquered the whole area in battle there should still exist armed and politically organized persons ready to turn against us in any emergency . . .

'The first phase of the operations in Croatia has been successfully carried out. We did succeed in smashing a substantial part of Tito's organization and in inflicting heavy losses in men and material on the invading troops. The extent to which the insurgents had already developed their organization is both alarming and instructive. It is high time we exterminated this movement if we do not want to incur the risk of being stabbed in the back the moment the Anglo-Saxons land in the Balkans.'

Unless the Axis disarmed both the Communists and the četniks and 'neutralized' the whole area, then revolt would break out, in the event of invasion, and all communications with Greece would be cut. The German divisions in the region would then have to fight the rebels—Communist and četnik—'and Italian troops will be unable single-handed to stave off an invasion of the Peloponnese or the Adriatic.

'I would be so glad, Duce, to discuss these problems with you personally. In the first place, I am familiar with all these regions and the mentality of their inhabitants, having studied the history of the country in which I was born and bred; in the second place the monitoring of telegraph and wireless

d. In October 1940.

communications, which it was found necessary to institute, provides irrefutable proof of the correctness of my views.'

The Allied alternative to a Balkan landing might be an assault on the Italian offshore islands. Hitler summed up this danger, which was the principal preoccupation of his ally, in brief and offhand terms. 'I consider it by no means impossible, Duce, that an invasion of Sardinia, Corsica and perhaps even Sicily will be attempted. Sardinia and Corsica seem to be particularly threatened. I look upon it as a matter of decisive importance to reinforce the defensive capacity of these two islands.'

The danger of Allied intervention in Spain was equally dismissed with a sad backward glance to the lost opportunities two years earlier. 'If in 1941 the Spanish Government had declared itself ready to resolve the Gibraltar problem once and for all—and unlimited troops and equipment were available for the purpose—the whole course of the war in the Mediterranean would have been different. There would have been no English or Americans in North Africa today, but only Italians and Spaniards. I have tried, Duce, to assist the Spanish army, as far as our own strained situation permits, in order to help counteract a threat of this kind, at least materially. The German Wehrmacht has naturally taken all dispositions itself to meet such an eventuality.'

It remained to review the war in the East after the fall of Stalingrad, and in the familiar apocalyptic rhetoric.

'Let me assure you, Duce, at least of this: the demands made on German soldiers have been immeasurable . . . The chief thing seems to me to be that soldiers should be trained to be hard as steel, especially towards an enemy who, if not driven out of Europe, will submerge the whole of Europe. And this, Duce, is what distinguishes the situation today from that of 1918. In the year 1918 Germany collapsed, only there was no military power in the East to fill the vacuum. But today we are faced with an immense military power which cannot be subdued by diplomatic sleight of hand, but can only be crushed by military might. We have captured a Russian general who, until he took over his present command, used to command the Russian home army. His information supplemented and confirmed our own observations. According to him, the losses of the Russian army up to the end of November in killed, missing, and so severely wounded as to be unfit for further service, amounted to some 11.3 million. German losses—killed, missing and severely wounded—total 1.4 million men. I therefore intend to continue fighting in the East until this colossus finally disintegrates, and to do it with or without allies. For I regard the mere existence of this peril as so monstrous that Europe will know not a moment's peace if, heedlessly balancing on the edge of the abyss, she forgets or simply refuses to face reality. Furthermore, Duce, I know how hard it is to take historic decisions. Whether anyone with the strength to do so will appear after my death, I cannot say. But I am resolved to complete the task which destiny has given me, and I am convinced that the battle in which I am engaged is not half so harsh and fraught with peril as that fight which Frederick the Great once waged, with his 3,700,000 inhabitants, against the whole of Europe. I am fully aware that I cannot aspire to be numbered among the great heroes of history, for they accomplished far greater things in much more difficult circumstances than we are doing now in fighting with our allies an enemy weaker in numbers and potential than ourselves. I have appealed to the population of Germany, including even sixteen-year-old boys, at least to take part in anti-aircraft defence and fight for their homeland, and also to work in industry and the factories without regard to social class or origin, former occupation, education, means and so on. The National Socialist Party will mobilize everyone, down to the last man and the last woman, in its inexorable resolve not to capitulate to our enemies in any circumstances whatsoever. I shall fight until the enemy himself admits defeat. And I believe, Duce, that Italy has no other choice either. I will not speak of our respective revolutions. It goes without saying that Fascism and National Socialism would be destroyed. But the fate of our peoples would be even worse. Quite irrespective of which emerged victorious, Western plutocracy or Eastern Bolshevism, International Jewry would triumph in the end, and would spare no efforts to extirpate our races, especially their élite. European culture would be doomed to destruction and ultimate annihilation. I thus regard it as a favour of Providence that it has destined me to lead my people in a conflict of this kind.'

On February 25 Ribbentrop was received by the Duce at Palazzo Venezia, in the presence of Mackensen, Alfieri, and Bastianini.[2] He handed over this personal letter from Hitler, and while Mussolini glanced through the Italian translation, read it aloud in German 'in a robust and emphatic voice'. [3] This document was his brief for the conference, and his exposition, together with Mussolini's comments, lasted for four hours.

Ribbentrop's commentary followed closely the lines of the Fuehrer's letter, though the points were developed in a different order. He began with the central theme of the Russian front. The Tripartite Pact powers were at the most decisive moment of the world conflict. 'The war could only be lost if Germany and Italy themselves gave in.' The stand at Stalingrad 'was of decisive importance for the conduct of the war'. It had saved the German army in the Caucasus. Germany would now, 'by the introduction of total war, bring her vast reserves into play for the first time'. A new offensive might be mounted in two and a half months' time when the muddy season was over and the German plans were complete. Hitler's plan was to paralyse Russian offensive power. He had no intention 'of launching an unlimited drive into the boundless territories of Russia . . . but would take up a position which, through the occupation of the Ukraine, would assure Germany food supplies and a substantial increase in war potential'.

Hitler did not believe that a political settlement with Russia was possible. 'In any case it would not be more than an interim solution, since the Russians of course were not to be trusted, and German troops would thus have to be held in readiness for use against them should occasion arise.' The German summer offensive aimed at paralysing Russian offensive power. Then 'there would be a switch to static warfare. The Fuehrer might have more far-reaching plans, with which Ribbentrop was not acquainted in detail, but the results which he had mentioned were the least that would definitely be achieved.'

Ribbentrop now turned to the questions of the neutrals, Spain and Turkey, whose reactions to the revolutionary changes in the balance of the war had been exercising both Berlin and Rome in the previous weeks.

Mussolini was told of the 'confidential protocol' recently signed by the German government with Franco, selling arms on the condition of a pledge by the Spanish government to defend the Iberian peninsula and the Atlantic and Mediterranean islands against any Anglo-American assault. Ribbentrop asked the Duce to treat this information as confidential, 'since its widespread dissemination would lead to unpleasant consequences for Franco. There already existed a secret protocol with Spain in connection with her accession to the Steel Pact: this too had hitherto been kept secret.'

As regards Turkey, Ribbentrop summarized his views on the Adana Conference. From various secret sources Germany could form a fairly clear picture of the talks. No binding agreements had been made with the British. Turkey would remain neutral, and was 'governed first and foremost by a strong fear of the Russians, and consequently hoped in her innermost heart for a German victory over Russia.

'In his Berlin talks with the Fuehrer,[e] Molotov had laid down his well-known four conditions: Finland, Roumania, Bulgaria, and the Straits for the Soviets, thereby revealing Russia's real aims. If Germany were weak, neither Britain nor America could block the path of Russia's advance. This was the reason why Turkey would stay out of the war, and hoped for an Axis victory over Russia. But just as she would not join us, neither would Turkey allow herself to be dragged into the war against us. She would remain aloof until the very last moment, and range herself with the victor only at the eleventh hour.'

A general pattern of German strategic thinking was emerging from Hitler's letter and Ribbentrop's remarks. A total effort by the Germans on the Russian front would produce conditions of static warfare by the summer,

e. In November 1940.

and revolutionize the economic position of Germany and consequently of Italy. The mounting submarine war would limit the power of the Western Allies to open a Second Front, and confine them to peripheral landing operations at points round the continent of Europe. In the Mediterranean theatre Franco would probably stay on the fringe of the war. In event of an Anglo-American action in Spain or her island possessions, German military aid might be increased to hold the balance. In the Eastern Mediterranean, Turkey would maintain her neutrality, and it was improbable that the British would press her further. There remained, as the threatened areas of Anglo-American operations, Italy and her offshore islands and the Axis-held territories in Yugoslavia.

Ribbentrop gave brief consideration to the former in terms which betrayed at once the perfunctory interest of Hitler in the Mediterranean war. 'Information was coming to hand according to which England intended to proceed against Corsica and Sardinia. In this connection the question of fortifying these islands became one of decisive importance. The engineer staffs, placed at the disposal of Italy, were of the opinion that the fortification of Sardinia was totally inadequate and that, in the event of a serious British landing, the island would be occupied. The Fuehrer believed that the enemy was aware of the fact that the transport problem was becoming more and more difficult for them, and they would therefore undertake landing operations as soon as possible.'

Having thus dismissed the direct enemy threat to the Italian ally, Ribbentrop felt free to concentrate on the main theme of his instructions. With the aid of a map he now explained in detail the German appreciation of the Serbo-Croat theatre. 'The Fuehrer's view was that we had to contend here with three distinct groups: the Communists, who had just suffered a severe blow, the followers of Mihailović, including also the četniks, and the irregulars. In the event of the British landing, all these groups would hasten to the aid of the invader.'

Hitler's analysis was confusing, and Ribbentrop's summary telescoped. The Communist forces of Tito had been driven southwards from Croatian territory in the direction of Montenegro as the result of joint winter operations by German and Italian forces, in which the latter had reluctantly taken part and had used as auxiliary troops the 'irregular' četnik bands based on Croatia. These units were nominally controlled by Mihailović whose main forces were operating in Serbia and Montenegro.

Ribbentrop was attempting to show that the 'irregulars' referred to by Hitler and the rest of the četniks were in reality one force, and the German Foreign Minister now handed to the Duce some material assembled by the Germans which showed that all these groups 'were secretly under Mihailović's command, i.e. that they were basically directed by the British General Staff'. German and Italian plans for maintaining control of the occupied regions of Yugoslavia had been sharply opposed since the initial campaign of April 1941, and it was the central purpose of Ribbentrop's present mission to sort out this sullen tangle.

The Italian military view was represented by General Roatta, now commanding the Italian Second Army in Croatia. According to him, the četnik 'irregulars' in those areas were serving a useful local purpose. They could be employed to destroy the partisans, and only then should be disarmed and disbanded. And as Mussolini retorted at this present meeting, 'German troops had also made use of the četniks in battle'.

The real intention of the Italian Command was to execute a gradual withdrawal of all their forces on Yugoslav soil in order to hold only a coastal belt against possible Allied landings, to withdraw as many troops as possible for the ultimate defence of the Italian mainland, and to leave četnik bands, armed with Italian weapons, to foment civil war in the interior against the partisans. The Italians did not accept the concept of a large-scale operation of 'pacification' which the Germans consistently pressed on them at all levels.

Bastianini summarized the Italian view in his only intervention in the conference. 'He contested the likelihood of a unification of all three groups in the event of a British invasion. The Russian-influenced partisans had nothing in common with the adherents of Mihailović. They regarded him as a traitor. Bastianini also rejected the idea of a military operation to extirpate the partisans. The war on the Serbo-Croat front had to be conducted on a pattern entirely different from that applied in the other theatres of war. It was not a question of the number of divisions. In mountainous terrain everything would be resolved by small-scale operations.'

And Mussolini added: 'No effective methods of combating the partisans had yet been found. The German and Italian regular troops were not up to guerilla warfare. This method of warfare was highly uncongenial, involved heavy losses, and had so far brought inadequate results. Altogether there were sixty thousand partisans and četniks. Ultimately they could of course not hold out, since—at any rate up to the present—they possessed no artillery or air force, and could obtain supplies only with difficulty.'

Ribbentrop felt the absence of his military experts in such a discussion and merely replied that 'the extent of the danger could be gauged, among other things, from one of Eden's announcements in which he openly described Mihailović's men as Britain's advance guard in the Balkans . . . The question of Mihailović and of pacifying the Croatian region was not a political but a purely military one. Once the war was won, Italy could settle her own political problems in this region. Germany had no axe to grind in the matter.'

He was well aware of Italian suspicions of German economic and strategic interests in Yugoslav territory, which remained the most sensitive subject of misunderstanding between the two governments, and was anxious on this occasion to confine the debate to the military aspects of these regions, which according to Hitler represented a major potential threat to the whole Axis position in Europe.

Ribbentrop was accompanied on his visit by General Warlimont, the Chief of Operations at the German High Command, and proposed that the whole issue should be discussed further in the presence of military experts.

Ribbentrop then swerved into an illuminating digression on his personal impressions of Stalin and his analysis of the war. 'It was a mistake to assume that Stalin would change. He (Ribbentrop) had twice negotiated with him and learned to recognize in him a tough fanatic and icy realist who dominated everything in Russia, and in whose presence none of his colleagues dared open his mouth. He was undoubtedly a man of historic stature. Ribbentrop mentioned that at the end of his second démarche in Moscow,[f] when a communiqué was being prepared that contained a few sarcasms at Britain's expense, he had asked Stalin, who was in a fairly expansive mood, whether Russia might not support Germany militarily as well. He was thinking in terms of, say, a Russian attack on Britain via Persia. Stalin had pondered for a long time before giving his reply, and had then said that Russia would never tolerate Germany's being weak in relation to Britain and France. Ribbentrop had not rightly grasped the full implications of this reply at the time. But in the light of subsequent developments he now realized that Stalin's whole policy was expressed in these words. Stalin had been preparing for war for fifteen years, he had then shared out Poland with Germany, and imagined that the Reich would have to wage a protracted war in the West. He had assumed that Germany would gradually wear herself out in the process and would finally be obliged to turn to Russia for support. Posing as a helpful ally, and having secured the Roumanian oil, he doubtless intended to bolshevize Germany from within and with the aid of this Communized Germany to extend his supremacy over the whole of Europe.' [g]

f. In September 1939.

g. These thoughts had been recently in Ribbentrop's mind, probably in searching for his own justification of Hitler's determined reactions to the fall of Stalingrad. On February 18 the German Foreign Minister had used almost identical language to the Turkish Ambassador in Berlin to that which he now employed with the Duce. Referring to his talks with Stalin in Moscow and the latter's remark that 'Russia would never suffer that Germany should become weak', Ribbentrop added that 'at the time he could not quite explain this remark: today he understood its meaning. Stalin knew how strong his army was. He thought that Germany would wear herself out in a long war against the Western Powers and become the booty of the German communists. With a Communist-led Germany he would then throw England, France and America out of Europe, and for this reason he stated that Russia would never allow Germany to become weak.' (German Collection. Ribbentrop-Arikan conversation, February 18, 1943.)

It now remained for Mussolini to allude to the points raised by Ribbentrop in his outline of German views on the state of the war. 'As early as December' the Duce had reviewed the present situation 'in a calm and sober spirit'. But he made no mention of his plea to Hitler at the time of the Goerlitz talks to consider a settlement in the East. Indeed he treated the present German exposition of the Russian front as cavalierly as Ribbentrop had in his reference to the Mediterranean theatre. 'What had to be done now was to erect this barrier (possibly on the Dnieper) and then await developments. The chief enemy in Russia had always been the country itself, for it was limitless. Not only was this the lesson to be learned from history, but he had also verified it by personal observation on the occasion of his visit to the Fuehrer, when he had flown over the vast plains and gained a deep and lasting impression of their unlimited extent.'

He continued: 'Until August of the previous year the Axis had held the initiative. But from that date it had lain with the enemy, both on land and in the air. This change had been brought about partly by transport and convoy problems.' Mussolini was referring to the African theatre, which had escaped attention in the German analysis. Rommel had not been able to continue his advance to Egypt because of the sinking by the enemy of his supply tankers. 'It had been a mistake not to retreat once it was clear that Rommel's offensive had failed. In particular the non-motorized Italian divisions should have been withdrawn. . . . It was incorrect to say that Rommel had left them in the lurch, but if they had been withdrawn in time and made available for later use, Cyrenaica would not have been lost.

'Italy was furthermore obliged to fight a sort of "proletarian" war. Italian troops were still fighting with arms left over from the last war. Italy had not had time to arm, having been fighting continuously ever since 1935, first in Abyssinia, then in Spain. True, her manpower losses in these wars had not been heavy, but her losses in arms and equipment had been much more severe. Spanish artillery, for example, had come for the most part from Italy. They were weapons handed over to the Spanish at the end of the Civil War, together with several aircraft.'

The Duce probed in one phrase to the root cause of the present loss of strategic initiative by the Axis. 'The Alamein offensive had misfired because the manoeuvre could not be based on the Caucasus.' In other words, there was no co-ordination or summit planning by the Germans and Italians, who continued to conduct and were steadily losing their 'parallel' wars, and in particular in North Africa.

Tunisia was 'the bulwark of Southern Europe'. It could be held, in Mussolini's view, on three conditions: 'First, if all the available submarines from whatever quarter were massed in the Mediterranean; second, if the appropriate artillery were made available; and third, if our air strength were at least equal to that of the enemy.' If Tunisia were lost 'the entire strategic position would be altered. An attack on Sicily, Sardinia and the Balkans would then become possible.'

As to the long-term plans of the British and Americans which Ribbentrop had so cursorily dismissed, the Duce personally did not fear an invasion of Italy, and merely thought that air attacks would increase in strength. As regards landings in Sardinia and Sicily, he thought that these would take the form only of 'commando' operations and not of a classical invasion backed by numerous warships and reinforcements.

Unlike the Germans, Mussolini placed greater emphasis on an eventual entry of Spain into the war, and such a move might restore a limited initiative to the Axis in the Mediterranean. Such was his private hope, which he now expressed with caution. 'The British might occupy the Balearic islands. This would be all to the good, as it would bring the Spanish question to the fore. He would let Ribbentrop have a copy of a letter from Franco to him, together with his reply. Franco had told him in his letter that he had no faith in British and American assurances and was making preparations for armed resistance. The Duce added that he presumed this attitude on the part of Franco was materially influenced by the fact that there were four American divisions on the border with Spanish Morocco, that the former Red President of Spain, Negrin, had turned up in North Africa and that Britain was propagating among the Arabs the notion of complete independence from Spain as well. Finally, there was still a great danger of Communism in Spain itself, since Franco had not carried through any kind of social reform and present-day Spain differed only superficially from the Spain of former days. Spain's entry into the war was unavoidable, and an enemy victory would also mean the end of Franco. Spain's entry into the war ought only to take place at a propitious moment, as otherwise she would become more of a burden than a help. He was therefore glad Germany was sending arms to Spain, the more so as he considered it out of the question that Spain should ever turn against the Axis.'

Mussolini did not expressly comment on the position of Turkey or on German confidence in her neutrality. He concluded his survey with a curt and sober note. 'The attitude of other countries towards the Axis was dependent on the situation in Tunisia and on the Russian front.'

It was agreed that the next meeting should be held together with the military experts and confined to the whole politico-military situation in Yugoslav territory.

In the interval the Duce and his advisers were able to study the contents of Hitler's letter of February 16, which Ribbentrop had delivered at the opening of the talks. To the Italians there was little new and nothing encouraging in this document. The twin disasters of Alamein and Stalingrad had not impressed on Hitler the need for that strategic revolution for which the new Italian High Command had hoped. The German war would still be essentially conducted on two main fronts: the war against Allied shipping at sea, and the destruction of the Soviet Union on land. All else was in effect secondary. There was little sign of a coherent plan of action in the Mediterranean, although the 'struggle in North Africa' was glanced at as having 'an equally decisive influence on the success of the war as a whole'. The repeated myth of wearing down the Allies on the sea route round the Cape was once again hopefully cited. And then, significantly, 'our enemies' counter-measures can, apart from the attempt to drive us out of Tunis and Bizerta, consist only in attempts at landing on the Continent itself'. And here lies the key to Hitler's thinking. He was not concerned about a major Second Front in the West in 1943, and mentions a series of possible Allied landings, or rather raids, stretching round the whole Northern and Western periphery of Europe from the Baltic to Portugal, but it is not in these areas that his interest lies; nor even in the outer defences of his Italian ally, Sardinia, Corsica, and Sicily. These are dismissed in five lines of the letter.

'I regard the situation in the Balkan peninsula with the gravest concern.' This was the historic invasion route into the heart of Europe, and the obvious point of concentration for the Allies. An enemy landing in the area, backed by local nationalist and Communist uprisings, might lead to the rapid control of the whole region, and the worst nightmare of all, to the exposing of the German southern flank in the East and an eventual gigantic turning movement—a joint Anglo-American-Russian enterprise—into Germany itself.

Mihailović and Tito, in ironic association, at the head of small bands of irregular guerillas, had become the symbol of the Fuehrer's main disquiet.

On the morning of February 26, the two delegations assembled at Palazzo Venezia. Ribbentrop was now accompanied by General Warlimont, and Mussolini was flanked by General Ambrosio and Bastianini.[4]

The Duce introduced the discussion on the central theme of the conference. Hitler had stated, in his letter, firstly that the Italian military authorities in the Balkans were supporting the četniks and delivering arms to them in order to use them against the partisans; and secondly, that the great danger lay in the 'unclarified conditions in the Balkans' in event of an Anglo-American landing on the Adriatic coast. He felt that there was no distinction between četniks and partisans, that all help should cease to the former, and that they should be disarmed. He had the impression that not many arms had been handed over to the četniks, as Italy did not dispose of many weapons. Something may possibly have happened, but the broad lines of policy, as laid down by him, were perfectly clear: to avoid substituting diplomatic solutions for military problems as long as possible, for such a move could only bring about misunderstandings and disagreeable surprises. The Duce had therefore called this meeting to clear up these matters with the help of military experts. 'General Ambrosio knew the conditions well and could be very helpful in this task.'

Ambrosio spoke with authority. He had commanded the Italian Second Army in Croatia until January 1942. There had at that time been no case for using the irregular 'nationalist' bands. 'But then the disturbances had spread, and under his successor, Roatta, certain subordinate military head-quarters had accepted the četniks' offer to fight the partisans, to whom they stood in strong opposition.' It was true that the četniks hated the Italians, 'but in spite of that one had to use them, because Italy had not enough troops available to deal with the partisans who were scattered everywhere.

'As to the general objective laid down by the Fuehrer,[h] the destruction of those groups operating in Serbia and the pacification of that region, no immediate solution was possible. As always in the Balkans, so this time too, long and bitter fighting and in addition a permanent and numerous occupation force, would be needed to pacify the area finally.'

Ambrosio agreed that the četniks should be disarmed, but by stages. Clearly both četniks and partisans were enemies of the Axis. 'But it was not possible to beat them both at once.'

The Duce interposed that an Allied landing on the Adriatic coast would be 'a very dangerous and complicated operation'. He believed however in the possibility of Commando raids, but not a regular invasion. 'The British had better opportunities elsewhere.'

Ribbentrop replied that he was not a military expert and, whether or not such a landing was feasible, 'it was in any case completely impossible to leave strong forces of četniks[i] and partisans in the rear of the German forces, if for instance a major landing took place in Greece. The Fuehrer was particularly disturbed by the latter possibility, for he knew that the disruption of the railway connections by rebels in Croatia at the moment of a British landing would have the most serious consequences.' Unless the area were cleared at least of the large bands, 'it might be necessary to bring divisions which ought to be protecting Greece from the British back into Croatia to fight the partisans'. Time played a very big rôle in action against the bands. In a life and death struggle one could not leave great masses of

h. In January 1943.

i. In reply to a question by Ribbentrop, Ambrosio had estimated the četnik 'irregular' forces in Crotia at 8,000 men. The Duce immediately added that this was certainly a small figure, but it gave an inexact picture, for the war in Croatia was not conducted as in the West. Neither the Italian nor the German army was in a position to expel the guerillas. For this, one needed troops drawn from the same regions and of the same race as the rebels. Thus 8,000 četniks represented for the Italian-German cause more than two or three divisions. In reply to a question from Ribbentrop, the Duce said the Italians had twenty-five divisions in Yugoslav territory. Ribbentrop then pointed out that, with a further six German divisions, there were in all thirty-one divisions available. With this not inconsiderable force, it should be possible in any event to master the rebels.

troops idle. The same measures must be taken in Croatia as in the East; as many partisans and followers of other hostile groups as possible must be liquidated. 'The report which General Warlimont had with him showed that more or less all the groups in Croatia were led by Mihailović, that is by the British General Staff.'

Ribbentrop then went on: 'To take the view that the area could not be pacified seemed to him to be a form of resignation that we could not allow ourselves in this war. It was possible that perhaps the whole region could not be cleared, but at least the larger bands . . . must be destroyed.'

General Warlimont was now called on to summarize the German military case. 'It was a matter of safeguarding the further requirements of 200,000 tons of bauxite, on which the carrying out of the German Air Force programme was dependent, and above all by destroying the main centres of resistance in the country to prevent the outbreak of a general revolt in event of a British landing . . .' He then described on a map the various operations in progress, and estimated the strength of the partisans at 15–20,000 men. Operation Weiss I [j] in the western part of Croatia had led to the liquidation of 5,000 men. 'But the Tito State (*sic*) had a considerably larger and wider woven organization than one had at first assumed. Most of the 15,000 men had got away in the direction of Mostar. Previously this situation had seemed very dangerous, but now certain advantages appeared. For the first time it was possible to surround and destroy the whole Communist force so that they could not take evasive action again.' He was prepared to agree that the četniks should take part in these coming operations, but not in contact with German troops. After the Communists had been destroyed, the četniks would no longer be needed, and could be at once disarmed. 'Then action could be taken against the centre of the Mihailović movement, namely in Serbia. The Fuehrer had therefore requested that firm directives should be agreed upon in Rome whereby these operations should ensue.' Warlimont then gave up to the Duce a draft of such orders which he had prepared in Rome on instructions from Ribbentrop.

While Mussolini was reading this document, Ambrosio continued the debate. The disarming of the četniks, 'which the German Foreign Minister had described as urgent, need not be precipitated so long as no actual British landing had taken place in Greece, and while Tunis still remained in German and Italian hands . . . a joint Italo-German military operation in Croatia would in Ambrosio's view not be successful. He thought that within a fortnight the same disorder would break out again. It was not possible, in the circumstances prevailing in Croatia, to mount long-term operational plans.'

j. The first operation of the combined military operation agreed in Italian-German talks in Belgrade in December 1942, for the destruction of partisan bands in Northern and Western Croatia.

In any event, new Italian divisions were not forthcoming. 'They were needed for the defence against an eventual British landing in Italy itself.' k

Ribbentrop retorted that it was not feasible to postpone or even not carry out all operations 'against the British auxiliary troops of Mihailović in Croatia simply out of fear that the British might perhaps carry out an operation somewhere else'.

The Duce remarked that the četnik problem was more political than military, and Ambrosio agreed that this was the case with 'the whole Croat question in general'. Ribbentrop had no intention of being drawn on to this delicate and contested ground, and he sharply countered. 'It was a purely military problem. Political questions could easily be settled when the war had been won.'

The tone of the meeting had risen, and Mussolini adjourned the discussion by agreeing with Warlimont's proposals, and instructing Ambrosio to work out with the latter the details at a separate military conference.

Even the dry official tone of Schmidt's record of these talks does not conceal the frustrated irritation of Ribbentrop. He had received categorical instructions from Hitler to reach a military agreement with the Italians to take joint operational measures to remove the menace of possible partisan activity in Yugoslav territory against economic targets and lines of communication in an area of vital concern to both allies. The Duce knew the problem, which needed no further explanation or exposition. He had been told by Goering in October and again in December. Ciano and Cavallero had been lectured on the same subject in the same month. The Fuehrer had now written a long personal letter as well, and sent Ribbentrop expressly to Rome to put an end to the delay and to clear up the matter once and for all. Yet there was clearly obstruction if not sabotage, both on the spot in the Balkans, and in Rome by the military authorities. Why should Ambrosio be so obstinate about abandoning Italian support to a few četnik bands operating on Croat territory?

Ribbentrop's exasperation exploded in a private talk on February 28 with that admirable listener, Alfieri.[5] The German and Italian military experts had met in the course of February 26. Early the following morning Warlimont had told Ribbentrop that full agreement had been reached, and the Italian High Command was preparing a joint memorandum. This document had now been received. 'It contained provisions about the Command arrangements, which did not coincide with the verbal agreements, whereby the

k. According to Dollmann, who was present with the German delegation as interpreter, 'Ribbentrop and Warlimont raised their eyebrows on hearing Ambrosio say . . . that henceforth he would consider military questions exclusively from the point of view of Italy's requirement'. (Dollmann op cit p. 189.)

German and Italian forces would operate separately, but with liaison staffs and the most precise co-ordination of joint plans. And further, the document —and this was the gravest point—omitted any mention of Mihailović.'

Ribbentrop 'expressed emphatically his astonishment at the activities of the Italian High Command. He must explain quite openly that during his meeting with the Duce he had detected a certain resistance on the part of the military gentlemen, which gave the impression that they were not convinced of the need for operations in Croatia, and they expressed the view that they did not have enough troops.' He 'had the feeling that behind Ambrosio's remark that it was a political question, something lay hidden. Perhaps in many circles of higher officers the connections between the different theatres of war were not well enough known . . . In the Italian High Command there were tendencies which one could not exactly describe as Fascist.'

Was this a veiled warning? Ribbentrop's view of the Italian military leaders had been marked by the demoralizing collapse of their armies on the Russian Front, and by what he regarded as the inability of the senior officers to fight an ideologically Fascist war. Sharing with Hitler the contempt and distrust of senior officers in Nazi circles, Ribbentrop, seemingly for the first time, began to reflect seriously upon the political consequences of military defeat, both on the structure of Fascist Italy, and upon the Italian High Command itself.

Ribbentrop later the following year referred to these frustrations, recalling 'how, as much as a year before the fall of Italy, when the measures to be adopted against Mihailović in the Serbo-Croat region were under discussion, Ambrosio had consistently sabotaged the talks with the Duce, even going so far as to oppose the latter in Ribbentrop's presence. The subject then being debated had been a decision of Mussolini's to issue forceful orders to the Italian Sixth Army to induce them to take rather more energetic action against the insurgents in the Serbo-Croat region. Ambrosio had made persisent efforts at the time to sabotage these directions of the Duce by insisting on getting the order in writing, and trying to distort what the Duce had said. Upon representations by Ribbentrop, Alfieri had then taken prompt action. He had hastened straight to the Duce, had obtained the written order and taken it to Ambrosio. Ambrosio had made one last attempt to express his disapproval to the Duce by refusing to sign the order to the Italian High Command in person and getting his deputy to sign it instead.' [6]

The final session was held on February 29 at Palazzo Venezia. Neither Ambrosio nor Warlimont was summoned and, presumably to give it an exclusively diplomatic character, only Mackensen, Alfieri and Bastianini were present. This was curious, as all decisions in regard to the Balkans— much to Ciano's annoyance in the past—had been taken exclusively by the Italian High Command.

Mussolini started the conversation with the 'question of Mihailović', and explained that 'he too regarded him as a dangerous and bitter foe of Germany and Italy'. Ambrosio had been given orders in regard to the necessary operations. 'Ambrosio was an excellent man who would make no promise that he could not keep, but who would in all circumstances carry out the Duce's orders.'

In reply to a query by Ribbentrop, the Duce said that in South-East Europe between Ljubljana and the Dodecanese, there were twenty-five to twenty-six Italian divisions. Ribbentrop pointed out tartly that 'once Mihailović had been liquidated, Italy would free a large number of divisions so that the destruction of Mihailović would bring great advantages to the Italian High Command'. He did not add that this figure of Italian forces represented nearly half the total Italian army, and might point to the original importance which the Italians gave to their Balkan interests.

At this point the Duce and Ribbentrop withdrew from the meeting to talk in private and without witnesses. There is no written record of this conversation.

There had been no mention in these talks of Bastianini's plan to sound the Germans on the advisability of some public declaration on the European 'New Order', both with the purpose of encouraging the occupied and allied countries of Axis Europe, and to test the reactions both of the neutrals and the enemy. According to Bastianini, however, the Duce in the course of the conference, and presumably during this last private conversation, obtained Ribbentrop's reluctant consent to the publication of an official communiqué which mentioned for the first time the ideals of liberty for all peoples and active collaboration between the nations. 'It was in substance the first and last official declaration of the basic principles of that New Order which the Axis up to that moment had avoided defining in any way.' [7]

In the event, the Germans suppressed any public comment, and the main effect of this preliminary show of independence by Bastianini seems to have been the neglect of Ribbentrop in making any protocol call at Palazzo Chigi at the end of his visit.

Mussolini himself showed little enthusiasm for the plan. As Prince Bismarck stated later: 'It is rumoured in Berlin that at the last meeting with Ribbentrop, Mussolini turned the discussion on to the problem of Europe. It was all limited to a few very vague phrases, and . . . my impression is that he has no clear ideas on the subject.'

It appears also that Ribbentrop did voice to Mussolini his criticisms of the Italian High Command, which had been aired in his talks with Alfieri, and on his return to Berlin told the Japanese Ambassador, General Oshima, who called to ask for his impressions of the Rome visit, that 'in the military sector the Duce wants to carry out certain reforms'. [8]

On February 27 Ribbentrop was received by the King of Italy. The German Ambassador, Mackensen, accompanied him, but did not enter the royal study.[1] After the audience, General Puntoni noted: 'the German Minister is full of optimism. He has no doubts about the success of the war in Russia, where, he says, the Germans will take the initiative as soon as possible. Hitler is placing his main cards on submarine warfare. According to Ribbentrop, the internal situation in Great Britain and Russia is far from cheerful. Turkey will not enter the war on the Anglo-American side, and Spain, in the event of her suffering any aggression by the Allies, will come in on our side. Germany understands the importance of Tunisia and will undertake the impossible to come to its defence and facilitate a rapid counter-attack. The content of these statements, made without any request on my part, makes me think that Hitler is disturbed at the lack of confidence which now reigns in many circles here.' [9]

1. There was apparently no reference to the ostensible reason for Ribbentrop's visit, the conferment of a decoration on the Prince of Piedmont, and there is no record of any discussion between the latter and Ribbentrop during his stay in Rome.

CHAPTER FOUR

SPRING TENSIONS:
RUSSIA AND TUNISIA

• •

'FROM WHAT I could understand, the Duce had succeeded in putting across our point of view in regard to three questions of fundamental importance: no more soldiers in Russia; Tunisia is of capital importance to us; it is essential to strengthen the air forces in the Mediterranean and the islands.' Such was the King's account to Puntoni of the audience of the Duce on March 1 on the talks with Ribbentrop.

These matters would be clarified in Mussolini's reply to Hitler's letter of February 16, and Ambrosio in particular hoped to influence this forthcoming statement of Italian policy. He had drafted a note for the Duce on the same day as the royal audience.[1]

'I think it advisable to bring again to your attention two concepts, already set out in previous memoranda,[a] because of their basic importance, and because from the military point of view it is of the highest interest to write them to the Fuehrer.

'To hold Tunis and defend our coasts we need German help in artillery, light naval craft, technical equipment, aircraft, and oil supplies in the measure as requested also through General Warlimont.[b] This aid is all the more necessary in that we have agreed to the operations in the Balkans, which will prevent us withdrawing from this region the troops we had counted on to reinforce the defence of the Mother Country.

'The German conduct of an offensive war cannot, in our opinion, lead to decisive results, at least unless the Germans succeed in pinning down and destroying the Russian army. This possibility is very chancy, while it is certain that offensive operations will lead to an enormous wastage of men

a. See pp. 166–9.
b. Presumably during the military talks on February 26.

and material. We also maintain that the Germans, being totally committed to an offensive in Russia, cannot effectively oppose the Anglo-Americans in other parts of Europe for lack of adequate reserves.

'The Ally must revise his plans and pay more attention to the Mediterranean theatre, because the danger does not come only from the East, but may well appear at any moment on the flank or rear of the German army.

'The Germans are not greatly worried about an Anglo-American attack because, in the first instance, it would take place far away from their territory. We are in the opposite position. One of the most likely objectives in the Mediterranean is Italy, and we shall end by bearing the weight of the struggle alone, a battle which will put our country to fire and the sword, and expose her to major damage. It may be that this thought forms part of the German plan, namely that they want to commit us to bear the brunt of the initial Anglo-American assault, with little regard to the fate of our population and cities.

'If we receive aid in respect of the necessary and indispensable flow of supplies, and if the operational views of the Germans both towards Russia and in regard to the vital Mediterranean theatre will be in conformity with a more positive vision of the strategic position of Europe, there will be more chance of holding Tunisia as long as possible . . . Otherwise the prospects cannot be equally hopeful and Italy will then have to consider how to avoid the consequences of irreparable mistakes which are not of her making.' [2]

This memorandum of the Chief of the Italian General Staff, written under the impact of the Rome talks, marks the first signs of his open revolt against the German attitude to the conduct of the war and of his anxiety as to the future of the Axis alliance. The meeting with Ribbentrop and Warlimont had been his first official contact with the German leadership. His reactions are revealed in this note. The last paragraph of the memorandum contains an early hint, as yet apparently unsupported from other quarters,[c] of the need of an independent Italian solution.

But for the moment the Duce, and he alone, could persuade Hitler to modify his position. It might even be that these common anxieties about the Russian war in certain German and Italian circles during recent weeks, of which Ambrosio was directly aware, in a sense delayed the elaboration of any counter action with the Italian Army Command against the continuation of the Axis alliance. On February 28 Ambrosio saw the head of the German Military Intelligence, Admiral Canaris. It is not known what passed between the two men.

The rôle of Mussolini as a possible arbitrator with Hitler had not yet been

c. It is perhaps significant that in the days immediately following Ribbentrop's visit, Ambrosio saw the Prince of Piedmont (March 1 and 3): Badoglio (March 2), Caviglia (March 5), and Bonomi (March 5). (Italian Collection. Ambrosio diary.) Was he seeking cautious support for such future action in the event of Mussolini refusing to face the realities of a war to the finish?

exhausted even though his performance with the German Foreign Minister had not been encouraging. The present concern of Ambrosio, however, was to press the Duce with every argument available in the direction of increased German aid to Italy in order to meet the enemy on more effective terms than hitherto in the Mediterranean theatre.

To this end Ambrosio drafted a series of points [d] to be considered by Mussolini in answering Hitler's letter of February 16. This reply was dispatched on March 8, and represented the considered comments of the Duce on the recent Rome talks. It followed the same general order of subjects as set out by Hitler, opening with North Africa.

'I am glad to note that you too regard Tunisia as an essential factor of the strategic campaign . . . We must remain in Tunisia, whatever the cost: in any case we must stay there as long as possible, since this will interfere profoundly, and perhaps decisively, with the execution of the plans drawn up by the Anglo-Saxons at Casablanca. In order to hold Tunisia, we must extend our bridgehead and not shrink it as Rommel wanted, since this would mean being overwhelmed and—in short—driven towards the sea, without means of escape, given the superiority which the enemy would gain from linking up his armies and being able to use all the airfields abandoned by us in Tunisia.

'I am convinced that we must resist on the Mareth Line. But in order to resist, and perhaps even counter-attack, our forces must be provisioned; and above all guns, tanks, and petrol must reach them.[e] Shipping on the short but compulsory route of the Sicily channel must be safeguarded. To obtain all this, Fuehrer, I will never tire of repeating it: the Axis air forces in the Sardinia, Sicily, Tunisia zone must be at least equal to the enemy aviation.

'As to the operation in Croatia . . . I find that the results, if not decisive, are at least satisfactory.' The 'četnik-partisan theme' had been discussed at length with Ribbentrop. The local Italian Generals in Montenegro had been summoned to Rome and instructed to cease deliveries of arms to the četniks, who would be disarmed 'as soon as the partisans have ceased to be a dangerous armed movement'. Agreement with the German commander in Yugoslavia would be reached 'on the subsequent action to be taken in regard to the movement of General Mihailović'.[f]

As to possible Allied landings, 'it is henceforward axiomatic that the

d. Italian Collection. 'Note for the Duce'. 'Points for a reply to the letter of the Fuehrer, February 28, 1943.' For these draft comments see the footnotes to Mussolini's letter.

e. Ambrosio's draft 'Problems of communications' and 'Struggle in North Africa'. 'Fully agree with what the Fuehrer says about "the decisive value" which communications have, in the actual struggle, especially as military success cannot be maintained if the rhythm of supplies is interrupted or lessened. Equally we are fully aware of the great importance of holding Tunisia, and in this respect we cannot pause in improving from day to day the organization and efficiency of the traffic.'

f. It is significant that General Roatta, the senior Italian commander, who was in Croatia, was not called back to Rome, nor did Ambrosio comment on this subject.

Allies must try to set up a Second Front in Europe. The demands of Russia are imperious. And when, as I firmly believe, the Russian initiative will peter out, the Anglo-Saxons will have to honour their engagements and land at some point in Europe . . . I foresee, and particularly if Tunisia were definitely lost, the following operations against Italy: mass bombing in the northern and southern regions of Italy; commando and parachute landings in Sicily and Sardinia, to improve the naval position of the Allies. A serious invasion of the peninsula is an operation which the Anglo-Saxons cannot carry out. Faced with these eventualities, all our defence preparations in the two islands have been stepped up.g

'Spain is still a card in our game, in spite of the oscillations of Franco's policy, and I feel that she could play a most important part the day on which she would allow us across her territory to take the whole Anglo-American position in North Africa from the rear. I get the impression that the enemy fear a move of this kind.'

On the subject of the Russian front, the Duce displayed unusual caution, and seems to have allowed his comments deliberately to be strengthened by Ambrosio's arguments, perhaps sensing too the opportunity to exert that element of personal persuasion on Hitler which, Mussolini realized, was expected of him in various quarters, both German and Italian.

The wording of this paragraph was sybilline. 'I have never doubted for a single moment that the armed forces of your Reich would restore the situation . . . I am sure that at a certain moment the Bolsheviks will find themselves up against an unsurmountable wall.

'But, Fuehrer, on the day when you accomplish the East Wall—with troops and fortifications—Russia, exhausted, will no longer represent the mortal danger of two years ago, and unless you are absolutely certain that you can destroy her forces once and for all, I wonder whether it is not too risky to repeat the struggle against the boundless space of Russia which is practically impossible to reach and grasp, while the Anglo-Saxon peril is mounting in the West? h The day when, one way or another, Russia will be eliminated or neutralized, victory is in our hands. But I hope to discuss

g. *Defence of the Italian Coast* (paragraph 5 of Hitler's letter). 'The view of the Fuehrer is shared about the possibility of an Anglo-American landing on our larger islands. We are now reinforcing the garrisons of these islands, and at the same time defence works are actively in progress. But to count on a defence which guarantees us against assault in force, not only in Sicily, Sardinia and Corsica, but also against the mainland, we need equipment, especially artillery, which we are asking from the Germans only in a strictly necessary measure. (These requests have now been renewed and handed to General Warlimont.)'

h. *Operations in the East* (paragraph 9 of Hitler's letter).
'The Fuehrer expresses his unshakeable will to fight in the East until the "Russian Colossus ceases to exist". He does not however refer to an operational plan for achieving this end. One would confirm here that the concept of an offensive in Russia, if it does not at least succeed in pinning down the Russian army and then destroying it, will be sterile of decisive results and expose the Germans less to losses of men and material.'

this thoroughly with you when I have the good fortune to meet you again.'

Finally, the future of the Italian contribution to the Russian war, which the King was so anxious to liquidate, was settled by the Duce's decision, apparently communicated to Warlimont by an unwilling Ambrosio during the Rome talks, that 'Italy cannot remain absent from the Russian front', and that the Italian Second Army Corps should stay in Russia. 'It must however be reformed and re-equipped with effective weapons, since with a threadbare deployment, like the Italian 8th Army on the Don, without reserves and with antiquated weapons, things could not turn out any differently from before . . . But allow me to express the wish that the Italian Army Corps will be used, not in duties in the rear, but in battle.' i

Behind this cussed insistence by Mussolini on retaining Italian military presence in Russia lay an intricate set of pressures. He was aware that such a contribution could only be symbolic. He could sense the catastrophic effect on Italian public opinion of the news of the military disaster in Russia in the previous January and the dissolving influence of the reports of the Italian soldiers repatriated from the Eastern Front.

Under the weight of the massive Soviet winter offensive the whole Italian front had collapsed. There had been no defence in depth, and the promised German reserve support of an armoured division behind the Italians never materialized, nor had the Italian transport received any supplies of petrol before the battle.[3] In many cases the Germans, like Rommel's forces in Africa, seized Italian lorries and left the shattered units to face a death march to the West.

On March 14, in a dispatch marked 'Behaviour of the Italian Army in Russia', Alfieri wrote to Bastianini that the tendency on the German side was to make one believe in the unworthy behaviour of certain units of the Italian Expeditionary Corps in the last Russian offensive and to insist that the disaster had happened solely owing to the fault of the Italian and Roumanian troops. This attitude of course was not new, and Ciano had complained of it at Goerlitz in the previous December. Alfieri, however, felt that there was need for a temperate reply, showing the failure of the Germans to produce reserves and supplies. This position could not of course be concealed from the Italian people and indeed the Germans themselves emphasized the point with every publicity. They had even ordered their cinematograph units to take films of the Italians in full flight.[4]

i. *'Our contingent in Russia'* (paragraph 9 of Hitler's letter).
'It has been decided that our Italian Second Army Corps shall remain in Russia. It is however relevant to clarify that our participation must be active and our troops used in the post of honour, namely at the front. Any other task, such as guarding the rear, is not compatible with our military prestige.

'The Germans must produce the equipment for such an active participation so as to reconstitute the units of the Second Corps, in the necessary quantities and quality for the struggle against a heavily armed foe. *Otherwise the Second Corps will also be withdrawn to Italy.'*

In Innsbruck, the Italian Consul-General reported in February that there were 'unsympathetic reports of the military conduct of the Italians on the Don and that there had been attacks on Italian shops in the Tyrolese capital'.[5]

In spite of this situation, Mussolini could not, for reasons of prestige, bring himself to recall the whole Italian armed expeditionary corps. He withdrew the shattered units, and, regrouped with reinforcements, this somewhat smaller military contingent remained, which the Germans now showed marked reluctance to equip.

At a military conference held by Hitler at the 'Wolf's Lair' at Rastenburg about this time. Jodl reported that the Italian High Command had sent a memorandum on the reconstruction of the Italian Army Corps in the East, stating that no more Alpine troops could be sent there. Perhaps, said Jodl, one should follow their wishes. There was need for a good Alpine division in Tunis.

As to rearming the existing Italian divisions in Russia, Hitler intervened, 'I shall tell the Duce that it makes no sense. We give them weapons and it is the same self-deception . . . If we want to equip our twenty-one divisions, we need our weapons . . . We cannot again equip 700,000 Italians . . . I shall tell the Duce that it would be much better to take these units away . . . and get them into shape here in Germany . . . It is no use giving the Italians weapons for building up "an Army", which will lay down its arms at the first opportunity in front of any enemy. It is equally no good equipping an army if one is not sure of its internal security . . . (text illegible) the Duce needs two, four, six, eight divisions gradually to be put at his disposal as a guarantee that nothing will happen internally in Italy. They will be no use outside Italy. I shall not let myself be taken in again.'[j]

The Don disaster was a turning point in the relations between the two countries and indeed the decisive psychological failure in 'Fascist' warfare. The lack of comradeship with the Germans was of course widely felt throughout the Italian armed forces, in particular after the North African campaign of Rommel, but the situation on the Eastern Front was more deep and grave than that. The Germans were fighting a fanatical crusade against Bolshevism, a concept which never really penetrated the Italian military mentality, and the lasting effect of contact between the Italian troops and the Russians was both to give the former a marked respect for the industrial potential of a society with which they were not familiar, and, as the Italian Consul-General in Innsbruck put it (in a dispatch of April 7) 'a feeling of

j. Hitler Military Conference, No. 32. Beginning of March, 1943. Badly damaged fragment. Original in the library of the University of Pennsylvania. Not printed in Gilbert *op cit.*

increased consideration for the (Russian) army and possibly even for Russia'.[6]

The point was even more forcibly made by a private letter written from the Russian front to Bastianini and read and initialled by Mussolini. 'Among the officers of both higher and lower rank a general feeling of rancour and distrust against the regime as responsible for every mistake is generally predominant here. A dangerous anti-Fascist spirit lurks and creeps . . . The majority do not understand that our frontier is today on the Don.' [k]

The recriminations between the two countries were not only confined to the Don disaster. 'Evidence has mounted as to the deterioration of the climate between the two allies' as Bastianini wrote to Alfieri on March 17. 'I am sending you a note [1] which speaks of the bad atmosphere towards us in Germany. I am sending it to you because it is not the only one of its kind, and it is in direct contrast to the idea we had here of Italo-German relations; or rather, of the German state of mind about us. What is the real truth?

'On the other hand we must note . . . that scarcely any of the war materials we asked for have been sent. Now comparing this with the situation in the enemy camp, where material is sent in bulk from the U.S.A. to Russia, and to England, this extreme parsimony about material in the face of our need, and in the common interest, does serious moral and material harm.'

The Germans tended to belittle the successes of their allies. 'I know very well that telling you all this is very like sending "coals to Newcastle" but I only heard these things half an hour ago. I have not yet read your latest reports on this subject, but they seem to be arcadian in comparison with many similar ones I am sending you, so that precise information on this score is particularly desirable.

'Think how very difficult it is to un-poison the minds of our comrades returning from the Soviet battle fields, who tell horrible tales of their sufferings during the full retreat, when they were retreating on foot and fighting, and the others were flying to safer places in motor vehicles (some belonging to the Royal Italian Army)—if, in fact, there was a flight . . . Anyway, I am sure you will know how to use your tact and the necessary sincerity in time to smooth out the atmosphere.' [7]

There was worse to come. On his return from Rome Ribbentrop had conveyed to Hitler the extent of his disquiet at the attitude to the war of the Italian High Command, even to the extent of hinting at the possibility of treason in certain Italian military quarters. It was indeed in part to meet such a threat that a summit meeting of the Fuehrer and the Duce must be

k. Italian Collection. Private letter to Bastianini, April 10, 1943. (Signature illegible.) It is not perhaps without significance that many of the officers and men, particularly from the Alpine divisions in Russia, appear as the leaders of partisan bands in northern Italy at the end of the year.

l. Not included.

held without undue loss of time, and on March 8 Ribbentrop summoned
Alfieri to tell him that Hitler wished to meet the Duce 'as soon as possible,
namely as soon as he could leave the Eastern Front; which would be in ten
to fourteen days or a little later if need arose. The Fuehrer wanted to talk
to the Duce on those specific subjects, which had sharply struck him, Ribbentrop, during his stay in Rome. . . .

'He (Ribbentrop) wanted to tell the Italian Ambassador quite openly that
he had formed a very negative impression of the attitude and mentality of the
Italian High Command. Certain other things had also struck him. The
Fuehrer was of the opinion that the situation could only be remedied by the
Duce if he carried out exceptionally drastic measures. In certain moments the
Fuehrer also had bowed to such a necessity in regard to Germany . . . The
mentality of the High Command was the incubus of the Italian Army. The
Duce had talked about this in confidence to Ribbentrop, and he could tell
Alfieri as an old Fascist and collaborator of the Duce that apparently also
the Duce appreciated the situation. The Fuehrer understood even better, as
he had found himself in similar circumstances. In the winter of 1941, certain
of his generals had come to tell him that it was impossible to hold the occupied regions, to which he had replied that the Army must stay at all costs
where it was, but that the generals must return at once to Germany. One
general, who did not obey the order, and who did not hold on to his position
with his Division, was brought before a court martial in Germany and shot.[m]

'In regard to the Italian army one must not be unfair, in spite of disappoint-
ments. The Italian soldier was fine if well led. The deficiency lay in the
senior officer corps . . . This matter was of vital importance, and Ribbentrop
asked Alfieri to raise the question with the Duce of drastic measures to be
taken after the meeting with Hitler. The old generals must be replaced with
young Fascist officers, even if the latter had not such a good military experience and training. Alfieri remarked that the Duce had often had such
thoughts. But the question was a very difficult one.'

Ribbentrop then revealed the subject of his main anxiety. 'It was only a
step from such a bad military spirit on the part of the generals to a bad
political state of mind. Failed generals mostly wanted to play politics . . . A
general, who is not spiritually one hundred per cent behind the Duce and
does not do everything to bring about the military triumph of Italy, is a
traitor.'[8][n]

There was also both humiliation and resentment on the Italian side. On
March 17, in a minute recording an interview of Alfieri with Steengracht in
Berlin, the latter noted that: 'From the conversations which the German

m. The following passage is deleted in ink from the draft of this minute: 'The Duce
had told Ribbentrop that he had not a single friend; to which the German Foreign
Minister answered that he had a great friend in the Fuehrer.'

n. The original text reads 'is more dangerous than an English agent'. This is deleted
in the draft.

Foreign Minister had had recently both with the Duce and also with Alfieri, it might be that the Duce would raise with the Fuehrer the subject of the Italian army and its achievements. Quite apart from the remarks of the German Foreign Minister, it should be stated that the feeling of the German army and public towards their Italian comrades in arms was subdued. The Duce was considering what could be done to re-establish complete and comradely confidence.' [9]

The 'Russian problem' between the Axis partners must now await discussion at the summit. The parallel issue of Tunisia, however, needed urgent review by military experts. It had been generally agreed, during the Rome talks, that this last African bridgehead must be held and that German aid, probably in the air, might be forthcoming. Mussolini's own conception was broadly that the Mareth line must be held, and the Axis forces built up for an eventual strike westwards in the direction of Morocco with the general hope of Spanish intervention on the Axis side. Rommel, who was still gloomily present in the North African sector, had never subscribed to such a strategic plan. On March 1 a report by him to his commanders was discussed at a meeting in Rome between the Duce, Kesselring, and Ambrosio. Rommel's general view was 'in favour of abandoning the Mareth Line, and retiring to a line further north'. Kesselring was opposed to this, and Mussolini was convinced that 'the loss of Tunisia would be a very grave blow and enable the Anglo-Americans to land on one or other of our own islands'.[10]

But the 'Tunisian problem' was to be discussed on a higher level. Just as Ribbentrop had been sent to Rome to raise the issues arising out of the Russian war, and in particular a possible Allied threat to South-Eastern Europe, now the visit of Goering was announced, presumably to initiate like discussion on the war in Africa.

The first Italian reactions to this familiar visitor were cool. At five o'clock on the afternoon of his arrival on March 8 ° he had an interview with Mussolini. The latter reported to the King that 'in substance Goering had neither added nor detracted from what Ribbentrop had promised. He (Goering) says that, by March 10, a German motorized regiment with much anti-tank equipment will reach Leghorn to be sent to Sardinia, and thence, as soon as possible, to Tunisia.' [11]

On March 13 the Duce mentioned to Kesselring rather cryptically: 'We have had a long talk with Goering on all problems on the agenda, distinguishing clearly between politics and the conduct of operations. At certain moments in fact the conduct of war should not be touched by politics.'

Goering had always regarded himself as the Italian specialist in high German circles, and apart from the problems of the war in Africa, he, like Ribbentrop—whom he had hoped to precede and not to follow in Rome—

o. There is conflicting evidence as to whether Goering arrived in Rome on March 5 or 8.

was anxious to form a first-hand view of the Italian political scene, particularly after the 'changing of the Guard' in February.

He seems to have had at least one private talk with the Duce during this March visit, of which there is no record. The subject of Russia was mentioned, as a letter of March 26 from Mussolini to Hitler shows. 'I have discussed this at length with the Reichsmarshal.'ᵖ

But the open purpose of Goering's visit was again to hector the Italians into a total war effort. As on previous occasions, a meeting was held with Italian technicians, with Goering in the chair. His usual protests against the failure to construct airfields, to repair bomb damage in the ports, to arrange convoy escort, were met 'with timid objections' on the part of the Italian military representatives. It fell to Count Cini, the new Minister of Transport and Communications, to answer sharply by listing the promised German supplies of war material, none or little of which had been sent. [12] Cini himself referred drily to this incident at a conference of ministers a day or two later. It had been 'an inconclusive meeting except for a few points of secondary importance'.[13]

On March 9 Rommel flew to Rome. At a meeting alone with the Duce he expressed his pessimism. 'The situation was very serious.' Enemy preparations against Mareth were far advanced, and the British attack could be expected after March 15. The Duce reiterated that, 'Tunisia must be held at all costs: it is the fortress of Europe and if this falls, the world situation can be definitely altered. The supply situation is first in importance, we are making every effort to get them there. I agree with the Fuehrer that Tunisia must be held. It may be that the enemy will attempt a landing in Sardinia, but more probably in South-East Europe: the enemy is making preparations also in Palestine and Syria. We must therefore resist. If we can improve the supply position, we shall improve the whole situation.'

According to Rommel, the Duce offered another Italian division for Tunis, but the former declined saying that it would be better to equip the existing troops. There were already 300,000 troops (of whom 116,000 were German) and 40,000 air force in Tunisia. [14]

The tone of the interview was cordial, if a little acrimonious at the end.[15] ᑫ Mussolini repeated that one must hold on, 'otherwise an American landing in the South-East—in Greece—may be inevitable'. It was a minor irony that Rommel himself, on the basis of such appreciations, would be sent to Greece at the end of the following July.

Rommel bore no rancour towards the Italian leader. 'Actually, I had always had a great regard for the Duce. He was probably a great actor, like most Italians. He was certainly no Roman, though he tried to act the part.

p. See pp. 216–17 below.
q. Their next meeting under very different circumstances was in October 1943.

Although of a high intellectual capacity, he was far too dependent on his emotions to be able to carry through his ambitious plans . . . Now the Duce saw his dreams crumbling, it was a bitter hour for him, and he was quite incapable of shouldering the consequences. Perhaps I should have spoken differently to him at the end, but I was so heartily sick of all this everlasting optimism that I just could not do it.' [16]

At the end of this interview, the Duce asked Rommel if he had seen Goering. 'I have to call on him later, but I want to leave at once unless I receive orders to the contrary.' But Goering wanted to see him. 'He seems noticeably anxious to come with me to the Fuehrer's Headquarters. I declined the offer as I wanted to make my report without Goering's continual interjections, which, being invariably of an optimistic tinge, were too attractive.'

The meeting between Rommel and Hitler took place on March 10 at the latter's advanced headquarters in Russia. The Fuehrer lay under the shadow of Stalingrad, and defeat increased his delusions. He rejected without discussion Rommel's guarantee to defend 'our southern European flank' with the 'African' troops re-equipped in Italy. 'I would beat off any allied invasion in Southern Europe. But it was all hopeless. He instructed me to take some sick leave and get myself put right so that I could take command later for operations against Casablanca.' [17] Hitler had been reluctant to remove the most popular German Field Commander, even though the conflict of policy in North Africa rendered the decision imperative.

On March 14 Hitler wrote to Mussolini that he had sent Rommel 'on leave for reasons of health as, in the opinion of the doctors, and it is also my personal impression, he needs this urgently . . . I want however to give you, Duce, a personal explanation of the definite reconstruction of the command in Africa. In any case I would ask you, Duce, especially that, on the sending on leave of Marshal Rommel and on the temporary changes in the African command, absolute secrecy is maintained . . . And specially in this case it would be very dangerous for us to divulge the news. I would ask you therefore, Duce, to give instructions in this sense to your various headquarters.

'What is more tragic is that this man, who is among my bravest officers, with exceptional gifts of bearing and courage, should have failed in the problem of supplies, which can only be solved by a massive increase in sea transport.' [18]

It is difficult to appreciate how such a problem at any stage was the responsibility of Rommel. But Hitler seems to have accepted such an unworthy judgment. A month later he told Admiral Horthy at Salzburg, 'The best German General has lost his reputation in Africa through lack of supplies.' [19]

The removal of Rommel had the indirect effect of forcing the unwilling Duce's attention back to the critical issue of supply convoys to North Africa. At the instance of Count Cini, the Minister of Transport and Communications, who was still ruffled at Goering's blustering on the state of Italian ports and communications, a special meeting of the Italian Service Chiefs on March 10 was held at Palazzo Venezia to review the state of the Italian Merchant Navy on which depended the future of not only the last foothold in North Africa, but also the maintenance of the Italian war effort itself.[r] This was the first attempt of a technical civilian minister of the February Cabinet to press for the efficient management of public affairs. Italy was facing a supply crisis, which, as Mussolini said in opening the discussion, 'can in practice paralyse the defence'.

The ensuing debate not only revealed the desperate nature of Italy's position, but also the rumblings of discontent, particularly of Count Cini, at the chaotic and amateurish direction of the war with an implied criticism of the Duce himself.

Cini's task was to open the review of the situation. The state of the merchant navy 'which constitutes the central problem of the war situation, is very grave'. It consisted of 3,300,000 tons in 1940; 560,000 was subsequently acquired from France; the losses as at March 1 stood at 2,200,000. This left 1,470,000: leaving out of account those ships which were laid up or under repair, and also tankers, 595,000 tons remained, and those were mostly slow ships.

'The number that can effectively be used is very small owing to lack of escorts, enemy air and submarine attack, lack of port installations, loading berths, warehouses and railway sidings, of loading and unloading due to the situation of the workers. Military requirements affect this by requiring irrational use of shipping. Sometimes ships have to leave half loaded and return empty. In such a situation we are further faced with an alarming rhythm of sinkings. The average of the last eight months is 50–55,000 tons a month. That of the last two months is 80,000. One should add to this rhythm, an increase in demands for shipping. There is also a transport crisis in being, or rather, should I say, it has been in being for some time.'

In the next four months it was hoped to replace the merchant fleet at the rate of 100,000 tons monthly, and taking into account sinkings, by June 30 the total figure available would be 450,000 tons. By more rational organization this estimate might be improved, but 'the situation cannot be substantially changed. One must consider it in its reality; one must relate programmes to possibilities. This, however, is the concern of the man conducting the war.'

The Duce commented on this survey that 'he is gratified for the clear and explicit exposition which only today, March 10, 1943, is shown in its full reality in contrast to the vague figures which have been hitherto given. We must also not forget that we have been at war for 33 months and have had to supply nearly 300,000 men in Libya. Our losses would have been smaller if

r. Italian Collection. Duce and Ministers, March 10, 1943. There were two such meetings, but there is as yet no record of the second.

we had been able to neutralize Malta . . . In February we carried out only three operations against Malta; these led to a concentration of enemy forces there with a consequent rise in our losses.'

The situation was now reviewed in relation to Italy's military commitments. There were nine theatres to be supplied, of which in present circumstances Tunisia and Sardinia were the most important. The total armed forces involved were 1,250,000 men, and they needed supplying at the rate of 337,000 tons monthly.

'The problem is most serious in Tunisia. 120,000 tons a month are required. Taking into account sinkings at a rate of about 30,000 one should dispatch 180,000 tons . . . Thinking in terms of convoys of ten ships each, we ought to send one convoy every three days, which is impossible.'

In Greece, transport was much delayed because the Balkan railways made a minimum contribution. They also had to supply Crete and the Aegean. They were run by Germany. There was no joint Axis agreement. The result was that the main burden fell on supply by sea.

The Duce interposed that one should increase convoys on the North African run and cut down on the Adriatic run. Use of Balkan railways must be improved. 'One must bear in mind that the forces in Greece will have to be increased.' The new problem was that of labour force and raw materials.

Cini spoke as an experienced leading industrialist. No revolutionary change in the situation could be expected. It would be interesting to hear, after these comments, who is responsible for the conduct of the war.

The Duce 'insists again that one should not think of a revolution in the situation; that would be a dream; it is a matter of keeping afloat, of holding out. He quotes a minute which he had kept, in which figures are given showing that in June, or the latest July, we would have remained without a drop of petrol and fuel. After which date we should have had to seek an armistice. On the contrary, we have remained afloat.

'At the worst today we dispose of 600,000 tons of shipping, and with a loss of 100,000 a month in six months we shall be left with only fishing boats. The essential is to protect our patrimony now while preparing to safeguard what we shall have later. Anyway no one can state that our losses will be at the rate of 100,000 a month.'

Cini 'points out that the present situation is already at the limit of our possibilities'.

It had taken the major disasters of the previous winter to bring about one such revealing meeting. It seems that this occasion created a kind of precedent, for during the following weeks a series of such discussions took place under the Duce's chairmanship to review the process in different departments of government.

On March 30 the Foreign Exchange situation brought to light similar chaos. Bonomi, the Minister involved, asked for further powers in dealing with the other ministries. There was no co-ordination in purchases abroad. For instance, tin from Spain was urgently needed. 'It is bought separately by the various service attachés.

'35 million lire were spent on "intelligence service abroad". There are also the expenses of air intelligence which are three times greater than that of the whole High Command.'

The Duce noted that each year in October/November the financial position had been reviewed at such a meeting. This habit had lapsed. The present deficit was 1,161,000,000 lire. The meeting closed with this remark of Mussolini: 'The important thing is to avoid anyone interfering in someone else's sphere.' s

A series of contacts between the Fuehrer's headquarters and Rome now took place as preliminary soundings on which a summit meeting between the two leaders would be based. Following Goering's return to Germany, Kesselring was also summoned to report to Hitler. On March 13 Kesselring had a meeting with the Duce. 20 The pending conference at Hitler's headquarters was to review the whole position in regard to preserving the Tunisian bridgehead and in particular to overhaul the vital machinery of convoys. As Kesselring told the Duce, 'Admiral Doenitz has also been summoned. He will then return to Rome with him on Monday or Tuesday. Given the presence of Admiral Doenitz, he assumed that the present Mediterranean situation will also be discussed. Before taking leave, Kesselring stressed once again the necessity of increasing by every means shipping for Tunisia.' He also asked whether the Duce had any message for Hitler and was told that it had already been suggested by Mussolini in his letter of March 8 that a meeting might take place at the end of the month or the beginning of April and that Mussolini wanted to discuss the whole situation.

'For my part,' he told Kesselring, 'I consider that the possession of Tunisia is a question of vital importance, and equally the problem of building up Sardinia as a defensive position. Here the Duce stressed his anxiety about an eventual Anglo-American landing in that island; reports from Gibraltar showed that preparations included 4,000 parachutists and other troops, the total of which corresponded roughly to the forces assembled at the time for West Africa.' t

A further Italian division had been sent to Sardinia, which the Duce thought was the most threatened of the islands. The enemy would 'in the next few weeks' launch their offensive in Tunisia. Kesselring's estimate was 'at the next full moon'.

s. There were further meetings on April 3 and 5 on the subject of rail transport.
t. Presumably the Allied expedition against Dakar.

The meeting at Hitler's headquarters took place on the following day, March 14. He gave a concise summary of the 'African problem'.

'Tunisia is strategically of prime importance. The conquest of Tunisia means a saving of four to five million tons and more to the enemy . . . The 80,000 tons per month cited as necessary by the Italian Supreme Command are entirely inadequate; rather, 150,000 to 200,000 tons monthly are needed. We estimate for each division about one train—500 tons daily. For the eight divisions in Tunisia, inclusive of the Italians . . . a total of 4,000 tons daily. It is impossible to supply armies by air . . . Protection of convoys by the Air Force alone is not possible; ships continue to be required. The Straits of Sicily must teem with patrol and escort vessels. Good organization is essential. Only the German navy can organize this . . . It is therefore necessary at the present time to confront the Italians boldly with the alternative of either making an all out effort to get through supplies regardless of personnel considerations, or to lose Tunisia, and with that also Italy.' [21]

Doenitz was to be authorized to present these views to the Duce, and they were embodied in a personal letter from Hitler, which Kesselring was to deliver before the German Admiral arrived. The letter, dated March 14, dealt both with the military situation in North Africa, especially the central nagging question of convoys and supplies.

'. . . Among the questions of great importance which engross me at the present time, the first, Duce, is the preservation, and possibly also the extension of your positions in North Africa . . . On the other hand I cannot refrain from holding the view that all this can succeed and is only possible if the supply problem is faced and resolved in a truly radical manner. This is the decisive factor, Duce; not so much the air weapon as the organization of escort protection . . .

'The solution of this problem, Duce, is of such importance that on it depends the fate of your North African possessions, and that, at the same time, is also an important condition for the victorious conclusion of this war. I am therefore sending to you perhaps the best naval officer that the German Navy has ever had, Grand Admiral Doenitz, to make proposals to you, Duce, which I would ask you to examine solely from the point of view of the necessity of adopting whatever measures are appropriate to settle this most important problem.' [22]

Admiral Doenitz's mission to Rome was to deliver an ultimatum. If the Italians were unable to handle the North African convoys effectively and independently, the Italian naval machine was to be penetrated by German 'experts' and in reality taken over.

The situation was reviewed at a meeting held by the Duce at Palazzo Venezia on March 15. Doenitz approached the subject cautiously by suggesting an exchange of experiences with the Italian navy on convoy work by attaching German naval advisers to the Italian General Staff and in certain ports. German anti-aircraft crews could be installed on Italian escort vessels. It was proposed to hand over seven or eight ex-French vessels now in Bizerta or Toulon, and Doenitz wondered whether they should not be grouped into an all-German convoy escort as an experiment.

The thought of German control by stages of the Italian navy, even though in the last resort the latter was totally dependent on German oil supplies, was inconceivable. Rather than produce counter-arguments, the Duce embarked on a glorious alternative. 'In event of an enemy attack on Sardinia, which I regard as more probable than that against Sicily, I want to bring out the fleet, including the battleships. There is however one great difficulty, lack of fuel oil. I would be very sorry if we were not given this opportunity of attacking the enemy naval forces . . . From reports received it seems that the Anglo-Americans want to land in Tunisia and therefore they will have to protect their convoys and accept battle when our ships appear on the scene. I am prepared to run this risk.' [u]

Doenitz's only limp reply was, 'I will get in touch with Berlin immediately; as I do not know exactly what we have available.' [23]

The Duce was suffering from a fit of optimism. Provided that 'the Russian chapter could be liquidated in some way or other', the Axis would turn to the West and regain the initiative lost the previous autumn. As he wrote to Hitler on March 26: 'It should be realized that the Anglo-American landing in North Africa has been a fortunate move in that it has created a new strategic situation, which allows them to think of carrying out plans which earlier would have appeared fantastic—namely, the invasion of the Continent. That such plans exist and that the enemy is preparing to carry them out, I have not the slightest doubt. Now we have the possibility of converting what was a happy conception and a lucky, not to say easy, enterprise into a catastrophe which could have incalculable consequences on the development of the war, especially in the United States. The Allied expedition to North Africa would become a disaster if the Axis resisted in Tunisia to the end. And it is to make this resistance possible that I have sent you an urgent request for air reinforcements . . .' [v] This must be coupled with a major operation in the rear of the Allies across Spain and into Morocco. The Balearic Islands were to be occupied to give the Axis control of the Western Mediterranean.

The revival of the discarded operational plans of 1940–1 on the creation of a Spanish theatre of war was now to be the magic Italian contribution to

u. Admiral Riccardi added, 'We shall need 18,000 tons of crude oil.'

v. Kesselring reported to the Duce on March 29 that in response to this request Hitler would be sending three air groups to Italy. (Italian Collection. Kesselring-Duce-Ambrosio meeting March 29, 1943.)

a revised Mediterranean strategy, though the mention of a practical Italian military contribution to such an extension of the war is not touched upon.

Mussolini's letter continued: 'The day when the first German armoured unit arrives in the rear of Gibraltar, the English fleet must move out and cannot go to Alexandria (if we still control the Sicily channel). Even without conquering the Rock of Gibraltar we would have—with long-range artillery —control of the straits, and from the air also of all the Atlantic ports which today serve the Americans. Cut off from supplies, the fate of the Anglo-American troops would be sealed. What I propose to you is a bold move, but you have given too many proofs of your audacity for this not to interest you. And after all—since Roman times it has been said—fortune favours the bold.

'It remains to consider—what will Spain do? Nothing. She will not oppose because she cannot, and because such a move is also to her advantage. Spain will let well alone. This manoeuvre, which should of course be like lightning, would restore to the Axis the initiative in that sea which will be decisive for the fate of the war, and will allow Italy to march with Germany to the end.' 24

The mirage of Malta in the previous summer was now replaced by the illusion of a successful operation against Gibraltar, which would decide the war in the Mediterranean.

At least one German witness however was sceptical of the Duce's powers of advocacy. Prince Bismarck, Counsellor at the German Embassy in Rome, told a senior visiting German official, who was preparing the ground for the forthcoming summit talks, 'I do not foresee, on the part of Mussolini, any particular embarrassing request. His fleet does not exist, his army is problematical. His future is even more so. He feels himself to be weak. Even in the past he has avoided raising questions of principle in his various meetings with Hitler, and it is unlikely that he will do so now. Hitler only thinks and talks of military matters, and this is not a favourable platform for Mussolini. One can say of Hitler that he has and does make mistakes, but he has also ended by being competent in military questions. Mussolini has remained a dilettante. Even in this field he sticks to generalities. I can say, since I have seen the minutes of the talks between Mussolini and Hitler, that the Duce has never taken the initiative and never raised general questions as to the political line to adopt.' ᵂ

The long awaited meeting with Hitler had to be postponed 'as a result of the opening of the Anglo-American offensive in Tunisia', but as the Duce explained in his letter of March 26, he ought to be able to get away 'during the coming week'.

w. Italian Collection. In Farinacci's papers in a parcel found in the German Embassy in 1945. Presumably a police or informer's report, dated March 25, 1943.

CHAPTER FIVE

THE HOME FRONT

• •

'THE ITALIAN situation must be carefully examined as far as the Home
Front is concerned, since we can only go on fighting if it holds. Moreover,
any new serious military blows can be borne only if the whole nation is
fully prepared for them.'

One of the Italian informants of the German Embassy in Rome began
with these words a long and comprehensive report on internal conditions in
Italy in February 1943.[a] The 'Changing of the Guard' at the beginning of
the month had but briefly affected the scene. 'It was with a real feeling of
relief that true Fascists heard of the ministerial changes, while anti-Fascists
did not hide a certain interest in the affair.' This dramatic move by Mussolini was intended to demonstrate the strengthening of government action at
the centre, but his solicitude for the retiring ministers, who were all provided
with honorary posts, 'gave rise to the comment that if the Duce had wanted
to throw them overboard he had not the courage to condemn them, and this
strengthened the belief that either he put up with them through weakness or
they really were implementing his wishes and commands'.

The Duce, as was his habit, had shelved responsibility for the darkening
scene at home. The situation was comparable to that of 1917, after the grim
military defeat at Caporetto, but with instructive and basic differences.
During the crisis of the First World War the country was governed under
a parliamentary and party system; in the Second, by a totalitarian régime.
Fascism alone would be responsible for a collapse on the Home Front, and
equally only the 'system' could take steps to prevent such a disintegration.
The Duce 'still enjoyed prestige in many circles', and if he adopted 'a more
energetic conduct, as the lower classes in particular demand', he could regain
'a respect which today is completely lacking'.

a. German Collection. An unsigned and undated report of thirty pages addressed to
Mackensen. From internal evidence it was written in mid-February. The author may
have been Buffarini.

In 1917, military defeat had led to the occupation of three Italian provinces and a direct threat to the vital industrial areas of the North. A million refugees from those territories brought the reality of war to the country as a whole. The disasters of 1942 at Alamein and in French North Africa were the decisive events in the loss of Italy's imperial position on the African continent. The war had not reached the shores of Italy whose metropolitan territory was still intact, and, apart from the demoralizing air bombardment of the main Italian cities, the ordinary Italian was relatively protected from the effects of the war. In 1917 the country was exhausted by general mobilization and her last military reserves and hopes lay in one age group—that of 1899. In early 1943 the bulk of Italy's man-power had not yet been called up.

'Since Fascism is a totalitarian régime it leaves no room for spontaneous patriotic reactions as in 1917. Therefore the régime alone can bring about a recovery, just as it alone can make the collapse of the Home Front fatal, and final defeat inevitable.'

The official war propaganda and measures of Fascist government had signally failed in their purpose. There had been no organized building up of morale. The uncertainties of the period of non-belligerency in 1939–40, the lack of clarification to the public of Italian war aims, the deliberate and hectoring underestimation of the strength of the enemy, and the late introduction of food rationing, together with its corrupt and ineffectual administration, created a general climate of absence from the conflict, and a lurking sense of unalarmed defeatism.

As Mackensen's informant wrote: 'People are saying that this is a transition government, and that Mussolini is going to choose better men. This is the wishful thinking of true Fascists. But they themselves cannot fail to wonder whether while the house is burning, anyone has thought of how to extinguish the blaze once the house is burnt down. For their part, anti-Fascists are taking advantage of the ever-increasing decay in the country, of the lack of authoritative intelligent leaders at the Ministries and in the Party, of a general slackening of public order, to raise a threatening head. And those who do not do so are spreading everywhere the corrosive poison of their defeatist, pro-democratic, anti-German campaign.

'Vidussoni's nomination only stirred a unanimous wave of ridicule from Fascists and anti-Fascists, who found themselves in agreement for the first time. In a country which has been making wars since 1911—the Libyan war—it is quite normal for an Italian to be a veteran, and the heroic loss of an arm is something worthy of great respect but not of political reward. What is more, after Fascism has preached the need for preparing men for posts of leadership however small, the sight of the supreme Party position in the country being entrusted to a young man who has not even taken his degree, as the communiqué announcing his nomination said, and who appears increasingly lacking culturally and mentally, has been and continues to be a cause of very great weakness to the Party. This boy, whom even true Fascists persist in not taking seriously—and therefore the Party whom he impersonates—is surrounded by other young men of no political colour, devoid of ideas and above all out of touch with the present moment . . . Their propaganda is of schoolboy standard, and leaves Fascists unmoved while producing quite contrary effects in other circles.

'The Party today is not respected, its strength is only superficial; Fascists of the old school or those who would like to bring it back to fighting condition are kept at a distance, and sometimes not even intentionally, but because young men who have become party leaders do not and cannot know anything about the Revolution and the men who made it. When the rumour was spread that not even the Duce is satisfied with Vidussoni, that he has been a disappointment to him, the Party Secretary lost his last follower, and with him the Party passed into the second rank, while it still keeps all the organizations which should today be functioning at full strength, so that Italy is facing the battle for the home front with no political organization at all. The regional situation reflects that at the centre. Everything leads one to suppose that at this rate the Party will shortly not even be in a position to keep its own members loyal, and discipline itself, superficial and choreographic, is tolerated with more and more impatience and less and less respect.

'Since the country's political and social activities are entirely incorporated in the Party, it is easy to imagine what an abandoned and decadent state they are in, with very obvious detrimental effects to resistance on the home front.'

This devastating analysis reveals the basic failure of Italian Fascism to capture the loyalties of the second generation. The same writer also gives a revealing picture of the effect of this cardinal weakness of the system as it affected in particular the élite of the 'second wave', the student youth, of whom Vidussoni, in spite of his academic failings, was intended to be the symbol. Despite their incorporation in the Fascist youth and university para-military organizations, which had been the pride of Starace and Ricci, these young men displayed 'very little Fascist feeling. The older classes up to 1910, whether called up or not, show a certain amount of seriousness and understanding. The really young, the students, are easily influenced by the atmosphere, which just now is not over-favourable to Fascism among the middle classes to which these students belong. When the figure of the Duce appears on the cinema screen, only the proletariat, young men in their thirties, and one or two from the lower middle classes, applaud. The very young are silent, more indifferent than hostile, even if that morning they were wearing Fascist uniforms. The widespread opinion of these youngest generations is that Fascism should be purely profitable: this mentality does not make for willing sacrifices. There are brilliant exceptions, but against these the mass of the young is at least detached from Fascism when it does not adopt—even if on the Party registers—Bolshevik tendencies favoured by the climate in intellectual circles.'

The responsibility for the maintenance of order and morale lay, however, with the machine and leadership of the Party rather than with the heads of the various ministries, and in the former sphere there was spreading a climate of frustrated alarm under the lengthening shadow of military disaster. Increasing reports of discontent in high Fascist circles reached Palazzo Venezia. The Duce was never short of information or informers. The files of his secretariat had accumulated, since the beginning of the régime, an indiscriminate mass of intelligence and gossip. The human game involved, and the individual weaknesses exposed, appealed to his sardonic humour, and his own intuitive judgment of men was rarely affected by the flow of denunciation and hearsay which passed daily across his desk. The Party dossiers, and the police reports which from an independent angle supplemented them, were among the most revealing comments on the climate of the régime.

On February 16 one such report was sent to Palazzo Venezia, drawing attention to disquiet in Party circles at Vidussoni's 'lack of capacity, which each day is further emptied of any meaning'.[1] The Party Directorate was the centre of strife: 'The poetaster Ravasio (one of the Party Vice-Secretaries) leaving Rome every now and then like an hysterical woman . . . making no mystery of the fact that he declines all responsibility, seeing that the Party comes to no decisions and is lost in idle chatter. The effect of this attitude of a Vice-Secretary, who was believed by all to have the confidence of the Duce—(he was the Dictator of the official Fascist review *Gerarchia*)—has a bad effect even among intransigent Fascists. Ravasio spends his time denigrating Vidussoni. His accusations are met with approbation and in effect they correspond to the truth. Vidussoni limits his functions to visiting the wounded in hospital, football and boxing matches. He does not know the business or the personalities of the Party. The questions which people are asking are: "Why does the Duce, who has so much human material at his disposal . . . keep at the head of the Party a boy of twenty-six, who does not know men or business or can make speeches or organize, and who has no ability of a political character?"'

'Why doesn't the Duce place in positions of leadership men who have already had a following in the provinces and in the nation? The Federal Secretary of Naples, for example, has no hold on the masses. He is one of the young men transferred from one province to another "like railwaymen". A possible answer has been the nomination of Tarabini and Scorza, both old members of the action squads, at the centre of affairs. But independently of the fact that Tarabini is regarded among the old leaders as a nullity, and Scorza has been given a secondary sphere from a political point of view, their inclusion has made a bad rather than good impression. Vidussoni and Farnesi, the senior Vice-Secretary, regard the two as possible candidates for their succession, especially Scorza, and are out to sabotage them. The picture presented is the reason why the Party does not exist.'

On a sterner and more practical note, another 'Memorandum for the Duce' referred to the Party directive of November 1942, calling on members to help with the grain harvest. A corps of inspectors had been supplied by the Party Directorate. This document throws an unusual light on the impotence and chaos resulting from conflicting jurisdictions in local administration in time of war.

'The President of the Fascist Confederation of Agricultural Workers has a programme of action, namely, a more energetic repression of breaches of the law, and the searching of farms for concealed stocks. The Party is against such drastic measures as yet, but proposes that: —
1. The Ministry of the Interior should give all Prefects authority to search homes.
2. The Ministry of Justice should order magistrates to be more severe in cases of hoarding.
3. The Ministry of Corporations should instruct its local offices to requisition transport and tyres.
4. The organizers and officers of the Fascist confederations should be used at least temporarily to organize collection of grain.
5. The Militia, the Military Police, and the Finance Guards should support searches.'

The passive resistance of the agricultural masses was matched with the failure of the Fascist industrial confederations to control the industrial workers. Although wages had been nominally blocked in 1940, labour was short, particularly in the war industries, and employers would pay illegal rates. The workers tended to ignore the syndicates and make their own terms.[2]

The whole structure of the Corporate State, so pompously advertised in the 1930's, was coming apart at the seams, and together with the failure of economic regulation of prices, productivity, and supply at the ministerial and Party level provoked the internal crisis on the Home Front parallel to, and accelerated by, the successive disasters in the military conduct of the war.

It was such a situation which was characterized even by the Political Police as 'the progressive degeneration of the State'.[3]

Intensive Allied bombing of the Northern industrial cities added to the disruption of economic life, and to the general spirit of defeatism and discontent. There had been rioting at the departure of certain troop trains for the

Russian front, and, between August 1942 and February 1943, sporadic strikes throughout the industrial centres of Northern Italy.

The rationing situation, placed fatally in the hands of the Party and its organizations, was alarming. Food prices had risen from an index of 100 in 1939 to 172 in 1942. At a private meeting of the Fascist Syndicate leaders in October 1942 in Milan, their leader Malusardi said, 'Wages are lower by not less than 5·80 lire a day in relation to the official cost of living.' And at the same period the Duce himself had telegraphed to the Milan authorities: 'In the great industrial centres the hardship from the point of view of food supplies is becoming increasingly acute.' [b]

At the beginning of March there was a sudden explosion. At 10 o'clock on the morning of March 5, the workers at the large Fiat Mirafiori factories downed tools. The prearranged signal was to be the daily testing at that hour of the air-raid sirens. The management had however been warned, and no test took place. But within a few minutes all work stopped throughout the plant, and the news spread through Turin. Although Fascist militia units had been standing by since dawn, as the authorities expected some planned demonstration, no immediate counteraction was taken. By that evening the strike had spread to seven other factories in Turin. On March 8 the local secretary of the Fascist Confederation of Industrial Workers had cabled the new Minister of Corporations in Rome, Tullio Ciannetti, that token strikes at 10 o'clock that morning had involved between 30–35,000 workers. By March 12 over 100,000 had come out.[c] The following day, secret meetings of the strike leaders were held in Turin at which economic demands of the strikers were discussed, and the drafting of leaflets decided, calling for a continuation of the movement and its extension to other regions. On March 14 the underground committee of the Italian Communist Party for Lombardy met in Milan to hear a report on the events in Turin and Piedmont. In the following days the agitation ranged through Lombardy. The call to strike was announced in Milan on the 24th, and the Pirelli and Falk works followed the example of Turin. Over 130,000 workers seem to have been affected, and the key war industries of the country were temporarily disorganized.

Behind the economic demands for a paid 192-hour month, a cost of living bonus, and increased rations, lay traces of concerted political agitation. The Fascist authorities had been aware of the increasing activities of clandestine

b. U. Massola, *Marzo 1943. Ore 10*, pp. 7 & 13 and *passim*. (The documents on which this book is based were drawn from the archives of the Fascist Confederation of Industrial Workers.) The author of this brief but detailed study was the underground organizer for the 'Internal Centre' of the Italian Communist Party. He had returned from Switzerland in August 1941. See also Luraghi, *Il Movimento Operaio Torinese durante la Resistanza, passim*.

c. This is a subsequent Communist estimate. Other sources mention a figure of 40–50,000.

groups during the course of the previous year. Although the main leadership of the illegal Communist Party was either in exile or under arrest, cells had been strengthened, and the underground press re-established.[4] The attention of the police had been particularly drawn to the intensive leaflet propaganda circulating in the previous January and February in the industrial areas of the North, and the Communist paper *Unità* had reappeared since June 1942. It was also logical that Turin should be the historic centre of a revival of political action again Fascism, with the memories of the civil conflicts of 1920. A National Action Front had appeared there at the end of 1942, and an appeal was published in *Unità* on December 27 calling for a separate peace and directed particularly towards 'soldiers, officers, militiamen and honest Fascists'.[d] This Front was in effect a liaison committee linking together the small groups of the old anti-Fascist parties, the Communists, Socialists, and 'Justice and Liberty'.[e]

The frame was established on Communist initiative, and their few cadres planned the militant strike action of March. The Front itself held no regular meetings and played no part, as such, in the strikes. It was primarily a symbolic signatory of leaflets, and an intermittent secret forum for exchanging ideas and programmes. The Italian Communists were particularly concerned to act as the initiators, and indeed organizers of a Popular Front, but not as an isolated group. Although the myth of these strikes appears in Communist historiography as an exclusive achievement, the figures from their own sources are a striking endorsement of their own tactical intentions at the time. The key strike, initiating the whole movement, which broke out at the Fiat Mirafiori works had been planned the previous month by the leader of the Communist cell there. Out of 21,000 workers, there was a cell of 80 members, none of whom paid regular party subscriptions until the following May, and in three other leading Turin factories the cell membership at that time was 30, 72 and 60 respectively.[5] The essential significance of the movement was that by the action of such small cadres a mass explosion was generated, with decisive effect upon the structure and prestige of Italian Fascism.

The reaction of the Fascist authorities revealed even more faithfully than the phenomenon of the strike movement itself the weaknesses of the régime. The Chief of Police, Carmine Senise, describes the situation in his memoirs: 'The strikes were proclaimed for economic motives, but with political aims, particularly as the factories where the workers folded their arms were all engaged in war production. We had wind of this strike some twenty days previously, as I had got hold of certain instructions issued by the Communist

d. On the whole subject of these strikes and the links with revived anti-Fascist activity see the brilliant and detailed study of Vaccarino 'The Strikes of 1943' in *Aspetti della Resistenza in Piemonte*, pp. 3–40.

e. The Socialist-Liberal group in exile in France founded in 1929 by Carlo Rosselli.

Party. I took these personally to the Duce, who read them carefully and kept them . . . Although forewarned, it was obvious that the Police could do nothing to forestall it. I do not know what action the Corporative organs took, but can only think that the Duce must have given some instructions, if only to observe the attitude and state of mind of the workers, all of whom belonged to the syndicates. The notable fact was that everyone took part in the strike, Fascist and non-Fascist, even those who were members of the Militia. At the Fiat in Turin there was a special Legion [f] composed entirely of workers in their factories, set up by agreement between the Party and the management with the aim of controlling the political behaviour of the masses. These militiamen took part in the strike like all the other workers, and one cannot possibly imagine that they did not understand the aims of a movement which had an obvious political character and was opposed to the war.

'The Head of the Government never summoned me to report during the strike, but only telephoned me every morning to ask for the latest reports from the local chiefs of Police . . . I do not know what instructions he gave . . . He did, however, consult Albini [g] every day, and the latter in turn conferred with the Prefects by telephone.'[6]

Such instructions as were given were not draconic. As the Vice-Secretary of the Party, Scorza was sent to Turin on March 17 and visited the party sections at Fiat, but had no contacts with the workers as a whole. All Fascist Party members were now ordered to wear black shirts at their places of work. On March 27 the leaders of the Fascist syndicates met in Milan, and were addressed by their local head, Malusardi, who stressed the political character of the agitation, and threatened the strikers that they would be treated as mutineers. In fact they were technically under military law. But the official attitude was 'soft'. Some strikers were mobilized and sent to Sicily. Some 300 were arrested in Milan. 164 were likewise picked up in Turin, and 87 charged. Directions to the Prefects were concentrated on Communist activities, and the police were instructed to keep watch on what lay behind 'the pretext of economic concessions', and to observe with particular attention military circles where the Communist movement 'hoped to set up armed groups'.[7]

The leader of the original Fiat strike was caught with some thirty com-

---

f. The Militia legion '18 Novembre'. See Vaccarino. Article on 'The Workers' Movement in Turin' in *Movimento di Liberazione in Italia*, No. 19, p. 13, footnote 14. (The historical journal of the Istituto Nazionale per la Storia del Movimento di Liberazione in Italia.) The Fascist militia had their own 'Political Investigating Office'. One of their reports, dated March 1943, on 'Political Subversion' is quoted by its commander, Galbiati, in his book, *op cit* pp. 159–161, and refers to the 'vast programme of mass agitation organized by Communists without hiding the political aims of the action, and aiming at creating a favourable atmosphere for disturbances of a clearer political nature'.

g. Mussolini was nominally Minister of the Interior. Albini had succeeded Buffarini in February 1943 as the Under-secretary.

panions. The police realized that they were facing an organization directly working for a collapse of the Home Front. In the report to the Chief of Police in Rome, the head of the Public Security in Milan stated: [8] 'The results of the operation, both from the capture of propaganda material, and from the confessions of the majority of the accused, prove objectively that the reconstruction of the Turin Communist Party has taken place, personally directed by an emissary of the party so far unidentified, and that the subversive work undertaken by it aims at destroying the national structure, inciting the working masses and even the army against the war and the German ally, to rouse the people against the régime, and against the powers of the State.' [h]

This emphasis on the role of the Communists in popular agitation was both a familiar tactic of the Fascist authorities, and an expression of the fear of a historic bogey created in the past by themselves to justify the original take-over of power. The response of the masses to action by a handful of conspirators was in reality more alarming than the party allegiance of that minority, and the consequent revelation of the weakness of the hold of the Fascist Party on those masses revealed more effectively than ever before during the history of the régime, the hollowness of the achievement of the Corporate State. Cianetti, the Minister of Corporations, and as such the most actively challenged of the members of the government, later described his visit to Milan:

'When as an old syndical organizer I confronted thousands of workers who immediately went back, although the Fascists showed themselves to be completely passive in the workshops and in some cases had even fomented the strikes, this latter phenomenon impressed me enormously and made me see that there was something which was wrong, and I returned to Rome with the precise conviction that one must put on the brakes a little.' [9]

But the significance of these March strikes is perhaps most harshly and clearly stated in a letter from Farinacci to Mussolini on April 1: 'I have seen the demonstrations of the workers in Milan though naturally standing in the background. I have remained profoundly embittered both as a Fascist and as an Italian. We have not been capable of taking either preventive or repressive action, and we have violated the principle of authority of our régime. In Milan

h. Another significant comment on the March strikes from the Fascist side is contained in a covering letter of April 15 from the Turin Police headquarters to the Special Tribunal in Rome, outlining the charges against 87 workers under arrest. 'Under the pressure of impelling circumstances it is relevant to mark down for severe repression with all the vigour of the law a real and proper seditious movement, staged with the pretext of bitter economic conditions in the different factories of this province, but in fact a movement which is without doubt the echo and the practical embodiment of the principles of disorder under the auspices of the enemies of the régime, as is clear from the manifestations of their propaganda.' (Quoted by Vaccarino from the Turin Police archives in his article *op cit* p. 19, note 4.)

events have deprived the local Party Secretary of any authority, though he is a fine comrade and brave fighter, but without the strength to dominate that situation. And then there is Liverani of the industrialists, and Malusardi of the workers [i] who did not know how to avoid what has happened, and then were unable to get themselves taken seriously by the workers.

'If they tell you that the movement has assumed an exclusively economic aspect, they are telling you a lie. The attitude of the workers at Abbiategrasso [j] in front of Cianetti is eloquent, as also the flowering of leaflets clandestinely printed, which give the demonstrations a deliberately and preordained anti-Fascist character. The few arrests do not count. One must have the courage to make an example which will give the workers in other factories and cities something to think about. We must not worry about what Radio London or Moscow may say, but about how to maintain the solidarity of the internal front and the prestige of the government.

'As to the State administration, you will admit that it does everything to make trouble for you. For the last three months the industrialists themselves have been saying how necessary it is to do something for the workers and you yourself were aware of this. But the Confederations, and the whole machinery, have moved at a snail's pace. And now I . . . take the liberty of proposing to you that you make an example both at the top and the bottom, but at least fairly high up, and do not always take on yourself the responsibilities for the mistakes of others.

'And do not rebuke me if once again I repeat to you that the Corporative experiment with all its innovators, improvisers, doctrinaires and demagogues has not succeeded in the spirit of our political faith and according to our aims. One must leap to the defence, and force the organizers of the war effort away from their grand ministries, among their secretaries, typists and assistants, into contact with the masses. Naturally for this we need capable and honest people who are able to make speeches and have a certain physical bearing. You know from experience that the masses want to receive a certain magnetic influence from their orator . . . If *you* were talking to a crowd of Bolsheviks or priests, you would get them to clap before you opened your mouth.

'The Party is absent and impotent . . . And now the unbelievable is happening. Everywhere, in the trams, the theatres, the air-raid shelters . . . people are denouncing the régime, and not only this or that party figure, but the Duce himself. And the most serious thing is that no one reacts. Even the police do not function, as if their work was now useless. We are facing a period when military events may become agonizing. Let us defend our revolution with all our strength . . .

'My dear Prime Minister, why do you not summon the Grand Council?

i. Representing respectively the Fascist employers and workers syndicates.
j. A small industrial town near Milan.

Let everyone give vent to his feelings, speak his mind, and come away comforted by your words.' [10]

Here was the first call to a review by the Fascist leadership at the summit, above the Party secretariat, of the internal scene in Italy. The 'system' was facing the greatest political crisis in its history since the murder of Matteotti and, as in 1942, Farinacci incarnated within the higher ranks of Fascism the demand for harsh measures.

His proposal for the summoning of the Grand Council was the first such move in 1943, and it was not until three months later, when the military situation reached the final edge of disaster, that Mussolini yielded to the request.

The National Party Directorate met on March 11 under the direct shadow of the strikes in Piedmont and Lombardy, of increased allied air attack on Italian cities, and of vague but verifiable signs of overt criticism of the régime. The Duce's traditional opening speech was more truculent than usual, and deliberately played down the unrest in the industrial North. He was perhaps not yet aware of its extent and implications. It was not a pungent oration, as he was not yet convinced of the need of another purge in the Party secretariat, and he was anxious to avoid drastic public changes, following so soon on the ministerial reshuffle of the previous month. He was also anxious not to increase still further the already lively preoccupation of the Germans with the Italian Home Front.

His speech was, however, as always a subtle amalgam of the gusts of public opinion, as seen through the prism of the gossip, rumours, and police reports which represented the information, scanned and selected by the Duce, and on which he based his political judgment.

'Some people complained recently of the Party's lack of activity in various manifestations of Italian life. Evidently many of these critics forget that 1,387,000 of the enrolled members of the Party are in the forces. It is clear that if these members were at home the general activity of the Party would be more intense. On the other hand, at times like the present the Party must have only one simple essential object—to keep the home front steady.

'At our last meeting [k] the main points of discussion were the following: the Russian campaign and the bombing of Italian cities. The Russian winter campaign has had various psychological effects, so have the American landings in Algiers. There were some people with weak nerves, and some people who are the scum of the earth, who thought that when the Americans disembarked they would be much nearer us in four or five days.

'Thus when the Russians overran first the Roumanian front, secondly the Italian, thirdly the Hungarian, and each time the German front, these people

k. On January 3, 1943.

thought that Stalin would arrive at Longatico.[1] This was absurd. I never doubted that the Germans would succeed in first halting the Bolsheviks and secondly taking the initiative . . . What happened then? A large number of Italians, who at first were afraid that the Germans would win, showed a remarkable instinct for self-preservation . . . Some Fascists wished to belittle the work of Fascism during this war; they seemed to say "this is not a Fascist war, that is an accusation brought against us by our enemies, this is Italy's war". We must react energetically against this attitude . . . It has been said that this is Italy's war because it is Fascism's war, and that it is Fascism's war because it is Italy's war. I reject distinctions of this kind. Even if they are made, do not believe that they will have any effect on our enemies: they will continue to say that this war was desired by me, Mussolini, because I am a friend of Hitler . . . As regards the spiritual attitude of Italians, if you look for enthusiasm among any of the people engaged in this war you will not find it. This war is one which goes behind individual feelings and thoughts . . . This demand for enthusiasm is idiotic. We must rather see that discipline prevails. It would be absurd to lament a few scattered events.

'Organized movements of any kind have only recently taken place. One at Milan was slightly serious because attacks on the régime were planned. Finally one was liberal-communist in character. Some people realized that a people cannot be content, consequently they invented a name, "liberal socialism" or "social liberalism".[m] Anyhow, just recently there appeared in Turin the first sign of a combined workers' movement. Here are the reasons for it. Evacuation pay was given to the families of evacuated workers. At a certain point workers who remained demanded an equal increase of wages. In general I have always been opposed to doing this, and at present I assert firmly that we must not give a single cent. We are not a liberal state which can be black-mailed by one hour's stoppage of work in a factory. I consider such payment as real treachery . . . Thirty years ago the programme which we have quietly carried out for the Italian workers was considered to be an extreme socialist programme. We do not ask for any gratitude for this . . . but if these men abandon their work at a time like this, when the whole life of the nation is at stake, if they do not pull themselves together in the shortest possible time, they will be treated as one treats those who leave their post of duty at the front.

'The Secretary of the Party has given the figures of enrolled members. Members are one thing, Fascists are another . . . We must purge the Party, because now, as in 1924,[n] individuals who have no courage think they win merit by disappearing so that they may be forgotten. However, it is certain that we do not forget them.

l. A small seaside resort near Rome.
m. The anti-Fascist movement associated with the names of the Rosselli brothers.
n. After the murder of Matteotti in 1924 there was a mass flight from the Fascist party ranks.

'As regards the young, we must be very careful. The great mass of young people is all right, but there are certain tendencies which demand our attention; for instance, this lack of interest in the history of world events and this listening to foreign voices. Further, it is essential that during and immediately after air attacks the Party should be present. Fascists must regard themselves as soldiers or rather as fighters . . . As for criticism, Italy is an extraordinary country. Newspapers can say what they like . . . Recently an article appeared in which attention was drawn to the possibility of a compromise peace with remarks addressed particularly to the Anglo-Saxons . . . This article made a great impression, and made people think that the Italian people were tired and hoped for a compromise peace. In peacetime I am indifferent to anything that may be said of me, of the régime, of Italy and of Fascism. But in war it is a different matter, because what is said may raise the morale of the enemy . . . The newspapers talk about everything; I do not object, but they must be intelligent. The Government does not consist of infallible beings . . . We sometimes make mistakes in our planning. Sometimes the people wait a long time for interesting plans of ours to be put into effect.

'What I wish to stress is that there is no substitute for the Party which constitutes the necessary link between State and People . . . The State must keep in touch with the People, for our State is not a police or absolute state, not a monarchy which says "This is my pleasure" . . . In war-time the people have justifiable susceptibilities, and non-fighting Fascists must not lay themselves open to criticism from the people who are suffering . . . That which belongs to the State is one thing, that which belongs to its citizens is another. Now there is a tendency among many people to confuse these things, to indulge in some small profiteering, making use of one's political career. This is a very bad thing. Sometimes it is not a negligible matter. For instance, there is this mania for trafficking . . . It is bad enough when it is carried on in Italy, but much worse when done by soldiers abroad as it was in Croatia, Dalmatia, Albania, and now is in France. It is very bad for the country's prestige . . . As a country we still suffer from the common phrases used to describe us three centuries ago . . . We have fought, we have built the swiftest ships in the world, we have built whole cities and produced heroes who would honour the greatest peoples, but we cannot free ourselves from the old epithets of sellers of statuettes and organ-grinders.'°

The impression of Mussolini's speech and of the situation which it reflected was less comforting to some at least of the Party leaders. Bottai noted in his diary on the same day, March 13: 'Rumours and more than rumours of an imminent crisis in the Party. One asks what man could, at the point which we

o. Italian Collection. These speeches of the Duce at the regular meetings of the Fascist Party Directorate were considered to be strictly private and were seldom prepared beforehand. This particular speech is also printed in Mussolini, *Opera Omnia*, Vol. XXXI, pp. 159 ff.

have reached, restore life and movement to this heavy and cumbersome body. "Both too late and too soon" was the answer of someone to whom I talked. And it is so; too late in regard to the war-time crisis, which does not allow those profound changes of direction and structure capable of persuading the country of the existing political and moral validity of Fascism; too soon for the post-war crisis which will involve a total transformation of men and ideas.' [11]

The German Embassy in Rome had for some time received a prompt if truncated report on each occasion of this valuable first-hand evidence of the Duce's appreciations of the moment. In so far as he ever expressed to an audience his unfettered thoughts, he seems to have done so on these occasions, and this series of speeches seems therefore to represent the most valuable evidence of all the current mood and preoccupations of the Head of the Italian Government.

On the next day, March 12, Mackensen sent the following telegram to the German Foreign Office: 'In spite of the strong rule of silence, a member of the Directorate of the Fascist Party, solely because of his friendly attitude to the Reich, has transmitted some information from yesterday's meeting of the Directorate on the improvised statements made by the Duce on Italy's internal and external position . . . The Duce's remarks are a clear proof that he has expressed, not only for us Germans, but also for that circle of men on whose co-operation he is primarily dependent his unbending will to fight the war to the end on our side, and his unshaken faith in a common final victory . . . In view of the absolute necessity to avoid giving this strictly confidential communication any office circulation at all, I ask that as an exception it should be transmitted as a direct report.'

This telegram was shown to the Fuehrer personally by Ribbentrop the next day, and the latter minuted by hand in the margin. 'The Duce is still the only *man* in Italy.' [12] But this unexpected phenomenon of the March strikes came as a disagreeable reminder to the Germans of the fragility of the Italian political front. Hitler, at a Military Conference,[p] expressed his dismay at the stoppage of work in Turin, 'Yes, and note—for wage increases'. Jodl interjected: 'Communist manoeuvres'. Hitler exploded: 'But that it is possible for people to stop work firmly in eight factories is for me unthinkable. And then no one dares to intervene. They have put a stop to it—but even so, after hesitating whether or not to intervene in a radical manner. I am convinced that if one shows the slightest weakness in such a case, one is lost. But that is what I am saying the whole time.'

p. Hitler Military Conference No. 32. Undated, but from internal evidence clearly the middle of March. The typescript is damaged by fire. Not published in Gilbert, *op cit*. The original is in the Library of the University of Pennsylvania, U.S.A.

The German Consul-General in Milan, reporting later on the strikes, noted that 'the impression is given that the movement has been centrally controlled'. German Collection. Milan telegram, March 29, 1943.

If the Fascist régime in Italy collapsed, were there extreme elements loyal to the Axis on whom the Germans could depend to maintain the war effort?

German penetration of Italian Fascist circles, and indeed intelligence on Italian political affairs, was superficial and uncoordinated. Himmler's organization, as represented by Dollmann in Rome, nurtured a circle of 'friends', mutually disloyal and of secondary importance in the hierarchy. It was not until the spring of 1943, and conceivably as a result in part of the March strikes, that the German Security Service was allowed to operate directly on Italian territory and was able to report from its own secret wireless station from Rome on the spreading signs of conspiracy against the personal régime of the Duce.[13]

CHAPTER SIX

THE ROYAL SECRET

'AS FROM January, 1943, I took the definite decision to put an end to the Fascist régime and to dismiss the head of the government, Mussolini. The carrying out of this precaution was made more difficult by the state of the war, and had to be both prepared in the smallest detail, and conducted in the utmost secrecy, which was also respected by the few persons who came to talk to me of the discontent of the country. You were aware of my decisions and personal directions, and you know that these alone, from January 1943 onwards, led to the following July 25.'[a]

In theory it should be possible for the King to dismiss his Prime Minister without disagreeable consequences, but although the constitutional myth of the Monarchy had survived the successive violations of Fascist legislation, no one knew in practice what would follow such an assertion of the royal prerogative. The Prime Minister was also the Duce of Fascism. The dyarchy of Monarchy and Party marked the point where the political revolution had stopped, and it was this dualism of loyalties which generated the confusion of the Italian scene.

If, when all else failed, the Crown should be forced to take political action, would the Party accept the decision? If the Monarchy was driven by external events into the centre of Italian political life, from which it had withdrawn in 1922, the whole balance of forces in the régime would be inevitably changed, and the beneficiaries of Fascism might in their turn revert, as twenty years earlier, to the panaceas of illegality. The retired revolutionaries might find themselves called up. This eventuality was ever present in the calculation of

a. This letter, purporting to be from the King of Acquarone, is undated, but if textually accurate, was written in the South after the event at the end of 1943. It is published in two pro-monarchist works, Ugo D'Andrea, *La Fine del Regno,* p. 406, and in Pietro Silva, *Io Difendo la Monarchia,* p. 160. It is also quoted by Paolo Monelli, *Roma 1943,* p. 83.

the entourage of the King, and the shadow of a Fascist counter-coup lies henceforth over each move and sounding of the Court.

Nor could the internal political scene be considered separately from the military. The fate of the régime was conditioned by the course of the war. The very problem of the intervention of the Crown was posed by the mounting threat of the greatest national disaster since the collapse of the Italian front at Caporetto in 1917. Only extreme circumstances, threatening military collapse and political chaos, which would involve the monarchy itself, could induce the King to act.

So long as there was any hope that the war situation could be restored, no such action would be envisaged. But in an atmosphere of rising pessimism, the whole range of possible solutions must be studied, and each related to the peculiar structure of the régime as conditioned historically by twenty years of Fascism. The historical significance of the present crisis was the undoing of the consequences of the March on Rome.

The political future of Mussolini depended on the successful conclusion of hostilities, which was remote unless, at least as a first stage, Hitler could be induced to liquidate the Eastern Front; or on the even more improbable negotiation of an acceptable compromise peace with the Allies, with or without German consent. The development of the internal political scene in the coming months would be governed by these postulates, and every move must be observed and studied within the privileged enclave of the Royal circle.

The Minister of the Court, Duca Acquarone, as the King's main adviser and confidant, would have to be the most accurately informed on the intricate interplay of political affairs both within the Fascist Party and machinery of government, among the retired elder statesmen and Army marshals, and to be aware of the lineaments of a clandestine opposition. And in particular he must keep in close touch with the General Staff and the governing circles of the Armed Forces. It might be that military events would force brutally on the Crown a decision in adverse internal circumstances, and some elementary precautions would have to be taken. In this sense it is possible to trace the rudimentary frame of an emergency royalist coup d'état.

Ambrosio, as Chief of the General Staff, reported daily to the Duce, on whose reactions everything depended, and there was always a hope that a top-level solution of the war might still be found.

In a subsequent statement after the event, Ambrosio said: 'It is not completely true that in the early days of my appointment as Chief of the General Staff I had already drawn up a plan for immediate action, or shall we say, forcible action. I certainly knew our military situation well: I realized that it was desperate. But my initial hope was to be able to persuade Mussolini to make a rapid "disengagement" from the Germans.' [1]

Among the officers attached to the Supreme Command was General Castellano. He had been involved in routine military planning since February 1942, but with the changes following on Ambrosio's appointment he undertook, in part on his own initiative, the task of keeping in touch with the world of politics. He already knew Ciano, with whom he had been in contact through another politically-minded young General, Carboni. After the February changes, Castellano came in closer touch with Acquarone.

Shortly afterwards the former drafted a plan for the removal of Mussolini, listing the measures to be taken to avert a Fascist counter-coup, the action to arrest Mussolini and the Party leaders, and the military plans to be put into effect against a German reaction. According to Castellano, both Ambrosio and Acquarone saw a copy of this draft, and Ciano knew of its contents. Castellano's superiors seem to have advised caution, and he settled down to cultivating political and diplomatic circles in Rome.

The corridors of the Fascist Senate in these weeks were the scene of active speculation. Here was one of the few places where the small group of ageing survivors of former governments and the commanders of other wars, the remnants of the political élite of the days before the March on Rome, could meet with impunity and exchange impressions of the increasingly fragile Italian scene. Outside the circle of the Court, here was perhaps the only place where a discreet club vintage anti-Fascism could be audibly voiced, although the open debates were unanimous in their sycophancy. Here in a fragmented prism could still be discerned the historical shape of an earlier political world, that of the Ultras of a future Restoration.

On February 23 the King received a survivor of this generation, General Zuppelli, who had been Minister of War in 1915, and was now a Senator. 'He is an old man of eighty-four, and a little afflicted with age. He spoke to the King in an excited and agitated manner, advising him to support a coup d'état and chase Mussolini out "on his two feet".' At the end of the audience, the King was 'rather annoyed' and told General Puntoni, 'The situation is serious, but not desperate . . . A new element could intervene and radically change situations from which there appears to be no way out. In any case a coup d'état at this moment against the Duce and the régime, with Germany in the house and at the gates, is completely inopportune.'[2]

Constitutionally, the Senate was the only surviving organ of the pre-Fascist State, and in theory could be the focus of a potential National Front. But behind the outward forms of an inviolate enclave within the 'system', lay the broad reality of senile subservience. The body had long been in the main infiltrated and packed by beneficiaries of the régime.

As Marshal Caviglia noted in his diary: ' . . . The present situation can be managed either within the Party or the Senate. If the Senate were more independent, if it were not so subservient to Mussolini, it could easily settle the situation. But as it is not independent, one would have to find a hundred senators, more concerned with the fate of Italy than of Mussolini . . . Let these hundred senators make a collective request to the President of the Senate to call on the government in plenary session to expound the conduct of the war, and to define what are the national interests which inspire the administration, for there is no doubt that the interests of the State must be clearly separated from those of Mussolini. But perhaps it will not be possible to persuade a hundred senators to adopt with courage such an attitude.'[3]

The possibility of a rift within the Fascist Party played an early part in royal calculations. An ideal but improbable solution would be the rejection of the Duce by the Fascist Party, thus enabling the King to act constitutionally, and untrammelled by a hint of illegality. It was more likely that leading elements, particularly those who had played a role in the events of 1922 in helping to establish the original compromise between Fascism and the Monarchy, might seek in declining circumstances the arbitration of the Crown.

A 'constitutional' Fascist administration might provide a temporary makeshift, or individual figures from such a grouping might strengthen an eventual coalition. Such a solution would cause the least disturbance of the political scene. The personal role of the Duce would be replaced by a 'National' government including 'moderate' Fascist elements—a reconstruction of the 'compromise' of 1922 without Mussolini. But it depended essentially on the eventual attitude of the Western Allies, and also on the co-operation of at least certain leaders of the pre-Fascist parliamentary groups, who still survived either in the Senate or in retirement.

The experience of Darlan in North Africa gave rise to a certain speculation in Italian circles as to the advantage of a 'Vichy' solution, though the Casablanca Declaration on unconditional surrender engendered more sombre thoughts.

The 'Changing of the Guard' in February 1943, however, was in effect the expulsion from the government of those very moderate elements of the Fascist movement, who might fit into such a royal design. Their acknowledged leader was Grandi, and, although dismissed from his post as Minister of Justice, he remained as President of the Chamber, and was thus strategically placed in a central position to initiate discussions with the politicians of the Party.

On February 12 Grandi was received by the King in audience on his retirement as Minister of Justice. On leaving he entered into conversation with General Puntoni, the King's military secretary. 'One must not have any illusions,' Grandi said. 'Italy should attempt little by little to unhitch her wagon from that of Germany to make the crash less painful. I have always been a supporter of a policy of understanding with Great Britain, and within the limits of my power have always sought to oppose the thrust in the direction of Germany . . . On the home front, in face of the apathy of the great mass of the people, a general lack of confidence in their leaders, there is the resentment of many of the old Fascist elements, who have been frustrated in this desire to make and serve the country. For them, Fascism should be an instrument of redemption. At any moment, in face of military disaster, a political movement could take shape with a social basis which the Communists would at once exploit. Only the King at the right moment could restore things in their place. It would, however, be a most difficult and dangerous operation. For my part, I am with the King.' [4]

The following month a more significant move was made on Grandi's initiative. In February he had sought the support of Mussolini in approaching the King on his behalf as a candidate for the highest Italian order, the Collar of the Annunciation, which made its holder the symbolic cousin of the Sovereign.[5]

The first reaction of the monarch was cool. The honour would have to be conferred in Grandi's capacity as President of the Chamber. The King would therefore be obliged to bestow it also on Suardo as President of the Senate 'and there is no chance of doing that after the recent gossip about Senators giving information to the Police'.

Within forty-eight hours, however, Victor Emmanuel abruptly changed his mind, and the order was bestowed on Grandi. 'Was the conferring of the Collar a part of the conspiracy, by any chance?' [b] This honour did however give Grandi, in principle, unrestricted access to the Crown.

The ministerial dismissals of February had, as was intended, outwardly dispersed the Grandi-Ciano circle. The former spent much of his time between Bologna and Rome. Ciano did not come out of the Vatican Embassy until the summer. Bottai busied himself with the Roman scene. Little or no continuous contact between these men can be traced until July. Ciano's removal from political office threw him into the shadow and his future role, if any, would be subordinate to that of Grandi.

In event of an open political crisis, and constitutional action by the Crown, the Army would inevitably be involved directly in politics. Not only would internal law and order have to be maintained, but the issue of the conduct of the war and relations with the German ally would have to be faced. The new administration, whatever the details of its composition, must be headed by a military figure. The ultimate choice of the Crown was limited to the thinned ranks of the surviving figures of the First World War, and in effect to two: Badoglio and Caviglia. The events of the previous winter had already posed in general terms the problem of the succession to the Duce.[c]

Both men had long been rivals and enemies, and each sought in private to strengthen his personal following in military circles and in the Senate.

Badoglio had not seen the King since his dismissal as Chief of the General

b. Mussolini *op cit* p. 142. It was also a certain protection against arbitrary arrest. See Badoglio's remarks to Grandi after July 26. (Montanelli interview with Grandi *op cit* February 10, 1955.)

c. See pp. 106–23.

Staff in December 1940, but he had for some months been increasingly active behind the political scenes. In December 1942 his 'proposition' had been made to Ambrosio, then Chief of the Army Staff.[d] At the turn of the year, the Marshal had made his own private soundings in British circles in Switzerland, which were presumably not unconnected with recent developments in Vichy France. The concept of transitional governments by reliable Marshals might have an appeal in certain Allied circles.[e]

In January Marshal Caviglia noted in his diary: 'Badoglio too is actively promoting his own succession to Mussolini. He has apparently prepared his ministry and indicated the ministers for the different portfolios.' [6] In the Senate, and in the military clubs of Rome, he had already been sniffing the atmosphere. According to Cassinelli, Badoglio had expressed on several occasions his anxiety at the lack of suitable candidates for a 'National' administration. 'Several times he consulted the list of senators, and the parliamentary year books. The good ones were over seventy and the young have not shown themselves.' [7]

The dismissal of Badoglio's rival and personal enemy, Marshal Cavallero, now gave rise to much speculation and there were few candidates on the top level for military appointments. Badoglio had already been in touch with the new Undersecretary of War, General Sorice, and, when consulted, had shown a direct interest in the appointment of a 'reliable' Commandant-General of the Military Police. In the event of internal political tension, the importance of this post, controlling the forces of public order, was considerable. It was with Badoglio's approval that General Hazon, who had served under him in Africa and was already in the confidence of the Court, was appointed.

The German Ambassador had been warned by an anonymous informer that Badoglio 'is busy bringing together individuals who do not see eye to eye with the government, and carrying on anti-Fascist activities in those sections of the army still loyal to him'. [8] Sorice had also alerted Badoglio that the King was displeased with him 'because he was creating a Fronde'. [9] This deliberate note of caution preceded a summons to the Quirinal. The royal audience appears to have taken place on March 6, and it is perhaps significant that four days previously Ambrosio, in his new capacity as Chief of the General Staff, had called on Badoglio.[f]

d. See p. 111 above.

e. Badoglio is careful in his Memoirs only to hint at these moves and gives no dates. See Badoglio *op cit* p. 36, and also Vailati *op cit* p. 362.

f. Badoglio barely refers to this meeting in his own memoirs. The interview is however summarized in a pamphlet written by his lawyer and political intermediary, Guido Cassinelli. He was also the legal administrator of the estate of Badoglio's late wife. Cassinelli, *op cit* pp. 16–17. General Puntoni refers to this audience without comment, but under the date of March 6. It is typical of the 'official' account of Badoglio's activities that the latter is supposed to have been in touch with Ambrosio after the 'late spring'. Vailati *op cit* p. 78. But see Italian Collection. Ambrosio Diary, March 2.

The latter had not seen the King since December 1940. He explained his impressions to the Sovereign in very general terms. 'When a war is made on the explicit calculation that it will be short and if the preparations are for a lightning war, it is lost as soon as the opposite happens. When the country is against war, the war is lost. Every month we descend one step more towards defeat.' The King answered: 'I am also of this opinion,' and here the conversation came to an end.

The police reports reaching Mussolini gave a different impression. Badoglio had been received by the King 'last Saturday'.[g] The conversation had lasted one and a half hours. It was rumoured that the King had asked him to take over the Supreme Command, and that the Marshal's terms were that there should be no interference in military affairs by the Duce, nor by the Commander of the Militia, which must come under the direct control of the Army.

In any event the King had made a significant personal link with one of the few military leaders with a national, if controversial reputation, and an active following in Army circles.

General Ambrosio told Puntoni after a royal audience on March 13 that the Duce ought to retire in favour of Badoglio. The King remarked: 'He (Ambrosio) is a gallant fellow, who does not mince words. He says what he thinks, but this is not always a good method.' [10]

On March 15 Caviglia sent a private memorandum to the King written, it would seem, under the influence of the March strikes. 'Politically what should one do? The duties of the people are distinct from the will of the Crown. It is not for the King alone to handle the situation, but Italians. It is they who forcibly brought Mussolini to power, thus violating the laws of the State. The King, in order to avoid civil war, accepted the revolutionary solution . . . At the most he gave his consent and advice. Today the question can only be resolved by Italians . . . One should not pay too much attention to the activities of various groups which have sprung up at this moment as a natural reaction, and which often show little historical or common sense. The conflict of views between parties was after all no less serious during the Risorgimento when they were struggling for the unity and independence of Italy. So long as the situation is handled under the aegis of the dynasty, its

g. March 5 not 6, as Puntoni records. See Italian Collection. Badoglio file, containing police reports. They also record 'several visits' of Ambrosio to Badoglio. It is impossible to comment on the historical accuracy of such sources. In view of the intricate and self-cancelling net of political espionage endemic in the Fascist 'style' of government, many such reports were clearly deliberately inspired by those under surveillance. It is possible, for example, that the police report on Badoglio, dated December 2, 1942, at the time of his 'proposition' to Ambrosio, is such a case. Badoglio is reported to have said to his lawyer Cassinelli: 'Now that I am alone, I must think of my old age. I am the only general who has to his credit two victorious wars: the war of '15–18 and the war in Ethiopia. I can close my eyes in peace, having given of my best to the Fatherland.'

solution will have a legal orderly character, and the troops will still obey their leaders. But if events take a different course and the troops do not obey, if there is an internal revolution with or without Soviet influence, there is no predicting what might happen. But, in order to avoid excesses, there should be twenty or thirty divisions in the country itself, the Militia must be incorporated in regular regiments and divisions, the organization of the Fascist Party must be handed over to the Military Police, in the early stages the senior officer in each province must take over the Federal Secretary (the regional head of the Fascist Party), and equally a non-commissioned officer in the place of the political secretary.' [11]

Caviglia, too, had his supporters among the survivors of the First World War. On March 16 the King had received Admiral Baistrocchi, who wished to hand to the King a memorandum. It was received with some scepticism. Baistrocchi proposed the setting up of a military government headed by the Prince of Piedmont, with Marshal Caviglia as Vice President.[12]

The ties between Caviglia and the heir to the throne may well have militated against the former. The Prince was not in the close confidence of his father, and his household was at times regarded as the source of a possible rival political solution.

Although the whole machinery of the opposition parties to Fascism had vanished after the totalitarian legislation of 1925, a number of politicians, particularly of the former Socialist and Liberal parties, remained in the country on the fringes of retirement, or with one foot in the Senate.

The military reverses in the winter of 1942 gave a spurt to these survivors of an anti-Fascist parliamentary opposition, and brought some of them together in secret conclave. By the end of the year regular meetings were being held in Bonomi's house at No. 4 Piazza della Libertà in Rome.[13] A discreet series of consultations took place between former colleagues. Their names recall a whole political world. The three leading Liberals in Rome were Alessandro Casati, the representative of his party in Mussolini's second cabinet, who resigned, after the acceptance by the Chamber of the legislation of January 1925 setting up the machinery of dictatorship; the Marchese Tommaso Della Torretta, Minister of Foreign Affairs in Bonomi's own government in 1921 and afterwards Italian Ambassador in London; and Senator Alberto Bergamini, a former director of the *Giornale d'Italia*. The group met each Sunday in the latter's apartment in Rome. These men formed an elementary 'shadow cabinet' maintaining links with other survivors, with Vittorio Emmanuele Orlando, the Prime Minister of the First World War, together with Marshal Caviglia and others.[h]

In the Via Cola di Rienzo in Rome, in the office of one of the former

h. Caviglia spoke to Bergamini about an eventual intervention of such a body. 'He excluded the possibility of such an action, but I want to talk to him about it again.'

secretaries of the Catholic Popular Party—also dissolved in 1925—the group held frequent meetings with Alcide De Gasperi and Meuccio Ruini, the acknowledged leaders of Christian democracy in event of a major political change, through whom discreet relations with the Vatican were established. The Socialists too, represented by Giuseppe Romita, came to meetings at this address, and an embryo coalition front came into being, representing the historical currents of constitutionalism and a party system. Here were the Guizots of an Italian Restoration, innocent of any revolutionary intent.

Early in their discussions, it became clear that any initial action against Mussolini could only be taken on the initiative of the Crown, and that these clandestine political groups could only represent isolated and unorganized traditional currents of opinion.

With the organs of political control exclusively in the hands of the Fascist Party, an effective opposition could act only under cover, as yet inviolate, of the Monarchy, and through the prestige of an Army with its traditions of loyalty to the Royal House. Unless such a line was pursued, the alternative would be a popular revolution, sweeping away not only Fascism but also the vestiges of a constitutional monarchy.

The Monarchist solution, to which Bonomi and his group were instinctively and temperamentally bound, met with obstinate opposition from the younger generation of anti-Fascist intellectuals, whom Bonomi and his friends in Rome now sought to approach.

In recent months another centre of private discussion appeared in Milan, grouping together businessmen, writers, and university professors round two young Southerners, Ugo La Malfa and Adolfo Tino.[i] From this group emerged a strong element of suppressed republican Radicalism, latent in Italian politics since Mazzini. As Bonomi put it: 'This current saw no other solution except a Republican one and deludes itself that a popular rising at one blow would rid Italy both of Fascism and Monarchy, setting up a democracy with anti-clerical tendencies, determined to punish the Church for its approaches to Mussolini enshrined in the Lateran treaties.'[14]

The Rome and Milan groups established regular links, and the debate between them initiated in clandestinity early in 1943 was to become the central political theme of the Resistance movement in Italy. By April, with external events moving fast, Bonomi felt it imperative to sound the Royal House, at the same time grouping as far as possible on a united programme the democratic elements in Rome and Milan with whom he was now in touch.

His first approach to the Court had already been made in the form of a secret meeting with the Princess of Piedmont in a villa near Rome. Bonomi

i. The main personalities were Guido de Ruggiero, Piero Calamandrei, Luigi Salvatorelli, Guido Calogero, and Ferruccio Parri.

gained the impression that the Crown had decided to remove the Fascist régime, and that the Army would follow the King. Clearly the second condition was decisive and, at the Princess's suggestion, he saw the Undersecretary of War, General Scuero, whom she had indicated as a leading anti-Fascist in military circles. The latter was less optimistic. 'The Army was not prepared for a coup against Fascism and its then head, Marshal Cavallero, was still closely tied to Mussolini.'[j]

At the same time, through intermediaries, Bonomi was kept in touch with the views of Acquarone, and although discouraged by what appeared to be an absence of any military preparation, these contacts remained in being.

At the beginning of April, two reports from the Vatican caused alarm in the Rome group.

'1. The British Minister to the Vatican, ably questioned by Professor Gonella, a friend of De Gasperi and a discreet and serious person, let it be clearly understood that England would prefer a monarchical solution and that the withdrawal at this moment of Italy from the struggle would lead to notable compensations from the Allies. But action must be quick and there should be no delays in seeking for more radical solutions.

'2. The efforts of Grandi and Ciano were not being rejected out of hand by the British Minister Osborne. This showed that the Anglo-Americans, in order to come to an early solution, would not only accept proposals from the Monarchy, but also the mediation of elements of Fascist origin, even if they were now dissident.' [15]

Bonomi and his friends feared that this information might signify the beginning of an understanding between the Monarchy and Grandi and Ciano, and they hastened to try to restrain their Republican friends, now grouped in the clandestine Action Party which had been formed in Milan in January.

The March strikes in the North had accelerated the formation of anti-Fascist groups, representing the varying strands of historical resistance to the régime, and in particular the Communists, in the Northern industrial cities. Some time later the first clandestine meeting to include a Communist delegate was held at a palace in the Piazza del Popolo in Rome. He was Professor Concetto Marchesi, Professor of Latin at the University of Padua. His intervention, on party instructions, was directed towards supporting for tactical reasons any decisive proposals which the Crown might make towards the overthrow of the régime. The Communists were ready to enter a 'new government even with a minister without portfolio'.[16]

It was now essential to have some first-hand impression of the intentions of the Crown. Apart from Acquarone, the King was rarely available to anyone. His two conversations with Marshals Caviglia and Badoglio had

j. The meeting took place presumably before Cavallero's dismissal on January 31, and before General Scuero was replaced by General Sorice on February 5.

therefore been an eager subject of discussion among these elder statesmen, but revealed no hint of the King's thoughts.

At a meeting at Bonomi's house early in April it was decided to approach the one man who had automatic access to the King—apart from the officials of the Court itself. As Chancellor of the Orders of Knighthood, the Duca del Mare, Thaon de Revel was alone in such a position. The old Admiral, Commander-in-Chief of the Italian Navy in the First World War, was a traditional Piedmontese aristocrat with an almost religious respect for the person of the Sovereign. With great reluctance he agreed, and having gone to church to pray for divine strength, he sought a royal audience. This led to no result. 'The King entrenched himself behind the usual constitutional fictions, asserting that only the Chamber and the Senate could provoke his intervention.' [17]

There was nothing to do but wait for a sign. The King had told Puntoni of his conviction that henceforward it was not a matter of concealing from oneself the need of a decisive gesture in regard to men and affairs. But he said that one must choose the right moment and avoid in the most absolute manner any headstrong action. 'A mistake in the choice of the moment,' he said, 'could be fatal to the country.' [18]

CHAPTER SEVEN

THE AXIS AND THE
SHADOW OF STALINGRAD

DURING THE February talks in Rome Ribbentrop had been instructed to oppose any 'political' solution of the Russian war. Hitler was determined at all costs to bring his anti-Bolshevik crusade to a successful conclusion. There could be no European community or a common political programme prior to a decisive military victory. Although any open opposition in high German circles to this rigid approach to the European situation could but vaguely be discussed, the Italians began to receive reports which showed that cautious doubts existed in diplomatic and military circles in Germany.

How far Ribbentrop himself shared these anxieties at the time is beyond precise analysis. If he felt any such hesitations, he was careful never to put any such hints on record. But at his post-war trial at Nuremberg, and in his posthumous memoirs, fragmentary references do occur, suggesting that he may have held at moments such a view:

'During the sad days which followed the end of the battle of Stalingrad I had a very revealing talk with Hitler . . . On this occasion and in a later memorandum I again suggested peace feelers to Moscow, but the document, which I asked Ambassador Hewel [a] to present, suffered an inglorious end. Hewel told me that the Fuehrer would have nothing to do with it, and had thrown it away. I mentioned the subject once again during a personal conversation, but Hitler replied that he must first be able to achieve a decisive military success; then we could see. Then and later he regarded any peace feelers as a sign of weakness. Nevertheless, I did make contact with Madame Kollontay in Stockholm through my intermediary, Kleist, but without authority I could do nothing decisive.' [b]

a. The liaison officer of the German Foreign Ministry with the Fuehrer's staff.
b. Ribbentrop Memoirs *op cit* pp. 168–71. See also *Nazi Conspiracy and Aggression* (Nuremberg Trial Documents, American Edition, supplementary Volume B. pp. 1203–4). *'It was not possible to get Hitler to a quiet discussion.'* Madame Kollontay was the Soviet Ambassador to Sweden. Peter Kleist was a German agent used for such missions on several occasions. See his book *Zwischen Hitler und Stalin 1939–1945* (Bonn, 1950). See also pp. 260 and 760 below.

Bastianini has since stated that he discussed privately with Ribbentrop in Rome the possibility of sounding the enemy with a view to a separate peace. He attempted to persuade the German Foreign Minister to make contact with the Russians, while he would seek to approach the British and possibly the Americans. Ribbentrop did not categorically dismiss the suggestion.[1]

At the end of the Rome talks, one of his advisers, Megerle, had a private discussion with Babuscio Rizzo, Bastianini's chef de cabinet. This seems to have been the first hint to reach the Italians that, behind Ribbentrop's official attitude, certain such hesitations existed. Although none of the German leaders could oppose Hitler openly on the issue of the Russian war, some of them thought, and possibly Ribbentrop himself, that the only person who could persuade Hitler to seek a compromise solution with the Russians was Mussolini. Goering also, during his visits to Rome, appears to have hinted in the same direction.

Megerle seems to have taken a calculated risk in his talk with his Italian colleague. According to him, the German people, although sorely tried by the war, were resolved to support unreservedly the Fuehrer's orders to mobilize all the material and spiritual forces of the country, so as to organize a formidable resistance to the bitter end in all areas. But Europe would never collaborate effectively in Continental resistance by the side of Germany unless not only German methods but her whole vision of the Europe of the future were profoundly and radically altered.

'It is impossible to think of continuing to govern with bayonets and violence, and it is essential to associate the people of Europe in the future order of the Continent through terms and forms which are roughly acceptable to each, or at least to the majority of them. This, in his opinion, is the central problem that the Axis has to face and solve today, in order to make resistance into something virile and active, capable of creating those material and spiritual foundations without which concepts of a "New Order" would be vain and sterile, since until now, all the European peoples without exception have associated it with undisputed German dominion.'

According to Megerle, the task to convince not Germany, but her rulers, 'of the absolute necessity of profoundly modifying their present vision of Europe, belonged and now belongs more than ever, to Italy, under pain of falling completely short of what has always been and continues to be her specific and extraordinarily important mission within the Axis, and which is, above all, the most valid justification of her presence in the Axis.

'Since the possibility of a total military victory of German arms is compromised, he knows that the actions of Fascist Italy are automatically destined to rise in the estimation of friendly European peoples, who have in effect now transferred their hopes from those arms to the spiritual and political resources, possibilities, and capacities, of the Italians. And Fascist

Italy must profit from this in order to speak to Germany with words now no longer solely Italian, but European, and therefore of much greater weight and importance, and to interpret those tendencies and demands which are the only living and vital things on the Continent today, and which alone can undo those *idées fixes* which move the peoples of the hostile coalition, and consequently diminish their capacity to create offence and resistance.

'Megerle did not know what the Duce had said yesterday or proposed to say to Ribbentrop, but he ardently hoped that he would speak with his authority, prestige, and wisdom. He said in these explicit words: "The Duce is the only man who can do it. Even we Germans think of him in our minds as our most effective interpreter with the rulers of Germany, who, too immersed and absorbed in the cruel war, are perhaps of necessity driven to see and appreciate only the military side of the problem too vast and too complex to be reduced exclusively to these narrow limits." There are many men who think in this way in Germany, but they have not yet reached the highest positions of command, although they are near them. At any rate, they are from now on building up around the German rulers that atmosphere which will facilitate every work of persuasion to this effect. Ribbentrop has certainly a strong personality. He is obstinate and stubborn. It is difficult for him to listen to other people. To exert an effective influence over his mind, it is necessary to choose the right moment, words, and circumstances. But, under these conditions, he is open to persuasion—this is what Megerle and his friends will continue to do.

'Megerle earnestly and repeatedly recommended that the source of these impressions should not be revealed in any circumstances: that is, that his name should in no event be mentioned. For this reason, it would seem that the time is not yet ripe enough. He spoke with conviction; and, at times, with an emotion which he did not trouble to hide.' [2]

A cryptic confirmation of such an attitude in certain German circles appears in a brief record of a talk between General Ambrosio and the head of the Italian military intelligence, General Amé, on the afternoon of March 6.[c] The latter reported on his conversation held recently in Venice with his German colleague, Admiral Canaris, who pointed out how the morale of the German population had been affected by recent events. 'In the main the situation on the Russian Front is still viewed with pessimism.' The fall of Tunisia was inevitable, and the submarine campaign could not produce decisive results.

What subtle ultimate motives Canaris may have had for his defeatism have not been clarified, but the future of an opposition forming within the German leadership to Hitler's insistence on a war to the finish in the East

c. Italian Collection. See also Abshagen. *Canaris* pp. 334 ff. It appears that Ambrosio saw Canaris himself on February 28 at the time of the Rome talks, but no record exists of this conversation. (Italian Collection, Ambrosio diary.)

might well depend directly on the future intervention of Mussolini with Hitler.

In this intricate and menacing climate, the rôle of Goering was obscure but not absent. Hitherto, the only shred of evidence as to his attitude had been his remark in private to Mussolini during his previous visit to Rome in December 1942 that the Duce's proposal of 'a new Brest Litovsk' would be 'Hitler's ideal'. And this was prior to Stalingrad.

Early in March 1943, following on Ribbentrop's *tour d'horizon*, Goering came again to Rome. Although it is not clear what was said in the talks between the two men, it was at this moment that Mussolini re-opened the whole subject. At a luncheon at Palazzo Venezia, Bastianini noted Goering's 'reserve' when the Duce stressed that the Russian front must cease to exist in order to concentrate an all-out effort against the British and Americans in the Mediterranean.[3]

A few days later, in his letter of March 8 to Hitler, Mussolini in a carefully worded paragraph repeated these arguments: 'I ask myself whether it is not too risky to repeat the struggle against the boundless space of Russia, which is practically impossible to reach and grasp, while at the same time in the west, the Anglo-Saxon peril mounts.

'The day when, one way or another, Russia will be eliminated or neutralized, victory is in our hands. But I hope to discuss this thoroughly with you when I have the good fortune to meet you.'

On March 17 the Italian Ambassador in Berlin, Alfieri, was instructed to press for such a meeting, and this prompted him to review in a revealing personal letter to the Duce three days later certain relevant aspects of the German political scene relating to such a solution. 'I have been able to put together the reactions in those circles of the immediate advisers of the Fuehrer and Minister von Ribbentrop to your letter of March 8, which has made a strong impression on the Fuehrer, and which has been received in responsible circles with deep satisfaction; it is particularly the paragraph relating to the war on the Russian front which has aroused the greatest interest . . . You have thus fed the hopes that your view, listened to by the Fuehrer, may influence radically his decisions.'

Before attacking Russia 'the Fuehrer had to overcome resistance to his plans from both the politicians and the military, the latter stressing the inexhaustible reserves of men and material at the disposal of Russia, and the former the spectre of the feared "Second Front".

'This resistance reappeared, particularly on the part of the generals, during the campaign regarded by the Fuehrer as a war between two ideological imperialisms which could not be ended except by the annihilation of one or the other, and in which successes of a political or moral character ought to have an importance much superior to purely strategic results.

'The will to carry through his plans triumphantly, the increasingly violent clash with the reality of things, and the mounting resistance of the enemy, gradually led to an increasing rigidity in the Fuehrer's spirit and a great inflexibility and intransigence, fixing his mind on one sector of the immense theatre of the war, making him forget perhaps that the Russian was not his only mortal adversary.

'The lack of success of the plans worked out by the generals in the first phase of the war, drove Hitler to impose the offensive against Moscow; the negative results of this action led him to take over personally the supreme direction of operations. The campaign of 1942 culminated in the episode of Stalingrad, which Hitler had conceived of as a clamorous political success and around which he subsequently wished to create a legend of epic military sacrifice.

'This series of operations, worked and carried out by the Fuehrer, the practical results of which have not come up to expectations, have made a noticeable dent in the German war potential and have ended in weighing down the strategic situation on the Russian Front . . . Hitler, feeling himself personally and gravely committed and compromised in the eyes of his people, does not know how to bring himself to give up his design of avenging, by victory of arms, the disillusion and suffering of recent months, and on the other hand, he cannot see any other objective than the Russian one.

'The lively interest, with which responsible circles here have received the doubts expressed by the Duce as to the expediency of a total offensive effort on the Eastern Front, is clearly a reflection of the doubts present in the minds of not a few German leaders. They hope that on the occasion of a meeting, which it is hoped here is imminent, the Duce talking alone with the Fuehrer with complete clarity and precision, will drag him out of this fanatical atmosphere which has made him lose the correct vision of things, and will liberate him from the goad of the Soviet sphinx which dominates totally his thought.

'If the Fuehrer would give up, at least for the moment, the idea of an all out offensive in the East and could be induced to concentrate on the sector in the Mediterranean, the forces thus available could possibly obtain, with infinitely smaller means, and with results probably even greater for the entire war economy, that decisive success which he conceives possible only on the Eastern Front.' [4]

The hopes of an Axis summit meeting before the end of March were however dashed by a general Allied offensive in North Africa. But Mussolini persisted with his arguments about Russia, and wrote again on March 26 to Hitler: 'In the meantime, permit me to return to the subject which I hold to be decisive at this moment—Russia. I have discussed it at length with the Reichsmarschal.[d] When we met at the Brenner on June 1, 1941, I told you that, with Russia, one had to choose between alliance or war. After the

d. In Rome at the beginning of the month.

long and tormented meditations of which you have often spoken to me—and which few are better placed to understand than myself—you chose war, informing me of your decision a few hours before your troops crossed the border. History has proved that you were right. Russia had deceived Europe and the world, in the campaign against Finland too, and constituted a formidable threat in the rear of the Axis. In almost two years of war, through heavy sacrifices and acts of heroism such as have never been seen before, you have succeeded in weakening Russia to such an extent that she cannot, at least for a long time to come, constitute any real threat.

'For this reason I tell you that the Russian chapter can be closed. By a peace if possible—and I think it is—or by a systematic defensive—an imposing Eastern wall—which the Russians will never be able to cross . . . The summer advances and winter retreats cannot be repeated without leading to exhaustion, even if mutual, to the exclusive advantage of the Anglo-Americans. I would add that relations between Stalin and the Allies are really bad and that the political moment is somewhat favourable to us. In my opinion Russia cannot be annihilated, not even through the improbable intervention of Japan, given the enormous distances. The Russian chapter must therefore be liquidated in some way or other. On that day, we can put out our flags as victory will definitely be within our grasp. Having deprived England of the last continental army—and the most powerful—on which she has counted, the Axis, with all its strength, will turn to the West and regain the strategic initiative which since last autumn has passed into the hands of the enemy both on land and in the air.'[5]

At last the Duce seemed prepared to face the menacing issue at the heart of the Axis conduct of the war. On March 30, on the eve of the forthcoming talks, he reviewed the situation with Mackensen in Rome, who reported the following day: 'The Duce concluded his survey, which he made with great calm and with no trace of nervous tension or anxiety, with the remark that victory would indubitably be ours if we succeeded in liquidating the Russian Front. As to "how?" he did not vouchsafe further. However, I had the impression that particularly on this question he was thinking of talking to the Fuehrer.'[6]

A private and cautious sounding, similar to that of Megerle in Rome in February, was reported two months later by the new Italian Ambassador in Ankara, Guariglia, in the form of a conversation between a German diplomat on military service in Russia with a member of Guariglia's staff, who had been a former colleague of his in Moscow.[e]

e. Italian Collection. Relli to Guariglia, Ankara, April 28. Guariglia to Bastianini, April 29, 1943. I am indebted to the former German Ambassador in London, Baron von Herwarth, for enquiring into the identity of this diplomat. He was Dr Hans Georg Pfleiderer who had been since the 1930's firstly a member of the German Embassy in Moscow, and later of the Consulate General at Leningrad. During the first years of the

This memorandum throws a rare light on certain circles of German opinion, and of a latent opposition in Germany to the Fuehrer's conduct of the war.

'I am taking the liberty of summarizing for you the conversation which I had with a German official just returned from the Russian front, where he had spent two years with various military headquarters. He is a member of the German diplomatic service, whom I had occasion to meet in Moscow in 1929. It appears that he is at present concerned with Russian questions, and is awaiting demobilization. According to what he told me, he had come to Ankara "to pay a visit to his colleagues"; but before returning to Berlin, he will wait for Ambassador von Papen's return from Istanbul.'

After stating firmly that he was expressing his own personal opinions, he said: 'My stay at the front, my study of Soviet problems, and of the fortunes of the war, convinced me as long ago as last winter that a military solution in Soviet Russia is impossible. The war production of the Soviet Union is in good working order, and perhaps even increased, compared with the pre-war period; the difficulties of supply, and those relating to the civilian population, are not such as to worry the Soviet Government: the human resources have been severely tried, but can still feed the Red Army, and are in any case superior to the German ones. The defensive possibilities of the Soviet Union are inexhaustible, and if ever the German army wanted to undertake another summer campaign, the Red Armies would repeat their tactics of retiring to the East, making the German advance beyond a certain point difficult and dangerous. Even if the Russians were driven to the Urals, their powers of active defence would not be broken, while Germany would still have to face a front of several thousand kilometres. The maintenance of such a front would demand a number of men exceeding German manpower. The numbers used in active defence on such a front would be greater than that of the annual military intake into the German Army.

'In such conditions we must pose clearly before us the problem of finding some other solution than the military one. Is it possible to come to an agreement with Russia? The political prerequisites for it, and the conditions which we must or could offer the Russians in order to reach agreement, exist. I think that Stalin would be satisfied with the old frontiers, or rather with the line of demarcation fixed with Germany before the conflict, with the annexation of the Baltic republics, and with eventual loss of interest by the Axis in the Straits. We could moreover push the Soviet Union towards Iran, and find in a programme for the industrial reconstruction of the

war he served as liaison officer between the German Foreign Office and an Army Group in Soviet Russia. In 1943, Pfleiderer, who was then a First Secretary in the Political Department of the German Foreign Office, stayed at Ankara on official business from April 14th to April 25th. According to Pfleiderer's dossier in the Ministry's files, the object of his journey is given as 'official discussions (Russian questions)'. He died in 1958.

Ukraine, those reciprocal compensations which should appear as the basis of the agreement. It would be a question of knowing whether Moscow would be willing to negotiate on these lines, since in holding out such a possibility to the German ruling circles, we would be taking a very grave responsibility on ourselves. I think, however, that we must do it; and I think that we should not put off sounding the temper of the Russian rulers any longer than the autumn.'

The Italian diplomat interjected that, 'knowing the political mentality of the men in the Kremlin, and particularly Stalin's, I had not excluded the possibility in the course of this war of an agreement with Moscow in certain defined circumstances. For some time past the Soviet attitude towards her Anglo-Saxon allies had confirmed my suppositions. In my opinion, however, these circumstances needed to ripen still further, and the Russians needed to feel the real impossibility of breaking German military power. Then, perhaps, Stalin would be willing to negotiate. As far as the Soviet territorial hopes were concerned, I shared his opinion: Stalin was dreaming of ending his political career by making Russia the dominant power in the Euro-Asian continent. As to the Straits, however, I had to point out that the Russian presence in the Dardanelles would mean, to a greater or lesser degree, her predominance in the Mediterranean, i.e. in the Balkans and all the region washed by that sea. Since Italy lives—literally speaking—on the Mediterranean, such a solution would visibly affect her. For the rest, Russian entry into that sea would mean, later on, the encircling of Western Europe, and therefore also a threat to Germany.

'My colleague then tried to explain that the offer of the Straits to Russia would only be a move in the political game. In his opinion, the Soviet Union would not realize this dream because she would automatically line up against her not only Turkey, but those same Balkan states which now look on Russia as an elder sister. The Anglo-Saxons would moreover feel bound to prevent the Soviet advance towards the Middle East. Germany must now consider if her blood-letting is not to the advantage of a third party. Let others think of building dams against the Bolshevik danger in their own areas.

'Without going into the merits of these political forecasts, I want in conclusion to express some personal impressions which might help your Excellency to judge the value of the conversation. From the way my colleague expressed himself, and from his reiterated requests to keep the exchange of views secret, I became convinced that he was not only expressing his own thoughts, but that he wanted to establish general ideas on a subject already discussed in responsible (German) quarters. His repeated references to the necessity of resorting to political action at a certain moment in the war, a need which, according to him, is now understood and demanded even in German military circles, seemed to me important. Moreover, he denied all possibilities of scaling down the national structure of the Soviet Union, judging useless even the attempts made to such an end at Berlin with Caucasian elements. When I asked him finally what were the possibilities of convincing certain German circles of the expediency of what he had disclosed to me, he remarked that *"only narrow circles of the Party now rejected such ideas, but that they were already understood and admitted by the majority of the German ruling clan".*

On this remarkable document, Guariglia made certain comments in his covering letter to Bastianini:

'Two points seem to me especially worthy of your attention. (1) The doubts which Germany has about reaching a military solution in Russia, now or later. These doubts are also distinctly present in German circles in Ankara, especially military ones, and they are not hidden from me in intimate conversations with my German colleagues, except naturally, by those tied to Ribbentrop, whom, by the way, the others blame most for the errors committed in Germany. (2) The desire for a political agreement with Russia, who would be offered "Axis disinterestedness in the Straits".

'When Relli informed me of this extraordinary idea of his German interlocutor, I instructed him to give the latter an effective picture of the consequences which Russia's entry into the Balkans and the Mediterranean would have not only for Italy, but also for Germany herself.[f]

'In fact the threat which Russia, as a Mediterranean and Balkan power, would then constitute to our country would at the same time menace Germany, not only as Italy's ally, but as making her liable to encirclement, in her turn, round her central European borders.

'The German diplomat replied to these observations that it was simply a question of a political "move", and that Turkey, the Balkan states, and . . . England, would see to stopping Russia! These ideas of German diplomats, and of Ribbentrop's "systems", are the very ones which have brought Germany to her present plight.

'Once Russian military power were firmly settled on the Straits, neither the Balkans nor Turkey would be a serious bulwark, while by closing the Straits, Russia would no longer be vulnerable to the British Navy. That leaves America—and although the North American penetration of the Mediterranean, the Middle East, and Iran, is being accelerated, it is now and probably will be for many years to come, only a primarily economic penetration, profiting from the present political and military contingencies, and completely indifferent to eventual Russian hegemony, provided that the latter leaves the ports open to American traffic.

'The Germans need to understand once and for all that they are making a great mistake in formulating war propaganda only round the Bolshevik dangers, and that they ought to make all Europeans and even the English

f. There must have been more than one conversation between Relli and Pfleiderer.

see the Russo-Slav danger, of which Bolshevism is only the ideological disguise.

'If this mask were torn away, the Russo-Slav danger would no longer enjoy all those sympathies and assistance which the Communists of all European countries are freely offering at present, or she would enjoy them to a lesser degree.'

The immediate fears, on the part of the Germans, were however of a defection of the satellites as part of general Allied offensive action in the Balkans, and possibly with Italian connivance. This possibility played an increasing part in German calculations in the spring of 1943. Stalingrad had broken the myth of German infallibility, and given substance to a general desire among the Axis partners for a negotiated peace.

The rôle of Turkey in developments in South-East Europe must always be of special importance. Her major consideration was simple: the ultimate danger was the spread of Russian influence into the Balkans and up to the Straits, and the defence of these regions against such a threat was paramount. In this sense the success of Germany's campaign in the East was in the direct interest of Turkey, but it was the danger of a German military collapse on the Russian Front after Stalingrad that caused the Turkish leaders to re-appraise the whole Balkan position, and accept the exploratory talks with the British at Adana.

As Papen later reported to Berlin. 'As previously reported, the possibilities of a preventive defence against a Russian thrust into the Balkans were discussed at Adana. The Turks took the view that the line of the Danube must be defended in time.'[7]

The Anglo-American commitments to the Soviet Union circumscribed any advantages, from the Turkish side, of safeguarding their vital interests by entering the war on the Allied side, and their realistic appreciation of this situation, as confirmed by the Adana conversations, led them to consider cautiously a line of action independent of either warring camp.

Since January, the Turks had begun soundings particularly with the Yugoslav and Greek governments in exile, with a view to resurrecting plans for a Balkan Federation under Turkish leadership in order to preserve the whole area from Great Power control. Such a project, concerning an area of vital strategic importance, must affect all the belligerents.

The Germans were at once aware of these moves through intercepting the messages of the Yugoslav and Greek representatives in Turkey to their respective governments in London. From similar secret sources, they also knew that this Turkish plan had been communicated to Churchill at Adana.

The British were less alarmed than the Germans and Italians by such a project, being solely concerned with accelerating the early break up of the Axis positions in South Eastern Europe. According to Papen, Churchill had pleaded 'for a Turkish-Bulgarian rapprochement, as Bulgaria is the only Balkan state intact for the protection of Turkey and Near East in event of a German collapse on the Eastern Front'.[8] And again: 'Numan told Churchill that in all circumstances he recommended that the British should work with King Boris, as he was the only guarantee against the growing bolshevization of Bulgaria in event of a German defeat.' [9]

Such intelligence caused immediate and common concern in Berlin and Rome. The Bulgarians represented the only mobile reserve for the Axis in event of an allied landing in the Balkans. If the British influenced the building of a Balkan bloc under Turkish leadership in a neutralist and anti-Axis direction, a critical situation would ensue.

Mackensen reported from Rome after talks with Bastianini. 'As I have learned in confidence from the Italian Foreign Minister, the development of Bulgarian-Turkish relations is being watched at the moment with special care in regard to rumours from an English source that there may be a question of Bulgarian-Turkish negotiations for a non-aggression pact.' [10]

The scare of a possible Bulgarian defection, however, was temporarily dispelled during the course of the month.

A German Foreign Office memorandum noted that the 'Bulgarian Ambassador in Berlin reports that in Sofia one is convinced that at the moment Turkey is not up to any intrigues. One noticed the anti-Russian tendencies at Adana. The English went as far as they could to the limit permitted without directly compromising themselves in Moscow.' [11]

There was always, however, the danger of communist penetration into Bulgaria, and of a Russian-organized coup. Such a threat was the decisive element in the adherence of Bulgaria to the Axis, and indeed, by common agreement, formal diplomatic relations were maintained between Sofia and Kuibychev.

At the end of March, King Boris was summoned to Hitler's headquarters. His visit heralded a further general series of conversations with the heads of the satellite states of the Axis, reviewing the post-Stalingrad scene. He was shown in confidence the Adana military protocols, which had been obtained by the German Intelligence. The Germans seem to have been reassured by the King's reactions, and he was not subjected to any pressures. 'The question of breaking off relations with Russia had been discussed during the King's visit in 1942, and the King had asked for the break to be postponed. This point of view was also supported by the German Legation in Sofia.'

The Turkish plan for a new Balkan bloc was also raised with him, 'but without any concrete results'.[12]

Although the fears consequent on a Turkish-Bulgarian understanding had been dispersed, approaches were made in March by Ankara in the Hungarian and Roumanian capitals. These moves were regarded with renewed anxiety, as a precursory sign of a possible defection of the minor satellites.

The Hungarian Prime Minister, Kallay, informed the German Minister in Budapest on March 10 of the Turkish démarche, and Ribbentrop immediately sought Papen's comments in Ankara.

'The Turks have approached Kallay with the suggestion of an anti-Bolshevik pact—to include also Roumania, Greece, Bulgaria, Serbia and Croatia.' It was difficult to approach Greece and Serbia formally as they are occupied territories, 'but Kallay told Turkey that he was very interested and asked for further details. Kallay thinks that the proposal might bring Turkey nearer to the Axis and strengthen Roumania internally.'

Ribbentrop added that, from secret sources, the Turkish project of resurrecting a Balkan Union, and of attaching Hungary to it, was already known. But no clear picture emerged from Kallay's statements. 'In regard to Greece and Serbia, is the exiled or the local government envisaged in the Turkish project?' [13]

On March 19, Papen replied after consultation with the Turkish Foreign Minister. The latter denied disingenuously that any instructions had been given in the sense reported by the German Minister in Budapest. But Turkey would leave nothing undone to prevent a Russian move to the south-east. 'The best means would be an agreement between the Balkan states.' Papen's own thesis was that 'if the idea of a Balkan Federation was conceived as a protection against Bolshevism, it could only be considered in closest co-operation with us'.

Numan thought that 'given the tension between the Anglo-Americans on the one side and the Russians on the other, this worldwide conflict held within itself all the elements of surprise. One could not overlook that one or other of the Anglo-Saxon partners might strengthen itself by a separate alliance with the Russians, or that one day Germany might come to terms with Russia. Turkish policy must take into account every eventuality, and remain friendly with all warring parties.' [14]

On March 23 Papen telegraphed again, that Numan had told the Hungarian Minister in Ankara that in the days of growing Bolshevik danger he had wanted to discuss Balkan federation, but there was no need now to 'activate' the question. Things were much better on the Eastern Front. The British Ambassador had also asked for the talks not to continue, even at the request of the London exiled governments.

There was a momentary and general retreat on all sides from the Balkan field.

These suspicions were the subject of an enquiry when, later in the year, the Germans seized the Italian Foreign Office archives. These files were analysed, and one report refers to these Turkish efforts to build up a Balkan bloc.

'On the soundings made by Turkey in Budapest and Bucharest directly after the Adana conference with a view to setting up an alleged anti-bolshevik Balkan bloc, in which also Hungary should be included, we were already informed by the middle of March through communications from the Hungarian Government and from secret sources. On the basis of these reports Ambassador von Papen discussed the subject thoroughly on March 19 with the Turkish Foreign Minister, who attempted to play down the Turkish initiative. The matter was also raised with the Bulgarian Minister in Berlin.

'The assumption that the Italian Government did not discuss with us at the time the Turkish initiative, is not borne out by our own archives. These show rather that, on March 23 and April 8, extracts from the relevant reports of the Italian representatives in Bucharest and Ankara were transmitted to us . . . and that the Italian Embassy in Budapest kept our Minister there informed in detail on Hungarian-Italian talks on the Turkish démarche.' g

Italy's relations with Hungary had always been specially close, and this had been the personal achievement of Ciano. German pressure on Hungary after Stalingrad to increase her war effort led Kallay, with the consent of the Regent, Admiral Horthy, to turn for support to Rome.

The German reactions in Budapest had also been sharply hostile to any Hungarian participation in Turkish plans. Kallay had professed astonishment at this attitude, and told the German Minister that he 'would seek clarification in Rome' during his forthcoming visit. 15

On April 7, the Italian Ambassador in Budapest, Anfuso, telegraphed an account of a talk with his German colleague just after Kallay's departure. The German Minister von Jagow 'read me a long sermon on the Hungarian Government's attitude which he defined as continually shifting and somewhat far removed from the complete war aims of the Axis. Hungary's latest attitude was not liked by his Government, and perhaps for the purpose of getting Hungary to collaborate more satisfactorily, it would be wise to invite the Regent to Salzburg to meet the Fuehrer who could reveal to him the expediency of replacing the present President of the Council by Imredy, who was noted for his strictly pro-Axis political ideals.' 16

Anfuso added that in his view Imredy was under German orders; he had practically no political following, the Regent openly opposed him, and his possible nomination would provoke a grave internal crisis.

This German pressure on the satellite allies reveals a certain coherent pattern. Hitler had decreed a total war against both the Russians and the Anglo-Americans, and having set the example of a complete mobilization of the resources of Germany, he directed, in the spring of 1943, that the same policy should be extended, if possible, by diplomatic pressure to the other Axis countries. This might even imply radical changes in the political struc-

g. See Appendix B to this volume on the captured Italian Archives. The above German report on their contents is No. 3 and dated October 18, 1943.

ture of each ally, and either the dictatorship of the extreme pro-Nazi elements, such as the Arrow-Cross in Hungary and the Iron Guard in Roumania, or direct military rule through a reliable officer of high rank.[h] But the conditions for such a revolution did not exist in practical terms in any of the countries concerned.

It was partly therefore to resist such pressures by the Germans on Hungary, and also to discuss the common possibilities of seeking at least a limitation of the war, that the Hungarian Prime Minister came to Rome on April 4.[17] The visit was originally fixed for January, but had then been postponed in view of the military setbacks in North Africa.[i]

According to Bastianini, the Hungarian Prime Minister 'begged Mussolini to undertake two operations: first to put himself at the head of the minor allies, and to bring decisive pressure on Hitler to bring him back to reality; and second to undertake in their name some diplomatic initiative in the event of Hitler persisting in his plans of an all-out war, seeking a victory by now unobtainable . . . Mussolini promised him to speak frankly to Hitler about the situation and to propose a conference of the heads of all the allied governments.'[j]

According to Kallay's own account, Mussolini made it clear that any move towards a separate peace was premature, but hinted cautiously that with regard to the Russians he would favour such a move, provided he could persuade Hitler to agree. 'We cannot even think of a separate peace. Firstly, because honour would not allow it. Secondly, because Italy would achieve nothing by it. Her position would not improve; her prospects would not become more favourable. She would become a battlefield. The Germans, too, would become her enemies, and the country would suffer terrible destruction. In any event, the Allies' insistence on Unconditional Surrender excludes the possibility of such a step. Thirdly, nobody has been able to show me that getting out of the war is a practicable possibility. He was not, however, rejecting my suggestion and was even sympathetic to it. Should his coming visit to Hitler fail to convince him that by autumn the war would be over or a separate peace concluded with the Russians, he would decide that the time had come for us to serve our own interests by independent action.'

Mussolini complained that Hitler was not giving him sufficient support in Africa, that the German leader underrated that theatre of operations and was seeking a decision only in the East. That was Hitler's great error. If the Allies won in Africa, they would open the Second Front in the south from bases in Turkey. Such an invasion would be very dangerous because the

h. The names of certain Hungarian and Roumanian generals had been canvassed in German circles.

i. No official record of the ensuing talks has yet been published.

j. Bastianini, *op cit* p. 90. At the Hungarian Legation in Rome, Kallay told Bastianini, 'We must get out of the conflict if we do not want to see our countries ruined.' *Ibid*, p. 90.

enemy would have to be engaged over a wide area, and the German and Italian forces would be faced with an almost impossible task. On the other hand, if the Western Allies were unable to attack from the south, they must do so from the west, and that would mean certain defeat for them. 'Hitler could hardly wait for that moment, which, he had promised himself, would entail the destruction of the American and British fleets and open the road to England for him.

'Perhaps Mussolini sensed my depression from my silence. He rose, walked up to me, placed his hand on my shoulder, and said: "Trust me. I am judging events correctly. If the promises which I have been given fail to materialize, and if things turn out as you expect, I shall know what to do, and your nation can always count on the Italian people.

' "I can only repeat," Mussolini went on, "that everything depends on whether we finish the war, or rather, on whether Germany finishes the Russians by autumn. Before these decisive questions are settled, one way or the other, nothing must be done which would weaken, if only morally, the strength and driving power of the Axis. If autumn fails to bring victory, then—but only then—your line of thought can be considered. But I am prepared to state now that I accept your point as worth keeping in mind. I shall remember it, and I myself will return to it at the proper time. I must ask you, however, to do nothing that could weaken our position before that time, or to shake faith in our unity." '

Kallay also had an audience with the Pope and alleges that the latter indicated that he was prepared to offer his services as a mediator at an appropriate time. Mussolini was informed of this conversation and said that everything depended on his forthcoming meeting with Hitler, but he 'clasped his hands and rolled over and over on the sofa' adding that he did not feel physically up to a row with the Fuehrer. [18]

CHAPTER EIGHT

THE SALZBURG MEETING
(April 7–10, 1943)

•-

ON THE AFTERNOON of April 6 Mussolini left Rome for Salzburg by 'the last special train of the real Duce'. [1] He was accompanied by the German Ambassador in Rome, Mackensen, Ambrosio and Bastianini with a team of Italian Foreign Office experts.[a]

The last summit conference between the Axis leaders had been held a year before at Salzburg. [2] The setting in April 1943 in the Castle of Klessheim was the same, but as Ribbentrop now told his Italian colleague on arrival 'much has happened' since the previous meeting. Behind this laconic understatement lay the brutal unfaced reality that a decisive Axis victory in the war could no longer be won. The hammer blows of Alamein, 'Torch' and Stalingrad had marked the turning point of the conflict. The strategic initiative now lay with the enemy on all fronts, and the survival of the Axis depended on a basic revision of military policy. The issue was stark. There was no way back for Germany and Italy to the favourable balance of forces of 1940–1; the conception of a 'Blitzkrieg' was dead; the menace of a Second Front in Western Europe, derided by the Axis leaders in 1942, was now a strategic possibility; the loss of all Italian North Africa, and the mounting threat to the fragile Axis foothold in Tunisia brought the war close to the Italian mainland. The continued presence of Italy in the war coalition depended on a decisive reinforcement by Germany of the Mediterranean theatre. Such a strategic revolution could only be carried out at the expense of the Eastern Front, which must either be reorganized on a defensive basis or closed down following the negotiation of a separate peace with Russia. If this crucial move could be made, an all-out effort against the British and Americans might

a. This chapter owes much to Bastianini's own account in his book, *op cit* pp. 92 ff, and to conversations with him.

lead to a negotiated settlement which would preserve something of the Axis position at least in Europe.

Such an analysis of the war situation in the spring of 1943 was in general shared both by German and Italian circles—with the cardinal exception of Hitler. The pervasive fear of total defeat had seeped into the leadership of both countries, and the awareness that salvation lay uniquely in the relics of personal prestige which Mussolini still held in the eyes of Hitler. Only the Duce could persuade him to consider the necessity of a strategic revolution by liquidating the anti-Russian crusade. In such a move lay the last opportunity of the Axis to avoid defeat, and all depended on the person of Mussolini. At such a decisive moment, all defeatist caballing in high circles both in Rome and Berlin was stilled. Such was the significance of this Salzburg meeting.

Throughout the journey northwards, Mussolini was doubled up with severe stomach cramps, but nevertheless spent some three hours with Bastianini discussing the agenda for the conference, 'repeating his suggestion to seek from Hitler a complete explanation on all points. I suggested that he should propose that two feelers should be put out; to the Soviet Union through one of those agents who had already been used by him for such a purpose in Stockholm; and by ourselves to England.' The Duce replied that the matter 'could be considered'.[b]

On the following afternoon the train drew up just beyond Salzburg, near the Castle of Klessheim. The meeting of the two delegations took place with the familiar ritual of martial music and press photographers. Those present were startled by the physical appearance of both leaders. Mussolini's doctor wrote in his diary: 'Hitler looks tired, his face is pale, he has great pockets under his eyes.' [3] His own patient had little reserve of strength. Mussolini was lodged in the pavilion of the Castle, where Mozart had once played for the guests of a former Cardinal prelate.

The Italian delegation had drafted a political plan before leaving Rome. Three days prior to the conference, Bastianini had proposed that Mussolini, during the forthcoming talks, should develop with the Fuehrer the theme of the Axis communiqué issued after the February talks with Ribbentrop in Rome on the future of Europe, as a preliminary move to the central issue of the Russian front. 'He instructed me to make a draft of a European Charter, which would be like a Declaration of Rights of the constituted European nations. . . . Three days later I took the document for which he had asked to him. It consisted of five points assembled together in some twenty lines. He read and re-read it, pondering each word and amalgamating two points. Then he asked me to have it recopied on official notepaper.' [4]

b. It appears that the Italians were aware of the activities of Kleist, Ribbentrop's agent in Stockholm: p. 244 above, and see Bastianini *op cit* p. 92.

Mussolini was now half persuaded by Bastianini that, if the Germans could comprehend and co-operate, he and only he could rally the Axis powers in Europe, together with some of the neutral nations, into a political community, an answer to the Allied pronouncements at Casablanca on Unconditional Surrender and to Churchill's speech of March 21,[c] and give some meaning and a programme to an Axis-controlled Europe. There should be a joint pronouncement on the rights of small nations and the principle of nationalities directed to the occupied territories in Western Europe, in the East, in the Balkans, to the satellite Allies and to Vichy France—a European charter as opposed to an Atlantic Charter.[5]

Having rallied a European front on such a diplomatic basis, the Italians would seek for military agreement with the Axis partner on a defensive strategy on the Russian Front, and, in order to redress the political and military balance in the Mediterranean, a renewed and pressing approach to Spain should be made to enter the war on the Axis side. These combined moves might then create the conditions in which peace negotiations on a compromise basis could be opened with Russia, America, and Great Britain. Italy was possibly better equipped diplomatically to initiate such negotiations through the Balkan states or the neutrals.

If Germany would not consider such a programme, she must urgently come to the military aid of her ally by a major reconstruction of the Southern Front. A new Army Group South must be formed, an effective air defence of the Italian mainland be built up.[6]

Such was the programme of the new Italian Foreign Office team, drawn up largely by Bastianini and his experts and in agreement with Ambrosio. The latter had also raised with Mussolini the subject of a separate peace with Russia during the previous month. It had been however 'a simple subject of conversation without any ulterior development'. But there was now a tacit understanding between the Italian diplomatic and military leaders to force the issue at Salzburg, and Ambrosio took part in last minute discussions on the train.

The forthcoming private talks between the Duce and the Fuehrer were reviewed in a preliminary three-hour conversation between Ribbentrop and Bastianini on the afternoon of April 8, in the presence of Mackensen and Alfieri.

The German Foreign Minister based his comments on Mussolini's letter of March 26 and the 'Italian Memorandum'.[d] Ribbentrop touched at once on the Russian theme, voicing the obsessive determination of his master. There

c. Churchill had spoken in the House of Commons to launch the idea of a post-war Council of Europe: see *Onwards to Victory*, pp. 36–7.

d. The 'Italian Memorandum', which has not yet been traced, was presumably prepared for the conference by the Italian Foreign Office experts, Pietromarchi and Vitetti.

'can be no compromise in the world battle'. The main aim was to destroy Russian military power and not occupy more territory. 'Germany had never expected Russia to collapse at once. She had never intended to occupy the whole of Russia, but to destroy her military and national power so that there could never again be a threat from the East. This has been and still is the aim of the war against Russia, and this will certainly be achieved.' [7]

A captured Russian general had given the figure of Russian losses as 11,300,000. Out of 190 million Russians, 70 were in German occupied territory; out of the remaining 120 millions, 14 had been destroyed. The military potential of a country was ten per cent of its population; therefore 12 million soldiers were still available, but this presented a severe manpower problem for the Russians.

When Ribbentrop had been in Rome, the Russian Front had not been 'stabilized'. Now the German armies were in the Donetz basin and the Russians had been pushed back two hundred kilometres. 'In any case the Russian problem could only have a military and not suddenly a political solution.' Perhaps as the consequence of a liquidation of the military problems a political settlement could find a place. Germany could not leave the Russians near her frontiers without running the danger of one day being bombed from the air. 'Besides she needed the Ukraine. Stalin was also not ready to make peace.'

There were now two objectives; the remaining third of Russian manpower must be destroyed; and then troops and air-force moved from the Russian Front and committed against the British Isles. Allied losses in shipping had been 1,100,000 tons in the last month alone. 'The Germans wanted no peace with England until the latter begged for it.'

Bastianini countered with an outline of the Italian thesis, stressing the danger of playing the opponents' game. The Duce took the view that the 'continuance of war with Russia was a source of great satisfaction to the British and Americans, as they felt that Germany would then have no strength left to fight England.

'As for the position on the various fronts, Italy was compelled to supply nine armies by sea. This provisioning was becoming more and more difficult. Not one convoy, large or small, reached its destination, so that ammunition had now to be flown to Tunis.

'The general food position is so serious, because of the Anglo-American submarine war, which is now directed against motor sailing vessels which one had hitherto not thought worthy of torpedoes, that Sicily, for example, had wheat supplies for only five days, and Sardinia for only three . . . Italy had only 400,000 tons of shipping available, since in March alone 180,000 tons had been sunk; she would soon come to the end of her shipping capacity. . . . How in these circumstances could one ensure the maintenance of 1,374,000 troops in the nine areas dependent on supply by sea? . . . In two to three months the Russians would again be beaten. But in the meantime what would happen to Italy in view of the difficulties just described?'

Mussolini was also concerned that the Italian army could no longer take any initiative, and must confine itself to a defensive rôle. 'One wondered how long that could go on, for an army without initiative is in the end condemned. In these circumstances therefore it was understandable that a wave of pessim-ism was passing through Italy . . . which must not be underrated, nor must one overlook certain manifestations such as the unofficial strikes in Turin and Milan. One always talked of the good old Italian people; but their good nature had its limits. He knew these splendid Italians, as for example after the last war when Fascists, among others, had been flung into boiling water.' Ribbentrop's supposition 'that the strike had been contrived by British agents' was energetically contradicted by Bastianini. It had been the work of Italian Communists, 'who still existed in Italy and who received their instructions from Moscow'.

The strikes in Northern Italy had cast doubts on the internal security of the Fascist régime. The whole matter would be discussed between the Duce and the Fuehrer. Ribbentrop stressed the general need for drastic measures in such cases. This had been successful in Norway and failed in Denmark. There was a special case for such action in France. The implied parallel with Italy, if tactless, is an unconsciously startling revelation of the German Minister's inner view of his ally. He continued by stressing the need for harsh measures in Greece! 'The dynamism of those nations conquered by the Axis was naturally directed against the victors. An understanding between Italy and Greece, for example, was simply not possible. One must confine oneself to setting up a government which would as far as possible be at the beck and call of Germany and Italy. Wherever independent governments were set up in countries occupied by Germany and Italy, they would immediately conspire with England.'

These remarks led Bastianini to bring forward his European programme. 'He wondered whether Germany and Italy were not attempting simultaneously to do two mutually contradictory things, and therefore delivering new propaganda material to England. The English set themselves up as the defenders of the small and weak nations, while Germany was branded as an oppressor at a time when she was in fact fighting Bolshevism in the common interest of all.'

Ribbentrop replied that he had discussed this problem at length with the Fuehrer, and had also written him a memorandum. The recent speech of Churchill had caused great unrest. 'But if the Axis were to make a declaration it could only happen at a moment when the military situation was one hundred per cent in its favour, otherwise the following difficulty would arise. The Fuehrer would have to take drastic measures in the occupied countries to mobilize their labour force . . . If one set up governments in these countries, such measures would be continually thwarted by them. If one were to promise independence to the occupied states at the present moment, the effect of such a declaration would disappear into thin air in a fortnight. One would have to offer clear and substantial concessions . . . If for example one had allowed Laval to rebuild in part the French Army . . . these French divisions would have marched with the Axis so long as things went well. But they would go over to the enemy in twenty-four hours if the situation changed. One had to be very careful in these matters.'

Bastianini agreed, but 'after Churchill's declaration a new political situation had arisen. The German Foreign Minister closed the subject with the remark that one would never again get rid of the ghosts which had been called forth.'

At this point Ribbentrop was summoned by Hitler at the conclusion of the latter's first talk with the Duce.

No direct records of the private conversations between the two Axis leaders during the Klessheim Conference have yet come to light. According to Bastianini, the first talk between Hitler and Mussolini took place in private in the former's apartments almost immediately after the arrival of the Italian delegation.

The conversations continued during the afternoon. Ribbentrop had meanwhile reported to the Fuehrer the substance of his talks with Bastianini that morning, and later told his Italian colleague 'that Hitler hoped to go into the political gesture proposed by me together with the Duce'.[8]

That evening Bastianini hastened to call on Mussolini. He was in constant pain, but refused to see a doctor. He had attempted to talk to Hitler, but, as he told Bastianini: 'Hitler only played the same old record. I let him go on, but tomorrow I shall do the talking and very clearly. The affair of the European Charter doesn't work. He told me that it was premature. He has given orders to the German Air Force to send massive reinforcements to Italy,[e] which I will in due course distribute. He will also send anti-aircraft batteries, and as to the rest of our military requirements, our General Staff must define their requests and naturally on an acceptable scale.[9]

'I insisted that he should find a way of putting an end to the war in Russia . . . He agreed, but as he is convinced that he will be able to deliver a decisive blow against the Russians in the very near future, I could not raise with him peace feelers of any kind.'

Ambrosio was summoned by Mussolini on the evening after the opening of the Conference and told that there would be no further discussion of a German offensive on the Eastern Front as Hitler had given way to all the Duce's arguments.

Ambrosio heard from Ribbentrop an opposite version of this conversa-

e. Hitler appears to have changed his mind on this point after consulting his experts.

tion: 'I learnt later that Mussolini, having referred with Hitler to the situation in Russia, provoked a lively reaction on the part of the latter who intended to demonstrate to him that Russia, in view of enormous losses, was on the eve of final collapse and to this end therefore the German offensive was directed.'[10] There was to be no further talk of a separate peace.

These statements are however somewhat modified by the following indirect evidence. That Mussolini did raise with Hitler the proposal of seeking some compromise with Russia appears from the following confidential report to Ribbentrop later in the month.[11f] The Japanese Ambassador, General Oshima, had been instructed to call on Hitler and seek information on the results of the Klessheim talks. 'The closest collaborator of Oshima claims to know that Mussolini, in his talk with the Fuehrer, pointed to the possibility that Japan could under certain conditions mediate at Kuibychev between the Axis powers and Russia, if Stalin had to be convinced of an absolute military deadlock in the course of this year. The Japanese diplomat believed that this view of Mussolini's was shared in Tokyo. He even hinted that Mussolini had possibly been strengthened in this view . . . from the Japanese side.'

On April 22 Oshima had told Alfieri that he had sounded the German Foreign Minister on the possibility of peace negotiations with the Soviet Union at a later stage, but that Ribbentrop had replied that the conditions proposed by Germany would not be acceptable to Stalin.[12]

That such conditions had been proposed is stated in one unique piece of evidence. Towards the end of April the Italian Military Intelligence forwarded a report to the Duce allegedly giving a summary of the Klessheim talks as transmitted by Oshima to Tokyo as a result of his interview with Hitler.[13] The latter is reported to have said: 'I am convinced that notwithstanding the fact that in Italy the people are fed up with the war and public opinion is hostile to us, Mussolini is decided to continue the struggle at all costs. We cannot in reality consider the two years of war against the Soviet Union as a success, and in order to save ourselves being dragged towards defeat we must this summer turn to a new "system" not from a technical standpoint, but a general one. To tell the truth, this war was begun too soon from our point of view. It should have been started five years later, so that we could have completed our preparations, especially at sea. We expect major help from Japan in this latter respect. I cannot ask you to launch your armies against Siberia. In the first instance, however, we need you to block the arrival of American supplies to the Soviet Union via Vladivostok. In addition, we need Japanese submarine activities in the Atlantic. As to the war in North Africa, we find ourselves in the situation of not being able to decide anything except the withdrawal of our troops.

f. From internal evidence Oshima would have seen Hitler 'at the weekend', between April 23 and 25.

'Oshima asked Hitler if Germany had made any peace offers and Hitler replied that one had been made to the Soviet Union only at the end of last year. It was proposed that the Germans should evacuate all occupied Soviet territories except the Ukraine, but the Soviets energetically turned down the suggestion.'

It is not impossible that this account, which is not confirmed by other existing evidence, was 'planted' on the Italians by Admiral Canaris, the head of the German Military Intelligence, as part of an attempt by certain German quarters to press and encourage Mussolini in his personal efforts with Hitler to seek a way out of the Russian war.

Both among the political and military members of the German delegation at Klessheim there was a climate of defeatism and doubt as to the successful issue of the Russian war, and this attitude was deliberately conveyed to their Italian colleagues.

The Italian Foreign Office officials, whom Bastianini had brought with him, 'had ample opportunities to talk at length with their diplomatic colleagues in Ribbentrop's entourage, and they formed a united impression that the bellicose and rigid intransigence of their chief found no wholehearted response in their minds. Some of them even expressed a completely contrary view and they all stated that they expected, as a result of Mussolini's visit, that there would be a change of direction based on the realities of the situation . . . The military men also expressed the hope that Mussolini, by speaking openly and even threateningly, might succeed in bringing Hitler back to the path of reason.'

Bastianini reported the gist of the conversations to the Duce 'who told me that even Goering appeared to him to be very pensive'.[14]

There does seem to have been apparent, during these Klessheim talks, a definite and significant body of opinion on the German side in favour of a negotiated peace with Russia, and even a conscious feeling that the personal intervention of Mussolini was the only means of bringing Hitler to accept such a solution. The rôle of Goering is unclarified, but he had at least one meeting with Mussolini alone in the Castle of Klessheim on the evening of the first day of the conference, and the latter told Bastianini at the time that they had discussed the Russian war 'which must be terminated at all costs as Goering himself affirmed'.[15]

The failure of the Duce to persuade Hitler to consider such a course meant the disintegration of such a climate in high German circles.

Even before the discussions between the military delegations had got under way, the Germans had drafted their communiqué for release to the press on the talks ostensibly in progress. On coming out of the Duce's room on the first afternoon, Bastianini was met by Ribbentrop, who handed him a verbose and meaningless statement to be given to the press on the talks hitherto conducted between the two leaders. Bastianini rejected the draft, and the issue was postponed until the military conversations had been held.[16] In the meantime, Mackensen minuted to Ribbentrop: 'Under-Secretary Bastianini spoke to me early this morning about what he had discussed in my presence with the German Foreign Minister regarding the communiqué to be given out on the Fuehrer-Duce meeting. He wanted to point out to me once again that in the present circumstances it was difficult for the Duce to return to Rome with a fulsome communiqué in the form drafted by us, but otherwise more or less empty handed. One must be clear that at this moment the whole Italian people had very special expectations about the present meeting. He, Bastianini, personally thought that the statement as drafted by us could be accepted by the Duce without further ado, if at the same time it brought with it the five hundred aircraft for which the Duce had asked in his telegram to the Fuehrer some five weeks previously. He asked me to have yet another word about these questions with the German Foreign Minister. They seemed to him to be of really considerable importance in the present critical time.

'I then brought the matter to the German Foreign Minister, who in my presence immediately raised it with the Fuehrer. The latter answered that the Italian request could not be met since, according to reports in front of him, the concentration of aircraft on the Italian airfields in Southern Italy, Sicily, and Sardinia was such that a single bombardment by the British or Americans would be enough to destroy fifteen, twenty or even thirty aircraft on the ground.'

Mackensen reported this decision to his Italian colleague, who answered that these conditions were not known to him. On the contrary, he seemed to think that these airfields were capable of receiving further aircraft, at least up to the quantity now requested. He was asked to obtain reliable evidence from the Italian air force.[17]

After such an episode it hardly seemed as if the Germans had any serious intentions of sending effective assistance to the Mediterranean theatre.

The general impressions gained during the course of the meetings of the military delegations, and the round table conference under Hitler's chairmanship, as recorded in Ambrosio's notes,[18] reveal the lack of any real progress at these talks, and of any co-ordination in Italo-German planning.[g]

'On the German side insistence on the need to liquidate the Russian problem. It is hoped to succeed in this—given the state of exhaustion of the Russians after the effort made—by adopting the method of trying to annihilate the enemy forces rather than occupying territory.

g. According to Bastianini, however, Keitel had received orders from Hitler to meet Ambrosio's requests. Bastianini, *op cit* p. 93.

'As to the Mediterranean problems, German concern is limited to what one might have for a theatre of secondary importance. They see the need of holding Tunisia at all costs; to pin down enemy forces as long as possible; they fear a landing in Sicily and in Sardinia, and are prepared to ensure all possible aid, but they have a tendency not to allot the available means to passive zones which are not expected to be attacked.'

The Italian proposals about Spain had last been raised in preliminary fashion by Mussolini in his letter to Hitler of March 26, and then embodied in the formal Italian memorandum to the conference, as part of a general set of proposals on the Italian side for an overhaul of the whole Axis position in the Mediterranean.

The subject was raised in the informal talk between Ribbentrop and his Italian colleague on the afternoon of April 9 at Klessheim. 'As to the question of Bastianini about Spain, the German Foreign Minister remarked, with reference to the Duce's letter, that Franco by his attitude in making impossible the operation against Gibraltar had done the Axis a bad turn. He had not only shown himself ungrateful to the Duce and the Fuehrer, but had also proved that he did not possess very great foresight. Whether one could now work out something with the Spaniards was dubious. It was not clear how this could happen, and there was always a great risk that the Spaniards would turn against the Axis. Historical examples showed how strong such a Spanish resistance could be. The Spaniards were also very good and able soldiers in defence.'

The Italian delegation were firm in pressing talks with the Spaniards, perhaps by offering them concessions in Morocco. Ribbentrop thought that if one could persuade Franco that his régime would be endangered unless he allowed Axis troops into Spain, perhaps one could embark on something with that country. But it seemed doubtful whether Franco could be thus convinced. One only had to reflect on what experiences one had had with him on an earlier occasion. He had already once let a favourable opportunity slip, when everything had been prepared to the last detail for the conquest of Gibraltar. The Italians had however received a reliable report that Franco had been surprised that after the Anglo-Saxon landing in North Africa, the Axis had not requested the right to march troops through Spain.

'The German Foreign Minister commented that he was not at all sure. Perhaps the Spaniards would not have opposed an Axis entry. Franco was a wavering man, who had no power of decision, such as the Duce and the Fuehrer possessed.'[19]

The Spanish problem was also raised at the formal sessions of the conference. The Italians hoped to implicate the German leadership in joint pressure on Franco 'to obtain, if not the military co-operation of Spain, at least authorization to cross her territory'. Italy would take part in such an operation with at least one division together with naval and air forces. The objective was not the capture of Gibraltar. Such a plan could only be conceived with Spanish agreement. Mussolini had already proposed a meeting with Franco to such an end, and was counting on the presence of Hitler. But the latter had not forgotten the rebuff of Hendaye in 1940, and had little confidence or interest in an extension of the existing German commitments in the Mediterranean theatre, which he was already unable to honour.

It was agreed at Salzburg that this Spanish conference 'was first foreseen as Tripartite—Fuehrer-Duce-Franco, and then at a later stage it was decided to make it a *tête-à-tête*—Duce-Franco'.[20]

Whatever military solution might be reached at Klessheim, Bastianini was determined to air his political programme of a European union which he and his advisers had been working on for weeks past. The Germans had already received a hint of such an Italian move when Alfieri had pressed in March for the Salzburg meeting. A German Foreign Office minute recorded at the time: 'Since the incident of Casablanca, and in view of the imminent major Allied conference in Washington, a counterweight on the side of the Tripartite powers would be of value and importance. Alfieri gave one to understand that he was not only speaking on his own initiative, but rather that the Duce was thinking in terms of a kind of European conference, without it as yet having any concrete conception.' [21]

It seems that the Duce had been almost convinced by Bastianini that, in a position of military stalemate, and as effective propaganda against the Allies, he could now play a diplomatic rôle in Europe 'as in 1938 he had been able to prevent at the Munich Conference the outbreak of war'. [22]

On the morning of April 9, therefore, Bastianini renewed with Ribbentrop those arguments, which had been abruptly cut short on the previous day. He began by taking up 'the theme of the small states', stressing in the case of the occupied countries their fear that in the event of an Axis victory 'they would become German and Italian provinces'. Ribbentrop's counter-view, as before, was that a decisive military victory must be the prerequisite of any such consideration.

'As to the question of some sort of European Declaration, he, Ribbentrop, supposed that the Duce and the Fuehrer would deal with it in their talks. He would today raise the matter with the Fuehrer . . . He however "had the intuitive feeling that such declarations, as the example of the Atlantic Charter now clearly showed, if they were not well thought out, only caused damage, and their success was anyway problematical". The Fuehrer was of the opinion that a military success must be aimed at, and, particularly with a view to the situation in Tunis, a premature publication of such a declaration would be exploited as a weakness and have the opposite effect.'

Bastianini made a vain and final effort at a private talk over the tea-table, without Alfieri or Mackensen being present, on the afternoon of April 9. Ribbentrop told him of the attempt of Laval 'to obtain a declaration from Germany on France and Europe'. Hitler had answered that he was busy with military matters, and did not think that the time had come for such a statement. 'Laval pulled out every stop in order to get concessions . . . European co-operation was to be understood in the sense that the small states, when the war was won, must understand that they have to follow the leadership of Berlin and Rome. For Italy and Germany had undertaken great duties in regard to Europe, and had therefore claims to the right to make major decisions. They had to defend Europe, and the others must therefore follow them.'

Bastianini replied that 'in international affairs the enemy has sought to throw sand in the eyes of the world through the Atlantic Charter, and has stated that Germany wants to destroy everything. Politically therefore the moment is favourable to repeat that the war waged by Germany and Italy is revolutionary in character. Bolshevism and plutocracy must be beaten . . . and it must thereby be visible that Fascism and National Socialism have not given up. This fight is against plutocracy, not against Europe.'

Behind this verbal fencing lay a more practical disquiet on the German side. The Italians had already hinted, and even threatened, as Bastianini had done at their first talk, at the 'wave of pessimism passing through Italy'. But the present suggestion of a European declaration might well lead not only to organizing the war weariness of the satellites, the Roumanians, the Hungarians, and the Finns, but might lead further to rally the whole bloc to seek a compromise peace, and even under Italian leadership. This was exactly what Bastianini had ultimately in mind.

The Roumanians had already nearly maimed such a plot, if it existed, by making vague soundings of such a nature in Madrid, which had been reported by certain Spaniards to Ribbentrop.[h] He had taxed Bastianini on this subject, and the latter promptly minimized the incident. 'The Duce does not believe it, and the papers are filed away.' And as if abruptly to change the subject, Bastianini drew attention to 'certain Turkish efforts apparently originating at the Adana Conference. It was a question of building up a kind of Balkan entente under the cover of a common protection against the Russians, but with the aim of loosening certain states from the Tripartite Pact. In Greece, Bulgaria, and Roumania people were convinced that in the long run Turkey could not stay out of the war, but must at least take part in the same form as Bulgaria, i.e. through making available airfields and other indirect assistance.' And Bastianini then remarked non-committally,

h. It had been particularly provoking. The Roumanian Minister in Madrid, Dimitrescu, had spoken on instructions to the Argentine and Portuguese envoys 'in relation to the apparent intentions of the Fuehrer to consider peace-feelers'. Independent confirmation showed that the Hungarians had made similar moves in Ankara. See German Collection, Klessheim. Ribbentrop/Bastianini meeting, April 8, 1943.

'One must regard the present position of Turkey with certain question marks.'

Ribbentrop added that from reliable sources it was known that Turkey had made 'agreements in certain contingencies' with England, and remarked that 'if Turkey entered the war one must act very quickly. Both Germany and Bulgaria were agreed that one must then take preventive action beforehand.'

Ambrosio's notes of the general and military conferences showed however little immediate anxiety: 'A landing in Greece is not thought to be imminent, and to be related to the attitude of Turkey. It is thought that the latter will wait long before making a move, inasmuch as Bulgaria, after the recent statement of King Boris, would enter the war against her. Besides Turkey is an element of manoeuvre in British hands against eventual excessive and dangerous Russian claims.'

In a conversation with Ribbentrop on April 10, Bastianini illustrated by an anecdote the attitude of Churchill to Italy in 1940[i] 'which he had learnt about from four different sources, for example, from an Italian head waiter at the Savoy Hotel who had overheard a conversation of Churchill's at a meal. The British Prime Minister had then taken the view that if Italy and Germany succeeded in conquering Egypt before America came into the war, England was finished, but that the Axis could be broken if they did not succeed before the American entry. One would then wear down Italy and finally, after three or four weeks, stir up civil war in Italy. Then the British, as in his time Allenby in Egypt, would be welcomed as saviours bringing law and order after a considerable blood-bath caused by the Fascists.'

Bastianini regarded such a programme as still feasible 'unless one could succeed in cleaning up the most serious situation in the Mediterranean and prevent the war reaching the island and leaping on to the mainland'.[23]

General Ambrosio and his staff had come to Klessheim prepared for orderly technical discussions, both on the future joint conduct of the war and on the lists of urgent requirements in materials and supplies to enable the Tunisian bridgehead to be held. Previous interchanges of correspondence, the visits of Warlimont with Ribbentrop in February, and Goering and Doenitz in March, as well as frequent discussions with Kesselring and Rintelen in Rome, led the Italians to believe at last, after a year since the last summit meeting and in view of the recognized critical phase in Tunisia, that the pending talks would constitute a thorough review of the situation.

As to the general conduct of the war by the Axis, Ambrosio had drafted in note form a minute listing the headings for discussion.

i. Bastianini had been Italian Ambassador in London up to June 1940.

'1. *General Conduct of the War*

Unified conception of the conduct of the war. General lines to be fixed by agreement with the Ally. Need to regard the Italian and Balkan peninsulas as equally exposed. The importance which the defence of our country also has for Germany.

Need to interrupt enemy traffic in Sicily channel both for the defence of Italy and also to assist the defence of the Balkans.

'2. *Army*

(a) *Defence of Italy*

Evaluation of probable intentions of the enemy. Situation of our divisions. "Coastal defence. Need of weapons, artillery, tanks, which we have requested and which are absolutely indispensable for the defence of our coasts. Need for us to withdraw troops from Croatia and from Greece."

(b) *Africa*

Examination of situation in Tunisia . . . Definition of position of Marshal Rommel. German units in Tunisia and those still to be sent. Requests for medium calibre guns . . . Concentration of all means of transport available—sea and air—for a joint effort.

(c) *Croatia*

German military policy in Croatia. Recent "Weiss" operation. "Italian contribution to 'Weiss' has been at least equal if not superior to German."

(d) *Montenegro* (Proposed operations against Mihailović.) "Operations in grand style, and consequent transition to a policy of force are not opportune." . . .

(e) *Russian Front*

Eighth Army. Development of Don battle. "Rectification of German tendency to attribute general retreat to collapse of Allies." Withdrawal of three Army Corps (including Alpine). Movement of the Eighth Army to alternative zone for re-forming. Reconstitution of Eighth Army in Russia.

(f) *German organs in Italy. "The tendency to exceed their functions."*

Sending to Germany of 150,000 Italian soldiers for training in anti-aircraft defence and release of relative material. Equipment and supplies to be released by Germany for bringing up to strength of Italy in Greece and Dodecanese. German assault brigades destined for Sardinia and Aegean.' [24]

In Ambrosio's formal memorandum on the results of the Klessheim Conference, it is possible to trace the decisions taken on some of these points which the Italian delegation had hoped to raise.

The urgent request for tanks for the defence of Italy was met with a refusal. None were available except for 'sectors immediately threatened'.

The Italian Army in Russia could not be found an alternative zone. The Germans therefore offered transport to Germany and Italy. It was later decided in Rome to liquidate this painful episode and to withdraw the Eighth Army Corps to Italy.

As to the proposal for a unified command in the Balkans, the Germans would only discuss this 'in an emergency. It was not possible to foresee in what sector, and how, the attack would come.' In Croatia the Italian garrisons would only be withdrawn from one zone, and the Germans gave no information regarding any military agreement with Pavelić. They also insisted on carrying through the Rome agreements of November 1942 regarding disarming Mihailović.[j]

The Germans asked for 150,000 men for anti-aircraft training in Germany. The first request had been made by Goering in March. This would imply a further call up, and the Duce was unwilling to agree. In naval matters, the vital question of sea transport to Tunisia was hardly touched. The Germans said 'the problem was one of method rather than resources'. The urgent requests for fuel oil met with the German response that 'they could hand over nothing', but hopes were expressed of stepping up Roumanian production. The Duce's request of March 25 for five hundred planes for the Italian Air Force was evaded, and the answer in regard to aviation spirit was the same as that to the Italian Navy.[k]

The tenor of the military conferences at Klessheim mirrors the reluctance of the German High Command either to consider a combined war strategy with their Italian ally or to face the supply issues involved in maintaining her armed forces in being for the defence of Tunisia, and, in the end, the Italian mainland.

German fears of the political collapse of Italy, and their distrust of Bastianini and Ambrosio, deepened. Sensing this atmosphere, and also wishing indirectly to sound the Germans on their views on the internal situation in Italy, Mussolini shrewdly appealed for advice from an unexpected quarter. He asked to see Himmler. The conversation is summarized by the latter's representative in Rome, Dollmann.[25]

Mussolini was particularly concerned with the internal effects of a prolonged war on the political structure of both countries. Himmler, while expressing satisfaction with the system of forced labour and concentration camps as a prophylactic against political disorder, did not recommend similar measures in Italy. He thought rather that special militia units should be formed on the model of the S.S. for security duties, and offered to send instructors and the latest equipment to set up a complete division. He considered that the actual commander of the Italian Fascist militia, General Galbiati, was probably not up to his task. Himmler had met him in 1942 in

j. According to Roatta *op cit* p. 182, these talks took place in December 1942.

k. The memorandum of Ambrosio on 'Subjects to be raised at the Conference', was confined to Army matters. There is no record of the points to be raised by the other two services. The naval demands had already been made during Doenitz's visits, and those of the Air Force through Goering and Kesselring.

Berlin, and had rated him 'as a good Fascist, but in my S.S. at the most a non-commissioned officer'.[26]

This proposal of Himmler's was almost the only practical result of the whole meeting. It aroused Hitler's renewed interest, and he also discussed with the Duce the position of the Fascist régime in Italy, and such possible safeguarding measures. [27] As he had expressed it, at a military conference during the previous month: 'The Duce once said to me, "I did not myself know how. I only know that if, in Italy, Fascism is not victorious, Italy is lost" . . . It is roughly similar in Austria and the Sudetenland, where the National Socialist movement never came to anything. Only in Italy . . . (text illegible) the personality of the Duce spans everything, and then there is the courage of his own actively Fascist military organizations. There is no doubt about that. But of course the ideological basis is not there. I have it in a letter from Farinacci.'

Jodl interposed: 'A personal bodyguard is important,' and Hitler retorted, 'I only hope that the guard does not string him up! ' [1]

There is also a subsequent reference by Hitler to the private conversations between the two leaders. 'At Klessheim the Duce made a remark while we were having dinner together. He suddenly said, "My Fuehrer, I don't know; I have no successor in the Fascist revolution. A chief of state can be found to succeed me, but no one will continue the Fascist revolution." ' [28]

On the morning of April 10, after a breakfast of milk and biscuits, Mussolini was able to attend a closing plenary session on the military situation. There was no further news from the Eastern Front. Hitler warmed to his departing guest. 'Duce, I guarantee to you that Africa will be defended. The situation is serious, but not desperate. Recently I read the story of the siege of Verdun in the First World War; Verdun resisted successfully the attacks of the best German regiments. I do not see why this should not happen also in Africa. With your support, Duce, my troops will make Tunis the Verdun of the Mediterranean.' [29]

The formal meeting was closed; the two dictators led the way down the staircase of the main hall of Klessheim Castle where the members of both delegations were assembled. Some of them saw Mussolini for the first time since his arrival, as he had not left his room except for this one brief public appearance. Both leaders 'were livid, with contracted features, and vacant eyes'. The Italian delegates saw them with alarm. 'They seem like two invalids,' said one. 'Rather like two corpses,' said Dr Pozzi, Mussolini's personal doctor.[30]

A private lunch was held in Bastianini's apartment, at which, apart from

1. Hitler Military Conference. Dated from internal evidence 'the beginning of March 1943'. Hitherto unpublished. Original in the library of the University of Pennsylvania, U.S.A.

the Fuehrer and the Duce and their respective Foreign Secretaries, only Goering was present. The only point of conversation recorded, apart from the familiar comparisons made by Hitler between himself and Frederick the Great, was the Fuehrer's offer of a free hand to Mussolini in dealing with Franco in an attempt to bring him into the war on the Axis side. But as Hitler remarked, in getting up from the table, 'I do not believe that he will do it.' [31]

The two leaders then went through the formalities of leave-taking at the train. The Duce was in intense pain on the journey back to Rome, though a further radiographic inspection on his return yielded no new symptoms. He said to Alfieri before leaving: 'My illness has a name: "convoys".' [32]

The Duce had arrived at Salzburg in an exhausted physical condition, and for one entire day all talks had to be suspended 'as he was not in a state to participate in them'.[33] Hitler failed to persuade his guest to be examined by German doctors. The egregious Dr Morell flitted expectantly in and out of the public rooms of the castle, dispensing pills. 'A face like a full moon, with gold pince-nez, a green jacket and long grey trousers. He gives me,' wrote his Italian colleague, 'the impression of an unsavoury person.' [34]

Both dictators seem nevertheless to have been satisfied with their encounter. The familiar, indefinable and mutual hypnotism generated at such moments had reasserted itself once again. 'The Fuehrer told me,' Goebbels wrote in his diary, 'that the Duce had been really restored to his old form during their four days' discussion. The Fuehrer did everything he could, and by putting every ounce of nervous energy into the effort, succeeded in pushing Mussolini back on the rails. In those four days the Duce underwent a complete change at which his entourage was also amazed. When he got out of the train the Fuehrer thought that he looked like a broken old man; when he left again, he was in high fettle and ready for anything. We can see by the policies which he is now pursuing that his regeneration is continuing . . . The Duce understands clearly that there can be no further salvation for him except to win or die with us. The Fuehrer is very happy that he will now adopt a tougher tone in Italy.' [35]

The Duce was, as always, susceptible to this treatment. Hitler had lectured him about Stalingrad, and of the need to stay in Tunisia 'until quarter past twelve'. His advisers, however, political and military, came back from the Klessheim talks in a sharply contrasting mood of frustration and distrust.

PART ONE

Book III

CHAPTER ONE

THE END IN AFRICA

• •

ON his return from the Klessheim conference, Mussolini reported to the King that 'he had found much understanding on the part of Hitler, who had promised help in the form of tanks and planes for Sicily, and had undertaken to send back our Second Army Corps from Russia'.[1] On the same day the Duce also told Kesselring, 'On my visit to the Fuehrer I saw the unanimity of everyone, . . . as to the importance of Tunisia. All possibilities are open to us if we resist and therefore we shall hold on.' Kesselring could hardly appreciate this note of optimism, and replied that 'nevertheless we need men, munitions and precisely at once'. The Duce added more realistically, 'We have sacrificed our fleet in the African war. The merchant navy has lost threequarters of its strength.' [2] Allied attacks on shipping and ports were increasing. Two Italian cruisers had been sunk in harbour. It was clear from the attitude of the Germans at the conference that they were unable to supply the Italian battle fleet to enable it to put to sea.[a] The Italians equally rejected any German control of the North African convoys, and Doenitz had concluded that the only solution of the naval war lay in an intense concentration on the submarine campaign. This had been put to the Italians during the conference as one of Germany's main strategic objectives.[b]

Neither Ambrosio nor Bastianini shared the Duce's optimism over the summit talks. As the former told Puntoni after an audience with the King on April 16: 'The Salzburg agreements have served no useful purpose.

a. The three battleships could only put to sea for twenty hours (six hours of fighting). Italian Collection. Bastianini. Conference with Chiefs of Staff, April 18, 1943.

b. See Italian Collection. Ambrosio's notes of the Conference. On April 11 Doenitz pressed for increasing the submarine campaign at a Fuehrer Naval Conference. He was also in favour of occupying the north coast of Spain (Operation 'Gisela') in order to secure U-boat bases for the Mediterranean run, but this could only be done with Spanish consent. (Fuehrer Naval Conferences, 1943, pp. 19–21.)

Germany is only thinking of "her" war and not of Italy's interests, which are henceforth decisively compromised . . . Only on the repatriation of the Second Army Corps from Russia has there been not too much argument, but the formula worked out for the return of our units seems to be somewhat vague. There is talk of a "reorganization to be carried out in Italy rather than Germany". I am not substantially in agreement with the euphoria of the Duce. We have got and shall get nothing.' [3]

Bastianini had already told the German Ambassador two days earlier that he 'had come away with the impression, and he could confirm that the Duce had too, that as things were the result was very reassuring, but now he heard from many different sides, and particularly from General Ambrosio, that in the question of fulfilling Italian military requests practically nothing had happened. The Duce took the opposite view, and was satisfied also on this matter. But he (Bastianini) had gained no clear picture of exactly what had come out of it.' Mackensen admitted that, on the German side, 'we ourselves had run up against certain differences of view and lack of clarity, which perhaps had not been tidied up'. In other words, the German High Command had no intention of fulfilling any programme of military deliveries to Italy. The German Ambassador hedged. 'These were military matters, and on our side, jurisdictions were sharply drawn.' He admitted however that since Bastianini had raised the subject it became a political question, and it was important that his Italian colleague 'should know exactly what had been done at Klessheim in the military sphere'. He had talked to Kesselring and it was proposed that a meeting of German and Italian political and military representatives in Rome should be held to reach 'complete clarity'.[4]

Bastianini summoned this conference at five o'clock on Sunday, April 18, at Palazzo Chigi. Ambrosio asked drily whether the meeting would simply duplicate the recent discussions, to which his political colleague replied: 'Today it is a matter of establishing exactly what was the outcome of the Salzburg talks.' Kesselring expressed his regret at not having been present 'as with his particular knowledge of the Mediterranean, many things could have perhaps been simplified'. Ambrosio then summarized the results of the previous military discussions; the written negative reply by the Germans to the principal request for tanks. 'All this in regard to a request for 1,250 tanks.'

Kesselring's attempted defence made the fundamental point of the German situation: 'If we had not had the disaster of Stalingrad a great part of the requests could have been satisfied, but the German General Staff has instead had to throw in all its reserves to stop the Soviet steam roller.'

Ambrosio pointed out that the Italian demands represented needs, and, with a thrust at Cavallero, 'the former Chief of the General Staff let them pile up and hence today the figures of the requests are so high'. Kesselring undertook to support all Italian requests during his next visit to Germany.[c]

There was no response from Berlin.

On April 30 Mussolini himself telegraphed to Hitler: 'If, as I have already several times represented, the air problem in the Mediterranean is not solved at once by sending air support to counterbalance the shattering air superiority of the enemy, it will no longer be possible for any warship, or supply-ship, or plane, to arrive in Tunisia. This means losing Tunisia at once, without saving anything. Attempts to use destroyers for transport are also doomed to fail. Three destroyers, two of which were laden with German troops and one with ammunition, were lost today as the result of continuous air attacks by huge enemy air formations escorted by 70–120 fighters.

'Fuehrer, the question is one of the utmost urgency. The troops in Tunisia are fighting splendidly, as the enemy himself is forced to admit, but if we cannot supply them their fate is sealed.' [5]

Hitler replied on May 2. 'The Second Air Corps had a strength on March 1 of 1,012 front line aircraft. During March a further 574 planes have been sent. Stronger reinforcements were sent in April. Last month alone 669 front line planes were dispatched. This number only includes the normal consignments of planes without counting those attached to the detachments transferred to Italy, and the transport planes. I am studying at the moment what can be done to strengthen our air forces further. For this purpose Marshal Kesselring will call on you today.' [6] The Italian Embassy in Berlin, who transmitted this telegram, saw at once its implications. 'The Germans today are not in a position to conduct a struggle on two fronts. They regard the Tunisian one as lost. They will not send again a single plane. The Fuehrer naturally does not say so, but it is easy to understand from his reticence.' [7]

The discontent within the Italian High Command at the lack of a consistent direction of the war by Mussolini, which was a leading element in the gathering opposition to the whole structure of his leadership, is seen in an unsigned and unheaded minute, dated May 2, and initialled by Bastianini.

'The order of the Duce to reinforce Tunisia at all costs with warships has produced a sharp reaction in the Italian High Command. The reaction at Navy Headquarters has been the most open and lively, and has in this regard clearly and insistently expressed a contrary view to the use of naval vessels for transporting troops.

'The three warships loaded with troops sunk recently by the enemy in

c. Italian Collection. 'Meeting at Palazzo Chigi about the requests for military material to the German side.' April 18, 1943. The Italian representatives were Ambrosio, Riccardi, and Fougier; the German, Mackensen, Kesselring and Colonel von Waldenburg. The latter was acting for General von Rintelen, who had been badly injured in an air accident, and only returned to duty the following day. (See Rintelen *op cit* p. 194.)

In a letter to the Duce, dated April 19, Bastianini gave detailed lists of Italian requirements, and German deliveries to date.

the Sicily channel have naturally exacerbated the discussions and criticisms of the person of the Head of the government, who in his capacity as Commander-in-Chief of the Armed Forces, issues directives on the conduct of the war and orders which are often contrary to the opinions expressed by the competent General Staff Officers.

'Lively resentment has also been provoked by the direct interference of Marshal Kesselring, whose influence on the Duce in the conduct of operations is a subject of open comment. The conduct of the war, which is a pre-eminently amphibious one, is confided to the exclusive direction of the General Staff Officers of the army, whose incompetence in such matters is well known.

'For some days, with the increasingly critical situation in Tunisia, unfavourable comments at the expense of the Duce and Marshal Kesselring have been openly, and often violently, expressed, and with a significant solidarity between Generals and Admirals, to such a point as to give rise to a suspicion that a "common attitude" between the leaders of the Armed Forces is under way, and also in agreement with certain German elements.' [8]

On May 4, at a meeting between Mussolini and Kesselring, there was still talk of reinforcing Tunisia, though no reference to the Fuehrer's message. The Duce pointed out that to use any further destroyers for such a purpose would prevent the main battle fleet putting to sea. But, as Kesselring said, the Duce must decide on the use or not of destroyers as emergency troop transports. '1,200–1,300 troops could be sent in ten days by air to Bizerta. But the three ex-French destroyers will not be ready till mid-May. Less than 200 men a day is much too few. At least a battalion and its equipment must be sent daily.' The Duce added plaintively, 'One sees clearly the value of control of the sea. If we could send two armoured divisions, we could revolutionize the situation in Tunisia. The crisis will be grave during the next eight to ten days.' [9] He was optimistic. Four days later, on May 8, Allied forces entered Tunis and Bizerta, and the last foothold in Italian Africa was lost, together with more than 200,000 German and Italian troops killed, wounded, or taken prisoner.[d]

The loss of Tunisia, 'the front line of Europe' as Mussolini had called it, heralded an early threat by the enemy to the Italian islands and mainland. The Allies would certainly strike in the first instance either at Sicily or Sardinia as a move to an assault on the Italian peninsula, either as a single operation or geared to an all-out offensive against the southern coasts of Europe at a number of points, ranging from Spain to France and the Eastern Mediterranean.

d. For a detailed account of the last stages of the African campaign from the Italian standpoint see the book written by Rommel's successor, General Messe. *La Guerra in Africa* (revised edition 1960), which aims at refuting the version of events given by Field Marshal Montgomery in his Memoirs.

Whatever the direction of the ultimate Allied strategic objective, both Sicily and Sardinia were now the immediate outposts of the Axis defences of the Southern coasts of Europe. Their protection must fall to Germany, and indeed the loss of Tunis forced on the German High Command the whole problem of the Mediterranean War, at a moment when a major German offensive in the East was planned to change the whole balance of the war.[e]

The Fuehrer's prime concern in the Mediterranean theatre was to keep the war as far away as possible from the borders of Germany, and towards this end the territory of metropolitan Italy must be regarded as a key strategic area to be defended, which might at any time become an operational zone. Such a defence implied the strengthening of the German military position, and this in turn raised issues, hitherto muted, of an integrated Axis command in Italy. Hitler had by now realized that he might have to go further and even 'take over the Italian positions with German forces, and keep—and this point was the decisive consideration—the war as far away as possible from the heart of Europe and thereby from the frontiers of Germany'.[10]

On May 5 General Rintelen reported from Rome on the state of the Italian Army which 'has up till now in the war not carried out its appointed tasks and indeed has failed everywhere to do so. The main reasons for this are its completely inadequate armament and equipment, the faulty training of the officer corps, the insufficient psychological preparation of most of the other ranks and the lack of enthusiasm owing to doubts as to the favourable outcome of the war.' The Italian troops fighting alongside the Germans in Russia and Africa were glaringly inferior both in weapons and equipment. 'This lowers the will to fight and the Italian soldier must regard himself only as a camp-follower and a second line soldier except for certain deeds of individual bravery . . . There was no question of any inner participation in the vital battle of our time. The mass of the Italian people, as well as the soldiers, had on the average little understanding of an "Italian Great Power" or a "Mare Nostrum". The inner driving force to carry through such an idea is lacking.'

The High Command under Marshal Cavallero 'has got the best out of the army and war industry', but, given their structure, not much could be done, and the effort would probably deteriorate. There had been no improvement in the production of arms and equipment for the Italian army during the course of the war, but only through German deliveries. 'It has been hindered by Allied air attacks, lack of organizing ability, and an economic system which is dishonest and considers only private gain.

'The core of the Italian Army has been destroyed in Africa, Greece and Russia.' Italian troops were now 'not up to the burdensome problems of a major struggle: they are only of value as a weak stop-gap of a strong ally.

e. The original date for this offensive against the Kursk peninsula was May 3, but with the pending fall of Tunis it was postponed until June 12.

The main question-mark will be the reaction of the Italian Army to the invasion of the Motherland. The result of the first days of the battle will have a real importance.' If the first invasion wave were successful, 'most unpleasant consequences may follow in view of the atmosphere of reigning fatalism'. The weakest point was the absence of any Italian mobile reserves. There was only one armoured division in existence in Sicily, and that equipped with old French tanks.

'In summary, it must be said that the Italian army alone is not in a position successfully to ward off a major assault on its metropolitan territory. This can only be expected with strong German support and central mobile reserves.' [11]

In spite of the warnings of Rintelen, Hitler continued to underestimate Italian susceptibilities, now pathologically sharpened by the realities and implications of the loss of Africa. On May 6 Kesselring informed his Italian colleague that three German divisions would be re-formed within a few weeks out of the survivors from, and reinforcements destined for, Tunisia, and would be available for the defence of Italy. Mussolini expressed an instantaneous reluctance. 'We need first of all tanks and planes . . . As to our defence, the three divisions will change nothing.'

On May 9 the Germans offered two further divisions. Four days later, Mussolini sent a message to Hitler thanking him for the German offer, 'but pointing out that the commitment of three German divisions in all in Italy would be sufficient, and asking instead for heavy air force reinforcements in Italy'. In a reply to the Duce, explaining to him the position, it was stressed that the divisions to be formed out of the elements from Tunis would be organizationally and in numbers so weak that one could not compare them with regular divisions. For this reason, as well as the two divisions now in Sicily and Sardinia (the forces available were lacking for the third), the 16th Armoured and the 'Hermann Goering' divisions would be sent to Italy.[f]

For the first time a note of personal alarm and mutual suspicion had been sounded between the two Axis leaders. In the presence of Rintelen, Mussolini declared that three divisions would be sufficient, that he would make use of the hitherto undeployed German units in Italy, and would not accept further troops in the country. There were increasing rumours and indications pointing to a deep crisis impending in Italian affairs. The German High Command had no confidence in either Ambrosio or Roatta. Mussolini had recently and inexplicably refused to accept German training personnel for the 'M' division now being formed, as a result of the agreement at Klessheim in April, for purposes of internal security.

In order to study these developments, to attempt to mobilize Italian re-

f. German Collection. German War Office Archives. Rintelen report July 19, 1943. The message from Mussolini to Hitler was dispatched on the evening of May 12. No text has yet to come to light, nor Hitler's reply.

sources, and gain their consent to joint defensive planning, Hitler decided to send Admiral Doenitz again to Rome. Control of the sea by a joint Axis effort might still delay the Allied assault on Italy and the off-shore islands.

He arrived on the afternoon of May 12. In a preliminary conference with Admiral Riccardi and the Italian naval chiefs, they stressed that an attack on the Italian islands must be expected 'any day'. Enemy air attack had destroyed rail communications with Sicily, which must now be supplied by sea from Naples, and the island had reserves for only seven days. A similar situation existed in Sardinia. The Italian navy estimated that Sicily would not be under attack until the enemy could clear and utilize the ports of Bizerta and Tunis and sweep the minefields between North Africa and Sicily, and that therefore the threat to Sardinia was more urgent. 'An enemy invasion of Spain or Southern France is not being considered. The main objective of the Western Allies is a free line of communication through the Straits of Sicily. To attain this objective, the Balearic Islands and Southern France are not essential; however, Sicily and Sardinia are important. The Italian Admiralty therefore believes that Sardinia will be the first to be invaded. An invasion of Sicily may be expected some time after June 22. If the supply system fails, Donitz interjected, the islands cannot be held. However, a defeat at sea would not be decisive for us.'[g]

All kinds of craft might have to be used, including submarines and cruisers. Harbour facilities must be ruthlessly exploited. As Doenitz said, 'The responsible Italian officer must have the right to draft civilians for this task. It must not happen, as it did in North Africa, that we are defeated because our supply system failed.' Air cover and support were vital, and he promised to support the previous and unsuccessful Italian requests for increased air power.[12]

On the following morning he called on Ambrosio. 'A polite but formal reception.' Doenitz repeated the thesis of the Italian navy that it was more important 'to supply transport than to engage the enemy in battle'. Ambrosio, whose relations with his naval colleagues were increasingly distant, commented that 'he felt that submarines and cruisers should fight'. To which the German Admiral answered, 'The naval forces have already ceased fighting.' Ambrosio disagreed with the Italian naval thesis, and thought that 'the problem of Sardinia will arise after that of Sicily. At Salzburg it was said that Sardinia would be more in danger than Sicily. I think however that today the latter is the more threatened.' He also disagreed that the main task of the Navy was a supply one. The enemy must be held away from the Italian coast, the defences of which were weak, unlike those constructed by the Germans on the Atlantic shores of France.

Later that morning Doenitz was received by Mussolini, who appeared 'well, optimistic, composed, very frank, sincere, and amicable'. The Duce at once

g. The Italian battle fleet consisted of only three large battleships, three cruisers, and light destroyers at La Spezia.

made it clear, to Doenitz's surprise, that he was opposed to Hitler's offer of May 9 of five German divisions for the defence of Italy.

'Since August of last year I have had the conviction that the battle has been lost at sea. I have always been aware of the problem of the air. In recent days our inferiority in this field has been strong. I look on all this with the greatest calm. However, we do not know the Anglo-American plans . . . But I maintain that with the air superiority of the enemy a landing is one thing; an invasion another. In the latter case one has to supply divisions fighting on foreign soil. As regards troops, we do not need men; we have them. The Fuehrer has suggested five divisions. I think this is too many; three are enough, provided they are well equipped and mobile, and armoured. In my telegram of yesterday evening (May 12) to the Fuehrer I have put down the details.' [h] He then asked the German Admiral for the main reason for his visit, and was told that it concerned the problem of supplying Sicily. 'I am ready,' said Doenitz, 'to place at the disposal of Admiral Riccardi all the German naval forces in the Mediterranean, including all the units at Marseilles, and submarines when bases would be available.' [13]

That evening a final consultation took place between Doenitz and Kesselring. The latter referred to Hitler's offer to send the two further divisions to Italy.[i] 'The fact that the Italian High Command had partially refused the Fuehrer's offer of five divisions was reported directly to the German High Command, without informing the Commanding General South (Kesselring himself) or General Rintelen. Kesselring considers this an act of political importance inasmuch as it proves that the Italians want to remain masters in their own house. Relations between him and General Ambrosio are not very cordial.' [14] But like Ambrosio, he felt that Sicily was more in danger than Sardinia. The Italian and German naval forces together were so weak that their role in an invasion attempt would be minor. Kesselring was going to recommend reinforcing the second German Air Fleet.

Doenitz returned to Germany on the afternoon of May 14 and reported to Hitler on these Rome conversations. He had concluded that 'the plan to hold the Italian islands will result in a purely defensive operation. It will consume much energy without getting the Axis out of its defensive position.' The only hope of breaking the deadlock on the naval side would be a drastic stepping up of the submarine war. At present the only outbound route for submarines was a narrow lane in the Bay of Biscay.

Hitler then voiced his central suspicions. He believed that 'the Duce partly rejected the offer of several German divisions under the influence of the Italian High Command in order to keep a free hand'. The Fuehrer asked also whether Doenitz thought 'the Duce is determined to carry on to the

h. There is no record of this telegram.
i. The 'Hermann Goering' and the Seventh Airborne divisions.

end'. The reply was that Doenitz 'accepts this as certain, but he cannot be sure, of course. He has gained the impression that the primary failing of the Italians is their lack of initiative.' Hitler added that 'he does not trust the Italian upper classes. He believes that a man like Ambrosio would be happy if Italy could become a British dominion today.' [15]

Kesselring had already stated on May 13 that 'he considers an attack on the Iberian peninsula the best way of bringing relief to the Mediterranean situation and intends to submit such a plan to the Fuehrer'.[16] Doenitz again pressed the same case at this conference at the Fuehrer's headquarters. In view of the critical situation in the submarine war, the occupation of Spain, including Gibraltar, would be the best strategic solution. This would constitute an attack against the flank of the Anglo-Saxon offensive, the Axis would regain the initiative, and a radical change would take place in the Mediterranean, and submarine warfare would be given a much broader basis.

Hitler answered: 'We are not capable of an operation of this kind, since it would require first-class divisions. Occupation of Spain without the consent of the Spaniards is out of the question, since they are the only tough Latin people and would carry on guerilla warfare in our rear. In 1940 it might have been possible to get Spain to agree to such a move. However, the Italian attack on Greece in the autumn of 1940 shocked Spain. The Axis must face the fact that it is saddled with Italy.'[17]

This conference at least showed that there was no separate naval solution to the Mediterranean theatre. Equally, the defence of Italy could no longer be treated as an exclusively military problem. In reinforcing the German units in Italy account must henceforth be taken of their ultimate rôle in the event of Italian defection or collapse, and in supplying the Italian armed forces one must reckon on their ultimate use against Germany in event of a political coup d'état in Rome, followed by the withdrawal of Italy from the war. On May 9 Keitel referred cryptically to 'approaches to the Duce in Italy, if the situation in Italy becomes grave'.[18] On May 10 Rommel called on both the Fuehrer and Goebbels. 'I took the opportunity to stress the small capacity to fight and readiness for battle of the Italians, and thus the very serious position in Italy.'

Between May 10–16 a 'Survey of the position in event of the withdrawal of Italy from the War' was drafted for consideration by the German General Staff. The dilemma would be how 'to hold the fronts on the southern periphery of Europe, how far German forces were sufficient for the task, and what allied forces could be employed'. Italy, the Balkans, and Southern France would have to be regarded as operational zones. [19] At the same time, under the code names 'Alaric' and 'Konstantin', detailed planning began to prepare the necessary counter-measures; the former to deal with the occupation of Italy, and the latter to take over the Italian positions in the Balkans. The original General Staff directives for these two operations do not seem to have been authorized explicitly by Hitler, who preferred to give top secret verbal instructions to the two commanders concerned. General Loehr, commanding the German Army Group South-East, was summoned to Hitler's headquarters for this purpose immediately after the fall of Tunis.

At a conference of advisers on May 15, Hitler spoke of probable developments in Italy and Greece. 'Prospects for an early commitment of forces exist.' [20] In regard to Italy, Hitler decided to entrust Rommel rather than Kesselring with this task, and by the middle of May the former was established with a skeleton staff in Austria.[j]

The forces for 'Alaric' and 'Konstantin'—and these two operations to take over military control of Italy and the Balkans were closely linked—could only come from the German Army Groups in the West and the East. Any premature allocations of such forces would mean the postponement of Hitler's Grand Design of seeking a solution of the war in Russia by the summer. The Russian operation was held up, and, for the first time since the outbreak of war, the Germans gave their full attention to the Italian scene, and to the assessment of future Allied strategic moves in the Mediterranean theatre.

j. German Collection. War Office Archives. Rommel's skeleton staff was set up at Wiener-Neustadt from May 14 to July 14. On May 16 Rommel noted, 'Staff must be assembled'.

CHAPTER TWO

DIPLOMATIC INTERLUDE

(April—May 1943)

THE KLESSHEIM talks in April between Hitler and Mussolini marked the opening of a renewed German diplomatic offensive in Europe. The Stalingrad disaster had not only immediate and fatal military repercussions on the conduct of the war, but cracked the prestige of the Axis, weakened German morale at home, and encouraged the Italians to seek support among the minor satellites and the neutrals to challenge German supremacy in controlling occupied Europe, and to explore the possibilities of a 'political' solution to put an end to hostilities. Hitler now moved to reassert German authority within the continental fortress and stifle any such Italian initiatives.

Following the departure of Mussolini from Salzburg, first Marshal Antonescu and then Admiral Horthy were called to the presence of the Fuehrer. To the former he delivered a requisitory on the subversive intrigues of the Roumanian Foreign Minister in hinting at alleged German moves for a separate peace with Russia, adding that his last peace offer had been made to England in July 1940, 'since when the Germans had initiated no further negotiations'. [1]

To Horthy, the theme of total resistance was expanded with a highly personal touch of historical rhetoric. In 1918 the German collapse had been grave, 'but in spite of this, the essential substance of Germany as well as that of Hungary, Bulgaria, the Baltic States and Finland had been saved and thereby the Baltic countries and the Finns had been rescued by Germany from Russian domination'.

This collapse had not been expected by anyone. In the West, Germany's enemies were at the end of their strength. 'This the Fuehrer had learned from Lloyd George personally in a conversation at Obersalzberg.[a] It would have

a. This visit took place in September 1936.

been inconceivable for them to have continued the war. In the East—and this was decisive—there was no power left . . . The Bolsheviks had unfortunately control of the Ukraine, but on the other hand they were driven out of the Baltic region. If there had been a firm government in Germany at the time, an energetic drive would have dispersed to the winds the completely unorganized Red forces.

'Today a collapse of the Central Powers in the East would no longer create a vacuum but the mighty strength of Bolshevism would immediately press westwards. It was very important that as a result of this situation, all the allies should be clear that at the moment it was a question of total war, and that there was no distinction between the East and West, Russian and Anglo-Saxon. No Balkan alliance of Turkey, Roumania and Hungary could hold out against Russia in the same way as the German Reich with its 240 divisions. It was therefore urgently necessary that there should be no distinction between East and West.

'One could say perhaps that one could go over to the defensive in the East but this would merely mean that the Bolsheviks, who had already been severely mauled, could recover. Also the proposal to build an East Wall was pure theory.'

Bolshevism represented a permanent danger. Strong leaders like Horthy, Hitler, Mussolini and Antonescu would one day no longer be alive; then the danger of Bolshevism, if it had not already been liquidated, would remain and bring with it severe consequences. 'This mighty struggle might go on for decades as with the Huns and the Turks in the past.' [2]

The main purpose of these April talks was to impress on the minor allies the determination of Germany to make no concessions and to fight to the end. The alarm expressed at Klessheim by Ribbentrop to Bastianini about Roumanian feelers in Madrid and similar Hungarian moves in Ankara took the form of bringing pressure on the Roumanian and Hungarian heads of state to dismiss Mihai Antonescu and Kallay,[b] their respective Foreign Ministers, and to seek Italian backing to such an end. But a further if more deeply concealed cause of German anxiety lay in the signs of an Italian 'design' for Europe. The Germans were, for instance, not clear what had passed during Kallay's visit to Rome early in April. Just as the Roumanians had hinted at impending peace feelers by the Germans in Madrid, the Hungarians had apparently, and perhaps on surer ground, insinuated similar intentions on the part of the Italian government. On April 14, therefore, Ribbentrop had instructed the German Minister in Budapest to give a formal summary to the Hungarian President of the Council of the Klessheim talks with the Italians. Both Axis partners were decided to pursue the war in the East to the end. Ribbentrop attached 'importance to informing him of this message because it

b. Kallay was President of the Council as well as Foreign Minister.

would be clear from it that Kallay's communications to you on his talks with the Duce do not seem to convey the real attitude of the Duce'.[3]

Ribbentrop energetically sought evidence of a concerted conspiracy against German hegemony in Europe. Did the clues all lead to Rome?

The German Foreign Minister sent Dr Paul Schmidt to Italy to hand personally to Mussolini alone—and significantly not in the presence of Bastianini —the list of complaints presented by the Germans to the Roumanians and Hungarians, at Klessheim.[c]

Schmidt reported, on his return, that he had explained verbally to the Duce that Hitler 'had spoken seriously to Marshal Antonescu about Mihai Antonescu and that we would keep the Duce informed of the results. I also spoke of the mistrust which Hitler had expressed to Horthy in regard to Kallay. The Duce remarked that he regarded Mihai Antonescu with great reserve. Kallay had made a particularly bad impression on him, because during his visit to Rome he had appeared as "the apotheosis of Hungarian parliamentarianism". In addition he had reported on his reception by the Pope, who had complained that the Axis powers had not made any peace proposals, to which the Duce had replied that there was no question of such a move. Kallay then reported further that the Pope had stated that he himself was not in a position to forward such peace proposals so long as Germany acted as harshly as she had done up to the present in the occupied territories. The Duce answered that this was not his business, but that soft measures were pointless as he had learnt from his own experience in Greece, Slovenia, and elsewhere.' [4]

Mussolini's pliant and evasive tact brought little satisfaction to Ribbentrop, who was further concerned at the forthcoming Roumanian visit to Rome, which was already long overdue. At the end of April Ribbentrop asked the Italian Government to postpone such an invitation. If the Roumanian Foreign Minister came at this juncture to Italy 'it will appear that Hitler's comments to the Marshal (Antonescu) are not taken seriously . . . Could not the Italian government make the excuse of the war situation in Tunis to postpone the visit? In a roundabout way the point could also be made that Hitler naturally would not receive any foreign statesman who did not possess the confidence of the Duce.' [5] Mussolini told the German Ambassador that it would be 'delicate'. He found Mihai Antonescu 'perhaps even more unattractive than the Fuehrer does', but this would be the fourth postponement, and further there was the question of oil supplies.[d]

The Duce bowed however to the Fuehrer's wishes, and in Mackensen's

c. Schmidt delivered three messages, but the one above represented the key purpose of his mission. There were two members of the German Foreign Office named Paul Schmidt; one was the indispensable interpreter and the other was head of the Press section. It was presumably the latter who came on this mission to Rome.

d. This was a sharp reminder of the failure of the Germans to meet the Italian requirements at Klessheim.

presence sent a cable giving the pretext of the battle in progress for Tunis in order to postpone the visit. [6]

On the same day as Ribbentrop approached the Duce on the Antonescu visit, Goebbels noted in his diary: 'From the Research Office's reports,[e] I learn that the Roumanians were by no means as enthusiastic about the meeting at Salzburg as we had imagined. They felt the clear lack of aim in our policy and our war effort. Mihai Antonescu seems to be especially busy pointing this out. He is very unreliable. In a diplomatic report, I read about a conversation of his in which he emphasized that the Italians knew all about his aims and plans. It looks as though Bastianini were playing a somewhat dubious game.' [7] The suspicions entertained by Ribbentrop during his February visit to Rome of the political reliability of the Italian High Command were extending to the circles of Palazzo Chigi.

In a discussion with Mackensen on April 22, Bastianini reverted to his arguments put forward during the Italo-German conference at Klessheim earlier in the month. The Allies were waiting for the Russians and Germans to wear themselves out. 'We must not take part in this game, but must try, by political means, to counter it. In answer to my question as to how, in view of the Fuehrer's clear and effective statements at Klessheim, he conceived of the practical possibilities of a political solution, Bastianini confined himself to referring to Ribbentrop's summer talks in Moscow in 1939, which had really brought about a miracle.' The German Ambassador pointed out how conditions had changed. 'Bastianini then enlarged on the theme that the position of the Axis powers today was different from their former one in so far as the initiative had been taken from them and was on the other side. There was also no prospect in the foreseeable future of winning it back, for that could only happen, if Africa had to be completely evacuated, either by operations in the West, in the direction of Spain; or in the East through Turkey.' [8]

The brief illusion of Mussolini, fostered during the Italo-German talks at Klessheim, that the military deadlock in the Mediterranean could be broken by Spanish intervention on the Axis side, was soon dissipated. Hitler had at this time suggested that the Duce should take the initiative in seeking a meeting with Franco. It appears however that, after his gust of optimism at the end of March, Mussolini had lost interest. His enthusiasm for the problematical Spanish operation wavered with the extent of his immediate fears of the end in Tunisia. The Fuehrer's harangue at Klessheim also temporarily restored the Duce's nerve.

When Schmidt visited Rome in mid-April, on Ribbentrop's instructions, he asked whether the Duce would meet Franco. He answered that 'he had in mind a conversation at the end of April at the Spanish border, and had proposed this in a letter to Franco. The Duce did not think that Franco would

e. Presumably summaries of intercepts.

be able to leave his country and therefore he was prepared to go to the Spanish frontier. But he was not certain that Franco would accept the proposal of a meeting, for he had recently become very cautious in these matters. Spain was on the way from "non-belligerence" to full neutrality, and the improvement of the internal economic position in Spain had increased the people's dislike of warlike undertakings.' [9]

On April 20, the new Italian Ambassador to Madrid, Marchese Paolucci de' Calboli Barone, presented his credentials to Franco,[f] and presumably the letter from the Duce proposing a meeting. Franco opened the conversation by stressing Spain's economic dependence on the Allies.[g] From the military point of view he was primarily interested in whether the Axis powers would succeed in holding Tunis, which he described as being at this time the most important strategic key position. When the Italian Ambassador assured him that the Axis forces were determined to defend Tunis, Franco was visibly gratified. 'He himself had no doubt that Tunis would be held. What the Bolsheviks had succeeded in doing at Stalingrad the Axis would find possible in Tunis . . . As to imminent landing operations in the Mediterranean, these would be aimed in the first instance, according to Franco, at Sicily and Sardinia. He did not believe in an attack on the Balearics.

'In authoritative circles in England, there was an almost panic fear that Germany and the Soviet Union might come to terms. Franco expressed only indirectly his well-known desire for a peace, by saying that perhaps in the autumn a situation might arise which would show that between the Axis and the Western Powers no final decision could be reached, while on the other hand the Soviet Union could be played out as a military factor.'

In view of Franco's mood, it is not surprising that the Italian proposal for a meeting between him and Mussolini was politely shelved.

f. The appointment of the new Italian Ambassador to Madrid was subsequently linked, somewhat mysteriously, with hints at peace feelers on direct orders of the Duce. According to Tamaro, *Due Anni di Storia*, I, p. 176, on March 23 Mussolini instructed Paolucci explicitly to make contact with British and American diplomats 'in view of a possible separate peace'. He told his Ambassador: 'We are seized by the throat by the Germans, see if you can find a way out.' He also thought that Franco might be considered as a mediator.

In spite of being under constant surveillance, Paolucci (who is presumably Tamaro's source), obtained the secret collaboration of 'a scientist'. The latter made a first contact with the British, and was told that the only way out was unconditional surrender.

Another subsequent account of a former vice-secretary of the Fascist Party, Alfredo Cucco, *Non volevamo perdere*, p. 119, reads: 'Today it is known and documented that Mussolini thought of breaking with the Germans at the end of March 1943. He had already opened a file on which was written in his own hand "List of German Treacheries". Even earlier he had given to our Ambassador in Spain, Marchese Paolucci de' Calboli Barone, instructions to make approaches for a separate peace.'

No first-hand evidence has as yet come to light to confirm or deny this one of many ex-post facto apologias.

g. German Collection. Madrid telegram April 22, 1943. A summary of this conversation as given by Paolucci to his German colleague.

'At this point in the conversation . . . I had the opportunity to suggest how much a frequent exchange of ideas between the Duce and himself would be of value to both countries. Franco made a polite comment of assent, as if he shared my view, but stressed that the international situation made personal meetings very difficult for him.[h] He could not forget the repercussions which his journey to Bordighera had occasioned, and which had taken the form of a hostile attitude by America and England. The delivery of raw materials essential to Spain had been stopped . . . At that time it had been possible to meet these difficulties and in due course to surmount them; but today the reaction would be stronger and more dangerous.' Spain only possessed reserves of petrol for road transport for a few weeks, and for aviation spirit for fourteen days. 'On the other hand, Spain could not count on deliveries from Europe, which in effect had not been fulfilled in spite of assurances and promises from Germany, who it is true had not great export possibilities, as could also be confirmed in regard to deliveries to Italy.

' "My heart is with you", continued the Caudillo, "and I desire the victory of the Axis. This is also in my interest and that of my country, but you must not forget the difficulties which I face both in the international sphere and in internal politics." ' [10]

The German Embassy in Madrid reported on May 5 a hint that Franco would accept a proposal for a meeting with Hitler 'but not with the Duce'. Two days later, Ribbentrop gave instructions only to encourage the proposal if Franco himself took the initiative. On May 8 the Allied armies entered Tunis, and Franco promptly made a pacific speech. As the German Ambassador in Madrid wrote, 'It is not impossible that developments in Tunis have strengthened ideas about the balance of power.' [11] When, on May 19, the Japanese Ambassador in Berlin, General Oshima, pressed for the occupation of Gibraltar by the Axis, Ribbentrop replied that 'Germany had had such a plan in mind for some time, but that Franco's policy of neutrality and peace makes it more difficult to carry out'. As Oshima observed, 'Spain judges the intentions of the Tripartite Powers with scepticism.' [12]

The last of the cycle of diplomatic encounters at Klessheim in the spring of 1943 was with the most wily 'European' of all, Pierre Laval. At least in the field of German and Italian relations with Vichy, Ribbentrop had some expectation of support from Rome. The maintenance of an actively neutralist and collaborationist administration at Vichy was a central and joint Axis interest, now heightened by the possibility of Allied landings in Southern France as one direction of an assault on the European mainland. The political position of Vichy must be strengthened before such a military crisis might break.

Reports of spreading opposition to Laval in Vichy circles had prompted the

h. To meet Mussolini in February 1941.

summons to this meeting. According to Bastianini's account, however, he received this unexpected invitation to Salzburg through the German Ambassador in Rome without any indication of the purpose of the summons, and he learnt of the presence of Laval at the forthcoming meeting only on arrival at the railway station.[13]

Ribbentrop and Bastianini met at Klessheim on April 29 before Laval's arrival. The former told his Italian colleague that he had 'been invited to come to Salzburg at such short notice because news had come in from France that certain elements were working for the retirement of Laval, just as on December 13, 1940 . . . Pétain was very old and therefore he was very easily influenced by his entourage as he did not any longer survey the scene. He was, however, not only very old but also an old fox . . . One could not therefore ignore the cross currents and intrigues in the entourage of the Marshal because this could lead one day to Laval being kicked out again, and for the purpose and aims of the Axis in France, there could not be a better man. He was shrewd, and . . . convinced that only an Axis victory could preserve France from Bolshevism.' From a French point of view there were perhaps better patriots with whom one could have more sympathy, but Ribbentrop favoured those who were of use to Germany and Italy. Hitler had therefore sent a letter to Pétain which contained a warning in no uncertain terms that Germany would not permit such a repetition of the events of December 1940. Reports from French intermediaries had indicated that Pétain intended to withdraw his confidence from Laval. The latter, on his side, had definite and confidential evidence that close friends of Pétain had contacts through Switzerland with enemies of Italy and Germany. 'In the long run Germany and Italy could naturally not put up with this. Ribbentrop believed that it would be better if it were somehow possible to leave Pétain in his present position. They must watch the above-mentioned contacts very carefully, and if necessary sever them at a later stage. If it were necessary to remove him in the end, they would in this way have collected decisive evidence against him which would justify a sudden move. They need take no action against his collaborators . . . At the moment it would be more useful to keep him to "lance the boil" at Vichy.'

The underlying German fear was a repetition, not so much of the internal events in France which led to the previous dismissal of Laval, but of the impact on French affairs of another Allied landing such as had followed in November 1942 at the time of 'Torch', and which, if repeated, might lead to a loss by the Axis of any semblance of political control of France. Pétain could be the symbol of collaboration or resistance.

If necessary the Germans and Italians would have to act overnight. 'For example, they could inform Pétain that they had heard of English plans whose aim was to assassinate him and they would therefore place him in German and Italian protection. The German Foreign Minister added that this question was, however, not yet urgent. Under no circumstances could they let Pétain leave France, therefore all his movements were very carefully watched, and the Germans had already arranged for him to be continually under the surveillance of the German security services wherever he went. He had recently protested a little against this action, but then gave way to the proposed German arrangements. In no case could they afford to trust Pétain. This Ribbentrop had never done.'

Laval was now due at Salzburg. 'He seemed rather nervous and wanted to know if Germany and Italy would still back him up.' Germany relied on him. Hitler would express this directly and personally, and Ribbentrop now wanted to know whether Laval also enjoyed the confidence of the Italians. He had naturally a whole list of requests. Above all, he wanted a declaration on the future of France. 'In this connection there was nothing to be done. Everything was too fluid. Until the war was won, in the German view no declaration about France could be made. What would one say for example about Tunis? Tunis, Corsica and Nice would go to Italy, but Ribbentrop thought it imprudent to make any such statement.

'In general the French had a kind of touching naïveté . . . On the evening of Montoire, de Brinon i had said to him in all seriousness that the French had in no way lost the war because they had not fought properly and had not wished to fight. If a statement about France were put out today, within fourteen days the French would come up with fresh demands . . . Under such circumstances one must regard the relationship with France in a very sober light. The real basis lay in the occupation of France by German and Italian troops as well as in the fact that Laval was shrewd enough to know it was also in France's interests to wish for an Axis victory. He was bound hand and foot to the Axis and there was no way back. In general the French police were strongly committed to the Axis. This was in a certain sense an ideal situation. Anything else was Utopian and led nowhere.'

Bastianini thought that Hitler's letter would be effective. Laval must be clear that he could count on German and Italian support. Italy 'was against any declaration on France's future position such as he was seeking. It would be impossible to make such a statement at the present moment until the position of France was assured. In addition the future position of France could not be established alone through an outside act of will. France must work out her own moral fate. At the moment she did not seem to appreciate the position. The French loved neither the Germans nor the Italians, but they had also not understood that they had been beaten by Germany and that their country was occupied by German troops. If they had understood the meaning of these facts they would not run over to a Giraud or a de Gaulle. In this respect the views of the leaders of the new Europe, namely the Fuehrer and the Duce, fully coincided.' [14]

i. The Vichy Minister representing the Pétain government with the German authorities in Paris.

According to Bastianini, Ribbentrop also added that Hitler had wished for the presence of an Italian representative that morning to show Laval that there was complete Italo-German agreement and 'to discourage him from repeating again the effort already made with Ciano to play on the imaginary possibility of a difference between the Axis powers'. Laval would however certainly press for concessions and the Fuehrer thought that 'one ought to move very cautiously, and keep Italian claims out of the discussion'.j Any increased Axis support for Laval, or any concessions to France, must be at the expense of Italy, particularly if the remaining part of the French fleet was handed back.

Laval arrived late that morning at Salzburg. He first met Ribbentrop alone. The German authorities at Vichy had just been instructed to confirm to Pétain that Laval possessed the confidence of both the German and Italian governments, 'but on the German side it was thought necessary that this fact should be officially known in Vichy, and the Fuehrer had therefore last night sent Marshal Pétain a letter clarifying the German attitude in unmistakable terms'. In this letter, which Laval had learnt about on his journey, the Fuehrer 'had made it clear once and for all that Germany would never again bow to intriguing elements, and would never again accept a change of government. Such a game of intrigue would have catastrophic results for France.' Laval would be received by the Fuehrer that afternoon, and Bastianini would also be present. The Italian attitude to the situation at Vichy was identical with the German. Laval then said that 'in order to forward his present policy, a clearly recognizable goal must be put in front of the French. The struggle against Bolshevism was not enough. One must give France an aim and security, and take French national sentiment into account. Germany wanted to create a new Europe. He wanted to help in this, but France must be accorded a place which suited her.'

Ribbentrop replied: 'At Montoire the Fuehrer had made France an offer of the closest collaboration in order to beat England and America. This offer had not been accepted. France had handled the situation with reservations. This had led to the greatest betrayal in history. North Africa had seceded, although France had always maintained that she would defend it, and had sought and received arms for its defence. Whenever the question of France's future appeared, Laval's policy was that Germany and Italy should sacrifice their blood to the end in order to protect French culture.'

Laval answered that 'he would not persist in his desire to obtain a declaration on the future of France. But he must stress that he had reached the limit

j. Bastianini *op cit* p. 287. His account assumes that all these talks were held at Berchtesgaden, whereas the German protocols make it clear that at least those between Ribbentrop, Bastianini, and Laval took place at Klessheim.

of his capacity. The Germans must for once see the situation from a French point of view. He had mobilized one age group after another for labour service in Germany, without being able to tell these mobilized Frenchmen why this was happening.' [15]

The two foreign guests were received that afternoon in Hitler's study at Berchtesgaden, where Laval was subjected to a catalogue of the Fuehrer's resentments against Pétain.[k] 'For a Germany at war, France constitutes no problem. Two gauleiters would do the job; a German in one zone, and an Italian in the other.' [16]

Laval began at once with an outline of his central political thesis: by creating a new Europe, Germany and by opposition, the Allies, would be forced to define their war aims, which would narrow to questions of frontiers which could be easily settled. 'In order to construct Europe you assume that first the war must be won. In my opinion it would be preferable to organize Europe in order to win the war.'

Hitler's reply was that he needed no Declaration of a European Order 'but 20,000 planes and 20,000 tanks'. Laval riposted, 'A Declaration of twenty lines would be worth 20,000 planes and 40,000 tanks. You ought to take me on as secretary, set me up in a corner and I would write it for you.' The dialogue petered out round the tea-table in front of the Fuehrer's fireplace in the 'Eagle's Nest'.[l]

A truncated communiqué 'recognising France's place in Europe' was the only result of this Franco-German dialogue. Laval returned with the renewed assurances of Axis support for a policy of collaboration with him, a repeated threat that the Germans would not tolerate his removal from power, and no concessions to make his tenure of office viable.

That evening Ribbentrop gave a dinner for the Italian and French delegations. Bastianini wrote later that Laval held the conversation. 'You talk of a New Order to be set up in Europe after your victory. There is a need to do so, but people are asking what you intend and you do not tell them . . . Explain what this New Order consists of. Maybe people will like it. Begin to install it, and for the first time the French will be convinced of your good faith. I wager that if I go to Rome and talk to Mussolini we will reach agreement on how to define it. But if you don't do it, the enemy will have an easy time with their propaganda against you.' [17]

k. There are several secondary accounts of this meeting. See Bastianini *op cit* pp. 287 ff, p. 160 ff. Mallet *op cit* Vol. II, pp. 128–30. Guérard, *Criminel de Paix*, pp. 115–19. Brinon *Mémoires*, pp. 162–4. Laval was accompanied by Rochat, the head of the Vichy Foreign Office, and two of his close collaborators, Guérard and de Brinon.
l. Guérard *op cit* p. 117. Apparently based on and embroidered from a translation of Schmidt's record, which was published in the pro-Vichy periodical *Écrits de Paris*, February 1948.

Late that night he and his advisers returned in Goering's special train to France. Ribbentrop's parting words, according to de Brinon, were, 'Now you must get rid of your opponents.' [18]

Bastianini had also used the occasion of this visit to press once more his own European plan. He had been, as he explained to his advisers, 'for some time seeking to convince the Germans to make some gesture . . . which would have the concealed purpose of preparing a "European Charter" fit to serve as a basis for possible peace negotiations'.

If he had been alarmed at the German attitude at the first Klessheim talks early in April, he received even less comfort from the second. 'The Germans suspect Pétain in France, they suspect Kallay in Hungary and Mihai Antonescu in Roumania. They suspect Franco and fear Turkey. Naturally they suspect us. And they are right. The whole of Europe is in revolt against the German attempt at hegemony, conducted with such bestiality. And Italy, to whom so many peoples are turning, hoping that a voice of common sense will reach them from that quarter, is allowing herself, like the others, to be drawn into the vortex of this madness. Throughout the whole day a leaden atmosphere weighed on our group, isolated from the Germans, in the halls of Klessheim.' [19] [m]

According to his own account, Bastianini had gone so far as to lecture Ribbentrop not only on the need for the reconstruction of Europe, but also for the inclusion of France. It was pointless to exasperate her national feelings. And on May 1 the Duce went so far as to instruct the official Stefani News Agency to issue a statement in this sense.[n] But even if a mild collusion— and it is very doubtful—existed between Laval and Bastianini at this moment, the rancours and frustrations in Italo-French relations lay too deep for any mutual understanding. As Bastianini told Mackensen some weeks later: 'It was laughable that Laval should now talk of empty hands, when at taking leave in Berchtesgaden he showed himself fully satisfied.' The argument had been that Laval's position should be strengthened by a continuation of the policy of collaboration. Mackensen added: 'As for so-called collaboration today, it was rather that the whole of France was only waiting for an enemy landing to throw off the mask.' [20] And what of Italy?

m. Simoni *op cit* p. 332. Even Goebbels had some sympathy with at least part of this view. 'It is a curious fact that we shun the phrase "European co-operation" just as the devil shuns holy water. I can't quite understand why. Such an obvious political and propaganda slogan ought really to become a general theme for public discussion in Europe. Instead, we avoid it wherever possible.' Goebbels, *Diary*, p. 251, April 12, 1943.

n. Wiskemann, *The Rome-Berlin Axis*, p. 297 and note, quoting documents published by Bastianini in *Il Giornale del Mattino*, October 10–11, 1945. I am much indebted to Professor Wiskemann's pioneer account of Italo-German relations, which is substantiated by the publication of subsequent documentary evidence.

The Italians had no illusions as to the German reception of their European programme. As Alfieri reported from Berlin on May 14: 'I asked Steen-gracht [Under-Secretary of State in the German Foreign Ministry] whether the idea of a "European Charter" had by chance made any progress in the minds of the German leaders, since, I added, I had the impression, which was confirmed by the last meeting at Salzburg, that, on the German side, one had accepted with extreme difficulty a small part of the Italian thesis and only to please the Duce. The respective positions remained unchanged. Steengracht admitted loyally and confidentially that my impression corresponded to the reality.' [21]

But more significantly, those German circles which had looked cautiously for the Duce's intervention with Hitler in regard to the Russian war, both in the previous March and in timid conclave at Klessheim in April, were now stilled. Hitler had dispersed the shadows of Stalingrad on the German home front, and none of his advisers would risk any form of criticism of his obsessive pursuit of the Russian adventure.

As Steengracht declared to Alfieri, 'Hitler is intimately and deeply con-vinced of having the equipment, weapons, and men, and sufficient possibilities to inflict the gravest blow on the Russians. Perhaps this is the reason why none of the direct collaborators (Goering, Ribbentrop, Himmler, Bormann, Goebbels), who could have some influence on him, dare talk to him about such a problem and of the negative possibilities which are inevitable in all human affairs.' Alfieri felt therefore that 'at this point . . . it is useless to insist. It only remains to await the results of the first German military successes and to choose a good moment to exploit the favourable situation, and then to take another step towards the formulation of a European Charter.' o

The worsening of the Italian military position after the fall of Tunis in May was as usual marked by an extension of her diplomatic and political cam-paign independently of her German partner. At the instigation of Bastianini the Italian Senate became a brief forum of discussion on foreign affairs. The debate was harshly viewed in Berlin. On May 19 Mackensen reported the leading speech of Senator Salata,p 'which as I learn reliably is based on Foreign Office material, and has been agreed with Bastianini'. It represented a full dress review of Italian foreign policy, and called for 'joint Axis action in the political and military fields'. In regard to Spain, although she remained a non-belligerent, she 'was anything but indifferent to the present phase in the Mediterranean'. The so-called Iberian Union met with great sympathy in Italy because of its influence in Southern Europe, Africa and South America.

Italian relations with Turkey were unchanged. They shared a common

---

o. Simoni, *op cit* pp. 340–1. Alfieri had written 'and then to take a decisive step in favour of a negotiated peace', but evidently lost his nerve and corrected the draft.

p. The former Italian Ambassador in Vienna, and spokesman of the Italian Foreign Office in the Senate.

anxiety at the renewal of Soviet aspirations towards the Dardanelles, and Turkey could not remain indifferent to the future New Order in the Mediterranean. In the Balkans Italy must secure the Eastern coastline of the Adriatic and control the Ionian Sea. Italian claims on France, Tunis, Nice, and Corsica, were markedly stressed. These conditions for Italy's entry into the war had always been recognized by Germany, and 'confirmed in the last talks between Hitler, Bastianini and Laval'.

Salata drew attention to the Eurafrican aims of the Axis against the imperialist and bolshevik powers. The policy of Britain was anti-European. Casablanca had shown the Allied intention 'to set up a dictatorship of four basically non-European powers'. On the other side, since the Hitler-Mussolini meeting at Klessheim, the programme of the independence and unity of Europe and co-operation of European peoples had been stated anew. Italy had set herself two historical aims: to create again the position in the Mediterranean which belonged to her, and 'to offer to the small peoples the leadership of Rome'. The Duce was 'the European'. 'The Europe of the Axis, which was resisting the assault on its fortress, must make every effort to see that the direction of Europe does not slip from the grasp of Europeans. This is the meaning and the commitment of the last meeting of the two statesmen and their mission to Europe.' [22]

On the following day, May 20, Bastianini made his contribution to the debate. He referred to the period of the previous three months during which he had been at the Foreign Ministry. Senator Salata had rightly stressed the meeting between the Duce and the Fuehrer which took place at Salzburg in April. 'But further emphasis should be laid on the importance of the basic problem stated at that meeting, to which Italy and Germany intend to cling, to prepare the conditions and premises for the future order of the world: no aggression on small states by the Great Powers, no elimination of the national individuality of the smaller states, but a guarantee of the free development of all nations, with their spontaneous collaboration assured. It was in this framework of firm decision and sincere European collaboration that last month's meeting with Laval took place. The principles laid down by Germany and Italy as the basis of European and world order are also at the basis of Italy's relations with France. No wish to destroy or humiliate France, and understanding of her vital necessities. But to take part in the work of reconstructing Europe, France must understand the need to make sacrifices and contributions not only to Axis production and war efforts, but also to settling the questions which still remain outstanding with her conquerors. This is the essential condition for Italo-French relations to find, in a framework of mutual understanding, their place in greater Europe.' [23]

This speech enraged Hitler, who read the text aloud at a military conference on May 20. He took exception in particular to the concluding remarks about France. 'How can he say such a thing! The French say that they were not beaten by the Italians . . . a very rotten speech and it strengthens my feeling that a crisis of the type which we have discussed q can develop there at any moment.' [24]

q. On May 19, the previous day

CHAPTER THREE

THE ITALIAN 'POLITICAL DESIGN'

•-•

'THE TWO military requisites for successful Italian diplomatic activity are: German destruction of Russian strength, and the defeat of the Allies in the Mediterranean. Such hopes however are tenuous . . . Today it is unreal to suppose that Stalin would make peace with Hitler, or Churchill and Roosevelt with Mussolini.'

Such was the view expressed in an Italian War Office minute written by one of Ambrosio's staff after the Klessheim Conference.[a] During the summer months of 1943 in Rome, as the military situation of the Axis deteriorated in inexorable stages, the Italian Foreign Office headed by Bastianini and his professional advisers sought with mounting desperation their own diplomatic solution to the war. The first stage in such a 'plan' was to be a firm private agreement with the satellite allies in Southern and Central Europe, Roumania and Hungary, before taking soundings in the West as to the chances of a negotiated peace. The opportunity for such moves seemed to appear after the visit of Churchill to Adana at the beginning of the year, and was based on reports that the British Prime Minister had expressed views which could be interpreted to mean that the Western Allies, in particular Britain, were anxious about the future post-war extension of Russian influence on the Straits and in the Balkans, which would bring the Soviet Union to the shores of the Mediterranean.[b]

This thesis, on which the hopes of Italian diplomacy came to be exclusively centred, is set out in a document transmitted to Berlin later in the year by the German Ambassador in Bucharest. 'Immediately after the Adana Conference the Turkish Minister here, Tanroier, made a contact with the Italian Minister,

a. Italian Collection. The minute is internal and unsigned, but clearly refers to the period just after Klessheim. It may have been written by Castellano.
b. These Turkish reports are not confirmed by the British minutes of the Adana Conference. See pp. 177–8.

which was strengthened in numerous talks. The plan of building up a bloc consisting of Italy, South-Eastern Europe, and Turkey was discussed, and Tanroier developed the idea, to which Bova Scoppa rallied, that these states should seek a way to an agreement with England and then, rifle in hand, take the defensive against an eventual Russian attack on the Balkans.'

This conception was carried further in talks between Mihai Antonescu and the Italian Minister. 'The need to find a political solution to the war compelled these powers grouped round the Axis sooner or later to reach an understanding with England. The bridge to such an agreement would be built up on Turkish-Roumanian relations. The aim of this activity must be to persuade the Duce, and through him the Fuehrer, of the necessity of such a way and its feasibility.' c

Italian leadership must be the prime element in such a scheme, which might also be extended from Eastern Europe to the neutrals of the West, Spain and Portugal, and even perhaps to the France of Pétain and Laval. This chimera lies henceforth at the centre of Italian diplomacy.

In timing any further moves, much depended on the German military situation in the East. The reports of Bova Scoppa from Bucharest since the beginning of 1943 proved to be not only invaluable in this sense, but also the only direct source of such intelligence; the Italian Embassy in Berlin being able in effect to comment only on such reports as the Germans chose to pass on them.

On May 12 Bova Scoppa wrote a private letter to Bastianini, based on such confidential information from the Roumanian Military Attaché in Berlin, General Gheorghe, as to German intentions on the Russian Front, and passed on to him by Mihai Antonescu under pledge of secrecy.

'The Germans do not intend to begin a large-scale offensive against Russia this year . . . At the German Headquarters they maintain that Germany will only be ready to launch a decisive offensive against the Russian Army in 1944, when the total mobilization of all the forces of the nation has borne fruit. . . . The Fuehrer and his colleagues speak of "the new Seven Years War"—affirming that after the Soviet Army is destroyed, two more years will be necessary to deal with and wipe out the Anglo-Saxon offensives on European soil. The Fuehrer likes this historical parallel, because during that war, Frederick II was in a very similar position to the present one, and made a later come-back.'

As Mihai Antonescu pointed out to the Italian Minister, 'If the German General Staff proposes to wait another year before launching a decisive offensive against the Russians, we must bear in mind that this year will be

c. German Collection. Foreign Office Minute, September 28, 1943, referring to a telegram from the German Minister in Bucharest, Baron von Killinger, and enclosing a memorandum by the representative of the Italian official news agency in Roumania, Trandafilo, who appears to have been well informed of these moves, and to have also acted as a German agent during this period.

used by our enemies, and that the time factor is certainly not on our side
. . . And if this winter the Russians begin another offensive like this year's,
what will become of our armies, if at the same time we have to deal with
the Anglo-Saxon threat in the West?' [1]

On May 14 Bova Scoppa wrote again to Bastianini, on this occasion
to summarize the views of the very active Turkish Minister in Bucharest,
who had been pressing hard from behind the scenes for a 'diplomatic' solution of the war. The excessive optimism of Tanroier in regard to an eventual
British attitude to peace feelers was to exert an unfortunate and misleading
influence in the future.

'As each day passes, the Allies' morale rises a stage, while that of the
peoples of Europe falls. Germany thinks she can win the war with the submarine war, but in many people's opinion this is a dangerous illusion. The
Allies feel in a position to cope with the serious threats of the battle in the
Atlantic.' There was one more dangerous illusion: Russia. 'By now the war on
that front has changed from a battle against space to a battle against time. It is
almost certain that the Russians will move against the Germans as soon as a
second front can be established in Europe. The possibility of Russia collaps-
ing must therefore be discarded, and, in my opinion, so must that of a
separate peace between Germany and Russia.'

In such conditions, the struggle in the Mediterranean became of decisive
importance. 'You are not unaware that the Allied programme is to put Italy
out of action, as the first act of the final battle against Germany. Now that
you have lost Tunisia, a violent air offensive will be launched against your
country: your cities will be destroyed, and my European heart cannot think
of this prospect without shuddering . . . It is now probable that the Allies
will try to land quickly in Sicily and Sardinia, and will seek to engage your
fleet. If ever they get hold of your islands' gigantic air bases—Italy would be
changed into a sea of ruins. Think too of the possibility of Italy herself
becoming the battlefield of the Allied and Axis Armies . . .'

Tanroier stressed that he was speaking personally. 'I am certain that, if
you were ready to negotiate peace, England would give you honourable
conditions. The reason is very simple. England is not unaware that Italy is
an essential balancing and stabilizing element for the Europe of the future.
Could you ever imagine that, having won the war, the English and Americans would stay on guard in Europe to prevent suffocation by the Slavs, and
the rebirth of Germany? Italy must have her place in Europe and in the
Mediterranean, and land for expansion. We Turks too want this to happen,
and we have not hidden it from the English. I am sure of what I am saying,
that if you agree to negotiate peace, with that historic courage which must
be shown in face of certain untenable situations, and if in doing so you
emphasized the essential function Italy could have in the Europe of to-

morrow, and you came to an anti-Bolshevik union with England, then Italy would save her fate, and perhaps her régime as well.

'Her régime as well?

'I think so. The Anglo-Americans will never negotiate with Hitler and the Nazis, but it is very probable that they will treat with the Duce and the Fascists.' [2]

On May 17 the Italian Minister reported a second and even more significant conversation with his Turkish colleague. 'He said very explicitly that at the moment England is worried about the Russian factor. We have numerous proofs of this anxiety. Russia shows no signs of weakening; rather, she shows symptoms of unexpected power in the air. In these circumstances, the men in London are looking to what might happen if the German armies are not capable of destroying the Soviet Army. The English are being extremely generous to us in supplying armaments. And when we asked why they were offering us so much material, they replied, "Because we want a strong Turkey capable of stopping the spread of anarchy at a certain moment in south-eastern Europe." But more explicitly this means, we want to prevent Bolshevism spreading in south-east Europe. It is clear therefore that England considers us, our power, and our possibilities, much more in anti-Soviet than anti-German terms.

'Moreover, the fact that England insistently encouraged us to take the initiative in a possible Balkan union is another clear proof of what I am saying. You must not forget that this initiative was taken at the moment the Soviet armies were advancing on the Dnieper and were threatening to overflow on this side of it. The Germans did not understand the courage of our initiative. Rather, it irritated them . . . If the Axis won the war, this Balkan union had no sense or aim; if they ran the risk of losing it, it might provide a means for saving Europe.

'I still hold firmly to my opinion that the British anxieties could be the basic element for making possible contacts between you and England.' [d]
These dispatches stimulated Bastianini's long maturing 'political' design.

On May 29 Bova Scoppa came to Rome to report and was instructed to draft a memorandum on the Roumanian attitude to be sent to the Duce. On June 5 the document was handed to Bastianini, who now presented the whole case to the Duce in a minute dated June 14, enclosing both this memorandum, and an equally significant dispatch from Anfuso in Budapest. [3] The covering note was headed 'The Collaboration between Italy and the Danubian Countries in seeking a political solution of the War'.

The dispatch from Anfuso showed clearly 'the irrevocable decision of the

---

d. Bova Scoppa *op cit* p. 100 ff. See also Bastianini *op cit* p. 113. It is significant that Bova Scoppa took a draft of this document to Acquarone, who showed it to the King. The latter was very anxious that it should be presented to Mussolini.

Hungarian government to cling tight to Italy in any future eventuality . . . and to place henceforward their full and definitive trust in the loyalty of our friendship. We have also had recent proof of this from other quarters. 'You will remember, Excellency, the ready and, I would say, almost impatient support which Hungary gave to the idea of a Balkan bloc outlined by the Turkish representatives in some of the Balkan capitals. Even before identifying it as an English manoeuvre, or as an attempt to detach countries from the Axis, she saw in it the possibility of reinforcing her position in the Balkans by securing herself beforehand in an anti-Soviet direction, against possible Axis military disasters. This Hungarian position is not greatly changed; her need for assurance about the future is only increased and strengthened.

'The ups and downs of her relations with Germany are, in this light, only episodes, and if the Hungarian government today decided on definite concessions, this is with the sole object of not compromising the most vital interests of the near future in impulsive and ill-timed decisions. This is why Hungary has listened to the advice of her friend Italy, but it is also for the same reason that she is still waiting for those directives which she declares herself ready to follow from this very moment.'

Bastianini recommended therefore that the moment had come to clarify to Kallay Italy's policy in the Danube basin 'which coincides precisely with that of our (Hungarian) ally. The general lines of direction of our political conduct . . . which consisted above all in the strengthening of existing friendships with the Danubian countries, Hungary and Roumania, and in seeking closer ties with Bulgaria, are confirmed for the first time in the attached report of Minister Anfuso.'

It was equally important to consolidate 'in a precise manner our friendly relations with Roumania'. From Bova Scoppa's memorandum it appeared that 'the political line' of Mihai Antonescu, the Roumanian Foreign Minister fitted in many respects that of the Duce. 'In any case, it appears to be indispensable to keep him in his pre-arranged course of conduct in such a way that Roumania does not make any compromising gesture, not even in reaction to certain excessive and harsh pressures on the part of the Germans.'

Antonescu's visit to Rome should therefore at last take place. 'These talks could be decisive for a comprehensive exchange of views on the present situation, and the future, and for the stabilization of the second link in that close political chain binding Roumania to Italy and thus to consolidate that transversal Danubian-Balkan Axis, which should be headed by yourself and should follow your directives, not only in our interests, but for the same reasons of the war which imposes the closest solidarity between the adherents to the Tripartite Pact.'

Bastianini asked for detailed instructions for such a visit both in political

B.F.—11

and economic terms. There was also the urgent question of Roumanian oil and wheat deliveries to be discussed.

The memorandum by Bova Scoppa represented a wide-ranging survey of the war as seen from a Balkan capital, and in particular by the Roumanian Foreign Minister. 'After winning innumerable battles, Germany is reduced to defending the European fortress: a similar situation to that of 1918 apart from the scale of the defence. Since she attacked Russia while she still had to conquer England, Germany is powerless to destroy the Soviet Army. Great Britain and America are defended by the sea; Russia by land. Without an internal revolution, which seems unlikely, Russia is invincible in the present state of affairs . . . All the reports we have had at Bucharest are agreed on this aspect of the problem, and it appears too that they are in entire accord with those from Turkey and even from Japan.

'Germany is going through a profound crisis due to lack of man power, to a crisis in war production both because of the lack of some essential raw materials, and because of errors in aircraft construction, and to the general conditions of the masses who are sorely tried by the increasing bombardments . . . German supremacy in the air has ceased on all fronts. You cannot with impunity hold a front of 10,000 kilometres from the North Pole to Salonika—says Antonescu—without reducing your defence to a minimum, nor can you hold down a mass of 90 million men—the population of the occupied countries—without denuding the war fronts, as happened in the Eastern theatre last winter. The German hope of winning the submarine war is belied by the results of the Atlantic battle in the last few months. With her industries bombarded without respite, her cities bombed ruthlessly, a Russian front which shows no signs of being decided soon, and where the Germans are suffering continued attacks, with her occupied peoples in ferment and ready to rebel, with tired and discouraged public opinions which have lost faith in victory, the "Festung Europa" offers—according to Antonescu—a tempting spectacle to the Anglo-American war leaders.'

The results of the Tunisian campaign, where superiority of planes and tanks was decisive, left Antonescu in no doubt that the Allied General Staffs could dictate their will through an enormous concentration of materials and men at given points on the European coast. 'Even if a first and second attempt to invade the "Festung Europa" did not succeed, the Axis successes would be temporary, and whatever happened our attitude would always be negative, i.e. that of defenders, not of conquerors imposing peace . . . It is a question of a mathematical calculation. It is a question of time, and time is against us.' Militarily the war could no longer be won. According to Antonescu, 'this is the last hour for returning to the political method. It is therefore the hour of the Duce; he could be immortalized once more in a "Munich of the War".'

In addition the frequent contacts which Antonescu had with German military and diplomatic circles in Roumania convinced him 'that this idea is by now widely held in Germany too, and within the Nazi Party itself. In some occupied countries, certain S.S. elements regard a change to political strategy as indispensable and urgent. Because of this, he considers that, if the Duce took the initiative through a shrewd, very cautious diplomatic action, he would not only save the Axis countries from a dramatic situation, but would render a signal service to Germany herself.'

Bova Scoppa referred in this minute to his earlier memorandum to Ciano 'in which I reported that Mr Mihai Antonescu, feeling that the position of the Axis powers and of Roumania was becoming increasingly precarious, proposed a co-ordinated action between us to "open the eyes" of a hallucinated Germany to the war in the East. Mr Antonescu's attempt was not followed up, but he considers that his ideas again have a place in present reality, with a historic sense of necessity . . .

'In the last few weeks Hungary and Roumania have shown in various ways and with tortured intensity their conviction that the present situation is intolerable. It is beyond their powers to convince Germany. The only possibility of finding a solution within the Axis that they see is in concert with Italy. And they consider that the possibility of co-ordinating this action is in the Duce's hands alone. I take the liberty of adding that this would be the only way of preventing these two countries from detaching themselves and gravitating towards our enemies at the first serious blow—which, unfortunately, can be foreseen. From this aspect too, the Duce would render a notable service to Germany, and would save the Balkans and Eastern Europe from chaos . . . In the end, even for the Anglo-Saxons, it is a question of saving European civilization, and of avoiding the spread of chaos in Europe, which would make Russian expansion easier. It is well known that the English are particularly interested in Italy's Mediterranean function.

'Once we have established that points of common interest exist above all between us and the English, who have always based their policy on the principle of Continental balance of power, it would be a question of identifying these points, of isolating them and directing diplomatic action to certain historical necessities which are of essential value to us and to our enemies.

'It is clear that if the reply to any peace feeler were unconditional surrender, the Axis peoples would have to go on fighting to the last man and the last stone. But Antonescu thinks that though this reply would be inevitable for Hitler, it would not be so for the Duce. If from a psychological point of view, the clause "unconditional surrender" would raise the morale of the Anglo-Saxon peoples and Allies giving the impression of sure power, and lower the morale of the Axis peoples, from a military point of view the problem is seen in a different light—i.e. for our enemies a possible negotiated peace would mean saving several million men, and as many air and naval fleets as would necessarily be consumed in the blazing furnace which would be created in Europe by the attempts to land. Finally it would mean for England: saving Europe from chaos, and stopping Russia, who will inevitably arrive on the Mediterranean if we are defeated. No one imagines that in the case of victory, England and America will stay on guard in Europe against the Slavs for several generations. On the other hand, a negotiated peace in Europe would allow the Anglo-Americans to regulate the situation in the Pacific with Japan.

'These are the concrete advantages which might induce our enemies to listen to our feelers, our requests for conditions. Naturally if the Allies made any discussion conditional on not negotiating with Hitler, Antonescu thinks that the Fuehrer, who, in his very words, "has to write the history of his people, not his own biography" would know how to find the formula to save Germany.

'In substance, Antonescu considered that we have nothing to lose in putting out a circumspect feeler in the correct manner. Finally Antonescu considers that if the Duce coordinated the action which he refers to, he would be the interpreter for all the little fighting peoples from Finland to Roumania, and the ideas Your Excellency expressed in the Senate on the destiny of the small European nations would furnish further conspicuous elements of political identity and possible understandings with our enemies.'

Bova Scoppa had been Italian Minister in Lisbon in 1940–1, and in his tireless search for a diplomatic solution to the struggle which he could propose to Rome, he had discussed with Salazar the prospects of a Latin bloc as a bridge towards a negotiation with the Western Allies. The attitude of Spain after the fall of Tunis and the refusal of Franco to meet Mussolini had, however, discouraged such a diplomatic initiative. But Bova Scoppa still saw the possibilities of broadening any Balkan design to include the neutral powers of the Iberian peninsula. 'In numerous reports from Lisbon between 1940 and 1941 I repeatedly referred to some of Salazar's ideas on the conflict, which are identical in conception. From the knowledge I have of the man, and from his repeated confidences in me, I am convinced that the Duce and Fascist Italy would find in this Portuguese statesman of tried discretion, a true friend to whom they could turn, and whom they could probably interest advantageously for an indication of the possibilities and feasibility of a diplomatic action intended to explore the situation to find some honourable outlet. In assessing these ideas, please keep in mind that Salazar considers the presence of a great powerful Italy in the Mediterranean as of essential interest to the Hispanic nations.'

The reaction of Mussolini to this evidence in support of a political solution of the war by joint action between Italy together with the satellite allies, Roumania and Hungary, is described later by Bastianini. 'The effect which I was seeking was achieved in part. Mussolini declared that he agreed that Hitler should be placed with his back to the wall, that a close understanding should be established with Bucharest and Budapest, that a conversation should be held with Mihai Antonescu. Within two months, he (the Duce) said, the position would be clarified.' [4] But as Bastianini added to Bova Scoppa, Mussolini 'says however that it is still too soon to take the diplomatic initiative'.[5]

Bastianini sought what advantage he could from the Duce's long delayed approval to the first step of a meeting with the Roumanian Foreign Minister on Italian soil, and on June 21 he felt able to tell Mackensen that he was planning to meet the Roumanian Foreign Minister in Venice.

'A further postponement, now the fifth, was no longer possible' in view of the importance of trade negotiations. 'Bastianini intends to discuss Roumanian-Hungarian relations in the sense of the policy of the Axis powers. If sufficient reason appears, he will take Mihai Antonescu incognito to meet the Duce.' [6]

On June 29 Bastianini received his Roumanian colleague in Venice. The economic questions between the two countries were discussed. The conversation with the Duce took place at La Rocca on July 1. The discussions lasted for five hours, both before and after lunch.[e] Mihai Antonescu 'wanted the Duce to know, first of all, how the Conducator and himself since 1941 had been concerned to define in a way which would be clear to all, allies and foes alike, the political war aims of the Tripartite Powers. Since that time, on the several visits which he had made to the Fuehrer and Herr von Ribbentrop in Germany, he had spoken with complete frankness of the evident need to conduct the war not only by military but also political weapons, both to strengthen the will to fight of the Tripartite Powers and to show the European peoples that the Axis New Order represented a "substantial improvement" for the future of the Continent and based on "fair and just principles" to which the neutral nations could also subscribe.'

According to Antonescu, these ideas had been accepted in general terms by Ribbentrop, and therefore the former had had a certain 'exchange of views' with Salazar on general questions arising out of a common Latin tradition shared by Roumania and Portugal and the 'function of a common Latin heritage in this war and after the conflict'.

Roumania was not preparing for a separate peace, 'which also from all evidence seemed geographically impossible', but rather hoped to define 'certain political issues on which . . . the adhesion of the largest possible

e. Bastianini's record, which is printed in Tamaro, *op cit* I, pp. 68–70. See Bastianini *op cit* p. 113 ff. and p. 322 ff. Bova Scoppa, p. 113 ff. For a Roumanian account, Barbu, *Memorial Antonescu*, pp. 202–3 (written by Mihai Antonescu's chef de cabinet). And also Hillgrueber *op cit* p. 171 ff.

majority of the European peoples could be assured, and against which in effect extra-European forces were fighting'. Antonescu therefore appealed to the Duce to further the action begun by him. 'Roumania intended to bind her destiny entirely to that of Italy, and he was stating this to the Duce in the name of the Conducator.'

Mussolini was cautious in his reply. 'He noted the wishes of Roumania, and the firmness which she showed . . . He would not fail to speak to the Fuehrer at their next meeting. The view that the war must also be fought with political weapons had led him to make a proposal to the Fuehrer. This had been put aside two months ago, but he intended to take it up again as soon as the military situation had had that indispensable clarification which was now in progress. The Duce assured Antonescu that he had no intention whatever of abandoning this line which he had begun some months ago, and indeed it was his precise view that this line should be repeated and defined at a meeting of all the governments of the Tripartite countries.'

In Bova Scoppa's phrase, Mussolini must be persuaded that 'it is the Duce's hour: he could be immortalized once more in a "Munich of the War" '. All hopes were focused to this end in the present meeting, but they were modestly fulfilled. As was his habit, Mussolini accepted the basic views of his audience, and promptly defined an escape clause. He agreed to the principle of a general conference of the Tripartite Powers, and would make such a proposal to Hitler, but within the next two months. In spite of Antonescu's pleading, both at the two formal meetings and during luncheon, Mussolini would not yield, nor listen to the Roumanian argument that Hitler in any case would never agree and that their two countries must in any event seek their own solution. He did however imply that after two months, if Hitler had not listened to him, he would call such a conference 'including the neutrals'. He made no reference to Mihai Antonescu's hints 'at eventual peace feelers towards negotiations' with the Western Allies.

After luncheon the party adjourned on to the terrace of La Rocca, and looking across the plain of Forli, the Duce remarked with little relevance that this was the area 'where he had fought Socialism'. During the afternoon the talks were resumed and on taking leave Mussolini turned to Antonescu saying, 'I hope that this meeting may have an historical significance.' Bova Scoppa assumed that the Duce had given way on the time limit of two months, but on the train to Rome learnt that Mussolini had insisted that 'one could not negotiate when one was under the blow of a military defeat like that in Africa'.[7]

At the end of the conversation Antonescu had asked whether during this two months' interval he could continue to act on his own account, and the Duce had 'authorized' him to do so.

Eight days later the Allies landed in Sicily. The slim chances of any such diplomatic initiative vanished.

Bastianini accompanied his guest to Forlì station. 'Antonescu told me that he had understood that, while the Duce had shown the most cordial comprehension and had promised to raise with Hitler questions of minor importance concerning Roumania, he had avoided undertaking commitments of major significance. There was however no time to lose as Bolshevik Russia was at the gates, and one could assume that America and England shared with us the common interest in preventing Bolshevism being established in half Europe. I said that I agreed——and we were both to be proved wrong——and he assured me that I could count on total Roumanian support for whatever initiative that I had taken [f] . . . I did not tell him that when I begged Mussolini to let me act on my own and on my responsibility he had replied that it was too soon.' [8]

The only positive result of this meeting was that Bastianini knew that henceforward he could count on the Roumanians if he could persuade Mussolini on a last gamble to seek terms from the West. Before initiating any such action, he must give some explanation to the Germans of these talks with the Roumanians and, if possible, blunt their inevitable suspicions.

On July 4 Mackensen reported: 'Bastianini took advantage of my evening call . . . to inform me in general terms of the meeting with Mihai Antonescu. The first talks took place according to plan in Venice, where above all, economic matters were raised and experts called in. In regard to commercial affairs there had been only a modest success in breaking the marked deadlock because Roumania could not deliver those raw materials particularly needed by Italy—he quoted in the first instance oilseeds. Also in regard to grain deliveries, things did not look good, and this in particular was of the greatest importance for Italy, for according to yesterday's report from the Minister of Agriculture to Bastianini, in spite of a normal harvest in Northern Italy, the results in the Centre and the South would be small, so that the total average would be far behind that of last year.'

Antonescu had spoken of political matters both in Venice and at the final meeting with the Duce at La Rocca delle Caminate. Antonescu had given formal assurances that Roumania would and must follow with the Axis powers to the end. There had been no question of any kind of peace feelers. 'For Roumania it was and could only be a question of going with the Axis powers to the end. The danger for the country was as always Russia, whether it was a Bolshevist Russia or another, behind which for Roumania the dangerous Panslav idea lay.'

Antonescu had thus been originally in favour of the Turkish plan of a Balkan union, but as soon as he had realized that the Axis powers had

f. Bastianini had so far made no such moves.

shown outspoken mistrust of the Roumanian consent to this project he had stopped, and Turkey also had not pursued the idea any further.

Antonescu insisted further on the need to support the military struggle on the political side 'and so the Axis powers should ask themselves, more clearly than America has done, what the Europe of the future should look like. The Duce agreed with him, remarking that at the present moment he could and would not take any initiative in this respect when Italy was awaiting the far from negligible enemy invasion moves . . . In general, Antonescu made an impression both on the Duce and on Bastianini of a sincere man. In particular they had both been struck by what he had said on the question as to why Roumania above all, if she wished to have any future, could not follow any other policy than complete co-operation with the Axis. Bastianini reiterated, at the end of his account, which had lasted nearly an hour, that it would be right in his view to strengthen Antonescu's position as far as possible, even if only because it was impossible, given the internal political conditions in Roumania, to find a personality to replace him . . .' [9]

The assurance given by Bastianini that there would be 'no separate peace feelers' might well be received with scepticism by the Germans. It is however significant that there had been no German reports of any such moves by the Italians since the previous spring.

On March 26 Mackensen had reported to Berlin that in his view the very concept of an 'Italian Government' engaged in secret negotiations was false. 'The Italian Government is the Duce; to attribute such a thought to him is absurd.' [10]

The German Ambassador was formally correct in this view. Mussolini had never permitted his Undersecretary to make any such soundings. But from the German point of view the danger still existed of a secret understanding between the Italians and the satellite allies sanctioned by Mussolini. It seemed however from Bastianini's account to Mackensen of the talks with Mihai Antonescu that the Duce had not encouraged any such move, and again this was strictly accurate.

From these discussions held by Bastianini with the Roumanians during the late spring and summer of 1943 had emerged a clear and erroneous image of the Western Allies, of their relations with Russia, and their strategic conception of the war. A set of misleading assumptions was produced, which coloured irrevocably the belated Italian approach to peace feelers towards Britain and the United States.

Within the circle of the Italian Foreign Office a certain mirage had been conjured up. The Western powers, fearing above all else the post-war domination of Europe by the Soviet Union, were planning as their major assault on the Axis-controlled continent a landing in South-Eastern Europe in order to contain in the last resort the advance westwards of the Russian armies. In such an operation the support of the Roumanian and Hungarian forces, together with the resources of Italy, would be of decisive value. If Italy as the senior member of such an Entente, and speaking also in the name of Bucharest and Budapest, could approach the Allies with the offer of military assistance in such an event, and thus escape the consequences of the Axis commitment, salvation might still be won. In spite of the Casablanca formula, the British would treat with a Fascist Italy but never with Nazi Germany.

The diplomatic activities conducted in these assumptions between April and July 1943 had led to the point at which Bastianini was now able to speak, in any secret talks with the Western Allies, on behalf of Roumania and Hungary. It now remained, as a final manoeuvre, to secure the approval of the Duce to undertake such a move.

CHAPTER FOUR

THE 'LAST WAVE'
OF THE FASCIST PARTY

DURING HIS visit to Klessheim the Duce had been reflecting on the creeping fissures in the Home Front and relating them to the international scene. The leadership of the second generation of Fascism, the young men who had fought in Abyssinia and in Spain, of whom the Party Secretary Vidussoni had been groomed as the symbol, had not revolutionized the position, much less halted its disintegration. The Party had also been noticeably 'absent' during the March strikes.

On his return to Rome Mussolini struck simultaneously in different quarters. His first act was, on April 14, to dismiss the Chief of Police, Carmine Senise, who was officially accused of neglect of duty in not taking effective action against the strikers in Northern Italy.[1] The German agencies in Rome had been reporting against him to Himmler, and the Fascist Party machine was also out for his head. He was replaced by Renzo Chierici, a career officer in the Forest Militia, and a former companion of Italo Balbo from Ferrara. Bastianini informed the German Ambassador of Senise's dismissal on the following day, April 15. He described Chierici 'as an old Action Squad member and specially trustworthy. A first step has now been taken.'[a]

After 'an intense gestation of rumours and indiscretions', three days later, on April 17, Mussolini now summoned the Party Directorate to Palazzo Venezia. The Duce issued his latest confidential directive. 'The applause with which you have greeted Vidussoni's report shows your opinion. It is with great regret that I have decided to accept his resignation from an office which he has carried on faithfully for fifteen months. Vidussoni is not an orator. In normal times this would be meritorious, for I am not of

a. German Collection. Rome telegram April 15, 1943. It was rumoured that he was the creature of the Undersecretary of the Interior, Albini, also from Ferrara.

those who believe in talking, but in times like the present the man who is number two in the régime must have this gift as well, because he must be able to get in contact with the masses, especially when there is uncertainty . . . I have chosen Carlo Scorza as his successor. I have known him for twenty years and perhaps more. I am certain that he will carry out my directives in a true fighting spirit . . . In order to indicate what these directives will be, I must refer to recent happenings—to be precise, to the happenings of March 10, the date of the disturbances among the workers in Turin, Milan and other smaller cities of Piedmont and Lombardy. This unpleasant and deplorable episode has suddenly plunged us twenty years back. We must relate these happenings to the general international situation, that is, to the fact that the Russian advance at that time seemed irresistible and that it appeared that the moustachioed man, which is what the workers call Stalin, would shortly arrive to "liberate" Italy . . . The importance of these events is not only due to its character but to the fact that it at once involved political speculation. The motive of economic discontent seemed to justify the disturbances, but this motive was adopted as a pretext by Communist cells and by other cells which were more or less liberal. The old questions of "a separate peace", "an increase in the bread ration" (as if we did not all want to increase the bread ration if possible), "release of prisoners" and other similar desires came out into the open. This is a rough account of the facts; it is not enough; now we must consider whether all the organizations worked as they should have done. I do not believe it. First of all an upheaval of this kind does not fall from heaven like a thunderbolt. It is clear that there must have been signs to warn us of what was brewing, signs which would give the alarm and would tell us to be on our guard as something was about to happen.

'On the contrary, Rome got no warning.[b] This raises the question of the close connection between the syndical organizations and the working masses. This connection is essential, otherwise we shall find ourselves faced by these unpleasant criminal surprises which convince the workers that if they go back to the old methods they will get what they want. It is useless to create large numbers of press offices, it is useless to rack our brains over statistics and to organize legal offices; all these already exist . . . The syndical organizer must live in daily contact with the masses whom he claims to represent, he must have courage to uphold their interests if they are justified, and to oppose them when he sees that behind economic discontent there exists political speculation. At Turin a most extraordinary thing happened. The workers were asked to return to work through a printed pamphlet. The impression was that no one had the courage to sign it, neither the Federal Secretary of Turin, nor the Mayor of Turin, nor the Prefect of Turin; some form of signature was necessary to assume the responsibility. This pamphlet was a pathetic docu-

b. But see Senise's comments, *op cit* pp. 171 ff.

ment not only in its contents but in the way in which it was handed out at Turin. When it was known that these people were going to strike at 10 o'clock, it was suggested that the siren should not be sounded; as if these people had not got watches. These are small tricks, but I call them serious deceptions by means of which people hoped to avoid existing difficulties. On the contrary, they must be resolutely confronted.

'Once again, the Party. We must recognize that the Party was not in command of the situation either at Turin or at Milan. Why not? Because the Fascists themselves were not unanimous in their behaviour. Some went on strike, some did not, some made an agreement with the strikers. We got the impression that the whole local Party apparatus had been taken by surprise. At a certain point an announcement was made: "All Fascists are to put on their Black Shirts." But nothing was said about for how long, or whether this was compulsory . . . Some put on their shirts, some did not. This also gave the feeling of there being a serious division of opinion. The Federal Secretaries went to their posts, both the Federal Secretary of Turin and the Secretary of Milan, but I have not got the impression that they succeeded in getting control of the situation. Why? Because at a certain moment recourse was had to the disabled service men. It seemed that the situation was so uncertain that only the disabled could go into the factories and recall these gentlemen to their duty of producing munitions while our comrades were fighting in Tunisia, and that only these disabled men had sufficient prestige to restore the situation.

'Therefore do not be surprised that I have given draconian orders to the Police Chiefs and Prefects. Here is another sector to be examined: I did not get the impression that the police forces were sufficiently alert, they did not act sufficiently severely to make an end of the troubles. You do not get any result by saying to the workers "you must go and be a soldier", as if that was a punishment, "you will lose your exemption, you will be sent back to your own districts". All this showed lack of obedience to the directives from Rome. If they had fired at the workers, I would have taken the responsibility. When Italian workers murder other Italians who are fighting, I have them shot. All this explains the change of the Chief of Police. We must have a Fascist police; not policemen who are Fascist, but Fascists who are policemen. This will make many people think again. This is only the first step in the direction of a policy which for the moment I will call a rigid policy, while reserving the right to adopt a word with a more severe meaning. As it has always been said that we did not have a revolution (although we did have a very real revolution which has left a mark on the country) because we did not resort to terrorism, these persons will obviously force us to adopt it. Then they will not be able to deny that our revolution has had all the attributes of a revolution.

'This brings me to examine the situation on the Home Front. I have reflected much upon it . . . On the Home Front there exist the following categories: The families of those who have fallen—their morale is very high. It is clear that no such family would desire to accept conditions of peace which would make their sacrifice of no avail. Families of the fighting men—morale excellent. Men returned from the war—morale excellent. Now for the masses of Fascists—this is the best class on the Home Front. But then there is the inferior category. It is composed of all those who are physically and mentally below par and who are blind, lame, toothless, feeble-minded, shirkers, people lacking in some quality. All these people who have not been engaged in war and never can be, find an alibi for their consciences by saying that this war ought never to have begun. It is a curious fact that there is always a class of Italians who, when we are at war on the side of France, want a war on the side of the Germans, and when we are fighting on the German side want to be fighting on the English side; that is, they want the kind of war which is not being waged.

'My thought turns to the middle classes and their attitude. This is a subject which enrages many Fascists. We must finally define the middle classes . . . The following is the simplest definition of a bourgeois—the bourgeois is a man who is rich and cowardly at the same time. . . . We must react against the voluble hysteria of the intellectual Italians. . . . I read an article the other day which seemed to say "This revolution has got to be made all over again" . . . Now I do not say that we must remain completely mummified in certain mental positions, but there is a big difference between doing that and adopting a regular whirligig of ideas.

'It is said that this war is an unpopular war. I should like to know what wars ever have been popular. None in Italy, not even the war of 1840–49 . . . There were a large number of people who said these people are mad. When the troops came back to Turin after Novara the officers broke the windows of the Ministry of War. Was the expedition to Crimea popular? Cavour was very unpopular . . . Not even the war of 1859 was popular, it was then said that Piedmont was exhausted. Nor was the war of '66 popular. The war of the conquests of the Empire was popular, the least unpopular, but a number of people came to me in November 1935 to say, "You have already done great things, now lower your sails." I read certain letters in the Council of Ministers from very high military persons who said it was a very risky undertaking . . . We may conclude that wars are only popular with the great mass of the people when they result in victory. To pretend that war is popular with the great mass of the people is to pretend something absurd. The mass of the people have to obey. They cannot judge; they have no capacity for judging. The war of 1915–18 was most unpopular; it resulted in the first part of the civil war which ended in 1922.[c]

c. Mussolini might have added that the second part of the civil war began, for similar reasons, in 1943.

'Events in Russia have led to a notable recrudescence of hatred towards the Germans and Germany. All kinds of rumours are abroad. Now there is talk of atrocities happening in Russia . . . It is true that unpleasant things have happened in Russia, but everyone whom I have questioned says that this was due to the rout in which everyone fled as quickly as they could, not only Italians who resisted rather more, but Germans too . . . There was terrible confusion. We must react against this habit of thought, we must admit that things of this kind happen in every army and every war . . . The Party must stop this kind of talk. Meantime, I must say that such episodes have not taken place in the Alpine Corps, which has been respected by the Germans . . . War will be won by the army which becomes a political army more quickly than its opponents. This is what is happening in Germany; the development of the S.S. tends to turn armed forces more or less well endowed with individual, political and racial sensibility into a mass of fighters. The epoch of the soldier has finished—the soldier as a paid recruit. Now we come to the age of the fighting man.

'The régime intends to strengthen all its organs. I have decided to review their composition and their working from the point of view of the people at the head, many of whom are no longer in command of the situation. The purging of the Party must go on. The press will be watched, athough our press is the most free in the world. It prints whatever it likes because the State comes in with its censorship after the printing. Local organs of the régime, the syndical organs as well as the administrative and political, must be directed particularly to helping those who have returned from the war and who have a right to everything. We must adapt our propaganda to circumstances, for it is one thing to talk to a gathering of professors and quite another to address a political assembly . . . We must have that courage, my friends, which all revolutions have had, to take defeatists by the throat and denounce them. In Russia the ambition of the Communist is to be a member of the O.G.P.U. and in Germany to belong to the S.S.; the Spanish revolution had its assault brigades. Now we, as a result of the past, are not altogether possessed by such ideas. This is wrong.' [2]

Carlo Scorza, the new Party Secretary, was a foundation member. Born in Paola di Calabria in 1897 of a poor and numerous family, in 1916 he joined an elder brother in Lucca, where he settled until he was swept into the war, and like many of his generation came back from the front uprooted and restless. He studied accountancy for a time at a technical institute, but by 1920 was wholly active in extremist politics, and became the founder of the Fascist organization in Lucca. His career followed the pattern of a regional Party official. He was political secretary, and editor of a weekly newspaper *Intrepido*, giving French lessons to supplement his resources. The Lucca Action Squads occupied Civitavecchia during the March on Rome. Scorza rose in the normal ranks of hierarchy to be Federal Secretary of his province, when he also commanded the Militia. He was alleged at this time to have been responsible for the fatal manhandling of the Anti-Fascist leader, Amendola. In 1924 he was elected deputy, and entered the national machine of the Party as inspector and in 1929 as member of the Directorate. After 1930 he played a leading part in organizing the Fascist youth movement and its para-military organization.

His newspaper widened its range, and, as the *Popolo Toscano*, became a leading extremist organ of regional Fascism. But, as elsewhere in the Fascist machine in the provinces, Scorza's local control was contested by rival ambitions. Between 1926 and 1932 he was the subject of five Party enquiries, ending in his dismissal from all offices and the closing down of his paper in 1932. His main enemy was Achille Starace, the Party Secretary, who in spite of the backing of Scorza by Farinacci and Ciano, succeeded in keeping the boss of Lucca out of national affairs. After 1940 Scorza joined the army, and began to work his way back into Party affairs, specializing in questions relating to the Militia. In December 1942 he returned to Party Headquarters as Director of the Press Office, and one of the Vice-Secretaries. This nomination had already been a hint that the younger generation was under fire. His present appointment indicated by implication the bankruptcy of the 'second wave', the second generation of the Fascist élite typified by his predecessor, Vidussoni. He represented the action squads of the early 20's, the pretentious world of provincial Fascist journalism, and the Party machine of the 30's.[3]

Scorza now charged into his task. The Party cadres were shaken up, and in the following weeks four senior Party officers and twenty provincial secretaries had been changed. He also had plans for an internal emergency, and pressed on Mussolini to create special squads, under the direct control of the Party, to be attached to each party office in the provinces.[d] It seems that the Duce first agreed and then retracted. He had already discussed such eventualities with Himmler at Klessheim in April, and embarked on another solution —the Armoured Division of Blackshirts which the Germans had offered to equip.[e]

On May 3 the new Party Directorate was summoned to Palazzo Venezia to receive the directives of the Duce. The phrases were familiar.

'We must look after the best sections of the people, while the police deal with the lower elements which can weaken the resistance of the entire Italian people. You have certainly noticed that from the moment a new direction was given to the life of the Party, the atmosphere cleared immediately. I am

d. Such a plan was ultimately extended and put into operation under the Salò Republic.
e. See Appendix to this chapter on the 'M' division.

convinced that if we hold to this line of absolute moral and political intransigence we shall obtain concrete results. It is not that the Italian people is estranged. We must remember that the best part of the population is not on metropolitan territory. There are 1,300,000 Fascists fighting in Tunisia, in the Balkans or in lands which will one day belong to the mother country. All Fascists must be convinced—and they must convince the people—that the destiny of Italy for the next generations is now at stake. And there must be no arbitrary, superficial distinctions between Fascism and Italy, because there is absolute, perfect identity between them.'

The mystic power of the Duce's oratory faded with the dispersal of the audience. The continuous flow of comment on the political scene, which reached Mussolini daily in the form of reports from various agencies and individuals, had for so long marked the gulf between rhetoric and reality. A report on his directives of May 3 underlined this phenomenon.

His speech was described as 'a supreme appeal to the whole structure of the nation to strengthen our resistance, and, as such, a sign of the danger which hangs over the country'. It was also 'a recognition of the bankruptcy of the system, political, industrial, and economic hitherto adopted. People found it strange that the main heads of accusation are apparently directed against the masses, when the responsibility of the deficiencies mentioned weighs on the spheres, which up till now have directed all national activities.' The appearance of Scorza, however, had not been ill-received. He had shown courage in raising certain matters, which involved the responsibility of people in high places. His warnings to the youth and their harmful and illogical interference in affairs, had also been regarded as pointed.[4]

On May 5, two days after the Duce's speech, the new Secretary of the Party held a mass reunion of Fascists in the Teatro Adriano. Unconsciously it was to be the final appeal of old guard Fascism on the edge of political disintegration, but it was momentarily, by its very recognizable familiarity, to give a brief sense of security, that all was well, and Scorza's words were greeted with a show of genuine enthusiasm.

This last set piece of Fascist rhetoric lasted from noon, with one hour's break, until four o'clock that afternoon. 'The first attribute of the Fascist must be honesty . . . He is a temperament, a definite individuality, unmistakable, clear, precise. The Duce said one day that the Fascist should also look physically different from others.' There was now a need to resurrect the 'figure of the old Fascist as created by the Duce . . . For long years we have made rhetoric and anti-rhetoric . . . And we have made such use of this rhetoric that we have reached a real form of inflation. If we merely did our duty, we immediately assumed the right to exceptional rewards.' The Party needed higher standards. Scorza had extended the closing date by which one could withdraw one's membership card to June 10. He hoped however that people would not do so . . . There was an old argument: should the Party be a mass or minority one? This was an idle discussion. 'The question is one of quality: an aristocracy of the masses, selected in the spirit of minorities.' The Party cannot be reduced to a caste or a clan because of its vast tasks. The question of cadres is the central problem of Fascism. The test is competence. There must be no improvisation. Another point to clear up: the profession of Party leader should be abolished (applause). Professionalism has lowered the level of the leadership.'

Purges must also be instituted against irresponsible denunciations. There would be no question of sacrificing innocent victims, but the authorities would be implacable against the unworthy. 'The necessity of defending the country has delayed the Fascist construction.' There was now a need to return to the origins of the Revolution. The Party was the link between the State and the people. 'As defender of the State, the Party reserves the right to supervise and control and intervene in all organs and institutions of the State.

'If we must die, let us swear to fall in style.' [5] [f]

The inevitable police report mirrored mercilessly and vividly the content of this general internal malaise. Although Scorza, in his speech, had returned to the basic postulates of Fascism, 'everyone says that not even he can bring the Party back to that original creed, because he can do nothing against the camarillas, which have formed in the bosom of the Party itself, headed by this and that Party boss . . . The Party has in twenty years lost the confidence and esteem of even its own followers, because of the excessive robberies of the bosses and the patent injustices which have been committed.' The activities of war profiteers attracted universal attention. 'Enormous progress has been made by Communism, which is undermining all branches of production.'

The report closes with the quip of a Roman working woman, 'But no one asked him whether he eats with the Party card.' [6] [g]

Later in the afternoon of May 5, and as if to complete the circle, the Duce addressed the crowds from the balcony of Palazzo Venezia for the first time since June 1940. It was the anniversary of the entry of the Italian troops into Addis Ababa. The square below him was crowded with exalted citizens many of whom had come from Scorza's speech on the new spirit of the leadership of the Fascist Party in the Teatro Adriano. The joint celebrations, with their familiar pattern of heady oratory, was the last public expression of the twenty-year dialogue between the dictator and the crowd. When the Duce withdrew from the balcony, the tall windows would never be opened for him or for such an occasion again.

Outside Party circles the reaction to Scorza's appeal to a Fascist Golden

f. In Italian *cadere in bellezza*. This phrase aroused much ironical comment.

g. There was also bitter popular criticism at the moving of the Party headquarters to Piazza Colonna. People were thrown on the street. The excessive cost could have been better spent on bombed out families. Italian Collection. Police report, May 11, 1943.

Age dissipated in general frustration. Dollmann reported one typical episode to Himmler: 'The latest and grave internal crisis of the country has been without doubt influenced in a positive sense by the new and extensively felt wave of energy from Palazzo Venezia.' With the nomination of Scorza 'a fresh wind has been blowing among the Fascists themselves'. This was noticeable at the recent celebrations of the twenty-fourth anniversary of the founding of the Roman Fascio. The usual well-worn phrases of the Federal Secretary of Rome about 'in the name of the People, everything for the People' etc. were interrupted with enraged shouted interventions of the old bemedalled party members. 'We want deeds not chatter. What have you done for the People? Only what remains over from the millions which have poured into your pockets.' Amid stormy applause, proceedings against Volpi, Cini, and Morgagni (the director of the official Stefani press agency and a well-known profiteer) were called for. Bottai, the Minister of Education,[h] wishing to defend his own kind, who for years had fed with him at the trough, entered the fray, and the meeting broke up in confusion.[7]

There was no escape from the established workings of the 'system'. The Fascist Party reigned by an uneasy shifting balance of forces within the hierarchy of rival clans.

An anonymous report, or summary of reports, presumably from the central offices of the Party, forms a sour commentary on the inescapable functioning of the machine from which Scorza too, as an early beneficiary, had no chance of dissociating himself.

'The nomination of Scorza as Secretary of the Fascist Party was no longer regarded so favourably as it had been for the following reasons: It had been proved that either from fear or friendship he was under Farinacci's orders. His actions were in complete contrast with his famous twelve points and with the tenor of his speech in the Teatro Adriano.

'He had attacked political professionalism and then copied former Party Secretaries who had installed the system. For instance, he had transferred federal secretaries from one province to another as if they were civil servants. Further, while it was clear from his speech and his twelve points that the Party Secretary, the Federal Secretary, and the Secretary of the Fascio were alone to form the backbone of the Party, he still nominated Party Inspectors. Their names showed clearly that he did this to find jobs for Party bosses turned out of other posts.

'The Fascist Directorate, although partly composed of true, and proved, Fascists, was completely the creature of Farinacci. Cucco, one of the new vice-secretaries, though most worthy of respect, must be grateful to Farinacci who insisted on his re-admission to the Party from which he had been unjustly expelled.' Tarabini, also a vice-secretary, was notoriously a Farinacci man, and in constant touch with the latter, who kept him informed of his wishes

h. He had been dismissed in February 1943.

on changes of personnel so that he could stir up Scorza to make these changes. 'The opinion of Fascists, who had hoped much of Scorza, had consequently completely changed because he had set his course towards that favoured by Farinacci. Everyone said that in a few months' time they would pay heavily for faults once again committed.' [8]

Although expelled by the Duce's persistence from the centre of power in the Party machine, Farinacci, who had destroyed the pristine provincial enthusiasm of the 'first wave' of Fascism, possessed the classic style of a Party boss, and, although himself the prophet of that centralized Party bureaucracy which he himself had built, had through the years become by skilled management the more powerful of the clan leaders precisely because he had sought his support among the regional elements of Fascism, which he had weakened and attempted to destroy when Party Secretary.

Scorza was undoubtedly committed to the whole style of Fascist Party rule, but, though circumscribed in action by his own past, he strove at least to assess the situation in realistic terms.

On June 7 he produced a private report for the Duce, written in the familiar style and tone of twenty years of Fascist political vocabulary, and cognisant of at least some of the causes of present discontents.[9] 'Duce, what I am about to tell you may appear to be pessimistic but basically there is a rock-like feeling of security in the strength of the régime, in the vitality of the nation, in yourself and in victory. I know you demand of me not a passive obedience so much as a faithful and mystical interpretation of your directives: rather a subordinate and intelligent collaboration founded on the assumption of the most complete sense of dedication. The nation is henceforward wholeheartedly convinced that, with the new direction given to the Party, you have not wished solely to set about changing the individuals, nor simply revise the directives. The conviction is that you have wished to give a new slant to the whole national life.'

Among the rich, anti-Fascism and hostility to Mussolini was only limited by the fear that the eventual triumph of such an attitude might favour a negative outcome of the war, and thereby, with a Bolshevik triumph, the loss of their material belongings. Among the middle classes in general, 'there is neither anti-Fascism nor any open attitude against Mussolini, but neither is there any exalted Fascism. There is only a diffuse and apathetic resignation, aggravated by economic restrictions which face them with the elementary problem of having enough food. Among the lower middle class and including the working class, there is a genuine honest Fascist feeling and absolute devotion to you. This enormous mass is really the one on which we could work by a lively operation of penetration and conquest.'

As to the Party, Scorza had no illusions that in the few days that he had been Secretary any radical transformation had taken place. Drastic measures were needed as to the necessary time to carry them out.

The Party suffered from several diseases: firstly, 'an elephantiasis, not only numerical but also spiritual, which dissipates the will to fight and aggravates the spirit of preservation. In general everybody tries to preserve something, a position either in the Party hierarchy or finance. Such conservatism has transformed the dynamic earlier "offensive" into a concept which I can call modestly and even miserably "defensive". Even if one talks of heroism it is not the heroism of the Arditi,[i] who despise their own trenches in order to take those of the enemy, but the defensive heroism of the besieged.'

Secondly, a distrust between Party leaders in and out of office 'who, rather than consider matters from the national, and consequently Fascist viewpoint, are more concerned with their personal relations and rather than yield a jot of their positions and prejudices, ruin everything'.

Thirdly, the exaggerated enrichment of certain leaders. 'The distrust of the Fascist masses towards the leaders derives from this, as they have naturally lost any substantial credit, even if they retain any formal one.'

The youth had 'a somewhat limited belief in Fascism for various well-known reasons. But in their vast majority they represent material which can be recaptured (only a few months more, Duce!) as soon as we have changed the climate of the Party.' [j]

Scorza now turned to the flaws in the structure of the administrative machine of government: 'The various Ministries are today a real tangle of seldom defined and even more often overlapping functions, which complicates the enforcement of the simplest measure. I would add that this overlapping is frequently eliminated, and the measures decided on the basis of a common, and nowadays current, private deal: which means that personal favours are exchanged and money is circulated. While the lower ranks of the bureaucracy are in general both honest and Fascist, the higher ranks are in general neither honest nor Fascist: with the result that while the Party penalties are applied to petty infringements, the major sins of the big men go unpunished. And this not so much because these men know how to "organize" their affairs better than their inferiors, as because they are defended, often in good faith, by the politicians. . . . The upper ranks of the bureaucracy are not to be feared only because they are not Fascist, but above all because, by means of their own experience and the subtle and often captious interpretation of the law, they dominate the men and therefore the affairs of the régime.

'The controlling organs set up by the government are a wild jungle where no one can find his way: the Committees and Commissions and Organizations, symbolized by incomprehensible initials, constitute so great a confusion that even the best experts animated by the greatest good will often go astray. Here

i. The front line commandos of the First World War.
j. As Federzoni wrote: 'The "second wave" remained, until July 25, the ghost or rather than the mirage of the Party.' (*Memorie op cit* XL.)

too it is urgently necessary to cut down, reduce, simplify with a savagely dictatorial hand, and with full personal responsibility.

'This is not flattery, Duce, because you know I am a soldier not a flatterer, but at this point in my reflections I cannot help thinking that simple obedience to your orders and directives in East Africa, North Africa and Greece, would have produced different results. When the history of this war is written, documents, some of which I know personally, will give incontestable proof of your intuitive foresight of necessities, dangers, possibilities. . . . Now the organs directing the war have failed. Since the tasks have changed, it is only natural to change the organs.

'Our war was and is directed not by one but by five bodies. By a confused High Command, whose strategy is uncertain, and which has neither panoramic vision, nor connected or co-ordinated plans; by an Army General Staff which has gradually swelled out with cumbrous powers; by a Ministry of War with reduced functions, or interfering in functions no longer within its competence; by a Ministry for the Navy and a Ministry for Air who often act, in the technical field, without co-ordinated contacts with the other Armed Forces, and without taking into account, in estimating supplies, the time factor, the terrain, enemy progress, or our productive capacity.

'I cannot help thinking, Duce, that if all this disorganized structure was not preordained (in fact, I deny the existence of this kind of preordaining intelligence) it was certainly first accepted and successively desired and made more difficult only because you are the Supreme Commander and the ultimate responsibility lies with you . . .[k] There is no one who does not grasp straightaway that it is industrial and technical experts more than generals who command this war, because it is only the weapon which makes sacrifice and valour fruitful, deciding the outcome of battles. What unity exists in the directives, demands and orders for war production? And, if it existed, to what unified use would it be put? This is where the military situation becomes unhinged.

'If you ordered an enquiry you would find that the relations between war needs and industrial organization are such as to justify doubts even as to the existence of good faith.

'The morale of the upper ranks in general is not only depressed, but completely resigned: it can be said that the generals and admirals either do not feel that they can win, or do not believe they can win, or, allow me Duce to be brutally frank, want not to win. The officers feel the effects of the influence of the higher ranks. However, this influence is reacted to more and more strongly the nearer one gets to the lower ranks; so that among the

k. It would have been enough, according to Scorza, to transform the General Staff of the Army into a Supreme Command, leaving the three Ministries of War, Navy and Airforce, with administrative disciplinary powers, and to create a technico-scientific, industrial organ to be entrusted to a 'brain' not to a braided cap.

troops, among non-commissioned officers, among officers up to captains and majors, we find a truly indomitable spirit which will stand any test.

'Everything can be remedied, Duce, but on one condition: that you begin from the top, not only by substitutions in the ranks. Two-thirds of our generals are old, sour, and incompetent. They need support, or hierarchical procedure, or red tape before they will take the slightest step. They are arm-chair not horseback generals.'

Under such conditions it was not surprising that the Germans had 'no respect for us at all . . . We were not able to show—during these three years, either that we knew how to organize ourselves for what we needed, or that we were strong. And it is permissible to think today that without you, without the weight of your will, Italy, involved just the same in the war which she could not avoid, would be occupied by German troops, and with our Military Authorities themselves convinced and happy about it.'

Only a total transformation of Italy in all walks of life would convince the Germans of 'our steady determination . . . The European fortress is not being defended on the Brenner, but at Trapani.[l]

'The Duce has supreme command of the war; he cannot therefore be the Condottiere and at the same time the Soleri and Gasparotto [m] of the situation. It follows, logically, that the Head of the General Staff of the Army, Navy and Air Force, included in the Duce's General Staff, must be separated from the person and function of the Ministries for the Army, Navy and Airforce.

'In conclusion, I think that the central powers should be organized in this way: —

(a) Outside Italy the Duce must resume the political direction of the Axis with all the initiatives deriving from it. Internally, he must continue to be the only supreme regulator of the moral, political, and social life of the country.

(b) The Duce must be the Supreme Commander, with his Head of General Staff helped by the three Chiefs of the General Staffs of the Army, Navy and Air Force.

(c) The responsible Ministers must answer for the administrative-disciplin-ary functioning of the three Armed Forces, and co-ordinate the Services (the Minister for Air preferably an industrialist, or a politician with great prestige and powers of organization).

(d) A Minister of War Production (preferably an industrialist or a poli-tician of good organizing powers) helped by carefully picked men from the Army, Navy, Airforce, and Industry: he must know what he wants and what is needed, and must exercise a dictatorial function over the whole production.

(e) A Minister of Economy who co-ordinates and unifies the two existing organs of Agriculture for food and Exchange and Currency for commerce.

'There are two basic necessities, Duce: —

l. In Sicily.
m. Politicians of the First World War.

(a) Decentralize, in the sense of *functions*, and centralize in the sense of *responsibility*. The best exponents of the Party, of industry, and of finance, must be called to co-responsibility for the war and carry out their precise tasks with the pre-knowledge of capital punishment—whatever their rank, if they do not fulfil your instructions. No one can or should remain outside the life of the nation at this moment, or attempt to avoid it with stupid alibis, however trifling and slight.

(b) Bring the Country to realize the reality of the situation, forcing on everyone a way and plan of life in conformity with the grave destiny which weighs on the nation. Besides, we have irrefutable and undoubtedly successful precedents in the prominent periods of the history of all countries. Whatever the enemy propaganda thinks or does is unimportant: it will be important and sufficient for the Italian people to strive in a spiritual and productive effort which is the only guarantee of victory.

'Duce, I am a wheel on your cart: but this wheel will go on turning until it drops off, as long as you think it of some use. And forgive me for daring to write all this.'

These brave words bore much truth. The real crisis of the régime was, however, that the power and the will to act and reform had long since atrophied.

This report by Scorza might be regarded as a comprehensive and perceptive round up of the defects of the 'system'. It might have been written by the Germans. In directing his main attacks on the Civil Service and the Ministries of the Armed Forces, Scorza failed to pursue the implication that it has always been conceived to be the duty of the Party to act as the nosing watchdog of the régime in all spheres of government. The Party, however, had already exhausted its prestige and its cadres.

Italian Fascism had never succeeded in being totalitarian, and its fate in the end was to be decided in those enclaves which it had failed in twenty years to penetrate and control—the Court, the Army, the Civil Service, and even the Police.

On the day when he dispatched his analysis of the Home Front to Mussolini, Scorza initiated a series of disciplinary measures. The immediate reaction was one of general approval, but as forecast in his own report, the higher officials aimed at were protected by the Minister concerned and 'gently admonished'. In general, if Party members were denounced to the judicial authorities they received Party protection and suspended sentences. [10]

The Party was now, in the eyes of its hierarchy, a law unto itself, and the very root from which the growing demoralization of the nation had blossomed. Far from being the vanguard of resistance, it was from the ranks of the Party itself that the precursory signs of a national collapse could be envisaged.

The Director-General of Public Security [n] sent a brief marginal note to the Duce headed 'Signs of alarmism and defeatism'.

'It has been reported that the group of persons composed of Party leaders, various senators and industrialists opposed to Fascism are of the opinion in favour of seeking a separate peace.'[o]

Scorza seems to have had the fitful backing of the Duce in such isolated gestures. On June 11 twenty-four prefects were dismissed, a further nineteen retired, and twenty new appointments made in the provinces. These moves presumably were made on Mussolini's personal instructions as Minister of the Interior.

On the same day the news of the fall of the Italian naval and air base of Pantelleria brought the reality of enemy invasion to the approaches to Sicily. In the Duce's words, 'Pantelleria is an alarm bell; I might almost say, a warning ring at the gate.' [11] As Mussolini later put it in his Memoirs, 'Following the perturbation caused by the staggeringly unexpected surrender of Pantelleria, there was born in high circles an attitude of mind tending towards capitulation. There was a fresh chorus of defeatism.' [12]

The shadow of imminent invasion pervaded the whole internal scene. Not only were strategic considerations under hasty review, but the dangers of political and administrative collapse loomed. Scorza even exceeded his functions. Following on the strictures in his report of June 7 to the Duce on the Service Ministries, he took it upon himself to hold at Party headquarters on June 15 a meeting of the three Under-Secretaries of the Armed Forces, harangued them on the menace to the Home Front, and the need for military command to take anti-sabotage precautions. Ambrosio was furious at this interference by the Party and instantly complained to Mussolini, who characteristically did not support his Party Secretary but scolded him. Scorza's reply was a plaintive minute to the Duce:

'We talked of the repercussions in the country of the fall of Pantelleria and Lampedusa. I made it clearly understood to the comrades present that the "directive" of the Directorate, approved by you, was definite in the sense that it was up to the Party to determine a new phase in the conscience of the country and in the evaluation of military information; that in effect Pantelleria and Lampedusa were to be considered as the lowest point of major depression in the descending curve and not as the continuation of a mentality of surrender.

'I said among other things that from today on it was necessary to overcome the formula which has been tacitly accepted, that of "yielding to superior force" and that "superior force" should only signify a sense of duty, of honour, and of discipline for the Italians.

n. He was under the orders of the Ministry of the Interior.
o. Italian Collection. May 28, 1943. Marked in the Duce's hand 'Party' to be sent to Scorza.

'I recalled once again that the Armed Forces had always received, during the twenty-three years of the régime, all that they had asked for, and that therefore the nation has the right to assume that they will not fail in their sacred task.

'Having declared that the Party is prepared to follow to the limit your orders in every sense and direction—from the moral to the economic plans, from the repression of an attempt at subversion to the reorganization of all the resources of the nation—I called for . . . the most active propaganda . . . as a drastic and continuous appeal to those virtues which have always constituted the basis of all those peoples who do not wish to go under.

'Comrades Riccardi and Fougier cited the need for the necessary means and Comrade Sorice p that of facing up to certain demands of a welfare nature, as for example a bonus for those who could not take advantage, for reasons of higher orders, of a regular period of leave.

'All three, however, when confronted brutally with the reality of the situation, agreed that it was necessary to intensify moral pressure so that the various Headquarters and the troops should feel that this round, already embarked on, is decisive and they agreed the dragging brake of discipline must be restored by every means.' 13

The 'alarm bell' also rang for the civilian ministers. De Marsico, Minister of Justice, and Count Cini, the leading industrialist, who since February had been Minister of Communications, both members of the new government team nominated in February 1943, had for some time felt the urgency of forcing the lurking political crisis into open discussion among their colleagues. In particular, the efficiency of the country's military resistance depended clearly on the maintenance of the interior lines of communication on the mainland of Italy. 'After Pantelleria, Cini and myself,' said De Marsico later, 'agreed to press Mussolini for a complete report on the effective possibilities of this country in face of the war, and to seize the first occasion of a meeting of the Council of Ministers to put forward our own views.' 14

This opportunity came on June 19, and both men spoke out. This was the first and last independent expression of view within the governing clan. Both Ministers appealed to the Duce, in this hour of crisis, to accept 'a more open and frank division of responsibility' and to take his collaborators into his confidence. 'The series of failures are the consequence of irrational and inappropriate use of the few means at our disposal.' 15

Mussolini merely commented, 'Any discussion is useless. Italy has only one alternative: to conquer or fall at the side of Germany.' And he closed the meeting. 16 In his eyes, this inner Cabinet had never assumed a collective action or responsibility. It was never summoned again during the following weeks of mounting crisis.

p. The three Undersecretaries respectively of the Navy, Air Force, and Army.

Three days later Count Cini wrote to the Duce to explain his initiative at this meeting, and to resign.

'I meditated at length and hesitated before taking the decision which I now submit to you. I am putting forward certain rash doubts which I could not express at the Council of Ministers of June 19 which ended before I had the time to speak a second time.

'At that meeting, I pointed out the gravity of the moment and stressed the need for changing those methods which had produced such unfavourable results. I proposed that one should make a profound study of the general situation in its various aspects and warned that I did not intend to anticipate solutions which could and should only result from an objective examination of the situation itself.

'You, Duce, did not accept my proposal. You dismissed its practical value by referring to it as "academic". On the other hand you lingered over the theme of "peace", as if I had started the discussion, whereas not only did I not raise the issue, but said clearly that no solution could be reasonably considered without the necessary elements on which to form a judgement. My reference to peace was made with the sole aim of giving a warning that we must not find ourselves unprepared as we were when war broke on us.

'You likewise rejected the value of the discussion as you viewed the situation as such that it did not permit any possibility of release, summarizing your thoughts in the resolute and peremptory phrase "Burn our boats behind us". I permit myself to think that such an imperative is valid only for individuals: one does not burn boats for whole peoples unless every alternative is excluded and one is at the point of desperation. But this is not our case.

'In any event, I repeat, my proposal was not aimed at opening a discussion on peace, but to find out whether you would admit at least your colleagues to that examination of general policy which I regard as indispensable for any conscious responsibility.

'But your intention was clear, to limit collaboration only to the technical field. I do not disagree, but I would be over-reticent if I did not express my dissent on this essential point. Almost everyone thought as I did. But no one dares to say so. But I prefer to displease you rather than to betray your trust.'

Cini ended by asking to be relieved of his post.q

According to one source, Scorza broached a similar view at this time to Mussolini on behalf of the Party. In the general uncertainty, Fascist circles in Rome were pressing for a lead from the Duce. Scorza apparently wrote two letters on the theme of transferring to other hands the military direction of the war, thus placing the person of the Duce 'above criticism'. But on both occasions was met with contemptuous rebuff. Instead, the national Party Directorate was summoned to an informal meeting by Scorza, who drafted

q. Italian Collection. Count Cini to the Duce, June 24, 1943. The Duce did not accept the resignation until July 24.

under nine headings its last expiring autocriticism. This document was sent to Mussolini to await a sign from him.[r]

On June 23 Scorza felt it necessary to write to Mussolini, who had summoned for the next day the monthly meeting of the Party Directorate, which had been delayed by military events.

'I am under the impression that tomorrow you are going to put a brake on my activities. I say "impression", but I should say more exactly "I am afraid", for I have been afraid of it since hostile comments began to be made against the Directorate's "directive".

'In every case I have acted in accordance with the directives which you laid down for me in your speech at the time of my appointment:[s] you read and approved my speech made at the Adriano; you read and approved the Directorate's "directive". What has been the result of all this? The nation and the Fascists understood clearly that acting through the Party you were imparting an atmosphere of greater severity to the régime, or rather, were creating an extraordinary, war-time attitude everywhere. The Party is much stronger in consequence, and the results are truly considerable, for in scarcely two months the Party has not only returned to its position as the central motive power of national life, but it is valued, and what is more important, feared.

'You have said that the Party is the natural link between State and people. In order to be this, the Party must put some pressure even on the State, especially in regard to such of its forms and manifestations as are not yet wholly Fascist. For the State is only Fascist because you wish it to be so, because you issued laws which transformed it into a Fascist state, and, above all, because you are at the centre. But in fact it remains non-Fascist at its core: Fascism must realize this fact. I am referring to the continued existence of old laws and institutions and to the persistence of a non-fascist mentality among the ranks of the civil service . . . In time of war what should have been the most formidable arm of the State has shown that it is not Fascist— the army and the armed forces. Only those institutions which have a political idea behind them will survive the storm which is buffeting the world. You have said this yourself.

'The Party has followed this path rigorously for two months. If tomorrow you were to "shoot down" the Party (an event eagerly awaited by those who are afraid of having to give an account of themselves or of having to walk more quickly in another direction than their present one), the "new fact" desired by the nation with its deep instinct for spiritual resurrection at this moment of military disaster would become a delusion . . .

r. Napolitano, *XXV. Luglio,* p. 265 ff. See also Cucco *op cit* p. 93. The former work may have relied on private contributions from Scorza for these statements. They are not confirmed as yet from other sources. The text of the document is to be found in Napolitano.

s. On April 17. The Duce seems at least to have authorized its publication, but with no display of confidence.

'You say that you are first and foremost Duce of Fascism and only secondly Head of the Government. It follows logically that everyone must be first Fascists and secondly hierarchs of every grade and office. But this must be clearly laid down. You alone can do this and make it a command. It is a strange law, Duce, and yet it must now be defined as being a real law, that a Fascist who enters the Government, or a Bank, or the Civil Service, or the Army, inevitably becomes a slave and succumbs to the environment in which he functions. . . .

'I have told you, Duce, of the anxiety which precedes the summoning of the Directorate, which in my opinion will be an important date in the history of the Revolution.' [17]

On June 24 the meeting was summoned to Palazzo Venezia. Scorza read what was to be the last report on the state of that Party, which had been the central organ of Italian political life for twenty years. The statistics were impressive.[t] 'These are the figures,' he concluded, 'but they will have no absolute value if they do not represent spirit and will. The will and the spirit which animate the forces mobilized under the banner of the "Littorio" are called—loyalty, discipline, resistance, and victory.' Such was the vacuous epitaph of twenty years.

The Party representatives awaited the commentary of the Leader. In his customary address, the Duce referred to the criticism of the Party which had been aired at the last meeting in May. He admitted that it had been too bureaucratized, but it was the spirit that mattered. The mass of the people were behaving well, and should not be confused with an unreliable minority.

'Those relics of the old parties will never be those who will succeed in ousting the régime . . . One should pour ridicule on the authors and distributors of such detective stories, the product of a sick imagination.'

There was no way out of the war, and no question of a 'dishonourable' peace. 'The enemy must play their card. They have talked too much about the necessity of continental invasion. They will have to attempt it, for otherwise they will be beaten without having fought. As soon as the enemy attempts to land, he must be blocked at the line which the sailors call the foreshore, the sand line where the water ends and the land begins . . . The duty of Fascists is this: to give that feeling, and, more than a hope, the absolute certainty, which comes from an iron unshakeable granite sense of decision.' [18]

Breaking with tradition, this speech was published in the Press on July 5, and with unfortunate results. It was intended to raise public morale on the eve of the Sicily landings.

---

t. 4,770,770 members, 1,217,036 in the women's organizations, 903,389 in organizations dependent on the Party, 4,500,000 in the Dopolavoro. (The Party institution for providing recreation after working hours.)

APPENDIX

The 'M' Division

•••

ON returning from Klessheim in April the Duce had sent for Dollmann and
took up this question. He wanted to know whether Himmler could send to
Italy by the end of May: 24 8·8 guns, 24 tanks—not necessarily the latest
type, 60 heavy machine-guns, 150 lorries to carry twenty to thirty men, 30
flame-throwers.[19] The commander of the Italian Fascist Militia, General
Galbiati, invited Chief of Staff of the SA, Lutze, to visit Italy, but when
Mackensen asked Bastianini whether such a visit was opportune the latter
replied that 'personally he thought that the timing was not a happy one,
that he did not know the Duce's view on this special case', but would ask
him. The answer was to postpone the invitation 'until the summer'.

On April 23 Mackensen reported that the Duce had told him that the
setting up of the Division was being energetically undertaken. All recruits
were being very carefully screened. It was a matter of 8–10,000 men. Quality
was more important than quantity. The first battalion should be ready by the
end of May. There was however a note of anxiety on the German side at the
lack of progress in this affair. On May 2 Ribbentrop telegraphed to Mackensen: 'On the occasion of his visit to the Fuehrer, the Duce invited the Reichsfuehrer S.S. to visit Rome. It is assumed that the Duce intended to discuss
with him the questions of setting up the training and arming of the "M"
battalions.' [20] Himmler would be available for such a visit as from May 10.
Mackensen was instructed to arrange a meeting with the Duce. An ill fate
seemed to be attached to the whole enterprise. Himmler's Chief of Staff,
Lutze, was killed in an accident. The Duce did not seem to be impatient to
continue his talks with Himmler, and suggested in reply to Ribbentrop's
enquiry that a convenient date for a visit would be early in June.

At the end of May, 36 Tiger tanks and the latest German artillery and
automatic weapons, together with thirty-three instructors arrived. The survivors of the Italian Militia units from Russia were to form the core of this

division on which the crucial duty of defending the Fascist Revolution at home was to be placed.

Marshal Caviglia noted in his diary on May 29, presumably on information from General Ambrosio, who was disquieted by the news of this episode: 'In the ranks of the Party leadership they are not preparing to overcome the foreign foe, but the internal enemy. If we compare this state of affairs with that in Lombardy-Venetia before the liberation from Austria, the moral and political repression of our country is evident.' [21]

This increased attention to the Fascist Militia was the direct result of the German prompting against the unreliability of the Royal House, and the doubts as to the Fascist loyalties of the regular armed forces. This dualism in the military structure of the régime had always been a source of controversy. Marshal de Bono, who had himself been a leading Commander in the Militia, later advised Mussolini to put an end to this situation. The latter's reply was to stretch out the fingers of his hand: 'This (the index finger) is the Party, and this (the thumb) is the Militia, in the middle is Italy.' [22] And now in 1943 the lurking mutual distrust of the Militia and the Army was sharpened. Although in June 1940 the Militia had been officially incorporated into the armed forces, Ambrosio had unsuccessfully opposed the recent return from the Balkans of five Militia battalions, which were now ostensibly posted to coastal defence.

It was hoped that the new 'M' Division would be ready by the end of June. Its commander, General Losana, was an old Fascist, who had recently led the Militia units in Croatia. The training programme was working well. The main difficulty was that there were no spare parts for the tanks. Mackensen intervened. 'Seeing the great political interest which we have in handing over this new instrument to the Duce in impeccable condition, perhaps it would be possible for the Foreign Minister to intervene with the German General Staff.' [23]

CHAPTER FIVE

ROYAL HESITATIONS

•-•

THE SURRENDER of the Italian First Army in Tunisia on May 12 closed the imperial episode of Fascism and the penultimate phase of the drama of the régime. The loss of the last foothold in Africa meant inevitably that unless a compromise peace, or an armistice, were negotiated with the enemy, an Allied invasion of the mainland of Italy would follow, bringing with it the certain collapse of the Fascist state and possibly the end of the Monarchy. In a series of memoranda in his own hand, the King now put together his views on the state of the war.[a]

'15 May, 1943. Note One

1. Germany in her fifth year of war is weary and discouraged; her forces in Russia are less numerous than those of the Soviets; she has to occupy France, Belgium, Holland, Denmark, Norway, Poland, Yugoslavia and Greece. If, in the summer of 1943, she launches a major offensive against Russia, it will end like in 1942 but on a larger scale, due to the exhaustion of the German Army. The failure of a new offensive in Russia could bring about an internal collapse in Germany.

2. Slovakia and Croatia will keep going as long as the Axis is alive; they are both useless in the present war.

3. Roumania and Hungary are militarily flattened. The internal position in Roumania is uncertain: in Hungary strong anti-German currents are developing.

a. These manuscript notes of the King (of which photostats exist) were apparently found on his desk in the Quirinal after September 8, 1943. They were first published on April 25, 1945—the last day of the existence of the Republic of Salò, in the review *La Vita Italiana*. (Edited by Giovanni Preziosi.) These papers presumably formed part of Mussolini's personal archives and were released as belated propaganda to show the 'treachery' of the Crown towards the Axis. They have been reprinted in a number of secondary sources.

4. Bulgaria fears Russia: her army is short of artillery and would only be of use in fighting the Turks.

5. Japan is completely occupied in the Far East and India: she does not seem to be able or want to act against Russia.

Countries Occupied by the Axis Forces

1. In Poland the struggle of the partisans against the Germans is far from over.

2. Yugoslavia is in a state of full rebellion.

3. Greece is about to revolt.

4. In France, Belgium and Holland there will be risings against the Germans in event of an Anglo-American landing.

5. In Denmark and Norway almost the whole population is anti-German.

Enemy States

1. England and America control the sea and know how to contain the Axis submarine campaign. They have considerable resources in raw materials and much money: their air forces become increasingly dangerous to the Axis.

2. Russia seems to be still strong, with plenty of raw materials, manpower, and good military and civilian leaders.

Neutral Countries

1. Turkey will probably remain neutral until the end of the struggle. She adopts a benevolent attitude to the Allies.

2. Spain will not aid the Axis; nor will she become hostile.

3. Portugal is subject to the English.

4. Switzerland and Sweden are sympathetic to the Allies, but fear of Germany keeps them neutral.

V.E.'

'15 May, 1943. Note Two

After the occupation of Tunisia, what action will the Anglo-Americans follow in the Mediterranean?

1. Land in Spain or the Balearic Islands to move against France.

2. Land in Sequania b or Provence?

3. Land in Greece (or Thrace).

4. Land in the large islands of the Tyrrhenian Sea (Corsica or Sardinia) or in the Italian peninsula.

The first operation would be of little use to the Allies. The second could probably be carried out if timed with simultaneous landings on the Atlantic coast of France.

The third would be easy and the most profitable for the Allies. It would

b. The region of Celtic Gaul round Besançon.

strike Roumania from behind and would prevent Russian intervention in the Balkans, a move which would certainly not be well viewed by the Allies.

The fourth operation should be ruled out, as the enemy could hardly want to disperse their resources by invading Germany through Italy and the Alpine chain.

It may be that the Allies might believe that Italy was in a low state and think of knocking her out by heavy aerial bombardments followed by landings.

To occupy Sicily the Allies would require not less than 200,000 men; for Sardinia possibly 100,000 and for Corsica about the same.

In Sicily we have four Divisions, in Sardinia three, in Corsica two: our resistance in the Islands could be considerable.

If the Allies occupied Sardinia they would be more easily able to move against the mainland coast.

In the Peninsula we have: Three Divisions in Piedmont and Liguria, which cannot be moved, as they are the reserve for the thin forces which are in occupation of Provence. One Parachutist Division in the process of formation at Florence. Three Divisions in Rome. One Division in Calabria. One Division in Apulia. Seven or eight Divisions re-forming in the Po Valley.

Of the Divisions in the Peninsula only two are up to strength, and five in an effective state; the other Divisions can hardly be counted on, at least until the end of June.

All these Divisions are on a six-battalion basis, barely provided with supporting arms; the divisional artillery is out of date. There are no armoured units, except for a few German tanks.

This state of affairs is certainly known to the Anglo-Americans, as also the miserable condition of our fleet (reduced to three battleships, four light cruisers and twelve destroyers) and of our air force.

The enemy could as from now attempt a landing in Southern Italy, on the Roman beaches, or in Tuscany. They possess very many landing craft, and if they should succeed in getting ashore an armoured group, one landing could be very dangerous for us . . .

We must prepare our limited forces dispersed throughout the Peninsula to offer a strenuous resistance so as to allow for the intervention in the struggle of our troops in the Balkans and for the eventual influx of German troops from Germany.

Our Balkan armies would arrive with much delay and their efficiency is low. One cannot count on the arrival of considerable German forces. Perhaps the enemy might act simultaneously against Germany and Italy.

Our military situation certainly is not cheerful and gives much food for thought.

V.E.'

'*15 May, 1943. Note Three*

One must do all one can to keep the country united and not make rhetorical speeches especially only of a Fascist background.

One must keep close contacts with Hungary, Roumania, and Bulgaria, who have little love for the Germans.

One must not forget to make every possible gesture of courtesy to the government leaders in England and America. One must think seriously of the possible need to detach Italy's armed forces from those of Germany, whose internal collapse might come without warning, as happened to Imperial Germany in 1918.   V. E.'

On May 19 the King said to the head of his military household, General Puntoni: 'I am afraid that at any moment the British government or the King of England may approach me direct in order to negotiate a separate peace. Such a move would cause me grave embarrassment. If it should happen, I would act without subterfuge. I would speak to the Duce and agree with him a line of action.' [1]

By the end of May, Acquarone had established direct relations with Bonomi and his friends. He was also anxious that these politicians should not gather too closely round the alternative focus of the heir to the throne, the Prince of Piedmont. 'Let us leave aside the young ones,' was his remark to Bonomi at their meeting on May 26. But the main purpose of this preliminary talk was to indicate the readiness of the King to receive at first hand the views of his surviving advisers of the days before the March on Rome.

This audience took place at the Quirinal on the morning of June 2. The two men had not met for some twenty years. Bonomi recorded the conversation. 'Passing to the present situation . . . I underlined the need for overturning the Fascist régime, the cause of all evil in Italy. The King, who alone possessed the prestige of supreme power and had the support of the Armed Forces, could, whenever he wished, dismiss the Prime Minister and Head of the Government . . . Naturally if the Duce were dismissed, he would have to be placed under arrest to avoid the chance that, backed by the armed Militia of the Party, he might plunge the country into civil war. The first act then must be to turn to a military government. The King had but to choose between his military chiefs. In this respect I put forward three names: General Ambrosio, Chief of the General Staff, Marshal Caviglia, and Marshal Badoglio. The King did not reply, except to observe that Ambrosio is a professional soldier only, and that Caviglia is too old.'

The second act must be the denunciation of the pact with Germany. On this subject the King had no wish to comment. Bonomi however pressed on, pointing out that the Axis pact was not an alliance between states, but as drafted in the preamble, 'between two régimes and two revolutions'. 'With the fall of the Fascist régime the alliance is no longer valid.'

The King followed the whole exposition in silence, and only added, 'The nation always has the right to what it chooses.'

Bonomi reported to his friends, 'I think it unlikely that such a design will be accepted. It may be that the King will decide to act at the last minute.'[2]

As Puntoni noted in his diary: 'His Majesty, who does not miss a note of what is happening, is not what he was a month ago. He is conscious of the gravity of the situation, and is reflecting on what to do, but I think that, at least for the present, he is still decided to support Mussolini's action. The plan which His Majesty is elaborating in his head is a mystery to everybody, and I think that not even Acquarone is informed.'[3]

One possibility had already occurred to the King: a 'constitutional solution' arising from a political crisis within the ranks of Fascism and along the lines feared by Bonomi and his friends, already in April. This may have been the reason why, on the day following his talk with Bonomi, June 3, the King received Grandi in audience.[c] According to the latter's account he repeated to the Sovereign the arguments which he had used on previous occasions. 'Your Majesty, there is no choice: either Novara, namely abdication; or a change of front in the style of Victor Amadeus II who, when he realized the mistake of the alliance with the King of France, saved Piedmont and the dynasty at the last moment by going over to the Imperial camp.' The King replied: 'The moment will come. I know that I can count on you. Leave your King to choose the opportune moment and in the meantime help me to obtain the constitutional means.' Grandi assumed that the King implied a vote by the Chamber or by the Grand Council, and that presumably it was in his capacity as President to the former body that he was being received.[4]

As from this moment Grandi carefully avoided the Roman scene, and retired to Bologna as if awaiting a second March on Rome.

The fall of Tunis in May had also re-opened speculation round the choice of a possible military figure, the indispensable leader of any action in the name of the Crown. Caviglia's name was mentioned more frequently in the clubs and corridors, but his personal contacts with the General Staff of the Army, apart from Ambrosio, were, because of his age, impersonal and distant. Badoglio felt that he could count on the inner group, who effectively controlled the Army: Ambrosio, Roatta, and Sorice.[d]

c. Their last meeting had been on February 12 after Grandi's dismissal from office. Grandi had called on Ambrosio on May 14, two days after the fall of Tunis. (Italian Collection. Ambrosio's list of appointments.)

d. Cassinelli *op cit* pp. 25–7. He was told by Badoglio, 'Roatta is in agreement with me.' It appears however that Ambrosio did not take Roatta into his confidence at this stage. The latter was appointed Chief of the Army Staff on May 29, and was replaced in Sicily by General Guzzoni.

Another former minister of the 1920's, Marcello Soleri, who was then living in dignified retreat in Piedmont, was received by the King at this time. Acquarone had a particular regard for him and had already held a preliminary discussion with him on the afternoon of May 31.

'He did not conceal from me,' Soleri wrote in his Memoirs, 'that he was engaged in trying to persuade the King to substitute for Mussolini's administration a military government entrusted to one of the Marshals Badoglio or Caviglia or to General Ambrosio.' According to Acquarone, it was conceivable that the King might act at the weekly Thursday audience with Mussolini on June 8. In any event Soleri was asked to stay in Rome, and await an urgent summons. He then called on Bonomi, with whom he had already been on several occasions in contact, and learned of the latter's unsatisfactory audience with the King. On June 7 Soleri met Acquarone again and was told that the monarch had been disappointed in Bonomi and that 'the King had decided not to intervene at once: and that without a new political or military fact, this would not come about, as it seemed to him otherwise to be committing in cold blood an act of treachery towards Mussolini'.[5]

Soleri had also been in close touch with Caviglia. On the same day the latter's aide-de-camp had called on General Puntoni to say that the Marshal had hoped to seek an audience of the King, but was obliged to leave Rome immediately, but also that 'the Marshal had expected a gesture from the King which would right the situation, and that he was against coming to Rome because he felt that the King had no desire to discuss with him urgent matters of moment'.[6]

Early on the morning of June 8 Soleri was received by the King for the first time since the outbreak of war. His theme, that of the need to give back to Italy her freedom of action by a withdrawal from the war and by setting up at once 'a political anti-Fascist government' to treat with the Allies, took more than half an hour to deliver to the Monarch.[e] Soleri was then thanked, and without further comment asked to come and see the King in Piedmont.

In reflecting on his two talks with Acquarone and his audience with Victor Emmanuel, Soleri wrote later: 'Subsequent events made one think that the "new fact", political or military, to which Acquarone referred, as necessary to determine the intervention of the King, could only be precisely that inner split in Fascism and that rejection of Mussolini which would necessitate the King, thus given no choice and in no danger of making a mistake, dismissing his Prime Minister. It is perhaps this "new fact", during the first week of June, the possibilities of which may have been glimpsed, if not its preparation begun, and thus for this reason the operation—if ever conceived at this stage in practical terms—was postponed.' [7]

e. The royal audience is described by Soleri, *op cit* pp. 233 ff. See also Raimondo Collino Pansa, *Marcello Soleri*, p. 237. Puntoni states in his Diary that this audience took place on June 7.

Badoglio was already aware of the views of Bonomi and his political associates. The first meeting between the two men took place on June 30.[8] Badoglio had been Chief of Staff a quarter of a century earlier when Bonomi had held the portfolio of Minister of War. They both knew that, in five days' time, on July 5, Ambrosio was proposing to put before the King documented evidence showing that the military situation of Italy was no longer tenable.

At the beginning of July a meeting took place at Badoglio's villa in Rome, with Ambrosio and Acquarone. The question of the necessary military measures to be taken in the event of the King dismissing Mussolini was discussed in some detail. Ambrosio said that he would need twenty days to assemble the necessary forces in and around Rome, and he painted an alarming picture of the general military situation which Badoglio summarized in a subsequent memorandum after the meeting.

'All our existing strength in men and materials has successively flowed into the colonies and disappeared. In particular Libya has swallowed up almost all our scanty reserves. In Russia, where we sent an entire army corps, we have lost two-thirds of the forces and almost all the material. In Libya the Air Force has received a real death blow. The Merchant Navy has been gravely damaged, and the Fleet badly hit, especially in the classes of cruisers and destroyers. Of the divisions of the army, thirty-six have been sent to France, Croatia, Montenegro, Albania and Greece. To defend the whole mainland of Italy there remained twelve divisions of which one, far below strength, consisted of tanks and was entrusted to the Militia. There were certain coastal divisions without artillery, with few weapons and no transport. They represent an unfortunate creation of little value. Our military forces in the peninsula were divided into three groups: one in the valley of the Po, another between Florence and Rome, and the third in Apulia, Basilicata and Calabria. General Ambrosio informed me that, because of the damage caused by allied air bombardments to our railway system, it was impossible to concentrate our forces. Nor could one think of movement by road given the fact that our military transport pool is so reduced, particularly because of the losses in Libya. The Germans have eight divisions in Italy, of which four are heavy armoured, and all equipped with the latest mobile transport which makes their concentration at any point very easy. In addition against about four hundred of our aircraft, there are more than eight hundred German planes.

'The General Staff have also information that, centred on Innsbruck, a large mass of German transport has been assembled, and that along the whole border Germany was in a position to send into Italy in a few days at least eight divisions, and such a move was precisely confirmed to begin as from July 26.'[9]

On July 5 Ambrosio was received by the King, who had returned to Rome for this audience. Puntoni records that 'it was on this occasion that His

Majesty spoke to me for the first time of the action which the Chief of the General Staff was developing in order to achieve the substitution of Mussolini. It seems that he has talked of this openly with the King and suggested the appropriateness of the military dictatorship with either Caviglia or Badoglio at its head. His Majesty, however, has not received either of these schemes with much enthusiasm. My impression is that he thinks the carrying out of such a plan both premature and dangerous, especially in so far as the military situation is concerned. He tells me, too, that the arrival in power of Caviglia would mean a decisive return to Freemasonry and a consequent drawing nearer to the Anglo-Americans. His Majesty is however of the opinion that in approaching the problem of removing Mussolini, Fascism will not allow itself to be overthrown at one stroke. Instead, one will have to modify the system by stages and in order to change those attributes which have proved damaging for the country. On the other hand, he admits that Badoglio, although he has a character which he does not like, has a certain following among the masses and this following could be the unique catalyst of the situation. "I have the impression," His Majesty stated, "that Ambrosio is uncovering himself too much and has too many contacts with elements outside military circles." ' [10] Two days later, on July 7, the King told General Sorice, the Undersecretary of War: 'In the other war (1914–18) one did not feel this sense of isolation. For example, the Central Powers, although engaged in fighting did not lack official contacts with the powers in the other camp. And I have no Prince Sixte of Bourbon-Parma.' [f] [11]

By the beginning of July, according to Castellano, pressure increased on military circles for action against the personal rule of the Duce. 'Albini, Bastianini, Cini, and Volpi, were among the most disturbed, and all turned to Ambrosio.' [12] Castellano was again in touch with Ciano. The latter had been under observation, and they had ceased to meet for some months. The General was in good relations with General Chierici, Senise's successor as head of the Police, and the Carabinieri were now under the command of General Hazon, who was both loyal to Ambrosio, and had formerly served under Badoglio in Africa.

During the course of the month Ambrosio instructed Castellano to redraft the project for Mussolini's arrest. The previous memorandum had been destroyed. This had contained a statement that one month's preparation was required before any plan could be carried out. The period was now reduced to twenty days. Certain general considerations had to be faced. Both Palazzo Venezia and Villa Torlonia, the Duce's personal residence, were heavily fortified, and his personal police guard, a special unit, was an unreliable element. The arrest must therefore take place elsewhere. Ambrosio took a draft plan, as drawn up by Castellano, to Acquarone, but both men

f. Prince Sixte attempted to negotiate in 1917 a compromise peace between the Central Powers and the Allies.

thought that it was premature and hoped till the last moment that Mussolini would act against the Axis alliance. Acquarone would only concede that the King would decide soon 'and that from that moment not more than twenty-four hours would elapse during which Acquarone himself, Ambrosio, the future head of the government, the Commander of the Military Police, the new Chief of Police, and myself must remain locked in a room in the Quirinal so that no one should let out a word'.[13]

An important personage in this list would clearly be the new Chief of Police. Although Chierici was on good terms with Ambrosio's staff, he was a Militia general and was not taken into confidence. The civilian technician to be employed in such an event had already been chosen by Acquarone. He was Chierici's predecessor, Carmine Senise, who had completed plans for an eventual coup d'état before his sudden dismissal from office after Mussolini's return from Klessheim in April.

Senise seems to have continued his activities unofficially with the connivance of the Undersecretary of the Interior, Albini, and with the 'supine acquiescence' of his successor. During these weeks, he made a series of visits. He warned Ambrosio that the Germans also were manoeuvring against him. He saw Castellano, who discussed with him details of the central telephone exchanges, an essential element in event of any coup, and he called on Ciano, who hinted that he might be required later.[14] He also appears to have met Acquarone frequently, and the latter's personal stenographer, who had been placed in this position by Senise the previous winter, continued to act as a private link.

According to a later report, Senise was received by the King at least five times between April and July, 'staying at least one and a half hours'.[15]

CHAPTER SIX

OPERATION 'MINCEMEAT'

THE GERMAN and Italian military intelligence services provided their respective General Staffs with a reasonably accurate picture of the build-up of the Anglo-American forces in the British Isles, and of Allied troop movements and concentrations in the Mediterranean. Any developments at Gibraltar in particular were well covered, and both Axis staffs were confident, and indeed complacent, about their ability to identify the enemy order of battle. The interpretation of such intelligence was less sure, and indeed there was no co-ordination on a technical level, and the available historical evidence consists of arbitrary and discordant statements at irregular intervals by Hitler or Mussolini or by their immediate military advisers.

Mussolini's general analysis concentrated on the imminent threat to Sicily or the gateway to the Italian mainland. Hitler, on the other hand, saw the main danger in Sardinia. His interpretation of future Allied strategy was more consistent than that of the Duce. He foresaw that from Sardinia the enemy could threaten Rome and the main ports of Genoa and Leghorn, strike simultaneously through Upper Italy and at Southern France, and thence at the heart of the European fortress. A logical consequence of such a move on the part of the Allies would then be to attempt to turn the South-Eastern flank of the German position in Europe by a large-scale landing in Greece and the Balkans. Such was the essence of Hitler's strategic thinking during these weeks on the Mediterranean war and future enemy intentions in that theatre.

On May 9 a startling and dramatic confirmation of this interpretation reached the German High Command. On April 30 the body of an unidentified British officer had been washed ashore at Huelva in Southern Spain. Attached to the wrist of the corpse was a briefcase, containing confidential documents.[a] The local German intelligence agent was able to extract photo-stat copies from the Spanish authorities, and it was a tribute to his efficiency that a telegraphic summary reached Berlin so rapidly.

The appropriate section of the German General Staff produced an appreciation of the material on the same day. The British order of battle in the Mediterranean, contained in one paper, was accepted as genuine. On May 11 the German Commanders of Army Groups South and South-East were informed of the existence of the documents, which were accepted in Berlin as genuine, and warned that a major attack on Sardinia, timed with a feint against Sicily and a secondary landing in the Peloponnese, was to be expected. On the same day a detailed analysis of this material was presented to the German General Staff.

On May 12 the German General Staff sent a signal to Kesselring: 'From a source which is regarded as absolutely trustworthy, an enemy landing attempt on a grand scale will be made in the Eastern and Western Mediterranean in the very near future.' A summary of the material followed, together with a message for Doenitz, at that moment in Rome. 'Army Group South is requested to inform Doenitz at once of this report so that he can formulate his requests in his talks with the Italian High Command with increased emphasis.' [b]

Meanwhile, a confirmation of this startling intelligence came through German Foreign Office channels from Dieckhoff, the German Ambassador in Madrid. His telegram was dispatched at 11.20 on the evening of May 12, and received in Berlin ten minutes later. 'According to information just received from a wholly reliable source, the English and Americans will launch their big attack on Southern Europe in the next fortnight. The plan, as our informant was able to establish from English secret documents, is to launch two sham attacks on Sicily and Dodecanese, while the real offensive is directed in two main thrusts against Crete and Peloponnese and against Italian mainland. The enemy's chief rallying-point in Eastern Mediterranean will be Alexandria, in Western Mediterranean, Algiers. It is clear from the document that the attack in Eastern Mediterranean will be launched mainly by British, and that on Italy mainly by Americans.' [1]

An hour later a second message followed. 'Information from confidential source . . . largely tallies with that just communicated to me in strict confidence by Jordana (the Spanish Foreign Minister) . . . He also spoke of wholly reliable news of impending sham attacks and major offensives; as regards the latter he did not refer to Italy but only to Crete and Peloponnese. Jordana begged me not to mention his name, especially as he wanted to

a. For a detailed account of this brilliant 'plant' by the British Intelligence, under the code name 'Mincemeat'. See Hon. Ewen Montagu, *The Man Who Never Was*, *passim*.

b. German Collection. German War Office Archives. There is no evidence that Doenitz told the Italians of the existence of this material.

B F.—12*

exchange further information with me in the future. He emphasized that having regard to his source he considered the information wholly trust-worthy, and felt it his duty to pass it on to us.' [2]

There is no record of the German General Staff meeting on May 11, or of Hitler's immediate reactions. But the next day he issued a general military directive in the following terms: 'Following the impending end of fighting in Tunisia, it is to be expected that the Anglo-Americans will try to continue the operations in the Mediterranean in quick succession. Preparations for this purpose must in general be considered concluded. The following are most endangered: in the Western Mediterranean, Sardinia, Corsica, and Sicily: in the Eastern Mediterranean, the Peloponnese and the Dodecanese islands.

'I expect that all German commands and offices which are concerned with the defences in the Mediterranean will co-operate very closely and quickly to utilize all forces and equipment to strengthen as much as possible the defences in these particularly endangered areas during the short time which is probably left to us. *Measures regarding Sardinia and the Peloponnese take precedence over everything else.'* [c]

This document represents a summary of the British document, which was promptly subjected to further expert analysis in two further German Intelli-gence summaries, both dated May 14.[3] 'The genuineness of the captured documents is above suspicion' is the opening of the first report, and the second contains an analysis of the material on receipt of the originals from Spain.

On May 19, Dieckhoff again telegraphed from Madrid, summarizing the most recent intelligence available through Spanish sources in Gibraltar and North Africa: 'The Navy Minister, Moreno Fernandez, with whom I had detailed discussion today, seems convinced that an Anglo-American offensive against Southern Europe is about to be launched. He told me that all his information indicated that strong forces would be concentrated in Alexandria, Benghazi, Tripoli, Biserta, and Algiers in preparation for an attack on Greece and Italy. In the past few days specially large convoys, heavily guarded by battleships, had sailed into the Mediterranean from the Atlantic and continued in an easterly direction. He could scarcely imagine that the operation would be long delayed, the more so as a powerful force of enemy battleships was now assembled that would hardly be kept in Algiers etc. unless an early operation were being planned.

'The Navy Minister regards an attack on Greece as especially likely, since, owing to the conduct of the Greek population, a landing there would probably entail fewer difficulties than an attempted invasion of Italy; but he thinks it by no means ruled out that a simultaneous attack might be

c. Hitler Military Directives. May 12, 1943. No time of dispatch. Author's italics.

launched on Italy as well, and in this case one ought also to be prepared for sham attacks.

'Jordana, who dined with me last night, also confidently expects an early start to the enemy attack on Southern Europe. He again yesterday insisted that there were still no grounds for inferring any threats to the Iberian peninsula; everything pointed to the fact that operations would be directed against Greece, and possibly Italy as well.' [4]

This intelligence was confirmed in part by a patchy and verbose summary passed by Kaltenbrunner to Ribbentrop, and placed before Hitler on the same day. 'Reports from reliable sources show that the enemy have collected in the Algiers area 800 transport vessels of every kind with a total tonnage of about $1\frac{1}{2}$ million. This leads one to suppose that preparations for a landing are already far advanced. In contrast to the reports for March and April which spoke in particular of operations planned against the French coast and the Iberian peninsula, reports now mention as the targets of enemy operations Italy and her islands as well as Greece.

'The head of the American Intelligence Service for Spain and Portugal has stated that for the moment a landing in Spain was not being considered. After the occupation of Italy, this country (Spain) would climb down of her own accord and freely let through the Allies.

'Generally speaking in American Embassy circles the view is that as soon as Tunis has fallen, the enemy will attempt to land in Sicily, Sardinia and the Italian peninsula. Italy will be attacked from two sides, in order to cut off the southern part. The British Embassy reports from Madrid confirm this information . . . The attitude towards Spain must depend on the position taken up by the Reich towards that country.

'A confirmation of the enemy intention to land in Sicily lies in the great interest shown by the American Military Intelligence in assembling reports from their European representatives on the political and economic state of Sicily and the morale of its population.

'The above reports also indicate that a second pincer movement against Italy will be mounted via Crete and Greece. The Turkish Ambassadors in Washington and London reported similarly at the beginning of May that the Allies wanted to advance into the Balkans through Greece. Italian reports give further details of the landing planned in Greece. The landing would be in Kavalla in order eventually to thrust up into Roumania. In this connection the Americans intend to occupy Roumania to prevent a further advance of Soviet Russia into the Balkans.

'Also from the Swiss Intelligence it is reported that the British and Americans intend to land in Thrace.' [d]

d. German Collection. Kaltenbrunner to Ribbentrop. May 13, 1943. Initialled by the Fuehrer on May 19. Much of this material was clearly planted by Allied agents on the German Intelligence services as part of a deceptive manoeuvre.

On May 14, at 5.30 in the evening, Hitler received Doenitz's report on his Rome visit, and referred for the first time directly in conference to the British material. 'The Fuehrer does not agree with the Duce that the most likely invasion point is Sicily. Furthermore, he believes that the discovered Anglo-Saxon order confirms the assumption that the planned attacks will be directed mainly against Sardinia and the Peloponnese.' These judgments were 'not new at this time', but it is clear that they were considerably strengthened by 'the papers found on the body of a British courier washed up on the southern coast of Spain'.[5]

Hitler's strategic appreciation of the future course of operations in the Mediterranean now assumed a sharper outline. Allied plans for occupying the Italian islands and Southern Italy were but a prelude to a wide ranging landing operation against the western coasts of the Balkans in the Adriatic. If this analysis was correct, the consequences of an Italian collapse would have direct, grave, and early consequences in South-Eastern Europe, and a stage later on the southern flank of the German armies in Russia. This situation was debated by Hitler on the afternoon of May 19 at a military conference,[e] and the movement of German troops to Italy to counter such an event was for the first time reviewed in practical terms. 'In the last few days, and particularly last night, I have again been giving much thought to the consequences which would follow if we lost the Balkans, and there is no doubt that the results must be very serious.' Keitel interjected 'And certainly much more difficult if we have to protect ourselves against this front from anywhere in Italy.' The satellite allies would be 'shaken', and the vital supplies of Roumanian oil, and Yugoslav bauxite and copper would be lost.

Hitler's first proposal was 'as a precaution to take a further preventive measure against an eventual attack on the Peloponnese'. There was only one division readily available in the West, and it was from this zone only that troops could in principle be withdrawn as 'at the moment I have no fears that anything will happen in the West'.

Hitler assumed that Italy could always be managed. 'The Italians are not to be relied on, while on the other side I am convinced that, with relatively small forces, in the event of any mess in Italy, we can handle it, particularly if the first advance guards arrive within ten days . . . Zeitzler says that these fighting units will be there within ten days for he will lay on sixty trains a day. One can therefore say, one division will arrive in two days.'[f]

According to the calculations of the German Operations Staff, the Parachute Corps from the West, and the main body earmarked for Operation

e. Hitler Military Conferences. Conversation of the Fuehrer with General Keitel, May 19, 1943. The meeting ended at 3.30 p.m. Hitherto unpublished. Original in the library of the University of Pennsylvania.

f. According to Zeitzler, the successor of Halder as the chief of the German Army Staff, the 16th Armoured Division was 'now coming to Italy'. At this time the division was not equipped with new tanks.

'Gisela' to move into Spain were available for Italy from the resources of Army Group West. 'Naturally I want to send to Italy first of all the three S.S. divisions, because they know Fascism best.' Hitler was against sending young troops to Italy. 'They have not the experience, politically speaking too, nor the adroitness of my old S.S. divisions, who are propagandists. I am convinced that, if the three best S.S. divisions are sent there, they will very quickly achieve the closest fraternization with Fascism.'

The nagging problem was how to divide the armoured reinforcements in an emergency as between the Italian and Balkan theatres. And harping back to the conviction obviously based on 'British courier' documents that the immediate Allied plan was a combined assault on Sardinia and the Peloponnese, Hitler again stressed 'the danger is that they will establish themselves in the Peloponnese'. Two armoured divisions from the Eastern Front had already been earmarked for transport to Greece in an emergency.[g]

On the basis of the memorandum which Hitler had received from the Italian High Command,[h] he had 'come to the conclusion that, even more dangerous than the problem of Italy, which in the worst case we can always somehow tidy up, is that of the Balkans. If a landing takes place in the Balkans, let us say in the Peloponnese, then in a foreseeable time Crete will go. We have now supplied it for six months . . . If we lose the Peloponnese, then any further supplies are out of the question. . . . There are two German formations now there. . . . The nearest other units are in action in Montenegro. If we run into any trouble, particularly if we have difficulties with the Italians, we cannot depend on these units. They will be lost and we shall never get them out. Then we shall have to occupy the Montenegrin-Dalmatian coast, and disarm the Italians.[i]

'I have therefore decided whatever happens to transfer one armoured division to the Peloponnese. As things are, it can only be taken from the West. For naturally I want to attack only in the East, if no other situation arises and even if an Italian crisis breaks. I mean to say, I do not want to attack her only on account of a landing. So long as the Italians sit on the fence I do not want to attack in the East. But as soon as the Italians show signs of folding up or of internal collapse, we must attack in the East . . . If the enemy are going to attack anywhere they will do so only in Italy and naturally the Balkans. . . . If anything should happen in Turkey, and we shall have in any case to move forces from the East, I have only one reservoir there, and that is the Bulgarians.' [j]

g. This involved 9½ days' train journey.
h. Referred to in Hitler's letter to Mussolini of the same day at this meeting (May 19). It related to the anti-partisan operations in Montenegro.
i. As happened in September 1943.
j. As Warlimont pointed out: 'We shall also need for the Italian case at least five reliable Bulgarian divisions in the coastal area, etc. (Montenegro and Dalmatia). That is what we reckoned on earlier.'

Warlimont appears to have made a separate report at this conference in his capacity as Deputy Chief of the Operations Staff, summarizing the Italian position, and elaborating in particular on the necessary counter-measures to be taken in event of an Allied attack on Sardinia (the first priority, according to the 'British Courier' documents). 'The task of the German Army Group South is the defence of Sardinia, Sicily, and Southern Italy.' The harbours are menaced by air attack. 'Sardinia is particularly threatened. . . . the state of the defences of Sicily is better. . . . The Italians jealously claimed control and sovereignty. There is no full mobilization, no authority, no sort of civil defence, and no workers in the ports.' He went on to explain in his report that, with the present 'system of alliances' the task was insoluble. The influence of German leadership and troops as a 'heavy corset' was the prerequisite for the defence of Italy.

'In the event of the loss of Sardinia, the threat to Northern Italy is extremely acute. This is the key point for the whole of Italy, "the Balkans", Southern France and the base for an allied air offensive against Southern Germany. The invasion gates are Genoa and Leghorn. Their defence by German forces must now be prepared. The build-up of supplies for the defence of Northern Italy in the area of Verona and Milan must now be got under way. The early move of an armoured division to the area of Genoa seems to be required.' k

This conception of Allied intentions plays an increasingly central rôle in future German planning for the Italian theatre. If Sardinia was the first Allied objective, this must imply, as the next stage, a threat to Northern Italy, through the Gulf of Genoa along the main lines of communication, and aimed ultimately at the southern borders of the Reich. The eventual plan of the Allied Command of climbing up Italy, punctuated by tactical landings 'of little operational or political advantage', was the least expected by the German Command.

During this military conference Hitler mentioned the memorandum from the Italian High Command which had been recently received in Berlin. It concerned the joint anti-partisan operations in progress in Montenegro. On the previous day, May 18, the German military representative in Rome, General Rintelen, had been instructed to protest to General Ambrosio at the continued lack of Italian co-operation in this theatre. Ambrosio was evasive and surly. These views had already been expressed in discussions with Ribbentrop in the previous February. There had been talk then of pacifying the region in two months. Operations were now in progress 'but one need not have excessive illusions as to the results'. The dialogue became unfriendly.

k. These above notes, from which Warlimont was speaking, are in the German Collection, and seem to relate to this same military conference, the text of which is fragmentary and damaged.

Rintelen remarked that 'it had been reported from Montenegro that there is "no co-operation between Italians and Germans" '. To which Ambrosio retorted: 'In practice your troops act independently . . .' there was 'no question of disarming nationalists in Montenegro unless we wish to augment the rebels by 100 per cent'.

Rintelen could only repeat the German thesis expounded by Ribbentrop in Rome. 'The formations of Mihailović should be liquidated as soon as possible simultaneously with action against the partisans.' Ambrosio's reply was unambiguous. 'This appreciation is my business.' Rintelen answered that the Fuehrer was sending a letter through Kesselring on the subject, adding. 'We have a maximum interest in the pacification of the Balkans.' [6]

This document, dated May 19, is the sharpest ever written by Hitler to Mussolini during the course of their relationship. Rintelen was so alarmed at its tone that he asked for confirmation that he should deliver it. The order was repeated.[7] The immediate occasion of the letter was the copy of the report of the Italian High Command on the operations in Montenegro. Hitler considered that the views which it expressed 'are entirely off the point, and for Germany militarily untenable. . . . I am anxious to send you these lines. . . . as it is not a question of the problems of the High Command, nor of the (Italian) Second Army, nor of the Governor of Montenegro, but of the common struggle for our future destiny.' The Italian command was now using a new expression for the irregular bands protected by them, namely, 'Montenegrin national formations'. Hitler had passed on numerous intercepted radio messages proving that 'without exception all these formations were collaborating with England'. It had already been agreed that if this were the case they should be disarmed after the destruction of the partisans. Instead the Italian authorities had deliberately favoured these bands, had failed to prevent the Communists from penetrating Montenegro, and in some areas Italian units were cut off and asking for German help.

The Italian High Command had completely misunderstood the situation. 'The observations which we have made from the air leave no doubt that the Allies are planning a large-scale invasion of the Mediterranean basin.' Hitler went on to allude to the British Courier material but without disclosing what it was. 'It is also clear from documents which have been found that they also intend to invade the Peloponnese and will in fact do so. Neither the High Command nor the Governor of Montenegro will be in a position to prevent such invasions single-handed. The Second Italian Army (in Croatia) is in no position, either from the point of view of equipment and armament or from that of training, to protect the Peloponnese and Greece in general from similar invasions. If the British attempts are to be prevented, as they must be at all costs, this can only be done by German divisions. To allow these troops to fight in an area exposed to the danger of losing its supply lines would, however, be a crime against soldiers who are risking their lives in the front line. This is true of Italian soldiers as much as of Germans. However, as long as the fighting there has to be done by German soldiers, I am not in the least interested in General Pirzio Biroli's views (the Italian Governor of Montenegro), which might well lead us into a situation identical with that which we saw end in such terrible catastrophe in the Mediterranean. The fact that, in spite of our exertions, we did not succeed in assuring supplies for North Africa resulted not only in our disaster, but also in the repeatedly established heroism of Italian and German soldiers being in vain. To let our troops in Crete, in the Dodecanese, in the Peloponnese and southern Greece be put in the same situation through the blindness and incapacity of the military leaders would be a crime against the human lives engaged there. However, if banditism and all this "Comitadji atmosphere" is not immediately and ruthlessly put down, this situation will inevitably develop. We have little time to lose in this situation.

'As soon as any real danger of invasion appears within the next few days or weeks, a large number of German divisions must be sent immediately to the Peloponnese. It is, therefore, absolutely necessary for the areas behind the lines of communication to be cleared up in the meantime, so that our formations can pass into the areas where they will have to be used. It is, in fact, the last possible moment for restoring order with the greatest urgency throughout this territory. Moreover, by exercising truly angelic patience I have frequently and repeatedly succeeded in arriving at real collaboration in the conduct of the war in this region. But my efforts have failed in face of the repeated sabotage—I must use this hard word—of the agreements reached on operations, and of the insufficient desire to establish order in a territory which is of vital importance to both of us. Without German intervention there would be no more talk of bauxite supplies, and besides, the Italian High Command desperately needs German aeroplanes. The economic supplies which you should be able to obtain yourself from this territory have become unobtainable solely because of the behaviour of the Italian military posts, since instead of providing promptly for the security and tranquillity which are indispensable to economic life, they have allowed the territory to degenerate steadily under bandit activity; and this need not have happened, for this relatively small country cannot be compared with the huge spaces of the Orient.

'If, however, the High Command wishes to conclude from this that Germany has no intention of collaborating with Italy, I reject such a charge with the utmost indignation. Even before General Ambrosio made his historic appearance, I had long left no possible doubt about my desire to collaborate with Fascist Italy. General Ambrosio and the Governor of Montenegro were unknown to me when Italy was at war with Abyssinia. But already at that time I led Germany to support Italy. Since then this collaboration—which began on the battlefields of Spain and continued until recently—has been sealed both by Italy and Germany with the blood of tens of thousands of men, and the present operations in the Balkans have no other significance than that of preparing the ground for German formations to bring immediate help in case of an Allied invasion, and therefore to shed their blood again in the common cause.'

Unless order was restored in Yugoslav territory 'a crisis as grave as that of North Africa must ensue', and Hitler begged that the Duce should give clear instructions which complied with the spirit not the letter of previous written agreements. He added that he was transferring an armoured division to Greece.

Hitler barely concealed his distrust of the Italian General Staff, not only in regard to their 'sabotage' of joint Axis operations in Montenegro, but in the general conduct of the struggle. 'Let me say once more that the German and Italian Generals were not all behind us at the beginning. . . . Whether this will recur in the future I cannot say, but at least I can and must reassure you, Duce, that whatever happens I will always stand by you.' [8]

The alarm expressed in this letter was heightened in the following hours. Kesselring, who had been present at the Fuehrer's military conference of May 19, asked for an urgent interview with Mussolini on returning to Rome. He bore an invitation to an immediate summit conference between the two Axis leaders to discuss the situation arising out of the loss of Tunisia, but also to enable Hitler to sound the Duce on the present attitude of the Italian military leadership. Kesselring was summoned on May 20 to Palazzo Venezia. In replying to the proposal of a meeting, Mussolini replied evasively that 'there is always a host of problems which deserve handling' and made no further comment. He then asked: 'What do they say at the Fuehrer's Headquarters on the possibilities of an enemy landing?' Kesselring answered: 'They consider one possible in Sicily, Sardinia, or Corsica.' The Duce agreed, particularly in the event of a German offensive on the Eastern Front. 'Stalin insists on the opening of a new front (in the West), but this time a proper one, and not a secondary front.' [9]

Mussolini's cautious question to draw out Kesselring at this meeting may have been tinged with sly humour. On May 20, the same day as this talk and probably before it took place, the Duce himself was in the secret of 'the British Courier'. As Mackensen telegraphed to Berlin: 'Bastianini asked me to call on him on instructions from the Duce in order to inform me of the following and with the request to send an immediate report.

'Ambassador Paolucci in Madrid, has information from an absolutely unimpeachable source [1] that the enemy intend landing operations in Greece in the very near future.' There was no doubt as to its reliability. Bastianini added that the Ambassador had sent the information through his wife 'who

---

1. The Spanish official concerned may well have been bribed twice.

had come by plane as he did not wish to entrust it to anyone else'.[10] The Italians must have known of this 'information' some days before passing it on to Mackensen, and the Germans seem to have had no intention of reciprocating this gesture.

In replying to Hitler's letter of May 19, Mussolini summarized in temperate and factual terms the discussions on the Yugoslav issue between himself and Ribbentrop in Rome in the previous February. It had been agreed that the četnik bands would be disarmed after the defeat of the partisans.

'As is known, the "Weiss" operations, whose aim was the annihilation of the partisans in Croatia, did not lead to any decisive results, in that the main body of the Communists fleeing from the jaws of the trap set by the Italian and German troops succeeded in escaping to Montenegro. The necessary conditions . . . for proceeding to disarm the četnik formations are thus lacking . . . Given the present state of affairs, it seems to me appropriate that we should reach speedy agreement on the further prosecution of our joint operation. . . .'

Hitler had also referred to 'other matters, not strictly relating to the present situation in Montenegro, and, on these points, I feel that there cannot be any difference of judgment between us'. German support in the Balkan and Greek campaigns of 1940 and 1941 was 'well known, but it is equally well known that the Greek army was worn down by the Italian troops during a long winter struggle'. It was true that North Africa had been lost because of supply difficulties, 'but it is known that these were made impossible by enemy superiority in the air, which was insufficiently countered.

'What really matters in these hard times, Fuehrer, is to keep up the prestige of our armed forces, and concentrate the efforts of the Axis on striking down our common enemies and bring victory to our peoples.' Mussolini had therefore ordered the Governor of Montenegro to clarify the situation regarding 'all those who were, are, or would be our enemies. We cannot run the risk of having rebel zones in our rear at a moment when the possibility of an enemy landing in Greece might be imminent.' [11]

This last sentence of Mussolini was the only oblique reference made to the source of 'information' shared jointly with Hitler, and which the latter seemed so reluctant to disclose to his ally, a reticence which marked the extent of the spreading distrust in high German circles of the Italian will and intention to resist.

CHAPTER SEVEN

THE MILITARY CRISIS OF THE AXIS

HITLER WAS waiting for news from Rome of Mussolini's acceptance of the proposed conference, and had left East Prussia to be near a meeting point. But on May 21 Mussolini told the German Ambassador, who had been instructed to repeat the Fuehrer's invitation, that 'owing to the latest extraordinary and extensive shipping movements in the Mediterranean, as the Fuehrer would understand, he could not leave Rome'. [1] The Duce also insisted on a 'rendezvous' in Italy, and as Hitler's advisers feared for the latter's personal safety in such an event, the idea of these talks was dropped. As the precursory signs of an Italian defection mounted, Italo-German relations had reached their lowest point since the signature of the Axis Pact. Reports that the Italians were fortifying their Alpine border (as at the time of the assassination of Dollfuss in 1934) increased the tension, and Hitler was not convinced by Mussolini's explanations.

But in the Fuehrer's thesis of treason in high circles in Rome the Duce was not the villain but the victim of the Italian military leadership, and poised in the wings stood the figure of the Sovereign. Within the Court and the High Command lay the elements, as yet unmobilized, of an alternative régime. This threat lay at the heart of the Italian scene, and at each crisis in the struggle it drew the anxious attention of the German leaders: after Alamein the visit of Himmler was directed in the main to probing the shadows of the Court and seeking for traces of a Royal conspiracy; in the days following 'Torch' Goering searched for further evidence; and after Stalingrad, Ribbentrop detected furiously the lurking dissidence of the Italian High Command. Hitler's own alarm was constantly reviewed in discussion with his advisers.

On May 2, while awaiting Mussolini's reply to his proposal for a private consultation, he reflected on an earlier talk during the visit of the Duce to the Russian front in the winter of 1941 'down in the Galician area where the big tunnel was'. The two men were discussing the Soviet 'system'. 'At night we spoke about the Russian commissars; how there could not be two powers . . . Then he became very thoughtful, and while I was eating with him on the train, he suddenly said to me: "What you say is true, Fuehrer, that one should not have two powers in one army; but what do you think, what can you do if you had officers who entertain reservations towards the régime and its philosophy of the state? They say they have reservations because they are officers, and the moment you reason with them by appealing to the idea of the state or the interest of the state they say: We are monarchists and obey the King. That is the difference." That was already his problem in 1941. And it was even more pronounced on October 28, 1940 [a]. . . Suddenly he said to me: "You see, I trust my soldiers but not my generals; I can't have confidence in them." The man told me this on the very day on which he started his offensive against Greece.'

By May 1943 this tension had mounted to a danger point. Hitler continued: 'The question is how he feels physically. If the Duce were fifteen years younger today the whole thing would be no problem, but at the age of sixty it is more difficult. But in my opinion those two worlds have always existed. The one world was not removed and so continued to spin its web.'

This conference revealed in still sharper outline the progressive undermining of the Italian scene. The meeting had been called to comment on a report from Baron von Neurath, the son of the former German Foreign Minister, who had been on a special mission of inspection in Italy. He had been told by the commander of the Italian army in Sicily, General Roatta, that 'he did not have too much confidence in the possibility of a defence of Sicily'. If the island fell to the Allies and a general Italian collapse or defection followed, the bulk of Kesselring's Southern Army Group might be trapped in the peninsula and the southern frontiers of the Reich directly threatened. If the Italian armies deserted the Axis, the vital Alpine passes would be the first point threatened. Their main defences were anti-aircraft units, and Hitler gave orders that their supply of ammunition 'must be handled in such a way that it can be stopped at any time'.

When Rommel, who was present at this meeting, suggested that Italian troops should replace the Germans in Sicily, Hitler's answer was: 'What does worry me is that they do not want to defend it: we can see this lack of determination. The Duce may have the best intentions, but they will be sabotaged.' Hitler's 'definite opinion' was that the war had been sabotaged from the beginning 'by a certain group' in Italy. 'Every memorandum I wrote to the Duce immediately reached England. Therefore I only wrote things I absolutely wanted to get to England . . .' Neurath pointed out that 'this sort of

a. This was the date of Hitler's suddenly improvised meeting with Mussolini in Florence to discuss the unheralded Italian attack on Greece, Gilbert. *Hitler's Military Conferences*, pp. 29–38, May 20, 1943.

trafficking with England is still going on. The night before last, on the train, the submarine commanders based on Spezia told me that they had proof that every morning from 8 to 10 o'clock there was contact between the battleship Vittorio Veneto and Malta . . . The Italian Crown Prince is there as commander-in-chief of the Italian troops. It is significant that he holds frequent inspections, and that General Roatta spends a lot of time with him . . . Personally I am convinced that Roatta is up to something. Officers down there agree that it has become noticeable how he increasingly makes use of the Crown Prince, how he tries to find some common basis with him that would be acceptable when the English descend on Sicily.'[2]

The rôle of the Prince of Piedmont at this time baffled the Germans. Their information was fragmentary and contradictory. Mussolini himself had persistently defended him, but from what motives was less clear. He had pressed Hitler to invite the Crown Prince to visit Germany. This proposal had been aired in April when Schmidt had been sent privately to Rome. According to the latter, the Duce welcomed such a suggestion 'because it would in a certain sense "compromise" the Crown Prince with the Axis . . . although I had told him beforehand on the grounds on which I had been instructed, that the Fuehrer put no store by such an interview'. [3]

A month later, however, the proposal was renewed by Kesselring, and it was coupled with the invitation on May 20 to the Duce to a summit meeting. The latter asked 'When would this be? Before or after my visit?' Kesselring answered, 'Rather before: possibly after.' [b] The German intention was not clear. Were they seeking a hostage from the Royal House or even an alternative figurehead in opposition to the King in the event of basic changes in the régime? But Mussolini was equally emphatic in encouraging the plan. On June 11 he asked Mackensen for news of the planned visit which he would welcome. [4] An entry in the War Diary of the German General Staff reads: 'The attitude of the Crown Prince of Italy, whose visit to the Fuehrer was repeatedly proposed by the Duce, was completely puzzling.' [5] Yet the one consistent theme which German reports from Italy in June underlined was the loyalty of the Royal House to Mussolini. Rumours that the Crown Prince was anti-German or anti-Fascist were discounted. On June 23, for example, Colonel Berger of the German Army Staff on a special mission in Italy reported that any such rumours were not true, and General Rintelen told him that he was in favour of the Crown Prince's visit to Germany which had been so often postponed. 'The Duce is the decisive factor and is loyal to the alliances. There is no question of disloyalty among the upper ranks of the Army to the Duce, so long as the Royal House is loyal to him. Any cleavage between the Officer Corps and the Duce is not to be feared. But he still over-estimates the fighting capacity of his people.' [6]

b. Italian Collection. Duce-Kesselring meeting, May 20, 1943. The same day as Hitler was discussing the problem of the Crown Prince with his military advisers.

But if the identity of the 'certain group' to which Hitler had referred on May 20 was not at yet satisfactorily clarified, the extent of their sabotage activities was increasingly documented. On June 3, for example, the head of the German counter-intelligence, Admiral Canaris, informed the German Foreign Office that he had acquired an intercept of a cable from the American Embassy in Berne revealing that the measures promised by Hitler to Mussolini for increased military aid had leaked. The German Army Command intended to report to Hitler that 'such information has reached the enemy from the immediate entourage of the Duce'.[7]

Evidence was accumulating that the group of high officials in the Italian Foreign Office, including Bastianini's closest advisers, were active in private intelligence with the enemy. This leakage was regarded by the Germans as an example of this alarming development, which, as a further German counter-intelligence report stated, was 'the main organization of treason which exists in Italy', and with which Ciano himself was closely identified.[c]

Against such a background the Italian government pressed with a deliberate air of innocence for the increase of German military support for the defence of Italy. As Mussolini had told Kesselring on May 17, 'Tell the Fuehrer that I have written to him. The principal theme is always that of the defence (tanks: anti-aircraft: anti-tank). I think that with three basic German divisions we can be tranquil about Italy, Sicily and Sardinia.' [d]

The Duce relied on Kesselring to press for these requests with Hitler, and at the same time Bastianini invoked Ribbentrop's backing. Alfieri was given instructions to this effect on May 20, stressing that the essential requirement was reinforcements for anti-aircraft defence, and with Ribbentrop's support was considered by the Duce to be 'of special importance'.[e] Little did the Italians realize that on that day Hitler had given instructions to keep down the supply of ammunition to the A/A batteries in Italy to a minimum. The Italian Embassy in Berlin was also showing signs of agitation at 'the startling flexibility in German supplies to Italy. If we remonstrate, they take refuge behind difficulties owing to air bombing. If we insist, they say that our work-

c. German Collection. Abwehr report headed Ciano Group and giving a list of Italian Foreign Office personalities, and their wives of foreign extraction, allegedly in contact with enemy countries. June 24, 1943. A German Foreign Office minute, dated July 5, connected this report with the leakage to Berne mentioned above, and regarded Vittetti, the head of the Western Department at Palazzo Chigi, as particularly suspect.
d. Italian Collection. Duce-Kesselring meeting, May 17, 1943. This letter has not been identified. Its substance, Mussolini told Kesselring, was 'defence against enemy air attacks on Italy in the first instance. Also fighter defence.'
e. German Collection. Steengracht minute on a discussion with Alfieri, May 20, 1943. The request was repeated again in a minute from Bastianini to Ribbentrop. *Ibid* May 26, 1943.

ers in Germany do not work. If we stick to it, they let us understand that they regard Italy henceforth as written off.' [f]

The formal requests from the Italian side however were maintained. On May 26 Alfieri delivered to the German Foreign Office a further note from Bastianini. Heavy enemy concentrations were reported in the North African ports. The air effort requested from Doenitz during his visit to Rome was now needed to stop or delay a landing in Italy. Would Ribbentrop also back this up? 'Thanks to his intervention last time three armoured divisions were on their way to Italy.' [8]

These notes from Bastianini were perhaps also intended for the record in order to show that every effort was being made to persuade a reluctant ally to produce the means to defend Italy against invasion, and to document a possible withdrawal from the war if the situation arose. 'Bastianini is assuming in regard to the Germans an increasingly tough and intransigent attitude. We have the impression that he is seeking intentionally to poison relations between the two countries in order to provoke an incident which would justify an eventual breach.' [9]

The issue on the German side was deceptively simple. If aid to Italy ceased her collapse would be accelerated, and the military consequences for Germany would have to be faced. If limited supplies were sent, the Fascist régime of the Duce might be preserved temporarily, in spite of the increasing signs of treason in military and diplomatic quarters, but equally even among those elements still prepared to fight a marked sensitiveness to an extended German control of the Axis war effort must be expected. There was no absolute solution, and the Germans could only play for time.

At the end of May, General Rintelen forwarded a penetrating study of the Italian problem in a report to his superiors. 'The loss of the last position in North Africa has put Italo-German co-operation to the test . . . While a section of the army and population under the influence of the unfavourable development of the military position has given way to defeatism, and only longs for a rapid end to hostilities, other circles in the Army, Government, and population, are even more determined to defend the mother country by all means. In the Italian officer corps this determination is somewhat limited by the realization of their own inferiority, particularly in weapons and air-craft, as the best has been lost in North Africa and Russia. Those Italians who wish to continue the war are hoping for extensive German support through the delivery of weapons and the availability of troop reinforcements. If this expected help does not materialize in sufficient quantities it will not be

f. Simoni *op cit* pp. 341–2. See, for example, Ambrosio's memorandum to Keitel of May 29 pointing out that 'German deliveries of certain products important to the war effort have fallen behind the agreements made'. See German Collection. Clodius minute, July 4, 1943.

possible to defend the mainland coasts, and it is to be feared also that those who wish to fight will lose all hope and every desire to fight.'

Rintelen continued with a masterly summary of the attitude of the Italian High Command to the development of the war since 1940. At the beginning they 'strove to regard the Mediterranean as their own military theatre and to reject every German influence and indeed participation. Then, as soon as the great contrast between the German successes and Italian failures became clear, they fell back on German help, and the increased German operational commitment also had a strong influence on the direction of operations . . . Over-all German control was established in Africa, and also recognized in France, while in the Balkans even after the end of the campaign in early 1941, the Italians went their own way and repeatedly announced their claims to supremacy in this region. This is doubtless connected with the fact that in the Balkans, German and Italian interests clash. It has been pointed out to me many times by Italians who are reliably pro-German, that the Balkans are the only subject of difference between the two Axis powers.

'In brief, one can say that in the war years 1941–42 the Italians blindly accepted German leadership and the fact that their inferior military achievements were overshadowed by German superiority. The defeat of the Italian Eighth Army in the East and the loss of Libya brought great disillusionment, and shattered the blind faith in German superiority. Marshal Cavallero, who for a long time was attacked for his pro-German attitude, had to yield his place. The Italian Army Command under Ambrosio sought to resurrect their equality of status although the prerequisite was lacking, namely, the ability to cover the defences of their own country with sufficient forces of their own. The desire to be as far as possible independent of German leadership clashed with the need to seek German support. This is the essence of the position.'

The Italian High Command had recently emphasized its claims to military leadership in the mother country itself. 'They still want to work further with the German Command, but to hold in their own hands their independent control, at least so that it should look so from outside . . . As a Roman, the Italian puts a decisive value on external appearances both at home and abroad. There must be no doubt that the leadership lies in Italian hands. Only by taking into account this particular mentality of the people can co-operation be worked out successfully in the future.' [10]

Hitler had already decided to give effect to the planning of German counter-measures in the event of a military breakdown on the Italian front. During May and early June, transport arrangements were made, as a result of the Fuehrer's military conference of May 19, for three S.S. divisions to be moved if necessary to the Italian Alpine border. One of these units was the crack S.S. 'Leibstandarte' which was to be assigned to the special political rôle as outlined by Hitler. A similar movement plan was worked out to transfer the armoured divisions from the East. It was calculated that the move to Northern and Central Italy would take eight to ten days. Part of this group might have to be switched to the Balkans. For a complete German operation in Italy, fourteen infantry divisions would be needed, including those already in Italy, and the remainder could only be withdrawn from the West.

On May 31 the German Army Group West offered two armoured and six infantry divisions for operation 'Alaric'. In addition, two parachute divisions were to be alerted in the event of an Italian coup to control the central Alpine passes. On June 4 there is a laconic note in the German General Staff files: 'The Fuehrer has agreed in general to the intentions and proposals of Army Group West for "Alaric".' [11] It was to be the duty of this command to occupy the Western Alpine passes in event of an emergency, and to watch and disarm the four Italian divisions in France. But this German Headquarters in France was faced with technical complications in planning for such an eventuality since, on Hitler's orders, they were not kept informed of any general strategic plan. At no stage did Hitler relinquish personal control over these operations ('Alaric' and 'Konstantin'). Indeed, direct orders in event of an Italian collapse would be given by Hitler verbally in order to prevent any leakage.

As Hitler had stated on May 19, his prime objective, subject to military and political conditions in Italy, still lay in the East. On June 18 he gave orders to launch operation 'Citadel'—the long-planned offensive against the Kursk peninsula.[g] This decision meant the end of any armoured reinforcements for eventualities in Italy and the Balkans. On June 19 the Operations Staff pointed out that, in view of this operation, it would be impossible to defend in an emergency the coastlines of Italy and the Balkans. The only troops now available to this end were the infantry and parachute divisions earmarked in the West. The modified proposal of the German High Command was to move as soon as possible the infantry units for plan 'Alaric' up to the Brenner and to consider a defence line in Northern Italy, withdrawing in the event of a crisis from the South to such a prepared position.

This had always been Rommel's view, but he immediately pointed out that he had no forces at his disposal for such a move. The troop reinforcements from the West would certainly be committed in the event of an Allied assault on Italy, and would not be available for the 'special task' confided to Rommel. Apart from his skeleton staff and the designation of Army Group B as his future command, he had in fact no troops immediately available. There were also no plans for reinforcing the German Second Air Fleet, in spite of promises to the Italians, and no adequate anti-aircraft defence of the vital Alpine passes. Nor had any preventive action yet been planned against the Italian fleet.

g. This offensive was opened at dawn on July 5.

Hitler hesitated. He had realized the extent of such a commitment in Italy. Pending the summer outcome of the offensive in the East he must continue to keep the Italian army in the field by limited doses of military aid, and seek every opportunity to reinforce the political position of the Duce on the Home Front.

At the beginning of May, Dollmann had sent from Rome an alarmist report to Himmler headed 'The Situation'. 'In these recent days requests have reached me from the circles among the older Fascist generation asking that German military equipment now in Italy . . . should not be handed over to Italian army units but held as an iron reserve to be available when the crisis breaks.' In event of a crisis the Duce had at his disposal about 150 private bodyguards armed with revolvers; the Militia, 'very badly led and ill equipped, who will go as a faithful flock to the slaughter'; the old Fascists 'who are hardly organized at all, but whose leaders now at last, even if hesitatingly, are aware of the danger of the hour, and of the vital need for mutual understanding; and a Police force, which is inadequately armed, overbureaucratized by Senise, and very badly paid.

'On the other side the King . . . has at his orders the well organized, disciplined, and reasonably armed military police. And then the Army: that is almost the whole of the higher and middle-ranking Officer Corps, which was always hostile to the Axis . . .' The Fleet and the Air Force would obey blindly from above. There was widespread passive resistance to any co-operation with the Axis.

The ultimate threat to the maintenance of internal order in Italy was in theory the special concern of Himmler. But with Mussolini's deliberate procrastination over the arming and training of the 'M' division, proposed at Klessheim, a well mounted political conspiracy could no longer be suppressed by a simple police operation. Nor, in spite of Farinacci's continual offers to organize a counter-coup, were 'the old circle of friends of the Reichsfuehrer SS', whom the latter had sounded during his Rome visit of the previous October, confident that they could ever produce an alternative Fascist government. Nor were they a united group. As Dollmann reported: 'Everyone is clear and agreed about the size of the danger. I have been able to confirm that under the pressure of the moment old differences are being overcome, the worst being between Ricci and Buffarini. All these are faithful to Himmler.' Buffarini was particularly committed 'personally and practically. His fanatical hatred of the Ciano clique has contributed to this', and he had kept Dollmann informed in detail on everything within his range. He wanted urgently to meet Himmler and was very pessimistic at the internal situation. The present Ministers were 'a Cabinet of God-forsaken mediocrities.

'Ricci has specially undertaken, in the sense of the Reichsfuehrer's suggestions, to work for a reconciliation among the older Fascists, which I have carefully explained to him in three visits . . . From a human point of view

Ricci is of all the most unreserved friend of Germany and Italy. Unfortunately the Duce will not bring himself to decide to entrust to him again one of the great commanding posts, for example, the Party or the Militia.' [12]

While the German Intelligence authorities handled the discontented Fascists, the Embassy analysed the more official reactions of the Roman scene.

On May 22 Mackensen reported in a contrasting vein to that of Dollmann. 'However, the deliberate and thorough measures adopted recently by the higher authorities have met with a considerable response . . . in the government changes of February 5, the disappearance of Ciano was considered to be crucial, since in the eyes of Italian public opinion his name was linked with many unfortunate aspects of the régime. In contrast to him is the lucid personality of its new Foreign Secretary, Bastianini, who embodies the best type of old Fascist, entirely loyal to the Duce, and who above all does not avoid expressing his opinion openly to him. Equally fortunate is the designation of Albini as Undersecretary at the Ministry of the Interior, the nomination of Chierici as Chief of the Italian Police with the task of making this body a safe political instrument in the hands of the Duce, and the appointment of the new Fascist Party Directorate and the replacement of the weak and completely a-political Party Secretary, Vidussoni, by the energetic Scorza.

'In general one can say that internal politics in Italy are passing through an indisputably critical phase. The population increasingly questions the purpose of the war following on the heavy defeats and the loss of the African empire, and in critically reviewing the situation, inevitably judges the régime's achievements negatively. The Party, which was earlier the driving force, has become in recent years a free-wheeling engine. Nevertheless one can say that it is not too late for a change for the better.

'We must in future organize our own measures so that, in the event of an increasingly probable local collapse of a separate Italian resistance, we can stifle the beginnings of anti-Fascist revolts at the threatened points, and in this respect too be of real assistance to the Duce. Naturally any further developments depend on his personality. His disappearance or a noticeable decline in his health would have unforeseeable consequences.' [13]

The Duce had already tuned to Hitler's more receptive mood. On June 5, in a conversation with Kesselring, who had again been summoned to Hitler's headquarters, Mussolini asked him to tell the Fuehrer that 'as regards the divisions which should be sent to Italy, I am content with three. They are enough to defend the islands and the peninsula. As to the situation, today it has been altered. The Anglo-Americans have bombed La Spezia and hit two battleships. To repair them up to full efficiency will require a few months.[h] Perhaps I am a little optimistic. This new situation means that we

h. Note in Ambrosio's hand: 'I told him two months.'

must reinforce our air strength. It has always been my idea that the best defence of Italy can be achieved with a strong air force. Only if we have at our disposal such a force can the danger of an enemy invasion of the peninsula be lessened . . . Tell the Fuehrer that as to the bombing of our cities, the morale of the population is good . . . But 70,000 tons of shipping have been damaged.' [i]

To add to the confusion, and perhaps the intention was deliberate, General Roatta, who had relinquished his Sicilian command at the end of May and was now Chief of the Army Staff, pressed on his own initiative for an extensive scale of German military support on Italian territory. Rintelen reported to the German War Office that 'on June 6 General Roatta expressed his views on the need for German aid as follows: for the defence of Italian home territory ten German divisions in all would be required, namely two each in Sardinia and Sicily, and three groups of two Armoured divisions in South, Central and Northern Italy. He particularly stressed that this request arose from a strictly military point of view.'

Both Ambrosio and Roatta told their German colleagues that the Duce would accept reluctantly the sending of the two further divisions for which the German High Command had been pressing and provided only that they were armoured. This would mean a total reinforcement of the Italian theatre by five divisions. When Kesselring proposed on June 18 that an additional two divisions should be requested by the Italians he was told that 'the Italian Chief of the General Staff had just had to intervene with the Duce to get his consent for the two further armoured divisions, and was not inclined to raise a new request with him, as he would counter with more hesitations and objections. General Ambrosio stated that the Duce had after lengthy resistance agreed to the sending of these two only because Italy possessed no armoured divisions.' [14]

Axis speculation on the direction of the overshadowing Allied strategic assault was unco-ordinated and groping. On June 1 Mussolini told the German Ambassador in Rome that the enemy 'will next go for Pantellaria, then West Sicily, and finally Sardinia, so as to attack France simultaneously or shortly afterwards'.[15] On June 7, General Marras, the Italian Military Attaché in Berlin, had a talk with Keitel which summarized the latest German appreciation of Allied strategic intentions in the Mediterranean theatre.[j]

'The Anglo-Americans are ready for one or more landing operations. In order of probability, the German Command considers that these landings could take place in Sardinia, Sicily, Greece, and the Dodecanese. The main

i. Italian Collection. Duce-Kesselring-Ambrosio meeting. June 5, 1943. At the end of this minute in Ambrosio's handwriting is noted: 'Optimism + Optimism = ?'
$$D(uce) \qquad H(itler)$$
j. Simoni *op cit* p. 346. The influence of the 'Mincemeat' documents is clear in this appreciation.

probability is Sardinia, after the occupation of which the enemy will probably pass on to Corsica . . . The possession of Sardinia, completed by that
of Corsica, would give the enemy, as has been repeatedly stated, an excellent
air base from which to hammer Italy and Southern France. The German
Command then considers that a landing operation could be carried out in the
Peloponnese, in Aetolia, Epirus, and the Gulf of Patras. A landing in Crete is
thought to be too difficult. The occupation of the Peloponnese and the
Dodecanese would permit the isolation of Crete. But the principal aim of the
landing in Greece would be to secure an air base whence to operate into the
Balkans: the main objective would be the Roumanian oil fields.'

The first disclosure of Allied intentions was the attack on the Italian naval
and air base of Pantelleria on June 10, in accordance with the Duce's intelligent guess of ten days previously. Rintelen was in Ambrosio's office when the
Duce telephoned instructions to telegraph Malta to inform the enemy that
owing to shortage of water resistance had come to an end. 'It is astonishing
that the Duce, without further enquiry, should have ordered the surrender.' [16]
Mussolini never referred to this action on his part.

The Germans still maintained their view that Sardinia, and not the Italian
mainland, would be the next objective. [17] But the abrupt fall of this defensive
outpost of Sicily sounded the alarm. On June 12 Ribbentrop telephoned to
Alfieri that the Fuehrer was sending Air Marshal Richthofen to Rome 'with a
strong air unit'. But on arrival the latter announced that he was on a tour of
inspection and that 'the High Command had not the slightest intention of
sending any air group, big or small, to Italy'.[k]

The Italian requests for increased military aid as formulated at Klessheim
had never been met beyond a token degree. They could not have been satisfied except at the expense of the Eastern Front. The wrangling between the
two allied Staffs between April and June 1943 is therefore primarily of interest
in revealing German suspicions and Italian intentions.

The crisis of Italian military demands now broke. On June 21 Ambrosio
told Rintelen, in presenting him with a detailed memorandum, that he realized
that Germany could not fulfil Italian requests, but that he must present the
maximum needs to make the Italian army capable of fighting to its full
capacity. As Rintelen said later, 'Keitel, to whom I forwarded these requests,
saw in this list a pretext for giving up the war.' [18]

Colonel Berger, of the German Army Staff on a special mission to Italy,
wrote in his report dated June 23 that the three arms of the German forces
in Italy came nominally under Italian High Command, and as he put it, 'the
more modest the achievements, the more important for the Italian matters of
prestige'. His mission was to report on the readiness of the German units in

k. Simoni *op cit* p. 353. The final offer was six groups (sixty aircraft) for which
twelve airfields would be needed, and this would take $2\frac{1}{2}$ months.

Italy in the event of an Allied assault. His alarming conclusion was that for the next six weeks no German unit would be fully on a war footing. On June 30 Rintelen pointed out in a dispatch that the core of the Italian army had been destroyed in Greece, Russia, and Africa, and with an essential loss of equipment. Out of eighty-five nominal divisions, only twenty were effective. The Italian army was not capable of supporting the burden of a major war as an independent commitment. And yet, as Italian military strength declined, the High Command increased their demands to control the Mediterranean war.[1]

On July 6 General Roatta made a formal request for the two German armoured divisions to be sent to Italy. Four days later, according to the War Diary of the German Army Staff, instructions were given that this demand was not to be met.

---

1. See also German Collection. War Diary of the German Army Staff, July 2, 1943. 'The Italians' claim to independence in the conduct of the war in the Mediterranean is again strongly in evidence, and in the Balkans the attitude of the Italians is impenetrable.' Three days later the Diary records the view that the Italian Navy is incapable of resisting any landing attempts.

Book IV

'Conspiracies are not made without the association of others,
and are thus most dangerous; since most men are imprudent
or evil, one runs too great a risk in being involved with such
people.'
Guicciardini

CHAPTER ONE

SICILY: 'THE WATER'S EDGE'

•••

'I HEAR on reliable grounds that information has reached the Spanish General Staff that major offensive operations by the Americans out of Algeria and Tunis are imminent. Direction of attack probably Sicily.' [a] The German Ambassador in Madrid telegraphed this report to Berlin on June 18, and it was confirmed six days later by the German Security Service. 'From a very reliable Spanish source comes another supplementary report that very strong Allied convoys have passed the Straits during the last week, and are steering a course along the African coast.' [1]

On July 9 the Italian Military Intelligence produced an evaluation of enemy intentions, which hardly clarified the situation. 'An Anglo-Saxon offensive in the Mediterranean is imminent. The enemy attack with massive quantities of equipment and men will be directed most likely against our islands, especially Sardinia, in the Aegean, on the French coast, the Spanish peninsula, where Portugal will only make a token resistance, and on the coast of northern Europe while Russia will launch a major offensive.' A landing in Greece was less likely owing to Axis reinforcements.[2]

Confusion as to the precise direction of the Allied assault obscured the Axis scene until the last moment.[b] During the night of July 9/10, however, Allied forces landed in strength at several points on the southern coast of Sicily.

The Duce was inspecting the 'M' division near Lake Bracciano, just north of Rome. The King was at his private estate of San Rossore near Pisa. Both men hastened back to the capital to study the first bulletins from the front.

a. German Collection. Madrid telegram, June 18, 1943. Dieckhoff was later to cite this message to defend himself against Ribbentrop's criticism of the 'gaffe' in May. See the Appendix to this chapter.

b. According to a staff appreciation from Kesselring's command dated June 30, the main difficulty in assessing enemy plans was lack of intelligence regarding Anglo-American landing craft. (German Collection. War Office Archives.)

The drawn-out crisis of the Mediterranean war was about to break, and both men would be faced in the next days with decisions involving not only the military position of Italy in the war. The loss of Sicily would inevitably provoke the crisis of the régime.

At noon on July 12, Bastianini telephoned to Alfieri in Berlin, in an excited voice, instructing him to approach Ribbentrop at once with a renewed demand for aircraft. 'We cannot hold on any longer in Sicily.' Ribbentrop was ill, and the Undersecretary of State, Baron Steengracht, was not available. At 2 p.m. a telephone call from Rome came through again to say that 'we will try to seek aid through other channels'.[3] A personal message from Mussolini to Hitler was therefore sent through General Marras, the Italian Military Attaché in Berlin. 'This morning (July 12) I asked Marshal Kesselring to inform you of the absolute necessity of an urgent and important reinforcement of the German air force to defend Sicily. Imposing naval convoys, tanks, and artillery in increasing numbers would constitute precious objectives for enemy air attack, whose intervention would be decisive. The existing air strength although exposing itself generously, is not sufficient either to hinder landings or oppose the enemy air force which is inflicting ever mounting losses on our divisions. The figure of available aircraft is infinitesimal in relation to requirements, and is increasingly diminishing. The moral and military effect of any enemy reverse at the first attempt to invade Europe would be incalculable.

'The state of the game is such that every effort must be made to end it in our favour, and this is only possible by a maximum and immediate German air reinforcement. The attack on Sicily can be cleared up in the briefest possible time, after which the air formations will be available for other tasks.

'I would ask you, Fuehrer, to give attention to the above, and give the maximum air support to the defence of Sicily, particularly with fighters. If adequate support is not forthcoming, the land, sea, and air strength of the enemy is such that the defence of the Sicilian theatre will be extremely difficult. I would add that one cannot exclude that the enemy will launch his attacks elsewhere, against which the operations of the air force, in its present condition, would be nil.' c

Mussolini had deliberately refrained from seeking direct German military aid at this critical hour. Hitler had already been forced to issue orders on July 11 for the immediate reinforcement of Sicily as a result of the Allied landings, although even as late as July the Italian High Command thought fit to ask that any such armoured units which might be sent to Italy should

c. Italian Collection. Mussolini to Hitler. Telegram July 12, 1943. Also printed in Rossi *op cit* pp. 39–40. On July 14 Alfieri was able to see Steengracht and ask for German Foreign Office support for the Duce's message. German Collection. Steengracht minute, July 14, 1943.

be incorporated in Italian divisions. A week later, Rintelen made a shrewd analysis of this attitude. 'The opposition to a further spreading of German forces throughout Italy comes from the Duce himself. The reasons for this are probably the following: the maintenance of Italian prestige in the country itself; the excessive economic burden through having many German troops; a considerable overestimation of battle-worthiness of Italian troops. In contrast to this, the Duce for months has been asking for a substantial increase of the German air force.' [4]

In the meantime, news from Sicily reaching German headquarters provoked a violent outburst. The immediate cause was the surrender of the naval base of Augusta, where the Admiral in charge blew up the coastal batteries without a shot being fired. Rintelen was ordered to convey to the Duce the indignation of the Fuehrer at this incident and at other examples of Italian military conduct. Rintelen saw Mussolini on the evening of July 12, and handed him a copy of the most savage of the German telegrams from Sicily. The Duce told Rintelen that he would have an enquiry held into the Augusta affair, but in private he appears to have made the cryptic comment: 'For me this telegram is at least a fifty per cent alibi.' [5]

On July 12, the same day, Alfieri sent a personal letter to Bastianini describing the first German reactions to the Sicily invasion. 'Shorn of side issues and polemics, the Italian-German situation, after the landing of the enemy in Sicily, can be summarized as follows: Germany is fully committed in her engagement with Soviet Russia, against whom she has offensive plans of a grand style, although actual needs have forced her to postpone this operation until next year. In the meantime she proposes to preserve her forces intact, to build up new ones, and put off as long as possible any eventual assault on the territory of the Reich. This is why she considers friendly and occupied countries as bastions of the German fortress, and nothing more.

'Italy constitutes in effect just one of these bastions. Anglo-American power, let loose against her, finds thus an outlet and an obstacle; otherwise this power could threaten areas more closely linked to the territory of the Reich. Germany cannot commit herself fully in Italy against the Anglo-Americans, because she must reserve her main effort against Russia. . . . One has the impression that she intends to aliment the heroic Italian resistance with limited concessions.' [6] As the Italian Minister in Berlin noted, 'the impression is forming that the Germans, by leaving us unaided to fight in desperate conditions, are pursuing a plan aimed at provoking a collapse in Italy in order to install a new government completely subservient to them'.[7]

Even Kesselring, who during recent months had almost alone pressed the military case to keeping the Italian ally in a position to continue the war, was not prepared to maintain with any confidence his attitude any longer. His hesitations were a measure of the hopelessness of the situation. On the evening of July 12 Mackensen called on him. The position in Sicily had 'sharpened'. There had been 'a complete collapse of the Italian coastal divisions. The Fieldmarshal had asked himself yesterday the question whether, under these conditions, he cared to be responsible for the further transport to Sicily of German troops, which might be more urgently required elsewhere, but nevertheless had answered this question in the affirmative, as the politico-military importance of withdrawing from Sicily was of extraordinary significance. He had therefore decided on a further strengthening of his forces there.' [8]

On the following day, July 13, at a meeting with Kesselring, the Duce reviewed the situation in Sicily. The former was prepared to recommend the transfer of two German divisions from the mainland to Sicily, but there was not even any question of holding the whole island, and in any event 'new forces would arrive too late'. The Italian commander on the island, General Guzzoni, however, had confirmed on the telephone to the Duce that with the two divisions he could hold on. Mussolini added: 'I consider the situation serious and delicate . . . but not desperate. From the political point of view, if we lose this large island the success for the enemy will be too great. The repercussions on the morale of the Italian people, and also the German, would be too grave . . . During the course of this week the situation will be decided.' [9]

On July 14 Ambrosio minuted to the Duce on the intervention by Rintelen two days previously. 'General Rintelen, on the evening of the 12th, told you, Duce, in the name of the Fuehrer, that certain Italian troops in Sicily had not fought adequately, and added that if the Italians did not intend to fight, the Fuehrer would send no further troops to Italy . . . The hypothesis advanced by the Fuehrer is unjustified, and must be rejected.' [10]

On the same day Ambrosio drafted his own appreciation in a 'Note to the Duce'. A covering minute in the file states tersely: 'The High Command outlined to the Duce the gravity of the military situation and the impossibility of continuing the struggle with honour, without a notable and immediate allied intervention with land and air forces.' [d]

This memorandum was a bleak survey of the operational prospects in the event of the loss of Sicily. 'The fate of Sicily can be regarded as sealed with a more or less brief delay. The essential reasons for the rapid collapse are: the absolute lack of naval opposition and feeble resistance in the air during the approach to the coast, the landing, the advance of the enemy, and our counter-offensive reactions; the inadequacy of equipment and grouping of the coastal divisions; the scarcity and weakness of defensive works; and the lack of efficiency, in weapons and mobility, of the main Italian force.

d. Italian Collection. Among the papers of the Italian High Command. 'Documents for eventual discussions with the Germans.' (File for Tarvisio meeting. August, 1943.) The covering note was probably written in August.

'It is useless to search for the causes of this state of affairs. They are the result of three years of war, begun with scanty means, and during which the few resources have been burned up in Africa, in Russia, and in the Balkans. The same serious situation exists in Sardinia, in Corsica, and in the whole peninsula. Once Sicily had been occupied, the enemy could operate, either against the Italian mainland methodically in a series of operations within the range of fighter aircraft from North to South, or strike a single blow aimed at dividing the peninsula in two, or in Sardinia and Corsica as a preliminary operation to one against the peninsula or the coast of Provence.' Ambrosio judged that the first hypothesis was more likely, it would be strange to attack Sicily 'in order to reach Leghorn, Genoa, or Toulon, with the prospect of facing three landings rather than two'.

In any event the Italians were not 'in a position to face the situation alone. After the experience of Sicily, the problem of Sardinia and Corsica was more or less insoluble, given our inferiority at sea and in the air.' The defence of the Italian mainland required 'immense quantities of equipment and of land and air forces, which we are not capable of getting ready ourselves. One must however consider the need to organize the flow into Italy of German land and air forces (motorized units other than those already arrived, and 2,000 aircraft), even at the cost of interrupting temporarily operations in progress in the East, in order to defend Italy, and reconquer a relative air superiority in the central Mediterranean.'

For this, the Axis must operate massively 'against the more dangerous enemy, represented now by the Anglo-Americans, who, through the occupation of the Italian peninsula, would create the conditions whereby they would reach a decision above all in the Balkans (Roumanian oil).

'It is urgent to break from the outset the attempt to create a stable Second Front on which, in a more or less brief space of time, the Anglo-Americans will succeed in having an absolute superiority.

'The very slight chances, outlined above, of our being able to resist at sea, which appear from the recent operations, may induce the enemy to accelerate his timing. It is therefore indispensable that the above-mentioned forces are concentrated at once in the peninsula.

'On the other hand, the ally cannot persuade us that victory for the Axis is probable if the constitution of a second land front is prevented as long as the war in Russia drags on.

'If one cannot prevent the setting up of such a front, it will be up to the highest political authorities to consider whether it would not be expedient to spare the country further sorrow and ruin, and to anticipate the end of the struggle, seeing that the final result will undoubtedly be worse in one or more years.'

As an analysis of the possibility of further Italian resistance, Ambrosio's memorandum would have met with approval at German Headquarters.

On July 13, the Fuehrer had already issued a military directive on Sicily. 'After the bulk of the Italian forces are eliminated, the German forces alone, even if grouped together, are no longer sufficient to push the invading enemy forces back into the sea. In addition, further enemy landings in the west of the island must be expected. It will now be the task of our forces to delay the enemy advance as much as possible and to bring it to a halt.' [11] Hitler was now reducing his commitment on the Italian front as far as possible without precipitating the inevitable.

On July 13 he replied to Mussolini's request for aircraft in the following terms: 'I completely share the judgment of the situation contained in your telegram which has reached me on July 13, 1943. The loss of Sicily would represent for the enemy the definite control of traffic across the Sicily channel and a base for the further assault on the Italian mainland.

'After the unexpected and rapid folding up of the forces employed in coastal defence, which, as I communicated to you through General Rintelen, at least in one of the most important sectors did not even accept battle, the principal task of the air force must be, in an even greater degree than previously, concentrated on the maximum destruction of enemy shipping. This can be of decisive importance for the subsequent development of the fighting in Sicily and for the beginning of further landing operations in the Mediterranean. In spite of all difficulties, I have decided to continue maintaining the potential of the German air strength in Italy. In July, 220 machines were dispatched, and a further 250 bombers and fighters will follow, as foreseen, by the end of the month. And in addition I have arranged for a further strengthening of the Second Air Fleet by one fighter and seven bomber groups. Two bomber groups recently assigned are specially equipped for action against naval objectives. To reinforce the battle against the enemy forces which have landed, I have in the first instance given orders that the First Parachute Division shall be transported by air to Sicily and that the 29th Armoured Division shall be transferred to the Reggio area.

'Allow me, Duce, to beg you to take immediately the necessary measures to remove such obstacles and further to ensure that your forces stationed in Sicily give their utmost in the defence of the island which can only be held by the joint efforts of our troops.' e

The letter was delivered to Mussolini on July 15 at a meeting at Palazzo Venezia with Kesselring. He had precise instructions. 'The Fuehrer has said that he is opposed to sending equipment and troops to Sicily until supplies of

e. Italian Collection. Letter dated July 13. Also printed in Tamaro I, *op cit* pp. 188–90, under date July 13 or 14. Tamaro assumes erroneously that Ambrosio's minute of July 14 is a comment on this letter, which was in fact delivered only on July 15.

ammunition, petrol, and rations can be assured.' It was more important to defend the lines of communication in Calabria. [12]

The reluctance of Hitler to move German troops to Sicily led to worried speculation on the Italian side. As Mackensen reported on the same day: 'From an unprejudiced source, I know that in a conversation today the Duce referred with some seriousness to the effect which the abandonment of Sicily would have in the country. Similar remarks in front of Germans have been made by Ministers Cini and Albini, linked with earnest requests for the strongest air support. The loss of Sicily would produce in the Italian people a quite different effect from that noticeable in the surprisingly calm acceptance of the news of the loss of Libya or later the surrender of Tunis.' [13]

Kesselring's proposal to send two German divisions from the mainland to Sicily, which he had made two days previously, had been overruled. He now announced, 'on Hitler's orders, that no movements of troops will be undertaken until supplies are assured in Sicily . . .' The pretext was also given that 'the Fuehrer is concerned about the Leghorn zone' at the moment covered by one of the two German divisions concerned. Kesselring added: 'I don't understand why the Fuehrer sees a danger in Tuscany. I don't know the reasons.'

Kesselring was not yet aware that an intrinsic part of the planning of operation 'Alaric' was the building up of a reserve supply base in Northern Italy, and on July 13 the German War Office had drawn attention to the need to send at least one German division to Northern Italy 'on the grounds of the danger of an Allied landing or assault in the area of Genoa and Leghorn'.[f] From the military point of view there might well be a risk of sabotage and Allied air attack on the main lines of communication through the Alpine passes. Marshal Rommel, with his embryo planning staff, was to move at short notice into Northern Italy, with the responsibility of assuring the German Front in the peninsula in event of a crisis. This advanced headquarters had been set up near Munich early in July, and with instructions that its existence must not be discussed in writing.

Hitler's own interpretation of future Allied plans on the Italian front was that they would make a series of landings in the Genoa-Leghorn region. Mussolini, in his talk with Rintelen on July 15, took a different view, perhaps in accordance with Ambrosio's judgment in his memorandum of the previous day. He felt that 'the enemy has a greater interest in liquidating the whole of the South'.

There is indirect evidence of Ambrosio's reaction to this meeting. 'He was astonished at the contemptuous tones used by the German and that

---

f. German Collection. Forces were to be earmarked to secure a supply base in the region of Mantua. Italian agreement was to be sought. German War Office minute on 'Alaric', July 13, 1943.

the Duce puts up with it. Rintelen complained, among other points, that the German divisional headquarters were badly received everywhere and not given facilities in their tasks of deployment. When he left, the Duce instructed Ambrosio to prepare the reply to Hitler. Ambrosio did so at once, but now fears that he has let himself go in strong language. The letter ends by saying that if our allies do not hurry to support us in the air . . . we will have to open negotiations with the enemy. Ambrosio will take the letter to Palazzo Venezia this evening, but is very much afraid that the Duce will not sign it. He has told the Duce . . . "that the war is lost because Germany is not in a position to bring us immediately the necessary aid (Russian front etc.). Whether from this hypothesis follows the enemy occupation of Italy, preceded by the destruction of our cities, will be seen in a matter of weeks. One must talk clearly, honestly and clearly, to Germany. Italy cannot accept the use of her territory, with no hope of salvation, as the outer defence of the Reich. All Italy is convinced of this. Even if the armed forces would attempt it, the country would not submit to it, seeing the uselessness of this terrible effort. Germany is, on the other hand, for geographical and industrial reasons, able to hold out against the enemy for another year, perhaps longer. In these conditions it is better for both sides that Germany allows us freedom of action, thus safeguarding by common agreement, and in the best way, German interests too . . . One must not hesitate but cross the ditch before it is too late. And if the Germans want to make Italy their battlefield, one should not altogether exclude the possibility that Italy should fight against these allies who have systematically failed in their word."

'Ambrosio is seeing the Duce this evening between 8 and 10 p.m. to give him the reply to Hitler, drafted along these lines. Ambrosio says that the Duce has not reacted in any way to this verbal stand of his. Ambrosio is keeping the King informed. It is a pity that Mackensen has left before the Duce received this draft telegram.g Ambrosio feels like resigning if the Duce does not agree with these conclusions.' 14

On the evening of July 17 the Duce redrafted Ambrosio's version of the telegram to Hitler with many watered down 'corrections', and it was presumably sent off the next morning. 'The rapid initial success of the enemy landings in certain sectors of Sicily is not due to the lack of combative spirit by the troops assigned to coastal defence, but to the preponderance of equipment which the enemy has been able to put ashore with the help of strong naval forces which have been employed with impunity close to the coast owing to the limited possibility of opposition from our weak air force, and our artillery. The coastal defence has done all in its power given its equipment and emplacements.

'My directives assigned to the air force, in event of the enemy landing, as

g. He had been summoned on July 16 to report to Hitler.

a principal task the assault and destruction of enemy shipping. The air force has always operated accordingly, acting beyond the limits of human possibility.

'But it is not with the modest forces available, faced with an air concentration of overwhelming strength, that one can expect results of a decisive importance against the Allied battle fleet and transports, which have been concentrated in the Mediterranean for an operation in which England and America have committed their prestige in the eyes of Russia and the world.

'In view of the importance and continued aggravation of the war in the Mediterranean, your aid, even if generous, has not been enough, and at times has been subjected to impediments which have vitiated its employment with a unified vision. The 29th (German) division has lost and is losing precious time. [h]

'I cannot accept your observations regarding the conduct of the Italian authorities, who have always done all in their power to assist their German comrades.

'All possible ground arrangements have been made, but enemy air attacks on our landing grounds have assumed an intensity which has seriously affected the efficiency of the organizations. This too is due to enemy air preponderance to which alone are due the losses on land. The ground organization in Calabria is rapidly being set on foot.

'I assure you, Fuehrer, that the Italian forces in Sicily, in accordance with my orders, have always been and still are firmly decided to defend the island to the last.

'The enemy has opened the Second Front in Italy, concentrating there the huge offensive resources of England and America in order not only to conquer Italy, but to open up the road to the Balkans at the very moment when Germany is engaged on the Russian front.

'The sacrifice of my country cannot have as its principal aim the delaying of a direct attack on Germany.

'Germany is economically and militarily stronger than Italy. My country, which entered the war three years earlier than had been foreseen, and was thus unprepared, has progressively worn itself out, bringing up its resources in Africa, in Russia, and in the Balkans. [i]

'I think, Fuehrer, that the moment has come to examine the situation together, in order to draw the most appropriate conclusions to the interests of both countries.' [j]

h. The division was stationed in Calabria.

i. This paragraph is taken verbatim from Ambrosio's memorandum of July 14.

j. The evidence as to the drafting of this letter, and as to whether or not it was finally sent, is confusing. The above text exists in two version:

(A) In a file in the Italian Collection, and dated July 18 together with Hitler's letter of July 13.

Meanwhile, on July 15, at a meeting at Hitler's headquarters, Jodl produced a challenging report on the Italian front and proposed urgent measures to be taken to avoid a further disintegration of the military and political scene. [15]

'On any admission Sicily cannot be held any longer. It is not clear what the next aim of the enemy will be; Sardinia and Corsica, the Italian mainland or Greece. Large landings in Norway and France are not to be expected. The higher leadership of the Allies is centrally constructed, and their political leadership is geared to military requirements. Anti-Fascist elements in Italy want to capitulate and are active in wide circles of the Italian officer corps but at the moment treason is still camouflaged. It may be the object of the Italian traitors to request more and more German support and in such a situation to bring about their destruction.

'If we wish to take into account southern Italy, which is indispensable to us for the defence of Greece, then we must have strong striking forces ready in Apulia and Calabria. But so long as the cleaning up of the Italian military command apparatus is not carried out and the strongest measures taken . . . against all signs of decomposition within the Italian army, one cannot be responsible for keeping German troops south of the Apennines. It is therefore necessary that this internal political decision should be implemented. As a pretext could be used the need to oppose to the united command of the Anglo-Saxons a strict and unified Axis command in the Mediterranean. As the Italians do not possess the necessary leadership, German commanders

(B) In Tamaro I, *op cit* 187–8 marked 'Copy sent to the General Staff of the Army Command in Sicily' and dated July 16.

Version (A) quoted above is presumably the final version corrected by Mussolini from Ambrosio's draft. In the notes of the anonymous staff officer at the Ministry of War quoted in Tamaro I, 186–7, it appears that Ambrosio was ordered on July 15 to prepare such a draft in answer to Hitler's letter (of July 13). In these notes for July 16 occurs the entry 'Mussolini has signed the letter of Ambrosio for Hitler, and says that he will send it off to-day. Ambrosio is still dubious.'

The notes passed to the Italian Ministry of Foreign Affairs by their liaison officer with the Supreme Command, and cited by Tamaro Vol. II, pp. 587–91, contain a statement by General Castellano on July 16 showing that Ambrosio had drafted a telegram, and on July 18 another note read 'Mussolini handed back yesterday evening the draft telegram to Hitler together with many corrections, so that it is devoid of its strong points; it is a smooth telegram that should be sent off today. It will have no effect, and will allow the Germans to tie us in knots once again with counter-charges and lies.'

Version (B), the Ambrosio draft, contains such phrases as, at the end of the first paragraph, 'I must therefore reject your statement of a rapid folding up, in some sectors, for failing to accept battle,' and at the end of the second paragraph, 'Nor will the reinforcements announced by you and which in any case will arrive late, bring about a major change in the situation'. Both these phrases are struck out in the version (A).

Mussolini says in his *Memoirs op cit* (p. 41) 'On July 18 I sent a cable to the Fuehrer' and quotes only one paragraph of the version of the above text. Rossi *op cit* pp. 41–2, states in quoting the same passage and the two following that the message was held up by Mussolini, but was certainly not delivered or discussed at Feltre. The fact, however, that the version (A) is included in the Italian Collection file, which formed the dossier of the Italian Supreme Command for the Tarvisio Conference in the following August, would lead one to assume that the letter was delivered at some stage.

must be placed at threatened points. These proposals will certainly meet with opposition from all anti-Fascist elements, and this in itself is a reason for a general clean up in Italy as a second stage of the Fascist Revolution. This must be prepared by placing in all Italian higher military positions reliable commanders, and must end with the removal from the Italian High Command and the local Commands of all opposition personalities in Italy. German commanders must be placed at all important points in the Mediterranean area. Marshal Rommel seems to be the only leader in the Mediterranean under whom numerous officers and other ranks would willingly serve.'

Preparations had already been made for setting up German military administration in those areas of Italy under Axis control, in other words, the whole metropolitan territory and the islands, excluding Sicily.

At the same time direct German administration in certain areas of the Balkans, in particular Montenegro and Albania, was also planned. On July 15, Hitler gave orders to strengthen the German military forces throughout the whole of South-East Europe, and on the assumption that the whole area might have to be occupied.

These military decisions assumed an imminent political collapse in Italy. Hitler alone however favoured caution at the last minute, and summoned a meeting on July 17 in order to 'have a clear picture of the political situation in Italy'. Mackensen was summoned hastily from Rome for this conference, which was to consider the 'far-reaching proposals' which Jodl had made two days earlier. 'The main question was to back up the Duce in his efforts to bring into leading military positions in Italy hard and in every way reliable men who are ready to fight to the end.' [k]

At a conference on the same day Doenitz agreed with Jodl's appreciation. From the naval point of view 'if we want to hold Italy, German troops and German naval coast artillery must take over the mainland ports. Otherwise Taranto and Naples may meet the same fate as Augusta.'

Hitler said that 'he himself has been pondering the question how this might best be done. The greatest problem is the demoralization of the Italian army about which nothing has been done. Only very severe measures, like those applied by Stalin in 1941 or by the French in 1917 will be of any avail. If only individual units were affected, we could appeal to their sense of honour by offering medals etc., but the whole army is in a state of collapse and only barbaric measures can help to save the nation. He believes that a sort of directorate, tribunal, or court-martial should be set up in Italy to remove undesirable elements. Some capable people must be left in Italy, for everything could not suddenly have turned evil.'

k. German Collection. War Diary of German Military Command. See also Fuehrer Naval Conferences 1943, p. 61. Keitel, Warlimont, Jodl, Mackensen and Prince Philip of Hesse were summoned to this conference.

Mackensen, who had left Rome after collecting a set of pessimistic reports on the internal position from Scorza, Farinacci, and others, could 'suggest no one capable of taking over the leadership'.

Doenitz believed 'that either we have to do without the Italian army altogether, or we must try to strengthen it with German troops'. Hitler replied 'that without the Italian army we cannot defend the entire peninsula. In that case we would have to withdraw to a relatively short line' and this move, as Jodl added, 'would have very serious repercussions in the Balkans'. Doenitz pressed for the infiltration 'of our men into the Italian army'. But who could take over the task?

Rommel then entered the meeting and was asked 'whether he knows of any really capable persons in the Italian army who are fully co-operating with Germany'. He replied that 'there is no such person'.

Hitler ended the discussion: 'Everything depends on a radical change in the Italian situation. If this can be brought about, it will be worth the risk. If not, there is no point in throwing in additional German troops and thus engaging our last reserves.' [16]

On July 17 Alfieri reported despairingly in a personal letter to Bastianini. German air reinforcements were clearly not arriving with the necessary speed. Alfieri proposed that the Italian High Command should ask the German authorities to indicate exactly and in detail how many aircraft had been sent to Italy, to what airfield and on what dates. 'All this in the form of a precise commitment. In military and political circles in Berlin (very confidentially for the moment), one is saying that if Sicily must be abandoned, an impregnable line of defence must be established on the Continent . . . I have not yet found out to what line they are referring; but putting together certain rumours and remarks, I have come to the view that they are thinking of the Apennines.' [17]

The Italian Minister in Berlin wrote later: 'The German plan in Italy, barely indicated in Alfieri's last letter to Bastianini, is taking shape in the form of a defence organized throughout the length of the peninsula, aimed at stiffening along the line of the Po. Marras (the Italian Military Attaché in Berlin) declares that, faced with such an eventuality, Mussolini, whether he likes it or not, will be forced to get out of the war. In the meantime we are noting alarming signs: the German divisions in Italy no longer obey the Italian commands; they manoeuvre on their own, with the evident intention of carrying out this plan.' [18]

On July 18 the German General Staff informed the Italian Military Attaché's office in Berlin that the major Russian offensive had begun along the whole Eastern Front. Any chance that the Germans might even be in a material position to aid Italy must now vanish.

On the same day, there is a laconic note in Rommel's diary: 'At the

Fuehrer's at midday . . . In the East the Russians are attacking along the whole front. They are held for the moment. But no chance of withdrawing a few divisions. I gather that the Fuehrer has been advised not to give me command in Italy because I would be ill-disposed towards the Italians . . . My mission to Italy has therefore been postponed. The Fuehrer is probably going to meet the Duce.' [19]

APPENDIX

The Epilogue to Operation 'Mincemeat'

Ribbentrop was not slow to realize after the Sicily landings that the top secret information reported in May 1943 from Spain in regard to Allied strategic intentions in the Mediterranean had been a brilliant fake.[1]

On July 29 he cabled Dieckhoff in Madrid, 'for the personal attention of the Ambassador exclusively. Upon considering the remarks of Foreign Minister Jordana, which you report in your telegram of July 15th, 1943, I am struck by his emphasizing that we must certainly have been prepared for the Anglo-American attack on Sicily, as the Spanish had repeatedly pointed out to us what was about to happen. Jordana apparently meant this as a reminder of the report you telegraphed to us in your telegram of May 12, 1943. But in this report it was stated that the English and Americans were only going to launch sham attacks on Sicily and Dodecanese, the intention being to launch the *main* offensive against Crete and the Peloponnese.

'This report has meanwhile been proved false, since the operation directed by the English and Americans against Sicily, far from being a sham attack, was of course one of their planned major offensives in the Mediterranean. It is therefore reasonable to assume that the report passed on to you by Jordana, which tallies with the information (referred to in your telegram of May 12) you received direct from a "wholly reliable source", was deliberately allowed by the enemy to fall into our hands in order to mislead us as to the military plans.

'I would add that about the same time as we received your telegrams, mentioned above, we were also apprised by another source, though again via the Spaniards, of the content of certain English military documents pointing in the same direction as the information communicated to you by Jordana and your informant. This information can apparently be traced back to familiarity with these documents. We should therefore reckon with the possibility that these documents are consciously misleading and were deliberately allowed by the enemy to fall into Spanish hands.

1. See German Collection. Madrid and Foreign Office telegrams: July 29, July 30, August 2, August 4, and August 9, 1943.

'In the light of this, I would ask you to undertake a most careful reappraisal of the whole matter, particularly of your earlier reports, and to consider in so doing whether the persons from whom the information emanated are directly in the pay of the enemy, or whether they are hostile to us for other reasons, by virtue of their Catholic affiliations for example.

'Kindly telegraph your reply.

RIBBENTROP.'

Dieckhoff took immediate refuge behind his correct forecast of the Sicily landings, contained in his telegram of June 18.[m]

'I do not think there was any intention to mislead. What I learned on May 12 from the Spanish Foreign Office regarding the imminence of a major Anglo-American attack on Southern Europe was based on documents which had been found some days previously on the body of a shot-down English officer, and handed over in the original to our Counter Intelligence here by the Spanish General Staff. The documents were investigated by the Abwehr and I have not heard that their investigations cast any doubt on their authenticity.

'When Jordana referred me on July 15 to the Spanish warnings he no doubt chiefly had in mind the communications from the Spanish General Staff of which I notified you as follows on June 18: "It is reliably reported to me that the Spanish General Staff tonight received news of a major offensive operation about to be launched from Algeria and Tunisia. Objective: Sicily."

DIECKHOFF.'

Ribbentrop was not content with this, and his suspicions ranged further afield to the possibilities of Spanish complicity in the whole operation:

'In your telegram of July 30 you express your conviction that there was no desire to mislead us by passing on the English documents dealing with English invasion plans; you say that these documents were also examined by the Counter Intelligence without any doubt being cast on their authenticity.

'Here again it is taken for granted that the documents really emanate from the British. But the fact that they say that only a sham attack on Sicily is planned and the main offensive was launched against Sicily, permits us to conclude with certainty that the documents were deliberately intended to mislead us. The idea was presumably that we should not adopt any defensive measures in Sicily, or that we should adopt only inadequate ones. It is thus practically certain that the English purposely fabricated these misleading documents and allowed them to fall into Spanish hands so that they might reach us by this indirect route. The only question is whether the Spaniards

m. See p. 371.

saw through this game and deliberately led us out on a false trail, or whether they were themselves taken in by the Intelligence Service.

'In order that we may judge of this will you kindly let me know whether those persons in the Spanish Foreign Office who originally circulated the information evidently derived from these documents are, in your opinion, directly in the pay of our enemies or whether they have themselves fallen victims to this British deception manoeuvre from some other cause, perhaps by reason of their informant's Catholic affiliations.

RIBBENTROP.'

Dieckhoff refused to be chastened:

'I have no reason to suppose that Jordana and Doussinague,[n] who on May 12 provided us with the information derived from the English documents, are in enemy pay, nor have I any reason to suppose that these two persons have themselves fallen victim to a British deception manoeuvre from any other cause such as their Catholic affiliations. Both the Navy Minister and General Munoz Grande spoke to me at the time, shortly after May 12, about the documents and pointed out their significance. Like the Spanish General Staff, which notified our Abwehr, they too evidently lent them full credence.

'In my view this was not a case of an English deception manoeuvre. I gave very close consideration at the time to the question whether the documents might not have intentionally been allowed by the English to fall into our hands in order to mislead us; but the circumstances in which they were found overwhelmingly refuted such an assumption.

'It is my belief that originally (i.e. at the end of April or beginning of May) the English and Americans had every intention of acting as laid down in the documents. Only later did they change their minds, possibly regarding the plans as compromised by the shooting down of the English bearer. The operational plans must have been finally settled at the Washington Conference at the end of April; this is evidently where the attack on Sicily was decided upon; the Spanish General Staff, acting on their own North African intelligence, gave us accurate forewarning of the attack on May 18, and it actually took place on July 10.

DIECKHOFF.'

On August 9, in exasperation, Ribbentrop terminated the argument, through a subordinate:

'The Reich Foreign Minister has instructed me to inform you that the British Secret Service is quite capable of causing forged documents to reach the Spaniards, by whatever means, with the object of deceiving us. He therefore concludes once for all that the possibility of a forgery exists, it being

n. The Secretary General of the Spanish Foreign Office.

merely open to question whether all the Spaniards through whose hands the documents passed believed in their authenticity.'

The head of the Italian Military Intelligence, General Amé, has added later his sibylline comment. 'It was not false documents written in the hand of the Vice-Chief of the British General Staff which served to give credit to our faulty appreciations, as a recent British publication would have it, but the concepts of the same Vice-Chief of Staff expressed in an authoritative manner, which came to the knowledge of the Italian Military Intelligence, and confirmed our exact valuation.' o

o. Amé, *Guerra Segreta in Italia* p. 304, *op cit* p. 137.

CHAPTER TWO

THE ROMAN SCENE

•-

ON JULY 10 the Duce inspected the 'M' division, armed and trained by the German S.S. as the mobile striking force of Fascism guarding the centre of government in event of internal disorder. The main precaution taken on the Home Front had been the creation in May of this Division. The equipment for which the Duce had asked was delivered punctually by the end of that month. The skeleton division, which had been forming near Chiusi, was now to be brought south to the lake of Bracciano. [1] The parade was held at Sette Vene about twenty miles from Rome on the Via Cassia, and was attended by military leaders and German representatives, curious to see an exercise conducted with the latest military equipment provided by Himmler. It made a good impression, but a brief one.

The previous night, and throughout the early hours of July 10, the Allies landed in force in Sicily. In the confusion of events, Mussolini handled in characteristic fashion the local issue of the 'M' division. General Ambrosio, during the manoeuvres at Sette Vene, had already suggested sending these 'Security' troops to the front, and before witnesses the Duce agreed. On the following day the commander of the Militia Galbiati and Ambrosio met and argued. The latter wanted to get these 'political units' away from Rome, and proposed sending the division to Messina. On July 14, making use of the Duce's name, Ambrosio ordered Galbiati to move his troops. That afternoon the latter went with a written protest to Mussolini, and it was settled that it might be technically impossible to move the division, at least until July 21. But Ambrosio achieved one decisive gain: as from that date, the division came under the direct command of the Army—a point of decisive significance in the following days. [2]

The machine of the Fascist Party had reacted in its turn to the invasion of Sicily. An emergency meeting of Prefects and Federal Secretaries from

Southern Italy was held at Palazzo Wedekind, the Party headquarters, at midday on July 13. Scorza also invited, among others, Bottai, Albini, Bastianini, and Chierici. As Bottai commented, 'I immediately had the impression of being at a small council of war.' The Party Secretary had a plan; to carry the Duce's message of a 'granite sense of decision' to the provincial capitals of Italy through a speaking tour of Party bosses. Scorza had particularly hoped that Grandi would take a lead, and had telephoned him in his capital at Bologna. Grandi refused. Scorza now approached Bottai with a request to go to Bologna to persuade Grandi to change his mind, for without his support the oratorial ranks of the senior Party leaders would thin rapidly. Bottai too was sceptical. 'You must put me in a position to tell Grandi what line to give to the speeches. A few days ago Mussolini said that the enemy would never set foot on Italian soil. People have long memories. What are your instructions to justify this tragic reversal of the situation? And what *is* the situation? So that at least those of us who have to illustrate it are aware of it in its true light.' Scorza made no reply.[3]

The Party meeting then listened to the reports of the regional officials, scattered incoherent fragments which gave no clear summary of events. Scorza broke up the debate, and hurried to Mussolini. He returned in half an hour. The regional reports were to be deferred, the list of orators was to be drawn up, and the Roman group of Party bosses would be summoned to the Duce before the end of the week. The course of military events might make this their last meeting, and final opportunity to propose a 'radical' solution to Mussolini.

Bottai stayed on in Scorza's office. The whole structure of the régime was rumbling under the approaching earthquake. The Party, if it were to survive, must be given a lead and a programme. Now was the supreme testing of its élite. But Scorza had on his shoulders the dead weight of past errors, and an increasing sense of operating in a void, out of all touch with the realities of a situation, the details of which were unknown to him, with a Party machine scarcely turning over in a vacuum, and a leader beyond reach in self-imposed and total isolation.[a]

On the following day Bottai drafted a note interpreting his own thoughts in view of the forthcoming meeting of Party leaders with the Duce. There were two possibilities: first, on the assumption that the political situation was completely in the hands of Fascism, and that Mussolini would act as head of the government within the rules of the Fascist constitution, he should nominate military ministers, allow the Chief of the General Staff to fulfil his duties unhampered, make the civilian ministers actively responsible for their departments, permit the Cabinet to function properly, summon the Grand Council,

a. In a typical and abrupt gesture, Mussolini on July 7 gave orders to the Ministry of Justice 'that all illegal actions by Fascists were to be severely punished'. Italian Collection. 'Note for the Duce.'

and propose a message from the King to the Nation followed by a manifesto of the Duce and the Grand Council. Second, in the event of a situation considered untenable partly or wholly by Fascism, this would fall within the competence of the Crown. 'It is up to the latter to decide on a form of Government: military? civilian? military and civilian? . . . Including Fascist civilians? or solely with non-Fascist civilians? or both? These are the two alternatives.'

Bottai took this note on the afternoon of July 14 to Scorza's office, and a discussion followed. The latter agreed that there was no third solution. 'Either everyone with Mussolini, even if he were forced to act with us, in a close and frank solidarity of intentions and acts, for the final attempt to produce a government for the defence of Italy: or everyone with Mussolini in leaving it to the King to attempt such a defence.

'We both say together: then there are the Germans. Mussolini, and he alone can do it, ought to obtain from them *in extremis* an undertaking not to torment the country; the King to do the same with the others, the Allies. To achieve a kind of neutrality. To get us out of everything . . . A risky operation whose outcome is uncertain.' [4]

Scorza now felt it essential to convey to the Germans the rising alarm in Party circles. He asked Bastianini to arrange an urgent interview with the German Ambassador for that evening. The two men went together. The conversation was reported by Mackensen to Berlin. 'Scorza thanked me for receiving him and asked me if he could speak openly and in confidence, as both of us were convinced of the indissoluble alliance of the Axis powers. Above all he wished to make the formal declaration that the Fascist Party was determined to fight in the common cause to the last man. So long as one Fascist remained alive, nothing else was thinkable. The loss of Sicily would have unforeseeable consequences for Italy.' In the name of the Fascist Party he begged both the Fuehrer and the National Socialist Party for help 'to the bounds of possibility in the battle for Sicily, which would be decisive not only for the future of Italy, but also for that of Germany, and even of Europe . . . The Italians alone had not the necessary means. To ask for such means from the Axis parties at this decisive hour was his sacred duty as Party Secretary, and was independent of all the military departments. This was not the moment in which to go into the why and wherefore of Italian weakness in armaments. But the Fuehrer could be assured that, if the next critical fourteen days could be overcome, he, Scorza, by ruthlessly exploiting the intrinsic full powers of his position would set in motion with every means at his disposal a basic revival of the Italian people, which would bear comparison with the year 1793 in France. Nothing would be untouched by such a revival; neither the Army, nor its leadership, nor war industry.'

Mackensen answered that the Fuehrer was certainly following events in

Sicily with the same attention. 'I stated personally to Scorza that we were fully aware of his services in bringing new life into a party which had lapsed into a complete free-wheeling, but that we were also clear that in war-time the omissions of years could not be made up from one day to the next.' Scorza did not deny this, but emphasized that he would act 'with an iron broom'.

Mackensen was impressed: 'With him (Scorza) and through him we should be able to achieve that change in the exercise of the powers of command, which hitherto seemed unrealizable.'[b]

Ribbentrop replied with a personal telegram the following day. The Fuehrer had noted with interest Scorza's appeal. 'Already all available units are on the move, and war material is rolling every hour in the direction of Italy ... All our thoughts and wishes in these days are with the Italian people and the Fascist Party, on whom the future of Italy depends.' [5]

But the Party Secretary, eager in his rally for the last stand, like other actors in the scene, created his own vacuum round him. At such a moment, inexplicably, he had abolished the liaison officers between the units of the Militia and the machinery of the Party. It would therefore in a supreme crisis be impossible to organize common action on a political level. And for the next ten critical days, Scorza was 'unavailable' to the Militia commander, General Galbiati. [6] The body of the Party had a tail, but no teeth. As the Chief of Police, Chierici, told Bottai, ' "One must act quickly", and then he told me of the landslide of the Party in the provinces. It would be ingenuous, he said, to reduce the present crisis to a police problem, even supposing that the forces available were sufficient to maintain order.' [7]

On the morning of July 16, Scorza summoned to his office at Party headquarters certain of the leaders designated for the grand tour of the provinces. He wished to go over the arguments to be put before Mussolini that evening at a meeting of the orators to which the Duce had reluctantly agreed. It was important to present a united front. The discordant note was as always sounded by Farinacci 'thundering as if at a political meeting, giving vent to his uncontainable rage against the Leader'.[c] But the majority were agreed that Mussolini must accept to govern within the limits of the existing Fascist constitutional legislation 'and the proper working of all the organs of consultation, control and decision'—in particular of the Grand Council—must be demanded of him. The meeting was temporarily interrupted by a visit from

b. German Collection. Mackensen telegram July 14, 1943. According to Bottai *op cit* p. 278, Scorza also asked the German Ambassador to tell Bormann 'that the Fascist Party is in danger'.

c. Bottai *op cit* p. 277. According to Farinacci's own account in his deposition before the Verona Trial, he also attacked Grandi for his refusal to attend, saying that he should be told to accept with discipline the orders of the Party. Cersosimo, *Dall' Istruttoria alla Fucilazione* p. 4.

the German Ambassador to tell Scorza that he was leaving by air for Berlin to press for immediate reinforcements for Sicily.

At 5.30 that afternoon Scorza and the orators, with the exception of Federzoni and Grandi who both refused to come from Bologna, called on the Duce at Palazzo Venezia. There were fifteen Fascist leaders in the group. 'He turned his head to us, one by one, slightly aslant as if he wanted, by looking at us sideways, at the same time to defend himself and to penetrate our intentions. I know so well this attitude of the fencer ready for the parry and the thrust. How well I know that smile which now twists his lips; it is born of a nervous twitch which tries in vain to become an open courteous smile and remains half way between a diffident grimace and dissimulated ease.' [8]

Farinacci spoke first with his usual violence, soon losing the threads of his discourse and plunging into detailed complaints, exposing himself to the favourite game of the Duce of involved interruptions. Why, for example, should the Duce deal with matters of detail such as the price of bread? The retort is swift: 'Napoleon . . . stated that there were no such things as details.' But Farinacci's argument was clear. In his own words, 'I began by saying that the situation was serious because I had no faith in the General Staff and particularly in General Ambrosio, who had told me some days previously that the war was lost, and that within fifteen days we would have to shut up shop. I asked Mussolini that all those present should be put in a position to assume total responsibility along with him, by summoning the Grand Council.' [9]

Another speaker 'brought the subject back to the theme which we had set ourselves: it was not a matter of neglecting details, but of passing them to . . . those responsible organs whose actions the Leader should co-ordinate. This had not happened, there were only institutions which did not function, and laws which were not applied.' Mussolini opened his eyes wide. 'What's that? What then have we done in twenty years?' [10]

Bottai pointed out that the constitutional organs of Fascism must be allowed to function. This was no formal matter. 'The clash between the spirit of the law and the conduct of government shows a crisis of authority and of command, harmful at the best of times, and at this moment dangerous. Convinced of such a danger, we are here to enunciate in constitutional terms a question, which is simply and solely political . . . We are asking that the régime puts its apparatus in working order again. We are not here to ask that your powers or power should be diminished or to divide or fragment your responsibilities. We are here to share those responsibilities. The constitution provides that you should be "the first" but not the only minister: the first in a Council of Ministers really operating in each sector.' He also suggested that a reformed Grand Council should be created, capable of debating and deciding on the problems involved in a major overhaul of the structure of government. The two Chambers must also be made to function and with them the syndicates and corporations.[d]

'From Mussolini's expression it appeared that he had made up his mind for some time. After a moment of silence he said, "Very well, I shall summon the Grand Council. They will say, in the enemy camp, that it has been assembled to discuss the surrender. But I will call it together." And he dismissed us. Nothing else. No taking into consideration of any one of our proposals; and we wanted something more than just this announcement.'

The idea of a Mussolini collaborating cheerfully with a happy and united band of loyal collaborators in making Fascism work ignored the whole historical experience of twenty years, and of the Duce's character.

The following day he said to Bastianini: 'Scorza in a little more than two months has brought me with his Secretaryship two speeches, one directive, and one pronunciamento.' And Bottai commented in his diary: 'The "pronunciamento" is our move of yesterday. To such a point is the situation destroyed. Talking to others he (Mussolini) sneered: "Who were those badly dressed gentlemen? What did they want? What authority had they? The authority of a speaker which lasts just as long as his speech." ' [11]

Mussolini wrote later: 'I did not much welcome this gathering, as I did not care for meetings not prepared in advance with a regular agenda . . . All the speakers, or nearly all, insisted on the necessity of convening the Grand Council if only to enable me to inform the members of the highest assembly of the régime of certain facts which could not be given to the general public. At the end of this discussion, which not having been prepared revealed nothing but a sceptical frame of mind all round, I announced that I would convene the Grand Council in the second half of the month.' [12]

Although the deliberate absence of Grandi and Federzoni weakened this Party deputation, its significance was clear. This meeting in the Duce's office had been the dress rehearsal. The arrangements, and in part the initiative, lay now in Scorza's hands.

Ciano also had been absent from this gathering. On the pretext of ill-health, he retired during these crucial days to his family house at Leghorn. That day, however, Mussolini summoned him to Rome. The news of his return

d. A curious episode is revealed in the following 'Minute for the Duce' dated July 7, 1943, from Bottai: 'I thought it my duty after the conversation which I had with you on July 3 to inform his Excellency Grandi of what concerned him, and I have had in reply this letter which he himself charged me to show you:

' "Bologna, 6 July, 1943. Dear Bottai, I have received your letter in which you told me of your conversation with the Duce. Kind as always, he told you that he wished me to be forewarned. I confirm what I said to you and Scorza. I have been President of the Chamber for four years. It is natural and just that the men who have served the Revolution should in turn hold this very dignified post. I need not tell you that I shall be particularly glad if you are called to succeed me.

Yours affectionately, Grandi." '

raised alarm in German circles. The Germans feared above all that Ciano was the main link between a Grandi-Bottai-Federzoni group and the Court.[13]

Dollmann wrote two notes for Mackensen on his own contacts with 'the circle of Villa Torlonia', which signified his main informant Buffarini, with whom he had been until three o'clock in the morning of July 16. As Dollmann reported: 'Villa Torlonia sees its salvation only in the taking over by us of at least combined military responsibility and leadership and has the greatest mistrust of Count Ciano.' That afternoon Dollmann had talked with Donna Rachele. 'I would like to stress the clear and pressing warning from her side against her son-in-law and his plans.' Ciano had arrived from Leghorn and 'has had a long talk with Bottai, and other members of his circle'.[14]

Ciano then sent a message to Mussolini saying that 'he had never felt so close to the Duce as at this moment, and that whenever the Duce thought it necessary he could come and talk to him'. He seems however to have hesitated and pleaded ill-health, and only on July 20 added in a further note that he was well enough to call 'at any time'. [15] It does not appear that the Duce sent for him.

The shock of the Sicily landings was also felt in the field of foreign affairs. Military defeat was now inevitable and the search for a compromise peace could not be postponed. Bastianini hoped that at last the opportunity had arrived to act on his own initiative. If Mussolini were to allow him such latitude, there was no time to lose and a plan must be ready. As Bastianini wrote later, 'Supreme decisions are not taken by an Undersecretary, but I can at least try to put them into effect rapidly.' [16]

On the evening of July 17, Bastianini called on the Vatican Secretary of State, Cardinal Maglione. It is revealing of the absence of consultation between the Vatican and the Italian Government that the two men had not met since 1924. In any soundings towards the Western Allies, a logical and historical starting place would be through the diplomatic channels of the Papacy, whose nuncios in neutral and belligerent capitals were in a sense the professional representatives of peace.

For months past, rumours of peace moves initiated by the Vatican, and supported by the Portuguese, the Spaniards, and the Swiss, had circulated in European capitals,[e] but no reliable evidence appears of any interest in such soundings on the part of the Italian Government. There seems equally no reason to believe that Ciano at the Italian Embassy to the Vatican had made

e. As, for example, the German Minister in Bucharest reported information from Mihai Antonescu, 'that Salazar, together with the Vatican, wishes to approach both Spain and Roumania to see whether conditions are favourable for some sort of mediation. I regard the whole thing as a *ballon d'essai*.' German Collection. Bucharest telegram, April 5, 1943.

any formal approaches either to the Cardinal Secretary of State or to the British,[f] American, or neutral Legations in the Vatican City. There are equally few records of his private activities in this direction. He was reported, for example, by the German Legation to the Vatican to have remarked cryptically to a Cardinal in April 1943 that the war would not last long and that 'new developments might take place on the Eastern Front'. [17] A month later a vague German report from Berne mentions evidence supplied by the Swiss Minister at the Vatican that negotiations were in progress between Ciano and the Allies, who, however, were insisting as a preliminary condition on the resignation of Mussolini. The Italian King feared apparently that there would be public disorders in such an event and on this issue negotiations were suspended.[18]

But these rumours lacked any confirmation, and if accurate seemed to relate to a personal initiative. Bastianini's present move was the first to come belatedly from the Italian Foreign Office.

As the basis of an exploratory discussion he handed a memorandum to Cardinal Maglione. This was a bald statement of Italy's position. The war might last 'for an undetermined period of time'. Germany was still strong, and, with each shortening of the front, she could concentrate her military resources. But Italy was the main target, and thus the whole of her position must now be examined within the general frame of the war. 'Rumours have reached us of steps which the Pope would not be unwilling to take, if he had the prior assurance of Italian and German concurrence.

'Italy cannot take any initiative on her own, both for moral reasons as she must safeguard the honour of the country, and for practical reasons as she must take into account that any unilateral move in drawing away from Germany would automatically transform her territory into a battlefield. If the military situation in Italy should deteriorate even further, the only person in a position to persuade Hitler to withdraw troops from Italian territory is the Duce. It was therefore essential that England and America should not raise the immediate issue of the removal of the Duce, as this would not be in their own interests. The Germans would withdraw first to the line of the Po, where the Anglo-Americans would confront them, and then to the line of the Brenner. The intervention of Mussolini with Hitler would thus save them having to engage the Germans twice on our territory.'

The formal purpose of this note was to seek Vatican initiative in sounding the Western Allies on their political intentions in Italy. With what persons would they be prepared to treat? Were they planning to set up an Italian government-in-exile? [19]

But there was also a more urgent and practical request. On the assumption

f. As Ciano well knew, the Italian Intelligence had broken the cipher of the British Legation to the Vatican, and such a channel was thus valueless for at least any unofficial soundings.

that he would obtain the Duce's agreement, Bastianini had conceived of sending a trusted envoy to contact the British, and placed his remaining hopes of a political solution on this one mission.

He had in mind for this delicate task a leading Roman banker, Luigi Fummi, who was connected with J. P. Morgan and Company, New York, and also with the administration of the property of the Holy See. Bastianini's plan was that Fummi should travel on a Vatican passport to Lisbon, and apply for a British visa there in order to go to London on financial business for the Vatican, but in reality to get in touch with the British Foreign Secretary, Anthony Eden, with a personal message from Bastianini.

Cardinal Maglione agreed without comment to issuing such a passport, but when Bastianini explained the task to be given to Fummi, namely to attempt to negotiate, on Bastianini's responsibility, the exit of Italy, Roumania, and Hungary from the war, the Cardinal 'looked at me with a paternal expression, and certainly thought that I was deluding myself'.[20]

The next morning Bastianini went to Mussolini in a last attempt to persuade him to sanction such a diplomatic initiative.[g] He proposed that he should take certain steps, and if they failed, and were discovered by Ribbentrop, the Duce should disown his Undersecretary. Mussolini did not reply in either sense, and this was the best that Bastianini could expect. He left hurriedly and returned to Palazzo Chigi. There was no telephone call from the Duce for the rest of the day.

Fummi was now briefed and sent by direct plane to Lisbon. Some months earlier, Bastianini had secured the appointment of three experienced career diplomats in the key neutral capitals of Lisbon, Madrid and Ankara for precisely such an eventuality.[h]

There had been inconclusive contacts with British agents in Lisbon at the end of 1942, which had been severed on Ciano's instructions. The Italian Minister, Prunas, was now hastily instructed to try to renew these links. Fummi was explicitly told to conduct no discussions in Lisbon, but to insist on access to Eden in London. His mission was to convince Eden that Italy was in a position to answer both for Hungary and Roumania in seeking peace terms from Britain and the United States, on the assumption that the withdrawal of these three enemy powers from the German alliance would be a decisive element in Allied plans for an invasion of the Balkans, on which indeed the whole project depended, so as to bar eventually the Soviet occupation of South-East Europe.

g. According to Bastianini, this would have been on July 18 when in fact the German proposal for a conference had arrived. There is some confusion as to precise dates in all references to events between July 17 and 20.

h. Prunas in Lisbon, Paolucci de' Calboli in Madrid, and Guariglia in Ankara. On this episode see Bastianini *op cit* p. 118.

Fummi left Rome on July 17 or 18, and waited in vain in Lisbon for the British visa. He was still there on July 25.[i]

In reply to his request to Cardinal Maglione, Bastianini was told that, after enquiry, the Allies did not seem to be planning to set up a 'puppet' Italian government. This augured perhaps well for Fummi's mission. Bastianini now informed Acquarone, and through him the King, of this démarche.

The final step was to create an alibi with the Germans in the event of a favourable Allied reaction. Ribbentrop was to be told that Italy could not continue the struggle unless immediate and total satisfaction of Italian requests for military aid were immediately fulfilled. On July 17 Alfieri received instructions in this sense.[21]

The Germans were not unaware of these moves in Rome. On the same day, July 17, Dollmann reported to Mackensen: 'During the last two days, the Duce has been under pressure from various quarters, in particular from members of the government, in the direction of an "honourable capitulation".'[22]

During the first week of July the King was away from Rome at San Rossore, but he had returned in haste on receiving the news of the Allied landings in Sicily. Anticipating the long awaited political crisis, Badoglio and Bonomi met again on July 14 to draw up a joint shadow cabinet, which the former would attempt to urge upon the Sovereign. Bonomi was alarmed at news that Acquarone was hesitating. 'One must go by stages; bring down Mussolini, yes, but not attack the whole Fascist movement frontally.'

The two men now agreed on a provisional skeleton plan of a politico-military administration which would carry out two simultaneous operations, the overthrow of Fascism and the withdrawal of Italy from the German alliance. Badoglio would be the head of the new government, and Bonomi Vice-President of the Council. They arranged that Badoglio should seek an urgent audience with the sovereign to 'draw the conclusion of these clear premises already outlined by Ambrosio'.[23] There was a certain element of historical irony in the situation. It had been in October 1922 that the then Prime Minister, Facta, had summoned Badoglio to his office to discuss the possibility of military action against the imminent Fascist March on Rome.

The King received Badoglio on July 15 at Villa Savoia. He was, as Puntoni noted, 'about to take grave decisions'.[j] On the following day Bonomi wrote in his diary, 'The King has not accepted Badoglio's scheme. He

i. His presence in Lisbon was reported by the German Embassy in Madrid on July 26. 'Two days ago a representative of the Italian Foreign Office arrived in Portugal, according to Spanish sources to treat with the Allies.' (German Collection.)

j. Puntoni *op cit* July 15. The last recorded royal audience of Badoglio had been on March 6. According to police reports, however, he had been summoned frequently to Villa Savoia during the second half of May. He arrived in the later afternoon, in civilian clothes, and by taxi. He usually stayed about an hour.

objected that prearranged action fixed for a certain date had no chance of succeeding. In Italy people were not good at keeping secrets; after a few hours the whole thing would be widely known, and the plans at the disposal of any-one who had any interest in them.

'In addition the King did not believe that if he intervened—an eventuality which he did not even yet admit—it would be well to form a political min-istry; it would offend too many people and things, and as it would consist of old men, would give the impression of a pure and simple return to the past.' [24] Here at last was the essence of royal counsel.

The following afternoon Bonomi called on Badoglio to hear the latter's account of the audience. The discussion opened with the presentation by the Marshal of a brief memorandum on the military situation showing that with sixteen ill-equipped divisions in Italy and practically no Air Force, there would be no effective resistance to the Allies. The thirty-four divisions in France and the Balkans could neither be withdrawn at once nor without German consent. To this picture, the King showed little reaction, but only responded in clear opposition to the proposal to consider a political ministry. The elder statesmen from Bonomi to Casati, from Soleri to Einaudi, from Rodinò to Ruini, were all ghosts, the King said in Piedmontese dialect. To which Badoglio answered: 'Sir, we two then also are ghosts.' [25]

The German Intelligence received another and perhaps more accurate version of this audience: 'A completely reliable informant and well-known political personality reported to me yesterday the following, which he had been told by Marshal Badoglio with whom he has close relations. The King has turned to Badoglio with regard to eventually taking over the administra-tion in Italy. Badoglio has explained to the King that he is in no way inclined to take over in any way the succession of Mussolini. He would be prepared to exercise the powers of government on the orders and full responsibility of the King, and would carry out to the letter his instructions. If the King ordered that one should continue to fight on the side of Germany, he would carry this out loyally; if the order was to initiate peace negotiations, this he would also undertake; and so on. In any event let the King bear the respon-sibility: he, Badoglio, was only prepared to carry out the latter's orders, whatever they might be, in the most loyal manner. The King wept, and has not yet come to any decision.' [26]

The same afternoon, July 16, Acquarone asked to see Soleri, and con-firmed, what the latter already knew from Bonomi, the King's insistence on a 'technical' administration of civil servants. This royal decision was firm, and Soleri was asked to propose names. Acquarone seemed nervous and uncertain. 'It seemed to me that the excessive power which Badoglio would concentrate in his hands was a source of preoccupation to him, and he particularly did not like the idea of the Marshal being also Minister of the Interior . . . A phrase escaped him (Acquarone), "If all goes well for him, who will stop him?" Perhaps ill-natured gossip had also reached Acquarone that Badoglio resented that the King had not backed him in the quarrel with Farinacci at the time of his dismissal in December 1940,k and had let him resign as Chief of Staff and that the Marshal aspired, in the not unpredictable event of the Sovereign's abdication and that of Prince Umberto, to become the regent of the little Victor Emmanuel.'

Soleri reported this talk to Bonomi and his friends. He found them excited and, in face of the King's refusal to agree to a political ministry, prepared to disown the monarchy. Before taking such a step, however, they would wait to confer with the Prince of Piedmont, 'to clear up definitely certain preliminary understandings which had been reached with him in a conversation held some days previously'.[1]

The discussion ended inconclusively, and Soleri left that evening for his home in Piedmont. This was the end of a parliamentary solution of the Italian crisis. Everyone reassumed his liberty of action. Badoglio would not resist the alternative suggestion of an administration of civil servants and experts, and as the King determined to move by stages, such a government headed by a military figure was to remove Italy from Fascist control before facing the issue of withdrawing from the war.

According to General Cerica, the future Commandant of the Military Police, the King wrote a private memorandum about July 12. 'They have proposed to me a lottery of three names: Badoglio, Caviglia, and Thaon de Revel. Caviglia has close Freemasonry links and must be kept out. Thaon is too old. One, Badoglio, is left, whether I like it or not.' [27]

k. Farinacci's press campaign against Badoglio in the winter of 1940.
l. Soleri *op cit* pp. 239–40. This cryptic phrase has not so far been elucidated.

CHAPTER THREE

FELTRE

• •

'ON THE NIGHT of July 17 Hitler had received an alarming report on the situation in Italy. Things were going so badly that they might seriously endanger the programme of the German High Command, who were counting on holding the enemy as far distant as possible, and above all to bar the road to the Reich.' Such was the information available at the Italian Embassy in Berlin.[1]

On Sunday, July 18, the German Ambassador in Rome, who had just returned from the crisis discussions on Italian affairs at the Fuehrer's headquarters, transmitted an urgent invitation to a summit conference. Hitler was prepared to come to Italy, and the meeting might last three days. This message seems to have been conveyed to Bastianini by Mackensen late that morning. The former enquired as to the agenda for such a conference, and was told by the German Ambassador that he did not know.[a]

The Duce seems to have made a brief display of anger at Hitler's message. He accepted, however, the rendezvous, and telephoned Ambrosio at four o'clock that afternoon instructing him to leave within three hours for the North.[2] Hasty protocol arrangements had been made for the two delegations to meet at the seventeenth century villa, with its magnificent park, belonging to Senator Gaggia, near Feltre, in the province of Venice.

On the late afternoon of July 18 Mussolini left by air for the coastal resort of Riccione with his doctor and secretary, without holding any meeting with Bastianini or Ambrosio as to the policy or procedure to be followed at the forthcoming talks. He would spend a few solitary hours of reflection before facing the ultimate crisis of the Axis alliance. Bastianini met Ambrosio

---

a. Mackensen had only returned to Rome from Berlin on the late morning of July 18, and was due to see the Duce that afternoon. It is not clear whether Mackensen called on the Duce in person. The accounts of Bastianini and Alfieri are at variance on a number of points. See Bastianini *op cit* p. 119. Alfieri *op cit* pp. 318–19.

at Palazzo Venezia, when delivering Hitler's message to the Duce,[b] and suggested 'that he should be ready to leave with documentary material which would be useful in sustaining a somewhat heated discussion'.[c]

Meanwhile, on the German side, a last minute discussion was held at Berchtesgaden on the evening of July 18 to draft the headings which would form the basis of discussion at the conference. This document had been drawn up by General Warlimont, and was starkly concise.

The situation in the Mediterranean area urgently required unity of direction. This could only be placed under the command of the Duce. In view of a strengthened military commitment in Italy, a German Command, under the Duce, must be set up, to which the Italian armies would be subordinate. If German units were to be sent to Southern Italy, further Italian divisions must also be moved from the North. The Italian High Command and the other Staffs must be so constituted that complete and trusting co-operation could be ensured. The Air Command must be transferred to the head of the German Air Force in Italy, Marshal Richthofen.[3]

The essence of the German plan was thus to preserve this nominal authority of the Duce to cover the assumption of total military control by Germany in the Italian theatre.

The two delegations now converged on the rendezvous at Feltre. On the morning of July 19, Bastianini and Ambrosio arrived by train at Treviso, the nearest railway station. Alfieri, who had flown from Berlin, sought anxiously for a short briefing from the Foreign Undersecretary. The latter told him in the car between the station and the airport that both internally and militarily the position was serious. 'Mussolini no longer shows any external reactions. He has shut himself up in an impenetrable silence, and it is impossible to guess his thoughts.' [4]

At 8.30 a.m. Mussolini arrived in his personal plane at the airfield of Treviso. None of his advisers had as yet been able to brief him on the latest developments, and Alfieri now attempted to give him a hasty summary of events as observed from Berlin. The scene was dominated by the violence of the Russian assault on the Eastern Front where the main attention of the German leaders was inevitably engaged, and the effect of which could only be to reduce to vanishing point any willingness on the German side to send aid to Italy. 'I also stressed the anxiety of the German High Command as to

b. Bastianini *op cit* p. 162. Ambrosio saw the Duce at noon, according to his diary.

c. In the Italian Collection is a bulky file containing the documents taken by Ambrosio to the Tarvisio Conference in the following August. This includes Ambrosio's notes on the Feltre Conference and a general survey headed 'The politico-military conduct of the war on the part of the Axis'. This important paper is undated, but from internal evidence seems to relate to a period prior to the dismissal of Mussolini by the King. It is a lucid summary of Ambrosio's general conception of the war, and seems to have been written before the Sicily landings. See the Appendix to this chapter.

the Italian situation. Bastianini interrupted to say that during the journey he had attempted to get confirmation from Mackensen and Rintelen as to the veracity of the confidential information that Hitler was proposing to place the Italian armies under the control of the German High Command, on the specious pretext of greater unity of direction and action.' [5]

Before Mussolini could react, the German delegation headed by Keitel interrupted the dialogue to pay their formal respects to the Duce. As he descended from his plane a few minutes previously, Keitel gave Rintelen a brief clue as to German intentions: 'All power to the Duce, elimination of the Italian Royal House, stronger German intervention under German command.' As Rintelen began to express his astonishment at Keitel's remarks, saying that the Duce had indeed all power in his hands but could no longer exercise it, the conversation was cut by the arrival of Hitler's plane.[6]

Alfieri describes the scene. 'At eight minutes to nine appeared in the sky the profile of the large machine carrying the Fuehrer: the plane made one large sweeping circuit of the airfield, as is usual, and then another . . . Someone murmured "What could be the reason?". Mackensen who was next to me observed, "It is three minutes to nine and the arrival is fixed for nine o'clock precisely." ' [7]

According to Mussolini's own account, 'the meeting was, as usual, cordial, but the entourage and the attitude of the higher Air Force officers and troops were chilly'. It appears that Hitler had announced that he had to return that afternoon to Germany, and that therefore 'the time had to be used to the best advantage'.[8]

The two leaders travelled alone by train to Feltre and thence by car to their destination, and 'merely exchanged trivialities'.[9] Meanwhile the Italian and German delegations, in anticipation of the meeting, were sparring in the same train, which took them from Treviso to Feltre. The unusual absence of Ribbentrop and Goering emphasized the strictly military concern of the Germans with the meeting. A brusque dialogue developed between Keitel and Ambrosio. The former was 'confident that the Russian drive will be held'. The latter retorted 'in effect you are reduced to the defensive. What are the chances of victory? And your plans for the future?'

Keitel answered that on the Russian Front the Germans would succeed in wearing down and weakening the enemy; in the meantime they would prepare new forces which would enable them to operate actively next winter on the Southern Front, in the Balkans, and in Italy. To Ambrosio this was not an active programme, 'but a renunciation of operational initiative. The Axis is under siege, closed in a circle. One must get out of it. What proposals have you for doing so?' This question was evaded. Ambrosio then examined the situation in the Mediterranean where, in view of the commitment in Sicily, the enemy would presumably persist in his operations against Italy, and not only by aerial bombardment. 'The Second Front has been opened in Italy, and one must provide for her defence; the Italian forces are not sufficient.'

Keitel accepted the view that the enemy would seek to cross from Sicily to the peninsula and agreed that it was necessary to take measures to defend Italy. Germany, however, could not send any air reinforcements other than those promised in the recent message of the Fuehrer,[d] nor had she any armoured divisions available. He maintained that the coasts must be defended on the shore, with infantry divisions ranged behind. Above all, one must have recourse to the Italian infantry divisions, which were nearer and more easily available. German reinforcements could not be available for a couple of months. As it was above all essential to defend the southern coasts, the Italian divisions now in Central and Northern Italy must be sent to the South, including the Alpine divisions and those being re-formed, and then one would make provision to send German divisions gradually into the North. Ambrosio objected that, for the defence of the peninsula, infantry and motorized divisions were needed. As the Italian army only possessed infantry divisions, it was for Germany to contribute motorized divisions. The Italian units would cover all the coasts, including those troops in the Centre and the North; while the German mobile divisions must move to the South as well as the North, but particularly to the South which was more exposed. This dialogue at least clarified the extent of German assistance which might be forthcoming. It remained to discuss the conditions.[10]

Villa Gaggia—a labyrinthine edifice described by the Duce as 'a cross-word-puzzle frozen into a house'—was now the scene of this confused, ill-organized meeting, confined by Hitler's time-table to a single formal session. The two delegations assembled at eleven o'clock; on the Italian side, Ambrosio, Bastianini, and Alfieri; and on the German, Keitel, Warlimont, Rintelen, and Mackensen. Apart from the last, no representative of the German Foreign Office was present.

The company, sitting in a circle in the main lounge, was confronted with a sweeping review of the war in a two-hour monologue from Hitler who held a large file of documents on his lap. 'Mussolini, perched on the edge of an armchair too broad and deep for him, listened impassively and patiently, his hands clasped on his crossed legs.' [11]

The Fuehrer began 'with some remarks on the war situation'.[e] The present

d. The message of July 13. See p. 376.

e. Three principal records of Hitler's speech at the Feltre meeting exist. (i) The Italian notes, which are a summary and were found on the table of the Duce after the events of July 25. They are printed in Hitler e Mussolini *op cit* p. 165 ff (ii). The verbatim Italian text, also printed in the Rizzoli edition, is to be found in the Italian Collection, Tarvisio file. This is a translation of the Schmidt minute. (iii) This latter document exists in the German Collection in draft together with handwritten corrections, some of which are of interest as showing Hitler's editing of the record. The corrected Schmidt minute was, at Mussolini's request, sent to him on July 23.

conflict 'was no isolated war like the Franco-German War of 1870–1, but a struggle to determine the fate of Europe'. Control of vital raw materials, 'the material aspect of the conflict', lay at the centre of the struggle. As regards iron and steel production, this was thoroughly assured in those territories controlled by Germany. Iron-ore supplies would suffice under all circumstances. Extensive deposits existed on German Reich territory, particularly in Lorraine. Coal was likewise plentiful, and there was also at the disposal of the Reich the additional supply of coal, steel and iron ore from the East European countries. Just as important as iron, however, was the large number of raw materials, particularly metals such as molybdenum, nickel, chromium and the like, supplies of which had to some extent been assured for the Axis armaments industry in sufficient quantities only during the war by occupation and annexation. These raw materials were quite indispensable to the conduct of the war. There was no particular need to stress the immense importance in this respect of the Balkans, with their important sources of raw materials. Equally important was oil. Hitler had intended for this reason to seize the oil resources of the Caucasus. 'This operation had unhappily not succeeded.' Roumanian oil was thus all the more essential.

The paramount importance of these basic raw materials made it necessary to move in troops to guard those regions whence they came. One must have some understanding of the industrial basis of warfare. In military circles this was often lacking. Hitler had, for example, had to explain in detail the importance to war industry of the Donetz basin before having it properly understood that no heroism could make up for the coal deposits won there should the Donetz basin once be lost. Without nickel and without chromium, production of aircraft engines would come to a complete standstill.

As to the problem of food supplies, this could only be overcome with the aid of the Ukraine, which was helping to feed the army of a million deployed in the Eastern territories. The Ukraine could also export more if more petrol were made available for agriculture, particularly for tractors.

'If we could safeguard all the regions containing raw materials of military importance that were now in our hands, from Northern Norway to the Balkans and from the Ukraine to France, the war could be carried on indefinitely. Its continuance would then be simply a matter of mobilizing the necessary manpower. *This was a question of willpower: if we were to save the nations from ruin we must shrink from no hardship. We should not adopt the totally mistaken attitude that present-day defeats could be made good by future generations.'* f Hitler 'was sacrificing the whole of his time and personal comfort to the task of bringing about a settlement in his own lifetime'.

At midday the conference was interrupted. The Duce's secretary came into

f. This passage, and those following in the text, were underlined by Hitler in the draft minutes of the conference recorded by Schmidt.

the room, holding a paper, which he handed to his chief. Mussolini read, translating aloud into German, a brief communiqué. 'At this moment the enemy is engaged in a violent bombardment of Rome.' But even this news was but an irrelevant interruption to the strident voice.

There would soon come a turning-point in the U-boat war, especially when the new types, equipped with the latest technical devices, were brought out. As regards the Air Force, mass production of aircraft had only just got into its stride. Hitler then mentioned 'two new weapons he preferred not to enlarge upon, which would be used against the British at the end of the winter and against which they would have no way of defending themselves. Even Germany possessed no means of defence against them apart from her geographical position.

'Turning to the military operations, the Fuehrer stated that the question on the Eastern Front was to weaken the opponent as much as possible before winter set in. The twenty-one divisions lost at Stalingrad and several others besides had been re-formed. In the past year 32 divisions, including 8 light armoured divisions, had been earmarked for an attack on Mesopotamia (sic). They had unfortunately had to be used during the winter in Russia to relieve the crisis there, so that the project for which they were originally intended had had to be shelved.

'Germany was also having to supply an air force on a vast front, beginning in the North, where cover had to be provided for the convoys transporting iron ore from Sweden to Germany. If there were no more iron, no more aircraft engines could be built. These communications had therefore to be protected. But this was done chiefly by means of first-rate ground organization of the airfields.

'If—as had happened in Italy—300–400 out of 500–600 machines were destroyed on the ground, it meant that organization was simply bad. One just could not afford to pander to private interests in such matters. Every hardship imposed now would be a minor matter compared to what would happen if we lost the war. Germany had drawn her conclusions. Private considerations would be entirely swept aside. Airfields would be enlarged, runways for the aircraft constructed and protective walls, to shield individual machines against bomb splinters, erected wherever this might be necessary, and without regard to objection from private persons. Nor should the question of compensation play any part. If the war were won, then compensation could be paid. But if it were lost it would no longer be necessary, since the claimants would no longer be alive.'

It was quite inadmissible that in Sicily and Southern Italy 27 machines should have been destroyed on the ground on one day, and 52 on another day, owing to the unprofessional, unmilitary conduct of the ground personnel. Italy herself must find the personnel to staff these airfields. A labour force of this kind could of course not be sent from Germany—there were simply not enough men. With proper organization losses through the destruction of machines on the ground could be cut to a small percentage. 'In Germany and the West it was generally only 1 or 2 machines per raid. If the German Air Force had lost as many aircraft on the Eastern Front as had been lost through ill-organized airfields in Italy, it would have succumbed to the Russians long ago.'

As to the strategic problem of convoys at sea, Hitler recalled that the German Navy had needed strong pressure on his part before consenting to use warships for transport purposes. He emphasized the need for using cruisers, too, as troop transports, since they were fast vessels and as such less vulnerable to air attack. He pointed to the example of the British mine-laying cruisers that had supplied Malta in the most difficult days of the struggle. All the arguments of prestige advanced by the Navy must be silenced. Fast transport craft of the type just mentioned were needed for Sardinia, Corsica and the Dodecanese. Emotional arguments should be dismissed.

'Turning to the question of Sicily, the Fuehrer said he was in two minds. If reinforcements could be ensured Sicily would have to be defended, and, at a given moment, defence would have to revert to attack. But this presupposed that the hinterland was safe. If this were not the case then it would be better to withdraw from Sicily, though it was clear to him that this would mean a heavy blow to morale. The best solution of course would lie in defending the island. This postulated the complete protection of supply lines, and in particular the safeguarding of the crossing from Messina.

'Strong and excellently equipped infantry divisions would be far better as a defence force than armoured divisions, which were suitable for attack but not for defence. What was involved here was the fundamental decision as to whether we should actually fight. If so we would have to bear all the consequences of our decision in a fanatical spirit. If we did not want these battles, every man we sent to Sicily would be sent in vain.' Reichsmarshal Goering was ready to concentrate a large number of anti-aircraft batteries at Messina to cover the reinforcements. Additional supplies could then be moved up from other parts of Italy, where they would of course have to be replaced immediately by equipment from Germany. 'What was definite, however, was that every soldier and every officer who deserted an army or naval battery while there was still so much as a single shot left in it, must be shot. This was a question of training, and as experience showed would take some time to inculcate. To begin with, therefore, Germany would accompany the batteries she supplied with tough, proven German personnel.

'For the purpose of warding off attacks on Southern Italy, far more Italian units must be also concentrated in the "toe" than there were at present.' Hitler was following closely the proposals of his military advisers.

'It was therefore of fundamental importance to establish whether we believed that the decisive battle would preferably take place on the Italian mainland itself. If so, then every man we sent to Sicily would be wasted. Armoured divisions took a very long time to replace once lost, for tank warfare was largely a matter of routine and experience, demanding lengthy troop training and exercise. If, however, we wanted to hold Sicily, we must bear all the consequences, down to the very last. In that event, Germany would send in crack units. But such a decision would entail considerable re-casting of plans. What had happened now in Sicily must not be allowed to happen again! Several German units had had to be sent down, to establish first a defensive front, then a full-scale offensive front . . . If we held the position in Sicily and concentrated the attack on the British supply lines, in a few months' time the British would find themselves in the greatest difficulties as a result of the renewal of submarine warfare mentioned before. The Sicilian operation might then turn out to be a catastrophic defeat for them . . .'

Hitler was opposed to saying that the Axis would not hold Sicily but only Southern Italy. That way they would end up by only being able to hold Central Italy, and in the end only the North. The more advanced the defence position, the more effective it would be, and it would also have favourable repercussions on those parts of the interior which were threatened by air attack.

'If we decided to hold out we must steadfastly abide by the consequences of such a step, in the same way as he (the Fuehrer) had intervened in Germany with the utmost severity. Fifteen-year-old youths had been posted to anti-aircraft batteries as Luftwaffe auxiliaries. The fire brigades in areas threatened from the air were composed of elderly and very young persons. Women had been enlisted for productive labour on a far-reaching scale; since peasant women were needed on the land, and many women were in any case already working in industry, these measures had affected all women, even those from the middle and upper classes of society. At the same time he had also intervened at the front, and personally dismissed any proven officers who had temporarily lost their nerve. Italy, too, had a fundamental decision to make: it entailed the most drastic consequences and made it necessary to overcome all obstacles.'

As regards Italian requests for war material, Hitler said that a demand for 2,000 aircraft was of course impossible for Germany to honour in practice, and in view of the airfield situation was quite pointless. Nor could air force units be simply transferred from the Eastern Front, as owing to the completely different tactics obtaining there they would need a month's training first. 'The war would be won in the first place by men, and then by tanks, anti-tank guns, aircraft and anti-aircraft weapons.'

Hitler turned to the situation in South-East Europe where he had just reorganized the German commands and was dispatching Rommel to Salonika. He announced that several more German divisions would be moved to the Balkans, particularly to Greece.

'Before lunching alone with the Duce, the Fuehrer once again stressed that Sardinia and Corsica could only be held if defence got under way the moment the landings took place. The Fuehrer expressed concern as to the behaviour of the Corsican population. At this point the Duce spoke for the only time during the meeting. He stated that the Corsicans were now reasonably quiet. He had been showing signs of uneasiness, shifting in his armchair, wiping his forehead, and appearing to be in pain.' [g]

The delegations dispersed for luncheon. The Italians were indignant and frustrated. They gathered round the Duce in a last attempt to persuade him to counter Hitler's stand in private. As he joined the group—Ambrosio, Bastianini, and Alfieri—his first remark was: 'I am very upset to be away from the capital at such a moment. I would not like the Romans to think . . .' As Alfieri commented: 'In the position in which he was, his only thought was that the Romans should not imagine that he had gone away on purpose! I must admit that at this instant my devotion for Mussolini was put to a severe test.' [12]

His advisers pressed for a frank and final approach to the Germans to seek a way out from the alliance and the war. Ambrosio in particular 'used stronger language to Mussolini probably than he had ever heard'. Having listened to Keitel on the train journey, the Italian Chief of the General Staff was certain, if he needed such a confirmation, that the Germans would not be able to reinforce the Italian front. According to Bastianini who was listening, Ambrosio now delivered without any introduction an 'ultimatum' to the Duce, to get out of the war within fifteen days.[h]

Mussolini controlled a brusque gesture of impatience, and told everyone to sit down. 'Perhaps you think,' he said, 'that this problem has not been consciously in my mind for a long time. Under a seemingly impassive mask there is a deep torment, which tears my heart. I admit the hypothesis: to detach ourselves from Germany. It sounds so simple: one day, at a given hour, one sends a radio message to the enemy . . . But with what consequences? The enemy rightly will insist on a capitulation. Are we ready to wipe out at one stroke a régime of twenty years and the results of a long bitter effort, to admit our first military and political defeat, to disappear from the world scene? It is so quickly said: detach ourselves from Germany . . . What attitude will Hitler take? Perhaps you think that he would give us

g. The above text is based on the Schmidt minute.
h. Bastianini *op cit* pp. 120–1. There is some confusion among the witnesses as to the order of events. This ragged conversation may have taken place after luncheon and before the last meeting of the two leaders on the return journey.

liberty of action?' [13] In this last phrase lay perhaps the wisps of a solution.

The Duce's secretary came to tell him that Hitler was awaiting him for luncheon. The only direct record of what passed between the two men appears in Mussolini's notes written down a month later. 'After the Fuehrer's speech, we had our first discussion in private. He gave me two most important pieces of information. (1) That submarine warfare was about to be resumed with new means. (2) That at the end of August the Reprisals Air Fleet would commence operations against London, which would be razed to the ground in a few weeks. Among other things, I told him that, in anticipation of reprisals, the air defences of Italy would have to be strengthened. I was again called away to the telephone, and in the meanwhile the time of departure had arrived.' [14] i

According to Rintelen, the Duce had promised Ambrosio to make a final attempt during the train journey to describe to Hitler Italy's desperate situation. 'He (Mussolini) only asked for further German help, especially in the air. He could not bring himself to admit that Italy could not fight any longer.' [15] j

The two leaders travelled alone on the train to Treviso. Mussolini wrote later: 'It was only in the train on the way back that I was able to make quite clear the following points: Italy, I said, was at the moment being called upon to bear the full burden of the onslaught of two empires, the British Empire and the United States. She was in danger of being overwhelmed; the air attacks were not only undermining the morale of the people, but were also causing grave damage to war production and to the whole social fabric of the nation's life. I repeated that the African campaign would have taken a very different turn if we had had superiority, or at least parity, in the air. Finally I told him that the moral tension in the country was very great. He replied that the crisis in Italy was a phase, and that he would send further reinforcements to strengthen the air and land defences of the peninsula. The defence of Italy, he declared, was of the utmost importance to Germany. The tone of our conversation was very friendly, and we parted

i. According to Bastianini it was intended to hold an afternoon conference. Was this postponed in the confusion and because Mussolini feared an imminent political crisis in Rome? See Bastianini *op cit* p. 165.

j. Mussolini later told his conducting officer, Admiral Maugeri, who accompanied him to Ponza, a more cloudy version: 'The talk at Feltre did not go off well. It was supposed to last three days and lasted three and a half hours. I was very vexed at not having been in Rome during the raid. As usual none of the questions on the agenda were dealt with at all, but only quite different ones. I repeated my old theme: peace with Russia. Impossibility of the Germans giving us any substantial aid.' Admiral Maugeri, who in July was head of the Italian Naval Intelligence, stated later: 'My agent there (at Feltre) reported that Hitler could be heard shouting and screaming several times, pounding the table with his fists. The Duce attempted to shout him down, but each time he was smothered beneath an angry abusive torrent.' Maugeri, *From the Ashes of Disgrace* (1948), p. 118. No other witness has confirmed or denied this version.

on the best of terms.' [16] The only recorded remark of Hitler was that 'during our last meeting at the station, the Duce suddenly remarked: "I do not know how my generals reason, where they want to defend Italy, and why they keep such strong forces in the North." ' [17]

On the return journey in the train from Feltre to Treviso, Ambrosio and Keitel held a second discussion in the presence of Warlimont and Rintelen. Keitel raised again the possibility of reinforcing Southern Italy 'in the sense that the Italians should eventually contribute at least two more divisions'. Perhaps these could be withdrawn from the Italian Eighth Army in France, but, as Ambrosio pointed out, 'the withdrawal of divisions from France would have political repercussions, and such a question should be consequently put in the first instance to the Duce'. Keitel continued, 'It now remained to decide if one wanted to defend Sicily to the last. The Fuehrer has said that in Sicily one is defending Italy. Naturally if one accepts to defend Sicily to the end, the actual forces are not sufficient. At the present time the Germans have not the means to make a unilateral effort. In order to move eventually troops from the West, they will first have to be replaced and the divisions earmarked for this purpose are still re-forming.' Ambrosio asked how long it would take for them to arrive.

Keitel replied, 'As quickly as possible. As soon as the decision about Sicily has been taken.' He then produced the final ultimatum of the German High Command.

(1) From the tactical point of view: increase of forces to enable the setting up of a robust line, withdrawing the mobile units to a second position. (Two divisions.)

(2) From the operational point of view: the assurance of supplies and the creation of strong defence in Calabria and Apulia in Southern Italy.

(3) From the organizational point of view: a rigorous application of measures to give full liberty and control to the military authorities in Southern Italy, in order to organize and make full use of the airfields, railways, roads, depots, etc. The war must be totalitarian, suppressing all private interests and everything devoted to the war and to defence.

Ambrosio added a fourth point. 'We have need of an adequate air force.' Keitel retorted. 'Only after everything has been directed in the sense of the above three points, can all the necessary material be sent to this sector.' But as regards the air force, seven air groups were on their way. In Southern Italy everything must be organized on a military basis and all civil activity placed under the command of the Italian Seventh Army. This was a necessary contribution towards victory. To facilitate the task of this organization the Germans were prepared to set up a liaison staff with the Seventh Army. It was naturally assumed that all orders were an Italian affair.

'If there is a perfect agreement on these three points, I do not doubt that the Fuehrer will make available as much as possible.' Here lay the essence of the German plan.

Keitel went on: 'There are only two alternatives: either to fight with every means to hold our positions in Sicily with the prospect of going over to the offensive, or if we do not intend to do this, it would be better not to send further reinforcements. This point must be cleared up as soon as possible . . . We can dispose of our two infantry divisions for the defence of Calabria, if the Italians do the same. But I repeat I cannot commit myself to obtain from the Fuehrer the dispatch of such divisions unless I have a formal undertaking from you on the three points which I have outlined.'

Ambrosio's answer was sharp. 'We have not such a luxury of divisions. Moreover I believe that we are considering possibilities too far ahead, while our situation requires absolute and urgent measures . . . I make the reservation of examining the question of the availability of our forces. As to the measures of a general and civilian character, the decision rests with the Duce.'

Keitel concluded by saying, 'It is necessary, however, for you to do everything to persuade him to take these measures. We too have had to make grave sacrifices: they are however needed on an even greater scale.' [18]

Rintelen has a summary account of this exchange between the two commanders. He describes Ambrosio as 'unforthcoming and monosyllabic', and adds that he protested again that the Italian Command was not allowed to dispose freely of the German divisions in Italy.[19]

The two leaders took leave of one another at Treviso airport at five o'clock that afternoon.[k] They were not to meet again until the following September and then in revolutionized circumstances. The main cycle of the Axis closed with this encounter.

Mussolini's only later comment was: 'On parting from Hitler I said to him, "Ours is a common cause, Fuehrer." ' [20] He then turned to Keitel and remarked, 'Send everything we require as quickly as you can and remember that we are in the same boat.' [21]

As Hitler's plane took off, the Duce stood with his arm raised at the salute and remained thus until the machine was out of sight. His advisers approached him on the runway. 'I had no need to make that speech to Hitler,' he said, 'because, this time, he has firmly promised to send all the reinforcements which we need.' And turning to Ambrosio, 'Naturally our requests must be reasonable and not astronomic.'[l]

Ambrosio and Bastianini travelled in the same car from the airport to Treviso railway station. The former suddenly burst out, 'Did you hear what he

k. Rintelen says 6 p.m., and that 'at the leavetaking Hitler gave him a mistrustful look'. Rintelen *op cit* p. 215. Presumably he regarded Rintelen as out of sympathy with the German ultimatum.

l. Alfieri *op cit* p. 317. See also Bastianini, *op cit* p. 166. He states that on hearing Mussolini's words Mackensen smiled wanly.

said to Hitler after my warning of this morning? He asked him yet again for
that war material which they will never send. He still deludes himself, and did
not take my words seriously. He is mad, I tell you, mad. What I told him is
serious, very serious.' [22]

All last minute hopes that Mussolini would take issue with his ally,
demonstrate that Italy was at the end of her resources and seek an exit from
the war with German consent, had now vanished. The Italian delegation had
been subjected to a two-hour period of instruction in German, a language
which they imperfectly understood. No simultaneous translation was
made, although the familiar figure of Paul Schmidt, Hitler's personal interpreter, was present. He commented later on the conference: 'This meeting
of July 20, 1943, was one of the most depressing in which I have ever taken
part. Mussolini was so overwrought that on his return to Rome he asked
urgently for my report: we were told that he had not been able to follow
the conversation, and could therefore only consider the defensive measures
agreed upon when he had my text before him. After Hitler had gone through
the report in East Prussia, it was dispatched to the Duce by special plane.' [m]

Rommel was present at these talks, and had spoken with the Duce. He
noted that the latter gave no clear decisions, and 'cannot act as he would
like . . . The Duce is aware of the political intentions of his collaborators.' [23]

This cryptic remark may throw some light on Bastianini's comments on
Ambrosio's attitude at Feltre. 'This brusque change of front by the Chief of
the General Staff, from the decision expressed in writing to fight to the finish
to the fixing of a delay of fifteen days to withdraw from the conflict, did this
neither alarm Mussolini nor make him suspicious? . . . Did it not cross his
mind that this threatening ultimatum revealed the existence of an atmosphere
of "pronunciamento" in high military circles?' [24]

Such an interpretation may be too subtle, and the fragmentary evidence
which exists of these events does not show that, prior to the Feltre meeting, a
date had been settled by the King for the dismissal of the Duce and his replacement by Badoglio, although this might have happened at the royal
audience of July 16 or shortly afterwards.

But the general significance of the Feltre meeting is clear. The Duce in
person bore the historical responsibility for the entry of Italy into the war.
The Sicily landings marked the approaching end of that Italian participation.
Unless, within a matter of days, a tidy formula could be devised releasing
Italy from her obligations under the Axis alliance, approaching military
defeat would be followed by the collapse of the régime. Only Mussolini could
conduct such an operation with German consent. As he had said to Alfieri
during the talks, 'Perhaps you think that he would give us liberty of action?'
Indeed, it might be possible to convince the Germans that their own strategic

m. Schmidt. *Hitler's Interpreter*, p. 263. The meeting had been held on July 19;
this text was not transmitted to the Duce until July 23.

interests lay in withdrawing their divisions intact from the whole Italian theatre, concentrating on the defence line of the Alps, and allowing Italy to treat with the Allies on the basis of neutralizing Italian territory. The future of the Duce's position in Italy depended on some such solution. The significance of the Feltre meeting was that no such formula could be reached or even discussed with Hitler. With this failure vanished any illusion about a tidy exit from the war.

APPENDIX

'The Politico-Military Conduct of the War by the Axis.[n]

The politico-military conduct of the present war is characterized on the German side by a completely continental strategy and a total incomprehension of the decisive importance of the Mediterranean theatre.

In fact, apart from the episode of the air assault on England, and the battle of the Atlantic—to which can probably in the main be attributed a secondary role in favour of the battle for Northern Europe—the whole German effort has always and only been directed against the continental Powers (France—Norway—Russia).

A like tendency is shown by numerous points of fact which are briefly recapitulated:

1. Armistice with France.

The armistice with France was accepted only by taking into account the military necessities of Germany; this has been clearly admitted even in German circles. In fact, General Guderian[o] in a *confidential* conversation with General Marras in April (1943) expressed himself thus. "In 1940 I had urged the Fuehrer to postpone the armistice: I could then have marched on Gibraltar and occupied North Africa with a couple of armoured divisions." [p]

The occupation of French North Africa in 1940—a problem not difficult to solve, given the total lack of preparation of the British and the overwhelming superiority of the Germans—would have permitted the unbarring of the western door of the Mediterranean with the consequent incalculable advantage for the Axis of:

– having the maximum liberty of action in Africa (the possibility of occupying Egypt and of operating in the Middle East and Italian East Africa, and also of exploiting the anti-British ferment in Iraq, and among the Arab peoples.

n. Italian Collection. In a file marked 'Documents for eventual discussion with the German side'. (Conference of Tarvisio.) No date.

o. The German armoured divisional commander in the French campaign.

p. This statement is quoted, without indication of source, by Rossi *op cit* p. 10.

– being able to save the main part of the forces and equipment committed to the defence of the southern frontiers of Europe, and avoiding the burdensome operation of conquest and subsequent occupation in the Balkans.

– exploiting all the resources of North Africa and the Middle East along the most economical sea route of the Mediterranean and without appreciable enemy interference.

– obtaining, perhaps, unforeseen developments of the conflicts in the direction of the Caucasus and India.

The justification (of the German view) that once France had fallen one could foresee the imminent conclusion of the war with England, and at least in a very brief space of time, does not hold. Official German circles, in fact, notwithstanding that they held this erroneous view, equally and rightly were concerned with occupying all the French Atlantic bases, up to the Pyrenees, for the requirements of an eventual continuation of the conflict.

2. *Armour for Italian North Africa.*

From 1940 onwards armoured equipment was requested for the Italian troops in Italian North Africa to put them in a condition to undertake a rapid offensive against the British forces in Egypt. The requests for material were not conceded, in spite of the fact that during the whole of the second half of 1940 and the first quarter of 1941 the German army was not engaged in any operations of war.

A few hundred tanks at that time would have probably been enough to occupy the zone of Suez.

3. *Relations with France.*

The relations with France, given the territorial conditions of the armistice (Mediterranean coast of France—Corsica—and French North Africa not occupied by the Axis) could but have direct and important repercussions on the conduct of the war in the Mediterranean theatre.

The attitude taken up by the Germans in such relations was sharply in contrast with that of the Italians, and often in contradiction to a rational conduct of the war: in fact,

(i) the various haphazard concessions in rearming French North and West Africa were made by the Germans in the main without taking into account the necessities of war in the Mediterranean theatre, and in opposition to the Italian point of view, which initially maintained the need:

– to strengthen Dakar to enable the French to defend themselves against British attacks, but without giving them the eventual possibility of using such material against the Axis;

– to be sparing, on the other hand, of concessions in favour of French North Africa, and especially of Tunisia;

– to pursue simultaneously a direct action to ensure the proper use of the material conceded: (removal of disloyal leaders, and principally of Weygand, for whose removal the Italian Armistice Control Commission had to fight a real battle against the German).

(ii) In December 1941 Italy, having realized that the attitude of wait-and-see which characterized the situation of France after the armistice could not last indefinitely, accepted at face value the good intentions of the French government to turn decisively in the direction of the Axis (Darlan-Vacca Maggiolini conversation in Vichy; declarations of Pétain: Ciano-Darlan meeting in Turin), and after careful consideration of the situation and of the French demands, decided to arrive at a regularizing of relations with France. (Verbal instructions from the Duce to Excellency Vacca Maggiolini.)

Such a solution, which must have brought about within a short space of time the alignment of France on the side of the Axis powers, would have reversed the position in the Mediterranean, and eliminated the harm done by the conclusion of the armistice in 1940. (Contribution of the French fleet, completely loyal to Darlan—use of the first-class bases of French North Africa—liberty of movement in the Mediterranean.)

The German side, to whom the question was put by the Duce, not only refused to accept the Italian point of view, but with a sudden and completely unjustified change of course, adopted an attitude of rigid hostility towards France, making the continuation of negotiations impossible and bringing about the fall of Darlan and probably also, in the long term, his defection.

(iii) In examining the successive demands for strengthening French North Africa, the Italian side, who were henceforward convinced that the French, after the failure of their attempt to draw closer to the Axis, would never again collaborate with the Axis itself, logically took up an attitude, which if not decisively negative, was at least procrastinating.

The Germans, however, sought by every means to meet French requests, declaring themselves convinced of the loyalty of the troops and commanders in French North Africa, notwithstanding the opposite Italian view . . .

4. *Occupation of Malta.*

In the winter of 1941–2, in order to resolve the burdensome problem of the Mediterranean and of supplies to Africa, Italy tackled the planning of the landing on Malta, notwithstanding her modest industrial potential.

The German side accepted the Italian point of view, and collaborated in a responsive manner in the air preparations for the operation and promised a notable assistance in the form of units and material to build up an Expeditionary Corps.

In May 1942, when faced with the chance of carrying out an offensive in Cyrenaica, the Italian Command tenaciously clung to the view that any initiative in Italian North Africa must be subordinated to the occupation of Malta with the aim of ensuring supplies for certain and being in a position to exploit to the full in the strategic field the eventual success of the initial battle.

The German side did not agree, and authorized Rommel to begin offensive operations which, after a brilliant initial victory, ran to ground at El Alamein, precisely from the impossibility of ensuring the necessary supplies.

In consequence of the advance on El Alamein, the German Command, in spite of the contrary view of the Italian, persisted in the conviction that the occupation of Malta was no longer necessary and that one must persist in the effort to reach the zone of Suez.

The Italian side, lacking the main air support which was part of the Expeditionary Corps (for Malta) and the petrol supplies, was obliged to accept the decision of the Ally and postpone *sine die* the operation for occupying Malta, the preparation of which was by then complete.

5. *Supplying of Italian North Africa.*

(i) In July 1941 Italy asked Germany for a loan of a milliard francs to be used mainly in buying various material in Tunisia for supplying the troops operating in Italian North Africa.

Germany, notwithstanding the fact that she was receiving 500,000,000 francs daily for expenses of occupation (in France), saw fit to refuse.

(ii) During the second British offensive against Libya, Italy began negotiations with the French regarding the use of Tunisian bases to supply the expeditionary force in Italian North Africa.

On that occasion also the Germans hindered the course of these negotiations by underhand manoeuvres, and openly declared that they did not wish to take part, although the question was also of interest for supplying the German troops.

(iii) And again, in order to avoid the serious consequences of failing to occupy Malta, the Italian side, following also on the experience of the El Alamein battles, insistently sought from Germany at least enough aircraft to gain sufficient control in the Mediterranean to keep within tolerable bounds the shipping losses between Italy and North Africa. The demands put forward in October, November, and December 1942 had no result.

6. *Reaction to the Anglo-American occupation of French North Africa.*

(i) During the Salzburg conference, in examining the counter-measures to be taken:

(a) Germany reverted to the mistaken idea . . . that a threat to occupy the so-called "free" zone of Metropolitan France would be sufficient to compel the French in North Africa to resist eventual Anglo-American aggression and proposed as a solution to occupy the Free Zone and eventually Corsica, but completely neglecting Tunisia; only as the result of the clear and peremptory Italian attitude was it decided to occupy Tunisia, the firm possession of which, apart from allowing us to continue the war in Africa, would evidently also resolve automatically the problem of the other two theatres.

In actual practice, however, the Germans raised various difficulties and tried to obtain the constitution of an expeditionary corps, consisting only of German troops, with the evident aim of damaging Italy in a region clearly the object of our claims. Such a manoeuvre had the sole effect of delaying the Axis landing in Bizerta and Tunis by 2–3 days, with the consequent and considerable reduction of the initial bridgehead, all to the advantage of our opponents.

(b) The Duce also proposed and tenaciously stressed the expediency of seeking Spanish intervention to cut off at Gibraltar the supplying of the Anglo-American expeditionary force in Algeria.

The Germans, not being able to deny the appropriateness and sense of the operation from a military and political point of view, agreed in the first instance to the Italian proposal suggesting a meeting between Mussolini, Hitler, and Franco. At a second stage they changed their attitude, and came round to the idea of a meeting of two—Mussolini and Franco—which was the equivalent of a polite but clear refusal.

(ii) On a series of occasions (November and December '42, March and April '43) Italy renewed her urgent requests to Germany for air reinforcements to feed the battle in Tunisia. No request was completely and satisfactorily met.

7. Defence of Italian Metropolitan territory. Second Front.

As the course of the battle for Tunisia took shape, Italy became increasingly concerned with the strengthening of the defence of the Mother Country, and as the Anglo-American intention of attempting operations on a vast scale in the Mediterranean became apparent (opening of Second Front), she sought German aid in:

– aircraft, to balance the growing enemy air superiority;

– arms (tanks, artillery, trucks, etc.) and troops to put the coastal defences of Italy in a state to face up to the expected massive enemy assault.

On such occasions we repeatedly pointed out to the Ally:

(a) the importance of the Mediterranean theatre, where having concentrated their main resources the Anglo-Americans were trying to open the Second Front, which if it succeeded would not only have deprived the Axis of the main chances of victory, but even of resistance;

(b) the need to put the defence of the sea frontiers of Italy in such a state as to meet the enemy attack even temporarily, to give time to the Axis reserves, which were ready in Germany, to hasten when needed to the battle zone (manoeuvre on interior lines).

Germany not only agreed partially and tardily to the request for troops and material to strengthen the coastal defences but, in spite of the specific appeals made personally by the Duce, took the initiative of new commitments in Russia whence she was obliged to send the reserves built up at home at the very moment when signs of an imminent landing in Italy were completely clear.

The decisions of the German High Command seem absurd even from a strictly military point of view. Indeed, on the basis of the experience of the campaigns of 1941–2, no decisive successes were foreseeable; whereas a victory in Sicily—an eventuality not improbable to achieve—would have inflicted such losses on the enemy as to make impossible another attempt in strength before the winter season or even the spring of 1944. To such a result must be added the favourable repercussions—also calculable in military terms—on the resistance of the home front, in occupied countries, in the neutral and in the allied countries themselves, repercussions which would be all the greater in view of Anglo-Saxon propaganda and the anxious awaiting of the announced Second Front.

8. *Various.*

(i) The responsible German agencies declared on numerous occasions that the solution of the actual conflict is bound up with the Russian—not with the Mediterranean—theatre.

(ii) In dealing with the problem of Spain, the Fuehrer asserted that he preferred to give arms to countries already fighting for the Axis (Roumania) rather than to those who might be able to fight in the future; which does not alter the fact that concessions of reinforcements to Italy, who was already fighting, were always a subject of haggling.

Arms and equipment were, however, conceded to Turkey, evidently because the Turkish problem directly impinged on the continental theatre.

(iii) The Germans neglected no opportunity to compete with the Italian economy in exploiting the occupied countries, and in utilizing the contribution of the minor allies, thus contributing to the weakening, if indirect, of the military possibilities of the Axis in the Mediterranean.

Although conclusive evidence is lacking, it is not to be excluded that Germany has, partially at least, followed an organic plan of despoiling Italy herself, by systematic purchase of valuable goods by troops in transit or stationed in the peninsula, who have been deliberately and generously supplied with Italian currency.

9. *Conclusion.*

It appears clear and indisputable, from what has been set out, that the Germans, in the conduct of the war, have never had a realistic and panoramic vision of the Axis war, but have let themselves be guided prevailingly by one particular aspect: namely, the German war.

The incomprehension and deliberate lack of appreciation of the importance of the Mediterranean theatre:

(a) can be explained, if not justified, in the politico-military situation of the years 1940–2, when the lack of preparation of the Anglo-Americans could leave out of account decisive enemy operations in the Mediterranean while the possibility existed of liquidating once and for all the Russian danger before the Anglo-Americans completed their preparations.

(b) find no explanation or justification in 1943, when the enemy preparations allowed one to foresee without difficulty that the Anglo-Americans would attempt an attack on the European fortress in the Mediterranean to open that second front whose realization implied almost certainly the military defeat of the Axis.'

CHAPTER FOUR

'FIVE MINUTES TO TWELVE'
The Eve of the Grand Council

ON HIS RETURN from Feltre on the evening of July 19, Marshal Ambrosio drafted a summary of the military questions raised with the Germans at the meeting and on the train journey.

'The Fuehrer does not intend to send the 29th Armoured Division to Sicily, or the 3rd Motorized Division (which anyway is not ready) to Calabria or to move further German forces to Italy unless Italy undertakes a greater commitment in the war. She must therefore dispatch her infantry divisions to Sicily so that the German mobile forces, the 15th and Goering Divisions, can be withdrawn and placed in reserve; send two infantry divisions to Calabria to secure its defence; and, above all, remove all obstacles placed by civilian and private interests in the way of military action, concentrating all authority in Southern Italy in the hands of the Commander of the Italian Seventh Army. In such an event Marshal Keitel takes the view that he can get the Fuehrer to send two German infantry divisions.

'In more general terms, given the fact that the German forces will not be ready for two months and seeing that it is urgent to build up the defence of Southern Italy, it will be necessary to transfer at once the forces available in Northern Italy to the South, and namely Italian divisions, including the Alpine and those re-forming. They will then be replaced in due course by German divisions moving in.'

Ambrosio concluded his report. In answer to the 'well-known Italian point of view . . . the German side recognizes that the Second Front has opened in Italy, but has stated that it cannot send considerable air or armoured reinforcements, and has even made conditions for the dispatch of the minimal reinforcements available'. Ambrosio had already pointed out to Keitel that these conditions were for the Duce to decide.[1]

At noon on July 20, Ambrosio made his routine report to Mussolini, and the situation created by the Feltre talks was reviewed. A rejection of the German ultimatum, for such it was, would inexorably lead to a collapse of the whole Italian front, and with it the régime. An acceptance would imply ultimate German control over the threatened areas of Southern Italy, the *de facto* German military occupation in due course of the North on the pretext of organizing the defence of the Po Valley and the Alpine regions against an Allied landing in the Gulf of Genoa, and the inevitable infiltration of German influence into the Italian High Command and government itself. The decision was stark in its simplicity.

At Feltre, Ambrosio had pressed for the course of rejection and a withdrawal from the war in fifteen days. Mussolini told him calmly, 'I will now write to the Fuehrer to tell him what you in your aggressive statement yesterday represented as being in the interests of the country,' and took a sheet of notepaper to draft a letter asking to be released from the alliance. Ambrosio interjected that 'this could only have been achieved verbally at the Feltre meeting, and pressed his resignation. This was curtly rejected, and Ambrosio withdrew to his work.' [2]

That afternoon Rintelen called on the Duce at Palazzo Venezia, having received instructions from the German High Command to demand an answer to Keitel's 'three points' made on the train journey from Feltre. Ambrosio was present. 'Both had dark looks. The demands of the German War Office were accepted by the Duce. As we left Mussolini's study, Ambrosio explained to me that he had asked to resign.' [3] On the evening of July 21, Rintelen reported to Berlin that the Duce, in the presence of Ambrosio, had said that Sicily would be defended to the last man, but that 'those questions are still open'. [4] As Rintelen reported a few day later, 'In all authoritative military and political circles since the conversations of July 19 exists the overriding doubt whether Germany is in a position to give sufficient aid to Italy in her defensive struggle against invasion.' [5]

If Italy continued as a member of the Axis, the Germans could not prevent her military collapse. The Feltre meeting had demonstrated beyond doubt that Hitler would not discuss the withdrawal of Italy from the war. The essence of his ultimatum was the maintenance of Mussolini as the figurehead of the existing Fascist régime to cover the temporary and limited reinforcement of the Italian theatre, militarily to gain time to organize an orderly withdrawal to a tenable front against the Allies in Central Italy, and politically to take counter-measures against a threat of a coup d'état in Rome. Having thus forced certain military measures on Mussolini after the Feltre meeting, which might serve to delay the Allied invasion of the Italian mainland, what political precautions, if any, did the Germans take in the event of the threat of a coup d'état against the Duce?

On July 19 Himmler had written to Bormann a letter enclosing a message from Rome. 'I have received the following report from reliable sources. It comes with absolute certainty from the circles of the Committee of Five and I would ask you as soon as possible to bring it before the Fuehrer . . . Thanks to Italian circles friendly to the Axis, a counter-movement to resist these developments has been set up in a loosely organized form . . . Riccardi has been designated as the leading figure. The movement is directed by a Committee of Five.[a] . . . This counter-movement aims at setting up a War Cabinet to carry out an anti-Freemason, anti-Jewish, and pro-German policy, the radical exclusion of traitors of every kind, the reconstruction of the Fascist Grand Council in permanent session, the creation of a unified military command for the Axis forces. They seek German support for putting the Duce completely in the picture, with the aim of immediate granting of full powers to Riccardi, together with one of his above-named collaborators.' [6] The name of Riccardi occurs frequently in German Intelligence reports from Rome. As Minister of Exchange and Currency from 1939 to February 1943, he had been involved heavily in financial dealings with the German authorities. After his dismissal he seems to have been one of the leading German informers in Italian circles, but in event of an extreme Fascist administration he had not the stature to head a government. The leading specialist in crisis situations, and also a member of this group, was Farinacci, as at the time of the murder of Matteotti in 1924.

On the afternoon of July 21 Farinacci requested an interview with the German Ambassador. He wished to 'speak out openly on the internal situation' and inform Mackensen 'about certain inner political events which have happened here during the last week'. Marshal Cavallero accompanied Farinacci 'as a friend . . . and almost exclusively as a listener'. Farinacci began by describing the meeting of the Party leaders with Mussolini on July 16. Joint proposals had been made to the Duce 'on the inadmissibility of the present methods of government, and at the same time pointing out that it was five minutes to twelve'. Farinacci and the others had been assured by Mussolini that the three Service ministries, in Farinacci's view the most important, 'would be filled with their own ministers, and that the Grand Council would be summoned by the end of the week'.

The conversation with the German Ambassador turned to the Feltre talks. Farinacci had learnt the results in general terms from Scorza, who had been told by Mussolini, but 'his information referred only to that part in which there had been talk of the extent of eventual German aid'. At this point Mackensen interrupted to say 'that in view of the confidence which I enjoy of the Duce and Bastianini, which is the . . . basis of my work, I must naturally inform Bastianini of the content of this conversation, and also I must ask him (Farinacci), when criticizing the person of the Duce, not to

a. According to this report, associated with them were Ricci, Farinacci, Rossoni, Preziosi, Bastianini and others, many generals and prefects.

forget that I was not only his personal friend but in the first instance the representative of the Fuehrer'. Farinacci answered that he would take this into account, but that in the situation in which Italy found herself today, he must nevertheless speak openly, as he wished the Fuehrer to see clearly the real attitude of Fascism which he and his friends represented. Mackensen then added his version of the Feltre meeting. 'The Fuehrer had not made any "conditions" to the Duce, but had sketched out plainly the prerequisites which must be fulfilled before German military help would make any sense, and only after that could it naturally be achieved. And in the first instance, that our troops stationed in Italy should not have difficulties placed in their way in regard to their installations, air bases, quarters, etc. from the Italian side by Prefects, Federal Secretaries, or mayors. Only a radical change in this respect, a removal of all bureaucratic frictions, and a rigorous supervision of the Duce's orders could bring about a change.' In developing his thoughts on this theme, Farinacci spoke in a manner 'which almost word for word corresponded with what the Fuehrer told the Duce at Feltre, and what the Fuehrer mentioned to me at his Headquarters'.

The main purpose of the interview was now unfolded. Farinacci 'produced the idea, not of a directorate, but of one man, with absolute powers to issue decrees, a sort of Minister of the three Armed Forces . . . My conception of what we would call a battle headquarters he seized on with enthusiasm and thought that this was the only right solution.'

In a swift analysis of the political scene Farinacci scattered a handful of judgments. The King was 'indissolubly bound to the Duce by conviction'. Next to the Crown Prince was 'a small question mark'. Badoglio was 'absolutely against the Duce'.[b] Grandi 'hoped to count for something by holding back', and Ciano was 'politically finished'. Farinacci then attacked the Italian Army and in particular the officer corps in a destructive way which was 'completely in line with that of the Fuehrer'. Up to this point Cavallero had not uttered a word, and now made his only contribution to the dialogue. He 'thought, although he was hesitant, that one must make reservations, but this did not alter anything, for he too recognized that in this matter much, if not all, needs overhauling'.[c]

b. Mackensen noted in brackets 'Bastianini agrees with this'. Farinacci also cryptically referred to Badoglio as being 'in close touch' with the Duke of Spoleto (the nominal King of Croatia), 'a frondeur sick with ambition'. It is not impossible that Badoglio toyed with the idea of seeking a royal figurehead within the divided family of King Victor Emmanuel.

c. In Cavallero's memorandum dictated after his later arrest, and dated August 27, 1943, he refers to this meeting, and seems to summarize accurately Mackensen's account. Cavallero only added that 'reference was made, I think by Mackensen, to a combined command, with a veiled tendency to make the German element prevail, to which I said clearly that this absolutely would not work, and in my view one should think of attaching to the Italian Command a subordinate German headquarters'. Cavallero also added, 'This is my only contact, and it is seen to be an anodyne one, with the German authorities since January until today.' Canevari *op cit* p. 12.

From this conversation, and from other reports, Mackensen formed a particular impression of the Roman crisis, namely that an energetic group represented by Farinacci in the higher ranks of the Party, and in league with Cavallero, had forced a meeting of the Grand Council which would call for the same basic military and administrative reforms as Hitler had pressed at Feltre. This action would be the decisive element in the next days, and, if all went according to plan, might provide the political counterpart to the military measures now being taken by the German General Staff.

A curious passivity henceforward overtakes German action in Italy, almost as if their plans were prepared for every eventuality. A strange leaking of Hitler's thoughts at this moment reached the circles of the clandestine German opposition. Just after Feltre Goerdeler wrote to Field Marshal von Kluge, 'Hitler has told his entourage that his aim is the partition of Italy. In the end, he said, Mussolini will be forced to turn to him and perhaps he will make him governor of Northern Italy and make the Apennines the German Frontier.'[8] This was a startling and unconscious prophecy.

The troop movements requested in Keitel's ultimatum on July 19 to Ambrosio would provide the immediate delaying action against Allied invasion in the South and, in the second stage, lead to the transfer of Italian divisions to Calabria from the North where they would be replaced by Rommel's new Army Group now in formation with the ultimate task of reconstructing the German front in Central Italy. Such measures would also ensure the taking over of Italian military commitments on Italian metropolitan territory in the event of a sudden collapse or coup d'état. It is also significant that 'for reasons of the impressions gained at Feltre' Jodl had ordered that the preliminary alert for operations 'Alaric' and 'Konstantin' should be called off. [9]

This complacency seemed justified when on July 22 Ambrosio formally requested the dispatch of the two German divisions to Northern Italy and the transfer of the 29th Motorized Division from Calabria to Sicily, stressing that 'it is indispensable that the German reinforcements sent into Italy be freely employed by the Italian High Command'. [10] These German troop movements began on July 23.

On July 21 Rommel had been suddenly switched from his skeleton command in Southern Germany, pending the setting-up of the German Army Group in North Italy, to take up the defence of Greece and the Aegean islands. The general assumption of German military planning had been that a major crisis in Italy would be followed on the Allied side by a landing in South-Eastern Europe.

'Already on July 19 the King conveyed to us (*sic*) the decision to liquidate Mussolini.' [11] Ambrosio had returned from Feltre only that evening, and had driven from the station with Colonel Montezemolo, the liaison officer of the

Italian War Office with the High Command, to his office in the War Ministry. There is no record of any audience with the King that evening. It is however significant that the King later stated that when he received Mussolini to hear his version, he 'already knew of the conversation at Feltre from what both General Ambrosio and Colonel Montezemolo had reported to me'. [12] The mention of the latter suggests that the two men drove direct from the station to be received by the King on the evening of July 19, and that during the conversation the latter did make at least a preliminary decision, and that in any event he seems to have made up his mind to act by the time he saw the Duce on July 22, and had planned to arrest him after the next routine audience on July 26.

Before going to report to Mussolini the following morning, Ambrosio received a visit from the Prince of Piedmont, and, perhaps more significantly, in the late afternoon Acquarone came to the War Ministry. [13]

On July 19, the day of the bombardment of Rome and the return from Feltre, in Anfuso's words, 'the conspiracy took definite shape: each character put on his mask and came onto the stage'. [14]

The news had seeped round Rome that the summit conference had produced no lightning and magic formula. A buzz of activity followed. Early on July 21, Bottai called on Farinacci at his hotel and both men went to seek out Bastianini in his office to learn what had been the outcome of the meeting with the Germans. The description was discouraging. 'An atmosphere of embarrassment, uneasiness and ambiguity had hung over the talks.' There was no sign from above. Bottai, who saw Scorza later in the day, records that the Party Secretary 'is waiting for Mussolini to confirm the meeting of the Grand Council and fix the date. He tells me that the boss has shown no critical reaction to the démarche of the sixteenth.'[d]

Grandi had hitherto kept aloof in Bologna from the Roman arena. He had refused to attend the meeting of Party leaders on July 16 in spite of an angry telegraphic summons from Mussolini 'to justify his refusal to obey'. While in Bologna Grandi had drafted a series of papers. He first sent a private letter to General Puntoni after the Sicily landings. 'Almost a hundred years to a day since a great King of Piedmont promulgated the Statute of the Realm and drew his sword to give Italy liberty, unity and independence, the fatherland is running towards defeat and dishonour.' He then wrote two letters 'of equal tenor' to the King and to Mussolini enclosing the substance of his ultimate motion submitted to the Grand Council, whose summoning had been accepted by the latter on July 16.[e]

d. The delegation of Fascist Party orators. See Bottai *op cit* p. 289.
e. For Grandi's account of the following days see his interviews published in the periodical *Oggi* (May–June 1959). His letter to Puntoni is mentioned in the latter's diary under the date of July 21. There is no trace of the letter to Mussolini.

The essence of Grandi's 'Programme' as now outlined was twofold: firstly, a thorough reform of the conduct of national affairs by reconstituting and resuscitating the existing organs of government. The Chamber, the Council of Ministers, the various Ministries, and above all the Grand Council itself must be allowed to function. The personal rule of one man had destroyed the administrative process, as both Cini and De Marsico had already pointed out at the meeting of the Council of Ministers on June 19. Secondly, the military conduct of the war must be separated from the control of political affairs and must revert to where it theoretically lay, until usurped by the Duce in 1940, to the Crown.

Federzoni was also at that time in Bologna, and the two men consulted together before leaving for the capital. Grandi now decided to return to Rome and enter the political arena which he had been avoiding since June.[f]

On the morning of July 21 he called on Scorza, who told him that Mussolini, 'descending from the train' on his return from Feltre had ordered the Party Secretary to summon the Grand Council for July 24.[g] During this talk at Scorza's office it seems that Grandi gave him the draft text of his motion, for according to Mussolini the latter received the Party Secretary the same morning at the hour of the usual report, and was handed a copy. 'I read the document—a pretty long one of more than three pages—and handed it back to Scorza declaring that the document was inadmissible and contemptible. Scorza put it back in his briefcase and did not insist further. It was on this occasion that Scorza made me a rather ambiguous speech in which he spoke of a "shocker" or "super-shocker" which might be in store, a speech to which I did not attribute great importance.' [15]

Grandi's document was in no sense revolutionary, and his solution was deceptively simple. It was the spirit of application, not the structure, of the Fascist State which was at fault. The régime was out of joint because of the political method, or lack of method, of the Duce. If he could not be persuaded of this, the only incalculable and untried sanction was the royal prerogative, and for its use there was no precedent in the twenty years of Fascist history. And here Grandi was as much at a loss as everyone else, and in the end equally deluded. With deliberate calculation, and using all his political capital, he set to work to rally support for his project, not as a conspirator, but essentially as a politician. He left Scorza's office at midday, and went first to Feder-

f. The chronology of these days is confusing and contradictory. According to Grandi's account he must have reached Rome at the latest on the 20th. Bottai states that he arrived the following evening.

g. In fact Mussolini returned by air to the capital. This announcement by Scorza of the decision to summon the Grand Council may have been premature. See Bottai, *op cit* pp. 289–90. He may however have seen Mussolini on the morning of July 20 at the usual daily meeting. According to Alfieri, Scorza was instructed to issue invitations 'on the morning after Feltre'. This is probably correct.

zoni's house where he also found Bottai. 'We all three thought alike. There was no need of discussion.'

Grandi's next move was to make a final attempt to persuade the Duce to accept his proposals, either after debate in the Grand Council, or without summoning that body at all. Grandi had never pressed for its summoning, presumably because of the danger of giving a focus to the Party machine either under the leadership of Scorza or Farinacci or both. The Grand Council was also the traditional forum where Mussolini asserted his personal authority over the leaders of the régime. Grandi's later thesis was that the final summons was only sanctioned after Mussolini had talked to Hitler and that it was the latter who provoked this step by referring to the 'treachery' of many members of the Grand Council. It was thus the Germans who were ultimately responsible for the meeting, and their real motives were to supply the setting for a dramatic move by Farinacci to initiate the German 'plan' for Italy as conceived at the Feltre meeting, and face the Duce with a *fait accompli*.

At five o'clock that afternoon (July 24) Grandi was received at Palazzo Venezia. The formal pretext for the interview was for Grandi to hand to the Duce a copy of a book on the London Non-Intervention Committee during the Spanish Civil War. On arrival, Grandi was shown by the usher the list of appointments: he was allotted twenty minutes. As he passed through the ante-room, which was the Grand Council room, and where the chairs were already arranged for the forthcoming meeting, Grandi was aware of a senior German officer seated. The usher explained that he was Field Marshal Kesselring, who would be received next by the Duce for a lengthy interview.

According to the Duce, in this conversation 'Grandi touched on various points, but said nothing of what was to come'. [16] Grandi has recorded that the ensuing conversation, which lasted 'at least three-quarters of an hour'[h] was not stormy as subsequently alleged.[i] 'I told Mussolini everything that I had to tell him, and which I later repeated to him in front of the Grand Council.' He listened patiently and at the end said in quiet tones, 'You would be right if the war had been lost.' The Germans would produce a secret weapon which would revolutionize the situation. Grandi then asked him to renounce the idea of summoning the Grand Council, and to carry out of his own free will the proposals put forward in the draft motion. At this point Mussolini hardened. 'I will not hand over the reins of command to anyone.' Grandi took his leave. It was the last time the two men were to meet alone.

h. See Mackensen's telegram of July 22, 1943, based on Kesselring's remarks to him.
i. Grandi had been accompanied to Palazzo Venezia by Mario Zamboni, a National Councillor of the Party, and a close friend. The latter's impressions have a stronger note. The atmosphere of the talk had been bad-tempered, Mussolini had shown 'a polemical aversion' to Grandi's order of the day, and both men had discussed the course of events 'without any possibility of clarification'.

There is little further evidence of this key conversation. Giacomo Acerbo, Minister of Finance, stated that 'at Palazzo Venezia I met Grandi just as he was leaving the Duce's office, and he confirmed to me that the latter, albeit with clenched teeth, had authorized the presentation of the motion'.[17] That evening Bottai noted in his diary: 'I returned to see Grandi who had just come back from Palazzo Venezia, where he had found Mussolini "roused like a lion but not too much so". He was able to talk to him and say some tough things. He had above all narrowed him down to the argument of a national government, and the complete return of the King to the command of the Armed Forces.' [18]

The next day Kesselring informed the German Ambassador of Grandi's visit. 'Field Marshal Kesselring tells me that when he called on the Duce yesterday (July 21) he had to wait a long time as Grandi was with him.[j] This latter interview lasted at least three-quarters of an hour. The Duce apologized for the delay due to receiving Grandi, whom he described as a "trustworthy man". In connection with what Farinacci told me yesterday, although Grandi has been called upon by him to take part in a joint approach to the Duce, he had kept away and excused himself on the grounds of ill-health. This interview of Grandi with the Duce seems to me to be highly significant.' [k]

This 'significance', and the danger from the German point of view, might well be a repetition of Mussolini's tactics of a 'Changing of the Guard', as in the previous February, but with the contrary object of forming an administration to seek a 'political' solution of the war. Grandi in such a case might be the obvious Foreign Minister.

Action by Farinacci and his friends was a matter of increasing urgency. In concluding his telegram to Ribbentrop, Mackensen wrote perhaps rather plaintively, 'The summoning of the Grand Council has, as far as I know up to the present moment, not yet taken place.'

It does not appear that Mussolini asked for, nor had the King proposed, a special royal audience after his return from Feltre, and he was received as a matter of routine on the morning of Thursday, July 22. Since coming to power twenty years before, he had been received in audience by the Sovereign at the Quirinal every Monday and Thursday. During recent months both men seemed to have avoided the mutual embarrassment of a serious discussion of the looming crisis. As Alfieri wrote, 'In such a manner a neutral zone between the King and the Duce had come into being which each for contrary reasons did not wish to cross.' [19]

Mussolini found the King 'frowning and nervous. "A tense situation," he

j. There is unfortunately no record of this meeting. The relevant collection of minutes in the Italian Collection ends on July 15.

k. German Collection. July 22, 1943. Mackensen telegram 'For Ribbentrop personally.' Farinacci's remarks about Grandi do not appear in Mackensen's previous telegram.

said. "It cannot go on much longer . . . We must tell the Germans our dilemma." [1] The King stated later that Mussolini 'came to talk to me . . . I listened to the account of the Prime Minister. At Feltre Hitler had done almost all the talking in order to prove that the war was not lost. I observed that the Germans in Russia, in Africa, and also in Sicily, without any regard to the Pact or to honour, had retreated and left us in the lurch whenever it seemed to them the right moment. The situation in Italy was such that the dilemma must be put to the Germans . . . I prefer to avoid ruin and distress to my country, rather than sacrifice everything to a now useless resistance . . . Mussolini started talking to me of the German secret weapons. I interrupted him: "The best secret weapons are those which are best known." He took leave of me. The rest is known.' [m] Puntoni records that he found the King, after Mussolini's departure, 'dark in the face and frowning. At first he seemed to find it difficult to speak and then finally, as if to free himself from a weight which oppressed him, he said: "I tried to make the Duce understand that it was his person, which was not only the target of enemy propaganda, but also was aimed at by public opinion, which prevented an internal recovery, and called in question a precise definition of our military situation. He did not understand or did not wish to do so. It was as if I was talking to the wind." ' [20]

The formal invitations to the Grand Council for Sunday, July 24 had been issued the previous day from Fascist Party headquarters, and Grandi and his friends had exactly two days to complete their political action. The intention was to gain the support of the majority of the members of the Grand Council before the meeting. The inner group agreed on a more simple draft of the motion, and the collection of signatures began. Grandi went from his meeting with the Duce to call on Scorza. He announced that he would present his motion, and returned to his friends, Ciano, Bottai, Federzoni, and others. Scorza was kept informed of their conclaves and their intentions. De Marsico, the Minister of Justice, called on Grandi that evening, and brought his legal knowledge to bear on the redrafting of the document.

On the morning of July 23, there was much coming and going at the Party Headquarters in Palazzo Wedekind. Towards midday Grandi arrived with Bottai, and there they found Ciano in discussion with the Party Secretary. Ciano stated later, during his interrogation before his trial, 'I found him

1. Mussolini *Memoirs op cit* pp. 52–3. He says that the meeting took place on Wednesday, July 21. It took place however on the following day. Puntoni's record is more reliable. It is strange that Mussolini should have incorrectly dated this important meeting.

m. Nino Bolla, *Il Segreto di Due Re*, pp. 74–5. This apologetic version, written by the Press Officer attached to the Royalist government in the South after September 1943 may be a somewhat imaginative reconstruction.

(Scorza) somewhat preoccupied and depressed; he thought that the situation was grave, but believed nevertheless that on the home front the Party had sufficient forces and means to control it. During the conversation Grandi arrived and spoke of the need to raise national morale and referred to a motion which he had drafted and to which in principle several comrades had agreed, among them Federzoni.' [21]

The arrival of Farinacci at Party Headquarters struck a different note, and brought back memories of past internecine strife within the Fascist ruling clan. The boss of Cremona had always been an untouchable. His conception of Fascism as a permanent revolution had nothing in common with the 'constitutional' version of Grandi, Federzoni, and Bottai. His presence was embarrassing at this moment, as his close connections with the German Embassy and agencies in Rome were no secret, and, for tactical reasons, Grandi and his friends were not anxious to reveal in their present political move any hint at this stage of disloyalty to the Axis. Their formal programme was one of political and military reconstruction in order to carry on the war. As Bottai notes: 'We all sensed the meaning and limits of his (Farinacci's) approval, which was understood as solidarity *jusqu'au bout* with the Germans.' [22] Farinacci was not fooled, and in any event had his own solution. At his house on July 22, after his talk with the German Ambassador, he had, together with Cavallero, drafted a motion which he in his turn intended to produce at the Grand Council.[23] He was by now aware of the text of Grandi's draft and may even have agreed to sign it, perhaps as a deception. There is no evidence to show that he revealed his present intention. The wording of his draft, which followed that of Grandi in nominally calling on the King to assume command of the Armed Forces, concentrated on 'standing fast in the observance of the alliances concluded, and the restoration of all the organs of State', including the Party and Corporations, omitted in Grandi's draft.

Farinacci's private tactics were planned in advance. He would force the dismissal of Ambrosio and the recall, on the very evening of the Grand Council meeting, of Cavallero as Chief of the General Staff. Farinacci himself would be nominated as Minister of the Interior, and the 'defeatist' Party bosses, or at least Grandi, would be arrested.[n]

On July 17 Ciano had returned, like Grandi from Bologna, from a diplomatic retreat at his family home in Leghorn. The two men now spent that afternoon together with Bottai, retouching the draft, first in Grandi's office and then at Bottai's house. It was there that Ciano formally adhered to their plan of procedure. He thought that the Grand Council was not the effective place for such an ultimatum 'as its composition was not purely political', but

n. Canevari *op cit* p. 30. This pamphlet in defence of Cavallero is the only serious attempt to analyse the reactions of Farinacci during these days.

realized that 'the day would be decisive for us all'.[24] His rôle during these hours is not clarified by the available evidence. Anfuso, who had arrived in Rome during the Allied bombardment of July 19, called shortly afterwards on Ciano, who had been watching the air attack. 'He was at home with a political ailment, attached to the many threads of numerous conspiracies.' The house was invaded by numerous Princesses and Countesses. At one point Cini arrived and disappeared in private conclave with Ciano.[o] On departing, the former—by way of explanation—said that Mussolini was mad, and that one must have the courage to remove him. Amid the bustle of visitors, Ciano took Anfuso to one side. 'You don't understand that everything is finished. I cannot tell you anything, but you must understand.' [25]

The final meeting of the group was at Grandi's office on the following morning, July 24. Scorza had been sent a copy of the final draft of the motion. Farinacci arrived, and appeared to agree with everything except freer powers to the King.[p] Alfieri, the Italian Ambassador in Berlin, had been summoned by Scorza to Rome. He too accepted without reserve the line taken in Grandi's document. Other signatures were canvassed.[q] Cianetti, the Minister of Agriculture, came and expressed his agreement. Cianetti's later account of this scene reads: 'Grandi said to me textually, "Dear Cianetti, it is a matter of liberating the Duce from the total responsibility of the conduct of the war; the monarchy to which *we* have given lustre and ornament must be implicated." '[26] Federzoni had sounded out the 'Old Guard', De Vecchi and De Stefani. They too agreed, but did not actually sign.

Shortly after his arrival in Rome, Grandi was invited to call on Acquarone, but decided that he would not do so until after the meeting of the Grand Council.[r] Grandi now sent his friend, Mario Zamboni, to explain his refusal. 'What we are preparing to do in the Grand Council is most dangerous, and

o. Anfuso noted: 'I have never understood to what part of the conspiracy Cini belonged or how much he knew.' *Da Palazzo Venezia al Lago di Garda* p. 284.

p. See Farinacci's version of this episode (Cersosimo *op cit* p. 204). There was a question of inserting 'Political' as well as 'Military'. See also Farinacci in *Regime Fascista*, September 30, 1943. 'When Grandi showed us his order of the day we pointed out to him that the substance was so far from the spirit of Fascism that every squadrista could have deemed it his right to stab him. Naturally if we had in the slightest suspected that there was a pact of treason between Grandi and other members of the Grand Council with Badoglio, the meeting would have had a very different ending.'

q. Annio Bignardi, President of the Confederation of Agricultural Workers, a friend of Italo Balbo from Ferrara, and through this connection in early contact with Grandi, was mobilized. Through the link with Balbo he obtained De Bono's signature. He then approached his two fellow townsmen, Gottardi and Pareschi, who, though favourable in principle, wanted to wait until the meeting. Pellicano *op cit* Article I.

r. In a later account Grandi produced another version. (See articles in *Oggi*, May–June 1959.) He states that, on July 20 he sought an audience with the King, but that Acquarone then asked to see Grandi. The latter replied that he would only be received by the Monarch, and not by the Minister of Court 'whom he distrusted'. On July 21, after leaving Scorza's office, Grandi did not think any more of going to the King. 'The sudden decision of Mussolini made the audience both superfluous and even for that reason we do not wish to expose the Crown. Our aim is to furnish the King with the "constitutional clue" which the Sovereign has always declared to be the indispensable condition to induce him to act. We do not intend to "conspire" with the Court, still less with the Army. The generals will never take any initiative except after the King has ordered them to do so. The key to everything is the King alone.'

On July 24, an hour before the meeting of the Grand Council, Zamboni again called on Acquarone to hand him a letter from Grandi to the King, and a copy of the text of the motion to be presented at the session. 'I have the honour to inform your Majesty that I shall be leaving shortly for Palazzo Venezia to submit to the Grand Council the enclosed motion, the text of which I would ask Your Majesty to read . . . I do not know whether the initiative, taken in agreement with other members, will have a majority of those assembled. We have thought fit to undertake the extreme attempt to postulate the constitutional conditions for a restoration of the statutory guarantees and of the prerogatives of the Sovereign.' s

The events of July 23, culminating in the discussions at the Party Headquarters on Grandi's draft motion, had created a deceptive atmosphere of unanimity in the higher circles of the Fascist Party. Scorza found himself sponsoring a political move of national importance, which reached far beyond the responsibilities of the Party secretariat, and had given the impression to the younger Party bosses, such as Bignardi, that the official leadership of the Party was backing Grandi, and even with Mussolini's knowledge.

About 8.30 p.m. that evening, he called to his office the four Vice-Secretaries of the Party and one of them has put down the gist of his remarks: 'You have seen in these last days that there has been much coming and going of Party bosses and high personages here at Party Headquarters. I tell you at once that some of them are thinking in terms of replacing the Duce. Well, I have told Grandi, who is the exponent of this group, that I do not take any part in their plan. To me, the idea of replacement of the Duce only aggravates the situation. For the moment they have all kept away from Party Headquarters, and from me. You will have noticed that since yesterday morning[t] none of them has been seen here. Now as in the face of every eventuality it is as well if each of us assumes his own precise responsibility, I have prepared my own motion which nobody knows about, not even the Duce, and I shall take it on myself to present it tomorrow at the meeting of the Grand

undesirable . . . Our duty was not to implicate the King in the final effort to give him those constitutional means for which he had asked.' See also Grandi, in Ugo D'Andrea's article (*Incom Illustrata,* July 26, 1952).

s. This previously unpublished letter was given by Grandi to the editor of a post-war weekly published in Naples, and it has been printed in an article with an historical commentary. (*Incom Illustrata,* August 2, 1952.) Presumably this letter had been drafted in Bologna.

t. Bottai *op cit* p. 291, under the date July 23. 'Towards midday we (Bottai and Grandi) called on Scorza.'

Council. I shall read it to you as I want to know the opinion of each of you.' [27]

This text, the third now to be presented at the forthcoming meeting, was composed in the vacuous phraseology of Party manifestos, but is of perplexing interest as throwing some light on Scorza's own reactions to the pending crisis of the régime. 'The Grand Council is convinced that the new situation created by the events of the war must be faced by new methods, and means.' It was urgent to carry out 'these reforms and innovations . . . in the Government, in the Supreme Command, and in the country's internal life'. The Grand Council 'salutes in His Majesty the King . . . the symbol and strength of the continuity of the nation'. There was in Scorza's draft, and most significantly, no reference to handing over military powers to the Crown.

The four Party officials expressed unanimous agreement and the following morning (July 24) signed a declaration to that effect. In the meantime Scorza had apparently seen Mussolini, who said that he was prepared to announce during his opening report at the Grand Council the reforms and innovations which Scorza had in mind.

The ultimate defence of the régime had lain for twenty years with the Party and its armed embodiment, the Militia. The rumours of plots were everywhere. Scorza himself told the Duce of one particular report of a secret meeting of generals at which it had been decided to arrest Mussolini and place Badoglio in his stead. The Duce had commented, 'Don't produce detective stories.' [u] It was nevertheless the duty of the Party to take counter-action, and make recommendations to the Duce.

Reliable evidence pointed to Ambrosio as the central figure in the coalescing conspiracy against Fascism. At a secret meeting of selected Party bosses on July 22 his removal was discussed. Scorza had suggested the name of Graziani, who was briefly Chief of the Army Staff in 1940 [v] to replace him. One of those present, Alessandro Melchiorri, was instructed to sound the Marshal through the latter's private secretary. It appears that Graziani came to Rome on the morning of July 24, and through these intermediaries it was agreed that he should hold himself at the disposal of the Duce. Melchiorri drafted a letter to be sent to De Cesare, the head of Mussolini's private office, before the meeting of the Grand Council. The pretext of this approach was that the writer 'had heard mention of Graziani visiting the King and meeting or coming to some agreement with Badoglio'. This information had probably been given to the Chief of Police in good faith because one of the very few persons whom Graziani visited lived opposite Badoglio's house and another near the royal Villa Savoia. Graziani denied that any such meetings had taken place, and Badoglio he 'considers as his worst

u. Cucco *op cit* p. 94. This episode probably took lace on the morning of July 24 at the regular report of Scorza to the Duce. Such a meeting of generals had just been held.

v. Graziani was still the subject of a pending military enquiry into his conduct of the Libyan campaign in 1941.

enemy.' He also told Melchiorri that should the Duce think it necessary or suitable, Graziani would always be at Mussolini's orders, and in a postscript hastily added to this letter Melchiorri wrote that Graziani 'still hopes that the war might be brought to a favourable conclusion', but it must be 'an honourable one'.[w]

The nomination of Graziani to succeed Ambrosio may have been the main item in Scorza's 'plan', and Mussolini was aware of this possible card before the meeting and also that Scorza intended to propose it under certain conditions at the Grand Council.

Each party had in fact his military figure: the King with Badoglio, Grandi with Caviglia, and now perhaps Mussolini with Graziani.

The Duce was aware of the manoeuvres developing around him. He knew of Grandi's motion and of the currents of opinion within the Party. On the evening of July 23, Chierici, the Chief of Police, informed him of the contacts between the various members of the Grand Council and gave his opinion that Grandi's motion had probably already the support of the majority of the votes.[x] He had been warned of conspiracies round every corner, at Court, within the General Staff. He had received similar reports for twenty years from the police, old Party members and by anonymous denunciation. The history of Fascism is shadowed by the perpetual theme of treason within and outside the régime. In such admonitions the specialist was Farinacci, with his favourite theme of 'the traitors of the General Staff'.[y]

As Melchiorri had also written in his letter of July 24, 'Marshal Badoglio has declared that he is not a Mexican General and will not act as such. This statement should be taken to mean, according to Graziani, that Badoglio will not carry out a piazza revolution in Mexican style, but will act or attempt to act constitutionally since most of the General Staff are for him and he hopes for the support of the House of Savoy.' This proved to be an accurate forecast.

It seems that, according to the Duce, Grandi was hesitant and alarmed during the last hours. 'There was much coming and going in Piazza Colonna, where the Party Headquarters was housed in Palazzo Wedekind, on

w. This letter of Melchiorri to the Duce of July 24, 1943, is cited as evidence in Graziani's post-war trial. (Stenographic record, vol III, pp. 1091–3.)

x. Pellicano *op cit* Article II. Chierici told Acerbo the next day that he had given this warning. The former died in prison in mysterious circumstances at Verona in 1944. His death removed a vital witness at these trials.

y. Bastianini's letter cited in Verona Trial. Cersosimo *op cit* p. 20. Farinacci Diary, June 27. Farinacci had talked to Mussolini of a plot headed by Grandi, Badoglio, Acquarone, and Ambrosio, but met with a similar response from the Duce. On July 24 Farinacci had a final talk with the Duce, who is alleged to have remarked: 'For the first time the independence of the nation is in danger. This must be the moment of maximum effort, of the union of all classes, castes, churches, and opinions. However, the Party has become too middle class.'

Thursday and Friday (July 22 and 23). At a certain point Grandi put forward the idea of postponing the Grand Council—a clever move to look like an alibi. Scorza telephoned to know if this were a possibility. I replied that it was now absolutely essential to reach a general clarification of the position. The date had been fixed. The invitations had been issued. Of all the constitutional organs the convening of which was envisaged that week, the Chamber or the Senate, the Grand Council was the most suitable for reviewing the problems of the war in the light of recent events such as the invasion of national soil.' [28]

Mussolini himself was calm, and as always at such a moment, in splendid isolation. The German Ambassador saw him for what was to be the last time on July 23. 'My interview with the Duce, in order to hand over the transcript of the Fuehrer-Duce conversation (at Feltre) only took place at midnight owing to the Duce's heavy commitments with the recent political crisis and then owing to an air-raid alarm. The Duce thanked me for transmitting the text, read through several passages, and then remarked that he thought that it was an almost exact stenographic record of the Fuehrer's remarks. He then embarked on a long explanation, referring to a map of Sicily, of the military situation which showed clearly how much the statement of the Fuehrer had impressed him. In describing . . . the prerequisites for a successful stand in Sicily he used expressions which were identical with those employed by the Fuehrer on this theme. This time his still very exaggerated estimate of the fighting value of the Italian divisions was noticeably different. The calm, assured, and confident way in which the Duce spoke in no way revealed that in internal politics he was in the middle of the gravest crisis with which the régime had been faced since Matteotti.' [29]

In the early hours of the same morning, Mackensen sent another telegram. 'In connection with the grave crisis through which the Fascist leadership is passing, the far-reaching importance of which is confirmed by Farinacci's communications to me, and from other reliable quarters, it seems to me highly significant that the Duce should receive Grandi in a long audience. He is a man whose attitude for a long time has been deliberately impenetrable in a situation which has been resolved by the collective move of Farinacci, Bottai, etc. He will not identify himself with the Farinacci group, although no lesser person than the Party Secretary, Scorza, belongs to it. It is not only my own opinion that the Duce under certain conditions wants to make use of Grandi in order to try to get out of a highly unpleasant situation, otherwise than by yielding to the Farinacci group. One of the main demands of this group he has in the meantime fulfilled. I hear from the best sources that he has summoned the Grand Council for tomorrow, Saturday.'

The German analysis assumed throughout that the initiative at the coming critical meeting of the leaders of the régime lay in the hands of Farinacci and his friends. 'The efforts of the group extend to producing not only ministers who will think and act for themselves, and not simply carry out the Duce's orders, which are not always based on complete information and thus lead to wrong decisions, but also who will administer their departments in a responsible manner on the basis of expert knowledge and the use of all sources of information.' [30]

The same day Rintelen telegraphed to the German War Ministry: 'The Fascist Grand Council meets on July 24. This session is being held under circumstances of great importance. It is rumoured that a group of the Council will demand a stronger and more energetic leadership of the State. There is talk that the Duce will be obliged to give up the personal control of the Ministries of the Armed Forces.' [31]

In the closed circles of the Italian Court and the High Command the preliminary technical plans to meet the possible consequences of the dismissal of the Duce by the King had reached their final phase.

According to the former Police Chief, Senise, he had received a summons to call on Acquarone, apparently on the afternoon of July 19.[z] For his own personal curiosity Acquarone asked for his view 'of the evident aspirations of the opposition Fascists like Grandi, Ciano, and Bottai, to take over the succession of Mussolini'. Senise thought that there could be no question of such an administration. Acquarone then asked how the Party and Militia would behave when faced with a Royal decision. The answer was that 'as for the Party, it would be enough to proceed with its dissolution without fear of any eventual resistance by the Fascists . . . The state of mind of the Militia was roughly that of the Party, but it would be dangerous to disperse armed men to their homes, and the best plan would be to incorporate all units into the Army under an energetic general.' Acquarone enquired what attitude should be adopted towards Mussolini at the moment of his dismissal from office. Senise replied that the King must summon the Duce to the Quirinal where the latter must be arrested 'within the Palace itself'. To allow him to leave the building 'would constitute a serious threat to public order and the security of the country'.

It appeared from this conversation that Acquarone touched on the composition of the administration which would replace the Duce. Senise claims that it was he who at this stage suggested consulting the veteran Prime Minister of the First World War, Vittorio Emanuele Orlando. Two days later, on July 21, Acquarone again sent for Senise, and told him that the King had decided 'to carry out the coup d'état'. Badoglio would head the new government, which would consist of senior officers and civil servants. The Germans were to be told that Italy would continue the war. The King

z. Senise *op cit* p. 192 ff. It is possible that the date is anticipated. It confirms, however, Ambrosio's statement that the King had given orders on that day to act.

wished Senise to take over the Ministry of the Interior, but the latter refused and it was agreed that he should resume his old post of Chief of Police.

The technical planning of the coup d'état, which had already been studied for months past, was to be the responsibility of Senise. This was to include measures for the arrest of the Duce, the occupation of the Central Telephone Exchanges, the dissolution of the Fascist Party, the incorporation of the Militia in the Army, and the possible call-up of the railway and postal workers. Senise, however, insisted that the arrest of the Duce must be carried out not by the Police, 'being still under the order of Chierici, who certainly cannot be brought into things', but by the Military Police, as this must be the responsibility of the new government, and technically Senise was not even an official on active duty. The list of Fascist leaders to be arrested had been drawn up for some time, and the other measures also envisaged could be handled by the Police. It was agreed that the two men should meet again 'within a few days'. That afternoon Senise received a message from Acquarone telling him to be ready by July 25. [32]

According to Castellano, Acquarone had told him on July 20 that the King had decided to bring in Badoglio 'within six or seven days'. The Duce would probably be arrested at the customary royal audience on Monday, July 26. With a delicate sense of legality Senise would not, as he had explained to Acquarone, have this operation carried out by the Police.

The element of force must therefore be found in the Military Police, the traditionally monarchist and Piedmontese body linked to the structure of pre-Fascist Italy. Their commander since February—General Hazon—had been close to the Court since the outbreak of war. He was however killed in the Allied air-raid on Rome on July 19. There was a hasty search for a successor. General Angelo Cerica from the Forest Militia was nominated. The new commander, who was on leave near Florence, only took up his duties on July 22. He was immediately approached by Ambrosio the following morning, and according to Castellano, the details of the Duce's arrest were worked out.[a]

In addition to the rôle of the Military Police, certain precautions against a possible Fascist counter-coup were taken by the Army. General Roatta, the Chief of the Army Staff, had already been warned by Ambrosio at the time of his appointment in early June, of an imminent change of government. 'Just

a. Castellano *op cit* pp. 58–9. It is not clear from Senise's account whether Cerica was brought into the plan on the 22nd or 24th. Cerica recently published material on these events which form the basis of a series of articles which appeared in the magazine *Tempo* (see particularly July 19 and August 2, 1956). He makes, however, no reference whatever to these alleged contacts with Senise and Castellano, and gives the implicit impression that he knew nothing of these plans until sent for by Ambrosio on July 25. However, Ambrosio's list of appointments shows that Cerica called on him at 10.30 a.m. on July 23.

before the meeting of the Grand Council, he was taken on one side by Ambrosio after a conference of the Chiefs of Staff, at which he made no reference to such questions, and ordered to bring into Rome certain mobile units "already designated".' [33]

On July 21, General Carboni, the enterprising and ambitious young General who had been 'launched' by Ciano in the campaign preceding the dismissal of Cavallero, was appointed to command a Motorized Corps in the process of being formed near Rome, with the mission to defend the capital against any German-inspired Fascist counter-measures. The following evening, at the routine meeting of the Italian Chiefs of Staff, Ambrosio gave the following formal order: 'To ensure the defence of the capital against eventual landing attempts, certain units in Lazio (the province adjacent to the capital) are to be brought nearer to Rome.' [34] For reasons of security Ambrosio had been giving verbal orders since July 10 at these meetings. After Feltre it was planned to concentrate the three divisions which constituted the Motorized Corps, now under Carboni, round Rome, and this move had precedence over all others 'including defence against the Anglo-Americans'. [35]

The news that invitations had been issued to a session of the Grand Council at 5 p.m. on July 24 electrified the whole political scene, and just as Grandi and his friends had two days in which to decide their course of action between the announcement and the meeting of the Grand Council, so Acquarone and his military contacts in the General Staff had to complete in the same period and quite separately their precautionary measures. The result of Grandi's action might well enable the King to dismiss Mussolini 'constitutionally', but the risk must be considered of revolutionary outbreaks by the Fascist Party Militia, to say nothing of hostile action locally by the Germans.

On the morning of July 24, Senise and Castellano visited Cerica, the new Commandant of the Military Police. It was agreed to call on the support of the police officer commanding the 'Internal Group' in Rome, and of the head of the Transport Centre. The technical details were left to Cerica, while Castellano and Senise checked together the list of Fascist party bosses to be arrested. These arrests should coincide with that of the Duce.[b]

The same morning Castellano accompanied Acquarone and Ambrosio to the house of Marshal Badoglio. They announced that the King had decided to remove the Duce, and call on the Marshal. He was shown a copy of the proclamation of the new government drafted by Orlando, on which he made no comment.[c]

b. Senise *op cit* pp. 99–200. Castellano says that the meeting took place on the 23rd (Castellano *op cit* p. 59).

c. Castellano *op cit* p. 61. There is no mention of this incident in Badoglio's Memoirs, nor in Cerica's series of statements. The latter maintains that no such conversation took place until the following day.

Later in the morning Castellano saw Carboni. 'As Cerica had not sufficient forces to parry an eventual move by the German S.S., I decided with Carboni to entrust to the Military Police only the task of the arrests, while Carboni would carry out the military occupation of the City with his troops.'[36]

It now remained to await the outcome of the Grand Council.

CHAPTER FIVE

THE MEETING OF THE GRAND COUNCIL

·—·–

'I INTENDED the meeting to be a confidential one,' Mussolini wrote later, 'in which everybody would have the chance of asking for explanations and receiving them; a sort of secret committee. In expectation of a long discussion, the Grand Council was convened for 5 p.m. instead of the usual hour of 10 p.m.'[1]

Both the setting and the hour were unusual. This inner cabinet of Fascism had always been held throughout its twenty-year history with full ceremony. The standards and insignia of the Party were brought under Militia escort to Palazzo Venezia, where the Musketeers of the Duce, the personal bodyguard, were on duty. But on this occasion even the outward trappings of power and unity were absent. De Cesare, the Duce's private secretary, telephoned in the morning to General Galbiati, the Commander of the Militia, with orders not to place the Musketeers on ceremonial guard. Only the private police squad was present at Palazzo Venezia,[a] and four sentries of the Militia paced outside the building. There was no Party banner on the balcony. The square in front of the palace was almost deserted on the hot summer afternoon except for a few plain clothes detectives. Many citizens had left the capital after the bombing of July 19. The last act of the régime was concluded austerely and without accompaniment.

The members of the Grand Council[b] began to arrive shortly before the appointed hour, parking their cars in the inner courtyard in order to avoid public attention. Several of them expected a violent outcome to the session. Some, like Federzoni and Grandi, had been to confession; others appeared

a. The 'special squad' under Police Inspector Stracca. Some 200 agents inside the Palace.

b. For a list of members attending this meeting of the Grand Council see Appendix A to this chapter.

to have concealed weapons on their persons. Grandi admitted later that he carried two hand grenades, and passed one to De Vecchi under the table.

The members gathered in small groups in the Council Room where the seats were placed in their usual order; that of the Duce on a raised dais covered with red brocade at the end, with De Bono on his right as the Senior Quadrumvir of the March on Rome; next to him De Vecchi the other surviving holder of this title; Scorza as the Party Secretary on the Duce's left, and beside him Suardo, as President of the Senate. The others were to sit at two long tables opposite each other and at right angles to that at which the Duce presided. There was no stenographer, and the stool in the centre of the room was empty.[c]

As those present waited, Grandi was to be seen hurrying from group to group canvassing last-minute signatures to his motion. At five minutes past five the chief usher, carrying a briefcase, appeared in the doorway and announced the Duce. He entered, dressed like all those present, in militia uniform. Scorza called for the ritual salute to the leader. The members moved to their places.

Mussolini opened a bulky file of documents in front of him, and began to speak. He had summoned the Grand Council at the express desire of those orators designated by Scorza on his orders to tour the provinces, and several of them had explained to him the significance of this move as 'a manifestation of conscious responsibility'.[d]

'Let us first of all consider the history of the High Command.' Political and military circles aim their sharpest criticisms at those who bear the responsibility for the military conduct of the war. 'Let it be said once and for all that I did not in the least desire the delegation of Command of the Armed Forces in the field given to me by the King on June 10. That initiative belongs to Marshal Badoglio.' Mussolini then read out three memoranda written by the latter dated May-June 1940, showing the proposals made on this subject. How did these arrangements function? 'Falsehood has dominated the conduct of this war', partly because of the difficulty of checking reports and details sent in from various fronts, all overseas. The strategic decisions in these far distant theatres of operations could only fall on the local commanders on whose initiative one had to rely. The action of the High Command was more of a technical nature.

c. There were thus no minutes of this historic meeting. The scattered and apologetic fragments of autobiographical accounts which have so far been published give no clear record of the texts of the speeches and interventions made. Nor is it possible as yet to establish the order and sequence of the orators.

According to Buffarini, all documents and notes concerning the session in the possession of Mussolini were brought back by him to Villa Torlonia, and destroyed on the afternoon of July 25 during the alarm at his failure to return from the royal audience. See Cersosimo *op cit* p. 43.

d. For the following extracts and the text of the documents read out by the Duce at this meeting see Mussolini *op cit* pp. 55-61.

And then with a faint emphasis of pride, 'Only once—in Cavallero's absence—did I personally direct a battle: the naval action off Pantelleria on June 15, 1942. That decisive victory was due to me . . . When I fell ill in October 1942, I contemplated giving up my military command, but I did not do so because it seemed to me unseemly to abandon the ship in midstorm. I postponed doing so until after a "sunny day", which has not yet appeared.' There was nothing further to be said on the subject of the command.

There followed a catalogue of errors: Alamein and the blunders of Rommel in North Africa, the premature evacuation of Tripoli; the shameful surrender of Pantelleria where Mussolini had to give the final order. And now the scene in Sicily, the flight of the troops to their homes, and the dispersal of units in rout all over the island, the first signs of anti-Fascism in the villages and hamlets. 'And what does the General Staff forecast for the immediate future? Perhaps an enemy attack on Sardinia where there are one hundred and sixty thousand men, or in the Dodecanese and other Mediterranean islands, in order to prepare not for a landing on our peninsula, which is thought improbable, but a long-range manoeuvre either in France or the Balkans.'

What about help from Germany? The extent of her aid had been questioned in certain circles. It was generous and substantial. And Mussolini recited a list of figures showing the raw materials imported into Italy from German sources since 1940.[2]

The Duce had reached the end of his military exposition, and turned to the essential point of this meeting, the challenge to his authority in the Grandi motion. Bottai watched him. 'Up till then he had been speaking with his head bent over his papers . . . But now he looked up in the strong light which shone on us all from above. The mask fell. His real face appeared on which I read the signs of a will resigned to the final settlement of accounts. His voice no longer had the provocative sneering tones of aggressive polemic. It was strangely quiet, and his usual form of phrase for effect sounded inert and without the warmth of conviction.' [3]

Mussolini continued: 'Another point of the capitulationists is that "the people's heart is not in the war". Now the people's heart is never in any war. Not even in those of the Risorgimento, as can be proved by unimpeachable documents. We need not disturb those great shades; let us remember more recent events. Was the people's heart in the 1915–18 war, by any chance? Not in the least. The people were dragged into the war by a minority which succeeded in winning over three cities—Milan, Genoa, and Rome—and some minor towns such as Parma. Three men launched the movement—Corridoni,[e] D'Annunzio, and myself. Even then there was no sort of "sacred

e. Filippo Corridoni. One of the syndicalist leaders who followed Mussolini in the interventionist campaign.

unity". The country was divided into neutralists and interventionists, and this division continued even after Caporetto. Was the people's heart in a war which produced five hundred and thirty-five thousand deserters in the country? The "people's heart" seems to have been far less in that than in the present one . . . War is always a party war, a war of the party which desired it; it is always a one man's war, the war of the man who declared it; if today this is called Mussolini's war, in 1859 it could have been called Cavour's war. This is the moment to tighten the reins and to assume the necessary responsibility. I shall have no difficulty in replacing men, in turning the screw, in bringing forces to bear not yet engaged, in the name of our country whose territorial integrity is today being violated. In 1917, some provinces of the Veneto were lost but no one spoke of "surrender". Then, they spoke of moving the government to Sicily; today, if we must, we shall move it to the Po Valley.[f]

'Now Grandi's motion calls upon the Crown. His is an appeal not to the Government so much as to the King.' The latter had two choices: either to ask Mussolini to carry on, or to take over complete executive power in accordance with the Constitution of 1848, still nominally in force, and liquidate the régime. 'Reactionary and anti-Fascist circles, the elements devoted to the Anglo-Saxons, will press for the latter. Gentlemen, beware. Grandi's motion may place the very existence of the régime in jeopardy.'[g]

The Duce had been speaking for nearly two hours, and without one reference to the recent talks with the Germans at Feltre.

Marshal de Bono followed, in order of precedence, with a brief unconvincing defence of the Army and its leaders in halting and emotional phrases. He was quickly interrupted by Farinacci, who observed that no technical discussion was possible unless General Ambrosio, as Chief of Staff, were summoned before them. Mussolini appeared to agree, but let the matter drop.

As De Bono sat down, he whispered to De Vecchi, the other surviving Quadrumvir of the March on Rome, 'Give me a hand.' The latter claims that he defended the Army against the Duce's slighting remarks, and blamed the failings of the Fascist education of the youth and the 'political appointments' of senior officers. 'Mussolini showed no reaction, merely shrugging his shoulders, and motioning with his hand to pass on down the table.'[h]

Grandi now rose in his turn and read the final text of his motion.[i] It was already known to most of the members present.

f. This was an unconscious prophecy of the events of the following September.

g. See this different version of the end of Mussolini's speech in Bottai *op cit* p. 303.

h. De Vecchi, *Mussolini Vero*. Extracts have recently appeared in the magazine *Tempo* (November 10, 1959–March 23, 1960). According to Mussolini (*op cit* p. 61) De Vecchi merely referred to the weary defeatism of senior officers.

i. For the texts of the motions presented at the Grand Council see Appendix B to this chapter.

'The Grand Council declares . . . the immediate restoration of all State functions, allotting to the King, the Grand Council, the Government, Parliament and the Corporations the tasks and responsibilities laid down by our statutory and constitutional laws.

'It invites the Head of the Government to request His Majesty the King— towards whom the heart of all the nation turns with faith and confidence— that he may be pleased, for the honour and salvation of the nation, to assume, together with the effective command of the Armed Forces on land, sea and in the air, according to Article 5 of the Statute of the Realm, that supreme initiative of decision which our institutions attribute to him and which, in all our national history, has always been the glorious heritage of our august dynasty of Savoy.'[j]

He was heard in silence. He then continued with a bitter requisitory against the personal rule of one man, which 'having lasted too long and with its degeneration has changed the face of its leader, has destroyed and killed Fascism. The real enemy of Fascism is the dictatorship. From the day when the old motto "Liberty and Fatherland" inscribed on the banners of the Action Squads was replaced by the other "Believe, obey, fight", Fascism was finished. The narrow absurd formula of the Fascist war has brought the nation to ruin. The responsibility for this disaster lies not with Fascism, but with the dictatorship. It is the latter which has lost the war,' and, turning to the Duce, 'It is not enough that you assume the responsibility. We are also in it, and so is the country . . . In the fifteen years in which you have held the military offices of state, what have you done? The initiative of the Crown has been suffocated and its prerogatives manhandled.'[4]

He attacked the administration of the Party by Starace and was disillusioned with the rule of Scorza, 'which had begun in promising fashion'. His own order of the day aimed at creating an 'internal national front, which until today has not existed in Italy because the Crown has taken up an attitude of prudent reserve'. Let the King assume his historic responsibility.[5]

Grandi had been speaking for nearly an hour. He concluded his attack by reminding Mussolini of the catchword of 1924: 'Let faction perish so that the Fatherland may live.'[6]

While he was talking, Mussolini sat aslant on his chair with his hands shading his eyes and showing little sign of reaction, except a sarcastic interjection: 'Tonight we can also debate that the Revolution is finished.'[7]

Bottai followed.[k] He, like Farinacci, thought that the presence of General Ambrosio at the meeting would be helpful to the military discussion. He was not talking as a military expert but as a politician, and as such had three points to make: 'First, the thesis of the General Staff, according to which

j. For the text see Appendix B to this chapter.
k. His speech, presumably from his own notes made beforehand, is quoted textually in his book, *op cit* pp. 304 ff.

B.F.—15*

the enemy, having occupied Sicily, will not direct his attention towards the mainland, does not seem to me plausible. The enemy will face a choice between a widely ranging strategic operation which would bring him either into the Balkans or Southern France, or alternatively, a strategic-political plan which would lead to an occupation of the Italian mainland. The first would doubtless be more profitable strategically, but longer term. The second would be quicker in results and more profitable politically. Will the enemy be able to resist the immediate advantages to his prestige of this latter move when not even Hitler, when his armies reached the Channel, was able to resist the attraction of Paris. Italy means Rome. And in a war which you have defined as "a war of religion",[1] this would offer him the right to occupy the leading capital of the opposing political religion in the field.'

Was Italy prepared for the shock? 'The question by itself gives concrete meaning to the other one asked by you: war or peace? . . . To the question which you have put to us you yourself have given a negative answer. Your report has been a sore blow to our last illusions or hopes . . . You have expounded to us, on the one hand, a series of mishaps, mistakes, and malfunctioning which characterize the structure of the General Staff, and the whole of our military machine; on the other, a succession of your judgements, proposals, and orders regarding those projects of construction, and for war materials or operational plans which those technically responsible have not carried out or taken into account. This means that between the two lobes of the brain of the nation at war there is no organic link, no accord or harmony, and the political section of the Command has not the necessary ascendancy to impose its decisions on the technical. And thus a worm is boring at the very fibres of our system of command.'

Bottai concluded: 'In addition to a manifest technical inability to meet an enemy attack against the peninsula we are confronted with an inefficient machinery of command.'

The next speaker was Ciano, who quietly and measuredly described the background of the alliance with Germany, the Pact of Steel, and Hitler's undertaking 'not to raise matters which might lead to war until 1942'. But he had already decided to occupy Poland before signing the Pact. 'In any event we are not the betrayers, but the betrayed.'[m]

There was a moment of silence, and Farinacci followed.[n] He first read the

1. Presumably Bottai was referring to Mussolini's speech of January 3, 1943, to the Party Directorate. See pp. 129–33.

m. No text or notes of Ciano's speech have come to light except those phrases in Bottai *op cit* pp. 309–10.

n. The following is taken from the probably apocryphal diary of Farinacci published in *Il Giornale* (Naples) in January and February, 1947. These extracts convey the general sense of Farinacci's view and of his style of speaking, but it is very possible that they were written up later and not by him.

text of his motion.° Its main emphasis lay on close collaboration with the
Axis, on the duty of all Italians to stand fast in the observance of the
alliances concluded.

The following clause is almost identical with Grandi's wording, except
for the significant inclusion of the Party in the list of ruling organs. 'It
declares that the urgent necessity for this purpose is the complete restoration
of all State functions, allotting to the King, the Grand Council, the Government, Parliament, the Party, and the Corporations the tasks and responsibilities laid down by our Constitution and legislation.' Finally, and also as
in Grandi's motion, the King should be pleased 'to assume effective command of all the Armed Forces'.

Farinacci went on: 'In my motion I call for an even closer union with
our ally Germany in the conduct of the war. And now since the Duce, in his
statement, has undertaken such a commitment, all those present have let it
pass, although they say that both in internal and external affairs they all
know that he alone does everything himself. But at this grave hour it is a
question of everyone committing himself in the face of the world, of backing
up our leader, and sharing with him a common fate . . . I am convinced
that in this room one could count on the fingers of one hand those who are
ready to commit themselves to a moral and political pact with the Duce to
the end, whatever may happen, and although we are convinced that our
cause is really just, as up to a few months ago even comrade Grandi showed
that he thought so.'

Farinacci continued violently, and closely in tune with the German 'programme' for Italy. 'In the second place, my motion calls for a severe enquiry
into the military leadership, into the unheard of collapse in Sicily, into the
conduct of Ambrosio, Rosi, Roatta, and Guzzoni.ᵖ I demand that General
Ambrosio be heard here in the Grand Council and that we, the political
leaders, can at least this once judge as to the means, the men, the weapons
and the methods adopted by the General Staff to defend our policy and our
country. I also call for the resignation of Ambrosio, a supplementary enquiry into the Generals' plot, and for an effectual amalgamation of the High
Command with the Germans. In this war our enemies, first the Anglo-French
and then the Anglo-Americans, have set up a unified command and politico-
military direction of the war. The Axis has reached this position in the
political field, thanks to the Duce and the Fuehrer, but in the military sphere
we are completely sovereign and independent and with the results which
we see.

'I also ask, as comrade Grandi has also rightly requested, that the King
and the Royal Household be brought onto the stage, and called upon to

o. See the text in Appendix B to this chapter.
p. The Chief of the General Staff, the former and present Chiefs of the Army Staff,
and the present Commander in Sicily.

share the honour and burden of the war, which, if it proves victorious, will serve to make the House of Savoy one of the most glorious reigning houses of Europe. I agree, comrade Grandi, about Article Five of the Statute.[q] But I would want to see in your motion, where it said "His Majesty should assume the supreme decision of initiative for the honour and safety of the country", that one word should be added—"Fascist". To put it clearly and bluntly to Victor Emmanuel: "For the good of the nation we Fascists return to Your Majesty the powers and prerogatives which belong to you under the terms of the Albertine Statute, but only because you are fighting at our side for the greatness of Fascist Italy." '

At this point Ciano interrupted: 'Subtleties unworthy of the moment.'

'That is not true,' Farinacci went on. 'With Grandi's motion today, if it is approved, the King could say: "The Fascists at the Grand Council have placed Mussolini, and with him the Fascist Government, in a minority. It follows that I can form a new government, even of anti-Fascists, since by your vote you have not bound me to Fascism, but only to the good fortune of the country." But, with one qualifying adjective, you would prevent the monarchist clique from creating this alibi.'

This was a curious refuge in the wording of a formula.

Farinacci continued, turning to Grandi: 'You have provoked the crisis of Fascism with the enemy invading national soil. You cannot continue this underground and cannibal war against us. Besides, in this supreme Fascist gathering, accusations have been raised not only against previous Party Secretaries, but also against Scorza and the Party in general.[r] Such attacks on the Party are also against the Duce, the methods, the system, the doctrine, and the rank and file. I demand that the Party be given means to defend itself, and its leader, and that it be given absolute powers up to six months after the end of hostilities. Only the Duce and the Fascist Party can have the responsibility and guidance of the Home Front.'

As Farinacci sat down, Mussolini intervened briefly in the debate. He deprecated the corrosive attack on Fascism and on the Party. And what was the meaning of this 'return to the Statute'? It was not with such criticisms and revisions that one confronted in war three imperial powers.

These remarks brought the Minister of Justice, De Marsico, to his feet. He had played an active part in drafting Grandi's motion, which he now supported. He argued that in effect 'the Italian State is in a crisis, and that the actual state of the war itself demanded a speedy overhaul of its structure, which culminated in the powers of the King and in his complete initiative of decision'.[s]

q. Defining the executive powers of the Crown in March 1848.
r. In Grandi's speech.
s. In an interview dated 1949, De Marsico referred to his intervention in this debate in the following terms. 'I said that Mussolini no longer controlled the direction of the war, but followed its course in a state of dramatic subjection. He must therefore give

While De Marsico was talking, the Duce was consulting in whispers with Scorza, and at the end of the speech he announced that the Party Secretary had proposed an adjournment of the Grand Council until the next day.

This brought an outburst from Grandi. 'On the Charter of Labour you kept us here for seven hours. Today, when it is a question of the life of the Fatherland we can, if necessary, go on discussing for a week.'[t]

The Duce yielded, and Federzoni rose to support Grandi's motion.[8] He took issue with the Duce on the latter's remarks about the unpopularity of all wars. This had not been true of the Libyan campaign or of the 1915–18 war. If the present war was unpopular 'this was due in great part to the formula of the "Fascist war" which divided Italians more profoundly than had already been done by the Party with its policy of organization'. Federzoni's speech was in effect repudiating that alliance of the nationalist middle classes with Fascism, which had made possible the March on Rome.

A short maiden speech by the President of the Confederation of Agricultural Workers, Bignardi, followed on the isolation of the rural masses from the administration of the economy of the country.

It was a few minutes to midnight. Mussolini brought the session to a temporary break. For the next quarter of an hour the Duce remained in his study 'to read the latest telegrams from the battle areas'.[9] He was joined successively by Alfieri, Scorza, and Galbiati. The latter was instructed to speak against Grandi's motion, and to be at Mussolini's disposal after the session. It seems as if, momentarily, the latter—still uncertain of the outcome of the debate—had thoughts as to the intervention of the Militia.

Alfieri had followed Mussolini from the conference room into the study. 'What is happening in Germany?' was the rather surprising question from the Duce. Alfieri gave a short version of what he had already said to Mussolini at Feltre, emphasizing the particular interest in Berlin in the internal situation in Italy and the impression created by the Allied bombing of Rome. He repeated the argument pressed at Feltre by himself, Ambrosio, and Bastianini that the Duce must make one final effort to persuade Hitler that Italy had reached the limits of loyalty.

Mussolini sat in distant silence, drinking slowly from a glass of milk, and after remarking. 'And you, the Ambassador in Berlin, talk like that,' Alfieri was dismissed 'coldly'. He was followed into the study by Scorza. Outside he found Grandi, who handed him, with neat timing, a copy of his motion with the signatures appended. Alfieri now signed. It was the nineteenth and last name on the list.[10]

up the command. For me, his prestige would always remain intact, as would the basic tenets of Fascism. It was necessary to see the situation realistically and without further illusions. What I and the others were proposing to do is in the text of the motion. Nothing more or less.' Pellicano *op cit* Fifth Article.

t. Federzoni, *L'Ultima Seduta*. ('Quadrante', October 19, 1946.) The Charter of Labour was debated by the Grand Council in 1927.

Buffarini, according to his own account, was also summoned and pressed for drastic action. 'Arrest them all. It is a plot. There will not be even twenty to put inside. And outside here we should pick up Badoglio and a dozen more . . .' Mussolini's only response was to tell Buffarini to keep calm.[u]

In the Council room, Grandi had been passing from group to group adding to the list of signatures to his motion.[v] The tension relaxed a little, but there was as yet no atmosphere of decision. The intervention of the Duce in the debate following his speech had been brief. Most of those present felt that his auto-defence was yet to come.

The session of the Grand Council now reopened. Albini referred to the grave internal position, pointing out that the conflict of tendencies in the Grand Council reflected the situation in the country.

Bastianini, although not a member of the Council,[w] was called on by Mussolini to speak. 'You have invited us to talk frankly and accept our responsibilities, and I will do so and not without saying first of all that everything I am about to say I have already brought to your attention on different occasions, either verbally or in writing . . . Today there is a profound division between the country and the Party. To the constant and progressive decline of our war production, to the tremendous deficiences of our armaments must be added the spiritual inefficiency of the nation.'

Mussolini interrupted with the retort that perhaps this division was due to the enrichment of certain individuals.

Bastianini went on that whatever the causes, the present need was to rally the nation. In these twenty years, you, Duce, have given to the nation deeds, words, ideas which have raised it high in its own estimation, and all cannot be lost in a few months. Even if Giolitti had been in your place the work of twenty years could not melt away in an instant. Ideas are not canaries to be kept in a cage.' All national forces must be rallied. 'Let the King speak to the people as in other grave moments of history. The enemy must be given proof of our will to resist.'[x]

Bastianini wrote later that he also stressed the need to 'form a bloc of those forces which would raise the flag of the united Fatherland against the invader. I said that the King, placing himself at the head of the army, would restore

u. Spampanato, *Contro Memoriale* I, p. 231. Buffarini explained subsequently to Galbiati that during the interval he asked the Duce for permission to speak at the next session, but this was refused. See Galbiati *op cit* p. 232.

v. Grandi was particularly anxious to obtain that of the President of the Senate, Suardo. He seems to have done so during this interval. See Dino Grandi, *op cit* p. 52.

w. Both Bastianini and Albini had been told by Mussolini to attend by virtue of their respective offices.

x. For Bastianini's speech see his book, p. 127 ff. Neither Albini nor Bastianini had the right to speak. They were attending as representing their respective Ministries, but were not members of the Grand Council. Bastianini had ceased to be a member seventeen years earlier.

publicly the feeling of total solidarity between the régime and the Crown, and would establish that sense of duty wherever it was lacking. I said this, and had the certainty that it would be promptly realizable from your own words which you uttered just before I spoke, and which I reproduce textually: "My relations with the King are perfect; no later than last Thursday the King said to me: my dear Mussolini, you are being attacked from all sides, but I am at your side to defend you." ' [11]

Bottai recorded in his notes that Bastianini spoke of the diplomatic scene in the following terms: 'Abroad there could only be a political solution of the conflict, as had been proposed in vain to the ally at the last Salzburg meeting. One way or another: but it is only politically that a solution is possible. And indeed it still is possible. Those contacts must be revived, which it was our mistake not to keep alive.' [12]

There followed a prearranged intervention by Galbiati.[y] 'I have not signed and will not sign Grandi's motion and will state the reason. The situation is so serious that no motion can mend it even in the slightest degree. All those statements which we have so far heard condemn the lack of preparation for war, the conduct of operations, and the incapacity of the generals. As to the failure to prepare for war, it is all too clear that the fault does not lie in the fact that Mussolini has been Minister of War for seventeen years, as has been insinuated here, but in the unforeseeable development of the conflict, which has assumed proportions absolutely unequal to the resources of our country . . . The conduct of operations is a problem closely linked with the gigantic one of the availability of logistic means.' As for the capacity of the commanders, one must be circumspect in judging. 'Why did we enter the war? Let us consider this. We entered the war, at the side of Germany, confident of winning . . . Who would have doubted our victory last September when our divisions stood opposite Alexandria? . . . Today it is evident that, with the enemy in Sicily, with the enemy staring down from our skies and threatening our coasts, Italy cannot talk of successes. But it is also true that Italy, like any other nation, must still exert herself to the full.

'You have spoken of the rupture between the Party and the country, between Fascism and the Nation. This is not true; no such break exists. It may be that there is a rupture between you and the country, between Fascists and many Party members . . . If there were a schism between Fascism and the Nation, it would also be more visible and crude in regard to the Militia, which is the armed element of the Fascist Party. On the contrary, the Militia enjoys high prestige in the country and, incorporated as it is in the other armed forces, has fought and is fighting in close comradely solidarity with the soldiers of the other services . . . The schism, if it exists, and I must repeat, is

---

y. There are brief notes of his speech in Bottai, *op cit* p. 313, and extracts in Galbiati *op cit* p. 226–9. What appears to be a full text exists in the Italian Collection, and this has been used above.

between Fascism and Party members infiltrated into its ranks, ever ready to betray; it is between the mass of good Italians and those who are soft in character, capable of every renunciation, even of honour.'

The tone and direction of Galbiati's remarks gave the signal for Mussolini to intervene again in the debate. He made no effort at sustained argument, but lapsed characteristically into personal invective. If there was a rupture it was among the Party bosses themselves. 'There should be a searching of conscience. If there was a schism, it should be said that it was caused by the financial situation of many party bosses, whose economic standard is too high in relation to their political activity.' [z] An outburst followed. 'And further, this motion raises the gravest problems of personal dignity. What does the expression mean "The head of the government requests His Majesty . . ."? And again, what will the King reply? Let us admit that he accepts the restitution of the delegated military powers. It is then a question of knowing whether I accept to be beheaded. I am sixty years old; and I know what certain things mean. It is better to talk quite openly.'[a] And as a note of final confusion, 'And what is more, I have in my head a key which will resolve the war situation. But I will not say what it is.'

These remarks of the Duce produced a natural and momentary hesitation. As Bottai noted: 'Artifices are not without effect on tired minds.'

This was the moment chosen by Scorza to speak. During the brief interval at midnight he had been in the Duce's study, but there is no reliable record of what passed between the two men, nor does there exist any complete and dependable text of the short speech which he now delivered.

If he had given Grandi and his friends previously the impression that he accorded them a circumspect support, he now attempted to assert a limited and somewhat fictitious independence. Perhaps, as Bottai seems to have thought, he was stung by attacks on the Party into a lame and brief defence.

Scorza announced that he too had prepared a motion similar in tone to that of Grandi, but at variance on certain essential points. In particular, there was no mention of the reassumption by the Crown of control of the Armed Forces. The essence of his text was to stress that 'the new situation, created by the events of the war, must be faced by new methods and means'. He called therefore upon the Grand Council to proclaim 'the urgent necessity of putting these reforms and innovations into effect, in the Government, in the Supreme Command, and in the country's internal life, which, through the full functioning of the constitutional organs of the Régime, may bring victory to the united effort of the Italian people'.[b]

Scorza's further recommendations were outlined in vague and cautious

z. Bottai *op cit* p. 314. See a different version of these remarks naming the leading Italian industrialists in Alfieri *op cit* p. 338.

a. Bottai *op cit* p. 314. Bottai places here a paraphrase of Mussolini's remarks about his relations with the King, to which Bastianini refers, as having been said earlier.

b. See the text in Appendix B to this chapter.

terms.[c] 'I do however wish to put forward certain demands in my capacity as Secretary of the Party. First, the position of the General Staff must be entirely overhauled. It is clear that there has been treachery, sabotage, and negligence, and lack of preparation in what should have been the brain of the Armed Forces. A severe enquiry will be undertaken.' Secondly, a Front of National Union must be realized, as has happened in Russia at the moment of supreme danger, and it must be based on the Party, the responsible guide of the future of the nation. 'In regard to the plots which have been mentioned here tonight,[d] any reliable evidence has already been previously passed by me to the Duce.' Bottai apparently interrupted: 'we also should be told about it'. But he obtained no reaction.

Scorza concluded his speech by a defence of the conception of the Party, calling for a purge of unreliable elements, and a rallying of all groups and classes, the Army, the middle classes, the peasants, the ecclesiastics, possibly by declaring martial law and handing over full powers to Fascism.

At this point Ciano interrupted: 'For goodness sake do not touch on the Church. We have had enough trouble with the Vatican over our recent policy.'[e]

It was nearly one o'clock in the morning of July 25. A ragged and imprecise division of opinion between those in favour of total support for the Duce, and those giving varying degrees of support to Grandi's motion had been clear for some hours to those present. There was also a growing, if dim, awareness, that each of them would be judged in remorseless fashion for his stand in this debate on the future of the Fascist régime itself. Even while the speakers followed each other round the Council table, there were last-minute shufflings of allegiance in the corridors, adjoining rooms, and in the adjacent small salon, turned into an orangeade bar for the occasion. Beyond this area of the Palace, access to the outside world was cordoned off by plain clothes detectives.

Galbiati describes the scene: 'I met other members who had absented themselves briefly and with whom I attempted to exchange ideas, but they all belonged to the group who opposed my point of view, and I felt myself being shunned. When I walked back the first time into the Council room, I noticed outside the door and comfortably seated were Chierici, De Cesare, Stracca, Agnesina (the complete staff responsible for the Duce's safety as well as the

c. Short references to his speech occur in Mussolini *op cit* p. 63. Bottai *op cit* p. 315. Farinacci, *Diary op cit* (Extract No. 7) purports to give a verbatim text, of which extracts are given above.

d. By Farinacci.

e. Mussolini also recorded this point, but places it earlier. 'After Scorza's motion had been read, Ciano rose to say that any mention of the Vatican would not be welcomed on the other side of the Bronze Door (the chief entrance to the Vatican).' *op cit* p. 63.

command of the Italian police and detectives attached to his person) and possibly others. They had evidently been following the entire session.' [13]

Round the table the debate spluttered on.[f] Having tried twice in vain to attract the Duce's attention, Alfieri now obtained leave to speak. 'In my view those decisions, which are both desired and awaited, and which the head of the government will see fit to take at the conclusion of this debate in the interests of Italy, must be in the first instance brought to the knowledge of Hitler. This is a precaution which seems to me to be indispensable in order to avoid our being taxed with treason. Since one has been insisting here on aid from Germany, I must confirm to the Grand Council what I have emphasized often in my detailed and precise reports, of which the Duce has certainly been aware: Germany will not send to Italy again either timely or effective reinforcements. It is therefore useless to continue deluding oneself . . . Quite apart from the manifest ill-will in helping us, she is too heavily committed on her various fronts to dispose her forces. What Germany wants is to make Italy her bastion in order to delay the occupation of German territory, and only that. There can be no doubt as to this programme. And yet one has been talking here of an Italian resistance at all costs, against everything and everybody. These are noble and generous plans, which however err in not taking into account the real situation in which our people find themselves. Every sacrifice has a limit. At the recent conference at Feltre, General Ambrosio declared to the Duce in my presence that the Italian army could at the maximum resist only for another month. Albini for his part has outlined the extreme gravity of the internal situation. In such conditions, it is absolutely vital to our country to find a solution. Only the Duce can do so, by dealing directly and personally with Hitler.' [14]

This intervention produced a visibly divided effect on the audience. The President of the Senate, Suardo, announced, sobbing, that he withdrew his signature from Grandi's motion. In this momentary confusion Bottai saw the need to rally the other supporters, and in particular the uncommitted. 'I sensed the ambiguity which such oscillations could bring to the vote which was so imminent. I asked to speak. I pointed out that Grandi's motion, to which I adhered, was divided into three parts. The first, consisting of four paragraphs is a complete and proud affirmation of the will to resist; on this point one cannot admit doubts or speculations. With differences of emphasis, motives, and phrasing, everybody is agreed, from us to Farinacci and Scorza, in their motions, that we want to resist. As to the ways and means, the responsible organs will decide. Everyone has his own rhetoric and uses words in his own "scholastic" sense. It may be that ours do not coincide with that of General Galbiati or that of the Secretary of the Party . . . Nevertheless

f. De Bono made a further short defence of the General Staff and the Army. De Stefani reiterated the distinction between the régime and the country, emphasizing that the latter alone was capable of inspiring extreme decisions.

we are all in agreement in calling for the "revival" as we and Farinacci say, or the necessary "reforms" as Scorza puts it, of those institutions capable of guaranteeing united and responsible action by the government. It is not a matter today of reforms, but of applying laws which exist.

'Now I come to the last part of the motion: the appeal to the King. Broad and complete in ours: unacceptably confined to the military sphere in that of Farinacci. This is a considerable difference, which however seems to cancel out when one considers that, having turned to the Sovereign, even a half appeal becomes total, embracing the sum of his prerogatives. Scorza, on the other hand, shows that he thinks a crisis involving the whole nation in its historic interests is soluble within the frame of the Party and régime, and cannot be looked upon as a whole by the supreme decision of the Crown. We want to see visibly and appreciably in this grave hour the realization of that unity of directives between the King and the Duce which is the guarantee of the combined safety of the nation and the régime.'[15]

Grandi followed, briefly. He then handed his motion to Mussolini. The names of the nineteen signatories was appended. The Duce put the paper in front of him 'with affected indifference'.[16] And then 'without another word or gesture and in a relaxed and resigned manner' he called on Scorza to put Grandi's motion to a vote.[h]

Scorza stood up, and starting in order of priority round the table with De Bono, he called the roll of the names of those present. In an oppressive silence, he counted. Nineteen in favour; seven against. Suardo abstained; Farinacci supported his own motion, on which no vote was taken. The Duce gathered his papers, and stood up. According to his subsequent account he said: 'You have provoked the crisis of the régime. The session is closed.'[17] Scorza attempted to call for the ritual salute to the Duce, who checked him, saying, 'No, you are excused,' and retired to his private study.

It was 2.40 a.m. on Sunday, July 25. The debate of the last meeting of the Grand Council had lasted, with a brief interval, for nearly ten hours.

h. Bottai *op cit* p. 318. According to Federzoni, Mussolini stated just before the vote: 'If this motion is approved, and tomorrow the King accepts from me the restitution of the delegated powers of command, I should also consider my political task at an end. Everyone should have his own dignity.' (Federzoni, *L'Ultima Seduta op cit.*) As another example of conflicting testimony on a minor point see Alfieri *op cit* pp. 340–1: 'He (the Duce) suddenly changed expression and in a harsh and hard tone declared . . . "The discussion has been long and tiring. Three motions have been presented. That of Grandi having precedence, I put it to the vote." '

APPENDIX A

List of members of the Grand Council
(July 24, 1943)

The Duce of Fascism

De Vecchi	Quadrumvir of the March on Rome
De Bono	Quadrumvir of the March on Rome
Scorza	Secretary of the Fascist Party
Suardo	President of the Senate
Grandi	Member. President of the Chamber
Acerbo	Member
Pareschi	Minister of Agriculture
Polverelli	Minister of Popular Culture
Galbiati	Commandant of the Fascist Militia
Ciano	Member
Farinacci	Member
Albini	Undersecretary at the Ministry of Interior (Present by invitation of the Duce)
Rossoni	Member and Minister of State
Frattari	President of the Confederation of Agriculture
Gottardi	President of the Confederation of Industrial Workers
Bignardi	Secretary of the Confederation of Agricultural Workers
Balella	Secretary of the Syndicalist organizations
Marinelli	Member
Buffarini	Member
Alfieri	Member. Italian Ambassador in Berlin
De Stefani	Member
Bottai	Member
Tringali-Casanova	President of the Special Tribunal
Bastianini	Undersecretary at the Ministry of Foreign Affairs. (Present by invitation of the Duce)
Cianetti	Minister of Corporations
Federzoni	Member. President of the Italian Academy
Biggini	Minister of Education
De Marsico	Minister of Justice

APPENDIX B

Texts of the Motions presented to the Grand Council on July 25, 1943

(1) *Grandi*

'The Grand Council, meeting at this time of great hazard, turns its thought first of all to the heroic warriors of every Service, who shoulder to shoulder with the proud people of Sicily, in whom the unanimous faith of the Italian people shines at its brightest, are renewing the noble traditions of hardy valour and undaunted spirit of self-sacrifice of our glorious Armed Forces.

'Having examined the internal and international situation and the political and military conduct of the war,

'It proclaims the duty of all Italians to defend at all costs the unity, independence and liberty of the Motherland, the fruits of the sacrifice and labour of four generations, from the Risorgimento down to today, and the life and future of the Italian people.

'It affirms the necessity for the moral and material unity of all Italians in this grave and decisive hour for the destiny of our country.

'It declares for this purpose the immediate restoration of all State functions, allotting to the King, the Grand Council, the Government, Parliament and the Corporations, the tasks and responsibilities laid down by our statutory and constitutional laws.

'It invites the Head of the Government to request His Majesty the King— towards whom the heart of all the nation turns with faith and confidence— that he may be pleased, for the honour and salvation of the nation, to assume, together with the effective command of the Armed Forces on land, sea and in the air, according to Article 5 of the Statute of the Realm, that supreme initiative of decision which our institutions attribute to him and which, in all our national history, has always been the glorious heritage of our august dynasty of Savoy.'

(2) *Farinacci*

'The Grand Council of Fascism, having learned of the internal and international situation and the political and military conduct of the war on the Axis fronts,

'Salutes proudly and gratefully the heroic Italian Armed Forces and those of our Ally, united in toil and sacrifice in the defence of European civilization; the people of invaded Sicily, today closer than ever to the heart of our people; the working masses in industry and agriculture who by their labours are strengthening the nation in arms, and the Black Shirts and Fascists in all Italy who are marching in the ranks with immutable loyalty to the régime.

'It affirms the sacred duty of all Italians to defend the sacred soil of the Motherland to the last, standing fast in observance of the alliances concluded.

'It declares that the urgent necessity for this purpose is the complete restoration of all the organs of State, allotting to the King, the Grand Council, the Government, Parliament, the Party and the Corporations, the tasks and responsibilities laid down by our Constitution and legislation.

'It invites the Head of the Government to request His Majesty the King, towards whom the heart of the whole nation turns with faith and confidence, to be pleased to assume effective command of all the Armed Forces and thus to show the entire world that the whole population is fighting, united under his orders, for the salvation and dignity of Italy.'

(3) *Scorza*

'The Fascist Grand Council, convened while the enemy—emboldened by success and rendered arrogant by his riches—is trampling down the soil of Sicily and menacing the Peninsula from the sea and from the air,

'Affirms solemnly the vital and incontrovertible necessity of resistance at all costs.

'Assured that all organizations and citizens, in the full and conscious responsibility of the hour, will know how to do their duty up to the supreme sacrifice, it invokes all the spiritual and material resources of the nation for the defence of the unity, independence and liberty of the Motherland.

'Rising to its feet, the Grand Council of Fascism:

'Salutes the cities razed to the ground by enemy fury, and their people, who find in Rome—mother of Catholicism, cradle and repository of the highest civilization—the most worthy expression of their resolution and discipline.

'It salutes in His Majesty the King and in the dynasty of the House of Savoy the symbol and strength of the continuity of the nation, and the expression of the courage of all our Armed Forces which, together with the valiant German soldiers, are defending the Motherland on land, sea and in the air.

'It associates itself reverently with the Pontiff's grief at the destruction of so many famous monuments dedicated for centuries to the cult of the Religion and Art.

'The Grand Council of Fascism is convinced that the new situation created by the events of the war must be faced by new methods and means. It proclaims, therefore, the urgent necessity of putting these reforms and innovations into effect, in the Government, in the Supreme Command, and in the country's internal life, which, through the full functioning of the constitutional organs of the Régime, may bring victory to the united effort of the Italian people.'

CHAPTER SIX

THE COUP D'ÉTAT

．．

THE DUCE returned to his study at the close of the meeting, where he was
joined by a group of those members of the Grand Council who had supported
him in the voting; Scorza, Buffarini, Tringali-Casanova, Biggini, and Galbiati. 'The question was raised as to whether all that on which we had voted
was legal, but I did not take any particular interest in the matter.' This was
Mussolini's only recorded comment on this desultory discussion.[a] He had
allowed the Fascist hierarchy to speak their minds. But he had not deigned
to disclose his own views on the critical situation confronting them. He
seemed interested neither in the manner nor the outcome of the vote. He had
been prepared in the past to summon the Grand Council at a decisive historical moment and to permit an informal debate on high policy. He had done so
in February 1939, when he himself made a considered review, drafted in
advance, of Italian foreign policy, precisely because he regarded the Grand
Council as the appropriate body to place his views on record, and as he said
in the course of his speech on that occasion: 'An autocratic and totalitarian
régime—that is, without opposition parties—should have the courage of
autocriticism.'[1] The body had last met in December 1939 to accept the
decision not to enter the war and to declare Italy's non-belligerency.

The attitude of Mussolini to the rôle of the Grand Council was clearly
stated in a letter to Farinacci in October 1925. 'My orders are not voted on,
but are accepted and acted upon without any chatter. The Grand Council is
not a small parliament: never, I repeat never, is there any question of voting
in it.'[2]

It was consistent therefore with this attitude that now, in his study in the
early hours of July 25 nearly twenty years later, he should pay scant attention
to the disjointed counsel of the small groups gathered around him. Scorza

a. *Pontine Notes*, dated August 2, 1943. There is no reference to this discussion in
his Memoirs. On these notes see the Appendix to Chapter Four in Part II.

nevertheless felt impelled to contest the constitutionality of the vote. As Buffarini noted with a touch of malice: 'He thought of it afterwards.'[3] But Buffarini himself, with the original texts relating to the function of the Grand Council in his head, pressed the argument that such a vote was in fact unconstitutional. [4] Grandi's motion was purely an internal affair of the Council, and need not be disclosed to the outside world.

Those present also seemed to have urged the Duce to order the immediate arrest of Grandi and his supporters. Mussolini did not trouble to answer, but picked up the telephone and spoke to the Prefect of Bologna ordering the publication of a message of encouragement to the people of that city, which had been heavily bombed some hours earlier. He then put down the receiver, and dismissed those in the room without a word. [5] Scorza stayed behind. He asked to accompany the Duce back to Villa Torlonia, and the two men left the building together, just after three o'clock.[b]

'The streets were deserted. But one seemed to feel in the air, now almost clear in the morning twilight, that sense of the inevitable which comes from the wheel of destiny when it moves and of which men are often the unconscious instruments. In the night which has come to be known as the "Night of the Grand Council" the discussions lasted for ten hours . . . It is quite likely that the crisis would have broken out even without the session, the debate, and the order of the day, but history does not take into account assumptions which are not confirmed.' [6]

Mussolini had apparently mentioned before leaving his study that he would seek an audience with the King 'the next day, and ask him to appoint "the military ministers", and to issue a royal message strengthening the union of all Italians'.[7] According to Farinacci, the Duce told him after the meeting, 'I accept your advice about Ambrosio and have contacted Graziani—I think he will accept.'[8] He was confident that the King would not demur at whatever political solution of the crisis might be suggested to him. Mussolini was without doubt thinking of such a private design. His natural secretiveness has covered any trace of his intentions.

'I was up at seven o'clock,' Mussolini wrote later, 'and at eight in Palazzo Venezia. My working day—the last one—began regularly, as for the last twenty years. There was nothing very important in the official mail, except an appeal for clemency for two Dalmatian partisans, who had been con-

b. Scorza seems to have inspired two versions of his conversation alone with the Duce in the latter's study and in the car. (See Canevari's article in *Meridiano d'Italia* September 7, 1952, and Cucco *op cit* pp. 99 ff.) In the former account, Mussolini is alleged to have said, 'These gentlemen are in a hurry to talk about peace. If it were only a question of myself, I would retire at once. But they do not understand that Churchill and Roosevelt do not want my disappearance, but the suppression of Italy as a Mediterranean power. It is not a matter of myself alone. In any event, without me any peace would be a Diktat . . .' There is no confirmation from other sources of either account.

demned to death. I telegraphed to the Governor in a favourable sense.' About 9.30 Scorza 'gave a sign of life' and telephoned to say that 'many of those who had voted for Grandi's motion were beginning to regret it. I answered that it was now too late. Almost at the same minute a letter from Minister Cianetti was brought to me, in which he informed me that he withdrew his vote. I did not attach the slightest importance to this fact.'

The Duce now sought to find Grandi. 'I wanted in fact to ask him why, when he came to see me on Thursday (July 22) . . . he had asked and even beseeched me not to summon the Grand Council. An alibi or a manoeuvre?' [9] Mussolini was told that Grandi had gone to the country, and had left no message as to his whereabouts. Subsequent speculation has not produced any valid explanation of this move by the Duce.[c]

Albini came into the study at eleven o'clock to make his daily report from the Ministry of the Interior. He was told that he had no right to vote the previous night, and answered by profuse demonstrations of loyalty 'which left me indifferent'.[10] Indeed the morning was devoted to routine business, and Mussolini showed no concern in seeking advice from his collaborators.

Scorza seems to have appeared at Palazzo Venezia at the customary hour at noon, and bearing a draft letter to be sent to each member of the Grand Council over the Duce's signature. It stated merely that, having summoned in conformity with the law that body 'to consult it on the actual political situation, he had noted the various orders of the day and statements'. As Mussolini commented laconically, 'It seems, from this communication which was not in effect sent and which it would have been useless to send, that Scorza envisaged a normal development of the situation.'[11] If he too had a private solution, it has as yet not been clarified. He returned to Party headquarters about quarter to four in the morning, where the Vice-Secretaries of the Party were awaiting him with impatience.[d] Scorza first described the conversation in the Duce's office after the end of the session of the Grand Council. He stressed that there was no doubt that the vote had no validity, and that the Council was legally only a consultative body. He also told those present that, in the car on the way home, the Duce had thanked him for his intervention in the debate, and that he, Scorza, had replied: 'You left me alone,' meaning that Mussolini had not publicly referred to 'the important events which they had agreed together'. This obscure hint seems

c. Grandi's earliest version states that he was summoned about noon by Mussolini, but advised not to go by the King. (*Dino Grandi Racconta*, p. 59). It has also been suggested that Mussolini might have been playing with the idea of some political compromise such as had followed his first grave clash with Grandi, after the Fascist Party Congress in November 1921. (Tamaro *op cit* I, p. 13.) According to a later version of Grandi (Article 5 in *Oggi*) Biggini brought the news to his office that Mussolini wanted Grandi as Foreign Minister and 'hoped to arrange everything with a ministerial reshuffle.'

d. For the following see particularly Cucco *op cit* p. 99 *et seq.* Cucco, as one of the Vice-Secretaries, was close to Scorza, and is the main witness of these events.

to be an oblique reference to a last-minute move, instigated just before the meeting of the Grand Council. In event of a crisis at that meeting over the miltary command, the question would inevitably arise as to the possible substitution of Ambrosio as Chief of the General Staff, or even of a military figure as head of a new government. In fact each interested group was already considering a candidate. Grandi had in mind Caviglia;[e] Farinacci was thinking of Cavallero; Scorza of Graziani.

For the moment, however, Scorza did not pursue this last-minute plan. His immediate concern seems to have been to minimize the effect of the vote of the previous night. He telephoned Farinacci to seek a meeting, but the latter was untraceable.[f] He then seems to have gone to his office as President of the Chamber at Montecitorio where among others he met Bastianini and Cianetti.

Bastianini, in his letter of November 9, 1943, to Mussolini, relates that Scorza told him that 'as a result of the vote of the Grand Council you were about to make changes in the government' and that Bastianini suggested certain names. [12]

On this fateful morning Mussolini, as head of the Government and of the Armed Forces, made no move to summon the Chief of the General Staff, General Ambrosio, to receive the latest reports from the war fronts. Nor did he conceive of the need for taking exceptional measures in relation to any threat to internal security. General Galbiati however appeared—and unannounced—with a memorandum. [13] He had thought of a series of solutions: to summon the Party Directorate, or the senior personalities of the Party and Militia, or to send himself to make unofficial contacts with Himmler in Germany. Again Galbiati, who had heard that Grandi was unavailable, pressed for his arrest, and that of the group who had voted with him. The Duce would not hear of it, and added rather obscurely: 'In a few hours I shall go to the King, and examine the position with him. Measures against a particular person must be preceded by his being first replaced in the office which he holds. It is a question of Ministers and Undersecretaries whom I cannot change without royal assent. And then there are the Collars of the Annunciation [g] whom I cannot treat in the same way as an ordinary citizen.'

In his secretive way Mussolini was moving towards his own solution of the crisis as so often in the past. He would minimize the implications of the events of the previous night, and would make no extraordinary move. For the past

e. See p. 466.

f. He was also sought by Tarabini, one of the Party Vice-Secretaries, and a senior Party member, Host Venturi, 'to agree with him a possible action of defence of Fascism' but with equal lack of success. See Host Venturi's later report on these events in Dolfin *op cit* p. 125 ff. Farinacci was in fact playing bowls in the country outside Rome.

g. The highest Italian Order, which made its holder the symbolic cousin of the King. Both Grandi and Ciano were members.

twenty-one years he had been received by the King at half-past ten every Monday and Thursday morning. As a small concession to the untowardness of the present situation, the Duce asked his secretary, De Cesare, to seek instead an audience at Villa Savoia 'or elsewhere' for that afternoon at five o'clock, and to add that he would appear as usual in civilian clothes. The appointment was confirmed with Puntoni by telephone. It would almost appear to be a visit on routine business.

Scorza knew of this move, and was possibly present when the appointment was made. Shortly afterwards he received Tarabini and Host Venturi, both leading and long-standing Party members. The latter suggested that there was no point in wasting time with repentant members of the Grand Council, but that he must act. Scorza told him that 'the Duce will see the King the next day, and that everything would be settled quietly'. [14] Such was Scorza's interpretation of the Duce's intentions. According to his later account, Host Venturi insisted that the 'M' division must be brought to Rome, and asked what Galbiati was doing with the Militia. Scorza replied that he did not know. Indeed he had no contact with Galbiati during these hours, nor had he been available when the latter asked to see him for the last ten days. And it was Scorza himself who had abolished the liaison officers between the Party and the Militia, thus making impossible any organized common action on a political level. [15]

It was clear that Scorza had no intention of instigating any precautionary move by the Party. There is no evidence that he was aware of any measures being taken by the Court, or of the need to take any revolutionary move in defence of the régime. He was not in the close confidence of the Duce, and the latter's subsequent comment is drearily relevant: 'When I think back on the attitude of Scorza to many things, strong doubts occur to me.' [16]

Whatever he may have known about impending events he was probably, like the Duce, immune to rumours of plots and counter-plots, and by instinct a believer in political solutions.

At noon the Duce received his next visitor, the new Japanese Ambassador, Hidaka, who had arrived in Rome late in June. He had already attempted to have an audience with Mussolini before the Feltre meeting. 'Without any connection with the interview which his government had asked him to seek, he was to have called on the Duce personally to gather information on the general situation in Italy. The audience was finally fixed for midday on July 25.' [h]

Bastianini, who was present, made a record of the interview. [17] 'The Japanese Ambassador asked the Duce, in the name of the President of the Council, Tojo, to give him as precise a picture as possible of the political and

h. German Collection. Mackensen telegram July 28. 'The Japanese Ambassador related . . . that as a result of a coincidence he had a conversation with the Duce on the critical Sunday.' The above quotation follows in the text of the message.

military situation of Europe, which Japan regarded with some disquiet, adding that the Japanese Government was ready to collaborate with the Italian Government in whatever way was thought to be the most opportune in leading towards an improvement. The Duce replied that . . . he approved of the policy followed by Japan in the Far East because he himself held the view that when armed force was not sufficient to deal with a situation one must revert to politics. He had repeatedly attempted, on various occasions,[i] to make the Fuehrer understand this, but nevertheless had not succeeded in persuading him . . . The Duce had therefore decided that in the course of the coming week, he would undertake an energetic approach to the Fuehrer to draw his most serious attention to the situation which had recently developed, and to induce the Fuehrer himself, as he had already attempted to do on previous occasions, to cease hostilities on the Eastern Front, and thus arrive at a settlement with Russia.[j] Once this had been obtained, the Reich would be able to bring the whole weight of its military potential to bear against the Anglo-Americans in the Mediterranean, and thus restore a situation which today was undoubtedly compromised.

'The Duce asked the Japanese Ambassador to inform the President of the Council, Tojo, that it was his earnest wish that he (Tojo) should do all he could to support such a démarche with the Fuehrer, with a view to arriving at a cessation of hostilities against Russia. In the present situation it was in fact no longer a matter of thinking obstinately of holding on to the Ukraine, which could not represent for the Reich a complete solution of her economic problem and her food supplies. The Duce addressed such a request to President Tojo because only in this way did he think that the situation could be modified in favour of the Tripartite powers. Otherwise the conditions in which Italy was fighting were such that she would, and in a short space of time, find herself absolutely unable to continue hostilities, and would be obliged to examine a solution of a political character.'

Hidaka later commented to his German colleague: 'The Duce had thoroughly put him in the picture and in half-an-hour's conversation in no way gave the impression of a man who was not sure of his position.' [18]

A few days later Mackensen was told by Bastianini, who also spoke of this meeting between the Duce and the Japanese Ambassador, that, 'in answer to the Ambassador's request for information on the situation, the Duce had in reply mentioned—as Bastianini says, for the first time in his

i. In a letter to the author, Hidaka writes that Mussolini referred to one meeting with Hitler at which he said, 'It is nonsense to play a see-saw game with the Russian army, moving each time backwards and forwards.'

j. Hidaka had seen Bastianini on July 23, and been informed that 'the Duce had some months previously expressed his opinion on the need for a political solution in the East'. (See the summary of a German minute on the captured Italian Foreign Office Archives dated October 21, 1943, German Collection.)

presence—the possibility that Italy might not be able to hold out come what may, but, should sufficient support be lacking, might be forced to give in. The Duce added that in the course of the next days he would approach the Fuehrer and bring it home to him that he must make peace with Russia and that the possibility of doing so existed.' [19]

It seems that, under the impact of the events of the previous night, the Duce was confidently—and as always in impenetrable isolation—conceiving a dramatic formula which would liberate him this time from the gravest impasse of his career, and enable him to reassert abruptly his personal domination over the Italian scene. In order to do this, he must clearly find a lightning solution simultaneously on the disintegrating military and home fronts. In relation to the former, he seized swiftly on the opportunity given to him by the Japanese Ambassador's request at such a moment for an interview, in order to press once more as his own the formula of a separate peace between the Axis and Russia as a central and immediate solution for the future conduct of the war, and to place this aim squarely if belatedly as the main and urgent issue in relations with the Axis partners.

The 'possibility' which presented itself, and which fitted tidily with that occasioned by the talk with Hidaka, was that on July 29 Mussolini would be celebrating his sixtieth birthday. It had been suggested previously that this occasion should be marked by a ceremonial visit from Goering. It would not be the first time that the envoy of the Fuehrer had arrived, and opportunely, on a personal mission to Rome. The relations between the two men remain unclarified. There may well have been some mutual understanding between them. The records which exist of their previous meetings strengthen such a view. Goering's position in Germany was to some extent bound up with his personal relationship with Mussolini, and with his own predominant interest as head of the German Air Force in the Mediterranean theatre of war. And, most striking of all, there is more than a hint that Goering shared the Duce's attitude to the Eastern Front,[k] and that each needed the other in campaigning in the Fuehrer's circle on this theme. Goering had never dared to raise the subject with the German leadership, nor had the Duce, when faced with Hitler in person, been able to press the argument. But Mussolini must have realized that by now such a move was the only and ultimate possible one, and Goering's co-operation might prove decisive in a final approach to the Fuehrer. But in view of the internal crisis provoked in the Grand Council, and the challenge to the Duce's leadership at home, Mussolini

k. In particular, the three-hour private meeting between Goering and Mussolini in Rome on December 8, 1942. 'The Duce believes that, one way or another, the chapter of the new war against Russia, which has no point, must be closed. If it should prove possible to arrive at a second Brest-Litovsk . . . it must be so provided that a defensive line is reached that destroys any enemy initiative, and with a minimum commitment on the Axis forces. *Goering says that this would be Hitler's ideal.'* See p. 85.

could not afford to wait four days. Co-ordinated timing between two solutions —abroad and at home—was vital.

On returning to the Italian Foreign Office from the meeting between the Duce and the Japanese Ambassador, Bastianini was telephoned by Mackensen to enquire 'regarding the visit of the Reichsmarshal for the Duce's birthday. He immediately transmitted it by telephone to the Duce and suggested that perhaps it was desirable, particularly at the present moment, to have an opportunity of talking to the confidential envoy of the Fuehrer. It should not be regarded as a visit for his birthday, but July 27 or 28 had already been mentioned as dates. The Duce at once agreed, for it would then be a matter not of congratulations, but of a talk which might be really useful. He could then talk to the Reichsmarshal about his ideas on a solution of the German-Russian question.' [20] [1]

The promise of such a solution of the external crisis of the war must have strengthened the Duce's optimism in his abilities to handle the internal deadlock when he saw the King later that afternoon. Faced with the supreme dilemma of his career, Mussolini was both subtle and simple. The pattern of his behaviour is familiar, but sharpened and clarified more than ever before by his feline awareness of the consequences of failure during the next hours ahead. If he could persuade Hitler to cease fighting on the Eastern Front, the Mediterranean theatre might still be held and stabilized. And if he could convince the King to resume command of the Armed Forces, 'a command which I had for some time past been thinking of relinquishing',[21] and to accept yet another routine reshuffle of Ministers, the Duce would again emerge triumphant, supreme, and alone at the summit of power. In the meantime there would be no private consultations, no clues as to pending dismissals or promotions, only the maintenance of impenetrable and even unnerving secrecy.

Before returning to Villa Torlonia, the Duce summoned Galbiati back to his office to accompany him on a tour of those quarters of Rome which had been heavily damaged in the Allied air bombardment of July 19. It seems that the Duce sought instinctively at this moment some psychological refreshment in a direct contact with the crowd such as he never gained in private and personal discourse. 'In the neighbourhood of the church of San Lorenzo, groups of young people who were engaged in their preliminary service training for the Navy organized a spontaneous demonstration for me.' [22]

On their way back in the car to Villa Torlonia, the two men discussed

1. Bastianini seems to claim the credit for this last-minute initiative, and added incidentally that these were the last words which he heard from the Duce. See also Bastianini *op cit* pp. 131–3.

the memorandum which Galbiati had given him that morning and they went over, one by one, the members of the Grand Council. 'These lily-livered creatures who accuse me of having replaced them from time to time in commanding positions, and of summoning them back too late.' Galbiati replied, 'They need to be sent to Chianciano m for a cure, and under strict supervision. And then one would see, and take further steps. In itself, Grandi's order of the day merely provides an alibi for tomorrow.'

Mussolini interrupted, 'They have sniffed the contrary wind, and felt the approaching storm, as happens with certain species of animals, and they fool themselves into creating an alibi. It never occurs to these pusillanimous creatures that when he who raised them up on his own shoulders is no longer here, they will feel pretty miserable in the mortal dust.' [23]

Galbiati left the Duce at the gates of Villa Torlonia. Mussolini insisted that he had complete confidence in the King. 'I have never done anything without his complete agreement. For over twenty years I have been to see him once or twice a week, and have consulted him on every matter of State and even private questions. He has always been solidly with me.' [n] The Duce referred again to the memorandum which Galbiati had brought to him that morning, and said categorically: 'As to our own riff-raff, do not do anything to aggravate matters. There is always the Party or the Police to deal with them. Make a detailed study instead of eventual clandestine military action.' [24] The Duce then promised that he would telephone after the royal audience.

It was already three o'clock. 'An oppressive sultriness weighed on things and people. It sank down on Rome from a motionless sky . . . I lunched as usual, and then spent an hour talking to Rachele in the music room. My wife was more than depressed. She was deeply disturbed in expectation of something which must happen in the next moment.' [25]

Meanwhile Scorza was trying urgently to reach the Duce by telephone, and succeeded only as the latter was leaving for his audience with the King. Scorza had met Graziani's secretary in the early afternoon, and seems to have pursued the proposal of considering the Marshal as the successor to General Ambrosio. The Duce merely replied: 'All will be well. Afterwards I will summon you either to Palazzo Venezia or to Villa Torlonia. Bring with you *that person*.' [26]

The Duce seems thus to have imparted to his collaborator the same illusory optimism which he himself dispensed around him.

The night's work at the Grand Council held a very different significance in other circles. As soon as Acquarone received Grandi's message on the late

m. A spa in Central Italy for liver complaints.

n. In his evidence during a post-war libel action Galbiati gives the following version. He was told to wait quietly at Militia headquarters 'as eventual changes in the situation would only be carried out within the structure of the government'.

afternoon of July 24, he had appreciated that the circumstances which he and Ambrosio had been awaiting in order to achieve the palace revolution, which had been so quietly and actively planned in recent weeks, might be now created by an adverse vote in the Grand Council itself against Mussolini. The latter would be forced to consult the King, who would demand his resignation. Prompt action must be taken, in such an event, to ensure against any counter-coup from the Party or the Fascist Militia, and a technical operation to this end must be mounted immediately.

The first step was to learn the outcome of the session of the Grand Council with a minimum loss of time. The obvious informant was Grandi. Having instigated the crisis, he would certainly have his own political solution to propose. Its essence lay in his motion, the draft of which Acquarone already had in his hands, and if this had been carried at the meeting, Grandi would inevitably have a more detailed plan to submit to the King. Not that the latter had ever shown any special concern or interest, in his confidential talks with Acquarone or Ambrosio in recent weeks, in a 'Grandi solution' in political terms as an alternative administration. Grandi's rôle in the eyes of Acquarone was to provoke a crisis of the régime from within, which if successful would thus place the King in a position to act constitutionally and decisively in removing Mussolini, and restore the Crown to a historic position from which it had been excluded since the March on Rome.

On leaving Palazzo Venezia, Grandi had gone to his office in the Parliament buildings. Here Acquarone went to find him and to hear at first hand an account of the session. It was 3.30 in the morning. The two men left at once for the house of Grandi's confidant, Mario Zamboni, in the Via Giulia, and stayed there talking for nearly three hours. Grandi handed to the Minister of the Royal Household the text of his motion bearing the original signatures of the nineteen supporters. Everything now depended on the royal will. In these early morning hours the whole structure of Italian government was in suspense. The man who had provoked the crisis of the régime had considered also its solution. His version of this conversation exists in summary form.[27] The King must forthwith accept complete responsibility and form a new administration. Grandi's candidate for the head of the government was Marshal Caviglia 'the only one of the old Marshals of the 1915–18 war who had preserved an attitude of dignity and pride in face of Mussolini and the dictatorship. His prestige with the Army is very high and he is the only person who can negotiate with head high with England and the United States.' Caviglia should form a transitional ministry of experts, both Fascist and anti-Fascist. Orlando, as the veteran leader of the nation in 1918, should draft a manifesto to the country appealing for a sacred union of all patriots. The King should issue a royal decree ° transforming the Fascist Chamber

o. Grandi submitted a draft text shortly after this talk to Acquarone.

into a Chamber of Deputies. Grandi assumed that as its President he should guarantee a two-thirds majority for a vote of confidence in the new government. Most Fascist Party members would follow the royal action, but no member of the Grand Council should serve in the new administration.

Acquarone asked about Badoglio, hinting that the Marshal might be summoned to power, and received the answer that he was unsuitable 'for obvious reasons' and in particular as bearing major responsibility for Italy's entry into the war.

'And yourself?' asked Acquarone. Grandi explained that all he wished was 'to leave tonight on my own responsibility for Madrid, and to make contact with my old friend Samuel Hoare . . . to explain to him the situation with a view to a peace offer, which can be handled by whomever you wish to designate'.p

The Minister of the Royal Household listened and made little comment. He asked one final question. How would Mussolini now react? 'I would not be surprised', answered Grandi, 'if he considered the voting tonight as a trump card in the disengaging manoeuvre which he intends to carry through on his own with Hitler. The only thing which would astonish me would be to see him oppose any decisions of the King.' [28]

Acquarone left to report at the royal villa. Extreme measures must now be set in motion. Plans had already been drafted to arrest Mussolini at the customary audience which was due on Monday morning, July 26. But events might now be precipitated.

At about seven o'clock Acquarone joined General Ambrosio at Supreme Command Headquarters. It was now only a matter of putting into action a preconceived plan. As Ambrosio stated later, it had been suggested that the summoning of the Grand Council had taken him by surprise and upset arrangements. 'This is not correct. I would say that Grandi's action . . . and the decisions of the Grand Council complemented our plan; besides, the verdict of the Grand Council offered the King the constitutional weapon for removing Mussolini.' [29] Ambrosio had already been told by the King on July 19 that he had decided to take such action at an opportune moment.q

Acquarone now told him, after talking to the King in the early hours of Sunday, July 25, that this moment had arrived.

At 10.50 a.m. Puntoni went to the Sovereign. 'I found him quiet and serene. We discussed the situation, and from His Majesty's words it was easy for me to understand that the replacement of Mussolini had been decided. The King will tackle the Duce tomorrow, Monday, at the usual

p. See Grandi's letter to the British Prime Minister, sent from Lisbon and dated October 12, 1943. 'On the early morning of July 25, and even before Marshal Badoglio was appointed head of the Government, I asked to be sent to Madrid or Lisbon to get in touch with British representatives there.' (See Appendix B, Part II, Chapter II.)

q. See p. 423.

audience.' r At 12.15 Puntoni was telephoned by Mussolini's secretary, and this upset the King's programme. 'De Cesare asked for a private audience for the Duce at 5 o'clock at Villa Savoia. I immediately telephoned to the Sovereign and replied to the Duce's private secretary that His Majesty agreed to Mussolini's request. I also warned Acquarone, and told him that the King wished to see him at four o'clock.' 30

Acquarone immediately telephoned this news to Castellano, and seems to have admitted that the King was still reluctant to give the actual order to arrest the Duce. Both men agreed to meet at Ambrosio's house.s The detailed preparations for the arrest of the Duce were made in the early afternoon. It had already been agreed by the inner circle of the palace conspiracy that the arrest must be carried out by the Military Police. Their new commander, General Cerica, who was then on leave near Florence, had only been appointed on July 22. On the morning of July 25 he was completing his formal calls, when just after midday he received an urgent summons to go to Ambrosio's office in Palazzo Vidoni.31 According to Cerica's own account, he was told that the King was about to dismiss Mussolini and appoint a new President of the Council. 'After the audience you must take steps to arrest Mussolini, who may try to contact his people and put himself at the head of a subversive movement.' In reply to Cerica's question as to whether 'we are acting constitutionally or outside the law', Ambrosio answered: 'Constitutionally. The order comes from the Sovereign.'

At this point Acquarone was announced. He was 'anything but preoccupied'. After repeating certain details of the meeting of the Grand Council, he turned to Cerica. 'You must act at once, as there is no time to lose. As Ambrosio will have told you, the two radio stations at Prato Smeraldo and at San Paolo must also be occupied, the offices of Italian Radio, the central Post Office, the telephone exchanges at the Ministries of the Interior and of War.' Cerica then took his leave. He wanted to go at once to General Puntoni in order to arrange the entry of the Military Police into the gardens of Villa Savoia. Acquarone interrupted. 'His Majesty has given orders that, apart from the commander of the Military Police, no one will be told of the plan. The personnel chosen for the operation will make contact with me direct.' As Cerica was leaving, he remembered the presence of the Fascist 'M' division with their thirty-six Tiger tanks sixteen miles away on the outskirts of Rome, and mentioned to Ambrosio that if they intervened, he could do little to press the plan. 'You think of the part of the operation which concerns you. I have already studied the military question,' was Ambrosio's reply. At the door of the office, Cerica met General Carboni,

r. Puntoni *op cit* p. 142. It is not clear from this entry whether or not the King had already given Acquarone authority earlier that morning to take all preliminary measures in anticipation of such action.

s. Castellano *op cit* p. 64, quotes the purported dialogue between them. The precise rôle of Castellano in these events is not clear.

who had been summoned for this very purpose. The latter's assignment was to take over the Rome garrison after the Duce's arrest.

It was, according to Cerica, precisely 12.25.[t] It was essential to prevent the different groups of Military Police in the city dispersing on Sunday leave. He hurried to the main headquarters in the Viale Liegi, and sent out orders to all barracks in the Rome area that leave was suspended until 4.30 that afternoon, as he intended to review each unit as their new commander. Cerica had at his disposal some eight thousand men. Then he picked three officers to carry out the operation, and also consulted a senior police official, Marzano, who was not only the liaison with the Police, but also commanded the motor transport section of the Ministry of the Interior.[u]

Together this small group worked out a technical plan. It was decided to use a motor ambulance, escorted by fifty Military Police in a truck. It was probable that the Duce would be accompanied by a personal escort, and there was a disagreeable risk of a scuffle in the open street outside the royal villa unless there was a clear decision to carry out the arrest within the precincts. It was essential to receive precise orders, but this final point would have to be left until the last moment. The senior police official attached to the royal household now appeared at headquarters to co-ordinate arrangements. The ambulance would be parked in the drive of Villa Savoia, and the truck with fifty men concealed in the bushes inside the grounds facing the main staircase.[32]

The King was preparing to receive Mussolini in this unusual audience. General Puntoni had been summoned shortly after three o'clock, and was told by the King that at the conclusion of the interview he had authorized the arrest of Mussolini 'outside Villa Savoia'. The King then added: 'As I do not know how the Duce will react, I would ask you to stand by the door of the drawing-room where we shall retire to talk. You can then intervene if need arises.' [33]

While the two men were talking and pacing up and down the drive, Acquarone joined them. He explained that Cerica was pressing to be allowed to carry out the arrest inside the grounds of the villa 'to avoid compromising the operation'. The King made a gesture of annoyance, and an obstinate dialogue followed. Mussolini was due at any moment, and the King reluctantly gave the verbal order for which Cerica was waiting.

Just before five o'clock the Duce's car drove up. He was accompanied by

t. If Puntoni's memory is accurate, it was only ten minutes since De Cesare had telephoned to him asking for an audience with the King for the Duce at five o'clock.

u. Marzano was the chief subordinate of Senise in the 'plot'. He had been summoned by the latter earlier in the morning, together with Acquarone's secretary, and told of the imminent collapse of the régime. It was apparently at this talk that Marzano produced the idea of the ambulance. (Italian Collection. Report on Senise dated September 14, 1943.)

De Cesare. Three cars, with his personal detectives and escort, remained outside the gate. The King received the Duce on the steps of the main entrance.

There are several versions of their last meeting.ᵛ The Duce was anticipating an uneventful discussion. He merely needed the formal approval of the Sovereign in order to solve in his own familiar way the temporary crisis provoked the previous night. 'I took with me a book containing the Grand Council Act, Cianetti's letter, and other papers from which it emerged that the Grand Council's resolution was not binding on anyone, in view of the consultative function of the organ itself. I thought that the King would withdraw his delegation of authority of June 10, 1940, concerning the command of the armed forces, a command which I had for some time past been thinking of relinquishing. I entered Villa Savoia therefore with a mind completely free from any forebodings, in a state which, looking back on it, might really be called utterly unsuspecting.' [34]

It was a shuffling and embarrassed dialogue. The Duce began, in a low voice, to give a short account of the military situation, and of the meeting of the Grand Council.ʷ He did not reach the point of offering any recommendations. The King did not propose to argue, or to prolong the interview. In a few disjointed sentences, interspersed as was his habit with phrases in Piedmontese dialect, he announced that the developments of the last few hours had forced him to take certain steps. He now asked the Duce for his resignation. He had already arranged for Badoglio to succeed him as head of the government. 'He was in fact practically in office.' [35] There was a silence in the room, 'broken only by a phrase which the King had repeated several times during the course of the conversation: "I am sorry, I am sorry, but the solution could not have been otherwise." ' [36] The audience ended in silence. The King accompanied the Duce for the last time to the front entrance. 'The conversation had lasted half an hour. As the King said good-bye to me on the threshold, he shook me by the hand with great warmth.' [37]

During the course of this short interview, the preliminary steps for the

v. Mussolini's own version in his Memoirs was written down some months later, and like the whole book is a journalistic account. In his notes written at Ponza on August 2, 1943, he merely says that the conversation lasted half an hour, and gives no further details. Two anonymous articles were published on April 6 and 20, 1947, in the neo-Fascist paper *Meridiano d'Italia*, which purport to be a verbatim account by Mussolini which differs substantially from the text of the Memoirs, but gives an impression of greater accuracy. They are printed in Tamaro *op cit* I. p. 75. In Bartoli, *La Fine della Monarchia* p. 234 is a version apparently based on remarks made subsequently by the King or by Acquarone. The only witness of what passed was General Puntoni, who was behind the open door of the drawing-room. His notes were presumably written down in his customary methodical way soon afterwards. Unfortunately he could not catch every phrase, and his account is, though vivid, very fragmentary.

w. The King seems to have reminded him of his disapproval of the legalisation of that body in 1928! See Tamaro *op cit*, pp. 30–1.

Duce's arrest were put in motion. His chauffeur was quietly taken in charge in the telephone room of the villa, and his car removed from the main entrance.

The Duce appeared on the front steps. 'My car awaited me on the right side of the palace. As I was walking towards it, a Military Police captain barred the way, and said to me: "His Majesty has ordered me to protect your person." As I made a gesture to get into my car, he forced me into an ambulance which had been standing there for some time.' His secretary, De Cesare, insisted on accompanying him, and the incongruous party drove at high speed to a Military Police barracks in the Via Quintino Sella. Mussolini was put in the Colonel's office, and an armed guard mounted outside the door. In such a manner the ruler of Italy for over twenty years was abducted abruptly and without trace from the public scene.

The arrest of the Duce was the essential prelude to the 'legal' revolution. The brisk execution of the long-prepared technical details formed a muted epilogue. Cerica had completed his appointed tasks by about five o'clock. Senise, with a body of some five hundred police had appeared at the Ministry of the Interior about an hour earlier, and all government communications passed into safe hands.

Buffarini arrived at Villa Torlonia just after five o'clock. Donna Rachele was awaiting the return of her husband from the royal audience. In mounting disquiet Buffarini telephoned round Rome. None of the numbers answered. Finally a call came through that Mussolini had been arrested. Buffarini stayed through the night in the isolated villa, and was placed under arrest the next morning.[38]

About five o'clock Scorza summoned the Vice-Secretaries to Party headquarters to await the results of the royal audience. A message was sent to Farinacci to join them. The time passed, and there was no news from the Duce. Scorza failed to get through on the telephone to Palazzo Venezia, and this seems to have been to him the first indication that an abnormal state of affairs had abruptly arisen. Panic spread rapidly among the small group at Party headquarters. He then telephoned to the central exchange at the Ministry of the Interior, and was heard to exclaim, 'Oh God: not that.' After an excited discussion with two of his subordinates, he left by car for Palazzo Venezia, giving instructions that if he did not return, the Rome headquarters of the Party should be alerted and mobilized.[39]

Scorza did not attempt to enter Palazzo Venezia, but drove to the headquarters of the Military Police, where he was received by General Cerica. Scorza explained that he had come to seek help in tracing Mussolini, but Cerica interrupted quickly that he was obliged with regret to place his visitor at once under arrest. 'I explained to him that Mussolini was no longer

President of the Council but was under detention outside Rome, and that he, Scorza, was the first on the list of persons to be arrested, which had been given to me by my superiors.'

Both men were at a loss. Scorza, according to Cerica, argued that his arrest would 'leave the Fascists without orders or a leader, and unleash civil war'. If he were allowed to leave, he would issue instructions 'so that Italians would not slaughter each other'. Cerica released Scorza on parole, and the latter 'gave such orders'.[x]

Scorza left, and instead of returning to Party headquarters went into hiding.[40] It is not clear whether he telephoned any instructions to his subordinates following his talk with Cerica.[y] When Scorza did not return, the Federal Secretary as head of the Party organization in Rome, who had already been summoned to headquarters, was told of Scorza's mobilization orders. This official replied that, being Sunday, he could not raise more than twenty comrades. At this moment the private secretary of one of those who had left the building with Scorza, returned with the news. The Duce had been arrested and removed to La Rocca delle Caminate.[z] Scorza was also apparently detained, and a similar fate awaited the leading Fascist personalities. The telephone rang, and it was answered by Tarabini who was now the senior Party official present. It was General Ambrosio on the line. 'Tarabini replied: "Good. I will see to it at once." And he took down notes of a text, dictated verbatim on the phone. At the end of the conversation he said so that all could hear: "This telegram has to be sent to the Federal Secretaries." He sat at a desk to copy out the text. When he had finished, he added: "It is better to sign it 'Scorza'." [a] As it was a Sunday, the Party telegraph office was closed; an official was sent to the central Post Office, and paid in cash for the cables at the counter.' [b]

The group in Scorza's office had completed their work, and dispersed. Later that evening, the building was occupied by the Army. Tarabini went home, where Host Venturi called on him at eleven o'clock that night, and

x. Cerica, in his speech to the Italian Senate on July 25, 1958. In his previous evidence at Graziani's trial, Cerica stated, 'He (Scorza) gave orders to the Fascists not to resist. He denied this at his trial, but he gave the order. That evening at eight o'clock Vice-secretary Tarabini sent me the complete text of Scorza's telegram.' Scorza was tried by the neo-Fascist government at Parma in the spring of 1944, see p. 649. For another account of this talk with Scorza see also the article by Cerica quoted above in *Tempo*, August 2, 1956.

y. A circumstantial version of the final decisions taken in his office is given by Cucco. See his book, *op cit* p. 104 ff.

z. This seems to have been the official 'cover story' which spread in Rome.

a. Cucco *op cit* p. 106. It is unlikely that the caller was Ambrosio. See the detailed list, every few minutes, of the latter's phone calls in his notes in the Italian Collection. See also Scorza's letter to Mussolini of October 28, 1943, quoted in Montagna *op cit* pp. 99–100.

b. Cucco *op cit*. According to Cucco, some of the Federal Secretaries suspected the telegram was not signed by Scorza, who always included his first name.

was told what had happened at Party headquarters. In the early hours of the morning, the latter walked through the streets to the city headquarters of the Party in Palazzo Braschi, 'to see whether the Party had made any move. Everything was deserted and complete calm reigned.'[41]

Meanwhile Galbiati seems to have decided on his own initiative to consult Himmler's representative, Colonel Dollmann, whom he summoned to his office at five that afternoon. He did not give Dollmann much information about the meeting of the Grand Council, but said that he had been ordered by the Duce to prepare for eventual military action, and asked for an appointment with Marshal Kesselring to co-ordinate such activities. Dollmann undertook to fix this for the following day as Kesselring was out of Rome.

Then, like Scorza at the Party offices in Palazzo Wedekind, Galbiati, surrounded by his staff at Militia headquarters, awaited further enlightenment from the Duce. As time passed the tension mounted. There was no reply to telephone enquiries at Palazzo Venezia. Dispatch riders reported no sign of the Duce's car at Villa Savoia. There was evidence of troop movements in the city. Buffarini telephoned repeatedly from Villa Torlonia but with no news, and mounting suspicions. Galbiati sent his chief of Staff to Chierici at police headquarters. The officer returned about seven-thirty with the news of Mussolini's resignation and apparent removal to La Rocca delle Caminate. Shortly afterwards, Tarabini arrived and repeated the description of the scene at Party headquarters.

At seven forty-five that evening the militia command in the working-class quarter of Trastevere reported that they were under fire from regular troops. Evidence of attacks by civilians on isolated militiamen in the streets began to come in. Galbiati gave instructions to all militia commands to avoid provocation but defend themselves if attacked, and then, in a despairing final attempt to keep some control over the situation by telephone, Galbiati attempted to put through calls to the headquarters of the 'M' division still idle at its base at Sette Vene, to Bologna, and to Milan. He was told by the operator that the exchange had cut all lines on orders from the Ministry of the Interior.

For the next two hours a chaotic dialogue followed in Galbiati's office. Everyone took part: staff officers, militiamen, drivers, and civilians. There was loose talk of another March on Rome. Galbiati was not prepared to consider any move. The 'M' division was dispersed on manoeuvres round Lake Bracciano to the north of Rome, and since early July was under the direct orders of the General Staff.[42] There were no Militia battalions on a war footing in the city of Rome, and the anti-aircraft units, formed by the Militia, were dispersed over an area of one hundred kilometres.

On the other hand, visible counter-measures by the Army were mounting, and the square in front of Galbiati's own headquarters was already occupied by tanks. After the arrest of Mussolini, Roatta received orders by telephone from Ambrosio to bring the 'Piave' division into Rome. By the following morning the capital was heavily garrisoned by motorized units.[43]

At 10.10 that evening, Galbiati managed to speak on the telephone to Albini, who was still at his desk at the Ministry of the Interior. He dictated a brief minute. 'I request you to inform whoever at this moment is responsible for the government that the Militia remains faithful to its principles, which are: to serve the Fatherland in the joint names of the King and the Duce.' [44]

Shortly afterwards Ambrosio telephoned to say that he had received this message, and that Badoglio, who had taken over as head of the government, requested to see him. Galbiati said that he did not wish to stay at his post, and asked for a successor to be appointed. At midnight he received a letter signed by Badoglio, telling him to hand over in due course.[c] This exchange of messages completed the history of the rôle of the Militia in these events.

The technical counter-measures planned by Ambrosio and Acquarone thus unfolded without resistance. The formal protocol arrangements proceded equally smoothly. Shortly after five o'clock Acquarone telephoned to Badoglio, summoning him to the royal presence. He had received a preliminary warning in the morning, and had spent the afternoon prudently playing bridge.[d] Badoglio arrived at Villa Savoia in Marshal's uniform. The King told him briefly of the Duce's arrest and of the nature of the task ahead. The immediate measures were the formation of an administration of military and civilian technicians, the maintenance of law and order, the issuing of the proclamation of continuing the war on the Axis side, which had been drafted by the veteran Orlando.[e] Badoglio departed in the car

c. See Italian Collection. Ambrosio's 'Notes on the events of July 25/6'. 'General Ferone sent at 23.15 hours to Excellency Galbiati.' See also Galbiati *op cit* pp. 252–3 for the texts of this correspondence. Cerica gives a different version of these events, stating that, after news reached the office of General Ambrosio that the Militia were threatening an armed sortie from their central barracks, Cerica, who was present, took the initiative in telephoning to Galbiati to desist. (See *Tempo* articles *op cit*, and Cerica's speech in the Italian Senate, *op cit*.) The 'honour' of 'liquidating' Galbiati is also contested by Badoglio's official biographer (see Vailati: *Badoglio Risponde*, pp. 89–90). The writer alleges that Badoglio was summoned urgently to the High Command at 2 a.m. to write to Galbiati a stern letter ordering his removal. According to the notes recorded almost minute by minute in Ambrosio's office, the letter was dispatched to Galbiati at 11.15 p.m., a quarter of an hour after Badoglio's arrival at Palazzo Vidoni, and the reply was received at 12.15 a.m., just after Badoglio had left to go to bed.

d. Badoglio's private secretary had been told by Acquarone at 11 a.m. that morning that the Marshal would be summoned during the course of the afternoon. Vailati, *Badoglio Risponde*, p. 86.

e. The account of this audience given by Vailati *op cit* pp. 87–8, is full of inaccuracies.

which had brought the Duce to the previous audience.

The first step was to ensure that all measures to avoid a Fascist counter-reaction had been completed.[f] The immediate responsibility had already been assumed by Ambrosio in consultation with Acquarone, and for the following hours the precarious seat of power lay at the headquarters of the Supreme Command. By seven o'clock the operation was completed. It was not until 11 p.m. that evening, however, that Badoglio cautiously appeared in Ambrosio's private office.

The three radio messages to the nation announcing the acceptance by the King of Mussolini's 'resignation', the appointment of Badoglio, the direct assumption by the King of command of the Armed Forces, and the continuance of the war, had been drafted by Acquarone and Orlando by 6.30 that afternoon.[45] They were broadcast at 10.45 p.m. just before Badoglio's carefully timed arrival at Palazzo Vidoni.[46]

Such was the style of the transfer of power.

Perhaps the most pertinent comment is in an intercepted telephone call the following day from a senior Party official to a lady. 'We have avoided civil war; we have submitted to insults without firing a shot, and without reacting. Tomorrow we shall dissolve the Party, and all will be over. Order will have been re-established by the Army.' [47]

f. There seem to have been some 850 arrests, including Buffarini. Party officials were called up into the Army (see Tamaro *op cit* I, p. 126).

CHAPTER SEVEN

RETROSPECT

• •

'THIS IS my Eighteenth Brumaire.' It is said that these words were murmured by the King as he was walking in the garden of Villa Savoia after the arrest of the Duce. It was in the same residence that he had received other Prime Ministers; Salandra at the time of the intervention crisis in 1915, and Facta in the hours before the March on Rome in 1922. On the present occasion, as previously, the shape of events was decisively marked by the personality of the Sovereign. The coup d'état which led to the fall of Mussolini was a personal and dynastic operation.[a] The prime objective was the preservation of the House of Savoy in its traditional rôle of the defender of those Italian constitutional liberties, which had been successively violated during the years of Fascist rule. It seemed that after the successive humiliations of twenty years, the King could now hope to establish his personal rule. The nature of the action against the Duce also mirrors the King's personality, diffident, cautious, and secretive, and aimed at a minimum disturbance of public affairs. In its preparation 'there was perhaps more distrust of others than self-assurance'.[b]

a. The interpretation of these events, central to the history of modern Italy, is the basis of extensive controversy among Italian historians. Professor Salvatorelli for example has stressed in particular this personal dynastic aspect of the crisis, while the Communist spokesman, Professor Battaglia, seeks to eliminate the individual element. To the latter the Italian crisis of 1943 is essentially the result of a long matured mass action against Fascism as exemplified by the March strikes and the reaction of Italian industrial and financial interests seeking a way out of the war, in order to forestall Socialist revolution. For a preliminary discussion of these points, see the reports of the Conference of the Italian Liberation Movement ('The Italian Crisis of 1943 and the Beginnings of the Resistance' in their periodical 1955, Nos. 34–35). Professor Battaglia has also developed his thesis in more detail in an article in the Communist Party fortnightly review 'Il Contemporaneo' Anno II, No. 5, January 29, 1955.

b. Leopoldo Piccardi *La Storia Non Aspetta* (1957) p. 42. A book of collected political writings. See the brilliant essay on 'The Twenty-fifth of July'. See also his intervention at the Conference of the Italian Liberation Movement cited in note (a) above.

The author was the civil commissioner for Corporations in the Badoglio administration.

In the maze of rumour, gossip, and delation in Italian political circles it is possible to discern two separate and opposing conspiracies, or perhaps rather private cabals, against the régime. The idea of a coup d'état originated around the personality of the Princess of Piedmont in the summer of 1942 in an atmosphere of pre-Fascist Liberalism and drawing-room politics.[c] From this restricted circle extended the network of clandestine consultation between the leaders of the traditional parties of order in the Giolittian system, and the leader and co-ordinator of these personalities and programmes was Ivanoe Bonomi. By the summer of 1943 the elements of an historic anti-Fascist opposition emerged with a plan of political action. As Bonomi him-self put it, his house by mid-1943 had become the centre of all anti-Fascist circles, including not only extremist elements whose views and intentions were known, but those from the old 'parties of order' which could properly set up a government 'capable of resuscitating the physiognomy of the demo-Liberal cabinets preceding the March on Rome'.[d]

These groups had established 'occult and assiduous contact with the live forces in the country'. Their programme depended, like that of any other pretender or pretenders to the succession of the Duce, upon the ultimate action of the Crown. Bonomi's plan was in essence simple: the King must get rid of Mussolini's government, carry out his arrest and internment to prevent a Fascist revival, place a General at the head of the new administra-tion for a very brief period, and then nominate a civilian cabinet of the older statesmen to negotiate with the Allies for the withdrawal of Italy from the war. It is significant that even the Communists were prepared to accept such a solution, and in particular with regard to the monarchy.

In the eyes of the King such a political manoeuvre was open to certain basic objections. The circle of anti-Fascist figures was connected in origin with the Princess of Piedmont, whose political activities had always been regarded with distrust by her father-in-law. Just as on the eve of the events of 1922 family feuds within the Royal House, at that time between the King and the Duca d'Aosta, so in 1943 such rivalries had their significance. The connection of the Princess with these anti-Fascist personalities in part alienated the Sovereign but also forced him to meet their representatives.[e] His confidence in these men was slight. His experience led him to believe that those forces which had failed to stop the rise of Fascism in 1922 could hardly form an effective alternative government in 1943. As he told Badoglio, who had originally acceded to Bonomi's plan and undertaken to press it upon the Sovereign, 'They are ghosts.' They had also never been able, in the prevailing climate of Fascist rule, to maintain the elements of an underground skeleton of a party organization. The only exception, and that a limited one, was the

c. Piccardi, *op cit* p. 40. He was actively engaged in these early clandestine dialogues.
d. See Ivanoe Bonomi *Il Colpo di Stato* (Il Mondo, April 23, 1949).
e. See the comments of Piccardi *op cit* p. 40 ff.

illegal Communist Party which had agreed to work with this embryo anti-Fascist opposition, and even in their case and in spite of their subsequent inflation of the significance of the strikes in March 1943, the real structure was modest. They had planned to move their organizational centre into Italy in August 1939 at a secret meeting held in Paris at which twenty-one delegates were present. The collapse of France destroyed the plan, and the first emissary arrived only in July 1941.[f]

Indeed, even if mass organizational support for an anti-Fascist government had existed, the King would have displayed even greater suspicion of such a political plan, which might not only provoke civil war and a Fascist counter-coup, but could well undermine in the course of the explosion the existence of the monarchy itself, thus creating a situation which the King was at all costs determined to avoid—the setting up of a republican régime. By the middle of June 1943 the King had however made it clear that the Bonomi programme was not acceptable, and that any royal action would be concentrated on the setting up of a military government, strengthened by civilian technicians for the take-over of power. The details of such an operation remained guardedly in the hands of Acquarone and Ambrosio.

Any overt move against the authority and control of Mussolini must be preceded by the undermining and fragmentation of the Fascist system itself. With the mounting tide of military disaster, the elements of a second Fronde took cautious and probing shape within the official ranks of Fascism. There was no conspiratorial group as such, nor organized plot against the régime. The leading elements of moderate and 'revisionist' Fascism, represented by Grandi, Federzoni, and Bottai, met from time to time in private conclave to seek another solution. It was these elements which had opposed the entry into the war in 1940, and had played, each in their own way, a restraining and moderating part in the political compromise which emerged out of the March on Rome in 1922. The activities of these politicians—they could not be described as an organized political group—sought to define a programme in which the monarchy would resume its constitutional prerogatives violated by twenty years of Fascist rule, and to construct a national front, governing through the revived powers of the Senate and the Chamber, of which Grandi was President, producing to the outside world the semblance of a constitutional régime and including all men of good will, and among them the moderate elements within the Fascist Party itself who, whatever opinion others might hold of them, regarded themselves as uncompromised by the errors of the personal rule of the Duce, and in particular the responsibility for the war itself.

Like Bonomi and his friends, the Grandi circle equally possessed no mass

f. For further details see, for example, Alicata. *Partito e Movimento Popolare intorno at 25 Luglio* (Trent' Anni di Lotta Antifascita, Special Number of the Party monthly, *Rinascita,* April 1955).

organization upon which it could rely and through which it could become a political force. The ultimate value of any proposal from such a quarter could only lie in the possible services to the Crown which the individuals themselves might render. Federzoni, as the elder statesman of the Italian Nationalist groups, still commanded considerable but completely unorganized support in certain Fascist circles. Bottai, the prime mover in the setting up of the Corporate State, and a tireless campaigner for Fascist revisionism, aimed at creating the licensed opposition within the ranks of the movement itself, seemed also on his past record to be an influential figure. Grandi possessed perhaps the strongest qualifications of all. Apart from his reputation after 1922 as a moderate in internal affairs, he had an undeniable and marked reputation as such in circles abroad. He saw himself, and not without reason, as the most acceptable negotiator between an Italian government reorganized on the initiative of the monarchy and the Western Allies.[g] His constitutional programme, which he elaborated in private conversation with Federzoni and Bottai in the spring and summer months of 1943, was essentially linked with a concerted peace-feeler towards the Western Allies.

There is no evidence as yet to show that at any stage the King was prepared to consider the Grandi plan as a political solution. In regard to eventual negotiations with the Allies, and following the historical precedents of the First World War upon which the education of the Sovereign was based, the only hope of a compromise peace might be worked out within the circles of the Court, and it would be perhaps the King alone, with whom, if at all, the Allies might ultimately treat. There could be no question, in the Royal view, of any peace negotiations prior to the overthrow or collapse of the personal

g. For the Churchill-Grandi letters see the Appendix B to Chapter Two in Part 2 of this book, pp. 522–7.

The attitude of the British Prime Minister to Italian peace feelers in general, and after the proclamation of Unconditional Surrender at Casablanca, is, however, illustrated in a minute to Eden dated February 13, 1943:

'I am entirely in agreement with your view (about various anti-Fascist elements in Italy). There can be no harm in hearing what they have to say, as long as we do not make any commitments. I hope you will bring the matter up again in Cabinet. At any rate, I must inform the President. I have not the slightest doubt that should "Husky" [the invasion of Sicily] succeed in its early stages the United States will insist, if the opportunity is forthcoming, upon an agreement being made which will put Italy out of the war. I shall support such a movement to the utmost. I am not going to take the responsibility of carrying on this war a day longer than is necessary to achieve full victory.' (Winston Churchill, *The Second World War* Volume 4, Appendix C., p. 828.)

rule of Mussolini. The activities of Grandi and his circle were rather of immediate value to the Crown and to the Minister of Court, Duca Acquarone, in accelerating the fragmentation of power of the Fascist system itself, and increasing the isolation of Mussolini within the Roman scene.

By the beginning of July the King seems to have agreed reluctantly to limited planning for a technical coup in Rome to be organized by the Army and the Military Police, to carry out the arrest of Mussolini and the leading Fascist Party bosses, and to set up an emergency military government under Badoglio. The timing must await events, and until the last minute he felt obliged to await the outcome of the last moves of Mussolini towards Hitler in the hope of securing by diplomatic means Italy's withdrawal from the war with German consent. Everything turned on this now almost hopeless enterprise. It was the ultimate failure of Feltre which precipitated the crisis, but not its shape. It was to be left to the élite of Fascism itself to initiate the destruction of the system.

The summoning of the Grand Council for which Scorza issued official invitations on July 21, as Mussolini put it at the meeting, 'precipitated the crisis of the régime'. In the view of most interested parties, and because it was the only form of effective and high-level debate which could be called into existence, the meeting of this body was the signal for intense and expectant agitation. But seldom has such a vital session been held in such confused circumstances. From the point of view of the Crown, the summoning of the Grand Council, if concluded with an adverse vote against Mussolini, gave the King the one weapon for which he was seeking—namely the constitutional means to dismiss his Prime Minister, thus reducing direct and violent action to a minimum. To Grandi it was a supreme risk and challenge, and it is hardly surprising that at the last minute he seems to have hesitated. If all went well at the session, Grandi could go to the Crown with the majority vote which would mirror the strength of his personal position within the ranks of the Fascist movement and perhaps his ability to lead them in a 'constitutional' direction. If he were outvoted, he would be the first victim of repressive measures.

The attitude of Mussolini throughout these critical days of June and July 1943 defies as yet accurate analysis. In a bland understatement he wrote later, 'Everything came down to understandable expressions of discontent.'[1] With his brilliant instinct for turning unpromising events to his advantage, he might derive positive results from the session. An adverse vote—and he never regarded the Grand Council as a voting body but a sounding-board—might give him the pretext to put sufficient pressure on Hitler to agree to the tidy withdrawal of Italy from the war which he was not prepared to discuss at Feltre. On the internal front, Mussolini as Prime Minister would be able to go, as he confidently did, to the Sovereign with routine suggestions for the reconstruction of the government to carry through such a plan; and by accepting the transfer back to the Crown of its military prerogatives, the burden of a break with Germany might perhaps be alternatively shouldered on to the King.

In the event, this historic meeting of July 24/5, 1943, voted unconsciously, and without conspiratorial intent, the fall of the régime. Its real significance was to obscure and confuse the ultimate responsibilities of power as wielded under Fascist rule. There were no organized parties within the Fascist system, due to the deliberate technique of the Duce's personal rule. The Grand Council itself was neither a cohesive body nor held together by strong group loyalties. The effect of this summoning in a supreme crisis was to blunt any possible rallying action by the Fascist Party and its armed embodiment, the Militia, in the defence of the régime. Everything was discussed in an air of bogus cabinet deliberation which was alien to the traditions of Fascist rule. The decision of the Grand Council, even if formally unconstitutional, seemed to absolve the Fascist leadership from its responsibilities, and the debate of the night of July 24/5 represents a complete abdication of the leadership, involving each individual member and including Mussolini himself.

A bitter and sharp comment comes from Federzoni: 'Only the Grand Council, by its very Fascist designation, could have neutralized in advance, as in fact it did neutralize, a possible reaction by the Party and the Militia in the defence of Mussolini. In reality the regulative act of the Grand Council (i.e. the vote), precisely because it emanated from that body, was acquiesced in by the Blackshirts and completely disorientated the Germans.'[2] But for the meeting of the Grand Council the Crown would have been obliged to take direct military action and might thus have provoked a counter-coup by the Fascists. This analysis ignores of course the basic demoralization of the whole movement, but as a tactical comment Federzoni's statement is historically valid.

It seems that even the Germans awaited with complacency the outcome of this meeting. To what extent they had planned in practical and detailed terms either to support Mussolini forcibly in event of open opposition to his rule, or to replace him in event of political defeat, is not clear.[h] The political atmosphere of Rome during these months was shadowed by ghostly threats, and the subsequent search for historical alibis confuses further any attempt to analyse the scene. The German Embassy seems to have overrated the

h. Mussolini appears at this time to have told one of his rare intimates of the old days, Senator Manlio Morgagni: 'The Germans are still strong and could intervene effectively to plug and possibly decide the situation in Italy, which is now gravely compromised. But they do not trust us any longer. To intervene, *they want henceforward effective command of the whole Italian front, including the internal one.* And this is a condition which neither the Italian people, nor the King, nor yours truly could accept.' Quoted by Pini and Susmel, *op cit* IV, p. 242–3.

Morgagni was the director of the Stefani News Agency, who made his career as the administrator of Mussolini's Milan paper *Il Popolo d'Italia.* He shot himself on July 25—the only casualty of the Fascist Party on that day.

activities of Farinacci and his extremist circle.[i] It may be that they assumed that the latter possessed the stature of a Stellvertreter in event of the collapse of the Duce's position, or at best could with ultimate German support inject a final dose of resistance into the crumbling system, with the Duce as a nominal figurehead. In any event, a strange quiet pervaded German official circles in Rome during the critical hours. It was not until July 24 that reports reached Berlin of the summoning of the Grand Council for that evening, and the events of the subsequent days seem to have caught the Germans by surprise. The general view on the following morning that there would be some routine reshuffle of the government seems to have stilled any anxiety. The Japanese Ambassador, Hidaka, had been in telephone contact with his German colleague during the morning of July 25, and had been told that Mussolini had personally indicated to Mackensen on the telephone that there was no cause for alarm. The German Ambassador was actually attempting to speak on the telephone to Ribbentrop when the news of the Duce's arrest reached him.[3] The representative of the German Security Services and the military authorities had some vague conception of plots against Mussolini, but this was endemic to the Italian scene and, from the existing state of the evidence on the German side, the extent of the crisis which broke upon them seems to have been missed.

Whatever manoeuvres or intrigues or plots possessed any political reality during these hours, the shape of the crisis must in the last resort be dominated by military events. Both Bonomi and Grandi, from their very different analyses and attitudes, shared the same view that the removal of Mussolini from office, and the re-transfer of all constitutional powers to the Sovereign, must be linked with negotiations to put an end to Italian participation in the war. Such a decision must lie however exclusively with the Crown, and thus far the King was not prepared to go. Having been forced by events to decide upon the arrest of Mussolini as a minimum operation, and certain precautionary measures against a Fascist rising, the King seems to have instructed the veteran statesman of the First World War, Vittorio Emmanuele Orlando[j] to draft the controversial radio announcement that 'the war continues', with its fateful consequences leading to the events of September 8, 1943, and circumscribing the actions of the Badoglio administration.

The justification, however, in historical terms of the royal decision depends upon the analysis of German strength and intentions in Italy in the event of the removal of the Duce. The opinion of the Italian military leaders must have been decisive in this event, together with the temperamental

i. Grandi was aware of Farinacci's plans of a Fascist counter-coup, and in later statements expresses his conviction that German intervention was imminent. 'It was necessary to break with Germany before the Nazi coup d'état already planned could take place in Italy . . .' (Articles in the periodical *Oggi op cit*).

j. There is little evidence, as yet come to light, on the rôle of Orlando in these events.

caution of the Sovereign. General Ambrosio's main concern, when pressing forward with the technical arrangements for the coup d'état on July 25, was with a possible German reaction. As has been seen, the defence of Rome was met with the ordering into the outskirts of the capital of the Italian Motorized Corps, and instructions were given to the Italian Chiefs of Staff to this effect on the evening of July 22. Ambrosio was also hoping to send at least two Alpine Divisions to Northern Italy to block any passage of German reinforcements into that area and to protect the vital Alpine passes. He had been unable to get a clear decision from Mussolini as to the German military proposals at Feltre for the reinforcement of the German armies in Italy ostensibly to defend the Leghorn area against an Allied landing in the North, and to strengthen the southern front against an eventual Allied invasion of the mainland.

The German order of battle in Italy in July 1943 contained the following main units: there were four divisions still fighting in Sicily, and two Armoured Divisions in Southern Italy (the 16th and 26th) which had been stationed in Calabria with a view to reinforcing the island, but had not moved originally because of the transport situation, and now, because of the military position, remained in their cantonments. In Sardinia there was one German division, formed (like the two in Calabria) out of the reinforcements and replacements originally intended for Tunisia. In Central Italy there was the 3rd Motorized (Panzergrenadier) Division, the only unit sent by unilateral German decision to Italy as part of Hitler's personal preoccupation with the ultimate defence of the Gulf of Genoa. It was originally stationed in the area of Tuscany and Latium (the province in the region of the capital); it was incompletely equipped and possessed no tanks.[4] In addition there were certain elements of a Parachute Division under General Student in the same area. These two units in theory represented the only immediate striking force at the disposal of the Germans for internal action in Italy.

During the course of July 24 Ambrosio, who had now made what military dispositions lay within his power to protect the capital, learnt rumours of certain suspect German troop movements. At 5.30 p.m., just after the Grand Council had opened its session, Ambrosio asked Kesselring to come to his office and opened the conversation by saying, 'I have disturbed the Field Marshal to bring to his knowledge a few points. During these last days German troops have entered Rome to take up quarters in the City . . . The Ministry of the Interior is protesting.' Kesselring replied that the forces consisted only of two companies of engineers who were working to repair the damage done to the railway by the Allied bombing raid of July 19. But Ambrosio's suspicions were not allayed, and he asked abruptly, 'Where is the Command of the 3rd Motorized Division?', and was told that it was near Lake Bolsena, barely twenty kilometres from the capital.

There was worse to come. Kesselring announced: 'I wanted to inform

you that it is agreed with Field Marshal Keitel that the two German divisions
—the 305th and 76th—are ready to be transported to Southern Italy.' [5] This
move had been the subject of discussion on the train between Feltre and
Tarvisio between Keitel and Ambrosio, and an uneasy and sybilline agreement had been obtained from Mussolini under pressure from Rintelen in
Rome after the conference. It is not clear from the minutes of this present
meeting between Ambrosio and Kesselring that the Italian Chief of Staff
expressed any comment or agreement on this proposed move of German
troops, which might have decisive implications in the pending crisis in Rome.
But one thing must have been clear to Ambrosio: he could not answer for
the military consequences of an immediate breach with the Germans, whether
or not he expressed any view about Kesselring's announcement. And this
decision must lie behind Orlando's draft radio broadcast on 'The War Continues', and thus any possible plan for a simultaneous desertion of the Axis
alliance at the time of Mussolini's arrest vanished.[k]

Writing after the event, Bonomi claims that he had consulted the military
experts in the weeks before July 25, and there were only three German
divisions in Italy at the time. Petrol supplies were in Italian hands and it
would be a feasible operation to block the Brenner. It was strictly accurate to
state that there were only three German divisions on the Italian mainland,
but there were four in Sicily and a further one in Sardinia. There were also
detailed German plans for immediate military action in Italy directed both
from France and from Southern Germany under Rommel's command in
event of a crisis (Operation 'Alaric'). Early on July 23, according to a
cryptic entry in the War Diary of the German General Staff, Hitler had issued
verbal orders to the 3rd Motorized Division now stationed on Lake Bolsena.[l]
Rather than the brief post-war comments of Bonomi, a study of the immediate German reactions to the events of July 25/6 in Rome might in the
final analysis strengthen his case.[m]

Such was the military background to the establishment of the Badoglio administration in Rome on the evening of July 25. The technical coup d'état
had taken place between the hours of 5 and 7 p.m. and in an atmosphere of
apathetic calm. The expected reaction from the Fascist Party and Militia
never came. And just as the now historical debate rages round such issues

k. Ambrosio had paid several visits to Badoglio during the months of June and
July. They had at no time discussed the question of military resistance against the
Germans, and both men accepted the view that there would not be at any foreseeable
stage sufficient Italian troops to prevent the entry of German reinforcements into
Italy.

l. The real significance of this entry is as yet difficult to elaborate.

m. See pp. 499 ff. For example, 'on the basis of his impressions at Feltre' Field
General Jodl had stood down both operations 'Alaric' and 'Konstantin'. On the
night of July 26, at 23.00 hours, on verbal orders from Hitler the preliminary phases of
the former operation were again set in motion. German Collection. War Diary of the
German General Staff.

as 'the war continues', and the merits of the plans and programmes both of
Grandi and of Bonomi; so, on the neo-Fascist side, it erupts in libel actions,
pamphlets, and autobiographies around the lack of aggressive action by the
remnants of Fascist power and has been the subject of bitter and interested
scrutiny.[n] The slow erosion of Fascist morale had reached the point of collapse, and the edifice toppled with no loss of life in a cloud of dust. The
ultimate responsibility of the Duce was total. He neither willed nor ordered
any resistance, and his letter to Badoglio on the evening of July 25 shows the
extent of his personal abdication. The controversies as to the relative strength
of the Fascist 'M' Division, the Militia, and the Party organizations in Rome
as against the Military Police and the Army are of some historical interest,
but not of central import.

The government of Badoglio was a Royalist restoration, set up in an
atmosphere of apathy and war-weariness where no mass organization or party
existed which was capable of organizing a revolution under such conditions.
The immediate act of the new régime was to declare a state of siege—an
event unprecedented in the thirty years of Italian political life—followed by
curfew and martial law. The expected reaction came not from the Fascists,
and only slowly from the Germans. A caretaker government of senior officers
from the three Armed Services and civilian technicians assumed, out of
individual loyalty to the Crown, the responsibility of office to face the burden
in such circumscribed conditions of extricating Italy from the war.[o]

n. The only units immediately available for such a move were the famous 'M'
Division quartered about sixteen miles from Rome and certain anti-aircraft batteries
stationed in and around the capital. There has been considerable subsequent controversy as to why they were never used for this purpose during the course of the events
of July 25. See, for example, the reports of Galbiati's libel action against Mussolini's
nephew, Count Vanni Teodorani. (Italian press reports, March 1956.)

o. For a list of the leading members of the new administration see the Appendix to
this Chapter.

APPENDIX

The Badoglio Administration

Marshal Badoglio	Head of the Government
Baron Guariglia	Foreign Affairs
Admiral de Courten	Navy
General Sorice	War
General Sandalli	Air Force
General Favagrossa	War Production

Of the civilian commissioners, the former Prefect of Trieste and Milan,
Fornaciari, took over the Ministry of the Interior, to be shortly followed by
another Prefect, Ricci. The other posts were also held by senior civil servants,
none of whom had hitherto played any political rôle.

PART TWO

THE FORTY-FIVE DAYS OF MARSHAL BADOGLIO

CHAPTER ONE

BADOGLIO: THE FIRST
GERMAN REACTIONS

●・・●

ON SUNDAY JULY 25 Hitler met in the late morning with his military advisers
at his Headquarters, and called for the latest news from Rome. Goering was
due to visit the Italian capital in a few days' time on a goodwill visit for the
Duce's birthday. Mackensen had however telegraphed that the trip 'is no
longer certain in view of events'.[1] He had been told that 'the Farinacci group
has finally persuaded the Duce to call a meeting of the Fascist Grand Council,
that was originally scheduled for yesterday, but has been postponed until
10 p.m. because no agreement on the agenda had been reached . . . the meeting was extraordinarily stormy . . .' One of the most persistent rumours was
that attempts were made to persuade the Duce to install as Prime Minister
the politician Orlando, 'who is eighty-three years old and who played a rôle
in the First World War: the Duce is then to become President of the Fascist
Grand Council (sic). This morning at ten o'clock the Duce and a number
of generals went to the King, and are still there. They are receiving one
celebrity after another. Among others, Buffarini is there [a] . . . It is also said
that the Duce, strongly under the influence of the meeting in Northern Italy,[b]
is firmly decided to continue the war.'

This jumble of inaccuracies summarized German reports from Rome on
the spreading crisis in Italian affairs. It was as if all sources of information at
the disposal of the German Embassy had either ceased by some abrupt
unseen mechanism, that the usual reporters were themselves overrun and lost,
or even that the network had been faulty for some time.

Mackensen, in his telegrams of July 22 and 24, had so stressed the part
played by Farinacci in the events leading to the summoning of the Grand
Council that it seems these messages were interpreted at Hitler's headquarters

a. Hitler asked: 'Who is that?'
b. At Feltre on July 19.

as implying that Farinacci, possibly with Cavallero, was in a position to play a major political rôle in the event of an abrupt weakening of the Duce's position.[c]

This was also Goebbels' interpretation on July 25. 'In the course of the day we received confidential information that a certain change was taking place in Italian domestic politics. Led by Farinacci, the Old Guard Fascists have requested the Duce to call a meeting of the Fascist Grand Council. At this meeting, according to Mackensen, the Duce is to be asked to initiate more energetic policies. He is to be persuaded to get rid of the burden of holding so many offices so that he may regain his initiative and strength for guiding the overall policies and war effort of Italy. If so, we could only welcome it, for Farinacci is not only an energetic man, but also a friend of Germany. We can depend on him blindly.'[2]

Hitler was less convinced. At this morning meeting on July 25, his first exclamation, on hearing this distorted and fragmentary interpretation of the Italian scene was: 'That fellow Farinacci is lucky that he pulled that trick in Italy and not on me. I would have handed him over to Himmler immediately. What is the use of councils? What do they do except jabber?'

There was no note of serious concern. Perhaps Goering should not go to Rome for the moment. Mackensen was 'still trying to get more information'.

As a rival informer to Farinacci in the circle of the German Embassy, the former Undersecretary of the Interior, Buffarini Guidi was somewhat differently placed. He had made himself the confidant of Donna Rachele, and was thus a valuable source at least of gossip from the entourage of the Duce. He also had, for what it was worth, his former connections within the Ministry of the Interior in the underworld of the police and administration.

On the eve of these events, Buffarini had told Dollmann that he was about to 'undertake an important internal political mission',[3] and as Dollmann regarded him as one of his key informants, it was not surprising that his name should appear in the first German reports from Rome.[d]

On July 25 the two men lunched together. Buffarini gave a picturesque account of the session of the previous night. In the early afternoon Dollmann took him to see the German Ambassador, who was so lacking in sources, to give the latter a first-hand account of events. Buffarini expressed alarm at the imminent royal audience of Mussolini, and unsuccessfully entreated Mackensen to intervene and dissuade the Duce from going.

With more aplomb than realism, Buffarini then speculated on the reconstruction of the Fascist government if the Duce returned unscathed from the royal audience. Scorza and Albini must clearly go. As a former Fascist Party

c. See pp. 421–3.
d. He was almost certainly the mysterious 'B' of previous German reports from Rome.

Secretary, Muti's revived reputation made him a serious candidate for office.[e] According to Dollmann, Mackensen made the suggestion that Buffarini should be given a special post with full powers to deal with economic and financial questions arising between Italy and Germany. When Buffarini left the Embassy, he arranged to meet Dollmann that evening. By then, however, he was under arrest.

About 6.30 p.m., while Badoglio was already seeking an interview with Mackensen to explain the events of the last hours, the latter drafted and sent a telegram to Berlin based on Buffarini's remarks. The first contact with Badoglio had been made by the Counsellor of the German Embassy, Doertenbach, who was simply told that the war would continue, and a brief summary of this conversation was passed by telephone to Berlin.[4]

That evening Hitler held a further military conference.[5] He told Keitel, 'The Duce has resigned. It is not confirmed yet. Badoglio has taken over the government . . . probably by request of the King . . . We have to decide immediately on a way to get our people to the mainland.' He was referring to the German forces in Sicily.

The fate of the two German divisions fighting on the island—and with them of the whole German military position in Italy—depended on the sincerity of Badoglio's intentions in continuing the war. As Jodl asked at once: 'Are the Italians going to continue fighting?' Hitler answered: 'They say they will fight. We must realize that this is open treachery. I am just waiting for information about what the Duce says.'

In the absence of a clear and prompt analysis of events in Rome, Hitler and his advisers hesitated to take far-reaching counter-measures. The bleak fact dominating the scene was that successful action against the Russian offensive in the East depended on the stability of the front in Italy. It was essential therefore in reacting to the coup d'état in Rome to attempt in the first instance to deal with it politically. The available German military resources in Italy must be concentrated for such a purpose. Rommel had already been appointed earlier in July to the eventual command of Army Group B to cover Italy, and Plan 'Alaric' for the occupation of Northern Italy in event of an eventual Italian military collapse had been brought up to date at the same time.[f]

By swift action in Rome, the need for revolutionary military intervention in Italy, and also in the Balkans to protect both these southern flanks of the German fortress, might be avoided.

e. This mysterious remark may connect Muti with yet another internal Fascist intrigue. His later assassination by the Badoglio police remains a mystery.

f. Rommel had been ordered to Greece. He arrived on July 25, and that evening had been summoned back to his Italian command. He returned to Germany on July 26. Rommel Papers, p. 431.

One solution therefore would be to destroy the Badoglio government before it could initiate the surrender of Italy to the Allies.

The only German unit at full strength on the Italian mainland and immediately available for a counter-move was the Third Armoured Division stationed just north of Rome.

At this evening meeting on July 25 Hitler at once thought of ordering these troops to Rome 'to capture the whole government'. But he was still awaiting news from Mackensen, and 'after that we can work out the orders'.

A simultaneous move would be made to withdraw the two German divisions northwards from Sicily and to fall back on a defensive line along the Po, a move which Rommel had always supported.

To Jodl's cautious intervention 'We really ought to wait for exact reports about what is going on,' the Fuehrer insisted on planning ahead. 'Undoubtedly, in this treachery, they will proclaim that they were loyal to us; but that is treachery. Of course they will not remain loyal.'

The Third Armoured Division was about two hours away from Rome, and Jodl was now given orders by Hitler to drive down into Rome. 'I want the Crown Prince above all . . . The climax will come at the moment when we have mustered enough strength to go in there, and disarm the whole gang. The motto of the whole operation must be that the traitorous generals and Ciano, who is hated anyway, are leading a coup against Fascism.'

The success of any such operation depended on the powers of resistance of the Italian Fascist Party and the availability of Mussolini. As Hitler said, 'I only hope that they did not arrest the Duce. But if they did, it is even more important to go in there.' But this would present a transformed situation from the military side, as Jodl immediately drove home. 'That would be a different story. In that case we would have to go in right away, and the important thing is to get our troops over the passes . . .That order was given yesterday—to the effect that everything should be moved into Northern Italy, even if it cannot be moved on, so that we will get as much as possible into Northern Italy.'

During the night of July 25/6 General Rintelen in Rome received the orders of the German General Staff. All German troop movements to the south must cease. All units and headquarters in Rome to be in a state of alert; preparations to be made to evacuate the islands.[6]

Shortly after noon on July 26 Hitler called together again his military advisers [g] to discuss further inadequate scraps of information which had reached him from Rome.

g. Only Field Marshal Kluge, who had flown in from the Eastern Front, and General Zeitzler, as Chief of the Army General Staff, were present at this meeting. (Gilbert *op cit* pp. 55 ff.) Hitler had summoned Himmler and Goering to a conference earlier that morning, but the stenographic record is illegible. Goering's position at this moment is unclarified. Hitler telephoned him on the previous day to tell him of the dismissal of the

General Rintelen had been absent from the capital on the Sunday inspecting German units of the armoured division to the north of the capital. It was not until 1 a.m. on the 26th that he had returned to hear the bare elements of news, and he telephoned to Germany. His information was based essentially on press reports.[7]

Hitler then summarized the latest position:

'The developments I feared, and which I hinted at during the conference of generals recently, have taken place. It is a revolt instigated by the Royal House and by Marshal Badoglio, that is, by our old enemies. The Duce was arrested yesterday. He was summoned to the Quirinal [h] for conferences, then was arrested inside, and was then abruptly dismissed by this decree. Then this new government was formed, which, of course, officially still declares that it will co-operate with us. Of course that is only camouflage to gain a few days' time in which to consolidate the new régime. With the exception of Jews and riffraff who are causing a commotion in Rome, there is no one behind the new régime, that is evident. But at the moment they are in, and it is absolutely imperative for us to act. I have always feared this development. That is the sole reason for my constant fear to strike prematurely in the East; because I always thought that the lid might blow off in the South. The English will take advantage of this, the Russians will cheer, the English will land; one might say that in Italy treason was always in the air. Under these circumstances, I considered it expedient to wait until several units were ready. After all, we do have units in the West. I am firmly determined to strike here with lightning speed, just as I did in the case of Yugoslavia. I would estimate Italian resistance as nil. The Fascists will come over to us. Incidentally, we brought Farinacci over; he is with us. He is already in Munich, on his way here. I don't know where the Duce himself is. As soon as I find out, I will have him brought out by parachutists. In my opinion that whole government is a typical putsch government, like that in Belgrade, and one day it will collapse, provided that we act immediately. I cannot take action unless I move additional units from the East to the West.' [8]

Hitler hoped that the withdrawal of one S.S. division from the East, of special political reliability, would hold the Italian position. Orders were given for the crack 'Leibstandarte' S.S. division to be transferred, starting on the following day.

The conference was now joined by Himmler and Goering and soon afterwards by Rommel, whom Hitler intended to place in total charge of operations in Italy.

The picture was changing hourly. Mackensen had been able to see

Duce, and Goering appeared shocked and amazed. He was told, 'Adjust yourself to the fact that it is true.' On July 26, when discussing military moves into Italy, Hitler remarked that great secrecy was needed, and added: 'I'm afraid, though, that Goering might give himself away.' Gilbert *op cit* p. 54.

h. In fact to Villa Savoia.

Badoglio that morning, and now telegraphed that there was no trace of the Duce. Badoglio swore that he was not aware of the position. It seemed that the King had acted personally.[9]

The moment had now arrived to consider in detail the possibilities of immediate German intervention in Rome as a result of the Royal putsch.

On the evening of July 26, and in almost continuous session for the next hours, Hitler summoned a general conference of the leading personalities of the Reich.[i] Each had his own theory in the absence of reliable information.

Four military, para-military, and naval operations were under broad review. 'Eiche', the rescue of the Duce; and 'Student', measures to occupy Rome and to restore Fascism. In event of an Italian armistice with the Allies being negotiated before a Fascist counter-coup d'état could be carried out, the two precautionary operations planned earlier—'Schwarz', the military occupation of a defensible line in Italy; and 'Achse', the capture or destruction of the Italian fleet—must be urgently considered. In the case of 'Achse' certain precautionary moves had already been taken.[j]

At a conference just after noon on July 27, the war situation was discussed with heads of the armed services.

Doenitz had no doubts that Italy must be held, but was not sure that a hasty coup against Badoglio would be successful. 'A removal of the present leaders by us might have an undesirable effect . . . if not skilfully engineered. I doubt whether Fascism still means anything. . . . It is not to be expected that we can superimpose conditions on the Italian people . . .

'All will depend on the correct timing of any contemplated action against the present Italian government. I believe that there is still time, and that it can be used by us for further strengthening our position in the Italian area by bringing in several more divisions.'

Jodl had no confidence in a Fascist revival, opposed any overt action against the Badoglio government, and agreed that reinforcing the German units in Italy was the main action required. Kesselring believed that the present Italian government was trustworthy, and was against any interference.

As usual the Fuehrer brushed aside the appreciation of the senior representatives of the armed services.

'We must act at once, otherwise the Anglo-Saxons will steal a march on us by occupying the airfields. The Fascist Party is at present only stunned, and will rise up again behind our lines. We must therefore restore it . . .

    i. The different leading figures came in and out in the confusion. It seems that four main meetings were held in succession. The first on the evening of July 26, a continuation of the one quoted by Gilbert. The second at 10 a.m. on the 27th, according to Goebbels (*op cit* p. 323) and two discússions of the war situation 'with a select few' at 12.30 p.m. and in the evening of that day (see Fuehrer Conferences on Naval Affairs, 1943, *op cit* p. 66).
    j. See pp. 499–500.

These are matters which a soldier cannot comprehend. Only a man with political insight can see his way clear.'

Hitler gave his decision, 'Operation "Student" will be carried out as soon as possible.' This would be followed by the evacuation of Sicily.

This latter proposal drove Doenitz into violent opposition. 'The best way of preventing the enemy undertaking new operations is by tying up their forces in Sicily . . . If we abandon Sicily we expose the route to the Balkans by way of Southern Italy. We must gain time to strengthen our position in the Balkans and Italy with reinforcements.'

Hitler admitted these dangers and agreed to wait before giving a final decision. But he rejected the naval view as to the dangers of the occupation of Rome and the arrest of the Badoglio government.

According to Doenitz, this operation 'might find some support in scattered places, but will certainly be opposed by the armed forces and the majority of the people. This would lead to a complete disruption of communications . . . Without the co-operation of the Italians, the evacuation of our troops from the islands is entirely out of the question.' [10]

In other words, if the 'Student' operation failed, the German troops in Sicily would be lost.

The success of this Rome operation, on the other hand, depended on the aggressive spirit of the Fascist Party, now decapitated by the disappearance of the Duce. The reports from Rome were not promising.

The German Ambassador had seen Alfieri on July 26, who stated that the main opposition within the Fascist Party had not been aware of the possibility of 'a Badoglio solution', and that the party itself 'has disappeared from the stage unsung and unheard'.[11]

On July 27 Mackensen gave his view that: 'The Fascist Party in Italy stood and fell, as events have shown, with Mussolini. The majority of the Fascist leadership had delivered a political death-blow to Mussolini, and without wanting to, at the same time committed suicide.' [12]

And on the following day: 'The question is still open as to what led to the resignation (sic) of the Duce on the afternoon of the 25th. Alfieri also admits that here one is faced with a riddle. The Japanese Ambassador is deeply struck by the complete collapse of the Party, which has been quietly swept away and nowhere in the country has made the slightest attempt to influence affairs on the side of the Duce.' [13]

The German military intelligence was able to contribute a confirmatory appreciation from the unexpected quarter of their Italian colleagues. On July 27 General Amé, the head of the Italian Military Intelligence sent the following soothing telegram to Admiral Canaris:

'Present developments are inevitably due to the conviction pervading not only the population at large but also leading Party circles that the continued existence of the Fascist régime would lead Italy rapidly and unfailingly into catastrophe. The change of régime which has taken place has gained the full approval of all sections of the Italian community; the more so as Marshal Badoglio and the newly-appointed Ministers, in contrast to their predecessors in government, are personalities who combine administrative competence and personal integrity. The calm and disciplined atmosphere in which the change of régime was accomplished is the best measure of how badly the old Government mismanaged affairs.' [14]

Farinacci was now to receive fleeting attention. He was the only senior Fascist personality on German soil. He had appeared by air in Munich, accompanied by Dollmann and dressed as a German pilot. He was at least a direct witness of recent events, and had been flown on at once to Hitler's headquarters.

The Fuehrer had not modified his first reaction to the inaccurate early reports on Farinacci's activities. He told a meeting on the morning of July 27 that 'the crisis was provoked by the session of the Fascist Grand Council. Farinacci had behaved there like a clumsy bear, and possibly with the best will and noblest intentions, had played a rôle which proved fatal . . . The whole coup had undoubtedly been prepared for a long time, and Farinacci had played a decidedly minor part in this high drama.' [15]

That evening Farinacci arrived, and was 'dealt with' first by Ribbentrop [k] and then by Hitler. If ever he had a chance to play a leading part in the reconstruction of Fascism, this was his historic moment. Goebbels' account reveals the extent of Farinacci's failure. His intrinsic value proved as so often before to be that of a superior informer.

'He behaved very unwisely during these talks. The Fuehrer expected that he would express profound regret at developments, and at least stand unreservedly behind the Duce. This, however, he did not do. His report to the Fuehrer consisted mainly in severe criticism of the Duce's personality and conduct. As he described events, the Duce was violently attacked by Ciano, Grandi, and several other defeatists . . . Farinacci . . . found fault with him more from the viewpoint of Fascist ideology . . . Farinacci, together with Scorza, later that Sunday conferred at length with the Duce, who was then called to the Quirinal and failed to return.'

But even his reporting created further fantasies. He announced for example that an armistice would be signed with the Allies within eight or ten days, and that the British would land in the Genoa-Leghorn area.[16] His version of events confused the German leaders already ill-served by their own agencies in Italy.

k. Ribbentrop had received a cryptic telegram that day from the German representative in Athens reporting a talk with his Italian colleague. The latter said that 'Fascism has no powers of resistance in Central or Southern Italy, but a strong man could pull together the North based on Milan. He suggests Farinacci.' German Collection. Athens telegram, July 27, 1943.

Goebbels continued: 'Farinacci's description proved that our interpretation is right. He still believes that the King acted loyally towards Mussolini, and that the Duce resigned voluntarily; but how then is one to explain that Mussolini, before driving to the Quirinal, knew and foresaw nothing of this whole development, gave no intimation of his decision to resign, and then failed to return? . . . From the Fuehrer's talk with Farinacci, it is evident that we cannot use this man on any grand scale . . . The Fuehrer handed him over to Himmler to look after for the present.

'Farinacci is a completely broken man. It is gradually dawning on him how he blundered . . .' [17]

That hopes had been placed in him is shown by Goebbels's talk with Hitler the following day.[18] The latter was tremendously disappointed in Farinacci, and Goebbels feared that 'the Fuehrer entertained grave illusions' about him.

These illusions were not confined to Hitler. In German political circles, the sequence of events in Rome bore no rational explanation. Goering was unable to believe that Mussolini could have been replaced; Ribbentrop had telegraphed on July 26 asking whether Scorza could be brought out in German uniform? Surely the Secretary of the Party must be a central figure in an organized countercoup. Ribbentrop also wanted to know the whereabouts of Bastianini, presumably for similar motives. The latter had already disappeared from view. Scorza, on the other hand, asked cautiously what was the present attitude of the Germans to the Italian Fascist Party. The sharp reply was to tell him to answer whether or not he would leave for Germany. With some reason he prevaricated, in alarm for his own safety, and arranged and then cancelled a secret rendezvous with Mackensen. He too vanished from sight, and wrote a letter of capitulation to Badogolio.[1]

The Italian army had backed the royal coup. The Party, except for the irrepressible Farinacci, had no figure to lead a renascent revenge. The Militia had been surrendered by Galbiati to Badoglio. There was no Fascist personality round whom a counter-move could be organized. The German network of supporters, informers, and agents within the Italian machine had collapsed as utterly as the régime itself. The symbol of the extinction of a whole set of such relationships was the arrival, as the sole colleague of Farinacci on German soil, of Giovanni Preziosi.

This unsavoury individual had started life as a priest, but was excommunicated in 1914. He had agitated for Italian intervention in the war in 1915 and ran a noisy anti-German paper *La Vita Italiana*. He joined the early Fascist party in May 1920. A factious and slanderous polemist, he haunted

1. German Collection. Series of telegrams July 26–9, 1943. A final message from Scorza in September said that he would seek asylum in Germany 'in event of an English landing'. Rome telegram, September 2, 1943.

the fringes of the movement during the ensuing years, attracting a sinister reputation in a persistent campaign against Freemasonry and the Jews as the arch-enemies of Fascism. It was this clamorous if unheeded platform which earned him a nominal reputation in certain Nazi circles.[m]

This disintegration of the German picture of the Fascist scene left as deep traces in the minds of the German political leaders in considering the setting up of a neo-Fascist state six weeks later, as did the progressive military collapse of Italy upon the German army. If the lesson could have been drawn in simple terms, it was that in so far as Fascism had existed for some time past in Italy it was exclusively represented by the personality of the Duce, and that behind him lay only the historical rubble of a political movement. But even to the end such a thesis could not be quite accepted either by Hitler or his immediate political advisers.

On July 28 Hitler was however 'still optimistic about the Duce, and the possibilities of a Fascist come-back'.[19]

The only hope for the Rome operation was therefore to secure the release of the Duce himself. Badoglio had already refused to disclose his whereabouts. Mackensen was therefore instructed to seek an audience with the King. This took place on July 29.

The King read out a telegram 'dated from Rome' saying that the Duce was well and content. When asked by the Ambassador why the Duce had sent no word to Hitler on his resignation, the King answered that it might be 'the Duce's state of mind', and added:

'In the quite long conversation which had passed as warmly and trustingly as untold others in the course of more than twenty years' work together, he gave the impression of a man struck to the heart, who was faced with the to him inconceivable fact of being rejected by the "faithful". The Duce was at that moment in the same position as the Fuehrer would be if he were suddenly abandoned by Reichsmarshal Goering or Dr Goebbels. The Duce was broken by his own Party, whose attitude the King considered unworthy.'

Arrangements for protection of the Duce had been made with the King's agreement and to secure his person against 'Party extremists'.

Mackensen asked to be permitted to take Hitler's birthday greetings to the Duce. The King evaded the issue and said he would consult Badoglio.[20]

Kesselring equally failed to elicit any information from the latter, and was told that the Duce was in the private custody of the King.[21]

---

m. On July 26 Preziosi was transported to Germany in a separate plane, but on the same day as Farinacci, and was received at once by Hitler about midnight. During the interview Preziosi claims to have listed the warnings of conspiracy among members of the Grand Council which he had uttered to Mussolini since the end of May. In essence it was the Freemasons, headed by Badoglio, who were the organizers of treachery. But the Duce was as ever blind to these manoeuvres, and fooled by the King. For this unconfirmed and marginal episode see Bellotti, *La Repubblica di Mussolini*, pp. 7 ff.

Without the chief actor, the performance had to be at least postponed. If there was to be no immediate restoration of the Duce, at least temporizing relations with the new Italian government must be established.

German military preparations to move into North Italy, and to take over control in South-Eastern Europe, had been suspended, on Jodl's instructions, 'on the basis of his impressions at Feltre'. It seems that, up to the last minute, the German leadership had expected the Feltre programme in its political and military aspects to be carried through by the Duce and 'reliable' Fascist elements at the meeting of the Grand Council. But the disappearance of the Duce disrupted German planning. To meet the new situation, Hitler assumed personal responsibility. At eleven o'clock on the evening of July 26 he had given verbal instructions to Jodl to put in motion the first stage of operation 'Alaric'. All further orders from the German High Command would be directed to taking over all Italian military commitments in their own country. Rommel had already been summoned back from Athens to take over command of Army Group B, with headquarters near Munich.[22]

The immediate German intention was clear. By a lightning counter-coup d'état, Hitler hoped to restore a Fascist government in Rome, and at the same time to ensure complete strategic control of Northern Italy in event of a betrayal by Badoglio.

The Italian High Command had been aware for some time of the danger of German action in event of a revolutionary change as the result of the removal of the Duce.[n] General Ambrosio, whatever his motives, had himself requested on July 24 the move into Northern Italy of the two German divisions destined to reinforce the Southern Front.[o] It was undoubtedly the express decision of the King to insist on the continuance, at any rate for the time being, of the German alliance, and even if his ultimate intention was to negotiate with the Anglo-Americans, he would need German military support in the South in order to hold the front long enough to be able to negotiate 'with honour'.

The extent of German military infiltration into Northern Italy, however, and above all the fear of a sponsored Fascist plot against the new government, called for a sharp protective reaction.

As the first German troop movements began, a revealing conversation took place on July 31 between Ambrosio and Kesselring.[p]

The two German divisions whose move into Italy Ambrosio had already accepted, were now, owing to an alleged misunderstanding, not welcomed by

n. See p. 343. Ambrosio appears to have told Badoglio early in July of German plans for a coup on July 26.

o. Rommel noted that these two divisions were moving into Italy 'as agreed with Mussolini'. (German Collection.)

p. For the full text, see Appendix to this chapter. Dated July 31.

B.F.—17

the Italian High Command. Ambrosio told Kesselring that he had ordered one of them, the 44th Division 'to stay put and wait until trains are available'.

Kesselring lamely countered that 'this is no longer, one might say, an Italian theatre of war. It has become an Axis theatre.' To which Ambrosio retorted 'It always has been', and expressed concern that German units had occupied all block posts south of the Brenner.

Ambrosio's main argument was that if and when the two German divisions moved, they must not be concentrated in the Leghorn-Genoa area, but moved at once to the South.

Ambrosio's tone was high. 'It is the manner which I don't like.' Kesselring answered that the problem of defending the South did not depend on two divisions. 'Either one must end the war, or bring in further divisions.' Ambrosio commented tartly: 'But this question arises suddenly this evening . . . and in any case, to finish, I do not want that division to cross the Brenner.'

Advanced units of this 44th Jaeger Division, however, had already crossed the Brenner. At 1.30 p.m. on July 27 orders to implement 'Alaric' were given to take effect on July 30, and on the following day when Ambrosio and Kesselring met, the general move began. [23]

In the meantime, the German units already dispersed throughout Italy were instructed to re-group in the Rome area, and to the alarm of the Italian High Command, two parachute units appeared partly by air and rail in the neighbourhood of the capital.

By the end of the first week of August, some seven new German divisions were on Italian soil.[24]

The Royal government now strove to avoid an open conflict with the Germans. On July 27 Badoglio had sent a telegram to Hitler, reiterating the determination of the new régime to continue the war, and asking him to receive General Marras, the Italian Military Attaché in Berlin on a special mission.[25] The Italian proposal was to arrange a meeting between the King and Hitler. But the latter was still under the first emotional impact of the disappearance of the Duce from the scene, and curtly refused.

A mounting disquiet pervaded the Italian capital. During the afternoon of July 28 'the fear of a German reaction was accentuated. His Majesty ordered me to arrange everything for an eventual departure from Rome. "I do not want to run the risk," he said, "of ending like the King of Belgium." ' [26]

The German military leaders were opposed to any 'political' solution of the Italian crisis. They had no faith in a Fascist revival, and doubted whether they could back up such counter-measures. Rommel, now at his new command, favoured delay, and in strictly military terms no high level decision had yet been reached whether to continue to defend Sicily or to withdraw to defensive positions north of Rome. Rommel had consistently supported the latter course. Both Keitel and Jodl preferred to rely on a gradual military infiltration into the Italian peninsula, thus reinforcing the German tactical position without an open clash.

On July 30 came a soothing report from Canaris of a discussion with his Italian colleague at Venice on the previous day. According to Amé, 'the conversation at Feltre had had no influence on the decision of the Grand Council. Sicily could not be held any longer, the will to resist both in the population and the army was unbroken. The present government was determined by stern internal leadership to pursue the war with every means. There was no question of peace negotiations and even the Pope had not undertaken any. On July 29 the rumour had circulated that Germany wanted to put the Duce back again by marching into Rome. Ambrosio however had not believed this. On the other hand there were fears in Rome of action by uncontrolled German units.[q]

An added argument in favour of delaying drastic measures was the danger of a loss of control by Badoglio of the internal Italian situation. The new régime had taken firm measures to maintain law and order, and both Kesselring and Rintelen urged that the Rome government should be supported, if only on these grounds alone. On August 2 Rintelen reported in person to Hitler in this sense, and stressed that Badoglio was the only bulwark against Communism, which represented a real danger in Northern Italy.[27]

The new Italian Foreign Minister, Guariglia, only reached Rome on July 29 from Turkey where he had been Ambassador.

The formal Allied reactions to the change of régime in Italy had been cold, particularly in a speech on July 27 by Churchill to the House of Commons.

The suspicion in German circles of prior and secret negotiations between the new Italian régime and the Western Allies appear from the interception by the German Intelligence Services of a long-distance telephone call between Churchill and Roosevelt at one o'clock on the morning of July 29.

Churchill: 'We do not want proposals for an armistice to be made before we have been definitely approached.'

Roosevelt: 'That is right.'

q. German War Office Collection. War Diary of the German High Command, July 31, 1943. Canaris had informed Rommel of this conversation. He saw Amé again early in August. (See Abshagen *op cit* p. 339 ff.) This was to be the last meeting of the two Intelligence Chiefs. Amé was replaced shortly afterwards in August by Carboni, whom he had succeeded in the previous year. Canaris was sacked in February 1944 and the Abwehr incorporated in the security organization of Kaltenbrunner. To what extent in general there was connivance between certain German and Italian military circles with a view to a secret understanding to seek a negotiated peace with the Western Allies has as yet not been clarified.

Churchill: 'We can also wait quietly for one or two days.'

Roosevelt: 'That is right.'

Churchill says he will contact the King of Italy, and Roosevelt answers that he too will get in touch with 'Emmanuel'. 'I do not know quite how I shall do this.'[r]

In the political as in the military field, there was little break in policy in Rome. Badoglio had been aware of Bastianini's attempt to contact the British through Lisbon just before the Feltre conference.[s] Any military arrangements with the Germans, and they were essential to the survival of the Monarchy, would be inevitably temporary, and were conditioned by the need to create favourable conditions in which peace negotiations could be initiated. And there was still the remote possibility of persuading the Germans to agree to such a step. The basic position of the Badoglio government was that of Mussolini after Feltre, and the proposal of a meeting between the King and Hitler had been conceived in such terms.

According to Badoglio, the decision to contact the Western Allies was taken at an audience with the King on the evening of July 28, and therefore before the arrival of Guariglia from Ankara.[28] The latter made a first approach to the British Minister to the Vatican on the night of July 30, and on August 2 D'Ajeta, Ciano's former private secretary, left for Lisbon.[t]

Such soundings can scarcely have escaped the attention of the Germans. At a Naval Conference at Hitler's headquarters on August 3 Jodl reported that 'the Italians have completely ceased resistance to our measures'. Hitler's view was that 'they may just be biding their time in order to come to terms with the Anglo-Saxons before breaking openly with Germany'. Both Jodl and Doenitz however thought that the Italians might be feeling 'helpless' and therefore 'want to rely more on us again'.[29]

It was decided therefore to postpone all the four operations: 'Achse', 'Eiche', 'Schwarz', and 'Student', until further notice.

r. German Collection. Quoted in the War Diary of the German High Command with the comment: 'This is complete proof that secret negotiations between the Anglo-Americans and Italy are under way.'

s. See pp. 395–6.

t. Another Italian official was sent on August 5 to contact the British diplomatic representative in Tangier where Badoglio's son was Consul-General. See this official's account in his book, Berio *Missione Segreta*. The Vatican was aware of D'Ajeta's mission. There is in the German Collection a telegram from the German Minister, Weiszæcker, dated July 27, reporting an interview with the Secretary of State, Cardinal Maglione. The latter openly stated that he did not believe in the Badoglio formula 'the war continues', and added that he had sent for D'Ajeta 'but does not want to see Ciano'.

APPENDIX

Ambrosio-Kesselring Meeting July 31 1943

Kesselring: 'I spoke to Marshal Badoglio in regard to the military question. But the Marshal replied that he had nothing to do with the military side and that I should approach General Ambrosio.

'I then took it on myself to examine the question in detail this evening with General Roatta.

'After having talked to him, I went by plane to report to the Fuehrer and had left with the impression that the move of the 305th and 44th German Divisions had been assured, and to be precise, in the proportion of fifty per cent between the two German divisions and the (Italian) Alpine Division.'

Ambrosio: 'There is evidently a misunderstanding. General Roatta could not have given this assurance. When I knew that the divisions must come, I said at once that it was better to stop them, as we could not transport them.

'The Field Marshal will be able to discuss this matter with General Roatta. I have been told that the 44th Division should move tomorrow. I have given the following order: to stay put and wait until trains are available.'

Kesselring: 'In this affair I share the opinion of the German Army Staff, namely that in such a case—or in other similar ones—it is not opportune to hold up a troop movement for ten or twelve days. This is no longer, one might say, only an Italian theatre of war. It has become an Axis theatre!'

Ambrosio: 'It has always been. And by the way, why have all the block posts south of the Brenner been occupied?'

Kesselring: 'I was not aware of this fact . . . But I think it as well to clarify the situation by speaking clearly. The Fuehrer, apart from these two divisions, has allocated others, and namely to ensure the possibility of holding Italian territory, including Sicily.'

Ambrosio: 'An added reason for not encumbering the country, which is already full of troops.'

Kesselring: 'I maintain that the two divisions, according to how the Italian High Command wishes to allocate them, could be concentrated in the area of Leghorn, to be embarked and then sent on. I have thousands of men scattered throughout Southern Italy without any contact with the North. A base . . . for example in the zone of Leghorn, would be justified. As and when required, these forces could then be moved elsewhere.'

Ambrosio: 'I cannot agree to this. These divisions must go to Southern Italy and therefore their stay in that zone is not justifiable.

'The Field Marshal maintains that this is necessary. As the Italian High Command, I say no! . . .'

Kesselring: 'We could transport another division, not the 305th or 44th.'

Ambrosio: 'We have been talking of the 305th and the 44th. Let us not now talk of other divisions.'

Kesselring: 'One must take into account the general situation! In fact days ago the matter was discussed with General Roatta, and it was stated that in order to increase security it would still be as well to have forces in the zones of Naples and Leghorn.'

Ambrosio: 'It does not matter what you said to Roatta. You should in the first instance come here.'

Kesselring: 'Your Excellency has told me many times to make direct contact with the Army Command.'

Ambrosio: 'Yes, but before bringing the whole German Army into Italy you have to talk to me.'

Kesselring: 'General Roatta had noted at once the proposals made and I was certain that he would have talked to you about them. However, if a mistake has been made, we can remedy it. For precisely that reason I have come here. If Your Excellency were in my position and had to reason as a soldier, you would see these needs as I do.'

Ambrosio: 'It is the manner which I don't like!'

Kesselring: 'The problem down there (in the south) is not settled with two divisions. Either one must end the war, or bring in further divisions.'

Ambrosio: 'But this question arises suddenly this evening!'

Kesselring: 'I was sure that General Roatta had informed the Italian High Command.'

Ambrosio: 'The matter is quite new to me, and precisely for this reason, I cannot allow the argument to be continued.'

Kesselring: 'There has obviously been a mistake and we can talk it over now.'

Ambrosio: 'In military matters one must be precise. There was always a question of two divisions: now others come to light. Let us not discuss them now.'

Kesselring: 'In the common interest I was dealing with the matter with the German High Command.'

Ambrosio: 'I would ask you then to come here with a complete table showing everything available and we can talk about it.'

Kesselring: 'At the present moment one cannot take decisions of definite value. One must fit decisions to the needs of the moment.'

Ambrosio: 'All right. But come here with a complete schedule. Instead, you talk to me and from time to time pull out a new division.

'Let us have the discussion because nothing will be settled. In the meantime the authorization is valid only for the two divisions, the 305th and the 44th. I would ask you instead to withdraw those now stationed along the railway.

'This morning I had complaints from His Majesty that paratroops, without any permission, had occupied a royal estate. At Viterbo other paratroops (there are thousands of them) are shooting like the wrath of God. You are the commander, and as such responsible.

'By the way, what are all these paratroops in the Viterbo area?'

Kesselring: 'They are three battalions destined to complete the units of the 3rd Armoured Division.'

Ambrosio: 'It must be something else, and you cannot be in the picture.'

Kesselring: 'I assure you categorically that these are the three battalions, whose movements have been regularly reported to the Italian Army Command, which incidentally is always done.'

Ambrosio: 'They are giving a lot of trouble because they are acting illegally.'

Kesselring: 'That is another matter. I am grateful to you for the information, so that I can deal with it . . .'

Ambrosio: 'Returning to the main argument, I will send for Roatta tomorrow morning. If the Field Marshal is available, I would like to clear the thing up.'

Kesselring: 'Certainly. I only ask that confidence should be mutual.'

Ambrosio: 'It isn't a matter of trust. We are worried that the behaviour of German troops leaves much to be desired and the population is complaining.

'In any case, to finish for this evening, I do not want that division to cross the Brenner.' [u]

u. Italian Collection. Ambrosio-Kesselring meeting. July 31, 1943.

CHAPTER TWO

ROMAN INTERLUDE

• •

FORMAL RELATIONS between Germany and the Badoglio government were now taken a step further by holding a meeting of political and military representatives on both sides. This elaborate probing of intentions took place at Tarvisio on August 6.[1] It was an appendix to Feltre under changed conditions, and an examination of those changes in an atmosphere of tense mutual distrust. Guariglia, the new Foreign Minister, had already instructed his envoy D'Ajeta now in Lisbon to warn the Allies of this meeting, and to minimize its significance.

The Italian delegation was led by Guariglia and Ambrosio. They were accompanied in the train from Rome by Mackensen and Dollmann.

The German party headed by Ribbentrop and Keitel arrived in an armoured train, festooned with machine-guns and with anti-aircraft cannon mounted on the roofs of the carriages. S.S. troops lined the platform as this apparition came to a halt.

The morning session was confined mainly to the political situation and the dialogue was dramatic in tone. The German Foreign Minister defined the purpose of the meeting. It was 'to discuss the situation resulting from the change which has taken place in Italy and which has had political and psychological repercussions', and he sought a 'clarification' from the Italian government.

Guariglia answered that the change was a purely internal matter and that the head of the government had declared that the war would continue. The situation was now normal.

The reaction to the Grand Council had been such that the whole Fascist organization had disappeared. 'It would not have been wise to entrust the government of Italy to those very men who overthrew the Duce.

'Personally I think that you should take such political action, which you have already discussed with Bastianini,[a] as to modify some aspects of your propaganda: you should give out more precise ideas on the future organization of Europe.'

Ribbentrop stressed the Communist danger which must follow the collapse of Fascism, and the pretext for its rise!

Guariglia answered: 'The Fascist Party won over the country in 1922 without great Communist opposition; and, if after 22 years it has fallen at a blow, almost without a tremor, this means that the relationship between Fascists and Communists has not created the kind of situation which would give rise to profound internal struggles. Resemblances between National Socialism and Fascism are theoretical . . . In the most turbulent moments Italy has gone through in domestic politics, we were never in really dangerous situations.' [2]

Ribbentrop then came to the point. 'He wanted to know whether conversations had taken place with the British and Americans.'

Guariglia replied: 'No. The only contact was the conversation with the Turkish Foreign Minister.' [b] The subject was not pursued.[3]

How did Italy intend to collaborate in the military field? Ambrosio reacted at once. The Italian High Command had been 'not a little surprised' that the German divisions had been now sent to Italy 'without previous agreement'.

'We have the precise impression that you are abandoning the forces in Southern Italy, that you have concentrated them around Rome against eventual attacks in the upper Western Mediterranean, and are deploying them from the Ligurian coast along the Apennines as if, having altered your operational concept, you consider Italian territory only as a glacier for the defence of Germany.' [4]

Keitel answered that the German command, given the need for an urgent and joint defence of Italy, had moved troops from the East as well as West and North, and in each case had informed the Italian frontier posts of these moves. He was amazed that Ambrosio should talk as if the Italian High Command 'was no longer master in its own house. There must evidently be a misunderstanding due to the actual state of Italian communications.'

To which Guariglia tartly retorted that the impression given by the way in which German troops had entered Italy was that they came not to collaborate militarily but to preserve public order.

'We have no troops available except for fighting' was Ribbentrop's rejoinder.

The German and Italian military leaders met shortly after 3 o'clock that afternoon. Both sides had one aim in common: the avoidance of an open break in order to play for time. Neither party had the conviction that a

a. At Klessheim in the previous April.   b. Hitler e Mussolini *op cit* p. 193.

B.F.—17*

united front could be held on Italian soil for long. The Germans concentrated essentially on implementing, as far as possible with Italian consent, the series of operations already planned to come into effect if Italy collapsed or signed an armistice.

The immediate purpose of the meeting, as Keitel stated, was the constitution of a mobile strategic reserve, and the problem of supplies and transport for Sicily. In strategic terms, the German High Command still regarded the main danger to their southern front to be a major Allied landing in the Gulf of Genoa, launched from Sicilian and North African bases, and probably coinciding with a thrust into the Balkans once a foothold on the Southern Italy mainland had been secured. Such a move would constitute a major threat to the whole Axis fortress in Europe, and since May German military planning had given a high priority to counter-measures to such a threat. These involved in particular extensive troop movements and the securing of vital communications under German control in the Alpine passes and Northern Italy. As a result of the Feltre talks three German divisions were on the move from the Channel.

As General Warlimont, the Deputy Chief of Operations, now explained at this meeting, one of these was to guard the Brenner, another to remain just across the Italian border in Carinthia and to be switched either to Italy or the Balkans. The third to be sent to the Ravenna area, where with two further German divisions, now on the French frontier and destined for the Genoa area and Liguria and Lombardy, it would form a central operational reserve. A concentration of at least these three German divisions in North and Central Italy was considered by the German High Command to be essential.

This plan filled the Italians with alarm. There were already ten German divisions in Italy. It would give the Germans control of all movements and communications throughout Northern Italy, and enable them to concentrate round Genoa to seize the Italian fleet in a moment of crisis. German units in Central Italy could be moved to dominate Rome, which was already masked by a parachute division ostensibly the mobile reserve in the South, and if such moves were carried out, German military occupation of the North together with the vital arc of the Alpine passes could be imposed in a matter of hours.

In the afternoon, the Chief of the Italian General Staff pressed for the last time for the return of the Italian Fourth Army from France, 'which could, if need be, be transferred to the South . . . I do not see the excessive threat to Northern Italy.' The Italians would also guard the Brenner, thus relieving one German division. Keitel immediately said that he must refer this request to Berlin. 'This evacuation (from France) I find disquieting from the political point of view . . . and I must therefore take the matter up with the Fuehrer.'

Ambrosio equally insisted on withdrawing at least part of the Second

Italian Army from the Balkans, and again his German colleague retorted that he must refer to Hitler.[5]

This dialogue represented the end of the long drawn out episode of Italo-German military co-operation, and it evolved in a lowering atmosphere of mutual suspicion and threatening political undertones.

On his return to Rome, Ambrosio disclosed his essential impressions to Puntoni for the ear of the Sovereign.

'Our only remaining hope is that, in view of the reinforcement of the Italian front, the Anglo-Americans will launch their next assault in the direction of the Balkans or France. If such an attack succeeds, German troops will almost certainly be withdrawn from the Peninsula and sent to the new front. Only in such a way could we regain a certain liberty of action.'[6]

On the evening of August 6, the two delegations held a final meeting. It appears that during the interval, Ribbentrop and Keitel had driven to the border, and ordered the German division stationed on the Carinthian frontier to cross into Italy, and that on their return Ribbentrop and Guariglia had a private conversation in the former's drawing-room on the German armoured train.[7] This talk was a summary, and for the last time, of the main themes of past diplomatic encounters since the outbreak of hostilities: the German determination to continue the war, and the Italian thesis of a separate peace with Russia.

At 7 o'clock the diplomatic and military representatives met. Ribbentrop made a formal unconvincing summary of the talks, voicing a perfunctory acknowledgment that both Allies would continue the war, but 'in to-day's conversation it had been necessary to re-establish shaken confidence; now in the near future one could talk on a broader basis'.[8] There had been thinking in terms of a meeting between the King and the Fuehrer, but the present clarification was an essential preliminary step. Personal contact was now required. Such a conference would be held between the King with the Crown Prince and Badoglio on the one hand, and Hitler with Goering and Ribbentrop on the other.

'The resignation of the Duce had struck Hitler hard from the human point of view. The Fuehrer thought that the present Italian government might be replaced by another, and for that reason a meeting between him and the King, together with the Prince, was opportune, in order to make general contact and take decisions.'[9]

The proposal for such a meeting had of course been made to Berlin by the Badoglio government immediately after the events of July 25 under the impact of fear of German counter-measures. The significance of Ribbentrop's present suggestion was obscure and sinister. Guariglia, who was thinking of his envoy D'Ajeta in Lisbon, noted, 'There was now no question on our side of discussing it when we had already made contact with the Allies.' [10]

The inclusion by Ribbentrop of the Prince of Piedmont in the proposed Italian delegation at such a meeting might mean the revival of the operation to arrest the Royal family,[c] or perhaps the exertion of pressure on them to dismiss Badoglio, and accept an administration imposed by the Germans. The intention was not clear and in the event without result.

The leave-taking of the two delegations was cold and correct. As the heavily guarded German armoured train drew out, Ribbentrop without warning ordered Mackensen to accompany him to Germany. The Ambassador left with a single suitcase. Such was the abrupt ending of the latter's mission to Rome, and the penalty for imperfections of reporting on the crisis of the Duce's fall from power.

The Tarvisio conference marked the end of formal German co-operation within the frame of the Axis pact with an Italian government in Rome still nominally at war on her side.

Ribbentrop remarked in a later conversation that he already felt clearly, when Ambrosio and Guariglia presented themselves at Tarvisio, that Italy wanted to abandon Germany. In confirmation of this conviction, he adds that immediately after the meeting at Tarvisio he telephoned the Fuehrer and said, 'Danger all along the line,' meaning by this that he had had the clear impression that Badoglio's government had decided to hand Italy over to the Allies. 'I returned to Headquarters', Ribbentrop continued, 'with this conviction, and it was on the basis of this impression that all available divisions were sent into Italy, the divisions which stopped the enemy first at Salerno, then at Cassino, and which enabled Rome to hold out until last June, and now, after fourteen months, the Apennine line . . . In August 1943, we already knew that the betrayal was at hand.' [11]

Both sides had gained time. As Guariglia put it, 'I succeeded . . . in obtaining a truce; this had to be used without delay in order to conclude the necessary agreements with the Allies.' [12]

The Germans accelerated their preparations against an Italian betrayal. The plans to seize the Italian Royal Family were dropped after Tarvisio, and the search for the Duce was intensified. On August 9 Hitler ordered the early execution of this latter operation, adding that the Italian government was 'capable of almost any kind of treason'.[13]

The events of the last fortnight of August appear as an elaborate chess game between the German and Italian authorities, overshadowed by the imminence of an Allied invasion of metropolitan Italy.

The first soundings of the Allies in Lisbon by D'Ajeta on August 4 showed that there was no hope of negotiations through diplomatic channels. D'Ajeta

c. See p. 492.

had reported that the British and Americans would only treat on the basis of unconditional surrender, and with military representatives.

General Castellano was therefore briefed to undertake such a mission, though he was not informed of the previous diplomatic feelers. He left Rome on August 12 with instructions drafted by Ambrosio and approved by Guariglia.[14] The essence of his instructions summarized the extent of hopes of the Italian High Command. He 'was to seek contact with officers of the Anglo-American General Staff, to explain our military situation, to learn their intentions, and above all to say that we cannot detach ourselves from our ally without their help. He was to advise an Allied landing north of Rome, and another in the Adriatic. A landing to the north of Rimini would by itself settle the whole situation, since the Germans, the flank of their own line of communications threatened, would be forced to withdraw from Central Italy to defend the Alpine passes.' [15]

It had been the last hope, and illusion, of Grandi that he would represent the Badoglio government in peace talks with the Allies. He had already proposed such a plan to Acquarone on the morning of July 25, and had called on Guariglia soon after the latter's arrival in Rome [d] to press his nomination as ambassador to Madrid. Guariglia was clear, however, 'that Grandi was too compromised with the Fascist régime to appear openly as the representative of the new Italian government to ask for the assistance of the Allies who still intransigently make use of anti-Fascism as a weapon of war and ideological basis of their own political conduct'.[16]

He was however prepared to allow Grandi to make unofficial contact with the British and Americans in Spain or Portugal as 'his presence in Italy could cause much embarrassment to the government'. He might well become the focus of a 'moderate' Fascist opposition. According to Grandi's own account, he received on August 14 a message from Acquarone: 'Badoglio is ruining us all. In a few days you will enter the government.' [17]

Such a mission would also distract German attention from the moves of D'Ajeta and Castellano. Even before Grandi's departure, the Germans were aware of his intended journey. On August 11 Hitler stated at a Fuehrer conference: 'The Italians will not show their true colours until the presumed trip of Grandi to Lisbon or the meeting of Churchill and Roosevelt in Canada has produced results. The Italians are going ahead with their negotiations at full speed. They will be taken in by any promise of the Anglo-Saxons if only the continued rule of the Royal House is guaranteed. Their negotiations are treasonable. They go along with us in order to gain time. The Italian Army cannot be used in combat against the Allies. In contrast to former occasions, they have not appealed to us for military support in connection with the meeting at Tarvisio, but remained completely inactive.' [18]

d. Probably on August 3. See Grandi's own account in his letter to Sir Winston Churchill from Lisbon October 12, 1943. The text is in the Appendix to this chapter.

Grandi finally reached Madrid on August 18 and travelled on to Portugal. As he wrote to Churchill, 'contacts had already been established between military authorities, thereby making of no further use any contribution of a political character'.[e]

In Grandi's view, the first ten days of the Badoglio régime had sealed the fate of Italy.

On August 15, the last conference of military experts between the Italians and Germans was held at Bologna.[19]

The Germans were already considering the evacuation of Sicily, and the only reason for the present meeting was to make a final attempt to put into detailed effect the German defence plan in Northern and Central Italy with Italian consent. Roatta represented the Italians; Jodl headed the German mission together with Rommel, whose functions as commander of Army Group B were now to be disclosed to the Italians.[f]

This final encounter took place in a villa outside Bologna, which belonged to Federzoni and had been confiscated after July 25.

The German party had arrived by air under the protection of an S.S. guard of honour in spite of Rintelen's protests. 'Jodl asked me if I knew the history of the Italian Renaissance.'[20]

The tone of the meeting was quickly set. Jodl agreed to the partial evacuation of the Italian Fourth Army from France, as requested by Ambrosio at Tarvisio, but asked whether they would 'be used against the English in Sicily or the Germans on the Brenner'.[21] Roatta refused to reply to this 'tendentious' question.

The main purpose of the talks emerged. The German defence plan, as drawn up by Rommel and Jodl at a Fuehrer conference on August 11, was to be based on an ultimate defence line running from Pisa eastwards to the south of Florence and across to Rimini on the Adriatic coast. Rail communications to the north and the Alpine passes were to be exclusively under German control.

Rommel was to be appointed commander of a new Army Group B embracing all German and Italian units in North and Central Italy and nominally, like Kesselring, under the control of the Italian High Command. There would be on paper a united and Italian command in Italy. In the Balkans, however, the Germans proposed a combined headquarters under their control, but would accede to the Italian request to withdraw three divisions from the area.

Roatta hesitated to make further comment. Instead he suggested a pause

e. See Appendix to this chapter. Grandi to Churchill October 12, 1943. The Germans kept a strict watch on Grandi's movements in Portugal. (See German collection, Ribbentrop telegram, September 2, 1943.)

f. Rintelen was also present. See his book, *op cit* p. 241.

for luncheon. Jodl answered that he must return at once by air. It seemed that Hitler had given orders forbidding any social occasion, but, at Rommel's instance, the meal took place, with a German colonel with a loaded pistol sitting ostentatiously at the Generals' table.

After lunch Roatta, cool and diplomatic, traced on a map his proposals for a combined order of battle and chain of command. This map was later published by Goebbels to prove the Italian intention to trap the German units in event of an Allied landing.[22]

Throughout the conference the villa had been surrounded by an S.S. Company, and there had been German sentries posted at the hotel in Bologna during luncheon.

Roatta, whose mission, conscious or otherwise, had been to seek a final *modus vivendi* with the German High Command either until the Allies landed, or in the event of a failure of Castellano's mission, could hardly have conceived that any positive result would follow this brief encounter.[g]

Events in the Italian theatre now followed their appointed course. Allied air bombardments of Milan and Turin on August 12, and of Rome on the following day, were a sharp reminder of Allied intransigence. On August 17 the German and Italian forces evacuated Sicily. The long awaited Allied assault on the Italian mainland must follow. Its probable direction was discussed at a meeting in Rome on August 21 between Kesselring, Ambrosio, and their respective advisers.[23] This meeting was the last stage of Italo-German military collaboration, and was merely a mutual probing of intentions. In practice, both parties were acting in complete and mistrustful independence of each other.

Rommel had set up his headquarters 'as if nothing had happened',[24] and, according to the German defence plan outlined at the Bologna conference, units moved in the direction of Rimini and Genoa. On the Italian side, following the Tarvisio meeting, the defence of Rome had been strengthened, two divisions were being directed into the Spezia area to forestall any German *coup de main* against the Italian fleet, and a further two divisions took up positions in the Alto Adige to watch German intentions along the Brenner route.[25] German military penetration south of their announced defence line was thus halted. Detailed orders were circulated to all Italian commands in event of an open break with the Germans.[26]

German precautions had also reached their culminating phase. The very machinery of contact, political and military, had ground to a halt. There was neither an Italian ambassador in Berlin nor a German ambassador in Rome. Alfieri had disappeared from sight after July 25, and Mackensen had been

g. Roatta had been proposed as Alfieri's successor in Berlin. Throughout the military contacts with the Germans in the previous July, he had appeared as the main protagonist of increased German military support in Italy. He was not aware of Castellano's journey, and his own mission to Bologna may well have been a deliberate cover invented by Ambrosio.

brought back by Ribbentrop from Tarvisio. The last meeting between Ambrosio and Keitel had been held. The close collaboration of the two Intelligence services had been broken with Amé's replacement by Carboni, although perhaps this link had served to mask rather than expose the real course of recent events in Italy.

The end of the phase of military co-operation was symbolically marked by the retirement at the end of the month of General Rintelen, who had been in constant touch with Italian affairs since his appointment as Military Attaché in Rome in 1936. His successor, General Toussaint, former military adviser to the German 'Protector' of Bohemia, arrived on August 31 with a letter from Keitel.

'The development of the situation as seen at the highest quarters calls for special measures . . . The Fuehrer has thus decided, in the personal field, to make a change in German political representation.' [27]

The whole policy of Germany towards her Italian ally had been under agitated and spasmodic revision since the fall of the Duce in July. As in the past, there were deep divergences of view between the German military and political leaders. The former were against any 'political' solution either in the form of a constrained revision of the Axis alliance in concert with the King and Badoglio, the backing of a neo-Fascist administration without the Duce, or the reinstatement of Mussolini himself. All measures proposed by the German High Command in regard to Italy were directly destined to lead to military occupation.

The political complications of this attitude were all too apparent to Ribbentrop and his advisers. The lessons of Poland and Bohemia were not encouraging. The French model, with all its obvious drawbacks, might be more applicable, and Badoglio's resemblance to Pétain was not without a certain crude relevance. Native Marshals were preferable to German Protectors, and the mirage of Montoire was not yet empty of all content.

It was not therefore without significance that Mackensen's successor in Rome should be a collaborator of Abetz. Dr Rudolf Rahn had risen in the German diplomatic service through the special agencies in the Foreign Office created by Ribbentrop.[h] He was a ductile Swabian, determined under a genial manner, full of ideas and imagination, a shrewd politician with a sharp legal mind. In August 1940 he had been appointed to Abetz's staff in Paris and involved in the intricate phases of Franco-German collaboration. He became an expert at delicate missions: in Syria to bolster up Vichy in 1941, and shortly afterwards on the adventurous fiasco of the Iraq rising in May of that same year. At the end of 1942 Rahn was in Tunis as political adviser to the German military command dealing with Vichy French and Arab

h. In 1939 Rahn had been in the special Information Office and the following year in the 'Dienststelle Ribbentrop'.

affairs, and was evacuated in May 1943 on the eve of the Axis collapse in North Africa.

This mission had brought him into indirect contact for the first time with Italian affairs. He had reported to Ribbentrop on his return from Tunis, and had been told that the German leadership still believed that Italy was loyal to the Axis.[i]

After July 25 Rahn had been summoned to Hitler's headquarters, and told that he might be sent on a diplomatic mission to Rome. In brief, Hitler explained that he was determined if need be by force to prevent an Italian withdrawal from the Axis alliance.

But after the initial shock of the disappearance of the Duce of Fascism, the German leadership moved cautiously in its reappraisal of the Italian scene.

A confidential memorandum circulated by Ribbentrop's office on August 13 maintained that, 'thanks to methodical and not unskilful propaganda, however, the notion has gradually started to gain ground among Italians that to end the war suddenly at the present juncture would be highly detrimental to creating a more favourable military situation. The sense of honour, long acknowledged by all leading Italian circles as a decisive factor, is now playing a part which, whilst widely misunderstood, ought not to be underestimated. Any solution which would be incompatible with Italian honour, and would again make this a subject for international debate, is rejected categorically and emphatically. The present moment, as all German authorities repeatedly confirm, is undoubtedly one of great importance. The new Government's reiterated resolve not to acquiesce in unconditional surrender in any circumstances, and not to permit Italy to be turned into a theatre for operations against her German ally, is most earnestly meant and will be translated into reality.

'However, the great question for the future is of course whether in face of the renewed heavy air bombardment, which has already begun, and of possibly grave military reverses the Government will succeed, by applying the draconic military measures already introduced, in preventing a sharp swing to the Left. The beginnings of a serious Communist revolt are admittedly already present in Northern Italy. Whether this will continue to be so in future is the great and anxious question of the hour. What is not in the slightest open to doubt is the well-founded assumption that should the Badoglio government fall, men of a radical Left-wing, even Communist, outlook would come to power who would subscribe to unconditional surrender, thus throwing wide the gates to the enemy for an invasion of Italy's shores. In these circumstances, the presence in Italy of German troops is a very positive and a very reassuring factor, which is beginning to make itself generally felt.

i. Rahn's notes to the author. He saw Ribbentrop between May 15 and 17. See also Rahn *op cit* p. 223.

However, no one at the present time dare predict the course of future events, even for a day ahead.' [28]

At a Fuehrer conference on August 19 Mackensen stated in summary his final analysis of the conditions in Italy. There had been dissatisfaction in Fascist circles and 'the Fascist Council voted without realizing the consequences. Not even the Duce was aware of conditions. It remained for the King to make the Duce aware of the state of affairs that even his Fascist Party had lost faith in him. Following this the Duce offered his resignation and asked for a guarantee of safety for himself and his family. The King agreed and the Duce then was allegedly placed in protective custody. Mackensen believes that Badoglio had no previous knowledge of the entire affair. He says that the longing for peace is widespread among the Italian people but that the present Government is willing to continue to fight because the impossibility of obtaining peace without making all of Italy a battlefield is realized. Mackensen states that present conditions do not warrant a pessimistic attitude; that the Fuehrer was seeing matters in a more pessimistic manner than, in his opinion, was justified. He could of course offer no proof that he was right and the Fuehrer wrong.' [29]

These remarks by Mackensen constituted his concluding report to Hitler on his diplomatic mission to Rome.

Towards the end of the month, as the German military measures culminated in the setting up of Rommel's command, and reports were reaching the German leadership of secret Italian talks in Lisbon, some positive approach on the political level had to be taken.

Rahn was summoned again to Supreme Headquarters. He had already seen Ribbentrop the previous day. The interview with Hitler took place on August 29.[j]

The immediate cause for alarm appeared to be Italian troop movements in the area of the Alpine passes, which might indicate an Italian plan, in secret concert with the Allies, to cut off an eventual German retreat to the North.

In the face of pressure by the German High Command for drastic measures of security, Rahn was instructed to avoid any abrupt breach with Badoglio, but to use his judgment in impelling the latter to 'show his flag'. Ribbentrop had not given up all hope of an ultimate deal with the King and the Marshal, nor was Hitler ready to force the issue.

Under the seal of secrecy, Hitler told Rahn of the plan to liberate Mussolini. It was likely that the Fuehrer's real motive was to avoid an open break with Badoglio before this revolutionary move, now under active consideration, of restoring the Duce could be made.

j. In Rahn's notes to the author, he says between August 27 and 29, but other evidence favours the latter date.

The pace of events was moving faster each day with each side half aware of the unfriendly intentions of the other. The Germans were more or less militarily prepared for an Italian surrender, but the Italians were less certain of the danger of a German-backed Fascist coup to forestall such an event.

Fear of a counterplot to restore the position prior to July 25, linked with an exaggerated assessment of a possible Fascist revival, was a constant and indeed obsessive concern of the Badoglio government, and the atmosphere of conspiracy haunted the inner ruling circles of Rome in these last August days, inducing a certain panic and hysteria, coinciding with the lack of news from Castellano in Lisbon and nervousness as to Allied reactions to a separate peace.

A symptom of this panic was the discovery of a real or invented plot in which the main protagonists were Cavallero himself and the former Party Secretary, Muti. Whether this episode was mere police frame-up, or the work of German agencies, may never be known.

Puntoni noted on August 22 in his diary: [30] 'Tonight, following a report of contacts which they are alleged to have had with German military elements, many leading exponents of Fascism have been arrested. In the Senate, Cavallero has again been arrested.'[k]

The latter was incarcerated at Forte Boccea, where, among others, he found Buffarini for company. A series of arrests followed. Muti, whose name had been mentioned in July as resistant Fascist leader and former Party Secretary with connections which could be used, was shot by military police while escaping from detention.

According to Senise, the conception of a Fascist 'plot' was the work of Carboni, who had succeeded Amé as head of the Italian Military Intelligence on August 21.[31] The mysterious assassination of Muti lent a certain credence to the existence of a plot, and aroused fears of a Fascist reaction. As Puntoni noted, 'It will create a "Muti" myth and thus the Fascists will have their "Matteotti".' [32]

There were no police reports to justify the operations carried out during the following night, but there were vague indications reaching the Italian Military Intelligence that certain individuals had been in touch with the German Embassy. Among the arrested were, apart from Cavallero and Muti, Starace, Soddu, Teruzzi, Bottai, Galbiati, Riccardi, and De Cesare. This list of former Fascist personalities detained coincided strangely with that compiled at times by the Germans as the hard core of latter-day Fascism. It included Teruzzi, a leading beneficiary of the régime, a member of the early Action Squads, a former Minister of Colonies; Riccardi, one of the key informers for the Germans on the Italian scene and a former Minister of

k. Cavallero had been arrested on July 26, an hour after the nomination of Badoglio as head of the new government, but released the following day.

Foreign Exchange; and De Cesare, Mussolini's keeper of secrets as private secretary. All found themselves in the civilian prison of Regina Coeli.

On the same day, Guariglia sent reluctantly a violent telegram to Ribbentrop complaining of German participation 'in the so-called Cavallero plot in which Muti was also implicated'.[33] Guariglia was uncertain of his case and Ribbontrop's reply was heavily ironic.[34]

This state of alarm produced three leading, and unrelated, victims: Muti, shot between the seaside resort of Fregene and Rome; Cavallero under close interrogation at Forte Boccea;[1] and ultimately, Ciano.

There may have been some contact between the first two men, as Guariglia's phrase implies, but Ciano's position was isolated and separate. He had not been in direct touch with the Badoglio authorities after the coup d'état. He resigned promptly from his Vatican Embassy, and sent a mutual friend to Guariglia asking for permission to leave Italy 'for an unspecified foreign country'. The latter approached Badoglio, who counselled delay as public opinion might be roused. There may possibly have been some collusion between Ciano and Grandi, who was now in Portugal, and Badoglio may have feared that too much attention would be attracted by the presence of both men in a neutral capital.

Following the emergence, or mounting, of the 'Cavallero plot', Ciano's villa in Rome was put under police surveillance. There had been a clamour for his arrest soon after the fall of the Duce. Ciano had been the main target of a committee set up to enquire into illicit gains by leading public figures under Fascism. Senise claims that he resisted these pressures, but now at the same time as the Cavallero-Muti 'scare' it appears that Badoglio in a handwritten note to Senise ordered Ciano's arrest and internment at Ponza.[35]

In this degenerating atmosphere of plot and counterplot, and possibly as the result of a leakage, Countess Ciano in particular became increasingly alarmed, fearing for the personal safety of the family. It appears that she had a meeting with Dollmann, and attempted at first to enlist his support to escape to Spain.[36]

An alternative plan, however, was worked out to go to Germany. The request was referred by the German services in Rome to Himmler, and by him to Hitler. The latter accepted the proposal in regard to the Countess and the children. Ciano could also go 'if the Countess put store by it'.[37]

On the morning of August 23, the day of the arrests of the Fascist 'conspirators', Ciano and his family were spirited out of Rome and flown to Germany. The operation was conducted by the German Police Attaché, Kappler.

How far Dollmann and Kappler were acting in good faith is not clear. The German Intelligence services were interested in Ciano's person and his diary,

1. On the so-called 'Cavallero Memorandum' see p. 649.

the existence of which he made no secret. The operation of his flight seems to have been a kidnapping by consent.[38]

As Guariglia wrote later 'Given Ciano's personal feelings and his lack of esteem for Cavallero, I immediately excluded the possibility that he could have plotted in any way with the latter . . . I was convinced that he would have remained hidden in Rome and awaited events. I would never have thought that he would have fallen so ingenuously into the trap laid for him by the Germans.' [39 m]

m. According to one German account Ciano was brought to Germany on special instructions from Himmler.

APPENDIX A

Confidential Report from the office of the German Foreign Minister. August 13, 1943

'THE FOLLOWING is confidentially reported from Rome. Nothing definite can at present be said concerning the new situation which arose on the night of July 25/6. The wealth of rumour circulating about the events which led to the overthrow of the Duce has so far made it impossible to form a clear picture of the essentials. Later developments are equally obscure and un-clarified.

'The crisis of July 25 undoubtedly has its origins in happenings of the already distant past. Grave signs of internal decay, especially corruption, the lack of a clear lead and above all the presence of totally unqualified persons in leading positions, had already long discredited the edifice of the Fascist régime in the eyes of the entire nation. The eleventh-hour attempt made by the Party Secretary, Scorza, to revive the spiritual forces and energies of the first revolutionary era came too late and was too thoroughly sabotaged by various vested interests, even including Party circles, to save the situation. Nevertheless, outright revolution seemed hardly feasible, for at no time had determined opposition to the Duce in fact existed, either in the Party, the Army or the nation at large.

'As Italy's predicament grew steadily graver under the pressure of military events in Sicily, an attempt was made in leading Fascist circles to persuade the Duce to abdicate certain of his powers. Originally the idea was only that he should hand over the six or seven ministries grouped under his control to competent and trustworthy men, in order to restore the nation's shattered confidence in the Government. But the Duce flatly rejected all the warnings, counsels and suggestions so repeatedly proffered of late.

'In the grave crisis which has befallen Italy, a very significant, if not de-cisive, part has undoubtedly been played by two factors: on the one hand, by the Duce's long-standing and insidious ailment, which undeniably exists, though details are unknown; and on the other hand by his inadequacy as a military leader, which has revealed itself ever more clearly from the first days of the war.

'In the days immediately preceding July 25 the Duce had finally yielded to the instances of leading Party members and convened the Grand Fascist Council for July 24. According to the Constitution, the Council is the supreme advisory organ of the Fascist régime on all decisive matters of national policy, both domestic and foreign; but after December 1939 the Duce no longer consulted it. The course of this extremely stormy session, which lasted for nearly ten hours without a break, can be regarded as largely known and explained. The majority agree in presuming that it was only Grandi and Ciano who were methodically and consciously working towards the Duce's overthrow. The overwhelming majority of the Grand Fascist Council evidently had in mind some kind of Neo-Fascism, a fundamental revision and rejuvenation of the Fascist régime through the introduction of new and competent Fascists. It is clear that Grandi's motion, which was circulated a few days before the session, was endorsed by most members merely with a view to prompting the Duce to revise his previous methods. Even when the session of the Grand Fascist Council was over, this remained the dominant impression among the participants until Sunday evening. The situation then developed with amazing rapidity. At this point there began a phase as yet unexplained, namely the crisis of July 25.

'No really reliable account exists of the events which took place during Sunday at Villa Savoia, the King's summer residence in Rome. Apparently, though this again is by no means clear, the Duce at no time tendered his resignation. According to the version generally current, the King caused him to resign immediately; but the manner in which this came about is quite unknown.

'What does seem to be a fact is that directly on leaving Villa Savoia the Duce was courteously arrested by a Police Colonel, and taken to a police station by ambulance. Here he apparently stayed for two days, being thence conveyed to a place the whereabouts of which are being kept strictly secret and are in fact probably known only to a very limited number of Government figures.

'Such in brief was the external aspect of the crisis. It cannot, however, be doubted that the leadership of the Fascist Party completely broke down and that practically no one was loyal to the Duce to the last. After the proclamation put out by the King and Badoglio the upper crust of the Party scattered to the four winds.

'When during the night of July 25 not merely the public but even the best-informed quarters learned to their astonishment of the deposition of the Duce and the assumption of power by Marshal Badoglio, unedifying scenes occurred in Rome. In the course of a single night, thirty-one Party headquarters in Rome were stormed by the multitude and their furniture smashed and set alight. Fascist emblems everywhere were destroyed.

'This situation was naturally exploited by Communist elements to spur the mob to further unrest and excitement. The Government at once intervened with draconic measures. A strict curfew from 9.30 p.m. was imposed; all key points in the city were occupied by the military. The police received orders to shoot at sight; these are still in force with the result that even to this day shooting is still going on at night in obedience to the order to nip in the bud any attempt at a demonstration or disturbance. A number of civilians, among them the wife of the Counsellor of the Turkish Embassy, have unhappily fallen victim to these stringent orders.

'In Northern Italy events took a far more serious turn. The demonstrations in Turin, Milan, Genoa and Bologna were explicitly Communist in character. The Government took very forceful action everywhere, and for the time being has the situation in hand. Life is beginning to get back to normal, but the military measures will continue to be sternly enforced.

'The process of liquidating the Fascist régime is going ahead very methodically. But it is doubtless a most interesting sign of the times that the constructive ideas and institutions of Fascism are being handled by the Government with kid gloves, and so far from being abolished are to be salvaged so far as is practicable for use even in the distant future. The process of spiritual fermentation set up by Fascism cannot of course be expected, after twenty years, to vanish from one day to the next. The present-day military leaders are fully aware of this. The very outspoken anti-Fascist sentiments nurtured by the broad masses are really directed first and foremost against the political form taken by the régime, the symptoms of corruption, the irresponsibility of former officials and the breakdown of the State apparatus.

'The political leaders of Fascism, for the time being at least, display all the signs of collapse and confusion. Even if the broken fragments are slowly being pieced together again, no unified group of leaders exists, at any rate for the present. In view of the general mood of the population any attempt to reinstate the Duce by force would, at least in the present phase, enjoy no prospect of success. The perils and exigencies of war take care of that. The broad mass of the population looks upon the revolt of July 25 as the prelude to peace.

'Thanks to methodical and not unskilful propaganda, however, the notion has gradually started to gain ground among Italians that to end the war suddenly at the present juncture would be highly detrimental to creating a more favourable military situation. Their sense of honour, long acknowledged by all leading Italian circles as a decisive factor, is now playing a part which, whilst widely misunderstood, ought not to be under-estimated. Any solution which would be incompatible with Italian honour, and would again make this a subject for international debate, is rejected categorically and emphatically. The present moment, as all German authorities repeatedly confirm, is undoubtedly one of great importance. The new Government's reiterated resolve not to acquiesce in unconditional surrender in any circumstances and not to permit Italy to be turned into a theatre for operations against her German ally is most earnestly meant and will be translated into reality.

'However, the great question for the future is of course whether in face of the renewed heavy air bombardment, which has already begun, and of possibly grave military reverses the Government will succeed, by applying the draconic military measures already introduced, in preventing a sharp swing to the Left. The beginnings of a serious Communist revolt are admittedly already present in Northern Italy. Whether this will continue to be so in future is the great and anxious question of the hour. What is not in the slightest open to doubt is the well-founded assumption that should the Badoglio Government fall, men of a radical Left-wing, even Communist, outlook would come to power who would subscribe to unconditional surrender, thus throwing wide the gates to the enemy for an invasion of Italy's shores. In these circumstances, the presence in Italy of German troops is a very positive and a very reassuring factor, which is beginning to make itself generally felt.

'However, no one at the present time dare predict the course of future events, even for a day ahead.'[n]

APPENDIX B

Churchill—Grandi Correspondence [o]

(1) *Mr. Winston Churchill to Count Grandi:*

October 26, 1939.

My dear Grandi,

I am very glad indeed to receive your most kind letter of October 11. It was a grief to me that events, against which you and I both strove, clouded a period in your memorable mission to this country.

I rejoice that the forward path now seems brighter for Anglo-Italian friendship, and you may be sure I am continually working to that end. I feel a solid confidence that we shall be victorious in this War, which we are resolved to pursue at all costs until Europe is freed from the German menace; and I do not feel convinced that it will take so long as it did last time. Anyhow, long or short, we shall persevere.

Yours very sincerely,

WINSTON S. CHURCHILL

n. German Collection. Confidential report signed 'L'. Marked by Hitler on August 15.

o. I am indebted to Sir Winston Churchill and to Count Grandi for permission to publish these letters.

(2) *Count Grandi to the Prime Minister.*

Lisbon. October 12, 1943.

Dear Prime Minister,

I trust that all which has happened during these four fateful years since I last saw you has not made you forget the friendly relations existing between us: as for myself I shall always cherish the recollection of the hours we used to spend together and of the invaluable help I constantly received from you during my long and happy stay in England as Italian Ambassador at the Court of St. James.

You will understand why I feel that I must let you know a few things about events in Italy both before and after July 25th and the part I have played in them, as inaccurate reports continue to be circulated on the subject.

1. As you remember, in June 1939 I was dismissed from my post in London soon after the signature of the German-Italian alliance. At first it was thought that a speech which against my will I had been ordered to deliver at the Italian and German colony in London could allay the suspicions of the Germans toward me and make it possible for me to continue my work in England. Lord Halifax, then Foreign Secretary, knows all about it.

But I was recalled just the same, not being, as Mussolini himself told me, 'persona grata' to the German government. I was even forbidden to come back to London to present my letters of recall and to shake hands with my English friends.

Later, without my previous knowledge, I was appointed Minister for Justice and President of the Chamber of Deputies, two offices which were both considered practically out of any political influence in the Government. In spite of that and overcoming all sorts of difficulties, I went on working with my friends for the survival of that policy and ideals which I had always championed during fifteen years and that you knew so well.

When on August 31st Germany invaded Poland I did my utmost to prevent Italy from being drawn into war at Germany's side. Later I went further and openly asked in a meeting of the Cabinet that the alliance with Germany be publicly denounced and full neutrality declared; but this Mussolini refused to do.

During the nine months of Italy's non-belligerency I tried, as Sir Percy Loraine is well aware, to encourage all efforts in favour of keeping my country out of war. Unfortunately all this was of no avail because Mussolini declared war without even communicating with the Cabinet and with those whom according to our Constitution he was obliged to consult.

Allow me to remember that only a few days earlier I had received from you a letter in which you were good enough to encourage me in my efforts. This was the last letter I received from England.

2. Dictatorship had proved once more to be the cancer of our political life.

Events of June 1940 confirmed me in the opinion that the only way out was to overthrow the dictatorship and the totalitarian system upon which the former was founded.

We wanted to restore the Constitution and to revive our Parliamentary system which formally had never been discarded. This had also been the original aim of those patriotic elements who contributed so much to the early rise and success of the Fascist movement.

'Liberty and Country' was the motto I wrote in 1920 on our banners: we wanted to save our free national institutions which were imperilled by communism and could not be rescued by our powerless political parties.

The first open clash between Mussolini and myself occurred at the Congress of Rome in November 1921 and this same position I maintained in my speeches in the Chamber of Deputies up to 1925 when I was kicked upstairs to the Foreign Office to the only purpose that I should keep completely out of home politics.

Only after my recall from London and my appointment as Minister for Justice and President of the Chamber of Deputies I could resume my endeavours for a gradual resurrection of constitutional methods, though these efforts of mine were largely thwarted by the overwhelming power of dictatorship.

My friends and I hoped that in this way it would be possible to disentangle Italy from a war for which the dictatorship alone was responsible. We were also afraid that Mussolini's dismissal would result in a condition of anarchy eventually paving the way to Communism under the pressure of military collapse, unless constitutional machinery were at hand to withstand the impact of the downfall of dictatorship. Such was also the opinion of the highest Church authorities on whose understanding and help I knew we could rely.

Both Houses of Parliament proved to be too cumbersome to provide H.M. the King with the vote which alone would enable him to change the Government. It was found necessary, under the circumstances, to make recourse to the only available body, namely the 'Gran Consiglio'. To prevent any such move on our part Mussolini had not convened the 'Gran Consiglio' ever since December 1939 when it had ratified Italy's non-belligerency.

It was indeed no easy matter to obtain from the 'Capo del Governo', who alone had the authority to call it, a meeting which at last took place on July 24th. I led the attack in a purely Parliamentary way asking for a vote on the motion which I had presented.

Afterwards it had been rumoured that I was doing all this to become dictator No. 2. I trust you know me and all I stood for throughout my political life well enough to see how preposterous all this is. My friends and I risked our lives on the night of July 24/5 to put an end to dictatorship and to Italy's alliance with Germany, thus interpreting the will of the Italian people as it later appeared. I was glad to see recently that Marshal Badoglio has publicly given us credit for the over-throwing of the dictatorship.

When at last we achieved what we had been working for, my only thought was to put an immediate end to hostilities between our countries. On the early morning of July 25th and even before Marshal Badoglio was appointed Head of the Government, I asked to be sent to Madrid or to Lisbon to get in touch with British representatives there.

3. I was firmly convinced that any delay would obviously strengthen the German hold on Italy and by diminishing our national possibilities of resistance to the Germans make more difficult our subsequent siding with the Allies.

On August 3rd I was entrusted by the Minister for Foreign Affairs, Baron Guariglia, on behalf of the new Government, with the mission of approaching unofficially the Allied governments. This mission had been fully authorized by H.M. the King.

Unfortunately time was lost because it was necessary for the Government to allay the suspicions of the Germans who were after me since July 25th. In addition to this the permit for my entrance into Spain, officially asked for by Baron Guariglia, in order that I should see Sir Samuel Hoare was delayed for nearly two weeks by the Madrid Government.

So when at last I arrived in Spain on August 18th and a few days later in Portugal, contacts had already been established between military authorities, thereby making of no further use any contribution of a political character.

4. After what I have already told you it is quite unnecessary on my part to emphasize that I am, as I have always been, with my King and that I fully approve all which is and will be done by His present Government in order to achieve our most effective participation to the war at the side of the Allied Nations.

There it is, dear Prime Minister, how things happened and the part I had in them. I feel satisfied in my conscience that I did my best, under the circumstances, to be of some service to my unhappy country to contribute, as far and as soon as I could, to save her from total disaster and anarchy and to allow her to resume that policy of full co-operation with Great Britain for which I had always striven both as Minister for Foreign Affairs and Ambassador in London.

Yours very sincerely,

DINO GRANDI

(3) *Count Grandi to the Prime Minister.*

Lisbon, August 18th, 1944.

You will forgive me if I allow myself to make this personal appeal to you.

On the 12th of last October, nearly a year ago, I addressed a letter to you to relate in brief events which took place in Italy on July 25th, 1943, and the part I played in them. You kindly let me know that my letter had been duly received.

From then onwards, I have lived aloof from everybody and everything, loyal to my King and to my Government, constantly refusing to satisfy newspapermen's curiosity, only following with growing hope all efforts made by my Government to bring Italy more and more to the side of the Allies in the war against Germany.

On January 10th, Mussolini condemned me to death for the crime of high treason (the sentence says: '. . . for having given help to the enemy, endangered the military resistance of the country, giving cause to a separate peace with the enemy'), and the whole trial gave evidence to the fact that I had been mainly responsible for the action taken for the overthrow of the Fascist Régime and of Mussolini's dictatorship. For a whole year, the Nazi and the Fascist Press, have persistently gratified me with violent attacks, denouncing what according to them had been my 'treacherous' attitude for 20 years. On the other hand, I cannot expect anything but persecution from those anti-Fascist parties which appeared on the political scene after Mussolini's downfall and which are now in command in Italy. They did nothing to overthrow Fascism, but waited for the victories of the Allies to do it, and for someone who would have the courage to face and oust the Dictator: now they seem animated only by a spirit of revenge.

I know how difficult it is to re-establish the truth and to ask for a fair judgment when a terrible and devastating war is still raging with all the passions and sufferings it arises in human hearts, and when so many political and personal interests are involved. This is why I am bold enough to send you the two enclosed memoranda which have been already presented to the British Ambassador in Lisbon.

What I meant to do on July 25th was to accomplish my last duty to my King and my Country, and I feel quite satisfied in my conscience. I did not think of building up any future for myself: there could be no political future for me, who chose to work within the Fascist Régime, even if I finally helped to destroy it, and even if I stood against Mussolini's policy in previous years, trying to have it modified and changed, when the whole world applauded it.

On the very night of July 25th, soon after I had succeeded in attaining what nobody, not even myself, had then thought possible, I advised the King to appoint as Prime Minister a military leader, preferably one who had not committed himself with the war and with the Fascist Régime. I urged also the King not to lose a single hour in putting the war to an end and in asking the armistice to the Allies, convinced as I was that any delay played in German interest, and that no possible modification was to be expected—as many hoped then—in the armistice terms which the Allies had already fixed and agreed upon. I am still sorry that my advice was not followed, and that consequently a good part of the benefit which we expected from what had been done on July 25th was lost.

In twenty-four years of political life, I have made many mistakes: the greatest was to believe that in spite of the setbacks I had been confronted with and of the difficulties found on my way, I would have succeeded in preventing my country from departing definitely from that policy of peace and of loyal co-operation with Great Britain, which I had always advocated and stood for. All my political life is there to prove what I am saying, and the difficulties I had to cope with are there too, as big as very few political men have ever come across in their life. But I think I was right in not giving up my hopes and struggle, as others did, and just to await from without for events to take their course.

I shall be always grateful to you for the invaluable help and for all the friendly encouragement you constantly gave me during the fifteen years I was Italian Minister for Foreign Affairs and Ambassador to the Court of St. James. I shall never forget the words of friendly appreciation for the work I had done, which you kindly sent me on October 26th, 1939, soon after I had been recalled on the request of the German Government and to my deep regret, from my post in London. You will forgive me if I recall this now. I do it only because I wish to tell you that your words, more than anything else, have given me, throughout the last four years of sorrows and of tragic experiences which I have lived through, the strength to believe that I could still do—alas, too late—what my English friends expected from me, proving to them that they had not been wrong in placing their trust in me for so many years.

I honestly believe that I did not fail them and that even in the obvious difficulties of my present position, I may still hope to be looked upon as one who did what he could to be of some service to his unhappy country, and to keep faith in those principles in which he had believed during his life.

DINO GRANDI

The Rt. Hon. Mr Winston Churchill,
Prime Minister,
London.

CHAPTER THREE

THE ITALIAN SURRENDER

• •

On August 28 Castellano returned from Lisbon with the Allied military surrender terms. The formal decision to accept them was taken by the King on September 1, and communicated by radio to the Allies that afternoon.[1] On September 3 the terms were signed by Castellano at Cassibile in Sicily, and it was planned that they should be implemented in five days' time by a wireless broadcast by Badoglio.

Meanwhile, on August 30, Rahn arrived by air in Rome as the political representative of the Fuehrer, and called immediately on Guariglia.[2] The two men were to maintain fragile and correct relations during the ensuing days, and the last act of the Axis was to be played out, with mutual skill and bluff.

According to Guariglia, the German chargé d'affaires [a] told him that the Fuehrer, contrary to what people thought, was neither an impulsive man nor a theoretician. The Fuehrer did not care whether Italy was Fascist or non-Fascist, nor, in spite of his strong personal feelings of friendship for Mussolini, who was at the head of the government. 'The Fuehrer was a realist and only one thing counted for him: to win the war. If the Badoglio government intended to continue the war . . . the Fuehrer would have the same confidence in us, and Italo-German co-operation would be more effective than before.' [3]

Rahn was clearly speaking to his brief. He appears to have also hinted that the Germans were aware of Italian negotiations 'in Spain or Portugal', and warned Guariglia that a one-sided decision to withdraw from the conflict would be met on the German side with force.[b]

a. The German government had not yet asked formally for the agreement of the Italians for Rahn's nomination as Ambassador. His mission had deliberately a provisional air.

b. Rahn *op cit* p. 227. Guariglia does not mention this point in his account of this conversation, but later states that he had been questioned by Rahn about Grandi's activities in Portugal. (See Guariglia *op cit* p. 744.)

Rahn now sought an interview with Badoglio which took place on the afternoon of September 3, at the moment of the signature of the armistice terms in Sicily. The Italian Marshal reaffirmed calmly the policy of his government to remain loyal to her Axis ally, and asked Rahn to restrain the German military authorities from 'provocative action'. The German diplomat was immediately struck by the resemblance in manner and appearance to Marshal Pétain. The mystique of the Marshals was almost convincing. 'I am Marshal Badoglio—the Marshal Badoglio. I belong to the three oldest Marshals in Europe—Mackensen, Pétain and myself . . . The distrust of the German government towards me is incomprehensible. I have given my word and stand by it. Please trust me.' [4]

Both sides were half convinced that each was successfully deceiving the other. Rahn had given the impression that the Germans were still not completely convinced that an Italian surrender was imminent.[5] He had assumed after his talk with Hitler that the latter had as yet made no irrevocable political decision, and that in the last resort he would rely on military sanctions to redress the situation—as in the event happened.[6]

Meanwhile the game of mutual deception covered two operations under way: the Italian armistice to come into effect on September 8, and the liberation of the Duce planned for the following day.[c]

Already on August 21 Field-Marshal Jodl had sent a highly confidential telegram to all Army group commanders involved:

'For political reasons nothing must be put on paper as to later measures intended to be taken in Italy and the Balkans in regard to action in face of Italy's attitude.'

And on August 30 Keitel issued more detailed and revised orders: 'The most important task is to disarm the Italian army as quickly as possible . . . The pacification of Northern Italy will be carried out by using the Fascist organizations.' [7]

On September 7 the German High Command issued orders for the disarming of all Italian units. Later that day came news that strong Allied forces had put to sea in the direction of the south-western coast of Italy.

The announcement of the surrender of the Badoglio government to the Allies was heard on the American radio by the German Chargé d'Affaires in Rome, Rahn, at 5.45 p.m. on September 8.[8]

The latter had been received by the King in audience at noon on that day, and received assurances that Italy would never surrender. 'At the end of the conversation the King stressed the decision to continue the struggle, to the end, at the side of Germany, with whom Italy is bound in life and death.'

On hearing the broadcast, Rahn telephoned to General Roatta, the Army

c. Rahn *op cit* p. 228–9. Rahn learnt on September 6 of the decision of General Student to launch this operation on the 9th.

Chief of Staff, and was told: 'This report from New York is a bare-faced lie of British propaganda, which I reject with indignation.'

At 7 p.m. Rahn called at the Italian Foreign Office at the request of Guariglia, Badoglio's Foreign Minister. The latter stated that, 'I have to tell you that Marshal Badoglio, in view of the desperate military situation, has been forced to ask for an armistice.' Rahn answered, 'This is treachery to a given word.' He had seen Badoglio on September 3, the day of the signature of the surrender, and had been assured that, on the word of honour of a Marshal, there would be no capitulation.[d]

The news reached Berlin in similar fashion, through a broadcast from London: 'an occurrence that undoubtedly is unique and without precedent in history'.[9]

The German military commands in the peninsula now moved harshly and at speed. The first German reactions were felt at Nice, Salerno, and on the Brenner, where patrol activity began within an hour of the news of the Italian armistice.

The Italian Fourth Army on the French frontier disbanded; the Alpine passes were already in German hands, units of Rommel's army were in Trieste by September 9, and established on the vital lines of communication to the Balkans through Venezia Giulia and Slovenia in the next hours, cutting off thirty-two Italian divisions to the South. By September 10 the Germans had forced the surrender of nearly all Italian units in Croatia and Dalmatia, and in spite of isolated pockets of resistance in Montenegro, Greece, and the Aegean islands, had asserted control of the Axis positions throughout South-Eastern Europe.

In central and southern Italy Kesselring rapidly regrouped his forces both to meet the Allied landings at Salerno, and to dominate Rome.

In the small hours of September 9 Badoglio learnt of heavy German attacks on the outskirts of Rome, and decided to leave the city, together with the King, in order to avoid the risk of the capture of the Royal Family and the government. In ragged fighting at the gates and on the outskirts of Rome, isolated Italian units saved their honour, but resistance ceased the following day. Kesselring negotiated on September 10 the surrender of the 'Italian troops round Rome',[10] and agreed to respect Rome as 'an open city' under the temporary command of the only Italian general with any coherent orders from the Badoglio government, Count Calvi di Bergolo, who with one division to keep public order within the city, was isolated from the rest of Italy pending a decision, military and political, as to the fate of the

d. Guariglia's own subsequent comment was: 'I am convinced that even if Rahn regarded Italy's exit from the war as inevitable, he was surprised at the news of the armistice as he hoped to be able to back up for some time yet the game of those German military leaders, who hoped to gain time to reinforce to the maximum their defensive dispositions in Italy.' Guariglia, *op cit* p. 711.

Italian capital.[e] The following day, September 11, Kesselring declared all Italian territory, including Rome, to be a theatre of war under German military control.

The military and political implications of the collapse of the Axis had been inherent in German planning for some months, but when the end came it must inevitably also have produced a major psychological shock. It was not only the loss of a leading ally, but the failure of a whole policy, with possible lessons and consequences on the German home front. This latter aspect was the speciality of Goebbels.

'The Duce will enter history as the last Roman, but behind his massive figure a gypsy people has gone to rot. We should have realized that sooner, but for ideological reasons we were always too accommodating to the Italians. Once again our old German inheritance, our sentimentality, has had evil consequences when applied to politics. Added to this was a totally inept German diplomacy, which did not have enough vision to foresee what has now taken place in Italy.

'All this must teach us a great deal. National Socialism must undergo a renovation . . . The National Socialist leadership must have no ties whatever with the aristocracy or with so-called society.' [11]

Goebbels urged Hitler to address the German people without delay. Reluctantly, as the details of the Italian scene were as yet unclarified, Hitler agreed, and two days later on September 10 recorded a speech to be broadcast from Berlin.[12] It was a review of Italian treachery followed by 'an admonition to the Nazi Party and the assurance that the Italian precedent never can and never will be repeated in Germany'.[13]

The Italian warning must not constitute an encouragement to others, and this Hitler had made quite clear.

His interpretation of the march of events in Italy was, as frequently, an inner dialogue with himself in order to clarify his own mind.

'I find that now the moment has arrived, when freed from the heavy weight of a long and crushing suspense, to speak to the German people without recourse to any artifice either in regard to myself or to the public.

'The collapse of Italy was to be foreseen for a long time, not for lack of adequate possibilities of an effective Italian resistance nor of the necessary German aid, but . . . rather because of a lack of will on the part of those elements who have provoked the capitulation as an end result of their methodical sabotage, thus completing what for years many men had aimed at—the passage of the Italian military command from the side of the Reich to the common enemy.'

Italy was bound by treaty to join Germany in September 1939. 'It is

e. Count Calvi di Bergolo was the son-in-law of the King and commander of the 'Piave' division.

known that Mussolini had decided to order immediate mobilization in Italy, according to the pact. The same forces, who have today brought about the surrender, succeeded in August 1939 in preventing the entry of Italy into the war.' Hitler was aware of the difficulties facing the Duce, and left him complete freedom of action. 'In June 1940 Mussolini succeeded in obtaining the internal conditions necessary for Italy's entry into the war on the side of the Reich.' Since that time, Germany had given every possible aid to her ally, in particular by saving the position in North Africa in the winter of 1940–1, and in the spring of 1941 in the Balkans 'in order to avoid a danger provoked by Italy's action, but which naturally also threatened Germany'.

It was only because Italy had at its head 'her greatest son . . . since the fall of the ancient world' that Germany had adopted such an attitude.

'The last act which brought about the coup d'état, which had long been decided, was the request by the Duce for wider powers for a more effective conduct of the war.[f] I have been and am glad to regard as my friend this great and loyal man.'

But he could not forgive the act of the Badoglio government in signing the armistice without prior accord with its allies, and he gave details of its behaviour to the German representatives in Rome two days previously. It was clearly Badoglio's intention also to involve Germany 'in the fate reserved for the Duce and for Italy'.

But the struggle would continue without quarter. 'The measures for the protection of German interests in view of the step taken by Italy are very severe . . . and they will follow methodically and efficiently The example of the treachery of Yugoslavia had already given us previously a salutary lesson . . .'

'The Fuehrer is firmly determined to wipe the slate clean in Italy.'[14] On the day of his broadcast to the German people, he issued a basic directive for the administration of those areas of Italy now under *de facto* German control: 'An order from the Fuehrer regarding the appointment of a plenipotentiary of the Reich in Italy, and the organization of the occupied region as on September 10, 1943.'[15] It was a secret order and not to be published.

The German Chargé d'Affaires in Rome, Rahn, was appointed plenipotentiary to handle political matters, but without as yet precise instructions particularly in regard to the military authorities.

From their standpoint Italy was divided into two zones, operational and occupied. The former, stretching from the enemy front to the south of Rome to the circle of the Italian borders, came under Kesselring's Southern Army. The latter, as yet not precisely defined but representing in essence the ultimate defence line of Germany's southern frontier, was the responsibility of

f. The source of Hitler's information for this statement is not known. Perhaps Mussolini told him this at Feltre.

Marshal Rommel's Army Group B. Within this area two special administrations were to be set up, based on the former Habsburg territories in South Tyrol and southern Carinthia, thus bringing under direct German control the Adriatic coastline and the approaches to the Brenner. The gauleiters of the existing German provinces of Tyrol and Carinthia, Hofer and Rainer, were to be responsible for the civil administration of these areas and directly responsible to Hitler.

Finally, a third authority was set up to control security and order within the occupied regions, and was to come under the control of General Wolff, until recently the liaison officer of the S.S. at Hitler's headquarters.

The relations between the German political, military, and police organizations in Italy remained henceforth a dominant issue in the months to come.

Three days later, Hitler signed blanket instructions for Speer, the dictator of the German war economy, concerning the 'safeguarding' of the Italian war industry.[16]

Hitler's plan for a brisk Fascist counter-coup to the events of July 25 had thus melted away in the disintegration of Fascism throughout Italy. As the belated news from Rome and elsewhere filled in this picture as seen from the Fuehrer's Headquarters, any political move against the new Badoglio government receded in German calculations. The arrival of Farinacci and Preziosi as the would-be precursors of a neo-Fascist reaction had merely illustrated the absurdity and completeness of the demoralization of the whole movement.

These two men were followed during the ensuing days by the Duce's eldest son, Vittorio Mussolini, and other members of the family clan. Alessandro Pavolini and Renato Ricci had also arrived in Munich. These two men were typical professional representatives of twenty years of Italian Fascism. The former joined the Party in Florence in 1920, and rose in the ranks of Florentine Fascism, ending as Federal Secretary of the province. His progress in central politics had culminated in his appointment as Minister of Popular Culture. For a time he received the patronage of Ciano, and was dismissed together with him in February 1943. Pavolini had then been placed in charge of the Rome newspaper *Il Messaggero*.

Renato Ricci came from a working class family employed in the marble quarries of Carrara. His career was symbolic of that of the Fascist élite. He had served in the First World War in the Bersaglieri, joined D'Annunzio in the Fiume enterprise and commanded his legionaries when they occupied Zara in May 1921. Shortly afterwards he founded the first Fascist squad in his home town and distinguished himself in the notorious 'punitive expedition' to Genoa in August 1922. He led a Fascist column in the March on Rome. He passed rapidly through the cadres of the Militia, and the Party, became a deputy in 1924, and was nominated Vice-Secretary of the Fascist

Party in 1925–6. In the following year Mussolini put him at the head of the Fascist Youth organization, a post which he held concurrently with that of Undersecretary at the Ministry of Education, and which made him a central figure in the Fascist hierarchy.

From 1939–43 Ricci was Minister of Corporations and was removed in February of the latter year in the general 'Changing of the Guard'.

In this office he was alleged to have been the centre of a series of financial scandals, in particular that connected with the building of the Mussolini Forum and the supplies of material from the Marble Trust created by him in his political fief at Carrara. Unlike Pavolini, he had been in contact with the Germans prior to July 25[g].

The very absence of competing colleagues from Italy gave this little group a sense of its own importance. Pavolini had a certain standing as a propagandist and journalist, and Ricci, through the Fascist Militia, had links with Himmler.

The obscurity of their existence in Germany, under assumed names and police surveillance, was untroubled until the announcement of the surrender of the Badoglio government to the Allies on September 8.

But now the total assault on the régime in Rome for which Hitler had hoped in July must be mobilized, even if only for propaganda reasons, and in spite of the failure to gather together in Germany an alternative governing élite.

The available personalities were collected in East Prussia, and on the night of September 8/9 a radio station was improvised on Hitler's special train. Goebbels noted that 'Pavolini, Ricci, and the Duce's son are now at Headquarters, drafting an appeal to the Italian people and the Italian armed forces. They have been selected to form a neo-Fascist government and to act in the name of the Duce. They are to take up residence in northern Italy as soon as conditions have been consolidated . . . Farinacci is to arrive in the course of the afternoon to complement the work of the triumvirate.' [17] The announcement that an Italian national Fascist government would be formed was then broadcast on a relayed service from 'Radio Munich'.[18]

This first formal step livened the intrigues of the exiles, each of whom had his presumed support in mutually rival German quarters. Pavolini had already taken the additional step of teaming up with Vittorio Mussolini with a view to pressing the Duce's son as a nominal figurehead.[19]

Himmler was 'very anxious . . . to have at least a semi-effective Fascist government in northern Italy. He has not got enough police troops there to govern by force.' [20] And Ricci had ready for submission a draft programme, which he sent to Himmler.

'Since the first radio transmissions alluded to a National Fascist Government, it is indispensable to give immediate and concrete form to this Government, the seat of which can only be Italy, by selecting to serve on it persons possessed of the necessary prestige and capabilities. These persons should be beyond reproach, especially in the moral respect, and their loyalty to Mussolini, which we regard as the essential basis for every enterprise, should be beyond question. With a view to forming this Government, qualified elements must forthwith proceed to Italy. They should establish contact with the appropriate circles on the lines agreed with the Reich Foreign Minister and put forward suggestions for the eventual formation of the National Government.'

This faithful rump would have the task of rallying Fascist and nationalist elements in unoccupied Italy, 'and brief them suitably on political and organizational matters'. Friends from former political information centres such as Preziosi's creation in Trieste for the study of the Jewish problem would be brought in to form a nucleus of collaborators.

The urgent task of these men would be to reorganize a Fascist Militia 'for the purpose of crushing any attempt at a Left-wing coup and of preventing acts of sabotage. This Militia would guarantee the security of the German troops fighting in Italy.

'The necessity and urgency of setting up an intelligence network must again be stressed. Such a network would be subordinate to a central agency which would keep permanently in touch with the highest Reich authorities and would supply them with detailed information on Italian personalities and conditions.'

Ricci produced for Himmler's approval a wide and naïve programme, which should be broadcast to the Italian nation. The German government would undertake to arm with the latest weapons the armed forces of the new Italian government; to bring about a radical improvement in the Italian food situation, particularly in order to defeat Communist propaganda; and to declare that 'the direct aim of the struggle of German forces in Italy is the restoration of the territorial integrity of our country and of national unity and sovereignty'.[21]

But, as Goebbels put it, 'The so-called provisional Fascist government is diligently at work for us in the Fuehrer's Headquarters, even though one or another of its members is getting cold feet because he does not agree with the general political tendencies which we advocate. But what else can these gentlemen do except work for us? . . .' And again, 'What the German people want is the publication of the names of the new Fascist government, whose members for the present are sleeping on the floor at Headquarters. The trouble is that we cannot publish these names, as they are too unimportant.'[22]

On September 12 a message from the German Police Chief in Rome announced that an important group of Fascists had been 'liberated', and were in the German Embassy. 'Is the setting up of a Fascist action committee desirable?' [23]

This group had been imprisoned in a military fortress in August by Badoglio as being a potential centre of conspiracy against the new Italian government. The latter, too, like the Germans, could not conceive of the total absence of any reaction from the Fascist side to the removal of the Duce, and the menace of counter-plot was, in their view, a real threat.

Among the prisoners now released from Forte Boccea, only two were of major political interest: Badoglio's own personal enemy and rival, Marshal Cavallero, and the former Undersecretary of the Interior, Buffarini Guidi.

The former was clearly regarded by the monarchist government as the most dangerous hypothetical leader of an anti-Badoglio conspiracy, and it was logical, therefore, that the Germans, and especially his old associate Marshal Kesselring, would now consider him to be an important ally.

It appears that Kesselring, on his own initiative, approached Cavallero that evening, September 12, with some proposition to rally the Italian Armed Forces to continue the fight on the Axis side, at least as an urgent and temporary measure.

After dinner, on September 13, after a second talk with Kesselring at the German headquarters at Frascati, Cavallero was found in the garden, shot dead, and with a revolver in his hand. The full extent of his personal dilemma remains a mystery. During his recent imprisonment, Cavallero at his own request had made a long statement on his activities against the Duce and the Fascist régime for the past eight months, outlining the lineaments of yet another conspiracy for which he claimed the leading credit. He must have known that this deeply compromising document must soon either fall into German hands, or be 'leaked' by Badoglio. In fact Kappler, the German Police Chief, who had just liberated Cavallero, seems also to have found this document on Badoglio's desk in the Viminale.[g]

---

g. Cavallero had been arrested on the evening of August 23. The mysterious death of Muti must have led him to think that Badoglio might arrange a similar incident in regard to himself. It seems that he told his military guard that he had an important statement to make. Carboni as head of the Military Intelligence was ordered by Badoglio to conduct the interrogation. (See Carboni *op cit* pp. 243 ff.) According to Cavallero's son, his father intended that the resulting document should reach the King. (Carlo Cavallero, *Il dramma del Maresciallo Cavallero* p. 159.)

This 'Memorial', as it was later called, is an interrogation written in successive fragments in reply to points made during the course of the interrogation centring on Cavallero's alleged contacts with Farinacci and with the Germans prior to July 25.

Cavallero's answers admit implicitly a plan to remove Mussolini from the military command, in other words, he had by a separate route conceived of a similar action to that carried out by Ambrosio with the connivance of Badoglio.

This document was taken by Carboni to the Viminale, and a copy handed to Badoglio.

According to Carboni's later account, the latter entrusted it to his son, Mario Badoglio who stayed behind in Rome on September 8. If the flight of the King and Badoglio failed, Cavallero's statement would 'prove' that the real author of the coup d'état of

Kesselring must have been aware of this unexpected drama. He nevertheless asked his political colleague, Rahn, to take Cavallero by plane to Germany.

Rahn himself proposed that all those released in similar fashion from detention in Rome should be invited to Germany in anticipation of the forming of a neo-Fascist government in Rome, and especially in order to avoid any uncontrolled and premature Fascist initiative.

On the following morning, September 14, Rahn waited in vain at the airport for his passenger.[h]

But any schemes for a shadow puppet government, which would mask a German military occupation, of Italy, were cut short by the dramatic release of the Duce himself from Gran Sasso by Skorzeny's commando raid on September 12.

That evening Vittorio Mussolini was told the news at Hitler's headquarters.

July 25 was Cavallero, behind the back of the Germans, and not Badoglio. (See Carboni *op cit* pp. 246–7.)

Canevari, in his pamphlet *La Fine del Maresciallo Cavallero* pp. 33 ff. states that Kappler found the document in Badoglio's office on September 8. It was presumably known to Kesselring before his meeting with Cavallero on September 12.

What passed between the latter and the two German representatives is not clear. The Marshal was later overheard to say to his wife, 'The plane which will take me to Germany will be the plane of dishonour.' (Canevari's article in *Il Tempo* February 5, 1960).

Kesselring, in a letter to Cavallero's son dated February 27, 1947, said, 'As the definite cause of the suicide I maintain that it was because he did not wish to take the post which I offered him of head of the new Italian army with Mussolini.' (Canevari's article in *Il Tempo op cit* February 6, 1960.)

h. Dr. Rahn's notes to the author.

CHAPTER FOUR

EXILE AND LIBERATION

•-•

AFTER HIS ARREST at Villa Savoia on July 25, Mussolini was taken to the Carabinieri barracks in the Via Legnano. That evening he was visited by a doctor, to whom he described his medical symptoms at some length. He refused to take any drugs, adding, 'My physical person interests me no longer, but only my moral personality.'

He talked quietly, and showed no emotion at recent events. As the medical officer recorded: 'He referred to the new government of technicians and civil servants; a good administration which will continue the directives of the preceding one . . . It may be that there will be pacifist manifestations in the Po Valley which will be easily put down. The Italian people is superficial in all its manifestations, even religious; it believes in the saint only when it is accorded the favour requested; it supports the slogan: "Do as is done unto you." It is covered with a veneer which is not deep and leaves no trace . . .' [1]

Shortly after one o'clock on the following morning, Monday, July 26, a senior officer of the Italian General Staff called at the barracks with a personal letter addressed to 'His Excellency Cavaliere Benito Mussolini'.[2]

'The undersigned Head of the Government wishes to inform Your Excellency that what has been done in your regard has been done solely in your personal interest, detailed information having reached us from several quarters of a serious plot against your person. He much regrets this, and wishes to inform you that he is prepared to give orders for your safe accompanying, with all proper respect, to whatever place you may choose.'

Mussolini promptly dictated to Badoglio's envoy the following reply, which the latter wrote down in his own hand.

July 26th, 1943. 1 a.m.

'I wish to thank Marshal Badoglio for the attention he is according my person.

'The only residence at my disposal is La Rocca delle Caminate, whither I am prepared to go at any moment.

'I wish to assure Marshal Badoglio, if only in remembrance of the work we have done together in the past, that not only will I raise no difficulties of any sort but I will co-operate in every possible way.

'I am glad of the decision to continue the war together with our allies, as the honour and interests of the country require at this time, and I express my earnest hope that success will crown the grave task which Marshal Badoglio is assuming by order and in the name of His Majesty the King, whose loyal servant I have been for twenty-one years and shall continue to be. Long live Italy!'

The historical significance of this letter has often been evaded, and has hitherto received little comment. Mussolini himself published them both in 1944 but Badoglio, during his period of office, never released either text. The tone and import of Mussolini's letter is identical with that of similar missives sent to Badoglio, both by Galbiati and Scorza, and shows a total moral abdication and acceptance of the King's action in dismissing the Duce, thus ending twenty years of Fascist rule and appointing a new administration. Mussolini's letter would appear by implication to absolve from all political responsibility those who had voted against him at the meeting of the Grand Council. It is not surprising therefore that there is no formal reference to this correspondence with Badoglio when the 'traitors' of July 25 were brought to trial the following year.

Throughout Monday, July 26, Mussollini was under the impression that he would be exiled, as he had requested Badoglio, to his own house at La Rocca delle Caminate. It seems that for security reasons the new government hesitated to make such a concession, and that the Prefect of Forlì had indicated that he could not answer for public order in the event of Mussolini being interned in the Romagna. It was decided therefore, at the first meeting of the new Council of Ministers, to transfer the former Head of State to the island of Ponza off Naples, which Mussolini himself had established as a penal colony.[a] The Duce was the last of a series of prisoners on the island: they included Tito Zaniboni who had failed to assassinate him in 1925, Pietro Nenni, the Socialist leader, and the Abyssinian Ras Imeru. The two former were still members of the community.

From the moment of his departure from Rome under escort on the evening of July 27, Mussolini disappeared from the public scene, and outside official government circles his whereabouts were untraced for nearly six weeks.

His days of exile have little historical interest, except in relation to his own

a. The settlement had been abolished in February 1939, but re-established in 1941 to house political internees from the Balkans.

personality. There is equally scanty reliable evidence of these days, apart from Admiral Maugeri, who escorted him to Ponza, and kept notes of their brief conversations.[3] Mussolini himself jotted down certain musings of a remarkable banality, which came to light after the war.[4]

It was characteristic of him that he was glad of any audience however humble, and he was in permanent need of being able to conduct a dialogue, however commonplace. Maugeri appears to have noted Mussolini's remarks made on board the corvette transferring him from Gaeta to Ponza in the early hours of July 28. He made plaintive references to the style of his present treatment. 'I did not behave like this in 1922. They take me to Ponza where Zaniboni is . . . who made an attempt on my life.'

Mussolini seems to have thought of compiling a Napoleonic Memorial in exile, and he clearly had no thought of a Restoration. As he said to Maugeri, 'I am politically dead.' His ill-fortune dated, as he put it, 'from June 28, 1942.[b] One ought after all to give a man who has lost his chance the time in which to recover it.'

The main interest of his conversation on the corvette lies in his references to his talks with Hitler at Salzburg and at Feltre. 'I advised Hitler to come to an agreement with Russia, and on recent occasions at whatever cost giving up all that had been conquered, including the Ukraine. I tried to play on his superstition; the first campaign had not been successful, then followed that terrible winter, and finally the disaster of Stalingrad. But it was to no purpose. I told him we had lost the initiative since June 1942, and a country which has lost the initiative has lost the war.

'At Salzburg [c] I told him this: we cannot return to Africa, there will be an invasion of the Italian islands, there is only one final chance and that is to make peace with Russia and transfer your whole potential to the Mediterranean. You cannot help us, not because you do not want to do so, but because you cannot until you have made peace with Russia. At Feltre the talks did not go well. They should have lasted three days: they were over in three and a half hours . . . As usual, the points which were on the agenda were not discussed, but others instead. I repeated my theme—peace with Russia, and the impossibility on their side of being able to give us any substantial aid.'

The party reached Ponza on the morning of July 28. The Duce was treated as an ordinary internee. He was without funds with which to buy simple necessities until his family sent him 10,000 lire a few days later. He was installed in a small dwelling where the Abyssinian Ras Imeru had been housed. On arrival the military police escort made off to lunch without

b. The failure of Rommel's advance to Egypt.
c. In April, 1943.

making any such arrangements for their prisoner. The wife of one of them prepared a rough meal while the Duce rested in his bare whitewashed room on the bare springs of his bed with his greatcoat as a pillow. During the ten days of his stay on the island the fire was never lit to cook hot food. He remained isolated from the other internees and guarded by two military police, who also acted as batmen. Orders were given that no one was to speak to the Duce.

Time passed uneventfully on Ponza. On July 29, the day after his arrival, Mussolini celebrated his sixtieth birthday. The only gesture from the outside world was a telegram of congratulations from Goering.

He spent his time translating the Odes of the Italian poet Carducci from memory into German, in reading a life of Christ, and occasionally writing to the local parish priest. [5]

The jottings which he made at Ponza are significant only as showing his early attempt to put into some perspective the developments leading up to the meeting of the Grand Council, and skeleton notes on the personalities who had formed his entourage which were later to be used in his Memoirs.

Throughout these fragments runs a revealing vein of complacent resignation. 'When a man and his organism collapse, then the fall is irretrievable, particularly if the man is over sixty.' And again, 'Bearing in mind the colouring with which the Public Security officials are wont to present their reports, I am able to arrive at two conclusions: that my system has collapsed; and that my overthrow was final.'

One revealing fragment illustrates Mussolini's analysis of the political events of the recent past.

'The more depressing the atmosphere became, the greater were the number of suggestions made to me for the reform of our internal administration. The most radical reform occurred in January, when I changed all the Ministers but two. The result was a less united and therefore a weaker Government than before. In it, defeatism was represented by Cini, who could not see how Italy could hold out longer than June. The effect of this shuffle did not last long. Other internal measures, such as the appointment of new Ministers to the Ministries which I myself had held and the handing over of a whole complex of questions to new organizations and so on, were to be put into effect immediately after some military success—a day which I called "the day of sunshine", a day that never came. The people were looking forward to it, and even relegated to secondary importance the eternally difficult problem of food.

'The people, who had counted on at least a halt of the enemy advance, was no longer satisfied with the "points" which Scorza made again and again. Even in Fascist circles there arose a slight suspicion that Scorza was not on the right lines, and I myself began to have doubts as to his loyalty. One single day of victory—on land, at sea, or in the air, would have restored the situation. That is clear from the enthusiasm with which the rumours that the attempted landings had failed were greeted on July 10 and 11.'

News of the fall of Syracuse and Augusta followed. 'Accusations and counter-accusations poisoned the atmosphere. People talked of treachery on the part of the Admirals, first at Pantelleria and then at Augusta. The "Twelve" [d] who were to have spoken in the capitals of the régime, were themselves thrown from the saddle by the defeat. Scorza summoned them to a Party meeting to consider what was to be done. Then, almost without exception, they came to me, and there followed an exchange of views, which could have had no other logical and practical result than my decision to convene the Grand Council. Friday and Saturday were spent in drawing up the agenda, obtaining the necessary signatures and in preparing for the attack—or should I say, the manoeuvre. Three or four knew what they wanted, and what they would achieve. The others had no idea of what was afoot, and they never dreamed that at this meeting the existence of the régime would stand in the balance.

'There was as yet no search for traitors, though for the first time the germ of such a line of thought appears: "Was there a 'conspiracy' against me?" Yes, there was—otherwise there can be no explanation for the letter which Marshal Badoglio sent me on the night of 25–26th, in which he wrote of a "serious plot" against my person.'

This germ was to spread, and later explode into a general vendetta against the whole group who had voted for Grandi's motion at the Grand Council.

The Badoglio government was well aware of the danger of a German raid to rescue the Duce from his place of exile, and throughout these weeks there was an intricate and persistent battle of wits between the German and Italian Intelligence Services, the details of which have not yet come to light.

The immediate responsibility for the safety of the prisoner lay with the Italian Navy. On August 6 it was decided to transfer Mussolini by sea to the island of La Maddalena, a small naval base off the coast of Sardinia. Admiral Maugeri was again sent to conduct the operation. He explained to the Duce that there was the risk of a German *coup de main*. 'This is the greatest humiliation which could be inflicted on me,' was the reply. 'That one should imagine that I could go to Germany and try to take over the government with German help.'

The same dreary routine was once more established, but in a private villa which was reasonably furnished. Mussolini seemed content to be cut off from the outside world. He received a gift from Hitler of specially bound volumes of the complete works of Nietzsche. His reading and meditations were however to be again interrupted. On August 18 a German reconnais-

d. The party orators summoned by Scorza on July 16.

sance aircraft flew low over the island. The purpose of its mission was later to become apparent.

Rome at this time was full of rumours of plots and counter-plots and the threat of German military action against the capital, and by now clandestine links had been established between the Badoglio government and the Allies with a view to surrender. The Germans had also made progress in their search for Mussolini's hideout.

Simultaneously with the discovery of the 'Fascist plot' in Rome which led to the shooting of the former Fascist Party Secretary Muti while 'resisting arrest', the incarceration of Cavallero, and the removal on Himmler's instructions of Ciano to Germany, measures were taken to transfer Mussolini to yet another place of detention.

In the early hours of August 28 he was flown in a Red Cross ambulance-plane from La Maddalena harbour to an Italian sea-plane base on Lake Bracciano, where a Carabinieri officer and a police inspector named Gueli took him by motor ambulance across country. His destination was a ski-ing resort high up in the Apennines above Aquila. He was quartered in a hotel at Gran Sasso with a military police guard of 250 men.

Mussolini was not allowed any newspapers, but for the first time could listen to the radio in the hotel, and form a fragmentary picture of the confused politics of Rome.

The immediate reaction of Hitler to the disappearance of Mussolini from the Roman scene had been to give orders to mount at once a special operation for his personal release, together with a further plan under the code name 'Student' to organize a political pro-Fascist coup in Rome, and arrest the nucleus of anti-Fascist supporters of the Badoglio régime and of the monarchy. The story of these operations is both intricate and confused, and also obscured by the personal vanity of certain of the direct participants.[6] As the rescue of Mussolini might restore the situation, this plan was given top priority, and its planning was confided jointly to the German Naval Staff and the Air Force as represented by General Student, who commanded the parachute units in the Rome area. On August 1 orders were given to both services to proceed with this operation. All fragmentary reports as to the Duce's whereabouts were to be referred to the Fuehrer in person.

In addition to these general instructions, Hitler sent for the commander of a special S.S. unit under secret training for just such an operation. Colonel Otto Skorzeny was entrusted with an Intelligence mission to seek out, by all possible means, the secret place of detention of the Duce. He had been summoned to Hitler's presence on the evening of July 27, and was placed under the general orders of General Student. Thirty men were picked by Skorzeny from his special unit, and transferred to Rome. The first conception of his mission seems to have included not only the tracing of Mussolini's whereabouts, but also the implementation of that part of Operation 'Student' which included the arrest of leading anti-Fascist personalities in the Italian capital, and in fact a list of some fifty such persons was compiled at the beginning of the mission. According to Skorzeny's own account, which contains a number of inaccuracies, he had precise instructions from Hitler to keep his mission secret, even from the German Military Command and the Embassy in Rome. But he seems to have had at least one meeting with Kesselring, but subsequently dealt only with General Student and the latter's Intelligence Staff. The German naval representative was also naturally aware of the operation, and the German Police Chief, Kappler, and Himmler's representative, Dollmann, were brought into the picture.

The story of the search for Mussolini revealed the usual competition and lack of co-ordination between the German agencies concerned, and also the skilled deception plans of the Italians. As the first unconfirmed reports reaching Hitler pointed to the penal colony of Ventotene as the place of Mussolini's internment, operational plans remained in the first instance a naval responsibility, as any rescue operation would have to be conducted by sea. The first two clues to reach the Fuehrer's Headquarters came from Gaeta; one German witness had seen a column of cars heavily guarded by military police, and the other, a Petty Officer in the German Navy Signals base, had seen Mussolini escorted on board a vessel. This man was summoned to report personally to Hitler, and it was discovered that a friendly Italian officer had given the 'information' that the Duce had been sent to Ventotene.

An elaborate bluff developed. There was on Ponza, where in fact Mussolini was at that moment interned, a German aircraft intercepter station. The officer in charge was now ordered to Ventotene to report on whether or not the distinguished visitor was there. His instructions came from General Student, and neither the German Air Force commander in Italy, Richthofen, nor Kesselring were from now on informed of the development of the operation. In the meantime the German Chief of Police in Rome, Kappler, had intercepted a letter from Countess Ciano to her father, who had by now been moved to La Maddalena. This gave the first real clue, which Edda Ciano seems to have confirmed.

The aircraft which Mussolini had seen flying over the island on August 18 had Skorzeny himself on board, and on the return journey the plane crashed in the sea, and some of the crew and passengers, including Skorzeny, were rescued by an E-boat.

The next move was to send one of Skorzeny's officers, who spoke fluent Italian, to make a secret reconnaissance on La Maddalena, and he confirmed the presence of Mussolini whom he saw at a window of the villa where he was under guard. A combined naval and paratroop operation was now mounted under Student's orders, but before any action could be taken the Italians moved Mussolini to the mainland, and for the moment all trace was lost.

It is not clear how the Germans finally tracked down the new place of internment.[e] Hitler was himself convinced that he had been taken to La Spezia, but this rumour seems to have been planted by the Italians who had at that particular moment cordoned off the whole harbour as a blind. A belated report came in that Mussolini had been seen at the Italian experimental sea-plane base at Lake Bracciano, and again it was Kappler who traced the party to Gran Sasso, probably through intercepting the messages between the Italian Ministry of the Interior in Rome and the police inspector, Gueli, in charge of security arrangements at the ski-ing resort in the Apennines.

The arrest by the Badoglio government at the end of the month of the leading Fascist personalities, who would have played a part in Operation 'Student', led to the cancellation of this aspect of Skorzeny's mission, and his party of thirty men were now solely available for operations in connection with the rescue of Mussolini. The Germans now knew his precise whereabouts and the forthcoming operation, which could only be technically conducted by paratroops, became the sole responsibility of General Student.

The final operation was mounted in circumstances of general confusion, culminating in the news of Badoglio's surrender to the Allies on September 8. On that day a German reconnaissance aircraft was sent over Gran Sasso to take the photographs necessary for the detailed planning of Operation 'Eiche'. Skorzeny and his second-in-command, Major Radl, conducted this operation, and as no proper aircraft equipped for the purpose was available, they were forced to take photographs hanging out of an open hatch.

Detailed planning began on September 10. Twelve gliders were allocated to carry a force of a hundred and twenty men. Although Skorzeny was detailed primarily for an Intelligence mission, he persuaded General Student to let him travel with the party, and take his own group of twenty-six S.S. troops on the mission. The striking force was under the command of one of Student's officers, and the airborne operation was supported by another group of paratroops whose task it was to seize the funicular station at the base of the Gran Sasso mountain linking the hotel with the outside world. This latter group was commanded by Major Mors, an officer of German-Swiss origin.[7]

The final briefing took place on the evening of September 11 in the presence of General Student. It was realized that Mussolini was guarded by a sizeable force of Italian Military Police and in order to limit bloodshed, a search had been made for a senior Military Police Officer in Rome to accompany the German parachutists in the first glider to land, and to give orders to his men on duty at the hotel not to fire on the German party. For this purpose the

e. There are, for example, unconfirmed stories of bribery of Italian officials on a massive scale.

Germans picked up early on the morning of September 12, General Soleti. The offices in the Ministry of the Interior had already been occupied by the Germans the previous day and all telephone communications taken over.[8] Soleti was brought to the German paratroop base on the airfield at Pratica di Mare. He admitted that Mussolini was on Gran Sasso, but that there had been no news since September 8. On that day Soleti had sent reinforcements to the hotel, and he would therefore certainly be recognized by these men. When informed of the purpose of his arrest and the functions which he was now to perform, the Italian General showed a natural reluctance to take part. He appears to have attempted suicide, holding a pistol in each hand, before being forced at gun-point into the leading glider. But he was quickly disarmed and bundled in just before take-off.

The operation went more or less according to plan. Major Mors and his party, travelling in lorries by road, occupied the funicular on time, and punctually at zero hour—two o'clock on the afternoon of September 12—the gliders were released by their towing aircraft over Gran Sasso accompanied by a small reconnaissance plane which would bring the Duce back to the German air base at Pratica di Mare. Eight gliders landed safely, although one crashed injuring most of its occupants. Three others missed the landing ground.

General Soleti fulfilled with promptitude and skill his appointed task. He shot out of the first glider 'as if fired from a pistol' and called on the Italian Military Police on guard outside the hotel, who had witnessed with some astonishment the whole proceeding, not to shoot. The only German casualties were caused in the crashed gliders.

Mussolini was seen leaning out of a third floor window, and a group of German and Italian officers clambered up the stairs to greet him.

There is a confusion of evidence as to exactly what took place, nor is it of historical importance. It appears that Mussolini asked if he could go quietly by road into retirement at his house at La Rocca delle Caminate, an attitude which was consistent with his first wish expressed to Badoglio after his arrest in July. But the orders of the German party were categorical: to bring the Duce back to their base. After some discussion Mussolini was persuaded to squeeze into the light aircraft which had landed for this purpose. Skorzeny, who was a heavy man, insisted on accompanying him. This nearly led to disaster on take-off in the thin mountain air, and the plane returned to Pratica di Mare 'without a word being spoken'.

On direct orders from Hitler, Mussolini was transferred immediately to a Heinkel plane and flown to Vienna together with the bewildered General Soleti, Skorzeny, and Gueli the police inspector guarding Mussolini at Gran Sasso. This flight concluded the long drawn out Operation 'Eiche', which had been originally mounted in principle on July 27.

It is not clear to what extent there was any connivance on the part of the Badoglio authorities in face of these German efforts to secure the person of the Duce. The confusion in the hours following the official announcement of the Italian surrender on September 8 was such that it is unlikely that any positive and active steps were taken in Rome. The arrangements for the security of Mussolini's person lay primarily with Senise, who had been reappointed Chief of Police after July 25. The only new evidence which has come to light is that contained in the subsequent report by Senise's representative, Police Inspector Gueli, who on arrival in Vienna put down at once on paper his account of these events. [9] According to the latter, he had telephoned Senise on the morning of September 8 for news of events in the outside world, and was counselled to show 'great prudence'. Events were moving fast, and no one wished to take supreme responsibility. Rumours seemed to have reached Gueli that a German column (that of the paratroops under the command of the Swiss Major Mors) had arrived in Aquila, and had asked the way to Gran Sasso. The Italian military commander in that town was also worried at the presence of the Duce in the neighbourhood. Gueli seems to have foreseen an inevitable German action, and refused any reinforcements to defend the funicular station at the foot of the mountains. At 10 a.m. on September 12 he met the Prefect at this station, and there seemed to be little doubt that some operation on the German side was imminent. At 1.30 p.m., half an hour before the appearance of the gliders, the police chief of Aquila telephoned Gueli to pass to him a telegram from Rome. The cryptic text was signed by Senise, and read, 'Recommend to Inspector General Gueli maximum prudence.' [10]

This official had previously been given general authority to move his prisoner in case of a state of alarm, but clearly decided to take no action. On the landing of the first glider, containing General Soleti, it was Gueli who gave the actual order not to fire on the Germans.

On September 13 Skorzeny spoke on the German radio and announced, 'I liberated Mussolini'. Major Mors sent a formal complaint to the headquarters of the German Air Force in Berlin, and received the reply that the text of this communiqué had been personally authorized by Hitler. [11]

APPENDIX

The 'Memoirs' of the Duce written in exile

Two documents written by Mussolini while on Ponza and at La Maddalena have subsequently come to light.[f]

f. Printed in Spampanato op cit II, pp. 471 ff; Hagen op cit pp. 406–32. The note on July 25 only is to be found in translation in the German Collection.

The first records his first impressions of the events of July 25 and is dated August 2. The manuscript was confided, according to a footnote at the end, to Colonel Meoli, commanding the Military Police on Ponza.

The second document, headed 'Pontine and Sardinian Thoughts', and described as 'the first notebook' seems to have been written at La Maddalena between 8–28 August. It consists of daily and disjointed jottings of a philosophical, literary, and political character.

Mussolini kept this material in a suitcase which was transferred to Gran Sasso. On September 12 it was brought to Austria and in the custody of the Police Inspector Gueli. According to the latter, the documents were then impounded by Skorzeny 'on orders from the Duce' [g] and forwarded to Berlin for analysis.

On January 27 1944 Rahn received the following telegram from the German Foreign Office.[h] 'Personal for Ambassador. As is known to you, Colonel Skorzeny rescued the Duce's memoirs and placed them in safe keeping. He would now like to give them back to the Duce without consulting the Italian authorities. I would like your opinion as to how the return could take place and whether this is an opportune moment. Assuming that to be so, it is intended that Skorzeny should deliver the papers personally and give an assurance that, apart from himself, no one has looked at them.'

On February 2 Rahn replied that he recommended that for the moment no action should be taken. 'The Duce would never believe that no one had glanced at them.' [i]

These documents were again the subject of a German Foreign Office minute dated April 9.[j] Rahn had now asked for their return to the Duce. The Italian originals which had been passed to Kaltenbrunner, were destroyed in an Allied bombing raid on Berlin. The German security service possessed photostat copies, and it was proposed that these should be given to Mussolini with an explanation of what had happened. 'Whether the Duce will believe this is another matter.' [k]

In the event these copies seem to have been returned to Mussolini as it is clear from internal evidence that he used the text in the compilation of his memoirs published in the form of articles in the *Corriere della Sera*, and then in book form under the title *Storia di Un Anno* in November 1944.

Early in 1950 German translations of the originals, purloined by an S.S. officer who had saved them from burning at a documents centre near Linz in Austria in the last days of the war, were published in the newspaper *Salzburger Nachrichten*.

g. Dolfin *op cit* p. 350 note.
h. German Collection. Steengracht to Rahn, January 27, 1944.
i. German Collection. Rahn telegram, February 2, 1944.
j. *Ibid*. Foreign Office minute, April 9, 1944.
k. Spampanato *op cit* II, pp. 471 ff.

PART THREE

SALÒ: THE SIX HUNDRED DAYS

'It is difficult to cross the Rubicon twice;
especially if there is blood in it.'

(Briand to Mussolini at Locarno, October 1925)

PART THREE

Book I

CHAPTER ONE

THE RETURN OF MUSSOLINI

MUSSOLINI ARRIVED at Vienna airport from the German base at Pratica di Mare near Rome shortly before midnight on September 12. He was accompanied by Skorzeny, and both men were taken by waiting security officials to the Hotel Continental. The Duce was too weary to attempt any adjustment to the outside world. He was already far away from the radio set in the hotel on Gran Sasso, and still unaware of the swift pace of events in Italy and their impact on his German friends. He retired to bed, unshaven, and without pyjamas. Within a short while, however, he received a telephone call from Hitler. Goebbels noted in his diary that the Duce 'informed the Fuehrer that he was tired and sick, and would first of all like to have a long sleep. On Monday he wanted to visit his family in Munich. We shall soon see whether he is still capable of large scale political activity. The Fuehrer thinks so.'[a]

It seems that the next morning Mussolini was able to learn scraps of news from the unfortunate Italian General Soleti, who was still with the party of 'liberators'. The General told him that, on orders from Senise, the Italian guards at Gran Sasso had not resisted the coup. The Duce then asked for news of events in Rome, and received a brief outline. He had already been told of the arrival of his wife and younger children in Germany, and, as arranged with Hitler, left about noon for Munich. He seems to have felt the need of the cushion of family intimacy before facing the political realities of what were to be his Six Hundred Days.

Donna Rachele and the younger children had been hurried from La Rocca delle Caminate on the previous day by a German S.S. escort, flown to Munich from Forlì, and housed for the night in the Vierjahreszeiten Hotel. Only then did she learn the meaning of this journey. Hitler had feared reprisals by the

a. Goebbels *op cit* p. 361. Goebbels had gone to Berlin on September 12. His evidence on this episode is thus not an eye-witness account.

Badoglio government as a reaction to the Gran Sasso raid, and ordered the family to be brought to safety.

On the afternoon of September 13 Mussolini landed at Munich airport to find his wife and family waiting. He withdrew quickly into the privacy of a villa which had been placed at their disposal. That night he and Donna Rachele sat up late listening to the broadcast of the Italian Fascist Radio, and recounting the events of the previous day. [1]

The Cianos were also in Munich. Their flight from Rome had been organized by the Germans at the end of the previous month.[b] It is not clear whether Mussolini saw them during these brief hours. Nor did he meet those Fascist leaders, headed by Buffarini, who had been released in Rome the previous day and also flown to the Bavarian capital and also housed in the Vierjahreszeiten Hotel.[2]

The next morning at 11 o'clock the Duce left for the North. He was without any reliable information on recent events in Italy. On the journey he settled down to study the newspapers of the previous weeks, stuffing into his pockets scribbled notes and marking the pages of the papers. He had as yet given no sign of any personal reaction to his release.

Early that afternoon, he reached his destination. Goebbels describes the scene. 'The mutual greeting was exceptionally friendly. The Fuehrer himself waited outside his bunker with the Duce's son Vittorio. Hitler and Mussolini embraced after their long separation. It was a deeply moving example of loyalty between men and comrades. . . .' [3]

This first meeting between the two men lasted two hours. About seven o'clock that evening the Duce received the exiguous Fascist group present at the Headquarters in the conference room in the Fuehrer's bunker. [4]

'Mussolini thanked those present for the faith which they had shown, and rapidly reviewed the events in which he had taken part as well as those of which he had learnt through a rapid perusal of the newspapers and certain second-hand reports. He was not thoroughly sure of himself and from his first sentences one could almost draw the conclusion that he considered himself out of the picture or at least wished to remain as such.'

Pavolini answered for those present. 'The Provisional National Fascist Government awaits ratification from its natural head. Only after this could the composition of such a government be announced.'

Mussolini was perplexed for a moment and then replied, 'Your work is worthy of praise. But, gentlemen, everything has to be done from scratch. One must begin at the beginning, in the political, military, and social fields. In the political field, after what has happened, the monarchy is disqualified. In the military field one must reconstruct, particularly the air force. In the social field, one should be able finally and decisively to turn to the people.

b. Ciano later denied the story and said that he left 'undisturbed' (Cersosimo *op cit* p. 81). The Cianos had departed from Rome on August 27.

To-day it is possible for you to carry out this programme in which I have not succeeded for a multitude of reasons, many of which are unknown to you.'

Pavolini reiterated the need for a leader, but Mussolini replied, 'At this moment I cannot take any decisions. I lack too many elements to form a judgment. Let us see to-morrow. I can do something for you, gentlemen.'

The meeting closed, but those present flocked round him while he told of his recent adventures, and asked for news, particularly of individual Fascist leaders.

He then shut himself up until late that night, sometimes alone and at times talking together with the leaders of the 'provisional government'— Pavolini, Ricci, Farinacci, and Preziosi. 'In these talks the bases of the new state were laid.'

The following morning the Duce had a second talk with Hitler, and it seems that afterwards he attended the Fuehrer's military conference and a series of meetings with the senior German ministers. [5]

During these two days, the whole future of Italian-German relations passed under review, and for Mussolini personally a cruel adjustment to circumstances of which he was as yet only imperfectly aware had to be made with a minimum of concessions on his part. The régime which he had personified no longer existed. The members of little Fascist groups, each backed against the other by rival German agencies and ministers, and who had formed a shadow administration in exile and barely in existence in name, now confused him with conflicting advice. Each claimed priority in his confidence, and an exclusive knowledge of German intentions towards Italy. The remnants of the prestige of Italian Fascism had vanished for ever in German eyes in a few hours in the previous July, and with inevitable consequences to the standing of the Duce himself.

In such a shifting world the only stable element, as in the past, was his private bond with Hitler, whose personal idea it had been to bring him back to such a scene, and in such a melodramatic fashion. And the Fuehrer's advisers had been by no means unanimous upon the merits of this operation. The Army Command, particularly Keitel and Rommel, would have preferred a direct military occupation of Italian territory. Goebbels was particularly dubious. 'However much I may be touched on the human side by the Duce's liberation, I am nevertheless sceptical about its political advantages. With the Duce out of the way, we had a chance to wipe the slate clean in Italy. Without any restraint, and basing our actions on the grandiose treachery of the Badoglio régime, we could force a solution of all our problems in regard to Italy.

'To me it had seemed that, besides South Tyrol, our boundary ought to include Venetia. That will hardly be possible if the Duce re-enters politics. It will be very difficult for us even to put in our claim for South Tyrol.

'Under the leadership of the Duce, assuming he becomes active again, Italy will attempt to start a national rump government towards which we shall have obligations in many respects.' [6]

But everyone knew that the fate of Italy would be decided behind closed doors between two men in an atmosphere of mutual hypnotism. The substance of their conversation can be pieced together, though no official record has yet come to light.

These September talks at Rastenburg, in their outward tone, revealed no formal change in the relationship of the two men.[c] It had been Hitler's obstinate loyalty to his friend which had been responsible for the planning of the Duce's liberation. The emotional link had survived the destruction of the Axis alliance, but it was against the background of a collapse of the political relations of the two countries that the discussions between the two men now took place. The reasons for the catastrophe had to be analysed, the limits and direction of future action traced.

Hitler had been deeply shaken by Italian events. He had for some time been possessed with doubts as to the strength of Italian Fascism, but a persistent belief in the personality of Mussolini blunted his disquiet. The brutal and lightning collapse of July inevitably broke a last illusion. As he appears to have told Goebbels just after these September talks, 'The Duce's personality did not impress him as powerfully this time as at their earliest meetings. The main reasons may be that the Duce now came to the Fuehrer without any power, and that the Fuehrer accordingly looked at him more critically.

'The Duce has not drawn the moral conclusions from Italy's catastrophe which the Fuehrer expected.' [7]

Hitler had his own thoughts and conclusions. 'What is this sort of Fascism which melts like snow before the sun?' he asked Mussolini. 'For years I have explained to my generals that Fascism was the soundest alliance for the German people. I have never concealed my distrust of the Italian monarchy; at your insistence, however, I did nothing to obstruct the work which you carried out to the advantage of the King. But I must confess to you that we Germans have never understood your attitude in this respect.' [8]

It is now known that Hitler had in consequence taken severe measures, on the Mediterranean front, against a threat to the whole security of the southern frontiers of the Reich.

The disintegration of Italian Fascism had brought dire losses to Germany but it is not clear how far he went in revealing German plans to Mussolini. The latter denied to Anfuso, in a later talk, any suggestion of a menace in

c. Goebbels describes in his diary the comments of Hitler to his inner circle. Anfuso notes the subsequent results of his questioning of Mussolini on his recollections. See Goebbels *op cit* pp. 360 ff, and Anfuso *op cit* pp. 320 ff. See also Tamaro *op cit* I, p. 560–2 for the comment of minor Italian personalities.

regard to German annexation or indeed occupation of the northern frontier provinces of Italy. 'When we talked of the Mediterranean at the General Headquarters Hitler always specified that nothing had changed in regard to Italy's rôle.' There was no need for any anxiety on this score, and even less in relation to the Adriatic. It was of course obvious that, since Badoglio's surrender, the strategic aims of Germany were such that certain questions had had to be resolved, as for instance in Albania, without taking into account special Italian interests. But, according to Mussolini, the Fuehrer never spoke of reparations or eventual claims by Germany on Italy. 'The war must be won,' Hitler said, 'and once it is won Italy will be restored to her rights. The fundamental condition is that Fascism be re-born, and avenged.' [9]

As Mussolini quickly urged, alongside Fascism a new Italian army must be created. But to Hitler the process must be different. As in the case of Germany, the army must be created out of a new Fascism. In any event Hitler appears to have made no commitments on this issue. He knew the distrust and hostility of his own General Staff and of his political advisers to the suggestion of reconstructing the Italian armed forces to continue the fight, but he had to encourage his friend, and, at this early stage, leave him with some sense of liberty of action.

Goebbels' comment was sharp: 'The Duce intends to call a new Italian national army into being from the remnants of Fascism. I doubt whether he will succeed. The Italian people are not equal to grandly conceived revolutionary politics. They don't want to be a great Power. That desire was injected into them by the Duce and the Fascist party. The Duce will therefore not have much luck with his recruiting.[10]

'Old Hindenburg was right when he said of Mussolini that even he would never be able to make anything but Italians of Italians.'

The question of the new army was thus by implied omission subordinated to the reconstruction of a Fascist state in those areas of Italy outside the control of the Badoglio government.

A Fascist renaissance implied a simultaneous break with an historical past, not only with the dyarchy of the Party and the monarchy, but also with the treasonable elements within Fascism itself. Reconstruction and vengeance must go hand in hand. And with revenge, a conscious and publicized break with the catastrophic and immediate past. 'The Fuehrer expected that the first thing the Duce would do would be to wreak full vengeance on his betrayers. He gave no such indication, however, which showed his real limitations. He is not a revolutionary like the Fuehrer or Stalin. He is so bound to his own Italian people that he lacks the broad qualities of a world-wide revolutionary and insurrectionist.' [11]

But Mussolini needed both time and proof in order to adjust himself to such a break. He had never been able to arrive by himself at brutal and rough decisions. And this time, conclusive evidence was not yet to hand. He needed to create his own historical myth of his fall from power. On his personal interpretation of that myth would depend the shape and form of the new political construction.

Hitler made little progress in attempting to widen the Duce's fragmentary knowledge of the extent of the treachery of his former adjutants. Mussolini seemed genuinely unaware for instance of Ciano's precise responsibility. 'It is so obvious that the Duce cannot start criminal proceedings against the traitors of Fascism if he is not willing to call his own son-in-law to account. . . . The Fuehrer had the greatest difficulty in convincing him that at least Grandi was a deliberate traitor to the Fascist party and to the Duce. The Duce at first would not believe that either. But the punishment of the Fascist traitors is indispensable to any resurgence of Fascism. The little Fascist out in the country cannot believe in the honesty of a new beginning of Fascism if those who led Fascism into this life and death crisis are not made to account for it.' [12]

But Hitler did not press too hard. 'I understand, Duce, your family feelings,' he said, and left it at that.[13]

There seems to have been little discussion of the war as a whole except in relation to the Italian collapse. Mussolini's last utterances on the foreign relations of the Axis had been to the Japanese Ambassador in Rome, Hidaka, on July 25. He now returned to the theme of a separate peace with Russia. According to Ribbentrop, in his posthumous Memoirs:

'After the treachery of the Badoglio Government in September, 1943, I again acted very energetically. This time Hitler was not as obstinate as in the past. He walked over to a map and drew a line of demarcation on which, he said, he might compromise with the Russians. When I asked for authority, Hitler said he would have to think the matter over until the following morning. But when the next day came, nothing happened. The Fuehrer said he would have to consider this more thoroughly. I was very disappointed, for I felt that strong forces had again strengthened Hitler's inflexible attitude against an understanding with Stalin.

'When Mussolini arrived at the Fuehrer's headquarters after his liberation, the Fuehrer told him, to my surprise, that he wanted to settle with Russia, but when I thereupon asked for instructions I again received no precise answer, and on the following day the Fuehrer once more refused permission for overtures to be made.' [14] And there the matter appears to have ended.

At the close of the second talk, on the morning of September 15, Mussolini agreed not to return to Italy for the moment, but to stay in southern Germany until the rudiments of a new administrative machine could be formed.

Goebbels noted Hitler's references to these conversations.

'The Duce intends first to rebuild the Fascist party. Next, with its help, he wants to start rebuilding the state, beginning with the lower administrative échelon. As the crown of this work he then proposes to call a constitutional convention. Its task would be to eliminate the House of Savoy. The Duce is still somewhat hesitant about taking this action as he is of course aware of the strong ties between the Italian people and the Royal House, and knows that these ties cannot be severed lightly. Besides, his measures will depend very much upon military developments.

' . . . On the whole I am very glad that the Fuehrer has stuck to his original intentions. Obviously sentimental, emotional considerations no longer influence him. The Italian problems must be considered and solved anew.' [15]

That evening the official Roman news agency broadcast a communiqué. 'Benito Mussolini has to-day reassumed the supreme direction of Fascism in Italy.' Five orders of the day followed; nominating Alessandro Pavolini as 'provisional' Secretary of the Party, which was now to be called the 'Fascist Republican Party'; ordering all those military, political, administrative and educational authorities which had been dismissed by the 'government of the Capitulation' to take over again their functions; instructing all the institutions of the Party to support actively the German army, to give immediate and effective moral and material help to the people, and to examine the position of all party members in relation to their behaviour at the time of the coup d'état and the capitulation. Finally the reconstruction of the Fascist Militia was proclaimed. Two subsequent instructions were broadcast, appointing Renato Ricci as the commander of the Militia, and liberating all officers of the Armed Forces from their oath to the King.

The essence of these Rastenburg talks was the agreement that such a government should be set up at all. This was perhaps the last achievement of the Duce's personal authority in his relations with Hitler. The old ties of loyalty had strained without breaking. Hitler was loath to minimize them even now; 'for after all it was thanks to the Duce that I had been able to bring about the rearmament of the Reich'. [16]

Unknown to the Duce, Hitler had taken severe measures in regard to Italian affairs on September 10, two days before the operation at Gran Sasso.[d] There was no question that these orders should be published, but their practical effect was to create a frame of control within which any Italian administration which might be set up would be obliged to function. The two frontier provinces of Venezia Giulia and Alto Adige were placed under two Gauleiters, Rainer at Trieste and Hofer at Innsbruck, who were to depend directly on the Fuehrer. The rest of Italy under German control was divided into two zones: one operational under the control of Marshal Rommel, and the other to be known as 'occupied territory' under the formal control of a

d. See pp. 532–3.

German military plenipotentiary. A parallel S.S. command was to be set up in Northern Italy, to be responsible for the security of the German forces through the area. Political relations with whatever Italian administration might take shape were placed in the charge of Rudolf Rahn, who had been since August German envoy in Rome. Three days later, on September 13, blanket instructions were issued to Speer to take whatever measures he wished to 'safeguard' Italian war industry in the North, in other words, he was to have a free hand to gear the output of Italian factories to the German war machine.

These general instructions were in essence henceforward to govern Italo-German relations, and it was to them that Goebbels referred when he wrote, on September 17, after Hitler's meetings with the Duce, 'All our political and military measures remain intact; the Fuehrer has insisted that no change be made.' [17]

The significance of these September talks between the two men is the breaking of a personal spell. Hitler had acquired a sad scepticism in regard to his friend and one time political mentor, whose future now seemed at least doubtful, but to whom, because of past services, limited benefits must be allowed.

On September 17 Mussolini took leave of Hitler and was flown to Munich. It was due solely to the personal decision of the Fuehrer that he was to set up any government at all. The German political and military authorities in Italy, as represented by Rahn and Kesselring, were firm in the view that a precipitate neo-Fascist experiment would be a dangerous fiasco.

Rahn himself had arrived at Hitler's headquarters on September 14 to present a first-hand account of the delicate situation of the 'open city' of Rome, and to stress the absolute necessity for some continuity of administration, at least for a transitional period, in the form of a 'technical' government on the lines, in effect, of the arrangements on which the Italian King had insisted after July 25, though for contrary reasons. The royal advisers had assumed the lowering threat of a Fascist reaction, and had no faith in a nascent anti-Fascist movement, whereas Rahn was convinced that there was no support whatever in the country in September for a Fascist restoration, and a grave danger that if such a move were attempted an effective anti-Fascist development might well take place.

After talks at Hitler's headquarters, Rahn found that he was unable to persuade Hitler, and more understandably Mussolini, whom he now met for the first time, not to proceed with a neo-Fascist experiment. But he had gained a certain prestige in Hitler's eyes for his rapid measures taken in Rome, in close understanding with Kesselring, to preserve law and order in the capital, and did succeed in preventing any suggestion that a Fascist administration should, at least at this stage, be allowed to function in Rome, and in pressing that its activities should be confined north of the Apennines.

This proposal was put to Mussolini in Bavaria a few days later, when the questions relating to the formation of such a government were discussed.

Mussolini expressed his annoyance at the transitional régime of the 'Open City'. He had already complained to Hitler, whose first reaction had been to remonstrate with Rahn, but ultimately to accept the latter's arguments. It was agreed to leave the situation in Rome as it stood and the administration of 'technical' commissars would remain in being until the general position was stabilized. There was to be no question of the return of the Duce himself, on the formal ground that his personal safety could not be guaranteed.

A reluctant compromise was reached in the form of a political mission by Rahn to Rome to rally collaborators for a neo-Fascist administration which would not be allowed to function in the capital, but under close German supervision in the occupied territory of Northern Italy.

Of the original exiled group in Germany, Pavolini had succeeded in achieving a certain ascendancy and his nomination as secretary of a new Fascist Republican Party was the first formal step in the creation of a counter régime.

Rahn agreed to take Pavolini to Rome on this strange enterprise. Both men would keep in constant contact by telephone with the Duce to whom Pavolini would be reporting on his assessment of the atmosphere of Rome, and on the progress in forming an administration. The creation of a list of ministers would be made with the approval of Mussolini, and on September 18 the two men left for Rome.[e]

Mussolini was now established, with his family, at Waldbichel, near Weilheim in Southern Bavaria at Hirschberg castle, once the residence of Bismarck's banker Bleichroeder. The presence of an S.S. liaison officer and 'guard of honour' was a reminder of the dependence of the Duce on his hosts.

His only link with the outside world was a German military telephone, which could connect him directly with Hitler's headquarters, and with Rome.

He had no personal staff or secretariat. Anfuso, who was the only Italian diplomat of note abroad to rally, left his Budapest legation and joined the Duce at Hirschberg on September 18. 'I ended,' he wrote, 'by taking on the duties of usher, secretary, and telephone operator.' And it was the telephone which symbolized this small world. As Anfuso put it: 'A telephone, first class, of the Rastenburg type, which put Mussolini in touch with the communications network of the Reich and of allied or occupied countries. It was on this telephone that my colleagues answered that they would have nothing to do with him, and on this telephone that the government of the Social Republic was formed in talks with Rome . . . When Mussolini returned to

e. For the above, the author has largely relied on the personal notes of Dr Rahn, and conversations with him.

Italy, the "system" did not supply an "A" telephone; it must have been category "B" or "C" . . . ' [18]

Such was the new Palazzo Venezia in the Bavarian pine woods.

Mussolini was as yet almost unaware of the measures taken by the German authorities in Italy since the surrender of September 8, and apart from scattered perusals of the Badoglio press, unable to secure a picture of the Italian scene on which to base any appreciation. Nor did his present isolation protect him from a revival of those feuding intrigues which had bedevilled Fascist politics.

Among his first callers was Ciano. His attitude to his son-in-law was already regarded generally as a test of the nature of the new régime.

Ciano stated later at his interrogation at Verona that during his stay in Bavaria, he had three talks with the Duce. 'I spoke to him of the question of the Grand Council, and he told me that he had no comment on the speeches which I had then made nor on my conduct: he would take it upon himself to speak to the Germans about it, and clarify my position.' [f]

On September 19, 'Mussolini told me that he had assured the Fuehrer that "he guaranteed with his head the correctness of Count Ciano's attitude" and added that he had found complete understanding on the part of Hitler, but open hostility on that of Ribbentrop.' [19]

Goebbels was even more violent in his attitude. 'Edda Mussolini has succeeded in completely reversing the Duce's opinion of Ciano. Immediately upon her father's arrival in Munich she had a long talk with him, which resulted in a reconciliation between the Duce and Ciano. The latter has again been accepted in the good graces of the Duce. That means this poisonous mushroom is again planted in the midst of the new Fascist Republican Party. It is obvious that the Duce cannot start criminal proceedings against the traitors of Fascism if he is not willing to call his own son-in-law to account. His son-in-law should have been the first to be tried. If he were a man of really great revolutionary calibre, Mussolini would have asked the Fuehrer to hand Ciano over to him and would personally have taken him to task. This he won't do, and that hampers him seriously in proceeding against the other traitors to Fascism.'

And again: 'The Duce is naturally very much handicapped by conditions in his family. His wife, Rachele, hates Edda from the bottom of her heart. One can easily understand that. The Duce, on the other hand, trusts Edda more than he does his wife. Edda visited the Fuehrer some days ago. On that occasion she created a very bad impression. All she asked for was permission to emigrate to South America via Spain. In this connection she tried to settle some money questions. Ciano has brought about six million lire

f. This conversation may have taken place on September 14 when Mussolini was on his way to Rastenburg, but see p. 554.

with him from Italy. She wanted to exchange these for pesetas and actually offered the Fuehrer the difference in the exchange rate, a tactlessness that nauseated the Fuehrer. Ciano intends to write his memoirs. The Fuehrer rightly suspects that such memoirs can only be written in a manner derogatory to us, for otherwise he could not dispose of them in the international market. There is therefore no thought of authorizing Ciano to leave the Reich; he will remain in our custody, at least for the present.' [20]

The Duce was, as yet, unaware of the extent of German hostility to Ciano, and the frustrated hates of the old guard Fascists in Italy had not yet manifested themselves. During these Bavarian days, Mussolini even seems to have fleetingly considered Ciano again as a possible Foreign Minister, and mentioned the idea to Rahn.[21]

Buffarini knew the strength of his position as one of the inner circle of informers at the disposal of the Germans, as the close adviser of Donna Rachele, and his peculiar knowledge of the workings of the political world of Fascism. He had been anxious to reach Mussolini's side at the time of their joint release from captivity, but was not received during the first hours in Munich. He put his ideas on paper therefore in a memorandum which was sent to the Duce:

'The armistice has brought to an end the situation which was created by the betrayal of the régime by the governing class and by the treachery of the King.

'The reaction of the German army which has been prompt and energetic has caused preoccupation and panic among large numbers of anti-Fascists in North-Central Italy and in those areas of the South which are not occupied by the enemy.

'The unexpected return of the Duce has brought hope and confidence to many faithful and devoted Fascists hitherto reviled, demoralized and scattered, and has aroused lively expectations even where public opinion is perplexed and confused, expectations justified by a natural if unconfessed belief in the creative power of the Duce and in his capacity to find a solution.

'I venture to suggest to you, Duce, that at this moment the immediate adoption of new, decisive, subversive, revolutionary measures, could cause a general upheaval in the political situation with obvious repercussions in the military sphere.

'In my humble opinion the following measures could be taken: A declaration of the decadence of the monarchy now stained in the general view by the shame of a two-fold betrayal; the betrayal of the régime with the unspeakable arrest of the Prime Minister, and the betrayal of the people with the ignominious flight of the King and his government in a moment fraught with tragedy for the country.

'A declaration regarding the new form of Government, the Social-Fascist Republic headed by the Duce, who would have under him a government perfectly united in a policy and administration suited to the exceptional circumstance of the moment.

'The legal historical basis of these measures lies in the investiture of the Duce by the people in 1922, an investiture which since the treachery of the dynasty is no longer confined by outward constitutional limits, but has recovered its original integrity and full revolutionary content.

'When the war ends the new form of government can receive formal sanction and develop accordingly.' [22]

Buffarini now went to Hirschberg after the Duce's return from Hitler's headquarters. [23]

Mussolini showed few illusions in his reflections on the events of July and the consequences which had followed. He told Buffarini, 'You were right that night. You said that we must get rid of them (the supporters of Grandi's motion) before their pronunciamento. But I had confidence in the King . . . Those gentlemen made a mess of things. Even over the betrayal, the last session of the Grand Council was a dilettante performance. In a country like ours, where conspiracy is an art, those gentlemen worked for Badoglio free. They enabled the Marshal and his accomplices to get where they would never have got on their own . . .'

But the present situation was grave not only 'because they have dismantled our régime, but the moral and political unity of the nation has been endangered'. One must return to the past 'and widen and perfect the social reform of the State. . . . I admit that the "system from on top" has failed; because the men have failed, not Fascism. A system "from below": we are considering the unknown; what if the masses also fail?'

It was with such thoughts that the Duce was preparing to address the Italian people on the eve of the formation of a new government. To help in the latter task Buffarini [g] left for Rome to join Pavolini and where Ricci and Vittorio Mussolini were also now installed.

Farinacci and Preziosi inevitably appeared in Bavaria with their gloomy prophecies; the former to press his claims for the Ministry of the Interior, having allegedly refused the Secretaryship of the Party; and the latter to pursue his vendetta against Pavolini,[h] Buffarini, and Freemasons and Jews in general.

On September 21 Farinacci wrote in his own hand to the Duce: 'I beg you to accord me a final interview—and before I clarify my position—loyal and unequivocal—with our German comrades.

g. It seems that he was now designated privately, and at the request of the Germans, as the new Minister of the Interior. See Tamaro *op cit* II, p. 5.
h. It was said that Pavolini had a Jewish sister-in-law.

'I meditated deeply last night on everything and have decided on my line of conduct: only to save my family from the inevitable disaster.

'Yes, Mr. President, your latest tendencies leave no hope for your old and loyal comrades.' [24]

With his sense of the occasion, Mussolini told Farinacci, 'Do not think that you are still living in the period of Dumini'—the chief suspect in the murder of the Socialist leader Matteotti in 1924. [25]

On September 18 Mussolini made his first broadcast from Radio Munich since his liberation, and, strangely, only the second of his career.

'After a long silence my voice reaches you again . . . I waited a few days before addressing myself to you because, after a period of moral isolation, it was necessary for me to re-establish contact with the world.'

A brief version of the events of July and the behaviour of the King followed. The total and planned treachery of the monarchy formed the essential gambit in proclaiming an alternative centre of government in Italy. 'As to our traditions, they are more republican than monarchist; the unity and independence of Italy were willed, more than by the monarchists, by the republican current and its purest and greatest apostle, Giuseppe Mazzini.

'The State which we wish to set up will be national and social in the highest sense of the word: that is, it will be Fascist, thus going back to our origins. While waiting for the movement to develop until it becomes irresistible, our postulates are the following: to take up arms again alongside Germany, Japan and the other allies; only blood can cancel such a shameful page from the history of the fatherland; to set about reorganizing our armed forces around the Militia formations without delay . . .; to eliminate the traitors and in particular those who up to 9.30 on the evening of July 25 had been active—some for years—in the ranks of the Party and who have gone over to the ranks of the enemy; to annihilate the parasitic plutocracies and at last to make labour the theme of our economy and the indestructible basis of the State . . .' [26]

On the day of his arrival in Rome, Pavolini, having reopened the old Party headquarters in Palazzo Wedekind, set about sounding such opinion as would risk being consulted. The political climate of the capital was one of uncommitted apathy. The old Fascists of the first days had either dispersed or were reluctant to come forward. The last Party secretary, Carlo Scorza, was said to have declared that he was in favour of a movement 'which would not show itself related to Fascism'. The leader of Italian Futurism and a foundation member of the Party, Marinetti, asserted that 'one must find new subjects of national unity, otherwise the Italian instinct for partisanship will prepare other and greater sources of grief'. [27]

It was not surprising that in such an atmosphere the resurrection of the

Party met with a damp response. The attempt of Ricci to reopen recruitment for the Militia was even more disappointing. Such an absence of prestige also cast a shadow on the search for candidates for ministerial appointments in the new administration, and the inevitable German pressures lowered the temperature further.

The scuffles round the key post of the Interior had been settled unobtrusively. Buffarini, with the support of Himmler through Dollmann, and having overcome Mussolini's hesitations on the telephone from Rome, received the appointment. [28] He was now able to contribute on arrival in Rome to the frustrating task of Rahn and Pavolini.

The Foreign Ministry presented a special problem. The only suitable candidates had to be found from the ranks of those career diplomats trained in the Foreign Service from the ranks of the Party in the 1930's to break the monopoly of the old school of Palazzo Chigi. This category of officials had however been groomed to promote a 'fascist' foreign policy now patently bankrupt, and it was very hard to visualize the attractions of such a ministerial post. Anfuso had been the only senior diplomat who had rallied to the Duce, and he was to be sent as Ambassador to Berlin, as only there would any serious business be transacted.

The expedient was attempted of nominating a minister on direct orders from the Duce, and Pavolini and Buffarini called on the unfortunate man accompanied by an S.S. escort. His prompt refusal ended similar experiments.[i] It was settled therefore that Mussolini himself would act as Minister, and a reluctant Undersecretary was found in the person of Count Mazzolini, who had been designated in 1942 as Italian High Commissioner in event of the Axis conquest of Egypt.

The very existence of the new régime depended on the creation of an effective Armed Force, but the quest for a suitable general foundered, and approaches made by the neo-Fascist clan met with equally negative results.

The other appointments were filled by clan patronage and reluctant technicians. The Ministry of Popular Culture with its key control of the Press, was placed, at Pavolini's instigation, in the hands of the young Umbrian, Fernando Mezzasoma, whose safe career had been made in the ranks of the very Party which had disintegrated in July.[j]

The ministerial list brought by Pavolini to the German embassy in Rome on the morning of September 23 confirmed Rahn's original appreciation of the parlous condition of the remnants of Italian Fascism. The whole prospect of setting up a neo-Fascist ministry would collapse unless direct and abrupt German pressure was exerted.

i. Consul-General Giuriati, who had been liaison officer between the Foreign Office and the Italian High Command prior to July 25.

j. Mezzasoma had at that time been in charge of the Press and was said to have asked Badoglio if he might retain the post.

At the same time, the temporary situation of the transitional administration of commissioners of the 'open city' of Rome itself, set up before the Duce's liberation, must be regularized, as also the position of Count Calvi di Bergolo, the Commander of the one Italian division, the 'Piave', allowed to exist in being by Kesselring to preserve order in the capital after the 'armistice' of September 10. This isolated military pocket represented the last unit on a war footing of the Italian army.

Rahn had already made his plans to complete his Roman mission. On the night of September 22 he telegraphed to Berlin:

'Regrettable weakness and incoherence of Fascist elements in Rome. Many of those followers of the Duce under consideration for ministerial posts are still hesitant. Ricci has not so far succeeded in recruiting members for the Militia. I therefore think it necessary to proceed at once with the proclamation of the new Fascist Republican government, and have undertaken the following:

'September 23 at 11.45 a.m. The German military commandant of Rome, General Stahel, sends for Calvi di Bergolo and the senior officers of the Piave division. He announces new government. Will they rally? No. Stahel then declares their functions at an end.

'12 noon. Announcement of the new government by radio. The High Commissioners will be ordered to continue temporarily or be arrested. The disarming of the Piave Division to be announced at 12.05.

'It is necessary that the new government, which here for the moment will not be able to command any authority, should be removed to North Italy as soon as possible, in order to avoid a situation whereby the police and civil service adopt passive resistance.' [29]

This message appears to have been relayed to the Duce, as a swift reply from Ribbentrop reached Rahn.

'Duce in agreement with planned action. He does not think that the Piave division will offer resistance. . . .' [30]

The outstanding gap in these arrangements was the appointment of a War Minister, and a personality of such seniority and prestige to be able to rally some support among the débris of the Italian army. The German military authorities were opposed anyway to the creation of a new Italian military machine, and the death of Cavallero had removed the one possible candidate whom they would have been reluctantly prepared to consider.

In desperation the name of Graziani was mentioned.[k] It evoked imperial memories of North Africa and Abyssinia and it had the perhaps decisive advantage of raising anew the reputation of Badoglio, whose Chief of Army

k. Rahn suggests that this was on his initiative, and that Pavolini then sought and obtained Mussolini's approval on the telephone. Notes of Dr Rahn to the author.

Staff Graziani had been, and whose relations with him could hardly be worse. As a counter figure to Badoglio at the present moment, Graziani was the obvious choice. It seems that he had, although subject to a military enquiry after his failure in North Africa in 1941, even been mysteriously considered as being suitable for a senior rôle in the Duce's plans for a reconstruction of the whole government machine in the hours after the meeting of the Grand Council.

On the morning of September 22, Graziani received a visit on his country estate from one of the new ministers, Barracu, the new undersecretary of the Presidency of the Council, with a personal message from Mussolini who had telephoned from Munich offering the Marshal the Ministry of National Defence.[31] Graziani refused. On the next morning he was in Rome, and was again approached by Barracu and two other ministers known to him and each of them with outstanding personal military records, a fact which it was hoped would strengthen their arguments.

They pointed out that all the new ministers were at that moment in session with Rahn at the German Embassy, and that he was expected at least to accept the German invitation to be present. 'Otherwise,' as Barracu said, 'your refusal would be taken for cowardice.' [32]

Graziani was temperamentally incapable of resisting such an insinuation and he accepted the challenge. Time was running short. Rahn had already told the Italian ministers designate that he would make a public announcement of the new administration at noon. It was then 11.30 a.m.

Graziani found Rahn, and the S.S. commander Wolff, now responsible for the German S.S. throughout occupied Italy, awaiting him. The former explained that a new government was being formed to re-establish the alliance between Germany and Italy in face of the world. 'You must remember that Italy has been declared a territory of war booty (sic) . . . and that what has happened in Poland could also happen to her. By setting up this government, this fury will be abated. . . .' [33] Unless Graziani with his prestige was now prepared to accept responsibility for the Armed Forces of the new republican régime, Rahn could not answer for the consequences. A few minutes before noon, Graziani consented, and the announcement of the new ministry was made according to plan.

That afternoon Rahn telegraphed that 'the operation was carried out according to plan. Reconstruction of the government completed at noon. . . . I was only able to persuade Graziani to enter the government one minute before the publication of the communiqué.' [34]

The German Consul-General in Naples, Wuster, witnessed these events on his way north, to report after being displaced by the Allied landings. The long distance calls between the Duce at Hirschberg and the German Embassy in Rome were made in his room. 'The formation of the new Republican Fascist government by Pavolini was a tragi-comedy, beset by disgusting intrigues for office, and old feuds.' Thanks to Rahn, some prestige had been added by Graziani's appointment.[35]

It remained to settle the affairs of the city of Rome. Immediately after the announcement of the new administration, Rahn summoned the High Commissioners of the 'open city'.

'The Duce has decided to form a provisional government and to summon next month a Constituent Assembly which will decide on the form of government in Italy. The seat of government will be in Northern Italy, and its activities will take shape according to the possibilities.'

Rome was a war zone, and Marshal Kesselring had instructed the commissars to remain at their posts. 'This is a military order.'[36] This unusual body would receive further instructions through the German Embassy in Rome, which would transfer its main offices to the North, together with the new Ministries of the Republican Government, leaving a branch office in the capital, now surrounded by a military operational zone, to deal with the affairs of this artificial enclave.

That evening the list of the new Fascist Republican government received the final approval of Mussolini in Bavaria.

CHAPTER TWO

THE DUCE IN ROMAGNA

ON SEPTEMBER 23 Mussolini flew from Munich to Forlì airport. He had a small German liaison staff attached to him, and was met on arrival by Rahn and Wolff, who had completed that day the Rome mission of controlling the setting up of the new Fascist administration. The former as his new political adviser and link with the German government, the latter as commander of the S.S. for Northern Italy.

General Wolff had been Himmler's senior liaison officer at Hitler's headquarters. At the end of July he was ordered to set up an advanced staff at Munich to establish an S.S. and Police command in Italy in the event of the defection of Badoglio. He had received telephonic instructions from Hitler on the evening of September 8 to act accordingly, and he left for Italy on the following day.

Wolff had made his career in the S.S. He had been in Rome in the 1930's and first met Mussolini in October 1936. He was responsible for the security arrangements for the latter's visit to Germany the following year, and accompanied Hitler to Rome in 1938 and 1940.

He now appeared again on the Italian scene in an enlarged security role which symbolized the total dependence of the Duce on German protection. It had been the S.S. who had had the honour of liberating Mussolini. They were now to symbolize the firm but indirect protection of the Reich, and this was emphasized by the permanent S.S. detachment of Hitler's own guard, which now appeared to render the honours to the Duce at his residence at La Rocca.[1]

During the next days the Duce gathered his first impressions of the extent of the disintegration of the Italian scene since his arrest in the previous July. The new Italian government of the Northern provinces was now a political fact, but without a capital, an army, or an administration, subject to enemy invasion from the South, and encamped amid the armies of a powerful and sceptical ally whose agencies, military and civil, were in effect in occupation of the territory of the new State, issuing their own currency, requisitioning factories and installations, and giving orders to those Italian civil authorities still in being.

On September 26 the Duce had a private conversation with Rahn at La Rocca. The latter reported that 'despite the optimism which he simulated in the presence of his colleagues, the Duce felt bound to tell me that his first impression was that Italy was in a chaotic state, like a punch-drunk man who has completely lost his bearings. The thing was to know exactly what one wanted. He could scarcely suppose that the diverse unsystematic ways in which Germany was interfering in every department of public life really served the German interest. Naturally he was realist enough to accommodate himself to circumstances as they were, but from Germany's point of view as well as Italy's it was meaningless to create a government that did not govern, to lay down regulations without having the means to enforce them, and to reorganize an administration which no longer had anything left to administer.

'It was a tragedy for the Italian people that Germany alone was left to fight. But seeing that such was the case Germany must have sole leadership in all matters relating to the conduct of the war in Italy. He would support this idea with the most rigid consistency, and for this reason he also wished to see the new Militia reorganized under virtual German leadership. . . . He regarded it as the task of the new Italian Government to maintain law and order in the rear of the German armies, and he would ask that at the earliest opportunity he should once again be granted the necessary means for doing so. Such means would include unified control of the administration, economics and finance.'

Rahn told Mussolini of the recent measures taken in Rome, and how the Ministries were being run by commissars, and that their offices were gradually being put into Fascist hands. 'The Duce approved those measures and reiterated his request that the matter of requisitioning currency and issuing it to the troops be clarified at the earliest opportunity, so as to avert an inflation that would be as dangerous to Germany as to Italy. I replied that now that the army had been disbanded Italy was relieved of a considerable part of her previous war burdens. I therefore proposed that Germany should receive from Italy a contribution towards war expenditure roughly equal to the German troops' demand for lire in Italy, other matters of commercial policy being settled in a similar fashion or by making credit available. The Duce agreed in principle with this suggestion. I refrained from enlarging on my proposals.

'In the sphere of internal administration the Duce means to do away with the dualism hitherto obtaining (Prefect—Local Party Secretary) and to appoint only one Party and administrative head in each province.'

The first Cabinet meeting was to be held the next day in La Rocca delle

Caminate. 'Afterwards the Duce will issue a Government proclamation, the wording of which has not yet been settled, and will then leave at once for the seat of government.' [2]

But even this last point had not yet been settled. The first and logical suggestion was that the Duce should be established securely in the neighbourhood of Marshal Rommel's new advance headquarters at Belluno, but on September 22 Hitler had sent a personal message to Rahn in Rome: 'The Fuehrer wants to know, before the Duce goes to Belluno, that Rommel has been asked his opinion as to whether the region is sufficiently safe.' [3]

The Duce himself had other thoughts in mind. Perhaps he could forestall the total absorption by the 'special' administration of Gauleiter Hofer of the strategic frontier province of Tyrol. On September 23 Rahn replied that 'the Duce would prefer Merano or Bolzano as the new seat of government'.[4]

The Tyrol represented the millennial struggle of German and Italian to control the Alpine gateway to the south. The territory was the symbol of the last remaining historical clash of interest between the two nations.

Such a despairing gesture of provocation on the part of the Duce could hardly be expected to meet with German agreement. Rommel and Wolff were told to choose a site, and it was hoped to complete preparations by September 29, and within speedy reach of Rommel's headquarters at Belluno, and that of Wolff at Verona.

On September 27 Mussolini summoned the first meeting at La Rocca of the new Council of Ministers. His opening survey of the scene was at once a polemical challenge and a directive. 'The situation of Italy at the moment when the Fascist Republican government assumes its task, can be defined without a shadow of exaggeration as one of the most serious in her history . . . On the morning of July 25, although martyred by Anglo-American bombing, Italy was a State and her territory, except for Western Sicily, was intact. The tricolour was still flying at Rhodes, Tirana, Ljubljana, Spalato, in Corsica, and on the Varo.[a] Today, two months later, the enemy occupies a third of the national territory, and all our positions beyond the frontiers and overseas have been evacuated.' The loss of these positions had been provoked by the armistice with catastrophic results, the surrender of the flag and collapse of the army, 'disorder in material and spiritual things and the continuation of the war on our territory . . .'

'Given this factual situation, the directives which guide the action of the Government can only be the following: to be faithful to the nations of the Tripartite Pact and thus to take up again our battle positions alongside the German armed forces through the most careful reorganization of our military

a. i.e. in the Aegean, Albania, Slovenia, Dalmatia, Corsica, and Nice. The Varo (Var in French) is a river which rises in Liguria and whose lower reaches marked the 1860 boundary between France and the Kingdom of Sardinia.

forces, beginning with anti-aircraft and coastal defence. Pending the organization of these units which has already begun, to extend a cordial and practical assistance to those German forces engaged on the Italian front. By a military effort we intend not only to cancel the page of July 25 and the even more disastrous one of September 8, but to achieve our objectives, which are the territorial integrity of our nation, our political independence and our place in the world.

'This new military effort . . . will be impossible if life in the provinces does not regain its normal rhythm, and if the citizens with their habitual discipline do not realize the needs of the moment.

'The present government has among its tasks the essential one of preparing a Constituent Assembly which must crown the programme of the Party with the creation of the Fascist Republican State . . .' [5]

The decisions reached at this meeting and summarized in a release at the end of the sitting gave some hint of the ministerial debate.

There could now be no question of moving to Rome. The intricate negotiations between the German military and civil authorities, the 'caretakers' left behind by the King and Badoglio, and the representatives of Mussolini had ended with the agreed declaration that Rome should be regarded as an open city, and thus in a sense politically neutralized. Skeleton staffs of the main ministries, the local prefecture, and a senior Italian officer, would deal with the German Military Command on all matters regarding the administration of the City.

The inability of the Duce to persuade the Germans that Rome must be the seat of the new Fascist Republic emphasized in the minds of Italians not only the immediate territorial, but also the historical disintegration of Italy. Where was the structure of national unity without the historic capital? Mussolini had already harshly and sarcastically opposed a more permanent project for a separate administration of Rome. In Graziani's words at his own trial after the war: 'Mussolini scotched the proposal with this expression "Rome an autonomous and open city; Rome a pontifical city; Rome the capital of a pontifical state . . ." He had in this period a great fear that Rome would fall again under papal influence. . . . His obsession was that one would arrive at a scission of Italian unity inasmuch as Rome could easily become the capital of a revived Papal State.' [6]

The press release of September 27 stated the decision. 'As a result of the declaration of Rome as an open city, the government is fixing its residence in another place near the General Headquarters of the Armed Forces.'

The task of building up a Republican army, divorced from the remnants of the royalist forces in the South, was inevitably from the outset conceived in terms of mobilizing human loyalties and integrating them in an entirely new military machine. Nothing existed except the prestige of Marshal Graziani, and the handful of officers who had rallied to him. The creation round this group of officers of a new force raised at once a familiar issue and a central thread in the historical experience of Italian Fascism. The control of a resurgent Army would be decisive for the shaping and the authority of the new state. Whatever forces controlled the military machine would dominate the political structure.

The events of July 25 had established sinister precedents and implanted in Italian public life the insidious model of a successful pronunciamento. A climate had been engendered in which all loyalties smoothly dissolved. Could a new Republican army be sealed against infection by the traditional royalist instincts of the old? What lessons should be drawn from the recent breakdown? Although the Fascist Party and its Militia had not moved at the time of supreme crisis, could the new Party allow without a struggle the setting up of a military machine independent of its influence? Perhaps the failure to create the 'M' battalions in sufficient numbers to protect the Fascist régime, as Himmler had foreseen and for which he had pressed, was the intimate cause of disaster. The old jealousy and distrust between Militia and Army was quick to burst into flame, and for the moment and as always the Duce prevaricated. The clash of 1924 was about to be repeated, not as an aftermath to the triumphant seizure of State power, but as the prelude to the painful patching together, with limited and demoralized human resources, of a new State machine broken from its previous roots and in the climate of national defeat.

Mussolini had already publicly committed himself to the principle of reconstructing the army on the basis of the Militia in the early broadcast directives from Germany. It even appears that the first concrete plan to be discussed was exclusively on these lines, and Himmler wrote a personal memorandum on 'Italian Militia Units' in sour reflection on the talks with the Duce on this subject at Klessheim in the previous April, and the fate of the unfortunate 'M' divisions of the previous summer. 'According to the wish of the Duce, S.S. units of the Italian Militia will be set up.' The main aim was to be to build up two 'M' divisions.[7]

Indeed one of the reasons given for the appointment of General Wolff as commander of the German S.S. in Italy was 'the desire expressed by the Duce in September 1943 at the headquarters of the Fuehrer to set up Italian S.S. with police functions and organized on the German system. The new organism would also have the task to make impossible an eventual repetition of July 25.' Wolff was to advise in the setting up of such units, the implication being that the only military forces allowed to the new régime would be for police duties.

The sudden appointment of Graziani, on Rahn's initiative in Rome, as Minister of Defence, had therefore aroused an immediate reaction at Hitler's Headquarters. 'The Foreign Minister asks for immediate telegraphic explanation of reasons which in your view induced the Duce to bring in Graziani again.' [8]

Rahn's office in Rome replied: the need for speed and because no other suitable personality was available. The duality Graziani–Badoglio would be advantageous. The Duce's advisers had been in favour of Graziani, and his relations with Mussolini were good. 'At the last meeting at La Rocca, they fell into each other's arms.' [b]

In this first cabinet meeting on September 27 Graziani had counter-attacked the conception of a Militia as the exclusive armed force of the new republic. 'I immediately put forward my concept, which was instead to set up an army on a national basis with solely voluntary cadres with a rank and file also largely voluntary, and incorporated in a State which would be as liberal and democratic as possible . . .' [9]

An unexpressed menace lay behind the discussion. Graziani had been appointed Minister of Defence and Chief of the General Staff. Could he carry out his duties effectively without further powers? As he had said at his trial, 'When a country is completely destroyed the control of the internal situation and of the armed forces must be in the hands of one person.' At an early stage, after talks with Kesselring, to whom he said 'I am taking over the Interior and the armed forces, and will give a united lead both to internal policy and to the police forces', Graziani seems to have tackled Mussolini. 'I reminded him of the case of the Russia of Alexander I after the great defeat. . . . He had nominated General Kutusov who, in one year, put the army on its feet and re-established the internal situation . . .' 'But the usual jealousies of the Party, of Buffarini Guidi and others prevented this act of unification which would have been providential.' [10]

The bitterness of this basic squabble was concealed in the communiqué. 'In the reorganization in progress of the armed forces, the land, sea, and air forces will be incorporated respectively in the Militia, the Navy, and Aviation of the Fascist republican state. Recruiting will be by conscription and voluntary enlistment . . .'

As for all practical purposes the Navy and Air Force did not exist, the meaning of these words was that the Party and the armed forces of the new State were co-existent and synonymous. But this minor verbal triumph would be meaningless, until the structure of the new Army had been established in agreement with the German ally.

The remaining shreds of debate on the future shape of the Government of the North appear in the other phrases of the communiqué. The Senate 'nominated by the King' was abolished. The former Fascist syndical organizations were

b. Moellhausen was in charge of a subordinate political office in Rome as a member of Rahn's staff. German Collection. Rome telegram (Moellhausen) October 8, 1943.

to be fused into a 'General confederation of work and technics' which 'would function in the ambit and climate of the Party, which brings to it its own revolutionary strength'. Finally, the Commission which Badoglio set up to enquire into the illicit gains of Fascist potentates was to continue to act. Pending the summoning of a Constituent Assembly, the Duce would assume the functions of Head of the Government.

That evening the Duce wrote his first letter since their recent meeting to Hitler.

'As you will have seen, the Fascist Republican government has held its first sitting and issued statements about its programme which have made a good impression. It is the figure of Marshal Graziani which gives character to the government and arouses vast hopes and sympathies.

'If we want to reconstruct the civil life of the country, the new government I have formed must have the necessary autonomy to govern, that is to give orders to the civil authorities subject to it.

'The Republican government, which I have the honour to lead, has only one desire and aim—to see that Italy resumes her place in the war as soon as possible. But to reach this supreme result, it is essential for the German military authorities to confine their activity to the military sphere only and, for all the rest, to allow the Italian civil authorities to function.

'If this is not accomplished, both Italian and world opinion will judge this government incapable of functioning, and the government itself will fall into disorder and, even more, into ridicule.

'I am sure, Fuehrer, that you will realize the importance of the points which I have put to you, and the gravity of the problems which I have to face, and their solution is not only an Italian, but a German interest.' [11]

The Axis satellites were instructed by Ribbentrop to recognize publicly the new Italian government and to antedate recognition to before September 27. Roumania, Bulgaria, Croatia, and Slovakia made such declarations, and Hungary under pressure. To preserve the tattered fragments of the Tripartite Pact, Japan also gave her public support.

German persuasion with the neutral powers, however, met with no response. The measure of the lack of regard for the shadow régime may be seen in the brutality of Franco's reaction to the German request. He told the German Ambassador in Madrid that he was prepared to grant *de facto* recognition only. Mussolini was 'to-day only a shadow'. The events of July 25 had been a mortal blow. There were now too few decent Italians behind him. Italians were split by the dynastic issue. There was 'no question of Mussolini being able to rely on any strong factors'. His power depended exclusively on the military strength of Germany. Only where German troops were stationed did the government of Mussolini exist, which anyway was not constitutionally set up; otherwise nowhere. 'Besides, according to reliable information, Mussolini is seriously ill, and presumably has not long to live.' Franco must therefore for the moment refuse formal recognition; like Portugal, Sweden, Switzerland, Turkey, Argentina and the Vatican.

Dieckhoff, the German Ambassador, stressed Mussolini's lack of hesitation in recognizing Franco in 1936. Franco made no comment.[12]

Ribbentrop instructed Rahn to tell the Duce of Franco's decision. The last of the Fascist 'triumphs' in the inter-war world, the Italian intervention in the Spanish Civil War, was revealed as dust.

Renewed contact with the Italian scene had by now revealed to the Duce the extent of the demoralization and chaos of the structure of the occupied regions, and of the boundless and all-embracing penetration of Italian life by rival and overlapping German military and civil authorities. He paused on the edge of a final and personal commitment to the task of a restoration of Fascist authority in accord with such allies, in such a mood.

On September 29 Rahn had an unvarnished talk with the Duce.

'The situation as a whole was well-nigh desperate, and his task almost insoluble. German military incursions into internal politics and administration were destroying all possibility of a co-ordinated joint effort. The destruction already accomplished and that which, according to his information, was yet to be accomplished, had led in many areas to the development of dangerous clandestine resistance to Germany and to the undermining of every vestige of the new Italian Government's authority. In so far as this destruction concerned definitely military targets or objects of military importance he not only understood but approved the German action. But he urgently requested that instructions be issued to spare gas, water and electrical installations as far as was possible. It would otherwise be impossible to avert civil disturbances and successfully continue recruiting for the Militia and the labour force.

'I advised the Duce to move into the Government headquarters provided at the earliest opportunity so as quickly to establish a workable instrument of administration. He agreed to do so as soon as accommodation, transport and means of communication had been guaranteed, besides his minimum requirements in the way of collaborators, officials and other personnel—some two thousand persons all told. Upon my recommendation that he should follow the German example, take only a small staff of close colleagues to start with, and let the rest evolve organically, the Duce agreed to the move being speeded up. General Wolff has been notified and will to-day proceed to the place finally designated, Belluno, to make the necessary preparations. . . .'

The Duce also proposed to assemble the local mayors, veteran Fascists, workers' and peasants' representatives for the meeting of the National

Assembly envisaged for the end of October or beginning of November. 'When I pointed out that such an assembly ought not to exercise an advisory, but only a confirmatory function, he replied that this was also his opinion. The Assembly must be convened with due pomp and circumstance, and he proposed to lay ready-made decrees before it, the text of the new Constitution in particular. This Constitution would be strongly socialist in character, providing for extensive socialisation of industrial enterprises, and workers' self-government. He had in mind something on the lines of the Turkish and Portuguese constitutions. . . .

'The Duce further stated that he had gained a very good impression from his talk with Graziani. Graziani was confident that with German support he could set up about ten Militia (sic) divisions by the spring of 1944. He would arrest and ship to Northern Italy all the old régime Generals and Admirals, who were still gadding about in Rome.' [13]

It looked as if Graziani would be charged only with raising Militia units under German command for police duties, behind the operational zone.

In terms of the German war effort, the value of Italy was still considerable, but its piecemeal exploitation in consequence of Hitler's draconian directives of September 19 was rapidly producing a situation bordering on chaos. Apart from the military requirements, exactions in regard to defence, and the *de facto* annexation of the two Northern and Eastern border provinces, the control in German interests of Italian war production and labour force, involved an increased network of civilian German agencies. Speer had received instructions to 'safeguard' Italian war industry, and a completely independent armaments mission under General Leyers was established throughout the whole occupied zone with headquarters in Milan and a free hand to interfere in the whole industrial structure of the country.[c]

It was now the turn of Sauckel, the labour boss of German-occupied Europe. As early as September 27 Ribbentrop warned Rahn that Rommel had apparently asked Sauckel to come to Northern Italy and to undertake 'the necessary steps to remove quickly for labour in Germany the members of the former Italian armed forces'. Rahn was instructed to support Sauckel 'in removing as many workers as possible from Italy', but only in close cooperation with Rahn, who 'must steer the affair properly with the Duce'. Rahn was to show Sauckel the terms of his own instructions from the Fuehrer as plenipotentiary, dated September 10, and to suggest to Sauckel that he appoint a 'special adviser' in Italy.[14]

But the Todt organization recruiting labour for military fortifications was already at work, and Sauckel's local offices for recruiting Italian civilian labour for German factories were opening throughout the region.

Italian manpower, and preferably unarmed, was the greatest and least de-

c. Ruestungs und Kriegsindustrie. Known under the initials RUK.

fendable asset of the nascent Republic, both in Italy and among the six hundred thousand prisoners of the Italian army rounded up after September 8. As Anfuso gloomily foresaw, there would be 'a fight between the German Labour Front, the Army, and the S.S. regarding the use of Italian prisoners'.[15]

In every field of German activity in Italy, an urgent overhaul and co-ordination was needed; the new Republic must be physically established without delay.

'The setting up of the new Italian government and the position of the German plenipotentiary'—Rahn was referring to himself—'make urgently necessary certain changes in the German administrative apparatus. . . .' [16]

Rahn feared that in the absence of any Italian political authority, the total occupation of Italy which would follow would increase unnecessarily and dangerously the burden on the German military authorities. And Kesselring, as commander of the operational front and thinking of the lines of his inevitable retreat northwards, could but agree. There was no problem, apart from territorial defence, which could be solved without the help of the Italian ministries.

On Rahn's instructions, his deputy in Rome, Moellhausen, had a talk with Kesselring on October 5, who assured his co-operation.

'There can be no comparison between the present and former Fascist governments. In the past Mussolini has been compelled to take into account the Royal House and the Army; also his collaborators were unreliable. Against this we on our side lacked the means to intervene. To-day our position is essentially different. Organized internal opposition has been eliminated; the government consists of men who are willy-nilly bound to Germany, and above all if need be we have the possibility of intervening. In addition we have delegates in each Ministry, whose task is precisely to bring our wishes before the Ministers and control their implementation in the Ministries. Every promise for constructive co-operation is thus assured. We can save ourselves a lot of trouble if we make use of the Italian government at our disposal.'

It was being always overridden by German agencies, and it could resign. Mussolini was very depressed and unsure.[17]

Kesselring reported in similar fashion to the German High Command:

'Minister Rahn informs me that signs are noticeable of a combined resignation of the Mussolini government. Reasons: No response from the people; no means of authority; practical exclusion by German might with full powers.

'The retirement of the government would, in Rahn's view, have intolerable political results. The need for more support than hitherto is thereby envisaged to launch the government and state administration, so that from outside they can appear as sovereign, whereas in reality the executive organs of Army Group B South remain.

'As chaotic conditions would ensue without the co-operation of the Italian administration and with the lack of German administrative agencies, I have for a limited period foreseen a stronger extension of the Italian administration and a deliberate withdrawal of my own person. The means at my disposal will when required be placed at that of the Italian officials. All requests relating to the conduct of the war naturally have precedence.

'German soldiers regard Italian territory as "occupied" . . . Full success can only be expected if the Fuehrer proclaims Italy under the new government as "an allied country".

'The new function "to defend Italy decisively" within the defensive position of Army Group B (Rommel) has consequences in other directions.

(a) The hinterland, above all Rome, must be kept pacified. In the first instance this means the safeguarding of food supplies, and means the prohibition of continual evacuation of all agricultural products and cattle from the area.

(b) So long as the hinterland is not and does not become a battle area, the autumn sowing must be carried out with all pressure.

(c) It is yet to be proved to what extent the industrial structure will come to a halt. The effort to collect about 200,000 men, who are swelling the ranks of the unemployed and bringing them to Germany has not yet had satisfactory results. One must build up a healthy relationship between assembling and removing them. Indiscriminate working of this plan increases the opposition of the people and the government against us.

'It should be considered whether the measures taken out of military necessity should not be legalised in a state treaty between the Fuehrer and the Duce, and eventual compensation could also be taken into account. . . .' [18]

Rahn now enlisted the aid of Rommel, and on October 8 called on him at his headquarters on Lake Garda. The latter accepted that the control of the civil sector should be left to an Italian 'as far as is compatible with military requirements'. These requests would be forwarded only through Rahn.

The Duce had agreed to issue instructions for the 'protection' of the German armed forces. He would call up the 1910–24 and 1925 age groups (the latter being reserved to Rommel for incorporation). Rommel would welcome new Italian units 'which will be incorporated in German units at battalion level'. The imminent move of the Italian government to the area of Garda, and Graziani's pending visit to Germany, would cause delays, but as a beginning both measures would be announced on the radio.[19]

But although the senior German representatives in Italy, Rommel, Kesselring, and Rahn [d] stressed, and even desperately, the need to establish the new Italian government in a workable manner, there was no united policy in regard to Italy at Hitler's headquarters. The influence of the High Command was normally paramount, and their distrust of civilian authority, German or Italian, unyielding.

d. The S.S. Commander, Wolff, shared the view of General Headquarters.

The Duce told Rahn on the evening of October 10 that 'Graziani informed him of the German intention of appointing a Military Plenipotentiary for Italy. He requested urgently that I should point out to the German government that such an appointment would gravely compromise the Italian government, thereby underlining that it was a shadow government. Naturally he recognized the need of a close identification of all Italian measures with the requirements of the German war effort in Italy.' The Duce asked for a military adviser or 'Head of German Military Mission'. 'I have the impression that he is less concerned with the duties of a Military Plenipotentiary than exclusively shocked by the name.' [20]

Anfuso wrote in his diary, 'Difference of opinion in official circles in Berlin on the Duce's liberation. On the one hand the Party shows its entire satisfaction for ideological and political reasons both internal and foreign; on the other, the soldiers consider that his liberation is a hindrance to their freedom of action in Italy, because without the Duce they could have acted as they would do in an occupied country.' [21]

This basic difference of view was henceforth never to be resolved, it governed the fate of the new Republic, and in the first stages bedevilled the workings of the German 'system' in Italy, finally it set the frame of the ultimate German surrender on the Italian front.

But quite apart from the intruding presence of this German 'system', the prospects of a Fascist revival, which was the *raison d'être* of the Duce's mission, were sombre.

The collapse of the whole Party machinery throughout Italy, silent and total, in the course of the morning of July 26, 1943, without a gesture in defence of the Duce and Fascism, had indeed been a decisive historic event. The symbols and the emblems of twenty years of a régime were swept away with ease by the Badoglio government. Deserted by the leaders, a whole political movement disintegrated. With the Duce in unknown confinement, and a handful of rival and pro-German party bosses in flight to East Prussia, the rank and file vanished out of sight.

With the unexpected and abrupt appearance of Mussolini in Germany in September, followed by the radio announcements of the imminent formation of a new government, and of the construction of a Fascist Republican party with Alessandro Pavolini as 'professional' secretary, a certain confused ferment of ideas and expectations was generated among the adherents and clans of the disbanded Fascist movement. The Duce was now publicly committed to a political revival of Fascism.

But the arrival of Pavolini in Rome on September 17, with instructions to draw up a list of ministers for a new party government, had at once revealed the extent of the shock to the prestige of the movement, which the coup d'état of July and the interregnum of Badoglio had caused in former party circles. It was natural that the disintegrating impact of these events had been sharpest in Rome itself, but disseminated too throughout the North. Even the most loyal Fascists doubted the sense of an automatic and uncritical Restoration.

Pavolini, by an immediate symbolic act, took over the former Party Headquarters in Palazzo Wedekind in Rome. The approaches and roofs were covered by machine-guns and two armoured cars, giving an aspect of an enemy garrison under siege.[22] The local party offices were also opened, and functionaries installed, and the Fascist Republican Party became a circumscribed reality. As the branch office of the German Embassy reported: 'Influence on the whole work of the Fascist Party absolutely assured. Contact with all Italian party offices only possible through Rahn's office.'[23]

With the announcement of the new government and the decision not to return to Rome, attention was transferred to the North. In these days of suspension, prior to the establishment of the seat of government, the regional clans of Fascism re-appeared. The original strength of the movement had in one sense always been based on the party machines of the cities of the North, and they had been the personal fiefs of individuals: Balbo in Ferrara, Grandi in Bologna, Farinacci in Cremona. Fragments of the 'system' survived the deluge. There was a bitter aspect of reality in the description of the new administration as 'the Grand Duchy of Tuscany'. The reconstructed Republican Fascist machine was in the hands of the Florentine Pavolini. Buffarini Guidi and Ricci were also Tuscans. The old regional battles for influence within the Party were in danger of reviving.

Following on the radio directives, the elements of a new party structure, based on the old provincial machinery, appeared. Already in October, some 250,000 members had registered, of whom 5,000 alone in Florence, the historic centre of the action squads in the '20's. But they rallied with mingled feelings of revenge for a past betrayal, desire for 'national union' and an end of monolithic party rule, and anxiety to safeguard jobs and careers. The old provincial factionalism of early Fascism quickly asserted itself, and in each regional capital an undirected and spontaneous debate arose in the absence of any assertion of central political control. A local press revived, and a noticeable movement for reconciliation and a 'new deal' appeared.

The first centre of these activities was in the province of Venice. At the end of September a Communist spoke at a Fascist Party meeting in the city. In Bologna, the Fascist elements, particularly Giorgio Pini as editor of the revived *Il Resto del Carlino* and Goffredo Coppola, Rector of the University. came out openly in favour of a national front. There were similar moves in Turin, in Savona, Verona round Castelletti's newspaper *L'Arena*, and in Milan where the blind war hero Carlo Borsani took the lead.

The reaction was not long delayed. On October 5 Pavolini instructed the party federations to take a stand against 'pacification'. 'In the field of internal politics and relations between opponents and ex-opponents it is, to say the least, useless to go on echoing here and there the positions taken up by Fascism in some provinces in the early days of reconstruction.' There was no need to indulge in 'too generic appeals to a universal embrace'. The special Tribunals would deal with traitors.[24]

A few days later, Mezzasoma issued a directive to the local Press. 'Newspapers must refrain from publishing appeals for the pacification of minds and concord of spirits, for the fraternizing of Italians. After 45 days of poisoning of public opinion, of scandalization, the preaching of hatred and manhunting, certain pietistic manifestations merely reveal pusillanimity and tepidness.' [25]

The unrepentant core of the old Fascist squads had found their acknowledged leaders in the 'Tuscans'—Pavolini, Ricci, and Buffarini, and indeed their geographical base, largely in Tuscany. One by one the official Party headquarters in Arezzo, Pavia, Milan, Turin and elsewhere came out against any form of 'collaboration' with moderate elements.

It was significant that in these days at La Rocca the Duce should be made aware of this familiar pattern of agitation. In the history of the Fascist movement, the rivalries of these city states had been a scourge and a convenience. They had been an outlet for the innate factiousness of Italians, and an indispensable means whereby the Duce should assert his own independent leadership by balancing these provincial clans against each other, and at times facilitating control at the centre.

The physical return to the Romagna, with its historical links not only with the Duce's family background, but with his early socialist associations, was at the same time a brutal return to the mental climate of early Fascism, to the violence and hesitations following the foundation of the political movement before the March on Rome. The significance of the meeting of the Council of Ministers in a country house in the provinces, and not in Palazzo Venezia in Rome, was a measure of the extent to which official Fascism had retreated from a central position of power to its regional bases. During this brief interlude of fifteen days in the familiar surroundings of La Rocca there were illusory signs of a fresh start, unhampered by the errors and omissions of the Fascist leadership during the years of triumph.

The old slogans of the early twenties were remembered. The new Republican State proclaimed by Mussolini was a personal defiance towards the Crown. Apart from loyalty to a personality, there must be a mobilization of opinion. In tracing over again the historical course of the Fascist movement, the early programmes and myths binding together the rank and file, had, under the impact of the responsibilities of power and the compromises which followed, been emptied of their content. The socialist and republican elements in the early Fascist movement had been quickly discarded in favour of an official conformity. Not only catchwords, but militants, were cast aside.

But the events of the summer of 1943 had obliterated official Fascism. An outstanding and vivid report on the political situation in the Romagna after July 25 was submitted by one of the prefects which, although written some months later, gives a balanced record, typical of other provinces at this time.

The writer shows that news of the fall of Fascism had caused stupefaction but not violent political agitation. Citizen committees were set up by members of the old political parties. These were split among themselves. The general wish was to secure liberties, and to destroy Fascism altogether. The problem was complex. Apart from the Communists, there were many members of the Committees, old Socialists, Republicans, honest modest people, who pursued a moderate policy between July and September 1943. They avoided violence, and there were no revolutionary outbreaks. Only in a few places, such as Forlì and Faenza, were there any serious disturbances.

The armistice came as a brutal shock. It brought the collapse of the country's military power, dishonour, and the destruction of international prestige. No authority, civil or military, was now recognized. The worst blow was the loss of Mussolini, but with his release the anti-Fascist orgy ended. There was however no enthusiasm for the creation of the Fascist republic. The people were too depressed, but it was well received. The rapid reconstitution of Fascist organizations was not very wise and had caused some disturbances. The Federal Police for instance went beyond Government orders, and made the Party responsible for the results. The reformed Party Militia often seemed to be at variance with the Government. The provincial Law Courts did not always live up to the ideas underlying their creation, and there were too many acts of revenge and too much Party violence. In Romagna, for instance, there was a great feeling for Mazzinian ideas of liberty and republicanism. Some Socialists should be approached and used to arouse the working people to a live interest in their problems, which are those of the whole country.[e]

As the Duce spent hours at La Rocca reading the newspapers of these months, lining the margins with his blue pencil, the extent and nature of this failure clarified. The challenge roused him a little. He had been morally deflated by his recent isolation from the world. But he was back on a job which he knew, and in an area filled with historical associations relevant to his platform.

Both ex-Socialist militants of the Left and extreme Fascists of the Right, pushed aside after the 'monarchical compromise' of 1922, showed signs of returning, under a Republican banner, to the leadership of a movement from which they had been discarded, and to a Republican Fascist State.

e. Italian Collection. This report is undated, but from internal evidence must have been written in March 1944.

It was characteristic of Mussolini to seize, as the first weapon of attack, on the reconstruction of a new Press, based as in the past on the regional papers. His own paper, however, *Il Popolo d'Italia,* was not to be reopened in Milan. His intuitive caution prevented him from committing his own personal prestige prematurely at a confused moment, in which the limits of German censorship were as yet unclarified. 'I can and must sacrifice myself in this tragic situation, but not my newspaper. For thirty years it has been a flag, and flags must be allowed to fly freely.'

But the machinery of propaganda, which the Duce had regarded always as a special and personal arm, had to be set up quickly. A network of papers, some new and some purged and re-established, spread through the North. Each editorial office, as in the past, became a cell and centre of political influence. Control of a provincial newspaper had always been the essential attribute of a successful Fascist politician.

On September 28 the Duce released to the Press the first of a series of anonymous political notes, which henceforward were to represent his contribution to the battle of words. It was entitled 'Let us talk clearly'.

'It is useless to indulge in recriminations. We must get out of this abyss; perhaps with broken bones but alive and capable of living. . . . In June 1940, when we entered the lists, there was not a single Italian who did not believe that the war would not end victoriously. But many did not do their duty . . .' [26]

Early in October he summoned to see him Giorgio Pini, a leading and close collaborator in the journalistic field who, for a long time after the death of Arnaldo Mussolini, had been his personal link with the newspaper world. Mussolini was now to appoint him director of the *Corriere della Sera* in Milan.

Pini had already, in the interregnum after September 8, taken over Grandi's old paper in Bologna *Il Resto del Carlino.* Round this editorial office the local opponents of Grandi had grouped themselves and the claims of a Republican Fascist organization in the capital city of the Romagna must now be pressed at this fluid moment, while the Duce was nearby, holding temporary court at La Rocca. In miniature the history of the Bologna Party machine was that of Italy of the previous twenty years, that of purges and Party enquiries, of plots and counter-plots. Now that Grandi was the main traitor of July 25, his defeated rival in Bologna politics, Leandro Arpinati became, after years in the shadows, one possible collaborator and counterweight to the provisional administration formed with German prompting in Rome at the end of September.

Pini's visit to La Rocca was for him an occasion to indicate such a possibility. Three days later, on October 6, Arpinati was invited to visit the Duce. The former was a typical and leading representative of the discarded

Fascist leaders of the '30's, obstinate in their regional independence, victims of successful local rivals in the battle for position in the central machinery of power. With the adhesion of such men Mussolini could renew his manipulation of politics and avoid exclusive dependence on one clan. He seems to have offered Arpinati the Presidency of the Council. The latter refrained from any references to the past, but was sharp in his refusal. He was not impressed by 'neo-socialism'; he was not a republican; he had an aversion to Germans. The Duce complained that they were oppressive, that the S.S. guarded him round the house, in the garden, and manned the telephone. But they were unbeatable in war. Arpinati commented that it was not enough to win, and the conversation was without results, except to reveal a private glimpse of the Duce's perennial tactics.[27]

But the political experiment, sanctioned by Hitler at Rastenburg, could not be delayed without the risk of total breakdown. The choice of the seat of government lay with the German military authorities. On October 5 Mussolini told the newly-appointed secretary of his private office, the Prefect Giovanni Dolfin, 'Tomorrow or the next day I shall move to the place which has been selected for my headquarters. I still do not know where it will be located. It is somewhere on the western shore of Garda.' [28]

On October 10 Mussolini left by car for Gargnano, on Lake Garda, accompanied by Renato Ricci, and Vito Mussolini, his nephew and additional secretary. The German authorities had picked the Villa Feltrinelli as the residence of the head of the new Republican State.

CHAPTER THREE

THE BATTLE FOR THE REPUBLICAN ARMY

●—●

AT THE FIRST MEETING of the Council of Ministers on September 27, Mussolini had shirked the issue as between the Party Militia as the frame of a new
military machine or the creation of a regular Republican army.

Graziani meanwhile had returned to Rome to consider the next step. He
called on the services of a former military intelligence officer and well-known
military commentator, Emilio Canevari, to draft a memorandum for submission to the Duce on the future shape of a regular force.

It was vital to avert civil war. The plan, announced by Mussolini on the
radio on September 16, to create a Party army out of the national Militia and
under the command of Ricci must be given up. 'The Militia is hated and must
be dissolved immediately: the army must be national and non-political and
under absolutely united command. Even the police forces of every kind must
be subordinate to the Ministry of Armed Forces.'

The cadres of the armed forces must be all voluntary. The troops, both
volunteers and conscripts, must be composed of the youngest age groups. It
was urgent to put into the field this small army, which must be equipped
and trained with the latest German weapons.

Such was the outline of Graziani's ideas: a small specialized regular force,
on the model of the German Reichswehr of 1920.[1]

On October 3 he returned to La Rocca to present this memorandum
to Mussolini. As usual the Duce agreed with his interlocutor of the moment,
who was now to prepare to open negotiations on these lines with the German
High Command.

On the same day Mussolini drafted the following letter to Hitler to serve
as a general brief for Graziani, and as a picture of the Italian scene.

'I am taking advantage of the forthcoming visit of Marshal Graziani to
inform you briefly, but precisely, of the Italian situation as it appears to me

since my return from Germany. . . . The bulk of the population is still stunned by the events which have taken place between July 25 and September 8, and they oscillate between a will to recover and a sort of resigned fatalism. . . .

'As I had occasion to tell you, Fuehrer, in the talks at your headquarters, when you extended to me such a comradely hospitality, the fundamental tasks of my government were and are:

'To reconstruct the civil life of the country so that all is quiet behind the front and every possible collaboration is offered to the German commands; and to prepare the new Republican army. On this latter point Marshal Graziani will give you a comprehensive and accurate exposition which I am sure will attract your attention.

'As to the first point the new government must have the necessary autonomy to govern and give orders to the civil authorities which are subordinate to it. Without this possibility, the government has no prestige, is discredited and thus destined to finish ingloriously. This is not in the common interest, will indeed have grave consequences and will feed those tendencies towards the newly reconstructed government of the traitor Badoglio.

'It is my duty, Fuehrer, to indicate to you the reasons which obstruct the reorganization of Italian life, and they are the following. The German military commands issue a continuous stream of orders on matters which concern civilian life. These orders are often contradictory from province to province. The Italian civil authorities are ignored and the population has the impression that the Fascist Republican government has absolutely no authority even in matters totally extraneous to the military sphere. Often the ordinances of the Northern German command contradict those of the South. . . . In the three provinces of Emilia, Piacenza, Parma and Reggio, the German military authorities have taken over the civil administration, and issued instructions that every request made by an Italian citizen must be accompanied by a German translation. In peasant provinces such as these, this is impossible to put into practice. Allow me to say, Fuehrer, that a joint Command would eliminate these inconveniences.

'I also have the duty to tell you that the nomination of a High Commissioner in Innsbruck for the provinces of Bolzano, Trento, and Belluno has created a painful impression throughout Italy. . . . The only person who will profit by this will be the traitor Badoglio . . .

'And now, Fuehrer, I would ask you to listen to what Marshal Graziani has to say to you. His ideas are clear and above all practicable.' [2]

Among Graziani's papers are two draft memoranda hitherto unpublished, which brutally outline Italo-German relations since the September armistice. The first is dated October 8.[a]

a. Italian Collection. Neither document is signed. They may have been drafted by Canevari.

. . . 'The German political authorities have nominated a Fascist government purely for the motives of German politico-internal interests.'

It was in effect really a puppet administration and it was the German military authorities who governed in Italy. 'As is well known and as history has shown, these latter are devoid of psychological sense and understanding, and contribute by their efforts to the ever deepening abyss between the two peoples. It is in the common interest to overcome this: both a contingent interest, to secure the base areas of the German Mediterranean front, and order, work, and tranquillity for the Italians; and also an interest in collaborating together in the Europe of tomorrow.

'The Italian government must be given the chance to be a complete one. It would be logical to place alongside such an administration a German liaison body with extensive powers and a professional capacity to gear Italian activities to German military requirements.

'The present hybrid situation should be cleared up as soon as possible and it should be officially laid down whether Italians are an "occupied nation" or "collaborators". In the first case, there will be clear opposition on the part of every Italian; and the Fascist government, being unable to govern, will have to resign. No Italian soldier will be able to continue to fight alongside the Germans. In the second case, after the necessary purges have been carried out, we shall be sincere friends and collaborators.

'If the government is allowed to govern, the function and tasks of the German general, or generals, now commanding in Italy must be defined precisely. We must at all costs avoid a repetition in Italy of the situation in France, where a German military command for the occupation of the territory was set up. Such a command would by definition exclude the possibility of the existence of an Italian government and also of a voluntary military and civil collaboration.

'These are the indispensable premises which must be defined precisely before we engage in talks or agreements on military co-operation.

'On this occasion it is up to the Fuehrer to decide whether the Italians will be able voluntarily to make their contribution to the formation of the new Europe or must for ever be an enemy nation.'

The second document was a brief for Graziani's forthcoming meeting with Hitler.[b]

The fundamental question was: 'Did the German government intend to treat Italy as occupied territory or to re-establish her political independence as soon as possible?' On the latter assumption it was urgent to give the Italian government freedom of action and the means to communicate with its political and military organs, without which the administration could not

b. It was headed 'Pro-memoria for the forthcoming meeting with the Fuehrer'.

function nor the new Republican forces be constituted. Graziani was planning a total army of 25 divisions.

Given the present condition of Italy, German weapons and equipment must be almost completely adopted, and German instructors would have to be employed in the units under formation.

The entire economic structure of Italy must be overhauled by agreement between the two countries, and vital decisions must be taken to define the control of Italian war production.

On October 9 Marshal Graziani left Guidonia airport, accompanied by Colonel Dollmann, and flew to Hitler's headquarters. They were met at the airfield by Keitel, and at lunch in the special train at the disposal of the High Command Graziani was informed, according to Dollmann, of their proposals to place occupied Italy in effect under military government.[c] In the afternoon Keitel accompanied him to Hitler.

Graziani had last seen the Fuehrer in 1938 during the latter's visit to Rome. The first meeting now at Rastenburg was brief. 'I am sorry that this ungrateful task should fall particularly to you' were Hitler's somewhat discouraging opening words to his guest.[3]

Graziani, at his subsequent trial, describes the course of the ensuing talks with the German military leaders.[4] 'The Germans seemed prepared to allow a modest army to be set up. It was agreed to constitute in stages, firstly four divisions, then eight, and then twelve . . . Mussolini and I had already examined this question of the reconstruction of the Armed Forces. There were two possible methods in relation to what Mussolini had said at La Rocca— a volunteer or a conscript force. We were both agreed on the impossibility of conscription at that moment. We had thought that the first four divisions should be formed from volunteers drawn from the camps in Germany where 6–700,000 unfortunates had been assembled as prisoners of war after September 8.

'I therefore asked that the men should be picked from volunteers from these concentration camps, and immediately requested to go there myself . . . Hitler was strongly and absolutely opposed.'

The German view was that the morale of these troops was too low, and there was nothing to be done with them. Graziani tried to argue: 'We had had a great drama in our army, that of 1917 at Caporetto. But then the opposite happened because the troops had been worked upon by anti-war propaganda while the leaders tried to counter this in every way. Whereas

---

c. It seems that Canevari was to have been with the party. But he arrived a few minutes late, and the German pilot refused to take him. Graziani gives the date as October 13. But German evidence conclusively points to the 9th. See Graziani *Processo I op cit* p. 261, and Dollmann *op cit* pp. 275–6.

this time, the soldiers had fought until September 8 in good faith against the enemy, and were suddenly told to turn their arms against yesterday's ally.'

But Hitler was firm. Graziani, according to his same account, said that he must therefore return and refer to Mussolini 'with whom you can take the relative decisions'.

Confusion and misrepresentation have surrounded the precise significance of Graziani's talks in Germany, upon which so much depended for the future stability of the new Italian régime. What exact commitments had Graziani undertaken?

On October 10, Rahn received a copy of the German summary of the talks held with Graziani at the Fuehrer's headquarters. 'It is important that Italy shall make the largest possible contribution in continuing the war. For this it is necessary that in so far as Italy should be occupied by us she will be treated as an allied and not an occupied country, and that the authority and independence of the new Italian government will be established and strengthened.

'In pursuit of this aim the operational area of the Southern Command and Army Group B (under Marshal Rommel) will be confined to a specified region behind the land front of the Southern Command and to certain areas on the North-East, North and North-West frontiers of Italy for the safe-guarding of communications with Germany and with France. The whole re-maining territory will be handed over to the administration of the Italian government, operational zones on the coasts being foreseen but will only be declared an operational area in event of an enemy landing. Until such a time the coastal areas will be under the administration of the Italian government.

'In the territory administered by the Italian government, a military pleni-potentiary will be appointed (General Toussaint) under the orders of the head of the German High Command. His duties will be to represent and execute the military requests of the German Army to the Italian government and the subordinate Italian authorities, and to support the Italian government and its officials both, in so far as is necessary, in its own administrative measures, and in its dealings with the German military authorities.

'The intended defence of the line hitherto envisaged is of decisive import-ance. If Rome were lost, Italy would in practice cease to be a country waging war on our side. All the resources of the country, therefore, must be mobil-ized to protect the deep flanks and long coasts, and considerably to relieve the German forces for battle on the main fronts.

'Subordinate Italian units consisting of volunteers under German command are required; for example, for coastal artillery, engineers, and ground per-sonnel for the air force.

'Military internees are not to be considered for incorporation in such units. In so far as volunteers cannot be procured through the means of the Italian

High Command, recruiting will also be carried out by the units. It must be so arranged that each unit of the above categories is aligned with a similar German one. Volunteers will be treated as German soldiers in regard to pay and rations. . . .

'The creation of larger Italian formations is envisaged at training establishments outside Italy.' [5]

Graziani now returned to report to the Duce at Gargnano. It was decided to send for Canevari, and brief him to go to Berlin 'to sign the protocols drawn up according to the agreements already reached by Graziani during his trip to Berlin'.[6] The Marshal, in subsequent accounts, does not refer to these 'agreements'.

On October 16 Canevari flew to Germany. He later stated that Graziani had instructed him to go to the headquarters of the German High Command to treat in detail the problems arising out of the formation of the four divisions. 'It is true that he told me that they would be drawn from the internees, but gave me no relevant details: I had no written directive, no piece of paper on which firm points were set down.' [7]

Before leaving, Canevari also saw the Duce, who added no new information. 'When therefore I arrived on October 16 at German headquarters I did not find it excessively strange that they proposed that such divisions should be formed from officers and non-commissioned officers drawn from the internees, and later brought up to strength with recruits. They assured me that such were the agreements made precisely with the Duce and Graziani according to stenographic notes . . . which were frequently quoted to me.' [8]

During the course of the day, Canevari negotiated with General Buhle, Chief of Staff to Fieldmarshal Keitel, 'on the basic points of accord for the reconstruction of the Italian Armed Forces'.[9] This protocol was drawn up 'in conformity with the agreements made on the occasion of the conversation between the Fuehrer and the Duce, namely in September at Rastenburg, and the Fuehrer and Marshal Graziani'.[10]

Mixed Italo-German units were to be constituted, including fifty batteries of coastal artillery, and by voluntary recruitment. 'In the proper sense of an Italian Army in Germany', three infantry and one Alpine divisions were to be set up, and ten groups of artillery and they would be trained in German camps and under German orders.

The Italian officers and the cadres of a rank and file would be recruited by a mixed Commission from the internment camps in Germany. The divisions would be brought up to strength by calling up three age groups in Italy. These recruits were to reach the training camps in Germany by November 15.

Such was the essence of this controversial document.

Canevari then spent several days in Berlin at the Italian Embassy, where he seems to have clashed with extremist Fascist elements, who had extracted themselves from the camps and had other plans for recruiting, on an S.S. model, the new Italian armed forces.

This was Himmler's solution, and following on the Graziani talks efforts were made to carry through this programme. The S.S. had already recruited some 10,000 men for their own plans of an Italian S.S. Canevari arrived unannounced at a meeting held by Anfuso at the Italian Embassy where Himmler's representative was engaged in addressing a group of Italian 'old' Fascists and damping down any enthusiasm for a new Italian Army. Canevari walked in with the protocols which had been signed with the German Army Command on October 16. In the report sent to Himmler of this episode, it is said that Canevari 'found the conversation very painful'. So did Himmler's deputy, who was unaware of the terms of these military talks.

And on October 19 at a further meeeting between Canevari and German S.S. representatives the question of the Italian S.S. Division 'constituted in accordance with Duce–Fuehrer agreements' was discussed.

The division was to consist of 13,000, and another 3,000 were to be trained as police. They had no weapons or training. 'Their military value is nil. It was agreed that such elements would not be the concern of the Italian Army in Germany, but only of the S.S.' [11]

On the afternoon of October 25 Canevari returned to Gargnano and was received by Mussolini in the presence of Graziani. In his later report Canevari wrote, 'No comment was made to me on the text of the protocol: on the contrary, everything was praised.' [12]

This programme was to be the signal for the first open and major clash between Graziani and the Fascist Party leaders. Everything was secondary to the central issue of the shape and control of the Armed Forces of the new state.

The Council of Ministers met the following morning, October 28. In his opening review the Duce put the position as follows: 'The agreements with the German General Staff, already drawn up and revised in detail, will allow us to form new units, whose contingents will be supplied to us not only from volunteers but also from the age groups soon to be called up. . . . On the basis of these fundamental outlines the new decrees concerning the National Republican Army, Navy and Air Force will be examined.

'As has been previously announced, the volunteer Militia for National Security will form an integral part of the Army, and, like the Alpine and Bersaglieri units, will form the Blackshirt Corps.' [13]

This mild and misleading statement provoked an immediate scene. In the absence of any recorded minutes, the closest account is that of Dolfin, the Duce's secretary, who wrote in his diary: [14] 'Mussolini had to intervene several times to calm down the heated contending parties. The profound objects of dissension were articles 18 and 19 of the decree, which by estab-

lishing the absolute "non-political" character of the Armed Forces, implied
the virtual dissolution of the Militia as such, since it is destined to become
just one specialist branch of the Army. The question has been discussed over
and over again during the last few days, and seems to have been definitely
settled in the statement which the Duce dictated to me. He and Graziani are
perfectly agreed on this. But Pavolini and Ricci have put up an improvised
and thorough-going fight, with all the old and new political arguments in
favour of their case. Graziani has not yielded, making it an issue of principle
from which he says he will not be deflected, as he claims that his project
coincides with the higher interests of the country.' It seems that Graziani
threatened to resign, and that he was thus able to insist that the offending
articles remained in the text of the decree.

Pavolini and Ricci were totally dissatisfied, and 'continued to repeat that
in this way Fascism is destroyed. Buffarini has followed the affair with luke-
warm interest. He is waiting his turn to join issue on the reform of the
police.' [15]

The following weeks were critical. On the outcome of this clash would depend the effective working or reduction to impotence of the new government.
The Duce hated such definite situations and retired grumbling to La Rocca.
Ricci and Pavolini were now in revolt. The former refused to accept any
orders from Graziani's chief of staff, or to dissolve the Militia. There was no
sign from Berlin that the German High Command would implement the
protocols of October 16.

On November 1 Mussolini sent a brief and disingenuous summary of the
Italian scene to Hitler by the hand of the S.S. General, Wolff.

'The situation has slightly improved. There are symptoms of recovery, but
the catastrophe was so complete and unforeseen that it will be a long time
yet before the masses recover morally and materially.

'I do not consider the phenomenon of the armed bands scattered here and
there on the slopes of the Apennines is very serious. They are mostly
disbanded soldiers (often from Southern Italy) and do not represent a
danger.

'I have however decided to cut short their activities, and will use for this
purpose the two thousand men who form the Italian African Police, and
strong detachments of Military Police . . . The former are in Rome, where the
situation is completely normal.

'Colonel Canevari had reported to me on the conversations which he had
in Germany. I think that it would be as well for him to be based on Berlin
until the first four divisions envisaged for the new Army have been formed.

'In a few days the young age-group of 1924 will report to the barracks. If
they do so in full force it will be a decisive sign that the crisis has been
surmounted. The General Staff is somewhat optimistic . . . The contacts of

Graziani and Gambara [d] with your Marshals are more and more cordial. As for Rahn, he is the man for the task, and my authorities are glad to co-operate with him.' [16]

Mussolini had not yet turned to the problem of armed resistance within the borders of the new State. This was another issue to be postponed. As to the army programme, there is no hint of the feuds and uncertainties in Italian circles. The casual mention of the forthcoming call-up of conscripts was both premature and misleading.

On November 6 Canevari went to La Rocca. He told Dolfin that 'the conflict with the Party and Ricci was in full swing and that those substantial differences as to what direction to take increased existing difficulties and particularly German mistrust'. According to him, if 'the Duce does not decide once and for all to stick to the directives agreed with Graziani, we shall accomplish nothing'.[17]

The following day Graziani telephoned from Rome to inform Canevari of Ricci's formal refusal to dissolve the Militia. When told by Canevari of this, the Duce's comment was 'the matter has already been decided. And now it is time to finish with Ricci. In essence it is a question of personal ambition. Tell the Marshal that matters remain as has been decided.' [18]

That evening Ricci arrived at La Rocca and the Duce capitulated. The latter's attention was slipping with ease away from the disagreeable issue of the Army versus the Party to the political scene, and 'the Duce, irritable and nervous, has postponed any decision on what he himself calls "The Ricci Case" until after the Party Congress'.[19]

It is not clear whether Mussolini, or indeed Graziani, had studied the protocols of October 16, when presented to them by Canevari on his return from Berlin. The agreement to call up certain age-groups and send them to Germany for training was the essential clause for consideration, and yet neither the Duce nor Graziani seems to have made any immediate comment. The insertion by Mussolini of a reference to an immediate call-up in his letter to Hitler of November 1 and in his speech to the Council of Ministers five days previously seem to imply their acceptance of this principle.

There is however no doubt that the Fascist Party leaders in their violent counter-attack on the whole principle of a Republican army on a non-political basis seized on the issue of conscription to destroy the whole plan. Their own motive was clear. Disposal of available manpower was the main weapon of the contending parties in the battle for the control of the State. If incorporated in the Army, from what sources would come the recruits for the police, which Buffarini regarded as his province and the essential basis of his position, or for the Militia, on which Ricci and Pavolini depended for the prestige of the Party? Above all, and this was the ostensible argument, what

d. Graziani's Chief of Staff.

would be the reaction of sending conscripts away from their homes to Germany, where already some 600,000 Italians were interned as prisoners of war? And there was the supreme if delicate point that a call-up might lead to widespread desertions, and even to the extension of armed opposition to the new régime of which there were already signs, and to which the Duce so casually referred in his letter to Hitler at the beginning of the month.

On November 10 the Duce received Graziani and Canevari. It was decided that the latter should leave at once for Berlin 'to assuage German mistrust' and to obtain from them the modification of the clause dealing with conscription. 'If the recruits knew that they were to go to Germany, there would be a "revolution", because the people would think that they were not being sent for temporary training, but to be interned.' In vain Canevari pointed out that the Germans had no confidence in these Italian disbanded troops already in camps in Germany who had 'thrown down their arms and were "Badoglio troops" '. Mussolini retorted that Hitler had agreed to the formation of four divisions to be drawn from the internees—which was not correct. As Canevari wrote later: 'I did not at this moment realize what was clear to me later; when the new class was called up all the Party bosses had prophesied a complete failure: they wanted . . . "a Fascist army" composed of the old Militia.' [20]

This state of affairs was astonishing. The call-up of these young men born within the last three months of 1924 and the whole class of 1925 had been publicly announced in Rome on November 9, the day before Canevari was ordered back to Berlin! They were to report during the last half of the month. In Graziani's own words at his trial: 'I received categorical orders from Mussolini to call up these classes.' [21]

Canevari arrived in Berlin on November 13, and saw Keitel, after preliminary talks with the latter's chief of staff. The Germans had already taken firm action. Voluntary recruitment in the camps had been stopped. The Todt organization had pressed a successful claim to use this dormant man-power for labour units. There could be no question of going back on the previous undertaking to introduce conscription in Italy.

The conversation reached a deadlock. Canevari telephoned to Mussolini and passed the receiver to Keitel. 'I would feel dishonoured,' the Duce said, 'if among so many internees 50,000 volunteers could not be found to form these four divisions. I cannot send the conscripts for political reasons.'

'I cannot enter into political arguments,' replied Keitel, 'and will refer at once to the Fuehrer. I should say, however, that for military reasons *we* do not want the internees; and therefore, if my opinion is asked, I shall give the Fuehrer—from the military point of view—a negative reply.' [22]

German opinion in regard to re-arming the forces of the new Italian government had hardened and clarified during the previous month. The insistence of Graziani and Canevari on a non-political force, drawn largely from what the German command regarded as 'unreliable' elements in internment camps, who had already served, admittedly in many cases unwillingly, under another and treacherous Italian Marshal, aroused increased mistrust.

The creation of an Italian Republican Army under the command of Marshal Graziani would in effect place the new Republic in theory at his mercy. Could he be relied on to resist such a temptation? The climate of treason was heavy in the minds of the German leaders, and the psychosis of September 8 had bitten deeper than even the Duce and his advisers had grasped. The argument of the constant danger of a second betrayal by 'someone' among the Italian leaders was henceforth familiar and constant in both political and military circles in Germany. As Ribbentrop, for example, later explained to a satellite minister, 'It was clear that the treason of the officer camarilla had begun at least two years before the collapse of Italy.'

But for this Germany could have conquered Egypt and Suez and neither Africa nor Sicily would have been lost, and no difficulties in Russia and at Stalingrad would have occurred. When treachery became obvious Germany had to withdraw divisions from Russia. 'If Germany had now to withdraw to shorter lines, for all this she had Italy to thank.' [23]

Canevari's contemptuous references to the collapse of Fascism in Italy and the need to break with the past increased this atmosphere of suspicion. How else could an Italian state, allied to Nazi Germany, be maintained in being except on Fascist lines? Ricci and Pavolini had not wasted their time. They had their agents in Berlin, and their political contacts with their German counterparts. In a sense their opposition to Graziani's military programme coincided with that of Keitel, and even more closely with that of Hitler. The German General Staff were therefore firm on the issue of conscription. Even at the lowest estimate the despatch of recruits to be trained in Germany was at least a partial guarantee against a repeated treachery.

In Graziani's own words at his trial: 'By agreement with the Germans, the reorganization of the first four Italian divisions was to take place in Germany. They wanted this for fear of threats in their rear . . .' and in case 'we might be faced with a new betrayal'.[24]

It was put rather more politely by the German liaison officer attached to Graziani's staff in his evidence at the same trial: 'German public opinion was very excited in regard to Italy. Ever since the first World War, public opinion had not completely forgotten that then there had already been a break.' [25]

On November 27 Canevari returned to Italy. Mussolini had already received reports from Berlin on the Italian General's 'anti-Fascist' utterances, but does not seem to have made use of them.[26] Canevari reported on the failure of his efforts.

The immediate effect of this breakdown on Mussolini was to brace him to decide against Graziani in the matter of the Militia. Rahn reported that the latter had called on the Duce on November 20 to press for the placing of the Militia under the Minister of Defence. The Duce gave 'a judgement of Solomon'. Out of the reliable remnants of the Militia and the Carabinieri a new Republican Guard was to be formed, and to be in the nature of a police force on the German model, answerable to the Ministry of the Interior, and only in special cases of war duty under the Defence Ministry.

On November 29 Dolfin records in his diary: 'The vexed question of the Militia has been resolved after a series of new discussions in a way which one foresaw, namely complete triumph for the autonomist thesis of Ricci, backed by the Party. The Militia passes *en bloc* to the Republican Guard, which will have its own statutes and budget, and whose commander will be directly responsible to the Duce. This means the setting up of another army. There is ironical talk of the "non-political" army of Graziani, and the "political" one of Ricci. But as the latter will also have the duties of the Military Police there will be new reasons for conflict with the Police. . . . Buffarini is making every effort to swell the ranks of the auxiliary police: the Party is doing the same for its squads.' [27]

This dispersal of strength, fatal to an effective military effort, mirrored the political weaknesses in the structure of the Republic.

An effective and detailed review of this central episode, on the outcome of which the whole future of the Salò republic depended, is contained in the first report of the German staff officer attached personally to the Duce.[28]

'If we consider the political line adopted by the Duce since his rescue, the most striking point as regards the exploitation of Italian defence potential would appear to be his radical switch of emphasis from the idea of the Militia to that of reconstructing the Army. One of the first orders of the day issued by the Duce from Germany stated that the Militia alone would remain in existence, and would be built up as the new Italian defence force. The Duce told me at the time that he regarded its reconstruction as his principal task, taking precedence over all other government business. The aim was for Italian units to replace the German troops at present wastefully employed on security and policing duties, thus freeing them for their real task of fighting. Ricci was chosen to organize this body. He at once began his work in Italy, set about it with great zeal, and despite formidable practical difficulties and the familiar Italian war-weariness has so far managed to round up some 40,000 men.

'Graziani's entry into the new Italian government brought about a complete volte-face on the question, and on October 4 the Duce broached to me for the first time the idea of subordinating the Militia to the new Army that was to be formed. The Army officers, headed by the former Colonel Canevari, had managed to rouse his enthusiasm for the notion of forming a large-scale new Italian army, and had succeeded in persuading him that this was the way to restore Italian honour and bring about a turning-point in the war.

'The ideas the Duce proceeded to form of the possibilities open to him were born of an optimism quite untroubled by any practical knowledge of the subject, and I telegraphically notified the Fuehrer's headquarters of them before Graziani's arrival there. Although the plans were substantially scaled down in the course of discussion with the German Army Staff, the Duce nevertheless greeted them with great satisfaction.

'The Italian army, whose leadership in the War Ministry still retains the greatest number of adherents of the old régime, have naturally been striving to assimilate the ever-hated Militia, and as things are going now will probably succeed.

'The Duce has taken up the following standpoint in the matter: The Army formerly took an oath to the King and not to the Duce, and there was therefore a need for a control organization loyal to the Duce or the Fascist party ideal. But after a preliminary purge of personnel the Army would now be reconstituted as a republican army and put on oath to the Duce as well. The existence of an independent Party guard would thus become unnecessary, and it would be possible, without misgivings, to put the ideal of a unified Army command into practice.

'The fallacies inherent in this deduction are obvious. The men who are to form the new army, particularly the officers, from the highest down, may be fewer in number but in all else will be the same as they were before. The revolution of September 8 was no spiritual change through which these people have been metamorphosed. The Badoglio-ites, the monarchists, the anti-Fascists and the war-weary have to a large extent remained in their posts, or are to be employed in new capacities. . . .

'Further discussions on the Militia question took place on the morning and afternoon of November 18, and again on the morning of November 19. Ricci advanced a new plan, details of which are not known to me but which was rejected. The discussions resulted broadly speaking in the following: The militia will be subordinated to the Army in all respects and without reservations. Ricci is to have no right to inspect them.

'A new body, the National Republican Guard, is to be set up under General Ricci, who will be responsible directly to the Duce; it will include the remainder of the Militia, whatever Military Police are left after the personnel purge, and the Italian African Police.

'The uniformed police are to be subordinated to Ricci, though the Ministry of the Interior will be responsible for putting them into operation; the plainclothes police will be subordinate entirely to the Ministry of the Interior.

'On the morning of November 19, following the discussions, Marshal Graziani turned up from Rome, presented himself to the Duce and demanded that the National Guard be put under the War Ministry. The Duce did not sanction this proposal . . .

'General Ricci asked to speak to me today . . . He told me that the important thing from his point of view was to know reasonably soon one way or the other whether he could count on the support of the German Army or Government for his task, for without it he could not continue his work. In fact, however, he had so far received hardly any support from any German quarter; on the contrary, he was always having to surmount obstacles, even in his dealings with the local German authorities. The explanation of this state of affairs is that, whilst Ricci was originally despatched from Germany with orders to become "the Italian S.S. leader" and turn the Italian Militia into an armed force, the situation in the meantime altered radically without Ricci's getting radically altered instructions or the Duce's issuing any orders to meet the case. Since the Militia had been declared an S.S. responsibility, the Germany Army naturally did not bother its head about it; and the S.S. in Italy was in no position to help, either from a numerical point of view or as regards methods, organization, the provision of uniforms from captured enemy stock, equipment and so on.

'I consider at all events that, largely on moral grounds, we should be well advised to strengthen Ricci's hand, if necessary even enlisting the assistance of the German military authorities . . . The concept of the Militia is the only one that still exerts the slightest power of attraction in Italy, however weak. As for volunteers! We shall soon see what practical results emerge from the Army campaign for volunteers, launched side by side with conscription. I for one do not expect anything to come of it. Fascism as a concept has hardly any support these days. But people do not identify the Militia with Fascism.'

Colonel Jandl also outlined in this report his impressions of the Italian Militia commanders. 'Ricci is a spirited character, and as such contrasts favourably with the other members of the Italian government, Graziani excepted. Unpromising as is Italy's present situation, he has gone about his task of reconstruction cheerfully and with wholly unbureaucratic zeal and tenacity. The virtues of will-power and character are in the forefront of his personality. Many doubt whether his organizing talents are equal to the task of building up an army in the present difficult circumstances; but this is a defect which could be made good by an efficient staff. . . . His manner is however too agile and unbureaucratic, by Italian standards, to have won him many friends among the other members of the Government.

'But the Duce has been completely won over by the Italian army representatives, who deceive him by grandiloquent talk of resurrecting a great new Italian army which shall atone by warlike deeds for Badoglio's treason. They are urging him to introduce a unified command, i.e. to liquidate the

Militia, as the essential condition and prerequisite for the fulfilment of this aim. Generals Gambara and Canevari are the two most powerful Army exponents of opposition to the militia. Gambara is widely regarded as an opportunist who sided with the Axis solely because of where he happened to be at the time of the Badoglio betrayal. His subordinates in the new "Ministry of National Defence" are in the main old Badoglio-ites and General Staff officers who missed their chance to jump on the enemy bandwagon. I am at present collecting evidence on this point so as to be able shortly to send in more concrete reports on the subject.

'Canevari, who makes himself out to be a thorough Germanophile, is a man who will do anything to satisfy his ambition and his passion for money. He is said to be a former anti-Fascist. However, after he was removed from the General Staff and from active service on account of "administrative irregularities", this did not prevent him from collaborating with Farinacci on the *Regime Fascista* and supplying the paper with military indiscretions in return for cash. We should undoubtedly keep a very close watch on this man. There is a growing impression that Canevari is the moving spirit behind the handling of all questions in defence policy in particular, and that in these matters he exercises a decisive influence on Graziani. In view of the present composition of the Italian War Office it would anyway seem appropriate to be on our guard against a second July 25. People may be hatching long-term plans in this direction. Still, so long as we keep our hands on the ammunition, new units are formed only with a German nucleus and under German supervision, and only small Italian formations, encircled by German troops, are sent into action, the danger cannot be regarded as acute. But we must certainly reckon with the fact that the Italian Army, supported by the Duce who is naturally acting in good faith, is going to attempt gradually to win back more and more of its independence. This is where we must exercise caution.'

The story of the first call-up of conscripts confused the scene still further. There was an almost complete response in Emilia, the traditional region of 'Red' socialism. Was it an implied reaction against the Fascist past? Graziani thought so.[29]

Elsewhere the numbers who reported varied, but the response generally was promising. But trouble came when, through widespread obstruction of the German military authorities in Italy, neither barracks, equipment, nor clothing were made available in an effective manner. Mussolini himself telephoned Anfuso in Berlin instructing him to point out that 'in some provinces difficulties are being made by the German army'.[30] The administrative breakdown was practically total, and the desertions began. In Graziani's own words: 'The recruits were to be concentrated at Vercelli. But many of them bolted during the journey, jumped from the trains and disappeared . . . The military police were in a state of disintegration in the North. Even if we had wanted to stop this flight, we could not have done so.' [31]

The internal struggle for the control of armed forces at the disposal of the Salò government led in practice to the creation of a series of private armies and police forces owing but tenuous allegiance to any central authority. In a sense this appealed to Mussolini, who could rely on an intricate pattern of balancing disloyalties, verging at times on treason, on which he could by a discreet push in one direction or another maintain a fragile initiative in the control of government.

By the end of the year, the medley of unco-ordinated armed bands at the nominal disposal of the Salò republic presented a chaotic picture.

The Germans had raised under their direct command 'autonomous battalions' after September 8. These originally numbered some ninety thousand men. General Wolff had recruited under his orders as S.S. commander certain Italian S.S. battalions, drawing on volunteers from the camps in Germany.[e] The Naval commandos of Prince Borghese had rallied directly to the Germans after the armistice, and with their high morale and voluntary recruitment might have formed a model for the future regular army, but beyond the reach of party control. But in the first call-up of November 1943, those who wished to join the Decima Mas were sent to Germany as the basis for one of the four planned divisions, the 'San Marco', and Borghese's organization was allowed to expand by only a small number of new battalions.

Of Marshal Graziani's regular armed forces on paper, certain anti-aircraft and coastal units, air and naval forces, provincial and administrative commands came nominally under a General Joint Staff, though in effect no serious operational troops were at its disposal until the return of the divisions in training in Germany.

Mussolini's decision to allow Ricci to set up finally a revived national Militia at the end of November increased the confusion and mutual distrust, and multiplied the recruiting offices. The bulk of the age-groups between 20 and 40 were scattered in camps in Germany, trapped in the Balkans, disbanded in the North and the South of Italy. In many cases the Militia recruits were between 15 and 17 years old.

Each commander competed with the other to increase his strength. And looming over the whole field of possible man-power were the blandishments and threats of the German recruiting agencies for labour units in Italy and factories in Germany.

Each military organization in addition tended to recruit its own police and information services, which added to the general chaos and climate of suspicion.

e. There were about 10,000 in these battalions, of which at the end of the war there were two. See Graziani *Processo op cit* I p. 367–8.

It was hardly surprising that Kesselring, in November, sent the following message to Hitler. 'We must put an end to all this and without further ado declare that Italy is occupied territory in the same way as has been done in Belgium and Holland.' [32]

The settlement of the military programme could however not be delayed indefinitely, if only because of the lamentable effect on relations with Germany. Both Mussolini and Graziani had placed themselves in an untenable position, the former by avoiding a clear position; the latter by failing to comment on the protocols of October 16 at the time, and by letting the assumption gain hold that there was no variation between his discussions with the Germans and those of Canevari.

On November 29 Rahn, on returning to Gargnano from a visit to Germany, reported to Berlin that, on his return, he found the following telegram which the Duce was intending to send to the Fuehrer.

'In the agreement signed in October last by General Canevari it was established that the first four divisions of the new Republican Army would be built up from the ranks of the military internees at present in Germany. For this purpose a permanent military mission in Berlin was set up under General Canevari. I am however now informed that the agreement has lapsed. I would ask you, Fuehrer, urgently to confirm this agreement, and namely that the first four divisions will be drawn from the best soldiers who are now in Germany . . . If you give these men, and others who voluntarily wish to do so, the honour of fighting, we will avoid the serious depression which must follow from the fact that while the traitors are creating an army for the Anglo-Saxons, Republican Italy cannot do the same.

'I am sure that with your profound political sense, you will meet my request . . . which will also strengthen the authority of my government and the confidence of the people . . .'

Rahn was immediately asked to call on Mussolini. He pointed out sharply that the German military authorities were alarmed at the internal situation in Italy and in particular, as Colonel Jandl had indicated in his report of November 19, drew attention to 'the circle round Marshal Graziani, which consists largely of officers from the former army, and whose reliability in regard to Fascist ideology and Germany is in many respects dubious, who are at the present time seeking to get in their hands all power in Italy. They aim to get control not only of military but social and economic spheres and to build up a state authority symbolized by Graziani and with no Fascist tendency.

'The remark of General Canevari to Marshal Keitel that there could be no question of a Fascist, but only a Republican army, his request that the new divisions should be recruited exclusively from the Italian military internees, his remark in passing that the troops should take an oath in the name of

Graziani, his desire to set up training camps in North Italy, his refusal to send to Germany the conscripts just called up but leaving them in Italy, all this gave the German military leadership just cause for anxiety.'

Rahn went on. Neither the Germans nor Mussolini wanted 'the experience of a second betrayal. He must understand that we had to pay dearly for the first treachery by being forced to withdraw German troops from the East, thus causing a Russian break-through into the German lines and severe German losses, and that we would meet any threatened repetition with the greatest suspicion and severe measures.' Germany appreciated the difficult position of the Fascist government, 'but could not idly look on'. Either a real Fascist state authority must be created, determined to accept all the consequences of the German alliance, or the work now begun must sooner or later collapse.

The Duce replied that the German government rightly regarded Italy with suspicion after Badoglio's treachery. 'But after very careful consideration he did not think that Graziani was personally disloyal. He had compromised himself too far in our direction for any possibility of understanding to exist between him and the other side.

'As to the question of the four divisions, he had no basic misgivings about sending the young recruits to Germany, but at the present moment there was a political danger that the new recruits, who up till now had not been sufficiently taken in hand owing to lack of barracks, equipment, and weapons, either did not report at all or ran to the partisans as soon as they heard that the intention was to transport them to Germany. This was backed up by the general state of mind of the population, who in great part were uncertain about the fate of the military internees in Germany and feared that the young recruits on reaching Germany would suffer the same fate.' It was most depressing that among some 600,000 military internees one could not find 50,000 who would be ready to fight.

Mussolini made the following proposals to the German High Command. The four divisions were to be set up from among the best elements now interned in Germany; these divisions would be trained by German instructors: they would come under the command of German generals with combined staffs; after training the first division would be sent immediately to the front and after its use in battle the second, then the third and fourth would be similarly engaged. Once the first division had been used at the front, there would be no misgivings about sending the recruits for further training in Germany.

As Rahn concluded: 'From this conversation I gained the impression that the refusal immediately to send the new recruits comes from the Duce himself, who fears for the moment the psychological effect of such a transfer on the Italian population.' 33

Two days later, on December 1, Rahn had another 'long and fundamental' talk with the Duce. It was agreed that the 'recruits will be sent to Germany, according to German wishes, in the second half of January' and that in the first half of the month several age-groups would be incorporated in the Militia and labour units for Sauckel. The Italian War Office would be purged, and Canevari dismissed.[34]

These concessions were confirmed and amplified at a joint Italo-German meeting summoned on December 4 at Gargnano. On the German side Generals Wolff and Toussaint, and Ambassador Rahn attended. Mussolini summoned Graziani and Gambara.

Canevari was excluded at the last minute after a violent scene with Graziani, who accused the former of misleading him. The blame had to be laid somewhere. Hence the casting of Canevari as scapegoat. Dolfin even suggests that the Duce and Graziani went and studied the Berlin protocols just before this meeting, which documents 'Graziani had not seen'.[35] He had had over six weeks in which to do so.

The discussion lasted five hours. According to Rahn's summary the following decisions were made: Canevari was to leave the Army. The new recruits would be sent to Germany for the four divisions. Requests for units in German army: 12,000 for the 10th Army, 18,000 for the 14th, 43,000 for the Air Force, would be met as soon as possible from the age-groups called up. 30,000 had so far been incorporated. Graziani was prepared to call up by military means all labour destined for Germany and under martial law.

Graziani called, after an argument with the Duce, for stern military measures under martial law in order to fulfil the contribution of manpower to Germany and offered to resign if the Germans had no confidence in him.

Rahn stressed that the setting up of the small Italian units was politically important and would have a good effect on recruitment for divisions and for labour.[36]

These joint talks merely registered the delayed formal acceptance by Mussolini of the Berlin protocols. 'The only serious fact is the commitment to send recruits to Germany. Mussolini and Graziani could not get out of it. They rightly fear that some of the young soldiers will . . . bolt at the moment of departure. The Marshal is even more exasperated than the Duce, because he does not see any way of changing things now without being accused by the Germans of disloyalty—which cannot fail to complicate further the difficult and intricate state of our relations with them.' [37]

Graziani now dismissed Canevari by letter. Mussolini received him on the evening of December 4. The Duce at least admitted that he had been at fault, and that the situation should never have arisen. But at once he characteristically attacked Canevari for the latter's anti-Fascist remarks at Berlin.[38]

The October protocols were abandoned in practice, and with them the only opportunity of an effective and independent military force in Northern Italy at the disposal of the new régime.

It was not therefore surprising that, some days later, Hitler's own comment at a conference of his advisers should have been:

'When asked about further plans for an Italian Army, the Fuehrer said that he does not believe anything will come of it. Germany is no longer interested in an Italian Army because her relations with Italy are too strained as the result of the events of last September and are bound to remain so. The organizing of Italian military units would therefore demand the greatest caution and watchfulness.' [39]

CHAPTER FOUR

THE DUCE AT SALÒ

•-•

THE SEAT of government chosen for the Duce by the German military authorities lay in a cluster of villas on the western shore of Lake Garda. The zone was cordoned off by road blocks, and the security arrangements were so strict that his own private secretary, Dolfin, had great difficulty in locating the area on his journey from La Rocca in the wake of Mussolini.[1]

The family clan had already installed themselves in Villa Feltrinelli at Gargnano, which was temporarily to be the Duce's residence. An S.S. detachment of thirty men from Hitler's own bodyguard were quartered round the house,[a] and an anti-aircraft gun mounted on the roof. The only contact with the outside world lay through a German field telephone exchange, with the irrelevant code name of 'Batavia'. Dolfin established his secretariat in a nearby villa; the nearest Ministry was the Cabinet Office under Barracu at Bogliaco.

Following the pattern set in the days of Palazzo Venezia, the control of access to the Duce was a subject of merciless contest.

The senior German representative attached to the person of Mussolini was Colonel Jandl, the liaison officer of the General Staff of the German Army. His first report to his superior contains an illuminating account of the Duce and his entourage.[2]

'. . . What is especially unique in the position of my staff is the fact that it forms part of the Duce's immediate circle, and this not merely in theory but, by virtue of the developments and experiences of the past several weeks, also in practice.

'We are billeted in a house adjoining the south side of the Duce's villa in Gargnano on Lake Garda, still within the security zone . . . I have one of my staff officers, Lieutenant Dyckerhoff, living in the Duce's house itself. This

---

a. An early compromise was reached by Mussolini's insistence with Wolff that an Italian picket should do sentry duty alongside the German unit.

affords me the best opportunity of keeping myself apprised of happenings inside the villa, the visitors received and the opinions current in the immediate neighbourhood of the Duce, and of informing the interested German quarters should the need arise.'

Colonel Jandl reported to Mussolini at noon every day. He received regular situation reports over the teletape from the German General Staff Headquarters. 'These enable me to select whatever seems expedient and compile a report; in so doing, I make a point of not showing the Duce the written particulars sent me by the sources mentioned, merely transmitting them verbally to him in Italian.

'This regular reporting not only brings me into comparatively close touch, intellectually speaking, with the Duce, but also allows me on each occasion to raise matters in the ordinary course of our discussions which would often not warrant my calling on him specially. The Duce is most candid in conversation and eager to discuss the most varied topics, including those having no bearing on purely military matters. With me, he is never in a hurry to end a conversation. I therefore have good occasion to sound him out each time on matters that might interest the various German authorities . . . and I can pass on any current information to the Duce in suitably modified language. Moreover, while I am waiting to report to him I naturally meet a number of callers also waiting to be received by the Duce, and this again affords opportunities for gathering information.

'. . . The Duce's closest staff could simply not have tackled its work had it not been for the German liaison staff. In face of the situation that developed after September 8 it was helpless. Supplying petrol and cars, interceding with the German authorities, instituting and maintaining a telephone and telegraph system, installing a telephone circuit between the principal Italian towns—these are but a few of the many matters in which we had to assist the Duce's headquarters staff.[b]

'. . . His state of health is generally agreed to have much improved in comparison with the time before July 25, and I myself can only say that he now makes a very good impression, appears for the most part very much alert and has latterly seemed to be experiencing no pain or inconvenience of any sort. His gait, demeanour, gestures and speech are by no means those of a broken man, but are vigorous and more or less lively, depending on his mood day by day.

'His wife, Donna Rachele, recently expressed herself as follows: "Even if the Duce is now no more than a shadow of his former self he can still be very useful to Germany."

b. The Germans controlled telephone communications through the territory of the new Republic. Even Marshal Graziani, as Army Commander, had no right to a private set until November 1943. 'Mussolini could not telephone to all the prefects . . . There was a complete ban on radio communications.' (Graziani *Processo op cit* II, p. 221.)

'The Duce's health is now being supervised principally by Dr Morrell's two deputies, namely Captain Dr Zacharias and physiotherapist Horn, who give him daily massage.[c] Some time back the Duce also consulted the Italian Professor Frugoni, who had already treated him earlier, without marked success.' The latter put his assistant, Dr Baldini, at the Duce's disposal to form part of his entourage, who periodically gave the Duce pain-killing drugs. 'As this was apparently quite at variance with the German doctors' methods of treatment friction ensued, and the Duce, as the patient involved, was characteristically unable to decide to entrust his case to one doctor only and rid himself of all other influences. The doctors have now made their peace with one another. I should like to mention in this connection that through Ricci and myself and in various other ways the Italians made repeated attempts to manoeuvre the German doctors out of the way, on the pretext that this was the Duce's own wish. The truth of this allegation has by no means been proved, however, and should rather be called in question.'

These minor clashes illustrated 'the multifarious intrigues that are constantly brewing in the Duce's circle, to which the presence of a whole tribe of relatives, even quite distant ones, contributes in a not insignificant degree. He has so far been unable to bring himself to make a clean sweep of this gang, dissociate himself from it and set some of its idler members to useful work. This laissez-faire, regarded by many outside observers—possibly with justice—as symbolizing that (when all is said and done) everything is still just as it used to be, can be explained in terms both of the very pronounced Italian sense of family solidarity and of the immense good nature, nay tender-heartedness, of the Duce himself.'

As Colonel Jandl concluded gloomily his first impressions: 'of the Duce's present position, it may be said in conclusion that he has only relatively few friends and supporters left among the population. Essentially the same reproach that is levelled at the King by the other side—namely that for twenty years he aided and abetted the Duce—is now levelled at the Duce himself: that he either failed to perceive or else turned a blind eye to long-standing treachery, and that for years he tolerated self-enrichment and other kinds of misrule on the part of Fascist Party members and collaborators, thereby sharing responsibility for them. This is of course not to say that the moment some military victory is reported from the front all will not be forgiven and forgotten, and the Duce be acclaimed as the saviour in the hour of need.'

The circle of the Duce, with the springs of power atrophied, settled down to a dreary and unreal routine. In December Colonel Jandl sent in his second report to Berlin.[3]

c. As Dolfin noted, Horn 'sleeps in the villa, goes backwards and forwards to Berlin: for us he is a member of the Gestapo'. Dolfin *op cit* p. 47. See also Zachariae's book *Mussolini si Confessa* (*passim*).

'The Duce makes a better impression outwardly than he did at the time of my last report. In particular, his desire to work and the daily amount of work he gets through have continued to increase noticeably. He now goes regularly to his office at 8.45 a.m.; soon after, he receives visitors, usually until 2 or 2.30 p.m. There is then a short midday pause lasting about half an hour, and in the afternoon he goes on working, usually until about 9 p.m. The Duce often works on his own at night. On one recent occasion he worked until 6 in the morning. It frequently happens that the Duce retires before midnight, wakes up about 4 a.m., does a little work until 5 a.m. and goes back to sleep again for a while. He always keeps paper and pencil at his bedside so as to jot down stray ideas, which he will then often elaborate on paper between 4 and 5 a.m. Harking back to his journalistic past, he writes for the press now and again: about a week ago, for example, he wrote a good article on the Teheran Conference.

'I am gradually getting the impression that the Duce is fully alive to the gravity of the situation and to his own unhappy predicament, and that he entirely realizes how weak is his position in the eyes of the population. Not that he is given to talking about it himself; rather is my instinctive impression in the matter confirmed by the remarks of some of the persons surrounding him. By nature very strong, both physically and morally, he does not allow his sensitivity to become superficially apparent. His ruling idea basically remains the creation of an Italian army, however small. He has said that his last task may well be to reconstitute an Italian army which should atone for the guilt of treason with its blood.

'. . . A month ago the Duce's private family accommodation was finally separated from his official quarters. Until then the living quarters of the Duce and his family had been located in Villa Feltrinelli along with his study and reception rooms. This house now only accommodates the Duce, Donna Rachele, the children and Dr Baldini. Lieutenant Dyckerhoff is still living there, though various intrigues had to be surmounted to ensure this. A villa in Gargnano, some 700 yards from Villa Feltrinelli, has been adapted as the Duce's official quarters for the transaction of government affairs. My staff is billeted about halfway between these two places. The more distant relatives have been "shaken up" a bit and are now scattered about the outlying districts.

'Donna Rachele has for some time been actively indulging in politics. She occasionally buttonholes individual Ministers. Recently, for instance, the Minister of the Interior, Buffarini Guidi, was closeted with her on two successive evenings for two hours each time. I am not conversant with the details of these interviews, but judging from the general attitude, conduct and character of this woman nothing prejudicial to our cause is to be inferred. I believe she chiefly exhorted Buffarini to intervene more decisively to restore order in internal affairs. I spoke in my last letter of Donna Rachele's pro-German attitude and of her deep-rooted aversion for Italian red tape . . .'

'There is a further not insignificant matter to report concerning Donna Rachele's intimate milieu and the Duce's private life, but that, I feel, had better be dealt with by word of mouth.'

Jandl was presumably referring to the disturbing presence of the Duce's mistress, Clara Petacci. She had been imprisoned at Novara by the Badoglio government and liberated by the Germans, who brought her with her family and installed them in a villa at Gardone. The usual German escort was attached to the establishment.[4]

Her presence on the edge of the world at Salò was a further element of strife in the Duce's circle and, as Goebbels put it, 'a source of much misgiving'.[5]

The skeleton private secretariat had been set up on October 5 by Dolfin's appointment, for which Buffarini had been responsible. On arrival at Salò, however, under family pressure and on the pretext that only close relatives could now protect the Duce from another 'betrayal', a 'political office' under Vittorio Mussolini, the Duce's son, took shape, and by the end of the month was formally established on the Duce's instructions with supervisory powers over the professional secretariat of Dolfin, and in spite of the latter's fierce opposition.[6]

The new body, apart from consisting of Vittorio's 'sporting friends', contained members of the 'committee of relatives' [d]—in Mussolini's phrase—and including his nephew Vito who had accompanied him from La Rocca, and Vanni Teodorani, the latter's brother-in-law. This clan moved into offices on the ground floor of Villa Feltrinelli, and it was here that all official callers were interviewed before being received by the Duce. Such a monopoly was, however, illusory in the face of German 'protection'.

As Colonel Jandl described it: 'The general picture is that the Duce has two kinds of Secretariat working for him: the "Special Secretariat", headed by the former Prefect of Ferrara, Consul of the Militia Dolfin; and the "Political Secretariat", exercising some kind of political supervisory function, and led by his son Vittorio Mussolini and a few relatives. Dolfin, a very lively, intelligent and energetic-seeming man who for reasons of a practical order, and no doubt of personal rivalry also, is anything but edified by the horde of relatives, is presumably using every available opportunity at least to check its influence. He is, incidentally, a creature of the Minister of the Interior, Buffarini. His attitude is shared by a number of other politicians and

---

d. This phrase originally applied to the horde of applicants for favours and financial support on the basis of claiming a family connection with the Duce. According to Dolfin the files contained 2,400 names.

Ministers, some of whom are vocal, others not. Ricci, for instance, belongs to the first group.

'The Duce's wife, Donna Rachele, whose origins, as is known, are of the humblest, is an admirable woman. She nurtures a quite un-Italian hatred for all this nepotism and does her best to combat it, though so far without visible success. She swears by the Germans, her experiences during her stay in Germany being no doubt largely responsible for this.' [e]

The elements of an administrative machine were being transferred from Rome to the Northern lakes, formed out of the remnants of a demoralized Civil Service, strained in their loyalties, diminished in number, and uncertain of the future. The Ministries were encamped without plan throughout the area; the Interior at Maderno on Lake Garda, and also the Secretariat of the Party, where the hotel restaurant was 'the waiting-room of politicians'; Foreign Affairs near the small town of Salò from which the new régime acquired its territorial epithet; and Popular Culture in the early stages in a former royal train on a nearby railway siding. The Ministry of Defence was installed at Cremona; Economy and Corporations at Verona; Agriculture at Treviso; Public Works at Venice; National Education at Padua; Justice at Brescia. Rome was now a distant enclave governed by the German military authorities, and with a small Italian 'office of co-ordination', headed by a nominee of Buffarini.

All communications were in German hands, both telephonic and transport. The writ of the government did not run beyond the road blocks of Gargnano, and it was the intention of the German military authorities that it should never do so.

The German agencies were installed through the region of the lakes; Rahn and his Embassy at the Villa Bassetti at Fasano; Wolff and his staff at Gardone and later at Desenzano; Harster and the Security Service offices at Verona; Rommel and his headquarters of Army Group B at Belluno until November, when he finally left the Italian scene for Germany. Kesselring remained at his headquarters at Frascati near Rome in command of Army Group South. General Toussaint as military plenipotentiary was near Verona; and General Leyers, who was in charge of the special mission of the German Ministry of War Production, was based on Milan and Como.

In addition to these main offices, there was a horde of German officials tramping across the Italian scene, from the Todt organization recruiting civilian labour to send to Germany, from Sauckel and the Ministry of Labour,

e. Even Donna Rachele did not escape German surveillance. A German Foreign Office minute reads: 'The Secretary of State requests that the letters of Donna Rachele are not directed through the usual postal censorship. The letters could not be opened so unnoticeably that under no circumstances the fact that they had been opened could be detected.' German Collection. October 1, 1943.

'advisers' on Agriculture and Communications and every field of public activity, and invading the scattered ministries, unco-ordinated in their terms of reference, adding effectively to the general confusion, and presenting Rahn as the Civil Plenipotentiary of the Reich with a further incubus.

The territory of the Salò Republic was nominally bounded on the West by the French frontier, northwards along the arc of the Alps, on the East by the Italian-Slovene administrative border as defined in 1941, and to the South by the war front now across the line of the Apennines south of Rome.

The events of September 8 had however torn up the map of Italy, not only by creating a basic disruption of the historic creation of Italian unity and a division of the country into two rival régimes of North and South, formally confirmed on October 13 by Badoglio's declaration of war on Germany, but also by the political and military measures taken on Hitler's orders by the German authorities.

The military security of the southern frontiers of the Reich made it essential to control the Alpine passes running through the Alto Adige, and the bastion of Venezia Giulia, which dominated the routes to the Balkans, must be urgently clamped to the German defence system. Apart from the military aspect, these areas were former Habsburg territory, and historically the frontier marches of the Austrian Empire. There were strong irredentist elements of Austrian stock in both regions, actively represented in high quarters in Germany, and the necessity of the military occupation of these areas raised at once that of political control. The price of Italian treachery would be the recovery of the Lower Tyrol (Alto Adige) and the Adriatic provinces of Austria with the port of Trieste lost to Italy in 1918.

These moves had been prepared during the course of the summer of 1943. A skeleton political staff had been working in Innsbruck, capital of the Austrian Tyrol, since July,[7] and another at Klagenfurt in Carinthia.

The gauleiter at Klagenfurt, Rainer, was in charge. Already on July 26 he had forwarded his proposals to Himmler:

'Given the turn of events in Italy, and the fact that the German frontier lies one hundred kilometres via Ljubljana from the Adriatic, the latter can become an English operational zone. Between Trieste and Ljubljana lies already an area controlled by partisans. They are supported by the Slovene population.'

Rainer's proposals were: an all-out struggle against the partisans 'in the old and new Italian territories' with full powers to be delegated by the Fuehrer to Rainer; military measures to fortify the Adriatic coast; the German military occupation of the former Habsburg territories in Istria and Venetia.[8]

At the beginning of August German units stationed in the Italian-occupied zone of Slovenia had moved in divisional strength to cover the approaches to Trieste.[9] Following on the news of September 8, all Italian units in the province of Bolzano, the key to the Alto Adige, had been disarmed by the German military authorities, 'not leaving in this province a carabiniere, or a police agent, and interning everyone in Germany'.[10]

On the night of September 9 Berlin radio had announced, 'Trieste has been occupied after a brief struggle and 90,000 Italians have been disarmed. The treachery is without parallel in history, and rebounds on to the traitors themselves, and what will remain everlasting is the contempt for the traitors.' [11]

The next day Hitler gave confidential instructions for the setting up of two German political administrations based on Trieste and Innsbruck. Two gauleiters were nominated, Rainer from Carinthia and Hofer from the Upper Tyrol, to be responsible direct to himself.[12] Both men were former Austrian officials from these territories before 1918, and regarded themselves as fulfilling an historic mission to annexe their regions once more to the Reich.

Goebbels showed himself to be an influential supporter of these moves. 'I then posed the very serious and important question to the Fuehrer as to how far he intends to extend the Reich. His idea is that we ought to advance as far as the Venetian border, and that Venetia should be included in the Reich in a sort of loose federation. Venetia would be all the more willing to accept this, since the Reich alone would be able after a successful war to supply it with tourist trade, to which Venice attaches the greatest importance. I regard such a boundary line as the only practical and right one. I only hope that the Fuehrer will not let anything, especially his reawakening friendship for the Duce, divert him from this decision . . .' [13]

The establishment of a new Italian government headed by Mussolini as a loyal exponent of the Axis alliance would inevitably lead to discord, and it would be more difficult to occupy these regions, particularly the Tyrol, owing to the precise engagements which Hitler had made to Mussolini in 1938. German violation of Italian sovereignty in these historic frontier regions, whose acquisition was intimately bound up with extreme nationalism in Italian politics, and with the rise of Fascism itself, would be henceforth a foremost issue in Italo-German relations.

During the September talks at Rastenburg between Hitler and Mussolini, the former seems to have avoided making any clear statement of ultimate intention in regard to these areas.

By the time that the Duce was able to turn his attention to this sensitive issue, a grave situation of fact had arisen through the whole northern and north-eastern frontier regions, and in the Adriatric and Balkan areas held by the Italians since 1941.

The territorial gains to Italy of two world wars were in jeopardy, with all the psychological and moral implications involved. Unless the Duce was able to use his personal prestige at Hitler's headquarters to modify German measures in these areas, his chances of heading a political revival of Italian Fascism were sorely weakened.

Throughout September and early October events moved fast. German officials in Trieste and the surrounding districts initiated a pro-Slav policy, building up anti-Communist units from the Slovenes, and reverting to the Habsburg technique of playing off Italian and Slovene elements. The Italian prefects and administrative organs throughout Venezia Giulia were nominated direct by the German authorities. All Italian commands in Slovenia were liquidated, and a Slovene civil administration set up with German 'advisers'. The Italian army in Northern Yugoslavia was cut off from Italy. There was chaos in the Slav areas of Venezia Giulia, and a large-scale partisan rising against both Italian and German authorities. It was put down by German troops in October with 8,000 Slav casualties.

It was not only in the North and on the Eastern Marches that the Germans imposed direct military control. German troops now occupied the bases of Zara, Fiume, Spalato and Cattaro, the symbols of Italian presence on the Adriatic. Brief, and in places, violent skirmishing with the Italian Army, of over thirty divisions, ended in mass surrender and their removal as prisoners to Germany.

The Italian 'conquests' of 1941 in Dalmatia, Montenegro, and Albania, so obstinately contested with the Germans in the winter of 1942 and the spring of 1943, evaporated before German military necessity, and the long-standing hostility of the Axis satellite set up in 1941—the Croatia of Pavelić.

As Anfuso noted in his diary:

'As regards Croat claims in Dalmatia and in the Balkans generally to territories formerly annexed to Italy or Albania . . . they had been made on precise orders from the Reich Government which wishes to secure the friendship of these Balkan peoples, who have recently wavered in their attitude, by means of concessions and a good propaganda campaign.' [14]

Rumours and mounting evidence of German special measures in Tyrol and on the Adriatic could not be concealed from the Duce. On October 7 Anfuso in Berlin asked for an official denial of a Reuter message that Germany had annexed the Italian provinces of Bolzano, Belluno, and Trieste, as there was unrest among the Italian Fascist population. A week later the setting up of 'the Adriatic coastal province' was announced.

Rahn hastened to arrange a meeting with the two gauleiters. The basic question was, how far the annexation 'can be disguised'. Rahn suggested that only decisions vital to the war should be made public. Other decrees should be negotiated through Rahn with the Italian government, whose prestige must be preserved in public.[15] He pressed for 'a friendly settlement'.

In October Pavolini managed to get as far as the province of Trento, and the significance of German policy throughout the frontal areas in relation to the existence of the new and fragile Italian régime was the subject of a report to the Duce.

'If you succeed in saving for Italy the Alto Adige, Trentino, Zara and Ljubljana, the government which draws its being from your authority, Duce, will already have an historical justification for its existence, however things may develop in the future.' [16]

Early in November, during a short stay at La Rocca, Mussolini was able to study a bulky file assembling the evidence of these German activities in Venezia Giulia and Alto Adige. All physical contact with these frontier provinces had ceased. On November 9 Mussolini telephoned personally to the Italian Prefect of Trieste, whom the Germans had nominated. The latter was moved to tears. 'Yours is the first voice to reach me from the Fatherland.' 'Hold on; Italy is behind you,' was the Duce's reply, on a telephone line tapped by the Germans! And to Dolfin afterwards, 'You realize that from now on we must defend ourselves daily from a series of threats. I often have the impression that the Germans have regretted allowing us to form a government, especially one presided over by myself.' [17]

The protests to Rahn on the frontier question were a constant source of friction. The German Ambassador himself was not unaware of the added blow to the prestige of the new Republic. It was perhaps the sharpest political psychological burden of all. But the Duce's lamentations to Hitler remained like the rest of the personal messages, unanswered,[18] and the violation of Italian sovereignty in these areas continued. It was perhaps the most bitter personal shock which the Duce had thus far sustained. In his early days he had been intimately bound up with pressing Italian claims to the Lower Tyrol, and as a violent leader of the irredentist campaign in Italy, both in that region and in the Julian March and Trieste, he was deeply and personally committed. He had fought in the trenches on the Carso. He had witnessed in Trieste in 1918 the wave of nationalist sentiment at union with Italy, and three years later had made one of his major speeches in the city on the foreign policy of his party.

The very roots of Italian Fascism lay in origin in this campaign of 1914–15, which had brought Italy into the First World War. The present attitude of the German authorities struck at, and threatened to destroy, an intimate theme of the movement.

'There is a clear tendency to create a fait accompli on both sides of the Alpine watershed and as far as the Quarnero.[f]

'This is a plan which is naturally based on the assumption that the war is already won. Their attitude can only induce the Italians to react against any collaboration on a war footing, and to await their fate with resignation . . .' [19]

All that the Duce was able to do was to maintain contact with Trieste by

f. The North Eastern frontier of Italy as established in 1918.

telephone, and the reports which he received increased his general sense of discouragement and impotence. Anfuso's dispatches from Berlin confirmed these impressions. On December 10, for instance, he wrote that there was a violent campaign against Italy 'by Austrians and some of the Army staff, who think it stupid to waste time on the Italians who are useless militarily; in regard to the frontier provinces, Austrian irredentism is active. The only Italian in whom the Germans still believe is Mussolini himself.' [20]

Towards the end of the year it seemed that the experiment of the Alpine and Adriatic special zones might be extended to meet increasing partisan activity in Piedmont. Rahn was alarmed.

'The creation of the Alpine and Adriatic operational zones constitutes the most severe political and psychological burden for the Duce and the Fascist government. Only with great difficulty has one succeeded in creating normal relations between this region and the operational zones, and a certain quietening down of the Italians and an understanding on their part of the need for setting up such zones.

'The official creation of a new operational area would in the present very tense situation lead to an unbearable aggravation of our political work and a serious endangering of the Fascist government, and to an exceptional strengthening of enemy propaganda. The Italian government gives way to all necessary military supervision and control measures requested from the German side.

'I regard the setting up of the new operational zone, in present conditions, as unnecessary and harmful, and advise strongly against it.' [21]

Within the remaining rump territory of the Northern régime, there was as yet no recognized Italian authority other than the symbolic physical presence of the Duce at Gargnano. The German military authorities were in *de facto* control, appointing as in Turin even the Italian Prefects; but, in spite of Hitler's original personal directive of September 10, the functions of the various German commands and agencies themselves remained unclarified.

On October 10 the German Army General Staff had issued, on Hitler's personal orders, a revised set of instructions.[22] 'The following areas of Italy are to be operational: the area south of the northern boundaries of those provinces immediately behind the battle front south of Rome.[g] In this area the Commander (South), Marshal Kesselring, has complete control.

'The Alpine region from the Croat to the French border will be divided into several operational zones, of which the "Adriatic coastal area" and the "Lower Alps" have been laid down.

'Commander Army Group B, Marshal Rommel, has complete powers. A further operational zone will be set up in event of an Allied landing.

'The Commander in each operational zone would be responsible for "law

g. Littoria, Frosinone, Aquila, Pescara.

and order, administration and the economy".' Commissars would be appointed as civil advisers.

A 'Military Commander in Upper Italy' would be appointed with authority to cover 'all unoccupied Italy which is not operational and to coincide with the area of sovereignty of the Italian Fascist government'. He would be senior territorial commander in his area. All German civil and military agencies would be under him, and he would represent their demands to the Italian government. 'He will help the Italian government in reimposing their authority and implement their instructions.

'Next to him are the plenipotentiary of the Reich, Ambassador Rahn, and the special adviser for Police matters, S.S. General Wolff. Both receive their instructions from their respective chiefs—Ribbentrop and Himmler. All requests from subordinate agencies will be forwarded to the Italians in consultation with these officials.

'As Military Commander of Upper Italy, General Toussaint is nominated. German advisers to each Italian prefecture will come under him.'

As the covering telegram to Rahn from the German Foreign Office pointed out, this was contrary to the previous instructions of September 10 in which they came under Rahn. The German military commands would now be the channel of liaison with the Italian prefects; the German civil agencies would not be controlled by Rahn nor would he be the chief link with the Italian government.

This order bluntly established direct German military government of Northern Italy, and confirmed Mussolini's worst fears.

On October 19 Rahn telegraphed his own protest.[23]

'The setting up of new operational zones means further extraordinary aggravation in the reconstruction of the administration and the safeguarding of the supply position; a greater piling up of German staffs implies a further decline in the reputation of the Fascist government. The desired practical results can, in my opinion, be achieved through police or military . . . control measures with the consent and support of the Fascist government, and without the setting up of new operational zones.'

'The new operational zones' signified a threat to treat Piedmont and Liguria as areas menaced by Allied invasion, according to the German military forecast that the Allies would eventually undertake a landing in the Genoa-Leghorn area, or after an invasion of Southern France, across the Alps. To remove these provinces from the infant neo-Fascist régime would strangle the experiment at birth.

The main task of Rahn and the German Embassy at Fasano was to make such an experiment viable in political terms.

This pattern of German control of the Italian satellite was the subject of a report by a personal envoy of Martin Bormann.[24]

The central figure was Rahn. 'He rules Italy by exploiting Mussolini and the Italian government. His aim is to exercise this power with a minimum display of people . . . I get the impression that he does not regard the military plenipotentiary as necessary, that he would much rather take over the administration himself and on a smaller scale . . . and would manage with military commands. The close link with the S.S. and Police Chiefs and their staffs would be quite sufficient for him.' [h]

There was no co-ordinated inter-services staff. Marshal Kesselring as operational commander of Army Group South gave orders in the rear areas through General Toussaint, the Military Plenipotentiary, who also controlled the local German military commands. The Air Commander, Marshal Richthofen, dealt direct with the Italian authorities. The German naval representative reported to Berlin.

Wolff as S.S. commander was also police adviser to the Duce. Fortunately his personal relations with Rahn, at least at the beginning, were close. Leyers at Milan was nominally under Toussaint but had his own subordinates in each province who were normally independent. Sauckel's representative set up his own recruiting offices.

In this administrative chaos the Italians had an easy task in playing off one German agency against another. The recommendation of Bormann's envoy was to suppress the functions of General Toussaint and to nominate Wolff as supreme S.S. and Army Commander in the rear zone.

At the beginning of November the Duce sent his son, Vittorio, to Berlin on an 'unofficial' mission.

Vittorio had a glum interview with Steengracht, [25] at which he pointed out that 'several measures taken by the German authorities in Italy give the population the impression that the Duce is really an executive organ of the

h. At Nuremberg Wolff described Rahn as follows: 'He is a career diplomat and one of the new brand, very gifted with a lot of ideas and imagination. He takes great delight occasionally in reaching his objectives with the help of Jesuitic means. I have observed on many occasions that whenever he wanted to get Hitler, or the Army chiefs, or Mussolini, or Ribbentrop, or anybody else to agree to a certain measure, he would deliberately represent himself as worse than he was. He would assume the position of a Jesuit, whose only consideration is the goal, and who does not care what means are used. As the Political Plenipotentiary of the Great German Reich, Rahn was in those days the recipient of many complaints from the Duce and other Italian dignitaries about excesses and incidents. For that reason he felt that he had to do something about the education of our troops in this respect. I know that considerable difficulties resulted for Rahn in his dealings with the Duce and the Italian Government from the existing mutual dislike of the Germans for the Italians and of the Italians for the Germans. As Rahn considered himself responsible for making the best of war production in Italy, he thought that matters related to this task to be his concern. I would like to mention that whenever Rahn felt that he had to use one of these immoral Jesuitic tricks, he would say to himself: "I have to act as the advocatus diaboli—the devil's advocate." ' Nuremberg Trial Documents, Supplementary volume B, pp. 1675–6.

German government'. This was particularly unfortunate as recently 'a change of feeling in favour of Fascism has been noticeable'.

Examples of such acts by the local German agencies were cited. In the various provinces the Duce had nominated prefects, only to be overridden, as for example in Trieste. He had no channel of communication with the prefectures except through German military links. The Italian security organs had no weapons. The Fascist newspaper in Brescia had been confiscated by the local German authorities. The Duce requested that German officials should deal with the Italian government, and not direct with the population. 'The present situation weighed heavily on his father, whom', Vittorio said, 'he had left in a very depressed state of mind.'

Steengracht answered that Hitler and the German government had no intention to influence the Duce in his personal policy. The German army had found no organized Italian administration in being, and the special conditions in the frontier provinces were due to the needs of war. Draconian measures were now required. Many Italian officials were unreliable. All Hitler's measures were calculated to be for, not against, the Duce, and good relations depended on the purging by Mussolini of the Italian administration.

On the following day Anfuso wrote an autograph letter to the Duce describing this interview. He stressed that there were 'ample assurances from the German side. I should add, for truth's sake, that . . . they specially emphasize that we have not taken up a more energetic position against defeatism and compromise inside the country. In one word, one does not see that the agnostics of today are the traitors of tomorrow. Evidently everything will be clearer when the Republican Army begins to fight.' [26]

The intrigues of the neo-Fascist exiles in Germany during the interlude of Badoglio were not quelled by the formation of the Italian Republican administration in September. The Duce himself seems to have regarded his ministry as provisional in the sullen perplexity of those days. As a neo-Fascist journalist wrote, 'After the storm all the corpses float to the surface.' [27] One such was Preziosi, whom even Mussolini described as 'repulsive, a real figure of an unfrocked priest'.[28]

On October 12 Preziosi called at the German Foreign Office to criticize the new appointments in Rome, and to stress that theme of latent treachery in the Duce's circle, which was best calculated to undermine any German confidence in the new régime.[29]

He talked 'against practically every member of the present Italian government'. They were all 'unreliable opportunists who will betray the Duce at the first opportunity'. His special target of hatred was Buffarini, 'the friend of Jews and Freemasons', and Preziosi headed a detailed memorandum on the subject for the personal files of the Fuehrer 'who is the only person who can break this circle'.

He then called on Goebbels who noted that Preziosi's 'report on Fascist Italy gave much food for thought. He even criticized the Duce very severely and blamed him for not having followed the right line in his treatment of Jews and Masons. That, he said, was the reason for his fall.' [30]

These manoeuvres succeeded in promoting the conception of the first of a series of plots which mark the dreary stages of the history of the Salò Republic. Both Rahn and Wolff were not unconvinced.

On November 16 Rahn reported that there were 'grounds for suspicion that Buffarini (after warnings from Wolff and Preziosi he has been carefully watched) is planning treachery, has got together gold, foreign currency and valuable documents, and plans to flee to Switzerland'. Rahn agreed with Wolff that 'owing to the extraordinary good nature of the Duce and the indiscretions of his entourage, he should only fix matters with him at the moment when the arrest takes place following the revelation of the plot'.[31]

Preziosi was then received by Hitler, and seems to have been encouraged by him. In December Jandl reported from Salò.[32]

'Preziosi, originally a professor by calling, turned up here about a fortnight ago after a long stay in the Reich. He is said to be one of the very few Italians who enjoy the Fuehrer's confidence, and has been received by him on several occasions. He is credibly described as a thoroughgoing Germanophile. He is regarded as an expert on Jewry and Freemasonry, and has already published a good deal on the subject, having lately had an article in the *Voelkischer Beobachter*. He belongs, generally speaking, to the category of the doctrinaire professor. Those connected with Canevari say he is an intimate friend of his, which does not say much for him. According to remarks made in confidence by General Canevari's adjutant, the latter's circle seems to be hopeful that a big ministerial reshuffle is imminent and will be effected mainly with Preziosi's help. This also corresponds with the drift of a conversation Preziosi had with Ambassador Dr Rahn. He then said that it was essential to substitute other men for (among others) Buffarini Guidi, the Party Secretary, Pavolini, and the head of the Police in the Ministry of the Interior, Tamburini.

'Preziosi further maintains that another great betrayal is being hatched in the Duce's immediate circle, more particularly in the Political Secretariat . . .

'In my view we ought to be sceptical about wholesale accusations of this kind, which are getting to be fashionable. After the experiences of July and September it is really rather too easy simply to dub this man or that a traitor and if he denies it to pose as a prophet enjoying personal protection— but this procedure naturally makes it very difficult to extract the best from our system of government. And that, after all, should be our endeavour: once we have set foot on this path we cannot simply abandon it without more ado. According to the view which has lately been prevalent, ostensibly at the Fuehrer's Headquarters and other high places, it is impossible to trust anybody at all; but that, to my mind, is to rush to the other extreme and throw out the baby with the bath water. At any rate we ought not to give the Italians the impression that we distrust them. We should rather see to it that the responsible German representatives in Italy keep their eyes and ears open so as to prevent any recurrence of treason, keep a watch on any such developments by appropriate methods of observation, and if necessary put a stop to them.

'It is common knowledge that Graziani, for example, has never been pro-German. But he himself is not a member of the Badoglio clique, a fair number of whose adherents still remain in his Ministry though he has already kicked out a good many. His personal vendetta against Badoglio is an important criterion for the judgement of his character. One can understand and indeed accept the fact that in the last resort he wants to get away from German influence and see Italy sovereign and free, and that he has no scruples as to how he gains his ends. But the Marshal, shrewd as a peasant, knows full well that for him, too, the condition for this can only be victory, however ephemeral. He also knows that the most effectual Italian contribution at present towards bringing about a victory consists in providing a labour force, not in some huge new Republican army dreamed up by a few visionaries. We should therefore harness the ruthless energy of this man, who has drive well above the Italian average, and whose capacity for action is not maimed, as is generally the case here, by corrupt embroilments; we should spur him on by giving him the feeling that we have confidence in him.

'The German authorities will not press for a new Minister of the Interior until the proceedings against Ciano and the others accused of political crimes are over. Thus, whatever the outcome of the proceedings (and incriminating moments are sure to abound) only the outgoing man will be incriminated. I therefore consider Buffarini's position fairly safe for the time being, although there are a good many rumours current about him. Besides, Buffarini's type, his reassuring, conciliatory, pacifying manner, suits the Duce who considers him useful for maintaining his internal balance of power.'

But Preziosi was also able to link up with his former colleague in exile in Germany, the head of the Militia, General Ricci. As Jandl reported at the beginning of January, the latter 'recently spoke very openly to one of my officers about Buffarini's character, accusing him of having foreseen the whole collapse and final breakdown of Italy during the seven years in which he was formerly Minister of the Interior, and having done nothing to prevent this. Ricci stated that Buffarini could not last much longer and that in two months at the latest he himself would have got so far that he could kick Buffarini out.' [33]

This parlous crisis never burst into the open, and merely poisoned the climate round the Duce's circle. As Jandl wrote: 'One group centres round the sly Minister of the Interior, Buffarini, who looks like a Jewish cattle-dealer; as his advance-guard near the Duce can be seen Dolfin, the Duce's private secretary, former Prefect of Ferrara, whom I mentioned briefly in my first letter. The Party Secretary, Pavolini, can also be counted in this group.

'In already fairly open opposition to this group stands the so-called political secretariat under Vittorio Mussolini (which could also be called a sort of family council, since it consists almost entirely of the Duce's relations), the Duce's wife Donna Rachele, and General Ricci with the Militia . . .

'Each of these two groups is trying to oust the other from the saddle, the "family council" group through a ministerial overthrow with the aim of destroying Buffarini; the Buffarini group through changes in the Duce's headquarters with the intention of separating the Duce from his family and political secretariat and of removing these influences, but simultaneously of freeing itself from dependence on the German information service (so far the régime's requirements are met by my intelligence detachments). The strength of both groups' influence over the Duce fluctuates; their further aims, apart from striving to eliminate each other, are very difficult to know. The above-mentioned ministerial overthrow, which a few days ago had become very imminent, suddenly went under again.' [34]

The crisis, if it existed in reality, was quickly dissipated.

Rahn reported on January 14 that Mussolini 'intended to remove those members of the government who represented a burden to Fascist Italy, among them the Minister of the Interior, Buffarini, the Party Secretary, Pavolini, and the Chief of Police, Tamburini. Buffarini and Tamburini will probably be interned in Northern Italy on January 14 with the co-operation of the highest S.S. and Police chiefs, and be subject to an enquiry as to whether the suspicion against them is founded: that they have made sure of a mass of gold, jewels, and other valuables and have hidden them in part in Switzerland. If there is any truth in these statements, they will be brought to trial. In the case of smaller misdemeanours, the Duce will ask for them to be interned in Germany for the duration of the war.

'As Buffarini's successor Zerbino, former Prefect of Turin, is envisaged, who has worked excellently with German agencies . . .' [35]

But the Duce was not deceived by these antics, and whatever the facile temptation might be of a meaningless 'Changing of the Guard', and in particular to distract attention at the moment of the Verona trials, no such decisions were made.

On January 25 a laconic German Foreign Office minute reads, 'Rumours about the person of Buffarini are not proved correct.' [36]

The Buffarini 'affair' was closed for a space. Preziosi was allowed to continue to broadcast from Munich radio against the 'traitors' of Salò, and was compensated with the post of Minister of State. His energies were switched to devising renewed paper measures in Northern Italy against the Jews.

The Duce's technique of rule pursued its familiar course.

CHAPTER FIVE

THE CONGRESS OF VERONA

IT HAD BEEN announced on a number of occasions since the new régime had been proclaimed that a Constituent Assembly would meet to debate and approve fundamental articles of a truly revolutionary character. The historical break with the monarchy and the construction of a socialist Republic must be sanctified by popular mandate. The technique of mass backing must be organized to consecrate a programme, which must rival successfully, on the plane of ideas and emotional support, the counter-appeal of the Badoglio government in the South and the coalescing resistance, ideological and military, of the partisan bands now impinging upon the Northern scene.

The framing of such a 'new deal' presented grave formal difficulties. As an anonymous writer of a memorandum on the preparation of such an Assembly put it, 'the fact that a good part of national territory is now removed from the possibility of control by the Fascist government raises the problem as to whether or not it is opportune to convoke urgently the Constituent'.[a]

But on the other hand, 'the formation of a Kingdom of Italy took place without a Constituent and on the basis of decrees applying only to Piedmont. The Russian Constituent functioned at the beginning of 1918 when much of the territory of the State was still in the hands of foreigners and rebels.'

On balance such a body should be summoned. The present administration was however *de facto* in every sense. Nominated by the Germans in Rome out of a chance group of former Fascist politicians and officials, ringed by German military control posts in the confined space of the Northern lakes, it was in tenuous contact with the provinces under its nominal control. The press and radio, both under German censorship, had made a start in rallying opinion, and had initiated a wordy and incoherent battle. Under such con-

a. Italian Collection. The document is undated and unsigned. The passages quoted above are heavily underlined, and from internal evidence, by Mussolini himself.

ditions there was an air of unreality in the whole debate. There was no constitutional machinery to serve for electoral purposes, and the appearance of new parties in the formal sense was inconceivable. The practical measures for summoning a Constituent Assembly must inevitably fall upon the cadres of the Fascist Republican Party. Such a position precluded from the beginning the calling into being of an effective constitution-making body, which in any event the outside circumstance of war and the ubiquitous presence of the Germans made unreal.

Mussolini realized the impossibility of any effective grand gesture. The idea of a return to the socialist republican origins of the Fascist movement, the revival of old slogans, anti-plutocratic and anarchistic, were one set of tactical tricks in the game of political warfare which the Duce understood so well. Twenty years previously he had marched to power against a state machine already dissolved from within and driven on to the defensive by the success of such tactics. The pattern was too familiar for repetition; both the magic and the prestige were lacking. The resistance elements in the North who were competing for the loyalty of the masses were by their very presence an increasingly effective reaction against the system which the Duce of Fascism symbolized. The political structure of the South, of Badoglio and the monarchy, while it might be sensitive to a genuine socialist revolutionary movement from within—and proved to be so—it could hardly be shaken by such slogans from such a quarter.

Mussolini's dilemma was absolute. In essence his concept of a socialist programme was a tactic of political warfare. It was to deny the support of the masses to the enemy. But to attempt to rally them to a neo-Fascist cause meant to alienate the industrial leaders of Northern Italy, who had in the past been the leading supporters of Fascism; to cause disquiet to the Germans, who were only too ready to intervene in the improbable event of a genuine rallying of the workers and peasants to a socialist theme; and to demoralize the extremist Fascist elements, historically rooted in the middle class elements of the Northern cities, and in the lower ranks of the old state administration.

In the absence of a spontaneous revolutionary movement in response to the abrupt reappearance of the Duce in Italian affairs, the last word in any constitution making must lie with the bitter remnants of the old Fascist 'squads', the only nucleus of any physical backing for the 'provisional' government, and not with the ex-syndicalists and the progressive journalists who rallied with their private anti-historical illusions to the idea of a 'new' Fascism of the left, purged of the experiences of twenty years.

There were, however, certain strong and genuine reformist tendencies within the Party itself, and signs of revolt against the nominated leadership of a clique bound up with the defects of the old party structure. Both such a criticism and such desire for a revision of past mistakes was as yet dispersed in gatherings in the provincial cities and articles in the local press. The exist-ing Party caucus was in danger of losing control. It was therefore for tactical reasons essential to centralize and provoke an outlet and stage an inquest, but under the direct leadership of the present bosses. This was the purpose of the Verona Congress, and it was the special task and responsibility of Pavolini to organize the debate round a written manifesto and to reassert the monopolistic authority of the Party.

Mussolini clearly had no intention of throwing his weight unequivocally behind his Party Secretary, but preferred to remain in sardonic isolation, ostensibly to allow an open debate, but in reality to avoid being at the ex-clusive mercy of one clan. As Buffarini remarked, 'he does not like clear-cut situations, and thus subjects his collaborators to a continuous and dangerous wearing down.' [1]

Characteristically he sent at this moment a special message of praise to Concetto Pettinato, editor of *La Stampa* of Turin, who as an anti-Fascist exile in Switzerland had returned in September to Italy and rallied to the new régime in order to play a part in attacking the conformist rigidity of Pavolini and his allies.

The agreed arrangements now went forward. On October 28, 1943, Pavo-lini delivered a speech on the anniversary of the March on Rome, and made this solemn announcement.

'By decision of the Duce, the Party will at a meeting in the near future lay down precise directives in the form of a programme on the most important problems of the State, and on the new realizations to be achieved in the field of labour, which, more appropriately than social, we are not ashamed to call socialist.' [2]

The delegates from the Party organizations throughout Northern Italy were now summoned to meet at Verona on November 14. This is the first time that the idea of the Constituent Assembly was publicly replaced by that of a Party Congress, and the new implication was very different.

The preparation of the directives for the forthcoming congress seems to have been in the first instance based on a rough draft put together by Musso-lini himself. He seems also to have taken into account the hybrid theories of a renegade socialist revolutionary, Nicola Bombacci, who had attached himself to Mussolini as a self-appointed adviser during these days, and who had adhered to the new régime as a sort of 'proletarian' spokesman. His record was unusually strange, and as he frequently appears in these months at Salò in proximity to Mussolini and up to the end, his career is of some interest.

He had been a small schoolmaster in the Romagna, and worked in the same district as Mussolini. The two men knew each other, and met at socialist gatherings. Their careers diverged at an early stage. Bombacci joined the

Italian Communist Party and was at one time a deputy, and, in an undefined capacity, worked at the Soviet Embassy in Rome. In 1927 he had been expelled from the Communist party, and in subsequent years drifted round the fringes of Fascist offices, at one time editing a small review, with a leftist outlook, supported with even smaller official subsidies.[3] A rootless and restless agitator, with an imposing shock of white hair and luxuriant beard he looked the part of the familiar anarchist from his native Romagna. His disjointed enthusiasms for a 'proletarian' Italy eternally struggling against capitalist imperialism found a slight but positive echo in the newly proclaimed socialist republic. His rather shop-soiled baggage of ideological catchwords had some resemblance to that of Mussolini himself, and with all the tenacity of a drifting renegade he bombarded his long-lost colleague with memoranda and advice. There is no doubt that some residue is traceable in the final document, which was passed from the Duce's secretariat to the Party. But the final political manifesto, which was to be read at the Congress, was put together in the Party offices at Maderno by Pavolini, and submitted to the Duce on his return from a brief stay at La Rocca.

According to Rahn, he himself also had a hand in the text. 'The Party manifesto was drawn up in cooperation with myself, and I was impelled to tone down the originally very sharp socialist tendencies in the interests of maintaining private enterprise in war production, and further to strike out a section inserted by the Duce on the preservation of territorial integrity.' [4]

The draft under review had also to meet conflicting requirements: to be the manifesto of a united republican socialist movement, to appeal to a long suppressed desire for social justice without conceding any democratic control by the masses in any real sense or weakening the political monopoly of the neo-Fascist Party.

The approved document was in the form of Eighteen Points. 'On constitutional and internal matters', the Constituent Assembly, 'the sovereign power of popular origin', would be summoned to announce the dissolution of the monarchy, to proclaim the social Republic, and appoint the Head. Its composition would be 'the synthesis of all the values of the Nation'. The Head of the State would be reappointed every five years 'by the citizens'.

No citizen under arrest could be held for more than seven days without an order by the judicial authorities. The magistrature was to act in its functions with complete independence. There must be 'some mixed system' for the future electoral machinery.

The organization to which it falls to educate the people in political problems was the Party, alone worthy of being the custodian of the revolutionary idea. Its membership card was not required for any office or employment.

The religion of the Republic is that of the Roman Catholic Church. Other cults not in conflict with the law will be respected. 'Members of the Jewish race are foreigners. During this war they belong to "enemy nationality".

'The essential aims of foreign policy are the integral unity, and the independence of the Fatherland, and the recognition of the necessity of vital living space for forty-five million inhabitants.

'Such a policy will be adopted to carry out the realization of a European Community with the federation of all those nations who accept the following fundamental principles: the elimination of worldly British intrigues from the continent; the abolition of the capitalist system internally, and the struggle abroad against the world plutocracies; the exploitation, for the benefit of European and native peoples, of the natural resources of Africa, with complete respect for particularly those Moslem peoples who, like Egypt, are already organized as a state and nation.

'In social matters, the Republic is primarily based on labour, manual, technical, and intellectual. Private property—the result of labour and individual saving, the integration of the human personality—is guaranteed by the State. Public services, and, as a rule, war industries must be run by the State.

'The trade unions will be amalgamated in a General Confederation of Labour. All the impressive social legislation realized by the Fascist régime in twenty years remains intact. The Charter of Labour is its consecration and starting point for a further advance.' [b]

Whatever he thought in private of this document, Mussolini's public comment appears in the form of an article distributed to the press on November 13. 'The social reform in progress . . . will be the highest realization of Fascism; exquisitely humanistic and absolutely Italian, linking itself again to the age-old traditions of our Humanism and Mazzinianism in its spiritual essence and completely and finally resolving the needs and aspirations of the working classes.' . . . And again, 'Fascism, liberated from so much tinsel which has slowed its march and from the too many compromises which were forced on it by circumstances, has returned to its revolutionary origins in all sectors, and particularly the social one.' [5]

On the morning of November 14, the delegates of the Fascist federations and syndicates, representing some 250,000 Party members, gathered in the main hall of the Castelvecchio at Verona, to hear the 'national report' of the presiding Party Secretary, Pavolini.

A message from the Duce was read, which emphasized the need to pass as rapidly as possible from political discussion to the military defence of the Social Republic, 'that is, Fascist in the original sense of the revolution'. This was the first time since September that such phraseology had been used.

In his opening speech Pavolini began by describing the recent wave of partisan terrorism. This meant that 'we are taking the situation in hand in the

b. This clause is presumably the work of Preziosi.

provinces and the country . . .' Behind these words lay a sense of isolation and fear as of a besieged minority. 'I heard at Novara, at the funeral of four members of the action squads who had been killed, a voice which said "those are the profiteers".' Pavolini assured the Assembly that special tribunals would be set up and that the present meeting was a model 'in the revival of Fascist activity'. Fascist reprisals had already begun as for example in Brescia. He himself was not bloodthirsty but 'I have the definite impression that either one acts in this way or one does not touch people's consciences'. Civil war had been intensified. In many provinces one found the phenomenon of industrialists financing the 'bands of Lenin'.

'The spring of our life is the action squads. Whoever has been a squadrista remains so for life. (Voice "Not all"). I am of course talking of those present, but the task of the action squads should be temporary. The Militia must take over the political and armed national police which would absorb the Squads. You will have read that the armed forces must be non-political.' (Interruption 'Bad').

'After the disastrous experience of the past', Pavolini explained that he was against obligatory membership of the Party.

This speech was made with continuous interruptions. When he asked whether the University Fascist Youth groups should be set up in the original form, there were cries of 'No, no. Abolition.' There were shouts of 'When is the Ministry of the Interior to be purged?'

Pavolini reported that there were 250,000 members of the new Fascist Republic Party and the Hall answered, 'Too many; we want to remain few.'

In the afternoon the various provincial Party leaders took the platform and the meeting of the Assembly took increasingly the form of a dialogue between the platform and the Hall. All the old themes of twenty years of Party history were ventilated in an atmosphere of bewildered anxiety. Many of the delegates were old Fascists removed from the fruits of office and authority in the successive regional purges carried out by Party Secretaries in recent years. There were also the young and dwindling band of militants who had passed through the Party schools and in particular University organizations. It was a muddled debate of generations and survivors of a broken machine, bitter and humiliated about the past and uncertain of the future now menaced by civil war. The situation revealed a sad irony. Veterans of the Action Squads, and there were still many such men at this strange Assembly, had themselves been the agents of promoting civil strife in the months before the March on Rome in 1922. Under present conditions in the north they were now under siege. They were scared and puzzled by such a climate and the reality, so alien to their mentality, of having to appear as broken remnants of a proud movement.

In some of the speeches made by the regional leaders an impression is formed of the state of the provinces in recent months. In Perugia, for instance, no police had been on active duty in the Province since September. In army circles, 90% of the former officers were unreliable (Voices, '98%'). Of the former 50,000 members of the Fascist Party in the Province, only 3,500 had joined (Voices, 'Too many'). As the same speaker also plaintively remarked, 'The question of the trade unions is so serious and vast but it cannot be settled in one or two hours,' to which Pavolini retorted, 'It has been settled for twenty years not two hours.'

In certain areas of the country after September 1943, there had been moves by the local neo-Fascist groups to make contact with those opposition elements to the régime which had come into the open with a view to signing local pacts for a common effort, but without any definite programme. As the speaker from Florence at the Verona Assembly pointed out, articles had appeared in the Tuscan press recently, stating that the new Fascist Republican Party recognized freedom of action to the other parties. Pavolini made signs of astonishment and dissent, but the Party Secretary from Florence continued. One could not separate the political problem from that of the trade unions 'if you admit that the worker . . . elects his representatives even outside the field of the Party, you will admit the collaboration of efforts outside the Party. There is no need for a Party ticket in order to be elected to a Workers' Committee. How do you control these elements?'

But the same speaker pleaded for a single Party whose prime task would be to control the army and the youth. 'The young have given us a tragic disillusionment' (violent disapproval on the part of the Assembly), but this was the fault of the leaders. 'The young must fight and die without arguing. In Padua they whistled at the cadet officers of the Militia, among them my son.' The students wanted the speech of the Rector of the University to continue, and they shouted, 'Shoot the swine.'

Ciano was a main target of abuse. Again the speaker from Florence urged for the setting up of a Special Tribunal without delay. Again he feared 'an attempt, more or less open, of rescue'.

There were several nostalgic appeals for a return to origins to the Action Squads of the Twenties. The Party Secretary of Como announced that he had started all over again with ten members. The Militia must establish posts in the small villages, particularly in the frontier areas to be garrisoned night and day. 'We do not want to be —— about any more.' Pavolini interjected, 'These are barrack-room expressions,' to which the speaker retorted 'This is a barracks.' There were also talks on the attitude of the Church: 'the papers and radio propaganda can do nothing against thousands and thousands of parish priests'.

At this point the deliberations of the Assembly were interrupted by Pavolini to announce that the neo-Fascist Party Secretary in Ferrara had been assassinated. The old Fascist cries of twenty years ago resounded in the Hall. 'All to Ferrara.' Pavolini bellowed back: 'One does not shout in the presence of the dead. One acts in a disciplined manner.' Fascist squads from Padua and Verona were sent on a punitive expedition in which seventeen anti-Fascists held in jail in Ferrara were executed. This event symbolized the weeks of hesitation after September, and the end of any illusions of pacts or understandings with the other side. The 'New Deal' evaporated into a vendetta.

One speaker expressed his disappointment at the absence of the Duce. There had been no photographs of him in the papers since July 25. There were also no Ministers present in spite of the urgent need to learn of the situation in each of the provinces.

There was also a desperate confusion of mind as to the structure of the new Republic and in particular of the essential role of the Party. The representative from Forlì exclaimed, 'Who actually governs Italy? The Government through its separate bureaucratic organizations, or the Party? I insist that all powers should be given to the Party which alone can carry out the revolution which for twenty years we say we have made and as yet have not done. Naturally the Party—no Government can do it. We all understand that these delays depend surely on Galeazzo Ciano.' That is in the delays in bringing him to trial.

The Party Secretary from Terni simply announced that he was sorry that he had come at all. Amid all the shouting, there were no ideas.

The only important speaker on the Government side apart from Pavolini as Chairman, was Renato Ricci, the head of the new Militia. He announced that both the Chairman and himself had been fighting for days to achieve in the ranks of the Militia an armed force capable of guaranteeing the state and public order. The programme of the Party was the constitution of a civic police force, which had the task of achieving within the Militia the transformation of the Military Police, and also a rural gendarmerie to guarantee orders in small centres with permanent garrisons.

'When the enemy were about to enter Byzantium the Senate was discussing the sex of the angels. In these times there is only one problem: the incorporation of the Militia into the Party.'

It was time to conclude the meeting. Pavolini spoke of the 'warmth of disorderly faith' which had been expressed. He had also made special note that the Assembly approved of the Special Tribunal and in effect the whole Verona Assembly was intended to be a popular demonstration for the punishment of the 'criminals' of July 25.

Pavolini concluded, 'Of the other questions which you have raised, careful note has been taken. The Duce told me to have here four good stenographers "as I want to know everything which the comrades from the provinces have had to say and have thought that they said".' [6]

Pavolini closed the discussion The Eighteen Points of the Manifesto were then read out by him, and hastily and uncritically approved by acclamation. The company broke up in a state of confused excitement.

The main purpose had been served. A torrent of discussion had been canalized in a formal gathering under the aegis of the Party Directorate, and dissipated. There had been no effective challenge to the authority of Pavolini or his brand of Fascism of the Action Squads. But nor was his own position strengthened.

In conversation with Dolfin, Mussolini made his own comment on the Verona Congress. 'It was a complete and utter mix-up. A lot of confused chatter, few precise and clear ideas. The most odd tendencies appeared, including Communist ones. One man even demanded the outright abolition of private property! We really could ask ourselves why we have fought Communists for twenty years. According to these "leftists" we could today bring off a universal embrace all round, including them. From all these verbose exhibitions it is easy to see how few Fascists there are who have any clear ideas about Fascism . . . And not one, not one I say, of all those who have a sack full of ideas to wave around, comes to me and asks me to fight. The fate of the Republic will be decided . . . at the front and certainly not at congresses.' [7]

But perhaps the most immediate result of the assertion of the supremacy of Pavolini over the Party at Verona was the acceleration towards civil war, and to emphasize the deep division of Northern Italy.

'The action of neo-squadrism, which provoked a chain reaction of assassinations . . . has congealed the current of sympathy which was strengthening around the régime.' [8]

The battles of 1920–1 were to be fought out again twenty years later. It was a long-delayed revenge. The partisan bands of 1943 were the successors of the victims of the Fascist squads, and situations were to be inexorably reversed.

CHAPTER SIX

THE VERONA TRIALS
(January, 1944)

•–

ACTION AGAINST the 'traitors' of July 25 had figured early in the programme of the new government. The moral shock to the Fascist movement, and the sense of violence and frustration in Party circles since September had to be dissipated. It was not only the urge towards a vendetta, but also towards a limitation of the responsibility of each and all for the collapse of Fascism. As the Duce expressed it: 'On the historical plane, the trial will be convenient to many, because it will limit in space and time the wider responsibilities which led, on July 25, to the fall of the régime.' [1]

Formal steps to set up the legal machinery of special tribunals were taken at the Council of Ministers on October 13. It was a familiar procedure of Fascist invention, originating in another climate of conspiracy which followed on the murder of the Socialist opposition leader Giacomo Matteotti in 1924. Two years later, a Special Tribunal was set up, following four attempts to assassinate Mussolini. The new court was to try crimes against the State under the military penal code as applied to the Army in time of war. Its activities were directed to the extinction of those anti-Fascist elements, which might still be active in Italy. The same procedure was now applied to those Fascists who had voted against the Duce at the last meeting of the Grand Council in July 1943. In the words of the preamble of the decree:

'The coup d'état of July 25 has faced Italy with the greatest betrayal in recorded history. A sinister plot involving the King, certain generals, Party leaders, and ministers, who more than any others had derived advantages from Fascism, struck the régime in the back, creating disorder and confusion in the country at the agonizing moment when the enemy was setting foot on the soil of the Fatherland.

'The treachery of the King can be left to the judgement of the people and of history; it is however only right that the treason of those who violated not only their duty as citizens but also their own oath as Fascists should be severely repressed . . .' [2]

Under this decree an extraordinary Special Tribunal was set up, and a similar body in each province. Their members were to be 'Fascists of proved loyalty', and in effect the whole machinery was in Party hands, and the precedents for such repressive action were linked closely with the Fascist past. The first Minister of Justice at Salò, Tringali-Casanova, had been President of the original Special Tribunal set up in 1926 and abolished by Badoglio. The examining magistrate of the new court, Vincenzo Cersosimo, had held the same position with the former body.

The express and exclusive purpose of the Special Tribunal was to bring to trial those members of the Grand Council who had voted against the Duce. Ciano was the special target of hatred, and he had unwisely taken the initiative in seeking to return to Italy. His wife had preceded him, but under the strain of seeking to rehabilitate them both had had a nervous breakdown and was, as Buffarini told Rahn, 'under safe guard' in a clinic near Parma. On hearing this news, Ciano, who was at the house placed at his disposal in Bavaria, telephoned to Anfuso in Berlin asking him to seek the Duce's permission to come back to Italy. Anfuso smelt the danger, and intended to tell Mussolini that there was no point in such a move.[3]

The telephone line was automatically tapped by the Germans, and it seems that they decided to expedite for their own reasons Ciano's request.

On October 17 a German Intelligence officer announced to him that, in view of the setting up of the Special Tribunal to indict those members of the Grand Council who had voted against the Duce in July 1943, he would be flown to Italy and handed over to the Italian police.[4]

On October 19 Ciano left Munich airport. He was accompanied by an S.S. escort, and a female agent of the German security service, who went under the name of Frau Burkhardt or Beetz. She had been attached to the Ciano family during their stay in Bavaria ostensibly as an interpreter but with the prime mission of discovering the hiding place of Ciano's diary and private papers, which were of special interest to the rival German Intelligence agencies.

Frau Beetz had been the secretary of the German police chief in Rome, Colonel Kappler, and was an agent of experience.

On arrival at Verona airport Ciano was arrested and placed in the Scalzi prison. Frau Beetz continued her mission at his side, and under the immediate orders of General Harster, the head of the German security service (Sicherheitsdienst) in Northern Italy.

When Anfuso telephoned to Mussolini a second time to ask permission for Ciano to return he received the laconic reply, 'Already seen to; Count Ciano has already returned to Italy.' [5]

The other members of the Grand Council who had voted for Grandi's motion were not all available.[a] Gottardi had been arrested in Rome at the end of September; De Bono, Pareschi, and Marinelli early in October; and Cianetti some days later. These other prisoners were now also brought to the prison cells of the Scalzi fortress in Verona. It was a convenient setting. Extremist elements of the neo-Fascist party were strong in the city, and Pavolini's headquarters was close by at Maderno.

In spite of Party pressure, however, there were delays. Mussolini hesitated to accept the exposure of Ciano to public trial. Tringali-Casanova died suddenly on October 30 and his successor as Minister of Justice, Piero Pisenti, was, as a lawyer of standing, opposed to a revival of special procedures to sanction political revenge.

But the impotent violence displayed at the Party congress at Verona in November increased the urgency for action. Both a blood-letting and a cleansing of conscience were essential if the fragile structure of Salò was to achieve any stability. There was growing dissatisfaction not only within but also against the leadership of the Party.

Mussolini was aware of the dangers inherent in such a political climate, and after weeks of hesitation, prepared to give way. At the council of Ministers on November 24, 1943, on Pavolini's proposal, the Special Tribunal was set up.

Dolfin records Mussolini's private decision that 'not to strike Ciano means that it would be impossible to touch anyone; "The Ciano Case" is the element which must clarify the atmosphere created by the fall of the régime'.[6]

The Duce himself sorted the files from his secretariat, which were to be sent to the Tribunal, and instructed Pisenti to make a preliminary study of them.[b]

The Minister of Justice reported tersely that 'proof did not exist of prior collusion between the members of the Grand Council, Badoglio and the Monarchy'. The Duce reacted sharply, 'You see in the trial only the juridical aspect. As a jurist you judge things by other standards.[c] I have to look at it from a political angle. *Raison d'état* submerges every other contradictory consideration. Henceforth one must go through to the end.' [7]

The prestige of the new régime in the eyes of Italy and Germany was at stake.

The composition of the court left no doubt what course the trial would take. The members were all formally appointed by the Party. The president,

a. Nineteen members of the Grand Council had voted for the motion of Grandi. At the time of the Verona trials, Grandi himself was in Lisbon, and apart from Ciano, and those mentioned above who were all arrested in Rome, the rest were discreetly untraceable.

b. The list is in the Italian Collection.

c. Pisenti stuck to his point in the sense that he never signed the decree setting up the Tribunal.

Aldo Vecchini, had been removed by the Badoglio government from the presidency of the Italian Bar. General Montagna, a senior Militia officer, had been imprisoned by Badoglio after July 25. He was now ordered by the head of the disciplinary section of the Republican Fascist Party to serve on the court.[8] The remaining members were professional Fascists with extremist records.

As Rahn reported on November 25: 'Members of the Special Court will be proposed by Pavolini and appointed by the Council of Ministers . . . They are men who are proven and fanatical Fascists of the old guard, and most possess the highest war decorations, and in Pavolini's view they offer the guarantee that particularly in Ciano's case the death sentence will be pronounced.' [d]

The task of assembling the evidence fell to the examining magistrate, Vincenzo Cersosimo. He had at his disposal only those files of the Duce's personal secretariat, which Pisenti had found so inconclusive.

His first move was to interrogate the former Party Secretary, Scorza, who had been detained in prison at Padua, but not brought to Verona as he was not in the category of those who had voted 'treacherously'. Cersosimo hoped to learn of the whereabouts of any notes or documents directly relating to the last session of the Grand Council. He was told that they were taken personally by Mussolini after the meeting to Villa Torlonia, and that thereafter there was no trace.[9] It appeared from a talk shortly afterwards with Buffarini that all these papers were destroyed there on the afternoon of July 25 when in a climate of panic the Duce failed to return from his audience with the King.

It remained to start the interrogation of those prisoners held at Verona.

On December 14 the examining magistrate installed himself in an office in the Scalzi fortress. His first act was to seek access to Ciano. It was then that he learnt of the close supervision, which the German S.S. command at Verona had placed round the principal accused. The two sergeants on duty refused to allow the Italian official to enter the cell, and it was only after the appearance of Frau Beetz, who telephoned to her superiors, that the interrogation was permitted to begin.[10]

Apart from this supervision by the German police of Ciano himself, there is no evidence to indicate any direct interference from Nazi quarters. In fact

---

d. The list of the remaining members is grimly symbolic of this neo-Fascist world: Celso Riva, metal worker, founder member of the Fascist Party and father of Luigi Riva, murdered in Turin after the setting up of the Fascist Republican party; Ugo Leonardi, Lieutenant General of the Militia; Riggio, consul of the Militia, and leader of the recent punitive expedition to Brescia and Ferrara; Casalinuovo, consul of the Militia and member of its central staff; Ottello Gaddi, Militia Battalion Commander and early Fascist leader in Southern Italy, representing the enemy-occupied provinces; Domenico Mittica, Commander of Militia in Turin; Vezzalini, lawyer, squadrist, one of the leaders of the punitive expedition to Ferrara. German Collection. Rahn telegram, November 25, 1943.

Rahn received precise instructions from Ribbentrop on this point: 'For your personal information . . . the Fuehrer has stated that the trial of Ciano is exclusively a matter for the Duce, and that on our side no pressure whatever shall be exerted in favour of a condemnation.' [11]

But Ribbentrop indicated that he expected to be kept closely informed. On the following day Rahn reported that Pavolini had expressed to a representative of the German Embassy 'the firm conviction that the three-day trial, which would open on January 8, would end not only with the death sentence, but its immediate execution'.[12] And again, on December 30, that the Duce, in spite of pressure from the family—with the exception of Donna Rachele—had decided 'as head of the family and of the State finally to disinterest himself from Ciano's fate, and has completely handed over to Pavolini the "mounting" of the trial'.[13] Pavolini had expressly told the judges of the Duce's *désinteressement*.

On the morning of January 8, 1944 the public trial opened in the great hall of the Castelvecchio, where in the previous November the Party congress had been held, thus symbolizing the intimate connection between the two events. The Republican police, recruited from local action squads, were on duty inside and outside the building. The Party held in reserve armed bands of the most extremist elements of the Fascist machine summoned to Verona from throughout the province of Venice. The public in the hall consisted only of trusted young Verona Fascists.

Just before nine o'clock the six prisoners were brought in. They had each been allowed to nominate a defending lawyer, but not to call witnesses.[e]

The Germans took no official cognisance of the trial. Rahn was absent from Italy,[f] and only a small group of German representatives was in silent attendance; an S.S. officer, two officials in civilian clothes, and the ubiquitous Frau Beetz.

After considering and rejecting a plea from certain of the defence lawyers regarding the competence of the Tribunal, the accused were heard briefly in turn. De Bono stepped first up to the table placed in front of the Tribunal at the far end of the hall. He repeated in brief the substance of his interrogation, emphasizing the advantages in asking the King to take over command of the Armed Forces, and adding, 'I have never thought that the Duce should

e. De Bono had cited the Duce in person.
f. Dr Rahn has since told the author that he flew to Hitler's headquarters at this moment to propose that Ciano should be allowed to escape to Switzerland as it would be dangerous in view of Itailian feelings on the subject of family loyalties if Mussolini were to allow his son-in-law to be executed. Hitler reiterated his instructions that the trial must be regarded exclusively as the affair of Mussolini, in which the Germans must not interfere, positively or negatively.

leave his post as Head of the Government: my devotion to Mussolini was boundless. I myself had taken up the question of creating the rank of first Marshal of the Empire, and spoke of it to the King at San Rossore.'

There were no questions.

Pareschi followed, and in the same sense. He too made the point that he thought that only the issue of military command was under discussion at the Grand Council, 'It never passed through my mind that the Duce should leave office.'

Cianetti then addressed the court in the tone of an orator at a political meeting, outlining his past services to the cause of Fascism, and stressing that he understood from Grandi that the sole purpose of the latter's motion was to 'relieve the Duce of complete responsibility for the war'. Cianetti referred to the letter, which he wrote to the Duce during the small hours following the meeting of the Grand Council, in which on reflection he withdrew his vote.

In the afternoon Gottardi took the stand. In answer to a question from the President of the Court, Vecchini, as to why he had voted for Grandi's motion, he said even more concisely, 'I had the clear impression that there was a split between the Party, the people, and the army, and that the morale of the nation was shaken. Since it emerged from the Duce's own account at the Grand Council that the army did not want to fight, I thought that, if the Crown took a direct part in the fortunes of the war, perhaps the army would be able to recover. I also remember the gesture of the Crown in the war of 1915–18, which had stimulated both the army and the nation. That is why I voted for Grandi's motion.'

Marinelli followed. He was ill, and scared. At the meeting of the Grand Council he had heard little of the discussion as he was deaf, and sitting some thirty feet away from the Duce. He had little to add.

Ciano was the last to be called. He had no comment to make on his deposition: he was not in favour of summoning the Grand Council in the first place 'because of the international repercussions which it might have'; by voting he had intended to 'bring the Crown into the war'. He did not regard the 'dilemma' which Mussolini had postulated as real, as he, Ciano, considered that 'the position of the Duce was beyond discussion'.

The formal evidence of certain witnesses present at the Grand Council was given either in person, in the cases of Scorza, Suardo, Galbiati, and Frattari, or in writing in the cases of Farinacci, Biggini, and Buffarini. They produced no remarkable revelations.[g]

None of the evidence produced under interrogation of the accused present, or by written testimony from others, gave a picture of a co-ordinated plot

g. See Cersosimo, *op cit passim*. This book contains the texts of the interrogations and of the letters of the Court written by the absentee members of the Grand Council.

among the members of the Grand Council, who had voted for Grandi's motion, nor, as the Minister of Justice, Pisenti, had pointed out before the trial, of their collusion with the Monarchy and Badoglio.

But when the court reassembled on the following day, an isolated document was produced and read aloud by the judge with dramatic effect. It was a statement signed by Marshal Cavallero the previous August at the time of his interrogation by General Carboni, who had been appointed head of the Italian military intelligence after July 25. The agony of Cavallero's own personal dilemma was irrelevant to the moment, but the effect of the document now read in court, irrespective of the veracity of the statements which it contained and which were not debated, was to supply the needed content of a myth of universal conspiracy in high circles against the Duce in the months preceding the coup d'état of the previous July. And this was the essential purpose of its presentation.[h]

The accused in the dock followed with sharp and shocked attention the reading of this memorandum. It was the climate which it invoked, and not the alleged evidence which it contained that struck home. Its purpose was quickly clear. As if by rehearsal one of the judges, Vezzalini, asked the court's permission to question the accused.

'Some of the accused have spoken insistently of the treachery of the General Staff, and the guilty disinterestedness of the monarchy; what then were they aiming at when they besought the transfer of military powers to such traitors?'

De Bono answered: 'The whole Grand Council was against the General Staff, and broadly speaking against all the generals; but no one produced names or details. One must however remember that all the generals on the General Staff had twenty years of Fascism on their shoulders and could not therefore all be traitors.'

Ciano simply replied that 'I voted for Grandi's motion because I wanted to commit the monarchy, and force it out of its nebulous state, by making the King take over the supreme command.'

Then came the final sarcastic question as to whether De Bono and Ciano as members of the order of the Collar of the Annunciation, which carried the title of the King's cousin, had intervened with the King after the Duce's arrest.

Ciano replied, 'I did nothing because I was the only Collar of the Annunciation who had no contacts with the Royal House . . .' The President of the

---

h. It is not clear how this document came into the hands of the Salò government. It had been found after September 8 in Badoglio's private office, and therefore presumably by Kappler, the Gestapo chief in Rome, when he searched the building. Rahn was told in November that the memorandum would be produced at the forthcoming trials. See German Collection. Rahn telegram. November 25, 1943. For the text of this document see the Appendix to this chapter.

Court interposed 'And as a relative?', to which Ciano answered: 'My wife was more concerned than myself.'

De Bono's only response was, 'It never occurred to me.'

It now only remained for the Public Prosecutor to speak. He underlined the existence of a plot involving the monarchy, the military leaders, and 'high finance', as shown in the Cavallero memorandum; and of the sabotage of the war by the General Staff. He equally emphasized the reality of a political conspiracy headed by Grandi and other members of the Grand Council 'in order to save themselves and re-fashion their virginity'. These men had been fully aware of the consequences of their acts, and their responsibility had been proved in evidence. He demanded the death penalty, and turning to the accused he ended his speech. 'Thus I have thrown your heads into Italian history; perhaps my own also, but in order that Italy may live.'

After a deep silence in court, the defence lawyers followed correctly and unimpressively. There was a brief session again the next morning when Cianetti's lawyer made an eloquent plea on his behalf. It was then announced that the sentence would be proclaimed at the afternoon session.

Just before 2 p.m. the President of the Tribunal, speaking from lengthy notes, and in a low muttering tone, delivered the verdict. [14] With the exception of Cianetti, who was sentenced to thirty years' imprisonment, the others, including those who were not under detention, were condemned to death.

The accused heard the verdict with shocked astonishment. To them there had been an element of farce in the trial from the beginning, and the enigmatic lack of any sign from the Duce had given them a certain encouragement.

De Bono and Marinelli had not properly understood or heard the sentence. The former leant over enquiringly to Ciano, who, pointing at Cianetti, answered, 'Only he is saved: for us it is finished,' and then he crossed himself.[15]

Marinelli turned to Ciano, 'And for me, what have they decided?' 'Death, as for the rest of us,' was the reply. Marinelli fainted.[16]

Crowds gathered outside the Castelvecchio as the news reached the city, and the prisoners were locked under guard in a room for some hours before returning to their cells, on the pretext that they might be lynched by the Fascist action squads.

Formal requests for an appeal to the Duce were signed by all, Ciano agreeing only under pressure from his lawyer, who begged him not to abstain and prejudice the position of the others.

The Duce's secretariat had been in constant telephonic communication throughout the trial with the Prefecture in Verona. Dolfin brought the news of the sentences to Mussolini, and stayed with him for an hour talking in his office. 'The dilemma which I put to the Grand Council was clear. The vote for Grandi's motion meant to open the crisis of the régime and of my succession: in other words, to throw oneself into the abyss. Grandi, Bottai, Albini and the others knew this very well, and had deliberately provoked the catastrophe . . . Ciano was not unaware of these aims either, and played the last round with them.' The Duce did however add that Marinelli, Gottardi, and probably De Bono were not conscious of what they were doing.[17]

But in any event Mussolini showed no sign of intervening. The personal issue was resolved before the trial began. 'For me Ciano has been dead for some time.' He showed no interest in the mechanics of the procedure now set in motion.[i]

It was the personal responsibility and intention of Pavolini and the Party to put the finishing touches to this political vendetta. It merely remained to set up the machinery. In theory the Special Tribunals acted under military law. It would therefore be logical that the highest military authority, in this instance the territorial command of the provinces of Venice, should give the orders to carry out the executions. This would have added the convenience of implicating the Army in the trial. The General commanding the local district was therefore summoned by Pavolini on the evening of January 11 to Verona, but rejected every argument. The Army was in the process of being organised, and the territorial command was merely concerned with recruiting!

Pavolini felt that, after this rebuff, he should call on the Minister of Justice, Pisenti, and drove to Brescia for this purpose. A strange scene took place. Pisenti, on learning of the refusal of the military authorities to touch the affair, said that he could accept the appeals for clemency, and it would then be his duty to take them immediately to the Duce. Pavolini intervened excitedly in the conversation, shouting several times, 'It is absolutely necessary to leave Mussolini right out of it.' [18]

Pavolini now faced the decision that as Secretary of the Party he would himself reject the appeals 'as the whole of this affair has always exclusively concerned the Party'. He felt, however, the need for a final consultation with Buffarini as Minister of the Interior, and, after midnight, drove to Maderno. After persuasion, Pavolini agreed that the political authorities as such in their civilian aspect could not carry out the formal responsibility of executions, and it was agreed to turn to the highest Militia authority in Verona, the Inspector of the territorial zone, a senior officer of the Republican Guard. The latter was roused by telephone and at first refused to get out of bed. Pavolini returned hastily to Verona, and after severe bullying in the Prefec-

i. On January 10, the German Embassy reported that the Fascist chief of Verona had informed them that 'he has orders to prepare for the executions early on the eleventh but expects only one death sentence'. German Collection. Bock telegram, January 10, 1944. Bock was chargé d'affaires in Rahn's absence.

ture, the Inspector signed the rejection of the appeals and the order to carry out the execution at the rifle range at Verona at 8 o'clock that morning.

It seems that Frau Beetz had become the confidant of both Count and Countess Ciano, and that she felt a sad and real conflict of loyalties. She continued to report once a week to her superiors on her conversations with Ciano in his cell, and at the same time she acted as a confidential link between the prisoner and his wife.

According to her superior, General Harster, she called on him in his office on December 28 with the following proposal. As the outcome of the imminent trial was not in doubt, the inevitable fate of Ciano would certainly provoke the publication in America and England of the diaries and papers which it was the mission of Frau Beetz herself to locate. There was no time to lose, and the only solution was through German intervention to barter Ciano's life for the documents. Harster claims that he cabled Kaltenbrunner and received the same day a favourable reply. An operation was to be mounted to kidnap Ciano from prison. Frau Beetz informed both Ciano and his wife, who at once accepted the plan.

The hidden material was collected by a friend of Countess Ciano from a villa in Rome. Certain documents were handed to Frau Beetz, and the rest retained by the Countess.

On January 6 Hitler telephoned personally to Harster ordering him categorically to suspend the kidnapping operation which was about to take place. Frau Beetz was obliged to inform Ciano. On the following day his wife arrived at the rendezvous in Verona fixed in the plan, and waited in vain. She finally discovered Frau Beetz in her hotel room, and learnt the news.[19]

Shortly afterwards Edda Ciano decided on an alternative plan—flight to Switzerland. Before leaving, she wrote letters to the German military commander in Northern Italy, to the Fuehrer and to the Duce, and it was to Frau Beetz that she confided them through an intermediary.

The last session of the court had closed on the morning of January 10. As Kaltenbrunner reported later to Hitler's headquarters, 'At this moment took place the attempt of the Countess to flee from Verona, and elude our observations. Through a confidant, she pushed under the door of my agent, Frau B(eetz) letters with the following text: [20]

1. *Letter to German Military Commander, Italy:*
'General,
For the second time I have relied on the word of the Germans, with the result which you know. This time it is enough. If what I was once promised is not done, I will unleash the most frightful campaign against the Axis and make use of all the evidence which I possess and all I know. My conditions: within three days from the moment these letters are handed over by

Frau B., my husband must be in front of the military station in Berne, and accompanied only by Frau B. between 10 o'clock in the morning and 5 o'clock in the afternoon. If this is carried out in complete loyalty, we will retire into private life and no more will be heard of us.

'Frau B. will be handed the diaries by my husband on the same day. I enclose two letters on the same subject to the Fuehrer and to the Duce. Forward them immediately together with a copy of this letter.'

2. *Letter to the Fuehrer.*
'Fuehrer,
For the second time I believed your word, and for the second time I have been deceived. Only the fact that our soldiers have fallen side by side on the battlefields has hitherto restrained me from going over to the enemy. If my husband is not released on the conditions which I have specified to your general, no further consideration will hold me back. For some time the documents have been in the hands of persons who are empowered only to make use of them if anything should happen to my husband or to me, my children and family. But if, as I hope, my conditions are accepted and we are left in peace in the future, you will not hear from us again.
'I am grieved to have to take this step, but you will understand.'
EDDA CIANO.

3. *Letter to the Duce.*
'Duce,
I have waited until today for you to show me the slightest feeling of humanity and friendliness. Now it is enough. If Galeazzo is not in Switzerland in three days according to the conditions which I have stipulated to the Germans, I shall make merciless and clearly documented use of all that I know. In the opposite case, if we are left in peace and security (from consumption to car accident) you will hear no more of us.'
EDDA CIANO.

End of telegram:
'The death sentences followed at 10 p.m. and will be carried out by shooting about 9 a.m. tomorrow.'
signed: KALTENBRUNNER.

Frau Beetz passed these letters at once to her superior in Verona, General Harster, who sent them on to General Wolff. The letter to Mussolini reached its destination during the night.

According to Wolff, the Duce telephoned him about 5 a.m. and asked for advice whether or not he should intervene. Wolff claims that he answered that he could not form any official opinion, but that privately he would be against any interference.

The German authorities had already received instructions to keep clear of the whole affair. Wolff's own final gesture was to withdraw the S.S. guards from Ciano's cell during the course of the small hours.

The scene during the last night in the prison at Verona has been described by the chaplain, Don Chiot.[21] He hastened to the cells on hearing that the accused had been brought back from the Castelvecchio. He found Ciano in his cell 'pale, but his pupils sparkling as if with suppressed rage'. Ciano asked to take communion. The S.S. guards intervened, and pushed the priest down the corridor. Perhaps they conceived of some suicide pact and concealed poison. It needed Frau Beetz's intervention to allow Don Chiot to minister to the prisoners who were released from their cells, and were able to congregate together. Some gathered round De Bono. Ciano kept to himself.

A German S.S. officer was instructed to attend at the Scalzi prison at 5 a.m. on January 11 'and to witness their execution'. In his subsequent report to his superiors, he described the final scene: [22]

'As the execution had originally been fixed for dawn the condemned men were already awaiting their removal from the gaol. The director of the prison had given them permission to walk about in the corridors and talk to each other. With the exception of Marinelli, who had broken down completely and lamented without cease, all the men displayed calm and self-control. Marshal de Bono and Count Ciano were particularly self-possessed. When the arrival of the Chief of Province, expected at 6 a.m., did not materialize and had been three hours delayed, mounting excitement became perceptible among the prisoners; it could evidently be ascribed to their assumption that a favourable reaction to their petitions for clemency must be causing the delay.

'Shortly before 9, the Chief of Province of Verona appeared in the company of officials and agents of the local Questura, members of the Special Tribunal and a handful of civilians who were unknown to me. The Public Prosecutor had revealed to the condemned men that their appeals for mercy had been refused. When Ciano had been taken over by the Chief of Province, and escorted from the prison, I declared our watch over and dismissed the guard.[j]

The final arrangements passed in sordid confusion. Judges, police officials, and armed guards began to throng the prison. The condemned men were thrust into their cells and manacled. An untidy procession, headed by Don Chiot, filed into the courtyard, Ciano was cursing loudly, and Marinelli in a state of collapse. At De Bono's instance, Ciano quietened, and turning to the chaplain said, 'We have all made mistakes, and we are all swept away by the same gale. Tell my family that I die without rancour against anyone'.

j. The German S.S. guard was mounted in the prison solely for the purpose of watching Ciano.

The final scene is described in the German report:

'I accompanied the Chief of Province and his retinue in the prisoners' vehicle to the scene of the execution, a shooting range in the Forte San Procolo, a suburb of Verona. I should note that on arriving at the prison the Prefect had asked me whether I would be present at the execution, and I confirmed this.

'The firing squad consisted of a detachment of militia some twenty-five men strong. The execution took place in the following manner. The criminals were made to sit back to front on a chair, i.e. with the back of the chair facing forwards so that their own backs were exposed to the firing squads. Their hands were tied to the back of the chair. In the case of Marshal De Bono, who was furthest away from where I was standing, I gathered from his head-shakings and reluctance that he was refusing to be bound and only agreed to it after some persuasion. The only prisoner who caused trouble was again Marinelli, who had to be bound by force by several people and shrieked and moaned the whole time. The others maintained a calm demeanour. The firing-squad took up their positions in two rows fifteen paces behind the prisoners, their small Italian rifles loaded and at the ready. At the word of command the men simultaneously opened fire on the five prisoners, the front row from a kneeling, the back row from a standing position. Just before the order to fire was given one of the condemned men, either Gottardi or Pareschi, shouted: "Long live Italy! Long live the Duce!" After the first salvo four of the prisoners fell to the ground, taking their chairs with them, while one remained sitting on his chair quite unaffected, to judge from his posture. From the distance at which I was standing I could not make out whether he had been kept erect by sheer equilibrium or whether he had not been hit at all.

'The men lying on the ground had been so inaccurately hit that they were writhing and screaming. After a short embarrassed pause a few more shots were fired from the ranks of the firing-squad at the man still on the chair and the others on the ground. Finally the cease-fire was given, and the men were finished off with pistols by the commander of the squad and a few other militiamen.

'When Ciano's death and that of the other prisoners had been confirmed I left the place of execution. Apart from the Chief of Province, his officials and the members of the Special Tribunal, the execution was witnessed by several militia officers, a number of civilians who were unknown to me and a few German anti-aircraft troops. The progress of the execution was filmed by a militia officer apparently attached to some propaganda unit.'

The news was broadcast, heralded by the playing of the Fascist anthem. The Duce was enraged on hearing the manner of the announcement. 'The

Italians love to show off on every occasion. They are either savages or buffoons.' [23]

His private desire for details of the executions and the behaviour of the condemned do not belong to history, and the accounts of his talks with Don Chiot and with General Montagna contribute little further to the study of his personality.

Some months later, at the end of May 1944, Mussolini received a personal letter from the former Spanish Foreign Minister, Serrano Suner, deprecating the 'political error' of Ciano's death. On June 11 Mussolini replied, 'I have sometimes thought that the end of Count Ciano would have particularly saddened you, and this I understand. In the many agitations of my life, what happened at Verona has been the most dramatic chapter. Sentiment and *raison d'état* have sharply collided in my spirit.' [24]

There was no formal German comment on the Verona executions, but only excited alarm at the disappearance of Countess Ciano. The machinery of the German security services was alerted by Kaltenbrunner throughout Northern Italy,[25] and particularly along the Swiss frontier. Wolff was even instructed to enquire of the Duce whether he had any information.

'I learn,' wrote Kaltenbrunner on January 12, 'that yesterday's conversation between General Wolff and the Duce passed off in an exceptionally friendly manner.

'The Duce declared that he had no idea where his daughter was, as contact between him and her had been completely broken off since just before Christmas. He asked that every effort be made to search for her, and that he should be informed of the success. In event of catching her, he asked for his daughter to be brought to him.

'Wolff answered that if she were caught, she must naturally remain under arrest for the duration of the war. The Duce thought that in any case she had not left Italy, but that she was staying with Spanish friends in Italy . . .'

The Duce seems to have taken a brief malicious pleasure in his daughter's disappearance.

Rahn also saw him on the day of the executions, and on January 14 was able to elucidate the remaining mystery of Edda Ciano.

'It can be taken as proved that Countess Ciano crossed the Swiss frontier on foot on January 9. She equally succeeded, through a priest, in bringing her children to Switzerland. Count Ciano, as the other condemned, was induced to sign a plea for mercy before his execution. The forwarding of these appeals was hindered by Pavolini and Ricci.

'On the night before his death, Ciano had expressed himself very impartially and quietly about Germany, but in terms of wild hatred about the Duce. The publication of his diaries deposited in Switzerland will unmask the Duce as the greatest traitor. He died worthily and well. I met the Duce himself on the day of the execution, and he was completely calm, sure, and composed. He stressed his intention to proceed with the punishment of guilty industrialists, generals, and members of the Fascist Party. They must pay for their conduct just as the responsible politicians had done . . .' k

On the same morning Frau Beetz sought an interview with the German Ambassador. She wished to make her report. She was in tears and near collapse.[26]

In a brilliant dispatch to the Duce from Berlin, Anfuso summarized the German official reactions to these proceedings.

'As I told you in person, the Verona trial was for the Germans a sort of touchstone of the possibilities of revolution in Republican Italy. Later, the responsible circles said that the Verona trial was an internal Italian question. It is clear, however, that the Reich political leaders considered that it could only end in a death sentence. In their eyes, the capitulation of Italy, which was a very great threat to the existence of Germany as a state, derived from the fact that some of the Fascist leaders had been found wanting. This had to be punished. It can be added that the two régimes were too alike, especially formally and externally, for the German people not to draw comparisons between the Italian and German situations. And since they reason along general lines, and according to a direct conception of the world in Germany, members of the Grand Council had to be punished as examples not only to the Italian masses, but also to the Germans.

'The Fuehrer and Ribbentrop had spoken to me of Count Ciano bitterly, but without hatred. For them, there no longer existed a Ciano case but a general phenomenon of a political nature which had to be resolved in conformity with their political interests, so that the only thing which amazed the German leaders was that public opinion in the new Italy treated the punishment of those responsible for the capitulation so circumspectly. The harm which Badoglio's *coup d'état* and the consequent events had done to Italy, the blood which had flowed because of her, the danger which European civilization was in, were, according to the opinion of the great German political organs, such that punishment was no longer a question of persons, but a reaction of the State in self-defence. In fact, when it came to the execution—that is, when the penalty had been paid for what was a very serious political crime—I heard many people who, referring to the terrible tragedy which was weighing our country down, uttered a few words of sympathy for Count Ciano, whose marked intelligence and handsome appearance were admired in Germany. The connection of his name with so

k. Dr Rahn has since told the author that at this meeting with Mussolini, the latter was very downcast at Ciano's execution and that if he had known beforehand of the appeal for clemency he would have granted it. German Collection. Rahn telegram, January 14, 1944.

many recent events in German history had created a halo of sympathy for him which in the heart of a people like this, had not faded away.

'I repeat on the other hand that the opinion of this ruling class on the political crime of which the nineteen members of the Grand Council were guilty, is different and resolute: that the crime is not only condemned, but they are asking here why it was not condemned before. The fact that the Italian people have reacted with such a severe sentence has amazed people here, because until the last moment they believed that the traditional Italian tolerance would move the hearts of the judges at Verona, also on this occasion.

'Vice versa, the execution proved how much the Italian soul has been upset and almost changed by the tragedy which has hit our country: and, besides respect for our misfortunes, a feeling of understanding has arisen in Germany for this great unhappy people, which is acting against its feelings and traditions in an attempt to recover its national life, and everything it has lost.

'The editions of the morning newspapers carrying the news of the sentence sold out very quickly: this is almost unheard of in Germany, where the public now reacts in exactly the same way to each day's events. There is no feeling of satisfaction or revenge, rather of deep commiseration for the condemned: but at the same time, of admiration for the Italian gesture which signifies the condemnation of a political class of its own blood, which had written an ungrateful, insouciant, and despicable page in Italian history. I have not heard one harsh word for the condemned men. Rather, all the Germans I have seen in the last few days were aware of the great grief every Italian had felt in seeing the traditional physiognomy of Italy distorted by her need to live, and the respect due to the dead.

'In any case, there can be no doubt that the Verona trials have revealed here that Republican Italy has cut its link with the past, and intends to be near to Germany always and in every way.' [27]

The Verona trials in January 1944 had been produced as a set piece both to assuage a vendetta and as a symbolic exculpation of those numerous beneficiaries of Fascism, major and minor, who, while not being directly guilty of active disloyalty to the Duce, had not fulfilled their duty in the critical hours of July 25. The choice of victims for sacrifice, apart from Ciano, had been arbitrary. It is of curious and unexplained significance that although they did not vote for Grandi's motion at the meeting of the Grand Council, the two most responsible of the Party figures—Scorza as Secretary, and Galbiati as Commander of the Militia—whose positions made them by their office the defenders of the régime and who had capitulated to Badoglio by correspondence during the course of July 25, were not included in these trials.

There is no clear evidence as yet on this matter. Galbiati was never even arrested, though in spite of his attempts at self-justification after September

1943 in memoranda sent to the Duce, he was never employed again under the new Republic. Scorza, on the other hand, had been arrested and was brought to trial at Parma in April 1944. Mussolini took a special interest in these proceedings, and told Rahn that although he was most anxious to review personally with Hitler the experience of the first months of the Republic, he must wait until the end of the case against Scorza.

According to Rahn, Mussolini was 'favourable to Scorza and thinks him honest'. He was also interested in what further evidence might come out on the events of July 25. After Scorza's acquittal, Pavolini explained to Rahn that the former had not been acquitted of 'political responsibility'. His motive was no different from that of Grandi in its demand for the continuance of the war. Scorza too had equally foreseen the criticism launched against the Duce and his removal. The main case against him was his telegram of July 26, 1943, ordering the Fascist Party organizations to take no action. According again to Pavolini, the break between Scorza and the Duce had dated already 'from April 11, 1943'. (sic)[1]

Rahn reported, however, that in conversation with the Duce it was clear that the latter 'wanted the acquittal of Scorza and even influenced it'.[28]

But the reasons for this attitude of Mussolini towards Scorza are not clear. It is not impossible that in the hours following the meeting of the Grand Council Scorza was party to some ingenious solution propounded by the Duce, or indeed that there was some previous collusion between them in provoking the immediate events leading up to the meeting of the Grand Council. There is also the unexplained possibility that Scorza knew too much and that the farce of his trial was a foregone conclusion. In any event, his acquittal closed the cycle of trials relating to the events of July 25.[m]

1. The date of his appointment as Party Secretary.
   m. It is equally unexplained why Scorza was not arrested along with the other Fascist personalities by Badoglio at the end of August.

APPENDIX

The Cavallero Memorandum

Forte Boccea.
27 August, 1943.

This document was included among the papers selected personally by Mussolini and which were passed to the President of the Special Tribunal, Vecchini, on December 2, 1943. Two manuscript copies are listed: (1) Deposition of Marshal Cavallero dated August 27, 1943 (from Forte Boccea?) on eleven manuscript pages in an envelope headed 'High Command of the Head of the Military Intelligence Service' and enclosed in another envelope inscribed 'Private Secretary of the Head of the Government' and in Badoglio's handwriting 'Deposition of Marshal Cavallero'.

(2) The same document written in General Carboni's handwriting.

The text, which has been published in several secondary sources, reads as follows: [n]

I

'. . . In November of last year, at the time when his Excellency Mussolini was seriously ill, the worst had to be considered. In my capacity as Chief of the General Staff, I was anxious about this, and gave instructions for such an eventuality to General Magli,[o] to the Chief of the Army Staff, General Ambrosio, and to the Undersecretary of War, General Scuero. There were two meetings for this purpose. I stated clearly that they were to be prepared to preserve order in the country, and first of all in Rome, so as to hand it over to the government, which would decide to whom to entrust the civil administration and the military command.

'I envisaged that such a person would be His Excellency Marshal Badoglio, and I told my subordinates that we would all place ourselves under his orders.

'An unexpected interference of the Militia in the affair spoilt things a little; and the situation was in any case settled by the recovery of the invalid. The question did not arise again during December and January when attention was concentrated on the war in Africa.

'At the end of January, I left the command.

'Nevertheless, the problem of the removal of H.E. Mussolini at least from the military command, continued to exercise me. It was my view that, when Tunisia had fallen, it would be the moment to clear up the situation. I remember having spoken of this to various people, and even with insistence. I also spoke to Lieutenant-Colonel Roberto di San Marzano, repeatedly. I must add here that . . . I had already talked to this officer in November about what I had been preparing. My relations with him were determined by the fact that he was attached to the staff of His Royal Highness the Prince of Piedmont. These contacts continued until the evening of July 25. The problem was also discussed with Marquis Giovanni Visconti Venosta, an old war comrade, well known to H.E. Badoglio, and we agreed that our thoughts must be passed on to the highest quarters. Visconti Venosta assured me that, for his part, he had seen to this.

'Then came the attack on Sicily. The situation became increasingly urgent. Visconti Venosta and I thought—and today I admit that we were wrong—that it would be useful to pass on our ideas to the top.

'These ideas took the following shape:

n. Italian Collection. File on Verona Trials. Vecchini's receipt for a set of documents received from the Private Secretary to the Duce. Cavallero's memorandum has been printed, for example, in an appendix in Cersosimo *op cit* p. 283 ff, and also, together with an exculpatory commentary, in Canevari *op cit.*

o. Officer attached to the Italian General Staff. See Cavallero *op cit* p. 62.

'His Majesty the King, who had delegated the military command to H.E. Mussolini, could revoke the delegation. By so doing, and by declaring a state of war throughout Italian territory, all powers could be handed over to the army. The rest would follow automatically. My friend Visconti Venosta and myself were in full accord in maintaining that the government could not be entrusted to any other than Marshal Badoglio.

'In order to pass on these thoughts to the top, Visconti Venosta asked me if I could talk to the Grand Admiral (Thaon de Revel). The latter had always been very well disposed towards me, and I therefore agreed. I had several conversations with the Grand Admiral, and found him completely of our way of thinking.

'I had the juridical and constitutional aspect of the problem studied by the Counsel at the Court of Appeal, Giovanni Provera, my childhood companion. The Grand Admiral kindly wrote down at my dictation a summary of this study and I understood that he would take the matter up at once (i.e. with the King). This happened about Whitsun. In the meantime I carried out a modest propaganda in the above sense. In order to limit the number of persons whom I quote, I would refer to Senator Luigi Burgo [p] . . . Over a period of three months Burgo was kept informed by me of the development of my thoughts, and also partly of the action which I was taking. He was enthusiastic about the programme and went so far as to tell me that, in case of necessity, he would put at my disposal the sum of one hundred millions and even more, to finance an eventual movement. Naturally, in thanking him for his generous offer, I replied that there was no need for any money.

'I learnt in the meantime of growing agitation in the ranks of the Army: I was terrified at this as I maintained, and still do, that any such movement was constitutionally illegal and would lead to disaster. I did not fail to express my view particularly to H.E. Ambrosio and found him fully aware of this point.

'A conversation with H.E. Ambrosio on the general theme dealt with here took place, I think, about May, when I went to see him at his request on a service matter. I opened my heart to him, and told him what I was doing, and forecast, as I was confident, that the desired event would take place. He told me that a warning of seven days would be required. I pointed out that it would be an hour's warning . . . as to the impatience of some, on which I had information, I found H.E. Ambrosio aware and determined to prevent it.

'H.E. Ambrosio came to my house at the beginning of July to visit the quarters which I had to hand over to him. On this occasion I returned to the subject and told him that the new head of the government would certainly be Marshal Badoglio and that I, in the meantime, placed myself at the

p. The paper magnate. These references to the unfortunate senator led to his arrest, and imprisonment, at the time of the Verona trials. For details see G. Silvestri, *Albergo agli Scalzi*, p. 161 ff.

orders of H.E. Ambrosio for any eventuality; for which he expressed his gratitude . . .

II

'I would point out incidentally that my relations with Farinacci originated in family contacts, when he was a young man, with my wife's relations . . .

'I would specify that I hardly saw Farinacci before my appointment as Chief of the General Staff, and equally during that period, except for the Albanian episode, when he was stationed there.

'When I left my post, we met a couple of times before July; our relations were somewhat cold. But at the time of Scorza's appointment as Secretary of the Party, I was very interested in his (Farinacci's) statement that Scorza was firmly against the Duce. Although I was concerned with following this up, I avoided making closer contacts. It was only after the stormy meeting of the Party leaders with the Duce on July 15 that Farinacci wished to see me, and put me in the picture.

'Farinacci was quite clear that the Duce must give up the military command, and that this should be resumed by the Sovereign. This was for me the essential point from which everything could spring. But as I was in the dark as to what was being planned elsewhere. I could not think of a more radical solution which no one expected. Into the other Fascist camp I could not penetrate, because the situation was dominated by persons hostile to me (Ciano).

'When, on the evening of July 25, I was able to see Colonel di San Marzano at my house, I explained the situation to him, and he took some notes, and then left my house a few minutes before my arrest. I thought that my arrest had been ordered by H.E. Mussolini. Only later did I learn the truth. My relations with Farinacci during this period were limited to working out, and strengthening in his mind, the idea of transferring the military command to the Sovereign.

III

'After leaving my post, my relations with the German authorities, direct and indirect, were simply cut off. Up to today I have not seen again either any German commander or subordinate . . . My only meeting with the German Ambassador took place at Farinacci's house a couple of days before the Grand Council at the request of Farinacci, and I was by deliberate intent only a passive onlooker.

'*Contents of the conversation.* Farinacci made a violent attack on the Duce: Von Mackensen parried. Farinacci went further, and Mackensen asked him to stop. Then he said that he had anyway made the same criticisms on his own account to the Fuehrer and that the latter had made them a subject of remark to the Duce at Feltre. Then Farinacci asked when one could expect reinforcements, particularly in the air, from Germany along the lines, not known to us, made by H.E. Ambrosio at Feltre. Mackensen was vague in replying, referring to the conditions, or rather prerequisites, which the Fuehrer had laid down as to be carried out before sending any troops or planes: he did not specify these conditions. There was reference, I think by Mackensen, to a joint command, with a veiled tendency towards the prevalence of the German side; to which I said that this could not possibly work, and that, in my opinion, at the most one might consider attaching a subordinate German command to the Italian.

'Mackensen said that he would refer the substance of the conversation to H.E. Bastianini.

'This is my only contact, and as will be seen quite harmless, with the German authorities from January until now.'

CHAPTER SEVEN

BANDENKRIEG

THE BEGINNINGS of resistance to the neo-Fascist régime set up at Salò in October did not immediately present a military problem. Small bands appeared immediately after the collapse of the Italian Army in September, and particularly in the area of Piedmont and the Alpine valleys, where units were early formed by enterprising officers and other ranks of the Royal Army. Alongside these embryo formations developed slowly a parallel and distinct organization of civilian origin, quickly breaking down into groupings of a political complexion. It took some months for the form of partisan organization in the hilly regions of Piedmont, and then a little later in the Apennines, to assume an operational character.

In the cities equally during the same weeks resistance activity developed and the problem faced of attempting to organize the industrial workers of the North as a central means of sabotage of any Fascist restoration. This was the task of the cells of the different opposition party organizations which had begun to take shape since the events of the previous July. Led in particular by the Communists, picked units in the cities and small towns of a handful of men began to carry out special terrorist tasks again the renascent Fascist Party organizations. The historical lessons for such kind of activity had already been demonstrated by the early action squads of Fascism itself against the Socialist and Communist structures in the months before the March on Rome in 1922.

It was not until the turn of the year, however, that the new Fascist Republican government showed concern at the internal threat of rebellion against the establishment of its authority. The first sign of alarm appeared in the more traditionally accepted field of strike action. At the end of November 1943, the Communist-led underground committees in Turin launched a dress rehearsal and succeeded in bringing out on strike some 50,000 workers in the

Fiat factories, exploiting essential economic grievances in regard to wages and rations and lack of transport.

Such an example might well be infectious, and the German authorities who were in effective control of Turin reacted quickly to this menacing phenomenon. The writ of the Duce barely as yet ran in the city, and even the Prefect himself had been nominated by the Germans. Law and order in the Piedmontese capital was thus essentially in German hands, and a special military representative of the German authorities in Italy, General Zimmermann, was in charge. But apart from a few armed units he had at his disposal only some 120 German military police to deal with a city containing over 200,000 industrial workers. There could be no question of any punitive action being conducted by the Italian authorities. As Ribbentrop telegraphed to Rahn: 'I agree that you should bring strikers before courts martial and arrest a thousand here and there as an example and send them as military internees to Germany. The Fuehrer further empowers you to arrest ringleaders and shoot them out of hand as Communists.

'As to the threat to remove machinery to Germany from the factories on strike, I ask you to desist, as such a measure cannot be carried out with the necessary speed.' [1]

The Turin strikes were also significant in drawing attention to the total lack of any effective military or police forces at the disposal of the new Italian government, and the lessons of Turin formed the subject of Mussolini's instructions to his Ambassador in Berlin, Anfuso, to request at once from Hitler a supply of weapons for the Italian police, and also to raise the release at least of some elements among the mass of Italian military internees in Germany for this purpose, and also—rather plaintively—the suggestion that on future occasions the German officials might work closer with the Italian authorities.

The German response was unsympathetic. The Commander of the S.S. in Italy, General Wolff, was instructed to take up the question of arming the police. Anfuso was told that Rahn had given the Italian authorities in Turin 'every chance to handle the strikes, but they totally failed. The Duce himself had been constantly informed of what measures the Germans had taken, and his own instructions often went astray and only worsened the situation.' As to the question of releasing some of the military internees in Germany, this would be examined.[2]

But even supposing that the equipment and man-power were available to set up an effective Italian police force and equip at least a few armed units, there was as yet no agreement in the Duce's entourage as to the ultimate control over any such formations.

Apart from the Turin strikes, the Communist action squads in the cities now concentrated on discouraging the restoration of the Fascist Party by attacks on leading members and officials. These increased precisely in the weeks following the strikes, and were also to coincide with the Verona Congress. For example, in late November twenty-eight leading local Fascist personalities were assassinated in this way, and Pavolini ordered armed countermeasures. As Rahn pointed out, these murders took place not in areas where the rebels were strong, 'but where the Fascist Party has made the most rapid progress in reconstruction. I regard the sharp reaction of the Fascists as an encouraging sign of their incipient energy.' [3]

These early partisan actions led to an increased flare-up in the activities of the rebel bands, particularly in Piedmont and the North-west, which could no longer be ignored by Mussolini if he had any intention of establishing an effective administration at all. On paper, his solution was as usual deceptively simple: The action squads of the Communists must be dealt with by their Fascist counterparts, on the same pattern as the civil war of the early 1920s.

The first reaction of this kind took place in the middle of the Verona Congress, when a punitive expedition of old Fascists was sent to Ferrara to avenge the murder of the local Party chief. The letting loose of the Fascist squads, now consisting of middle-aged men or refugees from those areas of Italy now under Allied control, heightened the confusion of authority and hindered the reconstruction of an effective Italian police force, a situation already bedevilled by the wholesale defection of the essentially monarchist Military Police after the fall of the Fascist régime in July. As the only administrator of any experience in the new administration, Buffarini Guidi pressed the consequences of this situation from the beginning. It was the Ministry of the Interior, not the Army or the Party Militia, or worst of all the Germans, who should be responsible for the maintenance of law and order, and this included the suppression of internal rebellion.

At the funeral in December of the Fascist Party chief in Milan, likewise assassinated by Communist punitive squads, Buffarini had the opportunity to report on this issue to Mussolini. It appears that two shots had been fired from a window at the funeral procession, and the Fascist action squads in the street fired over five thousand rounds indiscriminately during the next quarter of an hour. Buffarini pointed out that as yet these units had no legally constituted basis at all, but where they did exist as spontaneously recruited local formations the men were completely out of hand, and the neo-Fascist Party itself had neither the means nor the prestige to control them. One such autonomous formation named after the former Party Secretary, Muti, who had been assassinated by the Badoglio police in August, was particularly out of control.

Buffarini himself had gone to Milan to inspect the situation. Party officials dared not show their faces at the Headquarters of the Muti, who threatened 'a March on Garda to remove the government'. In order to preserve some semblance of order, other squads had been ordered by the Party into Milan, particularly from Cremona where Farinacci was sulking, as so often in previous years, in his former political fief. He had been asked to intervene in the affair, but on learning that his arch-enemy Buffarini was present in the city, he failed to come. The lesson which Buffarini drew from this characteristic situation was the need at once to arm the police of Milan. The existing force consisted of some nine hundred men, of whom one hundred were not armed at all, even with a pistol, of which the total reserve stocks available were less than eighty.[4]

If the action squads of the Party were unable to deal with their now developing partisan counterparts, the newly-created Militia of Ricci was even less likely to deal with the partisan phenomenon in the countryside. This did not, however, deter Mussolini from issuing his instructions. The National Republican Guard, as it was now called, had been set up at the end of November 1943 'as the fourth armed force of the Republic'.

It was formed originally out of those cadres left in the North who were prepared to work under the new régime and scattered elements of the old Fascist Militia disbanded in the previous July. But the basic dilemma of the construction of any armed force in the new régime was that by far the largest part of the age-groups between 20 and 40 were in internment camps in Germany, and although the new National Republican Guard recruited on paper, together with its original cadres, some 150,000 men, many of these were boys between the ages of 15 and 17 without any discipline and military training. This military force was under the command of General Wolff, and therefore under the German S.S., and its functions were to deal with the new and regional menace of partisan activity.

As Mussolini wrote to Ricci on February 9, 'From the reports of the National Republican Guard it appeared that the "rebel phenomenon" has now assumed in central Italy an aspect even more disturbing than that in the Alpine valleys. In the latter areas the phenomenon is a peripheral one; in Central Italy it lies in the immediate rear of the front line . . . and of communications between North and South, between the Po Valley and Rome . . .

'A plan of action is therefore needed, and mobile forces are necessary. . . . Any further delay would aggravate the situation.' [5]

In the desperate search for man-power, recourse had also been made to switching those few trained elements of the former Marine Commandos who were to play a rather special rôle in the development of the Republican armed forces. Already in December the head of the Republican Navy, a very nominal body, was instructed to place one thousand of these men at Ricci's disposal, 'to liberate certain provinces of Piedmont from the so-called partisans, allies of the enemy . . . There is no time to lose. By March the rear lines of communication must be in perfect order.' [6] This move by Mussolini had unexpected and disturbing effects in the intricate field of confused rival and overlapping pockets of authority in the Northern provinces.

The lack of prestige and control by a central administration was the main characteristic of the Salò régime throughout its brief history, and inevitably resulted in a persistent and continuous atmosphere of 'Affairs, Plots, and, in the old Fascist vocabulary, Marches'. The Naval Commandos now split up for the purpose of partisan warfare and, placed under Ricci, led to just one such affair.

These troops had been raised as a quasi-independent private force by Prince Borghese, who had a specially gallant reputation through his exploits against British ships, and in particular his raids on Alexandria and Gibraltar harbours before the collapse of July. The Italian surrender found Borghese at the naval base at La Spezia and with some 1,300 men under his command. The Germans accepted immediately his proposals for creating an independent force under their command, and at the end of September Borghese was sent to discuss arrangements with Doenitz in Berlin. At the end of the month he reported to Mussolini at La Rocca, the latter seems to have been welcoming to this latter-day condottiere, and when the two men met again in November Mussolini said, 'Your "San Marco" must be in the line by the spring.'

It was agreed that Borghese should try and recruit, alongside the nucleus of what he called the 'Decima Mas',[a] Marines for possible land operations under the old Venetian designation of San Marco. By the end of the year Borghese had succeeded in raising some four thousand recruits on the basis of his own personal prestige as a commander, and even got back from the Germans, during his temporary designation by Mussolini as Undersecretary of the Navy, a small token force of Italian submarines and motor torpedo boats. This in fact was the whole of the Italian Republican Navy, and together with the private Marine Commandos represented a certain element of power which could only arouse jealousy in rival circles.

The removal of the Marines to be placed under Ricci's orders inevitably provoked a crisis. This was a deliberate attempt to split up what in effect had become a private army, and Borghese's successor as Undersecretary of the Navy, Ferrini, attempted to go further and sent the recruits enlisted by Borghese for the new San Marco battalions to Germany, for training along with the early call-up. Borghese envisaged his mission essentially as an élite anti-partisan force, to be used immediately for that purpose and ultimately for the defence of the historic frontiers of Venezia Giulia. In a secondary but effective rôle, his original Decima Mas conducted espionage and sabotage activities south of the Apennine front.

A series of reports began to reach Mussolini of Borghese's undisciplined

a. The Tenth Motor Torpedo Boat Flotilla.

activities.[7] Borghese's organization followed familiar lines. 'He has a numerous Intelligence staff and also a political office which indulges in unknown activities and obeys exclusively his personal orders.' He had refused to take any orders from the centre, and his officers, referred to as the party of the holders of the Gold Medal, 'would seem to be assuming supreme command of the Republican Navy'. Several units were already prepared for 'unspecified action'.

Matters came to a head when Borghese's officers arrested the ministerial nominee placed in command of the new Marine battalions. Borghese was away at the time setting up an advance headquarters in Venice, but he immediately assumed responsibility for the action of his subordinates. He was summoned by telegram to report to the Duce, and arrested personally, in true Renaissance fashion, in the latter's ante-room on Ricci's orders before he was able to make his report.

Borghese's activities were the subject of a court of enquiry, the main report submitted being that of the Commander of the National Republican Guard now based at Brescia. Borghese was not only backed by the German naval authorities at La Spezia and the local Italian Prefect, but his own officers threatened to march on Salò and release him.

As usual, the affair fizzled out in mutual recriminations and the usual display of passivity by the Duce, Graziani seems to have mediated between Borghese and Ricci. The former returned to his command and concentrated on what in effect became an almost private war against the partisans ineffectively controlled both by the Germans and the Republican Guard. But he lost his too successful experiment of the San Marco battalions, whose recruits were from now on sent to Germany to form the cadres of a division under the same name under the overall agreement to raise these units in German training camps.

The German military authorities were on their side doing their utmost to prevent the formation of any independent Italian armed force, or indeed the construction of an independent civilian administration. At the end of January Mussolini wrote to Rahn, enclosing a circular which the German military command had sent to the Italian authorities in certain of the Northern provinces, 'without, among other things, informing me or the Minister of the Interior.

'I am sure that you are not aware of an initiative whose nature and breadth exceed the function and responsibilities of a Military Command, while constituting a serious diminution of the authority and prestige of the Fascist Republican Government. The Italian people must not be given the impression that there are two Ministries for every branch of the administration, and therefore two governments.' [8]

Quite apart from the question of the reliability of an Italian Republican military force, there was the inescapable dilemma of the limits of Italian man-power, which was the dismal subject of competition between competing German agencies; the German military authorities in Northern Italy for auxiliary units such as anti-aircraft batteries, the German S.S. Command for units directly under their control for anti-partisan warfare, the local Todt organization for constructing defence works and repairing communications, the local offices of gauleiter Sauckel for recruiting civilian labour for German industry, and the Armament Mission for General Leyers for maintaining an adequate labour force on the spot in Italian war production under German control.

It was not surprising that at the end of January, at a meeting between Rahn, Kesselring, and Graziani, the latter concluded that the German Army was not in favour of large Italian units but only small ones incorporated in the German forces, and, as Rahn pointed out, the recruitment of the four divisions agreed in principle to be trained in Germany would in practice prove difficult without extracting Italian labour from German factories, and such a decision would meet with strong opposition in other German circles.

In fact there was never enough man-power available for any one kind of operation envisaged. It was hoped that the call-up of the new classes in November would create a sufficient reserve for the new Italian Army.[b] Out of 180,000 who received notices to report, some 87,000 appeared; but half of these were immediately taken by the competing claims of the several German agencies, and because of Mussolini's temporary priority given to Ricci and the Republican National Guard, 25,000 men were taken over by him for the anti-partisan struggle 'which is becoming the fiercer—so much so that Ricci has called for the help of the Army', which of course was non-existent. In desperation Graziani attempted to persuade General Leyers to release men from the German-controlled Inspectorate of Labour and the Todt organization, and merely received a rude reply. The only solution, which was one the Germans were not prepared to accept on security grounds, would have been an attempt to recruit on a mass scale from the military internee camps in Germany.

During these early months of the new régime Rahn persisted in his attempts to protect his protégé against the unsympathetic and united attitude of the other German agencies concerned with Italian affairs. This attitude on his part earned him a sharp rebuke from Hitler himself.

'The Fuehrer thought that Ambassador Rahn should be told for God's sake not to be taken in by the Italian soul, and fall into the same mistakes as his predecessors. It was certain once and for all that Italian troops were no longer employable. The best that they could produce were noisy demonstrations which intoxicated the people themselves. A really reliable battleworthy formation could not be set up either by us or our allies. Ambassador Rahn, under

b. For a summary of the position see Appendix to this chapter.

the influence of his surroundings should not lose sight of this sober reality.' [9c]

But the dreary farce continued. At the end of March, with the rising menace of partisan activities, Graziani attempted to get some concessions out of the German authorities in Italy, particularly in terms of releasing clothing and equipment for the new recruits. But the figures produced showed that none of these men were in fact available to Graziani.

Leyers emphasized the low statistics of production. All the Italian arms factories were under direct orders from Berlin. Production of rifles and machine-guns had already ceased owing to lack of supplies and labour difficulties. The factories were being dispersed into the countryside in Northern Italy, but 'the existence of the bands makes production unreliable owing to lack of security'. In addition there were no funds to pay for the orders from the Italian factories, although the Italian Ministry of Finance had promised to settle half of the outstanding arrears.

Italian man-power, which under existing conditions was, on paper, under arms, consisted of 100,000 men incorporated in units under Kesselring's command; 51,000 with the German Air Force on ground and anti-aircraft duties, and a meagre 25,000 to supplement the cadres of the four Divisions under training in Germany. The National Guard possessed 150,000 men on paper, equipped by the German S.S. Command. In the general see-saw of authority, Ricci had been given temporary priority and what was left over of the first call-up, after direct German demands had been met, was taken by the National Guard.

In January one of Graziani's staff officers reported that 'the Republican Guard is generously being given everything at once, and whereas one sees their very youthful recruits clothed and armed from the moment they report, nothing is available, or perhaps after long discussions, for the Army. The continued requests from soldiers and recruits to serve in the German units, gives rise to doubt as to whether Germany wants the setting up of an Army, or at least to delay it as long as possible.' [10]

As Graziani himself put it: 'I have shut my eyes in order to let the Guard be created.' It was never cleared up by Mussolini whether in the last resort Ricci or Graziani was responsible for combating the partisans. His instructions alternated from week to week.

At the end of January 1944, Ricci told Graziani that he had not more than 3,000 men available for the 'struggle against the rebels'.[d] To confuse

c. A typical report to Graziani in January reads: 'It is sad and in no way dignified for us to see Italian soldiers employed on fatigue duties as, for example, tending the gardens and orchards of villas requisitioned by the German commands, pouring petrol and cleaning cars, and other such tasks.' Italian Collection. Report of a Liaison Officer, January 2, 1944.

d. In March, however, Graziani announced at a meeting with the German representatives that he had 'made an agreement with General Wolff to create an organization of 10,000 men against the bands'. 3,000 would be supplied by the Party: the 3,000 men indicated by Ricci by the Republican Guard, and 3,000 from the training depots.

the issue still further, Goering had now come forward with the completely unreal demand for 150,000 recruits for anti-aircraft units, 'to be dressed in blue, for psychological reasons'.[11]

The lack of definition of the specific functions of the various German military agencies in regard to anti-partisan warfare, produced the counterpart to the confusion on the Italian side. Control of anti-rebel operations became the subject of a stiff quarrel between Kesselring and Wolff, which went up to Himmler. The latter stated formally that 'fighting against strikes and bands is the main task of the S.S. and the police, and he sees it as his own original domain which he cannot give up.

'Kesselring on the other hand takes the point of view that in a separate theatre of war like Italy . . . fighting rebellion is closely connected with the conduct of the war, and there must be one command responsible for all areas of military activity. This can only be Army Group South-West, and the senior S.S. and police commander in Italy must remain or be subordinate to him in matters of fighting rebellion. This is all the more required, at least at the moment, as the fighting against the rebels must be, in the last resort, carried out by the Army.'

Rahn reported Kesselring's view in regard to ultimate responsibility, but suggested that Wolff should be responsible for carrying out the task under Kesselring's orders.[e] In areas where there were not enough police forces available, the Army must be responsible for fighting the partisan bands. 'Of particular importance in this connection is the build-up of the new Italian Army in co-operation with the Italian General Staff.'[12]

This was far from what Graziani had hoped would emerge from his conversations to create an independent military machine, and he continually attempted to evade the ultimate onus of combating the partisans.

At his post-war trial in 1947 Prince Borghese thus analysed the mutual responsibilities of the German and Italian Commands. 'In the Italian Social Republic, administrative military arrangements came under Graziani while operational functions in the employment of units came under the German authorities . . . The German commander, Wolff, was responsible for operations for the maintenance of public order. If we wanted to engage our units in war operations, we had to obtain the authorization of the German Command and the same applied in the case of punitive drives and anti-partisan operations, which were exclusively ordered by the above-mentioned German headquarters. I repeat that no unit could take part in the above actions without the orders and consent of the German Commands.'[13]

Quite apart from the limitations of man-power and the failure of recruits to report, the phenomenon of mass desertions to the partisans in the hills as

---

e. Ribbentrop had also pointed out to Rahn that there was a political aspect to fighting the bands and requested that he should be kept fully in the picture. German Collection, Ribbentrop to Rahn, April 19, 1944.

the result of the attempt to call up recruits by the Republican authorities, led to a deterioration of the whole security of the Republic. In April a rash step was taken to enforce brutal sanctions against deserters. These measures merely had the effect of swelling the ranks of the partisan bands in the hills.

These daily frustrations bedevilled Graziani's task as nominal commander of a non-existent army. It must have been a rare and fleeting escape into the realms of theoretical strategy to have discussions in April with the visiting Japanese military representative in Europe, General Shimitsu.

The latter stated that 'the present position on the German Eastern Front was due to the fact that it had long been insufficiently flexible'. Shimitsu conceded the Marshal's objection that the German Army, thanks to an inner cohesion attained by no other force, had so far mastered the situation and prevented the Russians from gaining a strategic victory.

'But he added that in the meantime the Anglo-American forces had succeeded by merely threatening invasion in tying down very powerful German forces in France, and in thus preventing their effective deployment on other fronts. Shimitsu was not convinced that the enemy seriously intended to launch an invasion on the Western Front.[f] In his view a large-scale strategic victory could be scored at the present time only in Italy, but the prospects for it here were extraordinarily good. How long did the Germans intend to keep all their available forces in the West? He was convinced that Germany could last out another ten years of war, but wars were won by offensive action, not through defence. In the long run you could not afford to wait until the enemy took the initiative.

'There was a great deal of talk about these extraordinarily effective new German weapons, rocket missiles of huge dimensions, and mobile weapons controlled by radio. Why were these not being used? People did not believe in them any more.

'Japan would never enter the war against Russia any more than Russia would do so against Japan. Peace was in the interests of both powers. True, Japan had stationed strong forces on all the Manchurian borders, but in view of the general war situation a conflict with Russia would be much too risky for Japan.' Shimitsu then continued:

'There remained the possibility of a separate armistice between Germany and Britain. To Marshal Graziani's objection that this would run counter to the treaties, he replied that in any war one had to be prepared for surprises. The possibility of a German-Russian armistice could also be mentioned. The question was: What kind of separate peace would it be easiest to negotiate?

---

f. Kesselring, however, had expressed the view to Graziani in January that the 'centre of gravity of the war is shifting from the Mediterranean to the Atlantic'. Italian Collection. Kesselring-Graziani meeting, January 21, 1944.

'The Marshal replied that as things now stood a separate peace with Germany would be less to Germany's advantage than to England's, for Russia's advance into the Mediterranean basin, achieved thanks to naval and base treaties with the Badoglio régime in Italy and the latter's recognition of Tito in Yugoslavia, must jeopardize Britain's Mediterranean interests in the highest degree.

'Shimitsu then returned to the allegedly favourable prospects for a German offensive in Italy, which at present offered the sole possibility for a large-scale strategic success and would enable us to regain the strategic initiative.

'Japanese statements of a similar tenor, clearly hinting at the necessity for a German-Russian armistice, have repeatedly come to my knowledge via Italian informants ever since 1942.

'As I see it, there are two main trends in Shimitsu's pronouncements: Anxiety lest Germany should conclude a separate peace with England, and an attempt to parry inclinations to do so by encouraging an offensive against the Anglo-Americans in Italy and simultaneously backing even the remotest chances of peace with Russia.

'He must certainly have taken it for granted that in view of the Marshal's trusted relationship with us his ideas would reach German ears; and he must furthermore have counted on their receiving support, since the Marshal is known to favour offensive action and since the interests of the Italian national government coincide with Japanese aims.' [14]

APPENDIX

Note on the State of the Italian Republican Armed Forces March 1944

A summary report compiled by Marshal Graziani's staff and showing the results of the call-up of the 1924 and 1925 classes in the previous November, gives the following facts and figures as at March 10, 1944.

Army	130,639
Air Force	38,734
	169,373

These included 9,440 volunteers and 18,107 men who had reported under the threat of penalties for desertion. Recruits in units under German command were not included.

It was noted that in the provinces of Umbria and Lazio (round Rome) only 10 per cent of the age groups called up had reported to the depots.

CHAPTER EIGHT

SALÒ AND SOCIALIZATION

•••

THE SOCIALIST REPUBLIC, as set up in September 1943, possessed no administrative structure. The Badoglio government had in the previous July abolished by decree the political institutions of Italian Fascism, and the task of setting up a new machinery of rule in these circumstances could hardly be separated, at least by implication, from a critical reflection upon the historical errors of the last twenty years. Both the institutions and compromises of the Fascist régime passed under a gloomy review.

A central part of the original system had been the Charter of Labour and the Corporate State. This whole organization had been dismantled after July 25, with the exception of the Fascist workers' syndicates, which had nominally remained intact, and it was only necessary to appoint new leaders. But apart from the resurrected neo-Fascist Party, the new Republic possessed no institutions whatsoever. On paper therefore, and ignoring external circumstances, one could experiment in each sphere of government from the beginning and take into account the mistakes and experience of the past.

The Salò Republic from its inception however was plagued by a discordant chorus of criticism from within of all its institutional aspects, and its ultimate failure was total. Such experiments could hardly be conducted when the régime existed in reality on German sufferance, with a shadowy provincial administration in a territory which, for German reasons, must be held as long as possible against the inevitable Allied military invasion of Germany itself.

This brutal fact was cheerfully ignored by those—and they were many in the ranks of the supporters of the new Republic—who believed in the possibilities of a second chance. The most vocal groups of opinion at Salò came from the discarded or defeated elements on the fringes of the original Fascist movement. The debate which raged over the future institutions of the new régime was in the main, therefore, conducted by historically discredited and fragmentary minorities.

Mussolini himself set the tone and direction of discussion in his early broadcast of September 18, and on his own responsibility gave a certain licence to open criticism of previous errors in and limitations of the original Fascist 'system'. In terms of political propaganda of which he was a master he strove to give some hope of an ideal and pristine world which had not been brought into being during the previous twenty years.

From the tactical point of view he was quick to seize on the opportunity to unload the responsibility for many errors on to the Royal government in the South. Events of July 25 had led to the first division of the Italian State since its formation in 1861. The early compromises of Fascism with the Italian monarchy were at one blow outdated. The new Republic could begin with a *tabula rasa*, and most important of all, in psychological terms, the treason of the Italian surrender became the exclusive guilt of the Sovereign. The Republic of Salò was to start its existence without a history, and un-burdened by all the errors of the previous régime. In the competition between North and South for the loyalties of the population, the inevitable central theme must be the issue of socialization. The new régime was republican, but also socialist and revolutionary. It would conduct this central task, which it had abandoned in the compromise with the monarchy in 1922 and failed to press at the time of setting up the machinery of the Corporate State. Here was the great opportunity, and round this subject was fought the main battle of words in the few months during which the new régime was permitted by events to survive.

The first debate was held at the Party congress at Verona in November, and in the speeches of the delegates to the new Party assembly appeared the echoes of those syndicalist, and indeed anarchistic, elements which had played a leading part in the early days of the Fascist Party before the March on Rome, and which had been so formally discarded subsequently. The Corporate State, as set up in the late '20s and early '30s, had avoided two cardinal issues: firstly, the principle of election to offices in the syndicates themselves, and secondly, the parallel existence of a machinery to discipline the relations of capital and labour, together with 'liberal' arrangements in the field of production over which there was no workers' control. The employers' organizations had successfully prevented, during the years of Fascist rule, the application of an 'integral' Corporate State, and the organs and machinery of this structure became in effect an exclusive field of Party patronage, corruption, and control.

On September 26 it had been announced that a single corporation would be set up, controlled by the Party and embracing 'all syndical federations'. Details would be worked out at Party Headquarters. The manifesto as drafted by Pavolini and presented at Verona, merely provoked unprepared and unreal discussion. A free debate could only produce chaos, and with the presence of the new Republican Fascist Party as the unique institution of the new Republic, the Party machine would inevitably take up the same attitude as that of the old, and strive for a monopoly of control over any corporate institutions which might be re-established.

After the Verona meeting the Council of Ministers accepted a decree setting up the new single body. It was significant that on the same day another decree was published establishing a special court to try the 'traitors' of July 25, thus emphasizing the break with a historical past and the unhampered concentration on new institutions.

The fate of this decree was typical of that of all the measures of the new government. Behind a heady debate on the significance and possibilities of the new Socialization lay the brutal reality that the only real asset of the republican régime was its labour force, the ultimate control of which was the only source of political power. Should this be controlled by a civilian bureaucracy, by the machinery of the Party, by the new Republican Army or Militia (and therefore under another guise by the Party), or by the Germans themselves? This was the central issue in the history of Salò.

The prestige of the Duce's rule depended largely on the reconstruction of the armed forces and the re-entry of Italy into the war as an effective ally. The struggle for control of Italian man-power in the provinces remaining to the régime took on inevitably the colour of the historical battle for power which had waged for twenty years within the machinery of the original Fascist Party. Mussolini's method of retaining some control of the situation underwent no change. His solution was to allow independent overlapping and competing organisms to be set up, with the inevitable result of a complete administrative break-down.

The decree setting up the new Confederation of Labour was not published after the November meeting. The real reason seems to have been that Mussolini intended to wait to see the effects on public opinion of the trials of the 'traitors' at Verona, which were held in January, and then to judge how much support could be rallied for a 'Socialist' experiment.

In the battle behind the scenes over eventual control of the new programme, Mussolini shifted his ground slightly from accepting total Party control to agreeing on the formation of a new Ministry of Corporate Economy, which would in fact place the main burden of authority upon a traditional Civil Service department. The man he chose for this ungrateful task was Angelo Tarchi, who was by training a chemical engineer. He was full of good intentions to put into practice a programme of moderate socialization by stages, and although he had close contacts with Italian capitalist circles he was confident that in this quarter he would meet with comprehension and, within limits, qualified support. On January 13 the Council of Ministers met again to consider a document drafted largely by Tarchi, headed 'A Basic Premise for the New Structure of Italian Economy'. This in effect set up the new Ministry, reduced Party control over any future programme, and modified certain extreme elements in the Verona manifesto.

The first move was to study German reactions. Their attitude would indeed be decisive to the success of any such scheme, as their interest was paramount both in the gearing of Italian industry to the war effort and in the supply of Italian labour to Germany.

On February 10 Tarchi called on Rahn, and the following day wrote a manuscript letter to the Duce describing this conversation. Rahn was personally in favour, but there were various interpretations of the 'Premise'. The German military authorities and the gauleiters Rainer and Hofer were frankly hostile. Rahn however had succeeded in interesting the Fuehrer personally, and told Tarchi that, if the programme and its objectives were examined critically, the obstacles might be removed. The latter reported to Mussolini that Rahn 'thinks it logical that after your "Premise" your social conception should finally be fulfilled, but since this must have repercussions beyond the Alps and in Germany, how much better it would be if it could also gain the consent of the high political and military authorities in Germany prior to its application in Italy'.

Rahn also felt that there was a danger of German military intervention to prevent the printing of the document in the press, and its application generally. Tarchi therefore recommended to Mussolini that the next Council of Ministers ought to debate the terms of the measure before its publication, and in the meantime Rahn might be able to help in overcoming the obstacles to which 'our intriguing plutocracy in Italy is certainly not extraneous'.[1]

Rahn reported this conversation in a personal telegram to Ribbentrop: 'The Minister for Corporations, Tarchi, called on me today, and in reply to German misgivings, of which he was aware, as to Italian plans for altering the structure of the economy, informed me that the publication of the basic demands of the Republican Fascist Party at its Verona Congress and the continued discussion in the Italian press of recent weeks now required that these plans be given legal sanction. The old Fascist Party had continually made promises which it had not kept. There should be no reversion to this state of affairs.

'The new law would represent a blow struck at the Communist and Bolshevist influences to which Italian workers, more than their German counterparts, were exposed. Germany herself must surely have an interest in supporting the Fascist government in its struggle against the plutocratic and Communist forces in the country.

'In reply to my question, Tarchi gave the following details of the projected legal regulations: All Italian enterprises, whether companies or individually-owned firms, will be included if they have an investment capital exceeding one million lire or employ more than fifty persons. The board of directors of a company will in future be so constituted that half its members are elected at the shareholders' meeting as representatives of the investors, while the other half will be made up of representatives of the staff, i.e. technical and clerical personnel and workers. The company director will be appointed by representatives of the investors elected at the shareholders' meeting, and cannot be voted down by the other members of the board of directors. The director is, however, responsible not merely to the shareholders' meeting, but first and foremost to the State for the management of the company and the fulfilment of the production targets allocated to his firm. If the director of an enterprise fails to live up to these obligations, the Minister for Corporations can order the board to elect a new director, and if need be appoint a deputy himself.

'In privately-owned firms the collaboration of the staff will likewise be secured by the formation of an advisory council consisting of one technician, one clerical employee, and one worker . . . Labour inspectors and the provincial economic councils can inform the Minister for Corporations if the activities of a concern give rise to serious misgiving; the Minister for Corporations can then intervene and if need be hand over the management of the firm to a member of the advisory council.

'In State enterprises half the board of directors will likewise consist of members of the staff.

'In all State or private concerns included under the new regulations, the net profit shown on the balance-sheet after deduction of profits to the owners, reserve funds and dividends to investors should be shared out among members of the staff in proportion to their salary or wages. Still under discussion is a proposal to limit the share of profits allocated to the staff, the surplus thus made available being transferred to a State compensation fund for the advancement of social institutions.

'My request to see the text of the bill before the Cabinet meeting passed its decree on it was waved aside by the Minister for Corporations on the pretext that the Duce had not given him authority to circulate it. The Duce looked on this measure as his own handiwork. He intended to lay it before the Cabinet in person and thereafter publish it without delay.

'In conclusion, I told the Minister for Corporations that I felt bound to protest against this unilateral action on the part of the Italian government. Radical legislation of this kind directly affected Germany's interests in the Italian arms industry, not to speak of labour relations in the country as a whole, and in the operational zones. Even if, judging from what he said, this measure was no more than an attempt to reform Italian commercial law, it might neverthelesss have such far-reaching political and economic repercussions in the country that the advance agreement of the German military authorities and senior representatives ought in all circumstances to be obtained. Failing this, the Italian government must in future expect to see the publication and enforcement of Cabinet decrees prevented by the Germans.' [2]

But Mussolini intended to go ahead and publish the measure without waiting for any German clearance. On the same day as Tarchi talked with Rahn, the latter received a personal letter from Mussolini.

'Tarchi has reported to me on the content of the talk which you had with him yesterday evening concerning the law on the socialization of factories which will be presented by me tomorrow, Saturday February 12, to the Council of Ministers.

'There appears to me to be in certain German quarters the tendency to over-dramatize the development of an historical process, which in Italy goes back to 1906 when Giovanni Giolitti was President of the Council, and which has been more or less fully realized in most countries of Europe, Germany included.[a]

'You know, my dear Ambassador, as well as I do, that many leaders of Italian industry are awaiting the Anglo-Saxons with open arms and in great part are responsible for the treachery of September 8. These people, who boast of influence in certain German circles, wish to underrate the Social Republic, discredit it in the eyes of the people and to favour on the one hand the return of the monarchy and on the other the more or less partisan action of Communism which they are supporting by all possible means. They ardently desire one thing only: the victory of the Anglo-Saxons allied with Bolshevism. Not to appreciate this is puerile!

'The law will now be approved and published immediately as has always happened in the case of decisions of the Council of Ministers for twenty years. Its publication will dissipate those rumours which have been artificially created, will clarify ideas and above all give us the means to assess the reactions which the law will provoke among the various interested parties.

'Its publication will not mean that it will be applied immediately. I hope that this method of procedure will be enough to re-establish a calmer appreciation of the situation and such as to convince everyone that in war ideas are the best allies of weapons.

'Forty years of political experience give me the right to make such an affirmation.' [3]

On February 10 Rahn telegraphed to Berlin: 'The Italian government's plans for the reconstruction of the Italian economy, which are the work of the Duce in person, have aroused considerable uneasiness in German military circles, notably among the associates of General Leyers and the experts assigned to him, possibly under the influence of Italian industrialists. I am continually being asked to prevent the furtherance of these Italian plans, and

a. It was proposed to nationalize the Italian railways.

more particularly the promulgation of the laws and regulations relative to them.

'As I know that the Duce has discussed his plans with the Fuehrer as well as with the Foreign Minister, and that they met with understanding, and as it would appear essential to rid Fascism of its plutocratic connections, I am loth to comply with the demands of the RUK[b] representatives in the radical manner they wish.

'During conversations with the Duce, in which I urged on him the necessity for the greatest caution and for reaching agreement with the German authorities before any fundamental decisions were taken, I encountered for the first time a resistance which, while friendly, was none the less very definite. The Duce pointed out that the behaviour of Italian industrialists, the majority of whom were secretly drawn towards Britain, was responsible for the inadequate results achieved by Italian industry. His plans for reform were today being countered by objections identical with those raised as early as 1906, when it had been a question of nationalizing the Italian railways (which was eventually done, with complete success). Over and above that, however, it was obvious that the Italian ironworks and dockyards now under government control and the concerns directed by the Italian Institute for Industrial Reconstruction had shown better results during the war years than the private concerns.

'The Duce also said to me verbatim:

' "I have always been extremely cautious about economic matters up to the present, and have expounded the view before now that whereas surgical methods may often be applicable to politics, where economics are concerned medical or even homeopathic methods should be applied. If we had long ago acquired direct State control over the whole of the Italian arms industry, we should not have been confronted with a situation in which industrialists secretly kept back raw materials from Germany essential to the war, and the manufacture of armaments, so as to have them handy when the war was over. I naturally intend to act in the closest possible harmony with Germany, but I would ask you to give my plans your support."

'His next move would be to nationalize electricity; this he wished to place under direct State control as a public supply undertaking, since the marked degree of confusion prevailing in this sphere was causing set-backs to industry. All his measures were aimed at raising productivity and bringing about a definite increase in war production.'

Mussolini told Rahn that a meeting of the Council of Ministers would be held on February 12, when the first of these decrees would be adopted. It would be on the following lines: No expropriation was to take place. In so far as State took over capital, suitable interest to be paid to the owners. Management committees were to be formed in the enterprises. These should

b. The German Ministry of War Production.

consist of representatives of the investors and management, technicians, and workers and employees. The management committee would be headed by the director of the enterprise. The director could not be outvoted. The workers' and employees' representatives should be elected by the workers and employees from a pool especially designated for this task by the Government commissioner. Government control of the enterprise would thus be assured by means of this link between selection and election, while the employees would yet have the feeling that they were directly represented on the management committee. The possibility of Communist representatives being elected would at the same time be avoided. Management committee, together with director of enterprise, would answer to the State for all measures taken in the enterprise, especially as regards production and raising of productivity.

In the Duce's own words, 'this new system should present the opportunity of awakening in the Italian industrial worker a sense of participation and an interest in his firm. This had hitherto proved impossible through the fault of the big Italian industrialists, who were for the most part typical representatives of high finance. One could not expect a positive attitude on the part of workers who had up to the present been neither trusted nor guided by their employers and had no other link with the enterprise. Without these measures which the Duce proposed to introduce there was a danger that the workers might plunge headlong into Communism.'

Rahn asked for 'a radical decision' from the Fuehrer. 'Should the Duce's plans meet with rigorous opposition from us, or should we on the contrary allow him to carry out this experiment under our leadership and guidance? In the latter case it would be on the hypothesis that military and armament production were in no way hampered.

'Should the decision just requested not be speedily obtainable, I shall proceed, in respect of the administrative autonomy granted the Duce by the Fuehrer, to adopt a non-committal attitude towards any decision taken at the Cabinet meeting. I shall in any case continue to do my best to impede any development that might be regarded as tending to Marxism.' [4]

Rahn's patronizing but sympathetic attitude to the new Italian régime, which he tended to regard as his personal responsibility, caused Hitler to administer a picturesque rebuke. On February 14 Rahn received the following personal telegram from Ribbentrop.

'The Fuehrer took the view that the socio-economic measures adopted by the Duce were no concern of ours. The Duce had discussed them with him, and he was of the opinion that the Duce could act in the matter as he thought fit, though he did not anticipate that the measures would prove a great success. We Germans would have to cure ourselves of the habit of thinking it incumbent on us to play the "Medicine Man" all over Europe. The question of a swing to the Left hardly came into it, since the swing had already occurred to such an extent that if our troops were withdrawn the whole of the present edifice would collapse. He was, furthermore, under the impression that the Duce's measures were chiefly directed against the industrialists and factory-owners, who bore the brunt of the responsibility for sabotaging his armament programme.' [5]

The first reaction of Italian industrialists to the new programme was cautiously positive. As Valletta, the managing director of Fiat, told Rahn, when the latter had explained to him that the programme of socialization of the Duce was to be accepted in full, 'The Duce's law on socialization will meet with the approval of all those who, rising above private interests, see in the social programme of Fascism not only the safeguarding of an orderly symbiosis of capital and labour, but also the possibility of asserting the personality and the initiative of the individual.' [6]

The local authorities in Turin also reported that the attitude of the workers to the new programme was less clear. The same source reported that the intelligent workers approved, but there was intense Communist activity to undermine the implementation of any Socialist programme by the régime.[7]

On February 12, again according to familiar procedure, the Council of Ministers accepted a decree on the nationalization of certain enterprises, but this was not yet to be published until the general reactions were clearer.

The effective implementation of the decrees on nationalization were in the event held up until the fall of the Republic. In spite of Hitler's directive, the local German economic officials in Northern Italy played a decisive part in sabotaging the intentions of Mussolini and Tarchi. The chances of carrying out a successful programme were also diminished by the counter-activities of the underground resistance organizations in the main cities of the North. The strikes which broke out on March 1 in Turin, and which spread to Milan and Genoa on the same pattern as the agitation of the previous year, but now on a quite different level of organization, disrupted the whole picture.

The Police branch of the Militia in Turin, through their agents, received warning between February 25 and 29 of a general strike to break out on March 1, which would have 'an apparently economic character but was in fact political and concerted with the partisan movement'.[8]

The strike action was called by the central 'Secret Committee of Agitation for Piedmont, Lombardy and Liguria', which represented in its majority the Communist elements of the resistance organizations.

On March 1, in three main sections of the whole Fiat network of factories, the strike was total, but not in the other major enterprises. The action of the strikers was co-ordinated with sabotage and interruption on the railways in the province of Turin, thus preventing the workers arriving at their places of employment. For the first time the co-ordination of the various resistance organs functioned efficiently, and as the result of detailed planning.

The first German reports emphasized that there were no unified economic demands behind the strike action. 'The movement has political aims of a Communist character.' In Milan and Turin some 60,000 had come out on strike, and the industrialists were adopting an evasive attitude 'so as not to compromise themselves with the workers'.[9] It appeared that the strike in Genoa had been controlled rapidly by the Italian Police.

The German authorities proposed counter-measures on the following lines: there would be a lock-out proclaimed for one week and the important factories would be occupied by Italian military units. The workers would be summoned publicly back on March 8, and those unwilling to report would be threatened with transfer as forced labour to Germany. On March 4 the several hundred key strike leaders would be deported without warning.

On March 6 personal orders from Hitler reached the German military authorities on the spot. Twenty per cent of the strikers from Northern Italy were to be deported and put at Himmler's disposal for labour service.[10] In the Fiat works alone it seems that over six hundred workers were arrested, and in the end the partisan Action Committee for the three North-western Italian provinces ordered a return to work. According to their later figures, over 200,000 workers had come out on strike in Northern Italy, and 32,600 of these in Turin.[11]

From the reports of the Fascist authorities to Mussolini it appeared that they were not only very well informed of the background of the strikes, but also were aware of its grave implications.[12] Contrary to the opinion of the other members of the Committee, the Communists took responsibility for ordering the strikes. According to police reports there were last-minute hesitations. 'At 9 o'clock this morning the Communist Party were still deliberating, one does not know for what reasons, whether to issue counter-orders to their agents in the factories suspending the strike . . . One does not know if this counter-order, in view of the initial success of the manifestation, will be implemented.' [13]

The Fascist authorities had attempted to forestall the strike by declaring the week beginning March 1 a special holiday period, and certain factories succeeded in closing for this reason. The Communist counter-order was in fact suspended, and the strikes went ahead in certain factories that afternoon.

The significance of the March strikes in Northern Italy was the revelation for the first time of the extent of progress made by the Action Committees of the National Liberation Committee of the partisan movement, and of the leading part played by the Communists in organizing the first mass action of the workers in the Northern Republic against the Salò régime. These activities also showed what little hold the régime had over the industrial workers and revealed the latter's total lack of interest in the nationalization plans of the government. Although Tarchi felt that the strikes as a whole had been a failure, he did note in a report to Mussolini that there had been connivance between the industrialists and the 'local Secret Action Committee'. He nevertheless wished to press ahead with his programme, and in particular to earmark the major electricity firms for nationalization.

The German authorities had acted with customary brutality and the implications of this widespread strike movement had not escaped them. As one of the leading members of the National Committee of Liberation put it later, 'The real deportations in grand style began after the March strikes . . . There had been a general strike under German occupation with precise political aims. I must say that if it had not been for the strike of March 1944, the question of the defence of the factories (against dismantling and transport to Germany, which now became for the Germans a definite objective) would have been different. It was only at this moment that the Germans realized that people in the factories were not joking, but meant what they were doing. For the first time strike leaders were deported to Germany on political grounds.' [14]

The conspiracy against the nationalization programme of Salò was persistent and effective, and throughout the spring and summer of 1944 any moves to put into practice the February decrees were postponed. In addition to the hostility of the German economic authorities in Italy, and through collusion with those industrialists hostile to such planning, there was also the negative view expressed by the Swiss, whose investments in Northern Italian industry —particularly in the hydro-electrical field—represented a quarter of the total capital invested.

On April 4, for example, the Swiss commercial representative to the Salò government, who was in fact the only official Swiss representative attached to the new régime, delivered a memorandum which sounded a note of warning. 'It is only necessary to remember the attraction which the economic and industrial development of Northern Italy has always had for Swiss investment and industrialists, particularly in the field of chemicals, textiles, and electricity . . . The participation of Swiss capital and labour in the considerable development of industry in Northern Italy assumes an importance of such a degree that the most lively reaction aroused in Switzerland at the measures proposed by the Republican Fascist government cannot in any way come as a surprise . . .

'Given this situation, the Swiss Federal authorities have no doubts that the Fascist Republican government will exempt Swiss enterprises from the measures which it intends to take.' [15]

It was not surprising therefore that the whole programme came to a halt. As Tarchi expressed it in a memorandum to Mussolini on 'The Workings of Socialization' which he wrote a year later: 'The Republican government found itself on the one hand conducting a struggle against those capitalist forces which at once lined up against the legislation, and on the other hand waging such a struggle alone without the adequate support and understanding of the working masses.' [16]

Tarchi gave details of the reactions of Italian industrial leaders to the proposed measures. 'They pointed out that in the present situation of the Italian system of production, the socialization of industry could paralyse production activity, and this bogey was waved in the faces both of the Italian authorities and above all of the German organs in charge of Italian war production, so as to exploit their psychological reaction and skilfully to create active opposition to the law, on principle.'

The extent of the reactions of the German authorities is clear from a circular sent by General Leyers, the head of the 'War and Armaments Commission' set up in Northern Italy. This document was addressed to the heads of all 'protected firms'.

'I am arranging to be informed of any attempts to apply the new law or any partial introduction of it, after the publication of the socialization decree. In the affirmative case, I would like to be given all relevant facts with the names of the people who have initiated or taken part in the action.

'I take this opportunity of declaring explicitly that the law on socialization is not at present in force. Article 46 of the law contemplates bringing it into force on a day to be fixed later by decree of the Duce. If you should observe any tendencies to socialization in any of your firms in future, do not hesitate to inform me in all detail.' [c]

In spite of all discouragements, Mussolini was persuaded to bring into force on June 30 the legislation on socialization agreed by the Council of Ministers in February. But here again, equivocal misunderstandings were perhaps deliberately allowed to arise.

On June 27 Rahn wrote to General Leyers: 'The Duce told me that he is decided forthwith to bring into force on June 30 the law on socialization. With due regard to any further decision of the Reich government, I asked that in no case should the protected firms be included without German agreement in the socialization plan. The Duce promised this, and stated that a beginning would be made first of all only with the nationalizing of the enterprises concerned with the press. In any case in carrying out these measures one would act with the greatest prudence, and only by stages.

'In addition I asked Dr Tarchi to come and see me at once, and asked him also for a statement that the measures of nationalization in the protected firms would in no circumstances be undertaken without our consent. He at

c. The comment of the Italian Ministry concerned on this document reads as follows: 'This is a circular sent very confidentially to the heads of all firms protected by General Leyers, head of the War and Armaments Commission, which an anti-Fascist organ calls "The German Society for the Organization of theft in our factories and Countryside". The copy of the circular bears no date, but it is evidently recent.' Italian Collection. May 17, 1944.

once declared himself in agreement with our wishes, and was willing to give us immediately the necessary assurances also in writing.' [17]

As Tarchi pointed out in his later report to Mussolini, 'The German Ambassador's letter constituted the basis on which the economic organs of the German War and Armaments Commission supported the thesis that the law on socialization could not be applied to the protected firms without German authorization.' [18]

Apart from German, Swiss and Italian capitalist opposition to such a reconstruction of Italian economic life in a Socialist direction, there was the almost universal passivity of the industrial workers, and so far as the partisan organizations were able to operate, signs of active hostility.

As one of the Fascist syndicate leaders wrote to Mussolini: 'The masses refuse to accept anything from us . . . This is a malevolent preconceived idea on their part.' [19] It was finally pointed out that between November 1943 and February 1944 interest had been aroused among the workers on the subject of nationalization. But this had been dissipated by the failure to apply the legislation. The workers assert there will be no nationalization . . . They think German influence has been decisively negative, and such as to postpone the solution of the problem at least until after the war . . . This has the effect of heaping onto us their contempt, as they said we were not in good faith and hold that the announcement of nationalization was the nth expedient to draw into our orbit the few mugs who still give us any credit.

'In brief, the workers consider nationalization as a mirror to catch larks, and they keep well away from us, and the mirror.' [20]

CHAPTER NINE

THE KLESSHEIM CONFERENCE

AFTER NEARLY six months of frustrating experiment, the 'operation' of Salò could only be justified by a review at the summit. At the end of March 1944, Rahn sent a personal telegram to Ribbentrop. 'From the Duce's entourage I am told, even more frequently and in more or less veiled form, that the Duce hopes to be received by the Fuehrer in the foreseeable future.'

Before such a decision was taken, Rahn pointed out that 'the Duce will probably raise with the Fuehrer the question of the status of the operational zones of the Adriatic coastal and the Alpine zones. It is known to me that the Duce has been busy with the problem uninterruptedly and with frequent violent outbursts of feeling. He has been following closely the German press in these zones and in particular the old Austrian tendencies . . . In some of the measures taken by the gauleiter, the Duce sees the preparation for the future annexation of these areas by Germany . . .

'I have succeeded up till now in steering the Duce and individual members of his government away from a too intensive preoccupation with the problem of the operational zones, and in making them understand the measures taken by the High Commissioner. But gradually the authority of the Italian government, and its contribution to the common war effort in various fields . . . has assumed an undeniable importance, hence the Duce's inclination to face us with *faits accomplis* and seek out "our real intention" by little experimental jabs . . .' [1]

This question of the frontier provinces represented for Mussolini the main historical humiliation to which his Republican administration had been subjected by the Germans.

Early in January, the Duce received at Gargnano a verbal report from the Prefect of Trieste. It was a catalogue of further instructions by the Germans on the administration of the provinces, such as the ban on the call up of recruits to the Republican army and of spreading activities by Slav partisans.

'In the province of Trieste the whole Carso is hostile. The situation is no better around Gorizia. The situation in . . . Istria is even worse after the events of September and also in the whole zone round Fiume.' [2]

But Mussolini had, for the moment, run out of protests. He told the Prefect of Trieste, 'The time has not yet arrived when I can ask for an alleviation of German pressure . . . The creation by the Germans of an operational zone has its justification. A possible recovery on the southern front could be the condition of a resolute intervention on my part.'

Even worse, an impression was spreading that the Duce had tacitly accepted the position. On February 11, 1944, he was obliged to write to Rahn.[a]

'I send you, as an enclosure, a message from a German Headquarters to the command of the National Republican Guard, in which it is stated that all Italian sovereignty in the Alpine provinces and littoral has been temporarily suspended as a result of agreements with the Duce.

'You know, my dear Ambassador, that I have never had prior, much less official, notice of the setting up of the two commissions of Voralpenland and Kustenland, and that, equally, I learnt the names of the two commissars after they had been installed, and had already expelled the Italian civil authorities.

'Four days after the official constitution of my Government I sent a letter to the Fuehrer in which I said, "The appointment of a supreme commissar in Innsbruck for the provinces of Bolzano, Trento, Belluno, has aroused a painful impression throughout Italy."

'Three days after my letter, Rainer took up his post in Trieste, and, with him, every residue of Italian jurisdiction has completely disappeared. Has the policy inaugurated by Rainer produced the promised results?

'The incident a few days ago, in which an Italo-German supply column was annihilated to the last man, shows that the Slavs—Communist or not— are against Germany and Italy. In Venezia Giulia there are evidently few troops. But why has Mister (sic) Rainer "prohibited" the call-up of the Italian age-groups?'

And there the matter had rested until a favourable moment should arise for Mussolini to raise the whole question directly with the Fuehrer.

Rahn now asked for instructions on these points before a conference with Hitler was fixed. 'I cannot recommend a complete refusal to hold such a meeting as in recent weeks the Italian government has made considerable contributions to the common war effort, and has declared itself ready, in spite of severe straining of its authority and capacity, to make even greater efforts. As I shall be compelled in the next weeks to stretch this readiness to

a. Italian Collection. Mussolini to Rahn, February 11, 1944. The original draft of this letter (enclosure not printed), with the corrections in Mussolini's handwriting, appeared as a Christian Democrat wall poster during the Italian elections in 1954 as an answer to the neo-Fascists who were attacking De Gasperi for 'betraying' Italy in accepting the arrangements for the Free Territory of Trieste.

the limit, it is in our real interest to back up somewhat more the Italian feeling of independence, and to mitigate the ever-recurring depressive tendencies
of the Duce by certain personal or practical satisfactions.' [3]

Behind this verbose language, Rahn was agitated at an imminent breakdown of the Northern Republic, and was himself pressing for a personal
decision by Hitler.

On April 1, Rahn summarized, with his own comments, Mussolini's views
on the main points at issue between Salò and the Reich. German military
agencies in Italy should be only concerned with the conduct of the war. They
should not bother with administration and economy. The Duce had twenty
years' experience and he would be responsible for a greater Italian war effort
'than can be reached by a military or half-military organization'.

In effect much of the administrative responsibility had been given back to
the Italian government; 'nevertheless a substantial part of the newly acquired
authority of the Italian government rests on the awareness of the Italian
people that German power lies behind it, supporting and advising. It would
be unwise to destroy these supports, at least so long as a considerable proportion of the governing class is, as before, bound to the Royal House or
Badoglio, and is ready for a further betrayal of Germany and Fascism.'

The Duce wanted to control industrial as well as war production, and to
deal with those countries with whom he was in diplomatic contact especially
for purposes of trade agreements.

But, as Rahn pointed out, a co-ordinated plan of war production was necessary to meet the European programme, and 'Italo-German economy cannot,
given the war situation, be separated any more'.

The Duce wanted the Italian army expanded as quickly as possible, but
'at least 300,000 Italians are already in uniform. This implies an enormous
risk if one is not absolutely sure of their ideological direction and leadership.
The units incorporated in the ranks of the German army, and S.S., receive
a careful training so as to avoid military and political set-backs.' He also
sought for administrative sovereignty in the operational zones or at least for
the right to nominate officials, and for free activity of Fascist organizations.

But these zones, as Rahn added in his telegram, 'are the most sensitive
areas for supply and intelligence, and also the decisive defensive positions
for Germany, and must be absolutely safeguarded'. The Italian administration could not pacify Slovene and Croat populations. 'Coldly opportunistic
tactics' are needed to deal with the partisan problem. 'For this reason caution
is needed in allowing any Fascist organizations to operate.' The Province
of Udine represented the only route so far free from partisans, from the
Reich to Trieste.[4]

The Fuehrer accepted 'with pleasure' the proposal for a conference to be
held at the end of April.

Before coming to this meeting, Mussolini was intending to close the cycle of Verona, and end the political vendetta of July 1943. The former Party Secretary, Carlo Scorza, was due to appear before a court in Parma to answer for his conduct at the meeting of the Grand Council, and the Duce intended on this occasion to interfere personally.

He also hoped to visit the Italian camps in Germany where the ghost army of the new Republic was undergoing training, and on whose anticipated presence in Italy the very future of the régime rested.

The Duce was so unsure of Hitler's reaction to such a request that he 'explained deliberately that this wish was not a *sine qua non*, but that he would be grateful if before leaving he could learn whether such a review would be agreeable to the Fuehrer'.[5]

In the event no objection was raised on the German side, and the arrangements for the meeting were made with every consideration for the Duce's former position, including the special train.

Mussolini was, however, all too aware of the disastrous changes since the full-dress conference at Klessheim a year earlier and hoped to avoid at least in part the devastating monologues of the Fuehrer.

On April 16 Rahn telegraphed that the Duce would make a detailed report on the military and political situation in Italy and 'that two days would be enough'. And again, 'The Duce asks that the meeting should be confined to business, and attaches value to having his meals as far as possible alone.' [6]

The conference opened on the morning of April 22 in the fabulous setting of the castle at Klessheim.[b] It was to be the last of a series to be held in such a world.

The task of Mussolini was to set the frame of the talks by commenting on the Italian scene. It was the only occasion on which he had ever opened such a meeting. Hitler sat chewing uninterruptedly the small pills of Dr Morrell. Graziani sat nearby taking lengthy notes.[7] Speaking in German and from a prepared brief, the Duce began: 'When he had taken over the administration seven months previously he had encountered absolute chaos . . . This state of disorganization had assumed proportions which he had no conception of in the period immediately after his liberation.' He was now faced

b. The sources of the several meetings are:
(a) April 22 Morning: Translation of German minutes in United States Department of State Bulletin, October 20, 1946.
(b) April 22 Afternoon: German Collection. Schmidt Minute; and an Italian version, presumably from Anfuso's notes in *Realtà Politica*, August 1, 1945.
(c) April 23 Morning: Translation of German minutes in Department of State Bulletin, December 8, 1946.
(d) April 23 Afternoon: *Ibid.*
Hitler's advisers present were Ribbentrop, Keitel, Rahn, Wolff, Toussaint and Dollmann. The Duce had brought with him Graziani, Mazzolini, Anfuso, and the Italian Military Attaché in Berlin, Colonel Morera.

with various difficulties. The first was the 'matter of the internment of the Italian troops'. This measure had been 'advisable' and 'necessary' as many of them 'had been misled by enemy propaganda'. But some six or seven million Italians, who were their relatives and dependents, were closely concerned with their fate. The morale of the Italian people would be raised if the situation of the military internees could be improved.

A further difficulty was due to the measures taken in the Alpine provinces and the Adriatic coastal area. These steps 'were necessary at the time'.

The Duce did not see fit to emphasize more strongly these two central points of friction in Italo-German relations. Graziani noted later: 'At the Salzburg meeting Mussolini spoke first. He was not incisive, and did not know how to speak clearly, particularly in front of Hitler.' [8]

Mussolini went on. Only a minority of the population favoured the Republican-Fascist régime. 'The great majority stood between scepticism and pessimism. Only the Republican Fascist Party . . . represented a source of strength among these numerous sceptics. It would therefore be a good thing for Germany to issue a declaration of solidarity with the Republican-Fascist Party.'

There was also an actively hostile minority among the Italian people. But the monarchy had been abolished. 'The Republic was already a very widespread concept. Only a few plutocratic aristocrats were against it. It was important that by means of truly social measures the whole population should be won over for the Republic. Measures on a large scale would have to be undertaken in the field of social legislation, for the structure of Italy had not yet been changed. No disturbance in production would result . . . Strikes were entirely under control. Only 200,000 workers out of many million had gone on strike for periods ranging from ten minutes to eight days . . .'

The Church was 'hesitant' towards the new régime. 'The clergy had adopted a reserved or even a hostile attitude.'

Mussolini spoke of the food problem in the North and in Rome. A thousand lorries would solve the whole matter.

He then emphasized the need to defend Rome, which was 'the spiritual centre of Italy'.

'The strengthening of the Italian Republic was in the interest of Germany . . . The recognition of the efforts which Italy had made since September 8 of the previous year' seemed important to the Duce. Sauckel had requested one million workers. Goering for his anti-aircraft batteries had asked for 200,000 Italians, Kesselring for 62,000 . . . a total of 1,300,000. He (the Duce) was prepared to supply these. In order to do so, he would call up the classes of 1919 and 1922.'

But the Italian people 'must also be given the impression that the new Italian government had an independent position and that there were certain fields in which it had complete control'. The new Italy 'was determined to march alongside the Germans to the end'. England and America had lost the war. The Russians might be content to defend their own boundaries. England was the enemy number one.

At this stage Mussolini asked the Fuehrer to listen to a statement by Graziani. The latter was prepared for this moment, and even the German transcript of this meeting reveals his sense of violent frustration. 'Marshal Graziani first reported that when he had taken over his command in September of the previous year absolutely nothing had been available for the re-organization of the Italian armed forces . . . For example, he had had no telephone or telegraph service, which, of course, were being used exclusively by the German Army . . . Of the seven months he had been able really to work only during the last three.'

Graziani described the painful building up of a loyal officer corps. 'The Royal Army had been dissolved; the new army was built up on a volunteer basis. Although all the officers were loyal Fascists, they were forbidden to engage in any sort of political activity during their period of service . . .[c]

'The classes of 1924 and 1925 were now being called up. And here a new difficulty had appeared . . . there were not enough police available actually to force those who had been called up to comply . . . Although 100,000 men had come in, there were still many slackers. For that reason the death penalty had had to be introduced, not only for deserters, but also for those who sought to avoid service . . . The consequence of this measure was that 60–70,000 had reported.' But enemy propaganda was active in encouraging group desertions of whole units. 'Propaganda to the effect that Germany had already lost the war, and the activity of the partisans operated in the same direction . . .

'The operations against the rebels were also of the utmost importance.' General Wolff was doing everything possible. This struggle was important 'for the increase of the prestige and authority of the Italian government. Ten to twelve battalions were already employed against the rebels.' But in comparison with the latter, 'who were well armed and equipped with everything', the Republican Italians were poorly armed and lacked transport. 'It was only with difficulty that they could properly fulfil their mission of defending the Apennine passes.' The Italian warehouses had been emptied after September 8, 1943. There were no longer any uniforms available for the recruits now being called up. Graziani proposed that General Leyers, 'who was in control of industry, should put several factories at the disposal of the Italians in which they could manufacture their own requirements. The Germans should exercise supervision.'

Graziani ended with a summary of the Italian military contribution in manpower to the joint war effort.

The Duce took up the subject of the partisan movement, which he esti-

c. The Duce interrupted at this point to emphasize these last words.

mated at about 60,000 men 'or somewhat more', and principally in Piedmont. But they were suffering severe losses, and General Wolff interjected that the movement was cracking up, and that 'in the valleys infested by the partisans, good results had been achieved by deporting the entire male population'. The Duce added that 'the partisan movement was most dangerous in the Apennines where only four roads led from North to South, but that operations against them were now in progress. It was proposed that a corps of 12,000 men should be raised and trained at Parma to be employed against the partisans. Among them were 3,000 men from the Party, and 9,000 from the army.'

This meeting was the first such occasion when Hitler had remained silent, and allowed the Italian allies to state their case. He now announced that he had an important military conference, and deferred the talks until that afternoon.

The Italian party lunched with Keitel, and the meeting was resumed at 5 o'clock. It was now the turn of the Fuehrer. According to Mazzolini, the Italian Undersecretary for Foreign Affairs, he gave an exposition of 'acute realism'. [9]

He announced that he would now deal from the German point of view with the questions raised this morning. For months on end he had given no sign of life, for he had been faced with the hardest task of his career, had had many troubles, and in the last seven to eight months the situation had changed in a kaleidoscopic manner.

'We did not know if and where an invasion would take place . . . We stand practically alone against the Russians: only the Finns hold a small section of the front. In addition we have a front in Norway, throughout the West, in Italy, in the Balkans, and then there are our divisions in Hungary. During the last two to three years we have formed 135 new divisions. And with this the limit of human and material capacity had been reached.

'. . . After the Duce had been arrested, the Fuehrer was faced with a hard decision, either to evacuate Italy or to attempt to resist south of Rome. He had been forced to take the harshest measures, which had to be carried through, and about which the Fuehrer would speak the next day. If nothing exceptional went wrong, it would be possible to hold the Italian Front.'

Hitler 'had been told, by the Roumanians too, that he wanted to keep the war as far from the German frontiers as possible. This was not correct. . . . The allies had not borne their share of the burden. Thus Italy had been found wanting: Roumania and Hungary had not committed their troops, but wanted to keep them back for a private war.'

Hitler had been forced to act against Hungary since, after not succeeding in making an agreement with Badoglio, she wanted to work with the British and Americans. 'This was the worst fallacy. England had no intention of protecting Central Europe from the Russians . . .'

The decision in this war would lie in the West. The English preparations for invasion 'could be kept going for six to eight weeks', but there would be a serious crisis in England if after that the invasion was not launched.

The enemy coalition was 'unnatural'; 'it was a question of two worlds', and there were points of eventual strife between the Allies.

The Duce agreed with this, and asked, 'How can it be accelerated?'

At noon the following morning, April 23, the two delegations met again.[d]

The Fuehrer continued his discourse of the previous afternoon.

In Germany the war effort was total. 'If we got additional workers from abroad, the result was that German labour would be set free for use at the front. It was clear that a country which was exerting itself so completely was entitled to judge other countries according to their joint conduct of the war.' In Italy, however, 'had come the collapse. The Fuehrer believed that countries and peoples at all periods could be represented by individuals. The Russians had their Stalin. It was the misfortune of France that no great man had been discovered there. To a certain extent Churchill was also a strong man, and one thought of Italy in connection with the Duce. The best evidence that Italy had succumbed to subversive influence was the march of events in Southern Italy. Italy's will to resist had been bound up in the person of the Duce. When he had been removed it became our task to stabilize the situation.'[e]

The Fuehrer realized that, in retrospect, the German counter-measures which followed the Italian collapse might appear from the outside to be harsh. 'Since the Duce was not there himself, people had not known where the treachery had arisen, and one could hardly have believed that the English would exploit the situation in such a timorous and irresolute fashion as they did. The Fuehrer exercised great authority in Germany, but he nevertheless had to listen to his Marshals and Generals, who told him that the expenditure of any further divisions in Italy was folly, so long as the supply routes were not definitely assured. The Fuehrer had based his plans on the Duce, and then it was suddenly reported to him that Fascism was no longer in existence. Thus had come about the need for very harsh and thorough measures.'

The Germans had first intended to withdraw to the Apennines 'or even only to hold the Alpine passes which could have been completely defended with some twelve divisions'. Such a move would expose South Germany to

d. Apart from the Heads of State, only Ribbentrop, Rahn and Keitel were present on the German side, and Graziani, Anfuso and Mazzolini on the Italian.

e. Mussolini was already a little tired of this line of argument. In January 1944, in private conversation with Mazzolini, the latter had asked him if a meeting with Hitler would not be valuable. The Duce's answer was that for the moment he did not think so, adding 'this position of privilege created for me annoys me at this stage. Why believe only in me, and not in this martyred Italian people?' See Mazzolini's diary. Quoted in Tamaro *op cit* II p. 370.

increased air attack, but the difference between South Italy and the Po valley as enemy air bases was not so great. But the essential consequences of such a retreat would have been 'the complete destruction of everything which might assist the enemy and the removal of material which we could use in our own conduct of the war'.

One very difficult question had also arisen: 'What was to become of the Italian army?' Some elements were willing to continue the fight with the Germans; others included 'our bitterest enemies, including the Alpini', who had sung the 'Internationale' and made insulting remarks about the Duce and himself.

The Italian troops had therefore been disarmed and interned because they were infected. Increased burdens had followed for the German people 'who rightly demanded that the Italians should at least be put to work in Germany'. Those Italian workers had the same rations as the Germans. In spite of this, at Linz, 'a strike and a shooting affray had even occurred. The Italian workers had appealed to their Ambassador, posing as Italian patriots who were persecuted by us, although in fact they were pure Communists.[f] It was shameful that even the French workers behaved better towards us.'

There was no doubt that the present situation of the Italians in Germany was unsatisfactory from both sides. 'We would set up for the Duce an outstanding unit, composed of the best not the average.' There were also difficulties of arming new units, and the Germans must have priority. 'Every German rifle must go to the front.' And then came a vicious outburst. 'If out of the 600,000 military internees 200,000 should sign up for active service, they would be doing it only to improve their own lot, and would not be the sort of troops to have made the sacrifices required . . . around Cassino.'

Hitler said that he regretted that he could not accompany his guests to Grafenwöhr, where the first Italian division was in training. The organization of the new Italian army must be based on one sound unit, and as soon as the four divisions were organized, these could then be doubled and finally tripled.

'Such rebuilding . . . took time, and if the military forces of a country had passed through a crisis like the Italian one, the matter was still more difficult. The Fuehrer wanted to provide the Duce with the foundation for an absolutely reliable military force. This was a prerequisite for the stabilization of the Fascist régime in Italy. But the Italian soldiers must be determined to fight for the Duce like a Roman Legion.'

As to the zone of operations, Hitler 'said that he could only make one

---

f. This passage made a sharp impression on Anfuso. 'In reply to our gesture of astonishment, and in particular to a few louder questioning remarks from Graziani. Hitler raised his voice in reaction . . . I had never heard Hitler so brutal and so like his legend.' Anfuso *op cit* p. 435.

remark, that in Germany there was a proverb: "A burnt child dreads the fire." After the events which had taken place in Italy, we found ourselves in a terrible situation . . . In Italy there were two bottlenecks for the Germans: one was the Apennines. If the roads crossing the Apennines were dominated by the partisans it would be impossible for us to hold a position to the South . . . The second bottleneck was the Alpine roads. If we were to go on fighting in Italy against overwhelming superiority in material, we would have to dominate and make secure the Alpine passes so as to be sure that no partisans would be able to threaten those narrow supply routes. Therefore, for military reasons, no alteration could be made in the arrangement concerning the zone of operations under any conditions.'

An enemy attack was expected at any moment from the Nettuno bridgehead. 'Under no circumstances should a crisis be permitted to occur in the rear areas. A gradual abandonment of the necessary military measures in those zones was dependent on strengthening the Fascist system. This process, however, would be based on the Duce, and it was of extreme importance that he should remain in good health. At one time Badoglio had said to Kesselring that the Duce had only two months to live because he was suffering from cancer. The Fuehrer was happy to learn from Morrell that the Duce's trouble was only a nervous one . . .'

Unfortunately nothing was perfect and there were no limits to stupidity or madness. 'Thus, for example, a great quantity of maps of Sweden had been shipped through Sweden (in 1940). Yet one could not conclude from that that military maps should not be dispatched to any military authorities in future. The same had happened in the zones of operations. Some mistakes had certainly been made there. Ambassador Rahn had been commissioned to bring these mistakes to a halt . . .' There could be no new system of regulation, only attention to individual cases. 'When the régime of the Duce was more firmly re-established, then one could proceed with the removal of such regulations.'

Hitler would do his best in the case of the military internees, and sort out the younger and more reliable men. 'His commanders believed that the reconstitution of the Italian divisions could be accomplished . . . We would supply the Duce with the yeast, the germ from which the future Italian army would be developed.' That army must serve one god, 'for if a soldier served two gods, then in his hour of need he would call on the god of peace, which with the Italian people might very well mean the King and his compromise government'.

Hitler finished his speech and left the room for a military conference.

The final talk was held at four o'clock that afternoon.[g] The Duce had been riled by Hitler's references to the non-existence of Fascism in July 1943. 'The

g. At this meeting Dollmann and Morera were also present.

strength of the Fascist Party,' he said, 'had at that time lain with various armies. At home were the women, the young, and the very old.' Badoglio, too, had lulled people with the fiction that the war would continue. The Duce himself had abruptly and unaccountably been removed from the scene. 'The Italian people had not known how to take the situation, and it had come to pass that after a twenty-one year control of the government, he had been dismissed like an unreliable servant. If the Italian generals had ever surprised the enemy as well as they had surprised the Italian people on that occasion, the Italians would perhaps have been able to occupy Egypt . . .'

As to the military internees, the Duce 'would be satisfied if they remained in Germany'. He asked only for better conditions in order to improve the morale of their relatives in Italy. He was content also with the reconstitution of the divisions in Germany, and with the Fuehrer's idea that the units should be fewer and more reliable. He would send recruits from Italy who were uncontaminated. 'The worst was the attitude of the people between 24 and 40 years of age . . . The work of conciliation was now in progress. There were, however, still a large number of desperate characters, for example all the students . . . who from a political point of view . . . were indifferent.'

The Duce was prepared 'to call up the class of 1914 for gauleiter Sauckel, the classes of 1916 and 1917 for Marshal Goering, and to place them at their disposal'. He further agreed 'that 20 classes should be called up and placed in labour battalions'.

'The morale of the Italian people was reacting sharply to the news of the war. He intended to start a propaganda campaign throughout the various cities. He wanted to speak himself, otherwise the people would believe that the Duce was dead, and, looking at it in retrospect, this was the case: for the Mussolini of yesterday was dead, and it was the Mussolini of tomorrow who was alive.'[h]

The atmosphere of the meeting had softened. Graziani pointed out that the German command in Italy was very satisfied with the Italian workers. Hitler confirmed that the Todt organization was very pleased with them. He also thought that 'it would be better if the Italian units were not used in combat immediately after their period of training, but were doubled and tripled, so that with these twelve divisions the basis of the State could be established'.

The Fuehrer had reached his summing up. He 'had decided once and for all to rely on the Duce, and he had broken off all other contacts with Italy (sic) . . . If Ambassador Rahn transmitted to the Fuehrer the Duce's wishes, the Fuehrer would see that they were fulfilled,' or if it were not possible, would say so frankly. 'The Fuehrer in this terrific historic struggle took

h. In February 1944, Mazzolini had recorded in his diary that the Duce had been told that people, particularly in Rome, doubted the very existence of Mussolini. He had commented, 'Perhaps they are not wrong.' In Vatican circles it was thought that Mussolini was not in his right mind. His comment was: 'They exaggerate.' See Tamaro op cit II p. 371.

a broader view than from a church steeple . . . Italy was the first, and even today the only one, of our allies who was closely bound to us in ideology. That was why the Fuehrer in his own interest understandably and naturally wanted to fulfil all of the wishes of the Duce. Neither was it any good standing alone. One must also think each of his own end. The Duce and himself were certainly the two best hated men in the world, and in case the enemy got hold of the Duce, they would carry him off with a cry of triumph to Washington. Germany and Italy must win, otherwise both countries and peoples would perish together.'

That evening the two leaders dined alone together. The only recorded comment on their conversation is that of Anfuso. 'When they parted company Mussolini confided to me that Hitler's affirmations as to the outcome of the war had seemed to him to be devilishly optimistic.' Anfuso also noticed that there was no question raised by the Germans about the Verona programme of socialization to which Mussolini had referred during the meetings. [10]

After taking leave of the Fuehrer, Mussolini and his group of advisers visited the first Italian division in training in Germany at Grafenroehr camp. Some 600 officers and 12,000 men composed this cadre of the future Republican Army, grouped as the 'San Marco' division. There was a happy pause amid constant disillusion. The Duce received a familiar and enthusiastic reception. 'He regained confidence in himself and the future of the Fatherland.' [11]

It was but a brief interlude.

CHAPTER TEN

THE MARCH FROM ROME
(June–July 1944)

• •

ON MAY 6, 1944, Hitler issued a directive to Kesselring on the continuance of the battle in Italy. 'The task of Army Group C remains the defence of Central and Southern Italy wherever possible and to safeguard the flanks of Liguria and the Adriatic, in particular Istria.'

It was essential to fight south of the Apennines. The defence of the Po Valley would be the last line, and for this time must be gained. 'In this way strong enemy forces will be kept away from an attack on the western coasts of the Balkans; an operation which the enemy intended to carry out at the latest when he reached the line of the Apennines.' Kesselring could 'expect no reinforcements in the near future except two Italian divisions'.[1]

A month later the shadow of a direct enemy invasion of the territory of Salò by an advance to the Po Valley, and the imminent Allied threat to Rome led Mussolini to write a memorandum on military affairs, now a rare occurrence.

'Marshal Kesselring's forces are retreating at so fast a pace that the holding of any kind of defence line between Rome and the Apennines appears to be excluded. The massing of seven hundred enemy aircraft in Corsica and Northern Sardinia could mean that the enemy intends to stage a sea and air invasion on the Italian coast, or the Southern coast of France.

'It seems clear that in order to rid himself of the dual threat to his flank Kesselring will have to entrench himself along the so-called Rommel Line, the line of the Apennines from La Spezia to Cattolica. This line is a naturally strong one due to the height of the mountains, the breadth of the range, the scarcity of roads and the fortification works carried out there since last September.

'It would however be a great mistake to suppose that this line would in itself suffice to halt the enemy finally and save the Po Valley. A mass attack by troop transport planes and parachute forces could take place on the plain of the Po, just as it is doing in France. Hence the Apennine line is in fact already threatened, largely because of the crushing superiority of the enemy air force, which will soon have at its disposal dozens of airfields in Central Italy and is moreover able to improvise by applying the familiar system of rolling out temporary wire-netting airstrips. The necessity therefore arises of holding in readiness a force capable of being deployed against parachute and airborne troops and of defending the region from enemy air attack.

'The present (Italian) local commands can and should in my opinion form the basis for this arrangement, which need not entail a special force but should demand a proper army designed for the purpose and competent to amass the experience which we are now witnessing. We must counter a massed attack by parachutists by a defence *en masse*.

'Such a force must operate in close collaboration with anti-aircraft units and police formations, must be heavily armed and above all equipped with means of transport to take them from one part of the country to another.

'Some organization of a regional and local character may be set up along-side this regular force. It is not my business to enter into technical details at this stage. That is a task which must be tackled by the General Staffs.

'In conclusion I must stress that the threat of parachute landings already exists, although operations have only been localized until now. The attention of the German commands must be drawn to this problem. There is not a moment to lose.'[2]

The battle for Rome, however, ended on the afternoon of June 4. The fate of the city since the previous September had been totally isolated under German military and civil command from that of Salò. At one time it seemed that the Germans might attempt a dramatic stand, but the final decision, influenced in part by Rahn's insistence, was left to Kesselring, who took the responsibility for retreating northwards.

Apart from the weakening of the military position, the psychological shock in the North was brutal. Declining confidence in a victorious end to the war struck the morale of the Republican government, and spurred forward the partisan movement of liberation.

On June 5 Mussolini, in an appeal to all Italians, referred specifically to those in the province of the Social Republic. 'We utter a supreme warning: the fall of Rome must not weaken our energies and even less our will to achieve the conditions of recovery. Every measure will be taken to this end . . . The Republic is menaced by plutocracy and its mercenaries of every race.'[3]

A sense of impotence and violence pervaded the North in this reaction of defeat, enflaming the civil war, and grimly symbolized by the trial of

Admirals Campioni and Mascherpa accused of obeying Badoglio and losing the Dodecanese in the previous year. Mussolini, unlike his attitude at Verona and contrary to that in regard to Carlo Scorza, intervened in demanding the supreme penalty which was carried out.

But the authority of the Republic was crumbling, and particularly at the edges, in the now threatened southern provinces.

There was the threat of administrative collapse in these areas, and a flight to the North of officials and Party organizations, thus infecting with defeatism the remaining territories of the Republic.

On June 13 Graziani and the Duce met to discuss the reports of indiscipline and mass desertions among the Italian army units under German command and the Republican Guard in Tuscany. Colonel Jandl, the liaison officer of the German Army Command attached to the Duce, was summoned to a subsequent meeting. Mussolini thought that the crisis would last until the end of the month. He stressed the urgent need for weapons for the 'old Fascists', the survivors of the March on Rome, now retreating northwards, as the sole reliable defenders of the Republic. Colonel Jandl was not enthusiastic. [4]

Pavolini now went to Florence to study the situation arising from the fall of Rome. On June 18 he wrote a long autograph letter to the Duce. He had as yet no clear idea of German intentions to defend or abandon Tuscany. But 'as to the political situation after the fall of Rome, and since the Allied advance towards Bolsena, this had been decidedly at its worst at the beginning at Grosseto and Siena, bad at Florence, Pistoia, and Arezzo; while Leghorn and Pisa had recovered reasonably well.' In Grosseto and Siena control had already passed to the 'rebels', and this collapse was contagious in the adjacent provinces. 'Everywhere has been confirmed the desertion—almost always with their weapons—of the Military Police; and a more serious fact. Almost everywhere a part of the Republican Guard has simply disintegrated, infected by the Military Police and the general situation. One can say the same with even more truth about the Army units.'

This disappearance of the forces of order increased the general mistrust. The Germans had ordered all units of the Republican Guard out of the province. 'The Fascists and the Fascists only have saved the situation . . . but concretely the problem is only that of the loyalty of the rank-and-file.' [5]

Pavolini was engaged on a rescue operation to salvage the core of loyal Fascist elements in the menaced provinces of Central Italy, and to evacuate them northwards to brace the frame of the Republic, and incidentally to strengthen the position of the Party at the centre of the political machine.

Dollmann was with Pavolini as the liaison with Kesselring's command. The draconian requisitioning of all forms of transport by the Germans was hindering the planned evacuation of the Fascist cadres. Dollmann had called on the German commander 'to put before him certain requests both for the

solution of most urgent problems and for the suggested timing of our proposed plan of action'.[6] On June 19 Pavolini wrote again to the Duce. Six
provinces in Central Italy were still under control; Fascist Party units were
now equipped and armed; but a temporary panic had been caused by the
Allied occupation of Elba, where the Italian garrison had promptly surrendered and gone over to the enemy, headed by a military band.

Three days later Pavolini visited Bologna where he received orders from
Mussolini to organize action squads. But the weight of twenty years of history
was against them both. The retreat in progress was not only geographical.
Political positions were irretrievably abandoned.

On June 24, in a further letter, Pavolini reported again. There was bad
news from Lucca. The Military Police had deserted and armed the prisoners
in gaol. In Florence the anti-Fascist parties had approached the Federal
Secretary—the highest local Fascist authority and a post once held by Pavolini himself—to arrange an eventual transfer of authority.

Within a few days the Allies entered the province of Florence. Pavolini
asked permission from the Duce to witness the end of Fascist rule in the fief
which he himself had created. On July 7 he wrote to Mussolini, 'As from
Monday we shall begin the gradual concentration of the squads in Turin.' [7]

The following day he wrote again on the situation throughout Florentine
territory, and in particular of Siena where the French had been welcomed
in the main square as 'liberators'.

'The circumstances must not be underrated that Siena is one of the Tuscan
provinces where, when I arrived, the premature and irreparable exodus of our
authorities and armed forces had already taken place. The capital town and
the country districts of the province—except for the purely figurative presence
of the head of the province, Chiurco, at the German headquarters—were left
to themselves, in a demoralizing absence of Republican and Fascist institutions, and an anticipation of the revival of the old parties. The direct and
determining cause—in Siena and elsewhere—was the melting away of the
Military Police and the Army, and the collapse of the Republican Guard . . .
Under the impact of the exodus from neighbouring provinces of Umbria and
Lazio and of imminent invasion, the fragile administrative and Party structures practically dissolved. Chiurco stayed in the province until the end . . .
but his modest political construction has proved extremely frail and almost
non-existent.'

Conditions in the province of Lucca were similar. 'It is difficult to imagine
the state of abandonment, of weakness, and squabbling, and contradictory
errors.' All the Fascist authorities in Leghorn had been withdrawn under
higher orders. In Pisa the commander of the Republican Guard had vanished
with his unit.

German military jurisdiction would now be extended throughout all these
provinces up to the right bank of the Po.

Within the shrinking frontiers of the Republic conditions deteriorated sharply. The fall of Rome, the Allied landings in Normandy, and the rapid advance of the Soviet armies in the East, had led to a severe shock to the already evaporating morale of the régime. The added loss of the provinces of Central Italy represented a particular blow to the historic base of Fascism, to the Tuscans of Pavolini's early action squads, whose remnants he now hoped to concentrate in Piedmont for what could only be a last stand.

It was not only in the threatened provinces of Central Italy that the administrative machine faced collapse. The control of the whole Republic, never firmly in the grasp of the Ministry of the Interior at Maderno or the Duce's secretariat at Gargnano, had been from the beginning a haphazard affair. Telephonic communications were effectively in German hands, as were in the early days even administrative appointments. The scattered government offices on the northern lakes could never be an effective substitute for an historic capital, and almost imperceptibly the Republic disintegrated into a series of provinces. The fall of Rome accelerated this process, and in an effort to recognize and halt the political fragmentation of the northern provinces, Mussolini decided in June 1944 to divide the shrinking territory of the Republic into four administrative regions: Emilia and Romagna, Veneto, Liguria, and Piedmont.[8] Each area was placed under a special regional commissioner, who had on paper absolute control over the prefects and all police functions, and was directly responsible to Mussolini.

In Piedmont the immediate situation was particularly acute. The active and open opposition of the partisan movement was based on the valleys leading to the Alpine passes and the areas controlling the approaches to the French frontier and produced a major threat to military security. The underground activities were strong in the industrial centres, and the capital city of Turin, in which the German authorities had a firm economic interest, had become a concentrated target of partisan attack.

As Hitler had stated at Klessheim in April, the control of Alpine passes was vital to the Germans. In the absence of any Italian Republican Army on a regular basis, it had been suggested that special anti-partisan units should be recruited and based on Parma under the command of General Mischi. [9] He was a specialist in such warfare in the Balkans. He had joined Graziani in September 1943, and was at that time placed temporarily in command of the Military Police in Rome.

And now in June 1944 he was to implement the undertaking given by the Italians at Klessheim to repress partisan activity as the first priority in the vital region of Piedmont. He was now ordered to expand the training centre for Special Units[a] up to 10,000 men in a series of units reunited from the remnants of the Parma depot, with such odd designations as COGU

a. Known by the initials CARS.

(Counter-Guerrilla), and RAU (Squads of 'Arditi' officers mounted on bicycles). The immediate purpose of these units was to protect from partisan molestation the interior lines of communication and the passes behind the 'Ligurian' army of Graziani, which consisted of German troops with scattered subordinate Italian units.

On June 15, General Mischi made a general report 'on the repression of rebel activities' [10] to a gathering of all the regional commanders of the Republican Army (who were without operational troops), selected Italian staff officers, and a senior German military representative.[b] It was a co-ordinated survey by the Republican military authorities of the impact of the spreading partisan movement through the provinces of the North.

Mischi opened the meeting. 'After the fall of Rome there has been confirmed a major depression of a spiritual character, a decline of faith and therefore of strength, and a strong increase in the number of deserters.' There must be no weakening and the military code must be severely applied in all cases. 'Our enemies display a notable and cold determination, which we must recognize and equal. We must act on our part towards the enemy with an equally clear vision of our aims.'

The regional commanders spoke briefly of the situation in their areas. General Montagna,[c] from Piedmont, said that here 'the rebels who already control almost the whole of Piedmont will finish by taking it over completely'. The recent call-up had been a grave mistake and only led to increasing the rebel forces. Mischi pointed out to the German representative the need to use at least certain age groups, not for civilian labour, but in the armed forces. 'He would ask that the volunteers of 1926 should be destined for CARS as for various reasons this force had only gathered 3,500 instead of the planned 9,000.' The partisan danger could be better met if there were greater autonomy of action on the part of such units.

The Army commander for Liguria said that 'the situation remained grave'. Active bands totalling 400–500 men were operating there, but the total partisan strength was about 5,000 men.

General Diamanti, the Milan commander, reported that in his region the situation was worse at Sondrio, Como and in Milan itself. All the military police posts throughout the province were closed. One night one thousand partisans had been able to enter the city. He had at his disposal a total of 1,100 men, of whom 500 were from the 'Muti'.[d] The main preoccupation was the 300,000 workers in the factories. There was always the possibility of an insurrectional general strike. Mischi suggested that it should be made known that in such an event the factories would be bombarded by the German air force.

b. Inspector-General Lungershausen.
c. One of the judges at the Verona trial.
d. An autonomous Fascist 'legion'.

The commander of the region of Padua said that the provinces of Vicenza, Verona and Treviso were the most 'disturbed'. The situation was particularly serious on Mount Grappa and the uplands of Asiago.

Mischi, in conclusion, explained to the German representative that all those present were decided to act, for 'henceforward our life is beyond any vicissitude, victorious or otherwise'. But arms and ammunition were required 'and within forty-eight hours'.[e]

The paramount need was to organize counter-action to the partisans, and to gain the initiative in what was now open civil war. The existence of the Salò republic depended on the security of the German lines of communication in Northern Italy. Apart from a handful of special units, operating under German orders, the scattered regional commands with troops from the regimental depots, and the Republican Guard, which was already a proven failure, there was no military organization at the disposal of the republican government. The only proposal made at the Klessheim conference was to set up the special units under General Mischi. He was able and energetic, but so far only had available some three thousand men and those were still under training. Meanwhile throughout the territory of the Republic even the nominal control of the Duce's administration was disappearing.

The possibility of using the Fascist Party cadres now being evacuated from Central Italy revived the idea, put forward already several times by Pavolini, to militarize the Party and create out of this material the shock troops of the Republic. On June 21, therefore, Mussolini authorized a decree setting up the new units to be known as the Black Brigades. It was described as 'an auxiliary corps of Black Shirts composed of action squads' constructed on the existing machinery of the Party. The central Party Directorate was to be transformed into a General Staff at the top, and the local political leaders were to appear as military commanders at the bottom level.[11]

Even Mussolini was aware of the disadvantages of yet further duplication, and postponed the enforcement of this decree, which would weaken irremediably the chance of building an effective regular military force round the division now training in Germany, and which would also finally place the Fascist Party in a commanding position in internal politics.

On June 25, four days later, Mussolini sent Graziani instructions to co-ordinate 'personally and directly' all military activities to 'meet and overcome the banditry of the outlaws'. A special inter-service committee was to be set up for this purpose.

These instructions were followed by a letter from Mussolini to Graziani, dated June 27, which was headed 'The March against La Vendée'.

e. The text of this report was set up in type by the partisans as a supplement to the ultra Fascist paper in Piedmont *Il Popolo di Alessandria*, and for a few hours sold as such on the streets of Turin. See Agosti's evidence in Graziani *Processo* II, pp. 383–4.

'The organization of the movement against the partisans to which you referred last night, must be such as to strike the people psychologically and rouse enthusiasm in our unified ranks. It must be the "March of the Social Republic against the Partisans" (La Vendeé).

'And since the centre of the monarchist, reactionary, bolshevist Partisans is Piedmont, after gathering all its forces at Turin the March must begin with Piedmont. It must radiate from Turin to all the provinces, clear them up radically, and then go on immediately to Emilia.

'I think the situation will be reversed, especially if the operations on the Italian front are favourable.' [f]

The following day Graziani summoned a meeting, which was also attended by Wolff and Rahn, and later he had a long talk with General Toussaint, the German military zone commander of the whole of North Italy, excluding the operational areas under Kesselring.

The German attitude to this burst of energy on the part of the Italians was discouraging. Graziani sent a minute to the Duce and quoted the remarks of Colonel Heggenreiner, the German liaison officer at Graziani's headquarters, at the meeting with Toussaint. 'In face of this psychological stiffening on the part of the Italians, there still remains our imperative interest in man-power for civilian labour . . . We must convince ourselves that a people before whom one had already dangled the prospect of peace is no longer fit to bear arms, but only to be exploited as labour. Marshal Kesselring, after the Elba episode, does not want to have any more to do with Italian troops, in whom he has lost all confidence.'

And as Graziani commented at the end of the minute 'And what will become of our divisions in Germany if this view is accepted without question by the German High Command?' [12]

Graziani now stated his views on Mussolini's instructions to him to co-ordinate anti-partisan activities in the form of a long memorandum. It was a private ultimatum, and a catalogue of frustrations. It is also a summary history of the Republic.

'On June 25 (1944) the Duce, with the letter in his own hand which is herewith attached, instructed me to co-ordinate the activities of the various Armed Forces, including the National Republican Guard, and the formation of the Fascist Republican Party, in order to decapitate the rebellion of the outlaws. To accept such an important and difficult task, I think it is necessary

f. Italian Collection. See also a slightly different text in Graziani *Processo* I, p. 374 dated June 27, 1944. Mussolini sent a copy of this letter to Rahn, with a covering note—'I beg you to give your co-operation, as always, so that the March against the Partisans ("La Vendée") can be put into effect as soon as possible.'
This political vocabulary has a curious parallel. On October 9, 1919, the militant Italian nationalists sent a delegation to D'Annunzio, who had just seized Fiume with his 'legionaries' in defiance of the Italian government, with the proposal that he should extend his activities 'first to Venezia Giulia, then to the other provinces, and thus in succession finally to Rome'. (Quoted by N. Valeri, *Da Giolitti a Mussolini*, 1956, p. 49.)

to diagnose the causes of the present situation and to establish the political and military premises of my task, otherwise I do not consider that I can undertake the responsibilities which the Duce has assigned me.'

(1) *Factors governing the present situation in Italy*

'The principal causes of the actual grave politico-military malaise in Italy, which daily assumes all the aspects of a real wasting disease, to such an extent as to make one regard as imminent a new and irreparable collapse, and consequently a complete disintegration of the political and military structure of the Italian Social Republic, can be summarized thus:

(1) *The military situation in the various military theatres, particularly the Italian.*

'The Italian masses are convinced that Germany has lost the war, and that the efforts of their soldiers . . . serve no purpose. There is also much scepticism as to the efficacy of the new secret weapons. In the Italian theatre, no serious reinforcements have arrived, and given the lack of air superiority and the weakness of anti-aircraft defence, it is very problematical for a halt of the front along the Tuscan-Emilian Apennines to be made. The possibility of naval landings, backed by parachute troops, such as have been used with conspicuous success in Normandy, made German resistance in Italy a precarious matter, and an enemy invasion of the Po Valley is very probable.

(2) *The spread of Communism.* Enemy propaganda, "by ably exploiting old slogans and adapting itself to the Italian mentality" had produced a harmless and attractive version of Bolshevism . . .

(3) *Distrust of Fascism.*

'The continued presence in key positions of men like Pavolini, Buffarini, and Ricci, committed to the past and thus, in the view of the masses, responsible for the solution which culminated in the disastrous events of July 25 and September 8, has alienated the sympathies of most Italians from the neo-Fascist Republic . . .

(4) *German occupation.*

'Although everyone recognized the absolute right of Germany, after the betrayal of September 8, to secure the position of her armies operating at the Front, it is equally deplorable that after more than nine months of countless proofs of absolute loyalty on the part of the Italian Social Republic the régime of military occupation has become even more oppressive and extended to every sector of national life.

'Everyone is convinced that the Government counts for nothing, and that the Germans are the real masters . . . All the splendid official statements, particularly those which followed the meeting of the Duce and the Fuehrer last April,[13] are commented on ironically . . .

'No one can understand for what reasons . . . a special régime is maintained in the provinces of the Adriatic littoral, now practically cut off from the rest of Italy.

(5) *Recruiting of man-power for Germany.*

'The sending of men to Germany is the most unpopular aspect of life in Italy today. The result is that call-up to the Army is practically void. The mass of young people prefer to take to the maquis . . . rather than go to Germany.

'It was a grave error to attempt to impose the Goering-Sauckel programme on Italy at such a time. The Germans have no conception of Italian psychology, as is simply shown by their treatment of the military internees.

(6) *The failure to reconstruct the Republican Armed Forces.*

'Is this Army a reality or an illusion? Why were the divisions in Germany not sent to defend Rome? . . . The position today can be summarized as follows. We have called up 400,000 men to the armed forces and as civilian labour, and we have been able to send to the front only four battalions of volunteers, the "Barbarigo" and the "Folgore" and two S.S. units. Naval and air co-operation has been derisory, though brilliant. The territorial commands in all contained some 3,000 men armed only with rifles and a few machine guns. There were four battalions of CARS inadequately equipped, and their deployment hampered by the German S.S. command. Apart from 60,000 men in training with the four divisions in Germany, there were no other soldiers but only workmen.

(7) *The Phenomenon of Rebellion.*

'In practice the government of the Italian Social Republic controls, and that only up to a point, the stretch of plain astride both banks of the Po. All the rest is virtually in the hands of the so-called rebels, who are supported by large sections of the population . . . All our "peripheral" organizations have been destroyed. The local centres and the countryside lack today any element of force which can carry out the orders of the Government, and make them respected.

'(II) *Military and Political Prerequisites*

(1) To stop all dispatch of man-power to Germany, other than on a voluntary basis. Rub out the whole Goering-Sauckel programme.

(2) There must be a thorough reconsideration of the whole position of the military internees in Germany.

(3) Increased propaganda activities to raise volunteers for the Army.

(4) Maximum liberty of action. "This is the fundamental point, and condition *sine qua non* of the whole new organization."

(5) The Germans must equip and arm the voluntary units under Graziani's command.

(6) Reorganization of the "Republican Party". This must be left to the

"political sensitivity" of the Duce and conducted parallel to the acceptance by the Germans of the above outlined proposals. The principal exponents of the past must be removed from office.

(7) Reorganization of the Republican Guard. Graziani demands complete liberty of action.' [14]

At his trial Graziani maintained that he handed this memorandum in person to the Duce, saying that he could not accept the task. As there was no other figure of standing who could organize 'the march against La Vendée', throughout the whole territory nominally under the Salò Republic, Mussolini had to be content with appointing a regional commissioner to Piedmont,[g] and assigning to him the forces of General Mischi as this region was the most gravely exposed to danger. This combined arrangement was to be a test pattern of anti-partisan warfare.

This was the only result of the grandiloquent programme contained in the Duce's letter of June 27.

This modest outcome of Mussolini's programme of a national reaction to partisan warfare strengthened inevitably the position of Pavolini, and increased the potential value of the Black Brigades, to whose formation the Duce had not yet given active assent.

On June 27 Pavolini made his comments to Mussolini on those recent moves. [15] He thought that Graziani would be stimulating as 'the head of the anti-rebel movement if he supervises its activities acting directly as a politico-military leader, but if he nominally is in charge, through the machinery of the General Staff, it will be an unhappy experiment.

'Recent experience has shown that, except for the divisions training in Germany, wherever the army exists on national soil it is directly represented by nuclei of officers and men ready to desert and pass to the other side.'

The real strength of the régime lay in the reorganized action squads. Pavolini had respect both for Graziani and Mischi, but if they were going to command units of the Party 'they come as Fascists among Fascists on a terrain which is that of armed politicians against armed politicians. Your order to set up within the Party a corps of Black Shirt squads was so splendid. *Lo Squadrismo* had always had its own dynamism. It was necessary to the Republic, now threatened by the dynamism of the partisans. The whole Party must be transformed into an armed corps.'

On July 19 Pavolini wrote again to the Duce. On his return from Tuscany he had been summoned by Wolff who ordered Pavolini 'not to begin the move to Piedmont without first talking to him'.

It was agreed that the German S.S. should arm the first units of the Black

g. He was Paolo Zerbino, an able administrator, who had held a similar post in Rome until June 1944.

Brigades, now in formation from the remnants of the Party machine from the Central provinces, and which were as yet not officially in being. [16]

An immediate clash between Pavolini and General Mischi followed for control of the dwindling paramilitary forces of the Republic. Mischi asserted that he was not only in charge of operations in Piedmont under Graziani, but was assuming direct command of the Party units and expressing arbitrary and disagreeable judgments on such formations.

In the meanwhile there could be no illusions as to the gravity of the Republican position in Piedmont, not only owing to the 'Vendéean' opposition, but within the ranks of the supporters of the Salò régime. Despair at the weakness at the centre of government and at the factionalism of the leaders had led to a spirit of protest and indiscipline.

The editor of the Turin paper *La Stampa*, Concetto Pettinato, who had already at the time of the Verona Congress come out fiercely against the monopoly in public affairs of the Fascist Party, published on June 21 a leading article[h] which echoed the local discontent, even in Fascist Party circles, with the leadership. Dissident movements had been vocal and widespread not only in Turin, but in Milan, Brescia, and other northern cities, but they had as yet no rallying point. Pettinato's article voiced these resentments, and there was every practical danger that his words might produce at least a muffled explosion.

In his article he attacked the Government's failure to act, and also questioned the power of the Germans to hold the Apennine line. Hitherto small groups of Italians had fought by the side of their German comrades, but where were the new Italian divisions? Rumours were going about that especially the officers could not be trusted, that many had enrolled from the German internment camps simply in the hope of coming back to Italy and then deserting. If this was not true, the divisions should be sent to fight in and for Italy, and the question of loyalty must be settled.

Inside Italy there were serious problems. For example, the question of the nationalization of industries which had been due to take place on June 30, 1944 (according to decree of February 13). Here too there was uncertainty. The owners showed no enthusiasm, the workers looked on ironically, ready to maintain that the Government would not keep to its promise and that it was useless to expect reform from the Republic. Owners and workers combined in spite of mutual dislike. The Government was as usual acting too late. Piedmont was further plagued by rebellion. Resistance to military duties was explained as unwillingness to be trained in Germany and sometimes 'to serve Fascism'—and worse—refusal to submit to any kind of discipline—whether of officials, family or clergy. Piedmont had become 'a nursery of crime, disorder, and desertions'.

h. The title of the article was 'If you are with us, strike a blow.'

The favourable reaction to Pettinato's attack on the Party leadership spread beyond Piedmont to Genoa and Milan, and the head of the political secretariat of the Party was sent from Maderno to Turin to make a confidential enquiry into the whole local climate. His report revealed that Pettinato had gone 'against the government in agreement with all the local authorities', and even with the consent of the Germans.

The local Fascist organization in the province of Turin was in a state of 'exasperation without élan'. There were eleven thousand Party members, but at a recent meeting five hundred appeared of whom one hundred were police agents. 'They felt that they had been abandoned as they had no directive on which to act and no weapons with which to defend themselves.'

The city of Turin was practically under siege. 'The rebels could occupy Turin any time they wanted.'

The report concluded: 'The situation of Turin Fascism is extremely precarious, in that the Fascists lack decision, orientation, ideas, and even courage.' [17]

The key to the situation in Turin lay in the hands of the Fiat works, whose management was playing a double game. 'Now again in June there had been further strikes. These had been announced by the factory committees a month previously but the authorities had done absolutely nothing to prevent the strike, the motive of which was known; the threatened transfer of machinery to Germany; but the agitation was fomented by the Fiat management whose prestige is ever increasing as they are at the head of the only organization in Turin capable of feeding a large number of people.'[i] These strikes had been carefully prepared and closely controlled by the Liberation Committee in Turin, which was predominantly Communist. For the first time a mass effort was initiated. As previously the issue of supplementary wages was a leading motive, but even more important was the spontaneous revolt of the Fiat workers against the German threat to transport machinery to the Garda region, ostensibly away from Allied bombing. This would inevitably involve the removal of the workers themselves from Turin.

On June 20, 12,000 men came out on strike at Fiat Mirafiori, and on June 21 50,000 at Fiat (central) and Lancia in spite of the intervention of Agnelli (head of Fiat) and the German RUK representatives. The workers petitioned Agnelli not to allow the removal of machinery to Germany. On June 21 the Germans began this operation. On the following morning Allied planes bombed the works, thus showing, according to this police report, 'the existence of a link between the strike and the enemy air force'. In spite of a general lock-out by the Fiat management under German pressure, the movement spread and 40,000 workers came out over a period of ten days. The reaction of the Fascist and German authorities was half-hearted,

i. Another Fascist report reads 'The strikes were provoked and financed by the directors themselves.'

and after concessions over wages and assurances as to the transfer of machinery, the strikers returned to work, having given a first demonstration of massed organization with all its political implications.[j]

It was as a direct result of this state of affairs that Zerbino was appointed Regional Commissioner, with powers to report direct to the Duce, and to co-ordinate anti-partisan activities with General Mischi. On the success of this experiment depended largely whether the frame of the Republic could be held together elsewhere.

Reports from other provinces of the effect of Pettinato's article were sent direct to Mussolini. In Genoa the local Fascists regarded it as disastrous and demoralizing. 'In fact the Genoese are disgusted with the Government and its officials and agree with Pettinato.' In Milan the impression was immense and 'expressed the opinion of most Fascists', as being not against Mussolini but the men who surrounded him. [18]

Mezzasoma, the Minister of Popular Culture, wrote to the Duce that the the article was 'the hardest blow yet dealt to the prestige of the Fascist Republican Government'. [19]

It was against such a background that Graziani set about the task entrusted to him by Mussolini of co-ordinating all forces against the partisans.[k]

Between June 27 and July 5 he held a series of meetings with his commanders and German military representatives to survey the whole position of the armed forces of Salò. [20] Unless the Fascist Republic could gain the military initiative against the spreading partisan movement, the whole experiment of Salò would dissolve into chaos.

The review was one of unrelieved gloom. The Italian Army had by now recruited some 400,000 men, who were almost all under German control. The real army consisted of the four divisions still training in Germany. In Italy Graziani had under his control only four battalions ('Chasseurs of the Apennines') and they were nominally under S.S. command. The Party had offered 50,000 men to the Army, and less than 1,000 had materialized.

In conversation with General Toussaint, the latter asked Graziani whether Mussolini intended to cut down the Ministries and concentrate authority in a few hands. Graziani denied any knowledge of such moves, but said that the only new feature was the transformation of the Party into 'an auxiliary Corps of Black Shirts'.

But 'no one would talk of Fascism any more . . . the failure of the last call-up showed the people's lack of confidence in the government . . . they also believed that Germany was doing badly in the war'. No more civilian labour should be sent to Germany. The young men simply took to the woods if re-

j. For an account based on unprinted Communist and Fascist sources see Luraghi, *op cit* pp. 222 ff.

k. Graziani denied at his post-war trial that he had any responsibility for these activities.

cruited. At least the Italian divisions should come back to Italy. Toussaint said that it was impossible to interfere with Goering's and Sauckel's labour programme.

Graziani enlarged on his views in a report to Mussolini dated June 28. Most of the younger generation were joining the rebels. Only the flat lands of the Po Valley were under Republican control. All the rest was virtually in the hands of the rebels. In the towns the Government was represented, but these centres 'are the most dangerous breeding grounds of rebellion'. The last hope of saving the Italian Republic lay in effective action against the rebels and under unified Italian command, in accordance with Mussolini's order of June 25.

In his meeting with the German commander of the S.S. in North-West Italy, General Tensfeld, the latter gave a gloomy account of the rebel strength, especially in Piedmont, and centred on Turin. Many of the rebels were ex-soldiers, and above all from the 'auxiliary police forces'. The industrial centres were threatened. The Germans wished to remove industries to the Aosta region, but the last German-Italian attack, with 4,500 men, was not really successful. The rebels withdrew to the mountains, disposed of considerable forces and were awaiting a regular assault. They were feeling their strength. They had considerable supplies of explosives, which were widely used. The first objective of the Germans and Italians must be Turin.

In conversation with Kesselring, the point was emphasized that the partisans 'and the population generally' were giving trouble to the Germans. There was general refusal to help in repairing roads and railways, and not even the promise of exemption from transportation to Germany had any effect.

Kesselring said that 'he had advised Hitler to send two divisions, the "Monte Rosa" and "San Marco", back to Italy'. He proposed that these divisions should be united in an army under Graziani 'to be used in routing out the rebels from their retreats'. All Liguria to be placed under Graziani including the two and a half German divisions there. This meant that Graziani would be under his, Kesselring's, command.

Graziani voiced one serious preoccupation about the divisions from Germany. They included many men who had not been home for years, having been formerly interned in Germany. If given leave to go home, they might not return, if refused leave they would certainly desert. Kesselring said Graziani must clear this up before the troops left Germany, otherwise there would be a catastrophe for Italy. If there was any risk it would be best to disarm them.

Graziani added that he would use them at once on arrival in Italy. He would go personally to Germany to speak to the troops. It was agreed also that Mussolini should make a short visit to the troops in Germany. There was need of good propaganda from him.

Graziani then spoke of the strength of the rebels, of the feeling that the Po Valley was surrounded by them, and also dwelt on the effect of the despatch of people to Germany causing increase in the rebel bands. The greatest effect on public opinion would be produced by announcing that no one else will be sent to Germany. Goering had already taken 80,000 internees for anti-aircraft defence.

Kesselring promised to speak to Rahn on the subject, also to raise the question of internees. Graziani said this last matter was in course of discussion between Hitler and Mussolini, but that Kesselring's support would be valuable. He expected an enemy land and sea attack—and thought that the Allies would land troops at Rimini and throw in parachute troops on the principal centres of the Po Valley, while rebels would come down from mountains all round it.

It was on these two cardinal points—the return of the Italian divisions and the problem of the internees—that preparations were being made for a personal meeting between Hitler and Mussolini.

TO THE 'GOERLITZ' STATION
(July 20, 1944)

- -

THE SUMMER OF 1944 was stained by the rising ferocity of civil war in Northern Italy. The psychological shock to the Salò régime of the Allied occupation of Rome, together with the spreading of the partisan rising, increased the disintegration of the Republic. The ultimate defence of the Po Valley by the Germans and the Italian Fascists depended on the prior suppression of rebellion along the lines of communication throughout the whole northern region.[a] Unless a striking force were at the disposal of the Duce's government, the whole structure of the Italian satellite would vanish.

Mussolini decided therefore to visit the camps of the four Italian divisions, which had now almost completed their training in Germany, and whose presence in Italy was essential to the survival of the Republic. The tour was to conclude with a meeting at Hitler's headquarters in East Prussia.

The Duce left Gargnano on July 15. He travelled by special train and was accompanied by Graziani, Mazzolini, Anfuso, Vittorio Mussolini, and Rahn. At each railway station, the stops were punctuated by the study of the most recent air bulletins and by solicitous messages from Hitler enquiring as to the progress of the journey. The German chief of protocol, Baron Doernberg, was responsible for the arrangements, and under strict orders not to expose the Duce to danger from air attack.

At Munich the train passed through clouds of black smoke discharged by anti-aircraft units to mask the city from the air. In the distance the sound of heavy explosions was heard. Doernberg told the Duce that military exercises were in progress. Mussolini lost his temper.

The journey took the Italian party on a circular tour of the whole territory

---

a. As the resistance leader Parri stated at Graziani's trial after the war, the latter had written to Keitel that 'the breaking up of the rebels was the prerequisite of effective military action'. Graziani *Processo op cit* II, pp. 197–8.

of the Reich. It was marked by air-raid alarms, and hasty descents from the train. As Keitel murmured to Anfuso, 'It is lucky that there are only four divisions'.[1]

The visit to the training camps was the Duce's Indian summer.[b] He was received amid scenes of exaltation and fervour. As Rahn wrote, 'Mussolini and Graziani were greeted by their young countrymen with frenzied joy, and roused in them all too willingly the hope that this mood could be solid and later shared by the Italian population.' [2]

The physical presence of the Duce had produced its old hypnotic effect, and, for a moment, stirred and restored his faith in himself. He had a deep need for such emotional contacts with the crowd, and equally his appearance among Italian soldiers in the alien surroundings of the German camps provoked a spontaneous response. Both Graziani and Anfuso were swept into the same brief euphoric mood.

The final ceremony was held on the afternoon of July 18 at the camp of Sennelager near Paderborn, where the Roman Legions of Varus had been annihilated by the Teutonic tribes in A.D. 9, and where the monument to the victor, Arminius, now stands as a symbol of German national independence. It was here that Graziani spoke to the assembled Italian officers. Carried away by his own oratory, he shouted, 'Since the days of our Roman forebears we have often been hard pressed and defeated. But we have always grimly hit back. Varus lost his legions . . .' And at this point he caught Rahn's eye, and realized the implication that the classic defeat had been at the hands of the ancestors of his present hosts. He paused at a momentary loss, and then in an even louder voice proclaimed, 'But now the Germans have given us back our legions', and sat down.[3]

Anfuso too, had been impressed by the significance of these receptions. 'The fate of the four divisions is linked to the history of Mussolini's personality . . . and our misfortune was to have lacked imagination. Could one have conceived of Mussolini fighting like Garibaldi at the head of his legions? And yet this was exactly what the Italians demanded of him during four years of war. They wanted to fight for someone not something.' [4]

On the final stages of the journey to East Prussia, there was some discussion in the special train of the course of the coming talks. According to Rahn, he persuaded the Duce to concentrate on bringing up to Hitler in a decisive form the question of the fate of the Italian military internees. This was one of the central points of friction between the two governments, and which Mussolini had unsuccessfully pressed at the last meeting at Klessheim. A note was drafted on the train to form a basis of discussion. [5]

---

b. The itinerary was as follows: July 16, the 'Monte Rosa' Division at Münzingen; July 17 the 'Italia' at Paderborn; July 18 morning, the 'San Marco' at Grafenwöhr; and afternoon, the 'Littorio' at Sennelager.

The party was due to arrive at Rastenburg on the early afternoon of July 20, but, as the train approached the 'Goerlitz' station,[c] it came to an abrupt halt at a siding. An hour passed.

The unexpected delay, and the visible agitation of Doernberg, perplexed everyone. It could hardly be an air-raid alarm as there would have been orders to take cover away from the train. 'The Germans who accompanied us,' wrote Anfuso, 'learnt that something serious had occurred at the Wolf's Lair [d] and sufficiently grave to force them to slow down the speed of the train and oblige us to arrive at Rastenburg with doors and windows hermetically sealed and blacked out . . . At last the train, still protected in this sinister fashion, reached Wolf's Lair, where, with every kind of precaution, Doernberg opened one of the windows of the compartment, where Mussolini and . . . one of the others were. From this window we saw drawn up as usual Hitler, Ribbentrop, Himmler, Bormann, Keitel, Doenitz, and other Nazi leaders.' [6]

The whole railway station was occupied by S.S. Troops. 'Hitler came forward to meet Mussolini as he got out of the train, and said to him literally, "Duce, an infernal machine has just been let off at me." ' [7]

The Fuehrer stood 'wrapped up in his wide black cloak . . . He appeared completely calm. Only a slight trembling of the arm, raised in a Nazi salute, revealed the nervous shock to which he had been submitted. On the back of his right hand a very slight scratch: that was all.' [8]

In a convoy of cars, through tense control posts, where the documents of the Italian guests were closely checked, the party reached the hutted encampment of the General Headquarters. Hitler disappeared at once with Himmler, and after an excited conversation the latter took his leave. His mission was to suppress the conspiracy in Berlin. The Fuehrer then conducted the Italians to the scene of the explosion and described the incident.

'When we entered the group of huts forming the centre of the camp, our curiosity was equalled by the embarrassment which our presence caused. Hitler ran continually to the telephone. He spoke to Goebbels just after rejoining us. We stayed a long time at the entrance to a small salon where tea was laid for us, witnessing the comings and goings of all the Nazi leaders; and trying to reconstruct the events from the excited phrases which reached us through the partition of the huts and from the most recent remarks of Hitler . . .' [9]

Certain members of the Italian delegation wondered whether, if the plot had succeeded, they themselves would not have been made prisoners by the conspirators. According to a later dispatch from Anfuso on his return to Berlin, 'As to the fixing of the date of the *attentat*, the visit of the Duce was

c. The code name for the small railway station near the German General Headquarters.
d. Wolfschanze, Hitler's General Headquarters.

not extraneous. He was to be arrested immediately on arrival in East Prussia.'

An astonishing tea-party now took place. The German leaders, unsure of each other, burst into mutual recriminations in front of their guests. They had not all been present at the fateful meeting, and now arrived one by one. Goering in particular had been elsewhere, 'lurking in his special train'. [10] As Graziani remarked later, 'Among all those now assembled round Hitler, he seemed the least moved. If I had had to identify, among them all, a Judas, I would have picked on him.' [11]

Fortunately Hitler wanted to begin the talks with his Italian guests, 'perhaps thinking that it would be the only way of getting us to leave'.

The official German record of the ensuing conversation gives little impression of the savage and disordered preoccupations of the Fuehrer, and the astounded and stunned reactions of his Italian guests.[e]

Mussolini began by congratulating the Fuehrer on his escape, 'which he described as a signal proof of divine intervention'. Hitler merely stressed that the circles behind the attempt 'consisted of a small clique of reactionary cranks, who had nothing in common with the Nation.

'He had had an unpleasant feeling, and a sense of foreboding, while still on the way to his headquarters. Scientists might scoff at that kind of thing, but he himself had often in the past had premonitions of impending danger. He still clearly recalled one occasion in World War I when, feeling positive that the next shell was going to land in the mine crater where he lay, he and a comrade had left it at the very last minute before the catastrophe he had predicted actually took place.

'The Duce replied that only a man who had luck could ever be the leader of a great nation, reminding him that Napoleon used to choose his generals according to whether or not their lives showed them to be lucky men.'

Hitler launched into a perfunctory discourse. 'The crisis now upon us could be attributed partly to personal, but basically to material, causes. Germany, for example, had not hitherto mass-produced tanks. But production had now been started up. The decisive factor, however, was the Air Force. Germany had entered the war with an air force markedly superior to that of the enemy. Then some technical blunders had been made.'

Hitler then touched on the long mooted subject of secret weapons, seemingly

e. The main sources for this conference are: (a) German Collection: Schmidt minute 'Record of a conversation between the Fuehrer and the Duce in the Fuehrer's Headquarters, July 20, 1944', from which this account is essentially taken; (b) Amicucci, op cit pp. 163 ff, which contains fragments of an Italian record taken presumably from Anfuso's record. This is also quoted in Spampanato, op cit III, p. 212.

The best general account of the July Plot and its background is the detailed and imaginative description of Sir John Wheeler-Bennett. *The Nemesis of Power, passim* July 20, 1944. See also Anfuso, op cit pp. 449 ff. Dollmann, op cit pp. 393 ff. Rahn, op cit pp. 258 ff. Graziani, op cit pp. 445 ff. Zacharias, op cit pp. 123 ff.

taking his Italian guests into his confidence on highly technical matters on whose successful solution the issue of the war might depend.

'On the subject of weapons of retaliation . . . work was still in progress on another, and heavier, weapon to succeed the V.1. Basically, this invention was perfectly satisfactory. As a result of its newness, however, a number of practical problems arose, the solution to which was still being worked out. One of these problems was the fact that the missile fell to earth from a height of 53 miles and on re-entering the earth's atmosphere from the stratosphere was braked by a drop in speed from 5,500 feet to 2,600 feet a second. This generated such heat that the missiles mostly exploded in the air. By the use of fibreglass and other insulating materials this difficulty had already been overcome to the extent that 65–70% of the missiles had returned to earth. He was therefore hopeful that this weapon could be brought into action before long. The power of the new missile could be gauged for instance from the fact that blank missiles made craters some 32 yards wide and 9–11 yards deep on hitting the ground.

'Moreover, the approach of these missiles to their target could not be detected in advance. Hence no warning could be given to the population.' Hitler stressed that London would be bombarded until the whole city was utterly destroyed. As the new weapon was four to six times as powerful in its effects as the V.1, the destructive effect of fire on the British capital when it was brought into action would of course be greatly increased.

Turning to the Eastern Front Hitler attributed the crisis 'in part to a failure of leadership', which was compelling him to bring twenty-five fresh divisions and ten tank brigades into the field in the shortest possible time. This was largely a question of man-power—a subject which was depressingly familiar to the Italians. He now asked Mussolini to co-operate by sending a contingent of new Italian volunteers to serve in the anti-aircraft units recently set up to protect German factories. 'If no Italian volunteers could be provided, he would, in view of the urgent need to bring up the new divisions, have to resort to the Italian divisions on the same basis as to the German forces.' The German air force, for example, had had to find 50,000 men for these new formations for the Eastern Front. 'If, on the other hand, Italian volunteers were forthcoming, the two above-mentioned divisions could remain intact. Together with the two divisions which had returned already, these could then form a compact unit of four divisions of the Fascist Republican forces, so that, with the addition of, say, four German divisions, Graziani would have a whole army under his command. If a proportion of the German officers remained with Italian units and the divisions went into action alongside German units, the military results were sure to be excellent, the more so since the Italian officer corps had also been rejuvenated by the promotion of non-commissioned officers. The Germans would just have to borrow part of the equipment of the two Italian divisions, circumstances permitting, for a very short time (three weeks). But the Italian divisions would in any event be left with sufficient weapons for training to be continued.'

Hitler referred generally to the situation in Italy, 'a country of military importance both as a shield for Istria, Albania and the Balkans, and for its rôle in tying down the enemy forces. He had ordered Kesselring to pursue his retreat, fighting to hold on south of Florence as long as possible and to stem the enemy advance to the best of his ability. Florence itself would not be defended, so as to spare its art treasures. The final defence position, however, would be taken up only after strenuous delaying resistance, which among other advantages would gain time to consolidate the position. He hoped that he would then be able to resume the war in the air with German superiority. . . . He planned to mass 2–3,000 of the new fighters on a single front, repeat the process on another front, and by thus establishing spearheads, regain his former superiority . . .'

Hitler had reached the climax of his monologue.

'It was clear from the experience of the war to date, and especially from recent developments, that the world was witnessing a technical revolution of the first order. So as not to lag behind in the production race, Germany would enlist the population to an even greater extent than before. Youths from fifteen years up would be conscripted to help on the work on anti-aircraft sites, and women up to fifty would work in the factories. He did not dream of capitulating. Such an occurrence as the misfired attempt to assassinate him merely reinforced his firm and long-cherished conviction that Providence tested men, and gave the palm only to such as pursued their path undismayed and undeterred by difficulty.'

Perhaps for the first time on such an occasion, and because of the special and macabre circumstances, Mussolini sensed a superior calm. After so many humiliations in German company, and accusations of treachery on the part of Italy towards her Axis ally, the present dialogue was taking place in a climate of treason emanating from German military and political circles. The grim humour of the situation could not be missed.

The Duce began his remarks almost condescendingly.

'In view of the strain to which the Fuehrer had been subjected he would be brief, limiting himself to the following remarks on the situation in Italy. In the months of January, February and March, a certain progress in the Fascist Republican régime had been discernible. Then, with the opening of the offensive in Italy on May 12, a "crisis of expectation" had arisen. With the fall of Rome, morale had naturally fallen a good deal . . .'

The partisan menace had spread. 'The general insecurity had finally infected even the police and administration, so that reliance could now be placed only upon the Fascist Republican Party and its organizations.' He had therefore set up the Black Brigades for use in the anti-partisan struggle. Since the members of these brigades were fighting not merely for their own lives but for the lives and property of their families as well, they could be trusted absolutely. They knew what to expect from the partisans, should the latter gain the upper hand. In Rome alone, for example, between the evacuation of the Germans and the entry of the Allies, one to two thousand people had been shot by the Italian Communists.

'As regards the Italian divisions, he had carried away the best impressions from his visit to them. The German officers had dedicated themselves to the task of training them with great enthusiasm and marked success. The Duce thought that the assignment of the two divisions to anti-aircraft defence was a technical matter which could be settled between Keitel and Graziani. He merely asked that the divisions be allowed to keep their names and the flags which he had given them. He had of course no objection to their being used in Germany.

'The arrival in Italy of the first two Italian divisions would have a most salutary effect on the morale of the population and on their willingness to go to Germany as workers and soldiers. For enemy propaganda had alleged that these divisions would never come back to Italy, and their actual return to their homeland had proved the best and most effective of refutations.'

At this point Mussolini handed to Hitler a copy of the memorandum on the military internees, which had been drafted during the train journey.[f] 'The Duce said that he would be especially pleased to receive a "present" from the Fuehrer in this connection. The Duce was highly gratified, and stressed that the internee problem affected some ten million Italians, particularly in Southern Italy, and that this relief measure would have important repercussions on the populace. The prestige of the Republican government would moreover rise considerably . . .' [12]

On handing this note to Hitler, Mussolini had suggested that he should read it at his leisure. 'The latter, however, at once read through the three pages and then said, "I entirely agree with the proposals which it contains." ' [g]

The meeting broke up. Hitler showed his guest over the room in which the attack had taken place. 'The room, completely destroyed by blast, with the ceiling caved in and débris lying about the floor, left a deep impression on the Duce. Considering the devastation it was an absolute wonder the Fuehrer had emerged practically unscathed . . .' [13]

Tea was served, and Hitler took his leave.

He was not concentrating on the subjects under discussion, and had closed

f. For the text, see Appendix A to this chapter.

g. A fragment of the verbatim text of what appears to be the Italian minutes of this meeting are quoted in Amicucci *op cit* pp. 163–4. See also Anfuso *op cit* p. 454 for a slightly different version of Hitler's words.

the interview with speed. Messages were coming in constantly while these talks were in progress, and the Duce was merely repeating the arguments already made at the Klessheim Conference in April.

Simultaneously with this meeting, Graziani and Keitel were engaged in the latter's office in attempting to reach agreement on the employment of the remaining two Italian divisions, which had now completed their training in Germany.

Colonel Heggenreiner, the German liaison officer attached to Graziani's staff, was present at this talk and acted as interpreter. He later gave evidence at the Marshal's trial on what took place. [14] In view of the serious repercussions of the Russian advance into East Prussia, Keitel wanted to retain these Italian divisions in Germany, and use them for anti-aircraft defence on the Eastern Front. Such a suggestion provoked Graziani to explode sharply and to threaten to resign. Vittorio Mussolini was eavesdropping at the door of Keitel's office. Graziani therefore shouted even louder for him to hear. Even Keitel was made to see that such a move would be the end of the Republican régime in Italy, and the matter was dropped. [15]

The Duce had at least managed to exploit the confusion at German Headquarters. He had rapidly secured agreement over both internees and their future treatment and on the immediate return to Italy of the two remaining divisions in training in German camps.

The Fuehrer accompanied his Italian guests to the train. It was just ten years—June 14, 1934—since the first meeting of the two men in Venice. [16] They were not to see each other again. Hitler's last words were: 'I know that I can count on you, and I beg you to believe me when I say that I look on you as my best and possibly only friend I have in the world.' And then came a cryptic aside to Rahn, 'Be very careful.' [h]

At about seven o'clock that evening, the train drew out of the station, and orders were given to close all windows.

On the return journey, the Duce and his party received over the radio the official German news statement to the world of the July Plot. 'Today a bomb attempt was made on the Fuehrer. Several of his entourage were severely wounded . . . Others were more slightly injured. The Fuehrer, apart from superficial burns and shock, suffered no injuries. He resumed his work without delay, and, as anticipated, received the Duce at a long meeting . . .' [17] The comparison with the events of the previous July in Italy could hardly yet be effectively drawn, but there was small, if grim, comfort for the Duce.

h. Was this a warning to keep a close watch on Mussolini for fear of another betrayal or a solicitous instruction to look after his old friend? See Moellhausen, *op cit* p. 194.

It was a natural reaction on the part of the Italians to compare the rifts in the structure of the German régime as revealed by the attempt on Hitler's life with the stresses within the Italian Fascist State which had led to the dismissal of Mussolini in the July of the previous year. Anfuso made later a savage and perceptive historical comparison.

'July 25, 1943, and July 20, 1944, are the two most significant dates of the Second World War in that, in the space of one year, the classes which were to gather up the succession to the dictatorships came out into the open. On the one hand, the middle classes, who had delighted in frequenting and profiting by the authoritarian régimes, retreated out of fear: on the other, the proletarian forces which practised Socialism and had for the most part cooperated with the dictatorships up to the moment of repudiation and were then overcome by the same fears which pervaded the middle classes, became convinced that they could get rid of the first and the second.

'Rastenburg, on the day of July 20, 1944, suffered the consequences of not having wanted to bring about a relaxation of tension in Europe, such as Mussolini had always proposed and wished, and of having striven more and more inexorably to administer *à la Prusse* the territorial conquests made in Europe. The Putsch was a middle class one . . . Hitler the Prussian was attacked by the Junkers who did not know where he was leading them.' [18]

The respective rôles of the Army and the Party in Germany were therefore an urgent and pointed subject of analysis by Italian observers, and on his return to Berlin from the astonishing meeting at Hitler's Headquarters, Anfuso assembled, in a dispatch dated August 2, the information at his disposal on the crisis within the German political and military scenes.

'As I had the honour of telling you verbally, on the eve of the attack against the Fuehrer, a difference in principles and methods could be noted here between the German Army and the forces of the National-Socialist Party, which sometimes amounted to real tension. The German Army here does not mean the Army proper, which is largely made up of National Socialist elements, but the whole bureaucracy which is partly made up of the professional army of the Republic, the Reichswehr of von Seeckt, partly of Junker and pro-monarchic elements.

'The German Army in this sense of the word, had accepted war as a purely professional fact, and dedicated itself to it through all the victorious campaigns of the first years, with the capacity and courage traditional in Prussia and the other Germanic countries. When about two years ago the war began to lose its ascendant character, taking on that of a fanatical struggle which at a certain point was only inspired by mystic-social belief in the words of the Chief, the German generals, except the National-Socialists, refused to accept war as something overriding their professional powers, and began openly to criticize the leadership, above all if they were not personally blessed with fortune in arms. Noted, even noisy, champions of this criticism of the Nationalist-Socialist régime were Generals von Falkenhausen, von Brauchitsch, and the ex-Head of the General Staff, General Beck, who has already been shot.

'Even a close observer could predict that this dissatisfaction would burst out in an outrage or a *coup d'état*: but such a detailed attack, which at the same time had few ramifications throughout the country, was not predicted. In fact, we have seen that the conspirators calculated only on the surprise and the outburst of feelings which Hitler's disappearance would provoke in the country, while they had not thought of the possible immediate reaction of the Nationalist-Socialist masses even if the attempt succeeded.

'About the realization of the attempt, its scene, and the immediate reactions of the German leaders you yourself, Duce, have had a life-like and historically exact position, so that from the very beginning you have been able to observe the feelings of the government and the Party. I am now told, and report here, that the date of the crime was fixed in connection with your visit, and that you were to be arrested as soon as you arrived in East Prussia.[i] There are indications that the conspirators had understandings with Moscow or London, but certainly with Moscow, and there is certainly no doubt that they thought there could be no better opportunity of freeing themselves at the same time of the creator of European Fascism, and the head of German National-Socialism.

'If the attack failed so readily, its internal effects are deplorable, because an attempt against the life of a Chief who has been waging a merciless struggle against all the world for five years cannot help but make the soldiers reflect on the fate awaiting them if they are defeated: and internally too, such decided opposition shown by Generals who until yesterday were the authors of Germany's war plans, can only create a depression which the National-Socialist Party is now trying to correct with all its propaganda resources, and by appeals to a class struggle which finds echoes in the traditions of German Socialism and anti-monarchism.

'The one positive proof offered by the plot is that the country possesses a National-Socialist ruling class, which reacted effectively on the fringes against the orders coming from the chief conspirators. In fact, it is clear that several generals who had received orders from the German War Ministry in Berlin to arrest the gauleiter and kreisleiter in the provinces, telephoned to these men informing them of the affair, but adding that they did not know why they had to arrest them, and that therefore they wanted confirmation of the order. In short, it appears that the clique involved is less numerous than was thought at first, but that the leadership wants to take this opportunity of removing any kind of desire for future *coups d'état*.

'You yourself, Duce, will have heard from the Fuehrer himself, and from

i. This passage is underlined in pencil by Mussolini.

the other National-Socialist leaders present, how from the very first moment they intended to take extremely severe action against those responsible or possibly responsible.

'All Germany has naturally noticed that the expressions already in fashion here since September 8 for the "Traitor Generals" and "Traitor bands" were largely applicable to the conspirators against Hitler. I would say that our co-nationalists have derived certain understandable relief from this, since in private conversation they have been able to give their German comrades the retort that the plant of treachery among Generals grows just as well in Germany as in Italy. Perhaps realizing this state of mind, Minister Goebbels has twice used unhappily worded phrases in his speeches to say that, if there have been traitor Generals in Germany, the attempt was not successful. It was different in Italy. I informed Doctor Goebbels that this remark had caused offence in our country, since all loyal Italians realize that the success of the attempt on the Fuehrer's life would, besides gravely threatening Europe, have done irreparable harm to the Fascist Italy which reveres in Hitler the ally and saviour of the Duce. I will say further that we Italians have appreciated the full horror of the attempt, since it is we who have suffered most from the capitulation of precisely a few responsible generals . . .' [19]

As Mussolini said complacently, in answer to a question put to him on his arrival at Gargnano, 'We are no longer alone in regard to betrayals.' [20]

APPENDIX A

A Note handed by the Duce to the Fuehrer
(July 20, 1944)

'The Italian situation during these last months has not allowed me to make the expected contribution of man-power to Germany.

'Some months ago Marshal Kesselring absorbed some 70,000 workers, while 60,000 have been given to Air Marshal Richthofen. Since then, the government of the Social Republic has been asked to supply almost a million workers.

'In the present state of things it is impossible to accede to such a request:

(1) by reason of the considerable diminution of the national territory;

(2) because of the demoralization produced in almost every social class in Italy by the fall of Rome and consequent invasion of Italian Territory. Added to the fact that the sick and invalided who have recently returned from the internment camps in Germany are in a miserable condition, this state of mind has led to a form of aversion to recruiting for labour in Germany.

'Whereas there is a keen desire on the part of the authorities of the Italian Social Republic to contribute to the productive effort of Germany, the recruiting of Italian manpower appears to be difficult.

'Things being as they are, it is my duty to propose:

(1) that the labour potential of the Italian internees should be fully exploited for the process of German production. In order to achieve this, their material position must be improved;

(2) those internees of peasant origin should be employed in agricultural work;

(3) the internees should be sorted out according to their professional capacities;

(4) they could then be classified into proper military categories, which would assist also Marshal Goering's programme for using certain elements for the Air Force . . .;

(5) from the Italian side there would be no question of demanding the repatriation of the internees to Italy, inasmuch as I too am convinced that it would be harmful to reintegrate into the Fatherland men whose state of mind could easily send them into the enemy camp.

'A solution of the problem of the Italian internees on the above lines would on the one hand yield some hundreds of thousands of workers to German industry and agriculture, and, on the other, considerably alleviate the internal political situation of the Italian Social Republic. The resolution of such a problem together with the battle now going on against partisan banditry in Italy would represent without doubt a decisive contribution to the revival and reinforcement of the authority of the Fascist government.' [j]

APPENDIX B

Extracts from a dispatch of Ambassador Anfuso dated Berlin, August 2, 1944

'I give below a copy of two notes drawn up by two of my colleagues, reporting impressions and information gathered in Berlin. Their lack of agreement gives in the end quite a faithful overall picture of the tragic moment which Germany has lived through.

'The first of them writes.

'Berliners who remember the events of June 30, 1934, found those which took place in the capital on July 20 very similar. As then, on the day of the attempt against the Fuehrer armoured cars and lorries full of armed troops, with helmets and chinstraps lowered, passed through the streets of Berlin; as then, machine-guns could be seen at the corners of the central factories, and, at least for two nights, the S.S. arrested those suspected of having taken part in the conspiracy.

'On June 30, 1934, the most radical Leftist members of the Party paid in blood for following Roehm, and daring to want to storm the citadel of

j. Italian Collection.

the Prussian officers' camp to install themselves there, and to make the people's Brownshirt army into the permanent army of National-Socialist Germany.

'Ten years later, it was the turn of precisely the "Offizierkorps" of this order, perhaps unique in the modern world for its caste spirit and the influence it has had until now in the history of the country, to be shattered in the unsuccessful attempt to bring down the political leadership.

'If naturally it is not as yet possible to know whether the majority of the German Party was implicated in the conspiracy it seems at any rate probable that the circle of conspirators embraced more people than the press has indicated so far, i.e. more than Generals of the Army Beck and Hoepner, General of the Army Corps Olbricht, and the would-be assassin himself, Colonel Stauffenberg. To these we must probably add General of the Army Fromm, who was immediately replaced by Himmler in the Command of the Home Army, and on whom Count Stauffenberg was directly dependent, while even the Chief of the General Staff of the Army, General Zeitzler, would seem to be numbered among the suspects, if only because of negligence.

'The rest is as yet still rumour, but all in common mention Baron von Neurath [k] as the Foreign Minister of the rebel Government, the Chief of Police of the capital, Count Helldorf, and the Commander of the Berlin fortress, General of Division von Hass.

'To what Goebbels has already made known in his speech on the details of the "putsch" can be added that Major Remer, Commander of the Berlin Wachbatallion, presented himself to the Propaganda Minister to arrest him, and then disobeyed the orders of the Government of the Bendlerstrasse after being assured by telephone that the Fuehrer was living.

'The population showed no signs of reacting to the events with particular manifestations and was in no way roused out of the apathy which has now characterized it for months.

'Apart from arrests and executions and Ley's speech to the workers not given in full by the papers, in which the orator burst out against the "blue-blooded swine", accusing them collectively of treachery and sabotage—the reactions of the Government are now limited to abolishing the old military salute in the Army, substituting the Roman one which is called German here, and to nominating Goebbels as Plenipotentiary for the total use of national forces to war ends. The first two orders issued by Goebbels in his new capacity—one for really putting to work people who until now have pretended a non-existent employment, the other to raise the age-limits of compulsory work for women from 45–50—will not appreciably raise the capacity of a mobilization which has been enforced in a totalitarian way, until the beginning of 1945. Moreover, the new weapons which are spoken of so openly, and on which the hopes of the Germans who are not indifferent

k. There is no evidence that Neurath was involved in the Plot.

to the future are based, would be far better for reversing the military situation than the predictable results of this mobilization.

'My second colleague reports:

'The Chief protagonists of the attempts of July 20 were three German Generals: Beck, Olbricht and Hoepner; a few leading German officers attached to the General Command of the Army were accomplices, while the actual executor of the crime itself was Colonel von Stauffenberg, attached to the staff of General Fromm. Part of the Berlin garrison, unaware of the intrigue, and obedient to orders received by telephone from the German General Staff, played the part of the innocent pawn.

'Colonel von Stauffenberg, having placed the bomb where the Fuehrer should have sat to take part in the military conference, left by air for Berlin. When he arrived, he went to the War Office in the Bendlerstrasse, where he informed the interested group of conspiring officers of what he had done. At the same time, he informed General Fromm that the Fuehrer had been the victim of an attempt on his life. General Fromm seems to have tried at once to contact Headquarters with no immediate success. Meanwhile, however, he did not oppose the Bendlerstrasse issuing orders for safety measures. These measures, taken only in Berlin between four and five o'clock on the afternoon of the 20th, involved primarily the "protection" of the Ministerial areas.

'About 5.30 in fact, numerous tanks were filing down the Ost-Westachse [1], making for the Brandenburger Tor, where the Party had already put machine-guns and anti-tank guns in position. The same can be said for the Potsdamerplatz and the Schloss-Platz. A few passers-by were struck by the fact that no S.S. detachments were taking part in these measures, and some of them deduced that the detachments being sent might belong to the "new Government".

'For the rest, everything passed quite calmly amidst the smiling curiosity of passers-by who were thronging the Tiergarten on that clear summer night. At 9 o'clock, the troops were withdrawn.

'In his speech, Goebbels has made known how events developed. Major Rehmer, who was commanding the detachments which had been sent, finding his orders a little odd, went to the Ministry of Propaganda where the Fuehrer himself gave him the necessary counter-dispositions by telephone. Meanwhile, at the German General Staff, it appears that Fromm had had the telephone communication he wanted, succeeding in talking to Keitel.

'The first step taken was to arrest the group of conspirators and shoot the most suspect. When the attempt failed, some officers preferred suicide.

'In the German provinces, nothing was attempted and the calm was not disturbed even for one moment. For the rest, the only shots which disturbed that July afternoon at Berlin were those which put the traitors to death. The

1. The arterial road running across the city.

plot was known to a very limited number of people. The officers who directed it, convinced that the National Socialist permeation of the German Army was so great that no anti-Nazist plot could have any large following among the ranks of the Wehrmacht, had thought to profit from the confusion arising out of the Fuehrer's death to take the apparatus of government into their hands, and to direct it to their own ends. A German who took part in the Kapp putsch immediately after the war told me that that putsch had been a masterpiece in comparison!

'The conspirators started from the point of view that, since the driving force of the Reich would die with the Fuehrer, and they had the levers of control in their hands, they would succeed in driving people in the required direction. They forgot that in spite of five years of a bull-dozing war, men have not yet reached such a point of mechanization. Since the two essential conditions of the conspiracy, the death of the Fuehrer and mechanical obedience, were lacking, it was stifled in a few hours. If the conspiracy itself had had a larger basis of stronger men it would have been impossible to wipe it out in such a short time, without shedding blood. It seems from the interrogations that the guilty officers had already some time ago tried to penetrate deeper layers of the Wehrmacht. But since their efforts were in vain, they had decided to act in the way they did.

'As to foreign collaboration, it seems that the traitor generals were, if not in agreement, at least in contact with the German Committee for National Liberation in Moscow. It seems therefore that there was to be Russian occupation and the creation of a military government on an anti-Nazi basis. In fact any observation of the reactions of the British and Russian radios after the attempt, reveals that the excited British tone shows absolute surprise, while the Russian reserve makes it clear that Moscow knew something about it.

'The Duce's visit was not foreign to the date chosen for the attempt itself. In fact, Mussolini was to be arrested immediately on his arrival in East Prussia.

'The fact that the actual author of the attempt was a member of the German aristocracy has given the National Socialist authorities an excellent propaganda weapon among the masses. Instead of having to direct feelings of revenge or hatred against the "officer corps" or the "Generals' Club", which would have been dangerous, they can indicate to the workers that the reactionary and aristocratic circles were primarily responsible for the attempt. Even Doctor Ley spoke very violently to this effect to a great crowd of workers. The speech, however, was not reported in full by the press, which has left out the most extreme points.

'This initial direction given to propaganda was later partially modified. Minister Goebbels insisted on saying in his speech that the crime of one member cannot disgrace a whole class. However, action by the Party against the large landowners is predicted, especially in the Eastern areas of the Reich, Pomerania and Silesia, where the German aristocracy holds much of the landed property. This fits in too with ancient aspirations of the provincial National Socialist authorities, whose realization Army circles too have fought to prevent in the past.

'About the arrests made so far, they are estimated at about 5,000, 2–3,000 of whom have already been killed. Many names are mentioned. It is difficult to find out the truth of these rumours. General Fromm, who was arrested at first, seems to have been freed. They say that von Beck, von Hass, the Commander of the Berlin garrison, von Mannstein, and others have been arrested.[m]

'My personal impression is that, as soon as permission to purge was given, the S.S. arrested all who had been politically suspect recently, leaving it until later to ascertain the guilt or innocence of each individual.

'All reports are agreed in stating that the circle of conspirators was very limited. It is not however ruled out that the authorities are profiting from the circumstances to expel people who have for some time been undesirable.

'Summing up, and without wanting to minimize the importance of the incident, I would say that it has however afforded an opportunity of testing how strongly National Socialism has penetrated the German Army, and that we must not rule out the possibility that the "cleaning up" will from the political point of view give the German General Staff a sympathy it has not so far had.'[n]

m. Mannstein was in fact not arrested.
n. Italian Collection: Anfuso dispatch, August 2, 1944.

CHAPTER TWELVE

THE LONG WINTER

FOR A BRIEF MOMENT the Duce seemed to have won a signal personal victory in his talk with the Fuehrer. On his return to Garda, a circular instruction was sent out, with a copy of Mussolini's note to Hitler, stating that 'these proposals had been approved by the Fuehrer, who has given special orders for the immediate implementation of the principle of transforming the Italian military internees into civilian workers or their drafting into military units'. [1]

If such a decision had been made a year earlier it might have contributed to rallying opinion to the Republican régime. But it was now an illusory gesture, conceded with indifference by a Hitler preoccupied with sedition within Germany, and rejected in spirit from the outset by the German military and civil authorities.

In the northern frontier provinces, for example, the real attitude of Germany to the Italian satellite could be observed. Here Italian sovereignty had been in effect suspended. As Mussolini wrote in a personal letter to Anfuso on August 2, the situation was temporary, owing to the needs of military security, 'but it remains a fact that in these provinces . . . a complete attitude is clear, on the part of the German authorities, which makes me think of a preconceived plan not only to undo whatever Fascism has done to adapt these provinces to the rest of Italy, but to destroy in them any Italian influence'. The real aim was to restore Habsburg administration 'at a moment when things are not going well for the Axis'.

'The problem is much more important, from a psychological point of view, than perhaps it may appear to a country which has occupied so many other territories and is rightly concerned with more urgent and important problems of war.' [2]

The immediate preoccupation of the Duce's government was the combating of the mounting partisan danger to the security of his régime, and close behind the tide of the Allied military advance northwards.

On Mussolini's return from his July meeting with Hitler, he nursed the fleeting illusion that there would be a revolutionary change in the military position of Republican Italy. The first two Divisions under training in Germany returned at the end of July and an Italian army would soon be operating alongside the German forces against the Allies on the Italian front. For the second time, and, in implicit contradiction to Mussolini's instructions to Graziani in June, anti-partisan operations would be conducted by special units, reserving Graziani's troops for a strictly military rôle.[a]

With this in mind, Mussolini now permitted the decree setting up the Black Brigades of the Party, which had also been drafted in June, to come into effect. This was in effect mobilization of the remnants of the action squads of the '20's under the banner of the Party, and permitted to take effect only because of the previous failure of the experiment with the resuscitated Militia in the form of Ricci's Republican National Guard.

The formation of the Black Brigades was the rhetorical answer to the Red units of the partisans. The former were to be constituted on the basis of the old Party organization and in effect meant the total military mobilization of the Party machine, a Brigade Command being identical with the local Party Headquarters, and the whole new machinery being controlled at the top by Pavolini himself. The first mobile Black Brigade, under his command, went into action in Piedmont in August 1944. Parallel to this new military structure the so-called special units in training under the command of General Mischi, which had been detailed as shock-troops for use against the rebel bands earlier in the year, were simultaneously to be put into action on the internal front. Here again was a total confusion in any ultimate chain of command. Did these troops come under the orders of Graziani, or the Germans, or neither?

At the end of July, General Mischi issued his operational orders for a cleaning-up operation in Piedmont. As Mussolini wrote to him: 'I am sure that deeds will follow words. We must get rid of this odious plague with fire and steel. Do not leave Turin until the operation has been completed.'[3]

A month later, however, Mussolini wrote again to Mischi that as a result of his operations against the partisans 'the situation has not much improved . . . and indeed, in certain zones has noticeably deteriorated. It has been recognized that after one month's activity the results are modest and not in proportion to the effort made nor to the initial programme.'[4]

In the late summer of 1944 the advance units of the divisions of Graziani's

---

a. The 'San Marco' division returned to Italy in July. The 'Monte Rosa' followed in August, and the 'Littorio' in September. The 'Italia' remained in Germany. According to one of the Resistance witnesses at Graziani's trial, the Littorio division was immediately deployed 'in a purely anti-partisan rôle'. (Graziani *Processo op cit* II, pp. 396–7.) As another witness put it, 'The Germans considered anti-partisan warfare as a military by-product, and thus assigned it to the Italians.' (*Ibid.* p. 468.)

army arrived at last on Italian soil. They were formed nominally into Army Group 'Liguria' together with three German divisions, with the ostensible duties of opposing a possible Allied landing on the coast of North-West Italy or alternatively an Allied attack over the Alpine passes from French territory.

These units were therefore grouped in the Alpine regions on a front stretching from Ventimiglia to the St Bernard Pass and round the coastal areas of Genoa and La Spezia. The intention, which Graziani was to defend violently at his subsequent post-war trial, was that the prime rôle of this Army Group was an anti-invasion and not an anti-partisan one. The historical distinction in fact was meaningless, as in preparing to meet an Allied invasion, the internal lines of communication must clearly be free from and protected against partisan activities, and the special arrangements which Mussolini had now twice instituted for this purpose having completely failed, units of Graziani's army were inevitably deployed against the rebel bands throughout the whole area. Certain token units did however appear in action on the Apennine front.

At the beginning of August Mussolini insisted on a long-delayed visit to his troops, in spite of German reluctance. As the senior German Liaison Officer on Mussolini's staff reported: 'The Duce will not be put off carrying out his plan of a trip by reference to partisans and low-flying fighters. He turns down such attempts by comparing Churchill's and the English King's visits to the front. I will, however, try to cut down the journey by limiting the tours of inspection.' [5]

None of these measures led to the initiative being restored by the new Republican government either in controlling law and order in its own territory or producing an effective contribution to the Axis war effort. Nor, in the absence of any effective Italian measures to suppress the partisans, did the Germans, on their own, succeed in suppressing this phenomenon. Anti-partisan actions were carried out sporadically and without any central authority or control by local commanders, both Italian and German, as and when the resources at their disposal permitted them to move, and usually without coordination between them either at the top—through Kesselring or Wolff—or at any stage in the military hierarchy.

A typical order was issued by Kesselring, and circulated by Wolff, at the beginning of August.

. . . 'In his appeal to the Italians, Field Marshal Kesselring gave notice of the very strong measures to be used in the struggle against the partisans, and to all soldiers and police soldiers under his jurisdiction he issued the following directives:

1. The announcement of the use of every means in the struggle against the partisans must not remain an empty threat. These measures must in fact be used.

2. Every act of violence must be followed immediately by appropriate counter-measures.

3. If there are a large number of bands in a district, then in every single case a certain percentage of the male population of the place must be arrested, and, in cases of violence, shot.

4. If German soldiers are fired at in villages, the village must be burnt. The criminals or else the leaders must be publicly hanged.

5. All the neighbouring villages must be held responsible for acts of sabotage to cables and tyres. The best precaution against such acts of sabotage are security squadrons made up of the civilian population of the villages themselves.

6. The people are to be informed of the repressive measures mentioned under numbers 1–5. This will be the task of the S.S. Commanders and the police.

7. The honour of the German soldier demands that every repressive measure should be hard but just.

8. Members of the Fascist Party should be excluded from every retaliatory action. Suspects in these circles should be pointed out to the Prefects. Relevant information should be given through the Supreme Commander of the S.S. and of the police to the South-West Operational District.

9. Every soldier etc. in the various villages must be able to defend himself individually, carrying a firearm.

10. The territorial Commanders will decide in which towns firearms should be carried inside the town itself.

11. Every kind of theft is forbidden and will be severely punished.' [6]

Shortage of German man-power, and a deepening of suspicion by the German authorities as to the reliability of the Italian ally, bedevilled the scene.

The manifest failure of the combined efforts of the German and Italian forces to master the spreading activities of the Resistance movement led to a familiar proposal from Wolff to the Duce. The former was now not only German S.S. and Police Commander in Italy, but since the July plot had succeeded General Toussaint as Military Plenipotentiary. As Anfuso put it in a dispatch to Mussolini repeating Steengracht's comments: 'This step seems to have been inspired by the convenience of avoiding the disposal of military and police powers which had been too evident recently, rather than dictated by the urgent need to purge the High Command after the attempt on the Fuehrer. Wolff is working in agreement with Rahn, and winning much sympathy even in Italian circles. We can predict that the unification of commands will be useful too in the struggle against the partisans.' [7]

Mussolini had been approached with a suggestion to form an Italian S.S. division, though it must have been apparent to Wolff that such a plan could only have been carried out at the expense of the training programme of the existing Italian divisions now partly in German camps or under Graziani's command. Behind this and subsequent proposals lay a lurking desire on the part of both the S.S. and German military authorities to fragment and break up the armed units of the Italian Republic.

On August 14 Mussolini wrote therefore to Himmler in person:

'A representative of General Wolff has been to talk to me about the setting up of a proper Italian S.S. division.

'You know that the experiments tried out with men taken from the concentration camps in Germany as a whole had negative results. I told your Colonel, and I repeat my remarks to you, that recruiting in Italy at the moment is impossible. As many internees have given their allegiance to the Republic and have declared their readiness to fight, I propose therefore a plan for creating an S.S. division in Germany . . .

'I take this opportunity, dear Comrade Himmler, to congratulate you on the high charge conferred on you by the Fuehrer, and to renew my expression of friendship.' [b]

On the same day Mussolini also wrote a personal letter to Goebbels, with a note of frustrated sarcasm:

'First of all, I would like to congratulate you on the important task which the Fuehrer has assigned to you, and through which he has given you solemn proof of his esteem and trust.[c] You deserve both, because of your unwavering loyalty, your strength of purpose, and your lively intelligence.

'You are one of the few Germans who recognize that certain moments demand "improvisation"—this was until recently a purely Italian characteristic.

'You have the task of ensuring the supply of new forces to your Army which is fighting so splendidly on all fronts, and you set to work immediately. I am taking the liberty of telling you that you should turn your attention to Italy too, where in a whole series of offices there are hundreds and thousands of Germans who could be better employed elsewhere. I am told that in Milan alone there are 73 German officers. There is a Military Administration, and this is understandable, but then there are other offices—economic, cultural, police, etc.—which constitute a superstructure, a series of small states within a state, with the result that there is division instead of unity; with the result that the Republic's authority is continually being impaired.

'In every province there is an economic headquarters which is completely useless since the Italian economy is now non-existent or exiguous. Italian industry has been shattered or destroyed by enemy bombing, agriculture is at the point of death through lack of machinery, fertilizers, fuel, cattle, and

b. Italian Collection. Mussolini to Himmler, August 14, 1944. Hitler had appointed Himmler Commander-in-Chief of the German Home Army after the July Plot. See Wheeler-Bennett *op cit* p. 656.

c. Goebbels had been given full powers by Hitler to mobilize all national forces for war purposes.

above all means of transport. Hundreds of thousands of tons of fruit are rotting, because the Prefects have not even a battered old truck to transport it elsewhere . . .

'My government controls the thirty or forty provinces of the Po Valley; this plethora of "offices" is therefore completely useless and harmful—to while away the time they send out to all the towns ridiculous, truly ridiculous, statistical questionnaires.

'My dear Goebbels, you will be doing both Germany and Italy a real service if you reduce the number of these offices to the absolute minimum since, too, many of these officials have shown no sign of Fascist or National Socialist sympathies.' [d]

At the end of the month, Mussolini addressed his Council of Ministers 'in accents of deepest bitterness'. He intended to tell Rahn that 'either he should be placed in a position to function, or the government will resign'.[8]

The continued functioning of the neo-Fascist administration, in view of the declining military scene, would also depend on a complete review of the joint defence plans of the Germans and Italians of Italian territory north of the Po, and establishment of a safe stronghold in the Alpine regions from which to conduct a last stand. There were only three main areas left to consider in military terms, the Western regions north of Como, the Central Alpine passes leading to the Tyrol, and the mountain regions on Italy's Eastern frontier leading to Central Europe and the Balkans. The choice involved basic political implications. Of these three areas, the latter two were under direct German military and civil control, and although there was a strong nostalgic historical case to fight out the last battle in the regions of Italy's military achievements of 1916–18—in Friuli and Carnia—and this was the Duce's private desire, it seemed unlikely that the German leadership would accept an Italian enclave established at a central point in the immediate southern defence system of the Reich. Equally an Italian redoubt in the central region would merely fall under the control of the gauleiter of Tyrol.

At the beginning of September, preliminary discussions began in both Italian and German circles at Fasano on these alternatives. As Pavolini wrote to the Duce on September 8:

'In the unfortunate eventuality of a final and almost complete invasion of Republican territory the plan of grouping ourselves, with our weapons and government with the Black Shirts, in a defensible zone such as the province of Sondrio and part of that of Como, appears to me the most logical and dignified solution.

'I learn . . . that the German outline would be for Merano or some area nearby. I need hardly tell you, Duce, how such a solution would take away

d. Italian Collection. Mussolini to Goebbels, August 14, 1944.

any value from our project of a last stand of Mussolinian Fascism in an Italian fastness. At Merano it would be a matter of a shadow government, lodged unwillingly by gauleiter Hofer.

'On the other hand, our resistance in the Valtelline . . . would protect the German flank in the Tyrol. From every point of view, it seems to me that the practical and ideal interests of the Allies coincide with ours.' [9]

Pavolini suggested that Mussolini should talk at once to Rahn. The latter had just flown back from Germany where he had reported on the whole Italian scene. On September 9 he called on the Duce, who kept his own record of the talk. [10]

According to Rahn, the Fuehrer 'seemed physically very well, calm and, although preoccupied, decided', and sent greetings 'and promises to write again'.

Mussolini came at once to the point. 'Regarding the successive zones of defence, I indicated that the studies so far undertaken excluded Piedmont and Western Lombardy. Three Alpine redoubts had been borne in mind with a view to setting up the government, together with the armed forces of the Republic, and to organize there the last desperate defence of the last shred of Italian territory, the Valtelline, the Cadore, or Carnia. The idea would not be considered, when the struggle was over, of establishing a shadow government in some place in Germany.'

Rahn replied: 'De Gaulle, who today is in Paris, remained for a long time a head without a government or territory and only at a second stage had Algiers as a base.' Rahn had already put these proposals to the Fuehrer, who was determined to defend the line of the Apennines at all costs.

As to the three proposed areas of defence, Rahn excluded the first (the Valtelline). 'Men are men, and after a little while the solution of internment in Switzerland will flatter even the stoutest and you will remain alone with a handful.' Little did Rahn know of the accuracy of his prophesy.

His solution would be to choose the third—Friuli. 'You will still be on Italian soil and in contact with hostile races and this will restore the military spirit of the Italians. One would have to bring into the line against Slovenes, Croats, and Morlachs [e] not only the two divisions now in Germany, but also those two now on the Ligurian coast. It is immaterial whether one fights on the Po or the Rhine; the important thing is to fight together.'

As Mussolini commented, 'I have the impression that the problem has been more than touched upon at Hitler's headquarters. The conclusion is that the Germans do not want the first solution, from a residue of distrust in our loyalty; they do not speak of the Alto Adige which they retain for themselves, and prefer the third solution which has the advantage of placing us on disputed territory [f] and to which our presence will establish Italy's claim.

'Rahn has confirmed that, as far as Italy is concerned, there is no ques-

e. The historic Venetian name for Adriatic pirates.   f. With the Croats.

tion of a counter-offensive to reconquer the lost territories but only a delaying defensive action, which will contest with the enemy every square yard of Italian soil.'

On September 17 the Duce set up a special committee—'The Republican Alpine Redoubt'—under the chairmanship of Pavolini.[g] A first step was taken, after a meeting of the Council of Ministers on the following day, by asking Rahn to telegraph to Berlin the case for a redoubt in the Valtelline. An early decision was requested in a personal telegram from Mussolini to Hitler.[h] Here the matter rested.

Apart from intermittent and screened talks with German officials in Italy, Mussolini's only direct source of news and impressions on the progress of the war was Anfuso in Berlin. And equally all communications of the Italian Foreign Office to posts abroad passed through that Embassy. Anfuso's dispatches had therefore a peculiar importance in the formation of Mussolini's judgment of affairs, and they never lacked a sardonic realism.

For example, on September 20, Anfuso reported from the German capital, where official propaganda was once more trumpeting the theme of the imminent use of secret weapons to restore the balance of the war. 'Faith in miracles is confused with the news of the day, and even becomes a substantial part of it . . .

'What are these new weapons? It is difficult to say exactly without entering the realm of adventure or contradiction. Some people say that this extremely effective new weapon consists of an explosive process brought about by splitting the atom, a method which, turning physical laws upside-down, and altering the properties of the substances, causes terrible damage. Some say that a missile has already been used experimentally on the Russian Front, which causes the atmosphere to become so cold as to cause death over a wide radius. All these details could easily be treated ironically, if you did not know that they are signs of the mentality of a people who fears to see the sacrifices of five years of war go for nothing, and who wants to survive at any cost.

'. . . It seems that distrust of us increases as the situation deteriorates. The German newspapers vie with each other in remembering the capitulation and in ascribing to us most of the responsibility for Germany's present situ-

g. Mussolini seems to have wavered again in favour of Friuli, after his talk with Rahn. See Italian Collection. Pisenti to Pavolini, September 24, 1944. Pisenti, the Minister of Justice, came from Friuli. He pointed out that at least before beginning to plan, German agreement must be obtained to extract Friuli province from direct German control. The establishment of the government there would be 'a great political success' and revive the memories of the First World War.

h. See Italian Collection. Pavolini to the Duce, September 24, 1944. There is no trace of either this telegram or any reply.

ation. Today, they no longer say "Badoglio's Italy", or "Southern Italy", but simply "Italy" to indicate the country which invented betrayal . . .

'If you draw up the balance of the first year of the Social Republic, you must note with bitterness that the great sacrifices of blood the German Armies have made to stop the enemy invasions of Italian soil have met with no corresponding ethnical-political visions from the German leadership, which would serve and strengthen the Italian national idea. Once the new Fascist Republican state was set up our ally did nothing to give a natural character to a national organism, which could only become a rallying symbol for Italians by taking root in the respect of a friendly neighbour. They have shown complete ingratitude for what the German historians call the "nature" of Italian national life, so that we have, in practice, been treated like the states who have today abandoned Germany in disgrace . . .

'All this is not simply an outburst, but the identification of a situation which after a year in Germany it is my duty to report, although adding that, in spite of all this, both I and my colleagues will keep faith with our words and the promises we gave Mussolini, to work for the military and political understanding of the two countries.' [11]

It may well be that Anfuso deliberately wrote this dispatch with the knowledge that it would be intercepted and read by the German authorities.

Such was the disillusioned summary of the errors of German policy towards the Italian Social Republic. As Anfuso wrote again to Mussolini on September 27, [12] the first anniversary of the Duce's message from La Rocca on his return from Germany, 'With a little effort the Ally could have given the imprint of a national revival to the new Fascist state'. The only comfort was that the Italians realized that only Mussolini stood between them and Germany, and that the German army would otherwise have taken over the military organization of Italy.

But there was no end to the catalogue. As Mussolini wrote to Rahn: '. . . Providence, the season, Destiny, Fate, have blessed the Republic with a favourable harvest which would allow a further increase in rations.

'Now it would be really unpleasant and full of consequences if the lack of a few dozen lorries caused shortages and therefore revolt. This *slight* problem has been under discussion for *ten* months without the slightest result. Fiat produces 50 lorries a day. Let them give us at least three of them, and in a short time we should have all we need to distribute foodstuffs regularly to the population. And do not let them requisition for us the few *old* vehicles which are still to be found.' [13]

At the end of September, the Duce spoke to the Japanese Ambassador of 'the tragic situation facing Italy because of German lack of comprehension'. Hidaka, who had just returned from Milan, was shocked at the extent of unrest among the workers at the threatened removal of Italian industrial equipment to Germany. [14]

It seems also that, as in July 1943, the conversation turned to the hope of still persuading Hitler to seek a compromise peace with the Russians, but the recent meeting on July 20 had afforded little opportunity for serious political discussion.[15]

In October Mussolini was obliged to write again to Rahn in the following terms:

'I would ask you very insistently to be so good as to dedicate ten minutes of your precious time to reading the enclosed report on the "situation of the partisan bands" for the whole of September 1944. From the report it is clear that the "bands" have become "brigades" and "divisions", regularly formed and commanded by professional generals, under a central headquarters. They are excellently armed and each unit disposes of the necessary equipment, primarily anti-vehicle.

'In many places the German military authorities have come to a *modus vivendi* with the partisans, i.e. real agreements have been signed, and this has increased the power and prestige of the partisans.

'Their organization in Italy, with a total of one hundred thousand men divided into sixty brigades, constitutes a growing danger against which no efficient action is being taken for many reasons, the first is the division of command, forces and responsibility between Italians and Germans.' [16]

On December 10 the Duce wrote again:

'I am taking the liberty of drawing your personal attention to an incident whose gravity, I think, you will realize. I heard that there had been a raid on innocent women at Udine. I ordered an enquiry, and in the following lines I give you the results.

' "At the beginning of October last the German Commander of the Security Police asked the Chief Constable for a list of secret prostitutes, so that he could have them arrested and put under sanitary control, since many German soldiers had been infected with venereal diseases. The Chief Constable gave the said Captain a list of twenty-six secret prostitutes from the office files. On the evening of October 14, forty German and twenty Italian soldiers . . . rounded up the said women. Of the twenty-six women included in the list supplied by the Chief Constable, only thirteen were arrested, because the others could not be found. The service was not confined to the women indicated, but, at the order of a Lieutenant, was extended to all women who were in the streets of the city from 18-23 hours. Thus eighty women were arrested, bundled into lorries, and taken to the barracks of the Eighth Alpine Regiment, whence . . . they were accompanied to the hospital for a medical inspection. All were found to be free of venereal diseases, and some of them were virgins."

'The rounding up of healthy honest women created an uproar in the city, and aroused infinite protests against the Italian authorities who had nothing to do with the action.

'Amends should be made to the city of Udine, with the immediate removal of the two German officers responsible for the scandal—I request this formally.

'. . . I think, my dear Ambassador, that you will agree with me in considering that what I have told you is not likely to convince the Italian people that the Republic is independent, at least as far as internal policy is concerned, and that it is therefore absolutely necessary for the German military and political authorities to leave the allied Republic government the power and responsibility of really governing.' [17]

Nor was there any sign that the vaunted divisions of Graziani's army would ever be allowed to operate as an effective allied force alongside the German army on the Italian front. On October 4, Mussolini wrote to Kesselring:

'Since August 24 your tireless and incomparable troops have been fighting to deny the possession of the Po Valley to the Anglo-Saxons. Since that date the Italian people has been waiting to hear that Italian troops too were being used in the decisive battle.

'They ask: "Where are the Italian Divisions which returned from Germany at the end of July? What are they doing? Why are they not used? Why are the enemy armies using the peoples of five continents to attack Italy, while the Italians, the best Italians, are not allowed to contribute to her defence?"

'I need not tell you that it is inaction which most rapidly leads to the demoralization of troops. When the divisions returned to Italy, they were truly fired by a brave spirit. They were scattered along the Ligurian Apennines to defend them against a disembarkation which was of no interest to the British after their conquest of the main Apennines and France. The result has been that the men have absented themselves and deserted and some have gone over to the partisans, who now number a good 94,000, organized in units up to the size of a division and well armed.' [18]

Even the potential man-power of these Italian Divisions was being continually bled by competing German claims. Goering now demanded another twenty-four thousand Italians for anti-aircraft units to be incorporated in the German air force. As Mussolini wrote to him on October 9:

'During my last visit to the Fuehrer's General Headquarters we discussed the need to reinforce the German air force with Italian contingents. In a comradely spirit you declared yourself ready to support my desire to preserve the integrity of the two Italian divisions which had remained in Germany, provided twenty-four thousand men were transferred to Germany. After my return I tried to fulfil your wish. Although, contrary to my hopes, the carrying out of this request has been somewhat delayed by the difficulties caused by the present situation in Italy, it has proved possible to assign eight to ten thousand men to the Second Air Fleet.

'I further agreed to the immediate transfer to the Reich of seven thousand six hundred Military Police through the agency of General Wolff, on the assumption that they would be considered as forming part of the contingent asked for. Further efforts to mobilize young Italians of call-up age who are working in protected industries and in the Todt organization, in order to transfer them to Germany, have failed hitherto, owing in part to the opposition of the said German authorities who fear social upheavals as a consequence of such mobilization . . .

'In spite of all this it seems, as I am informed, that there is an intention to break up the two Italian divisions stationed in Germany. I appeal to your friendly understanding of the problem not to allow this to happen. For a year in fact I have devoted all my energies, within the range of what is possible for the Fascist government, to mobilize all the human and material forces of Italy for the common war effort.

'It is reported to me that no less than eighty thousand Italians are in your anti-aircraft units. Every day a continuous flow of important war goods and materials reaches Germany from Italy. Every day the needs of the forces employed on fortifications and on the repair of railways, roads, and bridges must be met. In the course of a few weeks my Prefects have provided for new work on fortifications alone more than one hundred thousand men, who according to the Germans are working admirably. Remember too that our organization for fighting the partisans needs to be constantly reinforced. We must eliminate the partisans or unpleasant surprises will befall us.

'The authority of my Government would suffer a serious blow if the four divisions, to whose training as the nucleus of the future Republican army the Fuehrer agreed in such friendly and generous fashion, were to be broken up or had to be disbanded.

'I beg you once more, my dear Marshal, to examine the question particularly from the political aspect which I have stressed, and to make every effort to keep the two divisions intact. . . . For my part I shall devote all my energies to seeing that the six or ten thousand men still lacking are sent to the Reich as quickly as possible for assignment to the German forces.' [19]

By the end of October there were further stormy rumours circulating in Northern Italy, that the two divisions still in German training camps would either be disbanded or sent to the Russian Front, and that the Italian government would be moved to Austria and set up as a shadow administration in exile.

It is not surprising under these conditions that the morale of those elements of the original planned four divisions under training in Germany showed advanced signs of demoralization on their return to Italy. Mussolini called, for example, for a report from the local Italian civilian authorities on the movements of the 'San Marco' Division after its return at the beginning of August.

'This unit indulged in wide-scale requisitioning and rapidly created bad relations with the local population. At one artillery base, thirty-seven radio sets had been requisitioned from civilians, and it was the officers who set the example. Nor did the different elements composing the division mould together. Some were volunteers, some recruits, and others former internees. From these units alone already over one thousand men had deserted.' [20]

Nor did the Germans risk arming these Italian troops sufficiently to enable them to become an effective fighting force. When the last of the four Divisions, the 'Italia', arrived at the end of the year, Mussolini wrote to Graziani:

'As soon as you can, inform Kesselring personally that I will never visit the "Italia" Division until its armament is complete. I mean to visit a Division, not a gymnastic society . . . and also that if the anti-aircraft defence is not strengthened, neither railways, nor vehicles, nor foot passengers will be moving in Italy in three months' time.' [21]

Towards the end of October the Allied offensive on the Apennine front halted just south of Bologna, and the army was ordered to remain on its positions.

On November 13 General Alexander issued a proclamation to the Italian partisans calling on them to cease large-scale operations, to reduce their activities, and to stay on the defensive. [22] Whatever the military justification for such a decision, there can be little doubt as to its depressing psychological effects on the partisan bands in the North and on the Liberation Committee for Upper Italy. It also coincided with the last major effort by the Germans and the Black Brigades to break the resistance in large-scale mopping up operations, and Mussolini had fixed the date of November 10 for the expiry of his declared amnesty to all army deserters.

The Alexander proclamation implicitly provoked a crisis of the whole resistance movement, and together with the pause in the Allied offensive on the Apennine front, induced Mussolini to consider how to exploit this lull in hostilities both in military terms and on the disintegrating home front.

His first reaction was to renew his declining personal correspondence with Hitler in an attempt to persuade him that there was a chance to regain the initiative on the Italian front.

On November 12 Mussolini had received General Vietinghoff. The latter had temporarily replaced Kesselring, who had been injured in an accident, in command of the German forces in Italy, and he told the Duce that he was convinced that if he could be allotted six new divisions he could be certain of pushing back the Anglo-American armies as far as Naples.[23]

It was probably as a result of this conversation that on November 14, the day following Alexander's proclamation, Mussolini drafted such a letter, which was to be carried by Vittorio Mussolini to Germany.[i]

'Except for one or two telegrams on exceptionally urgent matters, it is a long time since I gave you my views on the general situation, as it is at present and in its most logical future developments. Allow me to do this now, on the threshold of the winter which—whether we like it or not—will at least cause operations to slow up in several sectors. But first of all, let me express once more my deep admiration—shared, I can say, by all Italians (including our opponents) for the unparalleled bravery shown by your Armed Forces. Only an Army like yours, i.e. National Socialist, could resist as it resisted an attack launched on the European fronts with greater forces and means, and could neutralize the consequences of the treachery in Roumania, Bulgaria, and Finland where the local armies had allied with our enemies to block your way and make your task more difficult. I dare say that no other army in the world could have got the better of such a difficult and complicated situation which engaged your troops from Egypt to Lapland, from Athens to Petsamo. The resistance of your garrisons in the French Atlantic ports was really epic. The way in which the July 20 crisis was settled shows that the mass of the German people is fundamentally sound and that the Armed Forces are at your side, Fuehrer, and firmly determined to hold out to the very end in your struggle for life or death.

'Since August 28, 1942, when for lack of means and fuel the great Marshal Rommel was unable to continue his attack against Egypt, the initiative has passed to the enemy. They have attacked at all suitable points, and have succeeded in invading Europe. You will remember, Fuehrer, that when we met in Salzburg in April 1943 I proposed that you should bring in Spain in order to neutralize Gibraltar and surprise the Anglo-American forces in North Africa from the rear—when these forces were very far from having their present military and territorial strength. The Caudillo would only have opposed this for the sake of appearances, he would have been acting in his own interests, and today he would not be in a situation which to all intents and purposes must be considered precarious. Today, as in the Spring of 1943, there is only one problem: to win, we must resume the initiative in operations by land, sea, and air. You, Fuehrer, were the first to be convinced of this necessity, and you said so when we met at Salzburg this year. Having established that we must resume the initiative, it is a question of deciding at which sector of the land front it is possible to take the initiative and get political

i. The only text of this letter which has come to light is a manuscript draft in Mussolini's own hand in the Italian Collection. It bears no date or indication that it was sent. Mellini, in his book however, under the date November 14, states clearly that on that day Mussolini gave a copy of such a letter to Mazzolini, which was to be handed to the Japanese Ambassador for safe keeping, and that the original 'had been entrusted to Vittorio Mussolini'. Mellini *op cit* p. 47.

and military results. With regard to this, I rule out the Eastern and Western fronts and the Danube front for reasons which I will not bother you with. The only front where it is possible to resume the initiative is the Italian front . . .

'I am sure, Fuehrer, that a thorough examination of the situation will convince you and your colleagues that my suggestion is not absurd, and that this operation must be carried out this winter, i.e. when the enemy's superiority in armoured vehicles and planes cannot be exploited to the full. An Italo-German massed force of eighty to a hundred thousand men would turn the situation upside-down, and if, as is likely, it forced the enemy to withdraw troops from other zones of operations, the task of your armed forces would be lightened. I *feel* that this operation would constitute the first longed for day of sunshine after so many months of fog.

'Since I have the opportunity of writing to you, I want briefly to mention the internal situation as I see it in its objective reality, without optimism or pessimism. In spite of the enemy's unceasing advance and their entry into the lower Po Valley, the situation has improved recently. The twenty-two million Italians in Liguria, Piedmont, Emilia, Lombardy and the Veneto, are no longer waiting for the "Liberators". Even the anti-Fascists are no longer waiting with their former enthusiasm. Thanks to the achievements of German and Italian detachments, the partisan phenomenon is dying out, and my recent amnesty brought several thousands of young men to the barracks and factories . . .'

A postscript followed: 'I think it is of supreme importance for us to defend the Po Valley. If we lost this, we would face a very serious threat in the East, where Tito's military organizations already have the whole of Dalmatia and are spreading North. From a general point of view, the loss of the Po Valley would signify the virtual disappearance of Italy as a Tripartite power, while the ideal thing would be to get back at least part of that territory so that we could play a greater part in the common effort.'

There is no evidence to show whether Hitler replied to this appeal, but Anfuso's dispatches from Berlin reflect a similar mood of cautious optimism in German circles. Whereas in October it was generally accepted that the war might be lost in a few weeks, there was now an awareness that the Allied time-table on all fronts, including the Italian, had been proved to be premature, and that if the Axis could hold out until the spring several courses were open which might alleviate total defeat. The most important of these might be the now notorious secret weapons.

There was also the growing mirage of dissension between the Western Allies, and particularly in regard to the diverging political aims of the Anglo-Americans and the Russians, which might even lead to the break up of the coalition, and create a situation which could be exploited by the Axis in the direction of a compromise peace.

In any event the German leadership intended to make a maximum effort to stabilize the war fronts and gain time during these critical winter months.

As Anfuso wrote on November 18: 'The military situation has passed from the crisis provoked by July 20 and the consequent loss of French territories to a phase of adjustment. In the middle of October the irresistible march on Berlin was to have begun not only for the Allies, but also for certain German circles who did not feel fit or did not want to continue the war. When the English dropped from the air at Arnhem, I heard Germans talk as if the game would be up in the space of a few weeks.

'Since then, in spite of the terrible blow of the Roumanian collapse which brought the Russians to the gates of Budapest, and to the nearby road to Vienna, a feeling of stability has returned not only on the operational front but also to certain German minds which seemed bewildered. It became clear that although concentrating all its efforts on all fronts to obtaining a victory before winter, and exploiting its propaganda resources, the enemy coalition has not succeeded in gaining the victory which was the essential aim of the Teheran and Quebec conferences. The recent declarations of Stalin and Churchill indicates clearly that one of the Allies could not have obtained any positive success against Germany without decisive help from the other. Both Stalin and Churchill admitted that only a combined effort of the three Allies can defeat the German military power. The imprudence of such an admission which establishes the life or death of the coalition, added to the other rash move of fixing an approximate date for reaching this aim, has provoked the conclusion that although Germany is in a far from rosy situation, she has gained a point over her enemies, showing that, in spite of the tragic surprise of the Bulgarian and Roumanian betrayals, she has managed to maintain her defence on all fronts. Apart from its real importance, this circumstance also serves to persuade those same Germans who considered that the game was up in October that a national effort can be co-ordinated not only with the help of the new recruiting drive, and the Home Guards, but also with the parallel progress of inventions which permit conclusions about the possibilities of going on with the war.' [24]

The fate of the Republican régime in Italy equally depended on the strengthening of morale, and an overhaul of the machine of government. Both however depended on German comprehension and concessions. The dreary rasping issues between the two governments remained clamped in a vicious iron circle.

The neo-Fascist government would have to face relying on its own meagre demoralized resources. As Anfuso put it, in a further dispatch on November 18:

'. . . Until political cadres of legionary and revolutionary officers are re-created, we need have few illusions. And as long as the Germans see that the Army of a country which has emerged from a tremendous government crisis is ruled by the same academic ineptness which ruled the Royal Army, it is improbable that they will trust us in a strategic front, which could decide the fate of a campaign. I, for example, am convinced that the Black Shirt is the only military experiment which will yield results in the end. The Black Shirts are people who are aware of why they are fighting, and of the need to defend their ideal. Even if they are of necessity very few, their contribu-tion will certainly be more decisive than that of the large units of good troops commanded by people who have no "Schwung" (dash) as they say here. This is the secret of the S.S. armies, and the reason for their military and political success. All this refers to the unsuccessful employment of our units, which logically frustrates operations, and at the same time hinders our governmental activity. It is for this reason that I can never recommend strongly enough that our divisions trained in Germany should be treated in the Fascist sense, and that all our officers' cliques who are even slightly sus-pected of monarchic weakness, or capitulationism, should be swept away. It is a question of the worst evil, and the Germans who suffered the conse-quences until September 8 were too much stung by it to want to begin all over again today.' [25]

Although the nagging question of the Italian military internees had been settled on paper on July 20, this release of vital man-power meant only that the competing German agencies and armed services would absorb this re-serve, and there would be no direct benefit to the Duce's government.

German administration of Italy's Northern and Eastern frontier provinces had caused more resentment than any one measure taken by Hitler since the establishment of the Salò Republic. But as Anfuso pointed out in the same dispatch on November 18, 'There is no possibility, above all in present cir-cumstances, and at a moment when the six provinces represent the vital routes of access to the Italian front, of inducing the German leadership to slacken the policy which they have pursued up till now.'

Indeed the German attitude to their Italian satellite showed every sign of hardening rather than relaxing. In the same dispatch, Anfuso reported:

' . . . I talked to Rahn too about how expedient it would be for Germany to make some kind of "declaration" confirming Italian sovereignty over these regions of ours. I told him frankly that the situation of the six provinces is what we Fascists find most degrading. Rahn replied that he did not see any obstacle to such a desire, at the right time and place. He only observed that, from a rough estimation, it did not seem to him that the inhabitants of the six provinces and the Fascists showed excessive enthusiasm to serve the Re-publican cause; rather, he added, it was not the fault of the German govern-

ment or the two gauleiters if the Italian peoples of the six provinces tried
to profit from the temporary German occupation to get out of labour and of
military service, and showed clearly by their passive attitude that they had
carefully planned to wait and see.'

The same attitude applied to German control over and interference in the
whole economy of Northern Italy. In essence, whatever elements of the semblance of an independent state existed at Salò, the German attitude to Italy
remained unchanged: the maximum exploitation, in whatever convenient
form, of the resources and man-power of the area in the exclusive interests of
the German war effort.

In the same conversation with Rahn, the latter unwittingly made the point
of the isolation of the Duce from the population. As Anfuso wrote:

'. . . To my sharp protests on the conditions of the Italian Government and
the difficulties it has not only in asserting its authority, but also in extending
it to dependent organs, protests which I have made at Berlin too at various
times, Rahn replied pretty much as follows: "You cannot expect the free
working of the Republican Government to be effected through a peremptory
order from the Reich Government to its dependent organs in Italy. The
authority of the Government stems from the moral influence it can exert over
the masses. The Republican Government is called Mussolini. Now Mussolini
is the only living Italian who can obtain something from his co-nationalists
by the fascination of his words. With this 'something' I refer too to the
authority of the Republican Government. I begged the Duce to speak at
Milan on the anniversary of the March on Rome. He replied that he would
not speak because he felt he had nothing to say. I understand his opinion, but
at a moment like this his mere appearance in the Italian squares, even if only
fleeting, could restore to the Italian people the idea that it has a government,
and is not abandoned. Autonomy can be obtained by regaining prestige, and
the German government would be happy if the Duce, who is indubitably
still master of Italian minds, would show himself and speak to his people. If
this happened, the autonomy and power of the Government would automatically be restored, because it is the Italians themselves who, a prey to
indolence, and waiting for new developments, do not feel strong enough to
believe in a Government who gives only intermittent or superficial signs of
life . . . Naturally I am aware of the risks this would involve. But it is worth
risking, if you think of the enormous advantage the Republic would gain
from the propaganda activity of the Duce" . . .'

In a conversation with Ribbentrop at the end of the month Anfuso made
the same point, probably with a view to preparing the way in German circles
for just such a demonstration on the part of Mussolini, and which might
have consequences not in direct accord with German intentions.

The purpose of this talk was to air 'certain matters of complaint' which had already been submitted to Ribbentrop in writing by the Italian Embassy in Berlin.

'The conversation then turned to the condition of the Duce, which according to Anfuso was good, from the health point of view. Anfuso however expressed the opinion that the Duce should display more political activity. He should appear more frequently in public and address the Italians more often. The Duce was still very much beloved in Italy. The people's affection was still further increased by what Italians in the northern half of the peninsula had learned of conditions in those parts of Italy occupied by the British and Americans. Sympathy for him was particularly strong in Milan, Cremona, and Venice.

'When Ribbentrop enquired what it was, in the circumstances, that was preventing the Duce from addressing the people, Anfuso remarked that the Duce maintained such a reserved attitude because he was under the impression that he no longer wielded any authority in the parts of Italy still left to him, more especially in the so-called operational zones. He (Anfuso) did not minimize the difficulties with which the Duce had to contend in this connection; but as already stated he took the view that Mussolini ought, nonetheless, to be more active. If the Duce had taken a bold decision and gone to Rome, much harm might have been avoided. He should not repeat his previous mistake now, and should make more propaganda.'

On the perennial issue of the Italian border provinces Ribbentrop gave the usual answer that they were now operational areas and added cryptically, 'The Fuehrer had always shown great consideration for the Duce personally. It might have been to the advantage of all of us if the Fuehrer and the Duce had talked openly with one another now and again.' But if the question would be raised whether Germany would contemplate a political settlement with Russia, then Ribbentrop would reply that if one did not think in terms of a political settlement but only of fighting, then a political settlement might come. [26]

This heightening of tone in such exchanges between German and Italian leaders did not escape the Duce. External relations with the Axis partner must follow their dreary predestined path. The joint conduct of the war would not be influenced by any action on the part of Republican Italy. The time had come for Mussolini to work out an 'Italian' solution.

On December 9 he announced to a Council of Ministers not only the intention to make, for the first time since the setting up of the régime, a public speech in Milan, but also to move the government from Garda to the Lombardy capital. Such an act could only be interpreted as a crisis of faith in his relations with the German ally.

CHAPTER THIRTEEN

MILAN AND THE LAST
'CHANGING OF THE GUARD'

THE DECISION to deliver a public speech in Milan was made by the Duce on December 13. Apart from the urge to appear at last at a mass gathering, the first since his return from Germany in September of the previous year, there was the pressing motive of reinforcing the position of his administration in regard to the Germans 'at a moment when this was particularly needed'. [1] The air was more than usually heavy with rumours of treason and plot, and the Germans were on the alert during these weeks.

The Borghese affair flickered up again towards the end of 1944 as the result of German complaints that 'Commandant Borghese is carrying on an independent war, ignoring German military operations in the province of Aosta and thus creating serious difficulties. According to the German command, Prince Borghese has tried to reserve to himself a strip of the Swiss frontier with no liaison with the other Italian and German forces. At Aosta everyone agrees in having serious doubts as to his loyalty to the Italian Socialist Republic, and fear a surprise . . .' [2]

It was also suggested that he had 'not yet defined his political position' and there were dark hints of conspiracy. But the fragmentation of power was so far advanced at Salò that Borghese, although his units had achieved a certain notoriety, in fact merely reflected the mounting confusion of the whole scene.

Himmler had, for example, written to Wolff at the beginning of December:

'I have received from Martin Bormann the attached summary of treacherous Freemason intrigues in the Armed Forces of the Fascist republic. I assume that you are aware of these things in general terms. But as I am not quite sure, I would like to send you the document.

'In regard to Prince Borghese, you have already spoken to me about him . . . At the present time we must be very careful.' [a]

The disintegrating control of the Fascist authorities had been also the subject of an unusually sharp letter to Mussolini from Cardinal Schuster of Milan. He drew attention to the seven unco-ordinated police headquarters in the city. Every official had his own band of some fifty agents. 'Listen to what the population has to say.' The government 'must have unity of control and responsibility, which is now fragmented into dozens of companies and autonomous squads, each acting on its own initiative.

'In the history of the Roman Empire there was a period of anarchy, which was called that of the Thirty Tyrants. Do take steps to see that it does not happen again, and abolish them.' [3]

But, in the Duce's mind, perhaps the most important purpose of his address to the Nation was the search for an Italian 'solution' aided by personal magic, for the lineaments of a political programme. It was to be the last of a cycle of such speeches stretching back more than twenty years.

The last mass meeting of Italian Fascism was held in the Lyric Theatre in Milan on December 16. Mussolini launched without preamble into the obsessive historical theme of past treasons.

'At sixteen months' distance from the tremendous date of the unconditional surrender, imposed and accepted according to the democratic and criminal formula of Casablanca, the evaluation of events poses once more for us these questions: "Who has betrayed? Who has suffered or is suffering the consequences of this treachery?" It is not a matter, let us be quite clear, of a judgment of historical revision, and even less in any form an exculpatory one.'

Who had betrayed? The King, the Court, the plutocratic circles of the middle classes, and the freemasons of the General Staffs in alliance with clerical forces.

'As early as May, more precisely on May 15, the ex-King noted in his diary—which has recently come into our possession—that one must "disengage" from the German alliance. Without a shadow of doubt, the ex-King ordered the surrender, and Badoglio executed it. But to arrive at September 8 there had to be a July 25, namely the *coup d'état* and the change of régime.

'One must in any event recognize that there were even more infamous treacheries in the summer of 1944, since the Roumanians, the Bulgarians, and the Finns, after surrendering ignominiously and one of them, the Bulgars, without firing a shot, twenty-four hours later overturned the front and attacked the German units with all their mobilized strength, thus making the

a. German Collection. Himmler Papers. Himmler to Wolff, December 4, 1944. Bormann's main source was the egregious Preziosi. On Borghese see also pp. 657–9. The summary referred to is not attached.

retreat both difficult and bloody . . . It is time to tell our Italian, German and Japanese comrades, that the contribution made by Republican Italy to the common cause since September 1943—in spite of the temporary reduction of the territory of the Republic—is far superior to what is commonly believed.

'For obvious reasons I cannot go into detailed statistics of the total contribution—in both the economic and military sectors—made by Italy. Our collaboration with the Reich in soldiers and workers is represented by this figure: on September 30, 786,000 men. This fact is incontrovertible since it comes from German sources . . . In face of such evidence, the Italians living on the territory of the Social Republic have the right—once and for all—to raise their heads and demand that this effort be fairly, and in a comradely manner, judged by all members of the Tripartite Pact . . .

'In 1945 the participation of Italy in the war will be developed further . . . In the tumultuous period of transition during the autumn and winter of 1943 more or less autonomous military units appeared under men who with their past and the appeal of their attraction knew how to assemble the first fighting nuclei. Recruitment took place on an individual basis. The old commanders sounded the reveille. It was a splendid initiative, especially in terms of morale. But modern war demands unification and we are moving in this direction. I dare to think that Italians of all shades of opinion will welcome the day when all the armed forces of the Republic are grouped in one organism and there will be one police . . . all living in the climate and spirit of Fascism and of the Republic . . . Still, as we shall always do, calling ourselves Fascists, dedicating ourselves to the cause of Fascism as we have done since 1919 until today . . . we have initiated . . . a return to original positions. It is on historical record that until 1922 Fascism had republican tendencies, and the reasons why the insurrection of 1922 spared the monarchy have been explained. From the social point of view the programme of Republican Fascism is but the logical continuation of the programme of 1919 . . .

'In October 1943 I drafted and revised what is known in Italian political history as "the Manifesto of Verona" . . . Let us look now at what has been done, what has not been done, and above all why it has not been done.

'The Manifesto began by demanding the convocation of a Constituent Assembly. This has not been summoned and will not be until after the war. I tell you with the utmost frankness that I found it superfluous to convoke a Constituent Assembly when the territorial extent of the Republic, in view of the development of military operations, cannot be regarded in any way as definitive. It seemed to me premature to create a proper legal State with complete institutions when there were no armed Forces to defend it.'

On the place of the Fascist Party in public life it had been laid down at Verona that the Party card would not be an essential prerequisite for office. 'In my telegram of March 10, 1944, to the Heads of Provinces this formula was repeated and better defined. Thus any discussion on the plurality of parties is completely unapt.

'While some points in the Verona programme have been "unhorsed" by the succession of military events, more concrete achievements have been realized in the economic and social field.' These had been elaborated in the famous 'Premises' of February 1944 'which are now in the course of being implemented'.

In the conduct of the war there were no miracles to report. 'It was not a matter of "secret" weapons but new ones . . . which are secret until they are used.' They were of such significance that they could in the first stage re-establish a balance of forces and successively enable the Germans to regain the initiative. This, 'as far as it is humanly possible to tell, is almost certain and not far distant . . .'

As to the enemy, 'without exaggerating one can say that the political situation today is not favourable to the "Allies".' The Casablanca formula by its rigidity means the indefinite prolongation of the war.

'One day the Soviet Ambassador in Rome said to me: "The first world war bolshevized Russia; the second will bolshevize Europe." This prophecy has not been fulfilled, but if it does turn out this way the responsibility, in the first instance, falls on Great Britain.'

British policy is now taking protective measures, such as liquidating the Greek partisans. 'Churchill wanted a zone of influence reserved to democracy in Western Europe backed by a pact between France, England, Belgium, Holland, and Norway, first in an anti-German rôle and then anti-Russian. The Stalin-De Gaulle agreements stifled at birth this idea, which had been put forward, on London's instructions, by the Belgian Spaak. The game has failed, and Churchill must wonder, thinking of the Russian entry into the Mediterranean and Russian pressure on Iran, whether the Casablanca policy has not for poor old England been one of bankruptcy.'

In his final peroration, the Duce called for supreme sacrifice. 'We want to defend the Po Valley tooth and nail: we want it to remain Republican while waiting for the whole of Italy to be Republican . . . And it is Milan which must give the men, the arms, the will, and the signal of insurrection.' [4]

The Milan speech of Mussolini generated a brief but marked euphoria, quick to dissipate, and perhaps too elusive to harness to practical policy. As a gesture of independence towards the German ally, it could but increase the pervasive suspicions of Nazi circles in Italy, their distrust of the now revived 'social' programme, and alarm at rumours of internal subversion. The fragile face-saving compromise laboriously built in particular by Rahn between the extreme demands of the German High Commission, which implied the treating of Northern Italy as occupied territory, and the Duce's case for a sovereign Republic, was approaching its end.

At a meeting of the Italian Council of Ministers on January 18 a resolution was passed. 'The internal situation . . . appears still to be influenced by the Milan speech, but for further results, this must be followed by action.'

It was decided to send a delegation of the senior members of the Salò régime to call on Rahn in order to survey the frustrations of the Republican administration.[b]

The delegation 'demands a clarification of relations since, fifteen months after the foundation and solemn recognition of the Republican government, it must no longer give the impression that Republican territory, population, and assets are still considered as "war booty" . . .'

In reporting on the Armed Forces, Graziani said:

'We now know, and it is now time to say it with all frankness, that the German watchword is that the Italians cannot and should not be used as soldiers but only as workers . . . I have the clear feeling that the Germans wanted to prevent the re-establishment of the Italian Armed Forces. At first we made five to six hundred thousand men available. They were dismissed because the recruiting centres had neither uniforms, weapons, nor food; dismissed, these forces drifted towards rebellion. It is not our fault. Every one of our demands falls on deaf ears. We sent meat for four divisions to Germany. Today we are asking for the divisions to be put in a condition to fight. The visits I can make, have made and will make, those that the Duce has made and will make, serve to raise the troops' morale but nothing more. I have sent the Ambassador numerous minutes on the representations we have made to General Leyers, for the necessary equipment. To clothe a few men we have had to resort to the black market, and Leyers is still leading us by the nose today. I do not hesitate to state that in my opinion Leyers is precisely one of those most responsible for the programme against Italian re-armament.

'The divisions are partly disarmed. Twenty-five per cent of the men of the Italia division are unarmed. What can a soldier do without weapons? I consider that those who have stayed at their posts in the ranks are real heroes. During one of my recent visits to the "Italia" division, while I was speaking to the troops, a volunteer with a mutilated hand raised his stump in the air to speak, and told me that both his arms were useless. When I asked why he thought his other arm was lifeless too he replied that a soldier without weapons has no arms. I asked if he had not at least a pistol. He said no. So I gave him mine.

'An artillery detachment of the same division changes its position. It has

b. The Italian delegation consisted of Graziani, Pavolini, Pellegrini (Minister of Finance), Buffarini Guidi, Barracu (Undersecretary of the Presidency of the Council), and Mazzolini. See the minutes in Italian Collection. January 20, 1945.

not the means to bring its munitions along behind. Attacked by rebels, the soldiers use up their individual ammunition, and when they have no more cartridges, are overcome and captured with all their equipment. Immediately, the Germans say that a detachment of the division has gone over to the rebels. The news is false. Is it the fault of those soldiers if they had to surrender because their ammunition was exhausted? Can they honestly be called cowards? The Germans say so, but it is not true. There was no desertion . . .

'What are the conclusions? The people say: the Germans are stripping Northern Italy, and won't even leave us our eyes to cry with. When they leave this area we shall not have a single gun to defend ourselves from the Anglo-Americans.'

Graziani ended by saying 'we must fight the attitude of certain German circles who persist in considering the Italians traitors, incapable of carrying arms'.

Rahn declared firmly that it was not true that Germany desired and wanted Italians as workers but not as soldiers, and protested strongly against such a statement. 'Germany has only one desire: to have in Italy a pugnacious, strong, fighting ally.' He understood and shared Graziani's grief over the scanty equipment and weapons of the divisions. 'Everyone knows how much I did for the return of the four divisions.' He was aware of the technical difficulties beforehand, because he knew that the arms promised to the Italian units had on the contrary been thrown into the battle in the West and East. But he knew too that the four divisions' return to their Motherland was a political problem, and, in agreement with Kesselring, he had supported their return.

'. . . It is ridiculous to think that we want to set a trap for our ally, and then walk off. We must overcome the German military mentality that distrusts the military qualities of the Italian soldier.'

Graziani retorted: 'In that case we shall never be done with it, because in my opinion the psychological factor will never be overcome. In fifteen months' experience, I have had occasion to perceive that we are always suspected.'

A sharp argument followed on the painful evidence as to the desertions from the returning Italian divisions. Graziani admitted that 'the two divisions together provided five thousand deserters'. To which Rahn replied that there had been ten thousand. The Italian commander answered that the Germans themselves had calculated beforehand on twenty per cent and that 'this percentage certainly was not reached'.

This unvarnished dialogue heightened in tone. Rahn insisted. 'If you are sure of the morale of your troops, I will do anything I can to help you.' Graziani came back at once: 'The morale of the troops depends on many factors: equipment is among the first.'

Rahn ended by saying 'when it is said that the Germans do not want the Italians to fight, I feel personally wounded'.

The remainder of the meeting passed in plaintive wrangling. The Italian Finance Minister stressed the burden on the new State of war contributions. Buffarini complained of the interference of the German policy throughout Republican territory, and called for a final explanation of the position in the German-occupied border provinces where even Graziani could not come in direct touch with Italian military units in those regions. On this note the conference closed.

On January 29 Graziani had an equally lowering talk with Wolff.

'On the subject of calling up the classes, Wolff considers the moment unsuitable because of the progress of operations on the Eastern front, which will certainly create a state of alarm among the Italian people and therefore the result of the call-up might well be to cause a new flight of young men to the partisan bands.

'As to the reform in the Todt and Ministry of War Production organizations, General Wolff expresses his anxieties here too on the repercussions it could have on the mass of those enrolled in them, and consequent flight, hiding, or going over to the partisans rather than enrolling in the ranks of our armed forces. This would do two kinds of harm: increase the partisan bands, and impoverish our labour and industrial organizations.

'He considers it more profitable on the other hand to include trusted members of the police force in the Todt and RUK organizations, in order to get real knowledge of the exact position of every worker from a military standpoint, and then at the right moment to make use of those elements suitable for possible deforestation work.'

Germany had now lost the Upper Silesian coal basin. Many Italian industries would have therefore to either close down or cut down their activities. Masses of workers would thus be available, 'and once they are unemployed it will be easier to get them to enlist in our Armed Forces'.[5]

For some time the Duce had been considering a last reshuffle of ministers, and reconstruction of ministries. He had hinted at changes in the previous September, and had been persuaded to desist by the Germans. In January he began finally to implement the socialization programme in the face of German opposition. Only in September had it been possible to obtain the approval of the German authorities to the socialization of a group of four firms controlled by the Italian Federation of Industries. In October the publishing and newspaper enterprises and the printing and paper industries were also socialized; together with the above four industrial firms, this represented the limits of the effective application of the whole programme.

Tarchi protested in vain against this overall German control. In a letter to Mussolini dated December 5, for instance, he wrote:

'For my part I have always assured both Ambassador von Rahn and General Leyers that the Italian government intended to inform the organs of the allied government beforehand of its intention to socialize protected industries; but I have never accepted the view of previous authorization which seems to me injurious to the sovereign rights of the Italian Social Republic. Socialization is in fact a purely internal affair, and we cannot admit any German interference in it. The anxieties of the RUK about the efficiency of war production if the protected industries are socialized are greatly exaggerated. I am sure that, by regularizing the relations of capital and labour, socialization will strengthen the rhythm of production. This anxiety, however, which is very probably fed by our capitalists and the parallel interests of German industrialists in RUK circles, could lead to assurances by the Italian government which is responsible to the allies too for the progress of production. But it cannot bind the government's activity for reform in the social sphere.

'I think it is necessary, Duce, for you to intervene energetically with the German Ambassador to clear up this important question for good.' [6]

In speaking on this theme, in his Milan speech, the Duce had said: 'Through nationalization the best elements among the workers will prove themselves. I am decided to proceed in this direction. I have entrusted two sectors to the working classes—those of local administration and rationing. These sectors, of the highest importance in present conditions, are henceforward completely in the hands of the workers.'

Such were the limits of the bold declarations at Verona in November 1943, and the paper legislation of the following February.

The very conception of creating a working class Fascist élite was a measure of the unreality of the whole political scene at Salò. In the weeks preceding the final collapse, the whole programme was overhauled in discussion between the interested parties and brave statements issued, but this time not as a working programme but as a historical position.

The dreary battle for control of the Italian working classes was nearly over, and as a final element of confusion Mussolini now agreed to set up a separate Ministry of Labour in January 1945 with functions overlapping those of Tarchi's Ministry of Corporations. The new body was given responsibility for all matters concerning the syndicates, and the reforms envisaged in the socialization programme. The Minister, Augusto Spinelli, came from the old ranks of anarcho-syndicalism of the early 20's. He and his staff operated in a world of total isolation from the situation which was fast getting out of control.

The new Minister of Labour reported to Mussolini after a visit to Turin: 'I am very worried about the socialization of Fiat. Moreover, I could not hope, with the contacts of a few hours, to turn upside down a situation which has been growing deep roots for some time, and in which the working masses, as usual, are only the tools of those interested in preserving capitalism which is everywhere corrupting and manoeuvring the minor leaders of the so-called leftist parties . . .

'While I was in Turin, the Liberation Committee issued a manifesto taking up a clear position against socialization, which it calls a swindle, and inviting the workers to abstain from the elections. I replied immediately with two more manifestos; one official and one attributed to anti-Fascist elements favourable to socialization.

'In order to sound the attitude of the masses and to avoid humiliation when the anticipated legal procedure is begun, we thought that, strictly in the syndicalist sphere—since there are no shop stewards committees at Fiat —we might set up a Committee of five hundred members composed of one worker elected for every three hundred workers or clerks of the various factories in the group, a Committee which would carry out a preliminary examination of the Statute prepared by the Company for setting up socialization.

'From the news which Prefect Fossa, Commissary of the General Confederation for Piedmont, gave me over the phone this morning, I learn that in the first factory, between thirty and forty per cent of the clerks have voted, while the percentage of workers voting does not amount to ten per cent. Both for workers and clerks, half the slips are blank, the other half have genuine marks as well as other various comments.

'This is all I know so far, but I do not think things will change much.

'Evidently when we thought we would make a great gesture and cut an excellent figure in the press, deciding the socialization of Fiat and the other great industrial combines in a simple decree, we ought to have reckoned with the reaction of the mass of the workers regarding its active collaboration in the measure. This so as to avoid a humiliation which, even if we have succeeded in limiting it to a simple exploratory manifestation, cannot help but be exploited by the anti-Fascist elements, i.e. primarily those who want to preserve industry.' [7]

Realizing that it was quite impossible to implement any programme such as had been under ill-tempered review since February 1944, the Germans now withdrew their opposition to the nationalization of the key war industries of Northern Italy.[c] A discussion was held in the presence of Rahn, and reported by Tarchi to Leyers on January 5. [8] It was agreed 'that the setting in motion of the law on socialization is a purely internal Italian question which

c. Nothing remained but to make the case for posterity that the Republic stood officially for a programme of complete nationalization of industry, but owing to circumstances beyond its control was unable to carry it out. The Fascist Party made a declaration in this sense in early April, followed by a decision of the Council of Ministers that the project in its entirety must be implemented by April 26. By that date, the Republic had ceased to exist.

does not concern German interests . . .' In so far as the Germans had a particular concern, in the case of the protected firms, 'it must clearly be taken into account whether, by nationalizing a particular firm, production would not decrease'.

Parallel with these plans to socialize Italian industry and, in the Duce's verbal imagery, 'to sow mines in the Po Valley' leaving behind his shadow rule the explosive myth of Fascist Socialism, he was considering a final 'Changing of the Guard', and the last shuffle in his ramshackle government.

The centre of Republican administration lay in the Ministry of the Interior, lodged in the school buildings just outside Maderno. This was the private realm of Buffarini Guidi, the only professional civil servant in office. His responsibility for maintaining law and order throughout the Republic was circumscribed and invaded at every turn by the rival agencies of the Party, the National Guard, the Duce himself with his circular instructions direct to the Prefects and Heads of Provinces, and above all by the German 'system' or rather, unco-ordinated set of 'systems'. In October, after a year of frustrated activity, Buffarini surveyed the internal scene in a report to Mussolini. [9]

The attempt to create a Fascist governing class, purged of 'compromised' elements, had failed. The main need had been for unity of control at the provincial level, but this aim 'had remained an abstract ideological aspiration, which had never been realized in practice. The central and local organs of the Party had opposed such a healthy development by every means.'

The Party had sabotaged the government. 'It must be noted that this has been due to ill-will, to preconceived ideologies and a misplaced sense of revolutionary pride on the part of those leaders called upon to carry out your directives.'

The National Republican Guard too had played its part. From the beginning of the régime, there had been complete failure to create a unified police force under the Ministry of the Interior. The Republican Guard was completely separate, and had 'vociferously affirmed its total independence and autonomy'. It contained 150,000 men as against 20,000 in the Republican Police under the Ministry.

'It is incontestable that the real disorder in the countryside began at the moment of the withdrawal of the Republican Guard garrisons in the rural areas of national territory, thus leaving three-quarters of the population deprived of protection and abandoned to the excesses of outlaws and bandits'

In addition, the local police headquarters had been stripped of all political investigative functions which came under the Guard, and in turn were closely controlled by the German police.

In matters of recruitment, the youth were absorbed by the Guard, the veterans by the Black Brigades, and the middle age-groups were interned in Germany. 'The Party had not furnished one man to the Police.'

Of the Heads of the Provinces, replacing the former prefects, 127 had been nominated (including in the Adriatic littoral and the Aldo Adige) and of these only 44 were effectively installed, and a further 26 were without any other post 'having been all denounced'.

In conclusion, Buffarini wearily wrote that he had the impression that the Duce himself wished to intervene more in the conduct of home affairs, and that therefore Buffarini had reduced his own initiative. On that very day, October 10, 1944, an Undersecretary had been appointed to the Ministry by the personal action of the Duce. This was Giorgio Pini, assistant editor of *Il Popolo d'Italia*, and now the sponsor of moderate non-party activity outside the Fascist Republican Party.

This was the first, and as it transpired, the only move towards a 'Changing of the Guard' within the limits of the modest resources of Salò.

The appointment of Pini as Undersecretary of the Interior was a warning sign to the Minister. The former was at once isolated from the main conduct of business, especially policy matters. Ministerial correspondence did not pass through his hands, and affairs were handled personally by Buffarini from his office in the government guest house at Maderno. Even if he was prevented from enforcing the elementary norms of internal administration, his function as the centre of all political intelligence was highly developed. This was his element. He had his own police units and agents. Every telephone exchange was tapped, including that of the Duce and of his own secretariat. [10]

Buffarini's recent career had been promoted mainly because of his cultivation of the Germans, especially Wolff whose principal agent in a sense he was. [11] But this ductile Tuscan, with his effusive bonhomie, was in appearance friends with everyone. He had cultivated and with success Donna Rachele, and his frequent association with the circle of Villa Torlonia, had in the past created an invaluable source of private gossip and news from the immediate entourage of the Duce, and which was of special value, particularly to Colonel Dollmann.

This link seems however by the winter of 1944 to have sagged, and Buffarini seems to have played some obscure part in promoting the activities of the Duce's mistress, Clara Petacci, and her family clan. But in this minor Renaissance court, female influences were seldom decisive, and the imminent fall of Buffarini was due to other causes.

Graziani and Pavolini had long opposed him, and on another level the 'moderates' such as Pini and Cione, with whom the Duce was temporarily flirting because of their cautious anti-German line, regarded Buffarini as the leading representative of the total submission to German control. But his main reason for dismissing Buffarini was connected probably with a more general private intention on his part to commence by careful stages a disengagement from German overlordship, and his decision was taken at a moment of mounting tension between the Germans and the Republic.

On February 16 he sent for Mellini. 'There is a matter of much importance. Relations with the Germans are not working out at all. I had some time ago decided to dismiss Buffarini Guidi, and they knew very well why. He is a man with many qualities, but is hated by all, anti-Fascists[d] and Fascist. He is even more loathed than I am.' [12]

Mussolini apparently warned his Minister of his intention, for when on February 15 Wolff telephoned to Buffarini asking him to lunch, the latter asked maliciously whether the invitation was to the person or the Minister, because 'as from today I am no longer the Minister'.[13]

Wolff telephoned immediately to the Duce, and asked for a delay. On this almost unique occasion Mussolini curtly refused, and the German S.S. Commander took counter-measures, which revealed both the extent of his fears, and the measure of the decline in Italo-German relations.

Mussolini had intended to broadcast the news of Buffarini's dismissal, and the Germans at once threatened to censure the announcement. Two Italian police officials, Tamburini and Appollonio, both active in intriguing against Buffarini, were arrested by German S.S.[e] These actions provoked a final crisis in the relations of Mussolini and the German military and diplomatic representatives in Italy.

In part, this action on the part of the Germans arose from the climate of plot and counter-plot which was endemic in the claustrophic atmosphere of Lake Garda. The only justification of these arbitrary arrests which Rahn could give to Mellini was that the entourage of Mussolini 'was definitely anti-German, and that the Duce displayed lack of understanding and confidence towards both himself and General Wolff'.[14] Apollonio, according to Rahn, was half Jewish and 'about to intrigue against the Germans', while Tamburini 'had secret links with the Allies in Switzerland without informing the Germans. . . . The Duce must realize that the state of mind in German military circles resembles that of September 8.' [15] As he told Mellini, 'The situation cannot continue.'

German circles expressed further alarm at the episode of the capture by the Italians of a British officer, Captain Tucker, together with a priest, and whose explanation of his mission in Republican territory was that he bore a verbal message from General Alexander to Graziani. Captain Tucker's un-

---

d. The Italian Committee of Liberation had declared him to be a war criminal on September 27, 1944. See Catalano *op cit* p. 254.

e. Tamburini had been prefect of Trieste in 1942–3, and early in his career a squad leader in Florence. At Salò he had been for a time Chief of Police. Apollonio was a police official attached to the Duce's secretariat. He was a native of Trieste.

The control of the Salò police was largely in the hands of officials from Venezia Giulia and Istria, who were swayed by a frustrated and violent irredentism.

welcome appearance coincided with the Buffarini crisis, adding another scarecrow to the scene.[f]

There was a heightening element of farce. As on previous occasions, Mussolini, when faced with a clash with the Germans, sought the nodding approbation of the Japanese ally, and the main function of their Ambassador, Hidaka, was to convey to his German colleague the grievances of the Italian partner when all other means had been exhausted.

The Buffarini affair was such an occasion. The Duce wrote to the Japanese Ambassador: 'I would ask you to remain at Salò for a few days until the Buffarini crisis has been resolved. And I count on your spirit of friendship of which I have several proofs.'[g]

No formal announcement of Buffarini's dismissal had yet been made, nor any charges preferred against him. As he himself wrote to Mussolini, protesting his absolute loyalty, he had been accused of Masonic connections by that 'unmentionable ex-Minister of State', Preziosi, and that the second accusation, 'equally infamous, is that I caused two well-known characters to be arrested by the German authorities'. [16]

Mussolini's last Changing of the Guard displayed the familiar style. Buffarini received a letter on the morning of February 21 informing him of his removal from office, and in which the Duce assured him that a fulsome communiqué would be issued 'after a leave-taking visit'. Instead, 'a bald harsh' communiqué was broadcast at 1 p.m., and Buffarini had no opportunity to warn the Germans in advance of this change.

Mussolini saw him on the evening of February 22, and offered him the post of Economic Ambassador as co-ordinator between the relevant Italian ministries and German agencies. The post never materialized.

There seems to have been some suspicion that Buffarini himself encouraged the German reaction to his dismissal, as a letter from Pavolini to the Duce seems to show.

'Last night, before leaving Maderno, I received Buffarini on a leave-taking visit. I took this opportunity to tell him, on my own initiative and as Party Secretary, that I thought it his duty as a Fascist to do everything in his power to limit or eradicate any kind of German reaction to the replacement of Buffarini himself, since its effect on Italo-German relations, and therefore also above all on German interests in Italy, would be negative.

'At first he reacted strongly to the suspicion—which moreover I neither voiced nor hinted at—that he was either the voluntary or contributory cause

---

f. See Mellini *op cit* p. 82, and note at the end of the chapter. Tucker was interrogated by Graziani on February 17. (See the latter's diary in the Italian Collection.) The English Captain was taken into German custody on February 26.

g. Italian Collection. Duce to Hidaka, February 26, 1945. Hidaka at this moment was at Bellagio, where most of the foreign diplomats were quartered.

of a similar reaction. He protested that he had nothing whatever to do with anything of the kind.

'Later, when I had made my request clearer and more insistent, he stated that he was always loyal to you in all circumstances, that he considered himself completely at your disposal in every sense, and that he did not wish to deviate from the line of orthodox Fascism.

'He added that, as far as Tamburini and above all Apollonio were concerned, he would waste no words in their favour, but repeated that he had nothing to do with their arrest. As to other probable measures, . . . he assured me that he will endeavour to eliminate friction and conflict, in view of the fact that he is trusted by the Germans; and he stated that when he undertook this position of collaborator it was at your request. I did not fail to point out to him that a position of loyal collaboration is implied for every Republican Fascist and in all your directives.

'But perhaps this conversation served some purpose in clinching the responsibility which Buffarini would take in pushing a further and highly unjustified German reaction to a purely internal Italian question, involving a matter which is anything but harmful to true Italo-German co-operation.

'During our conversation he did not want to argue about the fact of his replacement, but complained about the "method".' [17]

There seems little doubt that Buffarini's removal was part of a design of the Duce to cut down contacts with the Germans, and seek to withdraw from their control. On the German side, there was spreading fear of an Italian 'betrayal' of which they would have wind if Buffarini were in office, and equally of a leakage to the Italians of any feelers which they might make to the Allies.

As Wolff put it subsequently in disingenuous terms: 'Today I know that as from February 1945 Mussolini had begun, via the senior clergy, direct negotiations with the Allies and that in this situation Buffarini represented an obstacle.' [18]

It is perhaps ironical that the day following Buffarini's dismissal, Wolff gave full powers to his subordinate in Milan to negotiate with Cardinal Schuster.

Rahn too made his comment on this affair, which marked abruptly the end of comprehension and regular consultations between him and Wolff on the one hand and the Duce on the other.

The German Ambassador in conversation with Mellini on February 17 'regretted at the very moment when, together with Wolff, they were setting about initiating a policy of greater independence in regard to the directives from Berlin, and of greater pressure on the German military authorities in Italy to accept the idea of not sacrificing uselessly the interests and dignity of Italy, there should be taking shape round the Duce an anti-German current, and a tendency to take certain initiatives unconnected with any agreement with Rahn and Wolff. Berlin already had wind of such tendencies and initiatives.' [19]

Within a few days both Rahn and Wolff would be implicated in their own 'initiatives' in Switzerland, and the disappearance of Buffarini from the scene deprived Mussolini of the one highly trained director of intelligence, who might have penetrated the secret.

PART THREE

Book II

CHAPTER ONE

OPERATION 'SUNRISE'

• •

ON AUGUST 31, 1944 Hitler held a military conference. The meeting was charged with the atmosphere of the Plot, and heightened by the darkening military scene. The Russians had now bitten deep into the Baltic States, and were fanning out to the south along the Vistula. From the south-east came graver news. On the same day as the Liberation of Paris in the West, August 23, King Michael of Roumania, following a lightning coup d'état organized in Bucharest, declared war on Germany. Within twenty-four hours the Roumanian armies turned round to the Allied side, and on August 31, the day of the Fuehrer's conference, the Russian troops of Marshal Malinovsky entered the Roumanian capital. The whole Balkan front of the Axis was shattered. Bulgaria 'withdrew' from the war on the day following King Michael's declaration. By September 1 Roumania was cleared of German troops. The mass of the Russian armies on the south-eastern front could now thrust forward into the Danube plain, sweeping aside in their path the broken German front, and striking up into Central Europe.

This catastrophe brought with it the loss of the vital oil resources of Roumania, soon to be followed by the Russian occupation of the coal basin of Silesia.

Against such a background, Hitler confronted his military advisers.

'The time has not come for a political decision . . . It is childish and naïve to expect that at a moment of grave military defeats the time for political dealings has arrived. Such moments come when you are having successes. I have proved that I did everything to come to some understanding with the British. In 1940, after the French campaign, I extended my hand to them, abandoning all claims . . . but the time will come when the tension between the Allies will become so great that the break will occur just the same. All coalitions in history have disintegrated sooner or later. The only thing is to wait for the right moment, no matter how hard it is . . . Under all circumstances we will continue this battle until, as Frederick the Great said, one of our damned enemies gets too tired to fight any more.' [1]

Hitler's historical obsession with the break-up of the coalition against Frederick the Great, together with an apocalyptic vision of the destructive power of the German secret weapons to change the course of the military events, now pervaded his thinking.

Apart from Goebbels, the Fuehrer's other advisers shrank from the prospect of total and collective suicide, and shadowed by the fate of the July conspirators, as Hitler prepared in spirit the last Bunker, they sought cautiously their private solutions. In discussing the Fuehrer's absolute control of power, Ribbentrop said to his interrogators at Nuremberg: 'Perhaps in the last year or half year, things ran more out of his hands and into others. That is possible, but there were a number of people who had great ambitions to become the successors of the Fuehrer and more of them had their Foreign Minister ready all the time. Himmler had his own, Goering had his own, and Bormann had his own.' [2]

On the day before Hitler's conference of August 31 Ribbentrop claims that he pressed once again on the Fuehrer the need to seek a political solution.

'On August 30, 1944, I again submitted a memorandum to the Fuehrer, asking for authorization to put out peace feelers in all directions. The memorandum opened with these words: "The object of diplomacy is not to see that a nation goes down fighting heroically, but rather to see that it survives. Thus every road that leads to this goal is opportune and failure to take it must be regarded as a damnable crime." This was a quotation from *Mein Kampf*, which I had used on purpose as an opening, to remind Hitler in his own words of the task of diplomacy. I also wanted to remind him that we were about to go down fighting heroically, and that he had always held that diplomacy must try to prevent this. But this memorandum, too, failed: I did not receive the authority for which I had asked.

'Soon afterwards Kleist[a] let me know that the Russians, too, had expressed a desire to make contact. I passed on this news to the Fuehrer and was at least given permission to put out feelers in Stockholm. I was somewhat sceptical about my information, and felt that the wish was father to the thought. But all I wanted was to have Hitler's authority. In fact, no Russian negotiator appeared.' [3]

This move by Ribbentrop coincided, as on previous occasions, with Japanese pressure, patient and consistent, for a separate peace with Russia. Shigemitsu, the Japanese Foreign Minister, had proposed on August 28 to the German Minister in Tokyo the good offices of his Government for such a purpose.

---

a. A German agent in Stockholm who had been employed on previous such occasions. See pp. 244 and 260.

On September 4, Oshima, the Japanese Ambassador in Berlin, acting on instructions from Tokyo to advise the same course and after previous talks with Ribbentrop, was received by Hitler. The German reply was that the proposal was premature but the Japanese Ambassador had the impression that the opposition of the Fuehrer and Ribbentrop 'which had been very categorical before, had become somewhat more moderate, and he made clear to Oshima that this refusal did not close the door to the Japanese proposal'.[4]

There may well have been a tacit collusion between the two men.

It seems that Ribbentrop also made private soundings, probably with Hitler's connivance, in the Western neutral capitals and in particular in Madrid and Switzerland. This could be regarded as a routine measure to sense the temper of the Allied coalition, on whose imminent dissolution the Fuehrer and indeed the Duce now placed such wishful hopes.

As Ribbentrop took pains to explain to Anfuso, 'At the present time, while we reject any compromise peace, we are on the other hand concerned with what is being done or thought abroad about the possibility of a peace.' [5]

But these private feelers were a reflection also of the mounting dissolution of the German leadership, accelerated by the climate of treason after the savage events of July.

Himmler, in his turn, was drawn to seek his own solution. His interpretation, too, was coloured by the conception of a rift in the enemy coalition, but also by the need in extreme circumstances, as supreme head of the S.S., to treat as a quasi-independent authority and to seize the opportunity now created by the shift in the balance of power within Germany since the July Plot in his favour, and at the expense of the Army. It might be the rôle in history of the Reichsfuehrer S.S. to seize the initiative before the fatal crash, save the remnants of the Reich from extinction in a last-minute compromise with the enemy, and place the S.S. divisions at the disposal of the Allies in an anti-Soviet capacity.

The Italian front seemed to offer certain special advantages as a base for such moves. General Wolff held the only important S.S. command outside German territory. Since the end of July, he also held the post of military plenipotentiary in Italy. As Ribbentrop put it to Anfuso, 'This step was dictated not so much by the urgent need to purge the High Command after the attack on the Fuehrer, but rather by the convenience of avoiding the dispersal of military and police powers, which had been too evident recently.' [6]

The weight of the Allied assault was concentrated on the Western and Eastern fronts. In the South, however, with the slowing down of military operations in the autumn and winter of 1944, there was a significant pause which might be exploited.

The Italian situation contained two elements of special interest; the presence of a highly organized industrial complex in the Northern towns, the preservation or destruction of which could be used as a bargaining counter in any soundings, and, allied to these formidable assets, the danger of a Communist 'liberation' of Northern Italy with grave consequences for the political future of Western Europe. Himmler's line of reasoning led him to believe that the British and Americans might listen to such approaches.

As capitalist powers they had an interest in Northern Italian industry, and they were directly concerned with the future post-war political structure of the country. Such a 'realistic' and oversimplified analysis coincided with that of the Russians, and any German sounding on these lines, if taken up by the Western Allies, might have the added advantage of creating that very rift in the enemy coalition which had now become the obsessive hope of Hitler, and in momentary gusts of optimism, of Mussolini.

Another major power—the Vatican—had an equal concern and interest in this situation. The desire to save the population of Northern Italy from the final horrors of a last stand by Fascists and Germans, to protect the industrial structure of the country, and to prevent social chaos and revolution, might become the main historic mission of the Papacy in the closing months of the war. The preservation of the Northern Italian scene from such horrors might be a step towards preserving the balance of political forces throughout Europe. The imminent and massive invasion of Germany and Central Europe from the East and the West called in question the whole future structure of the Continent.

It seemed therefore that through Vatican channels the most likely preliminary approach might be made to the Western Allies and, on Himmler's instructions, Wolff set to work.

He had been received by the Pope in June 1944, but the Allied occupation of Rome shortly afterwards cut off all direct German links with the Vatican except for the isolated diplomatic mission.[7]

Wolff could now only approach the Vatican through the two archbishoprics of Milan and Turin.[b] In the Lombard capital, Cardinal Schuster reacted at once to such a move. During September and October the first signs of a more moderate German attitude towards Northern Italy appear in the intensification of contacts between the Milan Curia and the German authorities.

Not only could this channel lead to the Allied authorities either through the Vatican in Rome or the Papal Nuncio in Berne, but also to the partisan authorities in Northern Italy. It was essential to Himmler's plan that, in any possible negotiation with the Anglo-Americans, a preliminary understanding with the Committee of Liberation for Upper Italy for the eventual peaceful evacuation by the Germans of Northern Italian territory should be reached, and then presented as an earnest of German intentions.

b. On Wolff's abortive approach to Cardinal Fossati of Turin in February 1945, see Caforna's evidence in Ballola, *Processo Parri*, p. 90. The move was rejected by the Committee of Liberation for Northern Italy.

The first moves came from the Milan Curia, through the contacts of the German services, to Colonel Dollmann, still Himmler's leading political agent in Italy. The ecclesiastical link with the Germans was undertaken by Don Bicchierai, one of the Cardinal's secretaries.

On October 14, on the initiative of Cardinal Schuster, the latter sent a note to his German contact, pointing out the social dangers of the destruction of the industrial plants of Northern Italy by the Germans. The Cardinal offered formally to act as mediator between the German Command and the Liberation Committee, on the understanding that the Germans would abstain from any systematic destruction or neutralization of Italian industry, and that the Italian partisans would abstain from acts of hostility or sabotage against the German Armed Forces.

Dollmann was asked to sound Field Marshal Kesselring. Discussions of this initiative seemed to have taken place in German circles in Italy. Indeed the success of any move depended on the co-operation of the three leading personalities in that theatre—Kesselring, Wolff, and Rahn.

Don Bicchierai was also instructed by the Cardinal to approach the Vatican through the Papal Nuncio in Berne, and he left for Switzerland later in the month, bearing a document enlarging on the note handed to Dollmann, and referring to a further talk held at the Milan Curia at which Rahn was present.[8]

The essence of the plan was the drafting of a document to be signed by Kesselring and Wolff on the one side, and the National Committee of Liberation representatives on the other. The latter as represented in the North were, however, sceptical of German good faith and fearful of the reactions of their colleagues in Rome and Central Italy to any negotiations with the Germans. The main purpose therefore of Don Bicchierai's intervention in Berne was to seek Vatican mediation with the Liberation authorities in Rome to further the enterprise.

This same theme was elaborated in a further document drafted by Don Bicchierai on December 13.[9] It seemed that Rahn was prepared to answer for Kesselring, but that the main difficulty came from the Committee of National Liberation. The latter had committed themselves to a general insurrection in Northern Italy. 'In the Committee of National Liberation the positions are as follows: Collectively—against. On a Party basis: favourable with certain reserves, the Christian Democrats, the Liberals, and the Socialists. Against, but open to persuasion, the Action Party. Completely against, and threatening to break up the structure of the Committee of National Liberation, the Communists. The proposed agreement can only be reached and carried out if the Communists adhere.' [10]

These moves coincided with General Alexander's proclamation ordering the partisans to cease operations and disperse for the winter, and with a crisis in their leadership. There was a genuine fear of hostile manoeuvres to accelerate and exploit this crisis in the relations between the Allies and the Italian partisans, and Don Bicchierai's activities coincided with such a climate.[11]

By February 1945 the whole plan had collapsed for this reason, and because the central Liberation Committee in Rome had equally rejected the proposals. It was now clear that the Curia could not exercise any influence on the anti-Fascist leadership as a whole. Don Bicchierai was therefore now told by Cardinal Schuster 'to deal in his name with the German authorities to prevent the destruction decided upon'.[12] On February 22, Wolff gave full powers to his representative in Milan, Colonel Rauff, to handle equally in his name any negotiations with the Curia.[13]

Although this aspect of Himmler's plan—to reach an agreement with the Liberation Committee for Northern Italy on avoiding the 'destruction of plants' as a preliminary to peace talks with Western Allies—had broken down, useful contacts had been established.

Another German move had been made simultaneously and in a different quarter. The head of the giant Italian rayon combine, Franco Marinotti, had been arrested by Mussolini for his hostility to the socialization plans of the neo-Fascist government and released on the insistence of the Germans. With their connivance, Marinotti had escaped to Switzerland where he had made contact with the British services. General Harster, the head of the German security police in North Italy, had followed closely these activities. Marinotti had close pre-war links with British industry, particularly Courtaulds. He might well be the agent for whom Himmler was looking to make the first contact with the Anglo-Americans, and in particular to exploit the fear which allegedly existed in British capitalist circles of the destruction by the Germans of Italian equipment.

On October 25 Marinotti travelled to Italy with a *laissez passer* signed by Harster, and a meeting was held near the frontier at which he and a Swiss lawyer, together with Harster and Rauff, discussed a possible approach. Harster stated that he was authorized by Himmler to treat.[14]

On October 30 Marinotti reported this talk to the British authorities in Zurich, and two days later an abrupt message from London ordered the affair to be dropped on the grounds of lack of faith in German intentions.

Perhaps Himmler's thesis of a Western bloc based on the preservation of its capitalist interests and the thwarting of Communism in Europe was based on erroneous judgment of the situation.

Rahn had also acted on his own account. In November it appeared that he had made cautious soundings in Switzerland, and in January 1945 had sent one of his staff for this purpose across the frontier.[15] He had already approached Kesselring on the offer of mediation put forward by the Milan Curia, and had had 'many talks' with Wolff.

Reports of these activities had reached Allied circles in Switzerland, and combined with the various approaches by German political and military circles in Northern Italy, even if rebuffed in immediate practical terms, raised the possibility of testing German good faith as a step towards considering the implications and value of a German surrender on the Italian front.

By the beginning of January 1945, the Russians had crossed the Oder and were on East German territory, thus occupying the major source of German coal supplies in Upper Silesia, while in the West the Siegfried Line lay under major assault from the Anglo-American armies. In the Balkans the Russians were engaged in the battle for Budapest. On the Italian front, the Anglo-American forces drew near to Bologna in November, but the switching of reserves to meet the Allied landings in Southern France brought the campaign to a halt in the late winter months and a temporary pause on the Front.

The Germans had committed twenty divisions to Northern Italy. The heavy bombing by the Allied air forces of the main rail and road communications with Germany would make any massive evacuation of the German military forces in Italy northwards an impossible operation.[c] In the West the Allies were already in control of Southern France, and in the South-East the German armies from the Balkans, after their stand at Budapest, were being driven inexorably northwards into Central Europe. There was no practical chance of transferring, therefore, the German Divisions in Italy either to the North, to the West, or to the East, and their only hope lay in making a last stand in the Alpine regions on the Italian-German frontier, with or without the co-operation of their neo-Fascist allies; or possibly in the Julian Alps on the Slovene border, linking up with the remnants of the German armies now in full retreat from South-East Europe.

In any event military defeat was certain, and the alternative to the creation of an Alpine redoubt could only be surrender. Ever since September 1944, with the breaking by the Allies of the Gothic Line, desultory talks had taken place between German and Italian Fascist representatives in Northern Italy as to the creation of a fortified area in which to conduct the last stand. These discussions were to drag on in an increasing climate of unreality until the end.

With the turn of the year and the inevitable renewal of the Allied offensive on the Italian Front, it was natural that the senior German representatives in Italy should again confer together. It was also however a period of private and unco-ordinated peace moves of individuals and agencies on the German side throughout Europe. Ribbentrop, Himmler, and Kaltenbrunner had begun in deep secrecy and individually to instruct trusted agents to contact

c. In September 1944 Hitler had considered withdrawing nine divisions and evacuating a large part of Northern Italy. Wolff and Kesselring had successfully opposed this move.

Allied representatives in the neutral capitals. Other moves were made by enterprising individuals on their own responsibility.[d]

The main centre of these activities, inevitably, because of its central geographical and neutral position, was Switzerland. The general attitude of the Allied representatives there to such moves was to refer rigidly to the Casablanca formula of unconditional surrender. The Italian situation, however, presented a rather special case. Here, from the Allied point of view, the prize was worth special concessions. The surrender of twenty German divisions and their exit from the war would save lives and effort, and complete the occupation of Italy. During the course of January 1945 the American services in Switzerland became aware of increasing private talks between Kesselring, Wolff and Rahn on the hopelessness of the situation.

The delicacy of such negotiations was apparent to all, and the experience of the July plot in Germany in the previous summer provided a signal warning. The Allies would be prepared to initiate secret conversations only with fully accredited representatives of the German military and police forces controlling Northern Italy. There would be no talks, even locally, on a diplomatic level. The problem of securing the consent of their superiors in Germany, including Hitler himself, or equally of refusing to undertake such a task, was the sole concern of the German commanders in Italy. The Allied representatives would in no circumstances negotiate direct with any German leader in Berlin.

The hierarchy of the German Command in Italy presented immediate difficulties. The operational commander on the Front, General Kesselring, took his orders from the German General Staff. The air force commander, General Pohl, was under the direct orders of Goering. General Wolff was supreme S.S. commander in charge of German police forces and responsible to Himmler, and since the previous summer he held the post of Military Plenipotentiary in succession to General Toussaint, and in this capacity reported, as did Kesselring, to the German General Staff.[e] But parallel to Wolff, and not under his direct control, were the various German Intelligence agencies with

d. Such contacts were not unknown to Mussolini. On March 2 a report had reached him from Anfuso. The entourage of the Fuehrer had given up hope of a decisive military victory. They were rather relying on mounting divergences between the Western Allies and Russia.

'Regarding rumours circulating of the activities of German agents in neutral countries relating to peace negotiations, it was really a matter of more or less official envoys, according to Anfuso, who, on most secret instructions from Ribbentrop, were to spy out the land to discover what was the real state of relations between the Allied Western powers and Russia . . . rather than to initiate proper discussions.' Mellini, *op cit* p. 102. March 2, 1945.

e. The forces at Wolff's disposal were as follows: (a) as S.S. Commander: 15,000 Germans; 100,000 Italians; 20,000 Russians; 10,000 Serbs; 10,000 Slovenes; 5,000 Czechs; and an Indian legion; (b) as Military Plenipotentiary: 10,000 Germans and 55,000 German supply troops.

competing and overlapping functions, reporting to Kaltenbrunner or Schellenberg.

The success of any negotiation for a surrender depended essentially on the co-operation, either local or on the supreme level, between the German military and S.S. commands, but with the sinister complicating possibility of leakages to Germany which might, even in the final weeks, lead to another holocaust such as the July Plot.

As early as December the first sounding was made by Colonel Dollmann. The go-between was a Baron Parrilli, who had been discreetly travelling on business between Italy and Switzerland for some months, and who could supply the necessary link through the Swiss Intelligence.[f] At the end of February Parrilli met American representatives in Lucerne, and indicated that under certain conditions General Wolff might be prepared to discuss surrender terms. As the result of this first contact it was agreed that Dollmann, the mention of whose name aroused the interest of the Americans, should be sent to Switzerland together with Wolff's adjutant, Lieutenant Zimmer, to enable them to take further soundings.[g]

On February 28 a discussion took place at Wolff's headquarters at Desenzano on Lake Garda between Wolff, Rahn, Zimmer who reported on his Swiss trip with Parrilli, and the German police chief in Verona, General Harster. The latter came under the orders of Kaltenbrunner, and he immediately informed his chief that same night by telephone of this discussion and of Parrilli's proposals.[16]

That night Dollmann was sent for by Wolff. Their first reaction seems to have been that an opportunity now arose to bargain with the Western Allies on the employment of the German forces in the Italian theatre in an eventual anti-Russian rôle. Rahn claimed subsequently however that on the contrary he advised that the Allies should be told that the German leaders had no such illusions.[17]

It was agreed that Dollmann, together with Zimmer, should cross at once to Switzerland with the first task of setting up a sure channel of communications. The two men reached Lugano on March 3, and met Parrilli, the latter's Swiss intermediary, and an American representative.

Dollmann was told plainly that there was no question of negotiating a surrender on terms, nor of playing off the Western Allies against the Russians.

The Americans demanded as a test of good faith the immediate release of Ferruccio Parri, one of the Italian resistance leaders who had fallen into the

f. For details concerning Baron Parrilli and his activities see Ferruccio Lanfranchi. *La Resa degli Ottocentomila, passim.* This book contains Parrilli's own account of these negotiations. The Swiss were primarily concerned with the protection of their industrial interests in Northern Italy.

g. Zimmer had independently been in touch with Parrilli for some time. See Lanfranchi, *op cit* pp. 113 ff.

hands of the German police together with one of his leading military agents. If the handing over of these men could be guaranteed, the Americans would receive in Switzerland at the same moment General Wolff himself for further discussions.

On Dollmann's return a meeting was held at Wolff's villa at Fasano to hear the results of this first direct contact. It was clear that the Allies would only deal with military representatives, and that they had no preconceived plan which might modify an unconditional surrender. Rahn was told that there was no room for diplomatic talks. His own version suggests that he had already received such a reply through his 'Swiss agent'. It was therefore agreed that Wolff and not Rahn should handle future negotiations and the latter tore up his agent's letter on the spot.[18] Wolff left at once to see Kesselring.[h]

That afternoon Parrilli arrived at Fasano, and for nearly four days a discussion developed, and according to him, again on the theme of using German troops under Allied control eventually against the Russians.[19] At dinner that evening Wolff gave orders for the liberation of Parri and his companion.

These moves were carried out according to plan. On the evening of March 8, Wolff alone met Mr Allen Dulles, the head of the American Office of Strategic Services, and his chief adviser on German affairs Mr Gaevernitz, in Dulles' flat in Zurich. A second meeting, at which Gaevernitz and Dollmann were present, took place the next morning.

The sincerity of Wolff's intentions, in so far as his own command was concerned, was accepted. He gave assurance that Himmler knew nothing of his presence in Switzerland, and was told that in no circumstances were the Western Allies prepared to deal solely with the head of the S.S. in Germany.

Everything now depended on the co-operation of Kesselring as the senior German Army Commander in Italy. Wolff reckoned that he would need five to seven days in which to persuade his colleague.

It was agreed that Wolff should therefore approach Kesselring on his return. This he attempted to do, but to his dismay learnt that on the evening of March 8–9 Kesselring had left suddenly for Germany in Hitler's private plane. On the following day he was appointed to command the German Army Groups facing the Allies on the Western Front. With this news the first phase of the negotiations ended abruptly.

Wolff had already given the American representative in Switzerland to understand that he ought to be able to act with full and joint powers within a week, but the departure of Kesselring meant an unavoidable delay. On March 15 representatives of Allied General Headquarters in Caserta reached

h. Rahn claims that he also had seen Kesselring, who told him, 'I hope that your political plans succeed.'

Switzerland on a clandestine mission and in civilian clothes. They were General Alexander's Director of Military Intelligence, General Airey, and Alexander's American Deputy Chief of Staff, General Lemnitzer. Four days later, on March 19, Wolff again crossed the frontier for secret rendezvous with the Allied military representatives.

Rumours had reached the Americans that Wolff had been talking to Mussolini. He denied this on arrival, and said he had been at the inspection of some Black Brigades. He had had no conversation with the Duce on this occasion, nor did he regard the latter as of any importance in regard to his own immediate problems.

The essence of the meeting with the Allied Generals was to work out a time-table. The German command believed that the Allies intended to mount a major offensive by the end of March, and Wolff calculated that if he had five to seven days he might be able to make the arrangement in time with Kesselring, who had been briefed in general as to the position of the present contacts between Wolff and the Allies. Kesselring's successor in command of the German forces in Italy, General Vietinghoff, was expected to arrive on or about March 19, and Wolff explained that in order to win him over it would be of decisive help to have Kesselring's general approval of the surrender plans, even if the latter were no longer technically in charge of the German Army in Italy.

Wolff went to see Kesselring on March 23 at the latter's new Headquarters at Bad Nauheim on the Western Front. Kesselring apparently told Wolff to go ahead, but that he had no longer any responsibility and had no intention of joining in any general surrender arrangements to include the German Army Groups in the West.

By now more than one leakage about Wolff's activities had reached Berlin;[i] and there were indeed also further precursory signs of a German collapse. As Wolff had learnt at Kesselring's Headquarters, Ribbentrop had at last made definite soundings on his own account through Stockholm.

Almost simultaneously Rahn, who was aware of Wolff's plan and in agreement, was summoned back to Germany, but decided to make excuses and not to go.[20] To make matters worse, Himmler now telephoned on April 1 to Wolff ordering him not to move around, but to stay in Italy, and that he, Himmler, would telephone him periodically to make sure that he remained at his Headquarters.

On the same evening Wolff revealed to Vietinghoff the state of his negotiations with the Allies. Both men appeared to agree with what Kesselring had told Wolff at Bad Nauheim, which was that if one could last out for ten to fifteen days the chances were that there would be a total collapse at the centre in Germany, and that then negotiations with Switzerland could proceed.

Wolff was now told, through Parrilli as an intermediary, that the Allies

i. Harster had at this time been summoned to report to Kaltenbrunner in Germany.

insisted that orders should be given immediately to prevent the destruction of any Italian industrial plants or equipment, as a second and more severe test of German good faith. In the meantime the two Allied military representatives from Caserta would return to report to General Alexander.

On April 6 Wolff gave instructions to his commanders that they would be responsible for avoiding any damage to Italian factories and installations, and on the following day he had a decisive talk with Vietinghoff. All the German military authorities in Northern Italy were to be ordered on to the defensive. But the German military commander had certain reservations as to 'points of honour', and the Allied authorities suspected that there might be appeals and last-minute attempts to negotiate rather than to surrender outright. Regular communications in these days of waiting were established through an Allied wireless operator placed in the house of Wolff's own Intelligence office in Milan.

Wolff now hoped to complete arrangements within the next week unless some unforeseen disaster occurred. He had won over the commander of the German air force, General Pohl, and in the event of any emergency, such as the appearance of the retreating German forces of General Loehr from the Balkans in Northern Italy, which might decide to fight to the last, the Alpine passes were to be formally secured by Pohl's anti-aircraft units.[j]

On April 13 Himmler telephoned from Berlin ordering Wolff to report to him at once. On the following day he telephoned twice again to know why Wolff had not arrived. The latter seems to have sent a letter by special courier, saying that it would be better, in view of the fact that there was no question of holding the Western Front, that Himmler should come to Italy and avail himself of Wolff's Western contacts, and he himself had no intention of coming to Berlin.[21]

On April 16 Wolff's adjutant Zimmer appeared in Switzerland to explain these latest developments, and to add that his commanding officer intended to carry through his plan of surrender, irrespective of Vietinghoff's consent, and that he had already sounded the other leading Army commanders successfully in this sense.

On April 17 Wolff however changed his mind about going to Berlin, and decided to take the risk of facing Himmler. He sent a message through the Allied radio link to say that he intended to take this course.

On April 21 unexpected orders arrived in Switzerland from Washington ordering all contacts with Wolff to be broken. It transpired later that, at the summit level on the Allied side, there had been a personal intervention by Stalin to sabotage these negotiations in Switzerland, of which the Russians had been informed in principle and asked to take part. In the increasing confusion of the fronts in the European Theatre, the Russians presumably

j. About April 10 Hitler had placed all German forces east of the Isonzo under General Loehr; hence the need for these precautions.

feared, as both Himmler and independently the German leaders in Italy had originally hoped, that the Allies were only concerned with using the German forces in Italy to hold some regions in Central Europe against the Russian advance.

By now events were moving so fast that it was difficult to carry out these instructions on the spot. Within a few hours of receiving the message from Washington, the senior American representative in Switzerland, Mr Allen Dulles, learnt that Wolff had returned from Berlin at noon on April 19 having achieved his mission successfully and was on his way to Lucerne with full powers to treat; and on April 24 he arrived as planned, accompanied by a senior member of Vietinghoff's staff with powers to treat on behalf of Army Group 'C'. There was now a frantic delay while the Americans reported to Caserta and to Washington the most recent developments, and pressed for a reversal of the summit decision to break off all contacts in regard to Operation 'Sunrise'.[k]

Events in Italy were now reaching the last stages before a final disintegration of the whole political and military scene in Republican territory.

Meanwhile Wolff waited for the next forty-eight hours in Lucerne. On April 26 he decided however that he must return to his headquarters at Fasano before the roads in the area were cut by partisan bands or by Allied patrols. The main Anglo-American forces were by now across the river Po.

Just before leaving Lucerne a telephone call from Italy gave him the text of a message from Himmler dated April 23, which read: 'It is more than ever essential that the Italian front hold and remain intact. No negotiations of any kind should be undertaken.'

Three days previously, Hitler had ordered Kesselring to prepare and defend the Alpine Redoubt. But central control from Berlin had finally broken down, and the local commanders had nothing now to fear.

On crossing the Italian frontier Wolff was unable to move further than Villa Locatelli at Cernobbio, the headquarters of the German security services for the frontier area.

Graziani was searching anxiously for his German colleague. He had arrived from Como on the morning of April 26 having left Mussolini at Menaggio. 'In my capacity as commander of the Ligurian Army, and as the surrender has not yet taken place, it is clear to me that I cannot abandon my army command.' [22] In Como, he had met General Leyers, the head of the German Ministry of War Production mission in Northern Italy, and while the two men were talking Wolff telephoned from Cernobbio saying 'that the surrender negotiations should be concluded in the course of the day'.[23] He added that he passed this news to the Duce through the Prefect of Como.

At 6 o'clock that evening Graziani arrived at Villa Locatelli. 'General

k. The American code name allotted for this operation.

Wolff confirmed to me that negotiations were in progress through the Church (Cardinal Schuster) or directly with the American representatives in Switzerland. He must go back again tonight for these agreements which according to him would then be definite. I gave him a proxy also in my name to deal with the Republic troops and Fascist formations . . .'

On the morning of April 27, Graziani noted in his diary: 'Yesterday evening General Wolff invited me to stay until the armistice had been concluded, which he thought would be confirmed in the course of today and tomorrow. I have just been informed that General Wolff left during the night for Switzerland, but will not be returning here as he must get to Bolzano via Switzerland.' By now Villa Locatelli was under siege. 'Movements of small groups of partisans had been noticed round the house.' [24]

In his book, published two years after the event, Graziani maintains that he had reproached Wolff bitterly 'for having hidden from us all reference to the surrender negotiations'. The latter merely replied that it was a sad necessity 'but if he had first talked to Mussolini the secret would have been nil'.[25]

Later that morning, April 27, Graziani telephoned to the Cardinal's secretary, Don Bicchierai, in Milan and dictated to him a note for Cardinal Schuster on the events of the last hours.[26] His last decision as Army Commander remained to be taken. He was out of touch with members of the government of the Italian Social Republic 'who were in places unknown to him'. He had given a surrender proxy to Wolff. He was marooned at Cernobbio, and was unable to move to Milan. He had decided to surrender to General Cadorna, the senior military representative on the Liberation Committee, and asked the Cardinal to act as an intermediary, and at least arrange for a conversation with Cadorna on the telephone.

That afternoon Don Bicchierai communicated the latter's reply. The competent body was the Zone Command of the Committee of Liberation at Como, and Cadorna would arrange for them to accept the surrender of Graziani and his staff. Cadorna could not come himself to Como 'given the chaotic situation which exists'.[27]

In the event Graziani came into the hands of two Allied officers, one Italian and the other American. They brought him to Milan, where a bomb exploded in the car, blinding the Italian officer to whom he had surrendered.

Graziani passed into Allied captivity, and after the war appeared before an Italian tribunal.[28] He had been unable to achieve a formal surrender of the Italian Republican forces. No results followed his attempted intervention with the Allies through Wolff, and the armed units of the Salò Republic, except when they fell directly into Allied hands, were exposed piecemeal to the vengeance of the Italian partisans.

During the night of April 26 Wolff was rescued from Cernobbio by a small partisan body under the orders of the representative of the American Office of Strategic Services in Lugano, who was at that moment negotiating with the Committee of National Liberation. This body had already assumed authority in Como, and the American agent had been clandestinely in touch with it for the last two years.

In the small hours of the following morning Wolff conferred with Mr Dulles' deputy in a Lugano hotel. The Americans were given the assurance that if Himmler attempted at the last minute to take over supreme command on the Southern Front, Wolff would arrest him, and equally any German military commander, who attempted at the last moment to hinder the surrender operations.

It was agreed that Wolff should leave for his new Headquarters at Bolzano, where Vietinghoff was already established, and from there supervise and control the final stages, and that the two military representatives from himself and Vietinghoff should be sent to Caserta.

Before Wolff left Switzerland, instructions reached the American representatives from the Combined Chiefs of Staff lifting the ban on the 'Sunrise' operations which had been imposed on April 23. But four vital days had been lost between April 23 and 27. It has been suggested that the Russian veto had been abruptly imposed since a premature collapse of the German front in Northern Italy before the proclamation of a general rising by the Italian partisans, and the arrival of Marshal Tito at Trieste, might well hinder the overall politico-military plans of the Soviet government in that part of Europe. It may have also been significant that the general order from the Italian partisan command for an insurrection throughout Northern Italy was given on April 25, after the Russian veto and before Field Marshal Alexander succeeded in obtaining the consent of the Combined Chiefs of Staff to proceed with the 'Sunrise' operation.[29]

The journey of the two German military plenipotentiaries to Caserta proceeded without a hitch. At 2 p.m. on April 29 the formal instruments of surrender were signed, and it remained only to secure formal ratification from Bolzano.

Wolff had arrived at his new headquarters on the previous morning, and the vital radio link with its gallant operator, who had been established earlier by the American services in Milan, was at the same time transferred to connect Wolff directly to Caserta.

On the evening of April 30 the German envoys were speeded back to Switzerland from Allied General Headquarters after the surrender ceremony and put across the frontier to Bolzano.

Wolff in the meantime was faced with a drastic and perilous set of events. The delay of four days, and the news of the suspension of the negotiations by the Allies, caused confusion and alarm at Bolzano. The situation was discussed at a five-hour conference at which Vietinghoff, Wolff, Rahn, and gauleiter Hofer were present. The latter represented the main opposition. He was still hoping to preserve his political fief of the Tyrol from Allied occupation. The futile bickering ended in a formal decision to await the return of the two envoys from Caserta, but Hofer took it upon himself to risk wrecking the precarious enterprise by telephoning to Kesselring, warning him of the latest steps to conclude the surrender of Army Group South-West.

Kesselring had been appointed, on April 28, commander of all the German Southern Armies. Although he had been generally informed of Wolff's recent moves by Dollmann, who had visited his headquarters for this purpose two days previously, he had been under pressure from Hitler to issue orders for a fight to the finish. The failure to hold Berlin against the Russians, the fate of the German armies in the East under the shadow of Soviet captivity, and desperate musings on his 'oath of allegiance' to the Fuehrer caused Kesselring grimly to reflect and to give unexpected retaliatory orders. Vietinghoff was summarily dismissed and replaced by a General Schulz, who appeared at Bolzano at noon on April 30 after a meeting with Hofer. An official investigation of the whole proceedings of the surrender negotiations was ordered, and Wolff's own case was referred by Kesselring direct to Kaltenbrunner.[30]

After midnight on April 30 the German envoys from Caserta reached Bolzano. The surrender terms provided that hostilities were to end at 12 noon on May 2.

Wolff had no choice. Early on the morning of May 1 he placed General Schulz and the latter's Chief of Staff under arrest, and severed all telephonic communications between Bolzano and the Reich. During the following hours, Wolff struggled and argued with the two men. In the afternoon Schulz presided, despite his arrest, over a meeting of all Army Commanders and finally agreed, in light of the hopeless military situation which had been reviewed, to present a fair case to Kesselring for final decision.

At 9.30 that evening a radio signal arrived from Field Marshal Alexander demanding the honouring of the Caserta instrument. A frantic attempt to reach Kesselring on the telephone failed, and at 10 p.m. Wolff, Pohl for the Air Force, and two leading Army commanders gave the surrender orders to their units on their own responsibility.

An hour later the death of Hitler was announced over the radio. Even at this stage Kesselring refused to accept the situation. Orders were issued for the arrest of Vietinghoff and certain other officers. Wolff called out tanks and a special S.S. group to defend his headquarters.

At 2 a.m. he finally received a telephone call from Kesselring, and for over two hours an interrupted dialogue swayed back and forth, with even General Schulz intervening in favour of capitulation.[1] At 4.30 on the morning of May 2 final approval was given to implement the terms of surrender.

1. Kesselring's brief account (in his book) does not mention Wolff.

CHAPTER TWO

THE DUCE AND AN
ITALIAN 'SOLUTION'

⋆•⋆

IT IS NOT KNOWN whether Mussolini was informed of the first stages of these moves in Switzerland towards a capitulation of the German forces on the territory of the Salò Republic. They almost precisely and mysteriously coincided in time with a major crisis in Mussolini's relations with the German authorities over the dismissal of Buffarini as Minister of the Interior towards the end of February. Whatever the reasons were for this action by the Duce, it meant the removal of the one experienced and efficient administrator in the Republican Government. The very violent reactions of Wolff to the removal of Buffarini at this moment have never been satisfactorily explained. The latter's relations with the Germans had their vicissitudes, but at this particular moment his dismissal caused an inexplicable alarm in German circles, and led to a serious breach in the daily relations of Mussolini with the German representatives.[a]

The disappearance of Buffarini from the political scene in late February 1945 also deprived Mussolini of an expert collaborator in the vital field of police and intelligence work. If anyone could have penetrated the German moves in Switzerland it was Buffarini, though it is just possible that he knew about them and preferred for his own reasons to keep his counsel.

Mussolini, like the Germans, could not fail to appreciate the inevitability of military defeat, but he was also concerned and even obsessed by building up before it was too late the last myth of an Italian Fascism overwhelmed by an international conspiracy of the plutocratic and bolshevik nations. His attention was therefore absorbed primarily with the aspects of such a manifesto for the future; the conception of a last stand in the Alpine regions, with or without German support; the plans to protect Italian industrial plants from destruction or removal by the Germans in their last retreat; and the

a. For the Buffarini crisis, see pp. 751–5.

high-sounding programme, which could not be implemented, for a totalitarian Social Republic.

The only direct move which the Duce seems to have made to seek an Allied reaction to an offer of surrender can be traced in March 1945. In reply to a letter of the previous month from Cardinal Schuster, the Archbishop of Milan, requesting the Duce not to make a last stand in the capital city of Lombardy, the latter sent his son, Vittorio Mussolini, to call on the Cardinal to present the following document headed 'Proposals for Negotiations from the Head of State' and dated March 13, 1945.[b]

'In the event of military or political events forcing the armies of Kesselring to withdraw within their own frontiers, all the armed forces of the Italian Social Republic will in such a moment concentrate in pre-selected areas from which they will offer the most strenuous resistance against the enemy, the forces of disorder and of the Royal Government, since anti-Fascist hatred affords them no other way out except to fight to the last man and the last round of ammunition.

'However, to avoid inflicting further sufferings on the population of Northern Italy, to preserve what remains of the industrial and agricultural patrimony from total destruction, and to demonstrate that love for Italy which takes precedence over any interest of Party or ideas, the government of the Italian Social Republic proposes that preliminary agreements should be signed with the Allied High Command on the basis of which the two contracting parties would bind themselves on the following points:

'The armed forces of the Social Republic under the command of Marshal Graziani and all the other military formations of the Republic will maintain order for as long as possible in the cities and the countryside, until direct agreements are signed between the Allied Command and that of the Social Republic . . . Any uncontrolled and extremist action by irregular formations or local demonstrators (partisan bands, Communists, meetings, strikes, etc.) will be countered by the Republican armed forces, and those of the Allies. The Clergy undertakes from now on to pursue a work of propaganda in favour of a general pacification. The Allied Command undertakes to prevent partisan formations carrying out indiscriminate terrorist operations and looting, and will proceed to disarm them prior to calling on the regular formations of the Social Republic to do the same. In addition, the Allied Command will do everything to prevent the formations of the Bonomi government and the Royal Military Police entering the Po Valley, until order has been completely restored.

'An absolute condition for negotiations and the signature of an agreement is "that all those who have taken the oath to the Italian Socialist Republic,

b. Vittorio had called on the Cardinal on March 1 to read out the proposals, and the latter then asked for the document in writing.

both soldiers and civilians, should be exempt from any kind of persecution by the tribunal now functioning for this purpose in Rome". Equally one would be glad to learn the fate which will be reserved for members of the government and those who hold commanding positions in the Social Republic (arrest, concentration camps, exile).

'The Republican Fascist Party will be dissolved. It is understood that citizens will have equal rights and duties, and it is hoped that at such a moment a government representing all tendencies will be formed, and a Constituent Assembly summoned at the earliest opportunity.' [1]

Cardinal Schuster undertook to transmit these proposals to the Allies in Switzerland through the Apostolic Nuncio in Berne. It appears that almost simultaneously Mussolini made use for the same purpose of an Italian parish priest, Don Pancino, whom he had in the past employed as a confidential link with his daughter, Countess Edda Ciano, in Switzerland.[c]

Don Pancino had already been asked in December 1944 by the Duce in person to see if he could make some contact through Vatican channels with the Allies, but, for reasons unexplained, this move was postponed until March when, simultaneously with the interview between Vittorio Mussolini and Cardinal Schuster, Don Pancino also called on the Apostolic Nuncio in Berne.

The reply to this Italian attempt to treat with the Allies was eventually received in a Vatican telegram via Berne and dated April 11. 'It has come to the knowledge of the Holy See that the Allies do not intend to enter into negotiations, and insist on unconditional surrender.' [2] [d]

The liberation of Parri created a special security problem for Wolff. The Italian leader had been arrested by the Germans without the knowledge of the Salò authorities, and he had been in the custody of Harster, the German

c. According to Don Pancino, the Germans had contacted him on one of his journeys to Switzerland and offered him one million lire for Ciano's diary which was still in the safe keeping of the Countess. See his evidence at the trial of Graziani, *op cit* Vol. III, pp. 1106–9, and for the following. According to Pancino's evidence at Graziani's post-war trial, he was approached while in Switzerland on March 16 by agents of General Wolff 'giving him orders to restrain Mussolini so that he (Wolff) did not have to "shoot off in top gear" '. There is no confirmation of this evidence of Don Pancino. He also stated that Wolff was due to arrive in Switzerland 'the next day', giving the date of his talk with the latter's representatives as March 16. Wolff in fact went to Switzerland on the first occasion on March 8/9, and subsequently on March 19.

d. According to Leo Valiani, the Action Party representative on the Committee for Liberation for Northern Italy, he and General Cadorna, the military representative on the Committee, had a meeting at the beginning of March in Lyons with representatives of British services. The Italians were told that the Allies had received an offer of surrender from Mussolini through the offices of Don Bicchierai and that he had asked that the Fascist armed forces should maintain order until the arrival of the Allied armies. The British made it clear that such a condition was unacceptable and that they insisted on unconditional surrender. See Valiani's book: *'Tutte le strade conducono a Roma'*, p. 320.

police chief at Verona, which meant that Kaltenbrunner—already alerted as to Parrilli's proposals—would be informed of the release. The risk of a denunciation of Wolff's secret moves to Hitler was thereby heightened. It would also not be long before news of the episode would reach Mussolini, and the German conspirators had no intention of risking further leakages from Italian sources. The climate of the 'double game' was endemic at Salò.

For these reasons, Wolff attempted to disguise the handing over of Parri as an exchange for Hitler's favourite adjutant, who was a prisoner of war, and to mark the occasion of the Fuehrer's birthday which fell on April 20. This bluff, which in the event the Allied representatives ignored, was for the special benefit of Harster 'and also in regard to Mussolini'.[3]

According to Parrilli, the decision to order the release of Parri was taken at dinner in Wolff's villa at Fasano on the evening of March 4. One of the waiters at table was apparently a neo-Fascist police agent.[4]

It is at least odd that already on the following day Mussolini should have referred to this scheme in conversation with Mellini, his Undersecretary for Foreign Affairs.[e] 'Some time ago this man happened to be taken prisoner by the Germans, who soon afterwards released him in an exchange of prisoners. Notwithstanding the importance of the person of Ferruccio Parri as the leader of the struggle waged by the partisans against us, I am not opposed to his release, in the hope that this could facilitate negotiations intended to diminish the damage to life and property in Northern Italy, and to damp down the bitterness which now characterizes the civil war.

'For some time now, however, Rahn and Wolff have been very careful not to tell me what is going on, though I know that they are in touch with the Committee of National Liberation. This may be a good thing, but I think I have the right to be told what is happening. I could say the same for the confidential contacts which they are maintaining with Cardinal Schuster.

'And now I have also learnt that the famous English Captain, who was in our hands and about whom there has been such a fuss, has been released and given messages for the British High Command from them. On this matter too neither Rahn nor Wolff have breathed a word.'[5]

Mellini was sent to call on Rahn on the following day, March 6, and was told by the latter that the confidential links with the Committee of Liberation were in his hands and had only a 'local character'. Rahn added that there were no negotiations in progress with Cardinal Schuster, but only a general contact with a view to diminishing 'difficulties and war damage'. Mellini could therefore assure the Duce that 'nothing concrete was happening'. Rahn and Wolff were acting independently of Berlin, 'and therefore

e. Mazzolini died at the end of February 1945 of blood poisoning. Mellini Ponce de Leon, who had been his immediate subordinate, succeeded him as nominal head of the Salò Foreign Office.

with a certain autonomy'. Their efforts were directed towards 'doing everything possible to take into account the interests of Italy, the Duce, and
Fascism'.[6]

The rôle of Rahn in these delicate and perilous Swiss negotiations is not
entirely clear. His private feelers on his own initiative had been merely
exploratory. The first stage of Wolff's contacts with the Americans made it
evident that the Allies would only treat with the German military authorities
in Northern Italy, and there would be no place in subsequent talks for a
representative of Ribbentrop. The essential task of Rahn seems to have lain
henceforth in concealing from the Italians any clue as to the existence of
German surrender negotiations.

This soothing function of the German Ambassador was manifest in two
further conversations with Mellini, on March 15 and again two days later.[7]
Speaking of the general situation which would have to be considered in
Italy in the event of the withdrawal of German troops, Rahn stated clearly
that the most recent orders of Hitler stressed the decision to defend the Po
Valley at all costs. 'However,' the Ambassador added, 'I do not intend to
follow the example and the system employed by Badoglio with me. The Duce
can rest assured in the most absolute manner that I will not fail to inform
him of any decision to abandon territory or of any relevant negotiation with
the enemy or the rebels. In any case he has only to ask me at any time when
he is in doubt and I will answer with all frankness.'

This dialogue bears a strange resemblance to the battle of wits between
Guariglia and Ribbentrop at the Tarvisio meeting in August 1943. Indeed
the situation of the German conspirators in the Italian theatre in 1945, and
their conduct, may be closely compared with that of the Badoglio government two years previously.

The second conversation between Rahn and Mellini, on March 17, took
place at the former's request. Rahn was anxious to allay any suspicions that
might have been aroused on the Italian side to which certain recent incidents
might have given rise.

He told Mellini that he had spoken to General Wolff about the case of
Captain Tucker, who was alleged to have crossed the Italian frontier with
messages from the British High Command to Graziani, and who was being
held incommunicado by the Germans. Wolff had assured Rahn that he
intended to use the English captain to see whether the channel was worth
considering. 'If that were the case, the initiative might be used to separate
even further, at least in Italy, British policy from that of the Russians.' The
whole affair was, however, only at the exploratory stage and Wolff would
not fail to keep the Duce informed of further developments.

Rahn then related to his Italian colleague 'the complete history of his
relations with Cardinal Schuster. He had only seen him once, and found him

firmly anti-Fascist in outlook'. A vague correspondence had followed on humanity and justice. No reference was made to the case of Parri.

But the real cause of Rahn's worries now appeared. He expressed a 'certain surprise and anxiety' that it had been announced that the Italian government intended to transfer by March 23 its seat to Milan. Mellini said that the real intention was merely to hold a Council of Ministers in the Lombard capital.

The departure of Mussolini from Garda would inevitably weaken German supervision of his activities, and increase his chances of independent action. This was precisely what the Duce had in mind.

When Mellini reported to him on the conversation which he had had with Rahn on March 6, he noted, 'The reply of Rahn interested and re-assured the Duce very little. He seems completely taken up with the desire to move to Milan as soon as possible,' [8] and Rahn was to be kept guessing as to the precise timing of the transfer until the last minute.

On March 19, when Wolff crossed the Swiss frontier for his second meet-ing with American representatives, they taxed him with rumours that he had been talking to Mussolini. But the German representatives at Salò could not avoid indefinitely a formal meeting with the Duce. The Swiss talks were reaching a critical phase, and the very absence of contact between Wolff and Rahn on the one hand, and Mussolini on the other, could only increase the latter's suspicions.

On April 6, under pressure from Dulles, and after meetings between Wolff and Vietinghoff, orders had been issued to all German military commanders that they would be responsible for any destruction of industrial equipment on their territory.

This issue and bargaining counter with the Allies was, of course, of equal concern to the Salò authorities. Some weeks previously, Mellini wrote a minute to the Duce on a conversation that he had had with Rahn on this subject.

'I spoke to the Ambassador about the serious problem of the so-called putting out of action of electric plants. The Ambassador said that this prob-lem had always been one of the chief preoccupations of himself and General Wolff. Then it was too much talked of. Cardinal Schuster, Switzerland, even the Committee of Liberation were made to intervene.

'No assurance could be given any more by the German authorities, for they had no intention of letting the enemy know now what and how much the Germans were intending to destroy in case of need.

'The Duce,' the Ambassador added, 'can count on my "European feeling" in addition to my being a good friend of Italy's and can feel sure that I shall not allow any damage to be done beyond what is strictly necessary. But for the moment I must veil discussion in a smoke screen.' [9]

Anfuso, shortly after his arrival, raised the subject again and in the setting of its political implications for the Social Republic.

The discussion centred on German plans for the destruction of the port of Genoa. As Anfuso pointed out, 'The working classes in Genoa were deeply concerned and to carry out the proposed destruction might lead to dangerous outbreaks. Rahn told me how difficult it was to save even vital national possessions from the destruction caused by war and pointed to the irremediable destruction caused in France, Hungary and elsewhere, not to mention Germany, maintaining that Italy in comparison had saved a great part of her heritage. I answered that one of the fundamental aims of the Government of the Republic was precisely that of preserving this heritage intact for the Italian people: the less destruction was caused, the more easily could Fascism return to govern throughout Italy, the possibility of which had been shown by recent events whenever enemy armies had to leave our country. Rahn agreed wholly on this point.' [10]

At this moment, a press item, apparently broadcast over the Swiss radio, passed across Mussolini's desk.

'German troops in Milan received on Wednesday (April 4) orders not to leave their barracks. According to neo-Fascist and Nazi circles, this measure is connected with negotiations which have begun to determine the fate of the German Army in Italy. Two members of the Resistance have been liberated and taken to the frontier. Allegedly, they carried definite propositions. One of these personalities is Ferruccio Parri, head of the military section of the Liberation Committee for Northern Italy. Parri had been arrested in Milan, and imprisoned by the S.S. at Verona.' [11]

Mussolini sent at once for Rahn, and asked for an explanation.[f] The latter denied all knowledge of the incident, but that evening, April 6, sent a message to Wolff warning him of what had happened.

On the following day, the Duce received Wolff, Rahn, and Dollmann at his office. The official theme of discussion was the Italian plan to implement a final withdrawal to the Valtelline.[12] But the Germans present were preoccupied with their own problems. It was the day of decision in pressing Vietinghoff to agree in principle to participate in surrender talks. The Germans did not conceal their lack of interest in the Italian scheme, which would indeed have compromised irretrievably their own plans.

That afternoon Dollmann returned alone to see the Duce at the latter's request. He had been warned before leaving by Parrilli 'at the wish of the Allies' that under no circumstances must any hint be given to Mussolini of the surrender talks. Simultaneously with this conversation, Wolff was holding a decisive meeting with Vietinghoff to secure the latter's agreement to

f. See Lanfranchi, *op cit* p. 223. Mussolini knew anyway of Parri's liberation and had made no move at the time.

surrender terms, and later spent the afternoon trying to induce the Duce to remain 'in our immediate neighbourhood'.

On March 17 Anfuso had reported from Berlin that 'a revision of the German attitude was under way. The mission entrusted to Moellhausen, one of Rahn's staff, consisted, as far as one could understand, in seeking contacts in Spain with a view to a compromise peace . . . Other initiatives are probably in the course of being made . . . They show that the Fuehrer has authorized Ribbentrop to try a certain active political line.' [13]

Anfuso was the only experienced and skilled source of information available to the Duce outside Italy. In any possible moves that Mussolini might consider making, his Ambassador in Berlin would be his obvious adviser. The post of Foreign Undersecretary was empty. Anfuso was now summoned from Berlin for this task.

Such an appointment filled Rahn and Wolff with alarm. Anfuso's unique experience of German affairs at the centre, if transplanted into the climate of Salò, could be a fatal element for the conspirators. It was clear to all parties, except Hitler and some of his immediate circle, that there was no military solution to the conflict. At any moment, Mussolini too would seek his own formula of escape.

From the German standpoint, both in Berlin and at Salò, the main danger appeared to lie in the Duce's neo-Socialist programme, in the possible evolution of Republican Fascism into a political compromise which might form the basis of contact, through elements in the Italian Resistance, with the Western Allies. It was the very platform on which Mussolini too was to place his last hopes, together with encouraging belatedly those non-Party 'moderate' elements which had rallied to the Social Republic and which might just form a bridge to the rebels.

The dismissal of Buffarini had been in some way connected with such a private plan and marked the beginning of a deliberate campaign on the part of the Duce to avoid close routine relations with his German 'advisers'.

On March 23 Rahn informed Mellini that he had received a dispatch from Berlin 'drawing attention to certain attitudes of Mussolini, which had not failed to give the Fuehrer anxiety. It seemed in Berlin that the Duce was bringing Fascism towards social forms "which can be bluntly defined as to the Left", and in contrast to that identity of principle which ought to characterize the two régimes.

'Socialization had already been regarded in Germany with much suspicion, but now it appeared that one was going even further. The setting up of the National Republican Socialist group was not only a step towards the Left, but also a blow at the single party.' And Rahn concluded, 'In Berlin they blame me for all this.' In the crumbling of relations between Berlin and Salò, this reproach was also an alibi.

Mussolini's reaction was ill-tempered. Banging the table, he told Mellini that the Germans ought to get on with winning the war. Instead 'they find a way to fuss about the Social Group and what Cione will write. Let them get on with the war, and leave me to govern Italy.' g

The same theme had been presented by Ribbentrop to Anfuso, when the latter took his leave as Ambassador. He was told 'Mussolini seeks to contact Socialism—the European Labour movement.'

On March 26 Anfuso returned from Berlin to the seat of government at Salò. He immediately told the Duce of his last talk with Ribbentrop. On March 31 Mussolini sent for Rahn, and in Anfuso's presence 'initially with great excitement', he delivered a harangue which summarized the whole sorry state of relations between the two countries, and which lights up his own analysis of the Italian scene.

'I am deeply grieved and disturbed by the German Foreign Minister's statements, not so much because of the facts under discussion as because of the psychological assumptions which led to such statements. If my personal loyalty is doubted, then naturally ulterior motives can be read into all my actions, but the Foreign Minister surely does not consider me so foolish as to presume that Fascism and myself still have some kind of back door open to us through which we can escape from our present responsibilities, and he surely cannot suppose that I am now, at this late hour, still willing to sully my name and my own ideals.

'From the numerous reports I receive daily, it appears that our enemies have issued orders for every available means to be used to sow distrust of Fascism and its leading personalities in Germany. I personally am convinced . . . that the reports which gave rise to the Foreign Minister's statement can be traced back to the influence of the Liberation Committee. These reports are stupid, senseless, indecent, and personally insulting to me.

'Let us analyse the situation: We have here in Italy relatively few units large enough or strong enough to make any large-scale effective contribution to the German conduct of the war. Besides the material and economic contribution to the common war effort, I am left primarily with political expedients to keep Germany and the German troops free in the rear. Naturally in the general war-weariness we have numerous internal political opponents, who have flocked in increasing numbers to the Milan and Turin Liberation Committees. It is an old tactical rule of the game in politics that

g. Mellini, *op cit* pp. 128–9. It appears that Rahn himself called on the Duce on March 31. The conversation was mainly concerned with the German protests on the renewed emphasis in Italian government circles at Salò on the socialization programme, and German suspicions were aroused as a result. A further cause of alarm emerged from the meeting, namely, Mussolini's intention to transfer the whole government to Milan, where it would be less easy to supervise and control its activities than on the confined shores of Lake Garda.

you fight your opponents most effectively if you succeed in splitting them internally and playing them off against each other. You yourself, Mr Ambassador, have often successfully applied this tactic in Italy, in pitting Communist and non-Communist groups against each other. Major-General Wolff and various local military authorities have done the same.

'To take the wind out of our opponents' sails I let certain counter-currents have their say, as soon as I thought the New Fascism in Italy strong enough; among other things, I allowed the formation of an opposition group under Professor Cione. This group calls itself national, republican and socialist. Professor Cione is no great brain, and will have no success. But the people who are now seeking an alibi will gather around him, and will therefore be lost to the much more dangerous Liberation Committee. This Liberation Committee is furious about the new group, and already labels Cione and his friends all as the worst kind of traitors. On the other hand the members of the Fascist Party have been very excited over this new group, and are launching a full-scale attack against it. This suits me perfectly, since it is a further incitement to Fascists to take a stand and do something active. I have allowed the Cione group to put out a small weekly newspaper. If the Foreign Minister sees some danger in this, I will have it suppressed. But I should regret this, for it would take away from the new group part of its ventilating function (*sic*) which I consider extraordinarily important.[h]

'My own attitude to the question of Fascism is clearly and uncompromisingly expressed in my Milan speech with which the Foreign Minister is acquainted. I am astonished that the leftist policy I have pursued since September 1943 is still questioned. In doing this I was in practice only following Germany's example, and have had nothing to do with Socialization except to initiate and carry through consistently, and in accordance with Fascist principles, a development which has become a pressing matter for

h. Since the inception of the Salò régime a strident debate raged among the discordant groups which rallied to this last desperate experiment of Italian Fascism. The constant theme of the polemics which issued from these verbal clashes were the need to heal the breach between North and South, to build a bridge between Fascist and anti-Fascist, and to allow a licensed opposition to the official party machine controlled by Pavolini.

The nomination of Pini as Undersecretary of the Interior in October 1944 marked the only administrative triumph of the moderate elements which had rallied to the Republic.

Edmundo Cione, a former pupil of Croce, and self-appointed intellectual leader of this tendency, had persuaded Mussolini in February 1945 to allow the publication of an 'independent' newspaper *L'Italia del Popolo* as the organ of a small group seeking a rapprochement with Socialist elements in the partisan movement and known as the National Republic Socialist Group.

This move was harshly contested by Pavolini and the Minister of Popular Culture, Mezzasomma, and attracted the disapproving attention of the Germans. This newspaper, however, appeared in March. It was suspended on April 10, 1945. (See Cione, *op cit* pp. 305–33.)

Europe and probably for the whole world. This has nothing to do with a rapprochement with the second International. The second International is dead. Compromise between Fascism and Communism is unthinkable, and because of this I must take the wind out of the Communists' sails. I have clamped down immediately on all signs which appeared in the ranks of the Fascist Party of readiness to compromise with liberal trains of thought. I would remind you of the example of our leading journalistic brain, Pettinato, who after publishing an interview with Cione lost the direction of *La Stampa* [i] and was involved in a Party enquiry.

'Moreover, I am being reproached for concentrating the régime in Milan. I cannot understand this; it is rational in the present all-inclusive military crisis for the government to be drawn as close together as possible. It was formerly dispersed over fifteen provinces. The lack of fuel and the ever-increasing danger from low-flying aircraft make unified government activity impossible. Nevertheless, in view of the doubts of the Reich government, I am ready to keep my headquarters at Gargnano. But I shall then have to be something of a bird of passage, staying a few days in Milan or the other large towns of Northern Italy from time to time, for it has become technically impossible to maintain the absolutely indispensable personal contact with Prefects, Mayors, Provincial Commissioners, Trades Union representatives, workers' delegations, etc., in any other way.

'Finally I would like to say a little more about the case of Buffarini. Rightly or wrongly he had become intolerable to public opinion, and above all to Fascist circles. As you know, I had defended him increasingly against all attacks, which came particularly from Germany. It is nevertheless astonishing that all those who for months had dinned into my ears that Buffarini was allegedly conspiring with the British, the Freemasons, the Jews, or with Bonomi's régime, now state that his dismissal is proof that the Fascist government is drawing away from the Axis policy. This is absolutely ridiculous. Obviously from the beginning I have striven to administer the country as self-sufficiently as possible, without unnecessary interference from all the various military authorities. The German government, however, cannot deny that our co-operation was satisfactory on all essential points and has improved continually. And finally, the undeniable results of this co-operation must also form the criterion for the confidence which I demand from the German government.'

A lengthy discussion followed on a whole string of separate issues. Rahn explained to the Duce that the anxiety of the German authorities over the conduct of some members of the government or the civil service was not without foundation. 'When I alluded to the often equivocal behaviour of the Decima Mas the Duce replied that he had often discussed this problem with

i. The leading Turin newspaper.

me, and that he was watching the development of this group with great attention and suspicion, and although, apart from the "chauvinistic" attitude of Prince Borghese over the question of operational zones, he had so far been unable to find any decisive proof of Prince Borghese's disloyalty to Fascism and the Republican régime, he had nevertheless placed the Decima Mas under Marshal Graziani.'

Rahn summarized his impressions of the political climate at Salò at the end of this telegram. 'The whole conduct of the war is endangered by signs of internal disunity and tendencies to create an alibi through treacherous changes of front. This problem has been the subject of my special attention ever since the beginning of my activities in Italy. The numerical size of the rebels, and the anti-Fascist attitude of the population resulting from their war experiences, made it necessary, since German executive powers were lacking, to adopt elastic tactics and to establish the balance ... before we can make use of the area, by playing on all the emotional elements in the Italian character (religious feeling, family feeling, desire to dominate, superstition, vanity, fear of hunger and physical danger, etc.).

'On the other hand, I have always urged my colleagues never to be influenced by our own propaganda, and, given the volatile Italian character, to reckon daily with the possibility of a new, presumably deliberate, treacherous *volte-face*. My greatest difficulty in this tactical game arose from the increasing tendency of the German authorities to produce repeated proofs of an immediate Italian betrayal, to get thus an alibi for a possible unfavourable development so that if the betrayal actually happened they could say that they had predicted it accurately, and if it did not happen, that it had been averted by timely warning.' [14]

During the following fortnight Anfuso had almost daily talks with the Duce, and a vivid personal interpretation of Mussolini's analysis of the course of events emerges, and the lineaments of a legend for posterity.[j]

During the previous winter the Duce had sought refuge in the belief that there was a deep political significance in the military halt of the Allied armies in Italy on the Gothic Line. They might be preparing an anti-Soviet advance into Central Europe, and would therefore need, as a corollary, a stable Italian administration which must be anti-Communist and would include Fascist elements. In a transition of this nature from peace to war, the Allies would need Mussolini's name, and he might even exploit his earlier relations with the British Prime Minister to such an end.

The possibilities of an approach to Churchill were now among the points

j. Almost the sole source for such an interpretation is Anfuso, *op cit* pp. 462 ff, and it is also half deliberately the creation of a posthumous neo-Fascist case divorced from the immediate reality of impending collapse. See also Mellini (*passim*); the last Anfuso dispatch in the Italian Collection is dated January 1, 1945.

discussed with Anfuso. There had always been an escapist side to Mussolini's nature, a facile avoidance of brutal realities by subtle calculations bearing little relation to the real situation. He was capable at this stage of conceiving of himself as a mediator, of completing the rôle which he had briefly assumed at Munich in 1938. Having by his diplomatic genius delayed the outbreak of hostilities, he would now secure his political survival by playing a similar part at the close.

In these talks with the Duce, Anfuso gave a summary of his impressions of the climate of Berlin, where Hitler was now installed. It was 'a mad world of flames'. The German machine was grinding to a halt. Real power was now in the hands of the gauleiters in the 'principalities'. They were the Mansfelds of the Thirty Years War. Each Nazi leader would seek his own separate peace. Ribbentrop's agents were active in Sweden and Spain, and Anfuso thought that it was probable that the German Foreign Minister would seek contacts in London. The intrigues of Wolff in Switzerland were known to him, but 'he could not suppose that they were a prelude to a total surrender of the Germans and the abandoning of the Social Republic'.[15]

Mussolini now told Anfuso of his approach to Cardinal Schuster. In any further peace feelers the main cards at the disposal of the Italians resembled those already being played by Wolff and Rahn; the preservation of Italian industrial equipment in the North and the offer to maintain law and order on Republican territory during the chaotic period of transition.

The main theme of these daily conversations at the beginning of April between the Duce and Anfuso was thus the search for an Italian 'political solution' to the war. Any such moves could only be conducted in Milan, and if they failed the last resort must be a final historic stand either in the Lombard capital or on Italian soil in the Valtelline. In both cases, the initiative must be entirely Italian and the first essential move must be to secure without delay liberty of action from the Germans.

The scene was set for such a disengagement, and played out during these first two weeks of April 1945. This was the Italian 'Secret', which, together with Operation 'Sunrise', now dominated the several moves between the Italians and Germans at Salò.

In the forefront of Mussolini's plans reappeared the organization of the final stand in the Valtelline, as an essential preliminary to the ultimate move to Milan. The state of this operation, under intermittent discussion since the previous September, revealed the paucity of neo-Fascist resources in manpower, and the confused overlapping military jurisdictions of the Social Republic. The preparatory moves had been a subject of wrangle between Pavolini and Graziani since the inception of the plan.

The area of the Valtelline was being reinforced by the surviving fragments of the refugee action squads of Central Italy together with the demoralized remnants of the National Republican Guard. By March, some 700 of the latter were stationed in the Como area, the base of departure, but 'the Duce's orders for concentration were being avoided'.[16]

Pavolini's first contingent of old guard Fascist squads consisted of 300 men from Como, and 100 from Florence. Another 2,000 men were under training in Sondrio province to be ready to move by April 5. As he wrote to Graziani, this meant that no further recruits would be available for 'mobile brigades' in the Army itself. The zone was infested by partisans, and it was imperative both for the Salò authorities to protect the power stations in the area, and to keep open the route to Switzerland.

At the beginning of April, Pavolini left for a tour of the region, and on April 5 sent a handwritten report to the Duce.[17] There were active partisan units in the plain and on the hills, 'with a copious and good armament' together with a certain number of British officers. The small garrisons of the Black Brigades were rather alarmist. The urgent need was to undertake a clearing action in the direction of the Swiss frontier. The forces immediately available were 120 men of the Florence Brigade, 100 from Cremona, and 150 from the region itself.

He concluded: 'If the Allied Commands and our own do not put any spokes in the wheel, I reckon that I can perfectly well carry out your orders, namely: The cleaning up of the whole province by April 30; and by that date to have brought the forces available up to 5,000 men.'

This was the Duce's prerequisite for the move to Milan.

On April 9 Pavolini wrote again to Mussolini on his return to Milan, where the Party headquarters had been moved earlier in the year. His last mission was to be the bringing up to strength of the Valtelline defence force.[k] These were the elements available for the planned last fight of Italian Fascism.

On the same day Pavolini drafted a questionnaire for formal discussion with the Germans. Rahn should be asked the intentions of the German government towards the Italian Social Republic 'on the likely hypothesis that the Gothic Line gives way. What end befell the French government?'

If the Gothic Line were overrun, the enemy will secure the whole Po Valley, and 'in such an event the Republican government would become a nominal one. But its responsible elements must be kept alive, about ten to each ministry, to be ready for any eventuality . . .'

An Italian politico-military command must be transferred to the zone of Sondrio in collaboration with the German headquarters in the Tyrol. This command 'must be the absolute arbiter in the area on the lines of the German model in the Adriatic zone'.

---

k. The list was in itself a despairing revelation. Pavolini could raise 100 men from the Pisa brigade by April 14, and 100 shock police and 200 men of the 'Muti' special battalion during the course of the month. By April 20 the Varese brigade would total 320 men.

All irregular Italian units must be transformed into a regular Republican Army. It should thus be possible to assemble 30–50,000 men. Their families must be excluded, except for some five hundred of those of Ministers and of persons deeply compromised.

'It would be also opportune to send in driblets about thirty young and intelligent individuals to set up a Fascist centre in Switzerland,' and to build up a considerable fund in foreign exchange.[18]

On April 14 the last meeting of Italian and German senior representatives on Italian soil was held at Gargnano under the Duce's chairmanship.

The main concern of the Germans was to play for time. On the previous day Himmler had ordered Wolff to report to Berlin. There could be no question of any serious acceptance of the Italian Valtelline project, which would disrupt the secret arrangements under review.

It seems that Anfuso had pressed a reluctant Mussolini to hold such a conference after all. 'Although Anfuso had few illusions as to reaching concrete results, he did not want to give up this last attempt to arrive at a clarification of respective positions and in particular of mutual intentions, and to avoid the continuance of misunderstandings which had already done so much harm.'

Pavolini introduced his Valtelline plan. Graziani pointed out that his forces could only be moved in concordance with the German Command. Vietinghoff laboured the difficulties of making preparations in time for such a large mass of troops. Wolff agreed, but showed 'scarcely any interest in the project'. Rahn merely pointed out that such a redoubt must be so organized as to allow for an eventual withdrawal into Germany.[19]

It seems that, after this inconclusive dialogue, Wolff had a talk with the Duce, at which, to his annoyance, Anfuso was also present. The two men had not met since the Buffarini affair. According to Wolff's subsequent brazen account, he said firmly that the war was lost and that a political compromise must be sought.[20] Mussolini might be able to use his socialization programme as blackmail with the Anglo-American capitalists, and Wolff offered to sound the Allies as to 'what price the Allies would be prepared to pay for nationalization to remain a dead letter'. He would need five or six days in which to obtain a reply, and asked the Duce not to treat himself with the Allies through Cardinal Schuster. 'A second Badoglio betrayal would be fatal to Italian relations with Germany.' In any negotiations which he undertook, he would naturally look after Italian interests! He was against the Italian plan to move to Milan and Mussolini promised that he would not carry it out.

Dollmann has a different elaboration on the theme of this conversation. Mussolini asked, 'What card is left for me to play?' To which Wolff replied, 'Give up socialization, and bargain with Western capitalism'. Mussolini commented, 'Excellent,' adding that he proposed to turn Milan into a second Stalingrad. Wolff begged him to be patient.

The two men were not to meet again. On April 17 Wolff left to face Himmler in Berlin, and the following day the Duce put into effect his long delayed move to Milan, which he had just promised not to carry out.

On the day prior to this last conference the news was broadcast of the death of President Roosevelt. This announcement gave a fleeting flicker of hope to the Duce of a diplomatic solution of the war.

He had always regarded the President as the Western Allied leader most responsible for maintaining the Anglo-American alliance with the Russians, whatever the political cost. Mussolini was already satisfied that Churchill, though a more bitter enemy of Fascist Italy than Roosevelt, had increasingly grave doubts as to the continuance of an alliance with the Soviet Union at this stage of the war. Perhaps now there could be some dim chance of peace talks, either with the Russians, or with the Anglo-Americans in the new conditions which might develop after Roosevelt's death. Mussolini considered the possible repercussions of this event in a conversation with Rahn on April 14.

'It was established that the deceased President of the United States represented not only the guardian of Soviet interests in America, but also the trustee of the ideology which culminated at Yalta in the plans for destroying Germany, and the Duce agrees with Ambassador Rahn that in fact Stalin's policy could meet with greater resistance from the White House. This, added to the inevitable confusion of public opinion after the President's death, could also lead Stalin, whose policy has so far been so realistic, to seek dominion over Russia's Asiatic and European positions by other ways, since there is no doubt that England is preparing to carry on a struggle, political today, bloody tomorrow, to defend her position against a Slav-Communist hegemony. It is probable that the disturbance caused by Roosevelt's death might lead directly not to a new orientation in Russia's policy, but to her adopting a more attentive attitude. These are the, let us say, intangible facts . . .

'The thought of profiting from these circumstances is exceedingly difficult today, given the grave military situation in Germany. Nevertheless, they examined the situation, remembering that the Duce at various times since 1941 has maintained the following point of view: Firstly, to establish a map of Europe which would open up a series of political combinations; secondly, that it would always be exceedingly dangerous for Germany to fight on two fronts, and more so on more than two.

'For these reasons the Duce had clearly referred in the last two years to the possibility of the Axis coming to a truce with Soviet Russia, for a whole series of reasons, first political and then social. An attempt of this kind at this moment, given the Anglo-Americans' obstinate stand on unconditional surrender, would be difficult, and could only be tried with exceptional means; however, the immediate or remote possibilities were examined and the Duce could only confirm what he has said in the last few years, adding that such a step would be extremely dangerous not to say impossible today. However, Rahn said that he was willing to examine every possible combination incorporated in the statements he had already made at the time.' [21]

Little did Mussolini know that the immediate effect of Roosevelt's death was for the Allies, under Soviet pressure, to order the suspension of the negotiations with Wolff in Switzerland.

About the same time Anfuso records a strange talk with Rahn which bears on this theme. The latter seems to have raised the familiar suggestion that Mussolini should make a last approach to Hitler on the theme of a separate peace with Russia.[22] The matter was discussed with the Duce and a telegram drafted which was telephoned to Berlin by Rahn. The latter proposed that he should fly with Anfuso to Germany to press this plan. He claimed that he was acting on his own initiative. Anfuso was puzzled. Did Rahn conceive of himself as the successor to Ribbentrop, with the historic mission to negotiate that peace, which had so often been mooted, and with the remnants of Mussolini's authority as the main arbiter in talks with the Allies?

Was this the sense of Rahn's remarks a month earlier when he told Mellini that he hoped at some stage 'to play a considerable rôle . . . and that Mussolini could still have great weight as a balance, and as a rallying point of the struggle to halt the march of Communism in Europe'?[23]

Was Rahn dissociating himself from Wolff's manoeuvring and thinking in terms of a separate move of his own? If he was in agreement with Wolff, what was the point of this démarche? 'Does Rahn know more than he told us?' [24]

More likely Rahn was seeking an argument to secure the return of Anfuso to Berlin, fearing that the latter was the most likely person to penetrate the Swiss 'secret'.

Anfuso had in fact returned gravely disturbed to his office after the Italo-German conference of April 14 at which the Germans had clearly avoided any clarification or 'unmasking of their batteries'. Ribbentrop had asked for his urgent recall for consultations in Berlin. Anfuso feared that the summons 'had been provoked by Rahn and Wolff, because they wanted to remove him from the Duce at such a delicate moment in order to have their hands more free'.[25] The Duce yielded to this last pressure from his German advisers and Anfuso departed the following day.

He remained, in the event, blocked and impotent in the sad enclave of foreign diplomats accredited to the Reich at Bad Gastein, and in the last hours of April 24–5 he made vain attempts to rejoin the Duce.

CHAPTER THREE

'DUST AND ALTARS'

(Milan: April 18–25)

THE DUCE now decided to move to Milan. He was seeking at last that liberty of action and manoeuvre of which the Germans had deprived him since his liberation from Gran Sasso in September 1943. He was, as always, secretive and at the mercy of immediate impressions and changes of circumstance, but his reasoning and intentions were not obscure. As emerged from his conversations with Anfuso, he must find an 'Italian' solution to the war, either by negotiation with the Committee of Liberation, and with the Church possibly acting as an intermediary, or by the remote chance of a last-minute direct deal with the Allies. Mussolini had a fine sense of the unexpected. Something would turn up. He must be at liberty to exploit it, whatever form it might take.

If all else failed, there must be a last stand, but on Italian territory and played out only by Italians. Of the many proposals put forward, the idea of the Valtelline redoubt, as studied by Pavolini, had received priority, and the Party Secretary had formal orders from the Duce to clear the area and bring up its garrison, the symbolic remnants of the fighters for Fascism of the civil war of the 1920's, to a strength of 5,000 men by April 30. As Mussolini remarked to Graziani, 'After all, in a place like that Fascism should fall heroically.' [1]

Throughout his career, however, Mussolini had never thought in terms of last stands, and even under the shadow of final defeat, he would not admit the absence of other solutions.

On the morning of April 16 the Duce summoned a Council of Ministers at Gargnano, the last of the régime.[2] He announced the transfer of the government to Milan. German circles at Salò were in consternation.

Rahn, whose main task at this stage was to 'look after' the Duce, tried once more to persuade him to remain on Lake Garda, or alternatively to move with the German Embassy to Merano on the Brenner road amid the converging retreat of exiles and military units. But here the Duce would be under the ineffable protection of the Austrian gauleiter, Hofer, and in the prevailing climate of the wildest rumours, Mussolini may have thought, as Rahn speculated, that Hitler had a Wagnerian scheme of an Alpine redoubt in the Tyrol, with Mussolini playing an inferior and secondary part. As the Duce now told Rahn, if the war were already lost he intended to die on Italian soil. When Rahn pointed out to him that Milan was a trap in which he would be caught, he answered that he could always break through to the Sondrio valley in the Valtelline, and there make his last heroic stand.

As early as April 8 the German escort of the Duce at Gargnano had been alerted. On April 18 the S.S. Lieutenant on duty was told that the Duce was leaving for Milan at seven o'clock that evening 'and would be returning in two or three days'.

A convoy of five cars and a baggage truck, with a German security detachment, set out for the Lombard capital, and arrived at nine o'clock at the Milan Prefecture in the Via Monforte, where Mussolini took up residence.

German supervision was set up in the shape of S.S. sentries stationed permanently outside the door of the Duce's office. But the chief German protagonists were too preoccupied with the perilous crisis ahead of them. During these same hours, Wolff was closeted with Himmler, and then Hitler, in Berlin, and the fate of clandestine surrender negotiations lay in the balance.[a]

There was much coming and going in the Prefecture, now the only centre of authority in the Social Republic, and where for the next two days (April 18–19) the Duce was in conclave with the Milan notables: the Prefect Bassi; the Federal Secretary Costa; the military commander for Lombardy, General Diamanti; and those members of the administration who had arrived from Lake Garda.

Confused counsel swirled round the idea of a last stand. For a moment Mussolini seems to have flirted with plans put to him for a fortified Bunker in the area of the Prefecture itself: 'the Quadrilateral of Monforte'. There was the tidy historical symbolism of a Fascist gesture in the city which had seen the foundation of the early movement just over twenty years before.

But in practical military terms it would be impossible to extract the remaining Italian Republican army units from the disintegrating front along the Po and to disentangle them from the German forces throughout Lombardy. Graziani was therefore decisively against any such proposal. In the Duce's eyes, it had also a further and capital disadvantage. A last ditch defence of Milan, with its heavily populated centre, would alienate the

a. Wolff returned to his villa at Fasano on April 19.

Curia, whose mediatory rôle with the partisans and the Allies might be decisive in the coming hours.

Each member of the Duce's private circle had his plan of flight. The Petacci clan were as usual fertile in expedients. For some months Mussolini himself had given countenance to the mysterious activities of a young lawyer, Mancini, who was engaged to the sister of Clara Petacci, and who had certain links with Spain.[b] Their present plan was to fly the Duce there secretly. There was talk of using Italian torpedo seaplanes from a base at Ghedi. It is perhaps significant that Mancini saw the Duce twice on April 19 and 20. But at no time was Mussolini prepared to think in terms of such a personal solution of his safety.

Rahn now paid a final visit to the Duce in Milan. It took place on the morning of April 20 in the Milan Prefecture. Since his departure from Garda, Mussolini had not been in direct touch with any German authorities.

Rahn's purpose was to make a final attempt to persuade the Duce to return to Gargnano. The latter calmly refused, and stressed again the preparations in course for resistance in the valley of Sondrio. Both men avoided any mention of political issues. On the almost empty desk in front of the Duce lay an open book. It was the works in German of the romantic poet Moerike. Mussolini smiled as he caught the glance of his visitor. 'Yes, that is all that remains to us.' [3]

Rahn had some hope that he could persuade the Duce to come under German protection to the concentration area of the various German headquarters now being established in the Tyrol. Pointing to the crowded courtyard of the Prefecture, Mussolini answered, 'I feel at home here, it is here that I must stay, here that I must govern.' The German Ambassador sensed that Mussolini was now determined to stay in Milan as long as possible.[4] It is more probable that he had not yet made up his mind.

The fragmentary sheets of the Duce's appointments in his office at the Prefecture during these days form rough signposts to the activities, and at least to the timetable, of the last search for an 'Italian' solution.

All now depended on establishing means of communication between the Republican Fascists, and those elements of the Committee of Liberation who might be willing to parley. In these hours of confusion and menace, each Italian leader manoeuvred according to his private contacts with the other

b. Anfuso was for instance in December 1944 asked to find seats for 'the Mancini delegation flying from Spain to Germany', and to stress that 'the Duce had repeatedly urged this matter upon him'. Ribbentrop refused to take responsibility 'for entrusting to this flight persons in whom the Duce took such an interest'. German Collection. Anfuso-Ribbentrop conversation, December 3, 1944.

side in a climate of mutual deception and betrayal, provocation and fear. There was no common or co-ordinated approach, and these final negotiations were a microcosm of the disharmonies of the neo-Fascist world, now huddled round their leader in the offices and courtyards of the Milan Prefecture, like a Renaissance court, awaiting massacre by the victorious condottieri.

Of some of these moves Mussolini was aware, and a few were directly encouraged by him. On April 22 he had, for example, instructed Zerbino, Buffarini's successor at the Ministry of the Interior, and General Montagna, the Chief of Police who had been active in the Verona trials, to attempt to negotiate a formal hand-over of powers between the Salò authorities and the Committee of Liberation. This would be a formalistic and mundane transfer of authority, the very conception of which ignored the passionate savagery of civil war between Fascist and Partisan, which dominated and haunted the scene.

An inner historic contradiction was on the eve of being resolved: the liquidation by force of the consequences of the original March on Rome: the return to legality after twenty years of Fascist rule. The retreat from Rome could not end courteously at a conference table. Those elements, which had been mauled and beaten and bruised in the rise to power of Mussolini and his Fascists, and which had been driven underground, or into exile, were now waiting at the gates; the victors of a civil war initiated by the Fascists themselves in the 1920's. The partisans of 1945 represented in a sense the defeated of 1922 and the opposition of the years between. Whatever rôle of manoeuvre constraining 'moderate' elements on either side might play in the final settlement, or whatever pressures the overshadowing Allied authorities might attempt to exert, it was the extremists of both sides who were coming face to face. Events were governed by a brutal historical pattern: a *coup d'état*, carried out some twenty years before by elements which now faced destruction, politically, militarily, and morally, was being dismounted. In such a climate, the room for polite negotiation was meagre.

With his hypersensitive political intuition, Mussolini was aware of all these elements. His instructions to Zerbino and Montagna were essentially lip-service to the outward forms of legitimacy, which he had for long violated at will. By temperament, and by the nature of the 'system' of rule which he had created, he schemed and analysed events in isolation from those around him. He had the basic complexes of an outsider and a renegade rather than those of a true rebel. Fascism was an 'anti-system' and its supreme failure was that the movement could by its nature not command established loyalties. Contempt for his opponents Mussolini had also extended to include his followers.

But throughout the feline manoeuvrings by which he had held dictatorial power through the years of Fascist rule, this governing attitude of contempt fitfully clashed in his mind with a nostalgia for the 'establishment' which he had weakened and renounced, the cause of Italian Socialism. His character is inexplicable without some consideration of this inner contradiction.

His isolation as the Duce of Fascism was in part an unconscious and in part a deliberate compensation for his rejection of the normal and traditional sense of a militant identity with the masses, which forms the stimulating element in the character of a traditional Socialist party leader. This emotion of fraternal communion Mussolini had destroyed in himself when he broke with his Socialist colleagues, and its ghost was to haunt him to the end.

Out of conscience and egotism he could never really believe that a bridge could not be built between the Fascist movement created in his own image and the resurrected elements of the Left, equally in part his own work, strengthened and rebuilt in revolt against his dictatorship. This was his last illusion. The events of September 8 lent a frail consistency to this view. By an historical accident, the creation of a separate Badoglio 'system' seemed to have removed those early contradictions and compromises between Fascism and the Monarchy, which had militated against a mending of those breaches with the organized forms of the Left, which the March on Rome had, as it transpired, irretrievably made.

The construction of such a bridge was to Mussolini to be the historical mission of the Italian Social Republic. Such a task was sabotaged from the outset by the frustrated and unfulfilled violence of the remaining Fascist party bosses, those professional ex-revolutionaries obsessed with clinging to the rags and pickings of a monopoly of political power.

The dramatic significance of these last days in Milan, lived out in a political and military vacuum, is the revelation of the extent of the Duce's illusion, and its disappearance lights up in a final flicker the inner contradictions of a whole epoch.

Early in 1945, during the period of discussion in Salò circles, and particularly in the Press, of a non-party political programme and a 'bridge' to the rebels, Mussolini had received on a number of occasions a former Socialist journalist, who had been intimately associated with the vendettas of the past. He was Carlo Silvestri, who had achieved a considerable reputation for independence at the time of the murder of Matteotti in 1924, and who had been interned by the Fascist police for attacking the Duce for his alleged complicity in the affair. Although a victim of the régime, Silvestri, like many fellow journalists and political hangers-on, appeared on the fringes of this neo-Fascist world, and had drawn to the mirage of a grand reconciliation between Italians of all parties in defiance of the historical acts of the past twenty years.

According to Silvestri, from several talks which he now had with his former opponent, he learnt that for some years Mussolini had been conducting his own private enquiry into the Matteotti case. Much evidence had apparently been collected, and recently his private secretary, Gatti, the successor of Dolfin, and Bombacci, the close adviser of these penultimate days, had been studying the files. Silvestri claims that he was allowed to read this material, which convinced him of the Duce's innocence of the assassination of the Socialist leader.[c]

With the ghost of Matteotti thus laid, the historical myth which bedevilled any hope of even a tenuous link between Mussolini and the Socialists could be conveniently exploded, and this curious trio—Gatti, Bombacci, and Silvestri—devoted their efforts to persuading the Duce to probe the reactions of the new generation of Socialist leaders within the ranks of the Resistance.

This was precisely what Mussolini intended to attempt on arrival in Milan.

On April 21 he held a meeting of those members of the government who were available in the city. Graziani reported on the collapse of the Apennine front, and, during the course of that day, Allied advance guards crossed the Po. Every hour counted.

The following evening Mussolini sent for Silvestri.[5] A letter was drafted in the name of the Duce, though typically not signed,[6] and it was agreed that it should be delivered without delay. It is not clear precisely the manner in which it was transmitted, nor to whom.[7] It was rejected by the Socialist group on the Liberation Committee curtly and without comment. Their political representative, Sandro Pertini, wrote subsequently, 'When I was told . . . that Mussolini had arranged to send a letter addressed to the Socialist party in which he offered to surrender himself and those with him, I immediately sent an answer . . . that the letter must be given no consideration at all.'[8]

Silvestri seems to have met, in a drug store, on April 23 Riccardo Lombardi, a member of the Action Party on the Central Liberation Committee for Northern Italy, and handed to him also a copy of the Duce's missive. He was told by Lombardi who 're-read' the text that it had not even been taken into account.[d]

This whole episode had no bearing on future events, and subsequently both neo-Fascists and partisans united to minimize the import of this feeler.[9] Its interest however lies in the light which it throws on the mentality of Mussolini, for it had been on his initiative.

In the meantime, Graziani was pressing for yet another solution, which he had considered with Commandant Borghese, the only real condottiere of the Republic. While maintaining the German alliance, a military triumvirate

c. For this mysterious affair see the evidence given by Silvestri at the post-war re-trial of the surviving assassins and their accomplices, in particular Cesare Rossi. This evidence was published separately under the title *Mussolini-Matteotti*. None of these files has as yet come to light.

d. Spampanato *op cit* III, pp. 44–5. According to Leo Valiani, *L'Avvento di De Gasperi*, p. 9, Silvestri's meeting with Lombardi was by chance, and Valiani was with the latter at the time. After hearing from Silvestri of Mussolini's proposal, Lombardi consulted in a corner with Valiani, who was the secretary of the Action Party for Northern Italy, and then told Silvestri that anyhow the offer was too belated to be considered.

would negotiate a formal surrender of all Republican forces with the Allies. Graziani was enraged at the various suggestions made by Mussolini to treat on a political level with any elements of the Resistance leadership; in Graziani's language, 'with three bums who didn't know what they represented'.[10]

On the early afternoon of April 25, according to Cione, Mussolini told him that 'he was in the midst of dealing with the adversary through three channels'.[11] These were Silvestri, Zerbino and Montagna, and the Curia.

The Zerbino approach, again according to Cione, was serious. The links were with the Christian Democrats in the Committee of Liberation, and the plan of surrender had been worked out. The Fascist forces would be concentrated in one province. Graziani would sign a military capitulation on behalf of the Republic. But when Montagna brought these proposals to the Prefecture that afternoon, the Duce had already played his final card.

In the isolation of the Milan Prefecture, Mussolini and his following were not only out of touch with the Germans, but with events exploding throughout the territory nominally administered by the Social Republic.

An insurrectional committee of three had already been set up by the Committee of Liberation in Milan at the end of March.[e] Already at the beginning of April, the Partisans had taken the initiative throughout Piedmont. On April 18, the day on which the Duce moved from Lake Garda to Milan, a 'dress rehearsal' strike took place in the Turin factories.

The railway workers of Northern Italy, a key body in revolutionary planning in whose hands all vital communications lay, were called out on strike in Milan on April 23. It was an historical irony that this syndicate had been the special and successful target of the Fascists in the organization of the March on Rome. Indeed, the technical activities of the Liberation Committee for Upper Italy in April 1945 bear startling parallels with the planning of the coup d'état of 1922. A Partisan March on Milan would symbolize the long-delayed revenge for the March on Rome.

On April 18 Graziani had dined with Rahn in the latter's villa at Garda.[f] His host seemed anxious that he should also spend the night. It was a puzzling meeting. Rahn gave Graziani the present of a pistol with the irrelevant remark that the port of Genoa was not blown up by the Germans. There was no hint of the surrender talks in progress. It was in fact the evening when Wolff was facing Hitler in Berlin.

Did Rahn hope that Graziani, as Cavallero had done, would commit suicide during the night? [12] Graziani could find no explanation, and left after dinner.

April 20 was the Fuehrer's birthday.

e. Valiani for the Action Party; Sereni for the Communists; and Pertini for the Socialists.

f. The date is confirmed by Graziani's notebook.

The correspondence between Hitler and Mussolini, which had begun in 1938, had long since ceased to be a source of mutual inspiration and confidence. The last message from the Duce in his Salò retreat, imprisoned by rival and competing German agencies, had related to general issues of the struggle and dated from the late autumn of 1944. A draft letter, headed December 10 of that year, and sent through Rahn, lists a further series of German 'abuses' in Northern Italy, including the stealling of bicycles and forced recruitment of labour by the Todt organization. [13]

But from the beginning of 1945 neither of the two leaders seems to have made any move to keep alive that peculiar and subtle relationship which set the arbitrary and untidy pattern of the Axis conduct of the war. The moods of exaltation, which gave rise to this remarkable correspondence, not dissimilar in effect but immeasurably and decisively different in tone and style from that between the British Prime Minister and President Roosevelt, had long evaporated in the drawn out agony of approaching nemesis.

It was Hitler, in his final musings, who recorded the naked summary of the relationship. 'Judging events coldly, leaving aside all sentimentality, I have to admit that my unyielding friendship for Italy, and for the Duce, could be added to the list of my mistakes. It is visible that the Italian alliance rendered more service to the enemy than to ourselves. The intervention of Italy will only have brought us an infinitesimal aid in comparison with the numerous difficulties which it has created for us. It will have contributed, if we do not win in spite of everything, to making us lose the war. The greatest service which Italy could have done to us was to have kept out of the conflict . . . Her intervention in June 1940, to give the final kick to the French Army in disintegration, had the sole effect of tarnishing our victory which those who had been defeated had by then accepted in a sporting manner. France recognized that she had been beaten fairly by the armies of the Reich, but did not want to be defeated by the Axis.

'Our Italian ally has embarrassed us everywhere. In North Africa, for example, we were prevented from following a revolutionary policy. By the nature of things, this living space became an Italian monopoly and as such was claimed by the Duce. Only we could have emancipated the Moslem countries dominated by France. This would have had enormous repercussions in Egypt and the Middle East, both enslaved by the British. By linking our fate with that of the Italians, such a policy was made impossible.

'From the military point of view, things were hardly better. Italy's entry into the war at once gave our adversaries their first victories . . . Although incapable of holding out in Abyssinia and Cyrenaica, the Italians had the nerve, without asking our advice and even without warning us, to launch into an absolutely useless campaign in Greece. Their dishonourable setbacks aroused the ill-humour of certain Balkan states in regard to us. It was here and nowhere else that the causes must be sought of the stiffening and then *volte face* of the Yugoslavs in the spring of 1941. This led us, contrary to all our plans, to intervene in the Balkans, whence the catastrophic delay in unleashing the war against Russia . . . If the war had remained one conducted by Germany, and not by the Axis, we would have been able to attack Russia as from May 15, 1941. And strong in the credit of only total and undoubted victories, we could have finished the campaign by winter . . .

'My attachment to the person of the Duce has not changed . . . but I regret not having listened to reason which imposed on me *a brutal friendship* g in regard to Italy.'

The bonds between the two men never formally broke, but had sagged through the mounting misfortunes of war. They had never recovered from the delay in launching the Russian campaign in 1941. 'I only failed by a short head: exactly five weeks . . . and I lost them because of the confidence which I had placed in my dearest and most admired friend, Mussolini.'[14]

The posthumous Nazi myth for future generations, replacing the stab in the back of 1918, was shaping in Hitler's reflections in the Berlin Bunker in 1945 into the form of an Italian scapegoat.

Besieged in Berlin, like Frederick the Great in 1762, but without any sign of the collapse of the Allied coalition which had snatched that monarch from disaster, Hitler had ceased to have any control over events. On April 22 he gave orders to evacuate the shelter. One of his last acts was to close the correspondence with the Duce.

The following telegram reached Milan on April 24, and was published in the newspapers the following morning:

'The struggle for existence or non-existence has reached its climax. Using huge forces and materials, Bolshevism and Judaism have engaged themselves up to the hilt to assemble their destructive forces on German territory, to precipitate our continent into chaos. Nevertheless, with their obstinate scorn of death, the German people and all the others who are animated by the same sentiments will fling themselves to the rescue, however hard the struggle, and with their incomparable heroism will change the course of the war at this historic moment which will decide the fate of Europe for centuries to come.' [15]

Nothing remained but to build up those historical myths for future generations, which would conceal and blur the personal responsibilities of both leaders for the imminent and common disaster of the total defeat which awaited each of them and in grim irony was to form in the end their only and equal unifying bond.

On April 23 Mussolini telephoned his Foreign Office at Salò.

Mellini had called on Rahn that morning and, according to the former, was told of a 'jealous secret not even to be confided to the Duce'.

g. Author's italics. This phrase is the title of this book.

Secret negotiations with Field Marshal Alexander were about to 'come into port', a solution which would avoid a massacre and 'which would leave hope for interesting developments. It would make it possible to save Mussolini, who would be useful in the future for the struggle against Bolshevism. He was awaiting an emissary tomorrow with a reply which should allow him to put before the Duce concrete and satisfactory proposals already completely defined.'

Rahn had wished hitherto to keep the matter secret, because if any other separate move got in the way or Berlin learnt of the existing negotiations, everything could be shipwrecked. Rahn would get in touch again at the opportune moment, and would ask Mellini to accompany him to Milan. Mellini commented later, 'I do not know what to think of all this.' He telephoned the Duce in Milan. The latter asked for news. 'I replied that there was nothing special to relate. I told him that Rahn intended to come to see him in Milan during the next days to make an interesting communication to him. He did not seem to be interested.' [16]

The last formal communication between the representative of the German government and the Salò authorities closed the cycle of their relations in impeccably bureaucratic style. In a minute, dated April 25, Mellini wrote:

'Ambassador Rahn informed me yesterday that he had heard from General Wolff in Milan (*sic*) that the Minister of Finance is making difficulties in paying the known war contribution for the German Armed Forces for the current month. He has asked me to point out to you, Duce, how a refusal of the Italian government to pay the war contribution at this moment would, after so many efforts made in common, result in creating an unfavourable atmosphere in the whole German military circle at a moment when the Embassy and the military commands are seeking to do everything possible to avoid further unnecessary damage to Italian territory, and to defend it against invasion.' [17]

In the clash of civil war and contending armies, the neutral enclave of the Milan Curia might at some critical stage afford a haven for parley. Cardinal Schuster saw an historical rôle awaiting him as the mediator in the closing stages of the struggle in North Italy, and actively sought to pursue such a function. The Cardinal had busily established early contacts with the Germans. In February 1945 one of his personal secretaries, Don Bicchierai, had been instructed to initiate talks with the Germans, and on their side, Colonel Rauff, Wolff's subordinate in Milan, received similar orders. It was shortly afterwards that the 'Sunrise' negotiations started in Switzerland, and these ecclesiastical links were henceforth to serve the Germans both as a cover and a last resort, particularly in territorial arrangements with the Italian Resistance. It was however the constant hope of the Cardinal that the formal surrender of the German authorities on Italian soil would take place in his Palace in Milan.

On April 3 Don Bicchierai had handed a memorandum to Rauff for transmission to Wolff and Dollmann, offering the mediation of the Church. Parallel with these links with the German military authorities through Rauff and intermittently on his personal account with Dollmann, the Cardinal welcomed a separate contact with Rahn, whose staff approached another of Schuster's secretaries, Don Corbella, early on April 9, with a request that he should get in touch with the Committee of Liberation and sound them on possible surrender terms.[18] The Christian Democrat representative, Achille Marazza, was empowered to act on the Italian side with the knowledge of the Allies through their local military representatives now living underground in Milan. Indeed each of these feelers seems to have been known both to the German and Allied Intelligence services. It remains a mystery how far the Italian Fascist authorities had any warning, intent as they were on making their own approaches to individual Resistance leaders.

The visit of Wolff to Berlin was reflected in a momentary coolness on the part of the German subordinate authorities in Milan. If the Swiss 'plot' failed, there would be victims, and traces to cover hastily. The 'circle of the Hotel Regina', the German headquarters in Milan, became 'impenetrable and hostile'.

After the return of Wolff to Italy, events moved however with speed and in perplexing fashion. The several German contacts with the entourage of the Cardinal seemed to spring spontaneously to life, perhaps as a German diversionary action in regard to operation 'Sunrise', and a last-minute insurance during the transitional hours. The timetable was dictated, as for many months past, by the rising tempo of the Allied advance. The crossing of the Po on April 21 marked the beginning of the end, and the criss-cross of messages and private meetings was intensified.

The Committee of Liberation was showing impatience at the lack of any concrete move from the German authorities. Like the Cardinal, the Committee was anxious, for its own prestige, to treat as an independent agency with the Germans before the arrival of the Allies in Milan. Marazza had already warned Don Corbella on April 15 that, once broken off, negotiations could not be easily resumed. The same day, Rahn instructed his private secretary and also the German Consul in Milan [h] to keep these contacts open. The latter held a meeting with Don Corbella, who read out the terms of the Committee of Liberation, whose representatives were still prepared to meet the Germans in the presence of Cardinal Schuster.[19]

The essential point on the German side was to preserve just enough confidence on the side of the Church and the Liberation Committee to remain in contact. As Corbella was told, 'Today the German Ambassador is not in

h. Consul Wolf. Not to be confused with the commander of the S.S.

a position to negotiate directly with the Committee of National Liberation as the Nazi régime still exists in Germany.' One must wait for the moment when the German authorities in Italy could act on their own. Meanwhile there must be maximum secrecy. The Germans even suggested that rumours should be spread that no agreement would be possible, even for the defence of Milan.

As a German Military Intelligence report, dated April 15 from Milan, stated:

'Within the next few days Cardinal Schuster will submit the following plan to Major-General Wolff . . . The city of Milan will not be defended by the Germans, but in the course of eventual withdrawal operations will be methodically and promptly evacuated. It will on no account be made into a centre of resistance. If Allied troops advance right up to the city, any German troops still in Milan will not resist but surrender. No factories, electricity plants, etc. are to be destroyed in Milan: only lines of communication. No hostages will be taken and deported in Milan. The Germans will bring pressure to bear on the Fascist police to prevent their taking hostages. On the outskirts of Milan too, no factories are to be destroyed.

'If the Germans will give binding assurances on these points, the Cardinal is ready to do all he can (he is thinking particularly of a solemn public appeal) to influence the opposition groups and particularly the partisans not to take any action against the Germans before and during their retreat. This would apply only to Germans, not to Fascists.'

The German author of this report commented on the Cardinal's plan as related to the general scene in Milan.

'At the present moment it is useless to wish to negotiate with the National Liberation Committee. The Committee consists of ambitious individuals whose interests are determined—more and more strongly the longer they exist—purely and simply by the interests of the Party they belong to at the present moment. They are all thinking of securing their Party a suitable platform for the future, especially against Communism. Therefore none of them are inclined, even in the interests of unity and of the Italian people, to make compromises which might now or later bring public discredit on them and their Party—such as negotiating and coming to terms with the Germans at the crucial moment. The members of the Committee are already at loggerheads, suspecting, accusing, and spying on each other. However, if the Allies brought pressure to bear on the Committee, it would—though unwillingly—submit to them. The only thing to do therefore is to negotiate direct with the Allies.

'But it is different with the Party hangers-on. Apart from a relatively small number of confirmed Communists, the majority of the opposition parties' followers and of the members of the partisan bands, including the Communists, are not ready to commit themselves seriously and absolutely. An appeal such as that mentioned above would bring all the Committee's great plans to nothing at a single blow.

'In any case, actions against the Fascists are definitely to be reckoned with, particularly in Milan and more particularly in Turin. The Republican Army will break up: the Decima Mas has already made definite arrangements to go over at the decisive moment: the Muti Legion has done likewise. The proposed measures against the Fascist Party and Black Shirts will be extremely ruthless . . .

'The following rumours are circulating among members of the National Liberation Committee: The Pope has received the German representatives, and immediately afterwards the British and American representatives. The Pope proposed a settlement by which the German troops in Italy would disarm the Fascists and hand over Northern Italy gradually and methodically to the Allies. The arrangements are already being made. Ecclesiastical circles comment that it may be true that the Pope proposed a settlement of this kind to the German and Allied diplomatic representatives; but that it was probably rejected when presented to the highest German authorities.

'After the occupation of Berlin the Allies will agree to the constitution of a German government in Germany which will order the German troops in Italy to evacuate their forces from Northern Italy; the orders would then be obeyed as if coming from the regular government. The same circles comment that so far the Allies have only spoken of allowing a German government in Germany.

'A few weeks ago in my presence the Fascist Federal Secretary of Milan rang up the Prefect and demanded "a bit of terror" (lit: "*un po' di terrore*") in answer to the murders of Fascists, over and above harsh measures. (All bicycles forbidden in Milan, earlier curfew, severe patrol actions in the city.) He could no longer control his people. When the Prefect referred to General Diamanti as the commanding officer responsible for all military affairs in Milan, the Federal Secretary replied literally, "Oh, that fat creature in General's uniform: what on earth will *he* do!" We must reckon with an increase of this animosity in Fascist circles.

'In the embittered and irritated atmosphere in these circles certain characteristic rumours are circulating among Fascists, including those of high rank. For example, it has been said for some time that certain German individuals —the RUK headquarters and especially its leaders are named particularly— have made secret arrangements with the National Liberation Committee. There is also talk of the existence of a German Liberation Committee in Italy which already has numerous followers.' [20]

On April 22, the Liberation Committee formally warned that they would break off relations with the German representatives. By that evening the latter were unable to reach their superiors at Fasano, as all telephone lines were cut by the Allied entry into Bologna.

Unless therefore Wolff could be persuaded to come in person to Milan, this laborious chain of contacts would snap. On the following morning, the Cardinal's twin negotiator, Don Bicchierai, called Dollmann to an urgent meeting, and was told that Wolff would be in Milan 'by noon'.[21] The German general seems to have telephoned such a message himself during this conversation.[22]

For the next twenty-four hours Dollmann and Wolff appeared to have vanished. The former was waiting at Fasano, while the latter was in Switzerland.

According to Dollmann's later account, the Cardinal's proposals for unconditional surrender had been passed to Wolff, who accepted them in principle and ordered Dollmann to send a message through Don Bicchierai, saying that Wolff would come to Milan on his return. This information was transmitted to the Curia on the late afternoon of April 23. The alarming delays in Switzerland could not be conveyed to the Cardinal.[i]

The only firm point established seemed to be that without fail Wolff would call on the Cardinal as soon as certain negotiations with the Allies had been completed, of which the Milan Curia must by then have been aware in general terms.

Wolff's reassuring message had been handed to the Cardinal on the morning of April 24, but throughout that day every attempt to reach Dollmann on the telephone at Fasano failed.

That evening the Cardinal decided to send a message to Wolff. It was dispatched by courier on the morning of April 25, by which time Wolff was blocked, after crossing the frontier back from Switzerland, at Villa Locatelli near Como.

In the message, Cardinal Schuster stated that he could summon 'at any time' the other parties to implement the proposals of the Curia, which Wolff himself had accepted on April 23, but that the signature of the surrender could not be delayed any further. The meeting must be held at the latest by 6 o'clock on the evening of April 25. 'Please state the precise hour and the persons instructed to sign for the Germans. For the place: the Archbishopric will do.'[23]

In the event, there was no question of Wolff coming to Milan, even if he could have eluded the insurgent partisans. His presence at Vietinghoff's headquarters at Bolzano during the final signatures at Caserta was imperative. In the meantime, his representative in Milan, Colonel Rauff, had a vital part

---

i. The accounts of Dollmann and Bicchierai of these vital hours (April 23–5) are so contradictory that a clear record cannot be established. The telephone conversation on April 23 is however mentioned by both men. Dollmann says it took place at 4 p.m. and the Cardinal's secretary at 11 p.m.

to play. He must convince the Curia that Wolff would come to Milan, and for such a purpose he called on Don Bicchierai on the morning of April 25 to announce that Wolff would arrive that evening to sign the surrender.[24]

At some point during the day Wolff did telephone Rauff with instructions to surrender 'if necessary' to the partisans. The Cardinal might therefore justifiably suppose that a German representative would appear at the ceremony at the Palace on which he was counting.

On the side of the Committee of Liberation, Marazza had already told Don Bicchierai that General Cadorna, the Military Representative, would be available to sign the surrender instrument 'at two hours' notice'. The latter also had only returned late on April 19 from a secret mission in Switzerland!

The scene was therefore seemingly set for an historic surrender of the German armed forces in Italy through the mediation of the Milan Curia, to the representatives of the Italian Committee of Liberation for Upper Italy, and as a fitting corollary to certain unclarified negotiations between the German leaders and the Allied authorities in Switzerland.

In the fragmentary notes which serve as the record of the contacts between the Germans, the Curia, and the Committee of Liberation, there is no mention of any inclusion of the government of the Duce or the armed forces of the Social Republic in such a capitulation. The Germans had indeed taken every precaution to exclude any such participation. The Curia had taken no initiative, and the Committee of Liberation had only received a series of approaches from individual Fascist personalities, political and military, which had been met with mild interest.[25]

The latest had been that of Silvestri, which was rejected without comment. For reasons not as yet clarified, a separate approach met with a certain response. It came to Marazza on the morning of April 24 from a Milanese industrialist, Gian Riccardo Cella, who had bought the printing machinery and building of Mussolini's former newspaper *Il Popolo d'Italia*. The latter acted at first on his own initiative, although when the suggestion was debated at 8 o'clock the next morning by the Liberation Committee at the Salesian College, Marazza reported on Mussolini's proposals'.[j] The aim was to negotiate through the mediation of the Cardinal. On receiving a favourable answer, Cella rushed to the Prefecture.

According to Cella, he convinced the Duce at 10.30 that morning to agree to attend a meeting for such a purpose at the Archbishop's Palace later that

j. See Valiani *op cit* p. 357. This version varies in some details from that of an article 'The Last Conversation', based on conversations just after the event with Marazza by a Milan journalist, Bacino, and published in a post-war review *Mercurio*, p. 328.

According to this account, Cadorna told Marazza of Cella's initiative on April 23, and that Marazza met the latter in the offices of the city pawn-shop on the following afternoon, and advised the Duce to surrender in the Palace to the Resistance representatives.

day.[k] It seems in any event that the Duce's decision was sudden, and that the negotiations, which he had authorized Zerbino and Montagna to undertake for a direct transfer of powers, were abruptly dropped that afternoon.[26]

What terms he expected to discuss is not clear from any evidence on the Fascist side, which consists of a jumble of impressions received in a moment of rising panic. The confusion in the anteroom of the Duce had reached its height. It is not even possible to establish the time at which the Duce left for the fatal meeting. It appears to have been just before 3 o'clock on the afternoon of April 25.

The Duce left the courtyard of the Prefecture in an antiquated limousine sent by the Cardinal. He was accompanied by Zerbino; Bassi the Prefect; Barracu, of the Presidency of the Council; and Cella. At the last moment the German S.S. Lieutenant in charge of the personal escort forced his way into the car, 'half sitting on Mussolini's knee'.[1]

Graziani witnessed the scene by chance from a window looking out on the courtyard. He knew of the decision of Mussolini to go to the Palace, and had a few moments previously advised the latter not to go in person, but to authorize talks in his name.[27] Graziani was now approached by a dispatch rider with a message to follow the Duce's party.

The planning of the meeting on the other side had been excited and hasty. The Germans were also expected. Marazza had told Bicchierai that morning that the German representatives must surrender by six o'clock and unconditionally. He then went to the Palace where the Cardinal told him that Mussolini was due 'in a quarter of an hour' and that he must fetch Cadorna. A rapid search was made for the latter, and apparently some sort of meeting of the National Committee of Liberation took place about 3.30 which authorized Cadorna, Marazza, and Lombardi to treat with the Duce on the basis of unconditional surrender, a last minute appendix to the long awaited ceremony with the Germans. As Valiani recorded: 'The Germans promise to surrender at 5 p.m.' [28]

In the meantime the Duce had arrived at the Palace of the Archbishop, and was received alone in the latter's study, presumably to gain time for the Liberation Committee representatives to arrive.[29]

The Cardinal later noted down his recollections of this uncomfortable interview. 'I began by assuring him that I much appreciated his personal sacrifice in thus initiating by capitulation a life of expiation in prison or in exile, in order to save the rest of Italy from final ruin. I assured him that decent people at least would recognize the value of his posthumous gesture. I did not want to delude him. As I then reminded him of the fall of Napoleon,

k. See a recent account, Franco Bandini: *Le Ultime 95 Ore di Mussolini*, p. 15, which unfortunately gives no references. The confusion of subsequent evidence on the course of these events is dense.

1. Wolff, *Tempo* article, No. 7. This consists largely of Lieutenant Birzer's diary. The latter states that he was told to be ready to leave at 5 o'clock, but not for what destination.

Mussolini observed that his empire of a hundred days was also about to expire. It only remained to him to meet his destiny with resignation like Bonaparte.'

Both men avoided any discussion of the pending conference, and a desultory dialogue touched on past relations between the Church and the Fascist state.

'Seeing him somewhat depressed, I insisted that he accepted at least a little comfort. Out of politeness he was persuaded to accept a glass of rosolio with a biscuit.' As the Cardinal said, this was the manner in which St Benedict had received King Totila at Montecassino, and Mussolini was presented with a copy of the Cardinal's recently published life of the saint.

This conversation dragged out for an hour in anticipation of the arrival of the Resistance delegates.

On turning to the events of the moment Mussolini said that 'his programme consisted of two separate parts and timing. In the first stage, tomorrow, the Army and Republican Militia would be dissolved: then he would withdraw to the Valtelline with a band of three thousand Black Shirts.'

The Cardinal replied: ' "And so you intend to continue the war in the mountains?" The Duce assured me: "Only for a while and then I will give myself up".' The Cardinal pointed out that the figure of 3,000 Black Shirts was nearer 300, and Mussolini answered smiling, 'Perhaps they will be a few more, but not many. I have no illusions.'

At last the arrival of the Liberation delegates was announced. In closing the private conversation the Cardinal remarked that history would relate that the Duce, in order to save Northern Italy, had placed himself on the road to St Helena.

Mussolini answered: 'History? You talk to me of history. I only believe in ancient history, in that which is written without passion and so long afterwards. I do not on the other hand believe in books and the daily press.'

The Fascist leaders, Graziani, Zerbino, Barracu, and Bassi, were assembled in the antechamber. A desultory and stilted conversation with the Cardinal's secretary Bicchierai was in progress. The only direct account is that of Graziani.[30]

'A few moments before the representatives of the Committee arrived, Prefect Bassi informed me that he had just learnt from the secretaries of the Archbishop how, through his mediation, the Germans had for two months been negotiating the surrender of their troops in Italy.

'To my amazement, the industrialist Cella came up: "Courage, Marshal, today is the great day. General Wolff will also be coming here, and the armistice will be signed." "But where," I asked, "are the Anglo-American representatives?" . . . I asked myself whether one was not taking part in a tragic parody.'

At that moment the three representatives of the Committee of Liberation appeared. There were no salutes or presentations, and both parties were ushered immediately into the private study of the Cardinal where he and the Duce were sitting in conversation on a sofa. The delegates seated themselves facing each other at a long table. The Cardinal made a sign to Mussolini to open the proceedings.[31]

One of the Liberation Committee delegates answered the Duce's questions as to what proposals the Committee had to make to him.[m] Their terms were unconditional surrender, and within two hours. Orders had been given for a general partisan rising. But if the Fascists concentrated their forces in the triangle Milan-Como-Lecco, they could formally lay down their arms.

Mussolini appeared to be about to accept this communication, when Graziani burst into the conversation with the information which he had learnt in the anteroom a few minutes earlier about the imminent German surrender.[n]

The discussion collapsed at once. Mussolini expressed astonished surprise, broke up the meeting and, according to Graziani, threatened to broadcast a denunciation of German treachery on the radio.

The Cardinal appealed for patience, and Mussolini undertook to give an answer to the terms of the Committee 'within an hour', adding that the German gesture of disloyalty gave him complete freedom of action.

As the Duce and his party left the room, the Cardinal turned to Graziani imploring him to prevent any broadcast, which would cause 'immense damage'.[32]

This scene has been the subject of much elaborate and contradictory comment from the surviving witnesses on both sides. All parties had been in varying degrees duped, and by the Germans. Both the Palace and the Liberation Committee expected either Wolff or his representative to appear during the talks with Mussolini, and although both had up till that moment refrained from any direct contact with the Duce they might reasonably suppose that he had some knowledge of the two months old negotiations between the Curia on the one hand and Wolff and Rahn on the other.

As Lombardi stated in his evidence at Graziani's post-war trial:

'I am morally certain that Mussolini was deliberately told that negotiations were already going on with the Germans . . . it was my firm impression,

m. Graziani, Valiani, and Bacino record that Marazza acted as spokesman; Lombardi states that he spoke on behalf of the Liberation Committee. There is no agreed account of the ensuing dialogue.

n. Graziani *op cit* pp. 508–9. The Marazza version differs; he claims that in answer to a query of Graziani's as to whether the Fascist government could accept terms without loyally consulting their ally, he announced that the Germans had been negotiating 'for the last few days' (*sic*) and that doubtless the Social Republican authorities had been informed. Mussolini then asked to hear the terms, and Don Bicchierai was called in to read them out. (See Bacino article *op cit* p. 332).

indeed certainty, that the Cardinal and Don Bicchierai wanted somehow to force me to suggest that the negotiations with the Germans, which had no serious character, were going well so as to overcome resistance and difficulties arising out of this. Mussolini could alone decide, and he consulted no one . . . He spoke with bitter words when he learnt, or pretended to learn— because it was impossible that he did not know— . . . and said that he would protest.

'There were contacts between Cardinal Schuster and numerous German emissaries and also from Mussolini. They even reached journalistic circles: even the Fascist papers. It is impossible to rule out that Mussolini was informed reasonably accurately on the state of affairs. He had been in Milan for three days.' [33]

Graziani, at his trial, dissented strongly. The Duce's links with the Cardinal had been 'through others', and at no time did he believe that surrender talks were in progress. Graziani had himself offered to go to the Cardinal on April 18, and Mussolini had agreed. The purpose of the meeting, which took place on April 22, was 'to find a way out'. The conversation however did not touch on politics, and the Cardinal's 'indifference' was clear to Graziani at the conference on April 25.[34]

On leaving the Palace, Mussolini had undertaken to give an answer to the Committee within an hour.[35]

In the Cardinal's study, the rest of the company awaited the reply from the Prefecture.

Shortly after seven o'clock, the German Consul in Milan arrived to ask for an extension of the time limit for the surrender, adding that General Wolff confirmed that arrangements 'were being made'.[36] Apparently Colonel Rauff telephoned almost at the same time to say that he had also been in touch with the General, who would now reach Milan late next morning. The parallel deception on the German side was to be maintained up to the last.

Among the Committee of Liberation representatives, there was mounting confusion and doubts. The spectacle of Mussolini remaining at large during the last hours before a general insurrection, and uncertainty about whose hands he might finally fall into, produced considerable alarm.

Sandro Pertini, the Socialist representative on the Liberation Committee, rushed during this waiting hour to the Prefecture, hoping to be in time to oppose any surrender talks with Mussolini except on the basis of treating him as a prisoner of war, and 'then perhaps he should be handed over to the Allies. We must abide by what had been decided by the Liberation Committee at a previous meeting.' [37]

These remarks were apparently overheard by an emissary of the Fascist military commander in Milan, who had also appeared with the task of trying to negotiate a local hand-over. He hastened to the Duce's office with this unnerving report.[38]

The scene on Mussolini's return to the Prefecture had been witnessed, among others, by the Fascist Party Secretary for Milan.

'I saw Mussolini jump out of the car, and walk quickly towards the stair-case, where he suddenly stopped short and turned to the German officer com-manding his escort, and said to him in a loud voice: "Your General Wolff has betrayed us." The German officer made a gesture of amazement, stroking his chin.' [39]

Mussolini then shut himself in his office. The illusion that a certain liberty of action remained to him was hard to dissolve. His elemental fear was that of a trap, and the repetition of an arrest, as had happened nearly two years previously, in July 1943, at Villa Savoia. The smell of treachery was omni-present. As he told Graziani: 'an attempt has been made this very night in Milan to put me in the bag together with the whole government'.[40]

The partisan insurrection was now flaring across Lombardy and Piedmont. How could any guaranteed surrender of the Fascist armed forces and the Party formations take place in this climate of savage anarchy?

Two courses only seemed to remain open to Mussolini. A last stand in Milan, or a move to the symbolic redoubt of the Valtelline. He was now isolated both from any control over events, and from all contact with reality. A futile dialogue ensued in the emptying offices and corridors of the Milan Prefecture. The faithful were still gathered, loyal and without a lead.

With his usual and familiar abruptness, Mussolini ordered an immediate and unplanned departure for Como, and away from the city which suddenly appeared as a trap. A column of ten cars was hastily assembled by the reliable German escort. There were untidy farewells in the courtyard of the Prefecture. The Minister of Justice, Pisenti, was left to hold the crumbling fort.

Mussolini departed in the company of Bombacci. The two men had been revolutionary Socialist schoolmasters in the Romagna over thirty years before. The one had become the Duce of Fascism, the other a failed Com-munist agitator and latter-day adviser in adversity to his former colleague. Bombacci seems to have had a ferocious sense of the occasion. It is said that, when joining Mussolini in his car, dressed in striped trousers and clutch-ing a small suitcase, he suddenly turned to the Duce's son: 'What else would I need? . . . I am expert in such matters. I was in Lenin's office in Petersburg when the White troops of Yudenitch were advancing on the city and we were preparing to leave, as we are doing today.'[41]

The Italian and German escort followed with Graziani in the second car in the column. As he was leaving Mussolini released all members of the

Party and Armed Forces from their oath of allegiance. He wanted no bloodshed in Milan. He was leaving for Como. Pavolini would give any further orders.[42]

Graziani wrote the last sentence of the account in his notebook: 'Eight o'clock. Departure with the Duce for Como.' [43]

This exiguous convoy, which pulled out from the Milan Prefecture at eight o'clock on the evening of April 25, 1945, represented the last historical act of Italian Fascism.

A few minutes later, a telephone call came to the Prefecture from the Cardinal's Palace asking for the Duce's reply to the terms presented earlier by the Committee of Liberation. The Prefect Bassi answered. The Duce had left. There would be no surrender and no negotiation.

The rearguard of the Fascist authorities, the Minister of Justice, Pisenti, the Prefect Bassi and the Chief of Police, General Montagna, waited throughout the night in the darkened rooms of the Prefecture. At dawn on April 26 the building was occupied without incident by Finance Guards, a body which had long since rallied clandestinely to the Resistance and whose discipline and network of communications had rendered a decisive service in the hour of insurrection.

In the early hours the remaining Party formations, the last armed concentration of Fascism, assembled their transport in the main arteries of the city and pulled out in column towards Como, and to an ultimate and unknown destination.

At 8 a.m. on April 26 the Partisans broadcast for the first time on Milan Radio.

The German authorities in Milan played the tragic comedy to the end. At noon on April 26 Rauff came to the Archbishopric to report that Wolff was prepared to come to Milan, but needed an escort to take him on to Bolzano. His journey thence was indispensable in order 'to carry out the German surrender'. Cadorna sent a party to Villa Locatelli, but it failed to get through, and Wolff, with American help, was smuggled back into Switzerland.

That evening Rauff called on the Cardinal for the last time. The bluff was exposed. The Germans were treating with the Allies in Switzerland. There was no need any more for separate negotiations in Milan. 'I regret that His Eminence cannot preside as a direct mediator.' [44]

The Cardinal had prepared a speech to deliver to the world on the solemn occasion of the end of hostilities in Italy. It was to be delivered at 10 o'clock that evening. It had been prepared 'after General Wolff had asked the Cardinal to send him an escort to bring him that evening, April 26, to sign the capitulation at the Palace. He was awaited in vain. On the previous day, however, he had left for Switzerland.' In fact Wolff had gone during the night of April 26.

'Such circumstances did not escape the Curia, and provided a new argument for distrusting the personalities then conducting German policy in Lombardy.' [45]

CHAPTER FOUR

EXIT

Tutto cio che è entrato nella storia non si cancella.[a]
(Mussolini, March 3, 1945)

THE DUCE'S PARTY reached Como without incident about nine o'clock that evening. A group of some thirty persons jostled into the Prefecture, and an untidy bivouac formed in the courtyard. Donna Rachele and the younger children had been moved some days previously from Gargnano to a villa nearby. She now joined her husband. Buffarini, who had been since February living in retirement in the neighbourhood, was also on the scene.

That evening a discussion began over dinner. Mussolini had already abandoned all formal authority on leaving Milan. Henceforth no one, not even his Ministers and his immediate staff, owed him allegiance. There was no meaning nor solution in this bewildering journey. Mussolini sensed the engulfing chaos, and had turned days before against the apocalyptic vision of a last stand. He would give no orders, shed no blood, not even surrender his person. He was discarding the last rags and trappings of power, deliberately, seeking a private release without regard to those around him. Such an ultimate mood was beyond their understanding. They were witnessing the dissolution of a public image, consciously willed by the man himself. The Duce was seeking a mountain, and there might still be a posthumous message. But the immediate legacy and the physical end had no meaning, nor did they belong to any strictly historical process. He had been since his early days as a propagandist in Trento an ardent student of Nietzsche, whose works Hitler had sent to him for meditation in exile at Ponza. But the irrational violence of Fascism could not end reasonably.

The debate at table in the Como Prefecture whether to seek a final refuge in Switzerland (for which Buffarini now strove with all his forensic skill),

a. 'Everything that has entered into history cannot be erased.'

or to force a passage through to the Sondrio valley now anyway in partisan hands, was thus divorced from all reality. Graziani, as a soldier, was perhaps more aware of this than the others. To him all that mattered was to save his troops from massacre by the partisans, and his loyalty was divided between them and the Duce. But along the last road Mussolini was divesting himself with deliberation of all loyalties.

In the early hours of the morning of April 27, sudden movement in the courtyard of the Como Prefecture indicated yet another imminent departure. Mussolini took farewell of his wife. The ubiquitous German subaltern, alarmed that the Duce should be driving off without escort, which would be contrary to his standing orders, blocked the exit and was obliged to resort to force to include the two German lorries in the little column, which set out northwards up the road along the side of Lake Como towards Menaggio, pursued by functionaries and their families seeking safety in proximity to the leader.

From Menaggio, the road led to the Swiss frontier. It seems that Mussolini on leaving Como indulgently yielded to Buffarini's plea to attempt a passage at least for members of the government into Switzerland.[b]

Buffarini and Tarchi, the Minister of Corporations, made a probing excursion but failed to reach the Swiss frontier posts, and were arrested by Italian Finance Guards, whose mission was to control the zone under the orders of the Resistance. They were both released later. Buffarini was recaptured, and after taking poison, unsuccessfully, like Laval, he was shot later in Milan. Tarchi was able to go into hiding.

The halt at Menaggio produced no further plan of salvation. Graziani departed to find his headquarters, and separated his fate from that of the main party.

The surrounding country was now in arms. The Fascist columns, ordered by Pavolini to concentrate on Como for the eventual long debated stand in the Valtelline, had appeared,[c] but the city was in the nominal hands of the partisan authorities, and there was no lead from above. Behind the tiny column, now at Menaggio, the last remnants of Fascist authority collapsed.

During the night of April 26–7 a German anti-aircraft unit of two hundred men, seeking a way northwards to the Tyrol, arrived at Menaggio, and absorbed the Duce's meagre German escort. Pavolini, unable to move his columns from Como, in a last gesture of loyalty joined the convoy with an armoured car. Clara Petacci too had forced her way up the same road to play her part to the end.

The presence of a protecting German force, larger than the average roving

b. Graziani had opposed such a plan. There is an eloquent and indecipherable sentence in his notebook scribbled at the moment. 'April 26. Sleepless night . . . towards the frontier . . . for passage of whole government with the Duce. Arrival at Menaggio.'

c. On the night of April 25–6 they numbered some four thousand men.

partisan band, gave weight to their own practical intention of reaching safety in the German military concentration area of Merano in the Tyrol. The combined party moved before dawn on April 27, passing through the small township of Musso about seven o'clock. The column was halted by a road block manned by a small partisan band about fifteen strong. The German officers were in a mood for parley. The partisan leaders searched for higher authority. The hours passed. By three o'clock, six hours after the line of vehicles had been halted, the Germans agreed to the condition that they could pursue their journey provided that no Italians passed in the convoy.

The German lieutenant in charge of the Duce's escort performed his last duty. Mussolini was persuaded, without seemingly paying any attention, to put on a German greatcoat and helmet and to sit in one of the German lorries. The Italian partisans insisted on a final check of each vehicle, and one of the local commanders recognized the figure huddled in the back of the truck.

The German column started northwards. Mussolini was at last beyond their surveillance. He was taken to the town hall in the next town, Dongo, and his immediate followers were rounded up by the partisan bands now growing hourly in the areas bordering the lake.

After spending a night in a barracks outside Dongo, Mussolini was taken back through that town in the early hours of April 28, when Clara Petacci, with a shrill and touching persistence, managed to catch up with him. They both spent the next hours in a peasant house which the partisans had been using as a hiding-place, in the village of Giuliano di Mezzagra.

The news of the capture of Mussolini reached Milan, where general insurrection had broken out. The manner of his sentence, and the responsibility of individuals, are of little import, as are the details of his death. The controversy in Resistance circles about the formal legality of his execution and on whose orders is of little historical relevance. Mussolini died by a revolutionary act.

On the afternoon of April 28, 1945, together with Clara Petacci, he was taken from the custody of local partisans by a killer squad, acting under orders from Milan, and shot down without warning at the gates of a villa on the outskirts of the hamlet of Mezzagra.

The executioners, led by a Communist partisan under the cover name of Colonel 'Valerio', hastened to Dongo to complete their task. Here had been identified, from the last Fascist column, certain leading figures of the régime. 'Valerio' drew up a list. It included Pavolini, Zerbino, Bombacci, Gatti the Duce's private secretary, and several Ministers. A priest was accorded three minutes in which to give final absolution. A squad of local partisans carried out the execution of fifteen such persons, lined up against the parapet on the main square of Dongo facing the lake of Como.

On August 12, 1944, just before dawn, fifteen hostages had been shot in the Piazzo Loreto in Milan as a reprisal for a bomb attack by Italian partisans on a German lorry four days previously. The executions had been ordered by the German military authorities, and carried out by a Fascist squad of the 'Muti'. There were no witnesses present. The victims were under the impression that they were being sent to work in Germany, but realizing their fate sought to flee across the square. They were shot down in indiscriminate bursts of fire. The corpses lay exposed until the evening.

Reprisal executions in a proportion of three to one were carried out in the next days by the Committee of Liberation. Fifteen Fascist militia prisoners and thirty German and Italian soldiers were shot.

But the symbolic vendetta of civil war was not assuaged until the following spring. To mark the Roman triumph of the Liberation, and perhaps the fleeting ascendancy of one section of its leadership, a macabre ceremony was staged on the site of the executions of the previous August. At four o'clock on the morning of April 29, 1945, twenty-three corpses were unloaded from a lorry in the Piazzo Loreto. The victims were Benito Mussolini and his mistress Clara Petacci, the fifteen prisoners from the last Fascist column executed at Dongo as a repeated reprisal for the Milan shootings of August, by chance, in mathematical miscalculation, four unidentified bodies, and Starace, the former Party Secretary, caught and shot shortly before.

Mussolini, Clara Petacci, and others, were hung head downwards from the roof of a petrol station with rough placards of identification. The bodies were removed that evening.

BIBLIOGRAPHY

* * *

(A) *Unprinted Documentary Sources*

1. *Italian Collection*

Owing to the historical circumstances of the Second World War, in particular of the Armistice signed with Italy in September 1943 and the establishment of the Republic of Salò, only fragmentary collections of the Italian government archives fell into Allied hands. From the point of view of the historian, therefore, there is no comparable set of records such as those of the German Foreign Office and Admiralty which ended in English custody, and of the German High Command and War Office which were deposited in the United States.

The available Italian material falls into the following categories:

(*a*) Material deposited at the present time at St Antony's College Oxford, and referred to in this volume as the Italian Collection. This consists of a series of documents assembled in Italy during the course of the advance of the Allied armies northwards at the end of the war, and which came fortuitously into Anglo-American hands. The bulk of the material consists of files from certain ministries of the Republic of Salò, collected in an arbitrary fashion from the ministries in Rome between September 1943 and June 1944 when the city fell, and certain files relating to the Republican period itself. An unsolved mystery surrounds the fate of Mussolini's personal archives, which disappeared during the final exodus from Milan in April 1945, though some of the files in this collection, on circumstantial evidence, may come from this source.

This collection does also contain such valuable items as the dispatches of Anfuso, the Italian Ambassador in Berlin after 1943, correspondence between Mussolini and leading Fascist personalities such as Farinacci dating back to the early period of Fascist rule, and material on the socialization programme including correspondence between the Duce and von Rahn, the German Ambassador to Salò. Some of the Farinacci correspondence was found in the German Embassy in Rome in June 1944, where it was presumably deposited before his flight to Germany in the previous July. Other files seem to originate with the Ministry of the Interior at Salò, and a considerable amount of documentary material of uneven interest was found by the Allies in the vaults of the Ministry of Popular Culture in Rome in 1944.

(b) A separate set of documents, which contains certain papers of Ciano, and copies of the correspondence between Hitler and Mussolini, has been added to the above collection. These files were removed surreptitiously from the Italian Foreign Office in August 1943 on the orders of the then Foreign Minister, Baron Guariglia, and transferred to the Italian Legation in Lisbon, where they were handed over to the Americans at the end of the war. Much of this material has been printed either in the Diplomatic Papers of Ciano or the Italian edition of the Hitler-Mussolini Correspondence. But certain unpublished documents from this source have been published in this book.

The originals of all the above material have been returned to the Italian government, and are deposited either in the Foreign Office or the State Archives in Rome.

2. German Collection

The documents referred to under this heading are from four sources:

(a) *The German Foreign Office Archives* from which the microfilms of selected files have been deposited in the Public Record Office. None of this material has been previously published, and the author has drawn heavily on this collection, particularly for the German minutes of the Axis summit conferences of the war, minutes and memoranda of the German Foreign Office on Italian affairs, and the records of the German Embassy in Rome. The originals of this whole collection are now in the German Foreign Office.

(b) *Himmler Files.* These are fragmentary and small in bulk, and are of interest only as containing certain reports to and from Himmler and his agents in Italy. Copies of this material exist in the Institut für Zeitgeschichte in Munich.

(c) *Archives of the German War Office.* These are deposited at Alexandria, Virginia, U.S.A., and have been used primarily in relation to the military records of certain conferences and military reports, in particular from General von Rintelen, German Military Representative in Rome.

(d) *The Hitler Military Conferences.* Most of these records have been published in Gilbert, *Hitler Directs His War* (Oxford University Press, 1950), but certain unpublished extracts have been used in this book. The original documents have been deposited in the Library of the University of Pennsylvania, U.S.A.

(B) *Printed Documentary Sources*

1. *Italian*

Ballola, R.C. (Editor)	*Processo Parri*	Ceschina. 1954
Ciano, G.	*Diary (1939–43)* (English translation)	Heinemann. 1947
Ciano, G.	*Diplomatic Papers* (English translation)	Odhams. 1948
Graziani, R.	*Processo* (stenographic record. Three volumes)	Ruffolo. 1948
	Il dramma di Graziani (Edited by Argenti, G. P. Mastino del Rio, G. Carnelutti, F.; containing the speeches of Graziani's lawyers)	Zuffi. 1950
Hitler e Mussolini	*Lettere e Documenti*	Rizzoli. 1946
Mussolini, B.	*Opera Omnia* Volumes XXXI & XXXII. (Edited by Edoardo e Duilio Susmel)	La Fenice. 1960

2. *German*

	Fuehrer Conferences on Naval Affairs (Edited by the Admiralty)	1947
	The Goebbels Diaries (Edited and translated by Louis Lochner)	Hamish Hamilton. 1948
	Hitler Directs His War (The stenographic records of certain Military Conferences. Edited and translated by Dr Felix Gilbert)	Oxford University Press. New York. 1950
Hitler, A.	*Table Talk* (1941–1944). (English translation)	Weidenfeld & Nicolson. 1953
	The Testament of Adolf Hitler (English translation. Edited by Professor H. R. Trevor-Roper)	Cassell. 1961
	Nazi Conspiracy and Aggression (Documents presented at the Nuremberg Trials. 10 Volumes)	Washington, D.C. (1946–8)
	The Rommel Papers (English translation. Edited by Captain B. H. Liddell Hart)	Collins. 1953

(C) *Secondary Sources*

1. *General Works*

Begnac, Yvon de	*Palazzo Venezia. Storia di Un Régime*	La Rocca. 1950
Bullock, A. L. C.	*Hitler*	Odhams. 1952
Canevari, E.	*La Guerra Italiana*	Tosi
Churchill, W. S.	*The Second World War* (Six volumes)	Cassell. 1950–2
Faldella, E.	*L'Italia e La Seconda Guerra Mondiale*	Cappelli (Second edition). 1960
Germino, D. L.	*The Italian Fascist Party in Power*	University of Minnesota Press. 1959
Gigli, G.	*La Seconda Guerra Italiana (1939–1945)*	Laterza. 1951
Hinsley, F.	*Hitler's Strategy*	Cambridge University Press. 1951
Salvatorelli, L. e Mira, G.	*Storia d'Italia nel Periodo Fascista*	Einaudi. 1956
Tamaro, A.	*Venti Anni di Storia (1922–1943)*	Tiber, Roma. 1953
Trevor-Roper, H. R.	*The Last Days of Hitler*	Macmillan. 1947
Wheeler-Bennett, J. W.	*The Nemesis of Power (The German Army in Politics, 1918–1945)*	Macmillan. 1953
Wiskemann, E.	*The Rome-Berlin Axis*	Oxford University Press. 1949

(2) *Memoirs, Monographs, and Special Studies*

Abshagen, K. H.	*Canaris*	Union Deutsche Vertagsanstalt. 1949
Alfieri, D.	*Due Dittatori di Fronte*	Rizzoli. 1948
Amé, C.	*Guerra Segreta in Italia*	Casini. 1954
Amicucci, E.	*I 600 giorni di Mussolini*	Faro. 1948
Anfuso, F.	*Da Palazzo Venezia al Lago di Garda*	Cappelli. 1957
Badoglio, P.	*L'Italia nella Seconda Guerra Mondiale*	Mondadori. 1946
Bandini, F.	*Le Ultime 95 Ore di Mussolini*	Sugar Ed. 1959
Bastianini, G.	*Uomini, Cose, Fatti*	Vitagliano. 1959
Benigno, Jo di	*Occasioni Mancate (Roma in un Diario Segreto, 1943–4)*	S.E.I. Roma. 1945

Benini, Z.   *Vigilia a Verona*   Garzanti. 1949
Bolla, N.   *Il Segreto di Due Re*   Rizzoli. 1951
Bonomi, I.   *Diario di un Anno: 2 giugno 1943*   Garzanti. 1947
  —10 giugno 1944

Bottai, G.   *Vent' Anni e Un Giorno*   Garzanti. 1949
Bova Scoppa, R.   *Colloqui con Due Dittatori*   Ruffolo, Roma. 1949

Brinon, F. de   *Mémoires*   L.L.C. Paris. 1949
Canevari, E.   *La Fine del Maresciallo Cavallero*   Latinità (Collana: Documenti per la Storia)

Canevari, E.   *Graziani mi ha detto*   Magi-Spinetti. 1947

Carboni, G.   *Più che il Dovere (Memorie Segrete 1935–48)*   Parenti. 1955

Cassinelli, G.   *Appunti Sul 25 Luglio 1943*   Edizioni S.A.P.P.I. 1944

Castellano, G.   *Come Firmai l'Armistizio di Cassibile*   Mondadori. 1945

Catalano, F.   *Storia del CLNAI*   Laterza. 1956
Cavallero, U.   *Comando Supremo, Diario 1940–2*   Cappelli. 1948
Caviglia, E.   *Diario (1925–45)*   Casini. 1952
Cersosimo, V.   *'Dall' Istruttoria alla Fucilazione' (Storia del Processo di Verona)*   Garzanti. 1949

Cione, E.   *Storia della Repubblica Sociale Italiana*   Latinità (Second edition). 1950
Coceani, B.   *Mussolini, Hitler e Tito. Alle Porte Orientali d' Italia.*   Cappelli. 1948

Cucco, A.   *Non Volevamo Perdere*   Cappelli. 1940
Dolfin, G.   *Con Mussolini nella Tragedia (Diario del Capo della Segretaria Particolare del Duce 1943–4)*   Garzanti. 1950

Dollmann, E.   *Roma Nazista.* (Trans. Zingarelli, I) Longanesi. 1951
Esposito, G.   *Trieste e la sua Odissea*   Roma. 1952
Favagrossa, C.   *Perchè perdemmo la Guerra*   Rizzoli. 1947
Galanti, F.   *Socializzazione e Sindacalismo nella R.S.I.*   Magi-Spinetti. 1949

Galbiati, E.   *Il 25 Luglio e la MVSN*   Bernabo. 1950
Gorla, G.   *L'Italia nella Seconda Guerra Mondiale*   Baldini e Castoldi. 1959
Graziani, R.   *Io ho difeso la Patria*   Garzanti. 1948
Guariglia, R.   *Ricordi 1922–1946*   E.S.I. Napoli. 1950

Guérard, J.   *Criminel de Paix*   Nouvelles Editions Latines. 1953

Hagen, W.	*Die Geheime Front*	Niebelungen Verlag. 1950
Hillgrueber, A.	*Hitler, König Carol und Marshall Antonescu*	Steiner, Wiesbaden. 1954
Kallay, N.	*Hungarian Premier* (Trans. Professor C. A. Macartney)	Oxford University Press. 1954
Kesselring, A.	*Soldat Bis Zum Letzten Tag*	Athenaum, Bonn. 1953
Kleist, P.	*Zwischen Hitler und Stalin 1939–1945*	Athenaum, Bonn. 1950
Kordt, E.	*Nicht aus den Akten*	U.D.G.S. Stuttgart. 1950
———	*Wahn und Wirklichkeit*	U.D.G.S. Stuttgart. 1948
Lanfranchi, F.	*La Resa degli Ottocentomila*	Rizzoli. 1948
Leto, G.	*OVRA*	Cappelli. 1951
Macartney, C. A.	*October Fifteenth. A History of Modern Hungary 1929–1945*	Edinburgh University Press. 1956
Mallet, A.	*Pierre Laval* (Two volumes)	Amiot-Dumont. 1955
Manunta, U.	*La Caduta degli Angeli*	Editoria italiana. Roma. 1947
Massola, U.	*Marzo 1943. Ore dieci*	Edizioni di Cultura Sociale, Roma. 1950
Maugeri, F.	*From the Ashes of Disgrace*	Reynal and Hitchcock. New York. 1948
Mellini, A.	*Guerra Diplomatica a Salò*	Cappelli. 1950
Messe, G.	*La Guerra al Fronte Russo*	Rizzoli. 1947
———	*La Mia Armata in Tunisia. (Come Finì la Guerra in Africa)*	Rizzoli (Second edition). 1960
Moellhausen, E. F.	*Die Gebrochene Achse*	Alpha. 1949
Monelli, P.	*Roma 1943*	Migliaresi. 1946
Montagna, R.	*Mussolini e il Processo di Verona*	Omnia. 1949
Mussolini B.	*Memoirs 1942–3*	Weidenfeld & Nicolson. 1949
Mussolini, R.	*La mia vita con Benito*	Mondadori. 1948
Napolitano, V.	*25 Luglio*	Vega. 1944
Pansa, R. C.	*Marcello Soleri*	Garzanti. 1948
Pini, G.	*Itinerario Tragico*	Omnia. 1950

Pini, G. e Susmel, D.	*Mussolini: l'Uomo e l'Opera* (Four volumes)	La Fenice. 1953–5
Pozzi, A.	*Come li ho visto Io*	Mondadori. 1947
Puntoni, P.	*Parla Vittorio Emmanuele III*	Palazzi. 1958
Rahn, R.	*Ruheloses Leben*	Diederichs Verlag, Dusseldorf. 1949
Ribbentrop, J. von	*The Ribbentrop Memoirs* Trans. O. Watson	Weidenfeld & Nicolson. 1954
Rintelen, E. von	*Mussolini als Bundesgenosse*	Leins. 1951
Roatta, M.	*Otto Milioni di Baionette*	Mondadori. 1946
Rossi, F.	*Come arrivammo all' armistizio*	Garzanti. 1946
———	*Mussolini e lo Stato Maggiore*	Regionale. 1951
Ruinas, S.	*Pioggia sulla Repubblica*	Corso. 1946
Schuster, I.	*Gli Ultimi Tempi di un Régime*	La Via. 1946
Scorzeny, O.	*Missioni Segrete*	Garzanti (Second edition). 1951
Senise, C.	*Quando Ero Capo della Polizia 1940–1943*	Ruffolo. 1946
Silva, P.	*Io Difendo la Monarchia*	de Fonseca. 1946
Silvestri, G.	*Albergo agli Scalzi*	Garzanti. 1946
Silvestri, Carlo	*Mussolini, Graziani e l'Antifascismo*	Longanesi. 1949
Simoni, L.	*Berlino Ambasciata d'Italia 1939–1943*	Migliaresi. 1946
Soleri, M.	*Memorie.*	Einaudi. 1949
Spampanato, B.	*Contro Memoriale* (Three volumes)	Edizione di 'Illustrato'. 1952
Tamaro, A.	*Due Anni di Storia, 1943–1945* (Three volumes)	Tosi, Roma. 1948
Vailati, V.	*Badoglio Racconta*	Ilte. 1956
	Badoglio Risponde	Rizzoli. 1958
Valiani, L.	*Tutte le strade conducono a Roma*	La Nuova Italia
Villari, L.	*Affari Esteri 1943–1945*	Magi-Spinetti. 1949
Zachariae, G.	*Mussolini si Confessa*	Garzanti. 1950

(D) *Articles*

1. *Bibliographical*

Manunta, U.	'La Repubblica Sociale Italiana', *Italia che Scrive* (April–May 1949)

| Ravà, F. e
Spini, G. | 'Fonti documentarie e memorialistiche per la storia della crisi dello stato italiano' (1940–45). *Rivista Storica Italiana LXI* |
| Toscano, M. | 'Fonti documentarie e memorialistiche per la Storia Diplomatica della Seconda Guerra Mondiale' in *Questioni di storia contemporanea*, 1952 |

2. *Articles and contributions in 'Il Movimento di Liberazione in Italia'* (1949——).

This most valuable source, containing much documentary evidence, specialist studies, and papers read to conferences, is the publication of the National Institute for the Liberation Movement in Italy.

See in particular:

No. 5	'I tedeschi e l'esercito di Salò'
No. 7	'La repressione dello ribellismo nel IV gran rapporto del Generale Mischi alle gerarchie dell' esercito fascista'
No. 11	'Alcuni documenti delle gerarchie di Salò sull' industria italiana e sulla classe industriale del Nord'
Nos. 19–20	'Il movimento operaio a Torino. Luglio 1943–Marzo 1944'

This article by Dr Vaccarino is of special interest. See also his valuable contribution 'Gli Scioperi del Marzo 1943' in the collected volume *Aspetti della Resistenza in Piemonte*, April 1950.

| Nos. 34–35 | 'La Crisi Italiana del 1943 e gli inizi della Resistenza'. Papers presented to the second congress on the History of the Liberation Movement. |

3. *Articles from reviews and interviews in newspapers*

| Alfieri, D. | 'L'Ultima Seduta del Gran Consiglio' *Epoca*. May 24, 1952 |
| Ambrosio, V. | 'La parte dei militari nel 25 Luglio e nell' 8 Settembre' Interview in *Il Corriere della Sera* March 11, 1955 |

(See also a further interview with General Ambrosio in *Unità*, October 22, 1953.)

Bacino, E.	'Ultimo Colloquio'	*Mercurio*. December 1945
Bonomi, I	'Il Colpo di Stato. Luglio 1943'	*Il Mondo*. April 23, 1949
Cerica, A.	'Sull' arresto di Mussolini'	*Tempo*. July–August 1956
Chiot, Don	'Parla Don Chiot'	*Messaggero*. September 15, 1948
Farinacci, R.	'Diario'	*Il Giornale* (Naples). Jan.–Feb. 1947

Federzoni, L.	'L'Ultima Seduta'	*Quadrante.* October 19, 1946
———	'Memorie'	*Indipendente.* May–July 1946
Grandi, D.	Interviews in *Incom: Illustrata* July–August 1952, in *Il Corriere della Sera*, February 9–10, 1955, and in *Oggi* May–June 1959	
Maugeri, F.	'Mussolini mi ha detto'	*Quaderni di Politica Estera.* 1944
Mors, Major	'Le SS Otto Skorzeny a menti'	*Curieux* (Switzerland). December 14, 1950
Anonymous (possibly Pellegrini)	'C'è tutto da rifare'	*Meridiano d'Italia.* August 31, 1947
Pellicano, I.	'I superstiti del Gran Consiglio si sono decisi di parlare'	*L'Elefante.* 13–20 October, 1949
Pertini, S.	'I Socialisti e la resa di Mussolini nell' Aprile 1945'	*Avanti* (Rome edition). April 30, 1947
Soleti, F.	'Come Mussolini fu liberato da Campo Imperatore'	*Avanti* (Rome edition). July 19, 1944
Vecchi, de, C. M.	'Mussolini Vero'	*Tempo.* November 1959–March 1960
Wolff, K.	'Ecco La Verità'	*Tempo.* Feb.–March 1951

APPENDIX

The German authorities and the Italian Foreign Archives (1943–44) [a]

(a) *The Seizure of the Archives.*

During the course of researches into the German Foreign Office Archives and certain documents in the Italian Collection for this study, a number of references has come to light revealing in part the fate of those files from Palazzo Chigi, which were impounded by the Germans after the Italian armistice.

On September 12, 1943, Ribbentrop sent instructions to Ambassador Rahn in Rome to take all necessary steps to seize the archives of the Italian Foreign Office. [1]

At 10.30 on the morning of September 14 the senior official in charge at Palazzo Chigi, Ambassador Rosso, noted in a memorandum drafted on the following day, [2] that the personnel at the entrance to the building warned him that it 'was about to be surrounded by a cordon of German military armed with sub-machine-guns, who were taking up positions at the corners of

a. Professor Mario Toscano has published an article entitled 'Le Vicende degli Archivi Segreti di Palazzo Chigi' in 'Nuova Antologia' (No. 1923 March 1961), which is based in great part on the original draft of this appendix.

B.F.—27*

the edifice'. An S.S. officer, accompanied by an armed escort, was announced
in Rosso's office and introduced himself as Major Kappler, the German
Police Chief in Rome. He declared that he had instructions from the Fuehrer
'to take charge of all documents which could be of interest to the Anglo-
Americans if they should fall into their hands', Major Kappler appeared to be
well informed of the lay-out of the premises, and made an immediate search
of certain private offices. He then announced that he must impound and
remove certain files. As Rosso cryptically noted in his memorandum of
September 15, 'In fact one succeeded in avoiding that Major Kappler should
take away a great part of the archives',[b] but he did show particular interest in
the papers of Minister Vitetti, and those of Minister Pietromarchi from which
he also removed a portable radio transmitter.

Three lorry loads of documents in all were taken away that evening from
Palazzo Chigi. It was noted by the Germans 'that the shelves and the filing
cabinets in the Secret Archives Section were empty'. Considerable funds were
found, and Rahn suggested that these should be transferred to a new Italian
government. [3] On September 17, 41 packing cases of files were dispatched
under armed guard to Berlin. [4]

(b) *The preliminary study of the material by the German authorities.*

On September 23 Dr Stieve, of the German Foreign Office Archives, was
instructed to set up a team to study these Italian papers. [5] The preliminary
report was sent to Ribbentrop from Berlin on September 28. The 41 cases
contained some 2,000 files with 15,000 documents in 200 series. There had
been an 'unbelievably disordered keeping of the documents', which were
barely in chronological order, in loose folders, many of them not even tied up.
They consisted broadly of (1) Cabinet papers of the Foreign Minister (filed
under subjects) (1932 to August 1943). (2) Papers of the Directorate-General
of European and Mediterranean Affairs (1936 to August 1943). (3) A collection of ingoing and outgoing 'non secret' telegrams (1940 to 1943).

On about September 4, according to enquiries made subsequently by the
Germans in Rome, Guariglia had ordered each section of the Ministry to
destroy their secret files.

The papers in (1) above contained the main files during Suvich's period of
office as Undersecretary at the Italian Foreign Office (1932 to 1935) including records of his political conversations. 'For the period of Ciano and
Bastianini all papers are missing. It appears that these were kept in a secret
collection, and have either been destroyed or taken away.' [c]

There was almost nothing of value on the period after the fall of Mussolini,
or on the Lisbon negotiations with the Allies after August 15, and only one

b. See the list compiled by Rosso in his note of the material removed in the Italian
Collection.
c. Some of this material was removed clandestinely to the Italian Legation in Lisbon.
See Bibliography in Appendix A.

secret telegram revealing that these messages did not pass through the Foreign Ministry.

On general points Stieve reported:

(1) *Of immediate propaganda value.* Very little, except on Italo-Roumanian relations. This would be worked up at once. A few interesting details regarding Spain and Portugal. Fairly full reports from Italian missions in Germany and German-occupied territories. Conversations with Japanese diplomats and in Turkey.

(2) *Historical.* One could reconstruct in detail Suvich's period of office.

(3) *Personal.* A few individual notes of interest.

Stieve then summarized the first impressions of his team. The Italian reports from Germany after the autumn of 1942 were 'extensively negative, mistrustful, and unfavourable'. There was no sign of any reproving action by the Duce. Alfieri's dispatches 'in this respect are unbelievable'. Throughout 1943 there was a daily increase of defeatism in the Italian Foreign Ministry. [6]

On October 1, 1943, Steengracht, the Undersecretary at the Foreign Office, minuted that the file of Hitler's letters to Mussolini had been found in a folder made up for the use of Guariglia. The last letter was dated May 19, 1943, and two letters are missing—March 11, 1938 and February 5, 1941. [7] Ribbentrop showed great personal interest in this file and gave orders to look for copies of Mussolini's letters to Hitler. [8] On October 6 a Foreign Ministry telegram was dispatched to Rahn asking him to find out from the Duce if he has copies of the two missing Hitler letters, and also to make a further search. [9] On October 11 Rahn's subordinate, Moellhausen, reported that such a search had proved fruitless. [10] On October 23 a further report from Rahn stated that the Duce did not know where the missing letters were. [11]

(c) *Detailed reports by Strohm on Italian Archives*

A more thorough survey of the material was now undertaken by Consul-General Strohm. It appears that he drafted 16 reports numbered in order. These were passed to Ribbentrop by Dr Hencke of his Private Office with covering minutes. The German records contain three of these minutes, based on Strohm's third, sixth, and fifteenth reports and dated October 18, October 21, and November 20 respectively. [12] There is no trace of Strohm's original reports.

The three surviving Hencke minutes are:

(a) October 18, 1943.

'Herewith is submitted the enclosed report No. 3, which has been drawn up by Consul-General Strohm. It is concerned with the efforts made by Turkey to build up a Balkan bloc in early this year and certain steps taken by Roumania in the same sense in August 1943.

'As to the content of the Italian archives submitted herewith, attention is drawn to the following:

(1) 'On the soundings made by Turkey in Budapest and Bucharest directly after the Adana Conference with a view to setting up an alleged anti-Bolshevik Balkan bloc, in which also Hungary should be included, we were already informed by the middle of March through communications from the Hungarian Government and from secret sources. On the basis of these reports Ambassador von Papen discussed the subject thoroughly on March 19 with the Turkish Foreign Minister, who attempted to play down the Turkish initiative. The matter was also raised with the Bulgarian Minister in Berlin.

(2) 'The assumption that the Italian Government did not discuss with us at the time of the Turkish initiative, is not borne out by our (own) archives. These show rather that Minister Baldoni transmitted to us on March 23 and April 8 extracts from the relevant reports of the Italian representatives in Bucharest and Ankara, and that the Italian Embassy in Budapest kept our Ministers there informed in detail on Hungarian-Italian talks on the Turkish démarche.

(3) 'On the conduct of the Roumanian Government in early 1943 and the rôle of the Italian Minister Bova Scoppa, we were already informed through the reports of the former Stefani representative in Bucharest, Trandafilo[d] ... These reports are fuller than the only fragmentary Italian archives. The extracts from these documents also confirm Mihai Antonescu's readiness to respond to Turkish prompting, although he expressed his conviction that this could not have been made without British agreement.

'We know anyway from secret sources that the Undersecretary of State, Bastianini, warned the Roumanians some weeks later against following up the Turkish proposal, since he regarded it as an intrigue inspired by England.

(4) 'From these Italian documents, Turkish motives are clear. The Italian Minister in Ankara compares two alternatives:

    (a) Turkey is pursuing the plan of building up a definitely defensive line within the sphere of her special interests in the event of an Axis withdrawal from the Balkans becoming necessary.

    (b) The Turkish initiative is merely one link in a series of British attempts to drive Hungary, Roumania and Bulgaria out of the Axis.

'Ambassador von Papen has expressed the view that the Hungarians and Roumanians had attributed an exaggerated importance to the more theoretical Turkish démarche. The Bulgarian diplomats have also a similar impression. It is not firmly established in our documentation how far England has in fact inspired in detail this action by Turkey.

'The British Ambassador in Ankara has told the Yugoslav emigré representative there that, a week before the Adana Conference he had given Turkey

d. Trandafilo was the correspondent of the Balkan official news agency Stefani, and an informant of the German legation.

information on British plans for the post-war organization of Europe and for the various federation projects. On the basis of this move it seems therefore that the planned Turkish initiative was discussed in general terms at the Adana Conference. In any event, only a few weeks ago the Turkish Foreign Minister told our Ambassador that the British had put forward at Adana the idea of a Balkan Federation. Anyway, the British did not this time openly support the amalgamation of the small states of Europe into groups of states, as Churchill's broadcast of March 21, 1943, shows.

'Whether Churchill agreed to the Turkish proposals in every detail is doubtful. For example, the inclusion of Hungary does not seem to correspond to British intentions. The reports of the Yugoslav and Serb (*sic*) emigré representatives give the impression that England was rather thinking of an extension to the various Balkan states of the agreement of January 15, 1942, of the Greek and Yugoslav Governments in exile. One can also probably assume that London was not quite in accord with Turkish activity, since rumours soon appeared in the press which only stressed the anti-Bolshevik side of the plan. It appears from our archives and from secret sources that the Turks had already dropped the subject by March 22, and had never officially taken it up again. The Turkish Foreign Minister told the Hungarian Minister in Ankara that the British Ambassador had asked him not to continue conversations. From the reports of the Yugoslav and Greek emigré representatives in Ankara one can see likewise that the English had put the brake on the Turks as from mid-March, as they had to take into account a foreseeable opposition from the Soviet Union.

(5) 'As to the Roumanian initiative in Sofia in August 1943, we were immediately informed by Minister President Filov. According to the latter's communication to us, this initiative went further than the Italian archives reveal. Apart from a co-operation of the Balkan states, it was proposed in the event of a German collapse to bring in British and American troops, so that they could protect the Balkan states against Russia. The only new point for us is that Mihai Antonescu informed Bova Scoppa of his successful move in Sofia, and explained already on August 21, 1943, that the political action of Roumania must seek its inspiration in that of Italy. It is also noteworthy that Bova Scoppa gained the impression from a talk with Mihai Antonescu that the latter looked to an intervention by Turkey in the Balkans precisely in order that this would hold up the dreaded Soviet advance.

'I cannot join in the view that Bova Scoppa's telegram of August 21[e] offers proof that the Roumanians were informed of the Italian armistice negotiations.

'It might be expedient to inform our Minister in Bucharest of the content of these extracts as they are of interest to him for the attitude of the

e. Not quoted.

Roumanian Government in recent months. A corresponding draft is attached.

'These Italian reports, set out in the first pages of the report, on Churchill's efforts of the Adana Conference to induce Turkey to prepare an anti-Bolshevik advance post in the Balkans, could be exploited to disturb Anglo-Soviet relations.[f] I would therefore suggest that these passages are transmitted to Ambassador von Papen with instructions to play them, without revealing their source and in so far as he sees no objection, to Soviet agents with the comment that such information as is already known as to Churchill's attempts to whip up Turkey against the Soviet Union receives further proof.'

(b)   October 21, 1943.

'The report No. 6 on the Italian archives drawn up by Consul-General Strohm is herewith submitted, together with an appendix belonging thereto. The collection of documents contains particularly interesting extracts from reports and minutes of conversations between Japanese and Italian diplomats and statesmen, above all in the summer of 1943.

'Attention is drawn to the following points contained in the Italian documents under review:

'The extracts show that Japanese and Italian diplomats have repeatedly referred to a joint or parallel influence on German policy. This joint action is above all based on the fact that they were only in effect interested in Germany's war against England and America, and judged Germany's struggle against Russia primarily from the standpoint that it could hinder or endanger a victory over England.

'It thus resulted that:

(1)   'Both powers wanted a strengthening of the German war effort on the Mediterranean front. As, for example, the Japanese Ambassador in Rome, Horikiri, explained in a conversation with the Italian Ambassador in Madrid on June 15, 1943, it was a grave error that the Germans would not regard the Mediterranean as the main military theatre. On the other hand, Bastianini assured the Japanese Ambassador on July 23 that Italy had never failed to stress in Berlin in every possible way the importance of the Mediterranean front.

(2)   'Both powers are interested in the conclusion of a separate peace between Germany and the Soviet Union, and seek to influence Germany in this sense. Already in a conversation on October 21, 1942, Oshima spoke to Alfieri of the possibility that Japan would formally guarantee such a separate peace. On April 22, 1943, Oshima informed Alfieri that he had sounded the German Foreign Minister on the possibility of peace negotiations with the

f. It is reasonable to believe that this 'evidence' was planted by the Turks on the Italians. The British records give a very different picture.

Soviet Union at a later stage, but that the German Foreign Minister had replied that the conditions proposed by Germany would not be acceptable to Stalin. On June 16, 1943, the Japanese Minister in Madrid told the Italian Minister there that Japan had already made attempts at mediation, which had failed because of Germany's refusal to consider the condition of handing back the occupied territories to the Soviet Union. Horikiri complained, in the above-mentioned conversation of June 15, of the alleged refusal by Germany to give up the annexation of the Ukraine and the Caucasus, and remarked that "not enough pressure had been brought to bear on Germany to move her to give up the occupied territories."

'This Japanese standpoint finds a certain parallel in the statements of Bastianini and the Duce shortly before the latter's fall. On July 23 Bastianini stated to the Japanese Minister that already several months ago the Duce had outlined to the Fuehrer and to the German Foreign Minister his views on the necessity of a political solution in the East. The Duce himself informed the Japanese Minister at noon on July 25 that he had decided in the course of the following week "to undertake an energetic démarche with the Fuehrer . . . with the intention of moving the Fuehrer to cease hostilities in the East and reach a settlement with Russia". Mussolini requested the Minister in a very pressing manner to inform the Japanese Minister President that "it was his earnest wish that Japan should support with all her strength such an approach to the Fuehrer".

'It should be mentioned in this connection that at the beginning of September the Japanese government, following a telegram from the Italian Minister in Tokyo of September 5, considered as unlikely the possibility of a separate peace between Germany and Russia in view of the increase in Soviet aspirations.

(3)   'As a result of this pressing desire for the conclusion of a separate German-Russian peace, there appear various expressions of regret as to German territorial demands on the Soviet Union. This regret takes the form of unfriendly criticism of the above-mentioned remarks of Minister Horikiri. Also in the minute drafted by Bastianini on the draft statements to the Japanese Minister on July 25 there is a note of criticism.

(4)   'There is also a parallelism in Japanese and Italian policy in seeking from Germany greater concessions towards the small states of Europe. Thus the Japanese Minister in Rome reports on June 8, 1943, that Oshima had recommended to the German Foreign Minister "a policy in favour of the small states". Horikiri welcomed the well-known speech of Bastianini to the (Italian) Senate on the problem of Europe, and expressed himself in critical terms of Germany because she had not, like Japan in the Far East "given back to the small states their political and economic independence". On the other side, Bastianini assured the Japanese Minister on July 23 that the Duce had already repeatedly drawn attention in Berlin to the "fruitful and intelli-

gent" organization by the Japanese of the New Order in the Far East.

(5) 'The extracts from the documents show that many Japanese diplomats regard German foreign policy with a certain reserve and criticism. In particular this applies to the former Minister in Rome, Horikiri. On the other hand, it is clear from the documents under review that Minister Oshima is regarded by his Japanese colleagues as an unconditional supporter of collaboration with the Reich. This is expressed by Horikiri in the remark: "Oshima is a soldier, and has completely fallen for the German military."

(6) 'Bastianini stated as late as July 23 that no other purpose existed in Rome other than "to resist in every way and by every means in our power, great or small". The Duce, however, two days later, said that, unless one arrived at the cessation of hostilities with the Soviet Union for which one was striving "the conditions under which Italy is fighting *her* war are such that in a short time it will be absolutely impossible for her to continue hostilities. She will therefore be compelled to examine a solution of a political character."

'It should of course be realized that this statement was meant to emphasize above all the urgency of the request to Japan to support the planned démarche to the Fuehrer.'

(c) November 20, 1943.

· 'I attach Consul-General Strohm's report No. 15 on the Italian documents, in which he has put together all the findings about Italy's conduct at the outbreak of the war and during the French campaign. Report No. 16, also attached, examines on the basis of the evidence in report No. 15 the Foreign Minister's question as to whether the Italian documents give any indications that perhaps "Mussolini's conduct towards us was at certain moments doubtful." In conclusion the following should be noted on the contents of the report:

(1) 'The documents we have for 1939 and 1940 are so fragmentary that no reasonably definite picture of Italy's policy can be formed from them.

(2) 'The reports confirm, as we knew already and as was also apparent from the documents captured in France, that England had since the beginning of 1938 taken immense pains to cultivate her relations with Italy. Through these she was not only pursuing the aim—increasingly apparent in the Italian records—of effecting through Italian action in Berlin some postponement and modification of Germany's political initiatives. she was also striving in the long run to detach Italy from her friendship with Germany and to preserve Italian neutrality in the event of war. Therefore, as we know from the French documents, England sought during the winter of 1938-9 and right up to summer 1939 to induce France to make concessions towards Italy's Mediterranean aspirations—naturally without success. Italy must have welcomed England's conduct, since first of all it brought about recognition of the conquest of Abyssinia, and then opened certain prospects of realizing her aspirations *vis-à-vis* France on a peaceful basis. That the Italian government in

return, so to speak, for English recognition of the Empire definitely promised in spring 1938 to exert constant influence in Berlin for "modifications" in England's favour, seems to me to be an inference which so far is not fully borne out by the available material. (That on several occasions the Italians let English confirmations of their "peace-promoting" activity pass uncontradicted, is understandable for reasons of propaganda.) At any rate the Italian documents show, as Consul-General Strohm also concludes, that in spite of all England's efforts, under the Duce's personal influence the Italian government put friendship with Germany more and more before relations with England, although these were welcome in themselves. This led, as early as the beginning of June 1939, to Mussolini's unambiguous question to the British Ambassador in Rome, whether considering England's isolationist policy "the Anglo-Italian agreement was still worth anything".

'After the outbreak of war England continued in markedly friendly language to try to hold Italy to her neutral course, and even at the beginning of September 1939 with a reference to Italy's efforts at mediation held the prospect of playing the rôle of European peace-bringer before the Duce's eyes. The documents give no evidence that the Italian Government was influenced in determining its policy by such enticements. Rather, at the turn of the year 1939–40, Mussolini refused to receive the former Dutch Minister President Coljin whom the Dutch Government sent to Rome to sound out possibilities of peace. He informed the Dutch Foreign Minister explicitly that he did not intend "to make any peace initiatives in the present circumstances". Finally, the British Government's attempts at the end of May 1940 to induce Italy to preserve her neutrality, by being willing to start immediate negotiations on the basis of English and French political concessions, were wrecked: already in the middle of May, as is apparent from the American White Paper "Peace and War", Mussolini had given Roosevelt clearly to understand that he had decided to enter the war on the side of Germany. We already know from public explanations given by the British Prime Minister that these last English efforts took in part the form of letters from Churchill to Mussolini. It is merely new that on May 26, under the pressure of the defeats in France, Halifax told the Italian Ambassador in London that he was definitely prepared in Italo-English negotiations "to take Italy's special connections with Germany into account, i.e. in the comprehensive framework of a lasting and just European settlement for which the Duce had worked ceaselessly and untiringly". This basic readiness for general peace negotiations was however qualified by the corollary "as soon as a favourable and decisive opportunity for this should arise". Finally, moreover, on May 30 Daladier suggested to the Duce "making a peace initiative through a universal settlement of European conditions on a new basis".

(3) 'Since the end of 1939 Roosevelt had played an increasingly large part in the attempts to keep Italy neutral. Already on January 6, 1940, the

American President had suggested common "effective action" by the United States, Italy and the Pope "for the restoration of peace in Europe" and had even expressed the desire for a personal meeting with the Duce in the course of 1940. The Americans obviously expected that Sumner Welles' tour of May 1940 would open the way for further efforts in Italy; it appears that the results of the North American Undersecretary of State's visit to Rome did not come up to these expectations. We already know from the American White Paper "Peace and War" all the details of the four messages by which Roosevelt sought in May 1940 to hold Mussolini back from intervening in the war, and the Duce's answers.

(4) 'The Italian documents confirm the impression that in the first month of the war Ciano and Italian diplomacy strove to complete Italian non-belligerence with a policy of fundamental neutrality, and to place Italy at the head of a "Neutral Bloc", through which Italy's position especially in the Balkans and Spain would be decisively strengthened. Berlin should be made to infer from this that such an attitude was also in Germany's interests, since a "Neutral Bloc led by Italy" would hinder England's policy of extending the war. It was obvious, however, as the attitude of the Italian Ambassador in Berlin, Attolico, shows, that this influential Italian diplomatic representative considered that she should adopt this policy even without Germany's approval. At the same time a closer mutual friendship with Japan was being considered which, according to the documents, appears partly attributable to initiatives made by the Japanese Government of the time, under the first impact of the German-Soviet Treaty.

'All these plans for an independent Italian neutral policy were however obviously very soon dropped again. In any case as early as October 6, 1939, Ciano had explicitly informed the Spanish Government that he had never said that Italy would make a declaration of neutrality. In the documents at our disposal there are no indications of a later return to such tendencies.

(5) 'Apart from the theme of Italian policy towards Germany and the Western Powers, the contents of the documents contain the following notable details:

(a) 'Already on February 21, 1938, Chamberlain explained to the Italian Ambassador, Grandi, that the British Government looked upon Austria as lost and had no intention of making proposals or suggestions to other states in relation to the Austrian situation.

(b) 'A Polish attempt to urge Italy through the Vatican to use her influence in Berlin was answered as early as May 2, 1939, by Ciano, with instructions to the Italian Ambassador in Warsaw to make it clear to Beck that in the event of a crisis Italy would "take her stand clearly at the side of Germany".

(c) 'From a Spanish minute delivered in Rome on August 30, 1939, it appears that at the end of August Bonnet implored General Franco to call for a 10-day "armistice" in which to continue negotiations, France and England being willing. Franco asked in the minute for Mussolini's opinion, since he "was in direct touch with the Fuehrer". How the Italian Government reacted to this suggestion is not clear from the documents; probably it was superseded by the well-known Italian initiatives.

(d) 'This sentence from Ambassador Bastianini's report of October 24, 1939, on his first impressions in England should be noted: "Halifax, Vansittart and Cadogan have made no secret of their preoccupation about the progress Communism might make during and after the war." '

There is no further reference to this study of these Italian documents in the microfilmed records of the German Foreign Office except, in a minute of March 21, 1944, the German War Office appear to have instituted a detailed study of documents relating to Badoglio's 'betrayal'. Field Marshal Jodl instructed Professor Major Schramm to undertake the research, and the latter asked to see the material held by the German Foreign Office, and Steengracht in the above minute recommended that he should have such access.[13]

The subsequent fate of these Italian archives is unknown. One version states that they were destroyed in an Allied bombardment of Berlin. If this is the case, the three memoranda drawn up by Dr Hencke of Ribbentrop's private office constitute the sole surviving evidence of their contents.

NOTES

PART ONE

Book I

1 : THE FOURTH PUNIC WAR

1 Italian Collection. Speech of the Duce to the Grand Council, February 4, 1939
2 Quoted in Pini e Susmel, *Mussolini: L'Uomo e L'Opera*, Vol. IV, p. 161
3 *Hitler's Table Talk*, p 592
4 *Ibid* p 614
5 Nuremberg Trial Documents (German edition) Vol XXVI, D.798, p 339
6 German Collection
7 Italian Collection. Mussolini to Hitler, May 30, 1939. (Also printed in Toscano, *Le Origini Diplomatiche del Patto D'Acciaio*, pp 362–5)
8 *Ibid* Telegram from the King to Mussolini, September 17, 1939
9 *Ibid* Memorandum by the Duce, March 31, 1940
10 *Ibid* Minutes of meeting of the Duce with the Chiefs of Staff, May 29, 1940
11 Italian Minutes of the Munich meeting June 18, 1940, in Carboni, *Più che il Dovere* (Second Edition, 1955), pp 95 ff
12 Italian Collection. Mussolini to Hitler, June 22, 1940
13 Carboni, *op cit*
14 *Ibid*
15 German Collection. Rintelen report, September 11, 1940
16 Rossi, *Mussolini e lo Stato Maggiore*, p 21
17 Graziani, *Processo I* (stenographic record), p 132
18 Italian Collection. Memorandum by General Ambrosio (undated, but probably drafted for the Feltre meeting July 19, 1943), 'The Politico-Military Conduct of the War by the Axis'
19 Printed in Graziani, *Africa Settentrionale* (1940–1), p 279
20 Messe, *La Guerra al Fronte Russo*, pp 177–8
21 Quoted in Rintelen, *Mussolini als Bundesgenosse*, p 21
22 Rintelen, *op cit* p 165
23 See Faldella, *L'Italia e La Seconda Guerra Mondiale*, p 428
24 Cavallero, *Comando Supremo*, p 251
25 e.g. 2,700 tons of stores unloaded at Benghazi on May 13. Cavallero, *op cit* p 256
26 Quoted in Cavallero, *op cit* pp 274–6
27 Kesselring, *Soldat Bis Zum Letzten Tag*, p 169
28 Italian Collection. Hitler to Mussolini, June 23, 1942. An abbreviated version in Cavallero, *op cit* pp 277–8

29 *Ibid* Mussolini to Hitler, July 22, 1942
30 *Ibid* Hitler to Mussolini, August 4, 1942
31 Cavallero, *op cit* p 282
32 *Ibid* p 283
33 Alfieri, '*Two Dictators Face to Face*' (French translation), pp 255–6 (August 5, 1942)
34 German Collection. Hitler-Vidussoni conversation, October 7, 1942
35 Cavallero, *op cit* p 321
36 Official Italian War History. *Seconda Controffensiva Italo-tedesca in Africa Settentrionale*, p 388. Quoted in Faldella, *op cit* p 459
37 Italian Collection. Hitler to Mussolini, August 4, 1942
38 German Collection. Rintelen report, March 26, 1942
39 *Ibid* Rintelen report, February 13, 1942
40 Italian Collection. Alfieri to Ciano, September 14, 1942
41 *Ibid* Alfieri to D'Ajeta, September 30, 1942

2: TWENTY YEARS AFTER

1 Italian Collection. Duce memorandum, July 22, 1942
2 Quoted in Dante Germino, *The Italian Fascist Party in Power*, p 13. The author is indebted to this recent American study for background information in this chapter
3 *Ibid* p 85
4 Pini e Susmel, *op cit* Vol. IV, p 169
5 German Collection. Anonymous Italian report dated February 1943
6 Bottai, *Vent' Anni e Un Giorno,* p 96
7 Gorla. *L'Italia nella Seconda Guerra Mondiale*, pp 103–4
8 Italian Collection. Hitler to Mussolini, October 21, 1942
9 Hitler e Mussolini, *Lettere e Documenti*, p 125. November 1, 1942
10 Ciano, *Diary* pp 515–6
11 *Ibid*

3: THE PROBLEM OF THE SUCCESSION

1 Ciano, *op cit* p 504
2 Bottai, *op cit* p 231
3 See the biographical articles on Ciano by Susmel published in 'Tempo' October 1960–January 1961
4 German Collection. Dollmann to Wolff, February 16, 1942
5 Puntoni, *Parla Vittorio Emmanuele III*, p 31
6 Ciano, *op cit* p 226
7 *Ibid* p 242
8 Grandi, Dino Grandi Racconta p 36
9 Ciano, *op cit* pp 328
10 Grandi, *op cit* p 37
11 Bottai, *op cit* p 6
12 *Ibid* p 233
13 Puntoni, *op cit* p 40
14 *Hitler's Table Talk*, p 594
15 Puntoni, *op cit* p 34
16 *Ibid* p 96

17 Italian Collection. Police reports. September 1939
18 *Ibid* Farinacci to Mussolini, November 9, 1940
19 Italian Collection. Personal letter of Alfieri to D'Ajeta, Ciano's private secretary, September 30, 1942
20 Ciano, *op cit* p 510
21 German Collection. Dollmann to Wolff, November 1, 1942

4 : 'TORCH'

1 German Collection. Rome telegram, October 17, 1942
2 Italian Collection
3 German Collection. Rome telegram, October 23, 1942
4 *Ibid* Goering-Duce conversation. Schmidt minute and two Rome telegrams (Bismarck) October 23, 1942
5 Rintelen, *op cit* p 177
6 Cavallero, *op cit* p 368
7 *Ibid* p 371
8 German Collection. Rome telegram, November 7, 1942
9 Rintelen, *op cit* p 180
10 Cavallero, *op cit* pp 371–2
11 German Collection. Rome telegram, November 8, 1942
12 Cavallero, *op cit* p 377
13 Ciano, *op cit* p 521
14 *Ibid*
15 German Collection. Hitler-Ciano conversation, November 9, 1942
16 Ciano, *op cit* pp. 521–2
17 German Collection. Hitler-Ciano conversation, November 10, 1942
18 For details see Mallet, *Pierre Laval* II, p 108 and footnotes
19 Ciano, *op cit* p 522
20 German Collection. Hitler-Ciano-Laval conversation. November 10, 1942. Afternoon
21 Ciano, *op cit* pp 522–3
22 Cavallero, *op cit* p 384
23 *Ibid* p 387
24 Ciano, *op cit* p 523

5 : THE AXIS AND NORTH AFRICA

1 German Collection. Mackensen memorandum, November 13, 1942
2 *Ibid* Weiszaecker minute, November 18, 1942
3 *Ibid* Rome telegram, November 13, 1942
4 Italian Collection. Hitler to Mussolini, November 26, 1942
5 Hitler e Mussolini, *op cit* pp 120–1
6 German Collection. Madrid telegram, November 16, 1942
7 *Ibid* Note for German Foreign Minister, December 3, 1942
8 *Ibid* Rintelen telegram, November 14, 1942
9 Ciano, *op cit* pp 533–4
10 Rommel, *The Rommel Papers*, p 349
11 Italian Collection. Hitler to Mussolini, November 20, 1942
12 Rommel, *op cit* pp 361–2

13 *Ibid* pp 365–6
14 Ciano, *op cit* p 529
15 Cavallero, *op cit* p 403
16 *Ibid* pp 404–5
17 *Ibid* p 406
18 Rommel, *op cit* p 368
19 Gilbert, *Hitler Directs His War*, p 13
20 Rommel, *op cit* p 367
21 German Collection. Dollmann to Himmler, December 16, 1942
22 *Ibid* Schmidt minute. Italo-German Staff meeting, December 5, 1942
23 Ciano, *op cit* p 531
24 Rommel, *op cit* p 366
25 Ciano, *op cit* p 532
26 Rommel, *op cit* pp 368–9

6 : 'THE BERESINA WIND'

1 German Collection. Duce-Goering conversation, October 23, 1942
2 *Ibid* Rome telegram, November 7, 1942
3 Ribbentrop *Memoirs*, pp 168–9. See a slightly different version in the Nuremberg Trial Documents, Supplementary Volume B, p 1204
4 Bottai, *op cit* p 239
5 Ciano, *op cit* p 533
6 *Ibid* p 535
7 Italian Collection. Unsigned and undated note headed 'Policy 1943'.
8 Gilbert, *op cit* pp 4–5
9 *Ibid* p 12
10 German Collection. Schmidt minute
11 *Ibid*
12 Italian Collection. Ciano minute
13 German Collection. Schmidt minute `
14 *Ibid*
15 Ciano, *op cit* p 536
16 Simoni, *Berlino Ambasciata d'Italia* p 299
17 Italian Collection. Ciano minute
18 German Collection. Schmidt minute
19 Italian Collection. Ciano minute
20 Ciano, *op cit* p 537
21 Italian Collection. 'Special Military Questions raised at the Talks at German Headquarters, December 18 and 19, 1942'
22 Italian Collection
23 Ciano, *op cit* p 537

7 : THE WINTER CRISIS

1 Puntoni, *op cit* pp 193–4
2 *Ibid* p 104
3 See Dollmann's portrait in his book *Roma Nazista* (Italian translation) pp 71–5
4 Leto, *OVRA* pp 231 ff
5 Ciano, *op cit* p 392

6 Senise, *Quando Ero Capo della Polizia*, pp 51–3
7 *Ibid* p 238
8 Puntoni, *op cit* p 109
9 Italian Collection. Militia report dated March 6, 1943
10 Puntoni, *op cit* p 107
11 Vailati, *Badoglio Risponde*, p 76
12 Caviglia, *Diario, 1925–42*, p 341
13 Mussolini, *Memoirs op cit* p 26
14 German Collection. Lisbon telegram, June 7, 1942
15 Italian Collection. Public Security report, December 2, 1942
16 German Collection. German War Office minute, November 1942
17 Italian Collection. Farinacci to Mussolini, November 19, 1942
18 *Ibid* Farinacci to Mussolini, January 20, 1932
19 *Ibid* Farinacci to Mussolini, November 9, 1940
20 *Ibid* Farinacci to Mussolini, January 22, 1933
21 Galbiati, *Il 25 Luglio e la MVSN*, p. 177. Some time in December 1942
22 Caviglia, *op cit* p 388
23 Puntoni, *op cit* p 98
24 Galbiati, *op cit* pp 176–7
25 Puntoni, *op cit* p 107
26 Castellano, *Come Firmai l'Armistizio di Cassibile*, p 25
27 Puntoni, *op cit* p 103
28 Ciano, *op cit* p 527
29 Puntoni, *op cit* p 111
30 Ciano, *op cit* p 537
31 Carboni, *op cit* p 176
32 Puntoni, *op cit* pp 30–1
33 *Ibid* p 105
34 Ciano, *op cit* p 526
35 German Collection. Canaris minute, November 7, 1942
36 *Ibid* Madrid telegram, November 9, 1942
37 *Ibid* Weizsaecker telegram to Rome, December 3, 1942
38 *Ibid* Mackensen telegram, December 4, 1942
39 *Ibid* Bismarck telegram, December 19, 1942, quoting a report dated December 12 and presumably from Buffarini
40 *Ibid* Dollmann telegram, December 16, 1942

8 : The Political Recovery of The Duce

1 Bottai, *op cit* p 233
2 *Ibid*
3 *Ibid* p 234
4 Gorla, *op cit* pp 378 ff
5 Bottai, *op cit* p 235
6 Gorla, *op cit* p 380
7 Bottai, *op cit* p 235
8 Gorla, *op cit* p 381
9 Pini e Susmel, *op cit* IV, p 196
10 Bottai, *op cit* pp 237–8
11 G. Pini, *Filo Diretto con Palazzo Venezia*, p 223

12 German Collection. Rome telegram, December 21, 1942
13 *Ibid* German War Office Archives. Rome telegram (Naval Attaché) December 14, 1942
14 Italian Collection. 'Note for the Duce' from Vidussoni, December 5, 1942
15 German Collection. Himmler Files. Report from Dr Ehrlich, Rome representative of the German National Socialist Party, to gauleiter Bohle and forwarded by the latter to Himmler with covering note dated January 11, 1943
16 Italian Collection and *Opera Omnia op cit* XXXI, pp 34 *et seq*

9 : 'THE EXPULSION OF THE DISCONTENTED'

1 Pozzi, *Come li ho visto Io*, pp 122–8. See also Ciano, *op cit* p 544
2 Gorla, *op cit* p 388
3 Ciano, *op cit* p 544, January 8, 1943
4 Pini e Susmel, *op cit* IV, p 205
5 Italian Collection. Report to Duce from Party Headquarters, January 11, 1943
6 Ciano, *op cit* p 546, January 15, 1943
7 German Collection. Mackensen telegram, January 16, 1943
8 Bottai, *op cit* pp 246–7. See also Ciano, *op cit* p 530, December 1, 1942. The liaison officer was Scamacca, an Italian Foreign Office official.
9 See the long and interesting letter from Bova Scoppa to Ciano dated August 6, 1941, in the former's book *'Colloqui con Due Dittatori'*, pp 42 ff
10 This report is dated January 15. A copy exists in the Italian Collection of Ciano's papers, and it is also printed in Bova Scoppa, *op cit* pp 72–5. The latter's text differs from the original in several passages, and the summarized translation here is based on the former.
11 Ciano, *op cit* p 548, January 20, 1943
12 *Ibid* p 549
13 Italian Collection. Anfuso to Ciano, January 25, 1943
14 Bova Scoppa, *op cit* p 80
15 Puntoni, *op cit* pp 115–6, January 22–3, 1943
16 Bottai, *op cit* p 250, January 27, 1947
17 Caviglia, *op cit* p 388, January 26, 1943
18 Gorla, *op cit* pp 389 ff. See further details of this meeting in Bottai, *op cit* p 248
19 Canevari, *La Fine del Maresciallo Cavallero*, p 17
20 Ciano, *op cit* p 548. On January 23, the Italian Foreign Office liaison officer at the Italian High Command reported that, among his colleagues on the General Staff 'a final decision on Cavallero's dismissal was awaited'. (Italian Collection, Scamacca to Ciano.)
21 Italian Collection. Scamacca to Ciano, January 25, 1943
22 German Collection
23 Ciano, *op cit* p 554
24 German Collection. Rome telegram (Bismarck) January 31, 1943
25 Interviews in the newspapers *Il Corriere della Sera* March 11, 1955, and *Unità* October 22, 1953. For a slightly different version of this conversation see Castellano, *op cit* pp 22–7. See also Jo di Benigno, *Occasioni Mancate*, p 37
26 Ciano, *op cit* p 554
27 *Ibid* p 555
28 Italian Collection. Ciano to the Duce, February 7, 1943
29 Bastianini, *Uomini, Cose, Fatti*, p 79

30 Gorla, *op cit* p 397
31 Puntoni, *op cit* p 118, February 6, 1943
32 German Collection. Himmler Papers. February 16, 1943
33 Bottai, *op cit* p 253
34 German Collection. Mackensen telegram to Ribbentrop, February 5, 1943
35 *Ibid* Mackensen telegram 'For the Foreign Minister only' February 8, 1943
36 Hitler. Table Talk, *op cit* p 186. January 6–7, 1942
37 German Collection. Political Report of Mackensen, February 10, 1943, 'Reconstruction of the Italian Cabinet'
38 *Ibid* Press Section, German Foreign Office, February 11, 1943. 'As a draft for the Foreign Minister'

Book II

1 : THE MILITARY SCENE

1 Italian Collection. Meeting of the Italian Chiefs of Staff with the Duce, January 28, 1943. Also printed in Favagrossa *Perchè perdemmo la Guerra* pp 278 ff, but dated January 29
2 German Collection. War Office Archives. Rintelen report, November 18, 1942
3 Italian Collection. Army Programme for 1943, January 28, 1943
4 *Ibid* Duce-Kesselring-Ambrosio conversation, February 13, 1943
5 *Ibid* Ambrosio diary, February 7, 1943
6 Rintelen, *op cit* p 191. Ambrosio's first audience with the King as the new Chief of the General Staff was on February 2. See Puntoni, *op cit* p 117
7 Italian Collection. Ambrosio-Riccardi meeting, February 4, 1943
8 *Ibid* Ambrosio-Cini meeting, February 18, 1943
9 *Ibid* Duce-Kesselring-Ambrosio meeting, February 5, 1943.
10 *Ibid* Mussolini to Hitler, February 11, 1943
11 Rommel, *op cit* p 416
12 *Ibid* p 417
13 Italian Collection. Memorandum for the Duce, February 17, 1943, and 'Evaluation of the General Military Position by the Italian High Command' February 21, 1943. The text of this document also exists in German, and one can assume that a copy was passed to the German military representative in Rome.
14 Italian Collection. Duce-Kesselring-Ambrosio meeting, February 13, 1943

2 : THE DIPLOMATIC FRONT

1 Bastianini, *op cit* pp 80–1
2 *Ibid* p 83
3 German Collection. 'Memorandum on the possibilities of the future implementation of policy towards Spain.' January 20, 1943 (Hoffmann Memorandum)
4 *Ibid* Ribbentrop telegram to Madrid, January 25, 1943

5 *Ibid* Madrid telegram, January 24, 1943
6 *Ibid* War Diary of the German General Staff
7 Italian Collection. Duce-Kesselring-Ambrosio meeting. February 13, 1943
8 German Collection. Hitler-Arikan conversation. August 14, 1942
9 *Ibid*
10 *Ibid* Papen political report, November 20, 1942
11 *Ibid* Bismarck telegram, December 20, 1942
12 *Ibid* German Foreign Office memorandum on Jodl's report of conversation between the Fuehrer and the Bulgarian War Minister January 6. 1943
13 *Ibid* January 7, 1943
14 *Ibid* Papen telegram, February 2, 1943
15 *Ibid* Papen political report on the Adana Conference. February 7, 1943
16 *Ibid* Ribbentrop to Papen. February 3, 1943
17 *Ibid* Ribbentrop to Papen. February 6, 1943
18 *Ibid* Papen telegram, February 6, 1943
19 *Ibid* Papen telegram, February 8, 1943
20 *Ibid* Hitler-Antonescu conversation. January 10, 1943
21 *Ibid* Ribbentrop—conversation with the two Antonescus. January 11, 1943

3: RIBBENTROP IN ROME

1 German Collection. Ribbentrop-Alfieri conversation, February 21, 1943
2 *Ibid* Ribbentrop-Duce conversation, February 25, 1943
3 Bastianini, *op cit* p 272
4 German Collection. Ribbentrop-Duce conversation, February 26, 1943
5 *Ibid* Ribbentrop-Alfieri conversation, February 28, 1943
6 Italian Collection. Anfuso-Ribbentrop conversation, November 30, 1944. Anfuso was at that time Italian Ambassador in Berlin
7 Bastianini, *op cit* p 85
8 German Collection. Ribbentrop-Oshima conversation, March 6, 1943
9 Puntoni, *op cit* pp 121–2

4: SPRING TENSIONS: RUSSIA AND TUNISIA

1 Puntoni, *op cit* pp 122–3, March 1, 1943
2 Italian Collection. Ambrosio 'Note for the Duce', March 1, 1943
3 *Ibid* Report of the Italian Consul-General in Odessa
4 *Ibid* Minute of the Italian Ministry of Popular Culture to the Italian Embassy, Berlin. April 17, 1943
5 *Ibid* Report of the Italian Consul-General in Innsbruck, February 22, 1943
6 *Ibid* April 7, 1943
7 *Ibid* Bastianini to Alfieri, March 17, 1943
8 German Collection. Ribbentrop-Alfieri conversation, March 8, 1943
9 *Ibid* Steengracht minute, March 17, 1943
10 Italian Collection. Duce-Kesselring meeting, March 1, 1943
11 Puntoni, *op cit* p 125 March 8, 1943
12 Dollmann, *op cit* pp 132–3
13 Italian Collection. Ministerial conference, March 10, 1943
14 Rommel, *op cit* p 418
15 Italian Collection. Duce-Rommel meeting, March 9, 1943
16 Rommel, *op cit* p 419
17 *Ibid*

18 Hitler e Mussolini, *op cit* pp 146–7
19 German Collection. Hitler-Horthy meeting, April 16, 1943
20 Italian Collection. Duce-Kesselring meeting, March 13, 1943
21 Fuehrer Conferences on Naval Affairs 1943, *op cit* pp 13–15, March 14, 1943
22 Hitler e Mussolini, *op cit* pp 146–51
23 Italian Collection. Duce-Doenitz meeting, March 15, 1943
24 Hitler e Mussolini, *op cit* pp 151–4

5: THE HOME FRONT

1 Italian Collection. National Fascist Party. Report by Angelo Caruso, February 16, 1943
2 *Ibid* Fascist Party office. Memorandum for Duce
3 See, for example, Leto, *op cit* p 245
4 Massola, *Marzo 1943. Ore dieci* pp 50–1
5 Vaccarino, *op cit* pp 20 ff
6 Senise, *op cit* pp 171 ff
7 Vaccarino, *Aspetti della Resistenza in Piemonte*, p 28
8 *Ibid* pp 31–2
9 Deposition of Cianetti. In Cersosimo '*Dall Istruttoria alla Fucilazione*' p 97
10 Italian Collection. Farinacci to Mussolini, April 1, 1943
11 Bottai, *op cit* p 255
12 German Collection. Mackensen telegram. March 12, 1943
13 Hagen, *Die Geheime Front*, p 392

6: THE ROYAL SECRET

1 Ambrosio interview in *Il Corriere della Sera*, March 11, 1955
2 Puntoni, *op cit* p 121
3 Caviglia, *op cit* pp 396–7
4 Puntoni, *op cit* p 119
5 Mussolini, *Memoirs*, pp 141–2
6 Caviglia, *op cit* p 385
7 Cassinelli, *op cit* pp 17–19
8 German Collection. Anonymous report to Mackensen. Undated
9 Cassinelli, *op cit* p 16
10 Puntoni, *op cit* p 125
11 Caviglia, *op cit* p 395
12 Puntoni, *op cit* pp 125–6
13 For the following see Bonomi, *Diario di un Anno*, passim
14 *Ibid* p xxv
15 *Ibid* p. xxviii
16 For details see Catalano, *Storia del CLNA* pp 18–19
17 Bonomi, *op cit* p xxxvii
18 Puntoni, *op cit* p 126

7: THE AXIS AND THE SHADOW OF STALINGRAD

1 Bastianini to the author
2 Italian Collection. Babuscio Rizzo to Bastianini, March 1, 1943
3 Bastianini, *op cit* p 108

4 Simoni, *op cit* pp 324–5
5 Hitler e Mussolini, *op cit* pp 151–4
6 German Collection. Rome telegram, March 31, 1943
7 *Ibid* Papen telegram, March 9, 1943
8 *Ibid* Papen memorandum, February 6, 1943
9 *Ibid* Papen telegram, February 8, 1943
10 *Ibid* Mackensen telegram, February 17, 1943
11 *Ibid* Weizsaecker memorandum, March 3, 1943
12 *Ibid* German Foreign Office 'Notes for the visit of King Boris to Berlin', March 29, 1943
13 *Ibid* Ribbentrop to Papen, March 12, 1943, repeating Jagow's telegram from Budapest of the previous day
14 *Ibid* Papen to Ribbentrop, March 19, 1943
15 *Ibid* Budapest telegram, March 29, 1943
16 Italian Collection. Anfuso telegram, April 7, 1943
17 For a detailed study of Kallay's visit to Rome, see C. A. Macartney *October 15. A History of Modern Hungary*, Vol II pp 147 ff
18 Kallay, *Memoirs* (English translation by C. A. Macartney) pp 144 ff

8: The Salzburg Meeting

1 Dollmann, *op cit* p 144
2 April 29–30, 1942. The Italian record of this meeting is in Hitler e Mussolini, *op cit* pp 119 ff. The German minutes are published in English translalation in the Department of State Bulletin July 14, 1946, pp 57–63
3 Pozzi, *op cit* p 139
4 Bastianini, *op cit* p 92
5 Rintelen, *op cit* pp 192–3
6 Dollmann, *op cit* pp 145 ff
7 German Collection. Ribbentrop-Bastianini meeting, April 8, 1943
8 Bastianini, *op cit* p 95
9 *Ibid* pp 96–7
10 Italian Collection. Notes by Ambrosio
11 German Collection. Confidential Report, April 19, 1943 'From an informant in Oshima's closest entourage'
12 German Collection. Minute to Ribbentrop on Strohm's report No. 6 on the captured Italian Foreign Office Archives (dated October 21, 1943). For an account of these papers see Appendix B to this volume.
13 Italian Collection. Military Intelligence report, April (the day is illegible) 1943
14 Bastianini, *op cit* p 96
15 *Ibid* p 97
16 *Ibid* pp 98–9
17 German Collection. Mackensen memorandum, April 9, 1943
18 Italian Collection. 'Memorandum on the Klessheim Talks' dated April 12, 1943. 'General Conduct of the War, Impressions derived from the various discussions April 7–10, 1943'. These appear to be Ambrosio's own notes
19 German Collection. Ribbentrop-Bastianini talk, April 9, 1943
20 Italian Collection. Notes by Ambrosio on the Klessheim talks (see 17 above)
21 German Collection. Steengracht minute, March 17, 1943
22 Rintelen, *op cit* p 192

23 German Collection. Ribbentrop-Bastianini talk, April 10, 1943
24 Italian Collection. 'Klessheim talks, April 7–10. Subjects to be raised at the conference in question'
25 Dollman, *op cit* p 116
26 *Ibid* p 148
27 Rintelen, *op cit* p 193
28 Gilbert, *op cit* p 37. Hitler Military Conference, May 20, 1943
29 Dollmann, *op cit* p 151
30 Pozzi, *op cit* pp 147–8
31 Bastianini, *op cit* p 100
32 Simoni, *op cit* p 331
33 *Ibid*
34 Pozzi, *op cit* p 139
35 Goebbels, *op cit* pp 274–5, May 7, 1943

Book III

1 : THE END IN AFRICA

1 Puntoni, *op cit* pp 128–9. April 12 and 16, 1943
2 Italian Collection. Duce-Kesselring meeting, April 12, 1943
3 Puntoni, *op cit* p 129
4 German Collection. Mackensen telegram, April 19, 1943
5 Hitler e Mussolini, *op cit* p 154
6 *Ibid* p 155
7 Simoni, *op cit* p 334
8 Italian Collection. Foreign Office minute, May 2, 1943
9 *Ibid* Duce-Kesselring meeting, May 4–5, 1943
10 German Collection. War Office Archives. War Diary of German Army Staff, July 25, 1943
11 Rintelen report. May 5, 1943
12 Fuehrer Conferences on Naval Affairs 1943, *op cit* pp 22 ff, for Doenitz's Rome visit
13 Italian Collection. Duce-Doenitz meeting, May 13, 1943
14 Fuehrer Conferences on Naval Affairs 1943, *op cit* p 32
15 *Ibid* p 38
16 Italian Collection. Duce-Doenitz-Kesselring meeting, May 13, 1943
17 Fuehrer Conferences on Naval Affairs 1943, *op cit* p 39
18 German Collection. War Office Archives
19 *Ibid* War Diary of German General Staff. Entry for July 25, 1943. There is as yet no trace of the Survey
20 *Ibid* War Office Archives

2 : DIPLOMATIC INTERLUDE

1 German Collection. Hitler-Antonescu conversation, April 12, 1943
2 *Ibid* Hitler-Horthy conversation, April 16/17, 1943
3 *Ibid* Ribbentrop to Jagow, April 14, 1943

4 *Ibid* Schmidt report, April 20, 1943
5 *Ibid* Ribbentrop to Mackensen, April 22, 1943
6 *Ibid* Mackensen to Ribbentrop, April 23, 1943
7 Goebbels, *op cit* p 265, April 23, 1943
8 German Collection. Rome telegram, April 22, 1943
9 *Ibid* Schmidt minute on his interview with the Duce, April 20, 1943
10 *Ibid* Rome telegram May 1, 1943. Extract of report of the Italian Minister in Madrid handed to Mackensen by the Italian Foreign Office
11 *Ibid* Madrid telegrams, May 5, 7, and 10, 1943
12 *Ibid* Ribbentrop-Oshima conversation, May 19, 1943
13 Bastianini, *op cit* p 160
14 German Collection. Meeting between Ribbentrop and Bastianini, April 29, 1943. Alfieri and Mackensen were also present
15 *Ibid* Ribbentrop-Laval meeting, April 29, 1943
16 Guérard, *Criminel de Paix*, p 117
17 Bastianini, *op cit* pp 290–1
18 De Brinon, *Mémoires*, p 164
19 Simoni, *op cit* p 333
20 German Collection. Rome telegram, May 18, 1943
21 Simoni, *op cit* pp 335 ff
22 German Collection, Rome telegram, May 19, 1943
23 Bastianini. Speech in the Senate. Summary in the newspaper *La Stampa*, May 20, 1943
24 Gilbert, *op cit* p 35

3 : THE ITALIAN 'POLITICAL DESIGN'

1 Italian Collection. Bova Scoppa to Bastianini, May 12, 1943. This is the complete text. See also Bova Scoppa, *op cit* pp 96 ff
2 *Ibid* Bova Scoppa to Bastianini, May 14, 1943. Also partly in Bova Scoppa, *op cit* pp 90 ff but under the date of May 7
3 Tamaro *Due Anni di Storia* I, pp 66–8, prints the minute of Bastianini to the Duce and the memorandum of Bova Scoppa. (See also the latter's book, *op cit* pp 102 ff.) The dispatch of Anfuso is to be found only in the Italian Collection.
4 Bastianini, *op cit* p 113
5 Bova Scoppa, *op cit* p 110
6 German Collection. Mackensen to Ribbentrop, June 21, 1943
7 Bova Scoppa, *op cit* pp 114–5
8 Bastianini, *op cit* p 324
9 German Collection. Mackensen telegram 'For Minister Only', July 4, 1943
10 *Ibid* Mackensen telegram, March 26, 1943

4 : THE 'LAST WAVE' OF THE FASCIST PARTY

1 Senise, *op cit* pp 176–7
2 Italian Collection. Speech of the Duce to the Party Directorate April 17, 1943
3 Much of this information on Scorza's career is contained in Mackensen's two telegrams of April 20 and 23, 1943, in the German Collection.
4 Italian Collection. Police Report
5 *Ibid* Text by the official Stefani news agency

6 *Ibid* Police Report, May 11, 1943
7 German Collection. Dollmann to Himmler, May 9, 1945
8 Italian Collection. Police Report
9 *Ibid* Report by Scorza to the Duce, June 7, 1943
10 *Ibid* Police Report, June 12, 1943
11 Cucco, *Non Volevamo Perdere,* pp 84–5
12 Mussolini, *Memoirs,* p 32
13 Italian Collection. Scorza report to the Duce, June 15, 1943
14 Pellicano. Articles on the Grand Council published in the review *Elefante* in October 1949, No. 5
15 Bottai, *op cit* p 263
16 Pellicano, *op cit* Article 5
17 Italian Collection. Scorza letter to the Duce, June 23, 1943
18 See a summary of the text in Pini e Susmel, *op cit* IV, pp 233–4
19 German Collection. Rome telegram, April 14, 1943
20 *Ibid* Ribbentrop telegram, May 2, 1943
21 Caviglia, *op cit* p 408
22 *Ibid* p 379
23 German Collection. Rome telegram, June 20, 1943

5: Royal Hesitations

1 Puntoni, *op cit* p 132
2 Bonomi, *op cit* pp 3–8
3 Puntoni, *op cit* p 133, June 1–3, 1943. Puntoni does not mention Bonomi's audience
4 Grandi Interview in *Il Corriere della Sera,* February 9, 1955
5 Soleri, *op cit* pp 231–2
6 Puntoni, *op cit* p 133
7 Soleri, *op cit* p 237
8 Bonomi, *op cit* pp 15 ff
9 Memorandum by Badoglio after a private conversation with Ambrosio, at the beginning of July 1943. Vailati, *op cit*
10 Puntoni, *op cit* p 137
11 Benigno, *Occasioni Mancate* p 62
12 Castellano, *op cit* p 45
13 *Ibid* p 52
14 Senise, *op cit* pp 191–2
15 Italian Collection. 'Personal Note' on Senise's activities compiled for the Duce's Secretariat. September 14, 1943

6: Operation 'Mincemeat'

1 German Collection. Madrid telegram. May 12, 1943. 21.20 hours
2 *Ibid* May 12, 1943. 22.30 hours
3 See Montagu. *The Man who never was, passim*
4 German Collection. Madrid telegram. May 19, 1943
5 *Ibid* War Office Archives. May 14, 1943
6 Italian Collection. Ambrosio-Rintelen meeting. May 18, 1943
7 Rintelen, *op cit* p 202

8 Italian Collection. Hitler to Mussolini. May 19, 1943. Hitherto unpublished
9 *Ibid* Duce-Kesselring meeting. May 20, 1943
10 German Collection. Rome telegram. 'For German Foreign Minister personal.' May 20, 1943
11 Hitler e Mussolini, *op cit* p 156

7: THE MILITARY CRISIS OF THE AXIS

1 German Collection. Rome telegram, May 21, 1943
2 Gilbert, *op cit* pp 29–38, May 20, 1943
3 German Collection. Schmidt minute, April 20, 1943
4 *Ibid* Rome telegram, June 11, 1943
5 *Ibid* War Office Archives. War Diary of the German General Staff, July 25, 1943
6 *Ibid* War Office Archives. Report by Colonel Berger, June 23, 1943
7 *Ibid* Steengracht minute, June 3, 1943
8 *Ibid* Steengracht minute, May 26, 1943
9 Simoni, *op cit* p 343, May 30, 1943
10 German Collection. War Office Archives. Rintelen report, May 26, 1943
11 *Ibid.* War Office Archives. Staff memorandum, June 4, 1943
12 *Ibid* Himmler papers. Dollmann to Himmler, May 9, 1943
13 *Ibid* Rome telegram, May 22, 1943
14 *Ibid* War Office Archives. Rintelen Report, June 19, 1943
15 *Ibid* Rome telegram, June 1, 1943
16 Rintelen, *op cit* p 206
17 Simoni, *op cit* p 346–7
18 German Collection. War Office Archives

Book IV

1: SICILY: 'THE WATER'S EDGE'

1 German Collection. Schellenberg to German Foreign Office, June 24, 1943
2 Italian Collection. Military Intelligence report, July 9, 1943
3 Simoni, *op cit* p 358
4 German Collection. War Office Archives. Rintelen report, July 19, 1943
5 Extracts from the diary of an Italian Staff Officer at the Ministry of War quoted by Tamaro, *op cit* I p 186
6 Alfieri, *op cit* pp 298–9
7 Simoni, *op cit* pp 359–60
8 German Collection. Rome telegram, July 13, 1943
9 Italian Collection. Duce-Kesselring-Ambrosio meeting July 13, 1943
10 Tamaro, *op cit* I p 190
11 Fuehrer Directives, 1942–5 p 83
12 Italian Collection. Duce-Kesselring-Ambrosio meeting July 15, 1943. This is the last document in the series
13 German Collection. Mackensen telegram, July 15, 1943
14 Tamaro, *op cit* I p 186

15 German Collection. Report by Jodl July 15, 1943, and summarized in the War Diary of the German General Staff
16 Fuehrer Conferences on Naval Affairs 1943, *op cit* pp 59–62
17 Alfieri, *op cit* pp 300–1
18 Simoni, *op cit* pp 365–6
19 Rommel, *op cit* p 430

2 : THE ROMAN SCENE

1 German Collection. Rome telegram, June 1, 1943
2 Galbiati, *op cit* pp 192 ff
3 Bottai, *op cit* pp 269–70
4 *Ibid* pp 272–4
5 German Collection. Ribbentrop to Mackensen, July 15, 1943
6 Galbiati, *op cit* pp 214 ff
7 Bottai, *op cit* p 276
8 *Ibid* pp 281 ff
9 Farinacci deposition in Cersosimo, *op cit* p 5
10 Bottai, *op cit* p 282
11 *Ibid* p 287
12 Mussolini *Memoirs, op cit* p 49
13 Hagen, *op cit* p 391
14 German Collection. Dollmann to Mackensen, July 16 and 17, 1943
15 Italian Collection. Ciano to the Duce, July 17, 1943
16 Bastianini, *op cit* p 115
17 German Collection. German Legation to the Vatican to Berlin, April 14, 1943
18 *Ibid* Berne telegram, May 15, 1943
19 Printed in Tamaro, *op cit* I, pp 70 ff
20 Bastianini, *op cit* p 117
21 Simoni, *op cit* pp 362–3
22 German Collection. Dollmann to Mackensen, July 17, 1943
23 Bonomi, *op cit* pp 17 ff
24 Bonomi, *op cit* p 22
25 *Ibid* p 23
26 German Collection. German War Office Archives. Abwehr telegram, July 14, 1943
27 Cerica. Article in *Tempo*, July 19, 1956

3 : FELTRE

1 Alfieri, *op cit* pp 318–9
2 Italian Collection. Ambrosio diary
3 German Collection. War Diary of the German General Staff, July 19, 1943
4 Alfieri, *op cit* p 305
5 *Ibid* pp 306 ff
6 Rintelen, *op cit* p 212
7 Alfieri, *op cit* p 316
8 Mussolini, *Memoirs, op cit* pp 50–1
9 *Pontine Notes, op cit*

10 Italian Collection. Tarvisio file. Minute dated July 20. 'Summary of first conversations, Excellency Ambrosio-Marshal Keitel (in the train).' Extracts are quoted by Rossi, *op cit* pp 335 ff
11 Alfieri, *op cit* p 309
12 *Ibid* p 313
13 *Ibid* p 315. See also Rintelen, *op cit* p 214
14 *Pontine Notes, op cit*
15 Rintelen, *op cit* p 214
16 *Pontine Notes, op cit*
17 Fuehrer Conferences on Naval Affairs 1943. p 81
18 Italian Collection. Tarvisio file 'Summary of second conversations. Excellency Ambrosio – Marshal Keitel (in the train)', dated July 20, 1943
19 Rintelen, *op cit* p 215
20 Mussolini, *Memoirs, op cit* p 51
21 *Pontine Notes, op cit*
22 Bastianini, *op cit* p 121
23 German Collection. Rommel Diary, July 20 and 21
24 Bastianini, *op cit* pp 122–3

4 : 'FIVE MINUTES TO TWELVE'

1 Italian Collection. Feltre documents
2 Castellano, *op cit* pp 56–7. See also Vailati, *Badoglio Racconta*, p 363
3 Rintelen, *op cit* p 215
4 German Collection. Rintelen telegram, July 21, 1943
5 *Ibid* Rome telegram, July 24, 1943
6 *Ibid* Himmler to Bormann, July 19, 1943
7 *Ibid* Mackensen telegram, July 22, 1943
8 Goerdeler to Kluge. Between July 20 and 24, 1943. Wheeler-Bennett, *The Nemesis of Power* p 572
9 German Collection. War Office Archives. War Diary of German General Staff, July 25, 1943
10 *Ibid*
11 Interview in *Il Corriere della Sera* March 11, 1955. Ambrosio was precise in his statements. It is possible, however, that this date is not correct
12 Nino Bolla, *Il Segreto di Due Re* pp 74–5
13 Italian Collection. Ambrosio's list of appointments
14 Anfuso, *op cit* p 282
15 Mussolini, *Memoirs, op cit* p 54
16 *Ibid* p 53. Grandi has published in successive interviews varying versions of this meeting. See Indro Montanelli *Il Corriere della Sera* February 9, 1955; Giovanni Cavallotti *Oggi* June 4, 1959. The above account is largely based on the latter
17 Pellicano, *op cit* Article II
18 Bottai, *op cit* pp 290–1
19 Alfieri *L'Ultima Seduta del Gran Consiglio* reprinted from the magazine 'Epoca' of May 24, 1952, p 5
20 Puntoni, *op cit* p 141
21 Cersosimo, *op cit* pp 6–7. Ciano's deposition before his trial at Verona
22 Bottai, *op cit* p 291

23 Canevari, *La Fine del Maresciallo Cavallero*, p 28
24 Bottai, *op cit* p 291
25 Anfuso, *op cit* p 283
26 Cersosimo, *op cit* p 7
27 Cucco, *op cit* pp 97-8
28 Mussolini, *Memoirs, op cit* p 54
29 German Collection. Mackensen to Ribbentrop, July 24, 1943
30 *Ibid* Second telegram, July 24, 1943
31 *Ibid* Rome telegram (office of Military Attaché) July 24, 1943
32 Senise, *op cit* pp 197-9
33 Roatta, *Otto Milioni di Baionette*, p 262 note
34 Italian Collection. Meeting of Italian Chiefs of Staff, July 22, 1943. 6 p.m.
35 *Ibid*
36 Castellano, *op cit* p 62

5 : THE MEETING OF THE GRAND COUNCIL

1 Mussolini, *Memoirs, op cit* p 55
2 *Ibid* pp 58–9
3 Bottai, *op cit* p 302
4 *Ibid,* pp 307–9
5 Mussolini, *Memoirs, op cit* p 80
6 Grandi, *op cit* p 49
7 Federzoni, *Memorie,* Article V, published in *L'Indipendente* (as from May 30, 1946)
8 Bottai, *op cit* pp 311–12
9 Mussolini, *Memoirs, op cit* p 63
10 Alfieri, *op cit* p 336
11 Letter from Bastianini to Mussolini, November 9, 1943, quoted in Cersosimo, *op cit* pp 180 ff
12 Bottai, *op cit* p 313
13 Galbiati, *op cit* p 232
14 Alfieri, *op cit* pp 339–40, and the offprint of his article *'L'Ultima Seduta del Gran Consiglio'*
15 Bottai, *op cit* pp 316–17
16 Alfieri, *op cit* p 340
17 Mussolini. *Memoirs, op cit* p 64

6 : THE COUP D'ETAT

1 Text in the Italian Collection
2 *Ibid* Mussolini to Farinacci, October 13, 1925
3 Spampanato, *Contro Memoriale* I, p 232
4 Galbiati, *op cit* p 234
5 Pellicano, *op cit* Article 3
6 Mussolini, *Memoirs,* p 83
7 Spampanato, *op cit* I, p 232
8 Farinacci, *Diario, op cit,* July 25, 1943

 9 *Pontine Notes, op cit*
10 *Ibid*
11 Mussolini, *Memoirs, op cit* p 88
12 Bastianini, *op cit* p 131 and the text of his letter in Cersosimo, *op cit* pp 181–2
13 Galbiati, *op cit* p 235
14 Host Venturi's report in Dolfin, *Con Mussolini nella Tragedia*, pp 125 ff
15 Galbiati, *op cit* pp 214 ff
16 *Pontine Notes, op cit*
17 'Note on the conversation which took place between the Duce and the Japanese Ambassador' (July 25, 1943) quoted in Tamaro, *op cit* I, p 72
18 German Collection. Mackensen telegram, July 28, 1943
19 *Ibid* Mackensen telegram July 31, 1943. 'For the Foreign Minister personally'
20 *Ibid*
21 Mussolini, *Memoirs, op cit* p 80
22 *Pontine Notes, op cit*
23 Galbiati, *op cit* p 239
24 *Ibid* p 241
25 *Pontine Notes, op cit*
26 Cucco, *op cit* pp 102 ff. This is confirmed in Graziani's book, *op cit* p 324
27 Grandi. Montanelli interview, *op cit*
28 *Ibid*
29 Ambrosio in an interview in *Il Corriere delle Sera*, March 11, 1955
30 Puntoni, *op cit* p 142
31 Cerica has described his participation in the events of July 25 in three articles published in *Tempo* (July 19, July 26, August 2, 1956). See also his speech in the Italian Senate, July 25, 1958
32 *Ibid*
33 Puntoni, *op cit* p 143
34 Mussolini, *Memoirs, op cit* p 80
35 Article in the newspaper *Meridiano d'Italia*, April 6, 1947
36 Puntoni, *op cit* p 145
37 *Pontine Notes, op cit*
38 Spampanato, *op cit* I, pp 230 ff. See also Senise, *op cit* p 206
39 Galbiati, *op cit* p 243
40 *Ibid* p 244
41 Dolfin, *op cit* p 128
42 Galbiati, *op cit* p 248 note, and a map in Appendix H
43 Roatta, *op cit* pp 262–3
44 Galbiati, *op cit* p 250
45 Jo di Benigno, *op cit* p 83
46 For the text see Tamaro, *op cit* I, p 47
47 Italian Collection. Intercepts of telephone conversations

7: RETROSPECT

1 Mussolini, *Memoirs, op cit* p 92
2 Federzoni, *'L'Ultima Seduta' op cit*
3 Hidaka to the Author
4 Roatta, *op cit* p 25
5 Italian Collection. Ambrosio-Kesselring meeting, July 24, 1943

PART TWO

1 : BADOGLIO: THE FIRST GERMAN REACTIONS

1 Gilbert, *op cit* pp 39 ff, July 25, 1943
2 Goebbels, *op cit* p 319, July 25, 1943
3 German Collection. Rome telegram (Dollmann), July 17, 1943
4 Tamaro, *op cit* II pp 583–4 notes. Source 'a member of the German Embassy'
5 Gilbert, *op cit* p 47
6 Rintelen, *op cit* p 224
7 German Collection. War Diary of the German General Staff
8 Gilbert, *op cit* pp 55 ff
9 German Collection. Mackensen telegram, July 26, 1943
10 Fuehrer Conferences on Naval Affairs 1943, pp 65–9. See also Rommel Papers, *op cit* p 433
11 German Collection. Mackensen telegram, July 26, 1943
12 *Ibid* July 27, 1943
13 *Ibid* July 28, 1943
14 German Collection. War Office Archives. Canaris report, July 27, 1943
15 Goebbels, *op cit* p 323
16 Rommel Papers, *op cit* p 432
17 Goebbels, *op cit* pp 328–9
18 *Ibid* p 332
19 *Ibid* p 332
20 German Collection. Mackensen telegram, July 29, 1943
21 *Ibid*
22 German Collection. War Diary of the German General Staff
23 *Ibid*
24 For the Italian side see Roatta, *op cit* pp 271 ff; Faldella, *op cit* p 637
25 Tamaro, *op cit* I, p 128. See also Simoni, *op cit* pp 378–87
26 Puntoni, *op cit* p 147
27 Rintelen, *op cit* p 234. See also 'Confidential Report' of the German Foreign Office dated August 13, 1943
28 Vailati, *Badoglio Risponde* p 99
29 Fuehrer Conferences on Naval Affairs 1943, p 75

2 : ROMAN INTERLUDE

1 See the Italian record of this conference in Hitler e Mussolini *op cit* pp 190 ff and 'Notes on the conversations' in Rossi, *op cit* pp 378 ff
2 Hitler e Mussolini, *op cit* pp 192–5
3 Rossi, *op cit* p 379
4 *Ibid* p 380
5 Minutes of the military meeting in Hitler e Mussolini, *op cit* p 203
6 Puntoni, *op cit* p 152
7 Guariglia, *Ricordi 1922–1946* p 623
8 Hitler e Mussolini, *op cit* p 208
9 *Ibid*

10 Guariglia, *op cit* p 628
11 Italian Collection quoted by Anfuso in a dispatch dated December 1, 1944. It is also cited by Villari, *Affari Esteri*, p 112 note. See also Guariglia's comments, *op cit* p 630
12 Guariglia, *op cit* p 630
13 Fuehrer Conferences on Naval Affairs 1943, *op cit* p 80
14 For the details of these negotiations, which do not concern directly this account, see Castellano, *op cit* pp 80 ff and Guariglia, *op cit* pp 640 ff
15 Castellano, *op cit* p 82
16 Guariglia, *op cit* pp 742–4
17 Grandi interview in *Oggi* Article 5, May 1959
18 Fuehrer Conferences on Naval Affairs 1943, *op cit* p 81
19 Rossi, *op cit* pp 385 ff; Roatta, *op cit* pp 279 ff
20 Rintelen, *op cit* p 242
21 *Ibid* The Italian minutes are slightly differently worded
22 *Ibid* p 224
23 *Ibid* p 247
24 Roatta, *op cit* p 281
25 For details see Rossi, *op cit* pp 206 ff
26 For the post-war controversies on this subject see for example the works of Roatta and Rossi, *passim*
27 Rintelen, *op cit* p 249
28 German Collection. Confidential report. Marked by Hitler on August 15. For the full text, see the Appendix to this chapter
29 Fuehrer Conferences on Naval Affairs 1943, *op cit* p 91
30 Puntoni, *op cit* p 157
31 Senise, *op cit* pp 234 ff
32 Puntoni, *op cit* p 157
33 Guariglia, *op cit* p 651
34 Simoni, *op cit* p 408
35 Senise, *op cit* pp 227 ff
36 The German evidence on Ciano's flight is contained in Dollmann, *op cit* pp 194 ff and Hagen, *op cit* pp 432 ff
37 Hagen, *op cit* pp 432–3
38 Guariglia, *op cit* pp 691–2
39 *Ibid* p 691

3 : THE ITALIAN SURRENDER

1 A radio set had been brought back by Castellano for the purpose. For details of the final negotiations see, among others, the books by Castellano, Rossi, and Guariglia (*passim*)
2 Rahn, *Ruheloses Leben* p 227. Guariglia, *op cit* pp 695 ff
3 Guariglia, *op cit* p 696
4 Rahn, *op cit* p 228
5 Guariglia, *op cit* p 697
6 Rahn to the author
7 German Collection. War Office Archives
8 See the communiqué of the German Foreign Ministry published on September 11, 1943, quoted by Tamaro, *op cit* I pp 396 ff and giving extracts from Rahn's telegrams

9 Goebbels, *op cit* p 342
10 Texts in Tamaro, *op cit* I pp 442 ff
11 Goebbels, *op cit* p 349
12 See the extracts of the speech which relate to Italy in Tamaro, *op cit* I, pp 448–9
13 Goebbels, *op cit* p 357
14 *Ibid* p 344
15 German Collection. Fuehrer directive, September 10, 1943
16 *Ibid* Fuehrer directive, September 13, 1943
17 Goebbels, *op cit* p 343
18 The text of this broadcast is in Tamaro, *op cit* I, pp 447–9
19 For an embroidered and picturesquely inventive account of this 'Radio' government on the train see Bellotti, *op cit* p 55 and *passim*
20 Goebbels, *op cit* p 350
21 German Collection. Himmler Files. Ricci to Himmler, September 10, 1943
22 Goebbels, *op cit* pp 352 and 354
23 German Collection. Rome telegram, September 12, 1943

4: Exile and Liberation

1 Tamaro, *op cit* I pp 76–7. Notes by Major Santillo, July 25–8, 1943
2 In the Italian Collection there is a draft of the first letter, which appears to be in Ambrosio's handwriting. The texts of both documents are printed in Mussolini, *Memoirs* pp 83–5. In a recent and 'official' biography of Badoglio by V. Vailati, Mussolini's letter is quoted in full but not that of Badoglio
3 These were published in a periodical under the title *Mussolini mi ha detto, Quaderni di Politica Estera*, 1944. See also his ghost-written Memoirs published in the United States under the title *From the Ashes of Defeat*
4 For the history of these documents see Appendix to this chapter. They are usually referred to as: *The Pontine Notes*. In his Memoirs published in 1944 Mussolini also described, in his familiar journalistic fashion, his days of exile. The English translation of these Memoirs contains in appendices a number of eye-witness accounts of him during these days, which are of minor historical interest
5 See Dies, *Istantanee Mussoliniane a Ponza*, written by this parish priest. It is a small pamphlet of little historical interest
6 See Skorzeny's own account, *Secret Missions passim*. A detailed and more accurate account by his second in command, Major Radl, entitled *Befreiter fallen von Himmel* ('Liberators jump from the sky')
7 Major Mors has given his account, which is very hostile to Skorzeny, in a Swiss periodical. *Curieux*, December 14, 1950
8 For Soleti's account see his article 'How Mussolini was liberated from Campo Imperatore'. The newspaper *Avanti*, July 19, 1944
9 Italian Collection. There is also a summary of this report in Dolfin, *op cit* pp 233 ff. It was written in Vienna between September 14–16 and removed by Skorzeny together with Mussolini's *Pontine Notes* 'on the orders of the Duce'. Gueli reconstructed this first report from memory, and sent the second version to Dolfin in February 1944
10 See also Senise's own account in his book, p 259
11 Article by Major Mors, *op cit*

B.F.—28*

PART THREE

Book I

1: THE RETURN OF MUSSOLINI

1 The only details of Mussolini's stay in Munich are contained in Donna Rachele's ghost-written autobiography, pp 208–11
2 Amicucci, *op cit* p 23
3 Goebbels, *op cit* p 363
4 The evidence of this meeting is scanty. An alleged eye-witness account is given in an anonymous article in the *Meridiano d'Italia,* August 31, 1947 (apparently written by the future Finance Minister Pellegrini) and in Fossani *Diario* published in *Momento* February 8, 1947. See also notes in Tamaro I, *op cit* p 560
5 See Pellegrini article, *op cit*
6 Goebbels, *op cit* p 361
7 *Ibid* p 378
8 Anfuso, *op cit* p 326
9 *Ibid* p 327
10 Goebbels, *op cit* p 380
11 *Ibid* p 378
12 *Ibid* pp 378–9
13 Anfuso, *op cit* p 328
14 Ribbentrop, *op cit* p 170
15 Goebbels, *op cit* pp 366–7 September 17, 1943
16 *Ibid* p 390
17 *Ibid* p 366
18 Anfuso, *op cit* pp 322–3
19 Cersosimo, *op cit* p 82
20 Goebbels, *op cit* pp 380–1 September 23, 1943
21 Notes of Dr Rahn
22 Italian Collection: September 13, 1943. 'Note from Buffarini Guidi written in Munich on September 13, 1943, to Mussolini on the situation in Italy and on measures to be adopted immediately.' See also extracts from this memorandum in Spampanato, *op cit* II p 21
23 See an account of this talk in Spampanato, *op cit* II pp 31 ff. Spampanato, a leading Fascist journalist, had been interned with Buffarini and remained close to him in these early days of the formation of the new Fascist administration
24 Italian Collection: Farinacci to the Duce, September 21, 1943
25 See Cione, *Storia della Repubblica Sociale Italiana* p 124. Pini e Susmel, *op cit* IV p 330, based on Farinacci's probably apochryphal diary

26 Text in Tamaro, *op cit* I pp 590–3
27 *Ibid op cit* II p 5
28 Amicucci, *op cit* p 34
29 German Collection : Rahn telegram (Rome) September 22, 1943
30 *Ibid* Ribbentrop telegram September 23, 1943
31 See Graziani '*Io ho difeso la Patria*', pp 375 ff
32 *Ibid* p 377
33 Graziani's words at his post-war trial. See *Processo Graziani* (the stenographic record) I pp 203–4. See also Rahn, *op cit* p 240. He dates these events in error on September 27. See Moellhausen, *Die Gebrochene Achse* p 67. See also the collective work of Graziani's lawyers. *Il dramma di Graziani*, pp 55 ff
34 German Collection. Rahn telegram (Rome), September 23, 1943
35 *Ibid* Report by Wuster, October 30, 1943
36 Italian Collection. Diary of Ambassador Rosso, who represented the Italian Foreign Ministry

2: THE DUCE IN ROMAGNA

1   Wolff. Article in *Tempo* No 3
2   German Collection. Rahn telegram, September 26, 1943
3   *Ibid* Hitler telegram, September 22, 1943
4   *Ibid* Rahn telegram, September 23, 1943
5   Quoted in Tamaro, *op cit* II pp 47 ff
6   Graziani *Processo, op cit* II p 135
7   German Collection. Himmler files, October 2, 1943
8   *Ibid* Ribbentrop telegram, October 7, 1943
9   Graziani *Processo, op cit* I p 259
10 *Ibid* p 254
11 Abbreviated text in Spampanato III p 260, quoted from the newspaper *Unità* May 24, 1945 (Milan). See Dolfin, *op cit* p 147. See Susmel's muddled note, *op cit* IV p 576. 'The famous letter which he sent to Hitler three days after his return from Germany'
12 German Collection. Madrid telegram, October 6, 1943
13 *Ibid* Rahn telegram, September 29, 1943
14 *Ibid* Ribbentrop to Rahn, September 27, 1943
15 Italian Collection. Anfuso's diary, October 1, 1943
16 German Collection. Rahn telegram, October 5, 1943
17 *Ibid* Rome telegram (Moellhausen) October 6, 1943
18 *Ibid* War Office Archives
19 *Ibid* Rahn telegrams, October 8 and 10, 1943
20 *Ibid* Rahn telegram, October 10, 1943
21 Italian Collection. Anfuso's diary, October 1, 1943
22 Tamaro, *op cit* II pp 5 ff. Amicucci, *op cit* pp 32–3
23 German Collection. Rome telegram (Moellhausen), September 26, 1943
24 Tamaro, *op cit* II p 215
25 On October 15. Amicucci, *op cit* p 122
26 Pini e Susmel, *op cit* IV p 340
27 Tamaro, *op cit* II pp 203–4. Pini e Susmel, *op. cit* IV p 344, and notes p 577. Pini, *Itinerario Tragico*, pp 35–6
28 Dolfin, *op cit* p 28

3 : The Battle for the Republican Army

1 Canevari, *Graziani mi ha detto*, pp 285 ff
2 Tamaro, *op cit* II pp 205–8, October 4, 1943
3 Graziani, *op cit* p 431
4 Graziani *Processo*, *op cit* I pp 260 ff. A slightly different version in his book, pp 430 ff
5 German Collection. Rahn telegram, October 10, 1943
6 Dolfin, *op cit* p 39
7 Italian Collection. Report of Canevari dated December 3, 1943, 'Question of Canevari-Buhle protocols of October 16'. See also Canevari, *op cit* pp 298 ff
8 Italian Collection. Report by Canevari dated December 3, 1943, at Gargnano. The complete set of reports on these negotiations is in the Italian Collection. The documents appear to have been marked and read by Mussolini
9 Italian Collection. Memorandum by Canevari dated October 18, 1943
10 Italian Collection. Text of Canevari-Buhle Protocol, October 16, 1943
11 German Collection. Himmler files. Berger to Himmler, October 19, 1943. See also Canevari, *op cit* p 291
12 Italian Collection. Canevari report dated December 3, 1943
13 Text in Tamaro, *op cit* II p 247
14 Dolfin, *op cit* p 58. His date is erroneously October 28
15 Dolfin, *op cit* pp 58–9. Further details in Canevari, *op cit* p 292
16 Spampanato, *op cit* III pp 260–1. Certain significant passages are missing from this version. For full text see 'The Germans and the Salò Army'—documents published in the Italian Resistance Historical Journal *Il Movimento di Liberazione in Italia* No. 5, March 1950
17 Dolfin, *op cit* p 79
18 Canevari, *op cit* p 294
19 Dolfin, *op cit* p 95
20 Canevari, *op cit* p 297
21 Graziani *Processo*, *op cit* I p 265
22 Canevari, *op cit* p 298
23 German Collection. Ribbentrop-Mandić conversation March 1, 1944. The latter was Foreign Minister of Croatia
24 Graziani *Processo*, *op cit* I pp 272–3
25 Colonel Heggenreiner. Quoted in *Il dramma di Graziani*, p 27
26 Dolfin, *op cit* p 129
27 *Ibid* pp 116–7
28 German Collection. War Office Archives. Report by Colonel Jandl, November 19, 1943
29 Graziani *Processo*, *op cit* 272
30 German Collection. Foreign Office minute, November 15, 1943
31 Graziani *Processo*, *op cit* I p 274
32 Quoted in *Il dramma di Graziani*, pp 61–2
33 German Collection. Rahn telegram, November 29, 1943
34 *Ibid* Rahn telegram, December 1, 1943
35 Dolfin, *op cit* pp 131–2
36 German Collection. Rahn telegram, December 4, 1943
37 Dolfin, *op cit* p 133
38 Canevari, *op cit* pp 300–1
39 Fuehrer Conferences on Naval Affairs December 19–20, 1943, p 109

4: THE DUCE AT SALÒ

1 Dolfin, *op cit* p 30
2 German Collection. War Office Archives. Colonel Jandl to Admiral Burckner, head of the Military Attaché section of the German War Office. November 19, 1943
3 *Ibid* Jandl to Burckner, December 12, 1943
4 Pini e Susmel, *op cit* IV p 345
5 Goebbels, *op cit* pp 411–12, November 9, 1943
6 For this characteristic episode see Dolfin, *op cit* pp 61 ff. Vittorio Mussolini, in his book *Vita con mio Padre* makes no reference to this period
7 German Collection. Himmler files
8 *Ibid* Himmler files. Rainer to Himmler, July 26, 1943
9 General Esposito, *Trieste e la sua Odissea*, p 27. The author was the Italian military commander of the region
10 *Il Movimento di Liberazione in Italia.* No 15, pp 3–9
11 *Il dramma di Graziani,* p 37
12 German Collection. Hitler directive, September 10, 1943
13 Goebbels, *op cit* p 383. September 23, 1943
14 Italian Collection. Anfuso diary, October 1, 1943
15 German Collection. Rahn telegram, October 19, 1943
16 Italian Collection. Pavolini to the Duce, October 10, 1943
17 Dolfin, *op cit* p 86
18 *Ibid* p 90
19 *Ibid* p 90, and again p 104. November 12, 1943
20 Italian Collection. Anfuso dispatch, December 10, 1943
21 German Collection. Rahn telegram, December 25, 1943
22 German Collection. Hitler directive, October 10, 1943
23 *Ibid* Rahn telegram, October 19, 1943
24 *Ibid* Unruh to Bormann, February 15, 1944
25 *Ibid* Foreign Office minute, November 3, 1943
26 Italian Collection. Anfuso to the Duce, November 4, 1943
27 Quoted in Tamaro, *op cit* II p 199
28 *Ibid* p 370
29 German Collection. Hilger minute, October 12, 1943
30 Goebbels, *op cit* p 422
31 German Collection. Rahn telegram, November 16, 1943
32 *Ibid* War Office Archives, Jandl report, December 16, 1943
33 *Ibid* Jandl report, January 22, 1944
34 *Ibid*
35 *Ibid* Rahn telegram, January 14, 1944. Zerbino did in fact succeed Buffarini in February 1945.
36 *Ibid* Foreign Office minute, January 25, 1944

5: THE CONGRESS OF VERONA

1 Dolfin, *op cit* p 142
2 Quoted in Galanti, *Socializzazione e Sindacalismo nella Repubblica Sociale Italiana*, p 24
3 Italian Collection. Bombacci file
4 German Collection. Rahn telegram, November 16, 1943

5 Quoted in Tamaro, *op cit* II p 220
6 The minutes of this meeting are in the Italian Collection
7 Dolfin, *op cit* p 97
8 Mussolini to Mazzolini. See Tamaro, *op cit* p 229

6 : THE VERONA TRIALS

1 Dolfin, *op cit* p 115
2 Cersosimo, *op cit* p 29
3 German Collection. Doernberg minute, October 15, 1943
4 Susmel, Biographical articles on Ciano, No 14 in *Tempo, op cit*
5 Anfuso, *op cit* p 410
6 Dolfin, *op cit* p 114
7 *Ibid* pp 180–1
8 Montagna, *op cit* pp 87 ff
9 Cersosimo, *op cit* p 43
10 *Ibid* p 70
11 German Collection. Ribbentrop to Rahn, December 27, 1943
12 *Ibid* Rahn telegram, December 28, 1943
13 *Ibid* Rahn telegram, December 30, 1943
14 Text in Cersosimo, *op cit* p 237
15 *Ibid* p 238
16 Tamaro, *op cit* II p 354
17 Dolfin, *op cit* p 197
18 Cersosimo, *op cit* pp 276–7
19 Susmel. Articles on Ciano, Nos 14–15 in *Tempo, op cit*. The author interviewed Harster after the war
20 German Collection. Kaltenbrunner telegram, January 12, 1944. For further details see Wolff article No 2 in *Tempo, op cit*
21 Articles by Don Chiot in the newspaper *Il Messaggero*, September 1948. Another account is in Benini, *Vigilia a Verona*, pp 61 ff. Benini, former Undersecretary for Albanian Affairs, was in the same prison at the time
22 German Collection. S.S. report, January 11, 1944
23 Dolfin, *op cit* p 205
24 Italian Collection. Mussolini to Suner. The letter is also printed in Suner *From Hendaye to Gibraltar* (Spanish edition), p 324
25 For details see: German Collection. Kaltenbrunner telegram, January 12, 1944
26 Rahn to the author
27 Italian Collection. Anfuso dispatch, January 17, 1944
28 German Collection. Rahn telegrams of April 12 and 22, 1944

7 : BANDENKRIEG

1 German Collection. Ribbentrop to Rahn, December 15, 1943
2 *Ibid* Foreign Office minute, January 3, 1944
3 *Ibid* Rahn telegram, November 23, 1943
4 Italian Collection. Buffarini's report to the Duce, December 21, 1943
5 *Ibid* Mussolini to Ricci, February 9, 1944

6 *Ibid* Mussolini to Ferrini, the Undersecretary of the Italian Republican Navy, December 28, 1943
7 Italian Collection. File on the 'Borghese Case'. Reports by Ferrini, officers of Graziani's staff, and of the National Republican Guard. January–February 1944
8 Mussolini to Rahn, January 25, 1944
9 German Collection. Foreign Office to Rahn. 'Personal and Confidential'. February 14, 1944
10 Italian Collection. Report by an Italian Staff Officer to Graziani, January 2, 1944
11 *Ibid* Graziani-Leyers meeting, March 29, 1944
12 German Collection. Rahn telegram, April 14, 1944
13 Borghese at his post-war trial (1947) quoted by Algardi, *Processo ai Fascisti*, p 199
14 German Collection. War Office Archives. Report by Colonel Heggenreiner on conversation with Marshal Graziani, April 14, 1944

8: SALÒ AND SOCIALIZATION

1 Italian Collection. Tarchi's manuscript letter to the Duce, February 11, 1944
2 German Collection. Rahn to Ribbentrop, February 11, 1944
3 Italian Collection. Mussolini to Rahn, February 11, 1944
4 German Collection. Rahn to Ribbentrop, February 10, 1944
5 *Ibid* Ribbentrop to Rahn, February 14, 1944
6 Italian Collection. Memorandum from the Head of Turin Province to the Duce, February 15, 1944
7 Italian Collection. Memorandum from the Turin authorities to the Duce, February 15, 1944
8 See the documents quoted in an article by Vaccarino, 'Il Movimento operaio a Torino nei primi mesi della crisi italiana. July 43—March 44' in the review *Il Movimento di Liberazione in Italia*, September 1952, No 20, pp 134 ff. See also the recent study by Luraghi *Il Movimento operaio Torinese durante la Resistenza* (1958)
9 German Collection. Rahn telegram, March 4, 1944
10 *Ibid* Keitel telegram (copy to Rahn), March 6, 1944
11 Vaccarino, *op cit* p 41
12 Italian Collection. 'The Decision to strike in Milan and the Divergencies of view within the Committee of Liberation.' ('Strictly reserved for Mussolini.') Dated March 1, 1944. This document describes the ascendancy of the Communist elements of the Committee
13 Italian Collection. Police report, March 1, 1944
14 See the evidence of Riccardo Lombardi at Graziani's Trial, *op cit* II p 674
15 Italian Collection. Memorandum of the Swiss Commercial Attaché in Como, April 4, 1944
16 *Ibid* Memorandum by Tarchi, February 1945
17 *Ibid* Rahn to Leyers, June 27, 1944
18 Italian Collection. Report of Tarchi, February 1945
19 *Ibid* Report by Vaccari (head of the Fascist Federation of Commercial Employees) to the Duce, June 20, 1944. This document is heavily underlined and annotated in Mussolini's hand
20 *Ibid* Vaccari's report to the Duce, June 20, 1944

9: THE KLESSHEIM CONFERENCE

1 German collection. Rahn telegram
2 Coceani, *Mussolini, Hitler e Tito*, pp 74–5
3 German Collection. Rahn to Ribbentrop, March 27, 1944
4 *Ibid* Rahn telegram, April 1, 1944
5 *Ibid* Rahn telegram, April 12, 1944
6 *Ibid* Rahn telegrams, April 16 and 20, 1944
7 Anfuso, *op cit* p 433
8 Graziani *Processo, op cit* p 331
9 Mellini, *Guerra Diplomatica a Salò*, p 198
10 Anfuso, *op cit* pp 435 and 437–8
11 Mazzolini diary, quoted in Tamaro, *op cit* III p 30

10: THE MARCH FROM ROME

1 German Collection. War Office Archives. Hitler directive, May 6, 1944
2 *Ibid* Memorandum by Mussolini to Kesselring, June 1944
3 See Tamaro, *op cit* III pp 52–3. Mussolini also published an article in the press entitled 'Rome or Death', the battle-cry of Garibaldi
4 German Collection. Jandl report, June 13, 1944
5 Italian Collection. Pavolini to Mussolini, June 18, 1944
6 *Ibid* Pavolini to Mussolini, June 18, 1944
7 *Ibid* Pavolini to Mussolini, July 7 and 8, 1944
8 Graziani *Processo, op cit* II p 642 and Italian Collection. This arrangement excluded Lombardy
9 For details see *ibid* pp 307 ff
10 See the text in *Il Movimento di Liberazione in Italia* No 7, pp 24 ff
11 Text in Tamaro, *op cit* III p 241
12 Italian Collection. Graziani to the Duce, June 28, 1944
13 Text in Tamaro, *op cit* III p 58
14 The text of this memorandum is quoted in full in Graziani *Processo, op cit* II pp 31 ff. It was apparently drafted by his Chief of Staff, General Sorrentino
15 Italian Collection. Pavolini to Mussolini, June 27, 1944
16 *Ibid* Pavolini to the Duce, July 19, 1944
17 *Ibid* Report by Pavolini to the Duce, June 24, 1944
18 German Collection. Intelligence Report, June 26, 1944
19 Italian Collection. Mezzasomma to the Duce, July 19, 1944
20 Italian Collection. Records of meetings between Italian and German military representatives. June 27–July 5, 1944

11: TO THE 'GOERLITZ' STATION

1 Anfuso, *op cit* pp 455–6
2 Rahn, *op cit* p 258
3 *Ibid* p 259
4 Anfuso, *op cit* p 457
5 See Rahn, *op cit* p 259; Mellini, *op cit* p 37
6 Anfuso, *op cit* pp 449–50
7 *Ibid* quoting the phrase of Hitler's in German
8 Graziani, *op cit* pp 445–6

9 Anfuso, *op cit* p 451, and his later dispatch of August 12, quoted in Mellini, *op cit* p 37 note
10 Wheeler-Bennett, *The Nemesis of Power*, p 644 and for the whole meeting
11 Graziani, *op cit* p 446
12 Anfuso, *op cit* p 453. See also an embroidered account of the tea party in Dollmann, *op cit* pp 393–400
13 German Collection. Schmidt minute, *op cit*
14 Graziani *Processo, op cit* pp 1173–4
15 *Ibid* p 1174
16 See the excellent account in the pioneer work on Italo–German relations, E. Wiskemann, *The Rome–Berlin Axis,* pp 36 ff
17 *Juli 20, 1944, Dokumente und Berichte*, p 135
18 Anfuso, *op cit* p 460
19 Italian Collection. Anfuso dispatch, August 2, 1944
20 Spampanato, *op cit* II p 232

12 : THE LONG WINTER

1 Italian Collection. Foreign Office Circular, August 1, 1944
2 *Ibid* Mussolini to Anfuso, August 2, 1944
3 *Ibid* Mussolini to Mischi, July 29, 1944
4 *Ibid*
5 German Collection. War Office Archives. Report of Jandl, August 5, 1944
6 Italian Collection. Kesselring order, August 4, 1944
7 *Ibid* Anfuso to the Duce, August 2, 1944
8 Tamaro, *op cit* III p 270. Quoted from Mazzolini's unpublished diary
9 Italian Collection. Pavolini to the Duce. Manuscript letter, September 8, 1944
10 *Ibid* Note by the Duce on his talk with Rahn, September 9, 1944
11 *Ibid* Anfuso dispatch, September 20, 1944
12 *Ibid* Anfuso dispatch, September 27, 1944
13 *Ibid* Mussolini to Rahn, September 21, 1944
14 Tamaro, *op cit* III p 271, quoting Mazzolini's diary, September 27, 1944
15 Hidaka to the author
16 Italian Collection. Mussolini to Rahn, October 13, 1944
17 *Ibid* Mussolini to Rahn, December 10, 1944
18 *Ibid* Mussolini to Kesselring, October 4, 1944
19 *Ibid* Mussolini to Goering, October 9, 1944
20 *Ibid* Report by the head of the province of Savona, October 25, 1944 (noted and underlined by the Duce)
21 Italian Collection. Mussolini to Graziani, January 1, 1945
22 For this acrimonious controversy in Italian Resistance circles on this Allied action see for example Catalano, *op cit* pp 283 ff and the article entitled 'The Alexander Proclamation and the attitude of the Resistance at the beginning of the winter, 1944–5', *Il Movimento di Liberazione in Italia* No 26, September 1953, and further documents in *ibid* No 27
23 Mellini, *op cit* p 47
24 Italian Collection. Anfuso dispatch, November 18, 1944
25 *Ibid*
26 German Collection. Schmidt minute. Ribbentrop-Anfuso conversation, November 30, 1944. This memorandum is the last in chronological order in the collection of German Foreign Office documents

13 : MILAN AND THE LAST 'CHANGING OF THE GUARD'

1 Mellini, *op cit* p 54
2 Italian Collection. Report from Fascist authority in Piedmont, September 2, 1944
3 Documents published as a White Book by Cardinal Schuster in 1946 under the title: *Gli Ultimi Tempi di un Régime*, pp 66–7, October 30, 1944
4 For the complete text of this speech see *Opera Omnia*, Vol XXXII pp 126 ff
5 Italian Collection. Graziani to the Duce, January 29, 1945
6 *Ibid* Tarchi to Mussolini, December 5, 1944
7 *Ibid* Memorandum from Spinelli to the Duce, March 1, 1945
8 *Ibid* Tarchi to Leyers, January 5, 1945
9 *Ibid* Buffarini, Report to the Duce, October 24, 1944
10 Pini, *Itinerario Tragico*, p 129
11 See Hagen, *op cit* pp 467–9, but with caution
12 Mellini, *op cit* pp 69–70
13 Spampanato, *op cit* II p 303
14 Mellini, *op cit* p 73
15 *Ibid* p 79. Rahn in conversation with Mellini on February 19
16 Italian Collection. Buffarini to the Duce, March 5, 1945
17 *Ibid* Pavolini to the Duce, February 26, 1945
18 Wolff, Article in *Tempo*, No 3
19 Mellini, *op cit* p 82

Book II

1 : OPERATION 'SUNRISE'

1 Gilbert, *op cit* pp 105–6
2 Nuremberg Trial Documents. Supplementary Volume B, pp 1203–4
3 Ribbentrop, *op cit* p 171
4 Notes by Ambassador Hidaka to the author
5 Italian Collection. Anfuso dispatch, December 1, 1944. See also Anfuso, *op cit* p 491
6 Italian Collection. Anfuso dispatch, August 2, 1944
7 See Wolff's article in *Tempo* No 4
8 Quoted in Lanfranchi, *La Resa degli Ottocentomila* pp 24 ff. Not in Schuster's White Book
9 White Book, *op cit* pp 109 ff
10 *Ibid* p 112
11 For revealing details of a session of the Committee of Liberation for Northern Italy on this subject on March 29, 1945, see Catalano, *op cit* p 391 note
12 White Book, *op cit* p 114
13 *Ibid* p 115
14 For details see Lanfranchi, *op cit* pp 44–64
15 Rahn, *op cit* pp 282 ff
16 See *Processo Parri*, pp 182 ff
17 Rahn, *op cit* p 283

18 *Ibid*
19 Lanfranchi, *op cit* p 150
20 Rahn, *op cit* p 287
21 *Ibid* p 286
22 Italian Collection. Graziani's notebook
23 *Ibid*
24 *Ibid*
25 Graziani, *op cit* p 520
26 The text is in his notebook in the Italian Collection, and is transcribed in his book, *op cit* pp 524–5
27 Italian Collection. Graziani's notebook
28 For details see Graziani *op cit* pp 528 ff
29 For this somewhat speculative account see Lanfranchi, *op cit* pp 273 ff
30 See Kesselring's very general remarks in his book, *op cit* pp 418 ff

2 : THE DUCE AND AN ITALIAN 'SOLUTION'

1 Cardinal Schuster, White Book, pp 104–5
2 *Ibid* p 106
3 *Processo Parri*, p 175. See also Lanfranchi, *op cit* pp 143 ff
4 Lanfranchi, *op cit* p 153
5 Mellini, *op cit* pp 105–6 under the date March 5, 1945
6 *Ibid* pp 15–16
7 The texts of Mellini's memoranda are published in the review *Il Movimento de Liberazione in Italia* No 5, March 1950, from documents captured by the partisans in 1945
8 Mellini, *op cit* p 108
9 Italian Collection. Mellini to the Duce, March 14, 1945
10 Italian Collection. Anfuso to the Duce, April 9, 1945
11 Italian Collection. Press report, April 1945
12 Italian Collection. Graziani's notebook. There is no other reference to this meeting
13 Mellini, *op cit* p 123. On Moellhausen's mission to Spain see *ibid* pp 87–8
14 German Collection. War Office Archives. Rahn telegram, March 31, 1945
15 Anfuso, *op cit* p 466
16 Italian Collection. Graziani to the Duce, March 17, 1945
17 *Ibid* Pavolini to the Duce, April 5, 1945
18 *Ibid* Memorandum by Pavolini, April 9, 1945
19 Mellini, *op cit* pp 134 ff based on notes taken by him at the meeting. The Germans were represented by Vietinghoff, Wolff, Rahn, and Dollmann : the Italians by Pavolini, Anfuso, Zerbino, the successor of Buffarini at the Ministry of the Interior, Barracu, Undersecretary of the Presidency of the Council. See also Anfuso, *op cit* pp 470–1
20 Wolff. Article in *Tempo* No 5
21 Italian Collection. Duce-Rahn conversation, April 14, 1945
22 Anfuso, *op cit* pp 471 ff. The conversation apparently took place between April 10 and 15
23 Mellini, *op cit* pp 114–15. March 14, 1945
24 Anfuso, *op cit* p 473
25 Mellini, *op cit* p 137

3 : 'DUST AND ALTARS'

1 Graziani, *op cit* p 490
2 Mellini, *op cit* p 138. And Graziani, *op cit* pp 490–1
3 Rahn to the author. See also Rahn, *op cit* p 290; Zacharias, *op cit* p 201; and Moellhausen, *op cit* pp 323–4
4 Moellhausen, *op cit* pp 324–5
5 Mussolini's list of appointments shows that he received Silvestri at 6 p.m. on April 22, and at the same time on the following day. For this whole episode, see Silvestri. *Turati l'ha detto*, pp 34 ff and 78 ff. *Mussolini, Graziani e l'Antifascismo. Passim.* Spampanato, *op cit* III pp 40 ff. Cione, *op cit* pp 356–60.
6 See the text in Silvestri, *op cit* p 99. A discussion on this draft appears in Spampanato, *op cit* III pp 42–3
7 It seems to have been delivered to Lelio Basso, Pertini's Socialist colleague, or possibly to Corrado Bonfantini, Commissar of the 'Matteotti' formations in Milan.
8 Sandro Pertini. Article 'The Socialists and the Surrender of Mussolini' in the newspaper *Avanti*, April 30, 1947
9 E. Cione, *op cit* p 358
10 *Ibid* p 356
11 *Ibid* p 359.
12 Graziani, *op cit* p 495
13 Italian Collection
14 *The Political Testament of Hitler*, pp 69 ff. February 17, 1945. English version of Bormann's notes, Cassell, London, 1961
15 Quoted in Tamaro, *op cit* III p 514
16 Mellini, *op cit* pp 148–9
17 Italian Collection. Minute by Mellini, April 25, 1945
18 See White Book, *op cit* pp 139–41
19 *Ibid* p 140. The report of Don Corbella to the Cardinal.
20 German Collection. War Office Archives. Military Intelligence Report from Milan, April 15, 1945
21 White Book, *op cit* pp 156–7. Memorandum on Don Bicchierai's 'Relations with the German side'
22 Dollmann's version of this talk is at variance in several details. See his account, *ibid* pp 153 ff
23 *Ibid* p 157
24 *Ibid* p 150. Statement by Rauff. See also Lanfranchi, *op cit* pp 285–6
25 There are a number of conflicting accounts from both sides. See for example Spampanato, *op cit* III pp 97 ff. Valiani, *op cit* p 334
26 Cione, *op cit* p 360
27 Graziani, *op cit* pp 504–5
28 Valiani, *op cit* p 341
29 The only direct account of this talk is the subsequent memorandum by the Cardinal in his White Book, pp 162 ff
30 Graziani, *op cit* pp 506–7
31 The accounts of this remarkable conference are numerous and conflicting in details. The completely or partially first-hand versions are : the Cardinal's note in the White Book, pp 163–4; Graziani, *op cit* pp 507 ff: Lombardi at Graziani's post-war trial, *Processo, op cit* II pp 660 ff: also Lombardi on Schuster's account *Il Ponte* No 12, December 1946. Marazza to Bacino

article *op cit,* and in Valiani, *op cit* pp 344 ff; Cadorna's book, *La Riscossa,* pp 249 ff

32 Graziani, *op cit* p 510
33 Graziani *Processo, op cit* II pp 660 ff
34 On the meeting of April 22 between the Cardinal and Graziani see the White Book, *op cit* p 135; Graziani, *op cit* pp 495 ff. Graziani, according to his account, asked to be put in touch with Cadorna
35 Again it is impossible to reconstruct a precise timetable. Valiani, *op cit* p 345 states that Mussolini strode out at 7.15 p.m.
36 See Don Bicchierai's notes in the White Book, *op cit* p. 158
37 Pertini article *op cit* in *Avanti* April 30, 1947
38 See also Cione, *op cit* p 371, Note 542
39 Costa in Spampanato III p 7
40 Graziani, *op cit* pp 510–11
41 Vittorio Mussolini, *Mio Padre,* p 223
42 Spampanato, *op cit* III p 114
43 Italian Collection. Graziani's notebook
44 White Book, *op cit* p 151
45 *Ibid* p 159

NOTES TO APPENDIX

1 German Collection. Ribbentrop to Rahn, September 12, 1943
2 Italian Collection. Memorandum by Ambassador Rosso. 'The Withdrawal by the Germans of Political Archives' September 15, 1943
3 German Collection. Rahn to Ribbentrop, September 14, 1943
4 *Ibid* Rahn to Ribbentrop, September 17, 1943
5 *Ibid* German Foreign Office minute, September 23, 1943
6 *Ibid* German Foreign Office minute, September 28, 1943
7 *Ibid* Steengracht, October 1, 1943
8 *Ibid* Note from Private Office of the German Foreign Minister, October 2, 1943
9 *Ibid* Ribbentrop telegram, October 6, 1943 (signed Hilger)
10 *Ibid* Rome telegram (Moellhausen), October 11, 1943
11 *Ibid* Rahn telegram, October 23, 1943
12 *Ibid* Hencke memoranda for Ribbentrop: October 18, October 21, November 20, 1943
13 *Ibid* Foreign Office minute, March 21, 1944

INDEX

NOTE: In this index all references to institutions (Army, High Command, Ministry, etc.) are to those of Italy, unless otherwise stated.

223–9; King's decision to end, 233; expulsion of moderates in, 236; secret opposition meetings, 240–2; 'last wave' of, 316–34; purging of, 320–1, 323; Scorza made Secretary of, 320, 324; plan for special emergency squads, 321; mass reunion, 322–3; Scorza's analysis of, 325–9; disciplinary measures, 329–30; membership of, 334n.; Bonomi on need to overthrow, 340, 396–8; reaction to Sicily invasion, 387–98, 421; Grandi's 'Programme' for, 425, 428–9, 433, 440, 441, 442, 446, 452, 455, 520, 638, 639, 641; Scorza's reform plan, 431–2, 450–1, 453, 456; and transfer of power to Badoglio, 471–5; stunned by coup, 484–5, 494; Hitler aims to restore, 494–5, 498, 499, 533–7, 557; 'complete collapse' of, 495–6, 497–8, 506–7, 521, 556; supposed plot in, 517–19, 543; and formation of new Republican Party, 554–61, 565–9

Fascist Party Directorate: composition of, 30–1; meeting of (Jan. 1942), 34; meeting (May 1942), 35–6; reconstruction of, 128–9, 151; Mussolini's speech to (Jan. 1943), 129–33; monthly meetings to be held, 133; meeting of (Mar. 1943), 228–31; Mussolini's speech to (April 1943), 316–20; new directives for (May 1943), 321–3, 330, 333; last Party report to (June 1943), 334

Fascist Party Militia, 30, 31, 32, 109–10, 113, 116, 117, 437; importance of, 35, 36; rôle in Fascist crisis, 56, 336; and strikes, 225; Army distrust of, 336, 574; loyalty to Mussolini, 364, 432, 435, 474; Scorza's abolition of liaison officers of, 390, 461; incorporated in Army, 435, 436, 449; and coup d'état, 473–4; surrender to Badoglio, 497; Mussolini's reconstruction of, 559, 571, 602; difficulty in recruiting for, 566, 567; as basis of Republican Army, 574–5, 578, 587, 593, 598; to form new Republican Guard, 598–601, 657, 723

Fascist Party Secretary: functions of, 30–1, 32; Vidussoni as, 34

Fascist Republican Government (Salò

Republic): formation of, 554–61, 565–9, 570; ministerial appointments, 566–9; establishment of seat of, 572, 573, 577, 580, 586; first Cabinet meeting, 572–3, 576; programme of, 575–6, 626–32, 666–7; recognized by satellites, 576; German control in, 578–81, 608n., 612–13, 618–20, 624–5, 665, 694, 698–9, 747; private armies and police forces, 602; secretariat and régime of, 607–23; plots and crises in, 621–3, 658–9, 741, 752–3; partisan resistance to, 628–9, 654 et seq.; and Verona trials of 'traitors', 633–53; state of armed forces (Mar. 1944) 664, (July) 703–4; and socialization, 666–77, 701–3, 747–50, 782; defeatism after fall of Rome, 691–4, 706; territory divided into four administrative regions, 694; disillusionment with German attitude to, 730–1, 738–9; decision to move to Milan, 740, 780, 783n., 785, 788, 792; Mussolini's 'changing of guard' in, 750–5, 775; his surrender proposals, 776–7; at Milan, 793 et seq.; dissolution of, 811–12, 815; shooting of members of, 816

Fascist Republican Party: formation of, 557, 559, 565–7, 581–3; reappearance of regional clans, 582–3, 629; conflict over armed forces, 593–6; dissensions in, 625–6, 635, 665, 701; and Verona Congress, 626–32, 666–7, 743–4; calls for Special Tribunals, 630, 631, 633; action against 'traitors', 631, 633–53; Black Brigades of, 696, 700–1, 712, 723, 734, 751, 788; 'sabotage' of Govt., 750–1; Mussolini's offer to dissolve, 777; Cione opposition group, 784

Fascist Syndicates, 223, 225, 748; fusion of, 575–6

Favagrossa, General, 12, 86, 148, 155, 164

Federal Secretaries, 324; pressure on, 110, 115n.; in National Directorate, 129; and strikes, 318; Mussolini's aim to abolish dualism with Prefects, 571

Federzoni, Luigi, 122, 425, 428, 429, 430, 481; intimacy with Bottai and